The
University of
Chicago
School
Mathematics
Project

PRE·TRANSITION MATHEMATICS

Authors

John W. McConnell
Cathy Hynes Feldman
Deborah Heeres
Emily Kallemeyn
Enrique Ortiz
Noreen Winningham
Karen Hunt
Troy P. Regis
Mihaela Florence Singer
John Wolfe
Natalie Jakucyn
Zalman Usiskin

Director of Evaluation

Denisse R. Thompson

The McGraw·Hill Companies

Authors

John W. McConnell
Lecturer in Statistics
North Park University, Chicago, IL

Cathy Hynes Feldman
Mathematics Teacher (retired)
University of Chicago Laboratory Schools, Chicago, IL

Deborah Heeres
Mathematics Teacher
Northern Michigan Christian School, McBain, MI

Emily Kallemeyn
Mathematics Teacher
Park Junior High School, LaGrange Park, IL

Enrique Ortiz
Associate Professor of Education
University of Central Florida, Orlando, FL

Noreen Winningham
Everyday Mathematics *Curriculum Team Leader,*
CEMSE – University of Chicago

Karen Hunt
Mathematics Teacher
Foster Elementary School, Ludington, MI

Troy P. Regis
Mathematics Education Doctoral Student
University of Missouri, Columbia, MO

Mihaela Florence Singer
Senior Research Officer
Institute of Educational Sciences
Bucharest, Romania

John Wolfe
Professor of Mathematics (emeritus)
Oklahoma State University, Stillwater, OK

Natalie Jakucyn
Mathematics Teacher
Glenbrook South High School, Glenview, IL

Zalman Usiskin
Professor of Education
The University of Chicago

www.WrightGroup.com

Printed in the United States of America.

Send all inquiries to:
Wright Group/McGraw-Hill
P.O. Box 812960
Chicago, IL 60681

ISBN- 978-0-07-618569-6
MHID- 0-07-618569-9

1 2 3 4 5 6 7 8 9 VHJ 14 13 12 11 10 09 08

UCSMP EVALUATION, EDITORIAL, AND PRODUCTION

Director of Evaluation
Denisse R. Thompson
Professor of Mathematics Education
University of South Florida, Tampa, FL

Coordinator of School Relations
Carol Siegel

Executive Managing Editor
Clare Froemel

Editorial Staff
John Wray (lead),
Emily Mokros, Kathryn Rich,
Adam Shapiro, Evan Jenkins,
Kathlyn Nguyen Ngo,
Melissa Yeung

Evaluation Consultant
Sharon L. Senk
Professor of Mathematics
Michigan State University, East Lansing, MI

Evaluation Assistants
Sophia Zhang, Gladys Mitchell,
Julian Owens, Shravani Pasupneti,
Zhuo Zhang

Production Coordinator
Benjamin R. Balskus

Production Assistants
Rachel Huddleston,
Nurit Kirshenbaum, Alex Liu,
Dylan Murphy, Gretchen Neidhardt,
S. L. Schieffer, Yayan Zhang

Technology Assistants
Luke I. Sandberg, Sean Schulte

Prior to the publication of *Pre-Transition Mathematics,* the following teachers and schools participated in evaluations of the trial version during 2006–2007:

Karen Hunt
Foster Elementary School
Ludington, Michigan

Jenny Adesso
Kilbourne Middle School
Worthington, Ohio

Ruth Janusz
Nichols Middle School
Evanston, Illinois

Trisha Pendill
Willmar Junior High School
Willmar, Minnesota

Deborah Heeres
Northern Michigan Christian School
McBain, Michigan

Barbara Dennett
Sanborn Regional Middle School
Newton, New Hampshire

Katrina Salaam
North Kenwood/Oakland Charter School
Chicago, Illinois

Joshuah Thurbee
University of Chicago Charter School
Woodlawn Campus
Chicago, Illinois

Erika Mortensen
University of Chicago Charter School
Woodlawn Campus
Chicago, Illinois

Tracy Beard
Ben Franklin Elementary School
Indiana, Pennsylvania

UCSMP The University of Chicago School Mathematics Project

The University of Chicago School Mathematics Project (UCSMP) is a long-term project designed to improve school mathematics in Grades Pre-K–12. UCSMP began in 1983 with a 6-year grant from the Amoco Foundation. Additional funding has come from the National Science Foundation, the Ford Motor Company, the Carnegie Corporation of New York, the Stuart Foundation, the General Electric Foundation, GTE, Citicorp/Citibank, the Exxon Educational Foundation, the Illinois Board of Higher Education, the Chicago Public Schools, from royalties, and from publishers of UCSMP materials.

From 1983 to 1987, the director of UCSMP was Paul Sally, Professor of Mathematics. Since 1987, the director has been Zalman Usiskin, Professor of Education.

UCSMP *Pre-Transition Mathematics*

The text *Pre-Transition Mathematics* has been developed by the Secondary Component of the project, and constitutes the core of the first year in a seven-year middle and high school mathematics curriculum. The names of the seven texts around which these years are built are:

- *Pre-Transition Mathematics*
- *Transition Mathematics*
- *Algebra*
- *Geometry*
- *Advanced Algebra*
- *Functions, Statistics, and Trigonometry*
- *Precalculus and Discrete Mathematics*

Why a Third Edition?

Since the second edition of UCSMP, there has been a general increase in the performance of students coming into middle school due to a combination of increased expectations and the availability of improved curricular materials for the elementary grades. The UCSMP third edition is more ambitious and takes advantage of the increased knowledge students bring to the classroom.

These increased expectations and the increased levels of testing that have gone along with those expectations are requiring a broad-based, reality-oriented, and easy-to-comprehend approach to mathematics. UCSMP third edition materials were written to better accommodate these factors.

The writing of the third edition of UCSMP is also motivated by the recent advances in technology both inside and outside the classroom, coupled with the widespread availability of computers with Internet access at school and at home.

Another factor for the continued existence of UCSMP materials for middle school is the increase in the number of students taking a full course in algebra before the ninth grade. These students will have four years of mathematics beyond algebra before calculus and other college-level mathematics. UCSMP is the only middle school curriculum which is designed so that average students are ready to take algebra in 8th grade. Thousands of schools have used the first and second editions and have noted success in student achievement and in teaching practices. Research from these schools shows that the UCSMP materials work.

Why *Pre-Transition Mathematics*?

Since the first edition of the UCSMP curriculum for grades 7–12, some middle schools asked for a text to precede *Transition Mathematics* in the style of that book. This is that text. It takes advantage of what we have learned from the widespread use both of *Transition Mathematics* and of *Everyday Mathematics* grades 5 and 6. It is designed to take a student from *Everyday Mathematics* grade 5 or another strong 5th-grade curriculum into *Transition Mathematics* and for some students, it is an appropriate text to follow *Everyday Mathematics* grade 6 or another 6th-grade text.

The content and questions of this book have been carefully sequenced to provide a smooth path from arithmetic to algebra, and from the visual world and arithmetic to geometry. We have moved some of the material in earlier editions of *Transition Mathematics* into this course because students now enter 6th grade better prepared than in the past and can handle this material one year earlier. Among that material are the models for operations and work on measurement. At the same time we have organized the material to ensure that students finishing this course have had work with fractions, experience with technology, and dealings with data that are assumed in *Transition Mathematics*. It is for this reason that this book is entitled *Pre-Transition Mathematics*.

The previous editions of UCSMP courses introduced many features that have come now to be deemed essential in courses at this level. There is **wider scope**, including significant amounts of geometry, integrated with the applied arithmetic and algebra that is customary, to aid students who finish algebra and yet lack enough prior knowledge to succeed in geometry. These topics are not isolated as separate units of study or enrichment but are connected to measurement, probability, and statistics. A **real-world orientation** has guided both the selection of content and its applications. Applications are essential because being able to do mathematics is of little use to an individual unless he or she can apply that content. We ask students to **read mathematics**, because students must read to understand mathematics in later courses and learn to read technical matter in the world at large. The use of **new and powerful technology** is integrated throughout. *Graphing calculator* use is assumed and introduced early as a pattern-finding and a problem-solving tool. The use of *spreadsheets* and *dynamic geometry systems* is also found throughout the materials.

Four dimensions of understanding are emphasized: skill in carrying out various algorithms; developing and using mathematics properties and relationships; applying mathematics in realistic situations; and representing or picturing mathematical concepts. We call this the SPUR approach: **S**kills, **P**roperties, **U**ses, **R**epresentations.

The **book organization** is designed to maximize the acquisition of both skills and concepts. Ideas introduced in a lesson are reinforced through Review questions in succeeding lessons. This daily review feature allows students several nights to learn and practice important concepts and skills. Then, at the end of each chapter, a carefully focused Self-Test and a Chapter Review, each keyed to objectives in all the dimensions of understanding, are used to solidify performance of skills and concepts from the chapter so that they may be applied later with confidence. Finally, to increase retention, important ideas are reviewed in later chapters.

Comments about these materials are welcomed. Please address them to:

UCSMP
The University of Chicago
6030 S. Ellis Avenue
Chicago, IL 60637
ucsmp@uchicago.edu
773-702-1130

Contents

Chapter 3 Using Addition 

Chapter 4 Using Subtraction

Chapter 7 398
Using Division

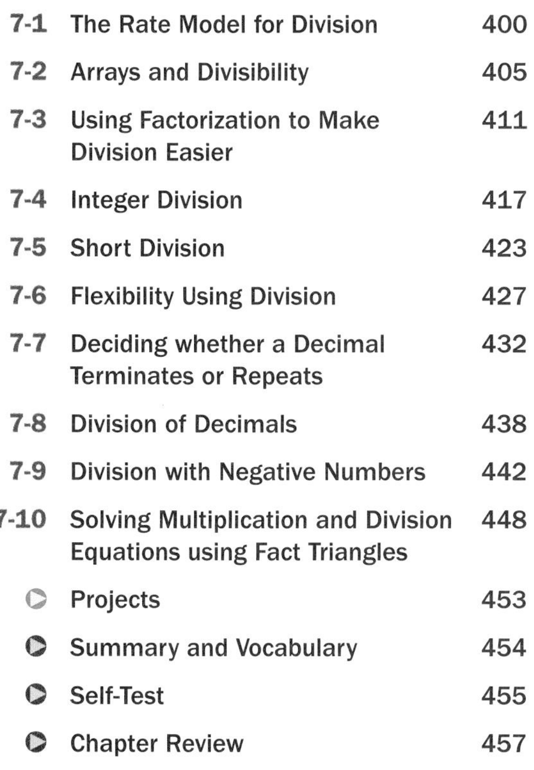

Chapter 8 460
Ratio and Proportion

Chapter 9 512
Area and Volume

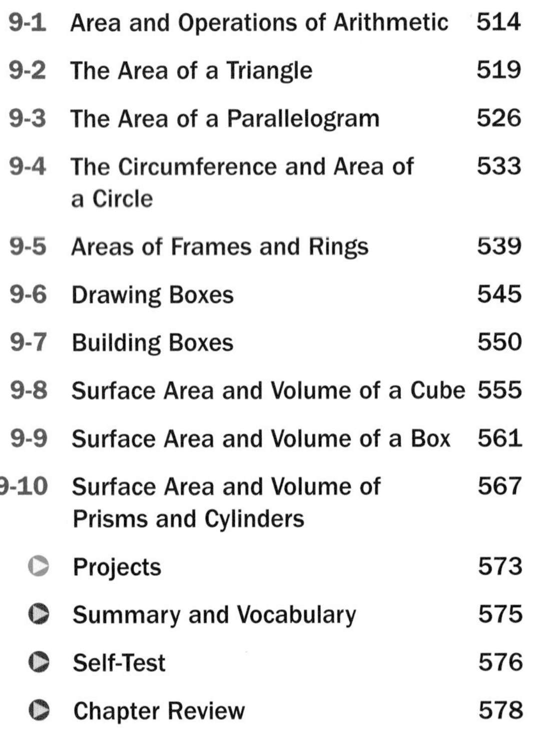

Chapter 10 584
Probability

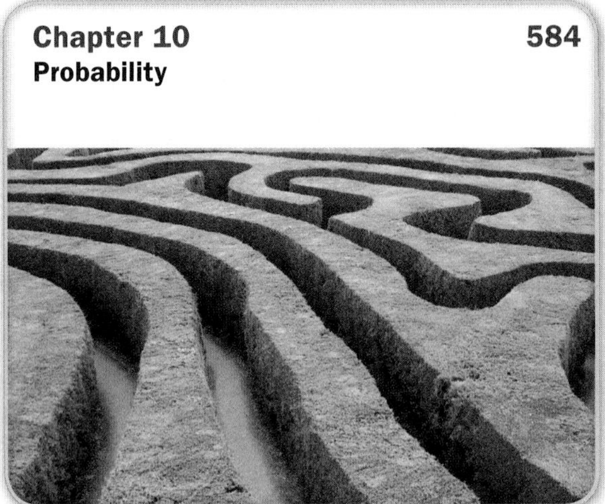

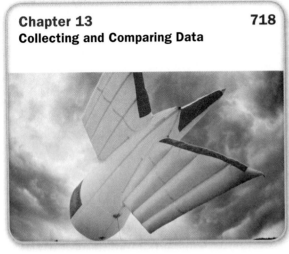

To the Student: Getting Started

Welcome to *Pre-Transition Mathematics*. It is a new book written as an introduction to middle school mathematics. It was written for you.

This year you will work with all kinds of numbers: integers and fractions, percents, and positive as well as negative numbers. You will see how numbers, measurements, and statistics are used in stories, in reports, on the Internet, at school, at home, and at people's work places. You will also continue to learn about geometric figures, and you will see some of the simple ideas of algebra.

Studying Mathematics

Learning how to learn mathematics is important not only in this book but in all the future mathematics you will study. At the end of this year, you should be able to learn mathematics more easily on your own. In previous classes, your teacher may have explained the ideas in a lesson. This year you will take more responsibility for learning mathematics by reading the book, by doing problems, and by working with other students. Of course, you aren't expected to learn everything all by yourself.

The word DART can help you learn.

Do
Ask
Read
Try

DO The more problems you do, the more math you will know. Each lesson has questions. Each chapter has review problems. Lessons include *Activities* and *Games* that you can work on alone or with other students.

ASK When you do not understand something, ask math questions of your teacher, your classmates, your friends, or your parents. You can learn to ask good questions. Explaining what you have already tried is a good start. Describing exactly what is puzzling to you can also be helpful. ("What does this mean?" is a good question. "Will you show me how to do it?" is not a good question.) Sometimes just thinking about how you would ask a good question is enough to give you the answer.

READ Reading a mathematics book is different from reading a novel, a newspaper, or a web page. You must be an active reader. Have pencil, paper, and calculator handy as you read. Try to write the solutions to examples, and take notes on new vocabulary. Pay careful attention to drawings and symbols. Do the "Quiz Yourself" questions (QY) and complete the Guided Examples.

TRY If you can't answer a question right away, don't give up! There are many things you can try. Read the problem again. Underline the part of the problem that states the question. Look back at the reading to see if there is a property, example, or explanation that gives you a clue how to start. If you still can't do the problem, go on to the rest of your math work. Sometimes working on a different problem will give you an idea how to solve the one that stumped you.

If you DART, you can hit the bull's eye!

What Tools Do You Need for this Book?

The first tool you need for this course is your brain. When you work, you should have your whole brain working on math, not part of it following a TV program, listening to lyrics of a new song, or talking on the phone.

You need some other tools to do any mathematics. The most basic tools are paper, pencils, and erasers. In addition you need equipment for drawing and measuring.

We recommend you have the following equipment:

- **Ruler** (marked in both centimeters and inches, clear plastic)
- **Protractor** (circular or semicircular, clear plastic)
- **Compass** (that tightens with a screw and holds regular pencils)
- **Graph paper**
- **Graphing calculator**

Getting Off to a Good Start

Spend some time looking through this book. The questions that follow will help you become familiar with *Pre-Transition Mathematics.*

Questions

COVERING THE IDEAS

In 1–5, look back at this introduction to find the answers.

1. What does DART stand for?
2. If you do not understand something, what is a good question you might ask someone for help?
3. List two things you should do if you can't solve a problem.
4. What is the most important tool for mathematics?
5. List three other tools you need for this course.

KNOWING YOUR TEXTBOOK

In 6–15, answer the questions by looking at the Table of Contents, the lessons, the chapters in the book, and the material at the back of this book.

6. In what lesson did you find circle graphs?
7. a. What are the four categories of questions at the end of each lesson?

   b. What word is formed from the first letters of each category?
8. Where can you find the answers to the "Quiz Yourself" (QY) questions?
9. What is a Guided Example?
10. Suppose you have finished questions in Lesson 2-7.

    a. On what page can you find answers to check your work?

    b. To which questions are answers given?
11. a. The review section at the end of each chapter contains what four parts?

    b. What word is formed from the first letters of each part?
12. Look at the Self-Test at the end of a chapter. What should you do after taking the Self-Test?
13. Where is the Glossary and what does it contain?
14. Find the Index. On which page would you find a picture of the dome of Santa Maria del Fiore in Florence, Italy?
15. Where in your book can you find the directions to the game referenced in a lesson?

REVIEW

16. List two math ideas you remember from last year.
17. What helped you learn math last year?

Chapter 1 Some Uses of Integers and Fractions

Contents

In *Romeo and Juliet*, Shakespeare wrote, "What's in a name? That which we call a rose by any other name would smell as sweet." This is a way of saying that you can name a thing in different ways without changing its meaning.

In mathematics, there are many ways to name the same quantity. For example, you can write and say the number $1\frac{2}{3}$ in different ways:

English	one and two thirds
Hebrew	אחד ושני שליש
German	ein und zwei drittels
Mandarin Chinese	一又三分之二
Spanish	uno y dos tercios
French	un et deux tiers
American Sign Language	(one) → (two) ↓ (thirds)

$1\frac{2}{3}$ can also be represented by graphs or pictures, as shown below.

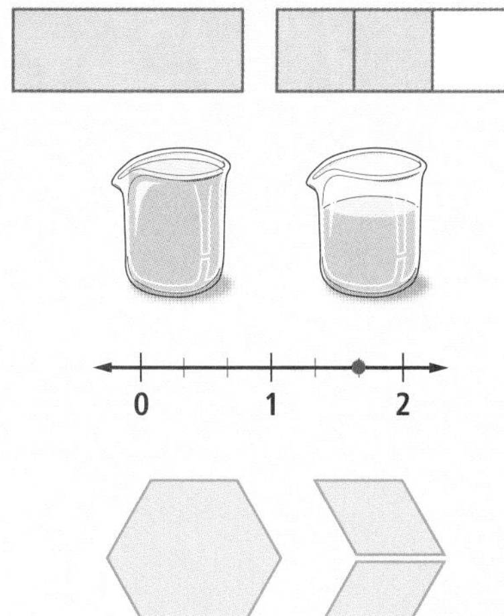

By using smaller units, you can rename $1\frac{2}{3}$ of things.

$1\frac{2}{3}$ years = 1 year, 8 months

$1\frac{2}{3}$ hours = 1 hour, 40 minutes

$1\frac{2}{3}$ feet = 1 foot, 8 inches

The mixed number $1\frac{2}{3}$ can also be written as $1.\overline{6}$, $\frac{5}{3}$, or $166\frac{2}{3}\%$, or as the expressions $2 - \frac{1}{3}$, $1 + \frac{2}{3}$, or $\frac{18}{27} + 1^2$. All of these are said to be *equal*.

What's in a name? In this chapter, you will explore how integers and fractions are named and used in different situations.

Lesson

1-1 Numbers for Counting

Vocabulary

whole numbers
decimal system
base-10 system
counting unit

▶ **BIG IDEA** The system of writing whole numbers as 0, 1, 2, ... 9, 10, 11, 12, ... 99, 100, 101, and so on, is called the *base-10* or the *decimal system*.

You probably learned to count using the numbers 1, 2, 3, 4, 5, . . ., even before kindergarten. Zero is also an important number. For example, a team may score 0 runs in a baseball game. The numbers 0, 1, 2, 3, 4, 5, . . . are called **whole numbers.** For example, 698 is a whole number but $1\frac{1}{3}$ is not.

Mental Math

a. What number is one more than 1,000,000?

b. What number is one less than 1,000,000?

c. What number is ten more than 1,000,000?

d. What number is ten less than 1,000,000?

The Base-10 Decimal System

The Greek prefix *deca-* means 10. Our number system is called the **decimal system,** or **base-10 system,** because any whole number can be written using the *ten* digits from 0 through 9. The first ten whole numbers require only one digit.

0, 1, 2, 3, 4, 5, 6, 7, 8, 9

The next ninety whole numbers require two digits.

10, 11, 12, . . ., 97, 98, 99

The next nine hundred whole numbers can be written using three digits.

100, 101, 102, . . ., 997, 998, 999

In the base-10 system, the position of each digit has a value. The place value of each digit is 10 times the value of the digit to its right. For example, in the 3-digit number 243, the 2 has a value of 200, the 4 has a value of 40, and the 3 has a value of 3. The base-10 blocks picture 243 below.

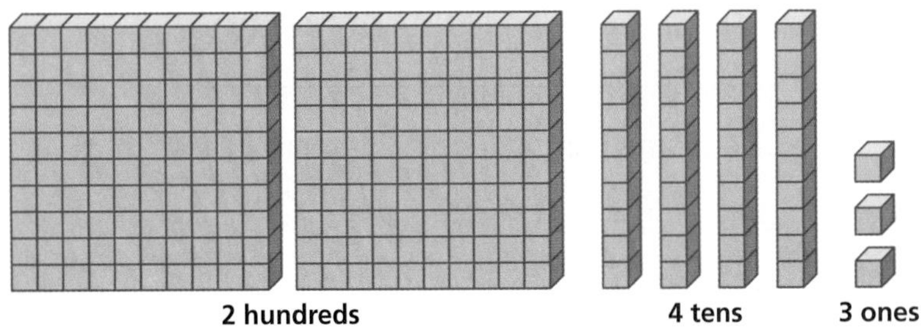

QUIZ YOURSELF 1

What is the value of the digit 7 in the number 372?

"Quiz Yourself" (QY) questions are designed to help you follow the reading. You should try to answer each Quiz Yourself question before reading on. They will appear in this main column or in the side column at the right. The answer to the Quiz Yourself is found at the end of the lesson.

By using more digits, very large numbers can be written. The Central Intelligence Agency cites the Chinese population in mid-2007 at 1321851888 people. To make this number easier to read, groups of three digits are separated by commas: 1,321,851,888.

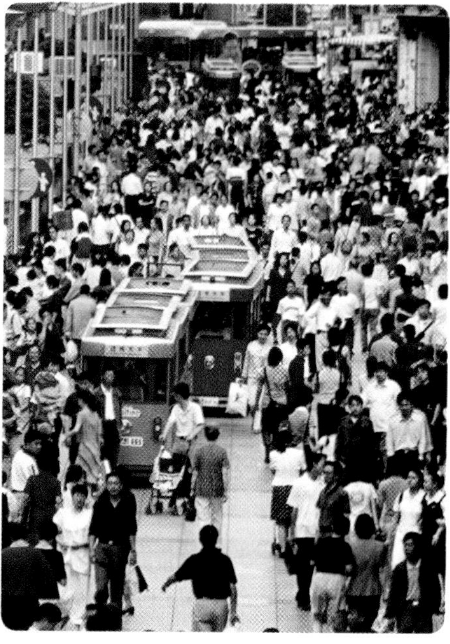
Pedestrians fill the crowded streets of Shanghai—China's most populous city.

Reading Numbers Written in Base 10

To read the population of China, or to write it in words, you need to include place value. Each digit has a place.

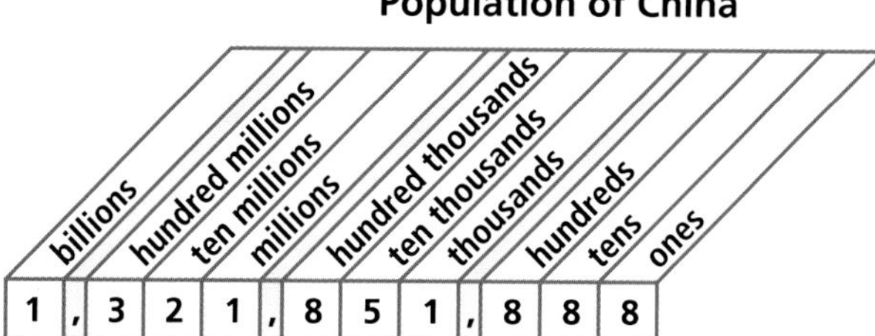

To read this number, read each 3-digit group as a regular 3-digit number. Then follow it by its group name. Here are the first seven group names:

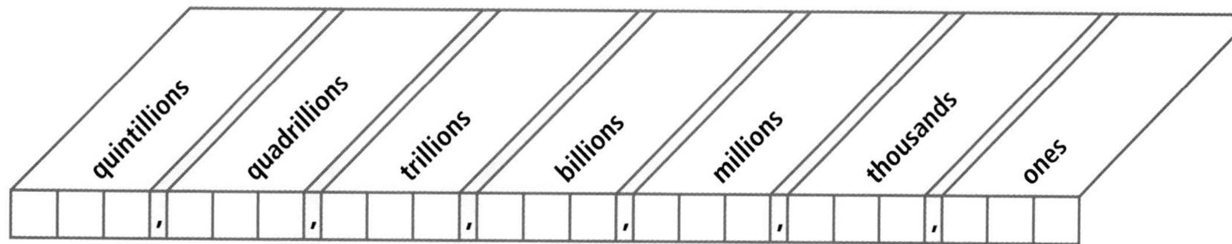

So the population of China is read, "one billion, three hundred twenty-one million, eight hundred fifty-one thousand, eight hundred eighty-eight." This is also how the population is written in words.

QUIZ YOURSELF 2

What is the value of the digit 5 in the population of China?

The population of China is an example of a *count.* The most basic use of numbers is a count. Counts are always whole numbers, never fractions. Every count has a **counting unit,** the object that is counted.

For population, the counting unit is *people.* For a box of 300 paper clips, the count is 300 and the counting unit is *paper clips.*

You write numbers using Hindu-Arabic numerals.

0, 1, 2, 3, 4, 5, 6, 7, 8, 9

But you are more likely to say a number in words.

zero, one, two, three, four, five, six, seven, eight, nine

Example 1

Write 56,440,623 in words.

Solution Think of the digits in each group.

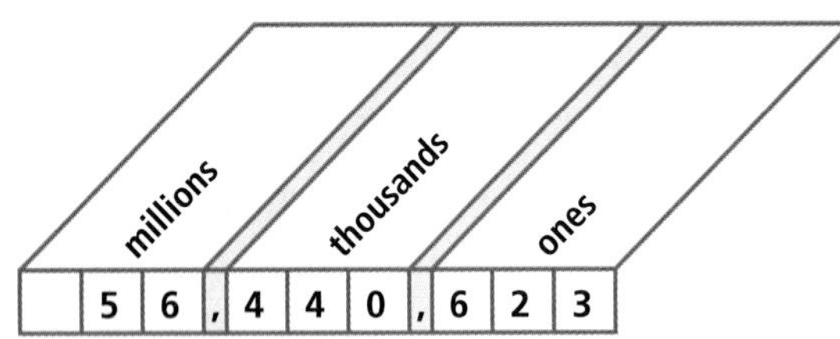

56 is in the millions group.
440 is in the thousands group.
623 is in the ones group.

So the number in words is fifty-six million, four hundred forty thousand, six hundred twenty-three.

▸ READING MATH

In the solutions to the examples, you will notice text that looks like handwriting. This is a sample of what you might write as a solution to the example.

QUIZ YOURSELF 3

What is 400,620,000 written in words?

Words for numbers are used in writing checks, in stories, and in legal documents. Sometimes you will read a number with numerals and words.

Example 2

According to *Number Freaking: How to Change the World with Delightfully Surreal Statistics,* the human body contains between 50 and 100 trillion cells. Write 50 trillion as a decimal.

Solution One trillion requires 12 places for ones, thousands, millions, and billions. So the decimal for 50 trillion is 50,000,000,000,000.

Now you can play *Number Top-It*. The directions for this game are on page G3 at the back of your book.

Questions

COVERING THE IDEAS

These questions cover the content of the lesson. If you cannot answer a Covering the Ideas question, you should go back to the reading for help in obtaining an answer.

1. How many digits are used in the decimal system?
2. How many whole numbers use exactly two digits?
3. Why might you write a number using digits instead of words?
4. Why might you write a number with words instead of digits?
5. **True or False** A number is always written with a decimal point.

In 6–8, write the number in base 10.

6. four thousand, eight hundred twenty-four
7. ten million, forty-six thousand, nine hundred eight
8. sixty-five billion

In 9–11, identify the count and the counting unit in the sentence.

9. There are about 9,700 species of birds in the world.
10. Many interstate highways have four lanes.
11. There are about 10 quintillion insects alive on our planet.

This is a Waxwing eating rowan berriers.

In 12 and 13, write each number in words.

12. 8,102
13. 56,000,000
14. Name the digit in the indicated place of the number 836,710,429.
    a. ten thousands
    b. hundred millions
    c. tens

APPLYING THE MATHEMATICS

These questions extend the content of the lesson. You should study the examples and explanations if you cannot answer the question. For some questions, you can check your answers with the ones in the Selected Answers section at the back of this book.

15. In the decimal system, write the largest whole number with
    a. four digits. b. five digits. c. ten digits.

16. In the decimal system, how many whole numbers have

a. exactly four digits?

b. four or fewer digits?

c. exactly five digits?

d. five or fewer digits?

17. a. Write the smallest whole number in the decimal system that uses each of the ten digits exactly once.

b. Write your answer to Part a in words.

18. The cost for television advertising partly depends on the number of households that watch a program. Here are the average number of households who watched several popular shows in June, 2007.

Television Show	Number of Households
Wheel of Fortune	9,868,000
America's Got Talent	11,818,000
Entertainment Tonight	6,791,000
Jeopardy!	8,048,000

Source: Nielsen Media Research

a. Which show should have the second highest advertising cost?

b. Which show should have the least advertising cost?

A crowd eagerly watches a taping of the popular TV game show, *Wheel of Fortune.*

REVIEW

Every lesson contains review questions to practice ideas you have studied earlier.

19. Suppose that $p = 20$ and $q = 4$. Find the value of each expression. **(Previous Course)**

a. $p + q$

b. $p - q$

c. $p \div q$

d. $p + 43$

e. $q \div 1$

f. $p \times q$

20. Students in a class were asked to name their birth months. Two students were born in January, six in March, four in April, three in May, nine in July, five in October, and four in November. **(Previous Course)**
    a. How many students were in the class?
    b. How many students were born in August?
    c. Display the given information in a bar graph.
    d. When Delsin read this problem, he felt that the numbers were unlikely to have come from a real class. Why do you think Delsin felt the way he did? Do you agree with Delsin?

EXPLORATION

These questions ask you to explore topics related to the lesson. Sometimes you will need to use references found in a library or on the Internet.

21. Each of the words below does not refer to a specific number. Look in a dictionary or on the Internet for the meaning of the word.
    a. zillion
    b. jillion
    c. bazillion or gazillion

22. Write the numbers from one to twenty in a language other than English.

23. The way we write numbers today comes from the ways that Hindus and Arabs wrote numbers about 1,200 years ago. Some people believe that the original shapes of their numerals were based on a square and its diagonals. The diagram below shows how the number 3 can be formed.

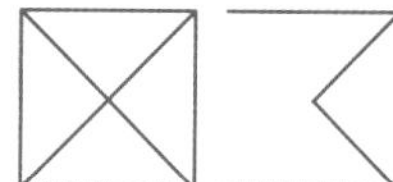

Use parts of the square and its diagonals to write the other digits.

QUIZ YOURSELF ANSWERS

1. 70

2. 50,000 or fifty thousand

3. four hundred million, six hundred twenty thousand

Lesson 1-2

Dividing Segments into Parts

Vocabulary

line segment
endpoint
midpoint
numerator
denominator

▸ **BIG IDEA** The fraction $\frac{n}{d}$ can stand for n parts of a segment that has a total of d equal parts.

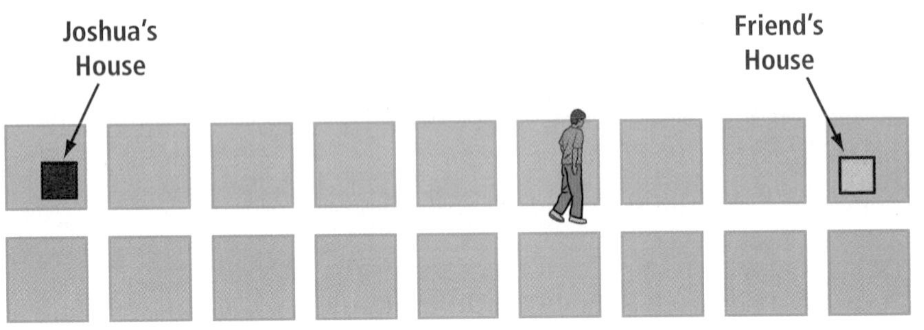

Mental Math

In a trip of 100 miles, what portion of the trip

a. remains if you have completed 30 miles?

b. remains if you have 75 miles to go?

Joshua leaves his house to visit a friend who lives seven blocks away. After walking five blocks, what part of the trip has Joshua completed? The answer is a fraction. It can be pictured using a line segment. Using line segments to represent fractions is explored in this lesson. You will picture Joshua's trip on number line in Quiz Yourself 2.

Splitting a Trip into Parts

A **line segment** (or **segment**) AB consists of two points A and B and all points on the line between A and B. The symbol for this line segment is $\overline{AB}$ and is read, "segment AB." A and B are called the **endpoints** of the segment.

Think of the segment below as a road that goes straight from Town A to Town B. When you are exactly in the middle, you have gone one-half of the way from A to B. This is the **midpoint** of $\overline{AB}$. You can indicate the midpoint by labeling it with the fraction $\frac{1}{2}$, as shown below.

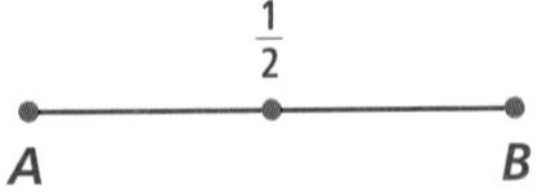

When the trip from A to B is split into 3 equal parts, each part is one-third of the trip. Two parts equal two-thirds of the trip. So we put $\frac{1}{3}$ and $\frac{2}{3}$ over the points that split the trip into three equal parts, as shown on the next page.

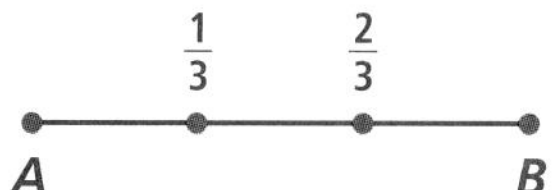

You can split a trip into any number of equal parts. Sometimes the separation into parts is shown with *tick marks.* Tick marks are small vertical segments similar to those shown on a ruler. Here $\overline{AB}$ is drawn with tick marks at every tenth.

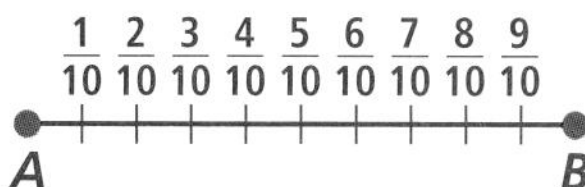

QUIZ YOURSELF 1

a. How many tick marks are needed to separate $\overline{AB}$ above into 10 parts?
b. How many tick marks are needed to separate $\overline{AB}$ into 100 parts?

Fractions and Parts of Wholes

Recall that the top number in a fraction is called the **numerator** and the bottom number is called the **denominator.** A fraction with a whole number as its numerator and a greater whole number as its denominator can be thought of as the part of a trip that has been completed.

$$\frac{\text{number of parts completed}}{\text{total number of equal parts}} = \text{fraction or portion of trip completed}$$

For example, if you have completed $\frac{11}{15}$ of a trip, you have completed 11 parts of a trip that has been split into 15 equal parts.

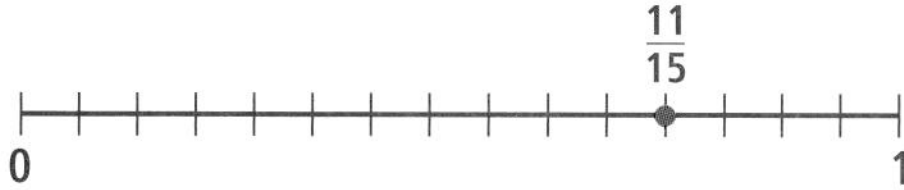

If you have completed $\frac{3}{8}$ of a trip, you have completed 3 parts of a trip that has been split into 8 equal parts.

QUIZ YOURSELF 2

a. Represent Joshua's trip from the beginning of this lesson with a line segment.
b. What fraction of the trip had he completed after walking 5 blocks?

Fractions Equal to 0 and to 1

Suppose a trip is divided into 5 parts. If you have not started the trip yet, then you have completed 0 parts.

$$\frac{\text{0 parts completed}}{\text{5 parts in all}} = \text{0 portion of trip completed}$$

When you have completed all parts of the trip, then the numerator and denominator of the fraction will be equal. So, if you have completed $\frac{9}{9}$ of a trip, you have completed 9 parts of a trip that has been split into 9 equal parts. This equals one whole.

$$\frac{\text{9 parts completed}}{\text{9 parts total}} = 1$$

What about fractions like $\frac{7}{4}$ or $\frac{100}{3}$, in which the numerator is greater than the denominator? You will explore these fractions in Lesson 1-6.

Finding the Length of a Part of a Segment

It is natural to want to find the length of a part of a trip. Suppose a trip is 54 miles long. When you have gone halfway, then you have traveled $\frac{1}{2}$ of 54 miles. This is the same as dividing 54 miles into 2 equal parts.

$$\begin{aligned}\tfrac{1}{2} \text{ of 54 miles} &= \tfrac{1}{2} \times \text{54 miles}\\ &= \text{54 miles} \div 2\\ &= \text{27 miles}\end{aligned}$$

The average vehicle in the U.S. is driven 12,494 miles per year.

Source: *The World Almamac*

To find the length of one-third of the 54-mile trip, multiply 54 by $\frac{1}{3}$ or divide 54 by 3.

$$\begin{aligned}\tfrac{1}{3} \text{ of 54 miles} &= \tfrac{1}{3} \times \text{54 miles}\\ &= \text{54 miles} \div 3\\ &= \text{18 miles}\end{aligned}$$

Dividing is easy when the number of parts divides evenly into the total length. But what should you do when the number of parts does not divide evenly into the total length? You will see how to answer questions like this when you study multiplication of fractions in Chapter 6.

QUIZ YOURSELF 3

a. What multiplication problem would you write to find $\frac{1}{4}$ of 60 miles?
b. What division problem would you write to find $\frac{1}{4}$ of 60 miles?
c. How many miles is this?

How Can You Accurately Split a Segment into Equal Parts?

You can use a sheet of notebook paper to split a segment into equal parts.

Activity 1

MATERIALS two thin straws or coffee stirrers, lined notebook paper, scissors

Divide a thin straw into five equal parts in two ways, first by guessing and then by using the lined notebook paper as a guide.

Step 1 Guessing as accurately as you can, divide a thin straw into fifths by putting four pencil marks on it. Carefully cut the straw at each pencil mark. Now stand the pieces on end to compare their lengths. Are the pieces the same length?

Step 2 Number the lines on a sheet of notebook paper starting at 0. Place another straw on the lined notebook paper. Hold one end of the straw on the top line 0 of the sheet. Move the other end until it falls on line 5. The lines of the paper now show how to mark the straw in five equal segments. Mark each fifth. Check your accuracy by cutting the straw at each mark and then standing the pieces on end to compare lengths.

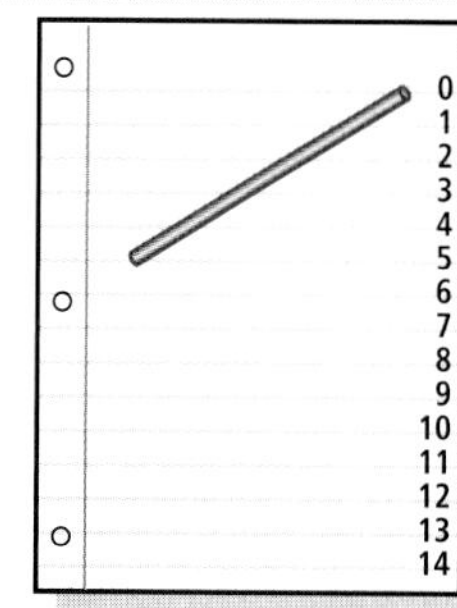

Was this method more accurate than the guesswork method? Each little piece of straw is $\frac{1}{5}$ of a full straw piece; two pieces would be $\frac{2}{5}$ of a full piece, and so on.

Activity 2 adapts the method of Activity 1 to divide a segment drawn on a sheet of paper.

Activity 2

MATERIALS lined notebook paper, unlined tracing paper

Samantha and Oscar disagree over which is greater, $\frac{2}{5}$ or $\frac{3}{7}$. Samantha says $\frac{2}{5}$ is greater. Oscar thinks $\frac{3}{7}$ is greater.

Step 1 To settle this disagreement, draw a line segment on a sheet of unlined paper.

Step 2 Place the sheet of unlined paper over the sheet of lined paper. Use the lined sheet as a gauge and mark $\frac{2}{5}$ of the segment.

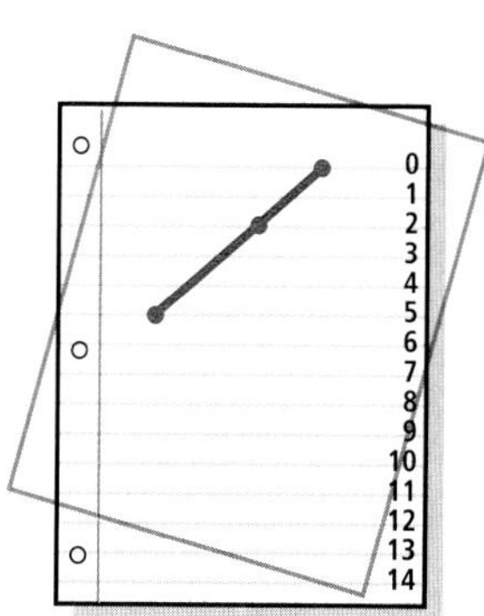

Step 3 Now mark $\frac{3}{7}$ of the segment you have drawn.

Step 4 Compare where the dots lie for $\frac{2}{5}$ and $\frac{3}{7}$. Who is correct, Samantha or Oscar?

Questions

COVERING THE IDEAS

In 1–3, trace the segment below. Using lined paper, divide the segment into the given number of equal parts. Use a different copy of the segment for each question.

1. 4 parts
2. 3 parts
3. 10 parts
4. A segment is divided into 12 equal parts.
   a. How many tick marks will there be between its endpoints?
   b. How many tick marks and endpoints will there be?
5. If the segment in Question 1 represents a length of 20 feet, what length does each part represent?
6. If the segment in Question 2 represents a length of 450 miles, what length does each part represent?

APPLYING THE MATHEMATICS

7. The Nelsons are going on a 200-mile driving trip. What fraction of the trip will they have completed when they have traveled
   a. 50 miles?
   b. 130 miles?
   c. What fraction of the trip will they have completed before they start?
   d. What fraction of the trip will they have completed when they have arrived at their destination?

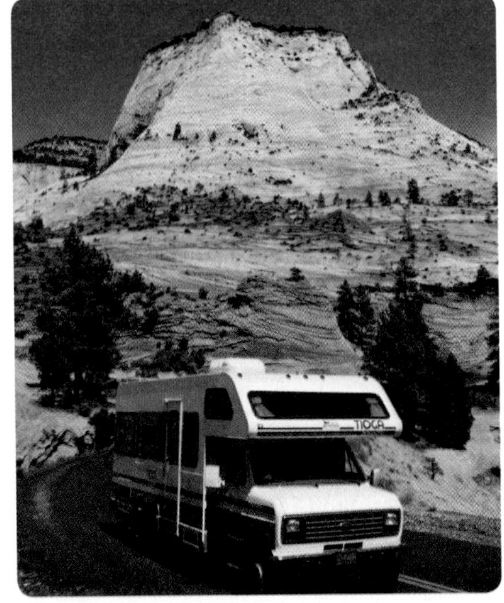

Zion National Park in Utah covers 229 square miles and is home to a wide variety of plant and animal life.

Source: U.S. National Park Service

8. A trip from Chicago to Boston takes about 18 hours by car.
   a. What fraction of the time of the trip would you complete after 11 hours?
   b. How many hours would you have traveled when you have completed $\frac{1}{3}$ of the time of the trip?

Four laps around a running track typically equals one mile.

9. Desiree and Alicia want to run one lap around the track. Desiree has run $\frac{1}{3}$ of the way around the track. Alicia has run $\frac{1}{4}$ of the way around the same track.
   a. Who has run farther?
   b. Explain why you think your answer to Part a is correct.

10. In Question 9, Desiree says that she still has $\frac{2}{3}$ of the lap to run.
    a. Is Desiree correct?
    b. How much of the track does Alicia still have to run?

11. On the circle below, there are 8 equally spaced points. The arrow indicates the *clockwise* direction (like a normal clock). The opposite direction is *counterclockwise*.

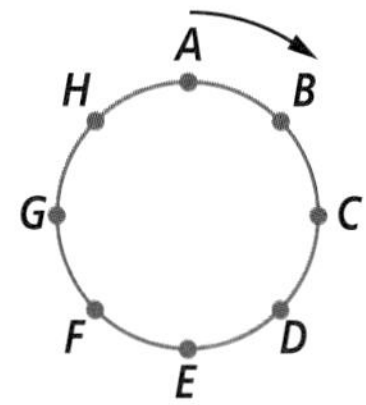

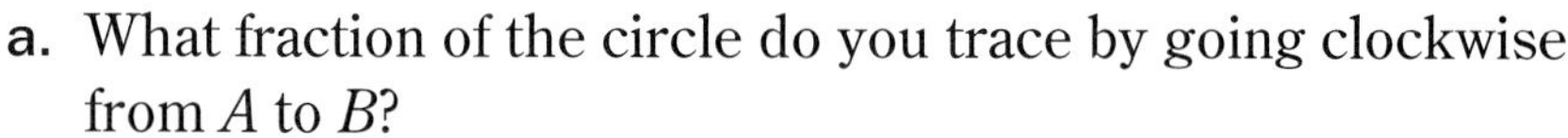

    a. What fraction of the circle do you trace by going clockwise from A to B?
    b. What fraction do you trace if you go counterclockwise from A to B?

REVIEW

12. Write the smallest whole number that does not have the digit 0, uses no digit twice, and has the given number of digits. **(Lesson 1-1)**
    a. 4 digits b. 5 digits c. 9 digits

13. A 2007 estimate of the populations of the countries of the world gave the results at the right for the 10 most populous countries (in alphabetical order). **(Lesson 1-1)**
    a. Order the countries from most to least populous.
    b. How many people live in the 5th most populous country? Write down this population in words.

Country	2007 Population
Bangladesh	150,448,339
Brazil	190,010,647
China	1,321,851,888
India	1,129,866,154
Indonesia	234,693,997
Japan	127,467,972
Nigeria	135,031,164
Pakistan	169,270,617
Russia	141,377,752
United States	301,139,947

Source: U.S. Census Bureau

14. Audrey and Basil collect stamps. Audrey has a stamps and Basil has b stamps. Answer the following in terms of a and b. **(Previous Course)**

a. How many stamps do they have together?

b. If Audrey collects 34 more stamps, how many will she have?

c. If Basil gives Audrey 20 of his stamps, how many stamps will each of them have? Include what Audrey collected in Part b.

The best way to store stamps is in a stamp album or on loose leaf paper in a binder.

Source: United States Post Office

EXPLORATION

15. Carmen's running coach assigns her an aerobic workout. The first 8 minutes Carmen runs 2,000 meters (2 km). The second 8 minutes she jogs half that distance. The third 8 minutes she power-walks half that distance. The fourth 8 minutes she walks half as far as that, and so on. The coach worries that if Carmen keeps up this pattern, she will never finish. At the end of an 8-minute stretch during which she covers barely a meter, she is still a meter from the finish line. Right then, she trips and falls over the finish line. For how long had Carmen been working out? How many kilometers do you think the coach required Carmen to cover?

QUIZ YOURSELF ANSWERS

1a. 9

1b. 99

2a. 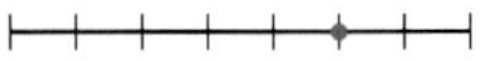

2b. $\frac{5}{7}$

3a. $\frac{1}{4} \times 60$

3b. $60 \div 4$

3c. 15 mi

Lesson 1-3 Measuring Length

Vocabulary

length

interval

mixed number

▸ **BIG IDEA** Short lengths in the U.S. Customary System are usually measured in multiples of $\frac{1}{2}$, $\frac{1}{4}$, $\frac{1}{8}$, $\frac{1}{16}$, or $\frac{1}{32}$ inch.

Mental Math

In each fraction below, tell whether the number 4 is the numerator or the denominator.

a. $\frac{4}{3}$

b. $\frac{2}{4}$

c. $\frac{4}{9}$

What is "Length"?

Length is the distance along a line or curve from one point to another. There are lengths of journeys, lengths of sides of rectangles, lengths of days, and so on.

Many words are used to describe lengths. Your *height* is the length of a segment from your feet to the top of your head. The *depth* of a swimming pool is a length from the top of the water to the bottom of the pool. The *distance* around your wrist is a length. The *width* of a sheet of paper is also a length! Any distance from one point to another is a length.

Rulers and tape measures are the most common instruments for measuring short lengths. Most rulers do not bend. This makes them reliable for measuring segments.

This ruler can measure short, straight segments.

Because tape measures bend, they can be used to measure the distance around your wrist or other curves. Lengths of time are usually measured with a clock or a stopwatch.

This tape measure can measure lengths around curves.

Measuring Lengths in Inches

A ruler can be thought of as a type of number line. The ruler below measures in inches. It is actual size. Recall that the marks on a number line are called tick marks. The distance between two tick marks is called the **interval** of the ruler.

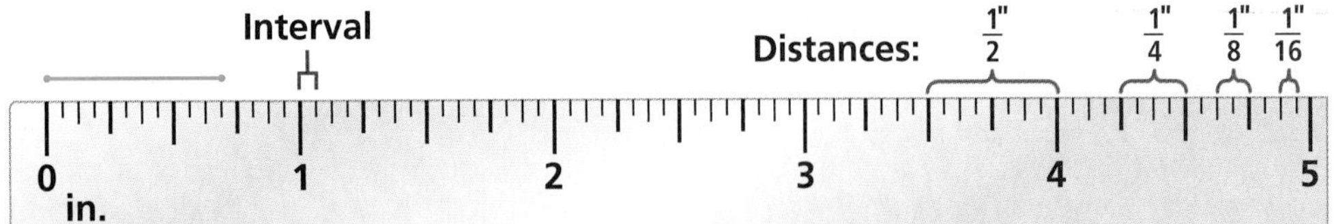

The tick marks on the ruler above divide each inch into 16 equal parts. Counting the number of parts, the length of the green segment above the ruler is $\frac{11}{16}$ inch. This means the segment is between 0 and 1 inch long; it is closer to 1 inch than to 0 inches.

Lengths and Mixed Numbers

A number that is written as the sum of a whole number and a fraction, with no symbol between, is a **mixed number.** Lengths in inches greater than 1 are often written as mixed numbers.

$$1\frac{1}{2} = 1 + \frac{1}{2}$$

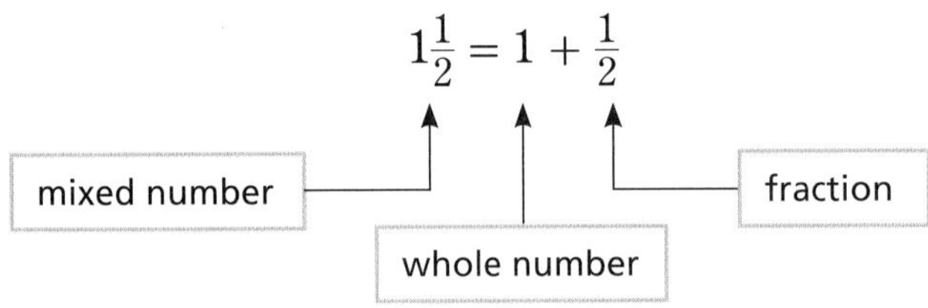

Example 1

Here is a segment whose length is longer than 1 inch. What is its length?

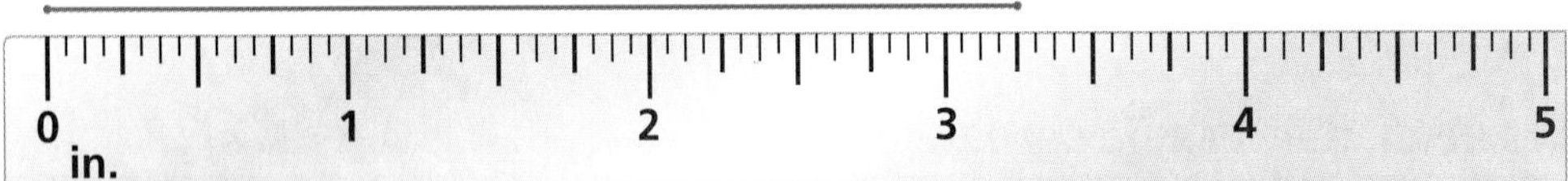

Solution The segment is longer than 3 inches, but shorter than 4 inches. It ends at the $\frac{1}{4}$-inch mark between 3 and 4. The segment is 3 inches plus $\frac{1}{4}$ inch long. It is $3\frac{1}{4}$ inches long.

The mixed number $3\frac{1}{4}$ is equal to $3 + \frac{1}{4}$. The number $3\frac{1}{4}$ is the sum of the whole number 3 and the fraction $\frac{1}{4}$. Every mixed number can be expressed as the sum of a whole number and a fraction between 0 and 1.

Measuring to a Desired Accuracy

Unlike a counting unit, a unit of measure can be split into smaller intervals. With intervals smaller than $\frac{1}{16}$ inch, say $\frac{1}{32}$ inch or $\frac{1}{64}$ inch, you can get a more accurate measurement. When you measure, first decide on the level of accuracy you want. This tells you what interval to use. Then pick the closest appropriate measure.

Example 2

Measure the segment below to the nearest $\frac{1}{2}$, $\frac{1}{4}$, and $\frac{1}{8}$ inch.

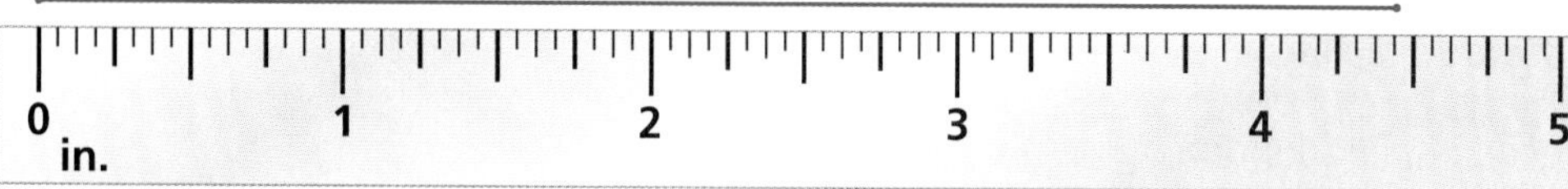

Solution To the nearest $\frac{1}{2}$ inch, the segment is $4\frac{1}{2}$ inches long. To the nearest $\frac{1}{4}$ inch, the segment is $4\frac{2}{4}$ inches long. To the nearest $\frac{1}{8}$ inch, the segment is $4\frac{4}{8}$ inches long.

STOP QUIZ YOURSELF

How long is the segment in Example 2 to the nearest $\frac{1}{16}$ inch?

Units of Length in the Customary System

In some situations, you may need to use a unit longer than an inch. In the United States, units of length longer than the inch are a *foot*, a *yard*, or a *mile*. These units are part of the *customary system of measurement.* You should learn the relationships among these units and their abbreviations.

1 foot (ft) = 12 inches (in.)
1 yard (yd) = 3 feet = 36 inches
1 mile (mi) = 1,760 yards = 5,280 feet

Because 1 foot = 12 inches, a foot divided into 12 intervals is marked in inches. Therefore, each inch is $\frac{1}{12}$ of a foot. Similarly, because there are 5,280 feet in 1 mile, 1 foot = $\frac{1}{5{,}280}$ mile.

1 inch = $\frac{1}{12}$ foot = $\frac{1}{36}$ yard
1 foot = $\frac{1}{5{,}280}$ mile
1 yard = $\frac{1}{1{,}760}$ mile

Measuring Length in Feet and Inches

Lengths are sometimes stated in feet and inches. The height of a person might be reported as "5 feet, 1 inch," rather than as "61 inches." Often this is written with the symbols for feet (') and inches ("), like 5'1".

$$5\text{ feet, }1\text{ inch} = 5\text{ ft, }1\text{ in.} = 5'1''$$

Example 3

A door is 90 inches high. What is this in feet and inches?

Solution Since there are 12 inches in each foot, divide 90 by 12.

There are different procedures for performing division. You have probably used one of the procedures shown here.

$$\begin{array}{rr|l} & & 7\text{ R }6 \\ 12) & 90 & \\ & -60 & 5 \\ \hline & 30 & \\ & -24 & 2 \\ \hline & 6 & 7 \end{array} \qquad \text{or} \qquad \begin{array}{rr} & 7 \\ 12) & 90 \\ & -84 \\ \hline & 6 \end{array}$$

This means that $90 \div 12 = 7$ remainder 6, or 7'6". The door is 7 feet, 6 inches high.

GUIDED

Example 4

A Guided Example is an example in which some, but not all, of the work is shown. You should try to complete the example before reading on. Answers to Guided Examples are in the Selected Answers at the back of the book.

Mrs. Chung is ordering a new countertop for her kitchen. The countertop measures 5 feet, 4 inches in length. How many inches is this?

Solution First find how many inches are in 5 feet. Fill in the blanks. There are __?__ inches in each foot, so multiply.

__?__ × __?__ in. = __?__ inches in 5 feet

Now add the 4 inches.

__?__ in. + __?__ in. = __?__ inches of countertop

Countertops for homes come in all sorts of materials like granite, ceramic tile, marble, or wood.

Example 5

You are flying in a jet when the pilot tells you that the plane is cruising at 35,000 feet above sea level. How many miles and feet is this?

Solution Since there are 5,280 feet in 1 mile, divide 35,000 by 5,280. Using a calculator that will display the answer with a remainder, you can see that

35,000 feet ÷ 5,280 = 6 remainder 3,320.

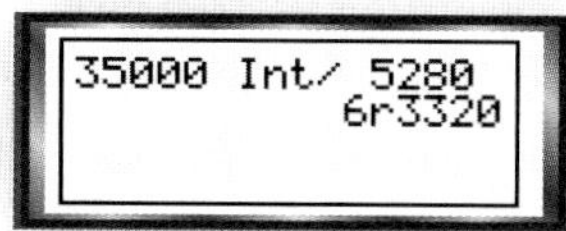

You are 6 miles, 3,320 feet above sea level.

A typical commercial airliner cruises between 30,000–45,000 feet above sea level. In 1976, a military jet set a world record for a sustained flight with an altitude of 85,069 feet above sea level.

Source: Lockheed Martin

Activity

MATERIALS inch ruler, inch tape measure

Work with a partner and complete the tables.

Measurement	Desired Accuracy	Value (in.)
Width of this book	To nearest $\frac{1}{8}$ inch	?
Height of this book	To nearest $\frac{1}{4}$ inch	?
Thickness of this book	To nearest $\frac{1}{16}$ inch	?

Measurement	Value (in.)	Value (ft, in.)
Height of your desk	?	? ft, ? in.
Width of the doorway	?	? ft, ? in.
Height of your partner	?	? ft, ? in.

Questions

COVERING THE IDEAS

1. Find the length of the segment just above the ruler to the nearest
   a. inch.
   b. $\frac{1}{2}$ in.
   c. $\frac{1}{4}$ in.
   d. $\frac{1}{8}$ in.
   e. $\frac{1}{16}$ in.

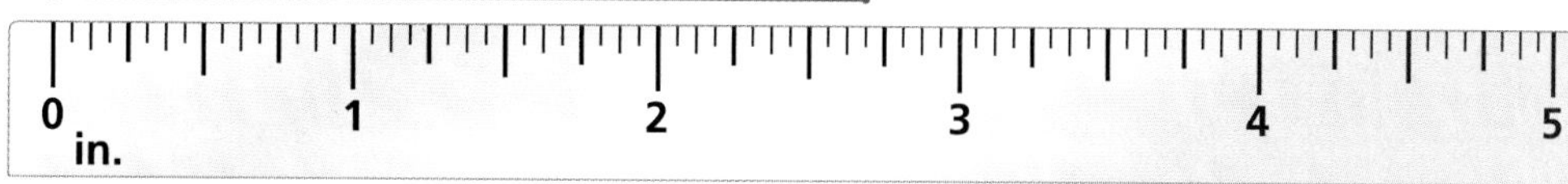

In 2 and 3, the given number is between which two whole numbers?

2. $4\frac{7}{8}$
3. $1\frac{1}{4}$

4. **Fill in the Blanks** The mixed number $2\frac{5}{8}$ is the sum of the whole number __?__ and the fraction __?__.

5. Name three customary units used to measure length.

6. One foot is what fraction of one yard?

7. One yard is what fraction of one mile?

In 8 and 9, measure each segment to the nearest

a. $\frac{1}{2}$ **in.** **b.** $\frac{1}{8}$ **in.**

8. 9.

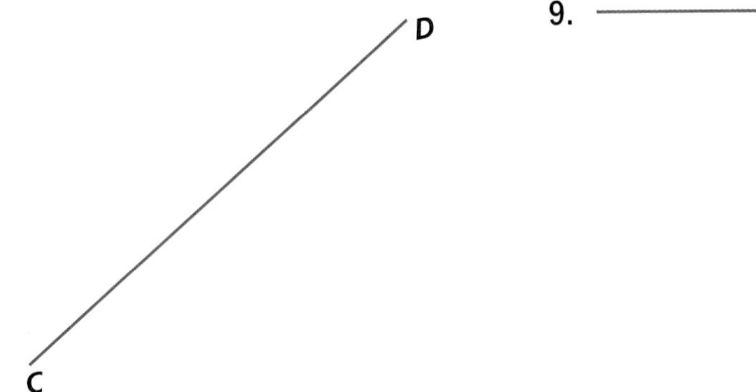

10. Malik is $63\frac{1}{2}$ inches tall. What is his height in feet and inches?

11. On your paper, draw a segment that is $1\frac{3}{8}$ inches long.

12. On your paper, draw a segment that is $1\frac{13}{16}$ inches long.

APPLYING THE MATHEMATICS

In 13 and 14, use a tape measure to measure each length to the nearest inch. Give your answer in

a. inches.

b. feet and inches.

13. the height of your bed

14. the width of your bed

15. Measure the length of one of your shoes to the nearest $\frac{1}{4}$ inch.

16. How many feet long is a 100-yard dash?

17. What is 1,000 feet expressed in yards and feet?

18. At some amusement parks, you need to be 52 inches tall to go on a ride. If you are 4 feet, 7 inches tall, can you go on the ride? Explain your answer.

19. **Fill in the Blanks** Many mountains in Colorado have peaks about 14,250 feet above sea level. This is between __?__ and __?__ miles above sea level. (Use consecutive whole numbers.)

20. Give an appropriate unit (inches, feet, yards, or miles) for each of the following.
    a. the length of a water slide at an aquatic park
    b. the length of a piece of shoelace
    c. the height of a 2-year-old child
    d. the length of all the hot dogs consumed in the U.S. in one year, lined up end-to-end

21. The wheelbase of one automobile manufactured in 2006 is approximately 107 inches. What is this in feet and inches?

Water slides are a huge tourist attraction in certain areas of the country.

REVIEW

22. A bathroom has 84 square feet of floor space that is to be tiled. How many square feet have been tiled when
    a. the job is $\frac{1}{4}$ done?
    b. $\frac{1}{3}$ of the job is still left to be done? **(Lesson 1-2)**

23. On a number line, what number is the same distance from 0 as it is from 1? **(Lesson 1-2)**

24. Write 489,726 in words. **(Lesson 1-1)**

25. How many digits are required to write the population of the United States, which is about 300 million? **(Lesson 1-1)**

EXPLORATION

26. There are many different units for measuring length. Where would these measures be used? How long are they?
    a. pica
    b. fathom
    c. cubit
    d. ell

QUIZ YOURSELF ANSWER

$4\frac{7}{16}$ in.

Lesson **1-4**

Mixed Numbers and Mixed Units

Vocabulary

mixed units

▸ **BIG IDEA** A mixed number is the sum of a fraction and a whole number; a mixed unit is the sum of two quantities with different units. You can add mixed units by using mixed numbers.

The customary system of measurement is in everyday use in the United States and in a few other places in the world. Here are some common units from that system and how they are related. Standard abbreviations are in parentheses.

Mental Math

Which is longer?

a. 30 inches or 2 feet?

b. 3 inches or $\frac{1}{5}$ foot?

c. $\frac{1}{2}$ inch or $\frac{3}{8}$ inch?

Customary System Unit Conversions

Weight
16 ounces (oz) = 1 pound (lb)
2,000 pounds = 1 ton

Liquid Volume
3 teaspoons (tsp) = 1 tablespoon (tbs)
16 tablespoons = 1 cup (c)
2 cups = 1 pint (pt)
2 pints = 1 quart (qt)
4 quarts = 1 gallon (gal)

The diagrams below may help you remember these conversions.

Gallon Splits Diagram

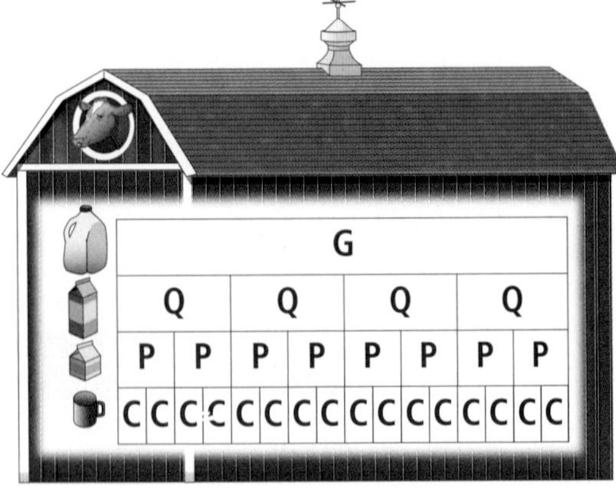

GQPC Diagram

The same common units of time are used all over the world. Here is how these units are related.

Time
60 seconds (sec) = 1 minute (min)
60 minutes = 1 hour (hr)
24 hours = 1 day
365 days = 1 year (yr)
366 days = 1 leap year

5:23 PM

STOP **QUIZ YOURSELF**

1. Refer to the Gallon Splits and GQPC diagrams for the following questions.
   a. How many quarts are in 1 gallon?
   b. How many pints are in 1 quart?
   c. How many cups are in 1 quart?
2. Try to answer these questions without looking at the Customary System Unit Conversions on the previous page.
   a. How many ounces are in 3 pounds?
   b. What part of a gallon is 2 quarts?

Mixed Units

In Example 1 below, the measure 6 pounds, 13 ounces involves *mixed units.* When two different units are used to write a single measure, the quantity is said to involve **mixed units.** When this happens, you may want to write the measure using just one of the units.

Example 1

A baby weighed 6 pounds, 13 ounces at birth.
   a. How many pounds is this?
   b. How many ounces is this?

Solution

a. 6 pounds, 13 ounces means 6 pounds + 13 ounces. Because there are 16 ounces in 1 pound, 1 ounce is $\frac{1}{16}$ of a pound, so 13 ounces is $\frac{13}{16}$ of a pound. Now add the 6 pounds.

$$\begin{aligned} \text{6 pounds} + \text{13 ounces} &= \text{6 pounds} + \tfrac{13}{16}\text{ pounds} \\ &= 6\tfrac{13}{16}\text{ pounds} \end{aligned}$$

b. Because there are 16 ounces in each pound, there are 6 × 16, or 96 ounces in 6 pounds. Now add the 13 ounces.

$$\begin{aligned} \text{6 pounds} + \text{13 ounces} &= \text{96 ounces} + \text{13 ounces} \\ &= \text{109 ounces} \end{aligned}$$

Example 1 on the previous page shows that there are three ways to write a measure with mixed units:

1. using both units (6 pounds, 13 ounces)
2. using the smaller unit (109 ounces)
3. using the larger unit ($6\frac{13}{16}$ pounds)

GUIDED

Example 2

Kesha has made 50 quarts of punch.

a. **How many gallons is this?**
b. **How many gallons and quarts is this?**
c. **A serving of punch is 1 cup. How many servings has Kesha made?**

Staying hydrated in warm weather is essential! A volunteer pours fruit punch on a warm day.

Solution

a. There are __?__ quarts in a gallon.
So, 50 quarts $= \frac{50}{?}$ gallons.
As a mixed number, this is __?__ gallons.

b. From Part a, you know the number of whole gallons.
1 quart = __?__ of a gallon
So the fraction part of the answer in Part a is __?__ of a gallon, or __?__ quarts.
Kesha has __?__ gallons and __?__ quarts of punch.

c. There are __?__ cups in a quart.
50 quarts = 50 • __?__ cups
= __?__ cups of punch

Questions

COVERING THE IDEAS

Fill in the Blanks In 1 and 2, fill in the blank with a number.

1. 2 gal = __?__ qt
2. 4,000 lb = __?__ tons
3. Use the Gallon-Splits Diagram on page 26. Paul brought 15 quarts of a sports drink for his teammates.
   a. How much is this in gallons and quarts?
   b. How many gallons is this?
   c. If a serving of the sports drink is 1 cup, how many servings did Paul bring?

4. If you can, find out how many pounds and ounces you weighed at birth. (Otherwise, use 7 pounds, 5 ounces.)
   a. Write the birth weight in pounds only.
   b. Write the birth weight in ounces only.
5. A baseball game lasted 2 hours and 45 minutes.
   a. How many minutes is this?
   b. How many hours is this?

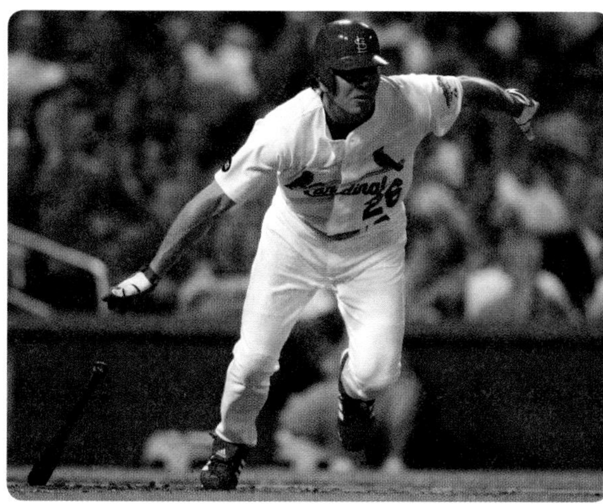

Scott Spiezio batted .272 in 2006, the year the St. Louis Cardinals won the World Series.

Source: Major League Baseball

6. One popular hybrid car is 175 inches long.
   a. How long is this in feet?
   b. How long is this in feet and inches?
7. It took Luis 255 minutes to get to his grandmother's house.
   a. How long is this in hours and minutes?
   b. How long is this in hours?

APPLYING THE MATHEMATICS

In 8 and 9, use the table of Customary System Unit Conversions.

8. How many teaspoons are in 1 gallon?
9. A stick of butter is typically 8 tablespoons. What part of a pint is this?
10. According to *Sports Illustrated,* in 1954, Roger Bannister became the first person to run a mile in less than 4 minutes. He ran the four quarters of the mile in about the following times: 57 seconds; 1 minute, 1 second; 1 minute, 2 seconds; 59 seconds. Find the total time
    a. in seconds.
    b. in minutes.
    c. in minutes and seconds.

11. Clem claims that 1 second is $\frac{1}{360}$ of an hour. Consider Clem's claim. Should Clem clam up, or should Clem exclaim his correctness? Explain your answer.

12. A grocery store has 159 pint-sized bottles of juice. How much is this in gallons, quarts, and pints?

13. The longest running race in the Olympic Games is the marathon. It is 26 miles, 385 yards in length.
    a. Write this length in miles.
    b. How many feet is this?

In 14 and 15, tell which is greater. Explain.

14. 3 cups or 45 tablespoons
15. 5 miles or 26,000 feet

In 16–21, give an appropriate unit for the quantity.

16. the recommended amount of water a person should drink each day
17. the weight of a semi-trailer truck
18. the amount of water in a bath tub
19. the length of time to download a song
20. the weight of a coffee cup
21. the amount of liquid cough medicine that is recommended per dose

Japan's Mizuki Noguchi completed the marathon in 2 hours, 26 minutes, 20 seconds to win a gold medal at the 2004 Summer Olympics

Source: The World Almanac 2006

REVIEW

In 22–24, use the segment and ruler below.

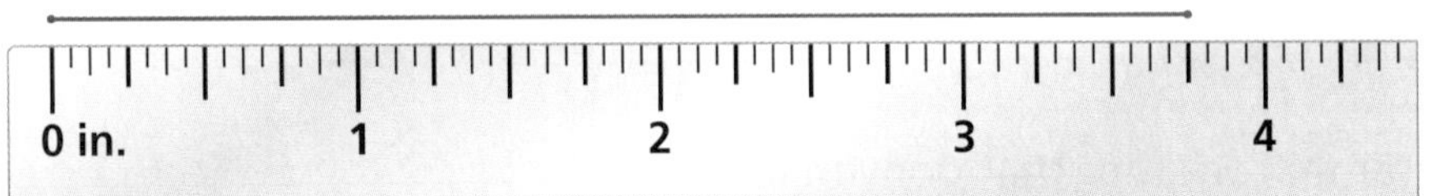

22. What is the smallest interval on the ruler? **(Lesson 1-3)**
23. What is the length of the segment just above the ruler? **(Lesson 1-3)**
24. Trace the segment and divide it into three equal parts. **(Lesson 1-2)**

25. a. Draw a horizontal line segment with length $3\frac{7}{16}$ inches. Call the left endpoint L and the right endpoint R.
    b. To the nearest quarter inch, what is the length of segment LR? **(Lesson 1-3)**

26. One laptop computer keyboard has 77 keys. What fraction of the keyboard is made up of alphabet keys? **(Lesson 1-2)**

27. Write the number five hundred nine million, sixty-seven thousand, three hundred twelve in the base-10 system. **(Lesson 1-1)**

The letters of the alphabet on a keyboard are generally laid out in a QWERTY pattern, named for the first 6 letters of the first row of alphabet keys.

EXPLORATION

28. It takes Earth approximately 365 days, 6 hours, 9 minutes, and $9\frac{1}{2}$ seconds to make one complete revolution around the sun.
    a. What is this length of time in seconds?
    b. What is this length of time in days?

The time it takes for Earth to revolve around the sun has been increasing at a rate of 0.0001 second per year.

Source: *The World Almanac*

QUIZ YOURSELF ANSWERS

1a. 4

1b. 2

1c. 4

2a. 48

2b. $\frac{2}{4}$ or $\frac{1}{2}$

Lesson 1-5 Equal Fractions

Vocabulary

equivalent fractions

lowest terms

simplifying the fraction

BIG IDEA By multiplying (or dividing) both numerator and denominator of a given fraction by the same number, you can create *equivalent fractions*.

Different fractions can represent the same number. For example, if you have traveled $\frac{2}{6}$ of the way to a place, then you have also traveled $\frac{1}{3}$ of the way. In symbols, $\frac{2}{6} = \frac{1}{3}$.

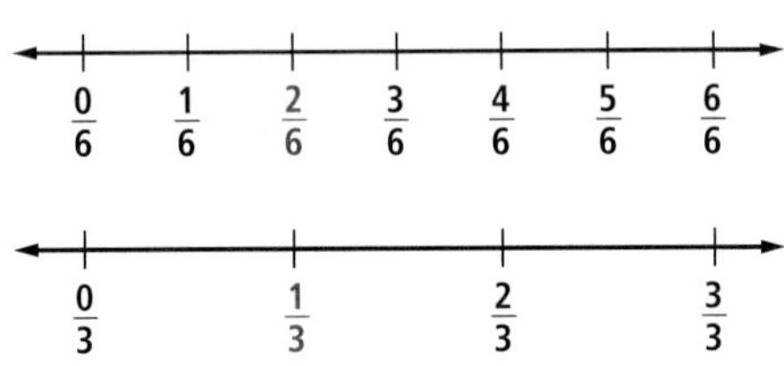

Mental Math

How many cookies does each child get, and how many are left over if

a. 4 children share 9 cookies equally.

b. 8 children share 18 cookies equally.

c. 12 children share 27 cookies equally.

The Equal Fractions Property

Below are four inch rulers. Ruler A shows $\frac{1}{2}$-inch intervals, Ruler B shows $\frac{1}{4}$-inch intervals, Ruler C shows $\frac{1}{8}$-inch intervals, and Ruler D shows $\frac{1}{16}$-inch intervals. On Ruler B, the dotted line marks $2\frac{3}{4}$ inches. This same location on Ruler C is $2\frac{6}{8}$ inches.

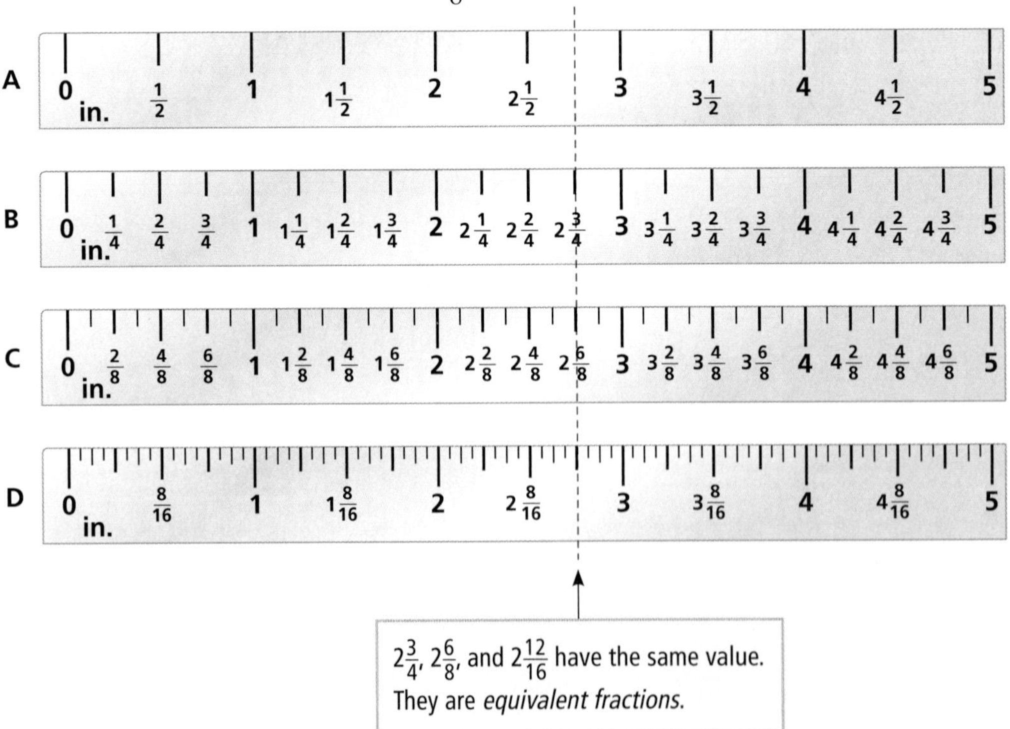

$2\frac{3}{4}$, $2\frac{6}{8}$, and $2\frac{12}{16}$ have the same value. They are *equivalent fractions*.

 See "Quiz Yourself 1" at the right.

The rulers on the previous page show different fractions that name the same quantity. These fractions are in the same position on a number line. The number of intervals on each ruler is double the number of intervals on the ruler above it. You can think of moving from one ruler to the ruler directly below as multiplying the numerator and denominator of each fraction by 2.

For example, the red dotted line crosses a location that is between 2 inches and 3 inches. On Ruler B, this location is $\frac{3}{4}$ of the way from 2 to 3, or at $2\frac{3}{4}$. On Ruler C, this location is $\frac{6}{8}$ of the way from 2 to 3, or at $2\frac{6}{8}$. Notice that $\frac{3}{4} \times \frac{2}{2} = \frac{6}{8}$. These fractions are known as equal fractions or **equivalent fractions.**

You can find a fraction equivalent to a given fraction by multiplying both its numerator and denominator by any number. So there are infinitely many fractions equal to $\frac{3}{4}$, and infinitely many mixed numbers equal to $2\frac{3}{4}$.

 See "Quiz Yourself 2" at the right.

You may be familiar with using this multiplication rule to find equivalent fractions. It is an example of a number property—a true statement that describes a numerical relationship. This general property is known as the *Equal Fractions Property.*

Equal Fractions Property

If the numerator and denominator of a fraction are both multiplied (or divided) by the same nonzero number, then the resulting fraction is equal to the original fraction.

Example 1

Use the Equal Fractions Property to find four fractions equal to $\frac{5}{7}$.

Solution For each of the four equivalent fractions, multiply the numerator and denominator of $\frac{5}{7}$ by the number chosen.

$$\frac{5 \cdot 2}{7 \cdot 2} = \frac{10}{14}$$

$$\frac{5 \cdot ?}{7 \cdot ?} = \frac{30}{42}$$

$$\frac{5 \cdot ?}{7 \cdot 11} = \frac{?}{77}$$

$$\frac{5 \cdot 200}{7 \cdot 200} = \frac{?}{?}$$

So $\frac{5}{7} = \frac{10}{14} = \frac{30}{42} = \frac{?}{77} = \frac{?}{?}$.

 **QUIZ YOURSELF 1**

What location on Ruler D is the same as $2\frac{6}{8}$ on Ruler C?

QUIZ YOURSELF 2

What number was used to multiply the numerator and denominator of the fraction $\frac{3}{4}$ to rename $2\frac{3}{4}$ as

a. $2\frac{9}{12}$?

b. $2\frac{300}{400}$?

GUIDED

Example 2

Write four fractions equal to $\frac{100}{150}$.

Solution To find four equivalent fractions, divide the numerator and denominator of $\frac{100}{150}$ by a different number each time.

$$\frac{100 \div 5}{150 \div 5} = \frac{20}{30}$$
$$\frac{100 \div ?}{150 \div 10} = \frac{?}{15}$$
$$\frac{100 \div ?}{150 \div ?} = \frac{4}{6}$$
$$\frac{100 \div ?}{150 \div ?} = \frac{2}{3}$$

So, $\frac{100}{150} = \frac{20}{30} = \frac{?}{15} = \frac{4}{?} = \frac{2}{3}$.

Writing Fractions in Lowest Terms

Of the fractions equal to $\frac{100}{150}$, the simplest is the one with the smallest possible numerator and denominator, $\frac{2}{3}$. The fraction $\frac{2}{3}$ is $\frac{100}{150}$ written in *lowest terms*. A fraction is in **lowest terms** if there is no whole number greater than 1 that will evenly divide both the numerator and the denominator. Rewriting a fraction in lowest terms is called **simplifying the fraction.**

To write a fraction in lowest terms, use the Equal Fractions Property to rename the fraction by dividing. Continue to divide until the only whole number that will evenly divide the numerator and denominator is 1.

▸ READING MATH

The word *simplify* has many meanings in mathematics. For fractions, *simplify* means to put in lowest terms. In other situations, it means something different. Sometimes, the simplified result is not the most useful.

Example 3

Rewrite $\frac{450}{600}$ in lowest terms.

Solution 1

$$\frac{450 \div 2}{600 \div 2} = \frac{225}{300}$$
$$\frac{225 \div 5}{300 \div 5} = \frac{45}{60}$$
$$\frac{45 \div 5}{60 \div 5} = \frac{9}{12}$$
$$\frac{9 \div 3}{12 \div 3} = \frac{3}{4}$$

No whole number greater than 1 will evenly divide both 3 and 4, so $\frac{450}{600}$ equals $\frac{3}{4}$ in lowest terms.

Solution 2 If you start with a greater divisor, you need fewer divisions to find the fraction in lowest terms.

$$\frac{450 \div 50}{600 \div 50} = \frac{9}{12} \qquad \frac{9 \div 3}{12 \div 3} = \frac{3}{4}$$

You can even do it in one step.

Fractions on Calculators

Many calculators can operate with fractions. However, different calculators deal with fractions in different ways. It is important for you to know how to enter and perform operations on fractions with your calculator. The screen below displays the answer to Example 3 in one step.

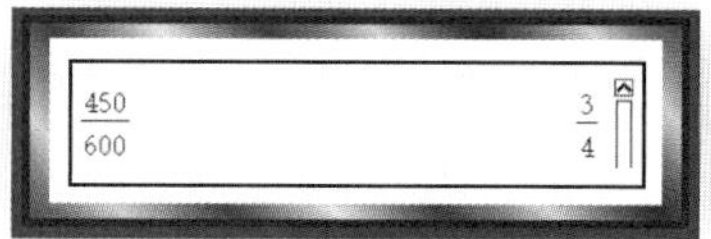

Activity

MATERIALS scientific or graphing calculator

Step 1 Display the fraction $\frac{600}{840}$ on your calculator screen and press [ENTER]. What fraction in lowest terms is shown? On some calculators you may need to use a decimal/fraction conversion key to display the output as a fraction.

Step 2 Find the greatest divisor your calculator used to arrive at the fraction in lowest terms.

Step 3 Repeat Steps 1 and 2 with the fraction $\frac{6{,}285}{47{,}640}$.

Questions

COVERING THE IDEAS

1. Draw and split a line segment in two ways to show that $\frac{2}{3} = \frac{8}{12}$.

In 2–4, find three fractions equal to the given fraction or mixed number.

2. $\frac{8}{12}$
3. $\frac{1}{7}$
4. $4\frac{10}{32}$

In 5–7, rewrite the fraction in lowest terms. Show each division.

5. $\frac{15}{18}$
6. $\frac{36}{48}$
7. $\frac{75}{125}$

8. Marta was working with fractions and wrote the following: $\frac{4 \times 0}{14 \times 0} = \frac{0}{0}$. Use the Equal Fractions Property to explain to Marta why her answer is correct or incorrect.

9. Derrick and Nat reduced $\frac{12}{24}$ to lowest terms.

Derrick's answer: $\frac{12}{24} = \frac{6}{12}$

Nat's answer: $\frac{12}{24} = \frac{4}{6}$

Who is correct and why?

APPLYING THE MATHEMATICS

10. Explain why 2 quarts is the same as half a gallon.

11. a. Simplify $\frac{66}{99}$.

b. Simplify $\frac{99}{66}$.

c. How are your answers to Part a and Part b similar? How are they different?

12. A circle represents one whole. Sketch two circles of the same size. Split one circle into eight equal parts and the other circle into four equal parts. Shade parts in the two circles to show $\frac{2}{8} = \frac{1}{4}$.

13. On a piece of graph paper, outline a large square that is 10 units on each side. Shade this 10-by-10 square to show that $\frac{25}{100} = \frac{1}{4}$.

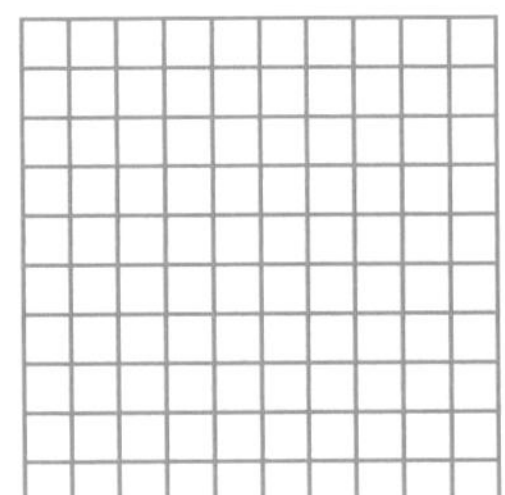

In 14 and 15, write the fraction in lowest terms. Then write the number in base 10 that is equal to the fraction.

14. $\frac{42}{14}$

15. $\frac{300}{25}$

In 16 and 17, you are asked to rewrite a whole number as a fraction. You can do this by writing it first as a fraction with the whole number as its numerator and 1 as its denominator. For example, $3 = \frac{3}{1} = \frac{15}{5} = \frac{24}{8}$.

16. Write four different fractions equal to 5.

17. Write three different fractions equal to 14.

18. Why do we rewrite fractions "in lowest terms" and not "in highest terms?"

19. Here is one way to rewrite $\frac{420}{720}$ in lowest terms.

$\frac{420 \div 10}{720 \div 10} = \frac{42}{72}$ $\quad \frac{42 \div 2}{72 \div 2} = \frac{21}{36}$ $\quad \frac{21 \div 3}{36 \div 3} = \frac{7}{12}$

By what number could you divide the numerator and denominator of the original fraction to do this problem in one step? Explain how you found your answer.

20. Jacqueline said to Andrew, "I'll meet you in three-quarters of an hour." Andrew thought to himself, "That's 45 minutes." What does this situation have to do with equal fractions?

REVIEW

21. a. $5\frac{6}{11}$ is between which two whole numbers?
    b. To which of these two whole numbers is it closer? (Lesson 1-4)

22. The tallest building in the United States in 2007 was the Sears Tower in Chicago. The top of the building is 1,450 feet above the ground. What fraction of a mile is this? (Lesson 1-3)

23. Stretch your hand. Measure the distance from the tip of your little finger to the tip of your thumb to
    a. the nearest inch.
    b. the nearest half inch.
    c. the nearest quarter inch. (Lesson 1-2)

24. On June 22, 2006 at 10:14 A.M., the total sum borrowed by the U.S. Government was over $8,339,000,000,000, according to the U.S. Treasury Department Bureau of the Public Debt. Write this number in words. (Lesson 1-1)

EXPLORATION

25. What is the largest number of digits your calculator will display as the numerator or denominator of a fraction? (*Hint:* Experiment with three-digit numerators and denominators, then use four digits, and so on.)

The Sears Tower graces the Chicago skyline.

QUIZ YOURSELF ANSWERS

1. $2\frac{12}{16}$

2a. 3

2b. 100

Lesson

1-6 Fractions and Division

Vocabulary

proper fraction

improper fraction

▸ **BIG IDEA** A fraction is equal to its numerator divided by its denominator.

Every Fraction Is a Division

All fractions share an important property. Every fraction represents the answer to a division problem.

Fractions as Divisions

The fraction $\frac{\text{numerator}}{\text{denominator}}$, or $\frac{n}{d}$ for short, equals $n \div d$.

For example, $\frac{4}{5}$ is equal to $4 \div 5$. Since $\frac{4}{5} = \frac{8}{10}$, $4 \div 5 = 8 \div 10$.

Mental Math

Which is greater?

a. $\frac{5}{6}$ or $\frac{5}{4}$

b. $\frac{6}{5}$ or $\frac{4}{5}$

c. $\frac{6}{9}$ or $\frac{4}{6}$

Example 1

As the ship Titanic was sinking in April 1912, the crew continuously loaded and fired 8 rockets, one at a time, hoping another ship would see the rockets. If the loading and firing of the 8 rockets took exactly 1 hour, how much time did it take to load and fire each rocket?

Solution 1 hour = 60 minutes; Calculating the interval is like splitting a segment of length 60 into 8 parts. So the answer is $\frac{60 \text{ minutes}}{8 \text{ rockets}}$, or $\frac{60}{8}$ minutes per rocket. As a mixed number, $\frac{60}{8} = 7\frac{4}{8} = 7\frac{1}{2}$. The fraction $\frac{60}{8}$ equals 60 divided by 8. This means a rocket was fired every $7\frac{1}{2}$ minutes, or 7 minutes, 30 seconds.

Check Check your answer by drawing a segment of length 60. Split 60 in half to get two segments of length 30. Then split each 30 in half to get four segments of length 15. Then split each 15 in half to get eight segments of length $7\frac{1}{2}$.

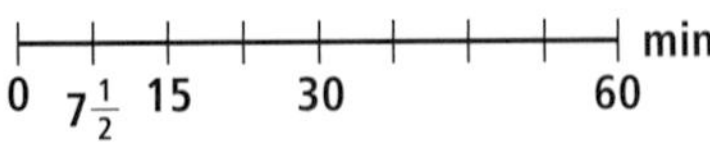

So you can see that $60 \div 8 = 7\frac{1}{2}$.

"All the News That's Fit to Print."

The New York Times.

TITANIC SINKS FOUR HOURS AFTER HITTING ICEBERG; 866 RESCUED BY CARPATHIA, PROBABLY 1250 PERISH; ISMAY SAFE, MRS. ASTOR MAYBE, NOTED NAMES MISSING

Col. Astor and Bride, Isidor Straus and Wife, and Maj. Butt Aboard.

"RULE OF SEA" FOLLOWED

Biggest Liner Plunges to the Bottom at 2:20 A. M.

RESCUERS THERE TOO LATE

The Lost Titanic Being Towed Out of Belfast Harbor.

PARTIAL LIST OF THE SAVED.

CAPT. E. J. SMITH.

Since discovering the wreck of the Titanic in 1985, American and French scientists have explored the ship repeatedly using manned and unmanned submersible machines.

Source: Encyclopedia Britannica

Suppose the Titanic had been able to fire 9 rockets in 1 hour. Then each rocket would have taken less time to load and fire.

$$\frac{60}{9} \text{ minutes per rocket} < \frac{60}{8} \text{ minutes per rocket}$$

$$\frac{60}{9} < \frac{60}{8}$$

You can verify this by converting the fractions to mixed numbers.

$$\frac{60}{9} = 6\frac{6}{9} \text{ and } \frac{60}{8} = 7\frac{4}{8}$$

$$6\frac{6}{9} \text{ minutes per rocket} < 7\frac{4}{8} \text{ minutes per rocket}$$

$$6\frac{6}{9} < 7\frac{4}{8}$$

The numerator in the fraction $\frac{60}{8}$ is greater than the denominator. In Example 2, the denominator is greater than the numerator, but the fraction is still a division.

Example 2

Suppose a board 2 feet long is cut into 3 equal pieces. Each piece is what part of a foot?

Solution 1 $2 \div 3$ is the same as $\frac{2}{3}$, so $\frac{2 \text{ feet}}{3 \text{ parts}}$ is $\frac{2}{3}$ foot per part.

(continued on next page)

Solution 2 Because 1 foot = 12 inches, you can substitute 12 inches for 1 foot.

$$\begin{aligned} 2 \text{ feet} &= 2 \times 1 \text{ foot} \\ &= 2 \times 12 \text{ inches} \\ &= 24 \text{ inches} \end{aligned}$$

You can divide 24 inches into 3 equal parts: $24 \div 3 = 8$. So each part is 8 inches long. But what part of a foot is 8 inches? Use the fact that 1 inch = $\frac{1}{12}$ foot.

$$\begin{aligned} 8 \text{ inches} &= 8 \times \tfrac{1}{12} \text{ foot} \\ &= \tfrac{8}{12} \text{ foot} \\ &= \tfrac{2}{3} \text{ foot} \end{aligned}$$

Check The line segment below illustrates the problem both in inches (on the top) and feet (on the bottom.)

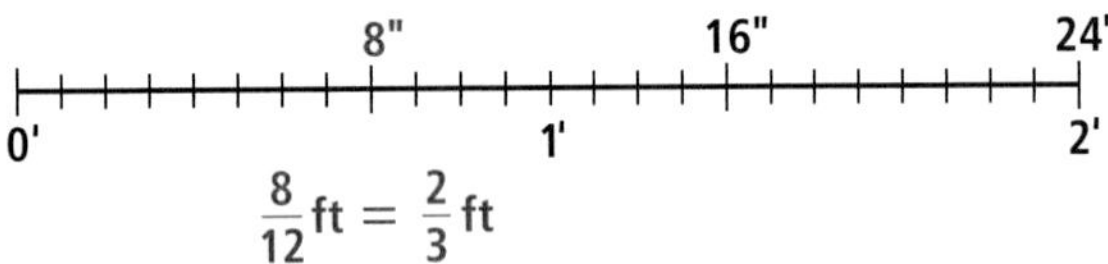

Proper and Improper Fractions

A fraction with whole numbers in its numerator and denominator is a *simple fraction.* (The denominator cannot be 0.) There are three types of simple fractions. If the numerator is less than the denominator, as in $\frac{2}{3}$, then the fraction is called a **proper fraction.**

If the numerator is greater than the denominator, as in $\frac{60}{8}$, then the simple fraction is called an **improper fraction.** Improper fractions can always be rewritten as mixed numbers: $\frac{60}{8} = 7\frac{4}{8} = 7\frac{1}{2}$.

A third possibility occurs when the numerator equals the denominator, as in $\frac{12}{12}$. Here is a way to think about this number: if 12 hours are divided into 12 time intervals, then the length of each time interval is 1 hour. As long as the fraction does not equal zero, any fraction with the same number in both the numerator and denominator is equal to 1.

Type of Simple Fraction	Example
proper fraction	$\frac{3}{7}$
improper fraction	$\frac{15}{9}$
numerator = denominator	$\frac{5}{5}$

Activity

MATERIALS scientific or graphing calculator

In this activity, you will compare fractions with the same numerator and increasing denominators. The constant numerator will be 15.

1. Enter $\frac{15}{4}$ into your calculator as a fraction and press ENTER or EXECUTE. Record the result.
2. Enter $\frac{15}{5}$, $\frac{15}{6}$, $\frac{15}{8}$, $\frac{15}{15}$, $\frac{15}{16}$, and $\frac{15}{25}$ into your calculator as fractions and press ENTER or EXECUTE. Record each result.
3. What do you notice about the resulting numbers in relation to the number 1?
4. Describe how to tell when a fraction is greater than or less than 1.

QUIZ YOURSELF

Which is greater?

a. $\frac{24}{4}$ or $\frac{24}{7}$ b. $\frac{4}{24}$ or $\frac{7}{24}$

GAME **Now you can play *Build It: Positive Fractions.* The directions for this game are on pages G4–G5 at the back of your book.**

Questions

COVERING THE IDEAS

1. Suppose you have 90 minutes to clean 4 drawers of a dresser. On average, how long do you have to clean 1 drawer?
   a. Write the division problem to answer this question.
   b. Write the answer to this question as an improper fraction.
   c. Write the answer to this question as a mixed number.
2. a. Write the division question that represents $\frac{12}{5}$.
   b. Make up a real situation that would lead to the fraction $\frac{12}{5}$.
3. The phone has to be answered at a company from 9 A.M. to 5 P.M. Three people will split the job evenly. How much time (in hours) will each person answer the phone?
4. Make up a real situation that would lead to the fraction $\frac{3}{7}$.

A tall chest of drawers is called a highboy. This highboy is 85 feet tall and marks the entrance to a furniture retailer.

Source: Furnitureland South

5. Give the value of $\frac{n}{d}$
   a. when $n = 100$ and $d = 5$.
   b. when $n = 100$ and $d = 10$.
   c. when $n = 5$ and $d = 100$.
   d. when $n = 10$ and $d = 100$.
6. Tell whether each number equals $\frac{6}{5}$.
   a. $6 \cdot \frac{1}{5}$
   b. $5 \div 6$
   c. $6 \div 5$
   d. $\frac{5}{6}$
   e. $5 \cdot \frac{1}{6}$

APPLYING THE MATHEMATICS

In 7–10, use the following information. A dram is a unit of weight equal to $\frac{1}{16}$ ounce.

7. A prescription calls for 20 drams of a medicine. How many ounces is this? Write your answer as both an improper fraction and as a mixed number.
8. **Multiple Choice** A furniture polish formula calls for 1 dram of perfume and 6 drams of olive oil, among other ingredients. How would you represent the amount of perfume in ounces?
   A $\frac{1}{6}$ B $\frac{1}{16}$ C $\frac{16}{6}$ D 16
9. Refer to Question 8. In lowest terms, how many ounces of olive oil does the furniture polish formula require?
10. A dram also equals $\frac{875}{32}$ grains. Rewrite this improper fraction as a mixed number. (*Hint:* Use division.)

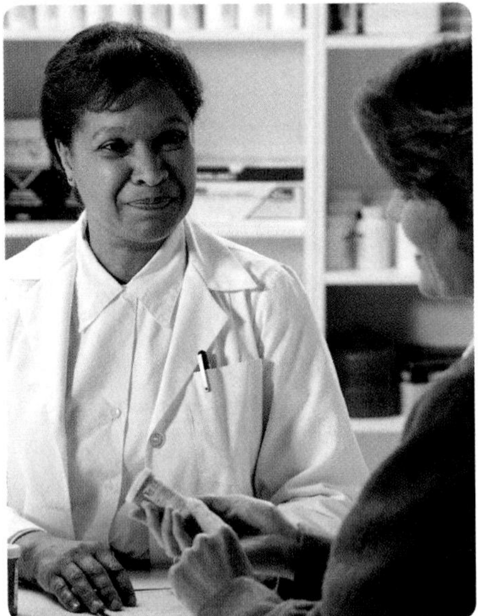

Pharmacists still use the measurements *grains*, *drams*, and *minims* when checking and filling prescriptions.

In 11 and 12, use the following information. In the fifteenth century, the Spanish silver coin called a peso could be broken into eight wedges, which came to be known as "pieces of eight."

11. Suppose a pirate ship sank with 9,234 pieces of eight in a treasure chest. How many pesos is this?
12. Another pirate ship returned to its harbor with 900 pesos to be divided evenly among 16 pirates.
    a. How many pesos did each pirate receive? Write your answer as a mixed number.
    b. How many pieces of eight did this pirate ship bring home?
    c. How many pieces of eight did each pirate receive?

13. Monique wanted to test her endurance and bike 84 miles in a 24-hour day. Throughout the day, Monique measured whether she was ahead, behind, or on pace. At each benchmark, tell whether she was on pace or not. (Use equal fractions to answer this question.) If she was not on pace, was she ahead or behind?

a. She traveled 14 miles after 4 hours.
b. She traveled 28 miles after 7 hours.
c. She traveled 32 miles after 8 hours.
d. She traveled 40 miles after 10 hours.
e. She traveled 42 miles after 11 hours.
f. She rested for 1 hour, so she traveled 42 miles after 12 hours.
g. She traveled 55 miles after 15 hours.
h. She traveled 70 miles after 20 hours.

Over 1,000 calories are burned per hour when cycling at a 25-mile per hour pace.

REVIEW

14. Write 3 fractions equal to $\frac{1}{7}$. (Lesson 1-5)

In 15 and 16, rewrite each fraction in lowest terms. (Lesson 1-5)

15. $\frac{55}{66}$

16. $\frac{24}{72}$

17. a. What fraction of the largest rectangle below is shaded?

b. What fraction is not shaded? (Lesson 1-5)

18. At swimming practice, Cesar swam 50 laps, each of them $\frac{1}{16}$-mile long. (Lessons 1-4, 1-3)

a. How many whole miles did he swim?
b. What is the total distance (measured in miles and fractions of a mile) that Cesar swam during practice?
c. What fraction of the last mile did he not complete?

19. On the first day of his journey up a 9-foot tall wall, a snail crawled one sixth of the total distance. On the second day, he crawled one more sixth of the total height of the wall. (**Lesson 1-2**)
    a. What part of the wall did he have left to climb after the second day?
    b. Write that distance in inches.

EXPLORATION

20. In the Broadway musical *Guys and Dolls,* an actor sings, "I love you, a bushel and a peck."
    a. A dry quart is equal to $\frac{1}{32}$ bushel and is also equal to $\frac{1}{8}$ peck. How many quarts of love does the actor claim to feel?
    b. An earnest actor, forgetting the words, improvised on her own, "I love you, ten gallons and an ounce." The actor claimed that her new lyrics professed "a bit more love" than the original. Was she right? Explain your reasoning.

The musical *Guys and Dolls* first opened in November, 1950 on Broadway. Since then, it has run 1,200 performances and enjoyed successful revivals all over the world.

Source: PBS

21. Start with a 2 inch-by-10 inch strip of paper.
    a. Fold the strip into 2 equal pieces. Without unfolding the strip, fold it again. Then fold it in half one more time. Open the folded strip of paper. What fraction does each section represent?
    b. If you could fold the paper 3 more times, what fraction would each section represent?

QUIZ YOURSELF ANSWERS

a. $\frac{24}{4}$

b. $\frac{7}{24}$

Lesson 1-7 Using Integers

Vocabulary

negative numbers
opposite
integer

▸ **BIG IDEA** The numbers ..., -4, -3, -2, -1, 0, 1, 2, 3, 4, ... are called the *integers* and are used in situations that have two directions (for example, up-down, gain-loss, before-after).

Mental Math

Order the following from least to greatest.

a. $\frac{1}{8}, \frac{3}{5}, \frac{1}{2}, \frac{8}{9}$

b. $-\frac{1}{8}, -\frac{3}{5}, -\frac{1}{2}, -\frac{8}{9}$

The lowest recorded temperature in the United States occurred in Prospect Creek Camp, Alaska, in January 1971. It was 80° below zero on the Fahrenheit (F) scale. To indicate a quantity below zero such as this, **negative numbers** are required. A thermometer shows temperatures above zero with positive numbers and temperatures below zero with negative numbers, indicated with a negative "-" sign in front of the number. The record temperature is written as -80°F.

QUIZ YOURSELF 1

a. What temperatures are represented by *x*, *y*, and *z* on the thermometer at the right?
b. What temperature is shown on the thermometer?

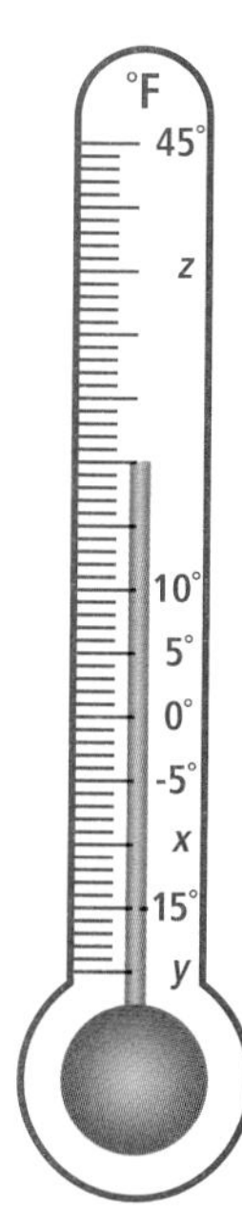

Zero is neither positive nor negative. In many situations, it is the starting or neutral point. For example, a player's golf score is given as a number of strokes above or below par. Two strokes above par would be +2 while three strokes below par would be -3. Mathematically, +2 and 2 are identical. Because it is shorter to leave off the + (positive) sign, positive 2 is usually written simply as 2.

When you say your basketball team is ahead, behind, or tied with another team, you are also using positive and negative numbers. For example, if at half-time your team is ahead by two points, you can represent this situation by the integer 2. If your team is behind by five points, you could represent the situation by -5. If the teams are tied, you could represent the situation by the integer 0.

Opposites

This table gives some situations that often use negative numbers.

Situation	Negative	Zero	Positive
savings account	withdrawal	no change	deposit
business	loss	break even	profit
time	before	now	after
elevation	below sea level	sea level	above sea level
football	loss of yards	no gain or loss	yards gained

The negative direction is the *opposite* of the positive direction. Earning \$4.50 is the opposite of spending or losing \$4.50. That is, \$4.50 is the opposite of -\$4.50. Three and one-half hours from now ($3\frac{1}{2}$ hr) is the opposite of $3\frac{1}{2}$ hours ago ($-3\frac{1}{2}$ hr).

The table at the right shows two correct ways to say the "–" sign.

Write	Say
-6	"negative six"
-6	"opposite of six"

Many people say "minus six" for -6. Technically, "minus six" is not correct because there is no subtraction. Most calculators have different keys for "negative" six and "minus" six.

The set of numbers that includes the whole numbers 0, 1, 2, 3, … and their **opposites** is called the set of **integers.** So the set of integers is {0, 1, -1, 2, -2, 3, -3, …}.

Example

Shania's dog Chunky was ill and lost 10 pounds. In the following weeks, he gained back 8 pounds. Over the next year, his weight stayed the same. Represent each change in the dog's weight as an integer.

Solution Losing ten pounds: –10
Gaining eight pounds: 8
Staying the same weight: 0

QUIZ YOURSELF 2

If today is 0, what day is represented by each integer?

a. 1 **b.** –1 **c.** –3 **d.** 8

Graphing Negative Numbers on a Number Line

Positive and negative numbers can be pictured on a number line. The number line below shows a graph of the numbers 2, 0, -1, and -4. When the number line is horizontal, greater numbers are to the right. When the number line is vertical, greater numbers are above lesser numbers.

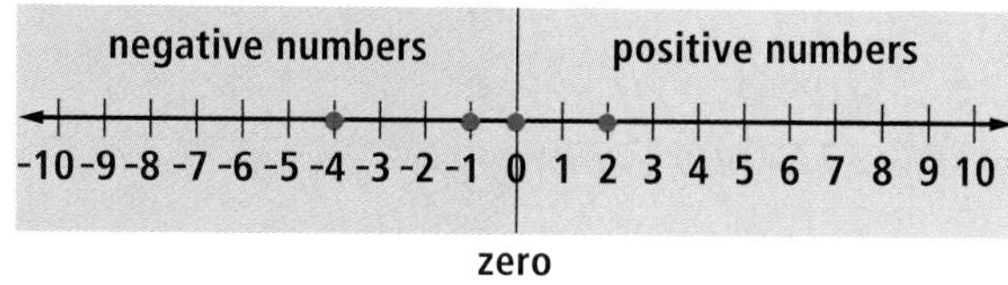

See "Quiz Yourself 3" at the right.

Which number is greater?

a. -1 or 7

b. -8 or -5

STOP **QUIZ YOURSELF 4**

The table below displays the record low temperatures for five states, according to the U.S. National Climatic Data Center.

a. Which of these states has the coldest record low temperature?

b. Which of these states has a record low temperature closest to zero?

Temperature (°F)	State
-61	CO
-2	FL
12	HI
-30	VA
-17	GA

All scientific calculators have a way to enter negative numbers. This is usually done by the opposite key [(-)] or [(+/−)] For example, [(-)] 4 results in a display of −4. Be sure you know how to enter a negative number on your calculator.

Questions

COVERING THE IDEAS

1. Translate -8 into words in two different ways.

2. Annika Sörenstam won a 2005 Ladies Professional Golf Association Tournament, finishing 15 below par. Another golfer, Jill McGill, scored +6. The best scoring amateur was Michelle Wie, who scored 0. If a par score for the four rounds of golf was 288, what were the three competitors' scores?

3. **Fill in the Blank** On a horizontal number line, the negative numbers are usually to the __?__ of the positive numbers.

Michelle Wie tied for fourteenth place in this tournament.

Source: Ladies Professional Golf Association

4. Graph 7, -2, 0, and -4 on a number line.

In 5–7, name an integer between the pair of integers.

5. 7 and 11
6. -3 and -10
7. 1 and -5

In 8–10, three words or phrases relating to a situation are given. Which word or phrase usually refers to positive? Which to negative? Which to zero?

8. Elevation: sea level, above sea level, below sea level
9. Time: today, tomorrow, yesterday
10. Football: losing yardage, gaining yardage, no gain or loss

11. a. Graph 60, -20, 40, -10, and -30 on a vertical number line.
    b. What interval did you use on your number line?

12. Landen records his expenses and earnings in a notebook.
    a. What number should he record if he buys a $12.88 CD?
    b. What number should he record if he earns $8.25 babysitting?

13. Name an integer that is neither positive nor negative.

14. **True or False** Every whole number is also an integer.

15. Give an example of an integer that is *not* a whole number.

APPLYING THE MATHEMATICS

16. Order -3, 17, 98, -100, and -2 from greatest to least.

17. The guests at a birthday party were asked to guess the number of times a piñata would be struck before it broke open. The piñata required 47 strikes before it opened. If a guess of 44 is scored as -3 (3 too low), what would be the score for each guess?
    a. 40 b. 3 c. 100

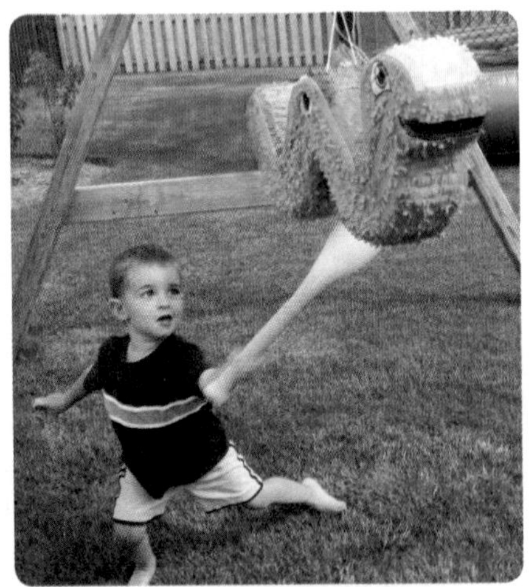

Although conventional wisdom holds that the piñata is a Spanish custom, many believe it first originated in China as discovered by Marco Polo.

18. **True or False**
    a. A negative number is always less than a positive number.
    b. A nonnegative integer is always a positive integer.

19. Write a rule for deciding which of two negative numbers is greater. Use a real-world example to explain why your rule makes sense.

REVIEW

20. If a doctor prescribes two pills every 3 hours, how many pills should you take from 9 A.M. to 9 P.M.? **(Lesson 1-6)**

In 21–23, a fraction is given. (Lesson 1-5)

a. **Identify each fraction as proper, improper, or neither.**

b. **Reduce the fraction to lowest terms.**

21. $\frac{630}{280}$

22. $\frac{625}{1,000}$

23. $\frac{427}{427}$

24. On May 9, 1984, the Chicago White Sox beat the Milwaukee Brewers in a 25-inning baseball game that lasted 8 hours, 25 minutes. Write the time in minutes. (Lesson 1-4)

25. Shawn had two $1 bills, 3 quarters, 6 dimes, 1 nickel, and 3 pennies in his pocket. (Lesson 1-4)
    a. What fraction of a dollar did he have in dimes?
    b. How much money did he have in all? Express your answer in dollars and cents.

26. Draw a vertical line of length $3\frac{3}{8}$ inches. (Lesson 1-3)

27. Draw a horizontal line of length $\frac{9}{16}$ inches. (Lesson 1-3)

28. Write three numbers between 2 and 3. (Lesson 1-2)

29. The total area of the United States is 3,794,085 square miles. Write this number in words. (Lesson 1-1)

EXPLORATION

30. Find an example of a negative number in a newspaper or magazine.

QUIZ YOURSELF ANSWERS

1a. –10°; –20°; 35°

1b. 20°

2a. tomorrow

2b. yesterday

2c. 3 days ago

2d. 8 days from today

3a. 7

3b. –5

4a. CO

4b. FL

Lesson 1-8 Negative Fractions and Mixed Numbers

▸ BIG IDEA Negative fractions and negative mixed numbers are used whenever situations with fractions have two directions (for example, up-down, gain-loss, before-after).

You can graph fractions on a number line by splitting intervals between integers into equal parts.

Mental Math

a. Name a number between 2 and 3.

b. Name a number between 2 and 2.1.

c. Name a number between 2 and 2.001.

GUIDED

Example 1

Graph $\frac{2}{3}$, $1\frac{3}{4}$, $3\frac{1}{6}$, and $4\frac{7}{10}$ on a number line.

Solution Draw a number line from 0 to 5 on a sheet of paper.

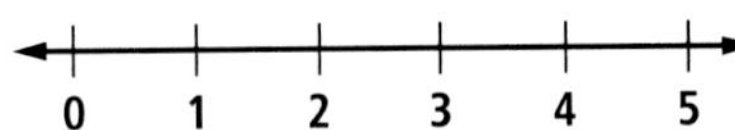

For $\frac{2}{3}$, divide the interval between 0 and 1 into three equal parts using two tick marks. Place a dot on the second tick mark.

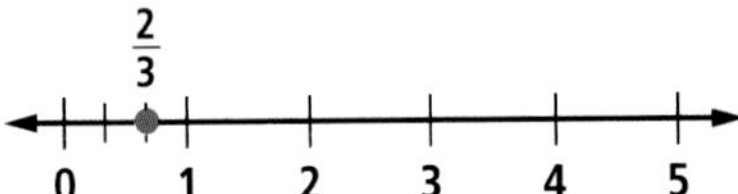

For $1\frac{3}{4}$, divide the interval between 1 and 2 into four equal parts, using three tick marks. Place a dot on the third tick mark.

For $3\frac{1}{6}$, divide the interval between __?__ and __?__ into __?__ equal parts, using __?__ tick marks. Place a dot on the __?__ tick mark.

For $4\frac{7}{10}$, divide the interval between __?__ and __?__ into __?__ equal parts, using __?__ tick marks. Place a dot on the __?__ tick mark.

Complete the number line.

Graphing Negative Fractions

A simple fraction is a fraction with an integer in the numerator and denominator. (Recall that the denominator cannot be zero.) The graph of a negative fraction is the same distance from zero as its opposite, but is on the other side of zero. A graph of $-\frac{2}{3}$ placed on a number line is shown on the next page.

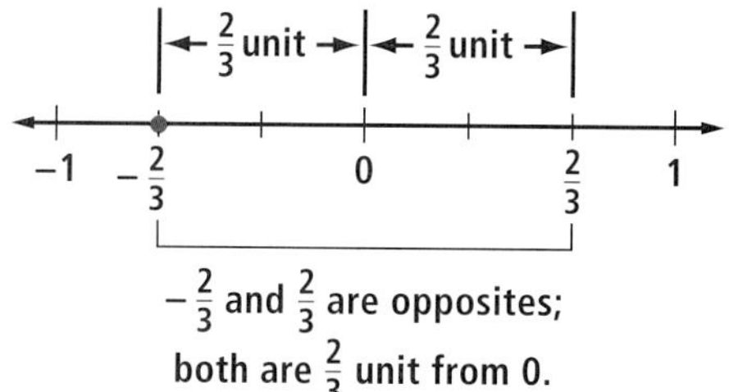

 See "Quiz Yourself" at the right.

 **QUIZ YOURSEFL**

Graph $-\frac{2}{3}$, $-1\frac{3}{4}$, $-3\frac{1}{6}$, and $-4\frac{7}{10}$ on a number line.

A number line can also help you find numbers between two fractions.

GUIDED

Example 2

Find a number between $-8\frac{3}{7}$ and $-8\frac{4}{7}$.

Solution Use what you know about equal fractions to rewrite $-8\frac{3}{7}$ and $-8\frac{4}{7}$ with a greater common denominator.

$\frac{3}{7} = \frac{3 \times 2}{7 \times 2} = \frac{6}{14}$, so $-8\frac{3}{7} = -8\frac{?}{14}$.

In the same way, $-8\frac{4}{7}$ = __?__.

Now you need to find a number between __?__ and __?__. A possible number to use is __?__.

The idea of Example 2 can be used to order fractions even when their denominators are different.

Example 3

a. Graph $-3\frac{3}{4}$, $-3\frac{1}{2}$, and $-3\frac{5}{8}$ on a vertical number line.

b. Order the numbers from least to greatest.

Solution

a. Rename the fractions so they have the same denominator. Then you can determine the number of parts in which to split the interval between −3 and −4. The numbers 4, 2, and 8 are all factors of 8, so use 8 as the denominator.

$$-3\frac{3}{4} = -3\frac{6}{8} \qquad -3\frac{1}{2} = -3\frac{4}{8} \qquad -3\frac{5}{8}$$

Like a thermometer, greater numbers are above lesser numbers. Divide the interval on the number line between −3 and −4 into 8 parts. The vertical number line is shown at the right.

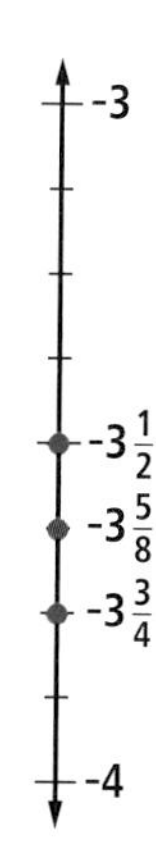

b. From the number line at the right, you can see that $-3\frac{3}{4} < -3\frac{5}{8} < -3\frac{1}{2}$.

Now you can play *Build It: Negative Fractions.* The directions for this game are on pages G4–G5 at the back of your book.

Questions

COVERING THE IDEAS

1. a. Graph $\frac{1}{2}$, $2\frac{4}{5}$, and $6\frac{1}{3}$ on a number line.

   b. Graph $-\frac{1}{2}$, $-2\frac{4}{5}$, and $-6\frac{1}{3}$ on a number line.

2. Give an example of a negative number that is not an integer.

3. Graph $-4\frac{1}{2}$ and $4\frac{1}{2}$ on the same number line.

4. The following numbers represent the change in the level of a lake measured in inches over several years. Graph these four values on the same vertical number line: $-\frac{3}{4}$ in., $1\frac{5}{8}$ in., $-4\frac{1}{2}$ in., and $2\frac{3}{8}$ in.

5. Order 3, $5\frac{1}{2}$, $-1\frac{4}{5}$, 0, and $-2\frac{1}{3}$ from greatest to least.

6. Order $-4\frac{1}{3}$, -4, $-4\frac{4}{5}$, -5, and $-4\frac{1}{2}$ from least to greatest.

7. **Multiple Choice** Which fraction is closest to 0?

   A $-\frac{1}{3}$ B $-\frac{2}{3}$ C $\frac{4}{3}$ D $\frac{2}{3}$

In 8–10, which number is greater?

8. -6, $-5\frac{1}{4}$
9. $-3\frac{1}{2}$, $-4\frac{1}{2}$
10. $-3\frac{1}{4}$, $-3\frac{1}{2}$

In 11–13, name a fraction between the two numbers.

11. -9 and -10
12. 0 and $-\frac{1}{5}$
13. $-1\frac{5}{9}$ and $-1\frac{2}{3}$

APPLYING THE MATHEMATICS

14. In 1954 at Rogers Pass, Montana, the temperature dropped to sixty-nine and seven tenths degrees Fahrenheit below zero. This is the lowest temperature ever recorded in the continental United States. Write this temperature as a mixed number.

Rogers Pass, Montana

15. Suppose hours are measured as a fraction of a day. Each hour is represented by $\frac{1}{24}$. Give each answer in lowest terms.

a. What number represents one hour from now?

b. What number represents five hours ago?

c. What number represents 12 hours from now?

d. What number represents 36 hours ago?

In 16–19, use the number line below. Which letter, if any, corresponds to the given number?

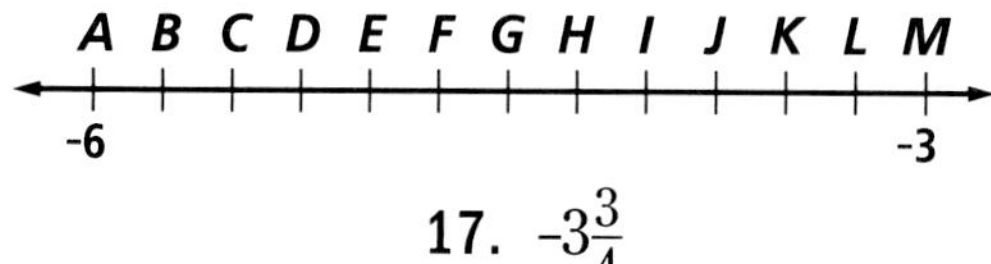

16. -5

17. $-3\frac{3}{4}$

18. $-4\frac{1}{4}$

19. $-6\frac{1}{2}$

20. Write the key sequence for entering $-3\frac{9}{11}$ on your calculator.

REVIEW

21. Graph 3, 4, -8, and -9 on a horizontal number line. **(Lesson 1-7)**

22. Represent the numbers in the following sentence as integers: I grew one inch, lost five pounds, met three new friends, and feel twice as happy as I ever have! **(Lesson 1-7)**

23. Use fractions to solve the following riddle:

Why do silent frogs live forever?

Fill in the blanks with letters from each word using the following clues. The first clue has been done for you. **(Lesson 1-6)**

Clues
first third of "Theocracy"
first third of "You"
first half of "Canteens"
first half of "Croatian"
last third of "Ask"

T H E ? ? ? ? ? ? ? ? ? ?

24. If you have 38 minutes to run 5 miles, write a fraction expressing the average time each mile would take. **(Lesson 1-6)**

25. Write four fractions equal to 8. **(Lesson 1-5)**

26. Many doctors say that adults should drink 8 cups of water per day to be healthy. A particular chemist likes to only measures things in small units. He drinks 386 teaspoons of water each day. How many cups does he drink? Is this enough to be healthy? **(Lesson 1-4)**

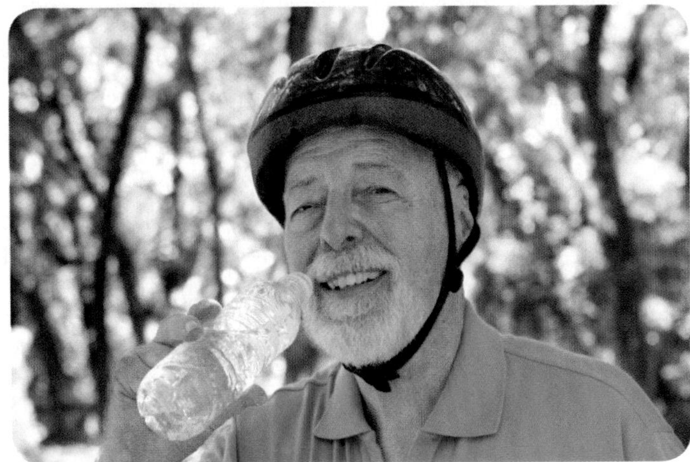

The National Academy of Sciences recommends a daily allowance of 1 millimeter of fluid for each calorie burned; a little over 8 cups for a typical 2,000-calorie diet.

EXPLORATION

27. From noon to 12:15 P.M., the minute hand of a clock turns $-\frac{1}{4}$ revolution. Give the fraction that represents the minute hand's movement from
    a. noon to 12:20 P.M.
    b. noon to 1:00 P.M.
    c. noon to 1:55 P.M.

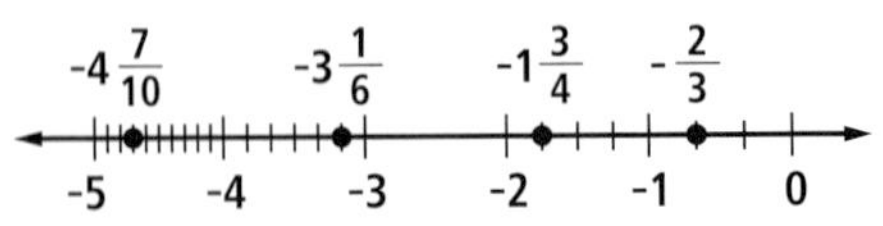

Chapter 1 Projects

A project presents an opportunity for you to extend your knowledge of a topic related to the material of this chapter. You should allow more time for a project than you do for typical homework questions.

1 A Cup Display

Create a display that shows the relationships between cups, quarter cups, tablespoons, and teaspoons. Use the gallon pictures on page 26 for ideas. A good display will help classmates remember the measurement relationships needed when cooking.

Spices are normally measured with spoons. Flour is usually measured with cups.

2 Other Number Systems

The decimal system is not the only number system that has ever been devised. You have probably seen numbers written in Roman numerals. Babylonian numerals were written in cuneiform on clay tablets using a stylus made from a reed. Cuneiform is a type of script and one of the earliest forms of writing. Write a report about one of these number systems, or any other non-decimal system. Include how to represent the numbers from 1 to 10, 25, 100, and two or three larger numbers.

The clay tablet shown contains an algebra/geometry problem in cuneiform script.

According to the Bureau of Labor Statistics, on an "average day" in 2006, persons in the U.S. age 15 and over slept about 8.6 hours. This is more than $\frac{1}{3}$ of the day!

3 Making a Schedule

Think about everything you do during the day: attending school, sleeping, eating, reading, socializing, and so on. Create a typical schedule for the day, divided into half-hour segments. Find what fraction of the day you use for each activity. When displaying your results, include the fraction in lowest terms and list your activities from most time-consuming to least time-consuming.

4 Large Numbers

Create a collage using at least ten large numbers (greater than 1 million) found in a newspaper, magazine, or on the Internet. Write the number as it was printed, and give it in decimal form (if it used a place-value name). Be sure to keep the original use of the number.

5 Absolute Value

Absolute value is a term used to describe a certain numerical value of a number without regard to its sign. Find a formal definition of absolute value. Research how absolute value is used in the real world, in graphs, and in equations with regard to length. Write a paragraph about your findings.

Chapter 1 Summary and Vocabulary

- The **whole numbers,** together with their opposites make up the **integers** ..., -2, -1, 0, 1, 2, ... Our standard way of writing whole numbers is called the **decimal** or **base-10 system.** Place-value names are used in reading these numbers.

- **Counts** have counting units that cannot be divided. In contrast, measures can always be split into parts. You can divide a **line segment** into any number of equal parts using lined paper.

- Numbers between whole numbers are needed for **measuring.** You can think of these numbers as part of the distance they are from one whole number to the next. For example, if the distance from 1 to 2 is split into 12 parts, then $1\frac{3}{12}$ is 3 parts away from 1 toward 2. You can be more accurate by using smaller **intervals,** such as using sixty-fourths of an inch instead of sixteenths of an inch.

- **Negative numbers** are used both for counting and measuring in situations with two opposite directions. You can represent **positive** and **negative numbers, fractions,** and **mixed numbers** on a **number line.**

- Every fraction is a **division.** The fraction $\frac{15}{12}$ is the division $15 \div 12$. An **improper fraction** that is not equal to an integer can be written as a mixed number: $\frac{15}{12} = 1\frac{3}{12}$.

- By multiplying (or dividing) the numerator and denominator of a fraction by the same number, you can create an **equivalent fraction.** For example, $\frac{25}{40} = \frac{7 \times 25}{7 \times 40} = \frac{175}{280}$. When the numerator and denominator have no common factor, the fraction is said to be in **lowest terms.**

- Some measurements have **mixed units.** For example, $\frac{15}{12}$ feet can be written as $1\frac{3}{12}$ feet, as 15 inches, or as 1 foot, 3 inches.

Theorems and Properties

Equal Fractions Property (p. 33)

Vocabulary

1-1
whole numbers
decimal system
base-10 system
counting unit

1-2
line segment
endpoint
midpoint
numerator
denominator

1-3
length
interval
mixed number

1-4
mixed units

1-5
equivalent fractions
lowest terms
simplifying the fraction

1-6
proper fraction
improper fraction

1-7
negative number
opposite
integer

Chapter 1 Self-Test

Take this test as you would take a test in class. You will need a calculator. Then use the Selected Answers section in the back of the book to check your work.

1. Write the number five hundred eight million, twenty-seven thousand, four hundred twelve in base-10 notation.

2. Write 9,123,083 in words.

In 3 and 4, use the segment below.

3. Measure this segment to the nearest quarter inch.

4. Trace this segment and divide it into three equal parts.

5. A surgical screw used to mend a patient's broken leg was $2\frac{3}{8}$ in. long. Draw a segment of this length.

6. The Tour de France is a bicycle race that is divided into 20 stages, with one stage raced each day.
   a. Draw a segment that represents the Tour divided into its 20 stages.
   b. In lowest terms, what fraction of the Tour is complete after 16 stages?

7. Order $1\frac{3}{4}$, $-\frac{2}{3}$, $-2\frac{2}{3}$, 0, $1\frac{5}{8}$, and $-2\frac{5}{6}$ from least to greatest.

8. The tallest player on the New York Liberty women's basketball team in 2007 was 6'5". How many inches is this?

9. Write three fractions equal to $\frac{9}{20}$.

10. Write three fractions equal to $\frac{5}{9}$.

11. **True or False** $\frac{7}{13} = 13 \div 7$

12. **Fill in the Blank** According to the Equal Fractions Property, $\frac{2}{3} = \frac{?}{18}$.

13. An 800-inch plank is to be sawed into 12 equal pieces.
    a. Write a division expression for the number of inches each piece will be. Divide and express the result as a mixed number in lowest terms.
    b. What is the answer to Part a in feet?

14. Express $1{,}280 \div 50$ as a mixed number in lowest terms.

15. Write $\frac{416}{35}$ as a mixed number.

16. Rewrite $\frac{66}{15}$ in lowest terms.

17. The high temperatures (in degrees Celsius) on the first five days of 2006 in Butte, Montana were 1°, 0°, -2°, -4°, and -3°. Graph these values on a number line.

18. **Matching** Match each number with a point on the number line below.

T U V W X Y Z

-2 -1 0 1 2 3

a. $-1\frac{1}{3}$ b. $2\frac{3}{4}$ c. $-2\frac{2}{3}$ d. $2\frac{1}{4}$ e. $1\frac{3}{4}$

In 19 and 20, represent the situation using positive numbers, negative numbers, or zero.

19. The highest peak in the world is Mt. Everest, cresting at 29,035 feet above sea level.

20. The snail on the wall didn't move an inch for days.

21. Explain why $\frac{100}{80}$ is equal to $\frac{5}{4}$.

Chapter 1 Chapter Review

SKILLS
PROPERTIES
USES
REPRESENTATIONS

SKILLS Procedures used to get answers

OBJECTIVE A Write word names for decimals, and vice versa. **(Lesson 1-1)**

In 1 and 2, write the number in words.

1. 91,402,725 miles: the closest Earth gets to our sun
2. 24,800,000,000,000 miles: the approximate distance to the nearest star other than our sun
3. A whole number is read "eighty-six thousand". How many digits does it have?
4. **True or False** Every seven-digit number is greater than every six-digit number. Explain.

In 5 and 6, write the number in decimal notation.

5. seven million, fifty-three thousand, one hundred ninety six
6. three billion, six million, one hundred twenty-four thousand, eighty-one

OBJECTIVE B Given a simple fraction, write other fractions equal to it. **(Lesson 1-5)**

In 7–10, rewrite the fraction in lowest terms.

7. $\frac{48}{72}$
8. $\frac{24}{20}$
9. $\frac{55{,}000}{35{,}000}$
10. $\frac{7{,}070}{42{,}420}$

In 11–14, write three fractions equal to the given number.

11. $16\frac{3}{4}$
12. $\frac{5}{7}$
13. $-12\frac{9}{12}$
14. $-\frac{26}{143}$

OBJECTIVE C Rewrite improper fractions as mixed numbers. **(Lesson 1-6)**

In 15–18, write the simple fraction as a mixed number.

15. $\frac{25}{2}$
16. $\frac{38}{5}$
17. $\frac{373}{200}$
18. $\frac{38}{9}$
19. Explain why $4\frac{2}{3}$ is equal to $\frac{14}{3}$.

OBJECTIVE D Write the answer to a division problem as a mixed number. **(Lesson 1-6)**

In 20–23, express the answer to the division problem as a mixed number in lowest terms.

20. $18 \div 12$
21. $63 \div 35$
22. $100 \div 60$
23. $150 \div 4$

OBJECTIVE E Order integers, fractions, and mixed numbers. **(Lessons 1-7, 1-8)**

In 24–27, order the four numbers from least to greatest.

24. -7, -17, 4, 7
25. $\frac{1}{8}, \frac{1}{6}, \frac{2}{7}, \frac{2}{9}$
26. $2\frac{1}{2}, 3\frac{1}{3}, -4\frac{1}{4}, -5\frac{1}{5}$
27. $-2\frac{1}{3}, -\frac{11}{3}, -5\frac{5}{3}, -\frac{19}{3}$

OBJECTIVE F Measure lengths in customary units. **(Lesson 1-3)**

28. Measure the length of the segment below to the nearest quarter inch.

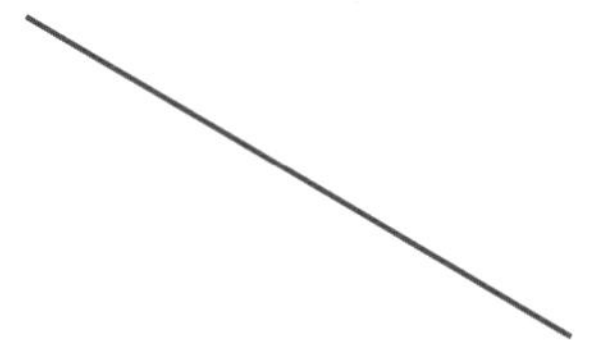

29. Measure the segment below to the nearest eighth of an inch.

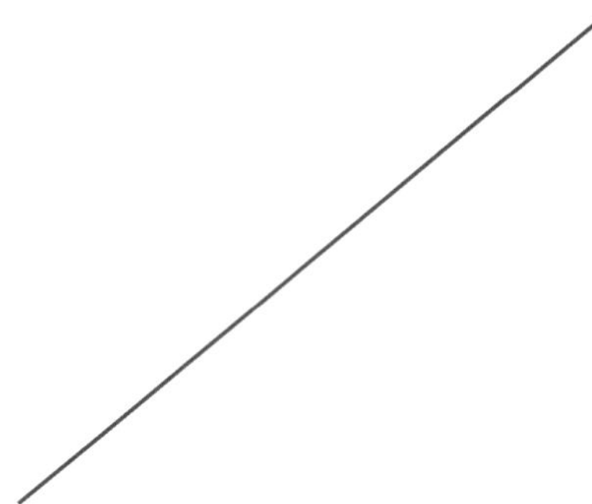

30. What is the volume of the liquid below?

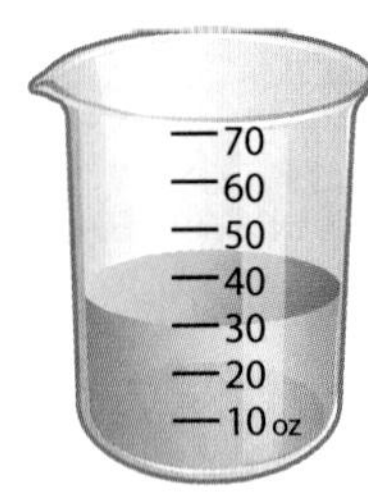

PROPERTIES The principles behind the mathematics

OBJECTIVE G Recognize the Equal Fractions Property and the meaning of a fraction in terms of division. (Lessons 1-5, 1-6)

In 31 and 32, state a property or rule that justifies the statement.

31. $\frac{7}{10} = \frac{7 \cdot 2}{10 \cdot 2}$

32. Two-thirds equals two divided by three.

33. What can be done to rewrite $\frac{1}{2}$ as $\frac{25}{50}$?

34. Multiple Choice Which of the following equals $\frac{11}{5}$?

A $11 \cdot 5$ **B** $11 \div \frac{1}{5}$ **C** $11 \cdot \frac{1}{5}$

USES Applications of mathematics in real-world situations

OBJECTIVE H Rewrite mixed units using a single unit. (Lesson 1-4)

35. Suppose a baby at birth weighs 7 pounds, 13 ounces.

a. How many ounces is this?

b. How many pounds is this?

36. Samuel stuffed 100 envelopes in 8 minutes, 3 seconds. Adriana stuffed 100 envelopes in 6 minutes, 38 seconds. How many seconds did it take them both to stuff 200 envelopes if Adriana started when Samuel stopped?

37. If a toy car track is four feet, three inches long, how many inches long is it?

38. The basketball player Dwyane Wade is 6 feet, 4 inches tall.

a. How many inches tall is he?

b. Write his height as a mixed number in lowest terms.

39. There are 1,760 yards in 1 mile. An Olympic marathon is 26 miles, 385 yards.

a. How many miles is an Olympic marathon in lowest terms?

b. How many yards is this?

OBJECTIVE I Correctly interpret situations with directions and amounts that are positive, negative, or corresponding to zero. (Lesson 1-7)

40. 450 meters below sea level corresponds to what number?

In 41–43, an auto mechanic estimates the cost to fix a car. What number stands for each estimate?

41. an estimate \$25 below the actual cost of repair
42. an estimate \$40 higher than the actual cost of repair
43. an estimate equal to the actual cost of repair

REPRESENTATIONS Pictures, graphs, or objects that illustrate concepts

OBJECTIVE J Graph simple fractions, mixed numbers, and integers on a number line. (Lessons 1-7, 1-8)

For 44 and 45, graph the given numbers on a number line.

44. $-\frac{1}{5}$, $-1\frac{1}{5}$, 2, $\frac{2}{5}$
45. -30, 20, 15, -10, 0

In 46 and 47, identify which letter corresponds to the given number.

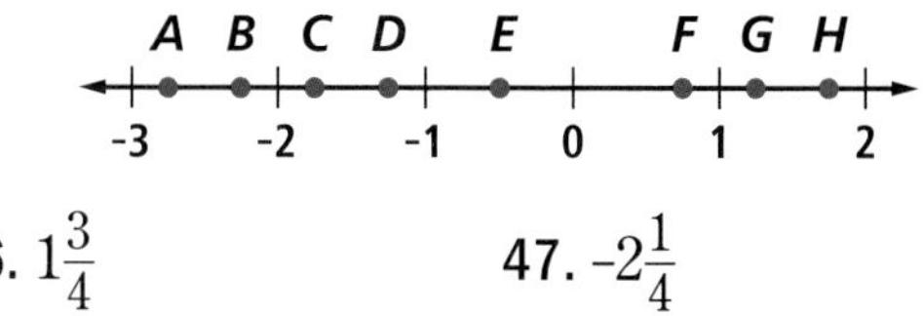

46. $1\frac{3}{4}$

47. $-2\frac{1}{4}$

OBJECTIVE K Draw a line segment with a given length. (Lesson 1-3)

48. Draw a line segment with length $3\frac{1}{2}$ in.
49. Draw a line segment with length $2\frac{1}{4}$ in.
50. Draw a vertical line segment with length $4\frac{3}{8}$ inches.
51. Draw a horizontal line segment with length $3\frac{5}{16}$ inches.

OBJECTIVE L Indicate parts of trips completed as points on a line segment. (Lesson 1-2)

52. Trace the segment below and divide it into
    a. four equal parts.
    b. five equal parts.

53. How many tick marks are needed to divide a segment into 13 equal parts?

In 54 and 55, Marissa and her friends are going on a road trip from Jacksonville, Florida to San Antonio, Texas. They will drive on the Interstate 10 highway, which is roughly a straight line about 1,066 miles long as shown below.

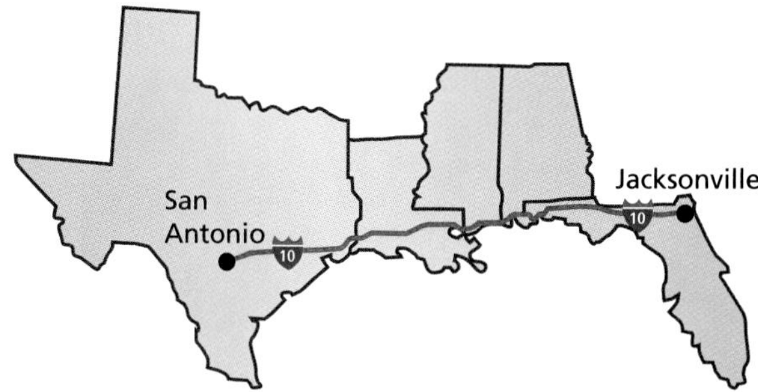

54. a. Trace the route and divide the trip into five equal segments.
    b. What fraction of the trip will they have completed when they have driven four of these segments?
55. a. Trace the route and divide the trip into eight equal segments.
    b. What fraction of the trip will they have completed when they have driven six of these segments?

Chapter 2

Some Uses of Decimals and Percents

Contents

Mathematical tools such as the protractor and compass have existed for hundreds of years. The idea of fractions dates back to ancient times. They are found in some writings over 3,000 years old. The use of decimals for numbers between whole numbers is more recent. The use of decimals in place of fractions was first popularized by the Belgian mathematician Simon Stevin in 1585. Thirty years later, the Scottish mathematician John Napier created a decimal-notation system like the one we use today, except that he separated the decimal part from the whole number part with a comma. In Europe, decimals are still written that way. Europeans write 2,03 where we in the United States write 2.03.

Many common everyday units are older than decimals. The *foot* was supposedly the size of Charlemagne's foot, who ruled France from 768 to 814 CE. The *yard* was the distance from the nose to the thumb of the outstretched arm of King Henry I of England. He reigned from 1100 to 1135 CE. By the 1700s, the measurement system in England was arranged into an assortment of lengths, weights, and money as shown in the table below.

In the 1780s, Thomas Jefferson and a group of scientists proposed a new system for measuring lengths, weights, and money based on the decimal system. Jefferson was only able to convince his fellow patriots to adopt this system for money. The new United States of America was the first country in the world to have a system of dollars and cents based on decimals.

The complete measurement system Jefferson wanted, the *metric system*, was first adopted in France in 1795 and is now used throughout the world. In this chapter, you will see how the decimal system of writing numbers and the metric system of measurement are related to each other and to percents and fractions.

Length	Weight	Money
12 inches = 1 foot	16 drams = 1 ounce	12 pence = 1 shilling
3 feet = 1 yard	16 ounces = 1 pound (lb)	20 shillings = 1 pound (£)
$5\frac{1}{3}$ yards = 1 rod	14 pounds = 1 stone	21 shillings = 1 guinea
1760 yards = 1 mile	2000 pounds = 1 ton	

Lesson 2-1

Decimals for Numbers between Whole Numbers

Vocabulary

expanded notation

one-place decimal

two-place decimal

▸ **BIG IDEA** All of the numbers of normal arithmetic can be written in base 10 as decimals.

In Chapter 1, you studied fractions. In this chapter, you will study decimals. Like fractions, decimals can describe part of a whole. They also describe numbers between integers.

Mental Math

Find each sum.

a. $4 \times 100 + 2 \times 10 + 8 \times 1$

b. $5 \times 1{,}000 + 4 \times 100 + 2 \times 10 + 8 \times 1$

c. $5 \times 1{,}000 + 2 \times 10 + 8 \times 1$

Different Kinds of Decimals

The place value of each digit in a decimal is ten times the place value of the digit to its right. Normal human body temperature is 98.6 degrees Fahrenheit. A decimal written to show all of its place values is said to be in **expanded notation,** as shown below.

$$\begin{aligned} 98.6 &= 9 \text{ tens} + 8 \text{ ones} + 6 \text{ tenths} \\ &= (9 \times 10) + (8 \times 1) + (6 \times \tfrac{1}{10}) \\ &= (9 \times 10) + (8 \times 1) + (6 \times 0.1) \end{aligned}$$

The number 98.6 is an example of a **one-place decimal** because it has one decimal place to the right of the decimal point.

The number 365.47 is a **two-place decimal** because it has two decimal places to the right of the decimal point. Money amounts are sometimes written as two-place decimals.

$$\begin{aligned} \$365.47 &= 3 \text{ hundreds} + 6 \text{ tens} + 5 \text{ ones} + 4 \text{ dimes} + 7 \text{ pennies} \\ &= 3 \times 100 + 6 \times 10 + 5 \times 1 + 4 \times 0.1 + 7 \times 0.01 \end{aligned}$$

A penny has one-tenth the value of a dime. A dime has one-tenth the value of a dollar. The value of each place is one-tenth the value of the place to its left.

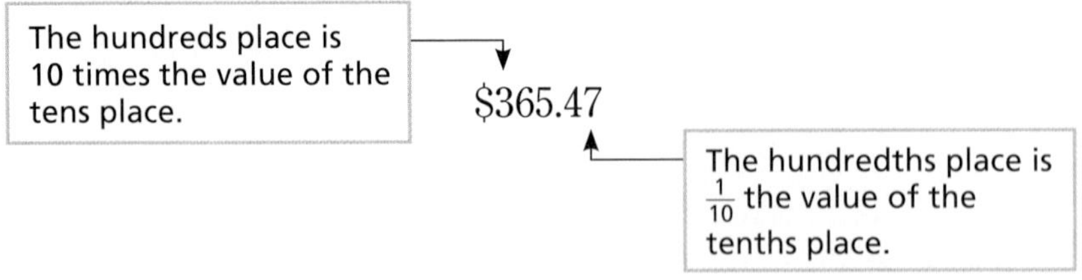
The hundreds place is 10 times the value of the tens place.
$365.47
The hundredths place is $\frac{1}{10}$ the value of the tenths place.

Graphing Decimals on a Number Line

Decimals, like fractions, can be graphed on a number line. In 1988, Florence Griffith-Joyner set the world record in the women's 200-meter run with a time of 21.34 seconds. This time is between 21 and 22 seconds. This interval is graphed on the number line below.

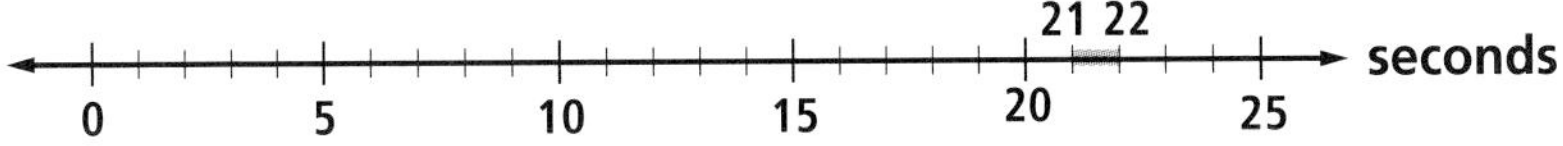

Changing the interval to between 21.3 and 21.4 allows for more accuracy. The tick marks now show tenths of a second. The value 21.34 is between 21.3 and 21.4.

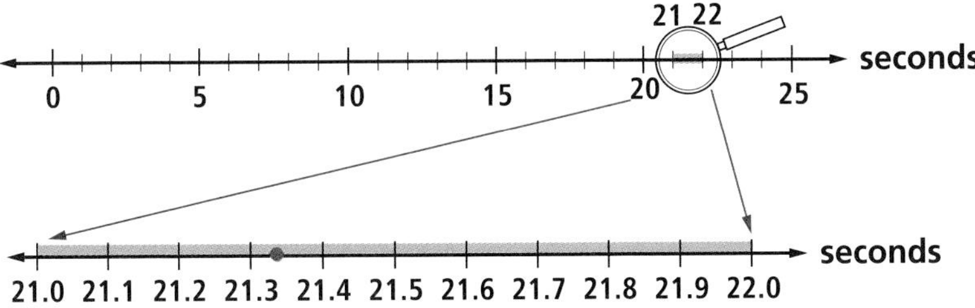

The interval from 21.3 and 21.4 can be enlarged. The tick marks now show tenths of tenths, or hundredths, of a second.

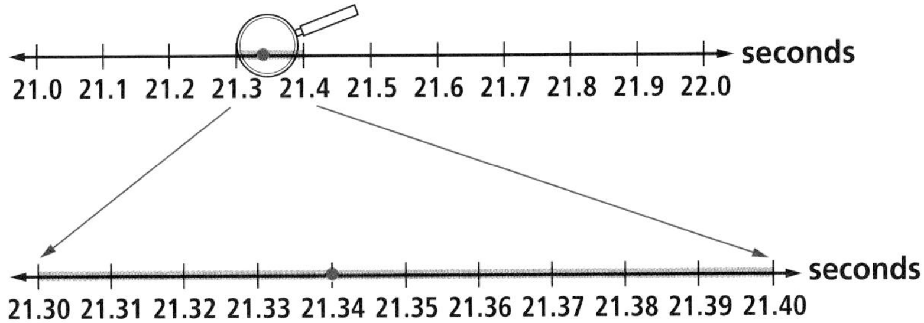

Names for Decimal Places

Some situations require decimals with more than two places to the right of the decimal point. For example, computers work at speeds often measured in nanoseconds, which are billionths of a second.

To remember the names for the decimal-place values, think of the ones place and the decimal point as the "center." The names to the right and to the left of the ones place and decimal point balance.

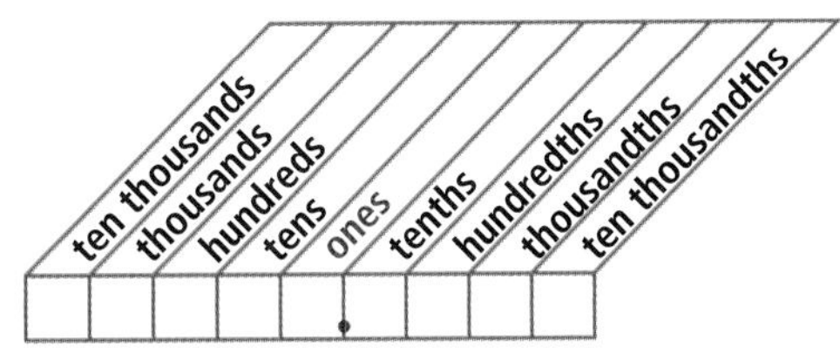

During the 1988 Olympics, Florence Griffith-Joyner also set the woman's world record for the 100-meter run with a time of 10.62 seconds.

Source: Sports Illustrated

The decimal 1.414213562 is part of the infinite decimal that represents the length of a diagonal of a square with sides of length 1 unit. This diagonal has a length equal to the ***square root of 2,*** written $\sqrt{2}$. The number $\sqrt{2}$ equals a non-ending decimal with digits that do not repeat in any pattern. Here are the first 30 decimal places of $\sqrt{2}$.

$$\sqrt{2} = 1.41421\ 35623\ 73095\ 04880\ 16887\ 24209\ldots$$

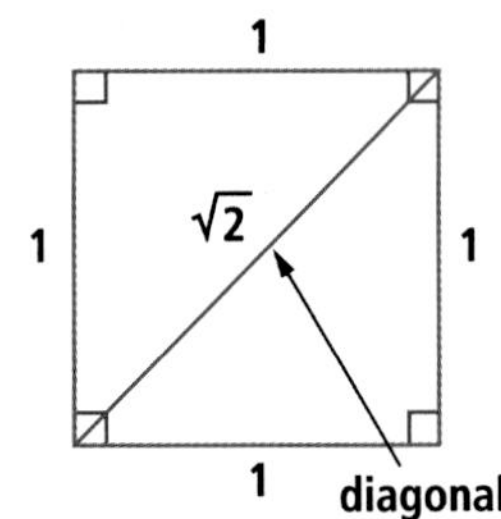

The digits above are separated into groups of five so they can be read more easily. Here are the names of first nine decimal places.

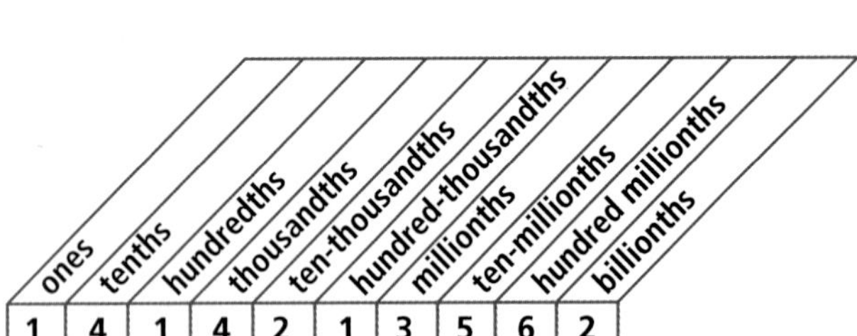

QY1

Find how many digits of $\sqrt{2}$ your calculator displays.

Comparing Decimals

Decimals are often easier than fractions to order and compare.

Example 1

Which is greater, 6.37 or 6.215?

Solution 1 Align the decimal points. (This means to write the numbers so the decimal points are above one another.)

6.37
6.215

Start at the leftmost digit. Move right, one place at a time, until there is a difference between the digits. As 3 is greater than 2, so **6.37 is greater than 6.215.**

Solution 2 Think about money: \$6.215 is between \$6.21 and \$6.22. \$6.22 is less than \$6.37. So **6.215 is less than 6.37.**

Below is a graph of the numbers showing which is larger.

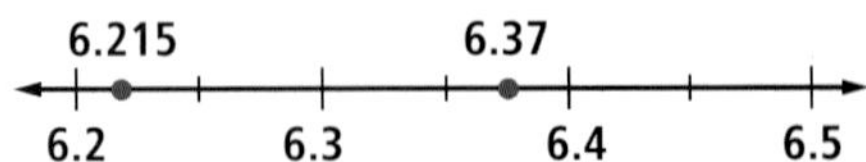

When you compare whole numbers, the number with the most digits is always greatest. This is not true for numbers that are *not* whole numbers. For decimals, the number with the most decimal places is *not* always greatest.

GUIDED

Example 2

Order 0.005312, 0.00579, and 0.0000009 from least to greatest.

Solution 1 0.0000009 is least because it has 0 thousandths, while the others each have ___?___ thousandths. 0.005312 comes next because it has 3 ten-thousandths, while 0.00579 has ___?___ ten-thousandths.

So the numbers from least to greatest are 0.0000009, ___?___, ___?___.

Solution 2 Align the decimal points. Then place zeros to the right of the numbers to make all the decimals have the same number of decimal places.

0.0053120
0.0057900
0.0000009

Using this method, you can temporarily ignore the decimal point and view the decimals as whole numbers in order to compare them. Now you can see that 0.0000009 is least, ___?___ is greater, and ___?___ is greatest.

Each number in Example 2 has a zero to the left of the decimal point. This zero is not needed. For example, \$.99 and \$0.99 have the same value. However, writing zeros to the left of the decimal point can make numbers easier to order and compare. It also draws attention to the decimal point and matches the display on many calculators.

STOP **QY2**

This is the first of several questions that will ask you to decode some words. Save your answers for the entire chapter for the table in Question 22 in Lesson 2-10 on page 126. Each letter is matched with a decimal. Order the numbers from least to greatest so that their corresponding letters spell two words.

N	4.891
S	4.91
I	4.909
O	4.89
E	4.9

Now you can play *Number Top-It: Decimal Variation*. The directions for this game are on page G3 at the back of this book.

Questions

COVERING THE IDEAS

1. Consider the number 31.665307.
   a. Between what two consecutive whole numbers is 31.665307?
   b. What digit is in the tenths place?
   c. What digit is in the hundredths place?

2. Consider the number 123,456.789078. What digit is in each place?
   a. thousands
   b. tenths
   c. thousandths
   d. hundred-thousandths

3. What digit is in the millionths place of $\sqrt{2}$?

4. Name a kind of measurement that can require accuracy to billionths.

5. Name one advantage of decimals over fractions.

In 6–9, put the numbers in order from least to greatest.

6. 0.02, 0.015, 0.0018
7. 4.321, 5.289, 3.8
8. 0.0001, 0.00001, 0.000000001
9. 0.34, 0.345, 0.3445

In 10 and 11, use the number line below.

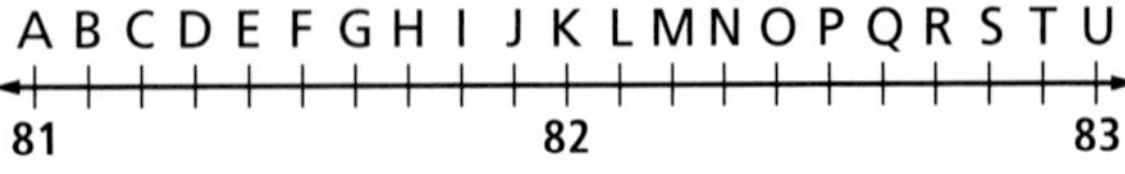

10. What is the length of each interval between consecutive letters?

11. Write the number that corresponds to each letter as a fraction and as a decimal.
    a. D   b. J   c. S   d. F

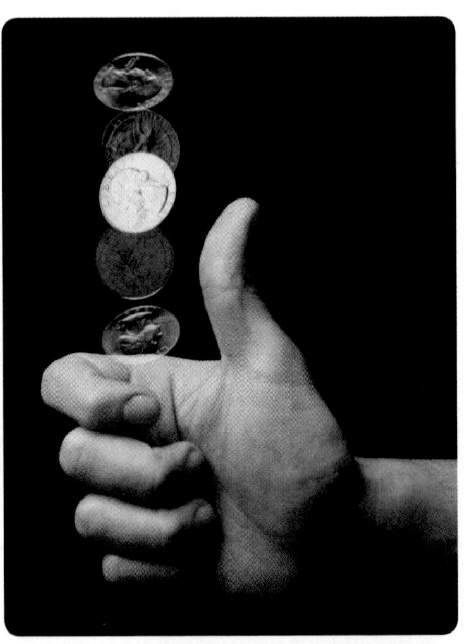

The George Washington quarter in circulation today was first produced by the U.S. Mint in 1932.

Source: United States Mint

APPLYING THE MATHEMATICS

In 12–14, write the number
   a. as a fraction.
   b. in words.

12. 2.54 (the number of centimeters in 1 inch)
13. 0.0625 (the probability of getting four heads in four tosses of a fair coin)
14. 79.6 (the average number of people per square mile in the United States in 2000)

15. You can find a number between 9.6 and 9.7 by first writing them as 9.60 and 9.70. Then, you can see that any decimal beginning with 9.61, 9.62, and so on up to 9.69, is between those numbers. Use this idea to find a number between 45.8 and 45.9.

16. A store sells 5 pairs of socks for $18. Malcolm wants only one pair. He uses a calculator to divide 18 by 5. The calculator shows 3.6. How much should Malcolm pay for one pair of socks?

17. In 2005, Asafa Powell set an unofficial men's world record of 9.77 seconds in the 100-meter dash.

    a. Copy the number line below, but enlarge it to show intervals of hundredths. Graph 9.77 on your number line.

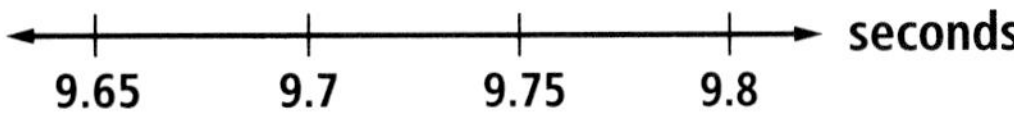

    b. If someone beat this record by one tenth of a second, what would the new record be?

    c. Graph your answer to Part b on your number line.

Asafa Powell

In 18 and 19, order the numbers from least to greatest.

18. five thousandths
    six thousandths
    five millionths

19. twenty-one thousandths
    twenty-one thousands
    twenty-one

REVIEW

20. Express the answer to $180 \div 25$ as a mixed number in lowest terms. **(Lesson 1-4)**

21. A commuter train leaves Central Station every 20 minutes from 6:00 A.M. to 9:00 A.M. How many possible morning trains could a commuter take? (*Hint:* Use a number line to represent this situation.) **(Lesson 1-2)**

Did you know that New York City has the largest fleet of subway cars in the world?

Source: Metropolitan Transit Authority

22. Consider the number in the following sentence: According to the Internet Broadway Database, the musical *Cats* ran for almost seventy-five hundred performances on Broadway. **(Lesson 1-1)**
    a. What is the count?
    b. What is the counting unit?

23. **Matching** Match each fraction to its percent. **(Previous Course)**

Fraction	Percent
a. $\frac{1}{4}$	i. 40%
b. $\frac{4}{10}$	ii. $33\frac{1}{3}$%
c. $\frac{3}{4}$	iii. 25%
d. $\frac{1}{3}$	iv. 75%
e. $\frac{1}{6}$	v. $16\frac{2}{3}$%

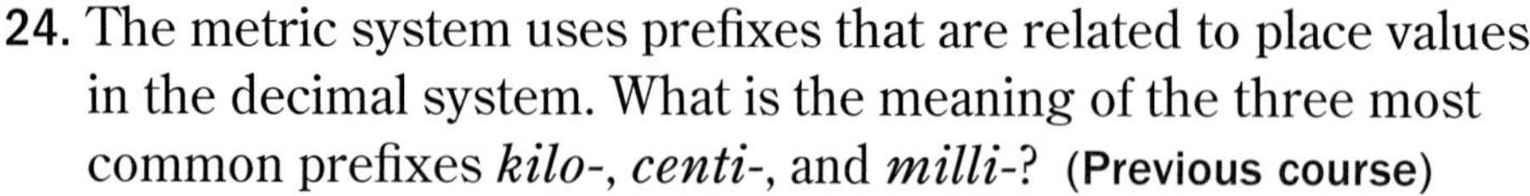

24. The metric system uses prefixes that are related to place values in the decimal system. What is the meaning of the three most common prefixes *kilo-*, *centi-*, and *milli-*? **(Previous course)**

EXPLORATION

25. Find the greatest number of decimal places to which $\sqrt{2}$ has been computed. To how many places was it computed? List your source.

QY ANSWERS

1. Answers vary. Sample: 10
2.

O	4.89
N	4.891
E	4.9
I	4.909
S	4.91

Lesson 2-2 Multiplying by 10, 100, ...

▸ **BIG IDEA** You can multiply a decimal by 10, 100, 1000, ... by moving the decimal point the correct number of places to the right.

Multiplying by 10

In 2006, the Chicago Cubs played their rivals, the Chicago White Sox, in a baseball game attended by 39,301 fans.

$$\left.\begin{aligned} 39{,}301 = {} & (3 \times 10{,}000) + \\ & (9 \times 1{,}000) + \\ & (3 \times 100) + \\ & (0 \times 10) + \\ & (1 \times 1) \end{aligned}\right\}$$

End place value is 10 times the place value of the digit to its right.

This expanded notation shows that each place value is ten times the value of the place to its right. This property of decimals makes it easy to multiply a decimal by 10. Each digit moves one decimal place to the right when you multiply by 10.

Rewrite 39,301 with a decimal point and a zero following it. Move the decimal point 1 place to the right.

$$\begin{aligned} 39{,}301.0 \times 10 &= 39{,}301.0 \\ &= 393{,}010 \end{aligned}$$

This is an example of a useful property of the decimal system.

Decimal Multiplication by 10

To multiply a number in decimal notation by 10, move the decimal point one place to the right.

This multiplication can be used in the following situation. Suppose the fans at the game spent an average of $10 per person on food. To find the total amount spent on food, you need to multiply 39,301 by 10. The total amount spent on food would be $393,010.

QY

a. Multiply 132.67 by 10. **b.** Multiply 0.007 by 10.

Mental Math

Bagels are sold in bags of one-half dozen. How many dozen bagels are in

a. 2 bags?

b. 3 bags?

c. 10 bags?

d. 5 bags?

Multiplying by 100

Because 100 = 10 × 10, multiplying a number by 100 is like multiplying it by 10 and then multiplying it by 10 again. So to multiply a decimal by 100, move the decimal point *two* places to the right.

$$86.774 \times 100 = 86.774$$
$$= 8{,}677.4$$

This same idea can be used to multiply by 1,000; 10,000; and so on.

$$10 \times 96.2 = 962$$
$$100 \times 96.2 = 10 \times 10 \times 96.2 = 9{,}620$$
$$1{,}000 \times 96.2 = 10 \times 10 \times 10 \times 96.2 = 96{,}200$$
$$10{,}000 \times 96.2 = 10 \times 10 \times 10 \times 10 \times 96.2 = 962{,}000$$

To multiply by a multiple of 10, move the decimal point as many places to the right as there are zeros.

Here is a way to think about certain types of multiplication problems so you can do them in your head.

GUIDED

Example 1

Compute in your head.

a. 20 • 15　　b. 31 • 300　　c. 25 • 40

Solution

a. Think 20 = 2 × 10.
20 • 15 = 2 • (10 • 15)
= 2 • 150
= 300

b. Think 300 = _?_ • _?_.
31 × 300 = (31 • _?_) • _?_
= _?_ • _?_
= _?_

c. Think 40 = _?_ • _?_.
25 × 40 = (_?_ • _?_) • _?_
= _?_ • _?_
= _?_

Multiplying by Decimals Written with Word Names

The word names for some large numbers are shown below.

Decimal Notation	Word Name
1,000	one thousand
1,000,000	one million
1,000,000,000	one billion
1,000,000,000,000	one trillion
1,000,000,000,000,000	one quadrillion
1,000,000,000,000,000,000	one quintillion

READING MATH

Look at the words *billion*, *trillion*, and *quadrillion*. The prefixes they start with *bi-*, *tri-*, and *quad-* stand for 2, 3, and 4. You will see these prefixes used in many words: biweekly means twice a week, triathlon has 3 sporting events, a quad is a rectangular area with 4 sides.

People often use the word name instead of writing so many zeros. For example, the made-for-television movie *High School Musical 2* was watched by 17.2 million viewers according to the *New York Times*. "17.2 million" means 17.2 *times* a million.

$$\begin{aligned} 17.2 \text{ million} &= 17.2 \times 1{,}000{,}000 \\ &= 17{,}200{,}000 \end{aligned}$$

You can check this by noticing that 17.2 million is between 17 million and 18 million. So 17,200,000 should be between 17,000,000 and 18,000,000, which it is.

You can replace the word *million* with the number 1,000,000 because of the *Substitution Principle*.

Substitution Principle

If two numbers are equal, then one number can be substituted for the other in any computation without changing the results of the computation.

This principle is very useful. It can be applied in the solution of many different types of problems.

GUIDED

Example 2

According to *The World Almanac*, 2.34 billion bushels of wheat were produced in the United States in 2003. Write 2.34 billion in decimal notation.

Solution 2.34 billion = 2.34 × _?_

= _?_

Check Because 2.34 is between 2 and 3, 2.34 billion must be between 2 billion and 3 billion. That is, your answer should be between 2,000,000,000 and 3,000,000,000.

In 2006, the United States was the world's fourth largest provider of wheat, producing over 50 million metric tons.

Source: USDA

Questions

COVERING THE IDEAS

1. In the number 18,745.062, give the value of the digit.
   a. 4
   b. 8
   c. 1
   d. 6
   e. 2

2. **Fill in the Blank** In the number 92,461, the place value of the digit 2 is __?__ times the place value of the digit 1.

In 3–6, multiply the number by 10 in your head.

3. 648
4. 5.6
5. 0.07
6. 97.03

In 7–10, multiply the number by 100 in your head.

7. 697
8. 0.66
9. 1,252.2
10. 0.151

11. a. Give a general rule for multiplying a decimal by 10.
    b. Give a general rule for multiplying a decimal by 10 million.

In 12 and 13, calculate in your head.

12. $1.01 \times 10{,}000$
13. $82 \times 1{,}000$

In 14–19, give the word name for the number written as 1 followed by the indicated number of zeros.

14. 3 zeros
15. 6 zeros
16. 9 zeros
17. 12 zeros
18. 15 zeros
19. 18 zeros

20. According to the *Oil and Gas Journal* and *World Oil,* in 2005 the United States had 204.39 trillion cubic feet of natural gas reserves. Write 204.39 trillion in decimal notation.

This section of natural gas pipeline is in Illinois.

21. The Federal Reserve stated that on May 31, 2007, there were 724,230.0 million dollars of money in circulation. On March 31, 1990, there were 257,664.4 million dollars in circulation. Write the both amounts in decimal notation.

22. Calculate the following in your head.
    a. $23 \times 3{,}000$ b. 52×200 c. $18 \times 200{,}000$

APPLYING THE MATHEMATICS

23. In December 2005, one million cars had been sold with built-in navigation systems. If the average car sold for $23,518.76, how much money was spent buying cars with built-in navigation systems?

24. 791.6264 times what number equals 7,916,264?

In 25–27, write the number as it might appear in a magazine.

25. 290,000,000 people

26. $3,430,000 in the budget

27. 26,500,000,000,000 miles to the nearest star

28. Use the graph below to estimate the world population for the given year to the nearest tenth of a billion. Write this number in decimal notation.

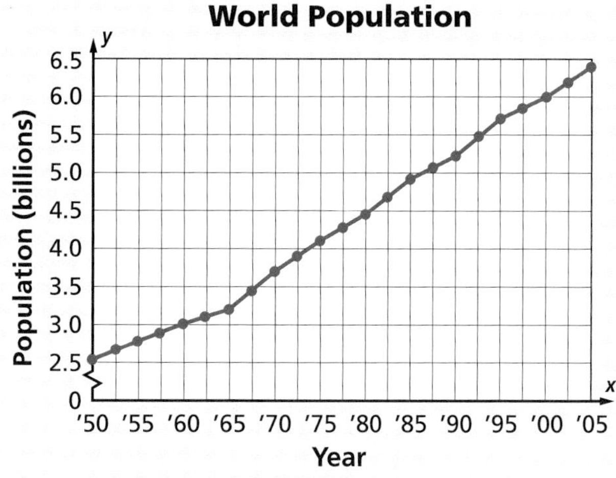

Source: U.S. Census Bureau

a. 1958 **b.** 1970 **c.** 1990 **d.** 2004

REVIEW

29. The tick marks on the number line below are equally spaced apart. Complete Parts a–c. **(Lesson 2-1)**

a. What decimal corresponds to G?

b. What decimal corresponds to J?

c. What letter corresponds to 0.4?

30. In 2005, at the DTM Hockenheimring race track, driver Jamie Green had the fastest qualifying lap time of 1:45.294 seconds. This was 76 thousandths of a second faster than Tom Kristensen, who finished in 2nd place. **(Lesson 2-1)**

a. Write 76 thousandths as a decimal.

b. What was Tom Kristensen's lap time?

Jamie Green won the Junior British Open Stock Car Championship when he was only 10 years old!

Source: Jamie Green Racing

31. Write the improper fraction as a mixed number. **(Lessons 1-6)**

a. $\frac{41}{10}$ b. $\frac{401}{100}$ c. $\frac{4,001}{1,000}$

32. One hundred small squares are shown below. Some squares are shaded. **(Previous Course)**

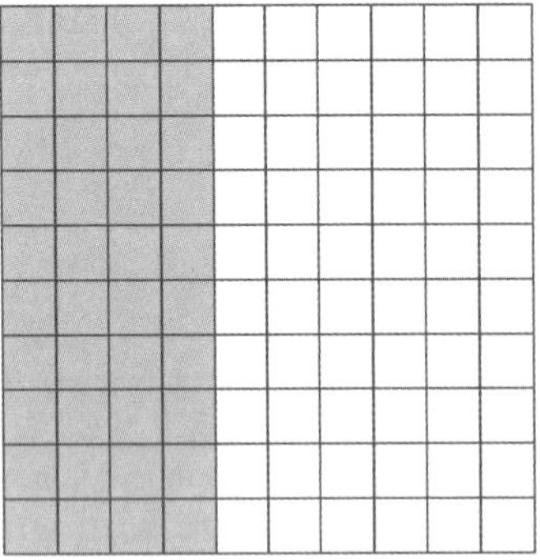

a. Express the shaded area as a fraction in lowest terms.

b. Express the shaded area as a percent.

EXPLORATION

33. A computer search of the number "17.2 million" led to about 1,170,000 hits! Do a search on this number or on another large number with a decimal and a word name. Pick the four hits that are most interesting to you. Explain why you find them interesting.

34. In England, the word *billion* does not always mean the number 1 followed by 9 zeros. What number does the word *billion* often represent in England?

QY ANSWERS

a. 1,326.7

b. 0.07

Lesson 2-3 Multiplying by $\frac{1}{10}$, $\frac{1}{100}$, ...

BIG IDEA You can multiply a decimal by $\frac{1}{10}$, $\frac{1}{100}$, $\frac{1}{1000}$, ... by moving the decimal point the correct number of places to the left.

As you saw in the last lesson, you can multiply a decimal by 10, 100, 1000, and so on, by just moving the decimal point. A similar idea works for multiplying a decimal by $\frac{1}{10}$, $\frac{1}{100}$, and $\frac{1}{1000}$, and so on. However, while the numbers 10, 100, 1000, and so on, get larger, the numbers $\frac{1}{10}$, $\frac{1}{100}$, $\frac{1}{1000}$, and so on, get smaller. This can be seen by looking at their decimal equivalents.

Mental Math

Find each product.

a. 50×11

b. 12×400

c. $3{,}000 \times 13$

d. 200×200

Fraction		Decimal		Word Name
$\frac{1}{10}$	=	0.1	=	one tenth
$\frac{1}{100}$	=	0.01	=	one hundredth
$\frac{1}{1{,}000}$	=	0.001	=	one thousandth
$\frac{1}{10{,}000}$	=	0.0001	=	one ten-thousandth
$\frac{1}{1{,}000{,}000}$	=	0.000001	=	one millionth
$\frac{1}{1{,}000{,}000{,}000}$	=	0.000000001	=	one billionth

Multiplying by $\frac{1}{10}$ or 0.1

To multiply a decimal by 10, move the decimal point one place to the *right*. Multiplication by $\frac{1}{10}$ undoes multiplication by 10. So, to multiply by $\frac{1}{10}$, or 0.1, move the decimal point one place to the *left*.

$\frac{1}{10} \times 50.692 = 50.692 = 5.0692$ *or* $0.1 \times 50.692 = 50.692 = 5.0692$

You can estimate to check your work. One tenth of \$50 is \$5.

Decimal Multiplication by $\frac{1}{10}$ or 0.1

To multiply a number in decimal notation by $\frac{1}{10}$ or 0.1, move the decimal point one place to the left.

Multiplying by $\frac{1}{100}$ or 0.01, and by $\frac{1}{1000}$ or 0.001

Multiplying by $\frac{1}{100}$ is equivalent to multiplying by $\frac{1}{10}$ and then multiplying by $\frac{1}{10}$ again. So, to multiply by $\frac{1}{100}$, or 0.01, move the decimal point *two* places to the *left*.

One year is 365.25 days, so $\frac{1}{100}$ of a year is

$$\frac{1}{100} \times 365.25 = \frac{1}{10} \times \frac{1}{10} \times 365.25 = 3.6525$$

or

$$0.01 \times 365.25 = 0.1 \times 0.1 \times 365.25 = 3.6525 \text{ days}$$

QY1

Find the product by moving the decimal point.

a. 0.1 × 12345.6789

b. 0.01 × 12345.6789

c. 0.001 × 12345.6789

You can estimate the weight of a very light object, such as a staple. You can do this by weighing a large number of them and then multiplying by the required fraction.

GUIDED

Example 1

1,000 staples weigh about 1.16 ounces. Approximate the weight of a single staple.

Solution Multiply 1.16 by $\frac{1}{1000}$ or 0.001. This is the same as multiplying by $\frac{1}{10}$ __?__ times.

0.001 × __?__ = 0.1 × __?__ × __?__ × 1.16
= __?__

One staple weighs about __?__ ounces.

GUIDED

Example 2

Compute in your head.

a. 0.2 × 43 **b.** 0.04 × 21 **c.** 0.003 × 150

Solution

a. Think 0.2 = 0.1 × 2.

0.2 × 43 = 0.1 × (2 × 43)
= 0.1 × 86
= 8.6

b. Think 0.04 = ___?___ × 4.

$0.04 \times 21 = \underline{\ ?\ } \times (\underline{\ ?\ } \times 21)$
$= \underline{\ ?\ } \times 8.4$
$= \underline{\ ?\ }$

c. Think 0.003 = ___?___ × ___?___.

$0.003 \times 150 = \underline{\ ?\ } \times (\underline{\ ?\ } \times \underline{\ ?\ })$
$= \underline{\ ?\ } \times \underline{\ ?\ }$
$= \underline{\ ?\ }$

 See QY2 at the right.

 **QY2**

Multiply in your head.

a. 0.3 × 15

b. 0.002 × 25

Multiplying by Decimals Written with Word Names

You have seen that large numbers, such as 7 million, are often written as word names. The same is true of small numbers.

GUIDED

Example 3

For jewelry to be called gold electroplate, the gold plate must be at least 7 millionths of an inch thick, and it must have at least 10-carat gold. Write the number 7 millionths in decimal notation.

Solution To write 7 million as a decimal, you begin with "7." and move the decimal point six places to the *right*. To write 7 millionths as a decimal, begin with "7." and move the decimal point six places to the *left*.

You need to add 5 zeros before placing the decimal point.

As a decimal, 7 millionths = 0.000007.

Gold electroplating is primarily performed on jewelry with intricate designs.

 **QY3**

Find the number missing from each equation.

a. 782.519 × ___?___ = 7.82519 **b.** 0.3218 × ___?___ = 32.18

 **Now you can play *Tens-Tac-Toe*. The directions for this game are on pages G6–G7 at the back of this book.**

Questions

Try to answer all the questions in this lesson without using a calculator, and without doing paper-and-pencil calculations.

COVERING THE IDEAS

In 1 and 2, write as a decimal.

1. one tenth
2. $\frac{1}{100{,}000}$

In 3 and 4, give a general rule for multiplying a decimal by the given number.

3. 0.1
4. $\frac{1}{100{,}000}$
5. Some people *tithe.* This means that they give one-tenth of their earnings to a religious organization or charity. If a family has total earnings of \$75,000, how much will they tithe?
6. Multiplying by $\frac{1}{1000}$ is the same as multiplying by what decimal?

In 7–10, write the product as a decimal.

7. $92 \times \frac{1}{10}$
8. 0.01×7
9. $\frac{1}{1000} \times 276.4946$
10. $0.0000001 \times 0.039800$

Fill in the Blanks **In 11–13, fill in the blank with a decimal.**

11. $\underline{\ ?\ } \times 25 = 0.25$
12. $350 \times \underline{\ ?\ } = 3.5$
13. $\underline{\ ?\ } \times 1{,}500 = 0.015$

In 14–16, multiply.

14. 0.02×42
15. 500×0.00003
16. $2{,}222 \times 0.004$

In 17 and 18, recall that the prefix *nano-* means one billionth. Write the number as a decimal.

17. A computer processes a calculation in 2.4 nanoseconds.
18. The wavelength of the color green is 510 nanometers.
19. 1000 postage stamps weigh 1.1 ounces. Approximate the weight of 1 stamp.

The world's first single-chip microprocessor, the Intel 4004, was created in 1971.

Source: CNN

20. Determine which number in the left column makes each equation true. Put that number's corresponding letter in the space to spell out a word. Save the word for the table in Question 22 in Lesson 2-10 on page 126.

T = 0.001	$7.984 \times \underline{\ ?\ } = 0.7984$
I = 10	$0.0562 \times \underline{\ ?\ } = 0.562$
N = 0.1	$\frac{1}{10} \times \underline{\ ?\ } = \frac{1}{100}$
Y = 0.01	$0.006 \times \underline{\ ?\ } = 6$
E = 1,000	$3.255 \times \underline{\ ?\ } = 0.003255$
	$120 \times \underline{\ ?\ } = 1.2$

APPLYING THE MATHEMATICS

21. Fill in the Blanks Fill in each blank with a number.

a. $10 \times \underline{\ ?\ } = 1$

b. $0.001 \times \underline{\ ?\ } = 1$

c. one millionth × ___?___ = one

22. a. Use the method of Example 2 to multiply 0.5 × 42.

b. Describe another way to multiply 0.5 × 42 in your head.

In 23–25, find the product.

23. 0.02 × 0.06 **24.** 400 × 0.03 **25.** 0.00008 × 0.00007

REVIEW

26. What is the result when you multiply 36.459 by the given number? **(Lesson 2-2)**

a. 100 b. 10 c. 1

In 27–29, fill in the blank with a number. (Lesson 2-2)

27. $\underline{\ ?\ } \times 45 = 45{,}000$

28. $2.86 \times \underline{\ ?\ } = 286{,}000$

29. $0.00067 \times \underline{\ ?\ } = 67$

30. Write the three underlined numbers as decimals. According to the International Program Center, the population of Asia grew from <u>two billion, four hundred sixteen million</u> in 1975 to <u>three billion, six hundred eight-six million</u> in 2000. It is projected to grow to <u>four billion, seven hundred fifty-four million</u> by 2025. **(Lesson 2-2)**

31. a. Order the numbers –1.7, –17, and 0.17 from least to greatest.

b. Graph the numbers on a number line. **(Lessons 2-1, 1-8)**

32. Name three fractions equal to $\frac{32}{48}$. **(Lesson 1-6)**

In 33 and 34, name the count and the counting unit. (Lesson 1-1)

33. A total of 513,561 guests visited the Nashville Zoo in 2005.
34. The U.S. State Department recognizes 192 independent countries around the world.

Guests enjoy a mild summer day at the Nashville Zoo.

35. **a.** What fraction is shown by the shaded area below?
    b. What percent is shown by the shaded area? **(Previous Course)**

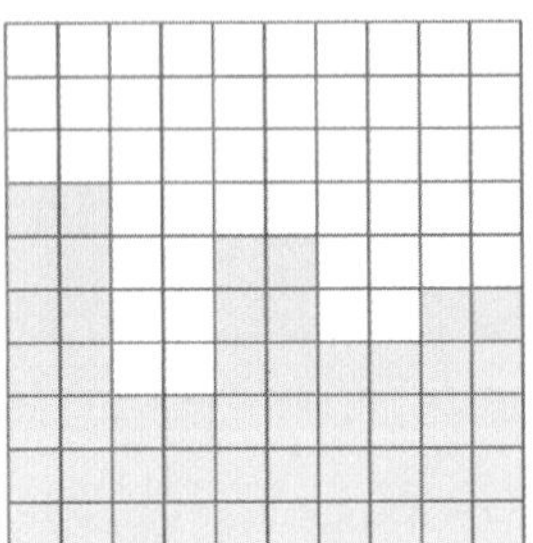

EXPLORATION

36. In Lesson 2-2, the largest place value name given was quintillion (1 followed by 18 zeros). Write the decimal number for 1 quintillionth.
37. Here are some other place values. Write each number in decimal notation.
    a. sextillion and sextillionth
    b. octillion and octillionth
    c. nonillion and nonillionth
    d. decillion and decillionth

QY ANSWERS

1a. 1234.56789

1b. 123.456789

1c. 12.3456789

2a. 4.5

2b. 0.05

3a. $\frac{1}{100}$

3b. 100

Lesson

2-4 Decimals and the Metric System

▸ **BIG IDEA** Because the metric system is based on the decimal system, converting between units in the metric system only requires multiplying by 10, 100, 1000, and so on, or by 0.1, 0.01, 0.001, and so on.

Vocabulary

metric system
kilo-, centi-, milli-
meter (m)
gram (g)
kilogram (kg)
milligram (mg)
liter (L)
milliliter (mL)
microgram

Mental Math

True or False

a. If the distance from your house to the store is 3 km, and the distance from the store to your school is 2 km, then the distance from your house directly to your school must be 5 km.

b. 12 kg of gold is heavier than 12 kg of feathers.

Inches, feet, cups, and ounces are everyday measures in the United States; however, other measures exist. For example, auto mechanics need to know how big a 13 millimeter (mm) wrench is. Nurses need to understand a 2 cubic centimeter (cc) injection. In fact, in medicine, auto mechanics, photography, science, and many other areas, almost all measurements are *metric.* The **metric system** is a system of measurement based on decimals.

Important Units of Length in the Metric System

The meanings of the prefixes of metric units are related to place values in the decimal system. The three most common prefixes are **kilo-** (1,000), **centi-** ($\frac{1}{100}$ or 0.01), and **milli-** ($\frac{1}{1,000}$ or 0.001).

Here is how these prefixes are used with length. The base unit of length is the **meter (m).**

kilo-	1 kilometer (km) = 1,000 m
centi-	1 centimeter (cm) = $\frac{1}{100}$ m or 0.01 m
milli-	1 millimeter (mm) = $\frac{1}{1,000}$ m or 0.001 m

QY1

a. How many grams are in 1 kilogram?
b. One millisecond is what part of 1 second?

A typical doorknob is about 1 meter above the floor. The kilometer is used to measure long distances; 1 kilometer is about the length of five city blocks, or a little more than $\frac{3}{5}$ mile. A circular aspirin tablet has a diameter of about 1 centimeter. A dime is about 1 millimeter thick.

Activity 1

MATERIALS meter stick or metric tape measure

Work with other students and measure the lengths of various things at your school. Here are some possibilities: perimeter of your classroom, length of a hallway, distance from home plate to first base on a baseball diamond, or length of a car or school bus.

Step 1 Find the length of each item in meters.

Step 2 Convert each length to centimeters.

Step 3 Convert each length to millimeters.

Measuring Length in Centimeters and Millimeters

The ruler below is actual size. The numbers indicate centimeters. The small tick marks divide the centimeters into millimeters.

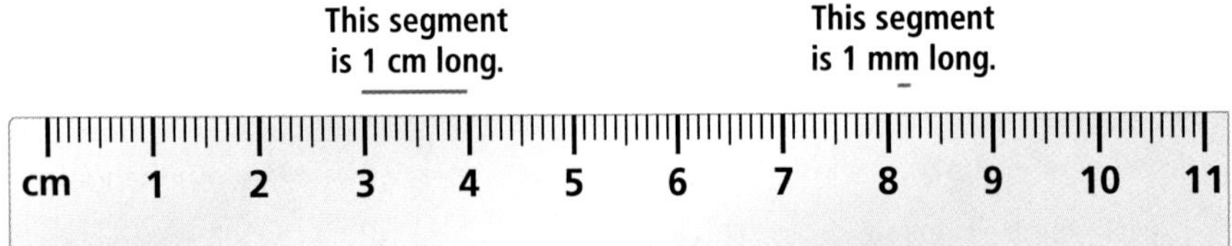

The segments below have lengths of 4 cm, $4\frac{8}{10}$ cm (or 4.8 cm), and 5 cm.

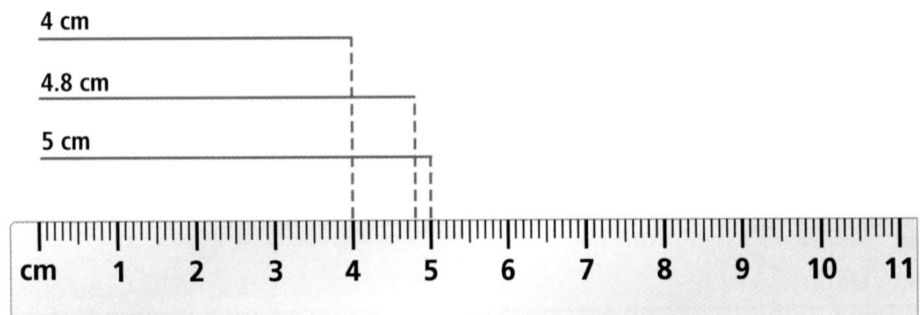

Multiplying by 10 converts these lengths to millimeters.

$$4 \text{ cm} \times 10 = 40 \text{ mm}$$
$$4.8 \text{ cm} \times 10 = 48 \text{ mm}$$
$$5 \text{ cm} \times 10 = 50 \text{ mm}$$

The segments have lengths of 40 mm, 48 mm and 50 mm.

Activity 2

MATERIALS metric ruler

Copy and complete this table.

Measurement	Length (mm)	Length (cm)
Width of this book	?	?
Height of this book	?	?
Thickness of this book	?	?

The ability to convert easily from one metric unit to another makes the metric system very useful. It is much easier than converting feet to inches, or miles to feet.

Example 1

How many meters are in 5.6 kilometers?

Solution Remember, 1 kilometer = 1,000 meters. Use the Substitution Principle from Lesson 2-2.

$$\begin{aligned} 5.6 \text{ kilometers} &= 5.6 \times 1 \text{ kilometer} \\ &= 5.6 \times 1{,}000 \text{ meters} \\ &= 5{,}600 \text{ meters} \end{aligned}$$

GUIDED

Example 2

Give the length of the segment in millimeters, centimeters, and meters.

cm 1 2 3 4 5 6 7 8 9 10 11

Solution From the ruler, you can see that the segment is about $4\frac{3}{10}$ or 4.3 cm, in length.

Because 1 cm = 10 mm, 4.3 cm = 4.3 × __?__
= 43 mm.

Because 1 mm = $\frac{1}{1000}$ m, 43 mm = 43 × __?__
= $\frac{43}{?}$ m.

So the segment is $\frac{43}{?}$ m, or 0.043 m, long.

Other Important Metric Units

Metric units of mass are multiples of the **gram (g).** In everyday use, the gram is also used to measure weight. An aspirin tablet weighs about 1 gram. One **kilogram (kg)** equals 1,000 grams. This book weighs about 1 kilogram. One **milligram (mg)** equals $\frac{1}{1,000}$, or 0.001, grams. A small staple weighs about 25 milligrams.

The most common everyday metric unit of capacity is the **liter (L).** Water is commonly sold in 0.5-liter, 1-liter, and 2-liter bottles. Smaller amounts are measured in *milliliters*. One **milliliter (mL)** equals $\frac{1}{1000}$, or 0.001, liters.

Kiloliter, liter, and milliliter, as well as kilogram, gram, and milligram, are related in a manner similar to the way kilometer, meter, and millimeter are related.

A skim milk latte has far fewer calories than a whole milk latte of the same size. Do you know why?

GUIDED

Example 3

A cafe latte has 412 milligrams of calcium. Change 412 milligrams to grams.

Solution Remember that 1 mg = 0.001 g.

$$\begin{aligned} 412 \text{ mg} &= 412 \times 1 \text{ mg} \\ &= 412 \times \underline{\ ?\ } \text{ g} \\ &= \underline{\ ?\ } \text{ g} \end{aligned}$$

QY2

Use a metric ruler to determine which letter is located at the given distance from the red, center dot. Decode a word by writing in the blanks the letters corresponding to that distance. Save the word for the table in Question 22 in Lesson 2-10 on page 126.

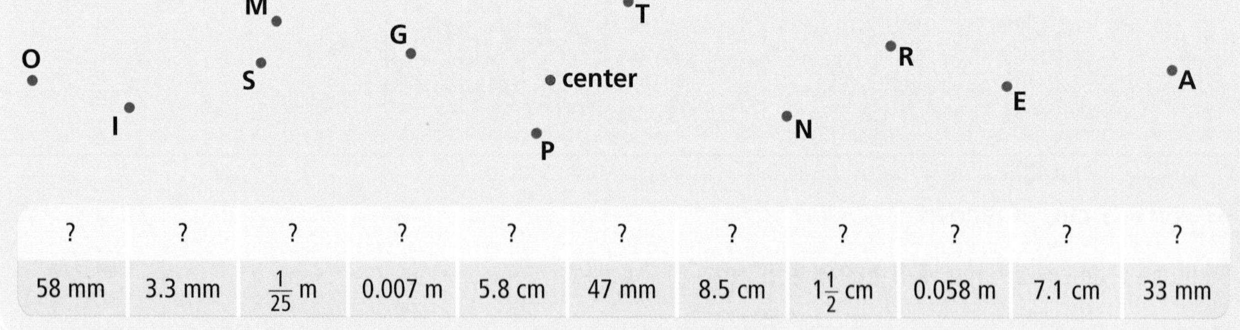

?	?	?	?	?	?	?	?	?	?	?
58 mm	3.3 mm	$\frac{1}{25}$ m	0.007 m	5.8 cm	47 mm	8.5 cm	$1\frac{1}{2}$ cm	0.058 m	7.1 cm	33 mm

Questions

COVERING THE IDEAS

1. **Fill in the Blanks**

   a. ___?___ cm = 1 m b. ___?___ mm = 1 m c. ___?___ mm = 1 cm

2. How are kilograms and grams related?

3. How are liters and milliliters related?

4. An abbreviation for a unit is given. Write out the name of the unit.

   a. kg b. km c. mm d. mL

In 5–7, name a real-world object with about the given length.

5. 1 centimeter 6. 1 meter 7. 1 millimeter

8. Measure the segment below in the following units of measure.

   ____

   a. millimeters b. centimeters c. meters

9. **Multiple Choice** A typical seventh-grade student is about how tall?

   A 1.5 mm B 1.5 km C 1.5 m D 1.5 cm

10. A bottle of water has a volume of 710 mL. Convert this to liters.

11. A 5K race is 5 kilometers long. How many meters is this?

Running five kilometers is the same as running approximately 3.1 miles.

APPLYING THE MATHEMATICS

In 12–15, select the best estimate of the weight of the object.

12. elephant: 6,487 kg or 6.487 kg
13. leaf: 1 kg or 5 g
14. football helmet: 54 g or 540 g
15. bicycle: 0.2 kg or 10 kg

16. **Fill in the Blanks**

a. 1 m = __?__ km

b. 1 cm = __?__ km

c. 1 mm = __?__ km

17. **Fill in the Blanks** An insect that is 4 mm long is __?__ cm long and also __?__ m long.

All insects have three major body segments: the head, the thorax, and the abdomen.

18. Draw and label a rectangle with dimensions 12.7 cm × 6.3 cm.

19. One inch is equal to 2.54 centimeters.

a. Use a centimeter ruler to measure a 1-inch interval on an inch ruler. Does the result support this?

b. How many millimeters is 2.54 centimeters?

c. What part of a meter is 1 inch?

20. The Institute of Medicine gives the recommended levels of vitamins in milligrams per day or *micrograms* per day. A **microgram** is one-millionth of a gram, or 0.000001 gram.

a. In 2000, the recommended level of vitamin A for girls aged 9–13 was 600 micrograms per day. How many grams is this?

b. In 2000, the recommended level of vitamin C for boys aged 9–13 was 45 milligrams per day. How many grams is this?

REVIEW

21. In 1786, the United States became the first country in the world to have a money system based on decimals. In our system, 1 dollar = 100 cents or, equivalently, 1 cent = $\frac{1}{100}$, or 0.01 dollars. **(Lessons 2-3, 2-2)**

a. Convert 3¢ to dollars.

b. Convert $135.67 to cents.

c. In May 2007, gasoline at many gas stations cost $3.199 per gallon. What is this cost in cents?

22. Multiply 4.765 by the given number. **(Lessons 2-3, 2-2)**

a. $\frac{1}{10}$ b. 10 c. $\frac{1}{100}$ d. $\frac{1}{1000}$

23. **Fill in the Blanks** To multiply a number by one hundred-thousandth, move the decimal point __?__ places to the __?__. **(Lesson 2-3)**

24. To find 10% of a number b, multiply $0.1 \times b$. Find each of the following in your head. **(Lesson 2-3)**
    - a. 10% of 25
    - b. 30% of 25
    - c. 10% of 80.4
    - d. 20% of 80.4

25. Graph $\frac{2}{3}$, 0, $\frac{1}{6}$, $\frac{3}{4}$, and –1 on a number line. **(Lessons 1-8, 1-2)**

26. Consider the improper fraction $\frac{108}{35}$. **(Lessons 1-6, 1-4)**
    - a. Use division to write this fraction as a mixed number.
    - b. Use the mixed number feature on a calculator to check your answer to Part a.

27. Measure the segment below to the nearest inch, half inch, quarter inch, and eighth inch. **(Lesson 1-3)**

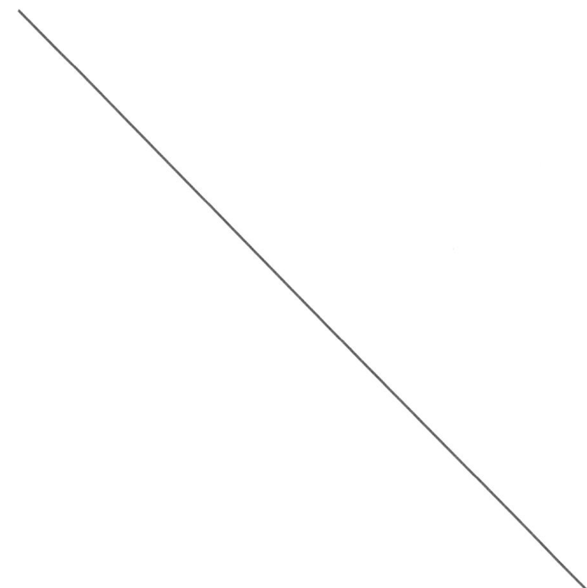

28. To show 32% of the area of a hundreds grid, how many squares would you need to shade? Sketch this situation. **(Previous Course)**

EXPLORATION

29. Below are eight metric-system prefixes in alphabetical order. Find the meaning of each prefix and put them in order, from greatest to least.

dec-	deka-	giga-	mega-
micro-	nano-	pico-	tera-

QY ANSWERS

1a. 1,000

1b. $\frac{1}{1000}$

2. INSPIRATION

Lesson

2-5 Rounding Up and Rounding Down

Vocabulary

round up
round down
percent circle
sector
truncate

▸ **BIG IDEA** In some situations you may need to round a number up to the next or down to the preceding decimal place value. Sometimes the answers you get from a calculation need to be rounded.

Two Kinds of Rounding

The 191 students and teachers at Jefferson School need buses to take them to a concert. Each bus can hold 60 people. To find how many buses to order, the principal divides 191 by 60 and gets $3\frac{11}{60}$. On her calculator, the display shows 3.18333333.

Mental Math

One mile is equal to 1,609.344 m. What is this, to the nearest

a. meter?

b. tenth of a meter?

c. kilometer?

QY1

How many buses should she order?

The principal could **round up** to the next whole bus and order 4 buses so that everybody could take a bus to the auditorium. Or, she could **round down** to the preceding whole bus and order only 3 buses.

 See QY2 at the right.

 **QY2**

How many people would have to find other ways to get to the auditorium if the principal ordered only 3 buses?

Businesses often must choose whether to round up or round down. When rounding prices, they usually round up. However, when calculating discounts, they usually round down.

Example 1

A carton of 6 bottles of chocolate milk sells for \$3.49. The store will sell you a single bottle. What is it likely to cost?

Solution Divide 3.49 by 6 to find the cost of 1 bottle. A calculator will show .5816666, which is between 0.58 and 0.59. These numbers are graphed on the number line on the next page.

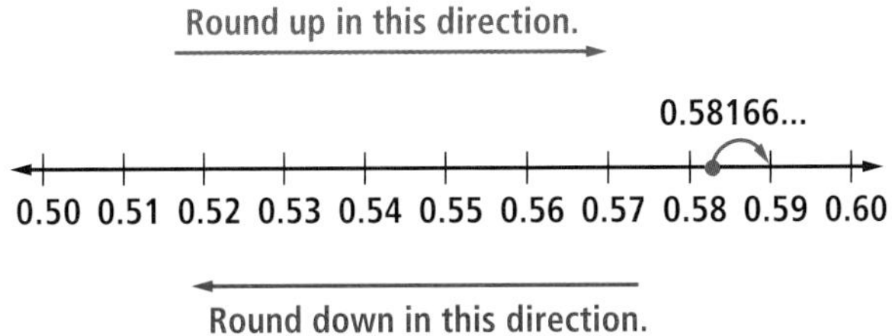

The store is likely to *round up* to the next cent, so a single bottle is likely to cost $0.59.

Example 2

On Saturday, the store in Example 1 runs a special. It sells the carton of 6 bottles of chocolate milk for the price of 5 bottles. What is the carton likely to cost?

Solution Dividing 3.49 by 6 shows the cost of one bottle is between $0.58 and $0.59. To discount the original price, the store is likely to *round down* to $0.58. With the discount, the carton is likely to cost $3.49 – $0.58 = $2.91.

 See QY3 at the right.

For most of its history, chocolate has been consumed as a drink. It was only a matter of time before it joined forces with milk!

 **QY3**

Suppose milk costs $6.25 for 2 gallons. What would you likely have to pay for one gallon?

Rounding Negative Numbers

You can also think of the number line when you round negative numbers.

Example 3

Round -247 down to the nearest ten.

Solution Draw a number line. Because you are rounding to the tens place, use an interval length of 10 as shown at the right.

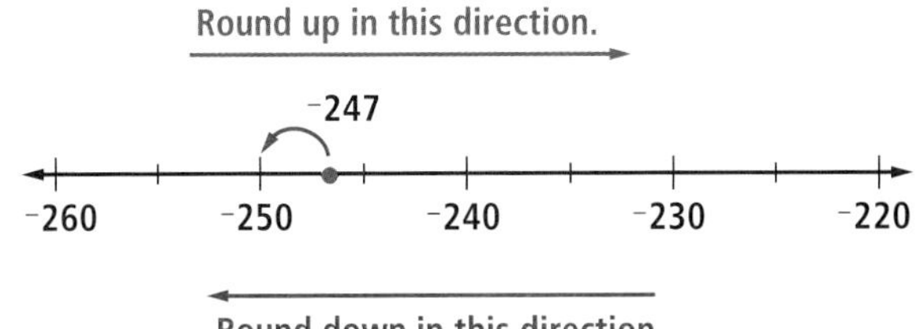

-247 is between -250 and -240. Rounding down would take you to the preceding ten. So, -247 rounded down to the nearest ten is -250.

Rounding With a Percent Circle

You have seen percents in the past. A **percent circle** is a circle divided into 100 equal intervals, as shown on the next page. Each interval is 1%.

A wedge-shaped piece of a circle and its interior is called a **sector.** The shaded sector in the percent circle at the right starts at 0% and ends at 33%. It is a 33% sector.

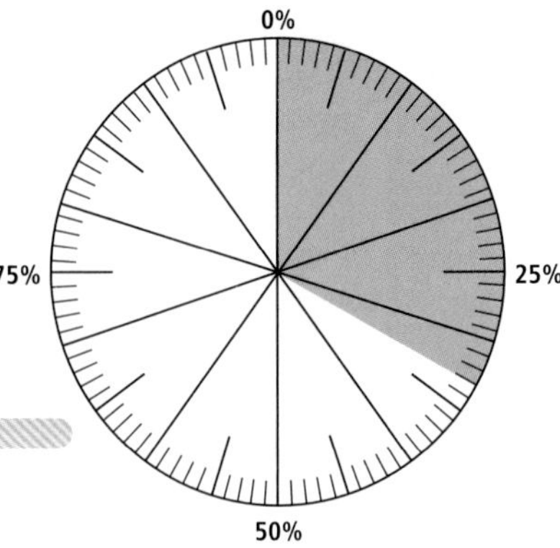

QY4

What percent is pictured by the non-shaded sector in the percent circle at the right?

Example 4

a. Round 33% up to the next 10%.

b. Round 33% up to the next 5%

Solution

a. Look at the tick marks for multiples of 10% (10%, 20%, 30%, and so on). 33% is between 30% and 40%. **Round up to 40%.**

b. Look at the tick marks that are multiples of 5% (5%, 10%, 15%, 20%, and so on). 33% is between 30% and 35%. **Round up to 35%.**

See QY5 at the right.

QY5

a. Round 33% down to the preceding 10%.

b. Round 33% down to the preceding 5%.

In the following activity, you will measure with a percent circle.

Activity

MATERIALS percent circle

Step 1 For circles a, b, and c below, place the center of the percent circle over the center of the circle.

Step 2 Rotate the percent circle so the 0% mark is lined up with one side of the sector.

Step 3 Read the marking over the other side of the sector. This tells you what percent the sector represents.

Step 4 Complete the table on the next page for the three circles.

a.

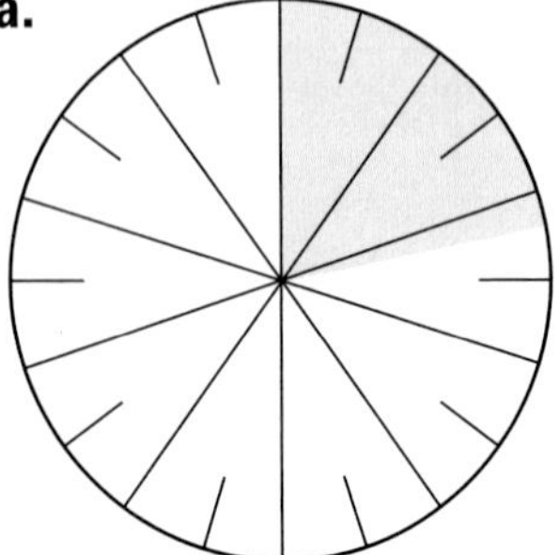

b.

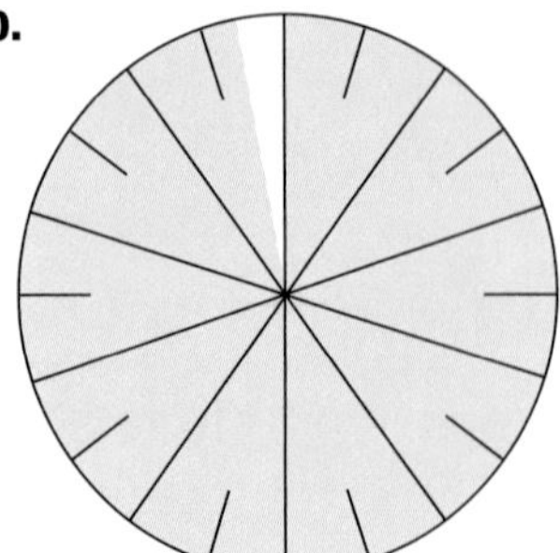

c.

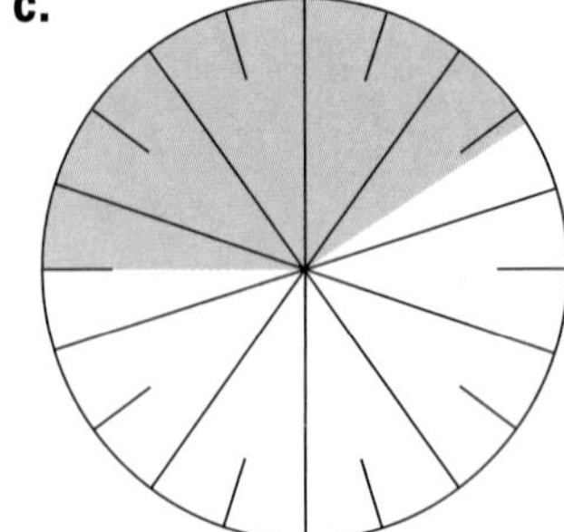

Sector	Circle		
	a.	b.	c.
Percent Shaded	?	?	?
Rounded up to the next 10%	?	?	?
Rounded down to the preceding 5%	?	?	?
Percent not Shaded	?	?	?
Rounded up to the next 10%	?	?	?
Rounded up to the next 5%	?	?	?

Questions

COVERING THE IDEAS

1. **Fill in the Blank** Destiny rounded 4242 up to 4300. She rounded up to the next __?__ place.

2. **Multiple Choice** Which is 3,629,610 rounded down to the preceding thousand?

   A 3,629,400　　B 3,629,000
   C 3,620,000　　D 3,630,000

3. Some pencils are sold in packages of 10. A teacher needs one pencil for each student in a class of 32. How many pencils must he purchase?

4. A store sells limes at 3 for $1. You want one lime, so you divide $1.00 by 3 to find the cost. Your calculator shows .333333. How much are you likely to pay for the lime?

5. A railroad plans to add extra cars to an existing train for 350 scouts and leaders returning from camp. Each car seats 75 passengers.
   a. How many cars should be added to ensure that all the scouts and leaders have seats?
   b. If the railroad rounds the number of needed cars down, how many scouts and leaders will have to find empty seats in the rest of the train?

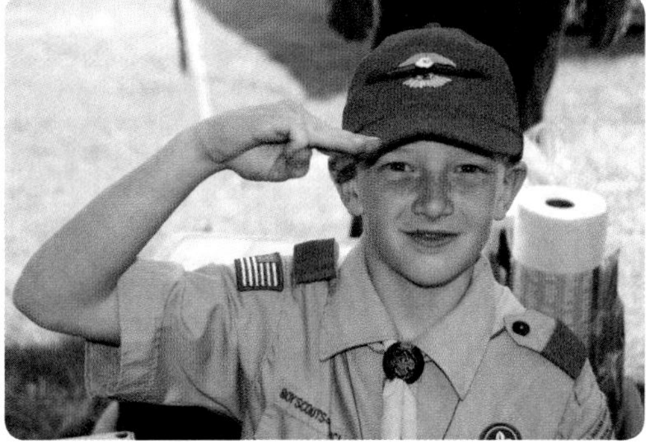

The Boy Scouts of America was founded in 1910 by William Boyce.

Source: *The History of the Boy Scouts of America*

6. A total of 143 students and teachers from Tubman School are going to a concert. If each bus seats 60 students, how many buses will be needed so that everybody can ride?

7. A store sells a dozen eggs for $1.09. You want a half dozen. To estimate how much you will pay, you divide $1.09 by 2. You get 0.545. How much would you expect to pay?

8. a. Round -351 up to the next 10.
   b. Round -351 down to the preceding 10.

9. a. Round -6,429 down to the preceding 100.
   b. Round -6,429 up to the next 100.

10. Refer to the percent circle below.

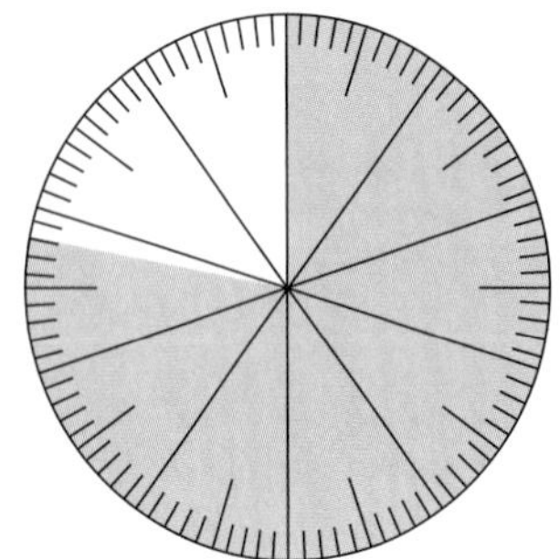

   a. What percent does it indicate?
   b. Round down to the preceding 10%.
   c. Round up to the next 10%.
   d. Round up to the next 5%.

APPLYING THE MATHEMATICS

11. Round the $23,295 price of an automobile up to the next
   a. ten dollars.
   b. hundred dollars.
   c. thousand dollars.

12. One foot is exactly equal to 30.48 cm. Round 30.48
   a. up to the next tenth.
   b. down to the preceding tenth.

13. It is about 455 km between the Turkish cities Izmir and Istanbul.
   a. Round 455 km up to the next 10 km.
   b. Round 455 km down to the preceding 10 km.
   c. Graph 455 km and your answers to Parts a and b on the same number line.

14. One mile is exactly equal to 1.609344 km. Round 1.609344
   a. up to the next thousandth.
   b. down to the preceding thousandth.

Istanbul has served as the capital city of many great empires, including the Roman Empire, the Byzantine Empire, and the Ottoman Empire.

15. **a.** Use a percent circle to measure the sector at the right.

b. Round up to the next 10%.

c. Round down to the preceding 10%.

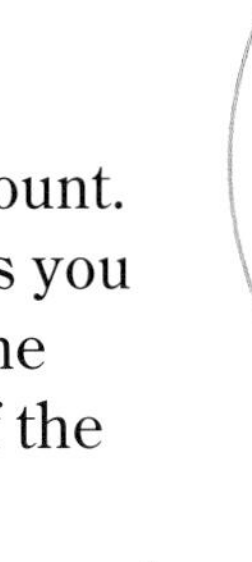

16. Suppose there is \$97 in your bank account. You would like to withdraw as much as you can using an Automated Teller Machine (ATM). How much cash can you get if the machine dispenses only

a. \$5 bills? **b.** \$10 bills? **c.** \$20 bills?

17. Round the temperature shown on the thermometer at the right down to the preceding whole degree.

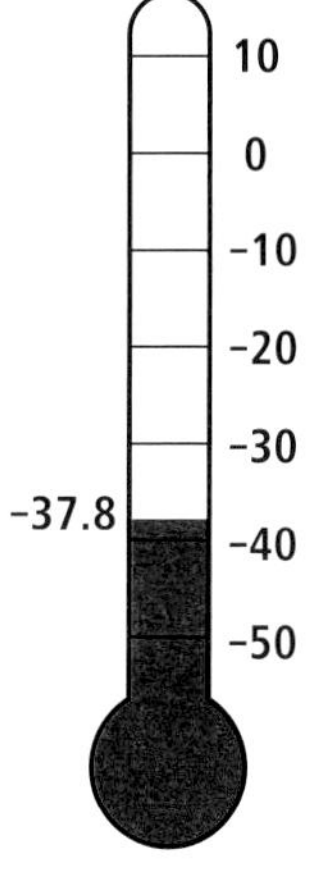

18. **a.** Measure the segment below.

b. Round the length up to the next quarter-inch.

c. Round the length up to the next half-inch.

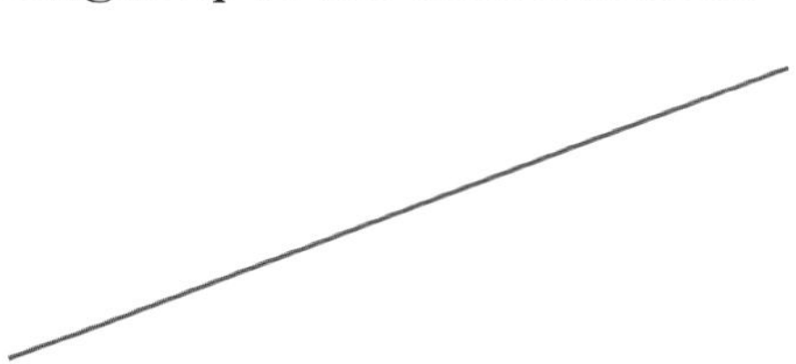

19. **a.** Find the percent represented by the shaded area below.

b. Round this percent up to the next 10%.

c. Round this percent down to the preceding 10%.

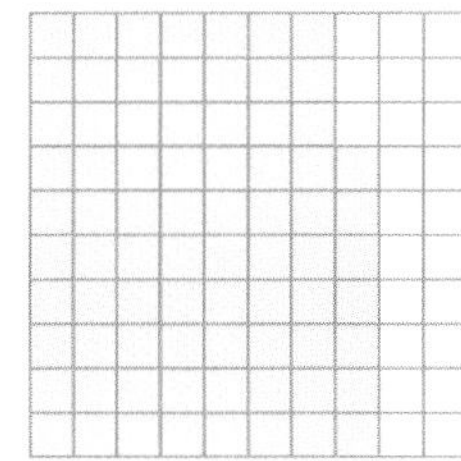

20. Another way to round decimals is to *truncate* them. To **truncate** means to cut off the digits after a particular place. To truncate 0.5816666 at the hundredths place, delete the digits after the second decimal place, 0.58~~16666~~. So, 0.5816666 truncated at the hundredths place is 0.58. Truncate 8.167217 to the

a. thousandths place.

b. hundred-thousandths place.

c. tenths place.

REVIEW

21. A race is decided by 30 milliseconds. How many seconds is this? **(Lesson 2-4)**

22. a. Draw a segment 10 cm long. Indicate each centimeter with a tick mark.
    b. Each centimeter can be divided into millimeters. How many millimeters equal 1 cm? **(Lessons 2-4, 1-2)**

23. By what number must you multiply 547.238 to get 0.0547238? **(Lesson 2-3)**

In 24 and 25, use the number line below. (Lessons 2-1, 1-2)

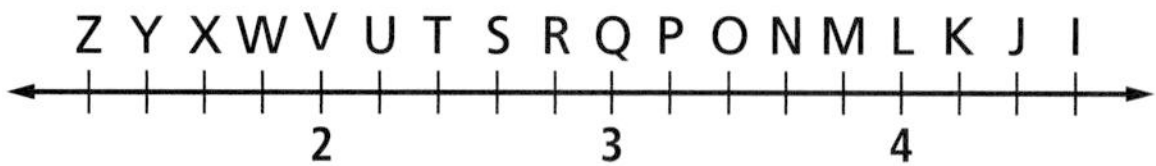

24. What is the interval on this number line?

25. Which letter corresponds to the given number?
    a. 3.0 b. 2.8 c. 1.4

26. **Multiple Choice** Which does *not* equal 0.86? **(Lesson 1-2)**
    A 0.860 B 0.86 C 0.086 D 0.860

EXPLORATION

27. Look through a newspaper.
    a. Find a number that underestimates the value it is reporting.
    b. Find a number that overestimates the value it is reporting. Write down enough about the examples to be able to report and define your findings to your class.

QY ANSWERS

1. 3 or 4

2. 11

3. $3.13

4. 67%

5a. 30%

5b. 30%

Lesson 2-6 Estimating by Rounding to the Nearest...

Vocabulary

estimate

rounding to the nearest

is approximately equal to ($\approx$)

BIG IDEA Many situations force a persion to estimate. Common ways of estimating are to round up, down, or to the nearest multiple of a decimal place value.

An **estimate** is a number that is close to another number. The other number is often the exact value.

Mental Math

A supermarket is selling yogurts for $0.49 each. How many yogurts can you buy if you have

a. $1?

b. $10?

c. $5?

d. $15?

Reasons for Estimating

There are times when an estimate may be more appropriate than an exact value.

Reason 1: An exact value may not be worth the trouble or expense required to find it. *The cargo plane held about 22,000 lb of packages.*

Reason 2: An estimate may be easier to work with than the exact value. *Instead of using $23.68 to calculate a waiter's tip, we used $24.*

Reason 3: It may be safer to use an estimate than an exact value. *Mrs. Torres allows an hour to drive downtown when she hears the radio announcer say "travel times to downtown average 42 minutes."*

Reason 4: The exact value may change from time to time. *The World Almanac stated that the population of New York City was about 8,143,000 on July 1, 2005.*

In 2004, approximately 28 billion miles were logged transporting cargo in American skies.

Source: Air Transport Association of America, Inc.

Reason 5: Exact values may be impossible to obtain. *The tourism industry is California's fourth largest labor market, supporting nearly 900,000 jobs according to the California Travel and Tourism Commission.*

Reason 6: A measure is always an estimate. (You can increase accuracy by using smaller units.) *Jonah weighed 6 pounds, 5 ounces at birth.*

Rounding to the Nearest

The most common method of estimating is **rounding to the nearest.** Sometimes rounding to the nearest requires rounding up, and sometimes it requires rounding down.

Consider the restaurant charge of \$23.68 on the previous page. Suppose you want to estimate this in dollars only. The bill is between \$23.00 (rounded down) and \$24.00 (rounded up). Because \$23.68 is closer to \$24.00, an estimate of the bill to the nearest dollar is \$24.00.

Example 1

The population listed for New York City on July 1, 2005, was 8,143,197. Because the actual number is constantly changing, round it to the nearest 100,000.

Solution Rounding down gives 8,100,000. Rounding up gives 8,200,000. The listed value is closer to 8,100,000.

To the nearest 100,000, the population of New York City on July 1, 2005, was 8,100,000.

Widely considered the tourism hotspot in New York City, nearly 1.5 million visitors pass through Times Square each day.

Source: Times Square Alliance

You can show that a number is an estimate by using the symbol $\approx$, rather than $=$. The symbol $\approx$ is read **"is approximately equal to."**

If p is the population of New York on July 1, 2005, then you could write $p \approx 8{,}100{,}000$ or you could write $8{,}143{,}197 \approx 8{,}100{,}000$.

GUIDED

Example 2

a. Round 2.73 to the nearest whole number.

b. Round 2.73 to the nearest tenth.

Solution

a. 2.73 is between the whole numbers __?__ and __?__. Because it is nearer to __?__, round 2.73 to __?__.

b. To round to the nearest tenth, consider the tenths that surround 2.73.

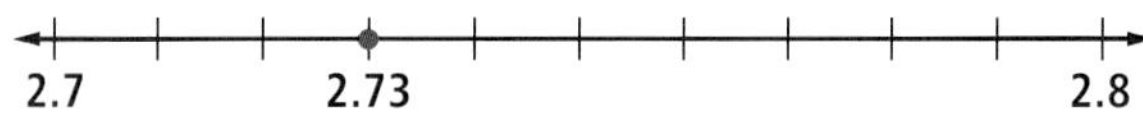

You can see that 2.73 is between __?__ and __?__. It is nearer to __?__, so round 2.73 down to __?__.

GUIDED

Example 3

On October 19, 1987, the Dow Jones Industrial Average had its worst point-loss in history, –508.32 points. This average is often rounded to the nearest integer. What is that integer?

Solution 1 –508.32 is between –508 and __?__. It is closer to __?__. So, –508.32 rounded to the nearest integer is __?__.

Solution 2 Label the tick marks. Then graph –508.32.

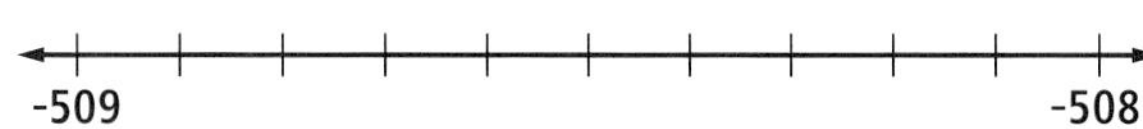

–508.32 is closer to __?__. So, –508.32 rounded to the nearest integer is __?__.

Note: This answer is rounded up since –508 > –509.

STOP See QY1 at the right.

STOP **QY1**

a. Round –483 to the nearest 100.

b. When –483 is rounded to the nearest 100, is it rounded up or down?

Activity

MATCHING The number 1,928.37465 has been rounded to each number below. Fill in the blank with the letter of the rounded number. The answers spell a word. Save the word for the table in Question 22 in Lesson 2-10 on page 126.

A: 2,000	__?__ To the nearest hundredth
E: 1,900	__?__ To the nearest hundred
I: 1,930	__?__ To the nearest thousandth
N: 1,928	__?__ Down to the nearest ten-thousandth
O: 1,928.4	__?__ To the nearest hundredth
P: 1,928.37	__?__ To the nearest ten
R: 1,928.375	__?__ To the nearest thousandth
S: 1,928.3746	__?__ To the nearest thousand
T: 1,928.3747	__?__ Up to the nearest ten-thousandth
	__?__ To the nearest ten
	__?__ To the nearest tenth
	__?__ To the nearest whole number

A Choice in Rounding

Suppose you are asked to round 1250 to the nearest hundred. It is exactly in the middle of your two choices, 1200 and 1300. How do you decide which to choose? There is no set answer. On federal tax forms, amounts that end in 50 cents must be rounded up. Some people have a method for rounding up half the time and rounding down half the time. You could alternate between rounding up and rounding down. Remember, this choice happens only for numbers exactly in the middle.

QY2

A number rounded to the nearest ten could be either 40 or 50. What is that number?

Questions

COVERING THE IDEAS

1. **Fill in the Blanks** Refer to the number line below. Round to the nearest ten.

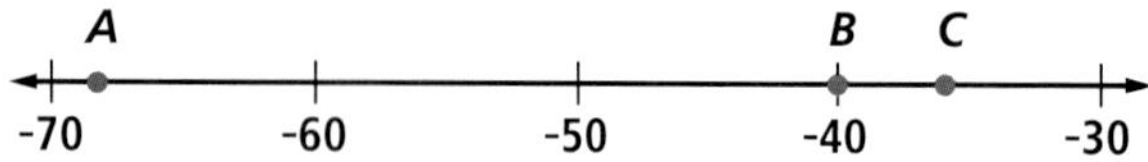

   a. The coordinate of $A \approx$ _?_.
   b. The coordinate of $B \approx$ _?_.
   c. The coordinate of $C \approx$ _?_.

2. a. Draw a number line from 0 through 40 with intervals of 10.
   b. Plot points at 18, 2.5, and 34.
   c. Round each number in Part b to the nearest 10.
3. Round 348 to the nearest 100.
4. Round -542 to the nearest 10.
5. A collector in Germany has 285,150 ballpoint pens.
   a. Round this number to the nearest ten thousand.
   b. Round this number to the nearest thousand.
   c. Round this number to the nearest hundred.
6. When rounding 34,500 to the nearest thousand, what choices do you have?

How long do you think it would take to collect 285,150 unique ballpoint pens?

7. Diamonds are graded based on color, size, and the way they have been cut. The highest color grade given to white diamonds is D. The largest known D-color diamond is the Centenary, which weighs 273.85 carats. Round the Centenary's weight to the nearest
   a. whole number.
   b. ten.
   c. hundred.
   d. tenth.

Because of their extreme hardness, "cutting" diamonds is a very delicate, extensive process.

8. Round all the numbers below to the nearest 10. Cross out each letter above a number that rounds to 1,010 or 1,030. The answers spell a word. Save the word for the table in Question 22 in Lesson 2-10 on page 126.

P	A	Q	U	N	R	D	O
1,012	1,024	1,029	1,033	1,040	1,006	1,016	1,026

APPLYING THE MATHEMATICS

9. The largest milkshake ever made had a volume of 6,000 gallons. Round the volume in gallons to the nearest
   a. whole number. b. ten. c. hundred.
   d. thousand. e. ten thousand.

10. Round all the numbers below to the nearest tenth. Cross out each letter above a number that rounds to 5.5 or 5.7. The answers spell a word. Save the word for the table in Question 22 in Lesson 2-10 on page 126.

S	L	N	C	I	F	N	B	H	E
5.52	5.74	5.61	5.68	5.44	5.49	5.76	5.53	5.66	5.60

In 11–14, estimate the answer to the nearest whole number in your head.

11. $8 \times \$5.98$
12. $30.4 \div 3$
13. $450.99999 - 9.1$
14. $3.09035 + 7.8922$

In 15–17, tell whether it would be best to round the value to the nearest hundred, ten, whole number, or tenth.

15. the weight of an automobile in pounds
16. a baby's temperature when his dad suspects he has a fever
17. the number of muffins made when a recipe is doubled

Refer to 18 and 19.

a. Estimate the percent of the shaded portion.

b. Use a percent circle to measure the percent of the shaded portion.

c. Round the measurement to the nearest 10%.

d. Was your estimate closer to the actual or rounded value?

18.

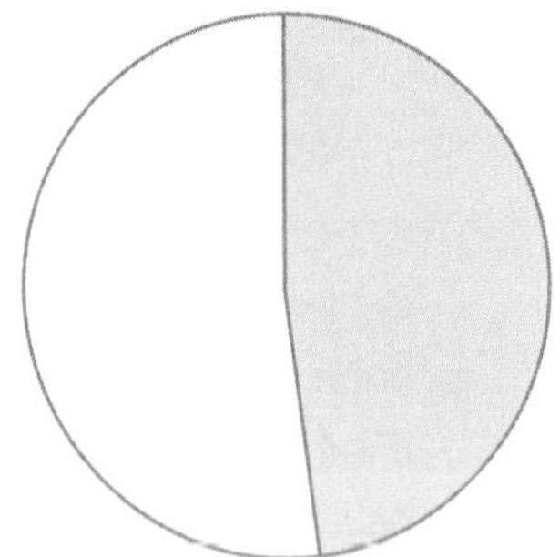

19.

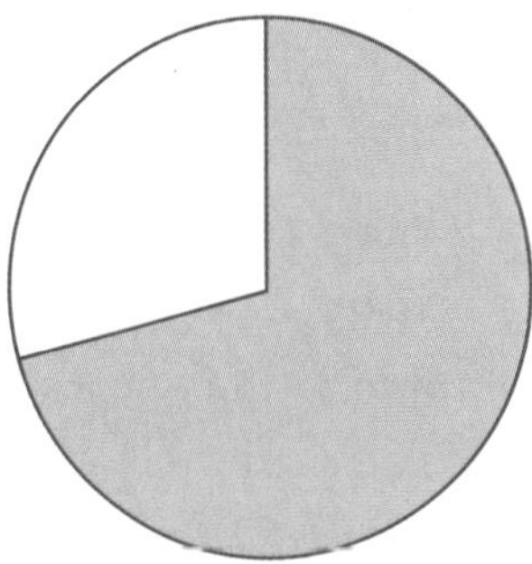

20. A gas pump shows $3.17[9] ($3.179) as the price for 1 gallon.

a. What would 10 gallons of gas cost?

b. Estimate the cost of 10 gallons by rounding the price per gallon to the nearest cent.

c. Estimate the cost of 10 gallons by rounding the price per gallon to the nearest 10 cents.

Gas prices reached an average of $3.22 per gallon during May, 2007.

Source: Energy Information Administration

21. Suppose n is an integer. Rounded to the nearest ten, $n \approx 80$.

a. What is the least possible value of n?

b. What is the greatest possible value of n?

22. At the beginning of this lesson, the number 900,000 is given as an estimate of the number of tourism jobs in California. Suppose j is the actual number of tourism jobs.

a. If this estimate is to the nearest 10,000, what are the greatest and least possible values for j?

b. If this estimate is to the nearest 1,000, what are the greatest and least possible values for j?

REVIEW

23. For each situation, decide whether it would be better to make a high or a low estimate of the value. **(Lesson 2-5)**
    a. the size of a cake for a 5-year-old's birthday party
    b. how much weight an elevator can hold
    c. the number of minutes it will take to do your homework
    d. how much spending money to bring on a trip

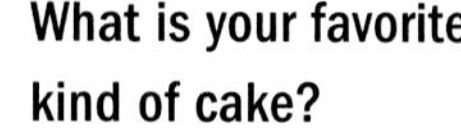

What is your favorite kind of cake?

24. Write two fractions equal to the given number. **(Lesson 1-5)**
    a. $\frac{5}{9}$ b. 1   c. 405
25. On Friday, Sarah worked for 7 hours and 45 minutes. **(Lessons 1-5, 1-4)**
    a. Express the time in hours as a mixed number in lowest terms.
    b. When she fills in her time-card, Sarah needs to express the time as a mixed number whose fraction part has a denominator of 100. What should she write?
26. Name a quantity between $3\frac{1}{4}$ lb and $3\frac{1}{2}$ lb. **(Lessons 1-4, 1-2)**
27. According to a 2005 Census Bureau estimate, there were 14.14 births for every 1,000 people in the United States. Express 14.14 as a mixed number. **(Lesson 1-4)**

EXPLORATION

28. The beginning of this lesson describes six reasons an estimate may be appropriate. Think of a different example of each reason.

QY ANSWERS

1a. 500

1b. rounded down

2. 45

Lesson 2-7 Converting Fractions to Decimals

Vocabulary

repetend

repeating decimal

terminating decimal

▸ **BIG IDEA** Using division, every fraction can be written as a decimal that either ends at a certain place or repeats forever.

While fractions are useful, decimals are often easier to order, round, add, and subtract. For these reasons, it often helps to find a decimal that equals a given fraction.

Mental Math

a. How many quarters are in 1 dollar?

b. How many nickels are in 1 dollar?

c. How many dimes are in 2 dollars?

Converting Fractions with Denominators 10, 100, ...

You can convert simple fractions with denominators 10, 100, 1000, and so on, to decimals using multiplication or division.

$$\frac{46}{1000} = 46 \times \frac{1}{1000} = 0.046$$
$$\frac{46}{1000} = 46 \div 1000 = 0.046$$

Remember, $\frac{46}{1000}$ and 0.046 are two different ways of writing the same number.

QY1

Write each number as a decimal.

a. $\frac{8}{10}$ **b.** $\frac{435}{100}$ **c.** $\frac{1612}{10{,}000}$

Converting Fractions that Are Whole Numbers

As you know, some fractions are whole numbers in disguise.

Example 1

Find the decimal equal to $\frac{117}{13}$ on a calculator.

Solution Key in 117 [÷] 13 [ENTER].

The result is 9. So, $\frac{117}{13} = 9$.

In Example 1, you can say that 117 is *evenly divisible by* 13. Sometimes people just say that 117 is *divisible by* 13.

Repeating Decimals

Simple fractions that do not have denominators of 10, 100, 1000, and so on, are not as easy to convert to decimals using division. For example, a soccer team has 11 players on the field during a game. Of these players, 2 play the forward position, so $\frac{2}{11}$ of the team plays forward. The fraction $\frac{2}{11}$ is equal to $2 \div 11$. It is the result of dividing 2 into 11 parts.

Soccer is commonly referred to as "football" in every country except the United States.

When you divide 2 by 11, your calculator shows a number with a repeating pattern of digits. If your calculator could display an infinite number of digits, you would see 0.18181818181818..., where the pair of digits 18 repeat forever. Below is a "shorthand" way to write this number.

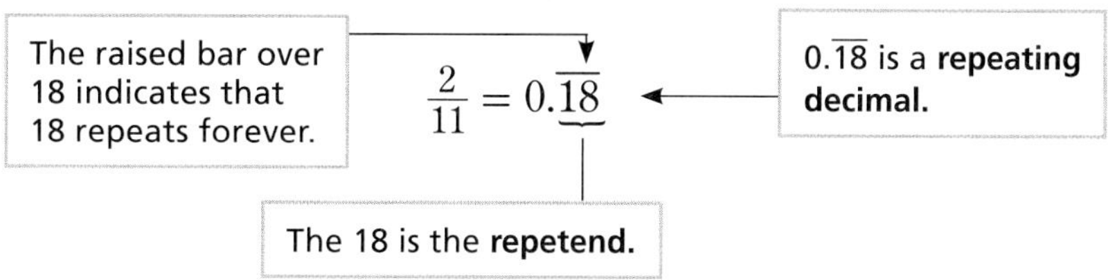
The raised bar over 18 indicates that 18 repeats forever.
$\frac{2}{11} = 0.\overline{18}$
$0.\overline{18}$ is a **repeating decimal.**
The 18 is the **repetend.**

You can check that $0.\overline{18}$ is reasonable by noting that $\frac{2}{11}$ is less than $\frac{2}{10}$, which equals 0.2. So $\frac{2}{11}$ should be a little less than 0.2, and $0.\overline{18}$ is a little less than 0.20.

QY2

a. Write the decimal equal to $\frac{5}{11}$.

b. Which does *not* equal the others? $0.\overline{18}$, $0.\overline{1818}$, $0.\overline{181}$

GUIDED

Example 2

Write the decimal equal to $\frac{65}{6}$.

Solution 1 Divide 65 by 6 on your calculator. The key sequence is _?_ [÷] _?_ [ENTER]. Depending on your calculator, the display will show 10.833333 or something similar. The 3 repeats, so $\frac{65}{6} = 10.8\overline{3}$.

Solution 2

$\frac{65}{6} = \frac{60}{6} + \frac{5}{6}$

$= 10 + \frac{5}{6}$

$= 10 + 0.8\overline{3}$ Use division to get $\frac{5}{6} = 0.8\overline{3}$.

$= 10.8\overline{3}$

Sometimes a repetend is long. For example, $\frac{5}{7} = 0.714286714286714286...$ or $0.\overline{714286}$. Many calculators will not show enough decimal places for you to see the repetition.

QY3

Divide 5 by 7 on your calculator. What does it show?

It is sometimes easier to compare and compute with decimals than with fractions.

GUIDED

Example 3

Drill bits are used to drill holes in wood or metal. Drill bits are measured by the diameters of the holes they drill. Suppose you go to a store and see drill bits with diameters $\frac{9}{13}$ in. and $\frac{3}{4}$ in.

a. Which bit will drill a larger hole?

b. How much larger will the hole be?

Solution

a. Change both diameters to decimals.

$\frac{9}{16} = \underline{\ ?\ }$

$\frac{3}{4} = \underline{\ ?\ }$

Which is greater, $\frac{9}{16}$ or $\frac{3}{4}$? $\underline{\ ?\ }$

The bit with diameter $\underline{\ ?\ }$ will drill a larger hole.

b. Subtract the lesser decimal from the greater decimal.

$\underline{\ ?\ } - \underline{\ ?\ } = \underline{\ ?\ }$

The hole would be $\underline{\ ?\ }$ larger in diameter.

The decimals for $\frac{9}{16}$ and $\frac{3}{4}$ are called **terminating decimals** because they end after a certain number of places. Other examples of terminating decimals are 386.4 and 0.00098765454. A decimal is either terminating or an *infinite decimal*. Some infinite decimals are repeating decimals and some are not.

Questions

COVERING THE IDEAS

1. Why is it helpful to be able to find a decimal for a fraction?

2. Consider the fraction $\frac{21}{8}$.
   a. What is the symbol for division in the fraction?
   b. Does it equal $\frac{21}{8}$ or $\frac{8}{21}$?
   c. Does it equal $8 \div 21$ or $21 \div 8$?
   d. Which is the divisor?
   e. Which is the dividend?
   f. Estimate a decimal equal to it. Check with your calculator.

In 3 and 4, consider two drill bits with diameters of $\frac{7}{16}$ in. and $\frac{3}{4}$ in.

3. Which bit drills larger holes?
4. How much bigger is the diameter of a hole drilled by the larger bit?

5. After rewriting these fractions as decimals, order them from least to greatest.

   $\frac{17}{23}$ $\qquad$ $\frac{7390}{9999}$ $\qquad$ $\frac{934}{1265}$

6. a. In $48.\overline{70}$, what is the repetend?
   b. Write the first ten decimal places of this number.
   c. Between what two whole numbers is $48.\overline{70}$?

7. a. In $0.26\overline{9}$, what is the repetend?
   b. Write the first ten decimal places of this number.
   c. Between what two whole numbers is $0.26\overline{9}$?

8. **Fill in the Blank** $\frac{171}{9} = 19$; Because 19 is a whole number, we say that 171 is __?__ by 9.

9. In a 365-day year, July 4 is the 184th day. Write the part of the year that has passed on July 4 as a fraction and as a decimal.

APPLYING THE MATHEMATICS

10. Carpenters often measure to sixteenths of an inch.
    a. Change $5\frac{7}{16}$" to a decimal.
    b. Is $5\frac{7}{16}$" shorter or longer than $5\frac{1}{2}$"?
    c. Explain how you found your answer to Part b.

11. Rewrite each number as a decimal rounded to the nearest thousandth.
    a. $\frac{1}{13}$
    b. $20\frac{1}{13}$
    c. $-20\frac{1}{13}$

Carpenters can add, subtract, multiply and divide fractions in their heads.

12. A softball team won 13 out of its 25 games. Write the fraction of games it won as a decimal.

13. **Fill in the Blanks** Insert = or ≈ to make a correct statement.
    a. $\frac{4}{9}$ ___?___ $0.\overline{4}$
    b. $\frac{4}{9}$ ___?___ 0.444
    c. $\frac{4}{9}$ ___?___ 0.4
    d. $-\frac{4}{9}$ ___?___ $-0.\overline{4}$

Over 80,000 teams participate in youth softball on an annual basis.

Source: Amateur Softball Association of America

14. Write a decimal, rounded to the nearest hundredth, to express the part of the day that has passed at each of these times.

    a. 8 A.M.
    b. 11 A.M.
    c. 8 P.M.

15. The United Fund wants to raise $25,000 in 1 month. After 3 weeks, they have raised $19,500. Write the part they have raised
    a. as a fraction.
    b. as a decimal rounded to the nearest hundredth.

REVIEW

16. According to many sources, the distance from the sun to Earth is 93 million miles. Do you think this distance is exact or an estimate? Explain your answer. **(Lesson 2-6)**

17. According to the Central Intelligence Agency, about 108,700,891 people lived in Mexico in July 2007. Round this number to the nearest hundred thousand. **(Lesson 2-6)**

18. Round 10.9876543210 to the nearest ten-thousandth. **(Lesson 2-6)**

In 19 and 20, tell whether it would be better to round the value up, down, or to the nearest and explain why. (Lessons 2-6, 2-5)

19. the number of bags of flour needed for a giant batch of pancakes

20. your dog's weight after eating these pancakes

21. What temperature does the thermometer below show? **(Lesson 2-3)**

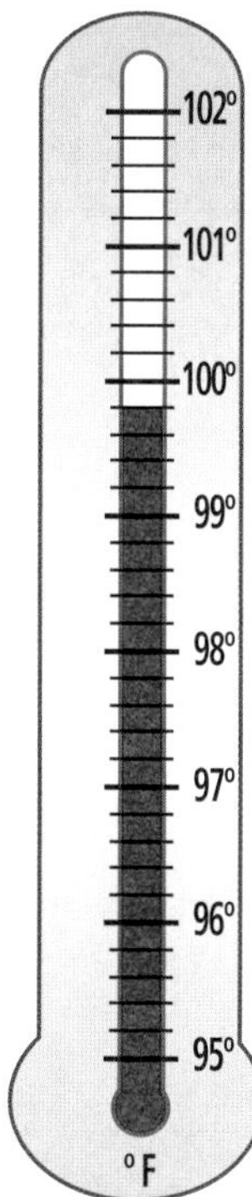

22. a. Multiply 9.979 × 7.779 with a calculator. What result does the calculator display?

b. Round your answer to Part a to the nearest thousandth. **(Lesson 2-2)**

EXPLORATION

23. a. Find the decimals for $\frac{1}{2}$, $\frac{1}{3}$, $\frac{1}{4}$, $\frac{1}{5}$, and $\frac{1}{6}$.

b. Which of the decimals in Part a are terminating and which are repeating?

c. Find the decimals for $\frac{1}{7}$, $\frac{1}{8}$, $\frac{1}{9}$, $\frac{1}{10}$, $\frac{1}{11}$, and $\frac{1}{12}$.

d. Which of the decimals in Part c are terminating and which are repeating?

e. Suppose you are to continue finding decimals for $\frac{1}{13}$, $\frac{1}{14}$, $\frac{1}{15}$, and so on. To what number would these decimals get closer?

24. a. Explore the decimals for all the simple fractions between 0 and 1 whose denominator is 13.

b. Use your results to give the first twelve decimal places for each of these fractions.

QY ANSWERS

1a. 0.8

1b. 4.35

1c. 0.1612

2a. $0.\overline{45}$

2b. $0.\overline{181}$

3. Answers vary. Sample: 0.714286

Lesson 2-8 Decimal and Fraction Equivalents

▸ **BIG IDEA** You should be able to convert back and forth between decimals and fractions with denominators 2, 3, 4, 5, 6, 8, and 10 in your head.

Memorizing Decimal and Fraction Equivalents

All simple fractions are equal to terminating or repeating decimals. The simple fractions in the table below often appear in mathematics and in real-life situations. Since they are so common, it is useful to memorize these equivalents.

Fourths and Eighths	Thirds and Sixths	Fifths and Tenths
$\frac{1}{8} = 0.125$	$\frac{1}{6} = 0.1\overline{6}$	$\frac{1}{10} = 0.1$
$\frac{1}{4} = \frac{2}{8} = 0.25$	$\frac{1}{3} = \frac{2}{6} = 0.\overline{3}$	$\frac{1}{5} = \frac{2}{10} = 0.2$
$\frac{3}{8} = 0.375$	$\frac{3}{6} = 0.5$	$\frac{3}{10} = 0.3$
$\frac{1}{2} = \frac{4}{8} = 0.5$	$\frac{2}{3} = \frac{4}{6} = 0.\overline{6}$	$\frac{2}{5} = \frac{4}{10} = 0.4$
$\frac{5}{8} = 0.625$	$\frac{5}{6} = 0.8\overline{3}$	$\frac{5}{10} = 0.5$
$\frac{3}{4} = \frac{6}{8} = 0.75$		$\frac{3}{5} = \frac{6}{10} = 0.6$
$\frac{7}{8} = 0.875$		$\frac{7}{10} = 0.7$
		$\frac{4}{5} = \frac{8}{10} = 0.8$
		$\frac{9}{10} = 0.9$

Mental Math

Suppose the area of a pool is 60 square meters.

a. If $\frac{1}{2}$ of the pool is covered, what is the area of the covered part?

b. If $\frac{1}{2}$ of the pool is covered, what is the area of the uncovered part?

c. If $\frac{1}{4}$ of the pool is covered, what is the area of the covered part?

d. If $\frac{1}{4}$ of the pool is covered, what is the area of the uncovered part?

QY

Every letter to the right equals a fraction shown. Match the fractions with their equal decimals. The answers spell a word. Save the word for the table in Question 22 in Lesson 2-10 on page 126.

?	?	?	?	?	?	?
0.875	1.75	$1.1\overline{6}$	$0.\overline{3}$	1.750	$0.1\overline{6}$	0.50

$E = \frac{7}{4}$

$T = \frac{50}{100}$ $R = \frac{7}{6}$

$P = \frac{14}{16}$

$N = \frac{1}{6}$

$C = \frac{5}{15}$

GUIDED

Example

Of the 96 seniors at Central High School, 60 stay in school for lunch, 12 go home for lunch, and the rest go to the mall for lunch. What fraction of the class is in each group? Write each answer as a fraction in lowest terms and as a decimal. Do not use a calculator.

In 2006, 65.8% of U.S. high school graduates enrolled in a college or university.

Source: U.S. Department of Labor

Solution Sixty seniors stay in school for lunch.

$\frac{60}{96} = \frac{30}{48} = \frac{5}{?}$, which is 0.625 as a decimal.

Twelve seniors go home for lunch.

$\frac{?}{96} = \frac{?}{?}$, which is __?__ as a decimal.

There are __?__ seniors who go to the mall for lunch.

$\frac{?}{?} = \frac{?}{?}$, which is __?__ as a decimal.

Check If you add the three fractions or three decimals, what should the sum be? Do your answers check?

Now you can play *Frac-Tac-Toe*. The directions for this game are on pages G8–G9 at the back of your book.

Questions

COVERING THE IDEAS

1. Find the decimal equivalent of each fraction. Try not to look at the table of equivalents at the beginning of the lesson.

   a. $\frac{1}{10}$ b. $\frac{2}{10}$ c. $\frac{3}{10}$

   d. $\frac{4}{10}$ e. $\frac{5}{10}$ f. $\frac{1}{5}$

   g. $\frac{2}{5}$ h. $\frac{3}{5}$ i. $\frac{1}{2}$

   j. $\frac{1}{4}$ k. $\frac{3}{4}$ l. $\frac{6}{10}$

   m. $\frac{7}{10}$ n. $\frac{8}{10}$ o. $\frac{9}{10}$

   p. $\frac{4}{5}$ q. $\frac{3}{8}$ r. $\frac{5}{8}$

   s. $\frac{7}{8}$ t. $\frac{1}{3}$ u. $\frac{2}{3}$

   v. $\frac{4}{6}$ w. $\frac{1}{6}$ x. $\frac{5}{6}$

2. Find a simple fraction for each decimal without looking at the table of equivalents at the beginning of the lesson.

   a. 0.4 b. 0.25 c. $0.\overline{3}$

   d. 0.60 e. −0.7 f. $0.\overline{6}$

3. Jamal knocked over his penny collection. 32 pennies fell out on the floor. 12 of them landed heads up. Write your answers to Parts a and b as fractions in lowest terms and as decimals.
   a. What fraction landed heads up?
   b. What fraction landed tails up?

In 2005, a man from Alabama cashed in 1.3 million pennies! How much is this in dollars?

Source: CNN

Fill in the Blanks In 4–7, fill in the blanks with decimals.

4. Since $\frac{1}{20} = 0.05$, $\frac{3}{20} = \underline{\ ?\ }$, $\frac{5}{20} = \underline{\ ?\ }$, and $\frac{7}{20} = \underline{\ ?\ }$.
5. Since $\frac{1}{25} = 0.04$, $\frac{2}{25} = \underline{\ ?\ }$, $\frac{3}{25} = \underline{\ ?\ }$, and $\frac{4}{25} = \underline{\ ?\ }$.
6. Since $\frac{3}{16} = 0.1875$, $3\frac{3}{16} = \underline{\ ?\ }$, and $-3\frac{3}{16} = \underline{\ ?\ }$.
7. Since $\frac{49}{50} = 0.98$, $1\frac{49}{50} = \underline{\ ?\ }$, and $16\frac{49}{50} = \underline{\ ?\ }$.

APPLYING THE MATHEMATICS

8. Miguel wants to make a table of decimal equivalents for twelfths. He does not need to determine decimals for all the fractions. For example, $\frac{4}{12} = \frac{1}{3}$, which he already knows is equal to $0.\overline{3}$.
   a. For which fractions will he need to calculate decimals?
   b. Use your calculator to find the decimal equivalent of each fraction you named in Part a. Use the raised-bar symbol where appropriate.
9. Erin wants to make a table of decimal equivalents for ninths.
   a. For which fractions does she need to calculate equivalents?
   b. Use your calculator to find the decimal equivalents.
   c. Describe a pattern for decimal equivalents to ninths.
10. You know that $\frac{1}{16}$ is half of $\frac{1}{8}$. Because $\frac{1}{8} = 0.125$, $\frac{1}{16}$ must be equal to $\frac{0.125}{2}$, or 0.0625. Use a similar method to find the decimal equivalent of each number.
    a. $\frac{1}{20}$
    b. $\frac{1}{40}$
    c. $\frac{1}{50}$

11. Miss Take wrote $\frac{7}{15} = 0.715$. Explain how you can tell this is incorrect without doing any calculations.

12. Use decimal equivalents to order $\frac{2}{3}$, $\frac{7}{10}$, and $\frac{3}{5}$ from greatest to least.

13. Compute $\frac{7}{8} + \frac{3}{4} + 1\frac{1}{2}$ by changing the fractions to decimals.

REVIEW

14. a. Estimate $\frac{4}{13}$ to the nearest ten-thousandth.
    b. Write $\frac{4}{13}$ as a repeating decimal. **(Lesson 2-7)**

15. A number rounded to the nearest thousand is 1,000,000. What is the smallest this number could be? **(Lesson 2-6)**

16. The circle graph below shows the distribution of the type of music of the top 100 hits of 2006. Estimate how many of the 100 hits were of each type. **(Lesson 2-5)**

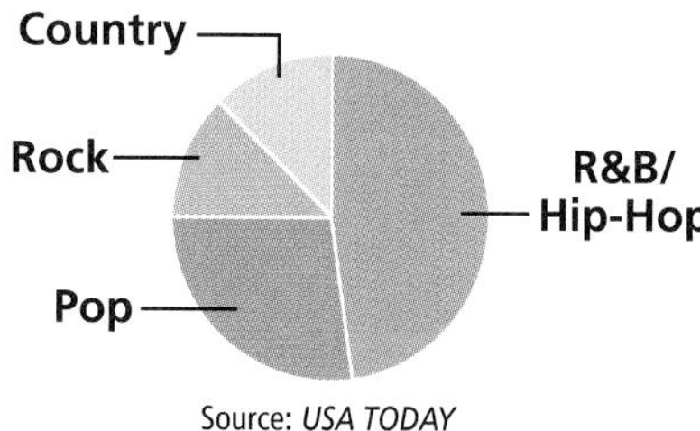

Source: *USA TODAY*

17. Which is greater, 862.000861 or 861.000862? **(Lesson 2-1)**

EXPLORATION

18. a. After entering a division calculation into your calculator, it displays 58.833333 as the answer. Name a division problem with this answer.
    b. After entering a division calculation into your calculator, it displays 58.833333 as the *exact* answer. Name a division problem with this answer.

QY ANSWER

PERCENT

Lesson

2-9 Percent and Circle Graphs

Vocabulary

percent sign (%)

circle graph

▸ **BIG IDEA** Percents can be used to create circle graphs in which each sector represents a part of a whole.

The word *percent* comes from the Latin *per centum*. The idea of percent originated about 2,000 years ago when the Roman Emperor Augustus imposed a tax on each group of 100 things sold at market auctions. In the middle ages, Italian merchants referred to "p cento," meaning "out of 100." Today we write 20% and say "20 percent."

Mental Math

Calculate.

a. 50 percent of 2

b. 25 percent of 4

c. 10 percent of 10

d. 100 percent of 1

Rewriting Percents as Decimals

The modern **percent sign %** means "multiply by one hundredth." To change a percent to a decimal, just multiply the number in front of the percent sign by $\frac{1}{100}$ or 0.01.

GUIDED

Example 1

Complete the table.

Solution

	Percent	As a Fraction	As a Decimal
a.	50%	$50 \times \frac{1}{100} = \underline{\ ?\ } = \frac{1}{2}$	$50 \times 0.01 = 0.5$
b.	63.1%	$63.1 \times \frac{1}{100} = \frac{63.1}{100} \times \frac{10}{10} = \underline{\ ?\ }$	$63.1 \times \underline{\ ?\ } = 0.631$
c.	4%	$4 \times \frac{1}{100} = \frac{4}{100} = \underline{\ ?\ }$	$4 \times 0.01 = \underline{\ ?\ }$
d.	12.5%	$12.5 \times \frac{1}{100} = \underline{\ ?\ } \times \underline{\ ?\ } = \frac{125}{1000}$	$\underline{\ ?\ } \times \underline{\ ?\ } = 0.125$
e.	100%	$100 \times \frac{1}{100} = \underline{\ ?\ } = \underline{\ ?\ }$	$100 \times 0.01 = \underline{\ ?\ }$
f.	125%	$125 \times \frac{1}{100} = \underline{\ ?\ } = \underline{\ ?\ }$	$125 \times 0.01 = \underline{\ ?\ }$

Note that a percent is greater than 1 when the number before the percent sign is greater than 100. For example, 125% > 1.

Changing Decimals to Percents

Recall that when a number is multiplied by 1, its *value* does not change. Because $100\% = 100 \times \frac{1}{100} = 1$, you can rewrite a decimal as a percent by multiplying the decimal by 100%.

Example 2

Ramón said that $\frac{1}{16}$ of the students in his class are left-handed. He found that $\frac{1}{16} = 0.0625$. Rewrite 0.0625 as a percent.

Solution Multiply by 100%.

$0.0625 \times 100\% = 6.25\%$

Check $6.25\% = 6.25 \times 0.01$
$= 0.0625$

QY

Write each decimal as a percent.

a. 0.38 **b.** 0.429 **c.** 1.3

Example 3

Susan asked 75 people to name their favorite color, and 33 said blue. What percent is this?

Solution Because 33 of the 75 people said blue, write the fraction $\frac{33}{75}$. First, convert $\frac{33}{75}$ to a decimal by dividing 33 by 75.

$$33 \div 75 = 0.44$$

Then change the decimal to a percent by multiplying by 100%.

$$0.44 \times 100\% = 44\%$$

44% of the people asked said blue is their favorite color.

Circle Graphs

As you saw in Lesson 2-5, you can represent percents visually with percent circles. You can use percent circles to make a *circle graph*. A **circle graph** uses sectors of a circle to show parts of a whole. You can use your knowledge of benchmark fractions and percents to sketch and to compare circle graph sectors.

▸ READING MATH

In everyday use, circle graphs are sometimes called pie charts. This is because the sectors look like slices of a pie.

Example 4

In 2004, about 34.24 million people living in the United States were born in another country. Of this number, 53% were born in Latin America, 25% in Asia, 14% in Europe, and the rest in other places. Display this information in a circle graph.

Solution Draw a circle. Keep in mind, there will be four sectors, one for each place of origin.

Step 1 Use a percent circle to draw a 53% sector. Because 53% is a little more than half, the sector for Latin America is a little larger than half of the circle.

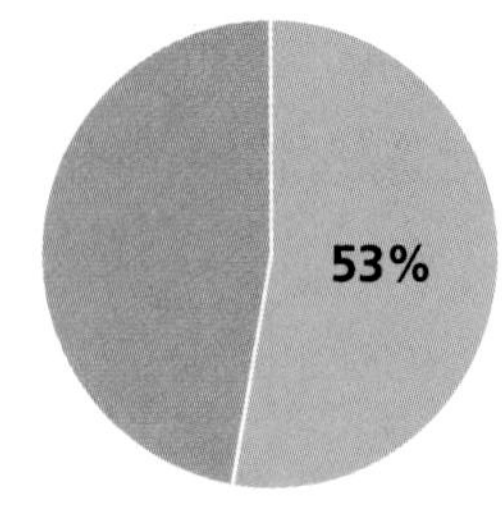

Step 2 Next to the 53% sector, draw a 25% sector for Asia. Because 25% is exactly $\frac{1}{4}$ of 100%, the sector for Asia is exactly $\frac{1}{4}$ of the circle.

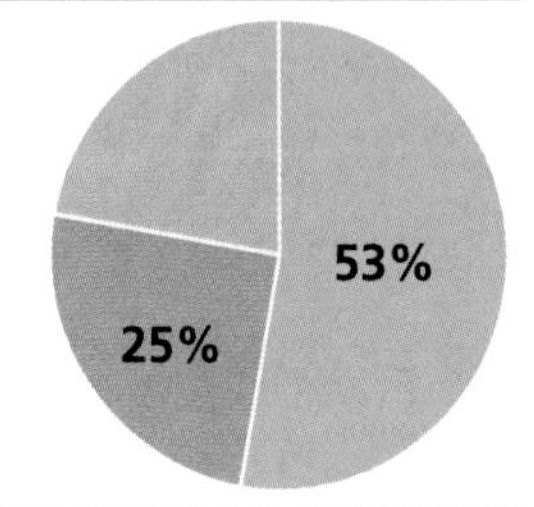

Step 3 Put a 14% sector next to the 25% sector. Because 14% is a little more than half of 25%, the sector for Europe is a little larger than half the sector for Asia.

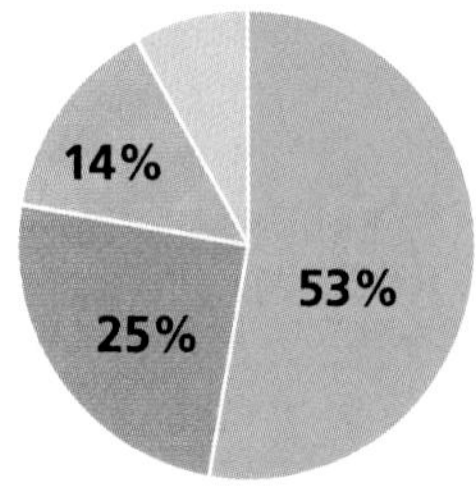

Step 4 The remaining part of the circle is for the fourth sector 8%, which represents people born in other places.

Step 5 Label each sector in the circle graph.

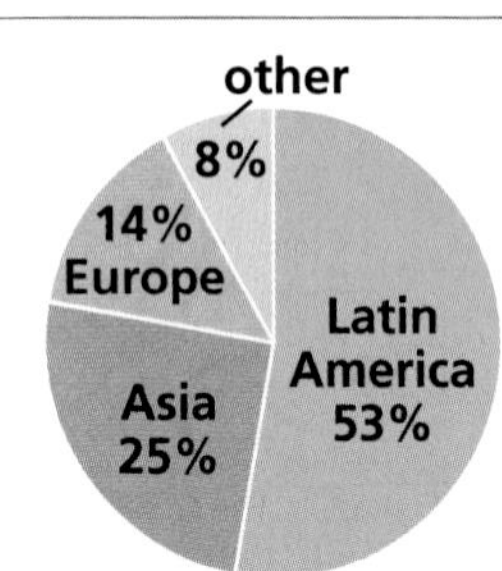

Check The sector for people born in other places represents $100\% - 53\% - 25\% - 14\% = 8\%$. This sector should make up a little more than half the sector for 14%. It seems correct.

Activity

MATERIALS percent circle

Step 1 Estimate the percent of each circle that is shaded on the next page.

Step 2 Compare your estimates with those of your classmates.

Step 3 Using a percent circle, measure the sectors to find the percent of each circle that is shaded.

a.

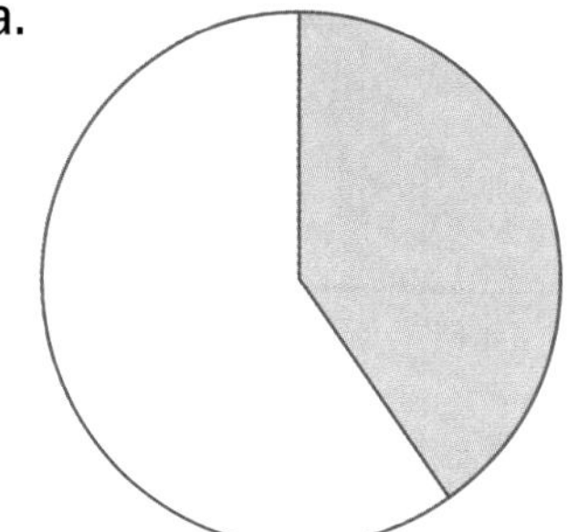

b.

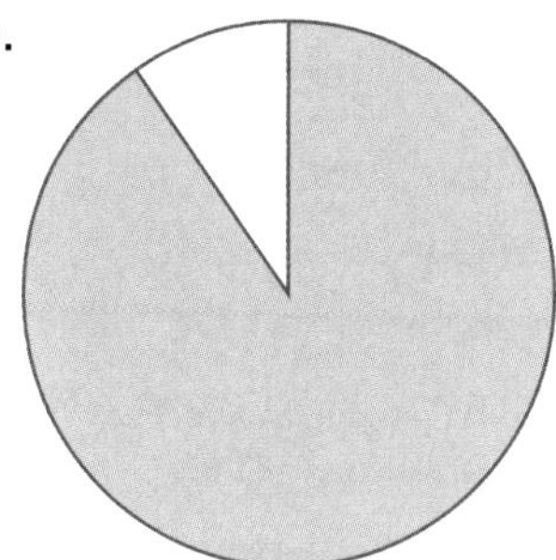

c.

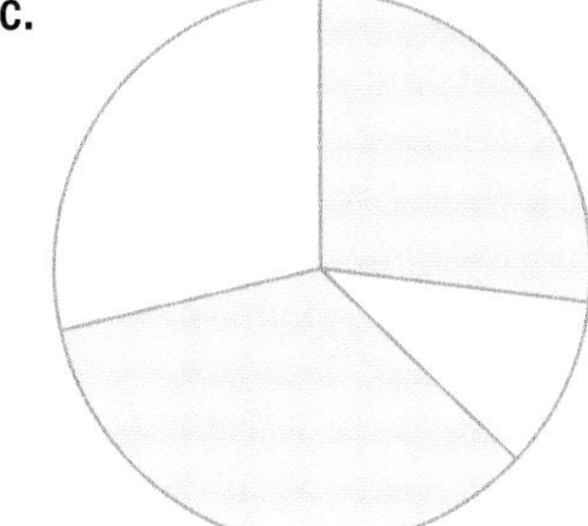

d.

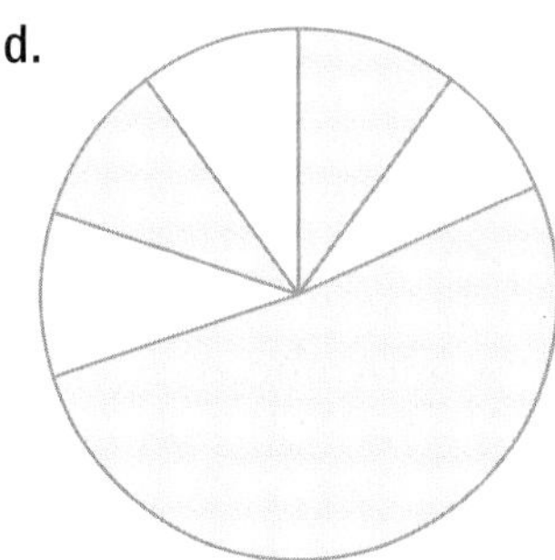

Questions

COVERING THE IDEAS

1. **Fill in the Blanks** The symbol % is read __?__ and means __?__.

In 2 and 3, explain how to do the conversion.

2. a percent to a decimal
3. a decimal to a percent

In 4 and 5, write the percent as a decimal and as a fraction in lowest terms.

4. 2%
5. 35%

In 6 and 7, write the percent as a decimal.

6. 100%
7. 150%

In 8 and 9, write the decimal as a percent.

8. 0.07
9. 3.25

10. The teachers at Liddle Middle School were buying food for the school picnic. Of the 120 students at the school, 15% wanted hot dogs, 45% wanted hamburgers, and 40% wanted barbequed chicken. Make a circle graph of this information.

In 2007, American Joey Chestnut set a world record by eating 66 hot dogs in 12 minutes!

Source: ESPN

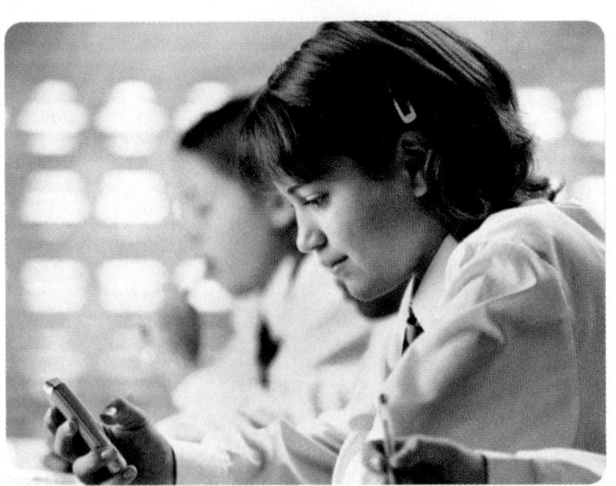

Personal digital assistant (PDA) technology is now incorporated into cellular phones.

In 11 and 12, write each underlined percent as a decimal.

11. According to the U.S. Census Bureau, <u>11.9 percent</u> of the 2004 U.S. population was not born in the United States.

12. The number of handheld computers sold increased <u>250%</u> from 1999 to 2000. The number of desktop computers sold increased <u>10%</u> during this time.

In 13 and 14, rewrite each fraction as a percent.

13. a. $\frac{1}{2}$ b. $\frac{1}{4}$ c. $\frac{1}{8}$ d. $\frac{3}{8}$

14. a. $\frac{3}{10}$ b. $\frac{3}{5}$ c. $\frac{3}{50}$ d. $\frac{3}{20}$

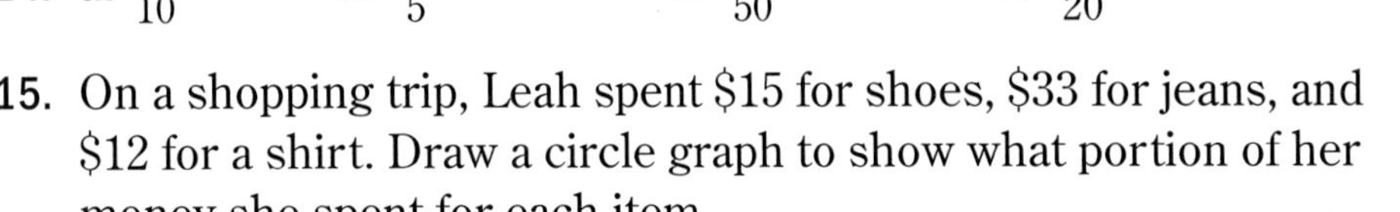

15. On a shopping trip, Leah spent \$15 for shoes, \$33 for jeans, and \$12 for a shirt. Draw a circle graph to show what portion of her money she spent for each item.

APPLYING THE MATHEMATICS

16. Over 20 years, Mr. Turner's income was multiplied by 5. What is this as a percent?

17. Graph 10%, 20%, 30%, 40%, 50%, 60%, 70%, 80%, 90%, and 100% on a number line.

18. If a cup is 20% full, then it is 80% empty. Tell how empty the cup is when it is
    a. 50% full. b. 55% full.
    c. 80% full. d. 6% full.

19. A survey asked high school students whether they use sunscreen if they plan to be in the sun for more than one hour. The results are shown in the table below. Compute the percent for each response. Make a circle graph showing these percents.

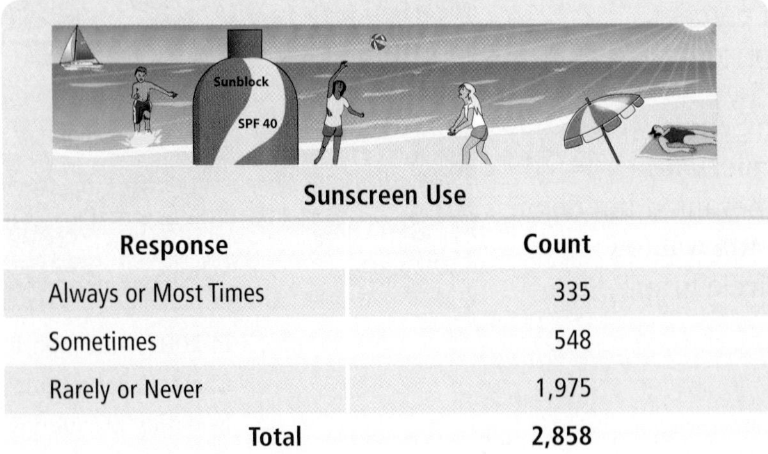

Sunscreen Use

Response	Count
Always or Most Times	335
Sometimes	548
Rarely or Never	1,975
Total	**2,858**

20. Between what two integers is 4.33%? Explain your thinking. (Be careful!)

21. Refer to the bar graph below. Automakers are represented by the letters A–F.

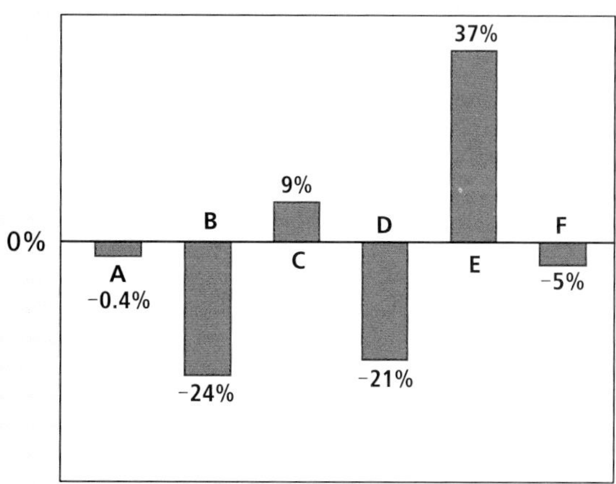

a. Which automaker had the greatest percent increase in production?

b. Which automaker had the greatest percent decrease in production?

c. Which automaker had an increase, but the smallest percent increase in sales?

d. What percent would indicate no change in sales?

22. a. Cecilia's punch recipe requires 2 cups orange juice, 2 cups lemonade, 8 cups water, and 4 cups of ginger ale. What percent is orange juice?

b. Shanté's punch recipe requires 3 cups orange juice, 5 cups lemonade, 14 cups water, and 10 cups of ginger ale. What percent is orange juice?

c. Shanté uses more orange juice than Cecilia, but the percent of orange juice in her punch is less. Explain how this is possible.

REVIEW

23. Write $\frac{1}{7}$ as a decimal to the nearest millionth. **(Lesson 2-8)**

24. Some polar bears weigh as much as 1760 pounds. Express this weight in tons as

a. a fraction in lowest terms.

b. a decimal. **(Lesson 2-7)**

25. Round 10111213.14151617 to the nearest
    a. million.
    b. millionth.
    c. hundred-thousandth.
    d. ten thousand. **(Lesson 2-6)**

26. **Multiple Choice** When a number is rounded to the nearest hundred, the result is 123,000. Which could *not* be the original number? **(Lesson 2-6)**

    A 123,000 B 122,957.2
    C 122,940 D 123,042

27. In the 2000 Olympics, Yang Xia of China set a weightlifting world record for women who weigh no more than 53 kg. She lifted 100.0 kg, beating the previous record of 97.5 kg. One kilogram is approximately 2.2 lb. **(Lesson 2-4)**
    a. About how many pounds did Yang Xia lift?
    b. Yang Xia weighed no more than how many pounds when she set the record?
    c. By how many kilograms did she beat the previous record?
    d. By about how many pounds did she beat the previous record?

28. Power is often measured in *watts* and *kilowatts*. Based on your knowledge of the metric system, how many watts are in 1 kilowatt? **(Lesson 2-4)**

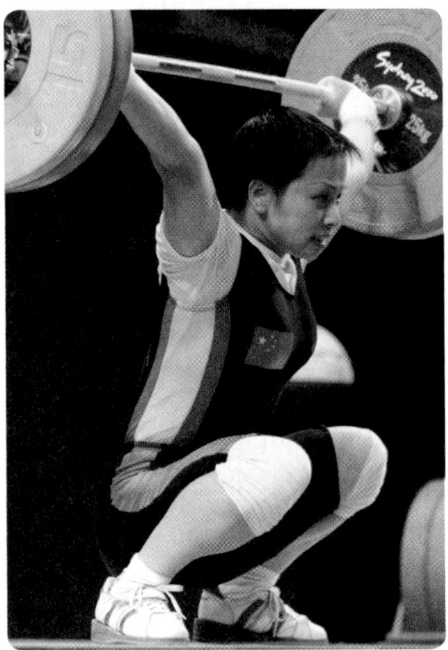

At the 2000 Olympics, Yang Xia also set the women's weightlifting world records in the clean and jerk and total lift competitions.

Source: *Sports Illustrated*

EXPLORATION

29. a. Find a use of percent in a newspaper or magazine that you think is interesting.
    b. Make up a question about the information you have found. Answer your question.

QY ANSWERS

a. 38%

b. 42.9%

c. 130%

Lesson 2-10 Comparing Fractions, Decimals, and Percents

Vocabulary

is less than $<$

is greater than $>$

▸ **BIG IDEA** By converting fractions and percents to decimals, numbers in any of these forms can be compared.

Two stores are having a sale on jeans. One store offers 30% off and the other store offers $\frac{1}{3}$ off. Which is a better deal? You are asked to answer this question later in this lesson.

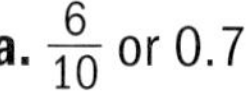

Mental Math

Which is greater?

a. $\frac{6}{10}$ or 0.7

b. $\frac{2}{3}$ or 0.8

c. 2.5 or $\frac{2}{5}$

d. 1.0 or $\frac{1}{1}$

Symbols of Inequality

Recall that these symbols are used to compare two or more numbers.

Symbol	Meaning
$<$	is less than
$>$	is greater than
$=$	is equal to

The symbols $<$ and $>$ are called symbols of *inequality*. You can remember which inequality symbol is which because the arrow points to the lesser number and opens to the greater number. For example, $1 < 2$ and $2 > 1$.

To compare decimals and percents, remember how they are placed on a number line.

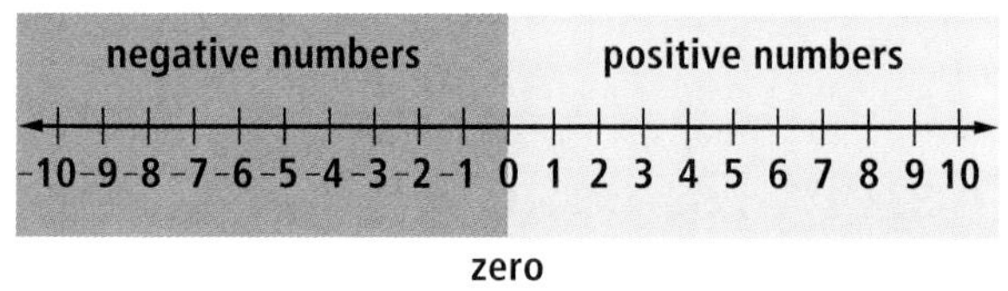

On this number line, smaller numbers are to the left. For example, -6 is less than both -2 and 2.

$-6 < -2$ $\qquad$ $-6 < 2$

Bigger numbers are to the right; 2 is greater than both -2 and -6.

$2 > -2$ $\qquad$ $2 > -6$

See QY1 at the right.

QY1

Fill in the Blanks

Compare the numbers using $<$, $=$, or $>$?

a. 1.45 __?__ 1.445

b. 6.21% __?__ 6.0%

Comparing Fractions with Equal Numerators or Equal Denominators

It is easy to compare fractions with the same denominator. For example, to compare $\frac{3}{7}$ to $\frac{4}{7}$, think of $\frac{3}{7}$ as 3 pieces each with a length of $\frac{1}{7}$. Think of $\frac{4}{7}$ as 4 pieces, each with a length of $\frac{1}{7}$. So, $\frac{4}{7} > \frac{3}{7}$ because 4 pieces is more than 3 pieces of the same length.

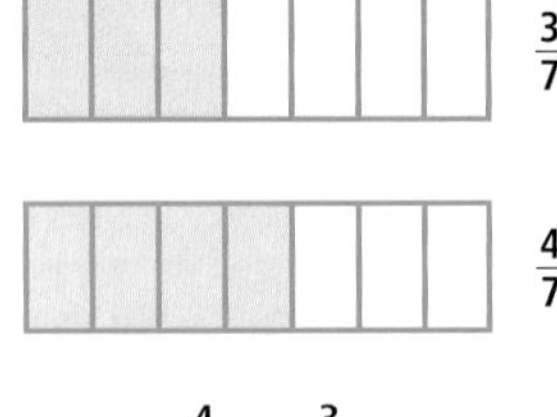

$\frac{4}{7} > \frac{3}{7}$

QY2

Ebony ran $\frac{2}{5}$ of the way to school before resting. Her friend Paige ran $\frac{3}{5}$ of the way before resting. Who ran farther before taking a break? Assume Ebony and Paige started at the same place.

Now we look at an example where the numerators are the same.

Example 1

Bill ran $\frac{5}{6}$ of the way to school before resting. Mary ran $\frac{5}{7}$ of the way. Who ran farther before taking a break? Assume Bill and Mary started at the same place.

Solution For Bill, the distance is divided into 6 equal parts. For Mary, the distance is divided into 7 equal parts. The more parts there are, the smaller each part is. So, Mary's five parts are smaller than Bill's five. Bill runs farther before resting, $\frac{5}{6} > \frac{5}{7}$.

The reasoning in Example 1 shows that when two simple fractions have the same numerator, the one with the smaller denominator is greater.

See QY3 at the right.

QY3

Fill in the Blank Compare the numbers using <, =, or >.

$\frac{11}{51}$? $\frac{11}{42}$

Comparing Fractions with Different Numerators and Different Denominators

Example 2

Ariana cut a pizza into 8 equal pieces and ate 3 of them. Tyra cut a pizza of the same size into 5 equal pieces and ate 2 of them. Who ate more?

Solution 1 Convert the fractions $\frac{3}{8}$ and $\frac{2}{5}$ to decimals. Remember the decimal equivalents or use a calculator.

$\frac{3}{8} = 0.375$ $\qquad$ $\frac{2}{5} = 0.4$

Because $0.4 > 0.375$, Tyra ate more pizza than Ariana.

Solution 2 Rewrite $\frac{3}{8}$ and $\frac{2}{5}$ with equal denominators. Because 40 is a multiple of both 8 and 5, use 40 as the common denominator.

$$\frac{3}{8} = \frac{3 \times 5}{8 \times 5} = \frac{15}{40}$$

$$\frac{2}{5} = \frac{2 \times 8}{5 \times 8} = \frac{16}{40}$$

$\frac{16}{40} > \frac{15}{40}$, so $\frac{2}{5}$ is greater than $\frac{3}{8}$. Tyra ate more than Ariana.

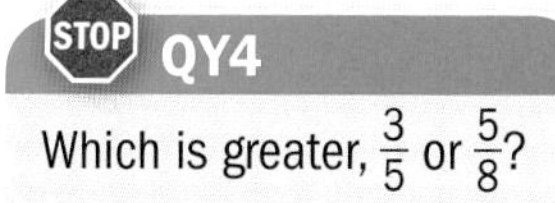

QY4

Which is greater, $\frac{3}{5}$ or $\frac{5}{8}$?

See QY4 at the right.

Example 3

Compare $\frac{1}{3}$ to 0.3, 0.33, and 0.333.

Solution As a decimal, $\frac{1}{3} = 0.\overline{3}$. The 3 repeats forever so $\frac{1}{3} = 0.3333...$. From this, you can see that $\frac{1}{3} > 0.3$. Using this same reasoning,

$\frac{1}{3} > 0.33$,

$\frac{1}{3} > 0.333$,

and so on.

QY5

How does this result of Example 3 help answer the question about the sale on jeans at the beginning of this lesson?

Now you can play *Match-It: Four-Way Conversion*. The directions for this game are on pages G10–G11 at the back of your book.

Using Percents to Compare Fractions

Percents and decimals are particularly useful when comparing fractions with large denominators. Here is a typical example.

As of 2006, Yao Ming is the tallest player in the NBA at 7'6".

Source: National Basketball Association

Example 4

The table shows the number of shots made and the number of shots attempted by two players during the 2004–2005 National Basketball Association regular season.

	Yao Ming	Shawn Marion
Number of shots made	538	613
Number of attempts	975	1,289

Who made a greater percent of his shots?

(continued on next page)

Solution Yao Ming made $\frac{538}{975}$ of his shots. Shawn Marion made $\frac{613}{1289}$ of his shots. Converting to decimals or percents makes these fractions easier to compare.

$\frac{538}{975} = 0.5517... \approx 55.2\%$

$\frac{613}{1289} = 0.47556... \approx 47.6\%$

Because 55.2% > 47.6%, Yao Ming made a greater percent of shots.

See QY6 at the right.

QY6

Arrange the numbers below from greatest to least. Then place the corresponding letter in the appropriate blank. The answers spell a word. Save the word for the table in Question 22 in Lesson 2-10 on page 126.

12.5% = S
0.75 = N
$\frac{1}{3}$ = U
90% = G
$0.\overline{6}$ = I
$\frac{7}{8}$ = E

Questions

COVERING THE IDEAS

1. a. Which inequality symbol means "is greater than?"
   b. Which inequality symbol means "is less than?"

In 2–4, rewrite using the correct symbol, <, =, or >.

2. 2.5 km is greater than 1.95 km.
3. 25 mm is shorter than 3 cm.
4. 5 ft is the same length as 60 in.

Fill in the Blanks In 5–10, compare the fractions using <, =, or >.

5. $\frac{7}{8}$ hr ___?___ $\frac{7}{12}$ hr
6. $\frac{3}{8}$ ___?___ 0.375
7. $\frac{4}{5}$ ___?___ 0.75
8. $\frac{3}{4}$ ft ___?___ $\frac{1}{2}$ ft ___?___ $\frac{1}{3}$ ft
9. 17% ___?___ 0.2 ___?___ $\frac{2}{9}$
10. $\frac{5}{6}$ ___?___ 0.833

APPLYING THE MATHEMATICS

11. Pedro, Juan, and Chloe each ordered a 10 oz steak at a restaurant. Pedro ate $\frac{2}{3}$ of his steak, Juan ate $\frac{3}{5}$ of his steak, and Chloe left $\frac{1}{4}$ of her steak uneaten. Who ate the most steak?
12. When she was born, Paola weighed $7\frac{1}{2}$ pounds. After 24 hours, she weighed $7\frac{1}{5}$ pounds. At three days old, she weighed 7 pounds, 13 ounces.
    a. Put these weights in order from least to greatest.
    b. Paola's weight pattern is typical of newborn babies. What does this tell you about the first few days of life?
13. a. Order $\frac{22}{100}$, $\frac{2}{9}$, and 0.222 from least to greatest.
    b. Order $\frac{-22}{100}$, $\frac{-2}{9}$, and -0.222 from least to greatest.

The average weight for a baby at birth is 7.5 pounds, or 3.4 kilograms.

Source: World Book 2001

14. At the end of the 1949 Major League Baseball season, Ted Williams had 194 hits in 566 at-bats, George Kell had 179 hits in 522 at-bats, and Jackie Robinson had 203 hits in 593 at-bats. The batting average of a player is found by dividing the number of hits by the number of at-bats and rounding to the nearest thousandth. Who had the highest batting average?

15. It is estimated that about 1 in 2,500 babies is born with some sort of liver disease. Is this greater or less than 1% of babies?

Jackie Robinson

REVIEW

16. A survey asked 150 people what TV show they watched from 7:00 P.M. to 7:30 P.M. last night. The table below shows the results. Sketch a circle graph of this information. Follow these steps. **(Lesson 2-9)**

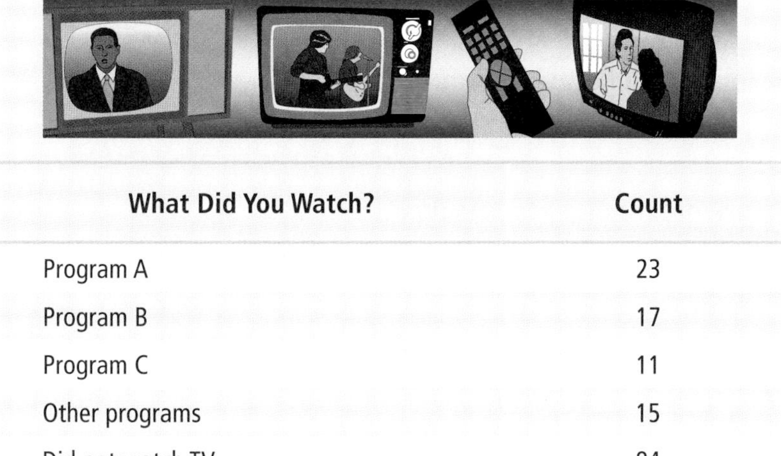

What Did You Watch?	Count
Program A	23
Program B	17
Program C	11
Other programs	15
Did not watch TV	84

a. Determine how many sectors the graph will have.
b. Determine the fraction of people each sector will represent.
c. Determine the percent of people each sector will represent.
d. Draw a rough circle graph.

17. a. What fraction of an hour is 3 minutes?
b. What percent of an hour is 3 minutes?
c. What fraction of a day is 3 hours?
d. What percent of a day is 3 hours?
e. What fraction of a century is 1 year?
f. What percent of a century is 1 year? **(Lessons 2-9, 2-7, 1-5)**

18. Copy this table. Fill in the missing equivalents. **(Lesson 2-8)**

Fraction	Decimal	Percent
a. ?	0.5	b. ?
$\frac{1}{4}$	c. ?	d. ?
e. ?	f. ?	75%
$\frac{2}{5}$	g. ?	h. ?
i. ?	0.6	j. ?
k. ?	l. ?	90%
m. ?	0.3	n. ?

19. A certain medium-sized jar of peanut butter has a mass of 456 grams. Convert this mass to the given unit. **(Lesson 2-4)**
    a. milligrams
    b. kilograms

20. a. Measure the segment to the nearest centimeter.

    ____

    b. Measure the segment the nearest millimeter. **(Lesson 2-4)**

EXPLORATION

21. When communicating information, people can choose whether to express numbers as fractions, decimals, or percents. For each example, explain why the number might have been expressed in the given form.
    a. Tomorrow's forecast calls for a 30% chance of rain.
    b. Before starting out on a trip, Félix discovered that he had only $\frac{1}{4}$ of a tank of gas.
    c. The average body temperature of human beings is 98.6° F.

22. a. In the table below, place the words you decoded from the QYs and questions from this chapter.
    b. Rearrange the words to form a saying by Thomas Edison. (One word is used twice.)

Table to Record Decoded Puzzle Words	
Lesson	**Word(s)**
2-1	?
2-3	?
2-4	?
2-6	?
2-6	?
2-6	?
2-8	?
2-10	?

QY ANSWERS

1a. > **1b.** <

2. Paige **3.** <

4. $\frac{5}{8}$

5. Answers vary. Sample: $\frac{1}{3}$ off is better than 30% off.

6. GENIUS

Chapter 2 Projects

1 Cubits

The *cubit* is an ancient unit based on arm and hand measurements. It is the length of the forearm from the elbow to the tip of the middle finger. Try taking measurements using the cubit system with your own arm. Measure things like the length of a wall, the width of your desk, and the length of a notebook. Make a chart comparing your measures with those of at least three other people. Write a paragraph about the advantages and disadvantages of the cubit measure.

2 Repeating Decimals

Investigate which fractions equal terminating decimals and which equal repeating decimals. Make a table of unit fractions $\frac{1}{2}, \frac{1}{3}, \frac{1}{4}, \ldots, \frac{1}{25}$ and their decimal equivalents. For the repeating decimals, be sure to find the entire repetend. It will never have more digits than the denominator of the fraction. If the repetend is long, dividing other fractions with that denominator can help. (For example, to find the repetend for $\frac{1}{7}$, look at $\frac{2}{7}, \frac{3}{7}$, and so on.) Try to determine a rule for predicting whether a given denominator will yield a terminating or repeating decimal.

3 Food Labels

Food products have nutrition labels. The labels report the amount, in grams, of several food components. Data is given for total fat, cholesterol, sodium, carbohydrates, and protein. Make a table that shows the amount of each of these components for at least five of your favorite foods. Compare the foods in your table. Discuss how the percent daily value is computed and whether the labels round up, round down, or round to the nearest.

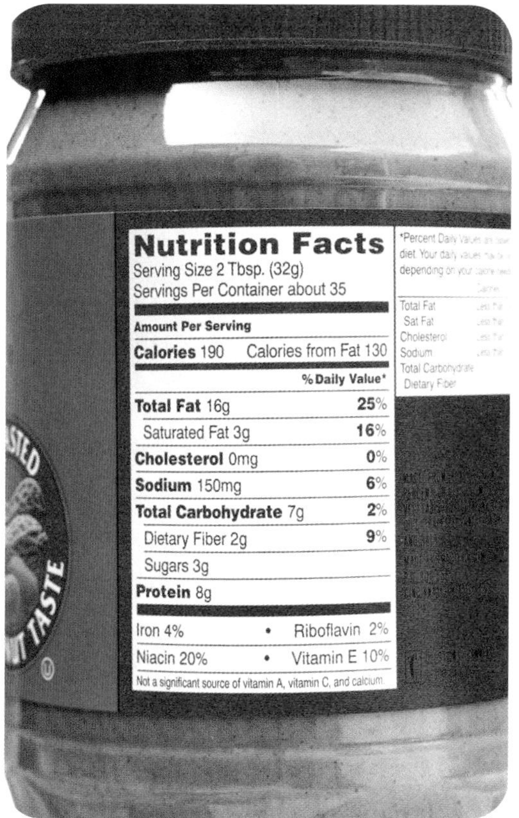

Most experts recommend consuming between 2,000 and 2,500 calories per day.

4 Circle Graph

Choose a topic that interests you, such as a hobby or sports. Write a question about this topic, giving at least four possible choices as answers. Your question should be designed so each person will choose one and only one answer. For example, you might ask, "Which of these sports do you like *best*?" and give the choices football, soccer, tennis, and golf. "Which sport do you play?" would not be an appropriate question because some people might play more than one. Survey 25 or more people using your question, and display your results in both a table and a circle graph.

Playing basketball is a good way to exercise and burn lots of calories.

5 Metric Units

There are metric units besides the ones you used in this chapter. Research the seven base units for the metric system. Identify all of the prefixes from 1,000,000,000,000,000,000, 000,000 to 0.000000000000000000000001. Then find at least ten real-world examples using these units. Your examples should not use common measures like kilogram or centimeter. Display your results in a poster or chart.

6 Caloric Values

A *calorie* is the amount of energy needed to raise the temperature of 1 gram of water 1°C at 15°C. The calories referred to on food nutrition labels are called *dietary calories*. A dietary calorie is equal to 1,000 true calories. Recall that the metric prefix "kilo" means 1,000. So 1 dietary calorie = 1 kilocalorie. Look at the labels on some foods around your home. Find how many real calories are in each food. Assume the average boy or girl eats about 2,000 dietary calories a day. How many real calories is this? To what temperature could you heat 1 gram of water with this amount of energy? Are you surprised by this?

Chapter 2 Summary and Vocabulary

- Many common numbers can be represented as **decimals.** Simple fractions may be represented as **terminating** or **repeating decimals.** To convert a fraction $\frac{n}{d}$ to a decimal, divide n by d.

- Representing numbers as decimals makes it easier to order them. Graphing decimals on a **number line** can also help. In real-life situations, it is often useful to **estimate by rounding** a decimal up or down or to the nearest value of a specified place.

- When a number is written as a decimal, each digit has a place value that is 10 times the value of the digit to its right. To multiply a decimal by 10, 100, 1000, and so on, move the decimal point to the *right* the same number of places as the number of zeros following the 1. To multiply a decimal by $\frac{1}{10}$, $\frac{1}{100}$, $\frac{1}{1000}$, and so on, move the decimal point to the *left* the same number of places as the number of zeros following the 1 in the denominator.

- The **metric system** of measurement is closely related to the decimal system. The units of the metric system are related to each other by **multiples of 10.** The basic units in the metric system are the **meter** for length, the **gram** for mass, and the **liter** for capacity. Other units are identified by prefixes. The most common are **kilo-** for 1,000, **centi-** for $\frac{1}{100}$, and **milli-** for $\frac{1}{1000}$.

- **Percents, decimals,** and **fractions** are all used often and sometimes interchangeably. The **percent symbol %** means to multiply by $\frac{1}{100}$, or 0.01. You should know the decimal equivalents for simple proper fractions with denominators 2, 3, 4, 5, 6, 8, and 10.

- To make a **circle graph** to picture data, you can express the data as fractions of a whole, and then convert the fractions to percents.

Theorems and Properties

Substitution Principle (p. 73)

Vocabulary

2-1
expanded notation
one-place decimal
two-place decimal

2-4
metric system
kilo-, centi-, milli-
meter, gram
kilogram, milligram
liter, milliliter
microgram

2-5
round up
round down
percent circle
sector

2-6
estimate
rounding to the nearest
is approximately equal to (≈)

2-7
repetend
repeating decimal

2-9
percent sign (%)
circle graph

2-10
is less than <
is greater than >

Chapter 2 Self-Test

Take this test as you would take a test in class. You will need a calculator. Then use the Selected Answers section in the back of the book to check your work.

1. Write the number 0.0009 as you would say it.

2. Write the decimal for 3.4 trillion.

3. Identify the place value of the given digit in the number 0.081672.
   a. 7 b. 8

4. Name three numbers between 27.895 and 27.8957.

5. Graph 1, $-1.\overline{3}$, 0, –0.875, and $0.1\overline{6}$ on a number line.

6. Write the fraction as a decimal and as a percent.
   a. $\frac{50}{75}$ b. $\frac{33}{18}$

7. Suppose you are flying from Detroit to San Francisco. The airline allows for a maximum of 40 pounds of carry-on luggage. In your luggage, you want to put an 11.5-lb CD player, clothes weighing 15.35 lb, cosmetics weighing 1.65 lb, and books weighing 9.45 lb.
   a. Estimate to the nearest higher pound the total weight of the items.
   b. Will you be allowed to take all of the items in your carry-on luggage? Why or why not?

8. Round 45.9725 to the indicated place.
   a. tenths
   b. hundredths
   c. thousandths

In 9 and 10, tell how to move the decimal point when multiplying by the given number.

9. 100 10. $\frac{1}{1,000,000}$

11. **Fill in the Blanks** Compare the numbers using <, =, or >.
   a. 0.005 __?__ $\frac{1}{20}$
   b. 1.78 __?__ $1\frac{6}{8}$
   c. 8.333333333 __?__ $8.\overline{3}$

In 12 and 13, write the repeating decimal using a raised-bar symbol.

12. 0.05050505...

13. 2.6666666...

14. **Fill in the Blanks** If you want to calculate $\frac{4}{5}$ of a quantity, you can multiply the quantity by the decimal __?__ or the percent __?__.

15. **Fill in the Blanks** Use the Substitution Principle.
   $\frac{1}{25} + \frac{1}{2} = 0.$__?__ $+ 0.$__?__
   $=$ __?__ % + __?__ %

16. Draw a segment 8.7 cm long.

17. Measure the segment below to the nearest millimeter.

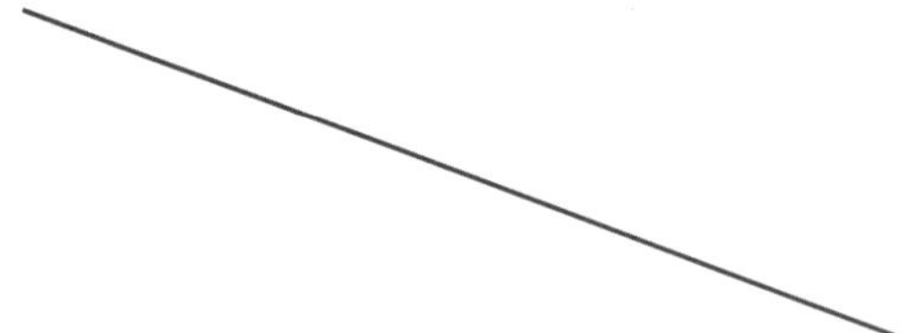

18. When Brianna was born, she weighed 3 kg, 576 g, and was 50 cm long.
   a. Convert her weight into grams.
   b. Convert her length into meters.

19. The table below gives the win-loss records of six college basketball teams at the start of the 2005 NCAA tournament. A win-loss record of 25-10 means that the team won 25 games and lost 10.

Win/Loss Record	School
27-6	University of Arizona
32-1	University of Illinois
20-9	Louisiana State University
24-6	University of Nevada
20-10	University of Texas
24-5	University of Wisconsin-Milwaukee

Source: NCAA

a. For each school, find the total number of games played and the fraction of games won.

b. Order the teams from first to sixth based on the percent of games won.

c. What percent of its games did the team with the highest percent win?

20. Consider the results of a North American survey that asked parents how much weekly allowance they give to their 12–17 year old child. Represent this information in a circle graph.

Amount of Weekly Allowance	Percent of Children Receiving that Amount
No allowance	29%
$5 or less	21%
$6–$10	23%
$11–$20	19%
$21 or more	8%

Source: www.kidsmoney.org

Chapter 2 Chapter Review

SKILLS
PROPERTIES
USES
REPRESENTATIONS

SKILLS Procedures used to get answers

OBJECTIVE A Identify place values in a decimal number. (Lessons 2-1, 2-2)

In 1–4, identify the digit with the given place value in 1,047,235.8964012.

1. hundred thousands
2. thousandths
3. tens
4. tenths

In 5 and 6, identify the place value of the underlined digit.

5. $0.087\underline{6}4$
6. $11,\underline{0}04,758.63$

OBJECTIVE B Translate back and forth from words into the decimal system. (Lessons 2-1, 2-2)

In 7–10, write the number as a decimal.

7. ninety-three ten-thousandths
8. nine hundredths
9. 4.7 million (the number of chickens quarantined at the outbreak of a flu virus)
10. 26.4 billion (the increase, in Euros, of the value of a company)

In 11 and 12, write the number in words.

11. 40.867
12. 122,000,000,000

OBJECTIVE C Compare and order decimals, fractions, and percents. (Lessons 2-1, 2-10)

In 13–18, order the numbers from least to greatest.

13. 0.0523, 0.523, 0.00523
14. 0.600000, $\frac{2}{3}$, 0.66666
15. 11.2774, 11.2779, 11.2764
16. -18.752, -20, -18.751
17. 30%, 4%, 0.35
18. 14.5%, 14.5, $\frac{3}{8}$

19. Find two numbers between 79.123 and 79.124.

20. Give three values between $8.20 and $8.90.

Fill in the Blank **In 21–24, compare the numbers using <, =, or >.**

21. $\frac{1}{7}$ __?__ $0.\overline{142856}$
22. $\frac{4}{5}$ __?__ $\frac{7}{8}$
23. $5.1\overline{6}$ __?__ $5\frac{1}{6}$
24. -2.709 __?__ -2.708

OBJECTIVE D Round any decimal to the indicated degree of accuracy. (Lessons 2-5, 2-6)

In 25–28, round 4,982.5149 to the nearest given place.

25. hundred
26. hundredth
27. whole number
28. tenth

29. Paco wants to buy groceries that cost $5.25, $6.68, and $7.99. He decides to quickly estimate the total cost.
    a. Round each of the original prices to the nearest dollar.
    b. What is the estimated total cost?

30. Demetrius's father drove 184.28 miles last week and 129.73 miles this week. Estimate to the nearest mile the total distance he drove over the two weeks.

OBJECTIVE E Draw and measure lengths in the metric system. (Lesson 2-4)

In 31 and 32, find the length of the segment below in the given units.

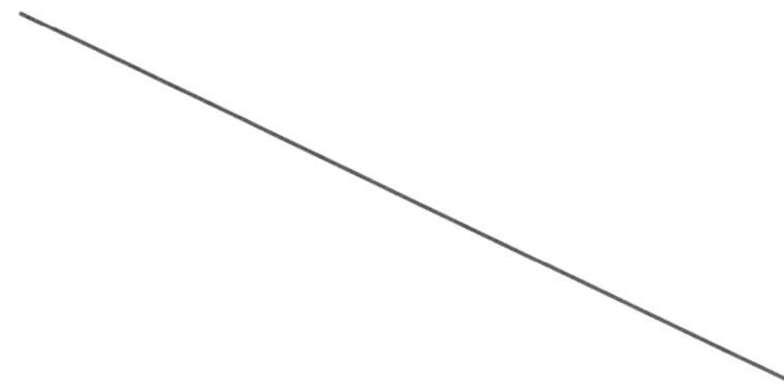

31. centimeters

32. millimeters

33. Find the sum of the lengths of the sides of the rectangle
 a. in millimeters.
 b. in centimeters.

In 34–37, draw a line segment with the given length.

34. 3.8 cm

35. 62 mm

36. 12 cm

37. $4\frac{1}{2}$ cm

OBJECTIVE F Convert among fractions, decimals, and percents. (Lessons 2-8, 2-9)

In 38–41, give the decimal equivalent for the fraction in your head.

38. $\frac{1}{3}$

39. $\frac{7}{8}$

40. $\frac{3}{4}$

41. $\frac{4}{6}$

In 42–45, give a decimal for the fraction or percent.

42. $\frac{5}{8}$

43. 1.44%

44. $9\frac{17}{50}$

45. $\frac{103}{33}$

In 46–49, give a simple fraction for the decimal or percent.

46. 25%

47. $0.1\overline{6}$

48. $33\frac{1}{3}$

49. $2.\overline{6}$

In 50–53, give the percent equal to the decimal or fraction.

50. $\frac{4}{5}$

51. $1\frac{2}{3}$

52. 8.2

53. 0.019

OBJECTIVE G Multiply by 10, $\frac{1}{10}$, 100, $\frac{1}{100}$, 1000, $\frac{1}{1000}$, and so on. (Lessons 2-2, 2-3)

Fill in the Blanks In 54 and 55, fill in the blanks and explain your answer.

54. 276 is __?__ times 2.76.

55. $1.365 \times$ __?__ $= 0.001365$

56. **Fill in the Blank** Multiplying a number by $\frac{1}{10{,}000}$ is the same as multiplying it by $\frac{1}{100}$ and then by __?__.

57. Multiply 36.742 by each number.

a. 10

b. $\frac{1}{10}$

c. $\frac{1}{100}$

d. $\frac{1}{10{,}000}$

PROPERTIES The principles behind the mathematics

OBJECTIVE H Correctly use the raised-bar symbol for repeating decimals. (Lessons 2-7)

58. Write the answer to $100 \div 3$ as a repeating decimal using a raised-bar symbol.

59. Rewrite $\frac{5}{6}$ as a repeating decimal using the raised-bar symbol.

In 60 and 61, write the repeating decimal using the raised-bar symbol.

60. 15.151515...

61. 1.63163163...

OBJECTIVE I Know and apply the Substitution Principle for decimals and percents. (Lessons 2-2, 2-9)

62. **Fill in the Blank** 0.15 of 5,000 is the same as __?__% of 5,000.

63. **Fill in the Blanks** To calculate 234% of a quantity, you can multiply the quantity by the decimal __?__ or the fraction __?__.

64. Bianca said that to calculate 87.5% of a quantity, she would multiply by 8.75 or $8\frac{3}{4}$. She wants you to check her work. What should you tell her?

65. $\frac{2}{5}$ of 60 is the same as what decimal times 60?

USES Applications of mathematics in real-world situations

OBJECTIVE J Find percents of quantities in real-world situations. (Lesson 2-9)

66. At Eva's birthday party, 16 of her 25 guests were from her school. What percent of the guests were *not* her schoolmates?

67. Brazil is the most successful soccer nation in the world. Of the 18 world cups held from 1930 to 2006, the Brazilians participated in 7 of the final matches, winning 5 of them. What percent of their final matches did the Brazilians win? Round your answer to the nearest percent.

68. Which sale gives a bigger discount, $\frac{1}{6}$ off or 16% off? Justify your answer.

69. The organizers of a bicycle race decide to shorten the length of the 10-mile race by 20%. How long is the new race?

OBJECTIVE K Convert among metric units for mass, length, and capacity. (Lesson 2-4)

70. If you divide a 2-meter long rope into five equal parts, how long will each part be in centimeters?

71. Today Roberto drank a 500 mL bottle of water at school, a 240 mL bottle of water at home, and a 240 mL bottle of water in the movie theater. How many liters of water did he drink?

72. Amy's dog weighs 48.3 kg. Jazmin's dog weighs 48 kg. How many grams heavier is Amy's dog than Jazmin's?

73. An adult Bengal tiger can run 55 km in 1 hour. At this speed, how many meters could it cover in 3 hours?

REPRESENTATIONS Pictures, graphs, or objects that illustrate concepts

OBJECTIVE L Graph and read decimal numbers on a number line. (Lesson 2-1)

74. Graph $-2\frac{2}{3}$, 1.8, 0, -2.200, and $0.1\overline{6}$ on a number line.

75. On the ruler below, a letter is given at every fifth tick mark. Determine which points correspond to lengths of 55 mm, 20 cm, 5 mm, and 10 mm, as measured from zero.

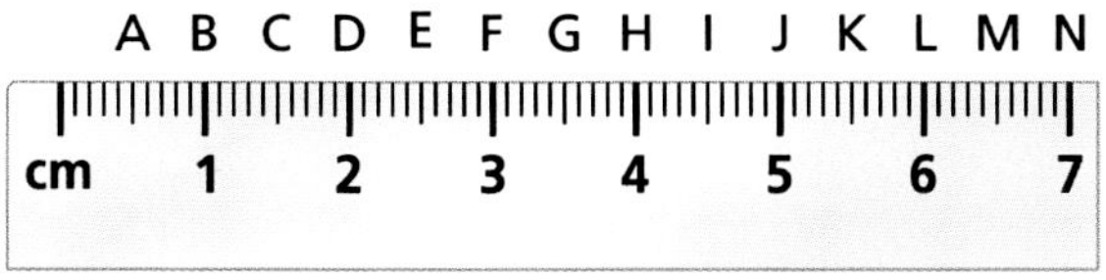

A B C D E F G H I J K L M N

cm 1 2 3 4 5 6 7

OBJECTIVE M Read and draw circle graphs. (Lesson 2-9)

In 76–78, use the following information about the favorite food groups of Ms. Holden's sixth grade class.

Food Groups	Students
Fruits	6
Vegetables	1
Dairy	8
Meats	3
Grains	6

76. Construct a circle graph of these data.

77. What percent of students like dairy best?

78. What percent of students like fruits or vegetables best?

Chapter

3 Using Addition

Contents

These are just a few of the tools a carpenter might use to build a home. In what ways do you think mathematics can help a carpenter? Why do you learn to add numbers of all kinds? The answer is simple. Addition gives answers in lots of real situations. These situations may involve whole numbers, decimals, percents, or fractions. They may use positive or negative numbers. Here are three situations leading to $\frac{5}{16} + \frac{3}{8}$.

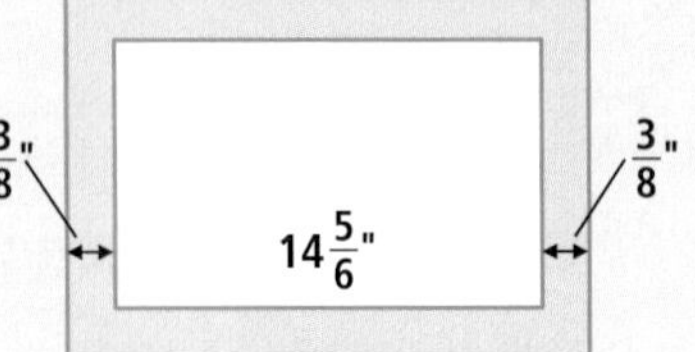

Building and decorating

Windows, drapes, molding, and most furniture are measured in parts of inches. Screws, nuts, and bolts are also measured in parts of inches. A picture is $14\frac{5}{16}$" wide as shown at the left. If you put a $\frac{3}{8}$"-wide frame around it, the width of the framed picture will be $14\frac{5}{16} + \frac{3}{8} + \frac{3}{8}$ inches. You have to add three fractions.

Parts of a whole

In a group of 16 people, 5 have blue eyes and 6 have brown eyes. What fraction has either blue eyes or brown eyes? You can find the result by adding $\frac{5}{16}$ and $\frac{6}{16}$. This is the same as $\frac{5}{16} + \frac{3}{8}$.

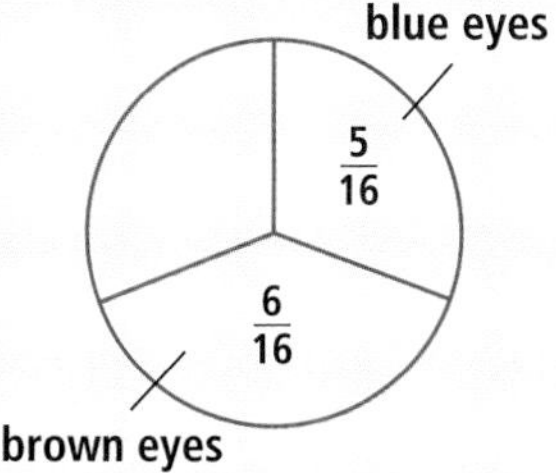

Cooking

You are making a batch of homemade granola. You need 5 ounces of dried cranberries and 6 ounces of almonds. You want to know how many pounds of fruit and nuts you need altogether. You can add $\frac{5}{16}$ lb and $\frac{6}{16}$ lb, which is the same as $\frac{5}{16} + \frac{3}{8}$ lb.

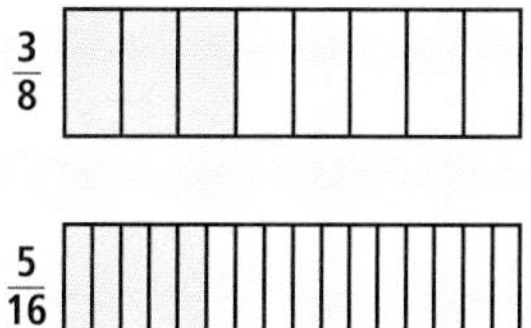

In this chapter, you will explore applications of addition in a variety of situations, and review and extend your knowledge of addition.

Lesson 3-1 The Putting-Together Model for Addition

Vocabulary

variable

▸ **BIG IDEA** The idea of putting together for addition can be applied to lengths, weights, times, and many other measures.

At Biddle Middle School, there are 134 sixth graders, 128 seventh graders, and 141 eighth graders. You can add the numbers 134, 128, and 141 to get 403, the total number of students in the school. When quantities are put together, addition is often used to calculate a total.

Mental Math

How many seconds are in

a. one minute?

b. two minutes?

c. three minutes?

d. half of a minute?

QY1

About 83,153 hybrid cars were sold in the United States in 2004. In 2005, 199,148 hybrid cars were sold. How many hybrid cars were sold in those two years?

It is impossible to list all the situations that involve putting together and addition. So we describe the general pattern using a variable. A **variable** is a symbol that can stand for any one set of numbers or other objects. We say that putting together is a *model* for addition.

The Putting Together Model for Addition

Suppose something with measure x is put together with something that has measure y. If there is no overlap, then the result has measure $x + y$.

The numbers that are put together may be large or small. They may be written as whole numbers, fractions, or decimals.

When a situation involves overlap, you cannot find the total just by adding. For example, the extension ladder pictured below has two sections that are 8 feet long. When they are put together, they must overlap by at least 3 feet so that the ladder can be used safely.

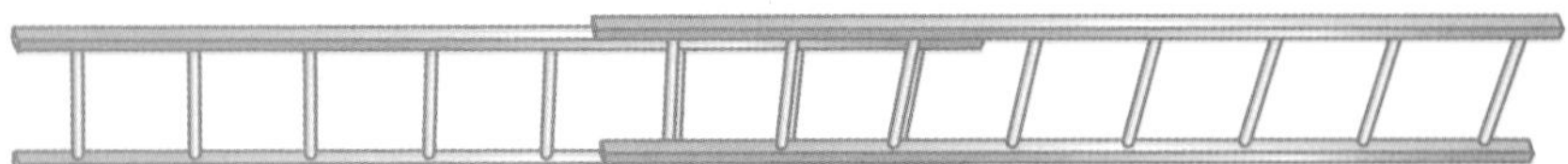

The maximum safe length of this ladder is *not* $8 + 8 = 16$ feet.

 See QY2 at the right.

 **QY2**

What is the greatest safe length of the ladder pictured on the previous page?

Using Variables

Sometimes you need to write a sum of measurements, but one of the measurements is not known. Use a variable for the missing measurement.

Example 1

A pizza costs c dollars. It also costs $5.00 to have a pizza delivered. What is the total cost of a pizza with delivery?

Solution This is an example of the Putting-Together Model. Add the cost of the pizza and the $5.00 delivery charge.

The total cost is $c + 5$ dollars.

Check Try some values for c. Continue to use $5.00 as the cost to deliver a pizza.

If $c = \$10.00$ then the total cost is $\$10.00 + \$5.00 = \$15.00$.

If $c = \$14.95$ then the total cost is $\$14.95 + \$5.00 = \$19.95$.

 **QY3**

In running a half-mile, Jan ran the first quarter-mile in t seconds and the second quarter mile in 90.38 seconds. What was her total time for the half-mile?

Putting-Together Measures with Different Units

When combining two measurements, they must have common units.

Example 2

A window sill is 3 feet above the floor. The 54-inch high window goes all the way to the ceiling. How high is the ceiling?

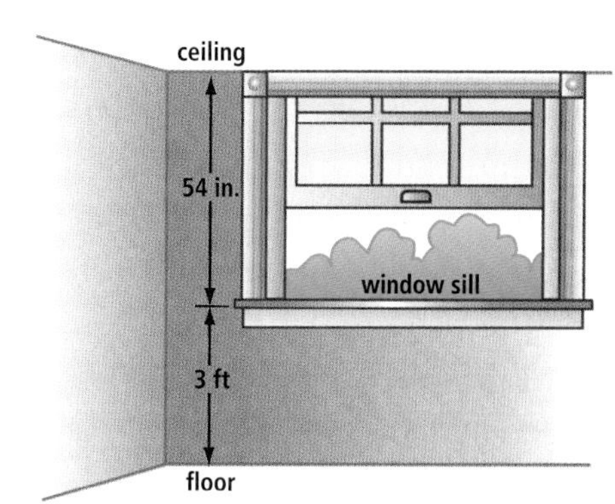

Solution 1 Change 3 feet to inches.

Multiply 3 by 12 to find the number of inches in 3 feet.

$$\begin{aligned} 3 \text{ feet} + 54 \text{ inches} &= 3 \times 12 \text{ inches} + 54 \text{ inches} \\ &= 36 \text{ inches} + 54 \text{ inches} \\ &= 90 \text{ inches} \end{aligned}$$

The height of the room is 90 inches.

(continued on next page)

Solution 2 Change 54 inches to feet. Divide 54 by 12 to find the number of feet in 54 inches.

$$\begin{aligned} 54 \text{ inches} &= \tfrac{54}{12} \text{ feet} \\ &= 4\tfrac{6}{12} \text{ feet} \\ &= 4\tfrac{1}{2} \text{ feet} \end{aligned}$$

$$\begin{aligned} 3 \text{ feet} + 54 \text{ inches} &= 3 \text{ feet} + 4\tfrac{1}{2} \text{ feet} \\ &= 7\tfrac{1}{2} \text{ feet} \end{aligned}$$

The height of the room is $7\frac{1}{2}$ feet.

Check The two measurements should be the same. 7 feet is $7 \times 12 =$ 84 inches and $\frac{1}{2}$ foot = 6 inches. So, $7\frac{1}{2}$ feet = 84 inches + 6 inches = 90 inches.

See QY4 at the right.

QY4

Add 4 days, 18 hours, and 15 hours. Give an answer in hours and an answer in days.

Finding a Common Unit

Remember to use common units when adding and subtracting. If you know a classroom has 14 boys and 16 girls, you know there are 30 students in the room because you mentally change the units of boys and girls to students.

When combining measurements expressed in mixed units, you can add the separate parts. For example, Rosa weighed 5 lb, 3 oz at birth. Her fraternal twin sister Maria weighed 7 lb, 12 oz. Add to find the combined weight.

$$\begin{aligned} 5 \text{ lb}, 3 \text{ oz} + 7 \text{ lb}, 12 \text{ oz} &= (5 \text{ lb} + 3 \text{ oz}) + (7 \text{ lb} + 12 \text{ oz}) \\ &= (5 \text{ lb} + 7 \text{ lb}) + (3 \text{ oz} + 12 \text{ oz}) \\ &= 12 \text{ lb}, 15 \text{ oz} \end{aligned}$$

The twins weighed 12 lb, 15 oz.

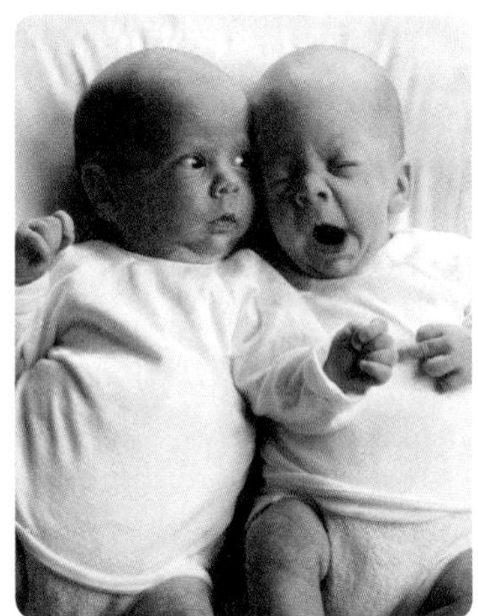

Do you know any twins? Are they fraternal or identical?

The Commutative Property of Addition

It does not matter whether you add 5 pounds and 7 pounds or 7 pounds and 5 pounds. Either way, you have 12 pounds total. The order in which two numbers are added does not change the answer. This important property can be described using variables.

The Commutative Property of Addition

For any numbers a and b, $a + b = b + a$.

The Commutative Property of Addition is probably not new to you. To add $\frac{5}{8} + 97.4 + \frac{3}{8}$ in your head, you might first add $\frac{5}{8} + \frac{3}{8}$ to get 1. Then you would add 1 to 97.4 to get 98.4. The Commutative Property of Addition says that the answer will be the same regardless of the order in which you add.

Questions

COVERING THE IDEAS

1. Chen swam the first 50 meters of a 100-meter race in 56.32 sec. He swam the last 50 meters in 58.4 sec. What was his total time?

2. Anoki rented two movies. One had a running time of 2:48 (2 hours and 48 minutes) and the other had a running time of 1:55. He'd like to know how much time he will need to watch the two movies back to back if he takes a 5 minute break between the two. His work is shown below. Anoki's result is not correct. Describe his mistake and find how much time he will need.

	1	1
	2 hours	48 minutes
	1 hour	55 minutes
+		5 minutes
	4 hours	08 minutes

3. A sandbox is 6 yards, 2 feet, and 10 inches long. How many inches is this?

4. Add 9,010 feet, 3 miles, and 1,270 feet. Write your answer in mixed units of feet and miles.

5. What property tells you that the total cost of the pizza in Example 1 can be written as $5 + c$?

In 6 and 7, find the sum in your head.

6. $\frac{100}{301} + 72 + \frac{201}{301}$

7. $97 + \frac{5}{8} + 3$

8. Megan's backpack weighs 10 pounds, 12 ounces. She adds a book weighing 1 pound, 9 ounces to her backpack. What is the backpack's weight now?

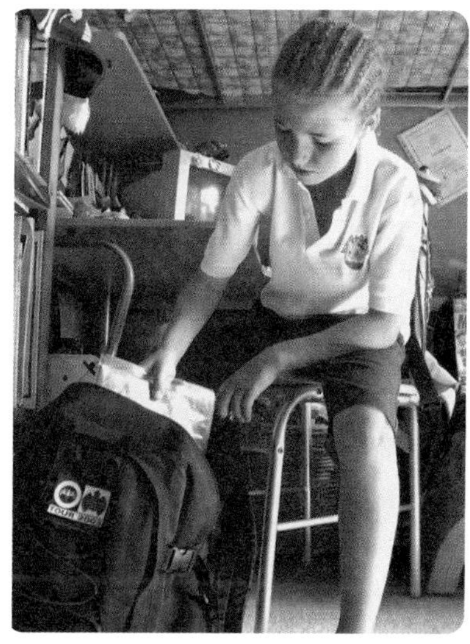

For a typical sixth grader, the maximum recommended total weight for a backpack is 15 pounds.

Source: American Chiropractic Association

APPLYING THE MATHEMATICS

9. In one of their cheerleading routines, Joy stands on Harry's shoulders. Joy is 5'2" tall. The distance from the floor to Harry's shoulders is 5'8". The bottom of a banner that hangs from the gymnasium ceiling is $10\frac{1}{2}$ feet above the floor. When Joy is standing on Harry's shoulders, does she fit under the banner? Explain how you know.

Don't try this at home!

10. Write an example of the Putting-Together Model for Addition different from those in this lesson.

11. At Diego's birthday party, his guests included b boys and g girls. Including Diego, how many people were at the party?

12. There are 35 sixth graders in band and 28 sixth graders in choir. If there are only 52 sixth graders in the school, how can this be?

13. On November 19, 1997, in Des Moines, Iowa, Bobbi McCaughey gave birth to the world's first known set of surviving septuplets. Here are the names and birth weights of the septuplets.

Kenneth Robert: 3 lb, 4 oz	Alexis May: 2 lb, 11 oz
Natalie Sue: 2 lb, 10 oz	Kelsey Ann: 2 lb, 5 oz
Brandon James: 3 lb, 3 oz	Nathaniel Roy: 2 lb, 14 oz
Joel Steven: 2 lb, 15 oz	

What was the total weight of the 7 babies?

14. **Multiple Choice** Which of the following is an example of the Commutative Property of Addition?

A $3 + \frac{1}{2} = 1\frac{1}{2} + 2$

B $5.6 \cdot 0.02 = 0.02 \cdot 5.6$

C $7 + -7 = -7 + 7$

D $2 + 2 = 2 \times 2$

15. Clowns who work for the Laughing Clown Company wear stilts that add 30 inches to their heights and funny hats that add an additional 18 inches. Copy and complete the table at the right to show the heights of the employees in their uniforms (including their hats).

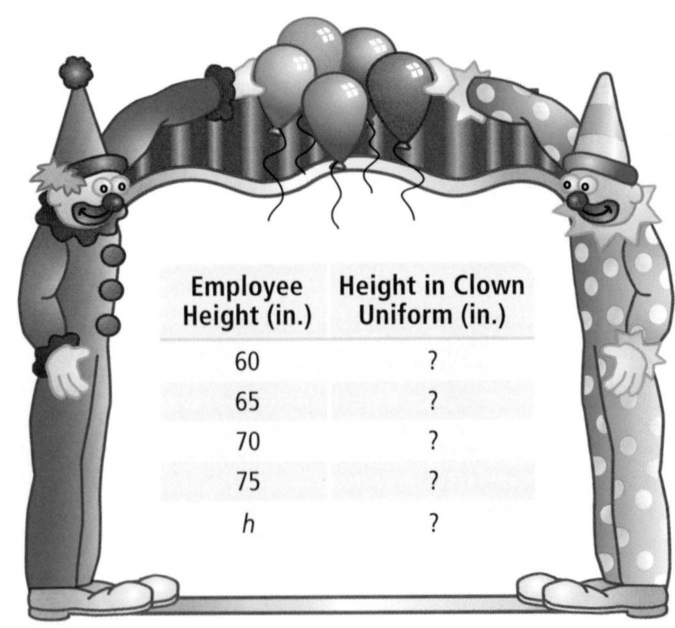

Employee Height (in.)	Height in Clown Uniform (in.)
60	?
65	?
70	?
75	?
h	?

REVIEW

16. Abigail bought a wedge of cheese, cut from a large wheel. The figures below show the wheel before and after Abigail's purchase. Estimate each answer below **(Lesson 2-9)**

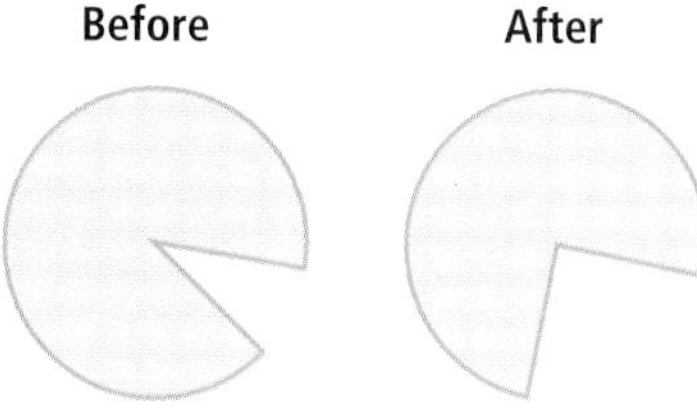

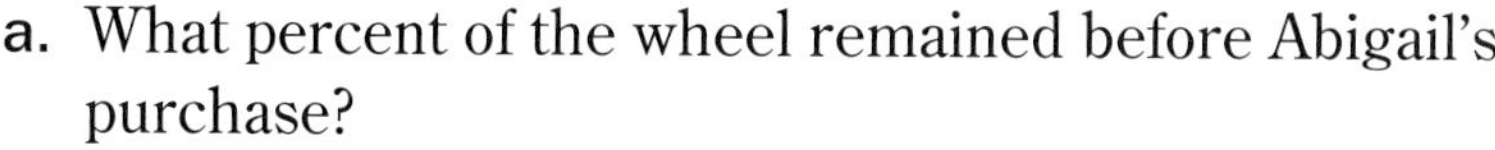

a. What percent of the wheel remained before Abigail's purchase?

b. What percent of the wheel remained afterward?

c. What percent of the total wheel did Abigail buy?

Holy cow! In 2006, Wisconsin produced over 25% of the cheese in the United States.

Source: USDA

In 17–19, round the price to the nearest dime. (Lesson 2-6)

17. \$34.87 18. \$19.95 19. \$3.233

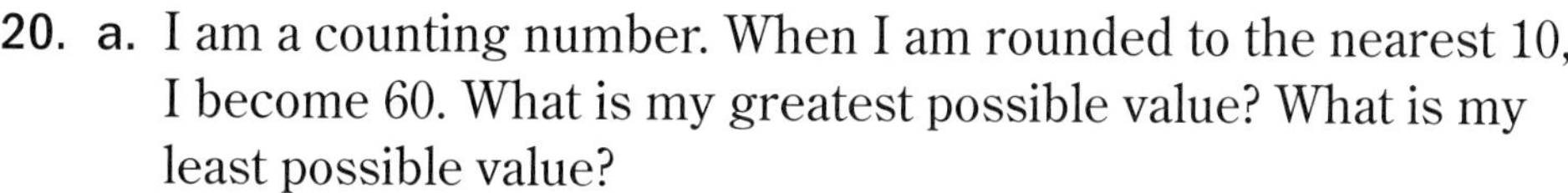

20. a. I am a counting number. When I am rounded to the nearest 10, I become 60. What is my greatest possible value? What is my least possible value?

b. I am a counting number. When I am rounded up to the next 10, I become 30. What is my greatest possible value? What is my least possible value? **(Lesson 2-5)**

21. a. Draw a $4\frac{1}{2}$-inch segment and label it $\overline{AB}$.

b. Draw another segment $\overline{CD}$ that is $\frac{3}{8}$-inch longer than $\overline{AB}$.

c. What is the length of $\overline{CD}$? **(Lesson 1-3)**

22. Add without using a calculator. Remember to line up the decimal points. **(Previous Course)**

a. $2.49 + 6$ b. $13.4 + 2.68$ c. $9.5 + 16 + 0.32$

EXPLORATION

23. Pablo and Precious have \$20 between them. Pablo and Priscilla have \$18 between them. Pablo has \$8 more than Precious. Can you determine how much money all three have together? Explain how you got your answer.

QY ANSWERS

1. 282,301 cars
2. 13 ft
3. $t + 90.38$ sec
4. 129 hr, or 5 days, 9 hr

Lesson

3-2 Adding Lengths

Vocabulary

polygon
sides
perimeter of a polygon
rectangle
integer rectangle
pentagon

▸ **BIG IDEA** The total length of a trip and the perimeter of a polygon are both the sum of lengths of segments.

Mental Math

a. How many sides of length 5 in. does a 5 in.-by-7 in. picture have?

b. How many sides have a length of 7 in.?

c. If an ant were to crawl around the outside of the picture, how far would it have to crawl?

The Total Length of a Trip

On the Internet, you can get directions for driving from one place to another. For example, here are the directions for driving from Capital Airport in Springfield, Illinois, to a hotel in downtown Springfield.

Step	Directions	Distance
1	Begin at Capital Airport, Springfield, IL.	
2	Go east on Capital Airport Drive for 160 feet to IL-29 S.	0.1 mi
3	Turn right onto IL-29 S and go south for 2.0 miles to Grand Ave W.	2 mi
4	Turn left onto Grand Ave W and go east for 0.48 mile to Grand Ave E.	0.5 mi
5	Turn left onto Grand Ave E and go east for 380 feet to 2nd St.	0.1 mi
6	Turn right onto 2nd St and go south for 0.99 mile to Washington St.	1 mi
7	Turn left onto Washington St and go east for 0.51 mile to Bus I-55.	0.5 mi
8	Turn right onto Bus I-55 and go south for 410 feet to Adams St.	0.1 mi
9	Turn right onto Adams St and go west for 0.14 mile to the hotel.	0.1 mi

QY1

What is the total length of the trip from the airport to the hotel?

Each part of the trip is called a *leg*. You can answer QY1 by adding the lengths of the eight legs. This is an example of the Putting-Together Model for Addition.

A salesperson living in Worcester, Massachusetts, needs to stop in Boston and Providence before returning home. At the right is a diagram of the situation, with the distances between the three cities labeled. The total of the trip is given by the addition $38 + 41 + 36 = 115$.

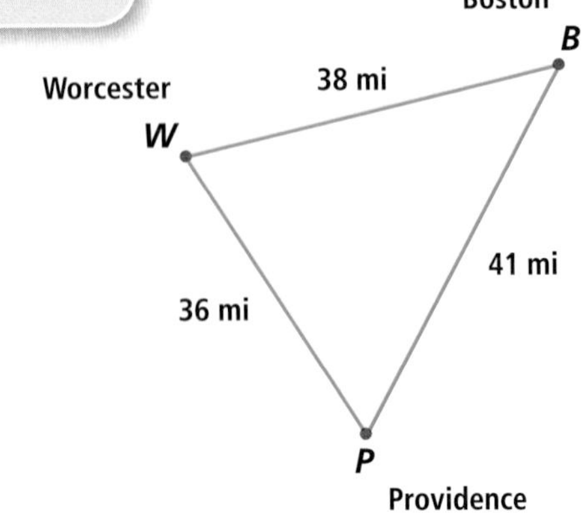

Associative Property

The sum 38 + 41 + 36 on the previous page can be computed in two different ways, shown below by using parentheses.

Do the left addition first.	**Do the right addition first.**
$(38 + 41) + 36 = 79 + 36$ $= 115$ mi	$38 + (41 + 36) = 38 + 77$ $= 115$ mi

The sums are equal: $(38 + 41) + 36 = 38 + (41 + 36)$.

The answer is the same either way. The order of additions does not matter. This basic property of numbers is called the *Associative Property of Addition.*

Associative Property of Addition

For any numbers a, b, and c, $(a + b) + c = a + (b + c)$.

GUIDED

Example 1

Do the addition problem 13.53 + .7 + .3 in the two ways using the Associative Property. Indicate which way you think is easier.

Solution

$(a + b) + c = (13.53 + .7) + .3 =$ __?__ $+ .3 =$ __?__

$a + (b + c) = 13.53 + (.7 + .3) = 13.53 +$ __?__ $=$ __?__

Which way was easier for you?

The Perimeter of a Polygon

Consider points that are connected by segments in order. The last point is connected to the first point, and no point is repeated. Below, D is connected to A, A to E, E to R, and R to D.

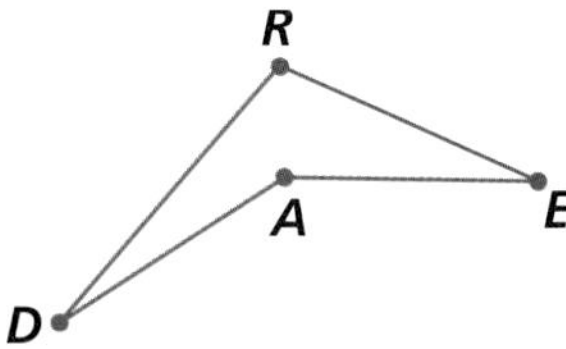

If, (1) the segments intersect only at their endpoints, and

(2) no two segments with the same endpoint are on the same line

then the segments form a **polygon.** The segments are the **sides** of the polygon.

 See QY2 at the right.

Every polygon has a perimeter. The **perimeter of a polygon** is the sum of the lengths of its sides.

On page 144, the total length of the sale person's trip is the perimeter of a triangle.

QY3

Find the perimeter of a triangle with side lengths 5 in., 7 in., and 9 in.

The way you found the perimeter in QY3 is expressed by the formula $p = a + b + c$. The variable p stands for the perimeter and a, b, and c stand for the lengths of the three sides.

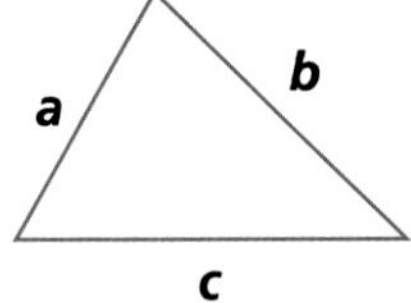

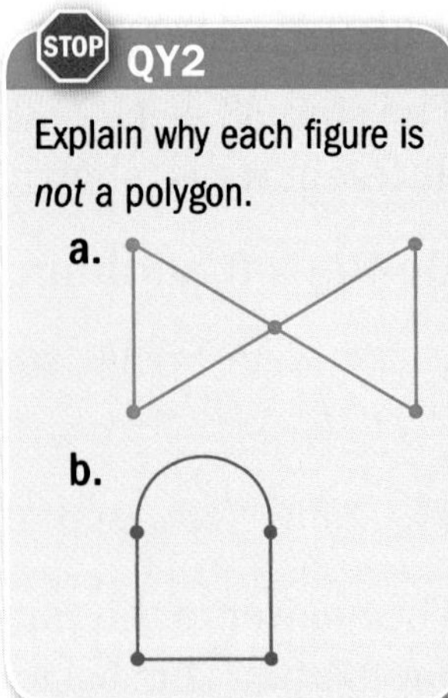

QY2
Explain why each figure is *not* a polygon.
a.
b.

Example 2

Use a formula to find the perimeter of a triangle with side lengths 7.1 cm, 2.8 cm, and 4.9 cm.

Solution Start by writing the formula. Then substitute.

$p = a + b + c$

$= 7.1 + 2.8 + 4.9$

$= 14.8$

The perimeter is 14.8 cm.

The Perimeter of a Rectangle

A **rectangle** is a 4-sided polygon with 4 right angles. The opposite sides of a rectangle are equal in length.

 See QY4 at the right.

Activity

MATERIALS centimeter grid paper

The perimeter of the rectangle below is $p =$ 4 cm + 6 cm + 4 cm + 6 cm = 20 cm.

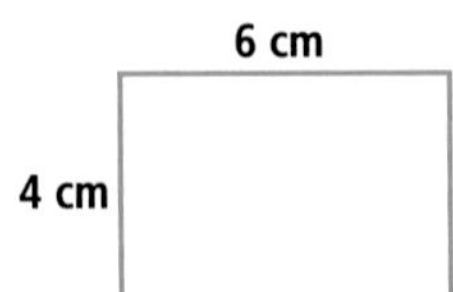

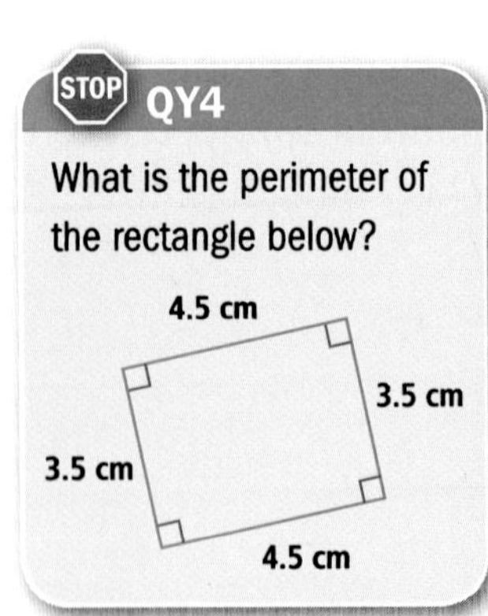

QY4
What is the perimeter of the rectangle below?
4.5 cm
3.5 cm
3.5 cm
4.5 cm

The perimeter of the second rectangle is
$p = 2\text{ cm} + 8\text{ cm} + 2\text{ cm} + 8\text{ cm} = 20\text{ cm}$.

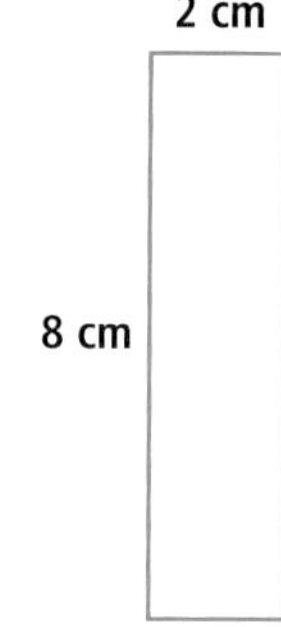

The perimeter is 20 cm for both rectangles.

These rectangles are *integer rectangles.* An **integer rectangle** is a rectangle with side lengths that are all whole numbers.

Working with a partner, draw as many examples of integer rectangles with a perimeter of 20 cm as you can on a sheet of centimeter grid paper. See if you can find all of them.

In the activity, you found that rectangles with different shapes can have the same perimeter.

Below is a rectangle with sides labeled L and W (for length and width). One formula for the perimeter p of a rectangle is $p = 2L + 2W$.

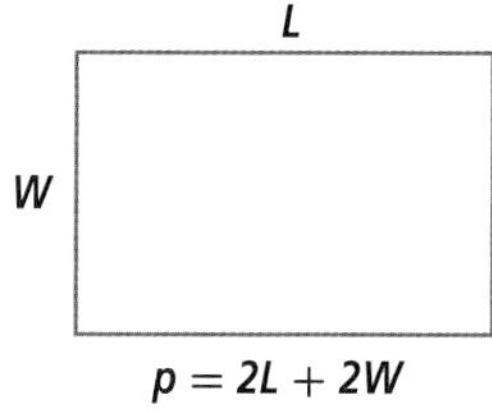

$p = 2L + 2W$

Does the formula make sense to you? Remember that when a number is written just before a letter, for example $2L$, this means multiply the value of the variable by the number. Remember that in expressions, multiplications are done before additions.

Example 3

You want to put a metal border around a rectangular wallboard with a length of 10 feet and a width of 3 feet.

a. Draw a picture. How long will the border be in feet?

b. Suppose you need to purchase the metal in yards. How many yards do you need to buy?

Solution

a. Use with the formula for the perimeter of a rectangle.

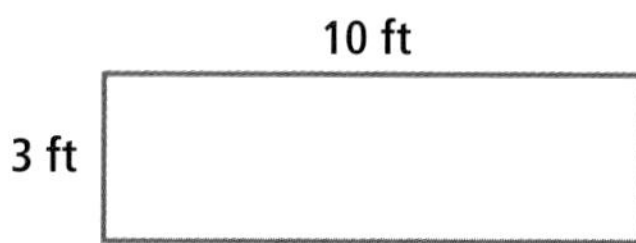

$p = 2L + 2W$
$= 2 \cdot 10 + 2 \cdot 3$
$= 26$

The length of the border will be 26 feet.

(continued on next page)

b. There are 3 feet in 1 yard, so divide 26 by 3 to find the number of yards.

$26 \div 3 = 8\frac{2}{3}$ yards

Round up to the next yard. You need to purchase 9 yards of metal border.

The Perimeter of a Square

All the sides of a square have the same length. So the perimeter of a square can be found just by knowing the length of one side.

GUIDED

Example 4

Write a formula for the perimeter of a square with side length s. Then use the formula to find the perimeter of a square with sides of length 6 cm.

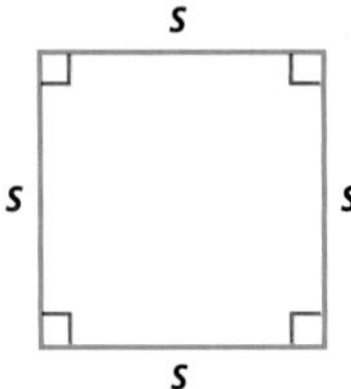

Solution Write the formula for the perimeter of a square.

p = s + _?_ + _?_ + _?_

= _?_ s

Substitute 6 cm for s. The perimeter is _?_.

Questions

COVERING THE IDEAS

1. A triangle has two sides of length 1.4 cm and one side of length 2.6 cm.
   a. Draw a rough sketch of the triangle.
   b. Find the perimeter of the triangle. Write the steps in two ways, as shown in Example 1.
2. a. Give the perimeter of $\triangle JKL$ below.

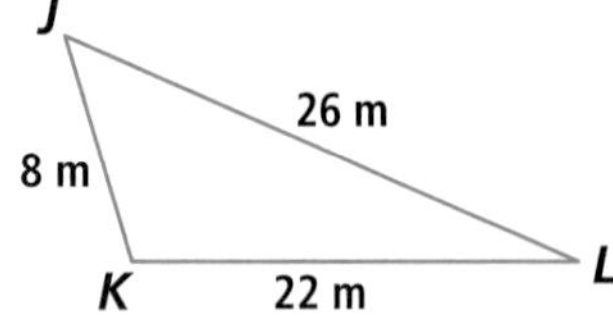

   b. If you walk halfway around the triangle, starting from J, how far from K on $\overline{KL}$ will you be?

In 3 and 4, use the following information. A family is returning a rental car to Newark International Airport after a visit to the Empire State Building in New York City. Here are the directions they received from the Internet.

Step	Directions	Distance
1	Begin on 5th Ave toward W 33rd St.	0.1 mi
2	Turn right onto W 31st St.	0.7 mi
3	Turn left onto 9th Ave.	0.05 mi
4	Turn right onto I-495 W/Lincoln Tunnel Expy.	0.1 mi
5	Turn slight right onto I-495 W/Lincoln Tunnel.	1.3 mi
6	I-495 W becomes NJ-495 W.	3.2 mi
7	Merge onto I-95 S/New Jersey Turnpike S.	6.3 mi
8	Keep right to take I-95 S toward Exit 14C.	0.4 mi
9	Merge onto I-78 W toward US-1/Newark Airport/US-22.	2.5 mi
10	Take the US-1-9 S exit-Exit 57.	0.9 mi
11	Take the ramp toward Rental Car Returns.	0.6 mi
12	Turn slight left onto Pitcairn Rd.	0.3 mi
13	Turn right onto I-495 W/Lincoln Tunnel Expy. End at Newark International Airport.	0.3 mi

When its construction was completed in 1931, the Empire State Building was the tallest building in the world.

3. What is the total length of the trip?
4. **Multiple Choice** After Step 5, the trip is in New Jersey. Which fraction best estimates the part of the trip that is in New Jersey?

   A $\frac{8}{14}$ **B** $\frac{12}{14}$ **C** $\frac{8}{3}$ **D** $\frac{3}{2}$

5. a. Copy $7639.7 + \frac{2}{7} + \frac{4}{7}$. Put in parentheses to show the easiest way to find the sum.

   b. Name the property that says that the answer is the same no matter which pair of numbers you add first.

6. Which step below uses the Commutative Property of Addition? Which step uses the Associative Property of Addition?

   $p + 11 + q + 3 = p + q + 11 + 3$ **Step 1**

   $= p + q + (11 + 3)$ **Step 2**

   $= p + q + 14$ **Step 3**

7. A rectangle has length 65 mm and width 3.2 cm.

   a. Draw the figure actual size.

   b. Find the perimeter. Use a formula to show your work, as in Example 3.

8. Find the perimeter of a rectangle with sides of length m and n.

9. a. **Multiple Choice** Suppose a triangle has 3 sides of length x. What is its perimeter?

   A $3 + x$ B $x - 3$ C $3x$ D $\frac{x}{3}$

   b. What is the perimeter of the triangle in Part a if $x = 12.4$ cm?

10. In the drawing below, A is connected to B, B to C, C to D, and D to A. Explain why the figure is not a polygon.

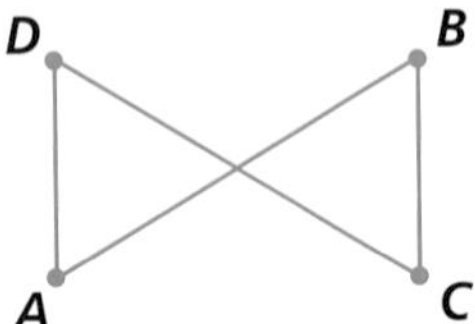

11. A square has a side of length 2.7 cm.
    a. Draw the figure actual size.
    b. Do you have enough information to find its perimeter? If so, find it. If not, tell why not.

APPLYING THE MATHEMATICS

12. Two sides of triangle SUN have the same length. $SU = 10$ cm and the perimeter of triangle SUN is 32 cm. What are the possible values of SN and UN? (Be careful!)

In 13–16, use this mileage chart of driving distances between four cities in Mississippi.

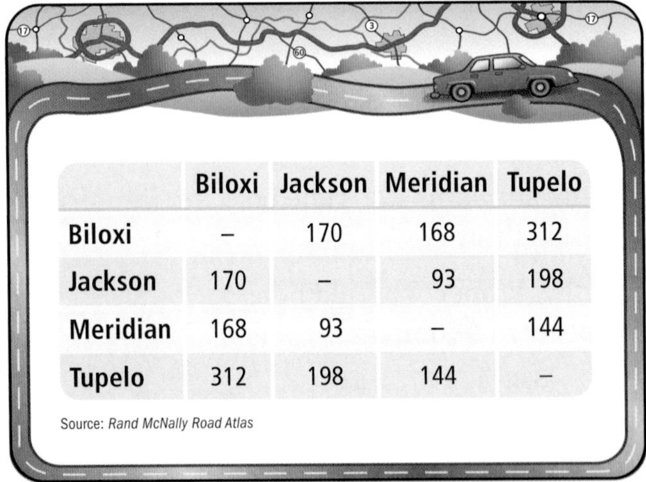

	Biloxi	Jackson	Meridian	Tupelo
Biloxi	–	170	168	312
Jackson	170	–	93	198
Meridian	168	93	–	144
Tupelo	312	198	144	–

Source: *Rand McNally Road Atlas*

13. a. Why do certain cells have no entry?
    b. What number could correctly be put in those cells?

14. Roshonda lives in Biloxi. She wants to visit the other three cities and return home. What route should she take to travel the shortest distance?

15. a. Sylvia said this mileage chart does not need the bottom row. Is Sylvia correct? Why or why not?
    b. Martin said the chart doesn't need one of the columns. Is he right?
    c. What is the fewest number of cells this chart could have and not lose any information?
16. What property tells you that the total distance from Jackson to Meridian to Biloxi will be the same as the total distance from Biloxi to Meridian to Jackson?
17. A **pentagon** is a 5-sided polygon. The Pentagon building in Washington, D.C. has a greater area than any office building in the world. Its outer boundary is a pentagon measuring 921.6 feet on each side.
    a. If you were to walk around the building, what is the shortest distance you could walk?
    b. Draw a pentagon in which all sides have length 1 inch.
    c. If all of the sides of a pentagon have the same length *L*, what is the perimeter of the pentagon?

The Pentagon is the headquarters for the U.S. Department of Defense.

18. Find the perimeter of the shape below.

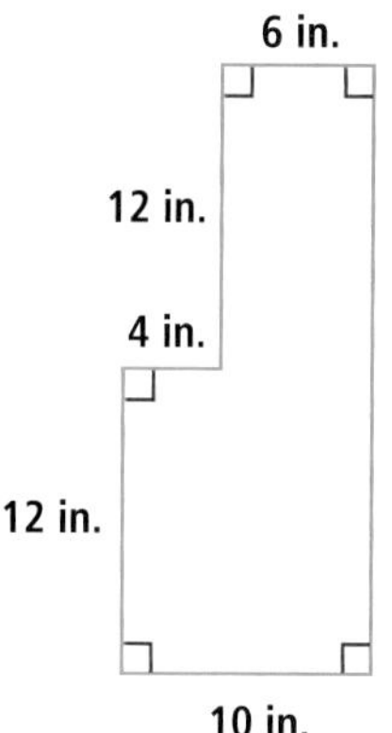

19. Speedway delivery service will only accept packages that meet both of the following conditions:
    i. The sum of the length, width, and height is less than 90 cm.
    ii. The length, width, and height are each less than 60 cm.
    Which of the packages below will be refused?

Package Number	1	2	3	4	5	6
Length (cm)	65	60	50	40	60	20
Width (cm)	12	25	30	10	19	20
Height (cm)	5	15	10	10	15	10

REVIEW

20. Yesterday, Jason read the first 52 pages of a book for his English class. Today, he read 48 pages, but this included 6 pages he reread because he had forgotten some of what he had read yesterday. With this he finished the book. How many pages long is the book? **(Lesson 3-1)**

21. Kiana started practicing the cello at 4:45 P.M. If she practiced for 1 hour, 40 minutes, at what time did she finish? **(Lesson 3-1)**

22. Compare the numbers using $<$, $=$, or $>$. **(Lesson 2-10)**

a. $\frac{253}{17}$ and $\frac{17}{253}$

b. $\frac{15}{16}$ and $\frac{61}{64}$

23. Give the decimal and percent equivalents of each number. **(Lesson 2-10)**

a. $\frac{1}{5}$ b. $\frac{2}{5}$ c. $\frac{3}{5}$ d. $\frac{4}{5}$ e. $\frac{5}{5}$

EXPLORATION

24. Find the side lengths of all integer rectangles with perimeter 40 cm.

The cello was developed during the Renaissance period of the 1500s.

Source: *Encylopedia Britannica*

QY ANSWERS

1. 4.4 mi

2a. Two segments with the same endpoint are on the same line.

2b. Not all sides of the polygon are segments.

3. 21 in.

4. 16 cm

Lesson 3-3 The Slide Model for Addition

BIG IDEA To add positive and negative numbers, think of each number as a slide in a direction, and the sum as the number where you end up after all the slides.

Remember that negative numbers are used in situations with two opposite directions. In a football game, the team with the ball attempts to move the ball forward (gain in yards). The other team tries to force the ball backward (loss in yards).

Mental Math

On Monday, the temperature at noon was 58°F. Find the temperature of the given days of the week.

a. On Tuesday, it was 7° colder than Monday.

b. On Wednesday, it was 13° warmer than Tuesday.

c. On Thursday, it was 6° warmer than Wednesday.

d. On Friday, it was 12° colder than Thursday.

Example 1

In a football game, the Panthers got the ball halfway through the first quarter. They gained 10 yards on their first play. On the second play, their opponents, the Lions, drove them back 13 yards. What was the overall change in position for the Panthers in the two plays?

Solution Think of the plays as slides on a number line. A gain can be represented by a slide to the right (or up), and a loss can be represented by a slide to the left (or down.)

The first play is shown with a blue arrow that has its endpoint at zero and is 10 units long, pointing to the right. The next play is shown with a red arrow that starts at 10 and goes left 13 units.

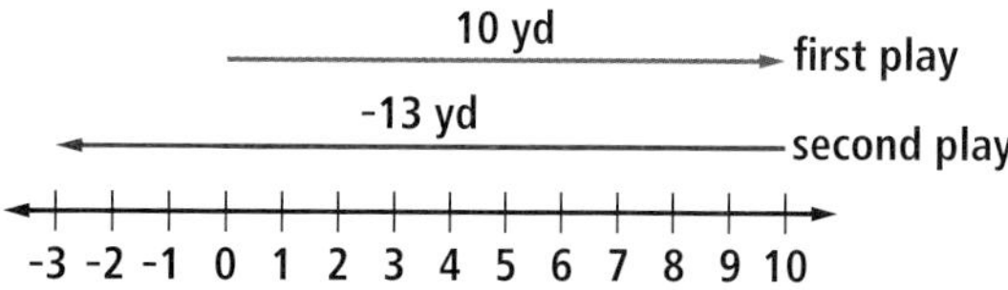

The second slide finishes at –3. Writing this in symbols gives an equation $10 + -13 = -3$. The Panthers lost three yards on their first two plays.

 See QY1 at the right.

 **QY1**

On the third play, the Panthers gained 4 yards. Copy the drawing above and add another arrow to represent the third play. Then write an equation for the total yardage on the three plays.

The football example illustrates the *Slide Model for Addition.*

Slide Model for Addition

If a slide x is *followed by* a slide y, the result is a slide $x + y$.

Example 2

Picture -5 + -3 on a number line. Write a number sentence to represent the result.

Solution

-3 -5

-8 -7 -6 -5 -4 -3 -2 -1 0 1

The result is a slide 8 units to the left, or -5 + -3 = -8.

The Slide Model for Addition is particularly useful to visualize adding positive and negative numbers.

GUIDED

Example 3

Spencer Spendalot had $432 in a bank account when his credit card bill for $581 arrived. How much more money does Spencer need to pay his full credit card bill?

Solution Use the addition problem 432 + -581. Think of it as an arrow ___?___ units to the right followed by an arrow ___?___ units to the left. The sum will be negative because the arrow going to the left is longer. How much longer? Find the difference of the lengths of the arrows.

432 + −581 = _?_ − _?_ = _?_

So Spencer needs _?_ more.

Check Use a calculator.

Key sequence: _?_ [+] _?_ 581 [ENTER]

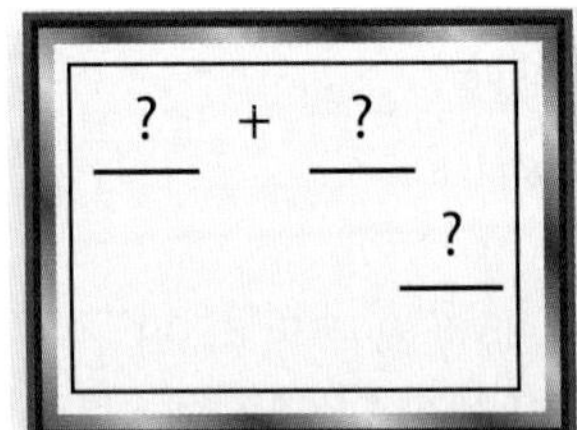

QY2

Find each sum.

a. -7 + -8

b. 7 + 8

c. -7 + 8

d. 7 + -8

Adding Several Positive or Negative Numbers

The Commutative and Associative Properties of Addition allow you to change the order of numbers in an addition problem. So, to add several numbers, you can group the positive numbers together and group the negative numbers together. Then, you can add those two sums.

Example 4

Simplify -1 + -5 + 14 + -7 + 18 + 6.

Solution Reorder the addends using the Commutative Property of Addition. Then add all the negative numbers together and add all the positive numbers together. You will be left with two numbers to add, one positive and one negative.

	-1 + -5 + 14 + -7 + 18 + 6
Reorder and group addends.	= (_?_ + _?_ + _?_) + (_?_ + _?_ + _?_)
Add the negative numbers and then add the positive numbers.	= -13 + _?_
	= _?_

STOP QY3

Simplify -0.5 + 4 + 3.6 + 0.6 + -7.9.

The slide model applies to data, too.

Example 5

Mrs. McGovern gave a 100-point test. The table below shows scores for 8 students. She decided that the test was too hard, so she told students she would add 5 points to each score.

a. Picture the original scores in a dot plot.

b. Calculate the new scores. Then picture them using a dot plot with the same scale, directly below the first graph.

(continued on next page)

Name	Score
Krystal	86
Ellen	62
Shaun	54
Diamond	83
Emilio	70
Ana	70
Jimmy	70
Sakari	86

Solution

a. Draw a number line that ranges from 50 to 90 points and plot the 8 scores.

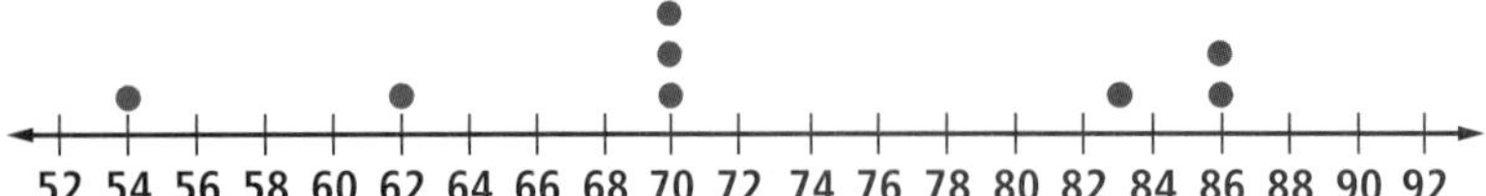

b. The updated scores are 91, 67, 59, 88, 75, 75, 75, and 91.

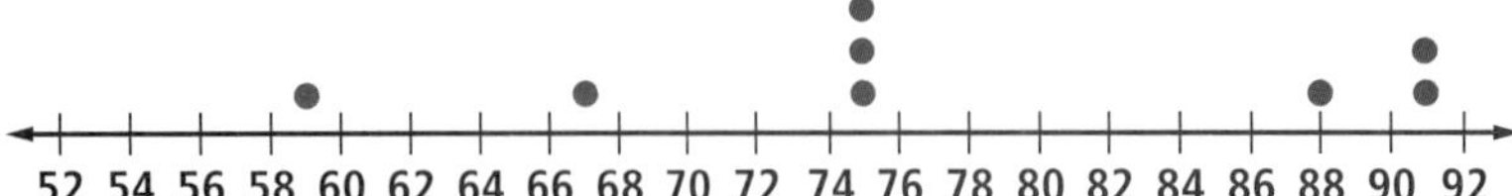

Compare the dots on the two number lines. You can see that the entire dot plot has been slid 5 units in the positive direction.

Now you can play *Sum-It-Up*. The directions for this game are on page G12 at the back of your book.

Questions

COVERING THE IDEAS

In 1–3, represent each situation as an addition. Then find the sum.

1. Margaret has \$4, and then earns \$5 babysitting. How much money does she have?
2. Quentin owes Raul \$3. Then Quentin gets \$5 from Esteban. How much does Quentin have now?
3. Brooklyn has \$18 in her wallet, and then she buys a \$5 CD. How much does she have now?
4. When addition is done on a horizontal number line, tell what each of the following stands for.
   a. an arrow pointing left
   b. an arrow pointing right
   c. followed by
   d. the endpoint of the final arrow
5. Over three weeks, Melvin lost 2 pounds, gained 3 pounds, and lost 3 pounds. How much did he gain or lose over those 3 weeks?
6. Draw arrows picturing $6 + -8 + 5$ as slides on a number line.
7. Without adding, tell whether the sum is positive or negative.
   a. $-56.7 + -72.3$
   b. $-56.7 + 72.3$
   c. $56.7 + -72.3$

In 2007, CDs accounted for about 85% of all music sold.

Source: *The Wall Street Journal*

8. Peter said that -45 + 46 is equal to -1. Marie said it is equal to 1. Who is right and why?

In 9–12, find the sum. Check using your calculator.

9. -8 + 21 + 17 + -30
10. 25 + 98 + 2 + -9 + -10 + -23
11. -4 + 8 + -7
12. 9 + 32 + -9

13. After a month of training, each member of the cross-country team ran the home course a minute faster than at the beginning of the season. If you were to draw dot plots of the earlier and later times, describe the relationship between the two graphs.

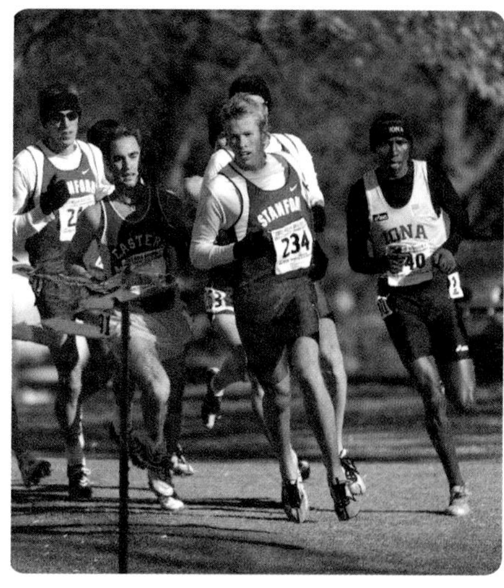

The American Heart Association recommends 30 minutes per day of aerobic activity such as running.

Source: American Heart Association

APPLYING THE MATHEMATICS

In 14–16, suppose *p* and *q* are positive numbers, and *m* and *n* are negative numbers. Tell whether the sum is *always, sometimes but not always,* or *never* positive.

14. $p + q$
15. $m + n$
16. $p + q + m + n$

17. Mrs. Castillo asked her class to represent 1 + -4 with a drawing. Her students gave her the following responses:

i.
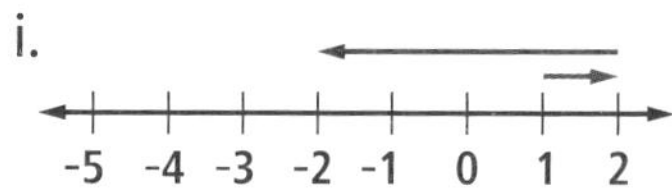

ii.
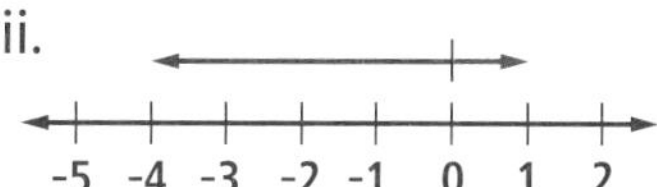

iii.
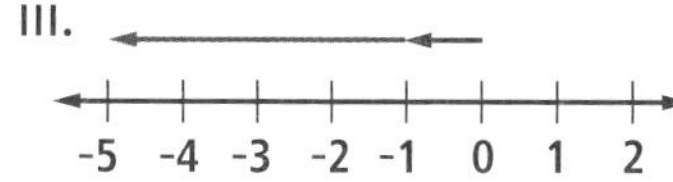

iv.
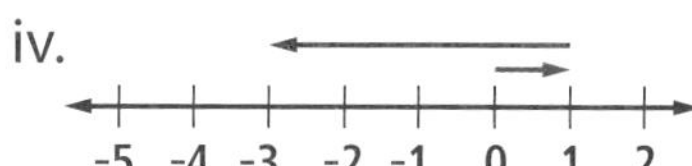

a. Choose the diagram that correctly represents the problem.
b. Explain why your choice is the correct one.
c. Explain why each of the other diagrams is incorrect.

In 18 and 19, write a mathematical expression to describe each situation. Then answer the question.

18. The temperature outside was -3°F. The temperature dropped 2°. What is the temperature now?

19. A submarine dives 143 meters below the surface of the water. Then it rises 38 meters. How deep is the submarine now?

In 20 and 21, four numbers are to be added.

a. Round each number to the nearest whole number.
b. Use the rounded values to estimate the sum.
c. Use a calculator to find the exact answer.
d. How accurate was your estimate?

20. $3\frac{1}{2} + -\frac{3}{4} + -4\frac{3}{8} + 1\frac{2}{3}$

21. $-4.8 + -8.2 + -6.73 + 10.58$

REVIEW

22. The Guerrero's garden is rectangular with dimensions 50 meters-by-30 meters. They built a 2-meter wide path around the garden and then built a wall around the path. Consider the outside *rectangle formed by the wall.* **(Lesson 3-2)**
   a. Give its length and width.
   b. Find its perimeter.

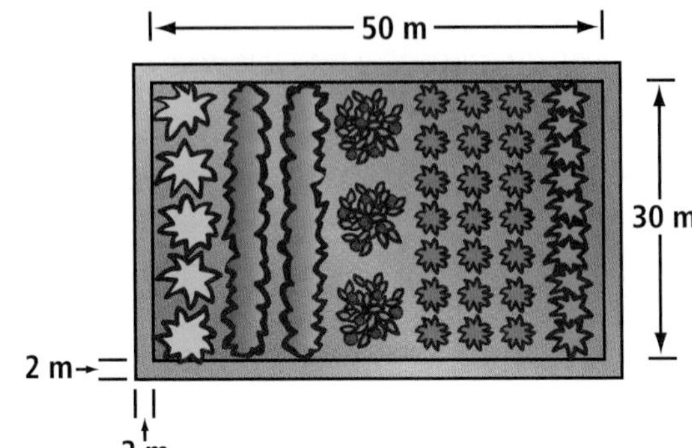

23. George and Ella arrived late to a contra dance. There was a row of dancers 30.5 feet long. They extended the length of this row by 3.75 feet. How long is the row of dancers now? **(Lesson 3-2)**

24. There are 16 tablespoons in a cup. If you add five tablespoons of freshly squeezed lemon juice to half a cup of water, how much lemonade will you have **(Lesson 3-1)**
   a. in tablespoons? b. in cups?

25. Which temperature is warmer, -13°F or -25°F? **(Lesson 1-7)**

26. Order -3, 4, 0, -4, 9, and -12 from least to greatest. **(Lesson 1-7)**

27. Is zero a positive number, a negative number, or neither? **(Lesson 1-7)**

28. Measure the segment to the nearest $\frac{1}{8}$ inch. **(Lesson 1-3)**

EXPLORATION

29. When 1 cup of sugar is added to 1 cup of water, the result is not 2 cups of the mixture. Why not?

QY ANSWERS

1.

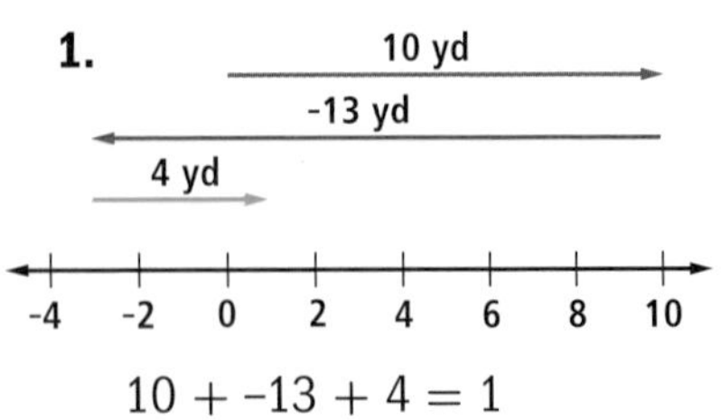

$10 + -13 + 4 = 1$

2a. −15

2b. 15

2c. 1

2d. −1

3. −0.2

Lesson 3-4 Zero and Opposites

Vocabulary

additive identity

additive inverse

▸ **BIG IDEA** Every number has an opposite, or additive inverse; and the sum of a number and its opposite is 0.

Mental Math

A grizzly bear weighs 350 lb.

a. If it gains 110 lb for winter, how much does it weigh?

b. If it then loses 130 lb during the winter, how much does it weigh?

This lesson discusses three properties of numbers and addition. QY1 demonstrates the first.

QY1

Add.

a. $-6\frac{4}{7} + 0$ **b.** 0.0003 km + 0 km

c. $0\% + 3\frac{2}{3}$ **d.** $0 + 0$

The *Encarta English Dictionary* defines *identity* as "the fact or condition of being the same or exactly alike." Your identity can be hidden, as when you wear a costume, but you are still you. Adding zero to a number, like $-6\frac{4}{7} + 0$, keeps its identity. For example, $-6\frac{4}{7} + 0 = -6\frac{4}{7}$. This is true for all numbers. This property is called the *Additive Identity Property of Zero,* and zero is called the **additive identity.**

Two teenagers are performing in a school play.

We can describe this property in words or by using variables.

The Additive Identity Property of Zero

The sum of any number and zero is that number. For any number x, $x + 0 = x$.

Recall from Lesson 1-7 that numbers such as 2.5 and –2.5 are called opposites. The dash (–) stands for *opposite of.*

If n represents a number, the opposite of n is written $-n$. Situations involving money are common examples of opposites.

- Receiving \$2.50 is the opposite of spending \$2.50.
- Spending \$2.50 is the opposite of receiving \$2.50.

Example 1

Rafael owes $15 to friends but then gets his $15 allowance. Use the Slide Model to represent this situation.

Solution Draw a number line and two arrows to show –15 + 15. Rafael's situation is represented by –15 + 15 = 0.

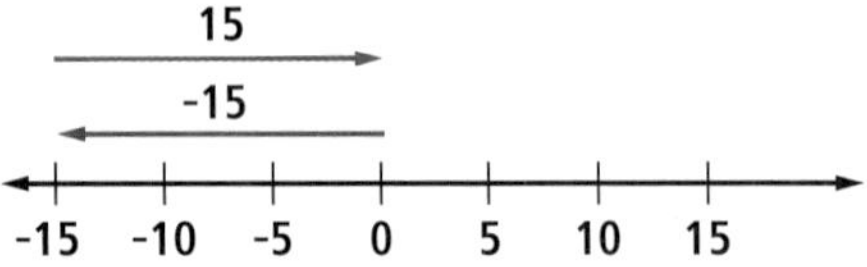

QY2

Copy and complete the table below.

Number	Opposite	Sum
–2.50	2.50	?
0.0001	–0.0001	?
$5\frac{1}{2}$	?	?
–12	?	?
x	?	?

The Additive Property of Opposites

The sum of any number and its opposite is zero. For any number x, $x + -x = 0$.

Another word for opposite is *additive inverse.* Because $x + -x = 0$, the numbers x and $-x$ are called **additive inverses** of each other. In other words, when two numbers add to 0, they are additive inverses of each other. For example, -8 is the additive inverse of 8, and 8 is the additive inverse of -8. You can write -(–8) = 8. The parentheses are used to make it clear that there are two dashes. This is read *the opposite of negative eight is eight.*

The Opposite of Opposites (Op-Op) Property

The opposite of the opposite of a number is the number itself. For any number x, $-(-x) = x$.

Example 2

Enter [(-)] [(] [(-)] 5 [)] [ENTER] into your calculator. What is the result?

Solution A calculator display is shown at the right.

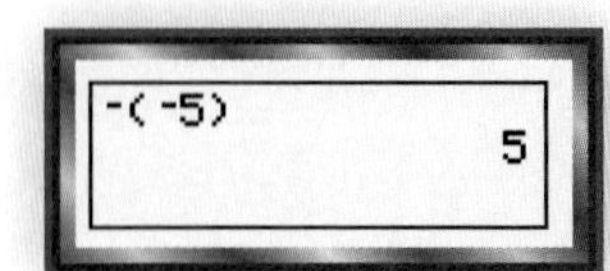

Caution When x is negative, $-x$ is positive! For example, if $x = -2$, then $-x = -(-2) = 2$. This will be easier to remember if you read $-x$ as "the opposite of x," rather than "negative x."

See	Read
-7	negative seven, or the opposite of seven
$-p$	the opposite of p

QY3

Simplify.

a. $-(4)$ b. $-(-y)$ c. $-(-(-16))$

Your answers to QY3 are *simplified* if they are written without parentheses. In Example 3, do any computation in parentheses first, working from the inside out.

Example 3

Simplify.

a. $-(4 + -7.5)$ b. $-(-(-(-11)))$

Solution

a. $-(4 + -7.5)$

$= -(-3.5)$ Add inside the parentheses first.

$= 3.5$ The opposite of -3.5 is 3.5.

b. $-(-(-(-11)))$

$= -(-(\ 11\ ))$ Work the innermost parentheses first. The opposite of -11 is 11.

$= -(-\ 11\ )$ The opposite of 11 is -11.

$= 11$ The opposite of -11 is 11.

So, $-(-(-(-11))) = 11$.

Questions

COVERING THE IDEAS

In 1–3, write an addition problem to answer each question. Then answer the question.

1. Last year Anisa was 66 inches tall. This year she grew 0 inches. How tall is she now?

How fast did you grow in the last year?

2. The population of Central City was 295,000 in 2001. It has not increased or decreased since then. What is the population now?
3. At a frog-jumping contest, Francis the frog did not move for the first four minutes. In the next minute, he jumped 0.75 meter. How far did he go in five minutes?
4. Name the property that is illustrated in Questions 1–3.
5. Why is zero called the additive identity?

American author Mark Twain may have helped popularize frog-jumping contests with his famous short story, *The Celebrated Jumping Frog of Calaveras County.*

In 6–9, write an addition problem to answer each question. Then answer the question.

6. Ten people came into a room, and 10 people left. What was the change in number of people in the room?
7. The water level behind a dam went up $3\frac{3}{4}$ feet because of heavy rains. It went down $3\frac{3}{4}$ feet when the water district allowed more water to go through the dam. What was the net change?
8. Linda bought a pair of shoes. The price was discounted $7.31, but the tax added was $7.31. What was the total adjustment on Linda's bill?
9. The Rockets football team started the second half by moving the ball forward 10 yards. On the next play, they were assessed a penalty of 10 yards. What was their net gain in yards?

10. What property do Questions 6–9 illustrate?
11. **Fill in the Blank** Another name for the additive inverse is __?__.

In 12–14, write the additive inverse of the number.

12. -$9.00
13. $\frac{5}{8}$ inches
14. $-w$

15. Find $-m$ if $m = -3.5$.
16. **True or False** $-c$ always stands for a negative number. Explain your answer.

APPLYING THE MATHEMATICS

17. Use the Slide Model to illustrate the Property of Opposites.

In 18–22, simplify.

18. $-(-4.2)$
19. $-\left(-\left(-\left(-\frac{4}{9}\right)\right)\right)$
20. $-(-(-d))$
21. $-(10 + -4 + -7)$
22. $-(-(x + -x))$

In 23 and 24, do the addition in your head.

23. $\frac{2}{3} + \frac{11}{9} + -\frac{11}{9} + \frac{5}{6} + -\frac{2}{3}$

24. $v + -w + z + v + -z$

25. a. **Fill in the Blank** Look for a pattern.

$$\begin{aligned} -1 &= -1 \\ -(-1) &= 1 \\ -(-(-1)) &= \underline{\ ?\ } \\ -(-(-(-1))) &= \underline{\ ?\ } \\ -(-(-(-(-1)))) &= \underline{\ ?\ } \end{aligned}$$

b. In Question 19, there are four opposite signs before the number $\frac{4}{9}$. Suppose that rather than four, there were fifty opposite signs. Is the resulting value equal to $\frac{4}{9}$ or to $-\frac{4}{9}$? Explain your answer.

26. On an architecture tour, suppose you walk 5 blocks north, then 3 blocks east, then 2 blocks north, then 2 blocks west, then 4 blocks south, then 3 blocks east, then 3 blocks south, then 1 block west. How far do you have to walk, and in what direction, to get back to where you started? (Grid paper may help you with this problem.)

Architecture tours are particularly common in large or historical cities.

REVIEW

27. Without adding, tell whether the sum will be positive or negative. **(Lesson 3-3)**
    a. -452 + -542
    b. -452 + 542
    c. 452 + -542

28. Find $-11.4 + \frac{32}{7} + -\frac{31}{7} + 11.4$. **(Lesson 3-3)**

29. Khalil wants to buy a computer game for $19.95, a comic book for $5.95, and a toy car for $4.87. His allowance is $5.00 per week. How many weeks will it take him to earn enough for all three items if he doesn't buy anything else during this time? **(Lesson 2-6)**

30. A soccer ball weighs 2 pounds, 4 ounces. **(Lesson 1-5)**
    a. How many ounces is this?
    b. How many pounds is this?

EXPLORATION

31. The room shown below has a light switch at each door. When the light switches are all off, the light in the center of the room is off.

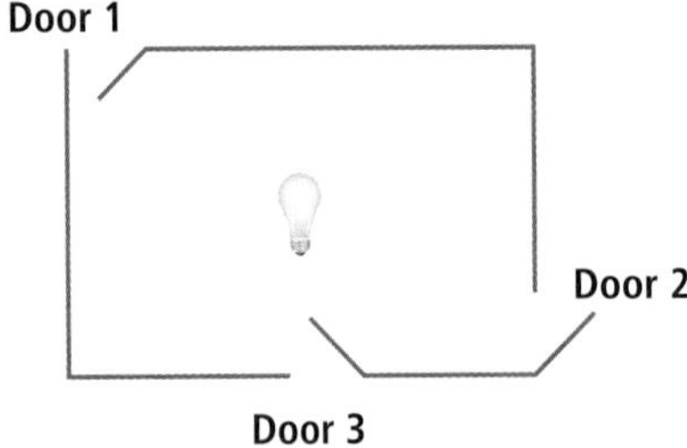

a. Complete the following table, giving all possible combinations of switches.

Switch 1	Switch 2	Switch 3	Light
off	off	off	off
on	off	off	on
on	on	off	?
on	?	?	?
off	?	?	?
?	?	?	?
?	?	?	?
?	?	?	?

b. How is this question related to the Op-Op Property?

QY ANSWERS

1a. $-6\frac{4}{7}$

1b. 0.0003 km

1c. $3\frac{2}{3}$

1d. 0

2.

Number	Opposite	Sum
-2.50	2.50	0
0.0001	-0.0001	0
$5\frac{1}{2}$	$-5\frac{1}{2}$	0
-12	12	0
x	$-x$	0

3a. −4

3b. y

3c. −16

Lesson 3-5 Measuring Angles

Vocabulary

angle
vertex of an angle
side of an angle
degree
arc
protractor

BIG IDEA Every angle has a measure that is a number from 0° to 180° and equal to the measure of an arc of a circle.

Shortly after construction began in 1173 of a tower in Pisa, Italy, the tower began to tilt. The Leaning Tower of Pisa is one of the world's most famous buildings. Engineers and scientists have reinforced the base and foundation to delay further tilting and are exploring ways to permanently protect the tower. To measure how far the tower leans, you need to know how to measure an *angle.*

An **angle** is the union of two rays with the same endpoint. The angle of the tower's tilt is formed from the horizontal ray *SA* (written as $\overrightarrow{SA}$) and the ray *SP* (written as $\overrightarrow{SP}$) from the center of the base through the center of the top story. The common endpoint *S* is the **vertex of the angle.** The rays are the **sides of the angle.** We put arrows in the picture to show that the sides $\overrightarrow{SA}$ and $\overrightarrow{SP}$ of the angle go on forever.

Mental Math

Estimate the percent of the circle that is shaded.

a.

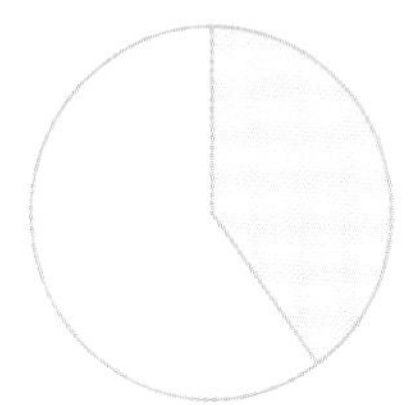

b.

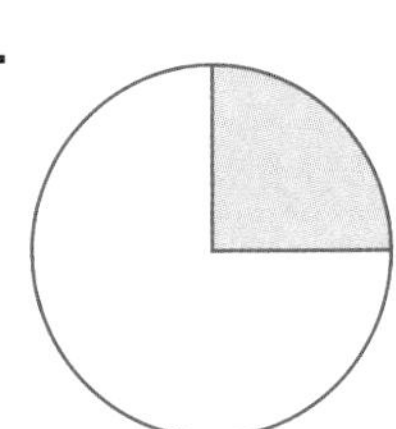

c.

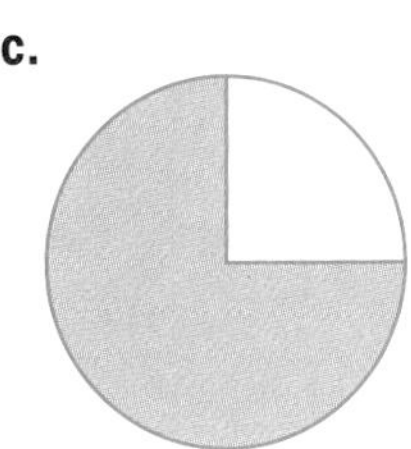

d.

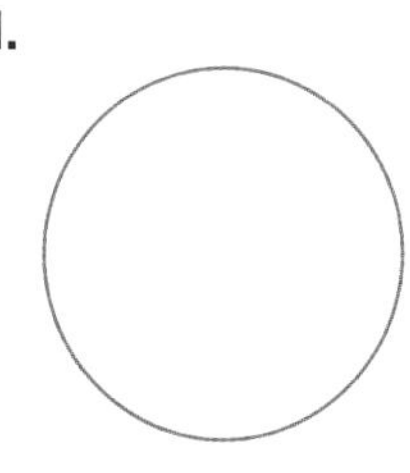

Naming Angles

The symbol ∠ means angle. You can name the Leaning Tower of Pisa angle with three letters, as $\angle PSA$ or $\angle ASP$ (with the vertex point in the middle). However, because there is no confusion about which angle you are referring to, you can also simply use the name of the vertex, $\angle S$.

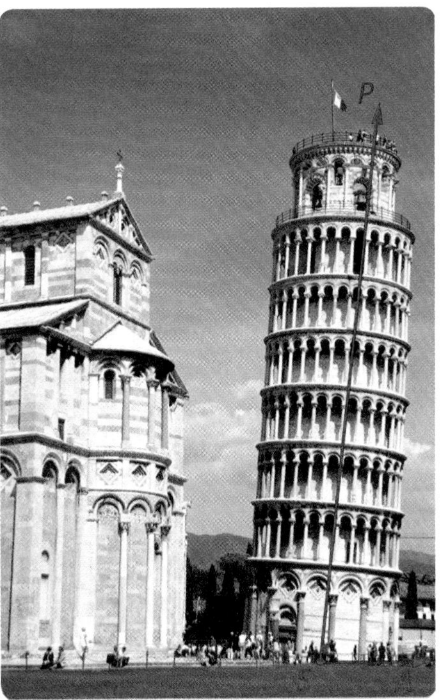

The Leaning Tower of Pisa

Sometimes a figure has many angles.

When there are many angles in a figure, you can use numbers inside the angles as short names. In this figure, $\angle ECB$ is $\angle 2$. So is $\angle ECF$.

QY1

Use the figure above.

a. What are two other names for $\angle ABC$?

b. What is another name for $\angle 1$?

The Measure of an Angle

A common unit for measuring angles is the *degree,* indicated by the symbol °. Think of a circle divided into 360 equally spaced parts. Each part is 1 degree, so 1 **degree** is $\frac{1}{360}$ of the way around a circle. The entire circle has 360°.

A part of a circle that connects two points on the circle is an **arc.** In the circle below, the part of the circle between points A and B and the part of the circle between points B and C are arcs. Arcs are named by their endpoints. The *smaller* arc between points A and B is named by the symbol $\overset{\frown}{AB}$ or $\overset{\frown}{BA}$.

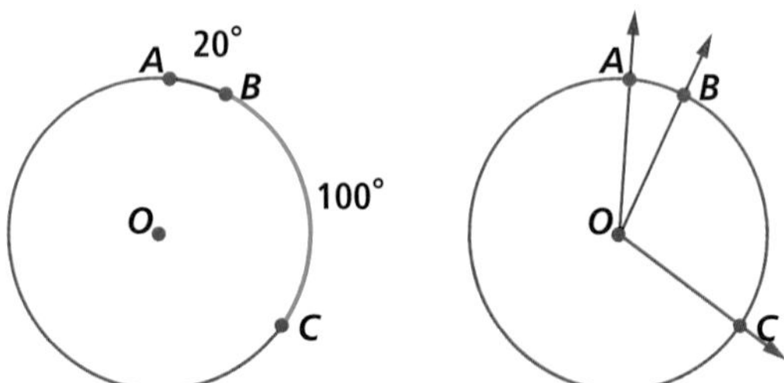

The measure of $\overset{\frown}{AB}$ is 20°. This is written $m\overset{\frown}{AB} = 20°$. *The measure of an angle with its vertex at the center of a circle is the measure of the corresponding arc.* Therefore, the measure of $\angle AOB$ is 20°, written as $m\angle AOB = 20°$.

QY2

In the circles above, what is the measure of

a. $\angle BOC$? **b.** $\angle COA$?

Here are some angles with their measures.

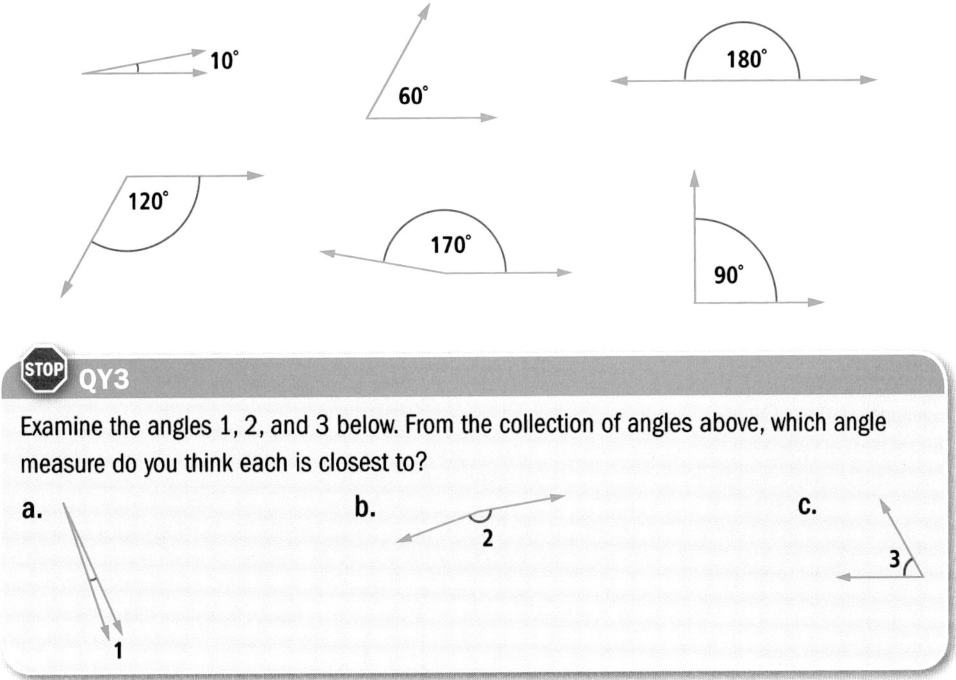

QY3

Examine the angles 1, 2, and 3 below. From the collection of angles above, which angle measure do you think each is closest to?

a. **b.** **c.**

Measuring Angles with a Protractor

You can measure angles by using a **protractor.**

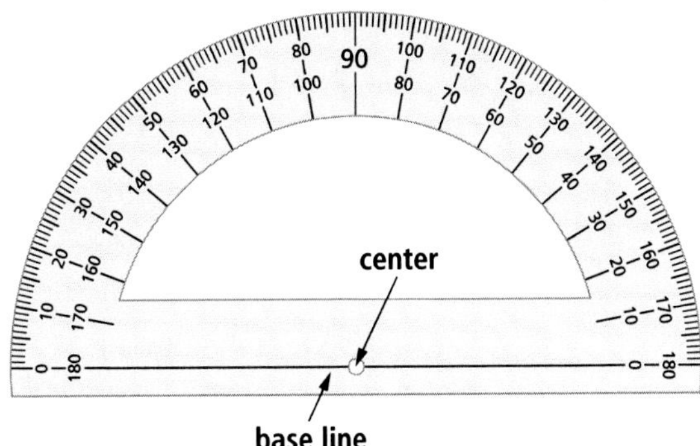

Every protractor has a segment that aligns with the 0° mark on one side and the 180° mark on the other side. This is the *base line* of the protractor. The mark at the middle of this segment is called the *center* of the protractor. Usually there are two scales on the outside arc of the protractor. Reading along the arc from left to right, one scale goes from 0° to 180°. The other scale goes from 180° to 0°.

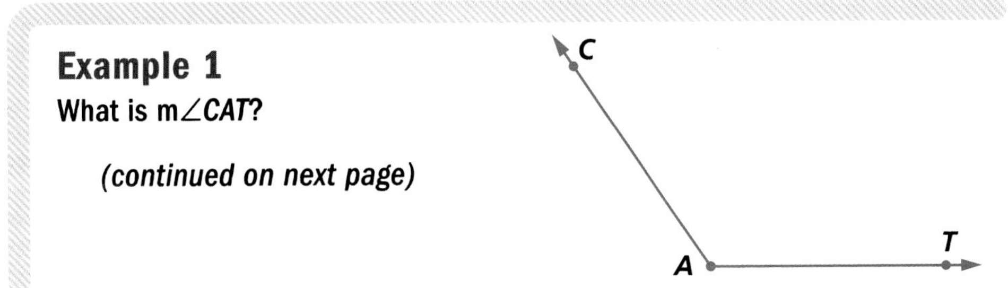

Example 1

What is m∠*CAT*?

(continued on next page)

Solution Put the vertex A of $\angle CAT$ at the center of the protractor. Put one side, $\overrightarrow{AT}$, on the base line. Examine where the other side, $\overrightarrow{AC}$, crosses the protractor. The two possible measures are 55° or 125°. Since $\overrightarrow{AT}$ crosses the inner scale at zero, use the inner scale. The measure of $\angle CAT$ is 125°.

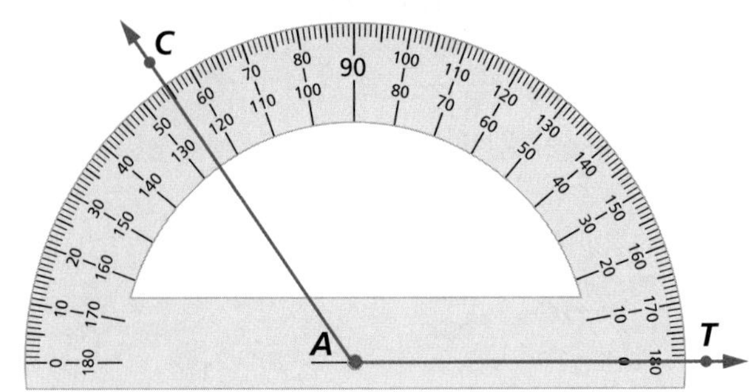

Check Since this angle opens more than a 90° arc, the correct choice is 125°. m$\angle CAT = 125°$

Caution: The measure of an angle has nothing to do with the length of its sides, which can be extended forever. It is determined only by the portion of a circle covered by an angle's arc.

 **See QY4 at the right.**

 **QY4**

Use the photo on page 165 to determine how much the Leaning Tower of Pisa actually leans.

Example 2

Draw $\angle FOG$ with a measure of 45°.

Solution

Step 1 Draw $\overrightarrow{OG}$ anywhere on your paper. Then place the center of a protractor at O, with the base line on $\overrightarrow{OG}$.

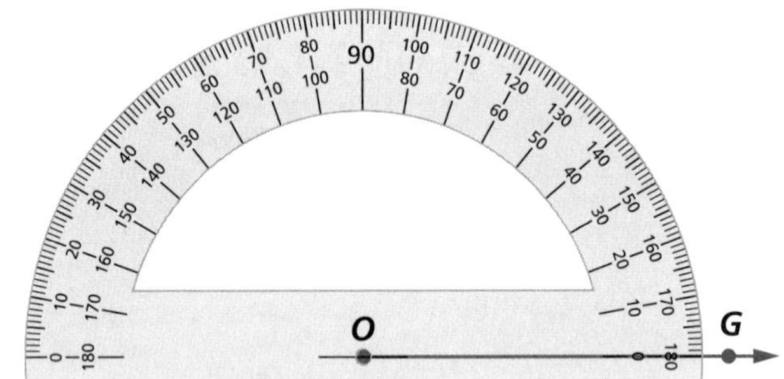

Step 2 Using the scale that crosses $\overrightarrow{OG}$ at 0°, put a point, F, at 45°. Use the straight edge of the protractor to draw $\overrightarrow{OF}$. m$\angle FOG = 45°$

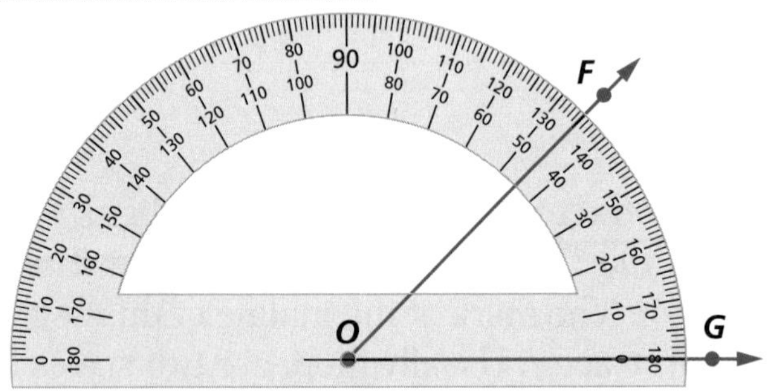

GAME **Now you can play *Angle Tangle*. The directions for this game are on page G13 at the back of your book.**

Questions

COVERING THE IDEAS

In 1–3, use the angle below.

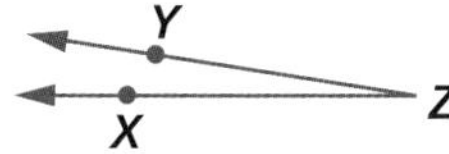

1. Name the sides of the angle.
2. Name the vertex of the angle.
3. Give three possible names for the angle.
4. Write m∠*BAT* in words.
5. Mark drew the figure at right to show that $\frac{2}{3}$ of a circle is 240°. He wrote m∠*APB* = 240°. What is wrong with this statement?

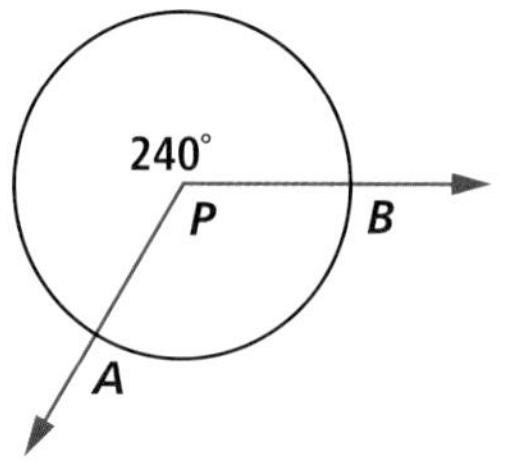

In 6–8, use the drawing below. Find the measure.

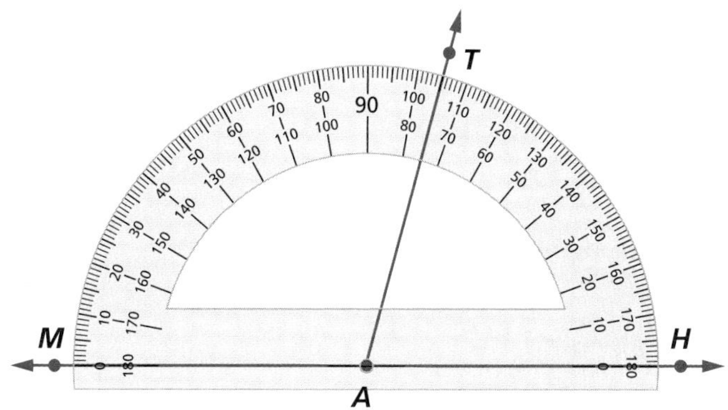

6. m∠*MAT*
7. m∠*HAT*
8. m∠*MAH*

In 9–11, use a protractor to measure the angle.

9.

10.

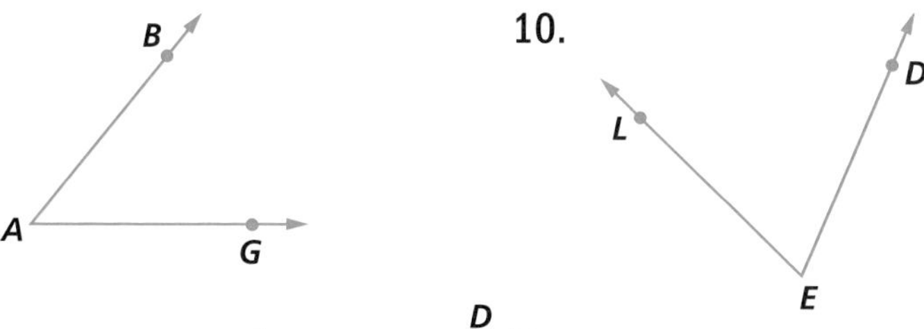

11.

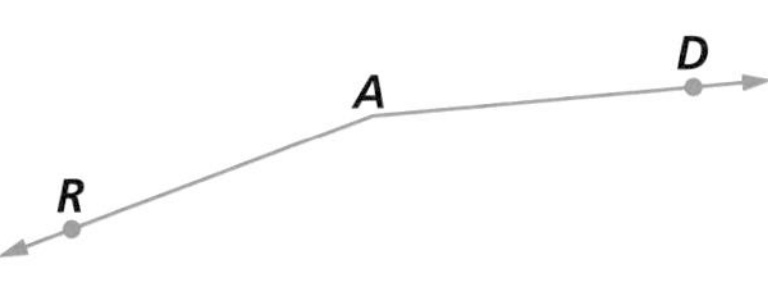

In 12 and 13, use a ruler and protractor to draw an angle of the given measure.

12. 38°

13. 126°

APPLYING THE MATHEMATICS

In 14–16, copy the drawing below. It represents compass directions with an airport at the center *O*. Compass directions are given as degrees clockwise from north (0°). So east is 90°, and west is 270°. $\overrightarrow{OA}$ represents an airplane departing at 120°. Use a protractor to add a ray to represent each situation.

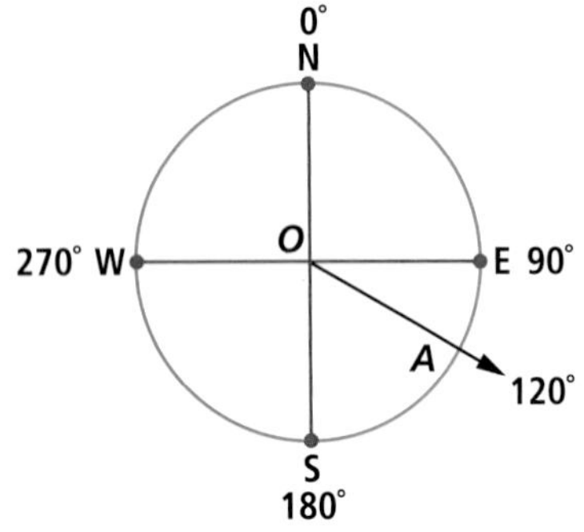

In 2004, the United States employed 24,000 air traffic controllers.

Source: U.S. Department of Labor

14. An air traffic controller sees a hot air balloon B at 50°.
15. A small plane P is approaching the airport from 310°.
16. The controller sees a crow C at 200°.

17. A percent circle divides a circle into one hundred equal arcs.
    a. How many degrees are in each arc?
    b. How many degrees are in 10% of a circle?
    c. 25% of the circle is how many degrees of arc?

REVIEW

18. **Skill Sequence** (Lesson 3-4)
    a. $-4.32 + 4.32$
    b. $2.9995 \times (-4.32 + 4.32)$
    c. $-12.395 + (2.9995 \times (-4.32 + 4.32))$

In 19 and 20, answer the question and tell which property is being demonstrated. (Lesson 3-4)

19. On the bus, Hassan lost 75 cents of his lunch money. Then he found 75 cents in his desk. By much did the amount of money Hassen had change?
20. Charmaine allowed 3 goals in the first half of the soccer game. She didn't allow any goals in the second half. How many goals did she allow in all?

21. Simplify the following sentence using the Op-Op Property: Selena's mom told her that if she did not eat her vegetables, she wouldn't not be unhappy. (Lesson 3-4)

22. Dennis paid off \$100 of a \$375 credit card bill. **(Lesson 3-3)**
   a. How much does he owe now?
   b. Write this situation as a problem involving addition of positive and negative numbers.

23. The table below gives the number of votes that two candidates received in the Student Council election. **(Lessons 2-10, 2-6)**

Candidate	Number of Votes from 6th Graders	Number of Votes from 7th Graders
Marcus	42	29
Catherine	27	42

   a. How many students voted in the election?
   b. How many 6th graders voted in the election?
   c. What percent of the votes were from 6th graders? (Round your answer to the nearest tenth of a percent.)
   d. How many students voted for Catherine?
   e. What percent of all the votes were for Catherine? (Round your answer to the nearest tenth of a percent.)
   f. Who won the election?

Every vote counts!

24. DeAndre multiplied 6 by $\frac{1}{1000}$ to convert 6 meters to 0.006 millimeters. Is this correct? If not, explain the correct way to convert from meters to millimeters. **(Lessons 2-4, 2-3)**

25. Write the answer to 138 ÷ 27 as a mixed number. **(Lesson 1-5)**

EXPLORATION

26. The Babylonians, a Middle Eastern civilization that flourished about 4,000 years ago, had a number system based on sixty. This system is still the basis for our measures of time and angles. Use the Internet or other sources to find information about the Babylonians and their number system. Write about what you discovered.

The Ishtar Gate was one of many fortified entryways into the ancient city of Babylon.

Source: Encyclopedia Britannica

QY ANSWERS

1a. ∠3, ∠*DBA*
1b. ∠*DCE*
2a. 100°
2b. 100°
3a. 10°
3b. 170°
3c. 60°
4. 6°

Lesson 3-6 Angle Measures and Addition

Vocabulary

diameter
semicircle
linear pair
adjacent angles

▸ BIG IDEA When two arcs are next to each other and do not overlap, the measure of the total arc is the sum of the measures of the two arcs. The properties of angles all follow from this idea.

Angle measures can be added. The three angle addition properties in this lesson can help you find angle measures in many different situations. Two of them use the fact that there are 360° in a circle.

Angles Around a Point

When you turn all the way around, you have turned 360°.

Example 1

At the right, four angles surround point *P*. The measures of three angles are given. What is the measure of the fourth angle?

Solution Think of a circle with center *P*. The measure of each arc is the same as the measure of its angle. So the three known arcs together cover 90° + 120° + 65°, or 275°.

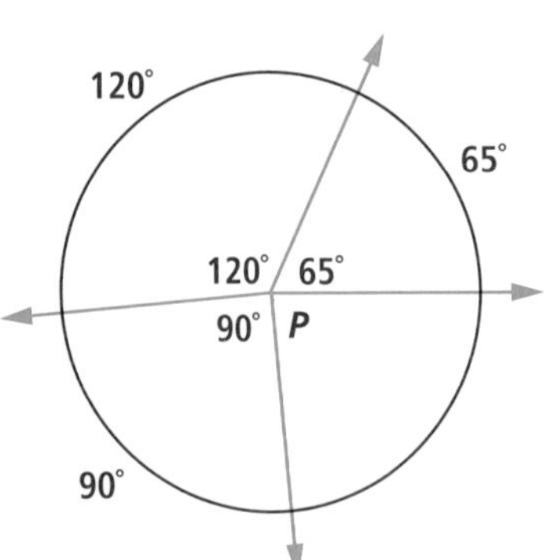

What arc measure, when added to 275°, equals 360°? The answer is 360° − 275°, or 85°. So the fourth angle has a measure of 85°.

The first angle addition property generalizes Example 1. It is due to the fact that a circle contains 360°.

Mental Math

Find the area of each figure, given that the area of the green figure is 3 square units.

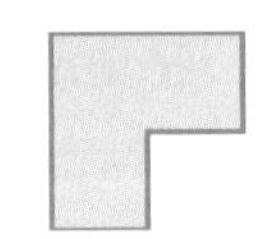

a.

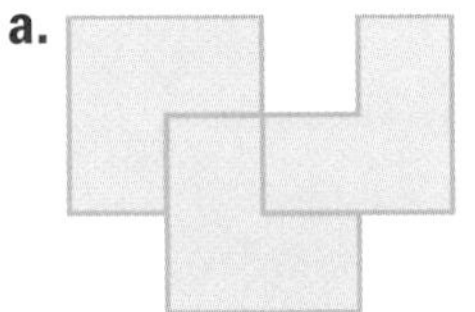

b.

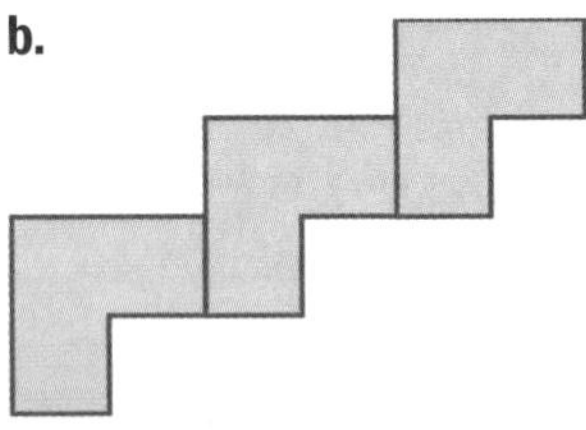

c.

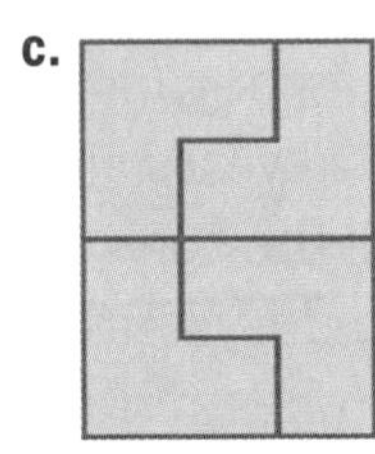

 See QY1 at the right.

 **QY1**

Three of the four angles around point Q measure $60°$, $70°$, and $80°$. What is the measure of the fourth angle?

Angle Addition Property 1

The sum of the measures of all the non-overlapping angles about a point is 360°.

Linear Pair

A segment that connects two points on a circle and contains the center of the circle is called a **diameter** of the circle. It divides the circle into two *semicircles.* A **semicircle** is an arc that has a measure of 180°. Notice that three letters are needed to name each semicircle.

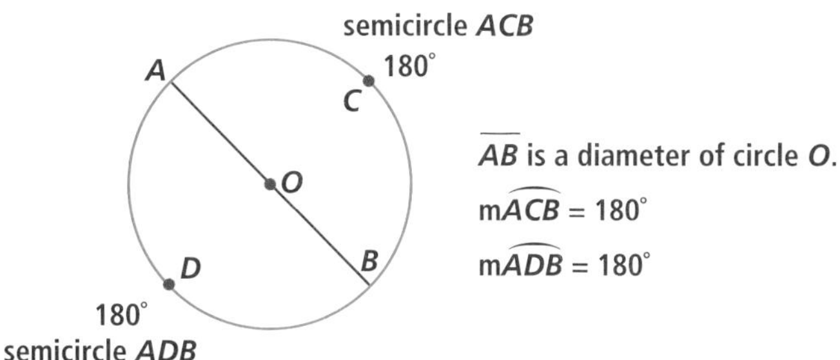

Examine circle Q below. A line through Q contains the diameter. Adding the ray $\overrightarrow{QM}$ creates two angles, $\angle 1$ and $\angle 2$, on one side of the line. These angles are called a *linear pair.* Two angles form a **linear pair** if they have one side in common and if their other sides are rays on the same line in opposite directions. Because together they form an arc that defines half a circle, together they must measure $360° \div 2$. So $m\angle 1 + m\angle 2 = 180°$.

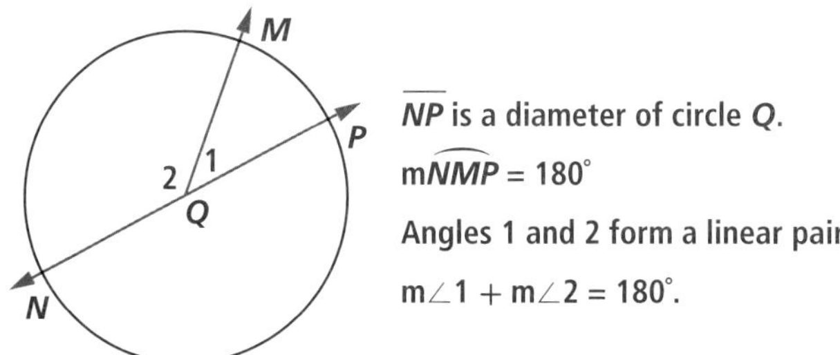

 **QY2**

Draw a linear pair that is *not* in a circle.

Angle Addition Property 2

The sum of the measures of the two angles in a linear pair is 180°.

Adjacent Angles

The angles of a linear pair are examples of *adjacent angles.* Two angles are **adjacent angles** if they have a common side, like $\overrightarrow{WY}$ in the figure below. Also, that common side is inside the angle formed by the other two sides, $\angle XWZ$.

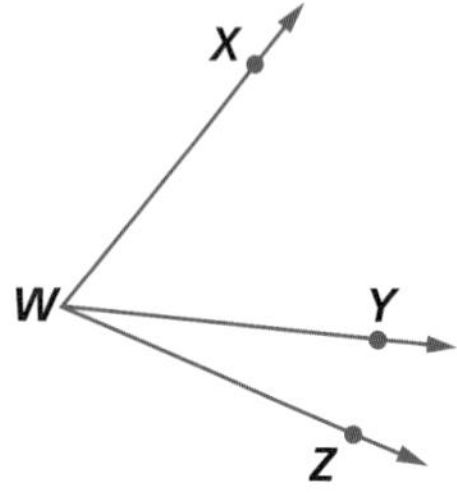

Adjacent angles share a common vertex. Think of that vertex as being at the center of a circle. You can see that the two smaller arcs can be put together to make the larger arc. In the figure at the right, $m\widehat{AD} + m\widehat{DB} = m\widehat{AB}$. So $m\angle ACD + m\angle DCB = m\angle ACB$. That is, $m\angle ACB = 13° + 124° = 137°$.

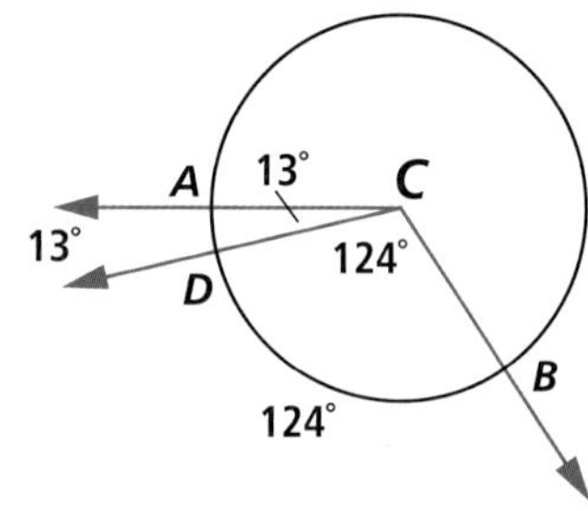

Angle Addition Property 3

If a ray $\overrightarrow{CD}$ is between $\overrightarrow{CA}$ and $\overrightarrow{CB}$, then $m\angle ACD + m\angle BCD = m\angle ACB$.

QY3

Draw adjacent angles *DOT* and *TOP*. If $m\angle DOT = 42°$ and $m\angle POD = 108°$, find $m\angle TOP$.

See QY3 at the right.

GUIDED

Example 2

The hubcap at the right has decorative pieces dividing it into equal sectors. The photograph is diagrammed at the right.

a. What is $m\widehat{AB}$?

b. What is $m\angle ALC$?

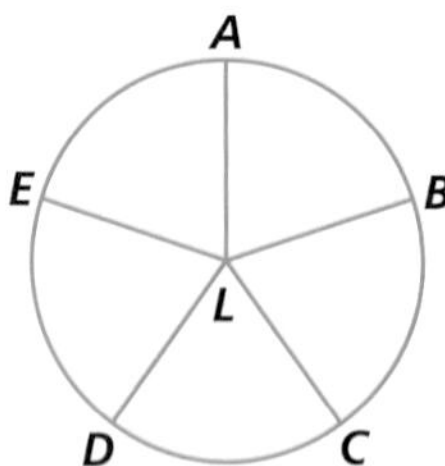

Solution

a. The five arcs in the drawing have equal measures. So the measure of each is $\frac{?}{?} = \underline{\ ?\ }$.

b. $\angle ALC$ is made up of angles of ___?___ sectors, so $m\angle ALC =$ ___?___ $\times$ ___?___ $=$ ___?___.

Questions

COVERING THE IDEAS

In 1–4, use the circle with center *C* at the right to name each figure.

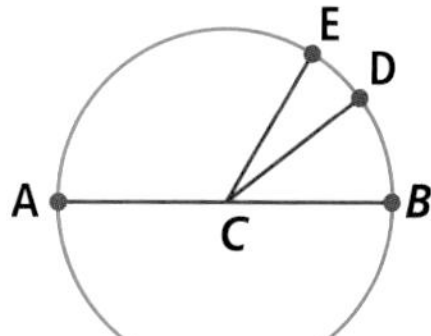

1. the smallest arc
2. the diameter
3. a linear pair
4. adjacent angles

5. Use the circle with center O below. What is $m\overset{\frown}{AD}$?

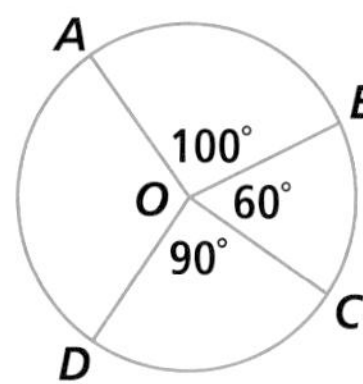

In 6–17, use the circles below. In each circle, the small arcs have equal measures. Give the measure of the angle or arc.

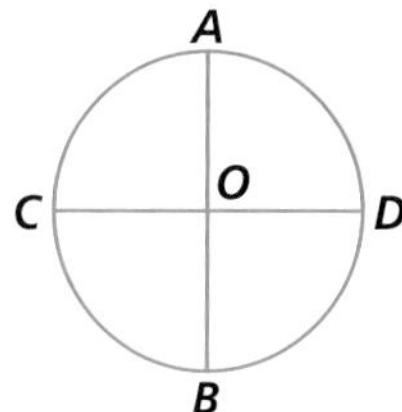

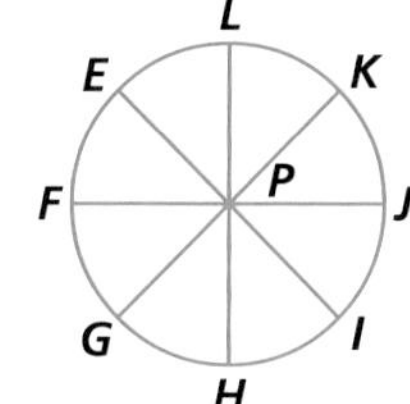

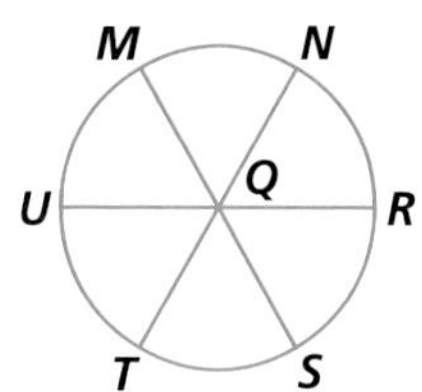

6. $\overset{\frown}{AD}$	7. $\angle BOC$	8. $\overset{\frown}{LJ}$	9. $\overset{\frown}{FG}$
10. $\angle FPG$	11. $\angle LPK$	12. $\angle JPG$	13. $\overset{\frown}{FJ}$
14. $\overset{\frown}{ST}$	15. $\overset{\frown}{TN}$	16. $\angle MQS$	17. $\overset{\frown}{NST}$

18. At the right, $\overline{UY}$ is a diameter of the circle with center W.
    a. Find $m\angle VWY$.
    b. Find $m\angle UWX$.

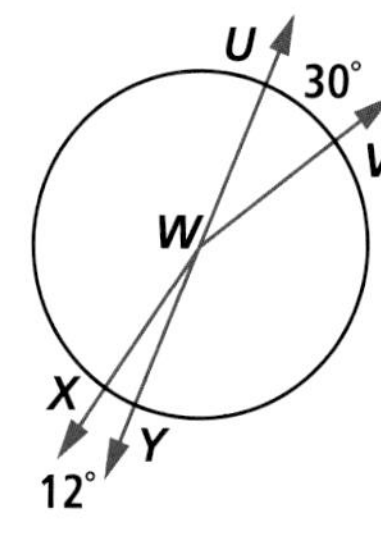

19. Joe Sneak was given a pie to cut into five pieces, as shown below. For some reason, Joe had crumbs on his face. What was the measure of the piece that Joe ate?

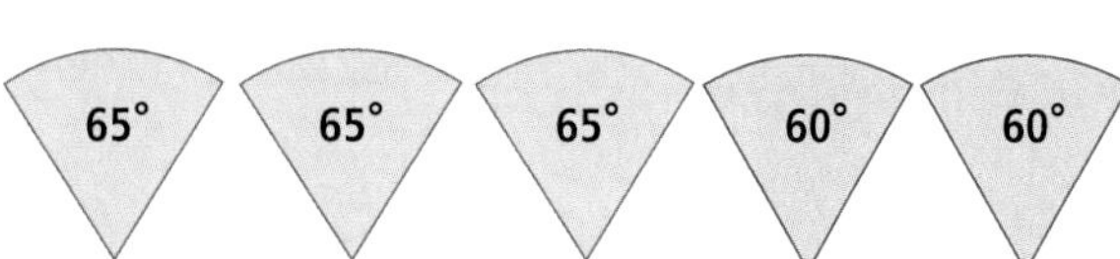

APPLYING THE MATHEMATICS

In 20 and 21, refer to the diagram below, which shows the intersection of two streets.

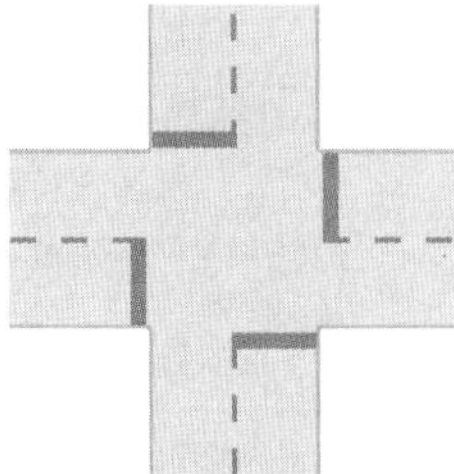

20. When you make a right turn, how many degrees do you turn?
21. Suppose you are asked to make a left turn, but you make a right turn instead. How many degrees must you turn to correct your mistake?
22. Use your protractor to draw angles in a linear pair that have measures of 35° and 145°. Label your drawing.
23. a. Use your protractor to draw angles with measures 25° and 115° that are adjacent.
    b. Why are these angles not a linear pair?
24. Two angles form a linear pair. Must they be adjacent angles?
25. All ten small angles below have the same measure. If O is on $\overleftrightarrow{AB}$, find the measure of each of the following angles.
    a. $\angle AOK$ b. $\angle JOB$ c. $\angle JOG$

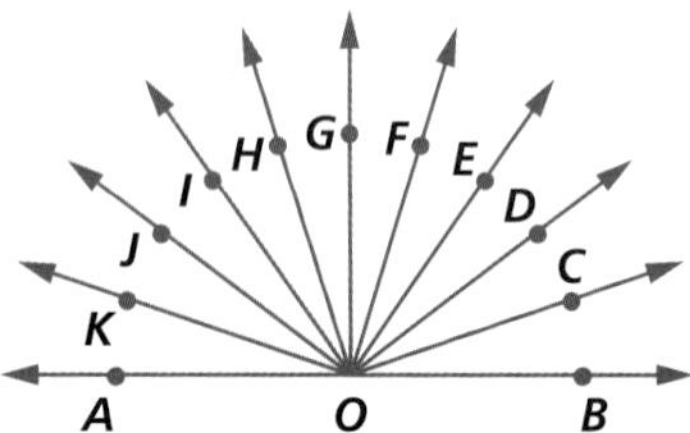

REVIEW

26. Use the figure at the right. **(Lesson 3-5)**
    a. Measure angle $\angle POQ$.
    b. Use the answer to Part a to find the number of degrees in $\angle QOR$ without measuring.

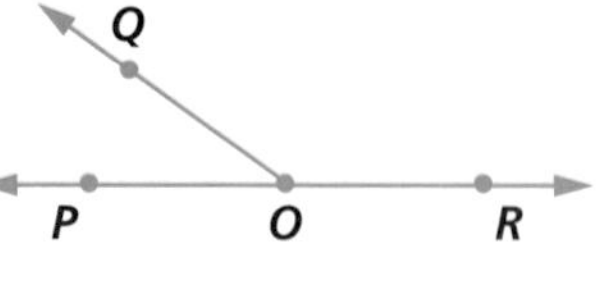

27. You make a 60° turn to the right and then a 60° turn to the left. How many degrees have you turned in relation to your initial position? **(Lesson 3-4)**

28. Michael's toy telescope is made of four tubes, each of length 20 cm. When extended to its full size, each tube has 5 cm of it covered by the next tube, as shown below. What is the length of the fully extended telescope? **(Lesson 3-1)**

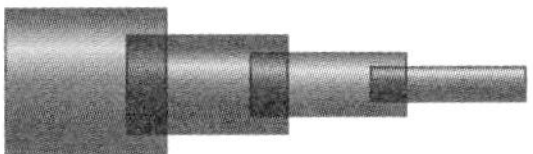

Galileo was the first person to use a telescope to study outer space.

Source: Encyclopedia Britannica

29. The graph below compares basketball participation at Biddle and Liddle Middle Schools. **(Lessons 3-1, 2-10)**

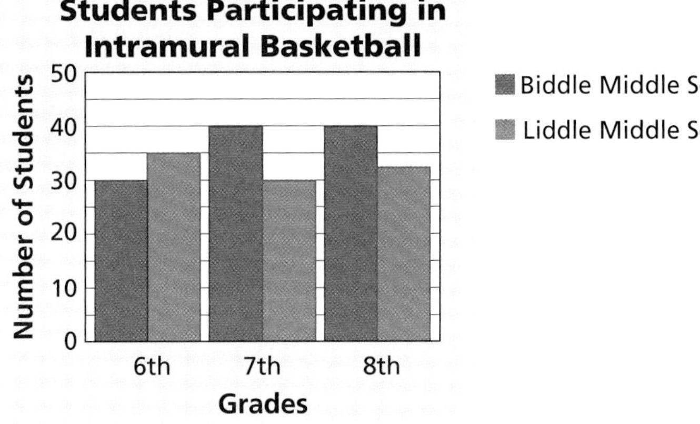

a. At which school do more 6th graders participate in basketball?

b. Does Liddle Middle School have more 6th graders or more 7th graders participating in basketball?

c. How many students at Biddle Middle School participate in basketball?

d. If Biddle Middle School has 250 students, what percent of all the students participate in basketball?

30. The first man to orbit Earth was Yuri Gagarin of the former Soviet Union. His flight, completed on April 12, 1961, lasted 1 hour, 48 minutes. Express this time in hours, as a mixed number in lowest terms. **(Lesson 1-5)**

EXPLORATION

31. The numbers on airport runways range from 01 to 36. What do these numbers signify? How are they related to angle and arc measure? Use a reference book or the Internet to find answers to these questions.

QY ANSWERS

1. 150°

2. Answers vary. Sample:

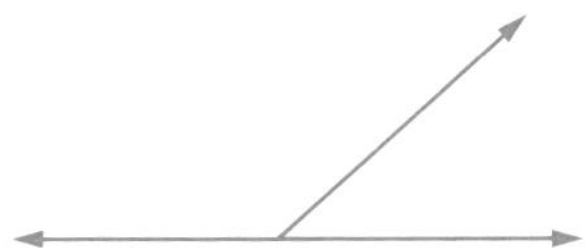

3. $m\angle TOP = 66°$

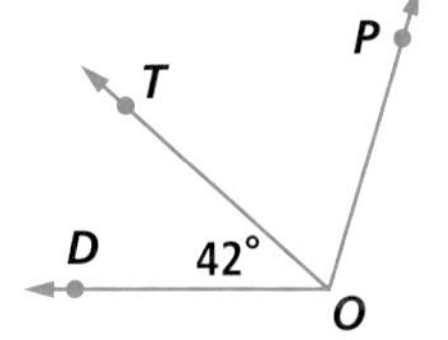

Lesson 3-7 Sums of Angle Measures in Polygons

▸ **BIG IDEA** The sum of the measures of the angles of a polygon depends on the number of sides of the polygon.

Angles in Triangles

In the following activity, you will investigate angle measures in triangles.

Activity 1

MATERIALS scissors

Step 1 In groups of four students, each person should draw a triangle of a different size or shape.

Step 2 Label the interior angles *a*, *b*, and *c*.

Step 3 Make six copies of your triangle and cut them out.

Step 4 Place angles *a*, *b*, and *c* from three of your triangles adjacent to one another about one point.

Step 5 Do the same thing with the other three triangles.

Step 6 Take both sets of triangles and try to fit them together to form a geometric shape around the same point or vertex.

Step 7 How many triangles can you place around a single point?

Step 8 Trade triangle sets with another person in your group.

Step 9 Repeat Steps 4–6 with the six new triangles.

Step 10 What might be a general rule about this activity? After Step 6 of the Activity, you might have a figure like the one below.

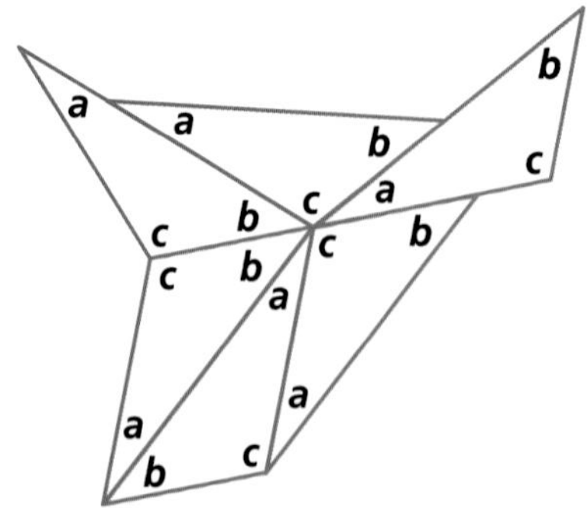

Mental Math

Find the sum of the angle measures in each figure.

a.

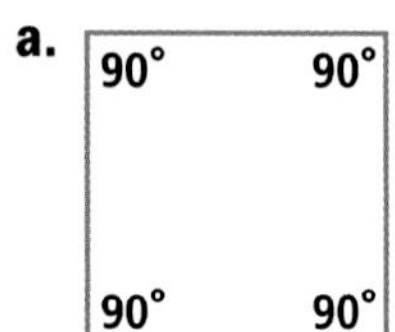

b.

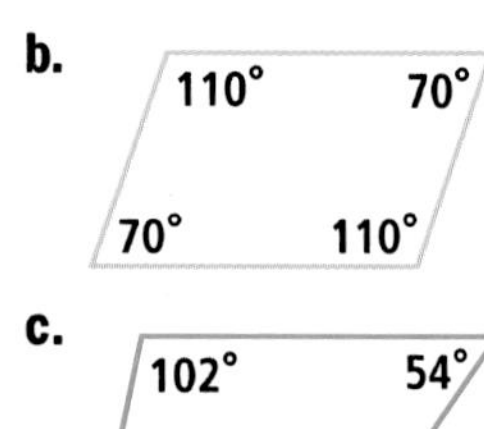

c.

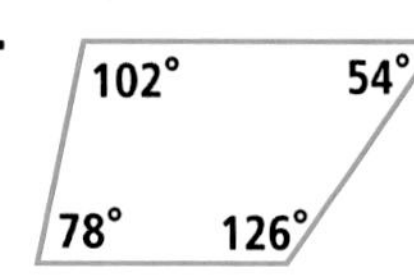

The Angle Addition Property for angles about a point tells you that $a + b + c + a + b + c = 360°$.

The left side of the equation is two times the sum of the angle measures in the original triangle. So the sum of the angle measures in a triangle is one-half of 360°, or 180°.

Triangle-Sum Theorem

In any triangle with angles having measures a, b, and c, $a + b + c = 180°$.

Example 1

Write an equation relating the sum of the angles in the triangle below.

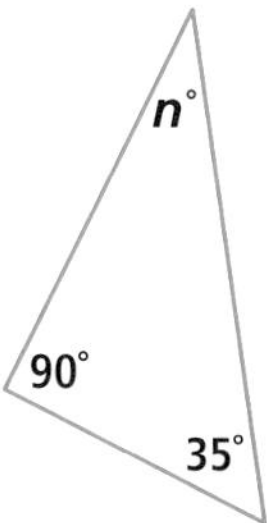

Solution Since the angle measures of the triangle add to 180°, write the sum and set it equal to 180°.

$$n + 90° + 35° = 180°$$
$$n + 125° = 180°$$

QY

What is the value of n in Example 1?

Angles in Quadrilaterals

You can use the Triangle-Sum Theorem and the Angle Addition Property to find the sum of the angle measures in other polygons.

Example 2

Find the sum of the measures of the four angles in the quadrilateral below.

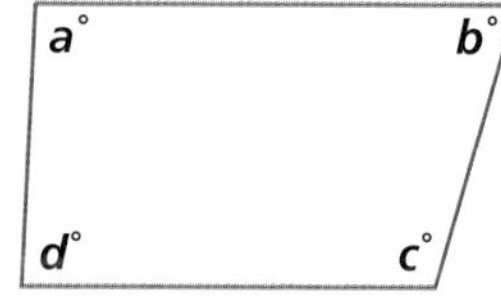

(continued on next page)

Solution Choose one vertex and draw a diagonal from it to the opposite vertex.

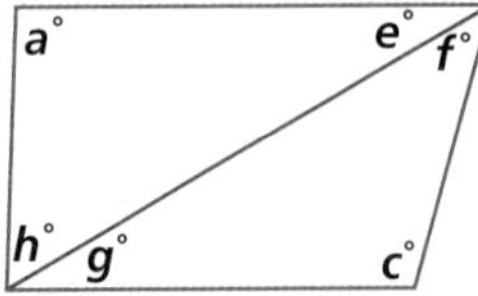

This divides the quadrilateral into two triangles. Notice that b in the original drawing is equal to $e + f$, and d in the original drawing is equal to $h + g$.

$$\begin{aligned} a + b + c + d &= a + (e + f) + c + (g + h) \\ &= (a + e + h) + (c + g + f) \\ &= 180° + 180° \\ &= 360° \end{aligned}$$

When the diagonals of a quadrilateral are inside the figure, the quadrilateral can be divided into two triangles whose neighboring angles are adjacent. So for those quadrilaterals, we can arrive at the following conclusion.

Quadrilateral-Sum Theorem

In any quadrilateral with angles having degree measures a, b, c, and d, and both diagonals inside the quadrilateral, $a + b + c + d = 360°$.

Activity 2

Complete the table. Find the sum of the angle measures for each polygon by splitting it into triangles.

Name of Polygon	Quadrilateral	Pentagon	Hexagon	Heptagon	Octagon	Dodecagon
Drawing						
Number of Triangles	2	?	?	?	?	?
Sum of Angle Measures	$2 \times 180° = 360°$	?	?	?	?	?

Caution: Be careful that all triangles share their vertices with the original polygon. Otherwise, you may get an incorrect sum.

Questions

COVERING THE IDEAS

1. Write an equation relating the sum of the angles in the triangle below.

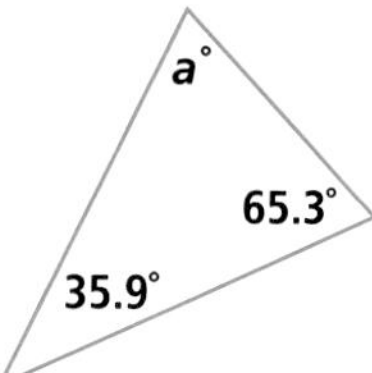

2. Write an equation relating the sum of the angles in the quadrilateral below.

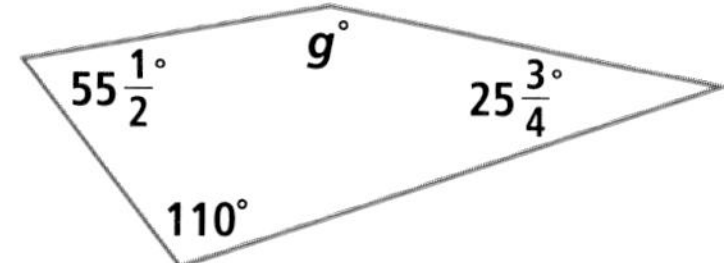

In 3 and 4, find the missing angle measure in the figure.

3. 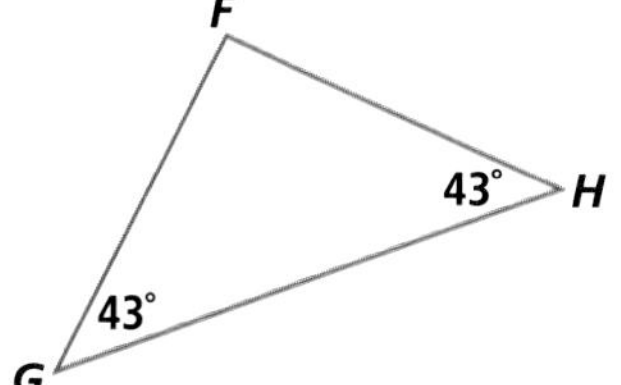

4. 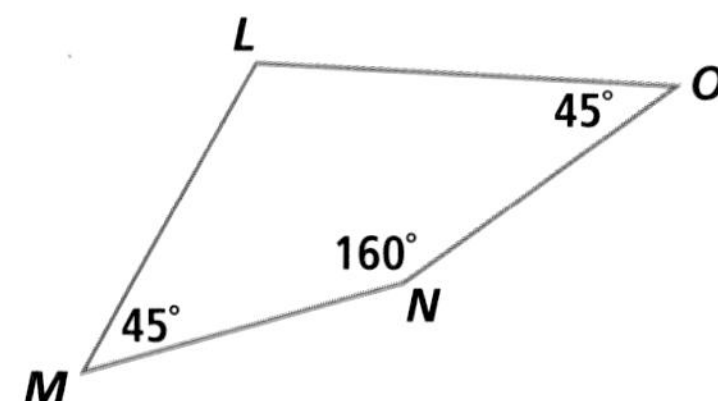

5. Split the hexagon below into two quadrilaterals. Use the divided figure to find the sum of the angle measures of the hexagon.

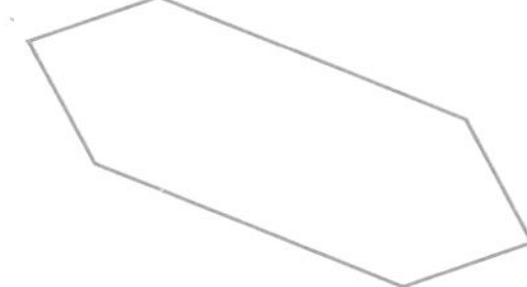

6. Find the sum of the measures of the angles of the octagon below by splitting it into four triangles and a quadrilateral.

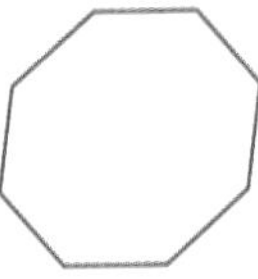

APPLYING THE MATHEMATICS

7. Pictured at the right is a *regular* pentagon. In a regular pentagon, all sides are the same length, and all the angles have the same measure. Find $m\angle A$.

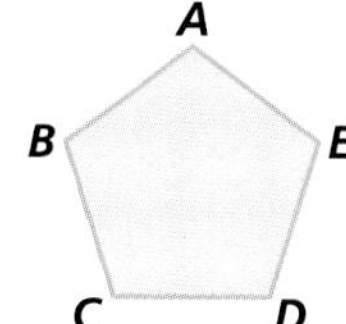

8. Find the measure of each angle of a regular heptagon. Give the answer as a mixed number.

In 9–11, tell whether the triangle is *possible* or *impossible* based on its angle measures. Explain your answer using the Triangle-Sum Theorem.

9. a triangle with two 90° angles
10. a triangle with two angle measures greater than 90°
11. a triangle with all angles having measures less than 90°

12. Charmaine said the diagram below shows that the sum of the angles in a hexagon is $6 \times 180° = 1{,}080°$. Is Charmaine right? Why or why not?

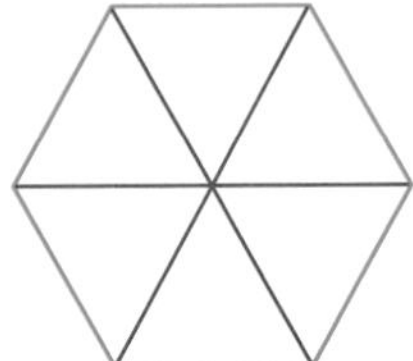

In 13–15, tell whether the following quadrilaterals are possible or impossible based on their angle measures. Explain your answer using the Quadrilateral-Sum Theorem.

13. a quadrilateral with two 90° angles
14. a quadrilateral with two angles with measures greater than 90°
15. a quadrilateral with three angles with measures greater than 90°

16. Find $m\angle I$ in the triangle below if $m\angle I = m\angle K$.

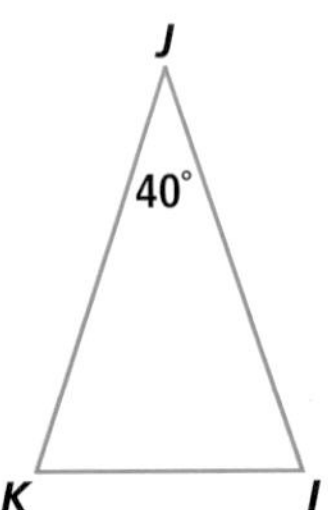

REVIEW

17. Find the measure of $\angle 1$ in the diagram below. **(Lesson 3-6)**

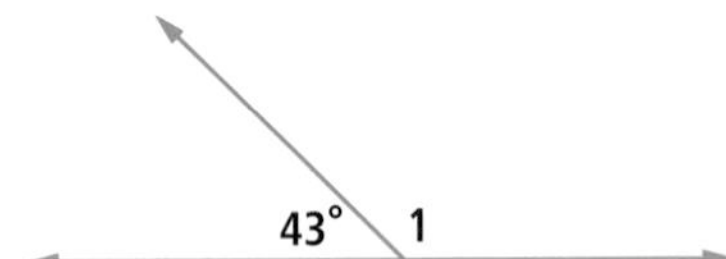

In 18 and 19, use a protractor to measure the angle. (Lesson 3-5)

18. 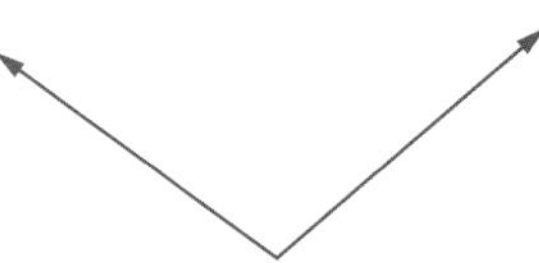

19. 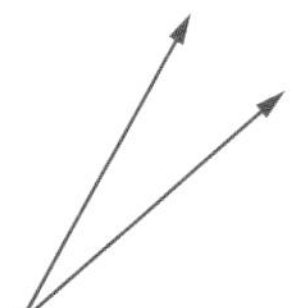

20. Describe a situation that demonstrates the Additive Property of Opposites. **(Lesson 3-4)**

21. Summit Plummet is one of the tallest waterslides in the United States at 120 feet tall. Suppose a trampoline were placed at the bottom of the slide. If you bounced 37 feet into the air, how many feet from the top of the slide would you be? **(Lesson 3-3)**

22. Suppose you live m miles from your cousin's house, and your cousin lives n miles from your favorite restaurant. Write an expression showing how many miles you must travel to pick up your cousin and go to the restaurant. **(Lesson 3-2)**

Have you ever slid down on a waterslide?

EXPLORATION

23. **a.** What is the sum of the measures of the angles of a regular 100-sided polygon?
    b. What is the measure of each angle of a regular 100-sided polygon?
    c. What is the sum of the measures of the angles of a regular n-sided polygon?

QY ANSWER

55°

Lesson

3-8 Adding Simple Fractions

Vocabulary

like denominators

unlike denominators

least common multiple

least common denominator

▸ **BIG IDEA** Fractions with different denominators can be added by renaming them so they have the same denominator.

In this chapter, you have added lengths, integers, and angle measures. The last two lessons cover addition with fractions and mixed numbers.

Mental Math

Add.

a. 0.5 + 0.75

b. 0.3 + 0.7

c. 0.6 + 0.2

d. 1.4 + 3.7

Many indoor tracks are $\frac{1}{8}$ mile in length. If Ima Runner ran three laps before stopping to catch her breath and then completed two more laps how far did she run? Finding the answer requires adding $\frac{3}{8} + \frac{2}{8}$. Notice that $\frac{3}{8}$ and $\frac{2}{8}$ have the same denominators, or **like denominators.** You can treat "eighths" as the unit. The sum of 3 eighths and 2 eighths equals 5 eighths. So, Ima ran $\frac{5}{8}$ mile.

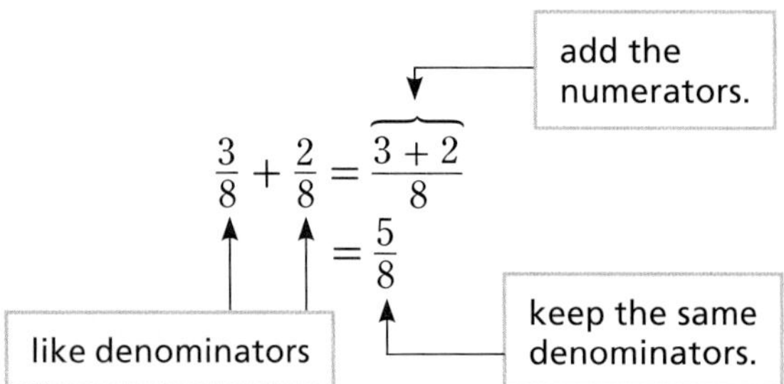

In general, to add fractions with the same denominator, add the numerators and keep the denominator the same.

The Adding Fractions Property

For all numbers *a*, *b*, and *c*, with $c \neq 0$, $\frac{a}{c} + \frac{b}{c} = \frac{a + b}{c}$.

Example 1

Simplify $\frac{2}{y} + \frac{5}{y}$ and check your answer.

Solution Since the fractions have the same denominator, simply add the numerators:

$$\frac{2}{y} + \frac{5}{y} + 2 + \frac{5}{y} = \frac{7}{y}$$

Check Substitute a value for y. Let $y = 10$ and the problem becomes $\frac{2}{10} + \frac{5}{10} = \frac{7}{10}$. Using decimals, $\frac{2}{10} + \frac{5}{10} = 0.2 + 0.5 = 0.7$. So, it checks.

Adding Fractions with Different Denominators

Fractions with different denominators cannot be added in this way. For example, $\frac{1}{6}$ and $\frac{1}{8}$ have different denominators, or **unlike denominators.** But you can rewrite the fractions to make the denominators the same. Then you can use the Adding Fractions Property.

GUIDED

Example 2

Alex used $\frac{1}{6}$ cup of flour in one recipe and $\frac{3}{8}$ cup of flour in another recipe. How much flour did he use altogether?

Solution 1 One way to rewrite $\frac{1}{6}$ and $\frac{3}{8}$ using the same denominator is to list multiples of the denominators.

multiples of 6: 6, 12, _?_, 24, _?_, _?_, _?_, 48, _?_, ...

multiples of 8: 8, 16, 24, _?_, _?_, _?_, _?_, ...

There are many common multiples of 6 and 8. The two shown above are _?_ and _?_. Since 24 is the smallest positive common integer multiple of 8 and 6, it is called the **least common multiple** of these numbers.

When fractions have the same denominator, that number is called a *common denominator.* The number 24 is the **least common denominator** of $\frac{1}{6}$ and $\frac{3}{8}$. Rewrite $\frac{1}{6}$ and $\frac{3}{8}$ with 24 as the denominator of each.

$$\frac{1}{6} = \frac{1 \cdot ?}{6 \cdot ?} = \frac{?}{24}$$

$$+\frac{3}{8} = \frac{3 \cdot ?}{8 \cdot ?} = \frac{?}{24}$$

$$\frac{13}{24}$$

Alex used $\frac{13}{24}$ cups of flour altogether.

Do you have a favorite kind of bread?

The figure on the next page illustrates the process of adding the fractions. One full bar represents 1 cup, and the shaded area represents the parts of a cup used in the recipes.

(continued on next page)

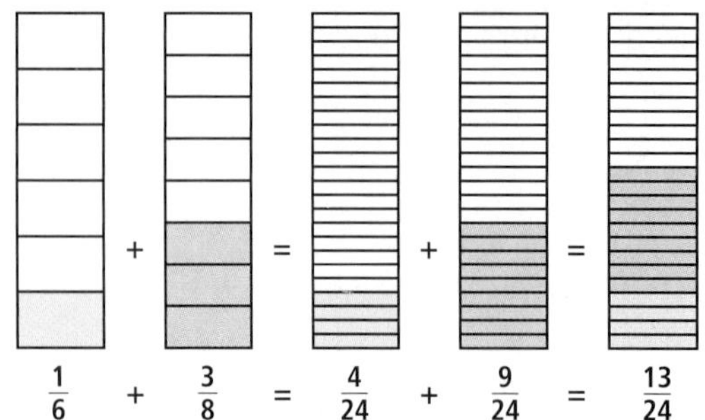

$$\frac{1}{6} + \frac{3}{8} = \frac{4}{24} + \frac{9}{24} = \frac{13}{24}$$

Solution 2 It is not necessary to use the least common multiple as the common denominator. You can always use the product of the denominators, in this case 48.

$$\frac{1}{6} = \frac{1 \cdot ?}{6 \cdot ?} = \frac{?}{?}$$

$$+\frac{3}{8} = \frac{3 \cdot ?}{8 \cdot ?} = \frac{?}{?}$$

$$\frac{?}{48} = \frac{?}{?}$$

Alex used $\frac{13}{24}$ cups of flour altogether.

Check Use a calculator.

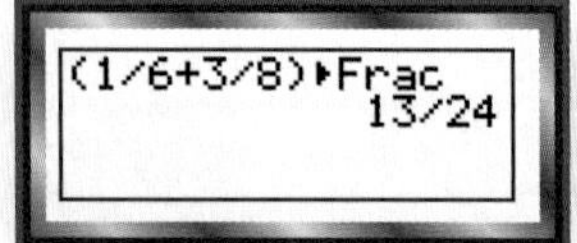

Some students prefer the method of Solution 2 when adding fractions with unlike denominators because it is easy to find a common denominator. However, the product of two denominators can sometimes be quite large. Because smaller numbers are easier to handle, it is a good idea to keep common denominators as small as possible.

GUIDED

Example 3

Find the sum of $\frac{13}{48} + \frac{19}{72}$.

Solution

multiples of _?_: _?_, _?_, _?_, _?_, ...

multiples of 72: _?_, _?_, _?_, _?_, ...

A common denominator for 48 and 72 is _?_.

$$\frac{13}{48} = \frac{13 \cdot ?}{48 \cdot ?} = \frac{?}{?}$$

$$+ \quad \frac{19}{72} = \frac{19 \cdot ?}{72 \cdot ?} = \frac{?}{?}$$

$$= \frac{?}{?}$$

 **Check** $\frac{13}{48}$ is a little more than $\frac{1}{4}$ and $\frac{19}{72}$ is a little more than $\frac{1}{4}$. So the answer should be a little more than $\frac{1}{4} + \frac{1}{4}$, or $\frac{1}{2}$, which it is.

 **QY**

Suppose you wish to add $\frac{17}{25} + \frac{41}{35}$.

a. Find a common denominator.

b. Find the sum.

GAME Now you can play *Scrambling: Fraction Addition.* The directions for this game are on pages G14–G15 at the back of your book.

Questions

COVERING THE IDEAS

1. On Monday, Deja ran 6 laps. On Tuesday, she ran 5 laps. If each lap is a quarter mile, how many miles did Deja run in total?

Do you think you can outrun a T-Rex? The Tyrannosaurus Rex would run at a speed of up to 18 miles per hour.

Source: CNN

2. Alvin used $\frac{5}{2}$ cups of broth in one recipe and $\frac{3}{2}$ cups of broth in another recipe.
   a. How much broth did he use altogether?
   b. Draw a picture to support your answer in Part a.

3. Use a ruler to draw a horizontal line segment $\frac{3}{4}$" long. Add a line segment $\frac{5}{8}$" long to it. What is the total length of the final segment?

In 4 and 5, find the sum.

4. $\frac{3}{8} + \frac{5}{8} + \frac{7}{8}$

5. $\frac{2{,}645{,}000}{10{,}000{,}000} + \frac{1{,}790{,}000}{10{,}000{,}000}$

In 6 and 7, find the least common multiple of the integers.

6. 4, 5, 6

7. 25, 75, 10

In 8 and 9, find the sum. Check your answer by substituting a number for the variable.

8. $\frac{1}{x} + \frac{5}{x}$

9. $\frac{14}{y} + \frac{3}{y} + \frac{4}{y}$

10. **a.** Find three common multiples of 4 and 10.
    b. Write $\frac{1}{4} + \frac{3}{10}$ as a single fraction. Show your work.

In 11–14, find the sum. Check your answer by converting the fractions and the sum to decimals.

11. $\frac{5}{8} + \frac{1}{2}$

12. $\frac{3}{4} + \frac{1}{5}$

13. $\frac{1}{60} + \frac{29}{30}$

14. $\frac{9}{10} + \frac{2}{20}$

APPLYING THE MATHEMATICS

15. **a.** What addition of fractions problem is represented by the following? A quarter and five dimes equals three quarters. (Remember that a dime is one-tenth of a dollar.)
    b. Find the sum of the fractions.

16. A nickel is $\frac{1}{20}$ of a dollar. Suppose you have 43 nickels in one jar, 125 dimes in a second jar, 30 quarters in a third jar, and 161 pennies in a fourth jar. Show how you can add fractions to determine the total value of this money.

Benjamin Franklin is frequently credited with the old saying, "A penny saved is a penny earned."

17. The student council is assigning auditorium seats for the honors assembly. Each grade (6th, 7th, and 8th) requires $\frac{1}{4}$ of the seats, and $\frac{1}{8}$ of the seats need to be reserved for parents.

   a. Represent this situation with a drawing.

   b. What percent of the seats will *not* be reserved?

   c. After the student council has reserved the seats, the principal asks the student council to reserve half of the remaining seats for members of the community. What fraction will be reserved for community members?

In 18 and 19, find the sum in lowest terms. Check your answer.

18. $-\frac{11}{100} + \frac{1}{20}$

19. $-\frac{1}{12} + -\frac{1}{6} + -\frac{1}{4} + -\frac{1}{3}$

20. a. Use grid paper. Divide a 5-by-8 rectangle into four polygons labeled *A, B, C,* and *D,* so that the following are true:
   - Polygon *A* is exactly $\frac{1}{4}$ of the rectangle.
   - Polygon *B* is exactly $\frac{3}{8}$ of the rectangle.
   - Polygon *C* is exactly $\frac{1}{10}$ of the rectangle.

   b. What fraction of the rectangle does Polygon *D* represent?

   c. What fraction is represented by polygons *A* and *B* together?

   d. What number is represented by all four polygons together?

21. Consider the addition $\frac{1}{k} + \frac{2}{k} + \frac{8}{k} + \frac{3}{k} + \frac{7}{k}$.

   a. Find the sum.

   b. Find a value for *k* that gives a sum that is a proper fraction.

   c. Find a value for *k* that gives a sum that is an improper fraction.

   d. Find a value for *k* that gives a sum of 1.

22. Consider the addition $\frac{11}{96} + \frac{7}{64} + \frac{13}{144}$.

   a. Should the answer be more or less than $\frac{1}{2}$? Explain.

   b. Find the sum.

REVIEW

23. What is the sum of the measures of the angles in a regular octagon? **(Lesson 3-7)**

24. Refer to the circle below. $\overline{RU}$, $\overline{QT}$, and $\overline{PS}$ are diameters of circle *O*. Suppose $m\angle POQ = 25°$. If $m\angle POQ = m\angle QOR$, find $m\angle POU$. **(Lesson 3-6)**

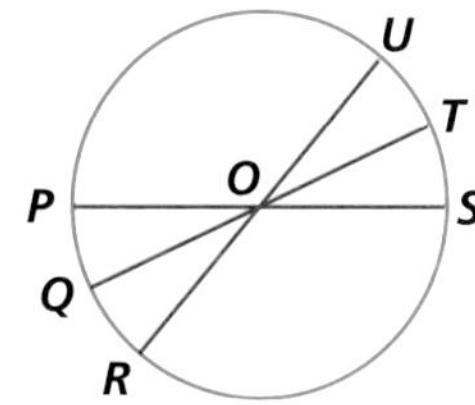

25. Find the perimeter of figure $ABCRQP$ below if the dimensions of rectangle $ABCD$ are $5\frac{1}{2}$" and $3\frac{1}{2}$". **(Lesson 3-2)**

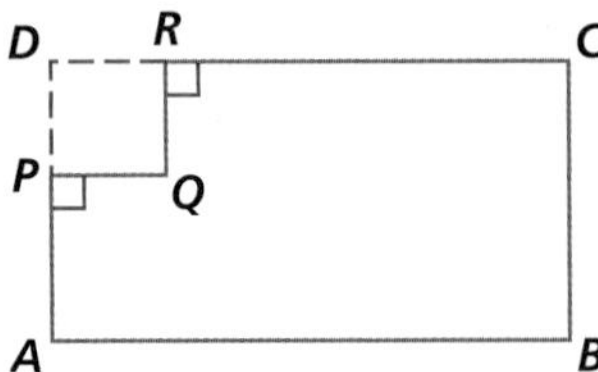

26. Compare the numbers using $<$, $=$, or $>$. **(Lessons 2-8, 1-6)**
    a. $\frac{11}{64}$ and $\frac{3}{8}$
    b. $\frac{8}{9}$ and $\frac{9}{10}$

27. Write an addition problem to answer the question. In the first round of a golf tournament, Boo Weekly was 2 strokes under par. In the next round, Boo was 3 strokes above par. In the third round, Boo was 2 strokes below par. After three rounds, where was Boo in relation to par? **(Lesson 1-8)**

EXPLORATION

28. a. Write three whole numbers and their sum. Here is an example: $12 + 43 + 61 = 116$.
    b. Now divide each of the three numbers and the result by another whole number. This whole number can be greater or less than the sum. For example, if you divide the sum in Part a by 47, you get $\frac{12}{47}$, $\frac{43}{47}$, $\frac{61}{47}$, and $\frac{116}{47}$.
    c. Is it true that the sum of the first three fractions equals the last fraction?
    d. Explain why this works or why it does not.

QY ANSWERS

a. Answers vary. Sample: 175

b. $\frac{324}{175}$

Lesson 3-9 Adding Mixed Numbers

▶ **BIG IDEA** You can add mixed numbers by converting them to improper fractions with the same denominator.

People who build or furnish homes work with measurements in halves, quarters, eighths, sixteenths, and, occasionally, thirty-seconds of an inch. When they need to put together lengths, they often need to find a common denominator large enough to enable the fractions to be easily added.

Mental Math

Find the total amount.

a. 50 cents and 2 quarters

b. 75 cents and 1 quarter

c. half a dollar and 3 quarters

d. a dollar and ten cents, 3 nickels, 4 pennies, and a quarter

Example 1

Arthur wants to frame a photograph that is $8\frac{1}{2}$" tall and $11\frac{3}{4}$" long. If the frame is $1\frac{3}{8}$" wide, what will be the length of the framed photograph?

Solution It helps to draw a picture.

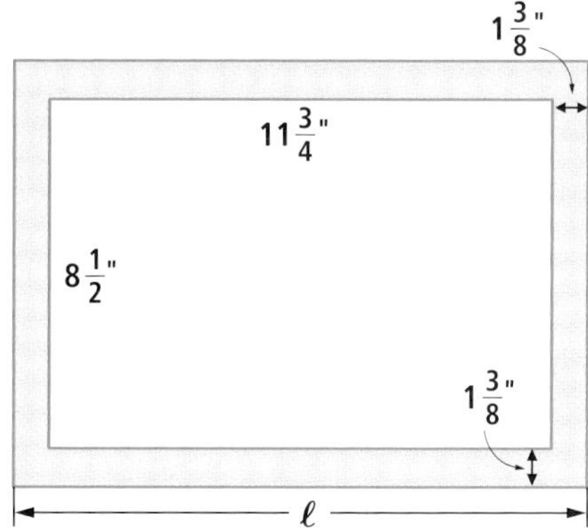

The width of the picture will be $11\frac{3}{4} + 1\frac{3}{8} + 1\frac{3}{8}$ inches. To add these fractions, rewrite $\frac{3}{4}$ as $\frac{6}{8}$.

$$11\tfrac{3}{4} + 1\tfrac{3}{8} + 1\tfrac{3}{8}$$
$$= 11\tfrac{6}{8} + 1\tfrac{3}{8} + 1\tfrac{3}{8}$$

The denominators are the same, so you can add the fractions.

$$11\tfrac{6}{8} + 1\tfrac{3}{8} + 1\tfrac{3}{8} = (11 + 1 + 1) + (\tfrac{6}{8} + \tfrac{3}{8} + \tfrac{3}{8})$$
$$= 13 + \tfrac{12}{8}$$
$$= 13 + 1\tfrac{4}{8}$$
$$= 13 + 1\tfrac{1}{2} = 14\tfrac{1}{2}$$

The length of the framed photograph will be $14\frac{1}{2}$".

Improper Fractions in Mixed Numbers

The addition $13 + \frac{12}{8}$ appears in the middle of Example 1. This sum can be written as $13\frac{12}{8}$. This number has an improper fraction as part of a mixed number. The last three steps of the solution to Example 1 are done to convert $13 + \frac{12}{8}$ into a mixed number without an improper fraction.

QY1

Simplify.

a. $6\frac{7}{3}$ b. $12\frac{10}{6}$

GUIDED

Example 2

What is the height of the framed photograph in Example 1?

Solution

Write an expression for the height of the photograph. $\underline{?} + \underline{?} + \underline{?}$

Rewrite the fraction with denominator 8. $= \underline{?} + \underline{?} + \underline{?}$

Add the whole number parts and the fraction parts separately. $= \underline{?} + \underline{?}$

Write the improper fraction as a mixed number. $= \underline{?} + \underline{?}$

Write the sum as a mixed number. $= \underline{?}$

Write your answer in lowest terms. $= \underline{?}$

Write a sentence about the height to answer the question.

STOP **See QY2 at the right.**

STOP **QY2**

Suppose the frame Arthur wants to put on the photograph is $\frac{7}{16}$" wide. What will be the length of the framed photograph?

Some people organize addition of mixed numbers in columns.

GUIDED

Example 3

Add $4\frac{2}{3} + \frac{3}{4} + 1\frac{1}{2}$.

Solution To find the least common denominator, first find the least common multiple of the denominators.

multiples of 3: 3, 6, 9, 12, 15, 18, ...
multiples of 4: 4, 8, 12, 16, 20, ...
multiples of 2: 2, 4, 6, 8, 10, 12, 14, 16, 18, ...

$$
\begin{aligned}
4\tfrac{2}{3} &= 4\tfrac{?}{12}\\
\tfrac{3}{4} &= \tfrac{?}{12}\\
+\ 1\tfrac{1}{2} &= 1\tfrac{?}{12}\\
\hline
5\tfrac{23}{12} &= 5 + 1\tfrac{11}{12} = 6\tfrac{11}{12}
\end{aligned}
$$

Check 1 Enter the addition problem into your calculator. Compare the calculator result with the answer.

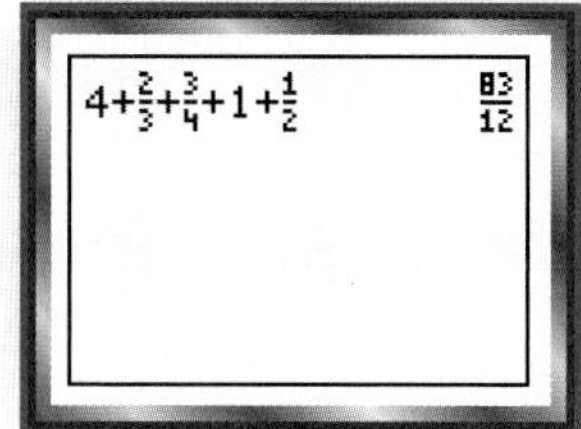

Does $\frac{83}{12}$ equal $6\frac{11}{12}$?

Check 2 Change the given fractions and the sum to decimals. The addition should check.

$4\frac{2}{3} = 4.\overline{6}$ $\frac{3}{4} = 0.75$ $1\frac{1}{2} = 1.5$ $6\frac{11}{12} = 6.91\overline{6}$

$4.\overline{6} + 0.75 + 1.5 = 6.91\overline{6}$

$6\frac{11}{12} = 6.91\overline{6}$

It checks.

Questions

COVERING THE IDEAS

1. Suppose Arthur from Example 1 decides he wants a frame that is $\frac{5}{8}$" wide. What will the dimensions of the framed picture be?
2. Write as a single mixed number.
   a. $17\frac{3}{7} + 4\frac{2}{7}$
   b. $17\frac{3}{23} + 4\frac{2}{23}$
   c. $17\frac{3}{1000} + 4\frac{2}{1000}$
   d. $17\frac{3}{y} + 4\frac{2}{y}$
3. A recipe calls for $2\frac{1}{4}$ cups of rice. A cook adds $\frac{2}{3}$ cup more. How much rice did the cook use in all?

In 4–7, write the sum as a mixed number in lowest terms. Show your work.

4. $9\frac{1}{2} + 14\frac{2}{7}$
5. $5\frac{4}{5} + 1\frac{5}{6}$
6. $2\frac{4}{100} + 1\frac{7}{10}$
7. $32\frac{8}{45} + 18\frac{8}{9}$

APPLYING THE MATHEMATICS

In 8 and 9, write the sum as a simple fraction.

8. $5\frac{7}{20} + 0.2$

9. $\frac{1}{6} + 1.5 + 1\frac{2}{9}$

10. a. Use a ruler to draw segments of length $1\frac{3}{4}$" and $3\frac{3}{4}$" as parts of one longer segment. What is the length of that longer segment?
    b. Show the addition.
    c. Check your answer to Part b by measuring.
    d. Check your answer to Part b by changing the mixed numbers and the sum to decimals.

11. Cynthia and Tyrone are cheerleaders. Cynthia is 4' 10" tall. Tyrone is 5' 9" tall. Tyrone's shoulders are 11" below the top of his head.
    a. When Cynthia stands on Tyrone's shoulders, how far is the top of her head from the ground?
    b. Check your answer to Part a by writing the heights as mixed numbers and adding them.

12. Add $3\frac{3}{10}$, $2\frac{21}{100}$, and $\frac{35}{1{,}000}$ by converting them to decimals.

13. Add $1\frac{5}{8} + 13\frac{6}{25} + 9\frac{17}{64}$ by converting each number to a decimal and then converting the answer to a fraction.

14. Consider $-1\frac{2}{3} + 1\frac{5}{6}$.
    a. Without adding, tell whether the sum is positive or negative. How can you tell?
    b. Find the sum.

REVIEW

15. A shelf is $35\frac{11}{32}$ inches long. Is this shorter or longer than $35\frac{1}{3}$ inches? **(Lesson 3-8)**

16. Add the following fractions and write the sum in simplest terms. **(Lesson 3-7)**
    a. $\frac{1}{9} + \frac{4}{9} + \frac{2}{9} + \frac{5}{9}$
    b. $-\frac{7}{12} + \frac{4}{12} + \frac{5}{12}$

17. **True or False** According to the Adding Fractions Property, $\frac{a}{b} + \frac{a}{c} = \frac{a}{b + c}$. **(Lesson 3-7)**

18. **Multiple Choice** Two angles of a triangle each have a measure of 35°. What is the measure of the third angle? **(Lesson 3-6)**

    A 20° B 35°

    C 110° D 290°

19. How many degrees are in a $\frac{3}{4}$-turn? **(Lesson 3-6)**

20. Write the addition problem and sum represented by the arrows below. **(Lesson 3-2)**

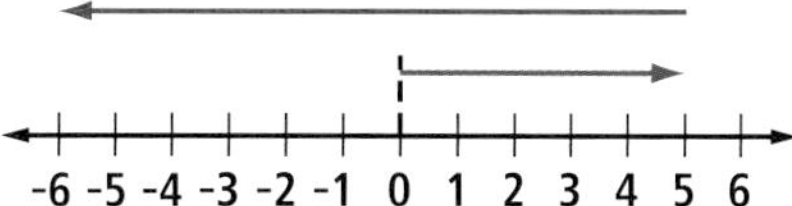

21. The number of solar power cells sold increased by 34% in one year. Is this greater than or less than an increase of $\frac{1}{3}$? **(Lesson 2-10)**

22. The Preakness, a famous horse race, is $1\frac{3}{16}$ mi long. Convert this to a decimal. **(Lesson 2-7)**

23. There are over six billion people in the world. There are six inhabited continents. What is the average number of people per continent? **(Lesson 2-4)**

24. Order $2\frac{3}{5}$, $5\frac{2}{3}$, and $3\frac{2}{5}$ from least to greatest. **(Lesson 1-8)**

Kentucky Derby winner, Street Sense, lost to Curlin at the 2007 Preakness.

Source: *Sports Illustrated*

EXPLORATION

25. Until the year 2000, stock prices were reported in fractions. In Parts a and b, convert each statement to an addition problem in dollars and cents.
   a. "Solar Company stock opened the day at $\$11\frac{1}{4}$, but closed $\$3\frac{1}{8}$ higher."
   b. "Tremble Tours started the day at $\$3\frac{1}{8}$. By midday it had gone up $\$\frac{1}{8}$. Company reports of a profitable month sent the price up $\$2\frac{3}{8}$ in the afternoon."
   c. Research to find out why the New York Stock Exchange changed from fractions to decimals in the year 2000.

QY ANSWERS

1a. $8\frac{1}{3}$

1b. $13\frac{2}{3}$

2. $12\frac{5}{8}$"

Chapter 3 Projects

1 The Harmonic Sequence

The harmonic sequence is the ordered list of numbers $1, \frac{1}{2}, \frac{1}{3}, \frac{1}{4}, \frac{1}{5}, \frac{1}{6}, \ldots$. This list goes on forever. If you add the first two numbers, or ***terms***, of the harmonic sequence, you get $1 + \frac{1}{2} = 1\frac{1}{2}$. If you add the first three terms, you get $1 + \frac{1}{2} + \frac{1}{3} = 1 + \frac{3}{6} + \frac{2}{6} = 1\frac{5}{6}$. Use technology to determine how many terms of this sequence you must add in order to get a sum greater than 2. How many terms must you add to get a sum greater than 3? Greater than 4? Greater than 5? Do you think that if you keep adding terms, you will get a sum as great as 100?

2 Casting Out Nines

"Casting out nines" is a method of checking the answers to addition problems. Find out how it works and write a description of the process. Include examples.

3 Toothpick Triangles

Given the lengths of two sides of a triangle, a and b, what are the restrictions on the length of the third side? Use toothpicks to investigate. Make as many triangles as possible using 8 toothpicks to construct the sides. Repeat the process using 12 and 15 toothpicks. Make a table listing all the triangles you are able to make. What restrictions did you discover about the length of the missing side?

4 Angles of Chairs

To measure the angle between a chair leg and the floor, consider the chair leg one ray, and the floor the other ray, with the vertex being the point where they meet. Use the smallest angle between the chair leg and the floor for your measurement.

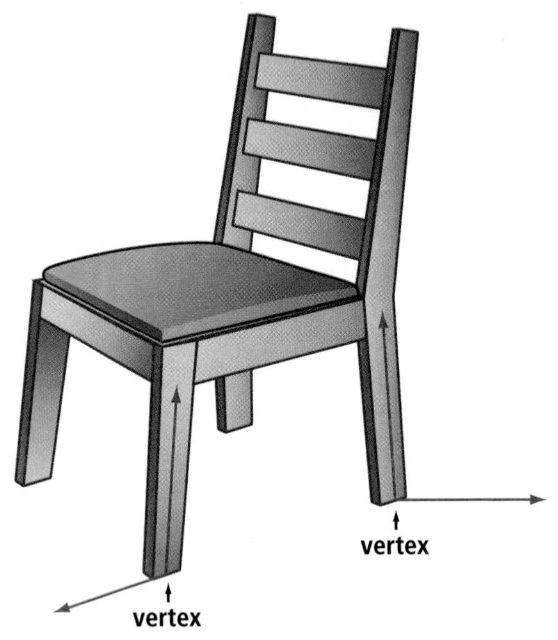

Find ten chairs of different styles. For each chair, measure the angle between a front leg and the floor. Then measure the angle between a back leg and the floor. Summarize your results.

5 Egyptian Fractions

The ancient Egyptians expressed all fractions as a sum of unit fractions (fractions with numerators of 1). So for example, they would write $\frac{3}{4}$ as $\frac{1}{2} + \frac{1}{4}$ and $\frac{2}{5}$ as $\frac{1}{4} + \frac{1}{10} + \frac{1}{20}$ (in hieroglyphics). The Egyptians also had a rule that the sum could not contain more than one of the same unit fraction. Fractions written according to these rules are called *Egyptian fractions.* A famous Egyptian fraction was often shown in its hieroglyphics as the Eye of Horus, shown below with the unit fractions labeled. The sum of these fractions is $\frac{63}{64}$. Find Egyptian fractions for ten non-unit fractions. Did you discover a good method for writing fractions in this form? Can all fractions be expressed as Egyptian fractions?

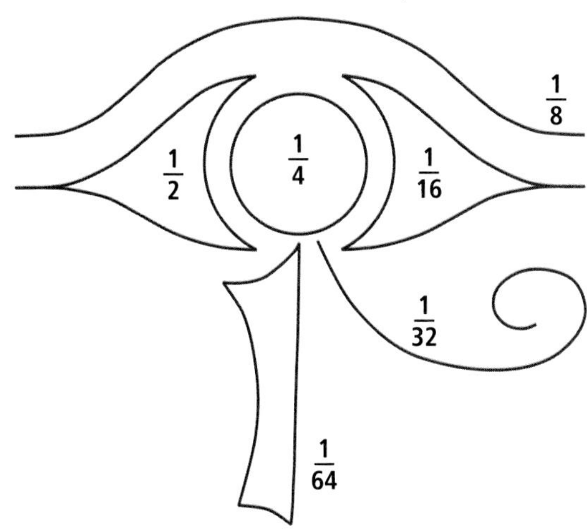

6 The Mayas

The Mayas, who are the first known people to have developed a symbol for zero, developed their own number system. Research this number system and write an essay on what you find.

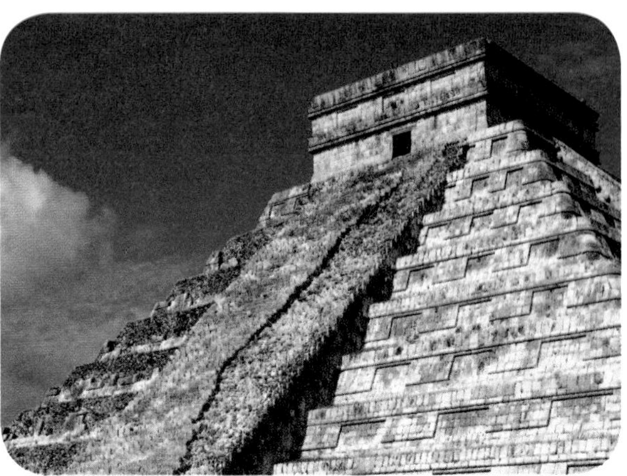

Some engineers believe the Mayas may have built their pyramids to create specific sound effects. For example, a handclap at certain pyramids will often result in a "bird chirp" echo.

Source: National Geographic

Chapter 3 Summary and Vocabulary

- The important applications of the operation of addition are mainly of two types: **putting-together** and **slide.**
- In a **putting-together situation,** a count or measure x is put together with a count or measure y. If x and y have the same units and there is no overlap, then the result has count or measure $x + y$. When the lengths of sides of a **polygon** are put together, the result is the **perimeter** of the polygon.
- In a **slide situation,** a slide x is followed by a slide y. The result is a slide $x + y$. Slides are appropriate in situations with two directions, such as changes up or down.
- **Angles** can be measured using **degrees.** One degree is $\frac{1}{360}$ of a circle. When **adjacent angles** form a **linear pair,** the sum of the measures of the angles is 180°. When the measures of all the angles around a point are put together, the sum is 360°. The sum of the measures of the angles in a triangle is 180°. From this, you can obtain the sum of measures of the angles of many polygons.
- Addition is **commutative** and **associative.** Zero is the **additive identity.** Every number has an **opposite,** or additive inverse. The sum of a number and its opposite is zero.
- Fractions with the **same denominator** are added just as you would add numbers with the same units. To add fractions with **different denominators,** you can rewrite them with the same denominator.

Theorems and Properties

Putting-Together Model for Addition (p. 138)
Commutative Property of Addition (p. 141)
Associative Property of Addition (p. 145)
Slide Model for Addition (p. 156)
Additive Identity Property of Zero (p. 159)
Additive Property of Opposites (p. 160)
Opposite of Opposites (Op-Op) Property (p. 160)
Angle Addition Properties 1, 2, and 3 (pp. 173, 174)
Triangle-Sum Theorem (p. 179)
Quadrilateral-Sum Theorem (p. 180)

Vocabulary

3-1
variable

3-2
polygon
sides
perimeter of a polygon
rectangle
integer rectangle
pentagon

3-4
additive identity
additive inverse

3-5
angle
vertex of an angle
side of an angle
degree
arc
protractor

3-6
diameter
semicircle
linear pair
adjacent angles

3-8
like denominator
unlike denominator
least common multiple
least common denominator

Chapter 3 Self-Test

Take this test as you would take a test in class. You will need a calculator and protractor. Then use the Selected Answers section in the back of the book to check your work.

1. Javier is building a fence for his chicken yard. The yard is rectangular, with length 30.5 meters and width 15.6 meters. How long must the fence be to surround the entire yard?

2. Akira wants to add a dog run against his house. The run will be 30" by 20'. How much fencing will Akira need for the three sides of the dog run?

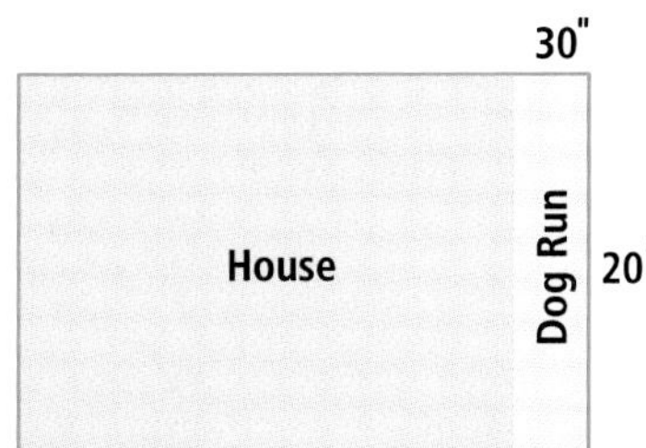

In 3 and 4, add.

3. 543 + -4,210

4. $-\frac{3}{5} + \frac{3}{5} + \frac{7}{5}$

5. The coffee shop is $3\frac{2}{3}$ miles from Shelby's home. If she runs to the coffee shop and back, how far will she have run?

6. Find the measure of $\angle SOX$, given the following information:

$$m\angle TOX = 110°$$
$$m\angle BOT = 80°$$
$$m\angle BOS = 75°$$

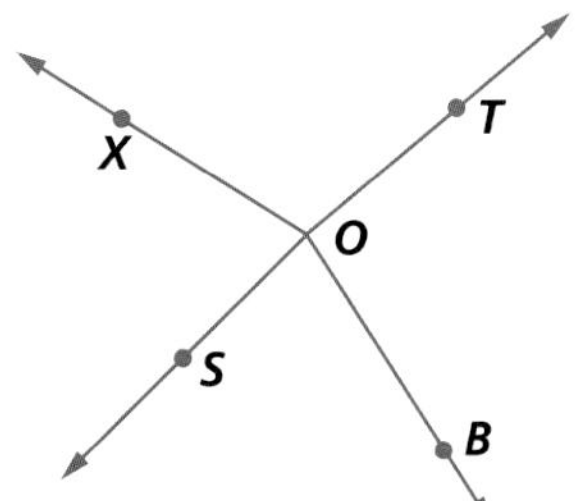

In 7–9, write the sum in simplest form.

7. $\frac{5}{7} + \frac{3}{7} + \frac{6}{7}$

8. $2\frac{7}{10} + -\frac{3}{5}$

9. $-3\frac{3}{4} + -2 + 0.75$

In 10–12, identify the property of addition.

10. $-(-(-x))) = -x$

11. $-a + a = 0$

12. $\frac{1}{4} + 5.73 + \frac{3}{4} = 5.73 + \frac{1}{4} + \frac{3}{4}$

13. Picture the following on a number line. On Friday, the temperature started at 0° and increased 13° by the afternoon, then cooled 7° by the evening.

In 14 and 15, use the angle below.

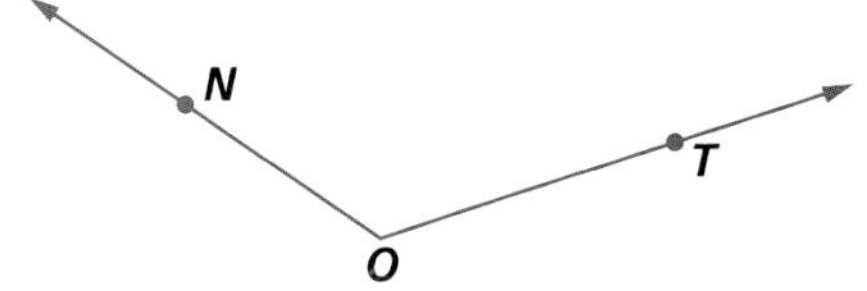

14. Name the angle in three different ways.

15. Measure the angle using a protractor.

16. Janae is 4'7" tall. She is standing 2.5 feet off the ground on a ladder. How far is it from the top of her head to the floor?

17. Picture -36 + -110 with arrows on a number line and find the sum.

18. What is the perimeter of a heptagon whose sides have lengths 6 cm, 7 cm, 13 cm, 8 cm, 2 cm, 6 cm, and 5 cm?

19. Find the perimeter of the square below.

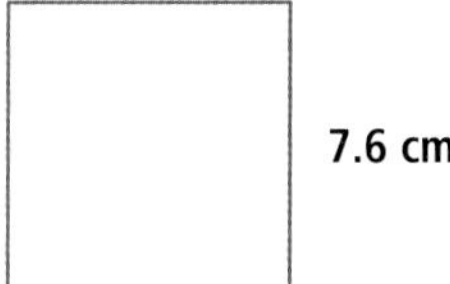

20. Reginald bought $4\frac{3}{4}$ lb of ground beef and $7\frac{1}{2}$ lb of chicken for a cookout. How many pounds of meat did he buy in all?

21. In the 2005 Tour de France bicycle race, Lance Armstrong trailed Jens Voigt by 2 minutes 18 seconds before a key stage. Armstrong finished the stage 31 minutes 41 seconds faster than Voigt. By how many minutes in all was Armstrong ahead of Voigt after this stage? Write your answer as a mixed number.

22. **Multiple Choice** $\angle LIT$ and $\angle TIP$ form a linear pair. Which could be the measures of the angles?

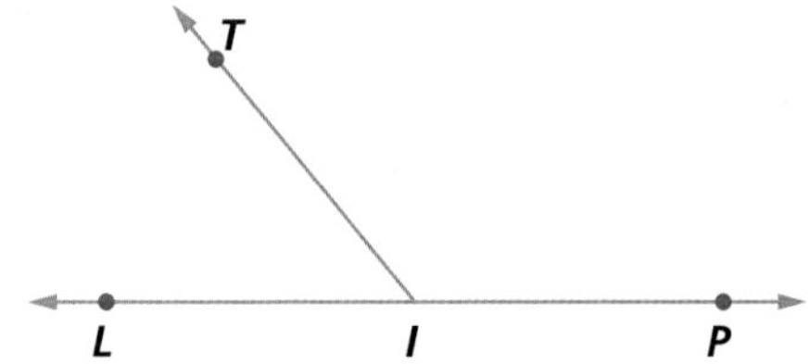

A $m\angle LIT = 50°$ and $m\angle TIP = 50°$
B $m\angle LIT = 180°$ and $m\angle TIP = 180°$
C $m\angle LIT = 50°$ and $m\angle TIP = 180°$
D $m\angle LIT = 50°$ and $m\angle TIP = 130°$

In 23 and 24, find the missing angle measure.

23.

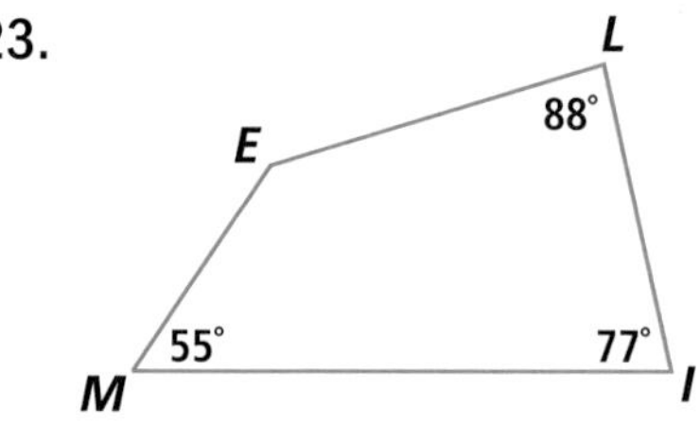

24.

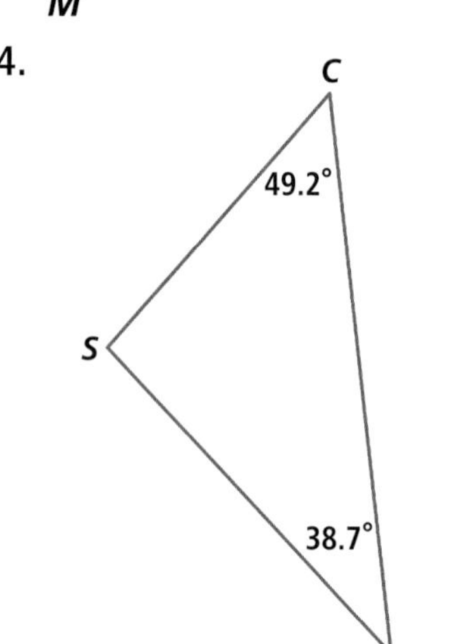

Chapter 3 Chapter Review

SKILLS
PROPERTIES
USES
REPRESENTATIONS

SKILLS Procedures used to get answers

OBJECTIVE A Find the perimeter of a polygon. (Lesson 3-2)

In 1–4, find the perimeter.

1. The figure is a rectangle.

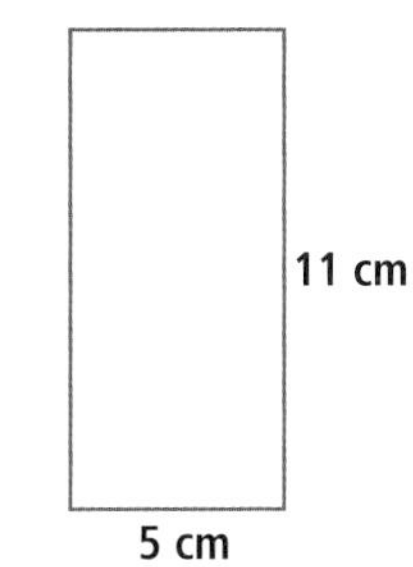

2.

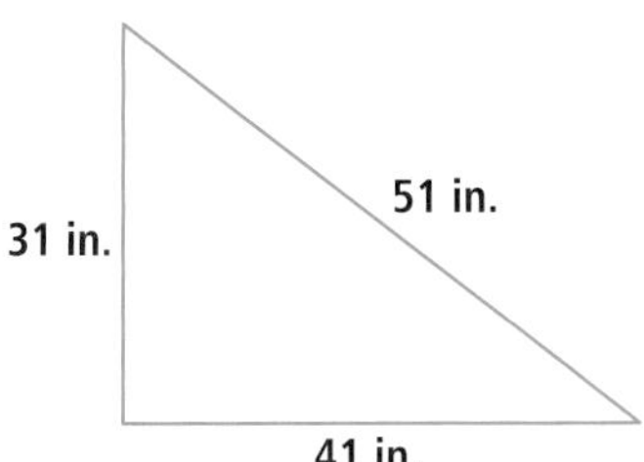

3.

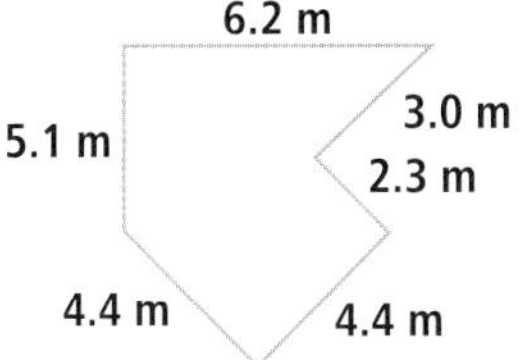

4.

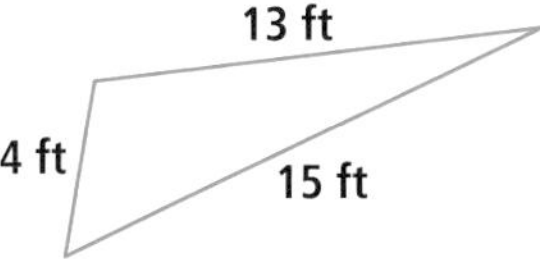

5. A square has a side length of 2.71 yards. Find the perimeter of the square.
6. A regular hexagon has 6 sides, each of which are 4 inches long. Find its perimeter.

OBJECTIVE B Add positive and negative numbers. (Lesson 3-3)

In 7–12, find the sum.

7. $-14 + 17.3 + -1$
8. $-13.2 + 15.4 + -5.4$
9. $-342 + 457 + 342 + 83 + -457$
10. $64 + -24 + 47 + -29$
11. $x + y + z + -x$
12. $15 + -2x + 2x + -18$

OBJECTIVE C Name and measure angles. (Lesson 3-5)

In 13–16, use a protractor to measure the angle in the diagram.

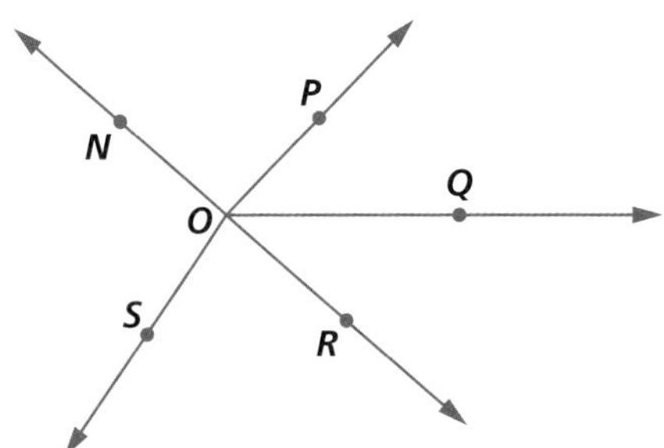

13. $\angle NOP$
14. $\angle QOS$
15. $\angle POQ$
16. $\angle ROS$

In 17 and 18, refer to the figure below.

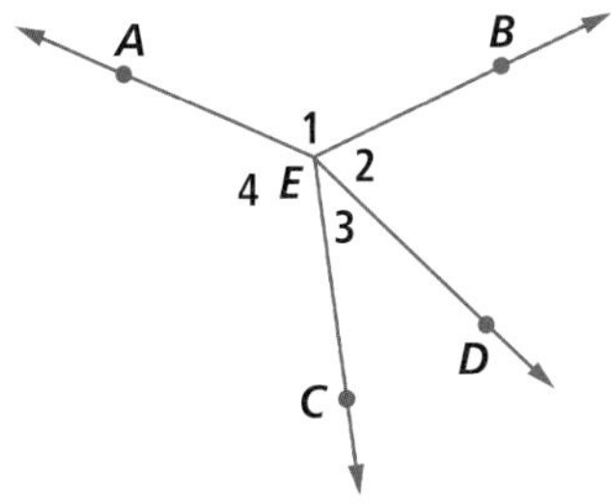

17. Give another name for $\angle 1$.
18. Give another name for $\angle 2$.

OBJECTIVE D **Add fractions and mixed numbers. (Lessons 3-8, 3-9)**

In 19–26, add and write the sum in lowest terms.

19. $\frac{4}{19} + \frac{4}{19}$

20. $\frac{31}{80} + \frac{61}{80} - \left(-\frac{13}{17}\right)$

21. $-\frac{1}{3} + \frac{1}{6}$

22. $\frac{1}{5} + \frac{3}{4} + -\frac{2}{3}$

23. $3\frac{3}{8} + 2\frac{5}{8}$

24. $4\frac{5}{6} + 5\frac{1}{6}$

25. $2\frac{7}{18} + 4\frac{5}{6}$

26. $8\frac{1}{3} + \left(-6\frac{4}{7}\right) + \frac{9}{17}$

PROPERTIES The principles behind the mathematics

OBJECTIVE E **Identify and apply the following properties of addition: Commutative Property of Addition, Associative Property of Addition, Additive Identity Property of Zero, Additive Property of Opposites, and Opposite of Opposites Property. (Lessons 3-1, 3-2, 3-4)**

In 27–30, simplify the expression and state which property you used.

27. $50 + 0$

28. $-(-(3))$

29. $-k + k$

30. $k + 0$

31. Use the Commutative and Associative Properties to add $-\frac{7}{8} + 15.2 + -\frac{1}{8} + 2.8$.

32. Simplify:
$-(-7y) + 7y + 0 + (7y + -7y) + -(-(-(-(-7y))))$.

OBJECTIVE F **Apply the properties of angle addition. (Lesson 3-6)**

In 33 and 34, refer to the circle below. $\overline{AO}$, $\overline{TE}$, $\overline{JF}$, and $\overline{BD}$ are diameters of circle C.

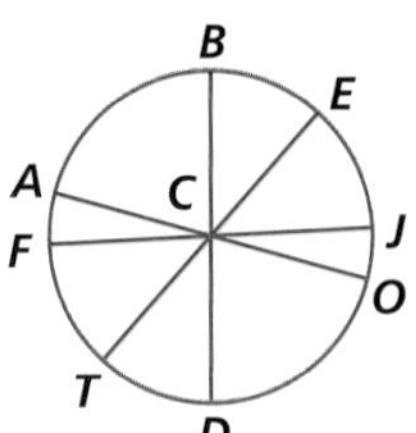

33. If $m\angle ACT = 64°$, what is $m\angle OCT$?

34. If $m\angle BCF = 95°$, what is $m\angle BCJ$?

In 35–38, refer to the circle below. The circle is divided into equal parts.

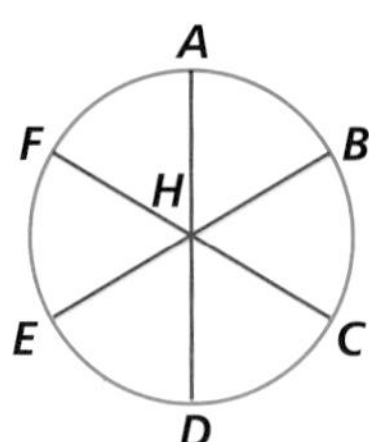

35. Find $m\overset{\frown}{AC}$.

36. Find $m\overset{\frown}{AB}$.

37. Find $m\angle AHB$.

38. Find $m\angle AHC$.

OBJECTIVE G **Apply the Triangle-Sum Theorem and the Quadrilateral-Sum Theorem. (Lesson 3-7)**

39. Find $m\angle A$ in the triangle below.

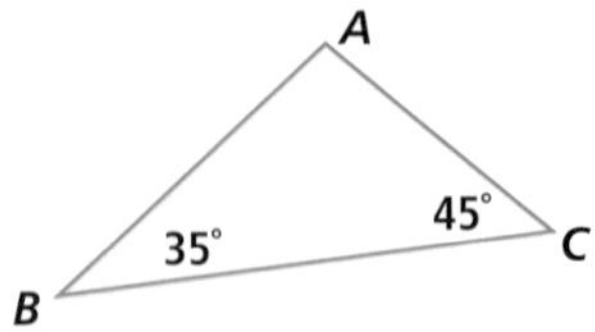

40. Find m$\angle O$ in the quadrilateral below.

USES Applications of mathematics in real-world situations

OBJECTIVE H Use fractions to add mixed numbers or numbers with mixed units in real-world situations. **(Lessons 3-1, 3-9)**

41. Alfonso rides his bike everywhere. On Tuesday, he rode $2\frac{3}{4}$ miles to school, $2\frac{1}{2}$ miles to soccer practice, and $3\frac{3}{4}$ miles home. How far did he ride his bike that day?

42. During the school day, Gloria spends 5 hours 28 minutes in class, 32 minutes at lunch, 32 minutes in advisory, and 36 minutes in the halls between periods. In hours, how long is Gloria's school day?

43. Felicia ran these distances in gym class. What was her total mileage for the week?

Day	Distance
Monday	$\frac{3}{4}$ mi
Tuesday	3,520 ft
Wednesday	1 mi, 1320 ft
Thursday	0 mi
Friday	2.5 mi

44. Keisha plans to mount curtains $\frac{1}{2}$ foot above a window frame. She wants the curtains to hang to the floor. The windows are 39 inches tall, and are 3 feet above the floor. How long (in feet) do the curtains need to be?

OBJECTIVE I Use the Putting-Together Model for Addition in real-world situations. **(Lesson 3-1)**

45. Denver is called the "mile-high city" because its elevation is 5,280 feet above sea level. If Andrea's bedroom floor is 15 feet above ground level in Denver, and her bed is 3 feet high, how far above sea level does Lori sleep at night?

46. In the Ironman Triathlon, a participant must swim 3.8 km, bike 180 km, and run 42 km. What is the total distance (in km) a participant must cover?

47. In a sprint triathlon, a participant must swim 750 meters, bike 20 km, and run 5 km. What is the total distance (in km) a participant must cover?

48. A bus leaves the terminal with 7 passengers aboard. At the first stop, d people board the bus. How many people are on the bus after the first stop?

OBJECTIVE J Add lengths in real-world situations. **(Lesson 3-2)**

49. In 1995, Inessa Kravetz of the Ukraine set a women's world record for the triple jump of 15.50 meters. When Alondra performed her best triple jump, she jumped 4.01 m, 3.84 m, and 5.29 m for the three jumps. How far is her total distance from the world record?

50. Suppose you need to tape all 12 edges of the box below. What is the least amount of tape you will need?

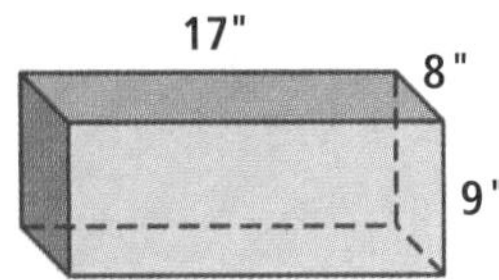

51. Hiking the Silver Knapsack Trail in Sequoia National Forest in California takes 6 days. The first day's hike has the following legs. What is the total length of the first day's hike?

Leg	Distance (mi)
The Summit Trailhead to Mountaineer Creek	1.7
Mountaineer Creek to Jacobson Meadow	2.3
Jacobson Meadow to Mowery Meadow	2.0
Mowery Meadow to Alpine Meadow	0.5

Source: National Park Service

52. Paloma bikes D miles to and D miles from the grocery store twice a week. She also bikes 3 miles each way to and from school five days per week. Write an expression for the total distance Paloma bikes in one week.

OBJECTIVE K **Use the Slide Model for Addition. (Lesson 3-3)**

53. In the 1986 Super Bowl, the New England Patriots gained a record –19 yards in the first half. In the second half, they gained 142 yards. What was their total yardage gained for the game?

54. Morgan was walking to the store 300 yards away. When she was halfway there, she realized she had forgotten her wallet and started to walk back home. After walking 100 yards, she remembered her wallet was in her pocket, so she walked back toward the store. After walking 70 yards, she looked down and realized she had dropped her scarf. She walked back 30 yards and found the scarf. How far away from the store was Morgan when she found her scarf?

55. Jack the rabbit is jumping into a strong wind. Every time he jumps, the wind pushes him backward 3 feet. He then walks forward 2 feet and jumps again. After 5 jumps and walks, where is Jack in relation to where he started?

56. In a board game, you roll a die to determine how many spaces you move. If you roll an even number, you move forward that many spaces. If you roll an odd number, you move backward that many spaces. Vanessa and Darnell start on the same space. On the first five turns, Megan rolls 3, 5, 6, 6, and 5. Darnell rolls 2, 4, 5, 2, and 2. After these five turns, who is ahead on the board? By how much is that person ahead?

REPRESENTATIONS Pictures, graphs, or objects that illustrate concepts

OBJECTIVE L **Picture addition of positive and negative numbers on a number line. (Lesson 3-3)**

In 57–60,

a. **graph on a number line using the Slide Model for Addition**

b. **give the sum.**

57. $5 + -5$

58. $4 + -8$

59. $-3 + 5 + -7$

60. $1.5 + -2.5$

In 61 and 62, represent the situation with arrows on a vertical number line, using the Slide Model for Addition. Then find the sum.

61. Tito is scuba diving. He jumps off the dive boat and descends 70 feet. Then he spots a sea turtle and slowly ascends 30 feet to get a better look. How deep is he now?

62. Javon was born weighing $7\frac{1}{4}$ pounds. At his first doctor's visit, his pediatrician announced, "Javon has gained $1\frac{3}{4}$ pounds!" The next day, Javon became sick for the first time and lost 8 ounces. What did Javon weigh after he lost the weight?

Chapter

4 Using Subtraction

Contents

As with addition, subtraction can be used to solve problems in a wide variety of situations. Here are three problems that can be solved by subtracting $15\frac{1}{2}$ from 20.

1. You buy a shirt for $15.50. You pay with a 20-dollar bill. How much change should you get?

2. A baby was $15\frac{1}{2}$ inches long at birth. At 6 months, she was 20 inches long. How much had she grown?

3. The Tigers football team gained 20 yards on one play. Then the quarterback was sacked $15\frac{1}{2}$ yards behind the line of scrimmage on the second play. What was the net gain in yardage for both plays?

Subtraction also has uses in geometric situations. It can tell you the size of one part if you know the size of a whole and the other part or parts. In each case below, the unknown amount can be found by subtraction.

Just as Chapter 3 started with models for addition, this chapter starts with models for subtraction. These models are used in a variety of applications, including geometric ones. The models also use all kinds of numbers, including decimals and fractions. At the end of the chapter, you will use addition and subtraction to solve simple algebraic equations.

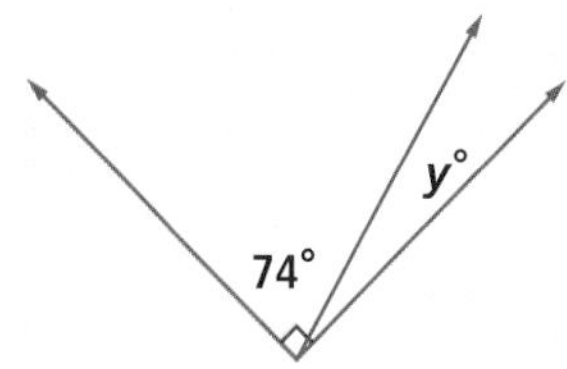

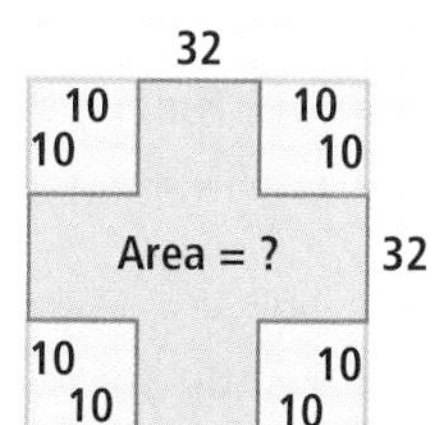

Lesson

4-1 The Take-Away Model for Subtraction

Vocabulary

minuend
subtrahend
difference

BIG IDEA The idea of taking away that you first learned for subtraction with counts can be applied to lengths, weights, times, and many other measures.

Mental Math

Calculate.

a. 4 + -3

b. -7 + 4

c. 25 + -38

d. -14 + -5

Cleveland's backpack and its contents weigh $18\frac{1}{2}$ pounds. The recommended maximum total backpack weight for someone his size is $16\frac{1}{4}$ pounds, so he removes a $2\frac{1}{2}$-pound book. Does his backpack meet the recommended maximum total now?

To answer the question, take the weight of the math book away from the total weight: $18\frac{1}{2} - 2\frac{1}{2} = 16$. Since 16 pounds < $16\frac{1}{4}$ pounds, Cleveland's backpack now meets the recommended maximum.

The general pattern of numbers in take-away situations is a basic model for subtraction.

The Take-Away Model for Subtraction

If a quantity y is taken away from an original quantity x with the same units, the quantity remaining is $x - y$.

GUIDED

Example 1

A rectangular poster measures 70 cm by 1.1 m. A solid frame 3.8 cm wide is placed over the poster. What are the dimensions of the visible part of the poster?

Solution Draw a picture. The picture shows that a 3.8 cm border takes __?__ cm away from each dimension.

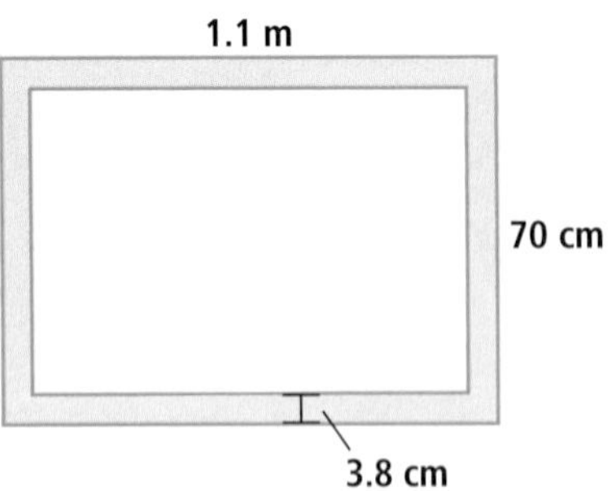

In order to use the Take-Away Model, the units must be the same. Because one of the measures is in centimeters, it is probably easier to use centimeters than meters. Convert meters to centimeters.

1.1 m = _?_ cm

The length of the poster is _?_ cm − _?_ cm = _?_ cm.

The width of the poster is _?_ cm − _?_ cm = _?_ cm.

The dimensions of the visible part of the poster are _?_ by _?_.

Example 2

According to the U.S. Census Bureau, in 2006, the population of Michigan was about 10,096,000. If *p* represents the number of people in Michigan who were 65 or older, what expression represents the number of people in Michigan under 65?

Solution To find the number of people under 65, take away the number of people 65 or older from the total population.

$$10{,}096{,}000 - p$$

QY

If there were 1,252,000 Michigan residents 65 or older, how many people under 65 were living in Michigan in 2006?

Taking a Larger Number from a Smaller Number

In a subtraction problem, the first (or top) number is called the **minuend.** The number being subtracted is called the **subtrahend.** The answer is most commonly called the **difference.**

$$\begin{array}{r l} 2.094 & \leftarrow \text{minuend} \\ -\ 0.284 & \leftarrow \text{subtrahend} \\ \hline 1.810 & \leftarrow \text{difference} \end{array}$$

In some take-away situations, the subtrahend is greater than the minuend.

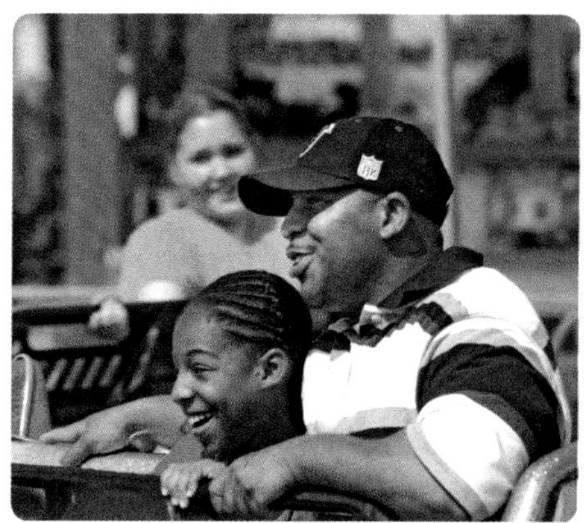

What is your favorite carnival ride?

Example 3

This year's school carnival earned a total of $5,760. The carnival committee had bills totaling $6,285 for game prizes and other supplies. How can you tell that the carnival had a deficit? How much was the deficit?

Solution Subtract what was spent from what was earned.

$$\begin{array}{r l} 5{,}760 & \leftarrow \text{minuend} \\ -\ 6{,}285 & \leftarrow \text{subtrahend} \\ \hline \end{array}$$

(continued on next page)

Because the subtrahend is greater than the minuend, the difference will be negative. This indicates a deficit. To see how much the deficit is, reverse the minuend and the subtrahend.

Original problem	Minuend and subtrahend reversed	
5,760	minuend	6,285
− 6,285	subtrahend	− 5,760
		525

The difference shows that $525 more was spent than earned. So, 5,760 − 6,285 = -525, for a deficit of $525.

Activity

Step 1 Fill in blanks in the table. (Use a calculator if necessary.)

Step 2 Look for a pattern in the two columns.

Step 3 Describe the pattern in words.

	Original Problem	Minuend and Subtrahend Reversed
	Example: 3 – 4 = –1	4 – 3 = ?
a.	6 – 2 = ?	? – ? = ?
b.	2.5 – 5 = ?	? – ? = ?
c.	? – ? = ?	6.2 – 8.1 = ?
d.	? – ? = ?	$5 - 3\frac{1}{3}$ = ?
e.	10,479 – 6,982 = ?	? – ? = ?
f.	? – ? = ?	0.003 – 0.048 = ?
g.	$17\frac{5}{8} - \frac{3}{4}$ = ?	? – ? = ?

The Opposite of a Difference Property

The general pattern in Example 3 and the Activity illustrates the *Opposite of a Difference Property.*

The Opposite of a Difference Property

For all numbers *a* and *b*, $a - b = -(b - a)$.

In words, if the minuend and subtrahend of a subtraction problem are reversed, the answer is changed to its opposite.

Order of Operations in Subtractions

Be careful when a computation has more than one subtraction. Consider this situation: Jesús had $20. He gave $5 to his sister. Then he had 20 – 5 dollars. Then he spent $4. Now he has 20 – 5 – 4 dollars.

Jesús showed this subtraction to his mother. She asked him, "Which subtraction do you do first? Does 20 – 5 – 4 mean

$(20 - 5) - 4$ or $20 - (5 - 4)$
$= 15 - 4$ $= 20 - 1$
$= 11$ $= 19$?"

You get different answers depending on which subtraction you do first. Jesús knew he had only \$11 left. Subtraction does not have an associative property. If there are no parentheses, always subtract from left to right.

Questions

COVERING THE IDEAS

1. After receiving \$16.50 for babysitting, Lamar went out and bought smoothies for everyone. If he had \$8.76 left, how much money did the smoothies cost?

The average price for a smoothie drink is \$4.

Source: Juice Zone

2. In the subtraction $2 - 1.75 = 0.25$, which number is the
   a. minuend?
   b. subtrahend?
   c. difference?

3. A picture is painted on a canvas measuring 60 cm by 40 cm. Jamila selects a frame that is 4-cm wide. What are the dimensions of the visible part of the canvas after it is framed?

4. Answer Question 3 if the picture measures 2 feet by 3 feet and the frame is 3 inches wide.

5. A wall in a kitchen is 6' long. A stove 30" wide will be placed along the wall. Cabinets will be installed along the rest of the wall. How wide will the cabinets be?

6. The sign in an elevator says the maximum weight it can carry safely is 800 pounds. Together, all the members of Albina's family weigh 928 pounds. Albina weighs 82 pounds, and her mother weighs 120 pounds. Can the rest of the family ride safely if Albina and her mother take another elevator? Justify your answer.

7. A person weighs 108 lb. Give the resulting weight if the person
   a. loses $\frac{1}{4}$ lb.
   b. loses $1\frac{1}{4}$ lb.
   c. gains 3.7 lb.
   d. loses 0 lb.
   e. loses n lb.

8. **Multiple Choice** $7\frac{1}{2} - 100\frac{3}{8} = \underline{\quad ? \quad}$

   A $-100\frac{3}{8} - 7\frac{1}{2}$ B $-\left(100\frac{3}{8} - 7\frac{1}{2}\right)$ C $-\left(7\frac{1}{2} - 100\frac{3}{8}\right)$

In 9 and 10, calculate.

9. a. $(50 - 10) - 3$ b. $50 - (10 - 3)$ c. $50 - 10 - 3$

10. a. $(4 - 17) - 17$ b. $4 - (17 - 17)$ c. $4 - 17 - 17$

APPLYING THE MATHEMATICS

11. a. **True or False** Subtraction is commutative.
    b. If you said the statement in Part a is true, give an example to support your claim. If you said it is false, give a counterexample (an example that shows the statement does not work).

12. A case of bottled water contains two dozen bottles.
    a. Travis and his friends drink four of these bottles. How many are left?
    b. Ernesto and his friends drink d of the original two dozen bottles. How many are left?

13. According to the U.S. Office of Management and Budget, the U.S. government received $2,407,300,000,000 in 2006. The government spent $2,655,400,000,000.
    a. Was there a surplus or a deficit in 2006?
    b. How much was the surplus or deficit?

14. **MATCHING** This is the first of several questions that will generate words for the quote for this chapter. Save this word for the table in Question 27 in Lesson 4-9 on page 260.
    Choose the best estimate. The letters matching the estimates form your first word.
    i. $8.28 – $10.89 ii. $1000 – $995.12
    A $3.00 B -$3.00 C $4.00 D -$4.00 E $5.00

15. A trip along the west coast of the United States from Los Angeles to Seattle took the Adams family through San Francisco and Portland. The trip is represented by the segment LW below.

L S P W
Los Angeles, CA San Francisco, CA Portland, OR Seattle, WA

Cape Blanco, Oregon

    a. If $LW = 1{,}190$ miles and $PW = 174$ miles, what other distance can you find? How many miles is this distance?
    b. If you also know that $LS = 382$ miles, find SW and SP.

16. Simplify $-(-b - a)$.

17. There are 162 games in the Major League Baseball season.
    a. If a team has a record of 51 wins and 45 losses, how many games do they still have to play?
    b. If a team has W wins and L losses, how many games in the season are left?

REVIEW

In 18–21, express the sum in lowest terms. **(Lessons 3-9, 3-8)**

18. $14\frac{5}{19} + 7\frac{3}{5}$

19. $-\frac{8}{45} + \frac{19}{25}$

20. Tina's skirt is $20\frac{3}{8}$" long. She wants to add a $\frac{3}{4}$" lace trim to the bottom. How long will the skirt be when she is done? **(Lesson 3-8)**

21. Every hour, the hour hand of a clock rotates 30°. How far will it rotate between 11:30 A.M. and 2:00 P.M.? **(Lesson 3-5)**

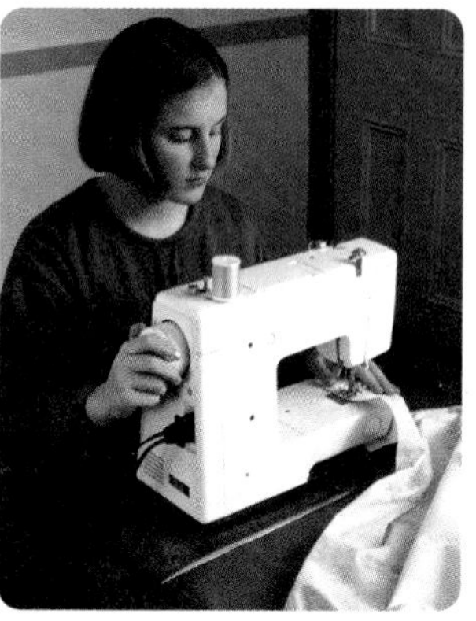

In 1818, the first American sewing machine was invented by John Adams Doge and John Knowles.

Source: International Sewing Machine Collector's Society

22. Emily tried to evaluate $-(-(-6 + 0) + 6) + 0$. She came up with a result of 0. Is this the correct value? Show all the steps necessary to evaluate this expression. **(Lesson 3-4)**

23. Sketch a circle graph from the following data. Seventy percent of students and faculty said "no" to adopting student uniforms, 5% were undecided, and the rest said "yes." **(Lesson 2-9)**

24. **Multiple Choice** Which value is closest to $2,156,906,000,000? **(Lesson 1-1)**
    A 2.2 million dollars
    B 2.2 billion dollars
    C 2.2 trillion dollars
    D 2.2 gazillion dollars

EXPLORATION

25. Here is the "same-change rule" for subtraction problems: If you add (or subtract) the same number to (or from) both the minuend and the subtrahend, the difference will not change.

$$\begin{array}{r} 5{,}907 \\ -\,3{,}698 \\ \hline \text{difference} \end{array} = \begin{array}{r} 5{,}907 + 2 \\ -\,3{,}698 + 2 \\ \hline \text{difference} \end{array} = \begin{array}{r} 5{,}909 \\ -\,3{,}700 \\ \hline 2{,}209 \end{array}$$

Subtracting 3,700 is easier than subtracting 3,698.

Show how you could change each of these problems to make the subtraction easier. Then find each difference.
    a. 189 – 97
    b. 6500 – 392
    c. 3462 – 2499
    d. 1111 – 998

QY ANSWER

8,844,000

Lesson 4-2 The Comparison Model for Subtraction

▸ **BIG IDEA** You can use subtraction to find how much bigger or smaller one number is than another.

Why do we call the answer to a subtraction problem the *difference*? It is because when subtraction is used to compare quantities that have the same unit, the answer tells by how much they differ.

Mental Math

Juice costs 50 cents. How much change should you receive if you pay with a

a. 1-dollar bill?

b. 5-dollar bill?

c. 10-dollar bill?

d. 20-dollar bill?

The Comparison Model for Subtraction

$x - y$ is how much more x is than y.

QY

The average high temperature for July 6 in Silver Spring, Maryland is 88°F. On July 6, 1990, the record high temperature was set at 100°F. How much warmer was the record than the average high?

Example 1

A contest is held to estimate the number of peanuts in a jar. Alicia guesses 1,338. Sierra guesses 1,090. Blanca guesses 1,200. If there are 1,138 peanuts, whose guess is closest?

Solution Compare each estimate to the actual number of peanuts in the jar.

1,338 – 1,138 = 200, so Alicia is 200 too high.
1,090 – 1,138 = -48, so Sierra is 48 too low.
1,200 – 1,138 = 62, so Blanca is 62 too high.
Sierra's guess is closest.

Notice in Example 1 that the subtraction not only tells by how much the estimates differ from the actual number of peanuts, but also whether an estimate is too high or too low.

Example 2

Two world records for the marathon were set in 2003. Paul Tergat from Kenya set the men's record of 2 hours, 4 minutes, 55 seconds. Paula Radcliffe from England set the women's record of 2 hours, 15 minutes, 25 seconds. How much faster is the men's marathon record?

Paul Tergat proudly displays his gold medal during the presentation ceremony at the Berlin Marathon.

Solution Subtract to compare the two times. Regroup the seconds by trading 1 minute for 60 seconds.

2 hr, 15 min, 25 sec	=	2 hr, 14 min, 85 sec
− 2 hr, 04 min, 55 sec	=	− 2 hr, 04 min, 55 sec
		10 min, 30 sec

The men's time is 10 minutes and 30 seconds faster, or $10\frac{30}{60}$ minutes faster, or $10\frac{1}{2}$ minutes faster, or 10.5 minutes faster.

Another comparison situation occurs when you want to find the amount that a quantity changed from one time to another. The quantities you are comparing can be thought of as a starting value and an ending value. The amount of change can be found by subtracting: ending value − starting value = change.

Example 3

The combined circulation of the nation's newspapers was 54,600,000 on February 1, 2005. On February 1, 2006, it was 53,300,000. What was the change?

Solution

change = ending value − starting value
= 53,300,000 − 54,600,000
= -1,300,000

The negative number indicates that the circulation went down.

So, 1,300,000 fewer newspapers were circulated in 2006 than in 2005.

Questions

COVERING THE IDEAS

1. Yolanda held her breath for 1 minute, 18 seconds. Rico held his breath for 33 seconds. How much longer did Yolanda hold her breath? Give your answer first in seconds, then in minutes.

2. The first Olympic women's marathon race was held in 1984. Joan Benoit of the United States won the race with a time of 2 hours, 24 minutes, 52 seconds. In 2004, Mizuki Noguchi of Japan won the race with a time of 2 hours, 26 minutes, 20 seconds. Which time was longer and by how much?

Joan Benoit brings home the gold for the United States.

3. Four friends estimated how many points their favorite football team would score in its next game. Mia guessed 15, Jacqueline guessed 27, Nina guessed 20, and Russell guessed 7. The team scored 23 points. Compare each guess to the actual score.

4. The first human to orbit Earth in space was Yuri Gagarin, on April 12, 1961. His flight was 1 hour, 48 minutes long.
   a. On May 5, 1961, Alan Shepard became the first American to go into space. His flight lasted 15 minutes. How much longer was Gagarin's flight?
   b. On August 6, 1961, Gherman Titov's space flight was 25 hours, 18 minutes. How much longer was Titov's flight than Gagarin's?

5. The men's individual pursuit Olympic track cycling record was set in 2004 by Great Britain's Bradley Wiggins. His time was 4 minutes, 15.165 seconds. A women's world record in the event was set by Sarah Ulmer of New Zealand. Her time was 3 minutes, 24.537 seconds. What is the difference in time between these two records?

6. The table below shows the five most widely circulated daily newspapers in the United States in 1995 and 2005. Calculate the change in circulation from 1995 to 2005 for each newspaper. Show each subtraction problem. (Be sure your answer is negative if the circulation went down.)

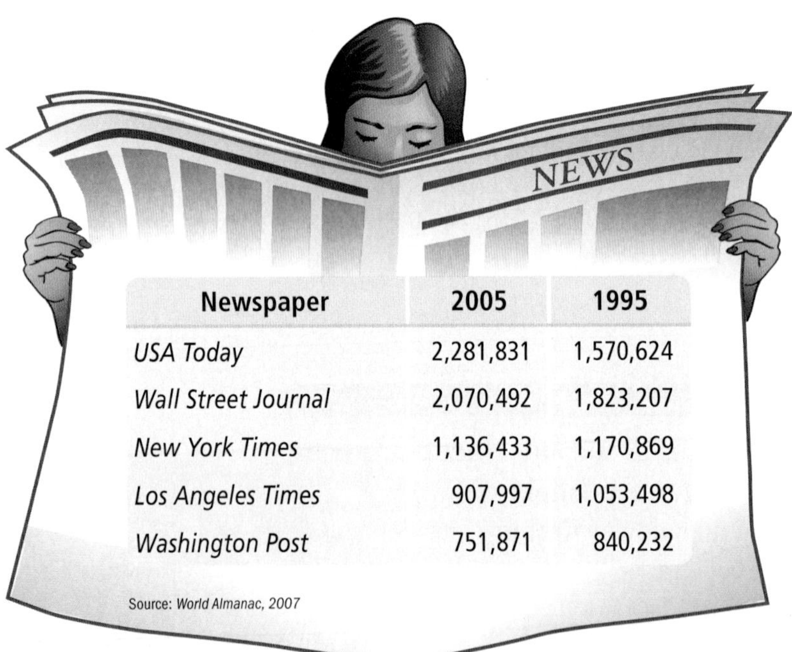

Newspaper	2005	1995
USA Today	2,281,831	1,570,624
Wall Street Journal	2,070,492	1,823,207
New York Times	1,136,433	1,170,869
Los Angeles Times	907,997	1,053,498
Washington Post	751,871	840,232

Source: *World Almanac, 2007*

APPLYING THE MATHEMATICS

7. Campers in the Grizzly Bear cabin ate seven 8-ounce packages of corn flakes. Campers in the Mountain Lion cabin ate four 15-ounce packages. Who ate more cereal? How much more?

8. Michelangelo Buonarroti and Leonardo da Vinci were two important Renaissance artists. Michelangelo was born in 1475 and died in 1564. Leonardo was born in 1452 and died in 1519. (*Hint:* There are two possible answers for Parts a and b.)
   a. How old was Michelangelo when he died?
   b. How old was Leonardo when Michelangelo was born?
   c. Who lived longer? Support your answer.

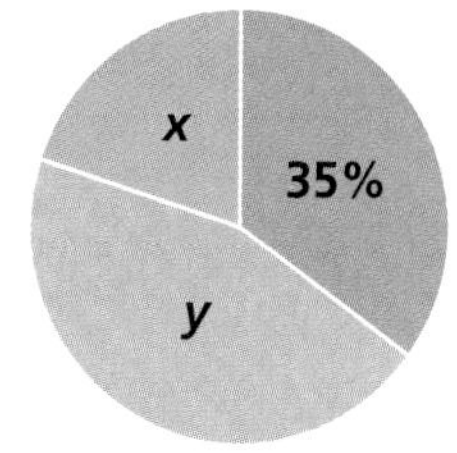

9. Examine the figure at the right. If $y - 10\% = 35\%$, what is x?

10. This table shows the air distances (in miles) between five of the largest cities in the world.

	Tokyo	Mexico City	New York	Moscow	Shanghai
Tokyo	—	7,021	6,740	4,647	1,097
Mexico City	7,021	—	2,094	6,663	8,022
New York	6,740	2,094	—	4,665	7,371
Moscow	4,647	6,663	4,665	—	4,234
Shanghai	1,097	8,022	7,371	4,234	—

Source: www.infoplease.com

   a. How far is it from New York to Mexico City? How far is it from New York to Moscow?
   b. How much closer is New York to Mexico City than to Moscow?
   c. How much farther is Shanghai from New York than from Tokyo?
   d. If you start in New York and travel to Moscow, Shanghai, Tokyo, and Mexico City, in that order, how long will the trip be?
   e. Find another route that starts in New York, flies through the other four cities, and that is longer than the route in Part d. How much longer is this route?

Moscow's sister city in the United States is Chicago. Does your city have a sister city in another part of the world?

11. A palindrome is a number that reads the same forward as it does backward, such as 101 or 2552. Harry read a book that was 317 pages long. Mollie read a book that was over 100 pages longer than Harry's. The difference in the number of pages in the two books is a palindrome. Give a possible number of pages for Mollie's book.

REVIEW

12. There are t problems in a math lesson. After you solve n of them, how many problems are left? **(Lesson 4-1)**

13. Inés was born on March 22, 1981. How many days old was she on January 1, 1982? **(Lesson 4-1)**

In the Japanese language, the word sushi means "snack."

14. Suppose you buy sushi for \$4.49 and zucchini bread for \$2.39. If you give the cashier \$7.00, how much change should you receive? **(Lesson 4-1, 3-1)**

15. Imani flew from New York to Singapore in several stages. First, she flew to San Francisco, where she waited $3\frac{1}{4}$ hours. Then she flew to Tokyo, where she waited another $2\frac{1}{2}$ hours before continuing on to Singapore. How long did she spend waiting? **(Lesson 3-8)**

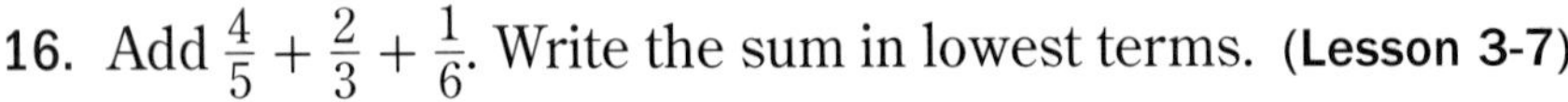

16. Add $\frac{4}{5} + \frac{2}{3} + \frac{1}{6}$. Write the sum in lowest terms. **(Lesson 3-7)**

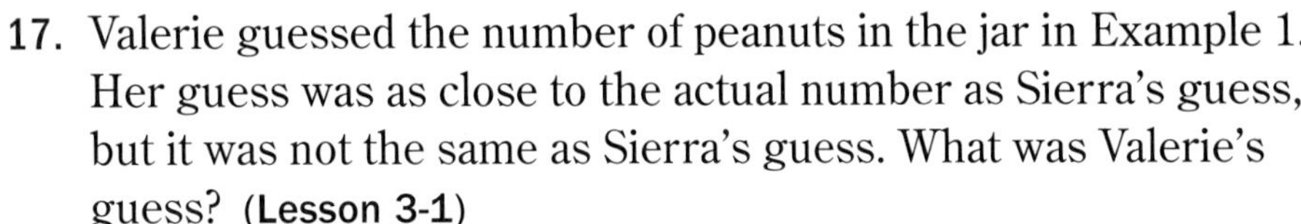

17. Valerie guessed the number of peanuts in the jar in Example 1. Her guess was as close to the actual number as Sierra's guess, but it was not the same as Sierra's guess. What was Valerie's guess? **(Lesson 3-1)**

18. Copy and complete the table. **(Lesson 2-10)**

	Fractions	Decimals	Percents
a.	?	0.32	?
b.	$\frac{3}{8}$	?	?
c.	?	?	80%
d.	?	1.25	?

In 19 and 20, round the amount to the nearest dollar. (Lesson 2-6)

19. \$53.49

20. \$4,599.98

21. Write four fractions equal to $\frac{14}{35}$. **(Lesson 1-5)**

EXPLORATION

22. a. How many whole numbers are between 10 and 20, not including 10 and 20?

    b. How many whole numbers are between 136 and 861, not including 136 and 861?

    c. How many whole numbers are between the positive integers I and J, not including I and J?

23. With some sequences, you can subtract each number from the next number until there is a common difference. For example, 1 is the common difference for the sequence 1, 4, 8, 13, and 19, as shown below.

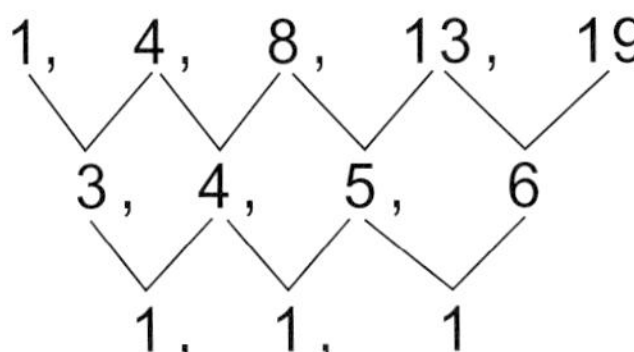

To find a word to use in the quote on page 260, start with the sequence below. The common difference tells how many letter Es are in the word. The other letters used in the word are L, N, D, W, K, O, and G.

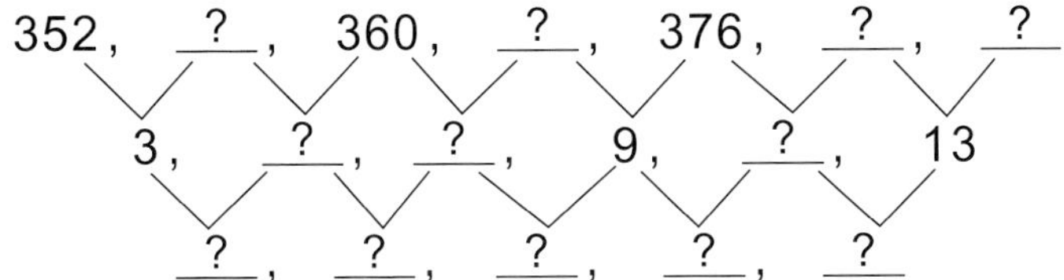

Unscramble all the letters and save the word for the table in Question 27 in Lesson 4-9 on page 260.

QY ANSWER

12°F warmer

Lesson 4-3 The Slide Model for Subtraction

BIG IDEA In a subtraction problem, you can think of the subtrahend as a slide of the minuend along a number line.

One December morning in Fargo, North Dakota, the temperature was 4°F. By noon, the temperature had fallen 6°F. This situation can be pictured on a number line. Start at 4 and move left 6 units.

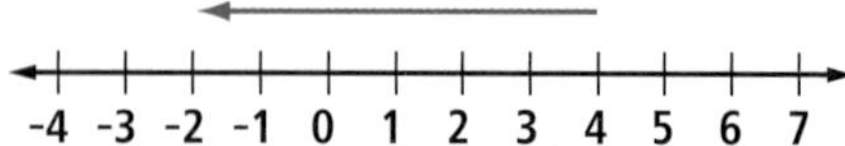

The resulting temperature is 2 degrees below zero, or -2°F.

You can also find the resulting temperature by computing 4 − 6. This situation is an example of the *Slide Model for Subtraction.*

Mental Math

a. How much more is 4 than 2?

b. How much more is 6 than 2?

c. How much more is 1 than 2?

d. How much more is –3 than 2?

The Slide Model for Subtraction

If a quantity x is decreased by y, the resulting quantity is $x - y$.

Recall that there is a slide model for addition. Results of sliding *up* are found by adding a positive number. Results of sliding *down* can be found either by adding a negative number or by subtracting a positive number.

Example 1

A hamster weighing 167 grams loses 19 grams. What is its new weight?

Solution 1 By subtraction: 167 − 19 = 148

Solution 2 By addition: 167 + -19 = 148

The hamster's new weight is 148 grams.

Running is a natural instinct for hamsters. That is why they love exercise wheels!

GUIDED

Example 2

The temperature in a freezer was -11° Celsius. After the temperature control was changed, it dropped 8°C. What is the current temperature?

Solution 1 By subtraction: ___?___ – ___?___ = ___?___

Solution 2 By addition: ___?___ + ___?___ = ___?___

The current temperature is ___?___.

These examples show a relationship between subtraction and addition. The formal name is the *Algebraic Definition of Subtraction.* It is also called the *Adding Opposites Property of Subtraction,* or the *Add-Opp Property* for short.

Algebraic Definition of Subtraction (Add-Opp Property)

For any numbers x and y, $x - y = x + -y$.

In words, subtracting y is the same as adding the opposite of y.

QY1

a. Write the Add-Opp Property when $x = 5$ and $y = 3$.
b. Write the Add-Opp Property when $x = 2$ and $y = -10$.

You can use the Add-Opp Property to write a subtraction problem as an addition problem. It is very useful when the subtrahend is negative.

Example 3

The record low temperature for Juneau, Alaska is –22°F. The record low temperature for Indianapolis, Indiana is –27°F. Which city has the lower record low temperature, and by how much?

Solution On a number line, –27 is to the left of –22.
Indianapolis has a lower record low temperature.

-30 -29 -28 -27 -26 -25 -24 -23 -22 -21 -20

Subtract to compare the temperatures. Use the Add-Opp Property.

$$-27 - -22 = -27 + -(-22) = -27 + 22 = -5$$

The difference of –5 indicates that Indianapolis's record low temperature is 5°F lower than Juneau's.

Glacier trekkers ascend Mendenhall Glacier in Juneau, Alaska. Did you know that Juneau is only accessible by air or sea?

In Example 3, suppose you had subtracted in the other order.

$$-22 - -27 = -22 + -(-27) = -22 + 27 = 5$$

The difference of 5° tells you that Juneau's record low temperature is 5° higher than Indianapolis's.

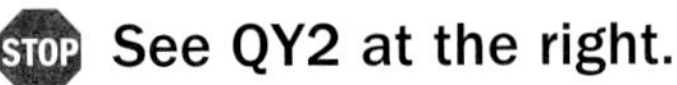
See QY2 at the right.

QY2

Rewrite each subtraction problem as an addition problem. Find the value.

a. –10 – –3

b. 15 – –6

Adding Several Numbers

Suppose you are given many numbers to add or subtract. Since subtraction does not have a commutative or associative property, you can start by using the Add-Opp Property to change subtractions to additions. Then you can rearrange numbers using the Commutative and Associative Properties of Addition.

GUIDED

Example 4

Simplify -7 — 18 — -5 — -25 — 8 — -1

Solution Start with the original expression.

-7 – 18 – -5 – -25 – 8 – -1

Convert all subtractions to additions.

= -7 + _?_ + _?_ + 25 + _?_ + _?_

Use the Commutative Property of Addition to rearrange the expression so that all negative numbers are together.

= -7 + _?_ + _?_ + 5 + 25 + 1

Use the Associative Property of Addition to group negatives together and group positives together.

= (-7 + _?_ + _?_) + (_?_ + _?_ + _?_)

Find the sum.

_?_ + _?_ = _?_

Uses of the – and - Signs

You have learned three uses of the – and - signs. Each has a different English word. Using the correct word helps make sense of the expression. For example, -11 — -*k* is read "negative eleven minus the opposite of *k*."

Where is — or - sign found?	Example	In English
Between numbers or variables	3 – 8	*3 minus 8*
In front of a positive number	-8	*negative 8*
In front of a variable or negative number	-*p* -(-6)	*opposite of p* *opposite of negative 6*

Now you can play *Top-It: Integer Subtraction*. The direction for this game are on page G16 in the book of your book.

Questions

COVERING THE IDEAS

1. Draw a number line and represent 3 – 5 using arrows.
2. State the Slide Model for Subtraction.

In 3 and 4, a question is given.

a. **Write a subtraction problem that will answer the question.**

b. **Write an addition problem that will answer the question.**

c. **Answer the question.**

3. The average November high temperature in Cheyenne, WY is 45°F. This average drops by 7° in December. What is the average December high temperature?
4. Team A lost 24 yards due to penalties. Team B lost 15 yards more than Team A lost. How many yards did Team B lose?

Cheyenne is the capital of Wyoming.

In 5 and 6, fill in the blanks.

5. $-68 - -17 = -68 + \underline{\ ?\ }$
6. $-p - -b - j = \underline{\ ?\ } + \underline{\ ?\ } + \underline{\ ?\ }$

APPLYING THE MATHEMATICS

7. The temperature is -19°C. What will the temperature be in each situation? Show the change as a slide on a number line.

   a. It falls 9°C.　　b. It rises 9°C.

In 8–13, simplify.

8. $-4 - 2$
9. $3.4 - -6.1$
10. $40 - 30 - 25$
11. $-803 + 461 - 212 - -68$
12. $6 + -8 + 5 + -12 + 0 + -1$
13. $-\frac{1}{2} - \frac{1}{3} + \frac{1}{4}$
14. Let $x = 25$ and $y = -10$. Give the value of each expression.

    a. $x - y$　　b. $y - x$　　c. $y - -x$

15. Anna has rewritten three subtraction problems as addition problems in the following way:

$$-4 - 8 = 4 + -8$$

$$-13 - -12\tfrac{1}{2} = 13 + 12\tfrac{1}{2}$$

$$47 - -20.5 = -47 + 20.5$$

   a. Anna wants to make sure she understands the Add-Opp Property. What would you tell Anna?

   b. Rewrite any equation that needs to be corrected.

16. Use a calculator to evaluate $-2\frac{2}{3} - -\frac{1}{6}$. What was your key sequence?

17. The top dot plot below shows a day's earnings (in dollars) of 7 taxicab drivers. The bottom dot plot shows the net earnings after the taxicab company deducted its daily service fee.

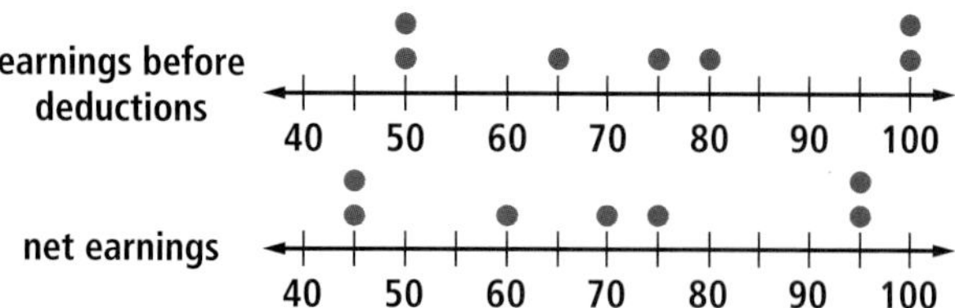

a. If a driver earned $150 before the fee was deducted, what would be the driver's net earnings?

b. Write an expression for the net earnings if m was earned by the driver before the fee was deducted.

Hailing a cab is easy in a large city such as New York.

18. The table below shows estimated populations of North Dakota for 2003–2006.

Year	State Population
2006	635,867
2005	634,605
2004	636,308
2003	633,837

Source: North Dakota State Data Center

a. Calculate the change from one year to the next.

b. Add the three numbers from Part a. What does the sum mean?

19. The absolute temperature scale uses the unit kelvins (K). Zero kelvins is called "absolute zero" because it is the temperature at which matter contains no heat, and all molecular motion stops. Absolute zero is about -273° Celsius.

Kelvins	Celsius	Letter
0	-273°C	G
273	0°	I
373	100°	H
383	?	T
100	?	N
300	?	S
d	?	

a. Copy and complete the table. (*Hint:* You can use a slide model to convert Celsius temperatures to kelvins.)

b. Below is a table with intervals of Celsius temperatures. In each blank, place the letter from Part a that corresponds to a temperature in the interval. Save the word formed by the letters for the table in Question 27 in Lesson 4-9 on page 260.

?	?	?	?	?	?
105 to 125	95 to 105	−10 to 10	−200 to −10	−283 to −263	15 to 50

REVIEW

20. Erik and Derek are fraternal (not identical) twins. Erik is 5'3" tall and weighs 105 lb. Derek is 5'1" tall and weighs 120 lb. **(Lesson 4-2)**
    a. Who is taller? By how much?
    b. Who is heavier? By how much?

Fraternal twins are born about twice as frequently as identical twins.

21. Every April 1, Marcie does spring cleaning. This year, she had B old magazines in her basement and took R of them to be recycled. How many did she keep? **(Lesson 4-1)**

22. Both Rita and Fidel brought egg salad to their company's picnic. Rita brought 75 ounces. Fidel brought 40 ounces. **(Lessons 3-8, 1-4)**
    a. How many *pounds* of egg salad did each bring?
    b. How many pounds of egg salad did they bring in all?

23. Raven and Dante are twins. At birth, Raven weighed 5 pounds, 10 ounces and Dante weighed 5 pounds, 8 ounces. **(Lesson 3-1)**
    a. What was the combined weight of the twins at birth?
    b. What was their combined weight in ounces?

In 24–26, fill in the blank. (Lessons 3-1, 1-1)

24. $10{,}000{,}000 + 30{,}000 + 60 = \underline{\ ?\ }$
25. $13{,}400 = 10{,}000 + \underline{\ ?\ } + 400$
26. $708{,}580 = \underline{\ ?\ } + 8{,}000 + 500 + 80$

27. **Multiple Choice** Which number has a 3 in the ten-thousandths place? **(Lesson 2-1)**
    A 0.72293 **B** 0.030303 **C** 0.323232 **D** 0.34513613

EXPLORATION

28. a. Find the hottest and coldest temperatures ever recorded in your community.
    b. What is the difference between those temperatures?

QY ANSWERS

1a. $5 - 3 = 5 + -3$

1b. $2 - -10 = 2 + -(-10)$ or $2 - -10 = 2 + 10$

2a. $-10 + 3 = -7$

2b. $15 + 6 = 21$

Lesson 4-4 Fact Triangles and Related Facts

Vocabulary

related facts

fact triangle

▸ **BIG IDEA** Whenever two numbers *a* and *b* add to a number *c*, then $c - b = a$ and $c - a = b$.

Putting Together and Taking Away

There are 12 boys and 11 girls in a class. Putting them together gives 23 students in the class. If you take away 12 from 23, you have 11. If you take away 11 from 23, you have 12. The Putting-Together Model for Addition and the Take-Away Model for Subtraction are related models. They produce four equations that we call **related facts.**

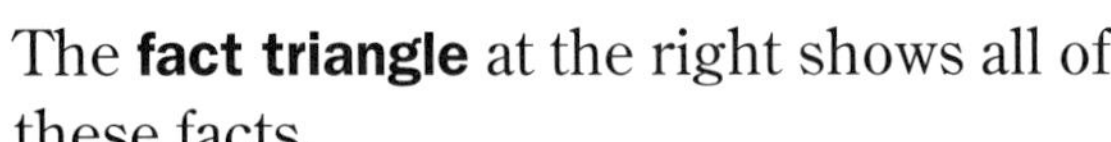

$11 + 12 = 23$ $\quad$ $12 + 11 = 23$

$23 - 11 = 12$ $\quad$ $23 - 12 = 11$

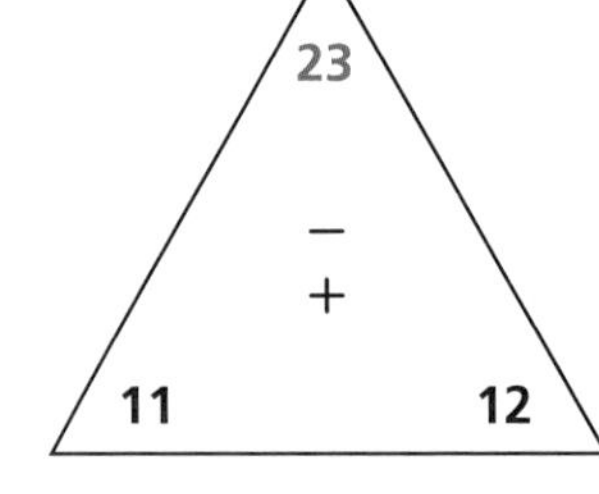

The **fact triangle** at the right shows all of these facts.

The + and − signs indicate that this is an addition and subtraction triangle. The number in the shaded corner is the sum of the other two numbers: $11 + 12 = 23$ and $12 + 11 = 23$. The subtraction equations begin at the top of the triangle and move down either side to a bottom corner and then across the bottom to the third corner. Thus, the triangle also pictures $23 - 11 = 12$ and $23 - 12 = 11$.

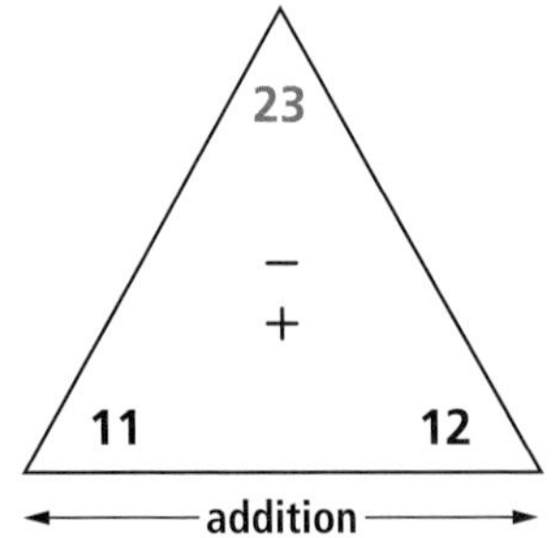

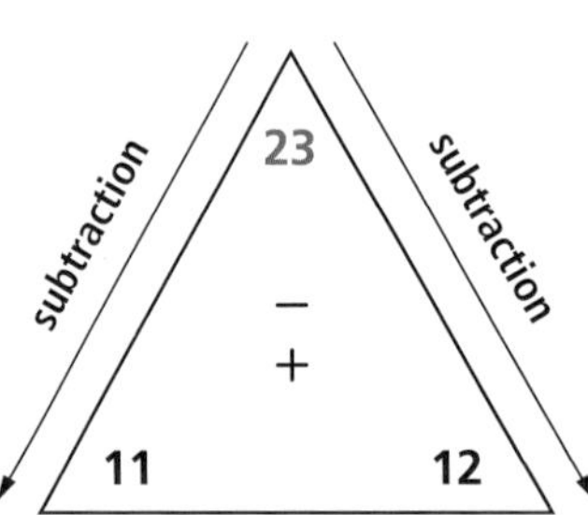

QY

a. Write four addition and subtraction facts relating 40, 50, and 90.

b. Draw a fact triangle showing these facts.

Addition and subtraction have related facts regardless of whether numbers are represented as whole numbers, fractions, or decimals.

Mental Math

A scale holding a box of weights reads 100 kilograms.

a. A 7-kg weight is removed. How much does the scale read?

b. Next, a 12-kg weight is removed. How much does the scale read?

c. Then, a 21-kg weight is removed. How much does the scale read?

d. The 3 weights removed are placed on an empty scale. How much will the scale read?

Example 1

A wooden box weighs 1.42 kg. The box is full of bolts. The total weight of the box and the bolts is 15.6 kg.

a. How much do the bolts weigh?

b. Use a fact triangle to check your work.

Most car tires are fastened with just four bolts.

Solution

a. This is a take-away situation, so subtract 15.6 − 1.42. When you subtract decimals, you may want to have the same number of digits to the right of the decimal point.

$$\begin{array}{r} 15.6 \\ -1.42 \\ \hline \end{array} \quad \text{is the same as} \quad \begin{array}{r} 15.60 \\ -1.42 \\ \hline 14.18 \end{array}$$

The bolts weigh 14.18 kg.

b. Make a fact triangle. Remember that the sum goes at the top of the triangle. 15.6 kg is the sum of the weights of the box and the bolts.

Does 1.42 + 14.18 = 15.6? It does.

The answer 14.18 checks.

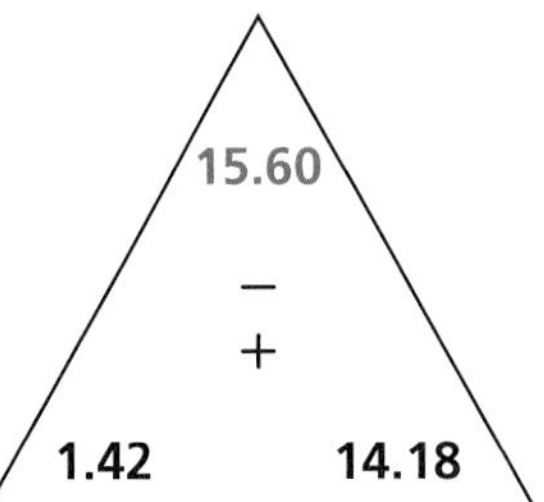

Activity

Use the fact triangle below to complete the table. First find *K*. Then arrange the sums or differences from least to greatest to form a word. Save this word for the table in Question 27 in Lesson 4-9 on page 260.

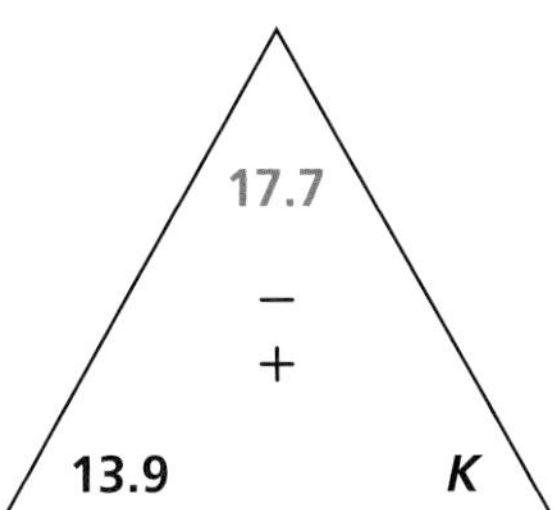

? + ? = ?	D
? − 13.9 = ?	M
? − 3.8 = ?	A
17.7 + 13.9 + *K* = ?	E

Fact Triangles with Negative Numbers

Fact triangles can be used with negative numbers as well as positive numbers. Consider the following example.

GUIDED

Example 2

The summit of Mt. Everest is about 8,848 meters above sea level. In contrast, the Dead Sea is about 418 meters below sea level.

a. What is the difference in elevation between these two locations?

b. Show the related facts for the computation of Part a.

(continued on next page)

Solution

a. This is a comparison model example using a negative number.

8,848 – __?__ = __?__

Mount Everest is __?__ meters above the Dead Sea.

b. The related facts are shown below.

__?__ + __?__ = __?__   __?__ + __?__ = __?__

__?__ – __?__ = __?__   __?__ – __?__ = __?__

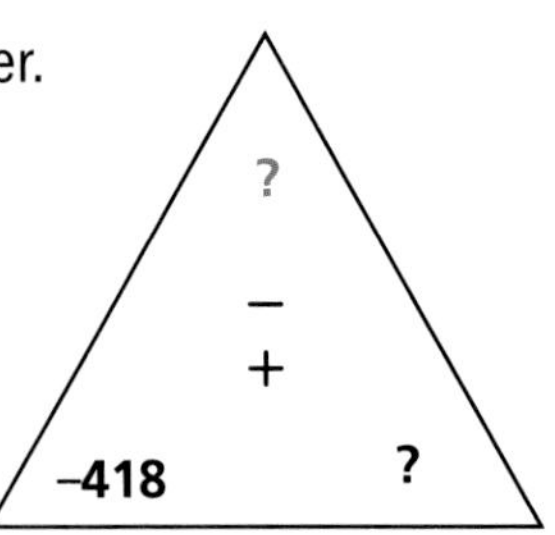

Questions

COVERING THE IDEAS

1. Give the four related facts from the fact triangle at the right.

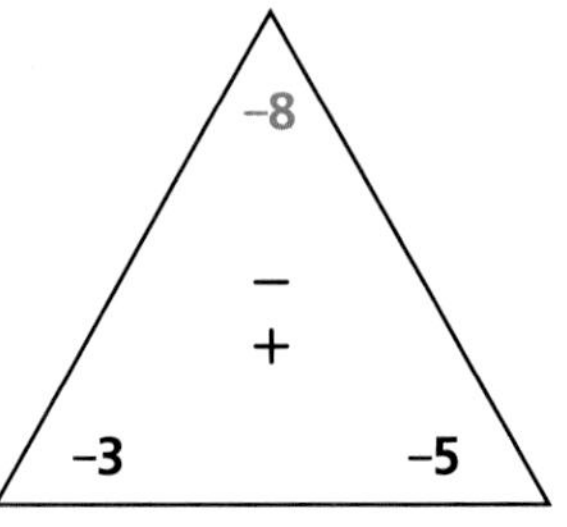

In 2–5, construct an addition and subtraction fact triangle from the given numbers, and write the four related facts.

2. 126, 133, -7
3. $\frac{3}{5}, \frac{7}{10}, \frac{13}{10}$
4. -19, -16, 3
5. 61, -29, 32

In 6–8, find the missing quantity. Use related facts if that will help.

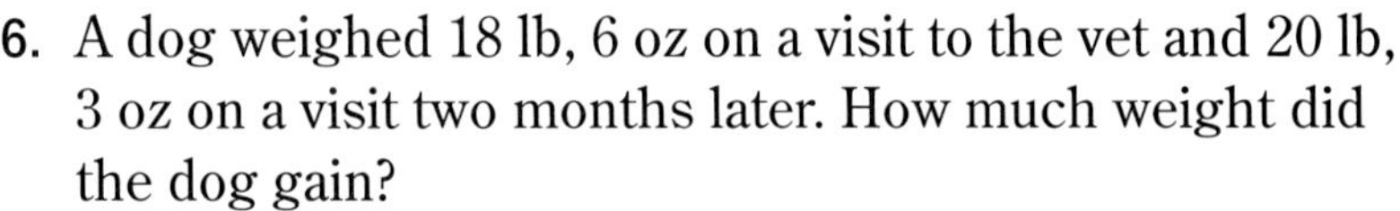

6. A dog weighed 18 lb, 6 oz on a visit to the vet and 20 lb, 3 oz on a visit two months later. How much weight did the dog gain?

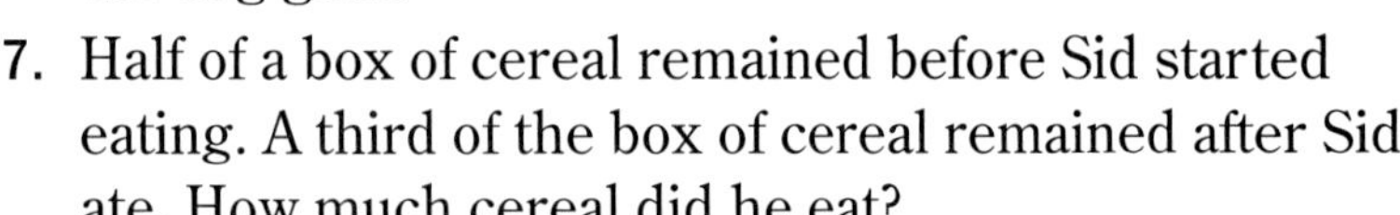

7. Half of a box of cereal remained before Sid started eating. A third of the box of cereal remained after Sid ate. How much cereal did he eat?

Dalmations typically weigh between 40 to 70 pounds.

Source: www.dogbreedinfo.com

8. On Feb. 27, 2007, the Dow Jones stock market index plunged 416.02 points to 12,216.24. What was the value of the index before the plunge?

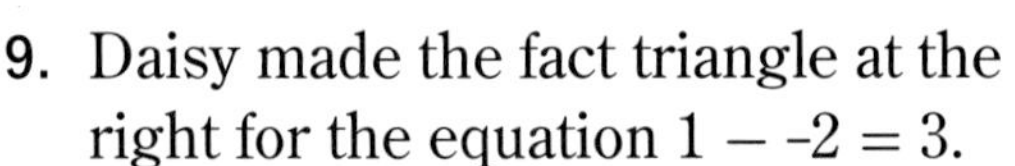

9. Daisy made the fact triangle at the right for the equation 1 – -2 = 3.
   a. What did Daisy do wrong?
   b. Write the correct fact triangle for 1 – -2 = 3.

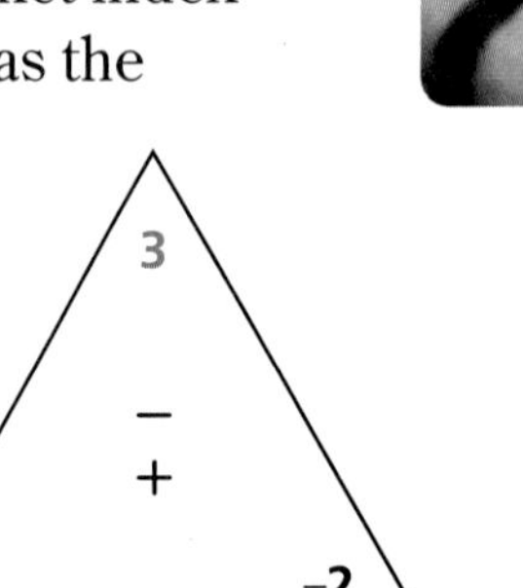

APPLYING THE MATHEMATICS

In 10–13, determine whether the difference is correct by using a related addition fact. If the difference is incorrect, correct it.

10. $\begin{array}{r} -486 \\ - \ -297 \\ \hline -289 \end{array}$

11. 6.4 – 0.22 = 0.420

12. $4\frac{1}{5} - \frac{1}{3} = 3\frac{13}{15}$

13. -46 – (11) = -57

14. At the right, $\angle FQP$ and $\angle NQP$ form a linear pair, with $m\angle FQP = 172°$, and $m\angle PQN = x°$.

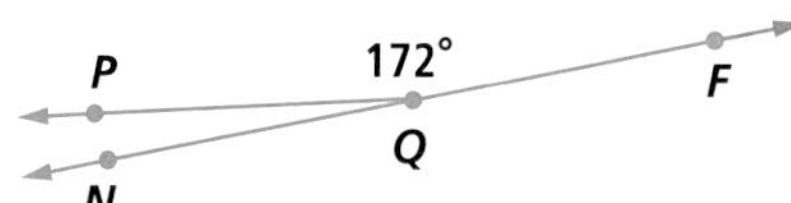

a. Write an addition equation using the Angle Addition Property for linear pairs.

b. Write the related facts.

15. **Multiple Choice** Suppose x, y, and z are three numbers and $x + y = z$. Make a fact triangle to help you decide which of the following are always true. (There may be more than one.)

A $y - x = z$ B $y + x = z$ C $z - y = x$ D $z + y = x$

E $y - z = x$ F $z + x = y$ G $z - x = y$ H $x - z = y$

REVIEW

In 16 and 17, evaluate. (Lesson 4-3)

16. 7 + -5 – -5 + -7

17. 13 – 7 + -8 – -4

18. Team A scored 12, 14, 17, and 19 points in the four quarters of a basketball game. Team B scored 22, 8, 11, and m points. Team B lost by 5 points. What is the value of m? (Lesson 4-2)

19. Ruth has a tiny backyard, but she has a garden, a path, and a kiddie pool for her son. In the diagram, each small square represents one square foot. (Lesson 4-1)

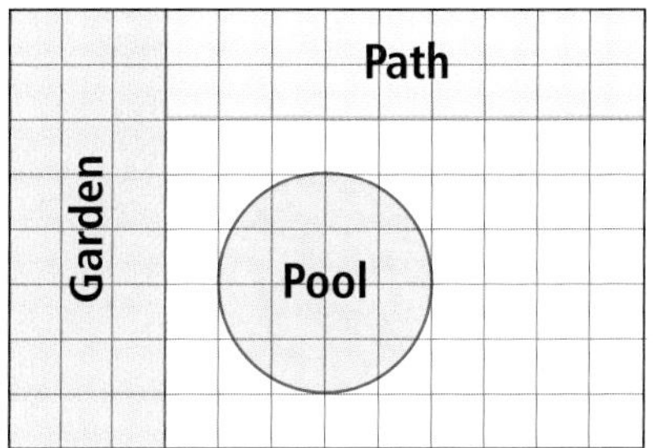

a. Estimate the area of the pool.

b. Ruth decided to put down sod in the part of her yard that is not a garden, path, or pool. How much sod does she need?

20. **Multiple Choice** Pine Street, Main Street, and Lemon Avenue intersect as shown in the diagram below. Which of the following must be true? (Lesson 3-6)

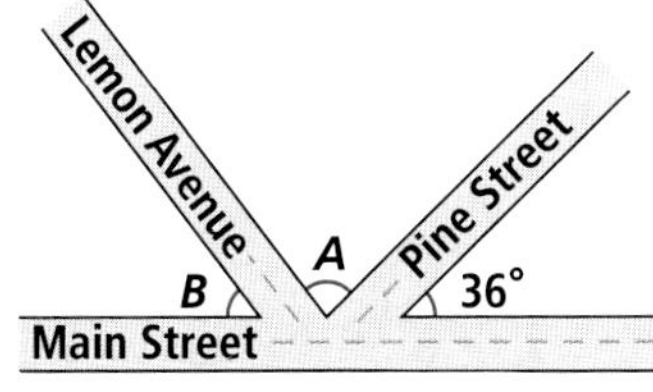

A $m\angle A + m\angle B + 36° = 360°$ B $m\angle A + m\angle B = 180°$

C $m\angle A + m\angle B + 36° = 180°$ D $m\angle A + 36° = 180°$

EXPLORATION

21. Gene thinks that if three numbers are in an addition and subtraction fact triangle, then the opposites of the three numbers can also be in a fact triangle in the corresponding positions. Is Gene right? Why or why not?

QY ANSWERS

a. 40 + 50 = 90
50 + 40 = 90
90 – 50 = 40
90 – 40 = 50

b.

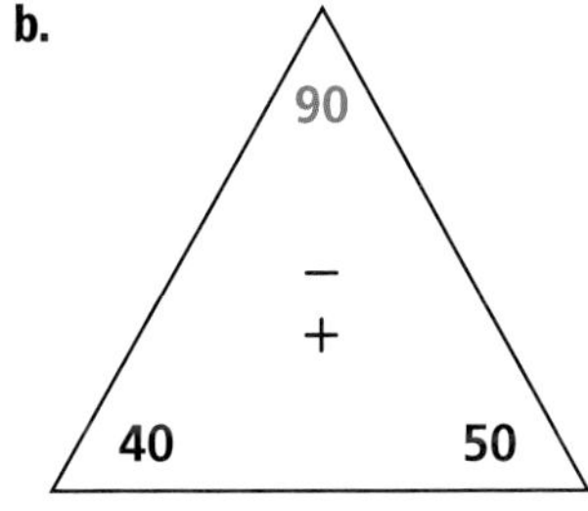

Lesson 4-5 Angles and Subtraction

Vocabulary

supplementary angles
vertical angles
bisect

BIG IDEA Because addition and subtraction facts are related, the Angle Addition Properties lead to situations involving subtraction of angle measures.

Recall the three angle addition properties from Lesson 3-6.

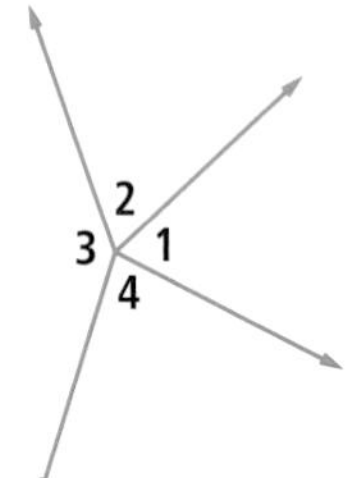

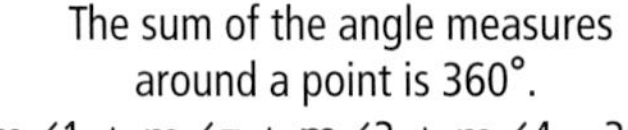

The sum of the angle measures around a point is 360°. ($m\angle 1 + m\angle z + m\angle 3 + m\angle 4 = 360°$).

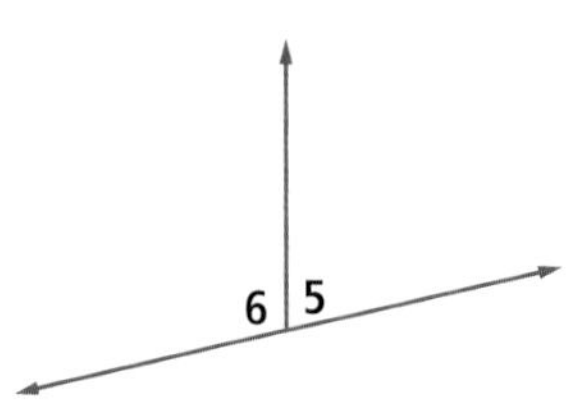

The sum of the angle measures in a linear pair is 180°. ($m\angle 5 + m\angle 6 = 180°$)

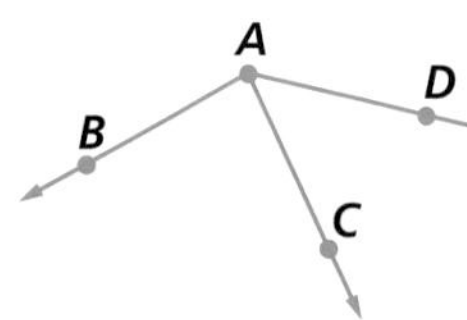

If $\overrightarrow{AC}$ is between $\overrightarrow{AB}$ and $\overrightarrow{AD}$, then $m\angle BAC + m\angle CAD = m\angle BAD$.

Because of the relationship between addition and subtraction, you can use subtraction to find the missing angle measure in a linear pair.

Mental Math

Find the missing angle measures.

a.

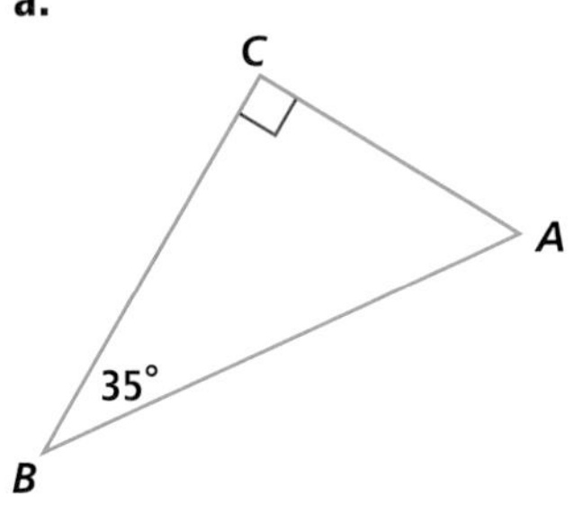

b.

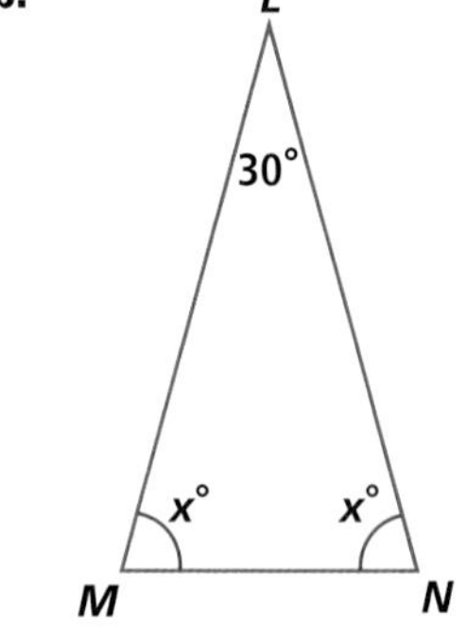

Activity 1

Copy and complete the table. Refer to the linear pair below.

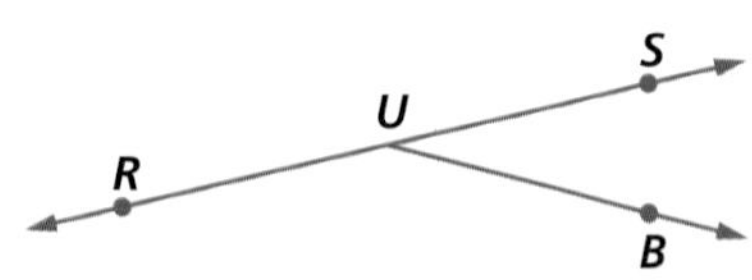

	$m\angle SUB$	$m\angle RUB$	$m\angle SUB + m\angle RUB$
a.	50°	?	180°
b.	?	125°	180°
c.	72°	?	?

Example 1

Archeologists make measurements to compare pyramids from different civilizations. To compare steepness, they measure the angle that the side of the pyramid makes with the ground. Since a pyramid is built from stone, the inside angle measurement cannot be made directly. The measure of the outside angle of the Pyramid of the Sun in Mexico is approximately 147.5°. What is the measure of the inside angle?

The Pyramid of the Sun is the third largest pyramid by volume in the world.

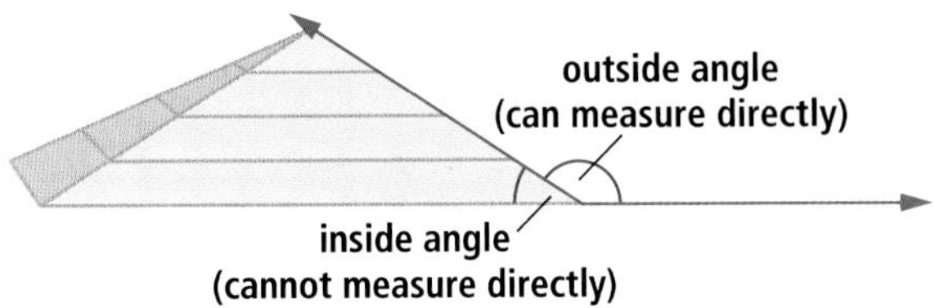

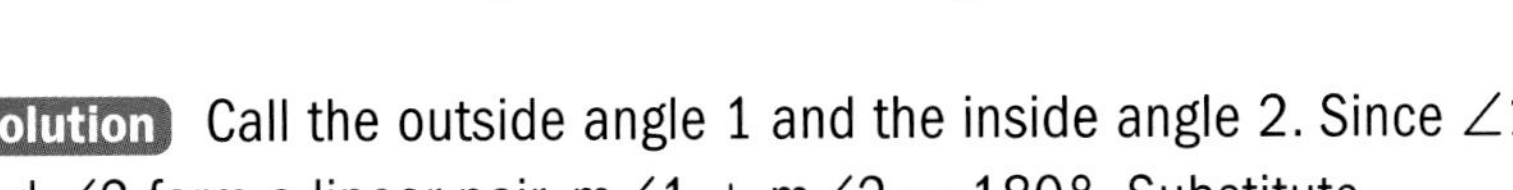

Solution Call the outside angle 1 and the inside angle 2. Since $\angle 1$ and $\angle 2$ form a linear pair, $m\angle 1 + m\angle 2 = 180°$. Substitute.

$$147.5° + m\angle 2 = 180°$$

Because of related facts, $m\angle 2 = 180° - 147.5° = 32.5°$.

See QY1 at the right.

QY1

The measure of the outside angle of the Great Pyramid at Giza in Egypt is about 128°. What is the measure of the inside angle?

When the measures of two angles add to 180°, the angles are called **supplementary.** The inside and outside angles of a pyramid are supplementary. The two angles of any linear pair are always supplementary. Pictured below are two examples of supplementary angles that are *not* linear pairs.

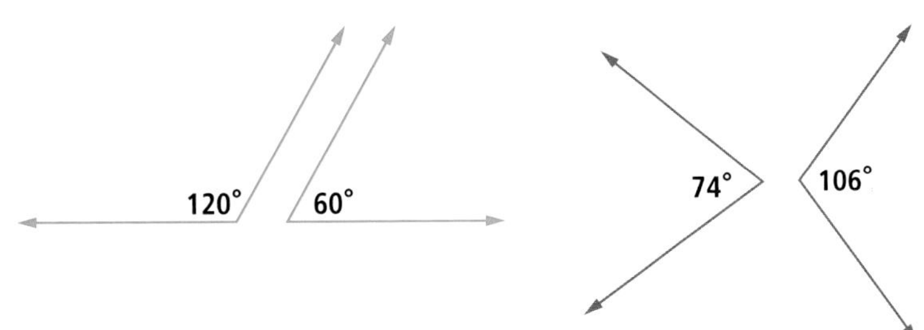

Activity 2

The figure at the right shows the intersection of two streets. Six angles are numbered. Angles 1 and 5 are supplementary.

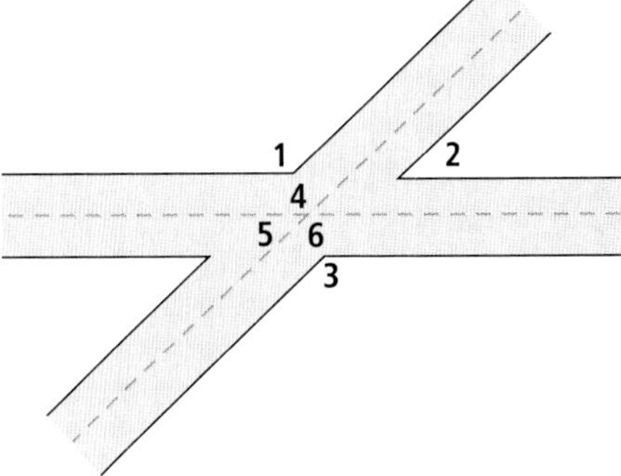

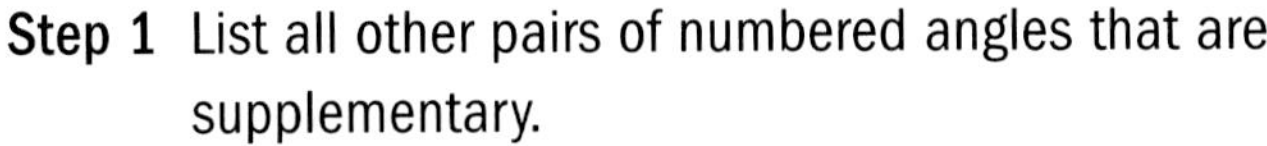

Step 1 List all other pairs of numbered angles that are supplementary.

Step 2 List those pairs that are also linear pairs.

When two lines intersect, the two angles that do not form a linear pair are called **vertical angles.** In the figure below, $\angle 7$ and $\angle 8$ are one pair of vertical angles. Angles $\angle 9$ and $\angle 10$ are the other pair.

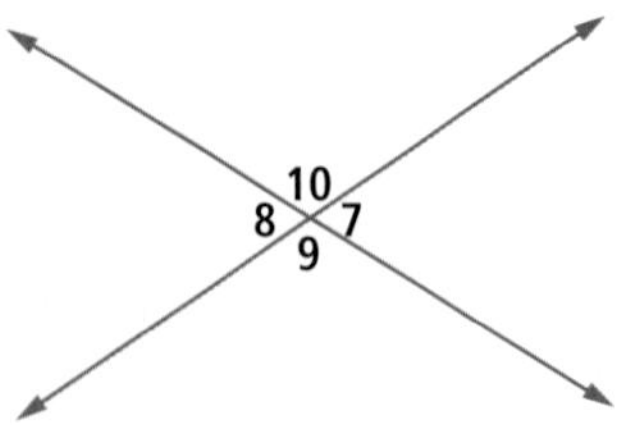

Activity 3

MATERIALS blank sheet of paper, ruler, protractor

Step 1 Draw two intersecting lines. Number the four angles.

Step 2 Find and record the measure of each of the four angles.

Step 3 List the two pairs of vertical angles along with their measures.

Step 4 Write a statement about the measures of vertical angles.

QY2

At the right are two intersecting lines. If the measure of $\angle 1$ is 35°, find the measures of the other three angles *without* using a protractor.

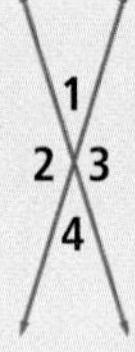

Remember that the sum of the angle measures for any triangle is 180°. You can use this fact, along with the angle addition properties and your knowledge of supplementary angles, to find the measures of angles in some figures without using a protractor.

GUIDED

Example 2

In the figure below, find *a* and *b*. Explain how you found each measure.

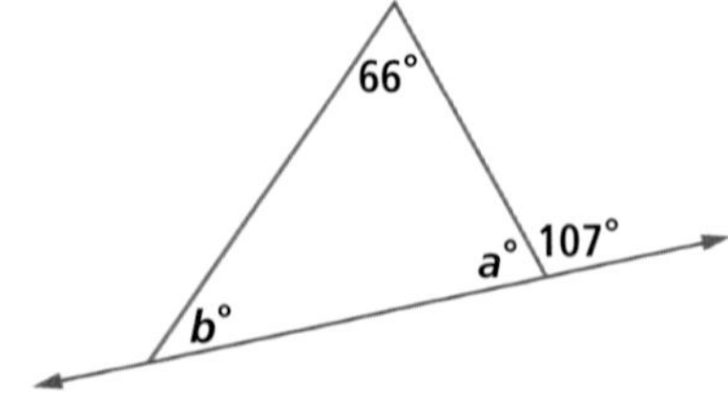

Solution $a =$ __?__; The angles with measures a° and 107° are __?__.
$b =$ __?__; The measures of the angles of a triangle must add to __?__.

Questions

COVERING THE IDEAS

1. The Red Pyramid at Dashur, Egypt, has an inside angle of $43\frac{22}{60}^\circ$. What is the measure of the outside angle?

The Red Pyramid is one of the few Egyptian pyramids that offers interior access to the general public.

In 2–5, fill in the blanks, using the diagram below. Points *X*, *Y*, and *Z* are on the same line.

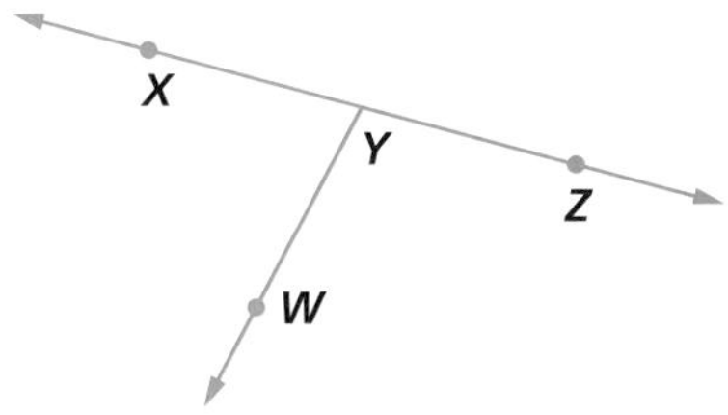

2. $\angle XYW$ and $\angle WYZ$ are a ___?___ pair.
3. $\angle XYW$ and $\angle WYZ$ are also ___?___ angles.
4. If $m\angle WYX = 75^\circ$, what is $m\angle WYZ$?
5. Why are there no pairs of vertical angles in this figure?

6. A director's chair folds for storage. When the chair in the picture at the right is unfolded, one of the angles formed by the legs measures 85°. What are the measures of the other three angles formed by the legs?

In 7–9, find the measure of a supplement to an angle with the given measure.

7. 45°
8. 132.7°
9. $\frac{1}{2}^\circ$

In 10–13, use the figure at the right to find the angle measure.

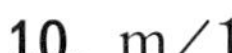

10. $m\angle 1$
11. $m\angle 3$
12. $m\angle 6$
13. $m\angle 7$

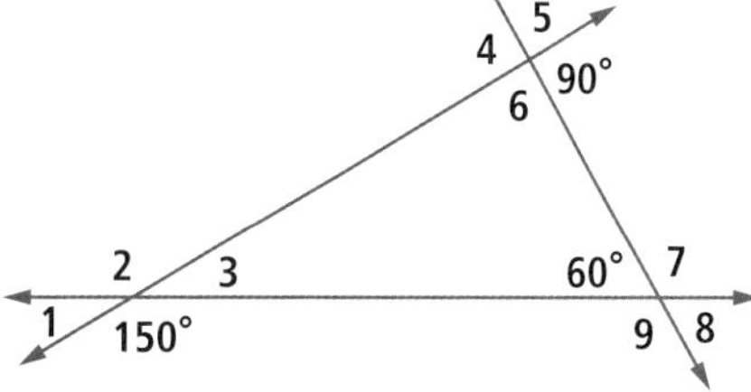

14. Without using a protractor, find the angle measures identified by variables in the diagram below. Fill in the blanks to form a word for the table in Question 27 in Lesson 4-9 on page 260.

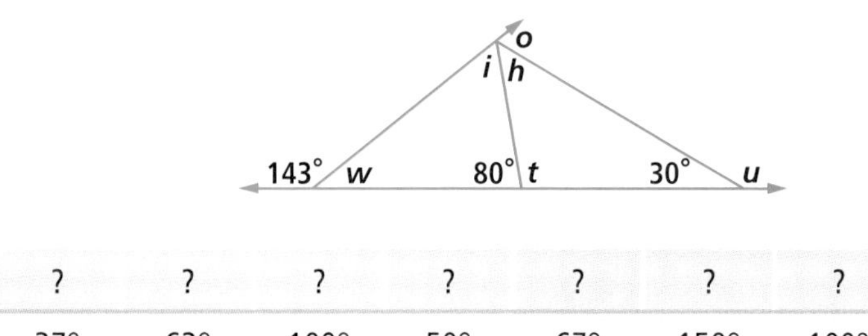

?	?	?	?	?	?	?
37°	63°	100°	50°	67°	150°	100°

APPLYING THE MATHEMATICS

15. If an angle has measure x, what is the measure of a supplement to the angle?

16. The U.S. Consumer Product Safety Commission (CPSC) recommends that ladders be set at about a 75° angle.

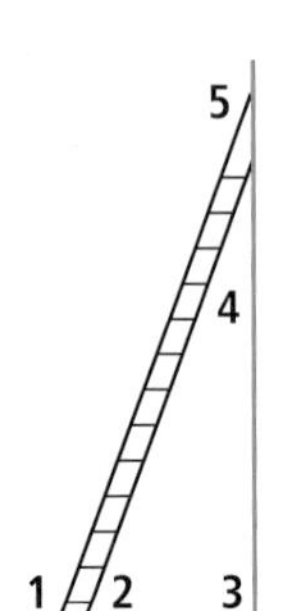

    a. To which angle in the drawing at the right is the CPSC referring?

    b. Is any angle in the drawing a supplement to the angle in Part a? If so, name it and give its measure.

17. In the figure below, $m\angle CAM = 87°$ and $m\angle PAM = 49°$. Suppose $m\angle CAP = x°$.

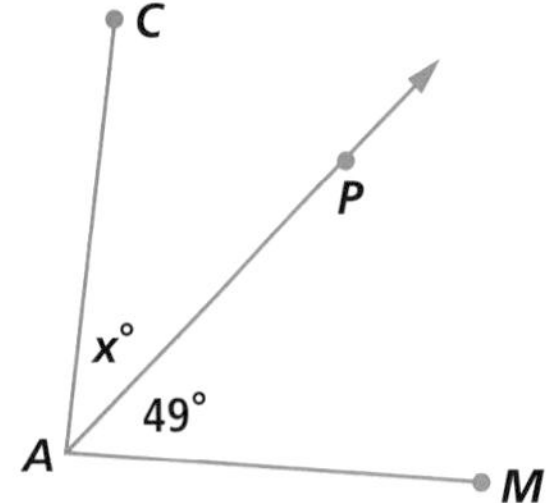

    a. Write an equation showing the relationship between the three angle measures.

    b. Use related facts to find $m\angle CAP$.

In 18–20, use the figure below. A ray *bisects* an angle if it splits the angle into two angles of equal measure. $\overleftrightarrow{SP}$ and $\overleftrightarrow{RT}$ intersect at point O. $\overrightarrow{OQ}$ bisects ∠POR.

18. If $m\angle POR = 41°$, what is $m\angle POQ$?

19. If $m\angle TOP = 152°$, what is $m\angle ROQ$?

20. If $m\angle POQ = 16°$, what is $m\angle TOS$?

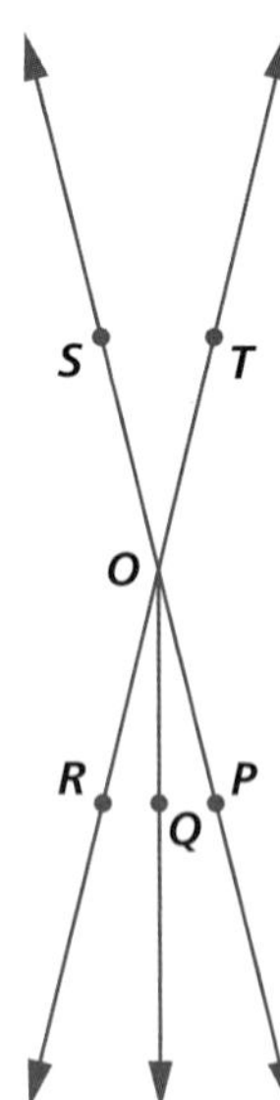

21. In the figure below, the four rays have a common endpoint.

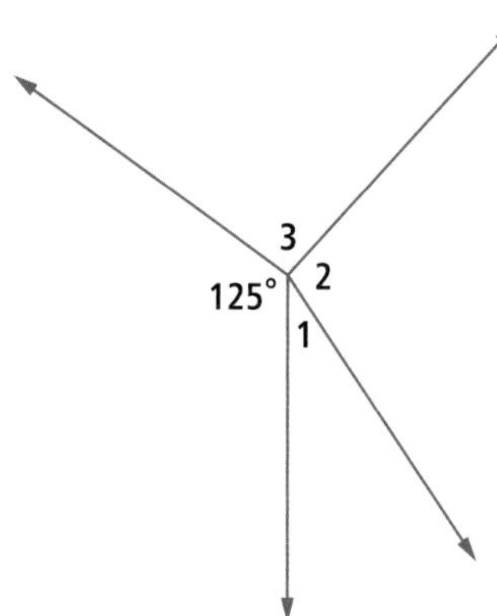

a. Is there enough information to find m∠1? If not, why not? If so, find m∠1.

b. Is there enough information to find m∠2? If not, why not? If so, find m∠2.

c. Is there enough information to find m∠1 + m∠2 + m∠3? If not, why not? If so, find m∠1 + m∠2 + m∠3.

22. In the figure below, what is the measure of ∠*A*?

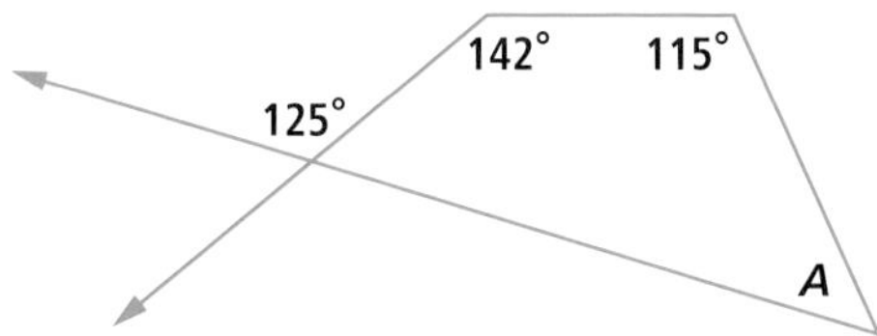

23. Refer to the figure below. If $m\angle AOB = 21.71^\circ$ and $m\angle BOC = 45.75^\circ$, find $m\angle AOC$.

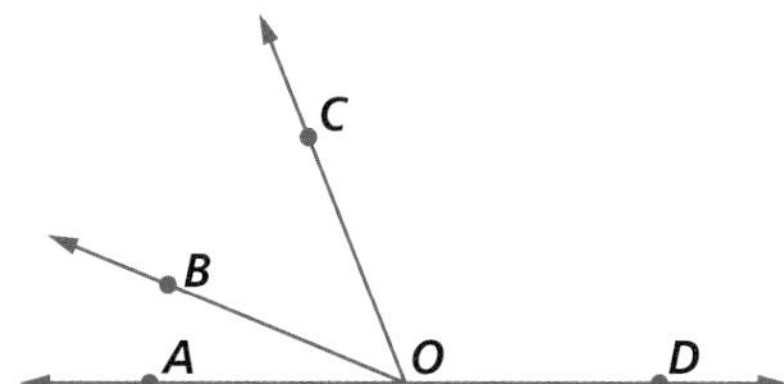

REVIEW

24. Joanna earned $30.60 babysitting last weekend. As a result, she had $56. **(Lesson 4-4)**

a. Suppose Joanna had *j* dollars before the weekend. Make a fact triangle to relate the quantities in this situation.

b. Using related facts and the fact triangle, find out how much money Joanna had before babysitting.

25. According to the U.S. Department of Transportation, there were about 7,953,000 licensed drivers under the age of 19 in 1980. By 2005, the number had risen to 9,331,220. How many more licensed drivers under 19 were there in 2005 compared to 1980? **(Lesson 4-3)**

In most states, the legal driving age begins at 16 years old.

26. a. Find the least common multiple of 2, 4 and 8.
    b. Calculate $3\frac{1}{2} + 2\frac{1}{4} + 4\frac{1}{8}$.
    c. Verify your answer to Part b by converting the fractions to decimals. **(Lessons 3-8, 3-4)**

EXPLORATION

27. You can use angle measures to indicate how steep stairs are.
    a. Measure $\angle ABC$, the inside angle of the stairs below.
    b. Find an angle that is a supplement to the inside angle. What is its measure?
    c. Are these stairs steeper than the stairs on the Pyramid of the Sun on page 231? Explain your answer.

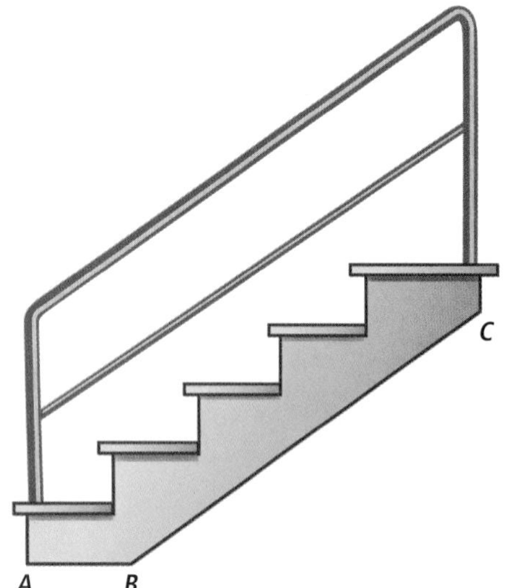

QY ANSWERS

1. 52°
2. m$\angle 2 = 145°$
   m$\angle 3 = 145°$
   m$\angle 4 = 35°$

Lesson 4-6 Kinds of Angles

Vocabulary

right angle
perpendicular
complementary angles
acute angle
obtuse angle
straight angle

▸ **BIG IDEA** You can classify an angle by its measure as acute (less than 90°), right (equal to 90°), or obtuse (greater than 90°).

Look at a corner of a page in this book. It is an example of a right angle. Angles measuring 90° are called **right angles.**

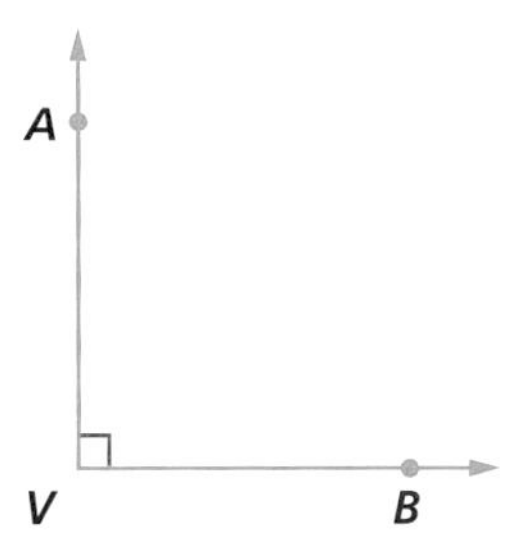

The measure of $\angle AVB$ at the right is 90°. That is, $m\angle AVB = 90°$. $\angle AVB$ is a right angle.

When lines, segments, or rays intersect at right angles, they are **perpendicular.** The symbol ⌝ in an angle identifies its sides as perpendicular and its measure as 90°.

Mental Math

True or false

a. If two angles make up a linear pair, then they are supplementary.

b. If $\overrightarrow{AB}$ is between $\overrightarrow{AC}$ and $\overrightarrow{AD}$, then $m\angle CAD + m\angle CAB = m\angle BAD$.

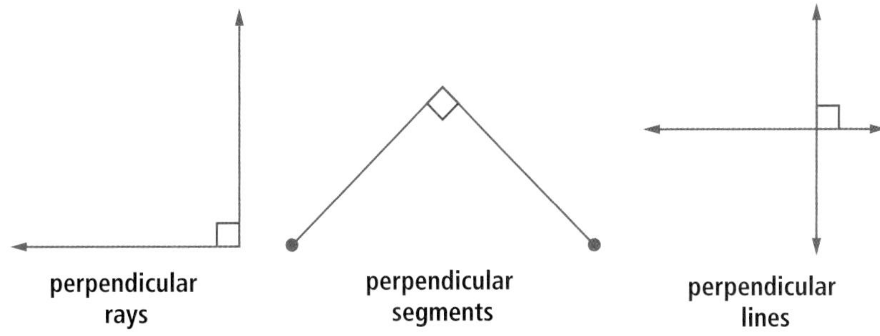

Traffic engineers prefer perpendicular intersections because they are safer. In the map of part of Chicago below, Drexel and Ellis Avenues make a bend in order to intersect South Chicago Avenue at right angles.

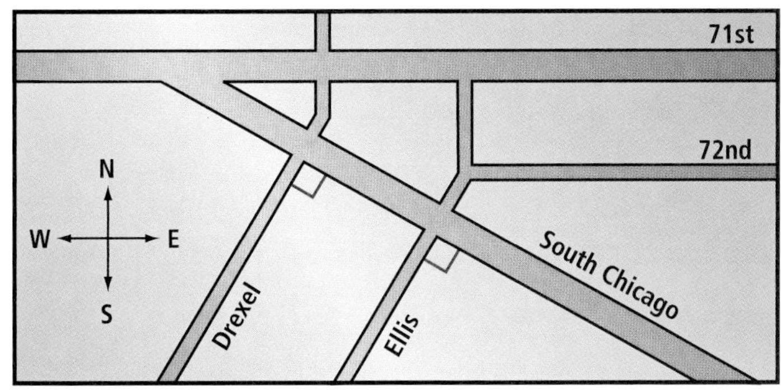

Can you imagine how bad traffic would be if it wasn't regulated with traffic lights and other signs?

Example 1

A tile-setter inserts a tile, cut at a 60° angle, into a corner of a rectangular room as shown at the right. At what angle must a second tile be cut to fit into the corner?

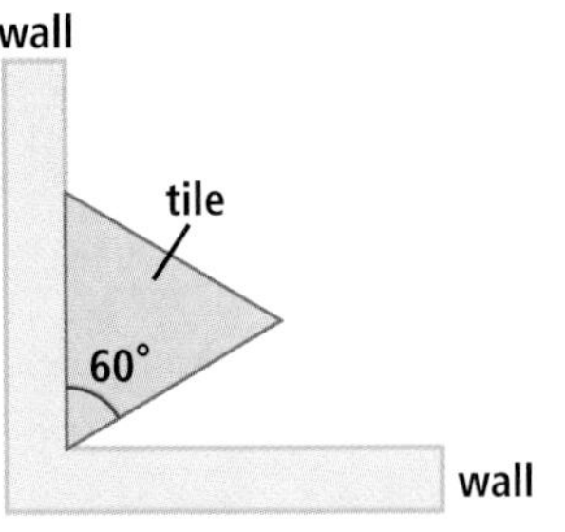

Very precise measurements are needed to accurately cut floor tiles.

Solution The diagram below represents the situation.

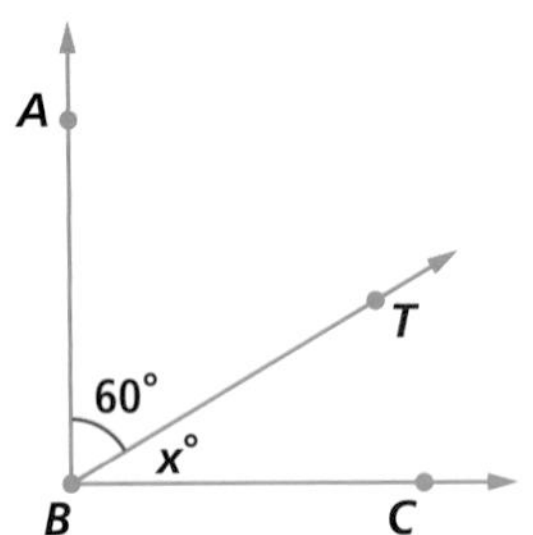

Because the room is rectangular, the walls are perpendicular, so $m\angle ABC = 90°$. By the Angle Addition Property,

$$\begin{array}{ccccc} m\angle ABT & + & m\angle TBC & = & m\angle ABC \\ 60° & + & x° & = & 90° \end{array}$$

Using related facts, $x° = 90° - 60° = 30°$.

The tile cutter must cut the next tile at a 30° angle.

Complementary Angles

Two angles whose measures add to 90° are called **complementary.** The angles *ABT* and *TBC* in Example 1 are complementary angles. Below are two more examples.

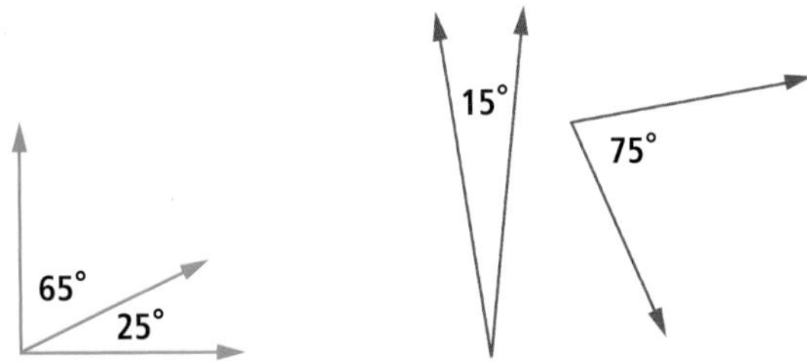

Notice that complementary angles do not need to be *adjacent*.

QY1

An angle *L* has a measure of 83°.

a. What is the measure of an angle that is complementary to $\angle L$?

b. What is the measure of an angle that is supplementary to $\angle L$?

Classifying Angles by Their Measures

Because right angles are so important, we classify angles by comparing their measures to right angles. An angle with a measure between 0° and 90° is called an **acute angle.**

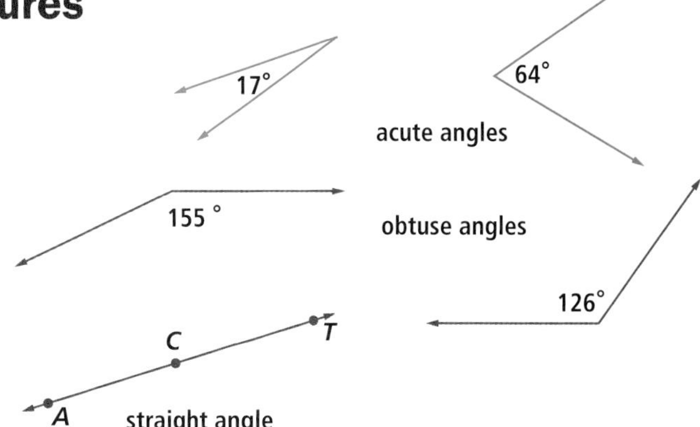

An angle with a measure between 90° and 180° is called an **obtuse angle.**

An angle whose sides are rays that form a line has a measure of 180° and is called a **straight angle.**

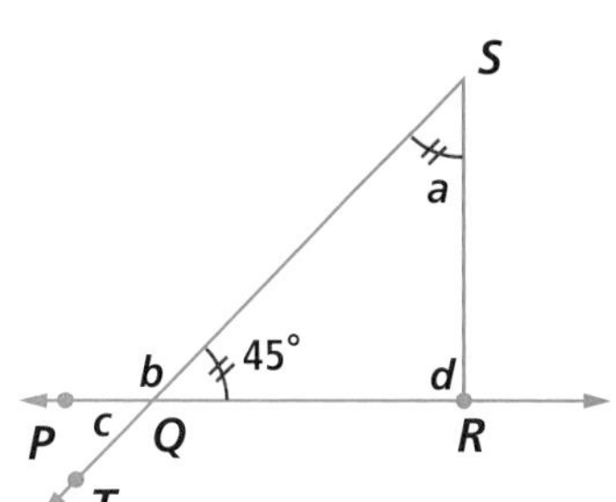

Example 2

In the diagram at the right, angles with equal measures are indicated with this marking ⸸.

a. Without using a protractor, find *a*, *b*, *c*, and *d*, and tell whether the angle is obtuse, acute, or right.

b. Is there a pair of complementary angles in the diagram? If so, what are the measures of the angles?

Solution

a. Because $m\angle S = m\angle RQS$, a = 45°, and the angle is acute.

Because $\angle PQS$ and $\angle RQS$ form a linear pair, b = 180 − 45 = 135. The angle is obtuse.

Because $\angle PQT$ and a 45° angle are vertical angles, c = 45°. The angle is acute.

Because *a*, *d*, and 45° are the measures of the angles of a triangle:

$$a + d + 45° = 180°$$
$$45° + d + 45° = 180°$$
$$d + 90° = 180°$$

Using related facts, $d = 180° - 90° = 90°$.

d = 90, and the angle with measure d is a right angle.

b. The two 45° angles are complementary.

STOP QY2

What are the values of *a* and *b* in the diagram below?

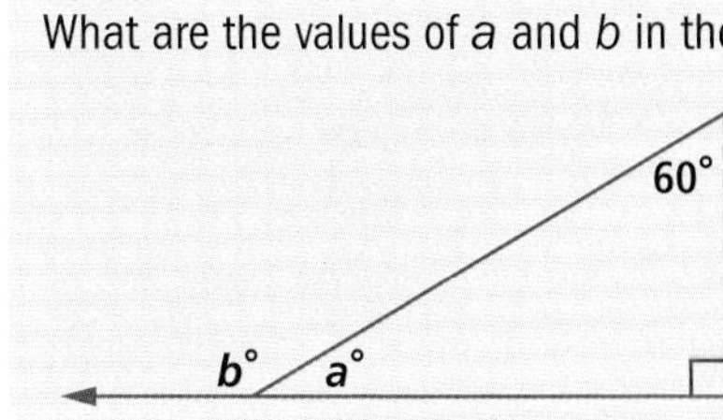

Questions

COVERING THE IDEAS

In 1–6, tell whether the angle appears to be right, obtuse, acute, or straight without measuring.

1. 

2. 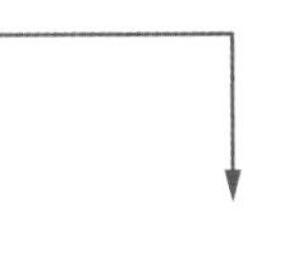

3. 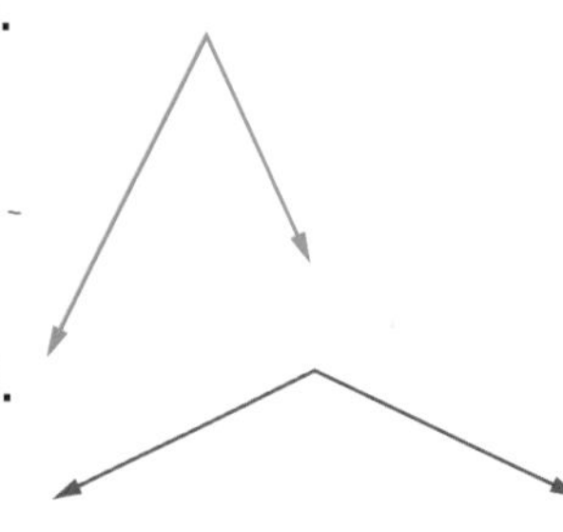

4.

5.

6.

In 7–10, use the map displaying part of Cambridge, Massachusetts at the right.

7. York Street is *not* perpendicular to which other street?
8. Name a street that is perpendicular to York Street.
9. Name a street that seems to have been "bent" to make a safer intersection.
10. Classify red angles 1–12 as acute, right, or obtuse.
11. One angle of the triangle shown below has measure 48°. What are the measures of the other two angles?

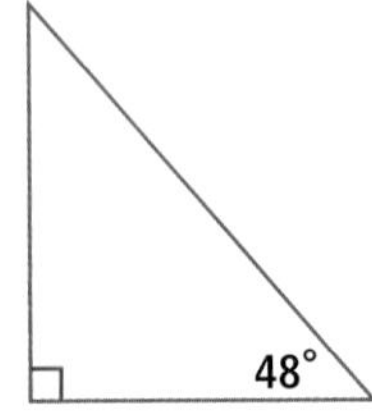

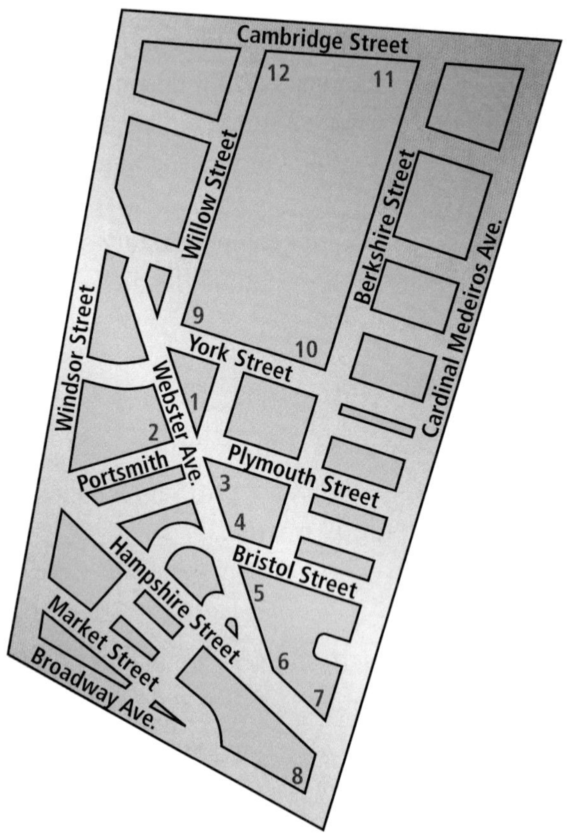

12. A stake is perpendicular to the ground. But it gets bent and forms a 56° angle with the ground. By how many degrees is the stake off the perpendicular?

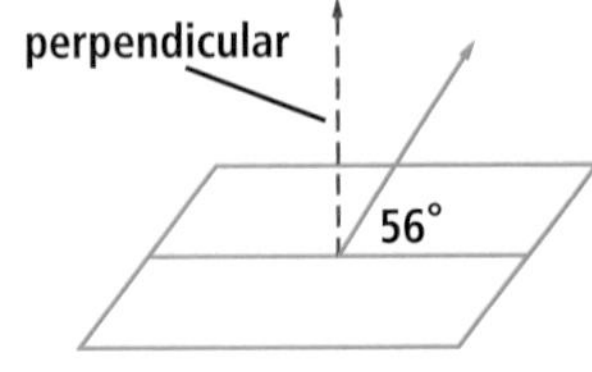

13. Refer to the figure at the right.
 a. Identify a pair of angles that are both adjacent and complementary.
 b. Identify a pair of complementary angles that is *not* adjacent.

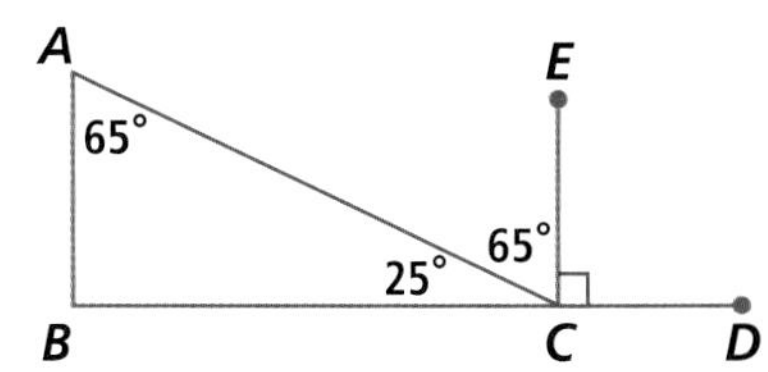

APPLYING THE MATHEMATICS

14. Copy and complete the table of angle measures.

	Angle	Complement
a.	15°	?
b.	39°	?
c.	?	85°
d.	*b*	?
e.	?	*y*

15. Refer to the diagram at the right. Find m∠1, m∠2, and m∠3.

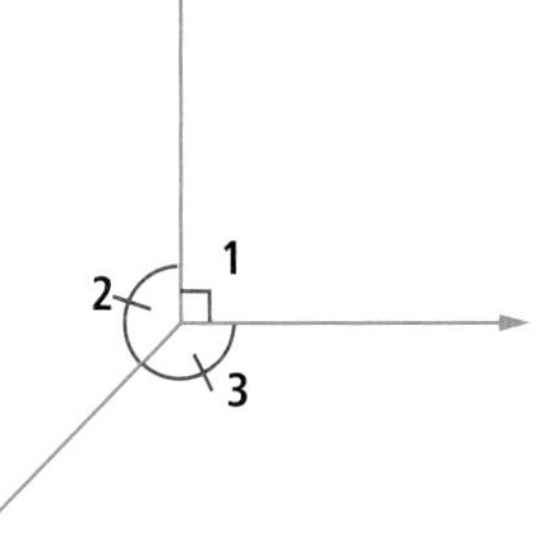

16. Without using a protractor, determine the angle measures marked with variables in the diagram below. Fill in the blanks to form a word for the table in Question 27 in Lesson 4-9 on page 260.

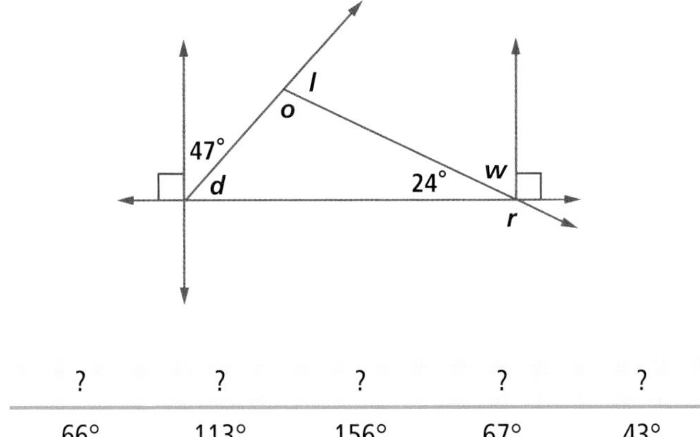

?	?	?	?	?
66°	113°	156°	67°	43°

17. In the diagram at the right, *b*, *c*, and *d* are all equal. Find *a*, *b*, *c*, and *d*.

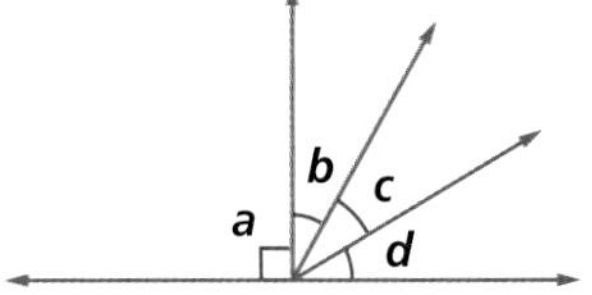

18. Julio made the following statement: *If two angles are supplementary, then one must be acute and the other obtuse.* Is he correct? Justify your answer.

REVIEW

19. Look again at the map for Questions 7–10 on page 240. Rana thinks that angles 11 and 12 are supplementary. Do you agree? Explain why you agree or disagree. **(Lesson 4-5)**

20. If three angles of equal measure surround a single point, what is the measure of one of those angles? **(Lesson 4-5)**

21. Construct a fact triangle with the numbers -4, 2.5, and -1.5. **(Lesson 4-4)**

22. Evaluate $37 - 5 + -25 - -4$. **(Lesson 4-3)**

23. Suppose you have a bunch of grapes. You eat half of them, and your sister then eats half of the remaining grapes. What fraction of the original bunch is left? **(Lesson 3-8)**

In 24–26, add, and give your answer in lowest terms. (Lesson 3-8)

24. $\frac{1}{3} + -\frac{1}{2}$

25. $-\frac{5}{6} + -\frac{1}{4}$

26. $5\frac{1}{6} + 3\frac{7}{5}$

27. Of 14 people waiting in a line for a bus, 7 are carrying umbrellas. Your friend says to you "Seven-fourteenths of the line has umbrellas." Say this in at least two other ways. **(Lesson 1-5)**

Studies have shown that a diet high in grapes may help prevent heart disease.

Source: The World's Healthiest Foods

EXPLORATION

28. Each of these words has a meaning outside of mathematics. Use a dictionary, if necessary, to find the non-mathematical meaning. Then tell if there is any connection between the meaning of the word in mathematics and its meaning outside mathematics.
    a. acute b. obtuse c. supplement d. complement

QY ANSWERS

1a. 7°

1b. 97°

2. $a = 30°, b = 150°$

Lesson 4-7 Subtracting Fractions

▸ **BIG IDEA** You can subtract fractions with different denominators by renaming them so they have the same denominator.

Subtracting Fractions with Like Denominators

Recall that when you add fractions with the same denominator, you can think of the denominator as a unit. You can also think this way when you subtract fractions with the same denominator.

Example 1

The track team practices on a $\frac{1}{4}$-mile track. At practice, Robin ran 14 laps and Matt ran 9 laps. How many miles farther did Robin run than Matt?

Solution This is a comparison problem, so subtract. One lap = $\frac{1}{4}$ mile. Convert the laps into miles. Robin ran $\frac{14}{4}$ miles. Matt ran $\frac{9}{4}$ miles. Think of *fourths* as the unit. Fourteen-fourths minus nine-fourths equals what?

$\frac{14}{4} - \frac{9}{4} = \frac{5}{4} = 1\frac{1}{4}$; Robin ran $\frac{5}{4}$ miles, or $1\frac{1}{4}$ miles, farther.

Check Since 14 laps − 9 laps = 5 laps, Robin ran 5 laps farther. 5 laps = $\frac{5}{4}$ miles

The general pattern for subtracting fractions is like that for addition. To subtract fractions with the same denominator, subtract the second numerator from the first and keep the denominator the same. This is the *Subtracting Fractions Property.*

Subtracting Fractions Property

For all numbers a, b, and c, with $c \neq 0$, $\frac{a}{c} - \frac{b}{c} = \frac{a-b}{c}$.

Example 2 presents two ways to subtract mixed numbers.

GUIDED

Example 2

Subtract $3\frac{2}{5} - 1\frac{4}{5}$.

(continued on next page)

Mental Math

Add.

a. $\frac{2}{3} + \frac{5}{3}$

b. $\frac{2}{5} + \frac{5}{5}$

c. $\frac{2}{-1} + \frac{5}{-1}$

d. Of Parts a–c, which has the greatest sum?

How quickly can you run a mile?

Solution 1 Change both mixed numbers to simple fractions.

$3\frac{2}{5} - 1\frac{4}{5} = \frac{?}{?} - \frac{?}{?} = \frac{?}{?} = 1\frac{?}{?}$

Solution 2 Subtract the whole number parts and the fraction parts separately. This may result in negative numbers.

Whole number subtraction: $\underline{?} - \underline{?} = 2$. Fraction subtraction: $\frac{?}{?} - \frac{?}{?} = -\frac{2}{5}$. You can show this in column form.

$$\begin{array}{r} 3\frac{2}{5} \\ -1\frac{4}{5} \\ \hline 2 + -\frac{2}{5} = \underline{?} \end{array}$$

Check Convert the fractions to decimals. $3\frac{2}{5} - 1\frac{4}{5} = 3.4 - 1.8 = 1.6$ and $1\frac{3}{5} = 1.6$. So it checks.

Subtracting Fractions with Unlike Denominators

To subtract fractions with different denominators, first find a common denominator.

GUIDED

Example 3

A recipe uses $3\frac{1}{3}$ cups flour. You have $2\frac{1}{2}$ cups. How much more flour do you need?

Solution 1 A common denominator is 6.

$3\frac{1}{3} - 2\frac{1}{2} = 3\frac{?}{6} - 2\frac{?}{6} = 2\frac{?}{6} - 2\frac{?}{6} = \frac{5}{6}$

You need $\frac{5}{6}$ cups flour.

Solution 2 The figure at the right illustrates this process. One full bar represents one cup, and the darkened area represents the amount of flour in the cup.

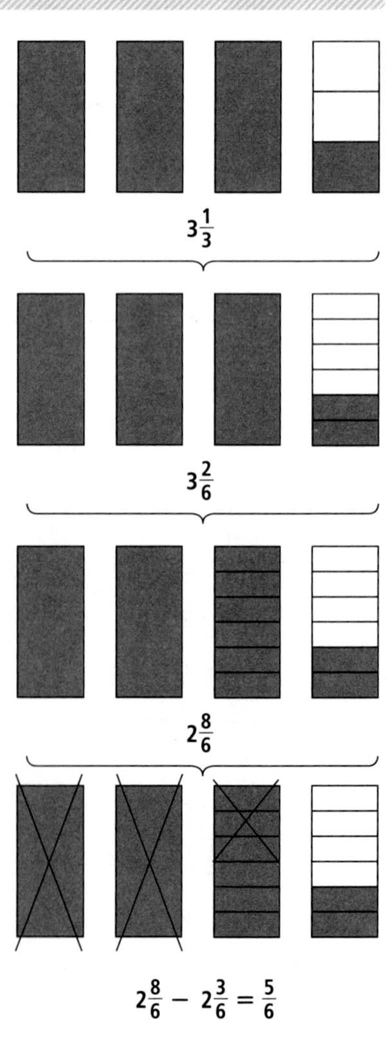

$3\frac{1}{3}$
$3\frac{2}{6}$
$2\frac{8}{6}$
$2\frac{8}{6} - 2\frac{3}{6} = \frac{5}{6}$

Check Make sure you know how to find $3\frac{1}{3} - 2\frac{1}{2}$ on your calculator.

Here is a key sequence and display for one calculator:

3 [UNIT] 1 [▼] 3 [▶] [−] 2 [UNIT] 1 [▼] 2 [ENTER]

The product of the denominators will always work as a common denominator, but by writing multiples of the denominators as in Example 4, you may find a smaller common denominator.

Example 4

Compute $4\frac{2}{3} - \frac{3}{4} + 1\frac{1}{2}$.

Solution 1 Rewrite the subtraction as an addition of the opposite.

$$4\frac{2}{3} - \frac{3}{4} + 1\frac{1}{2} = 4\frac{2}{3} + -\frac{3}{4} + 1\frac{1}{2}$$

Find a common denominator. The product of the denominators is 24. A smaller denominator is the least common multiple of the three numbers. Because 4 is a multiple of 2, you only have to find multiples of 3 and 4 to determine the least common denominator.

Multiples of 3: 3, 6, 9, 12, 15, 18, 21, 24, 27, 30, ...

Multiples of 4: 4, 8, 12, 16, 20, 24, 28, ...

Convert $4\frac{2}{3}$, $\frac{3}{4}$, and $1\frac{1}{2}$ to mixed numbers with denominators of 12.

$$\begin{aligned} 4\frac{2}{3} + -\frac{3}{4} + 1\frac{1}{2} &= 4\frac{8}{12} + -\frac{9}{12} + 1\frac{6}{12} \\ &= 5\frac{14}{12} + -\frac{9}{12} \quad \text{Add the first and third terms.} \\ &= 5\frac{5}{12} \end{aligned}$$

Solution 2 Write each mixed number as an improper fraction. Then find a common denominator.

$$\begin{aligned} 4\frac{2}{3} - \frac{3}{4} + 1\frac{1}{2} &= \frac{14}{3} - \frac{3}{4} + \frac{3}{2} \\ &= \frac{56}{12} - \frac{9}{12} + \frac{18}{12} \\ &= \frac{56 - 9 + 18}{12} \\ &= \frac{65}{12} = 5\frac{5}{12} \end{aligned}$$

Example 5

Calculate $18 - 4\frac{5}{6}$.

Solution Think of 18 as $18\frac{0}{6}$.

$$\begin{aligned} 18 - 4\frac{5}{6} &= 18\frac{0}{6} - 4\frac{5}{6} \\ &= 17\frac{6}{6} - 4\frac{5}{6} \\ &= 13\frac{1}{6} \end{aligned}$$

Check Use related facts. If $18 - 4\frac{5}{6} = 13\frac{1}{6}$, then $4\frac{5}{6} + 13\frac{1}{6} = 18$. Is this true? Yes, because $4\frac{5}{6} + 13\frac{1}{6} = 17\frac{6}{6} = 18$.

Questions

COVERING THE IDEAS

1. On Monday, Hector ran 7 laps. On Tuesday, he ran 9 laps. Each lap is a quarter mile. How many miles farther did Hector run than Matt from Example 1?

2. a. Find three common multiples of 4 and 10.
   b. What is the least common multiple of 4 and 10?
   c. Calculate $\frac{3}{10} - \frac{1}{4}$. Show your work.

3. a. Find three common multiples of 2, 3 and 5.
   b. What is the least common multiple of 2, 3, and 5?
   c. Calculate $\frac{41}{5} - \frac{7}{3} - \frac{5}{2}$.

4. One-eighth inch is shaved from a board $3\frac{3}{4}$" wide. What is the resulting width of the board?

Extreme caution must always be used when cutting with a mechanical saw.

5. Rewrite $11 - \frac{2}{5}$ as
   a. a mixed number.
   b. a simple fraction.

In 6–8, simplify. Give your answer in lowest terms.

6. $\frac{50}{7} - \frac{8}{7}$
7. $\frac{3}{z} + -\frac{9}{z}$
8. $\frac{2}{3} + \frac{5}{3} + -\frac{5}{6}$

In 9–11, simplify. Do not use a calculator.

9. $\begin{array}{r} 8\frac{2}{3} \\ -6\frac{3}{4} \\ \hline \end{array}$
10. $\begin{array}{r} 9\frac{5}{6} \\ -2\frac{3}{4} \\ \hline \end{array}$
11. $\begin{array}{r} 9\frac{1}{4} \\ -3\frac{2}{5} \\ \hline \end{array}$

APPLYING THE MATHEMATICS

12. Maurice used $\frac{5}{2}$ cups of flour in one recipe and $2\frac{1}{4}$ cups of flour in another. In which recipe did he use more flour? How much more?

13. Jessica, Pearl, and Yuma all ordered chicken pot pies. Jessica ate $\frac{2}{3}$ of hers, Pearl ate $\frac{3}{4}$ of hers, and Yuma ate $\frac{4}{5}$ of his.
    a. Order the three people by how much each ate, from least to most.
    b. How much more of a pie did the person who ate the most eat than the person who ate the least?
    c. Did the three of them eat more or less than 2 whole pot pies?

Chicken pot pies usually contain chicken and mixed vegetables like carrots, peas, celery, and green beans.

14. In triangle *SUM* below, $m\angle S = 22\frac{1}{3}°$ and $m\angle M = 33\frac{5}{6}°$.
    a. What is $m\angle U$?
    b. Is $\angle U$ obtuse, acute, or right?

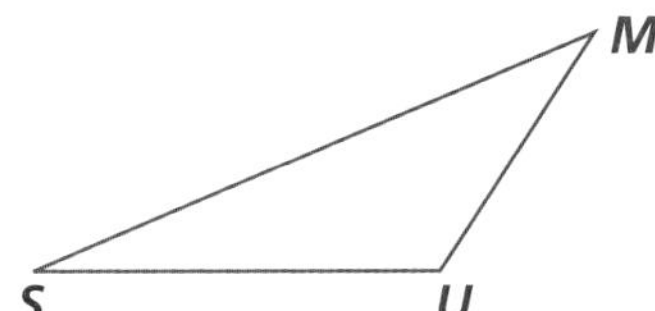

15. On Sunday, Santos was online for $1\frac{1}{4}$ hours in the morning and $\frac{1}{3}$ hour in the evening. Stephanie was online for 125 minutes. Who was online for a longer time? How much longer?

16. Each number in the box at the right is the answer to one of the problems below. When you can, solve these problems in your head. When you have the answer to a problem, fill in the blank with the letter corresponding to that answer. Save this word for the table in Question 27 in Lesson 4-9 on page 260.

A = $5\frac{1}{2}$	I = $\frac{4}{5}$
H = $-\frac{5}{6}$	T = $\frac{3}{4}$
C = $-1\frac{1}{4}$	S = $-\frac{3}{8}$
M = $1\frac{2}{3}$	E = $3\frac{1}{4}$

?	?	?	?	?	?
$2\frac{5}{6} - 1\frac{1}{6}$	$6 - \frac{1}{2}$	$1\frac{1}{2} - \frac{3}{4}$	$\frac{1}{6} - 1$	$3\frac{7}{8} - \frac{5}{8}$	$3 - 1\frac{1}{3}$
?	?	?	?	?	
$2\frac{3}{4} + 2\frac{3}{4}$	$1\frac{7}{8} - 1\frac{1}{8}$	$2 - 1\frac{1}{5}$	$\frac{3}{4} - 2$	$\frac{5}{8} - 1$	

REVIEW

17. $\angle A$ and $\angle B$ are complementary, and $\angle A$ and $\angle C$ are supplementary. If $m\angle C = 125°$, what is
    a. $m\angle A$?
    b. $m\angle B$? (Lesson 4-6)

18. Use the diagram below. m∠1 = 88°, m∠2 = 107°, and m∠3 = 45°. Find m∠4. **(Lesson 4-5)**

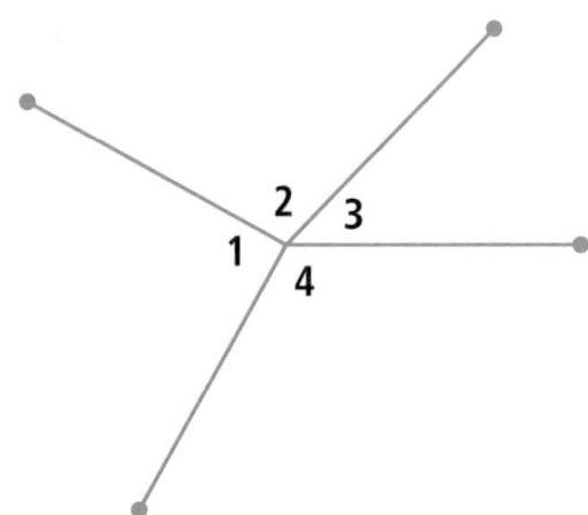

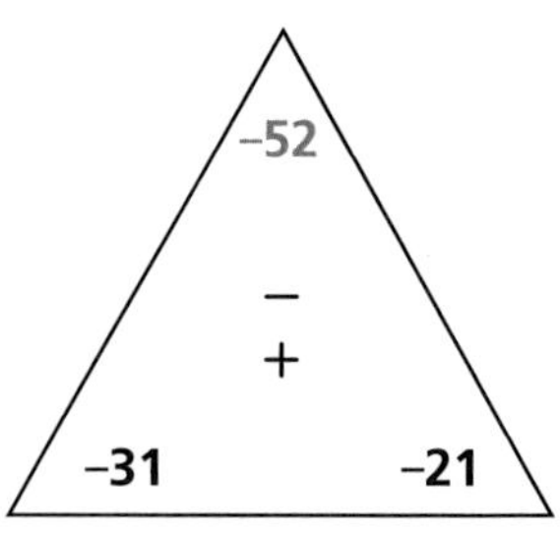

19. Write the related facts for the fact triangle at the right. **(Lesson 4-4)**

20. If you use a $20 bill to pay for a soccer ball that costs $17.53, how much money will you have left? **(Lesson 3-8)**

21. A computer program calculated the cost of some food items and rounded the total as shown in the table. Did the program round up, down, or to the nearest? Explain how you know. **(Lessons 2-5, 2-4)**

Item	Cost	Rounded
Milk	$2.48801	$2.49
Eggs	$0.3500	$0.35
Flour	$3.62192	$3.63
Sugar	$1.876773	$1.87

22. How many tiles are needed to cover the floor below? **(Previous Course)**

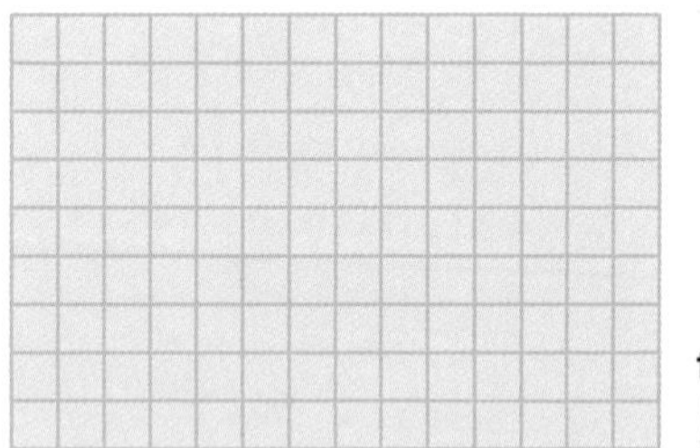

tile

EXPLORATION

23. Explore how close two fractions can be without being equal. For example, $\frac{3}{4} - \frac{7}{10} = \frac{1}{20} = 0.05$, so $\frac{3}{4}$ and $\frac{7}{10}$ are $\frac{1}{20}$, or 0.05, apart. Consider simple fractions between 0 and 1 whose denominators are no greater than 20. How close can you make the fractions?

Lesson 4-8 Solving Equations with Fact Triangles

Vocabulary

equation
sides of an equation
variable
open sentence
solve an equation
solution

BIG IDEA Many simple equations can be solved by using fact triangles.

Mental Math

Suppose two fractions have the same denominator. Fill in the blank with "larger" or "smaller".

a. The __?__ the numerators, the larger the sum.

b. The __?__ the denominator, the larger the sum.

An **equation** is a mathematical sentence with an equals sign. Here are four examples of equations.

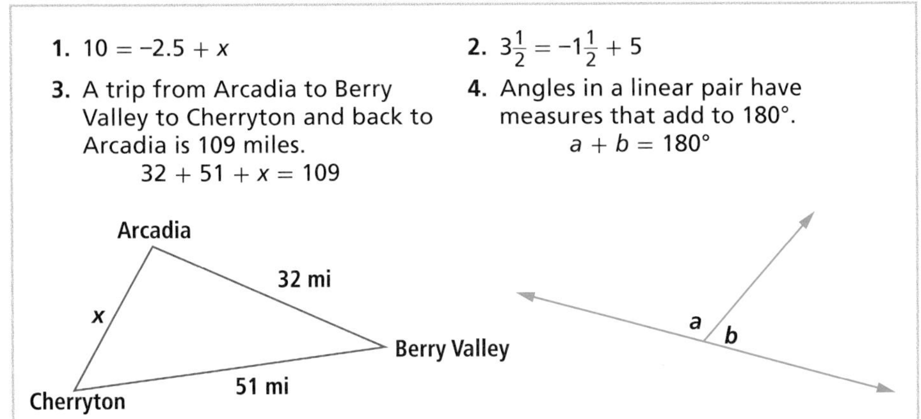

1. $10 = -2.5 + x$
2. $3\frac{1}{2} = -1\frac{1}{2} + 5$
3. A trip from Arcadia to Berry Valley to Cherryton and back to Arcadia is 109 miles.
$32 + 51 + x = 109$
4. Angles in a linear pair have measures that add to 180°.
$a + b = 180°$
Arcadia
32 mi
x
Berry Valley
51 mi
Cherryton
a
b

The expressions on either side of the = sign are the **sides of the equation.** An equation always has two sides.

The letters x, a, and b in the equations above are called *variables.* A **variable** is a letter or other symbol that may stand for any one of a set of values. Equations that have variables are called **open sentences.** To **solve an equation** means to find all the allowable values of the variable that make the sentence true. A value that makes the sentence true is a **solution** to the sentence.

$x + 5 = 7$ has only one solution: 2.

$n + 0 = n$ has an infinite number of solutions because n can be any value.

$y + 1 = y$ has no solution because no number equals 1 more than itself.

QY

Solve $x + 321 = 1{,}000$.

Some equations that contain one variable can be solved using fact triangles and related facts.

Example 1

Solve the equation $10 = -2.5 + x$.

Solution Make a fact triangle as shown below.

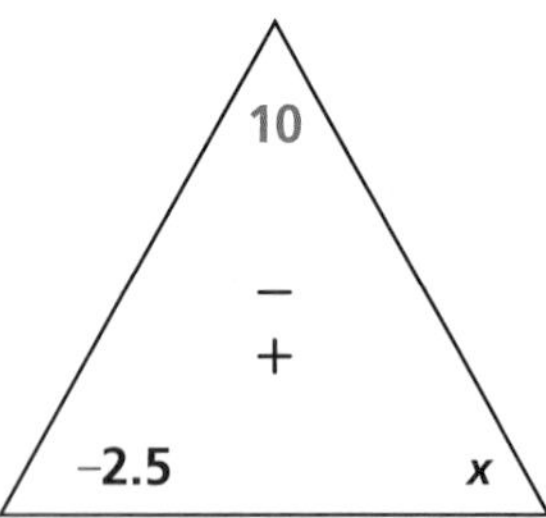

From this triangle, write the related facts.

$-2.5 + x = 10$ $\qquad$ $10 - x = -2.5$

$x + -2.5 = 10$ $\qquad$ $10 - -2.5 = x$

The first three related facts do not help you solve the sentence. But the last related fact tells you that $x = 10 - -2.5$.

$$\begin{aligned} x &= 10 - -2.5 \\ &= 10 + 2.5 \\ &= 12.5 \end{aligned}$$

Check Substitute 12.5 for x in the original equation. Does $10 = -2.5 + 12.5$? Yes. It checks.

GUIDED

Example 2

Solve the equation $9 - A = -3\frac{2}{5}$.

Solution First make the fact triangle. The facts related to $9 - A = -3\frac{2}{5}$ can be read from the triangle.

?$\qquad$?

?$\qquad$?

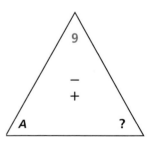

The fact that helps to solve the sentence is:

A = ? − ?

= ? + ?

= ?

GUIDED

Example 3

The temperature one January afternoon was 15° below zero. Later that day, the temperature was 3° above zero. What was the change *c* in temperature?

a. Using the variable *c*, write an equation that describes the situation.

b. Using a fact triangle, solve the equation.

c. Check the answer by substituting it for *c* in the original equation.

d. Describe the situation in the problem in a sentence.

Solution

a. -15° is the starting value, c is the change, and 3° is the ending value. So -15 + __?__ = 3.

b. Draw the fact triangle. The related facts are:

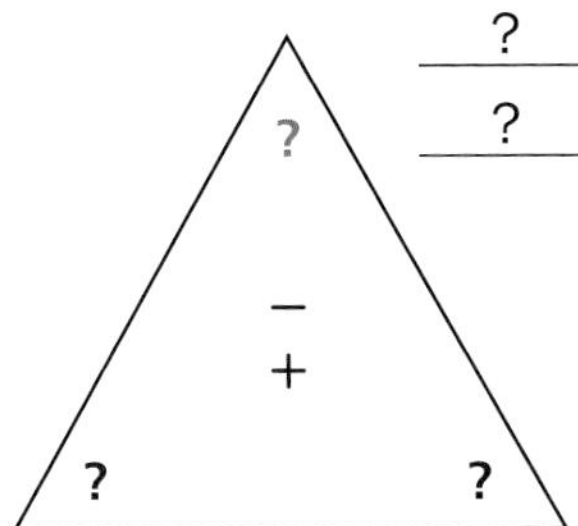

__?__ __?__

__?__ __?__

The related fact that shows the value of *c* is __?__.
The solution is __?__.

c. Check the solution: __?__ + __?__ = __?__.

d. Since 18 is a positive number, the temperature rose.
In going from 15 below zero to 3 above zero, the temperature rose __?__ degrees.

Questions

COVERING THE IDEAS

1. Is what is written an equation? Why or not?
   a. $x = y$ b. $3 + 2$ c. $4 + \frac{10}{2} = 9$ d. $y = 14 + 2.3$

2. **Fill in the Blank** In the equation $t + 16 = 32$, the letter t is called a __?__.

Multiple Choice In 3 and 4, choose all the numbers that are solutions to the equation.

3. $4 - x = -8$
   A -12 B 12 C 4 D -4

4. $y - 0 = y$
   A -70 B $8\frac{1}{2}$ C 8.8 D 1,591

In 5 and 6, an equation is given.

- a. **Draw a fact triangle for the equation.**
- b. **Using the triangle, write the four related facts.**
- c. **Use one of the facts to solve the equation.**
- d. **Check your answer by substituting it for the variable in the original equation.**

5. $m - 4 = -12.4$

6. $4\frac{33}{100} + q = 6\frac{1}{100}$

7. Angle A is a complement of $\angle B$, $m\angle A = 23°$, and $m\angle B = b°$.
   - a. Write an equation relating $23°$, $b°$, and another angle measure.
   - b. Draw a fact triangle for your equation.
   - c. Use one of the facts to find the value of b.

8. Antonia wrote these related facts for the equation $-5 + L = 20$:

   $-5 + L = 20$ $\quad$ $20 + 5 = L$ $\quad$ $20 - L = -5$
   - a. What is the fourth related fact, which is not listed?
   - b. Why is the fourth fact not needed?

APPLYING THE MATHEMATICS

9. Give at least three pairs of numbers a and b such that $a + b = 180$. Choose a negative number as one of the numbers in one pair.

10. Give three pairs of numbers p and q such that $p - q = -1$.

In 11 and 12, a situation is given.

- a. **Using a variable, write an equation that describes the situation.**
- b. **Solve the equation.**
- c. **Answer the question in a sentence.**

11. Josh started the day with \$80.00. He spent \$12.60 for a CD and then paid for a haircut. When he was done, he had \$52.90 left. How much did he pay for the haircut?

12. A hiker began the day at 20 feet below sea level. She walked for several hours and stopped to rest at 125 feet above sea level. By how much did her elevation change?

13. Darius was solving the equation $15 - x = -12$. He changed the equation to $x - 15 = -12$. His teacher told him the two equations do not have the same solution. Why not?

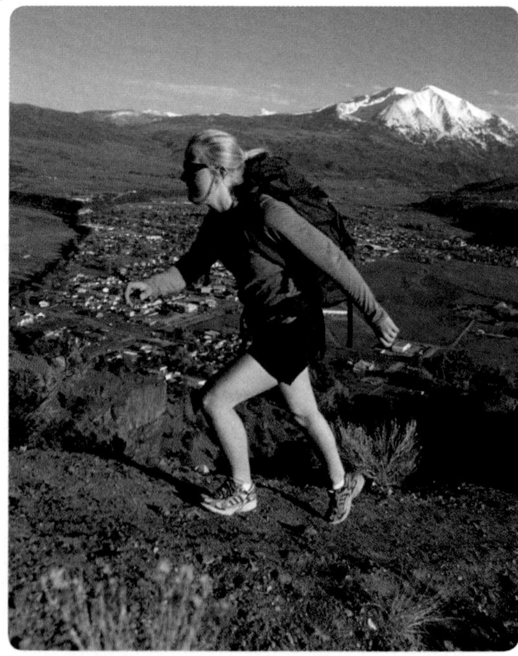

How long do you think it would take to hike a 2,000-foot tall mountain?

14. Write an equation and solve. The measures of two angles of a triangle are 31.3° and 87.7°. What is the measure of the third angle?

15. Solve the following equations. Then order the solution from greatest to least to unscramble the letters and form a word. Save this word for the table in Question 27 in Lesson 4-9 on page 260.

a.	$(-24) + C = 18$	$C =$?
b.	$O + 182 = 154$	$O =$?
c.	$-101 = T + (-52)$	$T =$?
d.	$-32.5 + 65.2 = A$	$A =$?
e.	$-\left(\frac{7}{10}\right) - 1\frac{1}{2} = N$	$N =$?
f.	$-26 - N = -43$	$N =$?

42	?
32.7	?
17	?
-2.2	?
-28	?
-49	?

REVIEW

16. Lola ate $\frac{1}{4}$ a corn casserole, and Genesis ate $\frac{1}{5}$. What fraction of the original casserole is left? **(Lesson 4-7)**

17. The circle below is divided into four sectors. The angles at the center are numbered 1, 2, 3, and 4. **(Lessons 4-6, 2-9)**

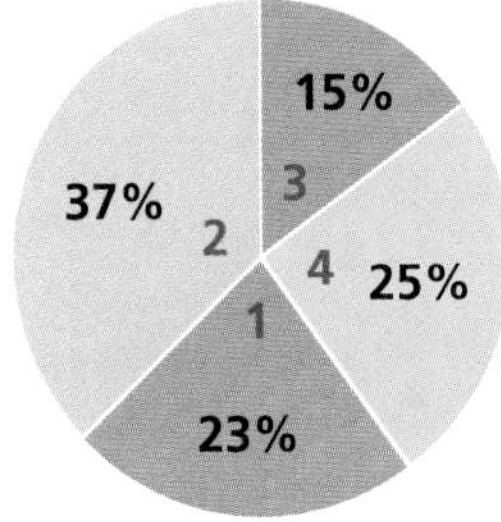

a. Name all the acute angles.
b. Name all the obtuse angles.
c. Name all the right angles.
d. Name all the straight angles.

18. The cafeteria manager had students sample two kinds of hot dogs to see which they preferred. The table below summarizes the preferences by grade. **(Lessons 2-5, 1-2)**

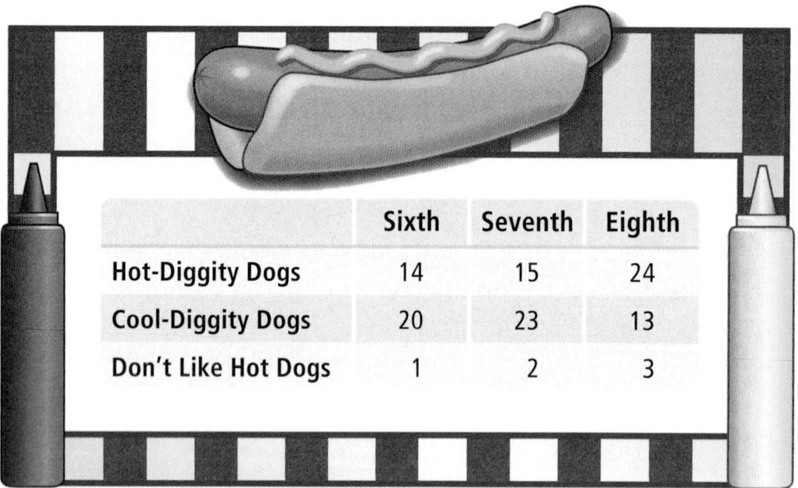

	Sixth	Seventh	Eighth
Hot-Diggity Dogs	14	15	24
Cool-Diggity Dogs	20	23	13
Don't Like Hot Dogs	1	2	3

a. How many students were surveyed?

b. How many 6th graders were surveyed?

c. What fraction of students surveyed were 6th graders? (Express in lowest terms.)

d. What percent of students surveyed were 6th graders? (Round to the nearest tenth of a percent.)

e. How many 7th graders were surveyed?

f. What percent of the 7th graders preferred Hot-Diggity Dogs? (Round to the nearest tenth of a percent.)

EXPLORATION

19. In the diagram below, the values of a, b, c, d, e, and f are -6, -2, 1, 2, 4, and 5, though not necessarily in that order. If the sum of the numbers in each circle equals 0, what is the value of each variable?

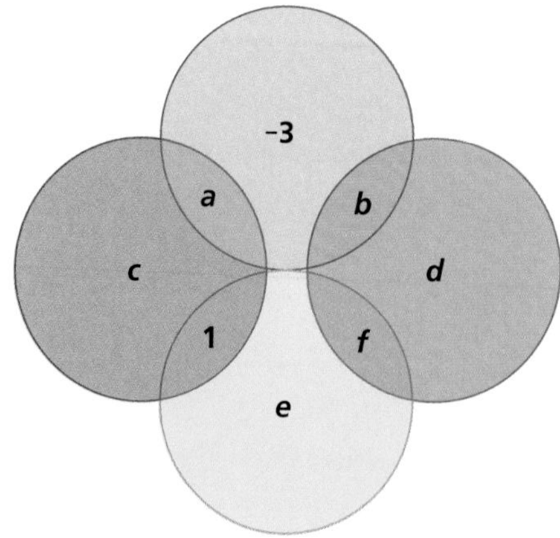

QY ANSWER

679

Lesson 4-9 The Addition Property of Equality

▸ **BIG IDEA** Many equations can be solved by using the Addition Property of Equality.

A mystery box is on the balance. How much does it weigh?

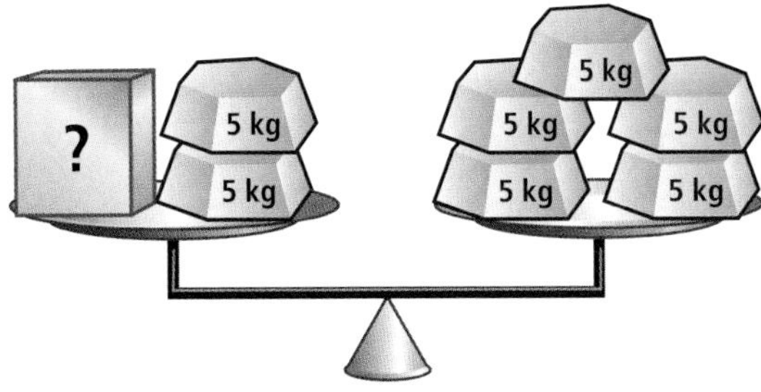

Mental Math

Find the value of the expression if $m = 7$ and $n = 4$.

a. $m + n$

b. $m - n + 8$

c. $\frac{m}{n} + \frac{5}{4}$

d. $\frac{m}{n} + \frac{10}{4}$

The objects on the balance can be represented by an equation. Let w be the weight of the mystery box. The pans balance when $w + 10 \text{ kg} = 25 \text{ kg}$. This is usually written without units when the units are the same.

$$w + 10 = 25$$

If you remove 10 kg from each side, the sides will be balanced, with the box by itself on one side. Then, you will be able to see how much it weighs. Removing 10 kg from each side can be shown by subtracting 10 from—or adding –10 to—both sides of the equation.

$$\begin{aligned} w + 10 - 10 &= 25 - 10 \\ w + 0 &= 15 \\ w &= 15 \end{aligned} \qquad \text{or} \qquad \begin{aligned} w + 10 + -10 &= 25 + -10 \\ w + 0 &= 15 \\ w &= 15 \end{aligned}$$

The box weighs 15 kg.

You might be able to solve $w + 10 = 25$ in your head, but you need a systematic method to solve complicated equations. That method is based on the Addition Property of Equality. Here are some numerical examples to illustrate the property.

The first line of each equation below is a true statement. When the same number is added to both sides of each equation, it is still true.

1. $\frac{1}{2} = \frac{1}{3} + \frac{1}{6}$

   $\frac{1}{2} + 1 = \left(\frac{1}{3} + \frac{1}{6}\right) + 1$

2. $5 + 6 = 11$

   $(5 + 6) + 3 = 11 + 3$

QY1

Check that the second equations in 1. and 2. on the previous page are true by finding the sums on both sides of each equation.

These examples illustrate an important property.

Addition Property of Equality

If $a = b$, then $a + c = b + c$.

The Addition Property of Equality can be pictured using a balance. If two weights a and b balance, then $a = b$. When the same weight c is added to both pans of the balance, the weight $a + c$ on one pan will balance the weight $b + c$ on the other pan.

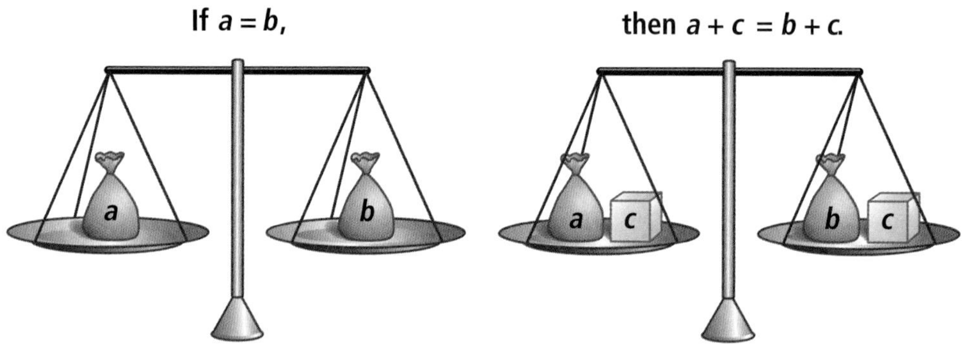

Note that the property does not say that c must be a positive number. To solve the mystery-box equation, we added –10 to both sides of the equation.

The Addition Property of Equality can be used to solve equations involving addition.

Example 1

Solve the equation $3{,}200 = x + -75$.

Solution You want to get x by itself on one side of the equation. To eliminate the –75 on the right side, add 75 to both sides of the equation.

$3{,}200 + 75 = x + -75 + 75$	Addition Property of Equality
$3{,}275 = x + 0$	Property of Opposites
$3{,}275 = x$	Additive Identity Property of Zero

Check Substitute 3,275 for x in the original equation $3{,}200 = x + -75$. It checks because $3{,}275 + -75 = 3{,}200$.

See QY2 at the right.

QY2

What number can you add to both sides of each equation to solve it?

a. $38 + X = -23$

b. $-5 = w + -18$

GUIDED

Example 2

Chen and Mario want to buy Rodney a present that costs $80. Chen has $25.75 and Mario has $41.34. How much more money do they need?

 Write an equation involving the given and unknown numbers.

Let m represent the amount of money they need to reach $80. Putting together m with the money they have must total 80.

$\underline{?} + \underline{?} + m = 80$

Add the numbers on the left side.

$\underline{?} + m = 80$

Solve your equation using the Addition Property of Equality.
Add $\underline{?}$ to both sides.

$\underline{?} + 67.09 + m = \underline{?} + 80$

$\underline{?} + m = \underline{?}$

$m = \underline{?}$

Check your solution. Then write a sentence answering the question.

 **Now you can play *X-Tac-Toe: x + a = b*. The directions for this game are on page G17 in the back of your book.**

Questions

COVERING THE IDEAS

1. **True or False** 8.5 is a solution to the equation $2.5 + x = 11$.
2. **True or False** -61 is a solution to the equation $39 - y = 100$.

In 3 and 4, the scale is balanced.

a. **Write the equation pictured by the balance.**
b. **Solve the equation.**

3.

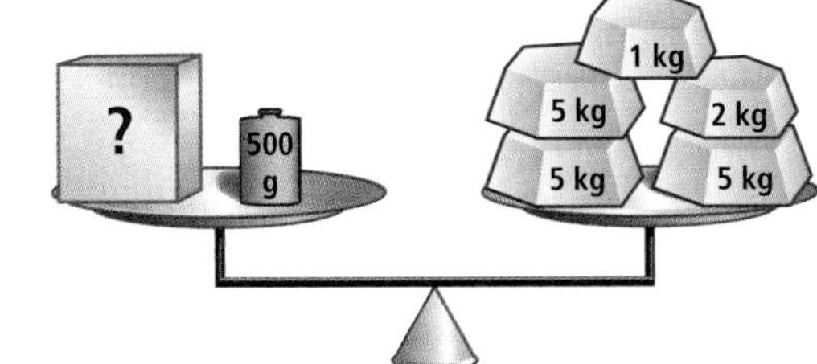

4.

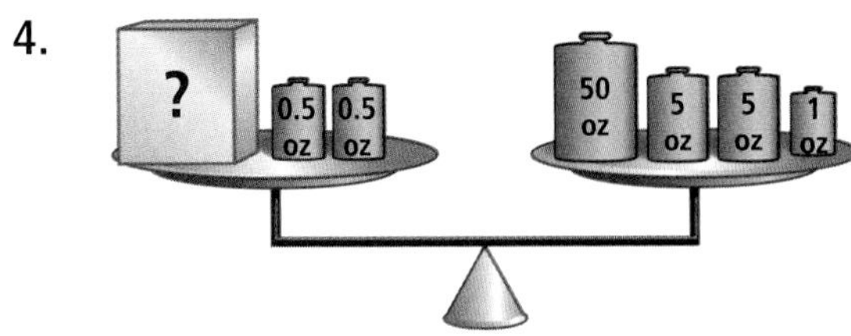

Multiple Choice In 5–8, which number is a solution of the equation?

5. $x + 3 = 8$
   A 11 B 24 C 5 D 4
6. $5 - y = 6.2$
   A 11.2 B -11.2 C 1.2 D -1.2
7. $z - 15 = 9.5$
   A 5.5 B -5.5 C -2.5 D 24.5
8. $3 + n + 2.5 = -7$
   A 12.5 B -2.5 C -3.5 D -12.5

In 9–12, an equation is given.

a. What number can be added to both sides to solve the equation?
b. Solve the equation.

9. $x + \frac{1}{3} = -\frac{2}{3}$
10. $y + \frac{1}{5} = 2$
11. $-46.3 + m = 82.9$
12. $\frac{1}{20} = n + -\frac{1}{6}$

In 13 and 14, a situation is given.

a. Write an equation to represent the situation. Use a variable for the unknown number.
b. Solve your equation using the Addition Property of Equality.
c. Check your solution.
d. Write a sentence answering the question.

13. Governor Mike Huckabee of Arkansas, pictured at the right, was diagnosed with diabetes. He went on a carefully supervised diet. After he lost 105 pounds, he weighed 175 pounds. How much did he weigh before he started his diet?
14. The land area of the United States is 3,794,085 square miles. The land area of Alaska is 663,267 square miles, and the land area of Hawaii is 10,931 square miles. What is the combined land area of the other 48 states?

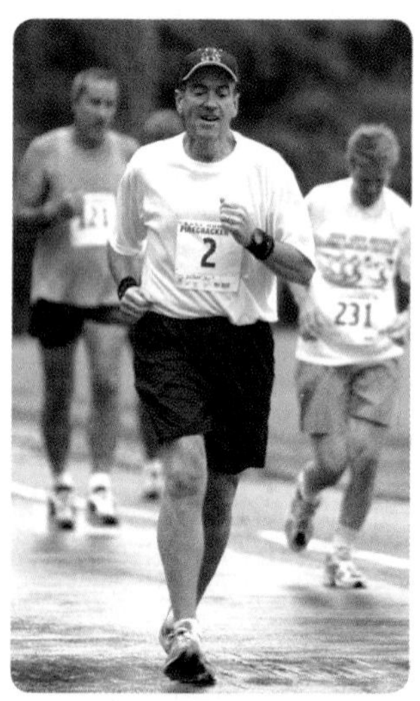

In 2005, *Time* magazine ranked Mike Huckabee as one of the best governors in the United States.

15. Solve each equation, and place the letter for the variable above the blank for its solution. Save this word for the table in Question 27 on page 260.

$3 + w = -2$ $k + \frac{1}{2} = 3$ $8.2 + o = 9$ $12 = n - 2$

?	?	?	?	?
$2\frac{1}{2}$	14	0.8	-5	14

APPLYING THE MATHEMATICS

16. On the balance below, which of the boxes, E or F, is heavier? How do you know?

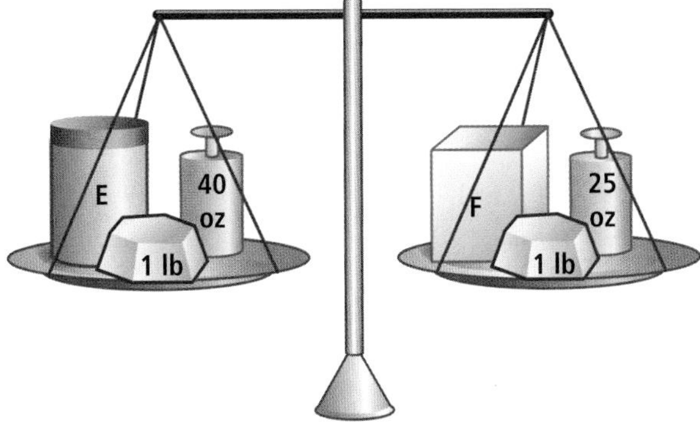

17. Find the weight of the box labeled y.

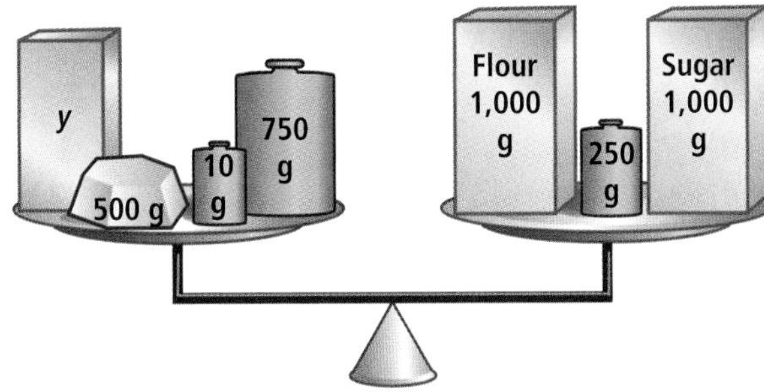

REVIEW

18. Consider the equation $-8 = y - 40$. **(Lesson 4-8)**
    a. Represent the equation using a fact triangle.
    b. Write the related facts for the triangle.
    c. Use one of your facts to find the value of y.

19. Your groceries cost \$5.83, and you want exactly \$0.25 in change. How much money should you give the clerk? **(Lesson 4-8)**

20. You buy three oranges for \$0.27 each. Your friend buys a pear for \$0.78. If you both pay with a dollar, how much more change does your friend get back than you? **(Lesson 4-8)**

Don't forget to always count your change!

In 21 and 22, find the missing numerator. (Lesson 4-7)

21. $6\frac{?}{5} - \frac{3}{5} = 6\frac{1}{5}$

22. $\frac{?}{8} - -\frac{5}{8} = 1$

23. Simplify $\frac{2}{3} + \frac{k}{3} - \frac{k}{3} + \frac{1}{3}$. **(Lesson 4-7)**

24. According to the U.S. Census Bureau, in 2005, the population of New York state was estimated as 19,254,630 while 8,213,839 people lived in New York City. **(Lesson 4-2)**
 a. How many people lived in New York state but not in New York City?
 b. How many more people lived in New York state outside of New York City than inside New York City?

25. Multiply 54.28 by each number without using a calculator. **(Lesson 2-4)**

a. 0.01	b. 0.1	c. 1
d. 100	e. 1000	

EXPLORATION

26. Imagine that you have a balance and several of each of the following shapes: square, triangle, diamond, and circle. Using the balance, you determine the following:
 3 triangles weigh the same as 2 squares
 4 squares weigh the same as 3 circles
 5 circles weigh the same as 4 diamonds
 a. Which shape weighs the most?
 b. Which shape weighs the least?
 c. Come up with a combination of 12 of these shapes that will balance on your pan balance. For example, you may have 9 shapes on one side, and 3 on the other.

27. Complete the table below using the decoded words from the lessons in this chapter. Rearrange the words to form a quote by Roger Bacon, the thirteenth century friar known as Doctor Mirabilis, which is Latin for "wonderful teacher."

Lesson	Word
4-1	?
4-2	?
4-3	?
4-4	?
4-5	?
4-6	?
4-7	?
4-8	?
4-9	?

"The __?__ of this __?__ __?__ __?__ __?__ __?__ __?__ a __?__ of __?__."

QY ANSWERS

1. $1\frac{1}{2} = 1\frac{3}{6}$ and $11 = 11$; Yes, they check.

2a. −38

2b. 18

Chapter 4 Projects

1 Nim

Nim is a game played using counters. There are several versions of the game. Two players or teams alternate turns. The goal is to force the other player to take the last counter. Play one of the following two versions of the game. After playing the game several times, determine if there is a strategy that will guarantee winning. Write a summary of what you learned.

Version 1: Start with 12 counters: a column of 3 counters, a second column of 4 counters, and a third column of 5 counters. On a turn, a player may take any number of counters from exactly one column, but must take at least 1 counter.

Version 2: Start with one column of 50 counters. On a turn, a player may take from 1 to 6 counters.

2 Nifty Nines

a. Start with a two-digit whole number. Add its digits, and subtract the result from the original number to obtain a new number. Then keep subtracting 9 from the new number until you get a number that is not positive.

b. Repeat Part a with several different numbers. Can you make any generalizations?

c. What happens if you start with a three-digit number?

3 Swimming World Records

Research the world records from 1970 to 2008 for men's and women's swimming events.

a. Find the difference between each new men's record and the one before it.

b. Find the difference between each new women's record and the one before it.

c. Compare the men's world record to the women's world record for 1970, 1980, 1990, and 2000. What do you notice?

In the 2004 Olympics, Michael Phelps won eight medals in swimming events.

Source: *Sports Illustrated*

4 Highest and Lowest Elevation

Use the internet or other source to find the places on each continent with the highest and lowest elevations. Record your findings in a table like the one below. When listing the highest and lowest elevation, include both the name of the location and the measurement in feet and in meters. Which continent has the greatest difference in elevation?

Continent	Highest Elevation	Lowest Elevation	Difference
Africa			
Antarctica			
Asia			
Australia			
Europe			
North America			
South America			

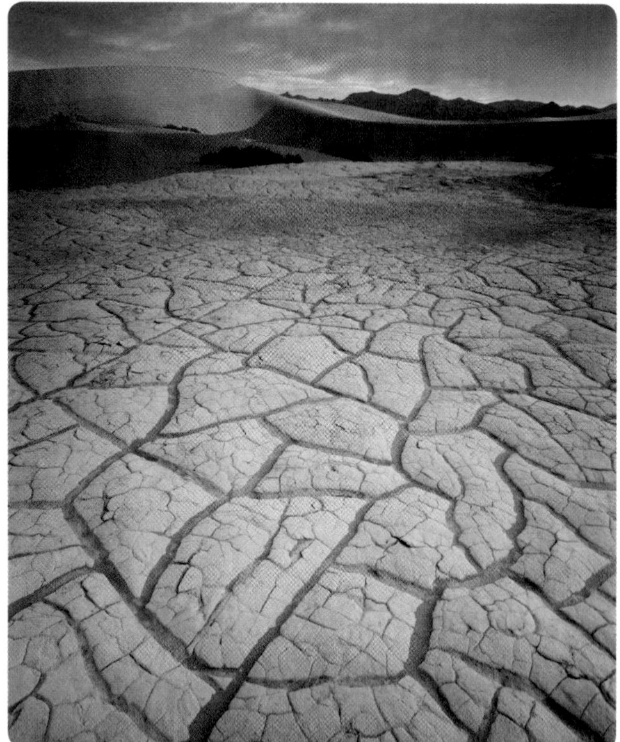

Death Valley, CA routinely tops 100°F during the summer months.

Source: *The World Almanac*

5 Card Toss

Rick Smith Jr., a magician and former college baseball pitcher, holds the Guinness World Record for the farthest throw of a playing card. He threw a single card a distance of 65.96 m (216 ft, 4 in.) at the Ohio State Wolstein Center in March, 2002.

a. Collect data on how far you and your classmates, or members of your family can throw a single playing card.

b. Organize this data in a table or other display.

c. What is the difference between the longest throw in your data and the world record?

Rick Smith Jr. tosses cards.

Chapter 4 Summary and Vocabulary

- Subtraction can arise from **take-away, comparison,** or **slide situations.**

- In take-away situations, $x - y$ stands for the amount left after y has been taken away from x. In the linear pair below and at the left, $m\angle BDA$ can be thought of as the amount left after y is taken from $180°$. So $m\angle BDA = 180° - y$. Similarly, with the perpendicular lines below and at the right, $m\angle EFG = 90° - x$.

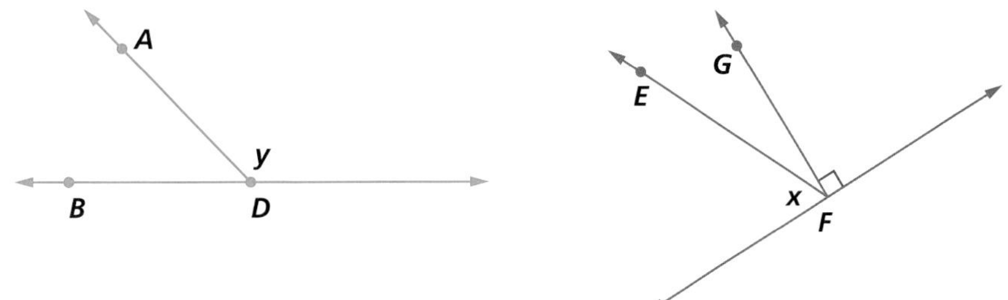

- In comparison situations, $x - y$ is how much more x is than y. The word **difference** for the answer to a subtraction problem comes from this use of subtraction.

- In slide situations, $x - y$ is the result after x has been decreased by y. In Chapter 3, we described this as an addition slide situation $x + -y$. Consequently, $x - y = x + -y$. This relationship enables any situation to be converted to an addition: instead of subtracting y, add the opposite of y.

- Another connection between subtraction and addition comes from **related facts:** $a + b = c$ means $b + a = c$, $c - a = b$, and $c - b = a$. Related facts, which can be represented by a **fact triangle,** can be used to solve simple equations involving addition or subtraction. The **Addition Property of Equality** helps with the solution of more complicated equations.

Theorems and Properties

Take-Away Model for Subtraction (p. 208)
Opposite of a Difference Property (p. 210)
Comparison Model for Subtraction (p. 214)
Slide Model for Subtraction (p. 220)
Algebraic Definition of Subtraction (Add-Opp Property) (p. 221)
Subtracting Fractions Property (p. 243)
Addition Property of Equality (p. 256)

Vocabulary

Lesson 4-1
minuend
subtrahend
difference

Lesson 4-4
related facts
fact triangle

Lesson 4-5
supplementary angles
vertical angles
bisect

Lesson 4-6
right angle
perpendicular
complementary angles
acute angle
obtuse angle
straight angle

Lesson 4-8
equation
sides of an equation
variable
open sentence
solve an equation
solution

Chapter 4 Self-Test

Take this test as you would take a test in class. You will need a calculator. Then use the Selected Answers section in the back of the book to check your work.

In 1–5, calculate without a calculator.

1. 15 – 42 – -5
2. -4.15 – -3.9 + 4.85
3. $\frac{5}{7} - \frac{3}{7} - -\frac{2}{7}$
4. $-\frac{3}{8} - \frac{2}{3}$
5. $5\frac{3}{4}$
   $\underline{-3\frac{4}{5}}$

6. Gina buys milk for \$3.49 and peanut butter for \$2.57. If she pays with a \$10 bill, how much change should she receive?

7. In an ice-skating competition, the winner had a score of 165.23. The last-place finisher had a score of 99.41. What is the difference in their scores?

In 8 and 9, refer to the diagram below. $\overline{AB}$ and $\overline{CD}$ intersect at *O*.

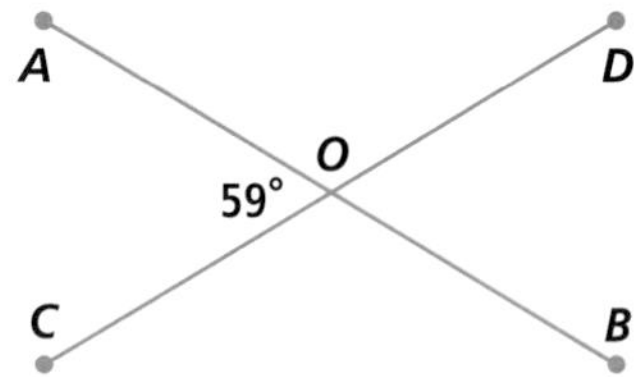

8. What is m∠*DOA*?
9. What is m∠*DOB*?

In 10 and 11, use the diagram below.

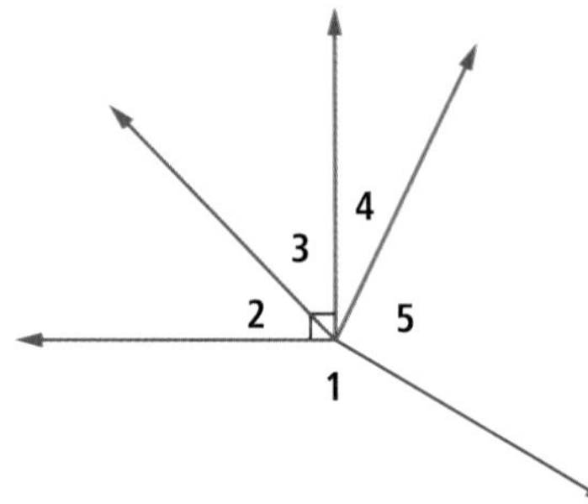

10. Which two angles are complementary?
11. Name one acute angle and one obtuse angle.

12. Solve the equation $x - -25 = -73$ using the Addition Property of Equality. Check your answer by substituting it in the original equation.

13. Consider this problem: Moses wants to buy a CD for \$5.70. He has already saved \$3.70. How much more does he need?
    a. Write an equation for the situation, using a variable to represent the unknown number.
    b. Solve your equation using the Addition Property of Equality.
    c. Check your answer.
    d. Write a sentence answering the question.

14. Tiara grew 3.7 inches last year. If she is 5 feet, 3 inches tall now, how tall was she one year ago?

15. In a recipe, Jamie mixes $5\frac{1}{4}$ cups of flour with $1\frac{3}{4}$ cups of cocoa. How much more flour does Jamie use than cocoa?

In 16 and 17, represent the subtraction expression on a number line.

16. 1.7 – 1.3
17. -4 – -5

18. Write the four related facts for the fact triangle below.

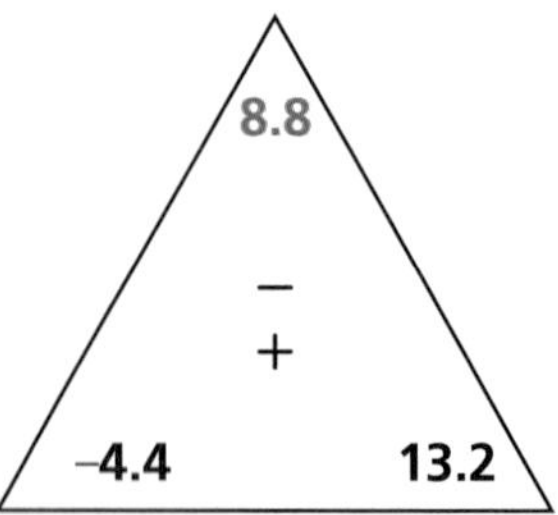

19. Consider the equation $-462 = -31 - x$.
   a. Draw a fact triangle for the equation.
   b. Using the triangle, write the related equations.
   c. Use one of your facts to find a value for x.

20. What is the weight of the mystery box below?

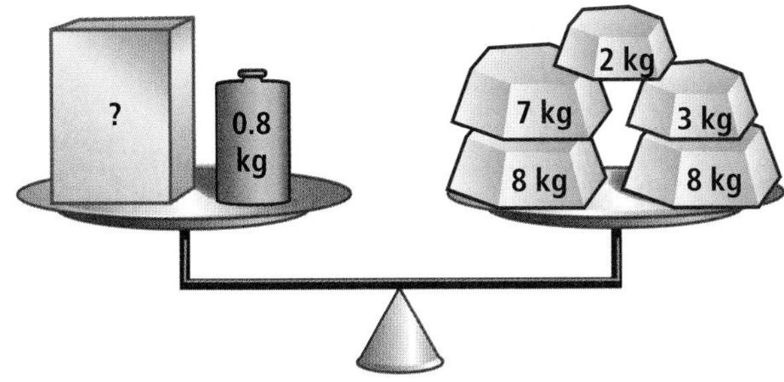

In 21 and 22, fill in the blanks.

21. $-3 - 5 = -3 +$ _?_

22. $-m - -s - -r =$ _?_ + _?_ + _?_

23. As of 2007, the record low temperature in Hawaii is 12°F. The record low temperature in Alaska is 92°F colder than that. What is the record low temperature in Alaska?

24. The measures of two of the angles of $\triangle PEW$ are shown. Find the measure of the third angle of the triangle and classify the angle as acute, obtuse, or right.

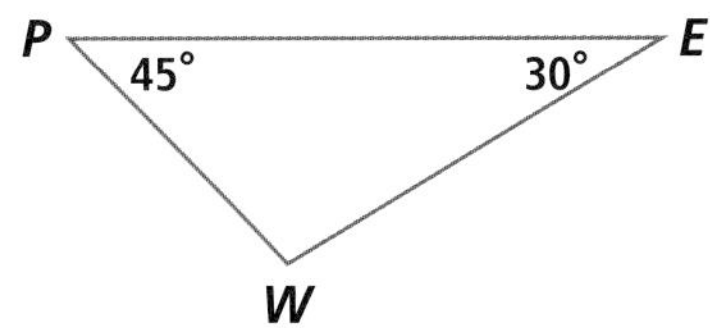

25. Solve for n: $2.7 - n = -5.3$.

Chapter 4 Chapter Review

SKILLS Procedures used to get answers

OBJECTIVE A Subtract positive and negative integers, fractions, and mixed numbers. (Lessons 4-3, 4-7)

In 1–4, calculate without a calculator.

1. $32 - -7$
2. $-45 - -3$
3. $-57 - 8 - 9$
4. $-92 - -12 - 170$

In 5 and 6, write as a single fraction in lowest terms.

5. $-\frac{8}{13} - \frac{7}{26}$
6. $-\frac{3}{10} - -\frac{1}{15}$

In 7 and 8, write as a single mixed number with the fraction in lowest terms.

7. $6 - 2\frac{3}{8}$
8. $-17\frac{5}{6} - 14\frac{2}{3}$

OBJECTIVE B Solve equations involving addition and subtraction. (Lesson 4-8)

In 9–12, solve for the variable.

9. $m - 11 = 7$
10. $n - -10 = -14$
11. $2.3 = -8.46 + x$
12. $p + \frac{2}{3} = \frac{1}{6}$

PROPERTIES The principles behind the mathematics

OBJECTIVE C Use the Add-Opp Property to rewrite subtraction problems as addition problems. (Lesson 4-3)

In 13–16, rewrite all subtractions as additions and evaluate.

13. $-3 - -9 - 5$
14. $12 - 4 - 6 - 5$
15. $3.5 - -2.45 - 1.28$
16. $4.9 - 8.75 - -0.234$

In 17 and 18, write each expression using only variables and addition.

17. $m - n$
18. $q - n - m$

OBJECTIVE D Know relationships among linear pairs and vertical angles formed by intersecting lines. (Lesson 4-5)

In 19–22, use the diagram below. $\overleftrightarrow{AD}$ and $\overleftrightarrow{BC}$ intersect at O.

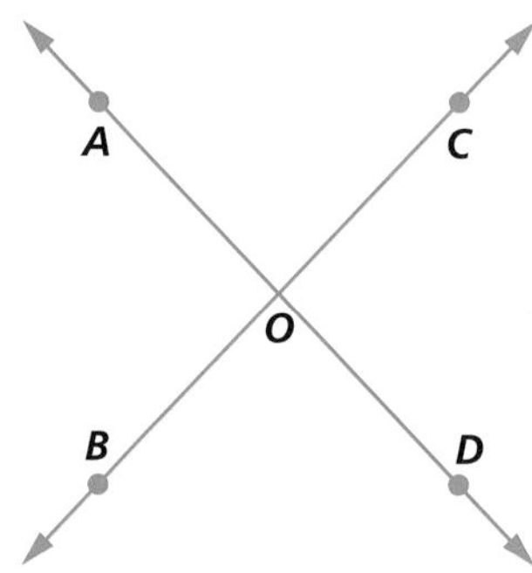

19. If $\angle AOC$ is a right angle, which other angles in the diagram must be right angles?
20. If $\angle AOC$ is acute, classify $\angle AOB$, $\angle DOB$, and $\angle DOC$ as acute, obtuse, or right angles.
21. If $m\angle AOC = 88°$, what is $m\angle BOD$?
22. If $m\angle AOC = 88°$, what is $m\angle COD$?

OBJECTIVE E Recognize acute, right, and obtuse angles, and complementary and supplementary angles. (Lessons 4-5, 4-6)

23. In your own words, explain when two angles are complementary.
24. In your own words, explain when two angles are supplementary.

In 25–28, use the diagram below. Without measuring, decide whether the angle seems to be acute, obtuse, or right.

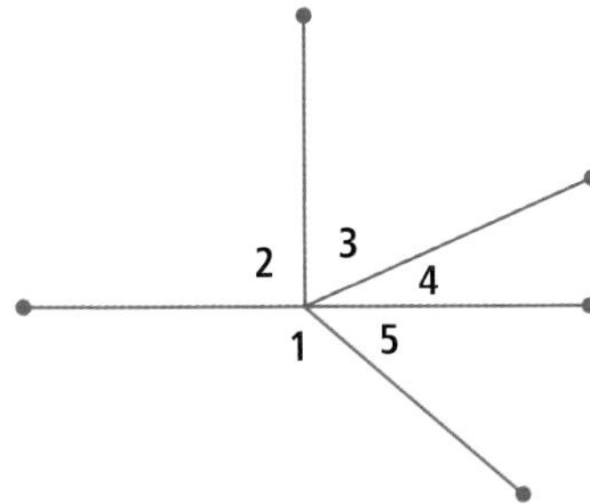

25. angle 1
26. angle 2
27. angle 3
28. angle 4

29. In $\triangle ABC$, $m\angle A = 41.8°$ and $m\angle B = 48.2°$. Find $m\angle C$ and tell whether $\angle C$ is acute, obtuse, or right.

OBJECTIVE F **Use properties of angles to find unknown measures of angles. (Lessons 4-5, 4-6)**

In 30–32, find the values of the variables.

30.

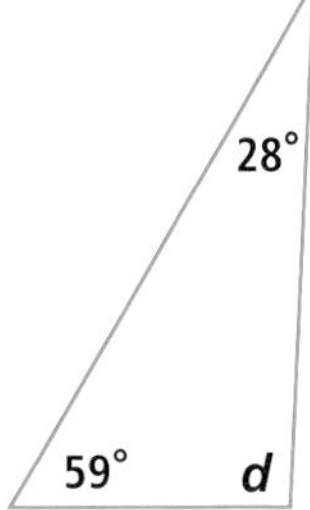

31.

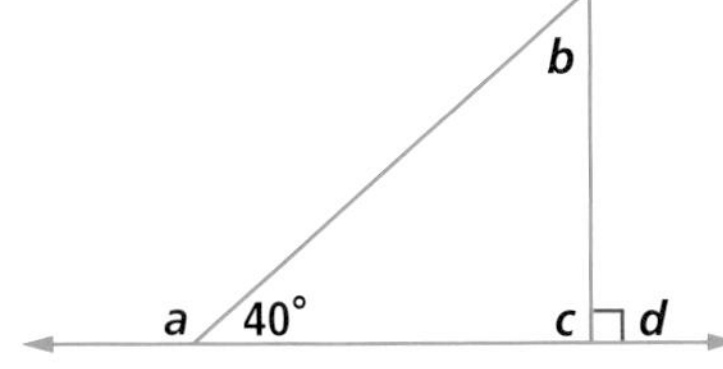

32.

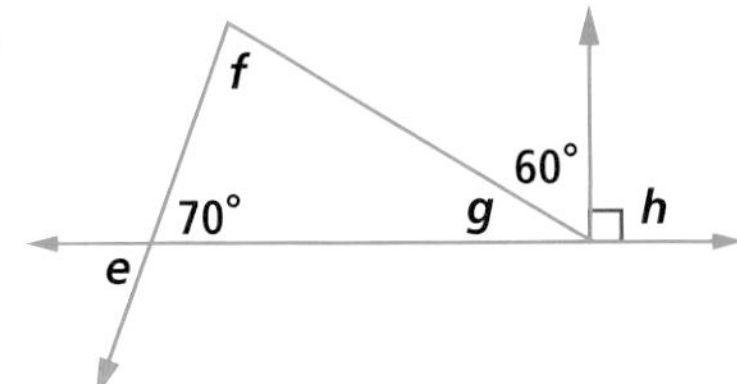

OBJECTIVE G **Use the Addition Property of Equality to help solve simple equations. (Lesson 4-9)**

In 33–38, tell what number can be added to both sides of the equation to solve it. Then solve the equation and check the answer.

33. $23 + x = 15$
34. $y + 298 = 423$
35. $1\frac{1}{2} = a + 3\frac{3}{8}$
36. $0.295 + b = -1.5$
37. $c - -3.2 = 1.8$
38. $5\frac{1}{16} = d - -1\frac{1}{3}$

USES Applications of mathematics in real-world situations

OBJECTIVE H **Use the Take-Away Model for Subtraction. (Lesson 4-1)**

39. If $\frac{1}{10}$ of the employees of a company left last year for another job, and $\frac{1}{20}$ retired, what fraction remained?

40. Two people are walking towards each other, having started 3 km apart. If each person walks 150 meters in a minute, how far apart will they be after 1 minute?

41. At the beginning of the 2007 season of Major League Baseball, Alex Rodriguez had 464 home runs. How many more home runs does he need to reach 800 home runs?

OBJECTIVE I **Use the Comparison Model for Subtraction. (Lesson 4-2)**

42. In 2006, there were 192 member nations in the United Nations. In 1962, there were 82 fewer members. How many members did the United Nations have in 1962?

43. In 1992, Edgar Martinez of the Seattle Mariners batted .343, while Ken Griffey, Jr. batted .308. How much higher was Martinez's batting average than Griffey Jr.'s?

44. In 1926, astrophysicist A.S. Eddington stated that there were about 3,000 million stars in the Milky Way galaxy. In 2000, the Encyclopedia Britannica stated that there were about 100 billion stars in the Milky Way. About how many more stars did the encyclopedia say there were in the Milky Way than Eddington?

45. The population of Philadelphia in 2005 was estimated as 1,463,281. What was the change in population if there were 1,517,550 people in Philadelphia in 2000?

OBJECTIVE J **Use the Slide Model for Subtraction. (Lesson 4-3)**

46. In Parsipanny, New Jersey, 14,987 people voted in a particular election. If voter turnout decreases by 5,248 people in the next election, how many people will vote in that election?

47. The temperature fell 10° to -4°. What was the original temperature?

48. Ramona lost 14.97 pounds in three months. She now weighs 107.03 pounds. How much did she weigh before she lost the weight?

OBJECTIVE K **Apply simple equations involving addition or subtraction. (Lessons 4-8, 4-9)**

In 49 and 50, write an equation to represent the situation. Use a variable to represent the unknown number. Then solve the equation.

49. When Alice's cat, Zephyr, was a new-born kitten, she weighed $\frac{5}{8}$ of a pound. Four months later she weighed $3\frac{1}{2}$ pounds. How much weight w did Zephyr gain?

50. Shayla took 35 seconds to make her first move in a timed chess game. If her clock shows 14 minutes, 25 seconds left, how much time t did she have at the start of the game?

REPRESENTATIONS Pictures, graphs, or objects that illustrate concepts

OBJECTIVE L **Picture subtraction of positive and negative numbers on a number line. (Lesson 4-3)**

In 51–54, picture the subtraction on a number line.

51. -5 – 8
52. -4.2 – 17.3
53. 5 + -7 – 10
54. -18.7 – -19 – 4.6

OBJECTIVE M **Use fact triangles to find related facts for addition and subtraction. (Lessons 4-4, 4-8)**

In 55–57, construct a fact triangle using the three numbers.

55. 4, -17, -13
56. $\frac{3}{4}, \frac{2}{3}, \frac{1}{12}$
57. 5.4, -2.2, 3.2

In 58–60, write the related facts for the fact triangle.

58.

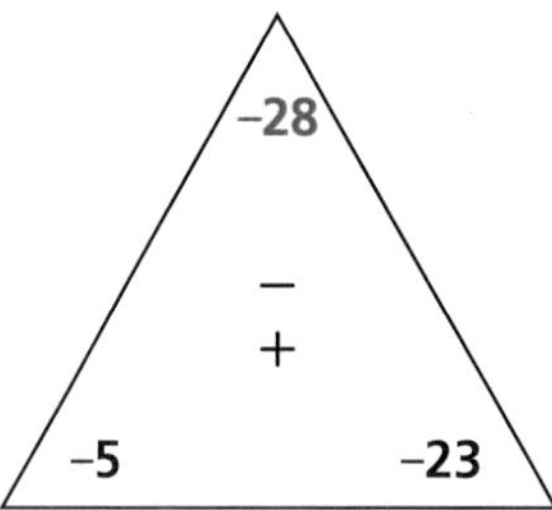

59.

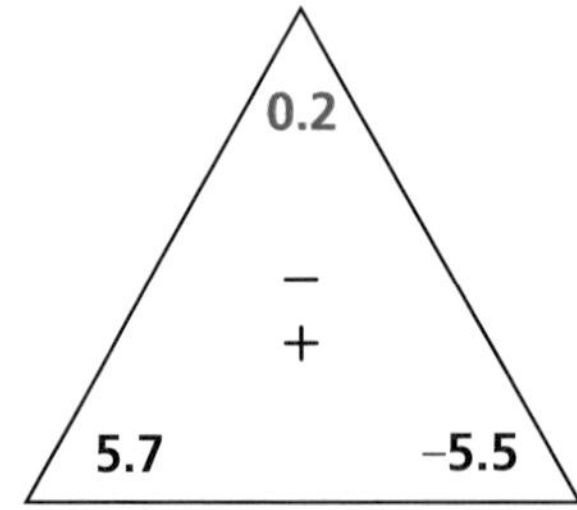

60.

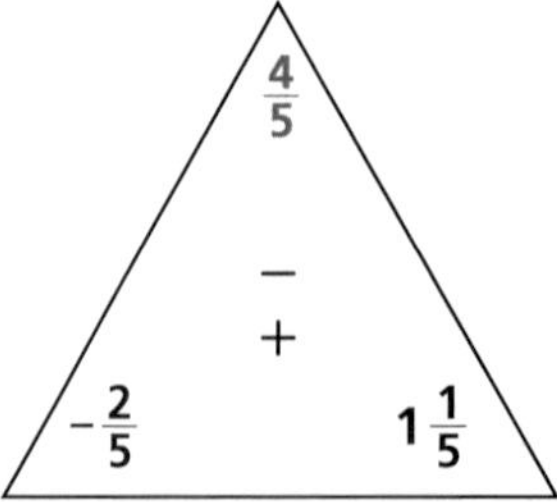

In 61 and 62, make a fact triangle to solve each equation.

61. $0.25 + x = 2.85$
62. $2\frac{1}{2} - v = 3\frac{1}{4}$

In 63 and 64, write the related facts pictured by the fact triangle and solve the equation.

63.

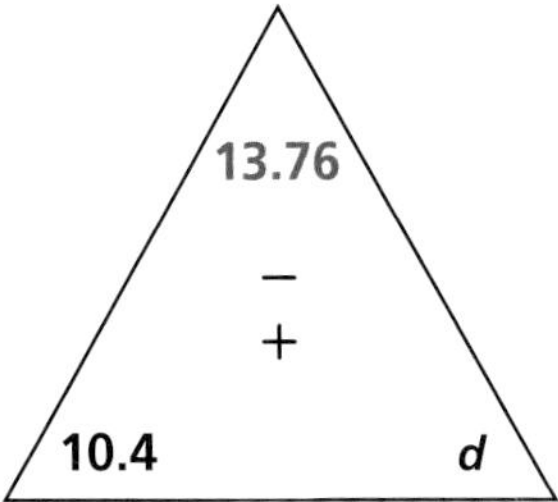

64.

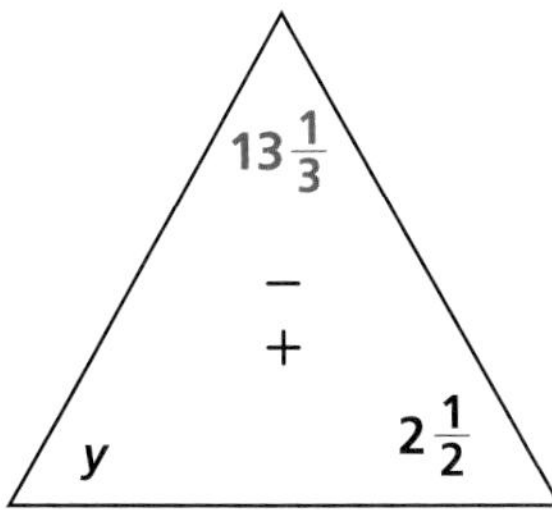

OBJECTIVE N Use balance scales to picture equations. (Lesson 4-9)

In 65 and 66, use the balance scale below.

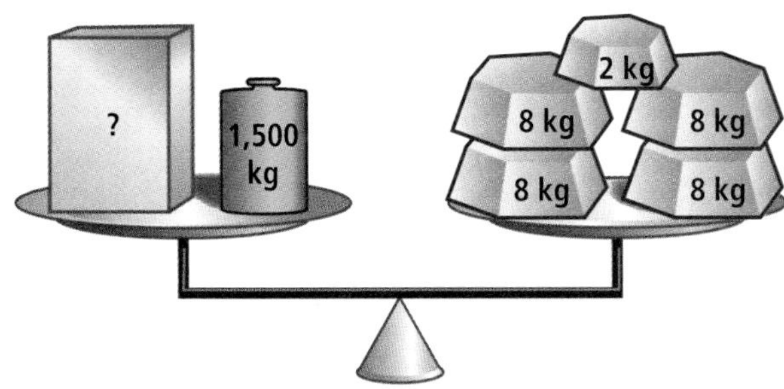

65. What is the weight of the mystery box?

66. Suppose a 5-kilogram weight is put on each side of the balance scale. What would the weight of the mystery box be now?

In 67 and 68, draw a balance scale to help solve the equation.

67. $m + 5 \text{ g} = 0.275 \text{ kg}$

68. $18 \text{ oz} + n = 4 \text{ lb}, 3 \text{ oz}$

Chapter

5 Statistics and Displays

Contents

The word *statistics* has two meanings. One meaning is as a field of study, like mathematics, biology, or history. **Statistics** is the science of the collection, organization, and interpretation of data. (A **datum** is a piece of information. **Data** is the plural of datum.) For example, statistics may be used to determine whether one medical treatment is more effective than another or to estimate the number of fish in a lake without actually catching all of them.

Statistic also means a single number used to describe a set of numbers. For example, you may already know about the mean, or average as a statistic describing the center of a set of data.

The table below summarizes data collected in 2004 about the birth places of people in the United States under the age of 18 who were not born in the United States.

Region of Origin	Number of Foreign-Born People 18 Years and Under
Europe	327,000
Asia	649,000
Latin America	1,836,000
Other	285,000

Source: U.S. Census Bureau

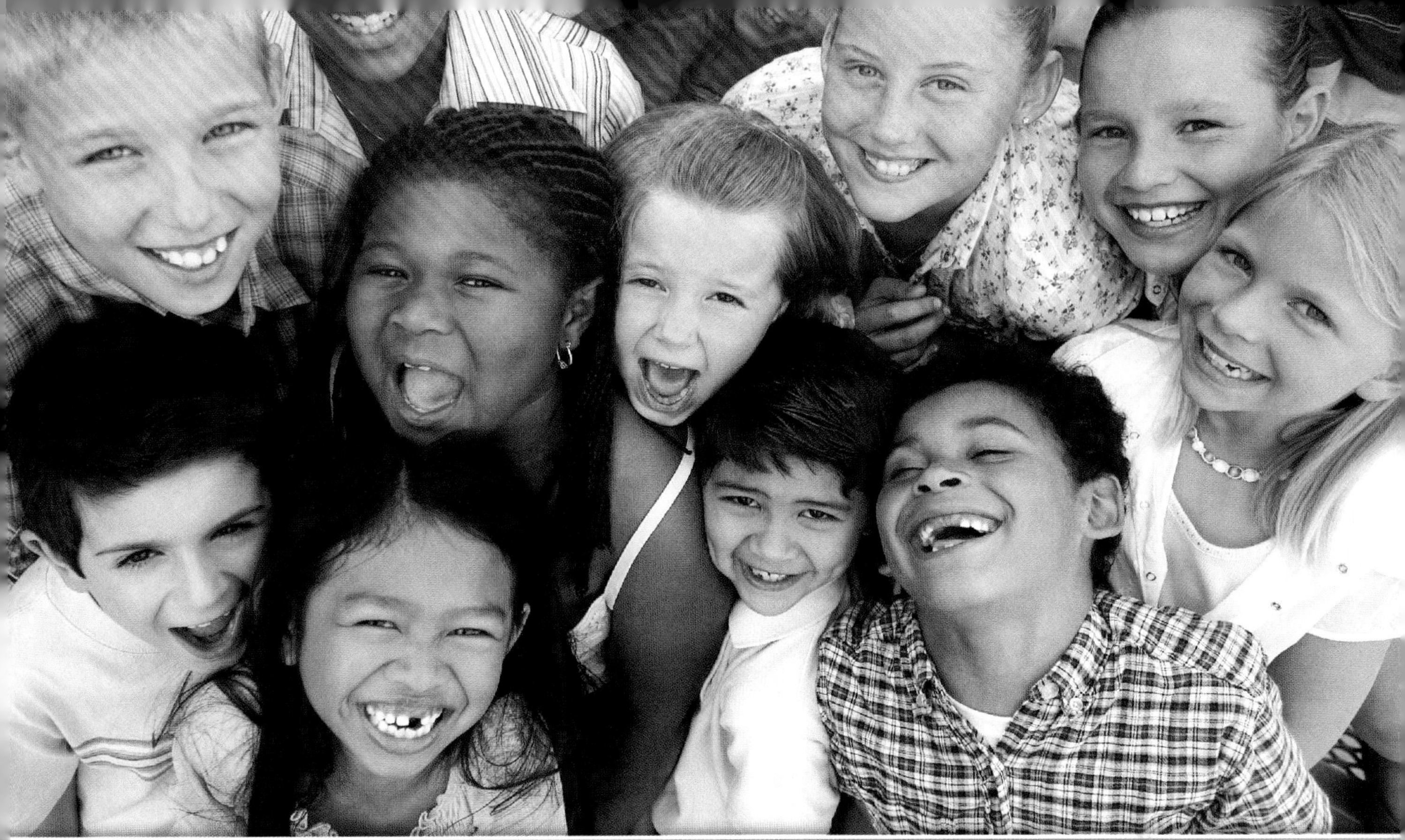

A *display* is a picture of data. Below are two displays of the data in the table on the previous page: a circle graph and a bar graph. Each display shows the data in a different way.

In this chapter, you will learn about different displays and how they present statistics and information.

Number of Foreign-Born People 18 Years and Under

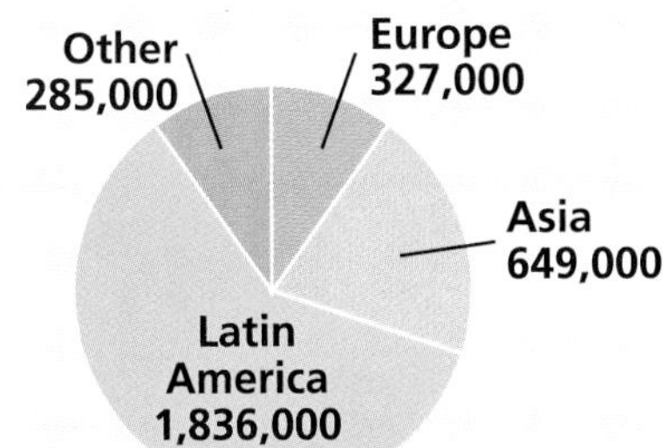

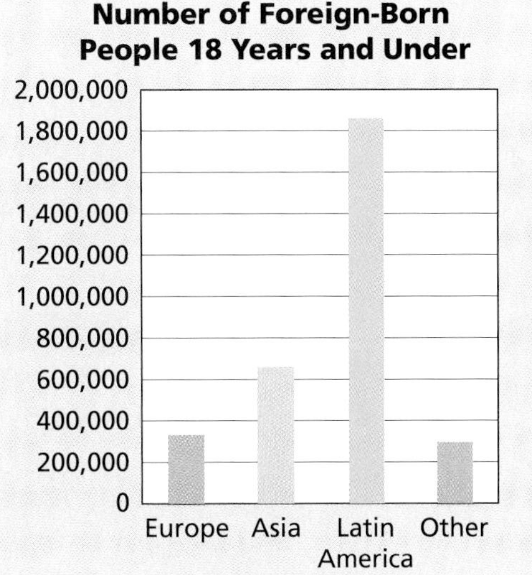

Lesson 5-1 Statistics

Vocabulary

statistics
minimum
maximum
mode
mean (average)
median
range

BIG IDEA Many different statistics are used in describing large sets of numbers.

Mental Math

Find the average of the two numbers.

a. 0, 2

b. 0, 1

c. 4, 10

d. $\frac{1}{4}, \frac{3}{4}$

Here is a table displaying data. Take a few minutes to study it.

Number of Teens Age 15–19 by State, 2003

State	Teenage Population	State	Teenage Population	State	Teenage Population
Alabama	317,306	Louisiana	347,200	Ohio	810,850
Alaska	57,058	Maine	93,767	Oklahoma	257,056
Arizona	389,565	Maryland	386,908	Oregon	244,825
Arkansas	195,362	Massachusetts	415,301	Pennsylvania	850,540
California	2,528,984	Michigan	728,381	Rhode Island	70,823
Colorado	315,934	Minnesota	376,843	South Carolina	288,841
Connecticut	234,892	Mississippi	216,778	South Dakota	60,909
Delaware	55,325	Missouri	412,683	Tennessee	392,372
Florida	1,100,327	Montana	71,149	Texas	1,668,884
Georgia	613,277	Nebraska	131,362	Utah	196,331
Hawaii	85,262	Nevada	145,450	Vermont	45,701
Idaho	108,976	New Hampshire	92,650	Virginia	508,355
Illinois	885,237	New Jersey	573,100	Washington	440,566
Indiana	442,311	New Mexico	148,512	Washington, DC	27,150
Iowa	211,983	New York	1,279,454	West Virginia	117,417
Kansas	204,865	North Carolina	554,623	Wisconsin	407,493
Kentucky	280,816	North Dakota	48,477	Wyoming	40,187

Source: U.S. Census Bureau

STOP QY1

What information is contained in the table?

Three kinds of **statistics** are most commonly used to describe data: *landmarks, measures of center,* and *measures of spread.* You have probably seen examples of each of these before.

Landmarks

We give the name *landmark* to certain statistics. The **minimum** value is the least value of the data. The **maximum** value is the largest value. The **mode** is the most common value. Sometimes there is no mode; other times there is more than one.

Measures of Center

There are two common measures of center—the *mean* and the *median.* The most common measure of center is the mean. The **mean** of a data set is the sum of all the numbers divided by the quantity of numbers. It is often called the **average.** However, because there are many averages used in statistics, mean is preferred. In the table, the mean number of teens age 15–19 in a state is found by adding all the populations and dividing by 51, which is the total number of states (including Washington, D.C.) in the data set.

The **median** is the middle number when numbers are ordered by size. In a data set with no single middle number, the median is the mean of the two middle numbers (their sum divided by 2).

See QY2 at the right.

QY2

Refer to the table on the previous page.

a. Find the maximum and minimum populations.

b. Explain why there is no mode.

c. The total population age 15–19 is 20,478,418. Use a calculator to calculate the mean.

Measures of Spread

There are many measures of how data is spread out from a mean, median, or landmarks. In this book, we discuss only one measure of spread. The **range** is the difference between the largest and smallest numbers in the data.

$$\text{range} = \text{maximum value} - \text{minimum value}$$

QY3

What is the range of the data in the table on the previous page?

Activity

MATERIALS metric tape measure

Step 1 Make a table of the heights of everyone in your class. Measure the heights to the nearest centimeter.

Step 2 Put the heights in increasing order.

Step 3 Find the three landmarks for these heights.

Step 4 Find the measure of spread and the two measures of center.

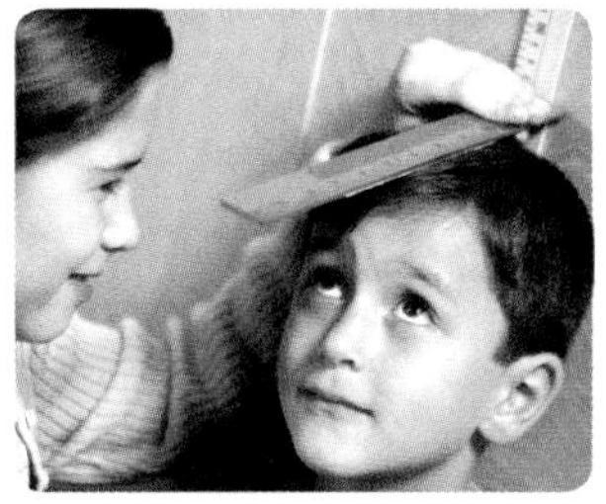

Do you remember how tall you were two years ago? How much taller are you now?

Now you can play *Let's Data Deal*. The directions for this game are on pages G18–G19 at the back of your book.

Questions

COVERING THE IDEAS

In 1–6, use the information on pages 270 and 271.

1. What are the two meanings of the word *statistics*?
2. In 2004, how many people under 18 in the United States were born in Europe?
3. What is the mean of the data?
4. What is the median of the data?
5. **True or False** Of the foreign-born people living in the United States in 2004, more than twice as many were born in Latin America than in any other area.
6. **True or False** In 2004, more than 25% of people in the United States born outside the United States were born in Asia.

In 7–10, each quote is from a report about the amount of money spent on food by families of four at a baseball game. Which statistic is being reported?

7. "On the average, a family of four spent $23.47."
8. "Families spent as much as $55 on food."
9. "More often than any other, a family of four spent between $20 and $25."
10. "A typical family spent about $20."

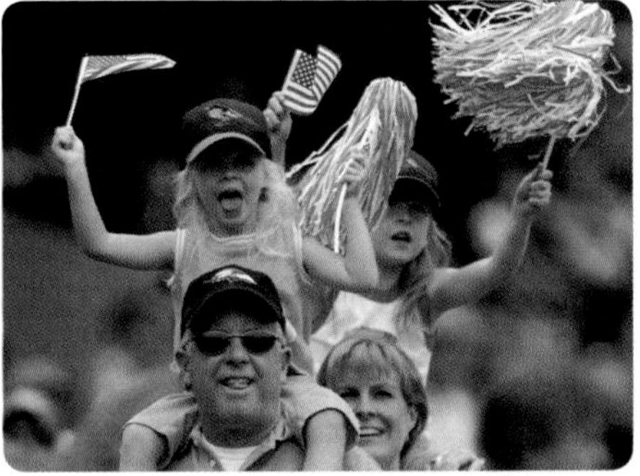

Major League Baseball closed its 2007 regular season with a record attendance of 79,502,524.

Sources: Major League Baseball

11. A class of 27 students was surveyed. Students were asked about the numbers of siblings they have. (A *sibling* is a brother or sister.) The results are shown in the table below. *Note:* A frequency of 3 for zero siblings means that 3 different students reported having zero siblings.
    a. What is the median number of siblings?
    b. What is the mode number of siblings?
    c. What is the mean number of siblings? (*Hint*: What is the total number of siblings?)
    d. What is the range?
    e. Which of these four statistics was easiest for you to calculate? Which was hardest? Why was that statistic hardest to calculate?

Number of Siblings	Frequency
0	3
1	8
2	8
3	5
4	2
5	1

12. A group of people were asked, "Which evening do you watch television the most?" Answers were tallied as shown here.

Day	Tallies
Monday	卌 II
Tuesday	卌 IIII
Wednesday	卌 卌 III
Thursday	卌 IIII
Friday	卌 IIII
Saturday	卌 卌 卌 II
Sunday	卌 卌 卌 II

a. How many people were questioned?

b. Find the mode of these data.

In 2005, the average American household tuned into television 8 hours, 11 minutes per day.

Source: Nielson Media Research

13. Five common statistics start with the letter *m*: maximum, mean, median, minimum, and mode.

a. Which are measures of center?

b. Which are measures of spread?

c. Which are landmarks?

APPLYING THE MATHEMATICS

14. Make up a set of data showing the ages in years of 10 students that satisfies *both* of the following conditions:

i. The median age is 12.5 years.

ii. The range is 9 years.

15. Create a set of ten or more numbers with *all* of the following characteristics:

i. range: 8

ii. minimum: 5

iii. median: 11

iv. two modes: 9 and 12

16. The table at the right gives the low temperature in New York City for the last ten days of a recent summer month.

a. Find the minimum, maximum, range, and median of these data.

b. Suppose another data set gave the *hourly* minimum temperatures in New York City for these same ten days. How would the minimum compare to the minimum in Part a?

c. How would the range of the data set of hourly temperatures compare with the range in Part a?

Date	Low Temperature (°F)
7/22	68
7/23	62
7/24	59
7/25	67
7/26	71
7/27	72
7/28	72
7/29	72
7/30	70
7/31	73

Source: www.weather.com

17. According to the Social Security Administration, the most popular names for babies in the United States in 2006 were Jacob (for boys) and Emily (for girls). Which landmark of data is reported in the previous sentence?

18. A reporter asked twenty people who bought lottery tickets what their income was per week. In dollars, the incomes were 0, 0, 0, 0, 0, 0, 0, 200, 400, 400, 500, 500, 500, 600, 800, 800, 800, 1600, 1600, and 7700. The reporter wants to describe the income of a person who bought a lottery ticket. Which statistic would the reporter have used if he reported the following statement?
    a. "More people who buy lottery tickets do not have a weekly income than people who earn any other specific amount."
    b. "The typical lottery-ticket buyer earns $450 a week."
    c. "On average, a lottery-ticket buyer earns $820 a week."

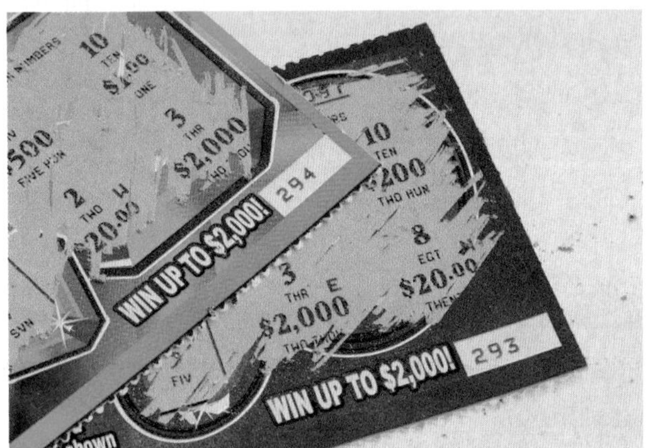

What would you do if you won the lottery?

REVIEW

19. What property says that if you add the same number to both sides of an equation, the equation will still be true? **(Lesson 4-9)**

20. Find the weight of the mystery box on the balance below. **(Lesson 4-9)**

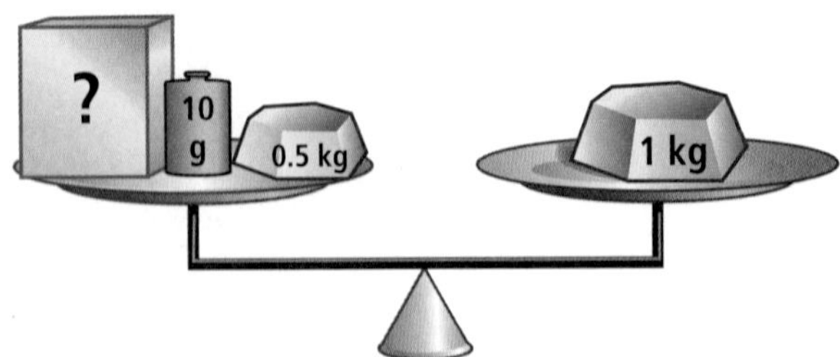

21. **True or False** If Pine Avenue and Main Street intersect and form a 60° angle, then they are perpendicular. **(Lesson 4-6)**

22. Write the related facts and use them to solve the equation $4.83 + m = 2.74$. **(Lesson 4-4)**

23. The table below gives the distances in miles between some cities in the world. Someone copied the table but forgot to copy the top row with the names of the columns. **(Lesson 4-2)**

Chicago	7,793	4,250	3,950	1,745
Hong Kong	0	5,549	5,982	7,195
Honolulu	5,549	0	7,228	2,574
London	5,982	7,228	0	5,382
Los Angeles	7,195	2,574	5,382	0
New York	8,054	4,964	3,458	2,451
Paris	5,985	7,438	213	5,588
Washington, D.C.	8,147	4,519	3,663	2,300

Source: www.infoplease.com

a. Name the columns.

b. Order the other seven cities by their distance from Los Angeles, starting with the closest city.

c. The number 7,195 appears twice in the table. Is this coincidence, or is there a reason why it appears twice?

24. Find the sum of $72\% + \frac{3}{5} + 0.14$. **(Lessons 3-1, 2-2)**

EXPLORATION

25. Two other landmark statistics are the 1st and 3rd quartiles. How are these statistics found? Give an example.

QY ANSWERS

1. The table gives the teenage population by state (and Washington, D.C.) in 2003.

2a. Maximum: 2,528,984 teenagers; minimum: 27,150 teenagers

2b. Each population value appears the same number of times: once.

2c. 401,538

3. 2,501,834

Lesson 5-2

Calculating Statistics from Lists

Vocabulary

list

BIG IDEA By putting data into a list, you can use a calculator or computer to calculate many statistics.

Mental Math

Find the median.

a. 1, 2, 3, 4, 5

b. 5, 8, 11, 28, 4257

c. 17, 2.8, 3.14, –5, 0

d. 9, –15, 42, 573, 46, 80

Before there were computers, it was very difficult to calculate statistics when there were lots of data. The first calculating machine was made by Wilhelm Schickard in Germany in 1623. Only a few were made. A later machine was made in 1642 by Blaise Pascal, a French mathematician, when he was 21 years old. Blaise did this to help his father, a tax collector, add long columns of numbers. About 50 of Pascal's machines survive today.

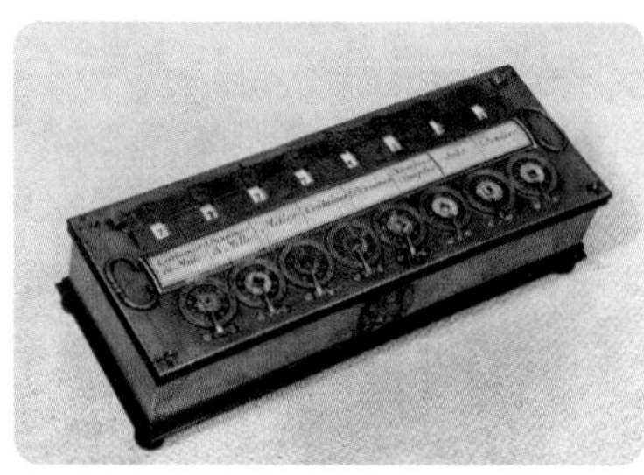

The first digital calculator invented by Blaise Pascal in 1642.

Around 1820, another Frenchman, Charles Xavier Thomas de Colmar, created the first mass-produced calculating machine, the Thomas Arithmometer. This machine could add, subtract, multiply, and divide. Through the 1800s and early 1900s these and other machines were used to calculate statistics. They were about as big as today's desktop computers and very bulky.

The first electronic computers were built in the 1940s. They were so big that one computer would fill a room. With the invention of the transistor, and then the silicon chip, computers became smaller and smaller. In the early 1970s, the first hand-held calculators appeared. In the late 1970s, the first personal computers were sold. Today's small calculators can do more than those first personal computers. Almost all people who work with statistics use technology to help them with calculations.

Organizing Data into a List

One way to organize data is to put it in a *list.* A **list** is a sequence of numbers. You can write a list in a row or column. For example, the table of numbers of teens on page 272 contains a list with 51 numbers. Each number is identified with a state.

Here is a list of recent costs (in dollars) of laptop computers.

350	550	400	500	1,660	1,200	850	1,100	2,540	1,070
530	400	550	630	500	1,200	960	1,300	1,250	760
470	1,700	680	1,050	900	1,000	580	1,360	1,500	840
400	940	2,700	810	600	1,060				

Some statistics about these data can be found without much work.

QY

Determine the minimum cost, maximum cost, and range of the costs of computers in this list.

Other statistics can be calculated by hand, but it may be quicker, and you may get more accurate results, if you use technology. Activity 1 shows how to create and use a list. The details may be different for your calculator or computer. Be sure you know the exact steps to use for your technology.

Activity 1

MATERIALS calculator or computer with spreadsheet software

Work with a partner. Use technology to determine the mean, median, and mode for the list of computer costs.

Step 1 Find out how to enter a list. On a spreadsheet, you enter the data in a column. On one calculator, you press [STAT], choose 1 : Edit, and press [ENTER]. This identifies a list called L1. The data will be put into that column.

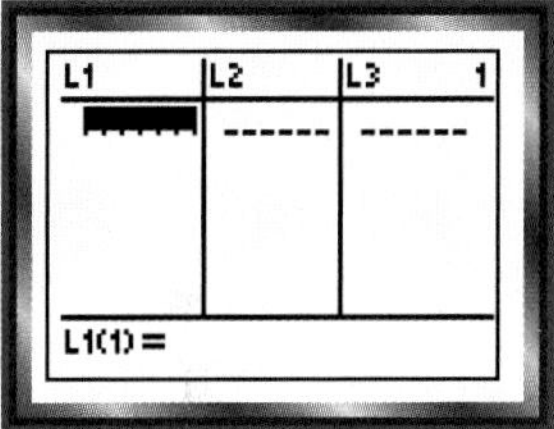

Step 2 Clear the list of any previous data. On one calculator, you can highlight L1, then press [CLEAR] and [ENTER].

Step 3 Enter the data. Have one person call out the numbers and the other enter them. Switch halfway through the list. On a spreadsheet, enter the data in column A. On a calculator, enter them in column L1. One calculator shows you the item being entered at the bottom. L1 (6) stands for the sixth number in L1.

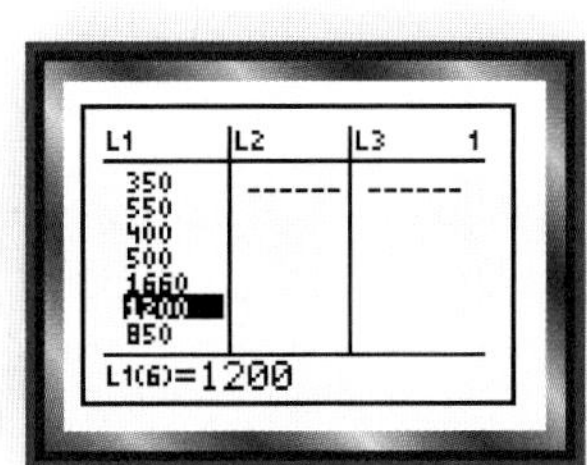

Step 4 Once all the data are entered, order them from least to greatest. Use a SORT command on a spreadsheet. On this calculator, press [STAT], choose 2 : SortA, and then press [2nd] L1 [ENTER].

Step 5 Check your list to make sure the data are sorted and entered correctly. The last entry should be in L1 (36), because there are 36 values.

Step 6 Read the ordered list to find the median and mode. The median will be the mean of the 18th and 19th numbers in the list. Because these numbers are 850 and 900, the median cost is $875.

(continued on next page)

Step 7 Use technology to determine the mean. On a spreadsheet, you may use AVERAGE(A1:A36). On one calculator, press [2nd][STAT], select 3:mean(under the MATH menu and press [ENTER]. Then, press [2nd][STAT], select 1:L1 under the NAMES menu and press [ENTER][ENTER]. Similarly, you can also find the minimum, median, and maximum values.

When you are finished with Activity 1, do not clear the data. You will use the data in Activity 2.

Exploring How Changes in Data Affect the Statistics

When you have data in a list, you can see how changing the data affects the statistics.

Activity 2

MATERIALS calculator or computer with spreadsheet software

Step 1 Use your list from Activity 1 to fill in the second row of the table.

Data	Number of Items	Minimum	Maximum	Range	Mode	Median	Mean
Original	36	?	?	?	?	?	?
Delete the minimum value.	35	?	?	?	?	?	?
Restore the original data. Then delete the maximum.	35	?	?	?	?	?	?
Restore the original data. Add a new maximum of 3,000.	37	?	?	?	?	?	?

Step 2 Complete the table, computing the statistics using technology.

Step 3 Which change in the data leads to the greatest change in the statistics in the table? Defend your answer.

Step 4 If someone asked you how much a laptop computer costs, what answer would you give? Why would you give that answer?

Now you can play *Let's Data Deal: Discard Variation*. The directions for this game are on page G19 at the back of your book.

Questions

COVERING THE IDEAS

1. a. How many years ago was the first calculating machine made?
   b. In what country was the first calculating machine made?
2. What two inventions enabled calculating machines to be made smaller and smaller?
3. In the technology you use, explain how you can put a list in order from least to greatest value.

In 4 and 5, use the calculator screen at the right.

L1	L2	L3 1
268	------	------
324		
580		
97		
286		
403		

L1(7)=191

4. Give the list location of the highlighted value.
5. What is the value of L1(3)?

In 6–8, use the data set evaluated on the calculator screen below.

6. What is the minimum of the data set?
7. What is the sum of the numbers in the data set?
8. What is the mean of the numbers in the data set?

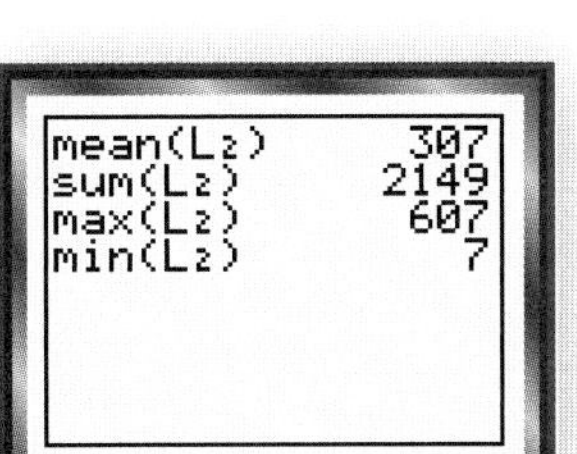

9. A group of 10 friends kept track of how many minutes they spent talking on their cell phones in one week. Here are the results: 20, 45, 10, 0, 30, 128, 75, 25, 180, and 40.
   a. Put these values in a list and order them from least to greatest.
   b. Find the maximum, minimum, range, and median.
   c. Find the mean.
   d. What is the total number of minutes these friends spent talking on cell phones during the week?
10. The friend in Question 9 who reported talking on the phone for 0 minutes meant to say 20 minutes. Without doing any calculations, determine whether each statistic will increase, decrease, or stay the same.
    a. maximum
    b. minimum
    c. range
    d. median
    e. mean

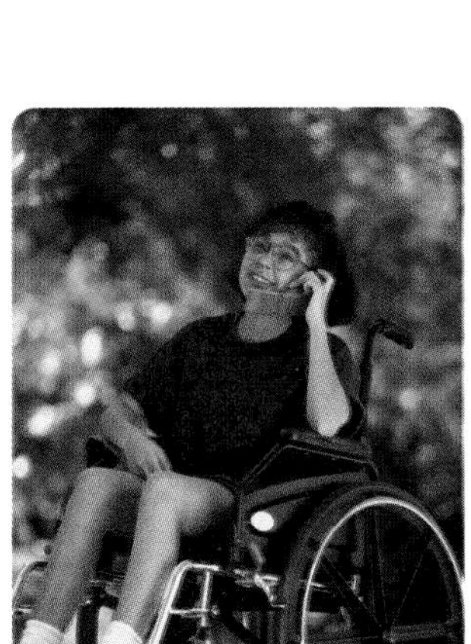

As of 2004, about $\frac{1}{2}$ of the population owns a cell phone.

Source: CTIA

APPLYING THE MATHEMATICS

11. Tamara's five test scores for this grading period are 87, 91, 85, 90, and 92.
    a. What score does Tamara need to get on the 6th test to have a mean score of exactly 90?
    b. What score does Tamara need to get on the 6th test to have a median score of exactly 90?

12. The state of Hawaii consists of 8 major islands and over 100 smaller islands and atolls. The 8 islands (one of which is called Hawaii, or "the Big Island") and their areas in square miles are shown in the table.
    a. Determine the mean, median, and range of these data.
    b. Which of those three statistics would change the most if the uninhabited island of Kahoolawe is deleted from the list?

Island	Area (sq mi)
Hawaii	4,028
Kahoolawe	45
Molokai	260
Kauai	552
Maui	727
Lanai	140
Oahu	597
Niihau	70

In 2007, over 7 million tourists visited the Hawaiian Islands.

Source: Hawaii Department of Tourism

In 13 and 14, use the tables below.

Ten Driest U.S. Cities	Annual Precipitation (in.)
Alamosa, CA	7.13
Bakersfield, CA	5.72
Bishop, CA	5.61
El Paso, TX	7.82
Las Vegas, NV	4.19
Phoenix, AZ	7.11
Reno, CA	7.49
Winnemuca, NV	7.82
Winslow, AZ	7.64
Yuma, AZ	2.65

Ten Wettest U.S. Cities	Annual Precipitation (in.)
Astoria, OR	69.60
Blue Canyon, CA	67.87
Hilo, HI	128.00
Miami, FL	59.55
Mobile, AL	64.64
New Orleans, LA	59.74
Pensacola, FL	61.16
Quillayute, WA	104.50
Tallahassee, FL	64.59
West Palm Beach, FL	59.72

Source: National Climatic Data Center

13. a. Find the maximum, minimum, range, mode, median, and mean of yearly precipitation of the 10 driest U.S. cities.
    b. Shayna said that she could remove 8 of the 10 numbers without changing the median. Is she right? If so, which 8 numbers could she remove?
    c. Hiroshi said he could remove 8 of the 10 numbers without changing the range. Is he right? If so, which 8 numbers could he remove?
    d. Marisa said she could remove 8 of the 10 numbers without changing the mean. Is she right? If so, which 8 numbers could she remove?
    e. Nicole said she could remove 8 of the 10 numbers without changing the mode. Is she right? If so, which 8 numbers could she remove?

14. a. Find the maximum, minimum, range, mode, median, and mean of yearly precipitation of the 10 wettest U.S. cities.
    b. Carla said, "Ignore everything on the lists but the numbers. I can add one more number to the list of the 10 driest U.S. cities and the median will be greater than that for the 10 wettest U.S. cities." Can Carla do what she claims?
    c. Fernando said, "Ignore everything on the lists but the numbers. I can add one more number to the list of the 10 driest U.S. cities and the mean will be greater than that for the 10 wettest U.S. cities." Can Fernando do what he claims?

Because Miami is located near two coasts, it is more susceptible to rainy weather than most cities.

REVIEW

15. Consider the measures of the four angles of a quadrilateral. What are all the possible values for the mean of these four measures? **(Lessons 5-1, 3-7)**

16. Give an example of a data set having at least five values in which the mean is an integer and the median is not. **(Lesson 5-1)**

17. a. Bags of oranges are on sale for $6.89 per bag. If Josephine buys three bags of oranges, how much money will she spend?
    b. If each bag of oranges has from 11 to 15 oranges, find the maximum and minimum total number of oranges she might have bought.
    c. Find the maximum cost and minimum cost per orange. **(Lessons 5-1, 4-1)**

18. In a soccer league, each team plays G games during the season. Suppose a team wins W games, loses L games, and ties T games. Write an equation that shows how these variables are related. **(Lesson 3-1)**

19. **Fill in the Blank** The laptop computer costs in this lesson were rounded to the nearest __?__. **(Lesson 2-6)**

EXPLORATION

20. On the Internet or in a magazine or newspaper, find at least 10 different costs of a particular kind of item. Calculate the landmarks and the measures of center and spread for these costs.

21. Al looked at Activity 1 and decided there was too much typing to make the list. So he didn't type any of the 0s that were the ones digits. That is, he entered 35, 55, 40, 50, and so on. What did Al have to do to each statistic he calculated, with his data in order, to get the right answers for Activity 1?

QY ANSWER

minimum: 350

maximum: 2,700

range: 2,350

Lesson 5-3 Stem-and-Leaf Plots

Vocabulary

stem-and-leaf plot

stem

leaf

▶ **BIG IDEA** Stem-and-leaf plots enable some statistics to be determined quite easily.

In the previous lesson, you organized data in lists. Another way to organize data is to use a *stem-and-leaf plot.* A **stem-and-leaf plot** is a tool for organizing data sets with about 15 to 50 numbers of similar value. Typical data of this type might be ages of people, temperatures, years, lengths, or prices of similar items.

In a stem-and-leaf plot, each number is split at a specific decimal place. For example, 135 might be split as 1|35 or 13|5. The digits to the left of the vertical line form the **stem.** The digits to the right form the **leaf.** The key to the plot is that each stem is written only once, while the leaves are listed every time they appear. For example, if both 135 and 136 appear and are split as 13|5 and 13|6, then you would write 13|5 6. If you made the split 1|35 and 1|36, then you would write 1|35 36.

The manager recorded the weights of a group of 24 sixth graders trying out for the middle-school football team. The coach used the data to make a stem-and-leaf plot with the ones digits as the leaves.

Weights of Boys Trying out for Football

Manager's List			
68	101	81	65
125	104	95	101
116	117	113	62
79	94	122	101
89	97	93	102
105	82	100	133

Coach's Stem-and-Leaf Plot

6	8	5	2				
7	9						
8	1	9	2				
9	5	4	7	3			
10	1	4	1	1	2	5	0
11	6	7	3				
12	5	2					
13	3						

Mental Math

Find the perimeter of the figure.

a.

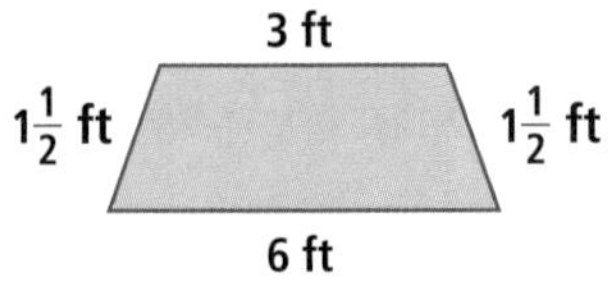

b.

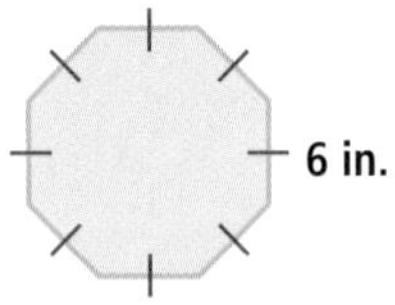

Why Is a Stem-and-Leaf Plot Useful?

Notice that a stem-and-leaf plot is like a bar graph on its side. But, unlike a bar graph, a stem-and-leaf plot shows all the data values. This allows you to determine statistics from a stem-and-leaf display that you can't determine from a bar graph.

GUIDED

Example 1

Determine the minimum, median, maximum, mode, and range for the stem-and-leaf display of weights on the previous page.

These football players are demonstrating a 3-point stance. Three points of their body are touching the ground (both feet and one hand).

Solution First, put the data in order.

6	2	5	8				
7	9						
8	1	?	?				
9	?	?	?	7			
10	?	?	?	?	?	?	5
11	?	?	?				
12	?	?					
13	?						

The smallest stem is 6 and the smallest leaf is 2, so the minimum is __?__.

There are 24 weights, so the median is the average of the __?__ and __?__ weights.

Counting from the top, these weights are __?__ and __?__, so the median is __?__.

The last entry, __?__, is the maximum.

The mode is the number that appears the most, which is __?__.

The range is __?__.

The stem-and-leaf plot in the next example includes negative numbers.

GUIDED

Example 2

The table on the next page has two numerical lists for each state. The first list is the record low temperatures (in °F) of the 50 states and the District of Columbia (D.C.). The second is the year the record occurred.

(continued on next page)

State	Low	Year	State	Low	Year	State	Low	Year
AL	-27	1966	KY	-37	1994	ND	-60	1936
AK	-80	1971	LA	-16	1899	OH	-39	1899
AZ	-40	1971	ME	-48	1925	OK	-27	1930
AR	-29	1905	MD	-40	1912	OR	-54	1933
CA	-45	1937	MA	-35	1981	PA	-42	1904
CO	-61	1985	MI	-51	1934	RI	-25	1996
CT	-32	1961	MN	-60	1996	SC	-19	1985
DE	-17	1893	MS	-19	1966	SD	-58	1936
D.C.	-15	1899	MO	-40	1905	TN	-32	1917
FL	-2	1899	MT	-70	1954	TX	-23	1933
GA	-17	1940	NE	-47	1989	UT	-69	1985
HI	12	1979	NV	-50	1937	VT	-50	1933
ID	-60	1943	NH	-47	1934	VA	-30	1985
IL	-36	1999	NJ	-34	1904	WA	-48	1968
IN	-36	1994	NM	-50	1951	WI	-55	1996
IA	-47	1996	NY	-52	1979	WV	-37	1917
KS	-40	1905	NC	-34	1985	WY	-66	1933

Source: U.S. National Climate Data Center

a. Construct a stem-and-leaf plot of the record-low temperatures.

b. What does the plot show?

Solution

a. The natural place to split the numbers is between the units digit and the tens digit. Think of a one-digit number as having a tens digit of 0. Since the smallest number is –80, which will be split as –8 | 0, the stems range from 1 to –8. List the possible stems in a vertical column.

Stem	Leaves
1	?
0	
-0	?
-1	? ? ? ? ? ?
-2	7 ? ? ? ?
-3	? ? ? ? ? ? ? ? ? ? ?
-4	? ? ? ? ? ? ? ? ? ? ?
-5	? ? ? ? ? ? ? ?
-6	? ? ? ? ? ?
-7	?
-8	0

Now put the leaves onto the diagram. For –27, a 7 goes in the –2 row to the right of the bar. For –80, a 0 goes in the –8 row. Proceed in this manner until all 51 units digits are entered.

b. The display shows that all but one record-low state temperature is negative. Also, by looking at the lengths of the stems, you can see that the most common lowest temperatures are in the –30s and –40s.

See QY at the right.

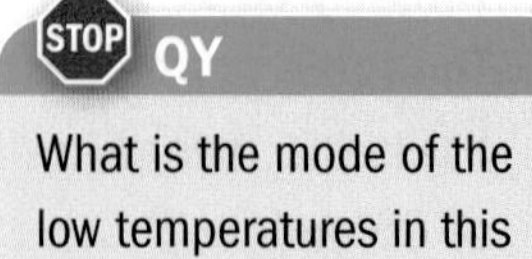

QY What is the mode of the low temperatures in this stem-and-leaf plot?

Stem-and-leaf plots are newer than other displays. They were developed in the 1970s by John Tukey, a professor of statistics at Princeton University.

Questions

COVERING THE IDEAS

In 1–7, refer to the stem-and-leaf plot in Example 2.

1. What do the two 7s to the right of -1 mean?
2. How many states have record low temperatures in the -40s?
3. How many states have never had a temperature below 0°?
4. How many states have had a temperature lower than -55°?
5. Why is there a 0 stem and a -0 stem?
6. What information is not in the stem-and-leaf plot?
7. What are two advantages of the stem-and-leaf plot over the table?

In 8–11, calculate the statistic for the low temperatures Example 2.

8. median
9. minimum
10. range
11. mean (use a calculator)

12. Explain why it is easy to determine the mode of a data set from a stem-and-leaf plot.

APPLYING THE MATHEMATICS

13. The table lists the number of passing touchdowns (TD) in the National Football League (NFL) for each team in the year 2006.

Team	Passing TD	Team	Passing TD	Team	Passing TD
Arizona Cardinals	17	Green Bay Packers	18	Oakland Raiders	7
Atlanta Falcons	21	Houston Texans	14	Philadelphia Eagles	31
Baltimore Ravens	21	Indianapolis Colts	31	Pittsburgh Steelers	23
Buffalo Bills	19	Jacksonville Jaguars	17	San Diego Chargers	24
Carolina Panthers	19	Kansas City Chiefs	18	San Francisco 49ers	16
Chicago Bears	24	Miami Dolphins	16	Seattle Seahawks	26
Cincinnati Bengals	28	Minnesota Vikings	13	St. Louis Rams	24
Cleveland Browns	15	New England Patriots	25	Tampa Bay Buccaneers	14
Dallas Cowboys	26	New Orleans Saints	27	Tennessee Titans	13
Denver Broncos	20	New York Giants	24	Washington Redskins	19
Detroit Lions	21	New York Jets	17		

Source: National Football League

(continued on next page)

a. Organize these numbers into a stem-and-leaf plot.

b. Find the maximum, minimum, range, median, and mode of these data.

c. To find the mean, would you prefer to use the data arranged in a stem-and-leaf plot or in a list? Why?

d. Find the mean.

e. Imagine you are a sports reporter. Write a sentence or two describing these data. Use the statistics you found in Parts c and e.

In the 2006–2007 season, Peyton Manning led the Indianappolis Colts to the Super Bowl title.

Source: National Football League

14. Use the table in Example 2.

a. Make a stem-and-leaf plot of the years for the record low temperatures. (*Note:* You will need stems with three digits.)

b. Use the plot to find the earliest and latest years and the mode year.

c. Use the plot to find the range of the years for low-temperature records across the states.

REVIEW

15. **True or False** If a maximum of a set of data changes, and the rest of the data stay the same, then the mean of the data must change. **(Lesson 5-2)**

In 16 and 17, consider the numbers 5, 7, 9, 11, and 13. (Lesson 5-1)

16. Change one number so that the mean of these numbers increases but the median stays the same.

17. Change two numbers so that the median decreases but the mean stays the same.

In 18–20, solve the equation. (Lesson 4-9)

18. $7 - x = 4$

19. $8.3 + m = 11.2$

20. $c - 5 = \frac{14}{9}$

In 21 and 22, find the value of *k*. (Lesson 3-7)

21.

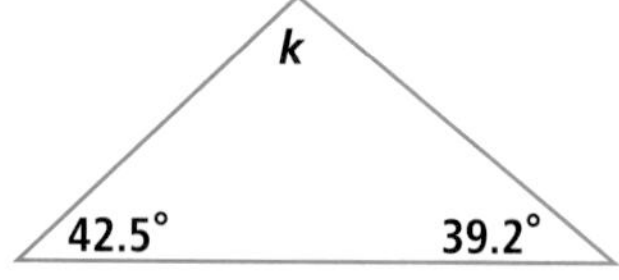

22.

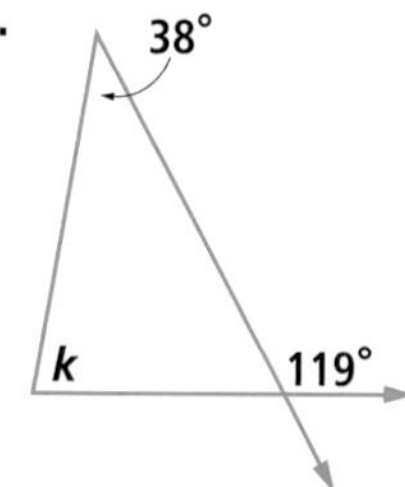

EXPLORATION

23. Find some data you find interesting.

a. Make a stem-and-leaf plot of those data.

b. Summarize what the plot shows about the data.

QY ANSWER

40°F

Lesson 5-4 Bar Graphs and Histograms

Vocabulary

bar graph
spreadsheet
cell, active cell
axis (axes)
histogram
relative frequency

▸ **BIG IDEA** Bar graphs and histograms are common ways of describing frequencies and relative frequencies.

When a list has just a few numbers, they may be represented in a *bar graph*. In a **bar graph,** the lengths of the bars correspond to the numbers that are represented. Below is a table created in a **spreadsheet** program. It shows the areas of the 8 largest Hawaiian islands. At the bottom of the page is a bar graph of these data.

Mental Math

Solve for the variable.

a. $5 + x = 11$

b. $5 + x + x = 11$

c. $5 + x + x + x = 11$

◇	A	B
1	Hawaii (Big Island)	4,028
2	Maui	727
3	Kahoolawe	45
4	Lanai	140
5	Molokai	260
6	Oahu	597
7	Kauai	552
8	Niihau	70

When you look at this bar graph, you immediately see that the "Big Island" of Hawaii is much larger in area than any of the other Hawaiian islands. Bar graphs allow you to see the relative sizes of the numbers in data and easily order them.

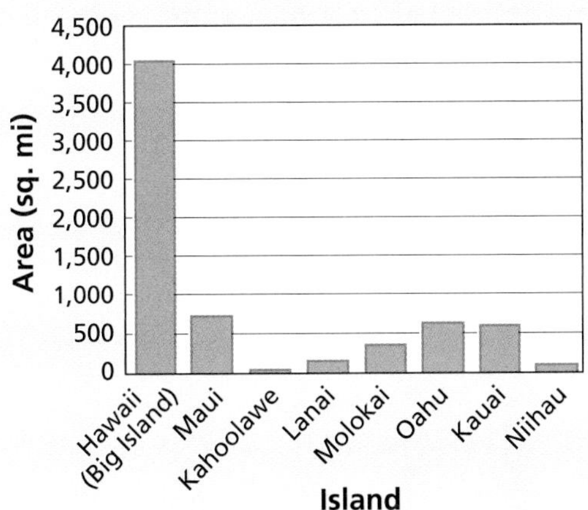

Source: *Encyclopedia Britannica*

Activity 1

MATERIALS computer with spreadsheet software

Use spreadsheet technology to create a bar graph like the one on the previous page.

Step 1 Open the spreadsheet application on your computer. One of the cells will be highlighted. It is the active cell and you can fill it with information. You can change the active cell by using the arrow keys, ▶, ▼, ◀, or ▲.

Step 2 Enter the names of the islands and their areas.

Step 3 Determine how your application works and have it draw a bar graph for these data. Some applications have a chart picture in the top menu bar.

Step 4 Find out how to title the graph. Add the title "Areas of Hawaiian Islands."

Step 5 Find out how to label the axes. Label the horizontal **axis** "Island" and the vertical axis "Area (sq mi)."

Step 6 Print your graph if you can. Show your graph to your teacher.

Histograms

To graph a list with 50 or 100 or 5,000 numbers, you would not want to have a bar for each number. The numbers are grouped into intervals. If

1) the intervals do not overlap and include all the numbers,

2) each interval is graphed as a bar, and

3) the bars are next to each other with no space between them,

the result is called a **histogram.** In a histogram, the vertical axis may show frequencies or *relative frequencies.* A **relative frequency** is the fraction or percent of the data that lies in a particular interval.

▸ READING MATH

The word "relative" in the term *relative frequencies* is used because you want to see how numbers "relate" to each other. Percents are often used for the comparison of numbers.

GUIDED

Example 1

Make a histogram of the relative frequencies of the weights of the boys trying out for the middle school football team (from Lesson 5-3).

Weight Interval (lb)	Frequency	Relative Frequency
60–69	3	$\frac{3}{24} = 12.5\%$
70–79	1	?
80–89	3	?
90–99	4	?
100–109	7	?
110–119	3	?
120–129	2	?
130–139	1	?

Solution First, add the frequencies to determine how many boys tried out.

$$3 + 1 + 3 + 4 + 7 + 3 + 2 + 1 + 0 = 24$$

Then find each relative frequency by dividing the frequency by the total number of boys who tried out. Copy and complete the table on the previous page.

Now copy and complete the histogram at the right.

The histogram resembles the stem-and-leaf plot of Lesson 5-3 turned on its side.

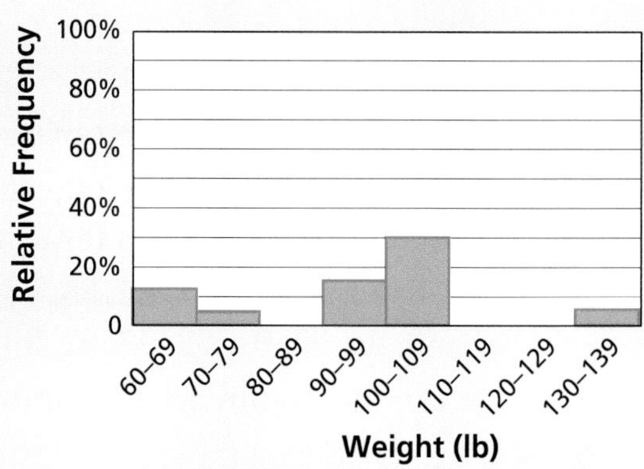

What Makes a Good Graph?

A good graph displays data clearly and accurately. It includes a title that tells what the graph is about, and the intervals on the axes have the same width and are labeled. When a graph is good, you can use all these things to give meaning to the data.

The histogram above is an example of a good graph. The title is clear and above the graph. The horizontal axis has intervals showing weight, in pounds, in the 60s, 70s, 80s, and so on. The vertical axis shows relative frequencies, with each interval representing 10%.

Watch out for misleading graphs that do not follow these rules.

Example 2

At the right is a graph from an advertisement for oatmeal. Identify three things that cause this display to be misleading.

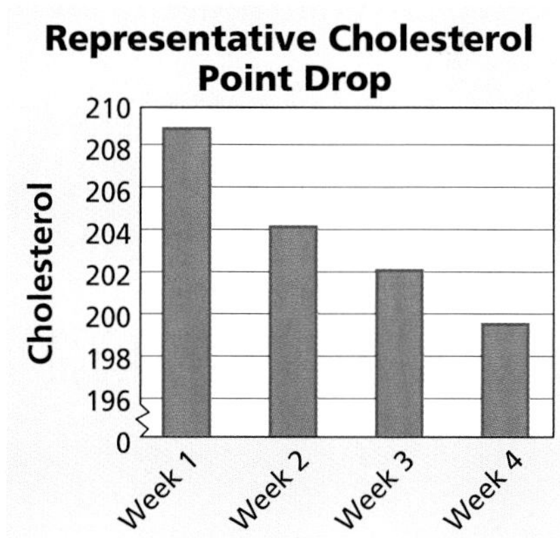

Solution

1. Look at the title. What does a "representative cholesterol point drop" mean? Does this refer to an average? A median? We do not know. "Representative cholesterol point drop" is not defined.
2. Look at the horizontal scale. Nowhere are we told what was done during the weeks. The labeling on the horizontal axis is incomplete.
3. Look at the vertical scale. It does not start at zero. This makes the numbers for the weeks look like they decreased more than they actually did. The numbers on the vertical axis do not start at 0.

 See QY at the right.

QY

True or False In the histogram data from Example 2, the cholesterol level from Week 4 is less than half the level from Week 1.

Questions

COVERING THE IDEAS

1. Thirty students received the following scores, ordered from least to greatest, on the final exam for a class.

   65, 78, 79, 79, 80, 84, 86, 86, 87, 87, 87, 87, 87, 88, 88, 88, 89, 89, 89, 90, 91, 92, 92, 92, 93, 93, 93, 93, 98, 100

   a. What are the minimum, maximum, and median values?

   b. Make a frequency table. Use test-score intervals of size 10, running from 61 to 100 (61–70, 71–80, and so on).

   c. Make a histogram from your frequency table. Remember to use a title for the graph and label the axes.

2. Name two differences between a histogram and a bar graph.

3. Explain why the histogram of Example 1 looks like the stem-and-leaf plot of Lesson 5-3.

4. Use the 16 test scores shown at the right.

   a. Make a relative frequency table for these data, as in Example 1. Use intervals of length 10.

   b. Draw an accurate histogram. Make sure it meets all the requirements of a good graph.

Average Test Scores

71.3	69.3	90.7	100.0
87.0	84.5	87.4	85.0
75.6	91.0	77.8	63.1
74.9	71.3	83.9	89.6

5. Claire has a collection of movies on DVD. In the collection, 45 are comedy, 20 are drama, and 15 are action.

   a. Which of the four bar graphs at the right is a good display?

   b. Tell what is wrong with each of the other three displays.

6. Draw a good graph using the data from Example 2.

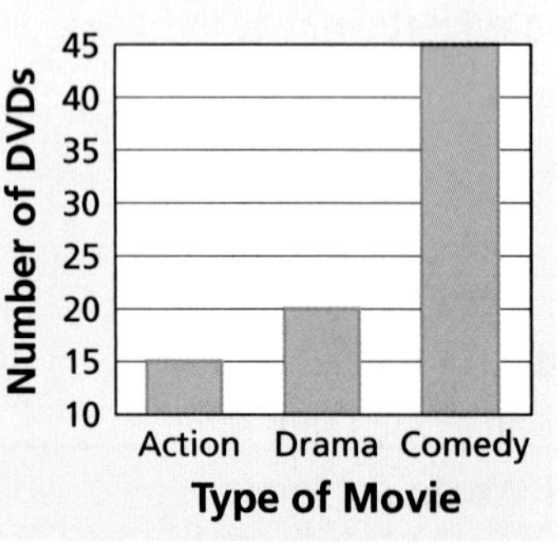

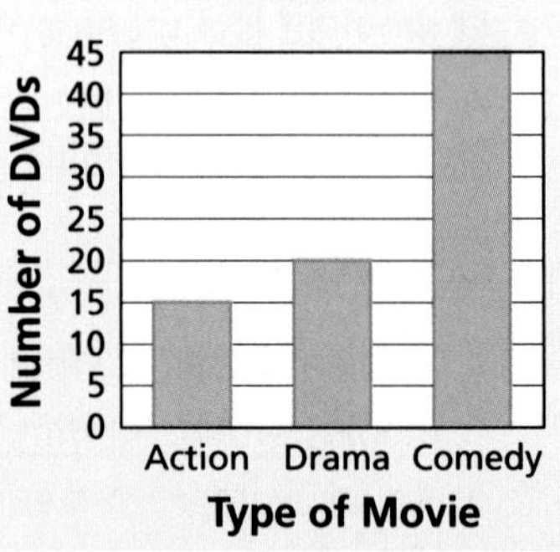

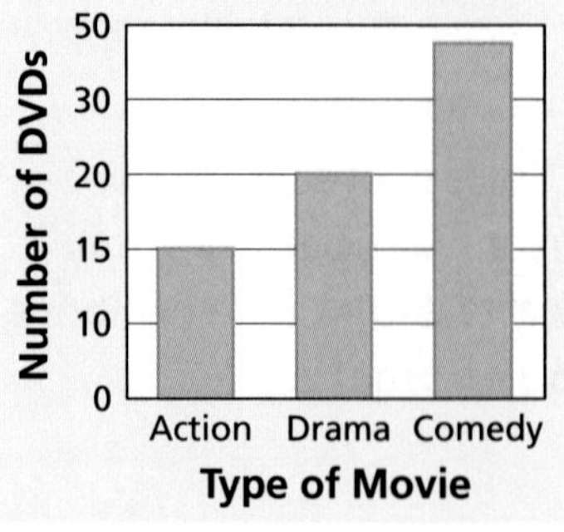

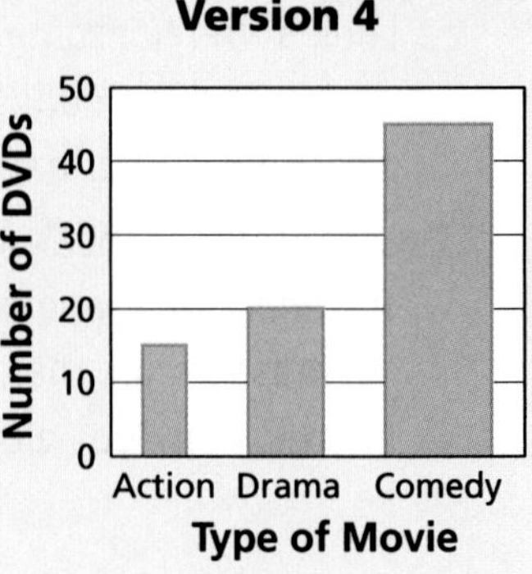

APPLYING THE MATHEMATICS

In 7–13, use the graphs below. The graphs were made from U.S. Census data like that in Question 19.

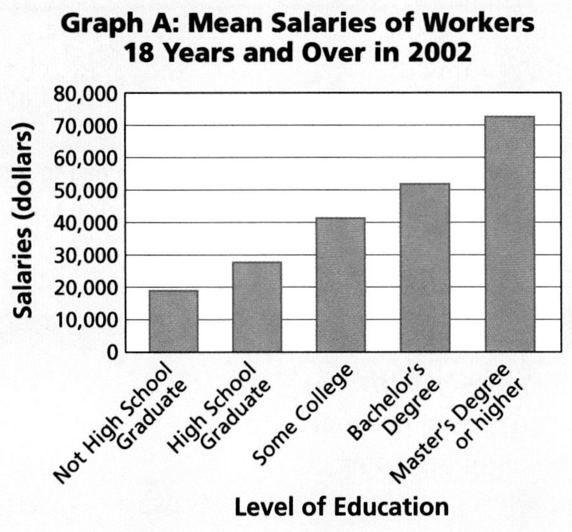

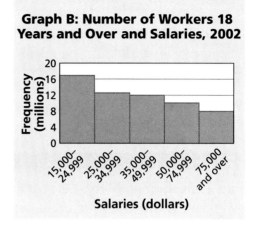

Graph B: Number of Workers 18 Years and Over and Salaries, 2002

Frequency (millions): 20, 16, 12, 8, 4, 0

15,000–24,999 | 25,000–34,999 | 35,000–49,999 | 50,000–74,999 | 75,000 and over

Salaries (dollars)

7. Describe what is shown in Graph A.
8. Describe what is shown in Graph B.
9. Estimate the difference between the mean salary for high school graduates and the mean salary for non-high school graduates.
10. What is the difference in mean salary between a high school graduate and someone who completes a bachelor's degree?
11. To the nearest million, how many workers earn from \$35,000 to \$74,999 per year?
12. Mr. Lopez has some college education and earns \$38,792 per year.
    a. In which bar on Graph A would his data be placed?
    b. Where would his data be included in Graph B?
13. Which graph would you use to determine how many workers earned less than \$50,000?

REVIEW

14. At the right are data on snowfall in Aspen, Colorado, in October and March for eleven years. Some data are missing. **(Lesson 5-1)**
    a. Compute the mean, median, and range for the listed years for October.
    b. Compute the same statistics for the listed years for March.
    c. Use the statistics you computed in Parts a and b to write a comparison of October and March snowfall in Aspen.

Snowfall in Aspen, CO (in.)

Year	October	March
1995	12.8	44.1
1996	22.4	–
1997	27.7	22.9
1998	–	33.1
1999	3.5	13.1
2000	0	29.2
2001	2.8	16.3
2002	13.1	26.6
2003	0	31
2004	9.3	11.6
2005	6.4	20.3

Source: Western Regional Climate Center

15. Solve for a: $a + \frac{3}{2} = \frac{2}{3}$. **(Lesson 4-9)**

16. Moises bought a sandwich. He handed the cashier a \$20 bill and received \$15.60 in change. Let S be the cost of the sandwich. Draw a fact triangle representing this situation, and find the cost of the sandwich. **(Lesson 4-8)**

What do you like to put on your favorite sandwich?

17. Jennifer tripped while carrying a glass filled with $1\frac{1}{2}$ cups of water. She was left with $\frac{2}{5}$ of a cup. How much water spilled? **(Lessons 4-7, 4-3)**

18. **True or False** If two angles form a linear pair, then their measures add to 180°. **(Lesson 4-5)**

EXPLORATION

19. Make up a question of interest to you that can be answered by using the data in the following table. Write your question, present the data you use in an organized manner, and make an appropriate display.

Mean Earning (in dollars) of Workers 18 years and Over: 1990–2005

Year	Total Mean Earnings	Not a High School Graduate	High School Graduate	Some College	Bachelor's Degree	Master's Degree or Higher
2005	39,579	19,915	29,448	33,496	54,689	79,946
2004	37,899	19,182	28,631	32,010	51,568	78,224
2003	37,046	18,734	27,915	31,498	51,206	74,602
2002	36,308	18,826	27,280	31,046	51,194	72,824
2001	35,805	18,793	26,795	30,782	50,623	72,869
2000	34,514	17,738	25,692	29,939	49,595	71,194
1999	32,356	16,121	24,572	28,403	45,678	67,697
1998	30,928	16,053	23,594	27,566	43,782	63,473
1997	29,514	16,124	22,895	26,235	40,478	63,229
1996	28,106	15,011	22,154	25,181	38,112	61,317
1995	26,792	14,013	21,431	23,862	36,980	56,667
1994	25,852	13,697	20,248	22,226	37,224	56,105
1993	24,674	12,820	19,422	21,539	35,121	55,789
1992	23,227	12,809	18,737	20,867	32,629	48,652
1991	22,332	12,613	18,261	20,551	31,323	46,039
1990	21,793	12,582	17,820	20,694	31,112	41,458

Source: U.S. Census Bureau

QY ANSWER

false

Lesson 5-5 Circle Graphs

Vocabulary

categorical data

numerical data

▸ **BIG IDEA** Circle graphs are a common way of displaying categorical data.

In Chapter 2, you made circle graphs by hand by using percent circles and fractions. Another way to make a circle graph is to convert the fractions to degrees and use a protractor to draw the angle of each sector.

Mental Math

Compute.

a. 10% of 500

b. 20% of 500

c. 50% of 500

d. 25% of 500

GUIDED

Example 1

Stuart Dent spent his day in the following way: 9 hours sleeping, 7 hours in school, 1 hour doing homework, and 2 hours at soccer practice. He also spent 5 hours doing other things. Use your protractor to make a circle graph to show what fraction of the day was taken up with each activity.

Solution

Step 1 Make a table like the one below. List the activities in the first column. Put the hours in the second column.

Step 2 Calculate what fraction each activity represents. For instance, 9 hours sleeping is $\frac{9}{24}$ of the day. Find the fractions for each activity.

Step 3 Multiply the fraction by the total number of degrees in a circle (360°). For example, $\frac{9}{24} \times 360°$ is 135°.

Step 4 Check your work so far. The fractions should add to 1 since together they make up the entire day. The degrees should add up to 360° to make a whole circle.

Step 1		Step 2	Step 3	
Activity	**Amount of Time (hr)**	**Fraction of Total**	**Calculation**	**Degrees**
Sleeping	9	$\frac{9}{24}$	$\frac{9}{24} \cdot 360°$	135°
School	7	?	?	?
Soccer	2	?	?	?
Homework	1	?	?	?
Other	5	?	?	?

(continued on next page)

Step 5 Draw a circle and use a protractor to determine the sizes of the sectors. For example, to make the 135° sector, place the center of the protractor on the center of the circle. Make marks on the circle at 0° and 135°. Label the sector as shown. Continue and draw the sectors for school, soccer, and homework.

Step 6 Measure the remaining sector. It should measure 75°. Label the last sector and put a title on your graph.

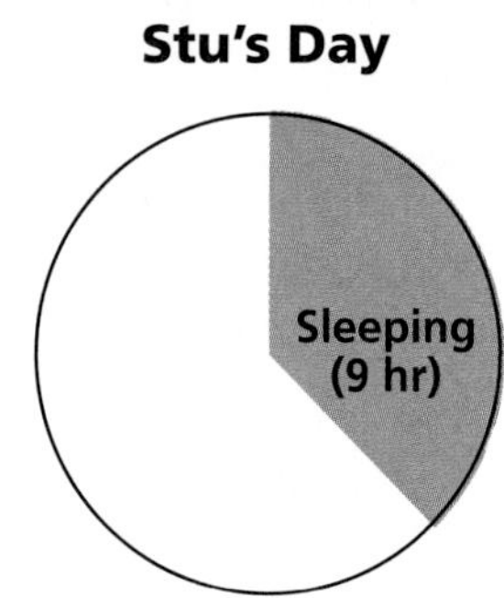

As with a bar graph, you can make a circle graph (or *pie chart*) with a spreadsheet or a calculator.

Activity

MATERIALS computer with spreadsheet software, protractor

Four students ran for Student Council President. The number of students who voted for each candidate is shown at the right.

Candidate	Votes
Trey	42
Erika	36
Mercedes	25
Tamia	50

Step 1 Enter the data in two columns, one for candidates and one for votes.

Step 2 Instruct your machine to make a circle graph. Your graph should appear on the screen.

Step 3 Add a title and category labels to your graph.

Step 4 Determine the degree measure of the sector for Trey. Does the computer graph appear to be accurate?

What Displays Can Be Used with What Data?

The data for the election results could be put into a bar graph. There would be four bars. However, a histogram cannot be used because the horizontal axis is a list of candidates, not a numerical measure.

The data showing the election results is **categorical data** because the votes are split into categories. Categorical data can be displayed in bar graphs (each category is a bar) and circle graphs (each category is a sector). In contrast, the data for the test scores of students that you saw in Lesson 5-4 is **numerical data.** Numerical data comes from measurements. Numerical data can be put into many kinds of displays, including bar graphs, circle graphs, stem-and-leaf plots, histograms, and line and other coordinate graphs. You will see line graphs and other coordinate graphs in the next two lessons.

Whether data you collect are categorical or numerical can depend on how you organize the data as shown in Example 2.

Example 2

The teachers in a school decided to collect data on how many books students have read since the beginning of the school year. Students are called *light readers* if they read from 0 to 10 books. They are *average readers* if they read 11 to 25 books. They are *heavy readers* if they read more than 25 books. Determine whether the data described in Parts a and b are categorical or numerical.

How many books do you read outside of school during the year?

a. The students are classified into three groups: light reader, average reader, or heavy reader.

b. The students are classified into three groups: 0–10 books read; 11–25 books read; more than 25 books read.

Solution

a. The groups do not involve numbers, so the data are categorical. Notice that it would not make sense to have a histogram with these data.

b. The groups involve a measure, the number of books read. So the data are numerical. You could make a histogram or circle graph with these data.

Caution: Sometimes categorical data appear as numbers, like zip codes or hotel room numbers. So if these data are numbers, how can you tell whether the data are numerical or categorical? Determine which displays you can create from the data and which statistics have meaning. If a histogram makes sense, or if you can describe the data with landmarks, the data are numerical.

QY

Tell whether the data collected would be categorical or numerical.

a. The eye color of each student in your room.

b. The birthdates of all the students in a school.

c. The area codes for 20 college students.

d. The minutes of battery life for a cell phone.

e. The bar code number on a library book.

Questions

COVERING THE IDEAS

1. In Mr. Numkena's class, 15 students ride the bus to school, 4 walk to school, and 5 ride in a car.
   a. How many sectors should a circle graph of this information contain?
   b. Determine the measure of the central angle for each sector.
   c. Complete a circle graph for the data.

2. Sophia's class sold fruit as a fund-raiser. They made $40 profit on the oranges, $45 profit on the apples, $15 profit on the grapefruit, and $20 profit on grapes. Make a circle graph to represent the data. Use a spreadsheet if possible.

3. What types of graphs have you studied that can be used to display categorical data?

4. Use a spreadsheet to make a circle graph of the areas of the eight biggest islands of Hawaii. Use the data from Lesson 5-4.

5. Listed below are the populations of the eight largest islands of Hawaii in 2000.

Island	Population (2000)
Hawaii (Big Island)	148,677
Maui	117,644
Kahoolawe	0
Lanai	3,193
Molokai	7,404
Oahu	876,151
Kauai	58,303
Niihau	160

Source: U.S. Census Bureau

a. Which island is uninhabited?

b. Make a circle graph showing the part of the total population that lives on each of the seven inhabited islands.

c. What are the major differences between the populations and the areas of these islands as listed in Lesson 5-4?

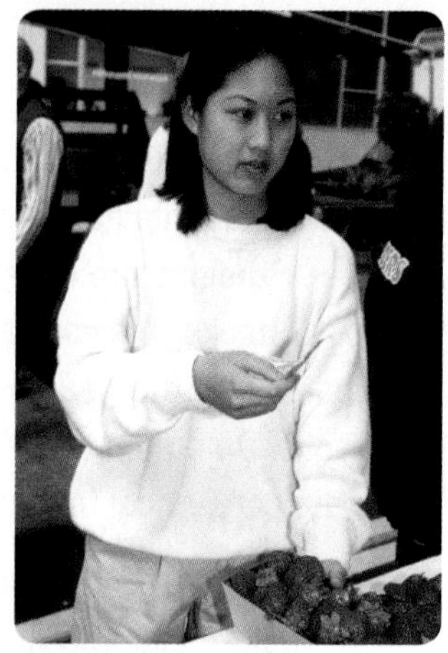

Fund-raising helps an organization raise money for trips, uniforms, relief efforts, special equipment, or service projects.

In 6–8, tell whether the data are categorical or numerical.

6. a. face showing (heads or tails) on 20 pennies that are tossed

   b. age of a penny

7. a. names of babies born in a particular year

   b. weights of babies born in that year

8. a. how many students are in a school

   b. whether a school is urban (in a city), suburban, or rural

APPLYING THE MATHEMATICS

9. Use the circle graph at the right.

   a. Find the measure of the central angle of each sector.

   b. Which type of livestock had the greatest value in 2002?

   c. **True or False** Over half of the value of livestock and poultry sold in 2002 came from cattle and calves.

Value of Livestock and Poultry Sold (2002)

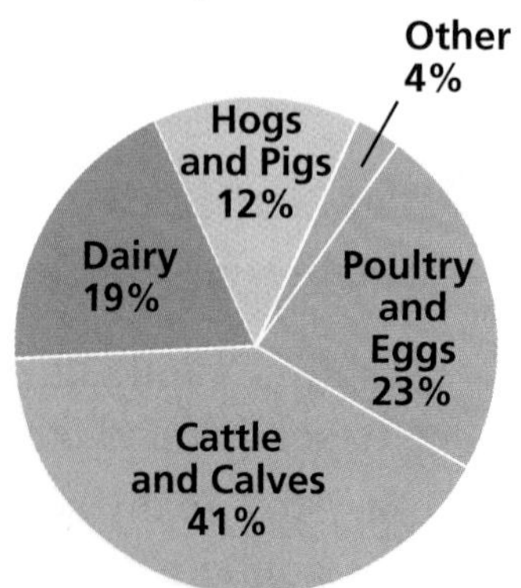

U.S. Total $105 Billion

10. Skyler surveyed the 26 students in her class about what pets they have. The results are Dog: 13; Cat: 10; Fish: 15; Hamster: 5. She tried to draw a circle graph of these data. She made a table to find the number of degrees for each sector. When she drew her sectors, she ran out of room. What did Skyler do wrong?

Pet	Fraction	Calculation	Degrees (rounded to nearest degree)
Dog	$\frac{13}{26}$	$\frac{13}{26} \times 360°$	180°
Cat	$\frac{10}{26}$	$\frac{10}{26} \times 360°$	138°
Fish	$\frac{15}{26}$	$\frac{15}{26} \times 360°$	208°
Hamster	$\frac{5}{26}$	$\frac{5}{26} \times 360°$	69°

11. The double bar graph below shows the number of three types of livestock on U.S. farms in 1900 and 2000.

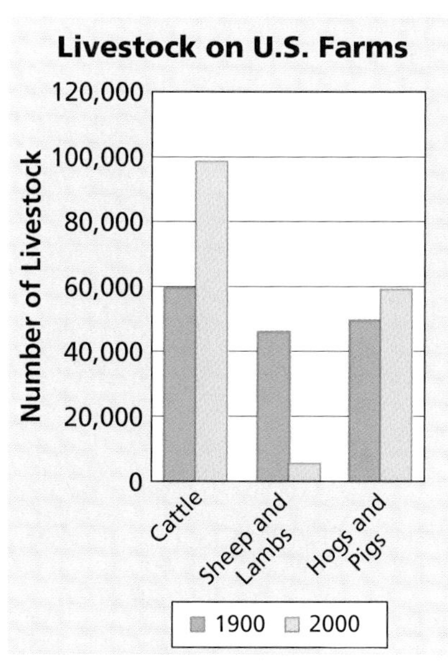

Source: *The World Almanac*

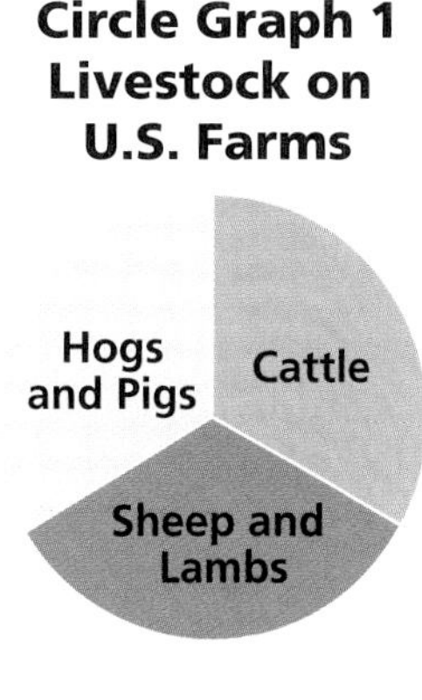

Source: *The World Alamanac*

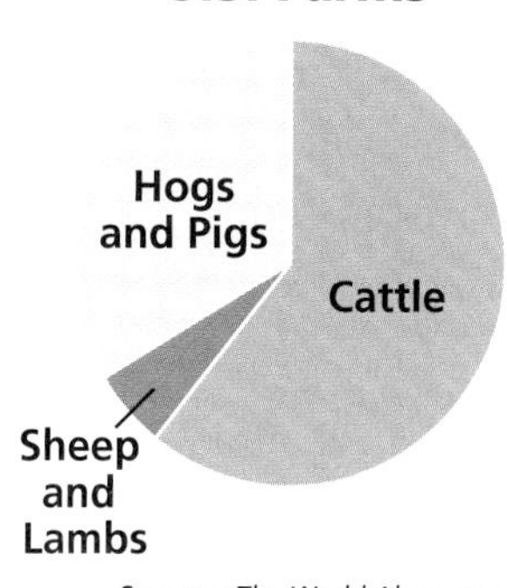

Source: *The World Alamanac*

a. Which circle graph above shows the data for 1900, and which shows the data for 2000?

b. **Multiple Choice** About what percent of the livestock on U.S. farms in 1900 was hogs and pigs?

A 0–20% **B** 21–40% **C** 41–60% **D** 61–80%

c. Tell how you determined your answer to Part b.

d. What was the biggest change between 1900 and 2000 in the types of livestock on U.S. farms? How can you tell?

12. a. Copy the table at the right. Estimate the percents on the bar graph, and use them to complete the table.
    b. Draw a circle graph with the data from this table.

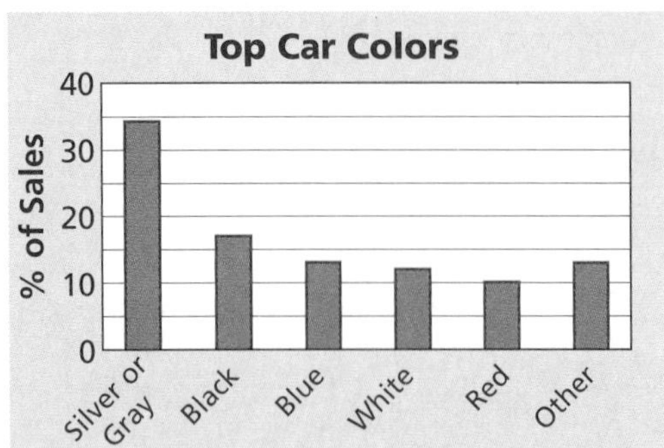

Color	Percent of Sales
Silver or Gray	?
Black	?
Blue	?
White	?
Red	?
Other	?

REVIEW

13. Trevon recorded the temperature outside his house every morning for two weeks. He recorded the following temperatures in degrees Fahrenheit: 61, 61, 64, 73, 72, 70, 72, 68, 67, 60, 63, 65, 63, 63.
    a. Make a stem-and-leaf plot of the temperature data. **(Lesson 5-3)**
    b. Make a frequency table. Use intervals of size 4, from 60 to 75 (60–63, 64–67, and so on). **(Lesson 5-2)**
    c. Make a histogram from your frequency table. Remember to use a title for the graph and label the axes. **(Lessons 5-4, 5-2, 5-1)**

14. The Rubio family's cell phone bill lists the following call lengths for the past week, in minutes: 1, 4, 1, 1, 1, 2, 9, 18, 1, 3, 5, 5, 1, 44, 1, 1, 2, 1, 1. **(Lesson 5-1)**
    a. Find the mean and median call lengths.
    b. Which statistic do you think is a better measure of the Rubio family's typical call length: mean, median, or mode? Explain.

15. In one stage of the 2006 Tour de France bicycle race, cyclists had to descend 1300 m from the top of the Col de Lautaret before climbing 1100 m to the top of the Alpe d'Huez. **(Lesson 3-3)**
    a. Picture the cyclists' change in altitude on a number line.
    b. What was the total change in altitude from the top of the Col de Lautaret to the top of the Alpe d'Huez?

This stage of the Tour de France is 187 kilometers. How many miles is this?

16. 1 ft = 0.3048 m. How many centimeters is this? **(Lesson 2-2)**

EXPLORATION

17. The Crimean War in the 1850s between England and France on one side, and Russia on the other, saw horrible conditions for wounded soldiers. Florence Nightingale, an English nurse, was one of the first people to collect statistics and use graphs to persuade people to change how they were treating the wounded. Find out and write a paragraph about the work that she did.

QY ANSWER

a, c, and e are categorical; b and d are numerical.

Lesson 5-6 Line Graphs

Vocabulary

line graph
double line graph
multiple line graph

BIG IDEA Line graphs show trends in data.

Reading a Graph

You should follow certain steps to make sure you understand any graph. First, read the title of the graph and any other words describing it. Then study the *scales,* if any, to be sure you know what is being measured. For example, are the scale numbers in percents? in millions? in dollars? in people? Where does the scale begin? Are the intervals on the scale uniform? All this information can help you determine the purpose of the graph.

A **line graph** is a graph of ordered pairs of numbers connected by segments in order from left to right. Like histograms, line graphs have horizontal and vertical axes with numerical scales on them. The display below contains two line graphs. Sometimes this is called a **double line graph.** A display containing more than two line graphs is a **multiple line graph.**

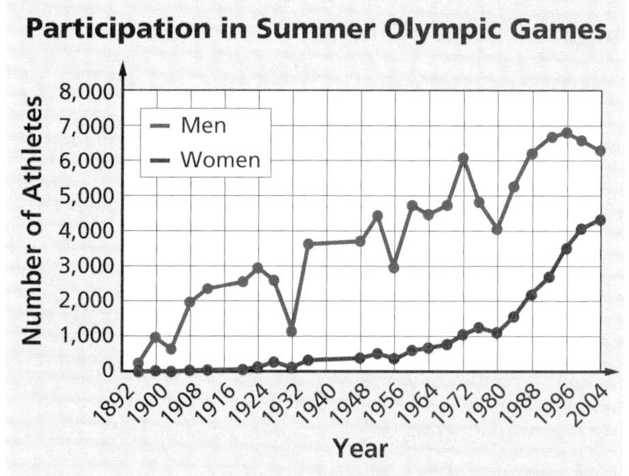

Source: *The Complete Book of Summer Olympics: Statistical Annexes of the Official Report of the Olympic Games*

Example

The line graph above shows trends in participation in the Olympic Games from 1892 to 2004.

a. What does this graph describe?

b. What label would you use on the horizontal axis?

(continued on next page)

Mental Math

Tell which angle looks to have the greater measure.

a. $\angle 1$ or $\angle 2$?

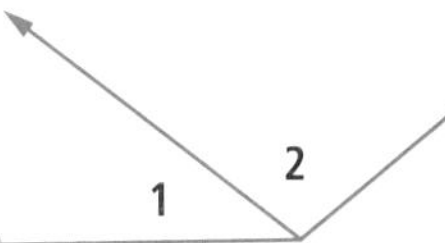

b. $\angle ABC$ or $\angle ABD$?

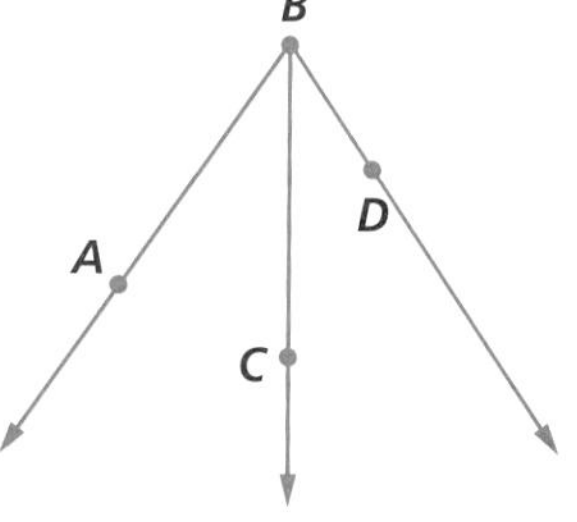

c. $\angle 3$ or $\angle 4$?

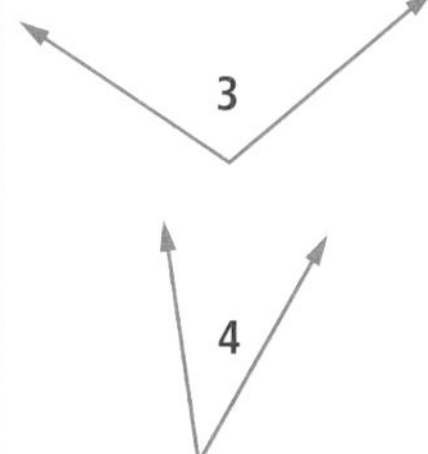

c. What does the vertical axis represent?
d. Give the ordered pair (year, approximate number of athletes) for the point on the men's line graph that represents the most men in an Olympics.
e. Give the ordered pair for the point on the women's line graph that represents the most women in an Olympics.
f. What trends are shown by the graph?
g. There are some gaps in the graph. Which years should have had Olympic Games but did not? Why do you think there were no Olympics those years?

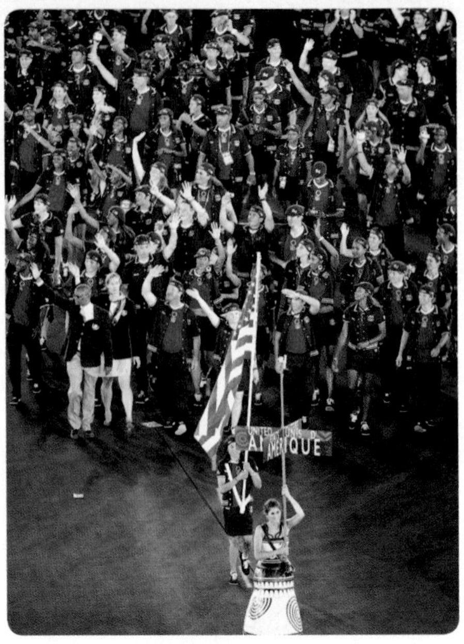

The 2004 Summer Olympics took place in Greece—the birthplace of the Olympics.

Solution

a. The title shows that this graph displays the number of male and female athletes in the Summer Olympics from 1896 until 2004.
b. Year of Summer Olympics
c. Number of Athletes
d. The highest point in the graph for men is at 1996. There were almost 7000 participants. (1996, $\approx$ 6,800)
e. The highest point in the women's line graph is at 2004. (2004, $\approx$ 4,300)
f. The number of male and female athletes has increased a great deal over time. In recent Olympics, however, the number of male athletes has decreased while the number of female athletes continues to increase. The number of female athletes has always been less than the number of male athletes.
g. 1916, 1940, and 1944; World War I was occurring in 1916, and World War II was occurring in 1940 and 1944.

Making Line Graphs with Technology

Calculators and spreadsheet programs can make line graphs.

Activity 1

MATERIALS calculator or a computer with spreadsheet software

The average high and low temperatures in Detroit, Michigan are listed for each month. Follow the steps to create a line graph for each set of temperatures. You may want to work with a partner.

Month	J	F	M	A	M	J	J	A	S	O	N	D
High Temp (°F)	33	36	46	59	72	80	85	82	75	62	49	38
Low Temp (°F)	20	22	29	39	51	60	65	64	56	45	36	25

Source: www.weather.com

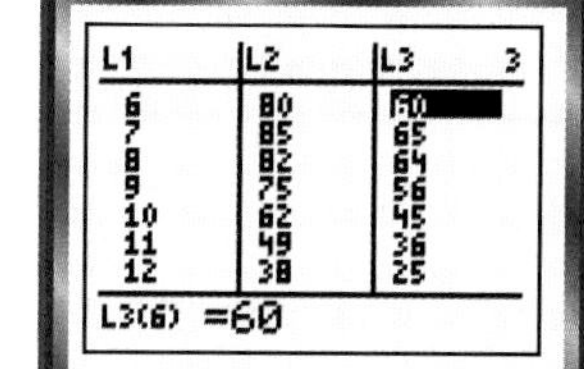

Step 1 Enter the months, 1 for January, 2 for February, and so on, in a calculator list or in a column of a spreadsheet. (On many spreadsheets, you can list the names of the months.)

Step 2 Enter the high temperatures in a second column.

Step 3 Enter the low temperatures in a third column.

Step 4 Choose the line graph display. On one calculator, you can do this as follows:

Press [2nd] [Y=] [ENTER]. Choose a line graph icon. Then enter L1 for *x* (the horizontal axis) L2 for *y*, and choose a point symbol. One calculator screen looks like the screen below.

Repeat for the second graph, using the third column, L3 for *y*, instead of L2 and a different symbol for the points.

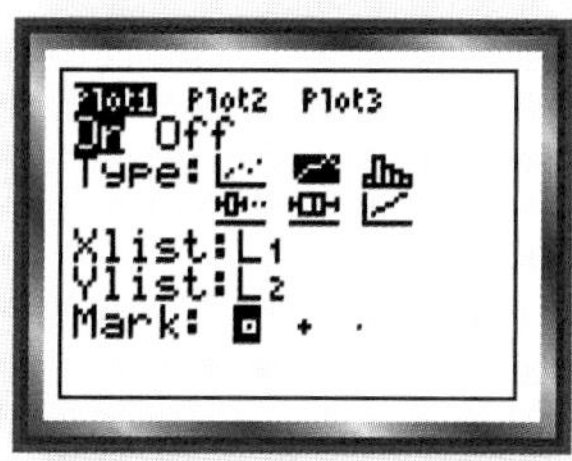

Step 5 Display the two graphs. On one calculator, you press [ZOOM], and choose `9:ZoomStat`. The result is a double line graph.

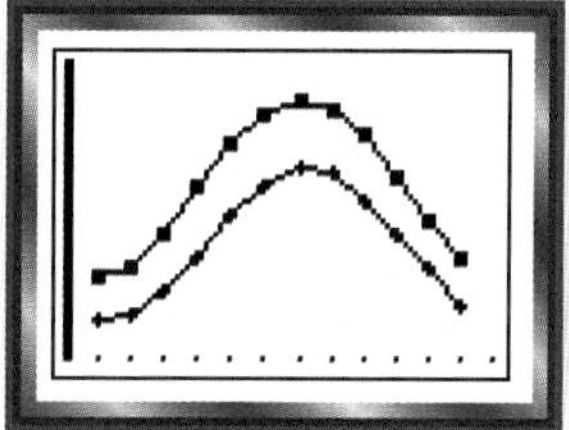

Step 6 You may be able to trace the points on the double line graph. The screen will display the coordinates of the highlighted point.

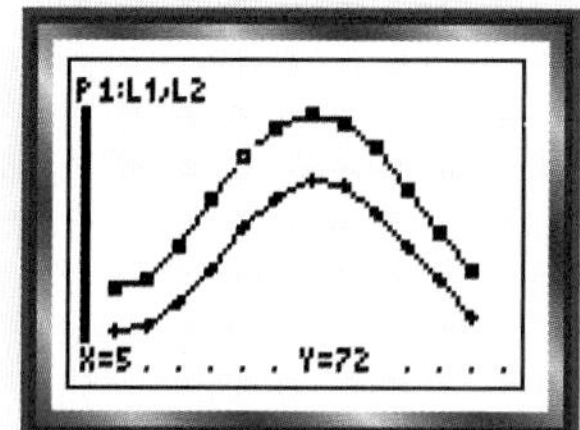

Questions

COVERING THE IDEAS

1. Give two reasons for using graphs and other displays.
2. Name at least two steps to follow when reading a graph.
3. What is a line graph?

In 4–8, refer to the graph on page 301. Describe how the lines in the graph lead to each conclusion in 4–7.

4. The number of female athletes has increased in each Olympics since 1980.
5. The number of male athletes decreased from 1996 to 2004.
6. The difference between the numbers of male and female athletes was less in 2004 than in any year since 1932.
7. There were more men participating in 1900 than women participating in 1968.
8. Predict the number of male and female summer Olympic athletes in 2020. Explain how you came to your prediction.

In 9–12, consider the multiple line graph at the right, which shows the per capita (per person) consumption of milk in the United States from 1970 to 1995.

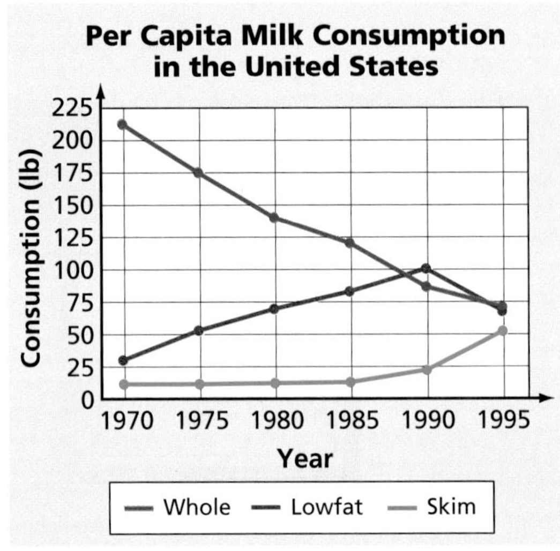

Source: USDA

9. In what year was lowfat milk the most consumed type of milk in the United States?
10. Make two observations about the trends shown in this graph.
11. What do you estimate the total milk consumption was in 2000?
12. Two of the lines intersect between 1985 and 1990.
    a. Estimate the coordinates of the intersection point.
    b. What does that intersection point mean?
13. Refer to the bar graph about paintball injuries below.
    a. Make a line graph for the data that is shown in the bar graph. Use technology if possible.
    b. Cassandra said, "The graph shows that it has become dangerous to play paintball." Quinton said, "That is not necessarily true." Why might have Quinton said this?

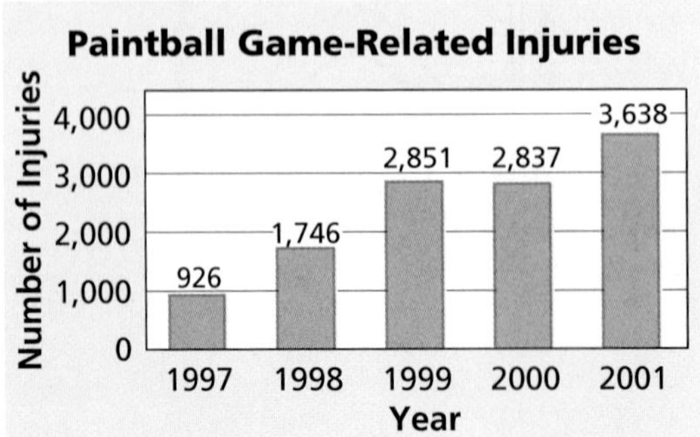

Source: *Injury Facts 2007*

APPLYING THE MATHEMATICS

14. Use this table, which gives the populations of the states of New York and California every 10 years from 1950 to 2000.

Year	Population of NY	Population of CA
1950	14,830,192	10,586,223
1960	16,782,304	15,717,204
1970	18,241,391	19,971,069
1980	17,558,165	23,667,764
1990	17,990,455	29,760,021
2000	18,976,457	33,871,648

Source: www.npg.org

a. Use technology to make a line graph of the data for both states, marking a different symbol for each state. On some calculators, you will need to adjust the window so that the points of the line graph will be seen. Use `Xmin=1940`, `Xmax=2010`, `Ymin=0`, and `Ymax=35000000`.

b. From the line graph, estimate when the population of California passed the population of New York.

In 15–17, tell which type of display (bar graph, histogram, circle graph, or line graph) you would use to represent data from the situation. Give at least one reason for your choice.

15. numbers of people subscribing to ten popular magazines

16. voter preferences for presidential candidates

17. relative frequency of heights of 8th graders in your school

REVIEW

18. Make a histogram for the data in the circle graph below. **(Lesson 5-4)**

Paintball Game-Related Injuries by Age Group, 1997–2001

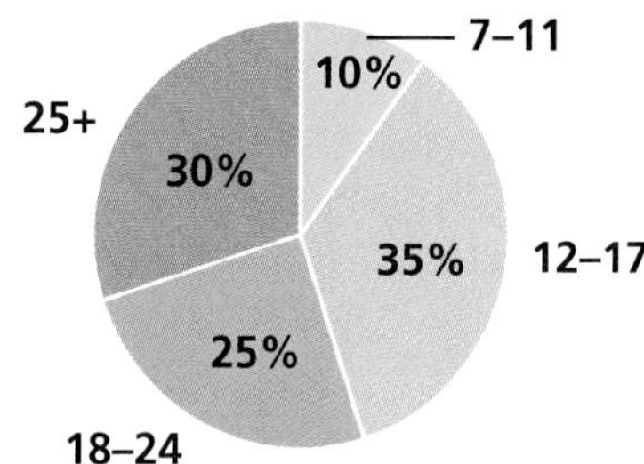

19. Subtract. **(Lesson 4-7)**

a. $\frac{1}{2} - \frac{1}{4}$

b. $\frac{1}{2} - \frac{1}{4} - \frac{1}{8}$

c. $\frac{1}{2} - \frac{1}{4} - \frac{1}{8} - \frac{1}{16}$

20. One batch of lasagna requires $1\frac{3}{4}$ cups of ricotta cheese. If Keiko is making two batches, how much ricotta cheese will she need? **(Lesson 3-9)**

The name *ricotta* comes from the Latin word *recocta* meaning "cooked twice."

Source: www.recipezaar.com

21. Find the sum. **(Lesson 3-8)**
   a. $\frac{1}{2} + \frac{1}{4}$
   b. $\frac{1}{2} + \frac{1}{4} + \frac{1}{8}$
   c. $\frac{1}{2} + \frac{1}{4} + \frac{1}{8} + \frac{1}{16}$

22. **True or False (Lessons 1-8, 1-7)**
   a. Every integer is either a whole number or a negative number.
   b. Every whole number or negative number is an integer.

EXPLORATION

23. You can find temperature data online for many places in the United States. Pick your home town or another favorite city. Find the data and create a line graph as in the Activity.

Lesson 5-7 Plotting Points on a Coordinate Grid

▶ **BIG IDEA** Coordinate axes are widely used to graph pairs of numbers.

When a flat picture is sent from one computer to another, the picture is stored by identifying each point on the picture with a pair of numbers. The most common way of identifying points with a pair of numbers use perpendicular lines to form **coordinate axes.** The horizontal axis is the ***x*-axis.** The vertical axis is the ***y*-axis.** The *x*-axis and the *y*-axis split the plane into four parts called **quadrants.** The four quadrants are labeled I, II, III, and IV.

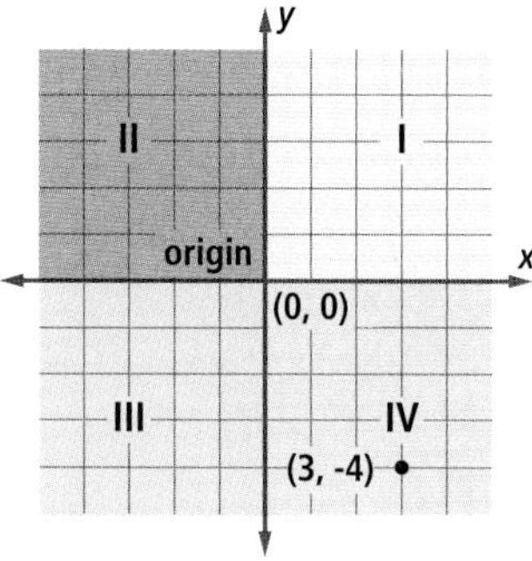

Each point can be identified by an ordered pair of numbers (x, y) called its **coordinates.** The intersection of the axes is the **origin,** which has the coordinates (0, 0). The first number in an ordered pair, the ***x*-coordinate,** tells how far to move left or right from the origin. The second number, the ***y*-coordinate,** tells how far to move up or down from the origin. To plot the point (3, –4) as in the above graph, start at the origin and move three units to the right and four units down.

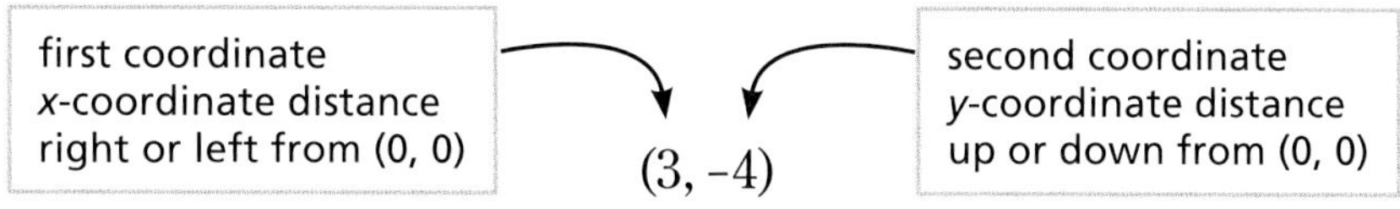

Activity 1

MATERIALS graph paper

Step 1 Draw and label coordinate axes with the *x*-axis from –10 to 10 and the *y*-axis from –8 to 8.

(continued on next page)

Vocabulary

coordinate axes
x-axis
y-axis
quadrant
coordinates
origin
x-coordinate
y-coordinate

Mental Math

Suppose apples cost \$4 per pound, and approximately 3 apples weigh 1 pound.

a. About how many apples can you buy with \$10?

b. About how many can you buy with \$20?

c. About how many can you buy with \$15?

Step 2 Plot these points: $D = (-8, 1)$, $E_1 = (-7, 4)$, $C = (-1, 6)$, $I = (2, 6)$, $M = (6, 4)$, $A_1 = (11, 3)$, $L_1 = (11, 1)$, $N = (4, 1)$, $U = (3, 0)$, $M = (3, -1)$, $E_2 = (4, -2)$, $R_1 = (5, -2)$, $A = (6, -1)$, $L_2 = (6, 0)$, $S_1 = (5, 1)$, $A_2 = (-5, 1)$, $R_2 = (-6, 0)$, $E_3 = (-6, -1)$, $F = (-5, -2)$, $O = (-4, -2)$, $R_3 = (-3, -1)$, $U = (-3, 0)$, $S_2 = (-4, 1)$, $D = (-8, 1)$
Notice that some of the letters have small numbers written below and to the right. These small numbers are called *subscripts*. They distinguish point E_1 from point E_2.

Step 3 Connect the points in order.

Activity 2

MATERIALS graphing calculator

You can also plot points using lists on a calculator.

Step 1 Enter the *x*-coordinates of the points from Activity 1 in L1 in order.

Step 2 Enter the *y*-coordinates from Activity 1 in L2 in order.

Step 3 Select the line graph display from the Stat Plot window. Use ZOOM 9:ZoomStat to make the graph.

You should get a picture that looks something like the one from Activity 1, but it may be distorted. To eliminate the distortion, go to the WINDOW menu and use a square window.

Plotting Data on a Coordinate Grid

Data can also be plotted on a coordinate grid.

Activity 3

MATERIALS graph paper

Follow the steps to draw a line graph of the average monthly temperatures in degrees Celsius in Anchorage, Alaska from January (month 1) to December (month 12).

Step 1 Draw the (horizontal) *x*-axis and the (vertical) *y*-axis on your graph paper. Make a scale from 0 to 12 on the *x*-axis to the right of the *y*-axis.

Step 2 On the *y*-axis above the *x*-axis, mark equally spaced tick marks for 2, 4, 6, . . . 16°C. On the *y*-axis below the *x*-axis, mark equally spaced tick marks for –2, –4, –6, –8, and –10°C.

Anchorage, Alaska

Month	Average Temperature (°C)
1 January	–9
2 February	–7
3 March	–3
4 April	2
5 May	8
6 June	12
7 July	14
8 August	13
9 September	9
10 October	1
11 November	–6
12 December	–8

Source: www.wrcc.drie.edu

Step 3 Plot the twelve pairs (month, degrees). To do this, locate the month on the horizontal axis. Then move up or down the required number of degrees.

Step 4 Connect consecutive dots from January to December.

Questions

COVERING THE IDEAS

1. What is one reason you would use a coordinate graph?

2. Graph the following points on the same set of axes. Connect them in order.
   a. (3, 2) b. (3, -3) c. (-3, -3)
   d. (-3, 2) e. (0, 5) f. (3, 2)

3. **Matching** Match the term with the best description.

a. x-axis	i. first number in parentheses
b. y-axis	ii. second number in parentheses
c. x-coordinate	iii. horizontal axis
d. y-coordinate	iv. (0, 0)
e. ordered pair	v. vertical axis
f. origin	vi. (3, 4)

In 4–9, use the graph below. Give the coordinates of the named point.

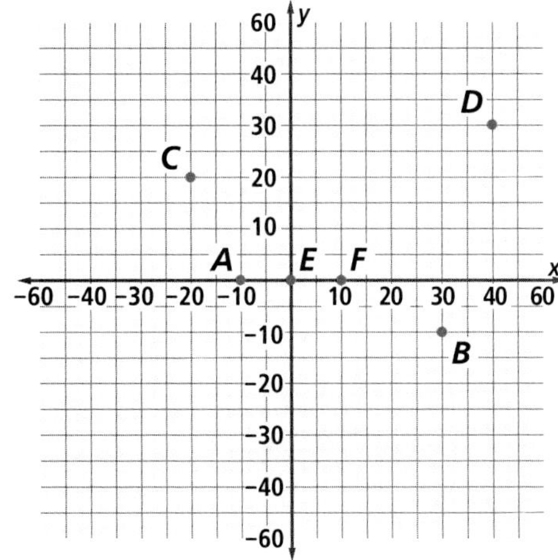

4. A 5. B 6. C
7. D 8. E 9. F

APPLYING THE MATHEMATICS

10. Change the coordinates of the points on the figure in Activity 1 so that the car is facing left instead of right.

11. If a point is in Quadrant I, its *x*-coordinate is positive and its *y*-coordinate is positive.
 a. What pattern fits a point in Quadrant II?
 b. What pattern fits a point in Quadrant III?
 c. What pattern fits a point in Quadrant IV?
 d. How can you describe the coordinates of a point on the positive *x*-axis?
 e. How can you describe the coordinates of a point on the negative *y*-axis?

12. The mean low temperature in °C for each month for Oklahoma City, Oklahoma are given in the following table. Graph these data in a line graph. (January = 1, February = 2, and so on.)

Month	1	2	3	4	5	6	7	8	9	10	11	12
Temperature (°C)	-3	-1	4	9	14	19	22	21	17	11	3	-2

Source: www.weather.com

13. Let $S = (-1, -3)$, $W = (2, 5)$, $I = (5, -5)$, $T = (-3, 2)$, $C = (1, 0)$, and $H = (0, -6)$.
 a. Reverse the coordinates of the points. Call the new points S_1, W_1, I_1, T_1, C_1, and H_1.
 b. Graph S and S_1 in the same color. Then, using a different color, graph W and W_1. Repeat for each pair, using a different color each time.
 c. Describe a pattern to the pairs in Part b.

14. a. Copy and complete the table below.

Original point	Add -3 to the x-coordinate of the original point.	Add 5 to the y-coordinate of the original point.
$G_1 = (5, -2)$	$G_2 = (2, -2)$	$G_3 = (5, 3)$
$R_1 = (5, 8)$	$R_2 = ?$	$R_3 = ?$
$A_1 = (-4, 4)$	$A_2 = ?$	$A_3 = ?$
$P_1 = (-3, -6)$	$P_2 = ?$	$P_3 = ?$
$H_1 = (0, -6)$	$H_2 = ?$	$H_3 = ?$

 b. Plot the points in the table on a coordinate grid. Use different colored pencils to connect the points in each column in order.
 c. Describe what happened with each change.
 d. How would you move $G_1R_1A_1P_1H_1$ two units down?

15. Study the graph at the right carefully.
  a. What does the origin represent?
  b. What is indicated on the axes?
  c. Estimate the coordinates of the position of the North Pole on each date: Nov 1, 2005; Dec 1, 2005; Jan 1, 2006; Feb 1, 2006; Feb 14, 2006.

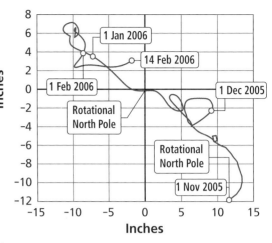

The North Pole Moves!

1 Jan 2006
14 Feb 2006
1 Feb 2006
1 Dec 2005
Rotational North Pole
Rotational North Pole
1 Nov 2005
Inches
Inches

REVIEW

16. Deonte's parents kept track of his height and weight every year from ages 3 to 10. **(Lessons 5-6, 5-2)**
  a. Enter Deonte's age, height, and weight as lists (L1, L2, and L3).
  b. Make a double line graph of these data with L1 as *x*-coordinates and L2 and L3 as *y*-coordinates.
  c. Make a line graph with L2 on the *x*-axis and L3 on the *y*-axis. Is there a general relationship between Deonte's height and his weight? Are there any exceptions to the relationship?

Age	Height (cm)	Weight (kg)
3	92	14
4	98	16
5	105	20
6	111	19
7	120	23
8	126	24
9	130	27
10	136	30

Multiple Choice In 17–19, what is the most appropriate type of graph to represent the data? (Lessons 5-6, 5-5, 5-4)

A circle graph B line graph C bar graph

17. changes in the average price for a gallon of milk from 1994–2004
18. results of a survey of Mrs. Frees's class on ice cream flavor preferences
19. average high and low temperatures for 12 months in Miami, FL

Aside from creating a picturesque view, Biscayne Bay in Miami is home to many endangered species.

Source: Florida Department of Environmental Protection

In 20 and 21, use the graph below, which shows the number of days per year with temperatures below 0°F at Madison Dane County Airport over the 66-year period from 1940–2006.

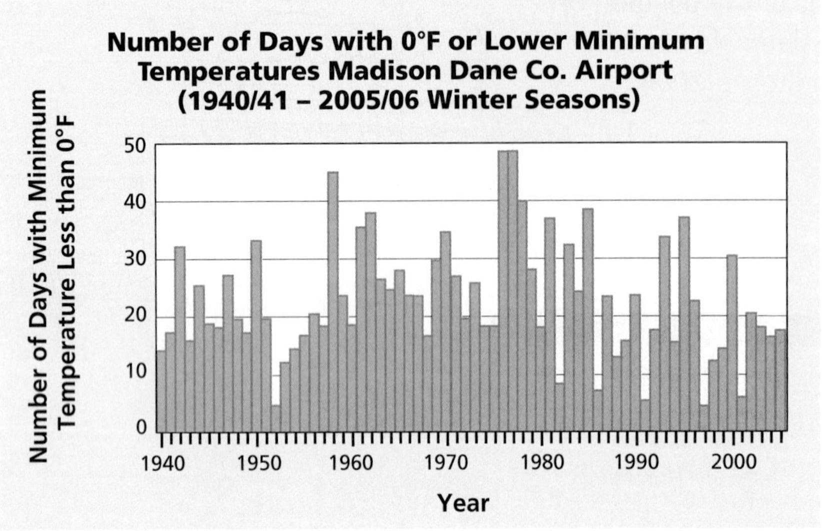

Source: *Wisconsin State Climatology Office*

20. a. Which year had the least number of days below 0°?
 b. Which year had the greatest number of days below 0°? **(Lesson 5-2)**

21. Estimate the mean number of days below 0° in Madison from 1940–2006? **(Lesson 5-1)**

22. Compute the mean, median, and range for the mean Anchorage temperatures given in Activity 3. **(Lesson 5-1)**

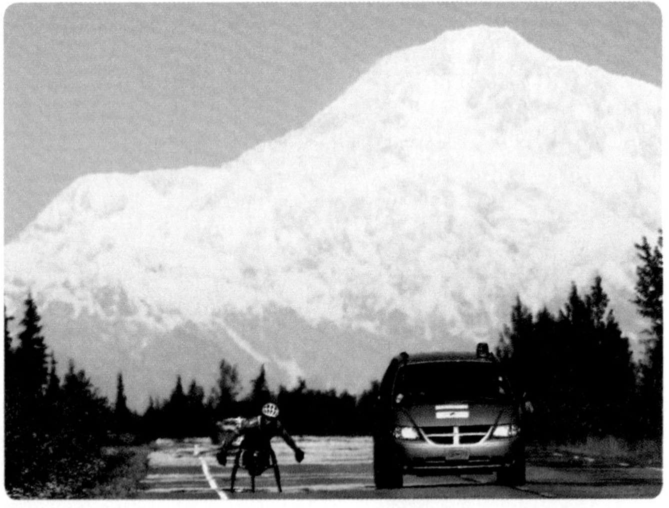

Six different mountain ranges can be seen from Anchorage, Alaska!

EXPLORATION

23. Suppose you have \$10 in quarters and dimes. Let q be the number of quarters and d be the number of dimes. For example, you could have 24 quarters and 40 dimes. Then $q = 24$ and $d = 40$, so $(q, d) = (24, 40)$. Graph this point and five other possible pairs (q, d). Describe the graph.

Lesson 5-8 Graphing Equations on a Coordinate Grid

▸ **BIG IDEA** Pairs of solutions to some simple equations can be graphed on coordinate axes.

Mental Math

Write the sum as a simple fraction in lowest terms.

a. $\frac{3}{10} + \frac{4}{10}$

b. $\frac{3}{10} + \frac{2}{5}$

c. $\frac{9}{30} + \frac{2}{5}$

Every Friday night, Lisa earns $16 babysitting for her next-door neighbors. She is saving all this money for a music system. To show how much money she saves over time, you can use a coordinate graph. Let the *x*-axis represent the number of weeks of babysitting. Let the *y*-axis represent savings. Here is a table with points to plot.

x-coordinate (weeks)	*y*-coordinate (dollars)
0	0
1	16
2	32
3	48
5	80
8	128

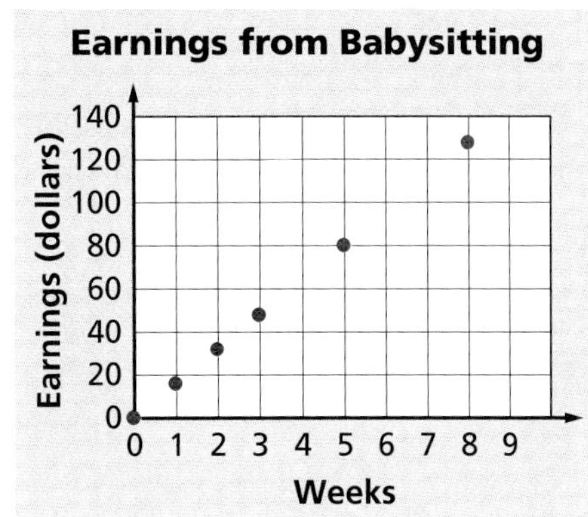

You can see that the six points lie on a straight line that passes through (0, 0) and goes up to the right. In this situation, the *y*-coordinate is 16 times the *x*-coordinate. This is written $y = 16 \cdot x$.

QY

In this situation, why are there no points in Quadrants II, III, or IV?

You can use the same idea to show the relationship between two variables in an equation.

Activity 1

MATERIALS graph paper

Consider the equation $y = x + 2$. This means you can find the *y*-coordinate by adding 2 to the *x*-coordinate.

Step 1 Study this table and then fill in the missing coordinates.

Step 2 Plot and connect the points. They should lie on the same line.

Step 3 Give the coordinates of two other points that would be on the line.

x	$y = x + 2$	(*x*, *y*)
3	5	(3, 5)
0	?	(0, ?)
−4	?	?
8	?	?
$2\frac{1}{2}$	?	?
?	−4	?
?	0	?
?	2.5	?

Activity 2

MATERIALS graphing calculator

In this activity, you will graph $y = x - 4$ using a calculator in two different ways: using lists and using the equation capability.

Using Lists

Step 1 Make a table of possible values for x and y.

Step 2 Put your x-coordinates in column A and your y-coordinates in column B on your calculator as shown at the right. Label column A "x" and column B "y".

x	y
-2	-6
-1	-5
0	-4
1	-3
2	-2
3	-1

B11

Step 3 Graph using `Quick Graph`, choosing the `xyline plot` option.

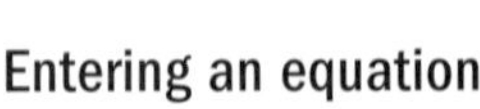

Entering an equation

Step 4 Enter the equation $f_1(x) = x - 4$. This is usually done at the bottom of the screen by entering X–4 for $f_1(x)$.

Step 5 Determine the window. Select window setting. The most common choice is `Xmin=-10`, and `Xmax=10`, and the same for the `Ymin` and `Ymax` choices. Then graph the equation.

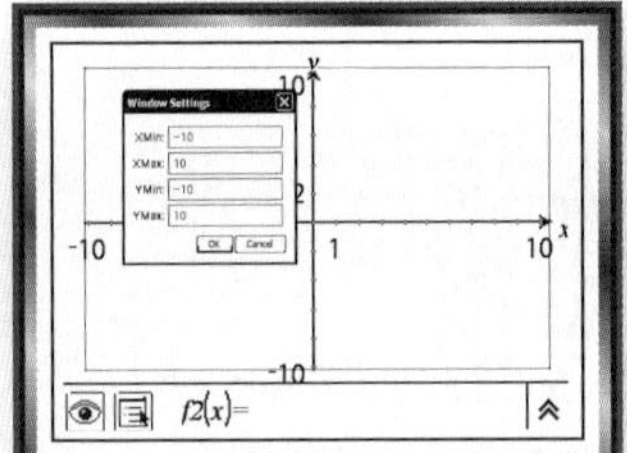

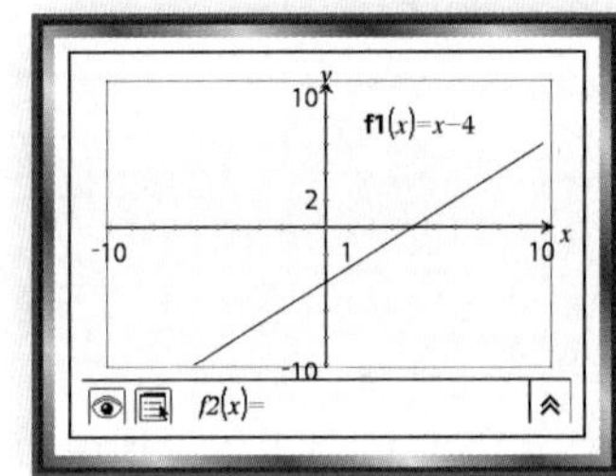

Activity 3

MATERIALS graphing calculator or graph paper

Step 1 Graph these four equations on the same set of axes:

$y = x - 2$ $\quad y = x - 5.5$ $\quad y = x + 3$ $\quad y = x + 4.5$

(If you do this on a calculator, make sure you know which equation goes with which line.)

Step 2 What is similar about the lines? What is different?

Step 3 Write a rule for a line that would go through the origin. Check your equation by graphing.

Questions

COVERING THE IDEAS

1. a. Felipe earns $2.50 per day by walking his neighbor's dog. Make a table of Felipe's earnings y if he works $x = 0, 3, 5, 9,$ and 10 days.
   b. Graph the points on a coordinate grid.
   c. Use the graph to determine how many days Felipe worked if he earned $20.

Dogs have the same five senses as humans; however, their sense of smell is considerably better than that of humans.

Source: *Encyclopedia Brittanica*

2. Graph $y = x - 1$ on graph paper. Use enough points so the graph goes through 3 quadrants.

3. a. Write a key sequence for graphing the equation $y = x - 8$ on your calculator.
   b. Sketch the display on your calculator after you graph $y = x - 8$.

4. Copy and complete th e table. Then graph the three lines on the same pair of axes.

x	a. $y = x$	b. $y = x - 3$	c. $y = x + 3.5$
−6.5	?	?	?
−3	?	?	?
0	?	?	?
2	?	?	?
4.5	?	?	?

   d. What is one thing that is the same about the lines graphed?
   e. What is one thing that is different about the lines graphed?

APPLYING THE MATHEMATICS

5. Find an equation for the line graphed at the right.

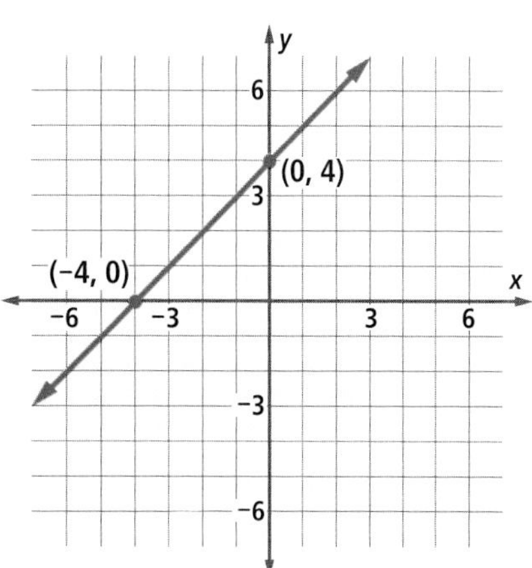

6. There are 68 sixth-grade students at Lincoln Middle School. During activity period, they must be in one of two rooms.
   a. If the number of students in one room is x and the number in the other room is y, how are x and y and related?
   b. Make a table of possible ordered pairs (x, y).
   c. Graph the line through all the possible ordered pairs.
   d. Are there parts of the line that are not meaningful in this situation?

7. Match each graph with its equation.

a. $y = x + 3$ b. $y = x - 3$ c. $y = 3 - x$ d. $y = -3 - x$

i.

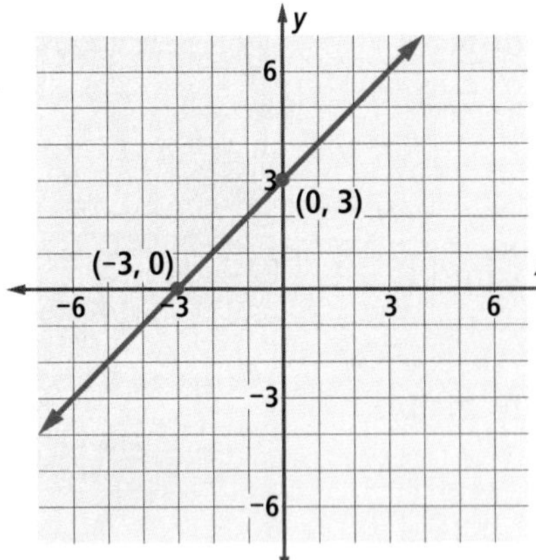

ii.

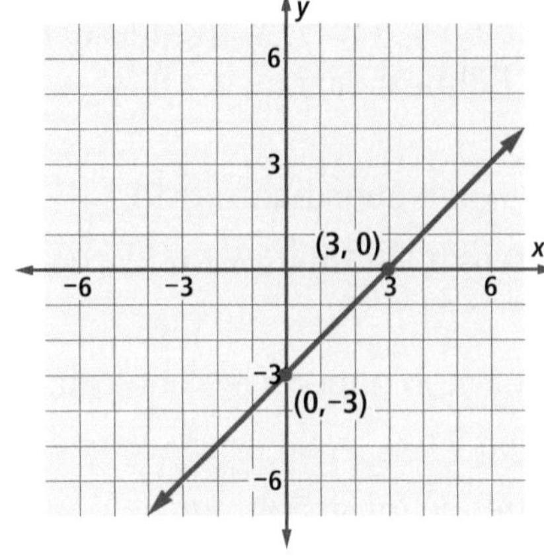

iii.

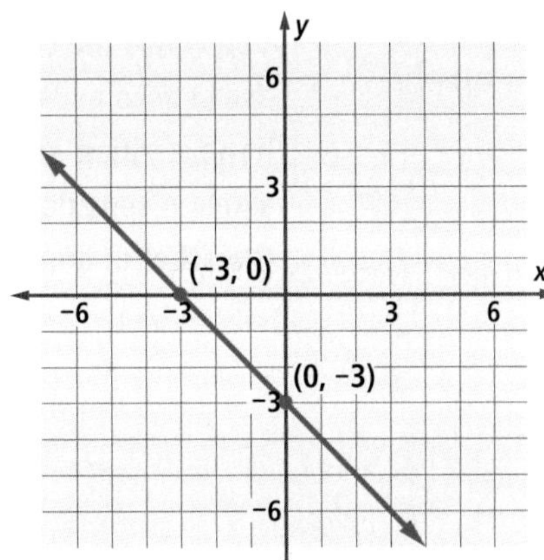

iv.

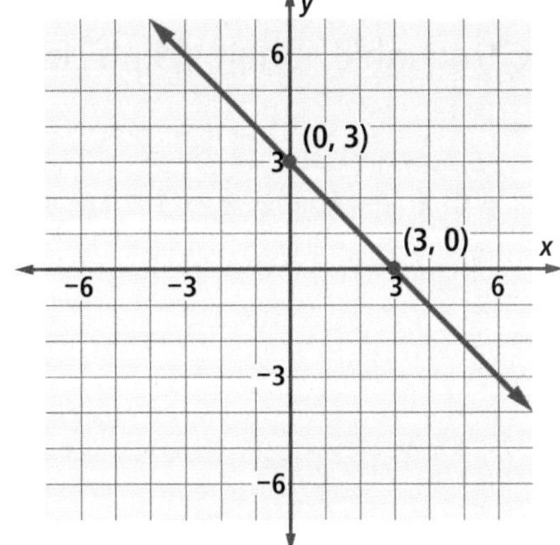

8. a. Graph these equations on your calculator, and sketch the calculator display showing the graphs.

$$y = -x \qquad y = 4 - x \qquad y = -3 - x \qquad y = 6.5 - x$$

b. How are these lines different from the ones in Activity 3?

c. What do you think accounts for this difference?

9. a. The graph at the right shows the relationship between the measures x and y of complementary angles. Give the values of (x, y) at points A and B.

b. What should be true about the x and y coordinates?

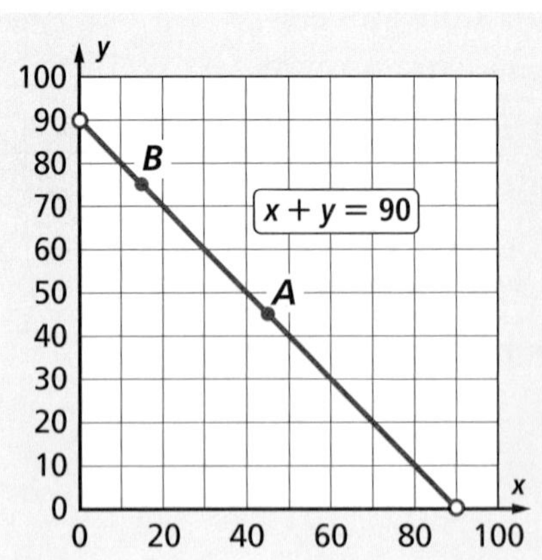

REVIEW

10. Graph the following points on the same set of axes. Connect them in order. **(Lesson 5-7)**

a. (0, 3) b. (3, 0) c. (0, –3) d. (–3, 0)

11. The table at the right lists the yearly number of visitors at Yellowstone National Park in certain years. Make a line graph of these data. **(Lesson 5-6)**

Year	Attendance
1915	51,895
1925	154,282
1935	317,998
1945	178,296
1955	1,368,515
1965	2,095,509
1975	2,239,483
1985	2,226,159
1995	3,125,285
2005	2,835,649

Source: National Park Service

Old Faithful in Yellowstone National Park

12. In a school survey, 44% of students said their favorite food was pizza, 32% said their favorite was hot dogs, and 11% said there favorite was hamburgers. **(Lesson 5-5)**

a. What percent of students said their favorite food was something other than pizza, hot dogs, or hamburgers?

b. Make a circle graph of the data with four sectors. Label the fourth sector, "Other."

c. If 200 students took the survey, about how many prefer hot dogs?

13. a. **Fill in the Blank** To multiply a number by 100, you move the decimal point __?__ places to the right.

b. **Fill in the Blank** To multiply a number by $\frac{1}{10}$, you move the decimal point __?__ places to the left.

c. **Fill in the Blank** To multiply a number by 100 and then by $\frac{1}{10}$, you move the decimal point __?__ places to the __?__. The result is the same as multiplying the original number by __?__. **(Lessons 2-3, 2-2)**

EXPLORATION

14. Graph ten points that satisfy $y = x^2$. (*Hint:* The points do not all lie on the same line.) Make a table including positive values, negative values, and zero.

QY ANSWER

Negative values have no meaning in this situation.

Chapter 5 Projects

1 Spreadsheets

Compare and contrast different spreadsheet software. Write an essay describing ten things each of these spreadsheets can do.

2 World-Record Rates

Look in an almanac or other reference book for all the world records in a speed skating, swimming, or track event for men and for women, from 1972 to the present. Present your data in a table and a double line graph. Describe any trends you find.

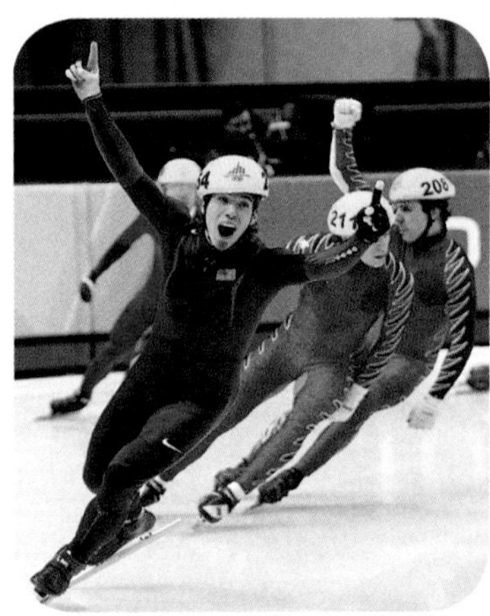

Speed skater Apolo Ohno won a total of five medals in the 2002 and the 2006 Winter Olympics.

Source: United States Olympic Committee

3 Graphs in the Media

Find a minimum of five graphs in newspapers, magazines, or on the internet. You should have at least one line graph, one bar graph, and one circle graph. Write a summary explaining each display. Be sure to include a description of what is being presented and what conclusions you can draw. Is the graph a good graph? If not, state why it isn't good.

4 Statistics

Explore more about the field of statistics. When and how did it get started? Why was it developed? Describe one or two important uses of statistics. What makes the use important, and what did the statistics show?

5 The Cartesian Coordinate System

The *x*-*y*-coordinate graph was invented by Rene Descartes. For this reason, graphs of this kind are called Cartesian coordinate graphs. Who was Descartes? Why is he famous? Why did he invent coordinate graphs? Write a page about the work of this man.

Because of his renowned intellect in so many matters, Descartes is commonly referred to as the "Father of Modern Philosophy."

6 Graphs at Work

Ask your parent or another adult you know to bring you a graph from work. Describe why the graph was created and the importance of the data for the job.

Chapter 5 Summary and Vocabulary

- Seven ways to display **data** were discussed in this chapter: a table (or chart or list), a stem-and-leaf plot, a bar graph, a histogram, a circle graph, a line graph, and coordinate graphs. Choosing the right display can make data much easier to understand.

- A **table** is made up of horizontal rows and vertical columns. It can show a lot of detailed information exactly, but it can be hard to see relationships quickly and easily. **Spreadsheets** are electronic tables. **Lists** serve as tables on graphing calculators.

- **Bar graphs** or **histograms** are useful for displaying the **frequencies** or **relative frequencies** of data values. They are good tools for comparing categories or data intervals. A **stem-and-leaf plot** is like a histogram but has the advantage of showing individual data values.

- A **circle graph** is useful when you want to show parts of a whole. It is easy to tell the relative size of the parts by the size of each **sector.**

- A **line graph** is composed of line segments that connect points on a graph. It can show a lot of information in a small space. Line graphs can show trends, particularly when the **horizontal axis** represents time.

- A **coordinate graph** provides a way to picture an **algebraic equation.** Points are plotted as **ordered pairs (x, y).** It is possible to find points that satisfy an equation by choosing different values for x and then determining the corresponding value of y. When an equation has the form $y = x + a$, the graph is a line.

- It is possible to draw many displays in this chapter by hand or using technology. You should choose the most efficient and clearest method for making a display. Good graphs have a clear title and well-labeled and uniform **scales.**

Vocabulary

5-1
statistics
minimum
maximum
mode
mean (average)
median
range

5-2
list

5-3
stem-and-leaf plot
stem
leaf

5-4
bar graph
spreadsheet
cell
active cell
axis (axes)
histogram
relative frequency

5-5
categorical data
numerical data

5-6
line graph
double line graph
multiple line graph

5-7
coordinate axes
x-axis
y-axis
quadrant
coordinates
origin
x-coordinate
y-coordinate

Chapter 5 Self-Test

Take this test as you would take a test in class. You will need a calculator. Then use the Selected Answers section in the back of the book to check your work.

In 1–3, use the following list of numbers.

30	47	61	25	43	52
52	29	47	58	31	36
26	18	22	38	48	59
54	7	28	86	42	

1. Construct a stem-and-leaf plot of the data.
2. Find the median of the data.
3. Find the median of the data if 78 is added to the data set.

In 4 and 5, refer to the histogram below. It shows how long how many students in a class could hold their breath under water for various times.

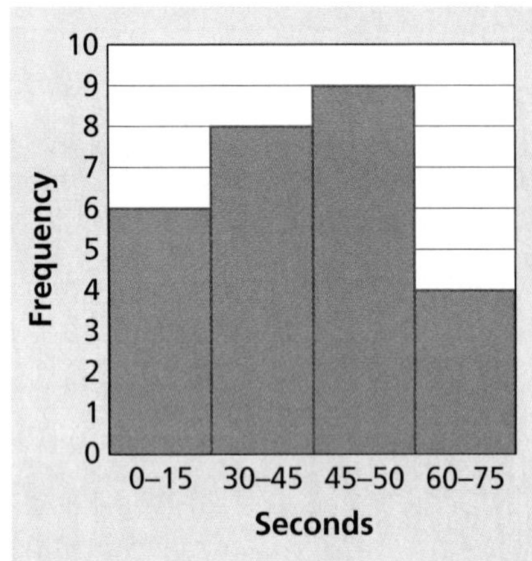

4. What is wrong with the histogram?
5. Determine appropriate intervals for the histogram.
6. **a.** Give an example of a type of graph that would be appropriate for displaying categorical data. Explain your reasoning.

   b. Give an example of a type of graph that would be appropriate for displaying numerical data. Explain your reasoning.

In 7–11, refer to the table below listing the number of students in a grade having various numbers of pets.

Number of Pets	Number of Students
0	5
1	15
2	12
3	9
4	5
5	3
6	1

7. How many students were in this survey?
8. How many students have more than 3 pets?
9. Construct a circle graph of the data.
10. What is the measure of the central angle of the sector representing students who own three pets?
11. Construct a relative-frequency histogram of these data.
12. **a.** Name coordinates of two points on the line with equation $y = 7 - x$.

    b. Graph the line $y = 7 - x$.
13. The point (4, -2) is in which quadrant?
14. Suppose the origin of a graph is where you live. Plot the following points of interest according to their location in relation to where you live. Label each location on the graph as an ordered pair. (North is up and east is right.)

    School: 3 miles west, 1 mile north

    Lake: 2 miles east

    Soccer field: 2 miles south, 8 miles west

    Art museum: 4 miles east, 4 miles south

In 15 and 16, use the following data on the times of sunrise and sunset in Helsinki, Finland on the first day of each month in a recent year.

Month	Sunrise	Sunset
January	9:24	15:23
February	8:35	16:33
March	7:20	17:47
April	5:46	19:04
May	4:18	20:18
June	3:08	21:29
July	3:00	21:47
August	3:59	20:52
September	5:14	19:25
October	6:25	17:53
November	7:42	16:24
December	8:56	15:22

Source: srrb.noaa.gov

15. Construct a double line graph of the data. On the x-axis, let January = 1, February = 2, and so on.

16. What trends do you notice in the graph?

Chapter 5 Chapter Review

SKILLS
PROPERTIES
USES
REPRESENTATIONS

SKILLS Procedures used to get answers

OBJECTIVE A Calculate the maximum value, minimum value, median, mode, mean, and range of a set of data. (Lessons 5-1, 5-2)

In 1–6, use the following table of data about the eight major planets in our solar system. Mass, gravity, and distance are given in units set so that Earth has a value of 1. (For example, the mass of Neptune is 17 times that of Earth.)

Planet	Radius (mi)	Mass	Gravity	Distance from Sun
Mercury	1,515	0.06	0.37	0.39
Venus	3,760	0.82	0.88	0.72
Earth	3,963	1.00	1.00	1.00
Mars	2,108	0.11	0.38	1.52
Jupiter	44,362	318	2.64	5.20
Saturn	37,280	95	1.15	9.53
Uranus	15,800	15	1.15	19.19
Neptune	15,300	17	1.12	30.06

Source: solarsystem.nasa.gov

1. Find the maximum gravity of the planets.
2. Find the minimum radius of the planets.
3. Find the range of the radii of the planets.
4. Find the mode gravity of the planets.
5. Find the median gravity of the planets.
6. Find the mean radius of the planets.

In 7–10, use the following information on the dwarf planet Pluto.

Planet	Radius (mi)	Mass	Gravity	Distance from Sun
Pluto	715	0.0022	0.08	39.48

7. Does the range of the planets' radii change if Pluto is included?
8. Find the median distance of the planets from the sun including Pluto.
9. Find the mean gravity of the planets including Pluto.
10. Find the mode gravity of all the planets including Pluto.

PROPERTIES The principles behind the mathematics

OBJECTIVE B Describe properties of points graphed on a coordinate grid. (Lesson 5-7)

11. A point with two negative coordinates is in which quadrant?
12. A point whose first coordinate is negative and whose second coordinate is positive is in which quadrant?
13. The points with first coordinate –3 form what kind of figure?
14. The points with first coordinate –3 and second coordinate 7 form what kind of figure?

OBJECTIVE C Differentiate between categorical and numerical data. (Lesson 5-5)

In 15–19, decide whether the given data are categorical or numerical.

15. serial numbers on home computers
16. favorite foods of different family members
17. average speed of the riders in a bike race
18. number of hours of sleep of different mammals
19. zip codes of everyone in the sixth grade

USES Applications of mathematics in real-world situations

OBJECTIVE D Locate, use, and draw conclusions from data in a table. (Lesson 5-1)

In 20–24, use the data table from Questions 1–6.

20. Which planets have a larger radius than Earth?

21. Which planets have a greater mass than Earth?

22. Which planets have more gravity than Earth?

23. a. What is the total mass of the 8 major planets in the solar system?

b. What is the total mass of the major planets in the solar system except Jupiter?

24. Which is larger, the median or the mean gravity of the 8 major planets in the solar system.

OBJECTIVE E Interpret information displayed in a histogram or stem-and-leaf plot. (Lessons 5-3, 5-4)

In 25 and 26, use the histogram below.

University of Iowa Wrestlers

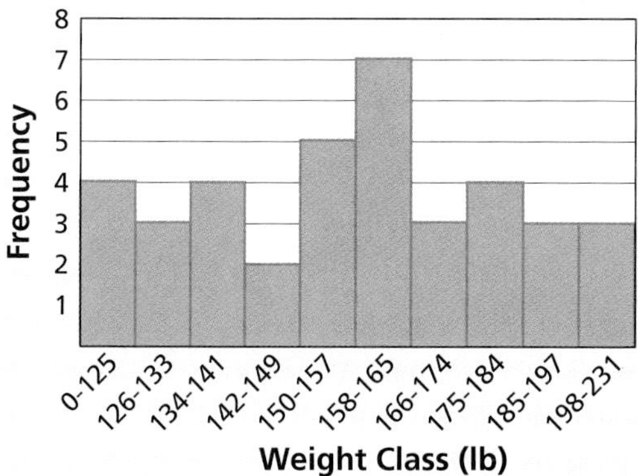

Source: University of Iowa

25. Which weight interval has the greatest number of wrestlers? How many wrestlers are in this weight class?

26. Which weight class would a wrestler who weighs 168 pounds wrestle in? Why?

In 27 and 28, use the stem-and-leaf plot below. It displays the populations of the 10th–29th most populous countries in the world in millions.

Stem	Leaves
12	7
11	
10	7
9	
8	9 4 2
7	9 5 0
6	9 5 3 1 1
5	8
4	9 7 7 4 4 1

27. What is the median population of this plot?

28. Add one population to the plot that does not change the median.

OBJECTIVE F Interpret information displayed in a circle graph. (Lesson 5-5)

In 29–32, refer to the circle graph below, which displays hair color of the students in a class.

Hair Color of Students

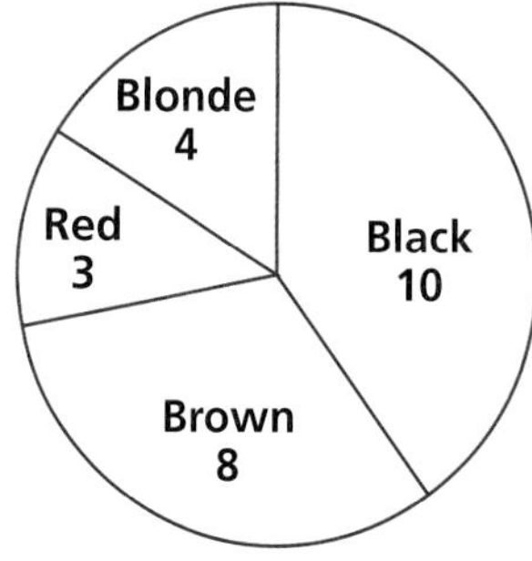

29. Which hair color is the most common?

30. What percent of the class has red hair?

31. What is the measure of the central angle of the blonde hair sector?

OBJECTIVE G Interpret information displayed in a line graph. (Lesson 5-6)

In 32–35, refer to the line graph below, which displays the number of new students at a school each year.

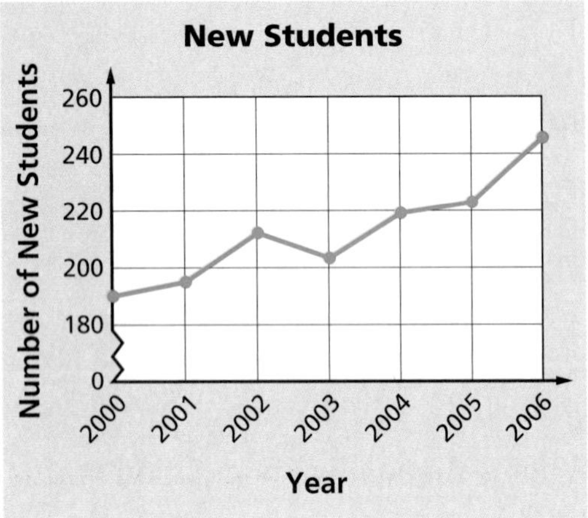

32. Does the number of new students seem to be increasing or decreasing?
33. Predict about how many new students there will be in 2007.
34. Explain how the overall population of the school could stay the same despite the changes in the number of new students.
35. During which years did the number of new students increase? During which years did the number of new students decrease?

REPRESENTATIONS Pictures, graphs, or objects that illustrate concepts

OBJECTIVE H Construct a histogram or stem-and-leaf plot. (Lessons 5-3, 5-4)

36. Construct a histogram of the number of copies of each of the top-ten-selling computer games as of 2006: 16.08 million, 11 million, 9 million, 8 million, 7.6 million, 5.21 million, 4 million, 4 million, 4 million, and 4 million. Use intervals of 0–3 million, 3–6 million, 6–9 million, 9–12 million, and over 12 million.

37. The following are the final exam scores for 24 students in a math class: 75, 43, 82, 94, 76, 78, 81, 88, 73, 88, 98, 91, 85, 70, 80, 61, 68, 79, 95, 87, 84, 82, 91, 90. If you were to put this information into a histogram, what intervals might you use?

38. Suppose the scores of Question 37 were multiplied by 0.1. What intervals would you use for your histogram now?

39. Construct a stem-and-leaf plot of the data in Question 37.

OBJECTIVE I Construct a circle graph by hand or by using technology. (Lesson 5-5)

40. At the shoe store there were 500 pairs of shoes sold during the month of January. Of these, 153 were Basics, 77 were Rebounds, 98 were Mikeys, 124 were Amoebas, and the rest were other brands. Construct a circle graph of these data.

41. Suppose there was a defect found in the Rebounds of Question 40, and all of them were returned. Now construct a circle graph of the remaining data.

42. Use technology to construct a circle graph with the following properties: There are a total of five sectors, the first sector is twice as big as the second, the third sector is three times as big as the fourth sector, and the fifth sector is the smallest.

OBJECTIVE J Construct a line graph by hand or by using technology. (Lesson 5-6)

43. Create a line graph of the data in the table at the right, which shows the number of students in a high school who work during the given months.

Month	Number
January	50
February	52
March	53
April	55
May	62
June	98
July	137

44. A new CD was released in January. Starting in January, the monthly sales of this CD over the following 10 months were 460, 665, 704, 518, 290, 313, 228, 159, 183, and 177. Create a line graph of these data.

45. When plotting a double line graph on a calculator, how do you distinguish between the two lines?

OBJECTIVE K Graph points on a coordinate grid. (Lesson 5-7)

In 46–49, use the table below of low temperatures for a week as recorded by a sixth grade class.

Day	Temperature (°C)
Sunday	-7
Monday	4
Tuesday	-3
Wednesday	8
Thursday	-1
Friday	12
Saturday	14

46. Plot these data on a coordinate grid, with the days of the week on the x-axis, represented by positive or negative numbers. (Wednesday should be represented by 0, Tuesday is –1, and so on.) Connect the points.

47. What trends do you notice in the graph?

48. This table shows the high temperatures of each day. Use a different color, and graph these data on the same grid as the low temperatures graph. Connect the points.

Day	Temperature (°C)
Sunday	7
Monday	14
Tuesday	8
Wednesday	23
Thursday	12
Friday	32
Saturday	31

49. On what day was there the greatest range in temperature?

50. Plot the following points on a coordinate grid and connect them in order: (2, 1); (–1, 2); (–2, –2); (5, 1); (–2, 4); (–4, –3); (5, –1).

51. Write the coordinates of the following points in the graph below.

a. A b. B c. C d. D e. E

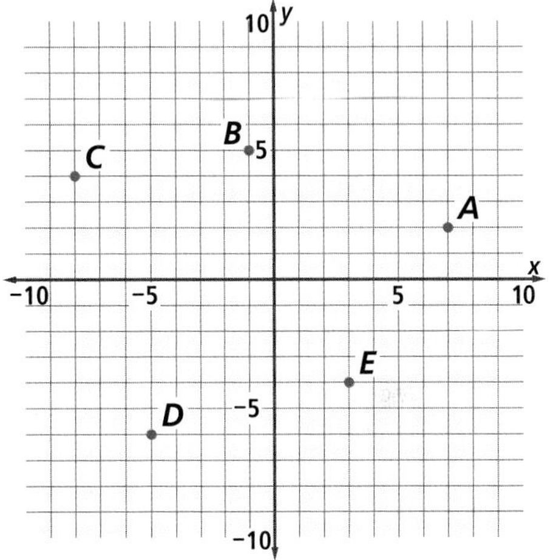

OBJECTIVE L Graph simple equations involving addition and subtraction on a coordinate grid. (Lesson 5-8)

In 52–55, graph the equation. Identify three points on the line.

52. $y = x + 4$

53. $y = x - 4$

54. $y = 4 - x$

55. $y = x - 2.25$

Chapter

6 Using Multiplication

Contents

You may remember being told to "learn your multiplication facts." At that time, you may not have realized why multiplication is so important. Multiplication is important because it has so many uses.

For example, here are a few of the things you can find by calculating $13\frac{1}{2} \cdot 12$:

- the area of a hall that is $13\frac{1}{2}$ meters long and 12 meters wide
- the total cost of 12 shirts when each shirt costs $13.50
- the number of inches in $13\frac{1}{2}$ feet
- the distance biked in 12 hours by someone averaging $13\frac{1}{2}$ miles per hour
- the distance biked in $13\frac{1}{2}$ hours by someone averaging 12 miles per hour
- the number of eggs in $13\frac{1}{2}$ dozen eggs

It is also common to see three or more numbers multiplied together. For example, here are a few of the things you can find by calculating $5 \cdot 4 \cdot 3$:

- the number of tennis balls in 5 packages that each contain 4 cylinders with 3 balls in each cylinder
- the volume (in cubic units) of a box that is 5 units wide, 4 units high, and 3 units deep
- the number of different outfits you can make from 5 hats, 4 shirts, and 3 pairs of slacks
- the cost of 4 yards of wood trim that is \$5 per foot
- the number of 3-digit whole numbers that can be written with 3 different odd digits in base 10 (such as 197 or 351)

Its many uses make multiplication as important an operation as addition. In this chapter, you will use multiplication of positive and negative numbers, fractions, percents, and decimals in a wide variety of situations.

Lesson

6-1 Multiplication and Arrays

Vocabulary

rectangular array

▶ **BIG IDEA** The product of two whole numbers can be pictured with a rectangular array whose dimensions are those numbers.

Mental Math

Calculate.

a. $3 + 3 + 3 + 3$

b. $1.5 + 1.5 + 1.5 + 1.5 + 1.5 + 1.5$

c. $7 + 7 + 7 + 7 + 7 + 7 + 7 + 7 + 7 + 7 + 7$

d. $3.9 + 3.9 + 3.9 + 3.9 + 3.9 + 3.9 + 3.9 + 3.9 + 3.9 + 3.9$

A picture models a situation by organizing the information. One way to picture multiplication is with arrays.

Rectangular Arrays

Eggs are arranged in rows and columns in a container. Multiplication tells you how many eggs are in the container.

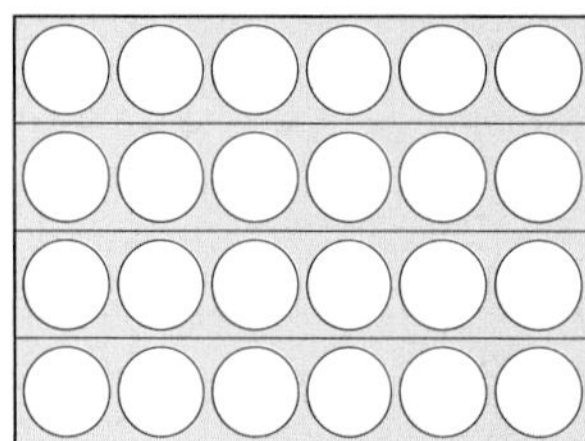

$$4 \text{ rows} \cdot 6 \frac{\text{eggs}}{\text{row}} = 24 \text{ eggs}$$

or

$$6 \text{ columns} \cdot 4 \frac{\text{eggs}}{\text{column}} = 24 \text{ eggs}$$

A box of watercolors has wells for different colors of paints.

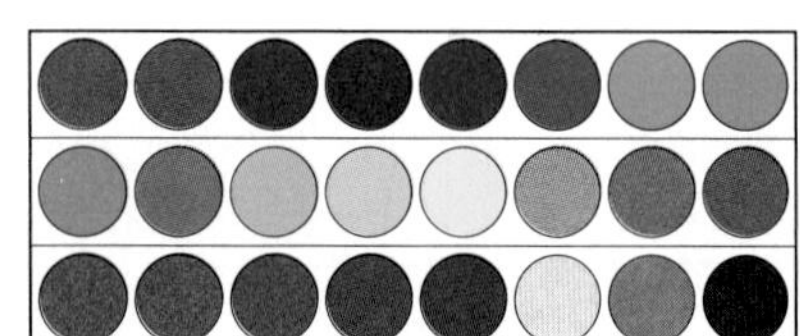

$$3 \text{ rows} \cdot 8 \frac{\text{wells}}{\text{row}} = 24 \text{ wells}$$

or

$$8 \text{ columns} \cdot 3 \frac{\text{wells}}{\text{column}} = 24 \text{ wells}$$

A large package of AAA batteries has 24 batteries lined up in one row in the box.

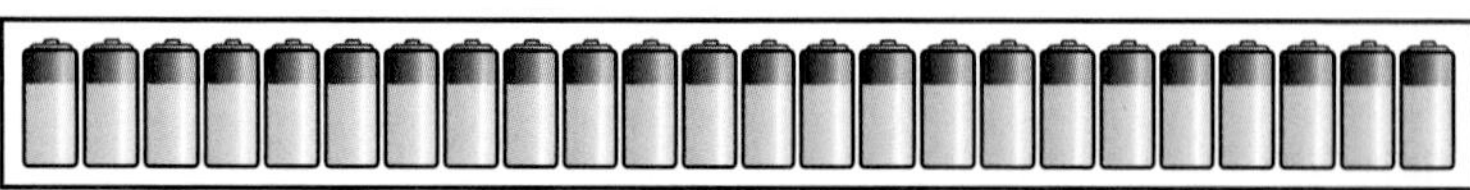

$$1 \text{ row} \cdot 24 \frac{\text{batteries}}{\text{row}} = 24 \text{ batteries}$$

or

$$24 \text{ columns} \cdot 1 \frac{\text{battery}}{\text{column}} = 24 \text{ batteries}$$

Each of these packages organizes 24 items in a different *rectangular array*. **Rectangular arrays** are arrangements with the same number of items per row and the same number of items per column.

QY1

Describe a way that 24 items could be organized in an array that is different from any of those shown here.

The boxes, or cells, in a table also can form an array. Mrs. Donigan recorded the chess club attendance in a table that has a row for each student and a column for each day the club had a meeting. The array is the arrangement of the 24 cells where she marks an "A" if a student was absent.

The United States Chess Federation has over 80,000 members and more than 2,000 chess clubs and organizations.

Source: The United States Chess Federation

Club Attendance	Tuesday	Wednesday	Thursday	Friday
Joshua		A		
Nelville				
Morika		A		
Sam				
Maria				A
José				

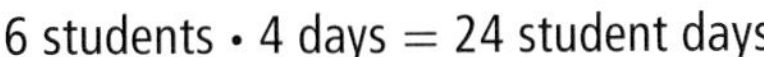

6 students • 4 days = 24 student days

In each of these arrays, the total number of elements can be found by multiplying the number of rows by the number of columns. We call this general pattern the *Array Model for Multiplication*.

Array Model for Multiplication

The number of elements in a rectangular array with r rows and c columns is $r \cdot c$ or rc.

Recall that for the multiplication x times y, x and y are called factors and the answer is called the product of x and y. To indicate multiplication with variables, the multiplication sign is usually not written. "The product of 5 and p" is written with a multiplication dot ($5 \cdot p$) or with no sign at all ($5p$). Do not write $5 \times p$, because $\times$ is easily mistaken for the variable x.

QY2

Write the product of the factors 30, *a*, and *b* with and without using the dot for multiplication.

Finding Parts of an Array

In some situations, an array can picture multiplication by a fraction.

Example 1

Jesse's dog Godzilla sat on a grocery bag with 15 peaches. He crushed two-thirds of the peaches. How many peaches did he crush?

Solution 1 You want to find $\frac{2}{3}$ of 15 peaches. Draw a picture of 15 peaches, arranging them into 3 equal rows. Circle two of the three rows to represent the crushed peaches. Godzilla crushed 10 peaches.

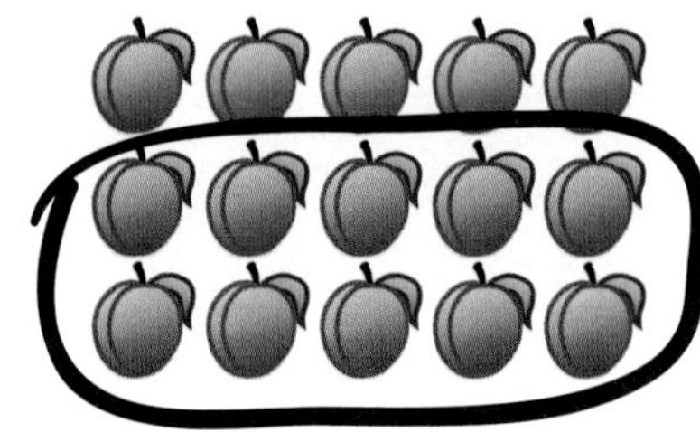

Solution 2 Divide 15 into thirds. $15 \div 3 = 5$, so $\frac{1}{3} \times 15 = 5$. $\frac{2}{3}$ will be twice as many as $\frac{1}{3}$, and 2×5 peaches is 10 peaches. Godzilla crushed 10 peaches.

Arrays can sometimes picture multiplication by decimals or percents.

Example 2

What is 20% of 15?

Solution Think of the array of 15 peaches and remember that $20\% = \frac{1}{5}$. Now $\frac{1}{5}$ of the peaches can be found by circling one of the five columns.

$$20\% \text{ of } 15 = 3$$

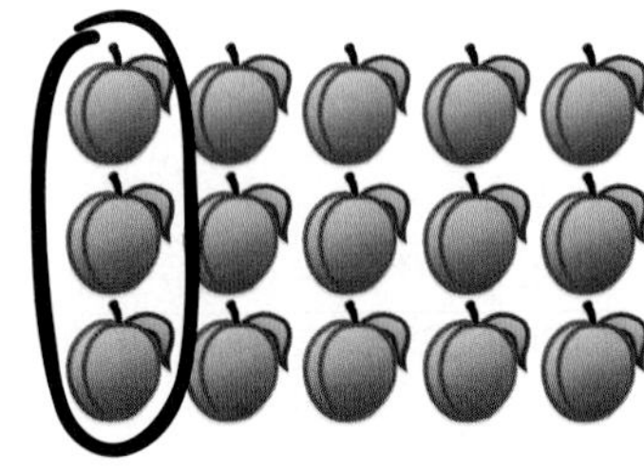

Arrays with Three Factors

The Array Model for Multiplication can be applied to three factors by using 3-dimensional arrays. For example, think of a sheet of 20 postage stamps, arranged in 4 rows and 5 columns. If six of these sheets are stacked on top of each other, the total number of stamps is the product of 4, 5, and 6: $4 \cdot 5 \cdot 6 = 120$.

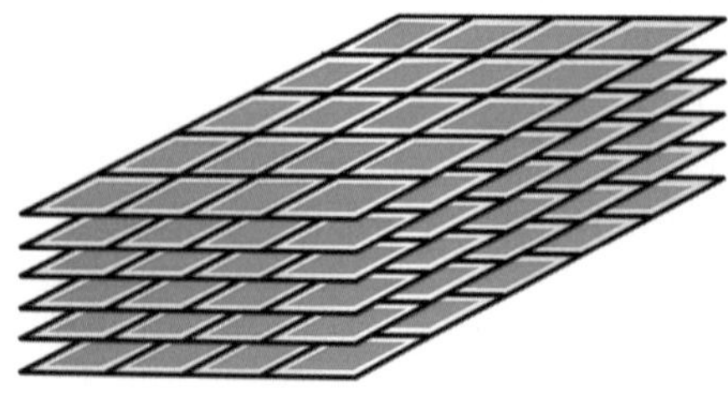

Activity

MATERIALS counters

Step 1 Work with a partner. Start with 36 counters. Arrange the counters into a 2-dimensional rectangular array that has more than one row and more than one column. Draw a picture of your array.

Step 2 Now use the 36 counters to make a 3-dimensional array by placing counters on top of one another. Picture this array.

Step 3 Use the 36 counters to find two other arrays that picture a product of 36 with 3 factors. Give the dimensions of these arrays.

Questions

COVERING THE IDEAS

1. a. Draw a rectangular array with 7 rows and 5 columns of dots.
   b. How many dots are in the array?
2. Kendra arranged her DVDs in a rectangular array similar to the one below.

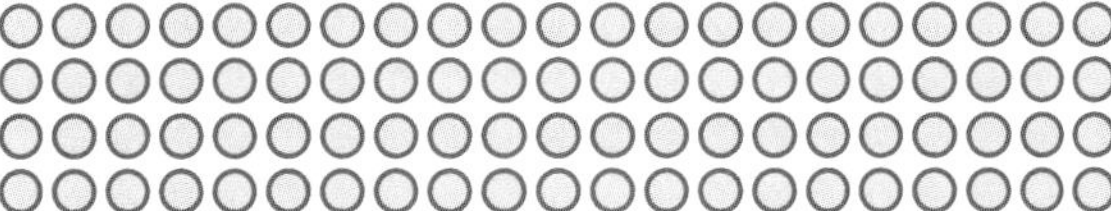

   a. How many rows are in this rectangular array?
   b. How many columns are in this rectangular array?
   c. How many DVDs does Kendra have in all?

In 3 and 4, refer to Example 1.

3. a. How many peaches did Godzilla *not* crush?
   b. What multiplication answers Part a?
4. Suppose Jesse went back to the store and bought 24 more peaches. This time, Godzilla crushes $\frac{5}{6}$ of them.
   a. Draw a picture of this situation.
   b. How many peaches did Godzilla crush this time?

Godzilla crushed some peaches.

In 5–7, calculate the product by using an array to visualize the multiplication.

5. $\frac{4}{7} \cdot 21$
6. $36 \cdot \frac{8}{9}$
7. $25\% \cdot 20$
8. Mrs. Delgado needs space on her bookshelf for 40 calculator manuals. Each manual is $\frac{5}{8}$ in. thick. How much space does she need?

9. Zachary earns \$88 for an 8-hour day of work. On Tuesdays, he leaves an hour early, so he is paid only for $\frac{7}{8}$ of a day of work. How much does he earn on Tuesdays?

Properly pruned shrubs and trees look more attractive, and grow healthier and more vigorously.

APPLYING THE MATHEMATICS

10. Hannah and An went out for lunch. They split a lasagna dish that cost \$6.60. Hannah ate $\frac{2}{3}$ of the lasagna and paid $\frac{2}{3}$ of the \$6.60.
    a. How much did Hannah pay?
    b. How much did An pay?

11. Use arrays to explain why $4 \cdot 5 = 5 \cdot 4$.

12. a. Draw a segment $\overline{AB}$ that is 2 inches long.
    b. Draw a segment whose length is $\frac{3}{4}$ the length of $\overline{AB}$.
    c. Draw a segment whose length is $1\frac{3}{4}$ times the length of $\overline{AB}$.

In 13–15, evaluate the expression.

13. $8a$ when $a = 6$
14. $\frac{4}{5}m$ when $m = 45$
15. $(2L) + (3W)$ when $L = 5$ and $W = 6$

16. There are 330 students in a school. Without multiplying, tell whether the answer to each problem is *greater than*, *less than*, or *equal to* 330.
    a. $\frac{2}{3}$ of the students ate at school on Tuesday. How many students was this?
    b. The Parent's Association bought $1\frac{1}{2}$ donuts for each student. How many donuts did they buy?
    c. 80% of the students have gym class on Friday. How many students is this?

17. A digital camera captures pictures by using little dots called picture elements, or *pixels* for short. Pixels are arranged in rows and columns. A million pixels equals one megapixel. Gerald's digital picture has 2,272 rows and 1,704 columns of pixels. How many megapixels is Gerald's image, rounded to the nearest megapixel?

In 18 and 19, refer to pages 326 and 327.

18. How far have you traveled if you have biked for 12 hours at an average speed of $13\frac{1}{2}$ miles per hour?

19. How many outfits can you make from 5 hats, 4 shirts, and 3 pairs of slacks?

20. Without actually multiplying, order the expressions from greatest product to least product. The letters underneath the reordered expressions will form a word. Save this word for the quote in Question 24 in Lesson 6-10 on page 389.

a. $25 \times \frac{2}{3}$ ib **b.** $\frac{9}{10} \times 25$ s **c.** 3×25 pos **d.** 0.05×25 le

REVIEW

21. Use the table below. It shows the number of regular-season wins by the winner and loser of the Major League Baseball World Series from 1996–2006.

Year	Winner	Loser
2006	83	95
2005	99	89
2004	98	105
2003	91	101
2002	99	95
2001	92	95
2000	87	94
1999	98	103
1998	114	98
1997	92	86
1996	92	96

Source: Major League Baseball

a. Find the median and mean of the values in the Winner column.

b. Find the median and mean of the values in the Loser column.

c. Was the team with the better regular-season record more likely to win the World Series? Explain. **(Lesson 5-1)**

22. ***Skill Sequence*** Calculate. **(Lesson 3-8)**

a. $\frac{1}{6} + \frac{7}{8}$

b. $13\frac{1}{6} + 5\frac{7}{8}$

c. $13\frac{1}{6} - 5\frac{7}{8}$

d. $5\frac{7}{8} - 13\frac{1}{6}$

23. Venus loves fractions so much that she labeled the price stickers at her garage sale in fractions of dollars. Rewrite the prices in dollars and cents. Round to the nearest cent if necessary. **(Lesson 2-7)**

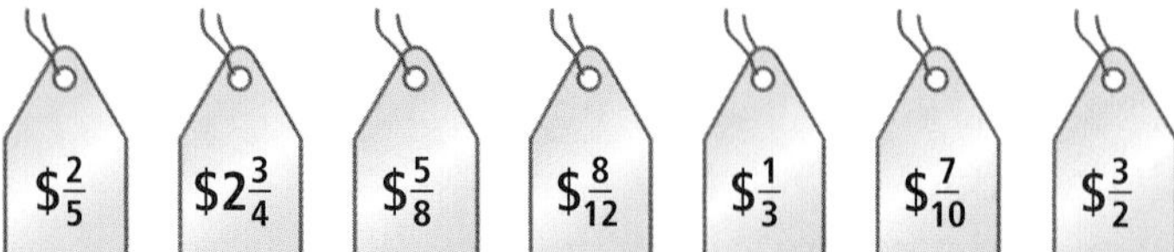

24. Find each product in your head. **(Lessons 2-3, 2-2)**
   a. $\frac{1}{100} \times 5623$
   b. $1{,}000 \times 0.04$
   c. $0.0001 \times 1{,}000{,}000$
   d. 20×23

25. Express 80 centimeters as a fraction of 1 meter. **(Lesson 1-6)**

26. Express 45 centimeters as a fraction of 2 meters. **(Lesson 1-6)**

EXPLORATION

27. The kindergarten class at Lori's school was having an apple festival. One of the recipes that the kindergarten students wanted to sample used $\frac{1}{6}$ of $\frac{1}{3}$ of an apple for each serving. The kindergarten students asked Lori's sixth grade class to help them.
   a. Draw a diagram showing how to cut an apple into pieces that are $\frac{1}{6}$ of $\frac{1}{3}$ of an apple.
   b. How many apples would they need to serve 30 students? Explain your answer.

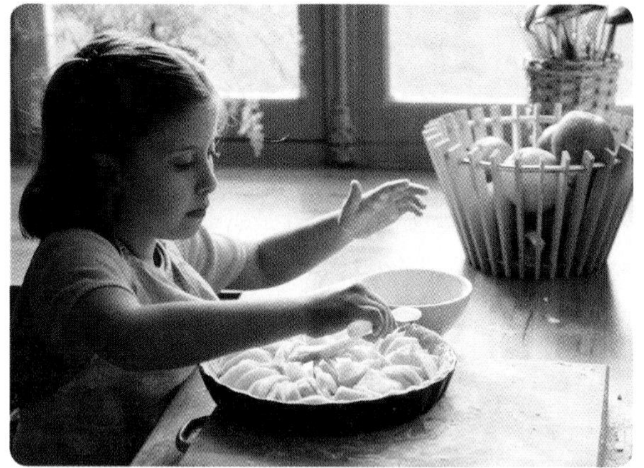

Apple pies were first created in the 14th century, but they did not contain sugar or the pastry.

Source: whatscookingamerica.net

QY ANSWERS

1. an array of 2 rows of 12 dots

2. 30 • *a* • *b*, or 30 • *ab*; 30*ab*

Lesson 6-2 Multiplying Fractions

BIG IDEA The product of two simple fractions is a fraction whose numerator is the product of the numerators of the simple fractions and whose denominator is the product of their denominators.

In Lesson 6-1, you multiplied a whole number by a fraction, as in $\frac{2}{3} \cdot 15$. What happens when you multiply two fractions?

Mental Math

Calculate.

a. $5 + 5 + 5 + 5 + 5 + 5 + 5 + 5 + 5 + 5 + 5 + 5$

b. $\frac{1}{2} + \frac{1}{2} + \frac{1}{2} + \frac{1}{2} + \frac{1}{2} + \frac{1}{2} + \frac{1}{2} + \frac{1}{2} + \frac{1}{2} + \frac{1}{2} + \frac{1}{2} + \frac{1}{2}$

c. $5\frac{1}{2} + 5\frac{1}{2} + 5\frac{1}{2} + 5\frac{1}{2} + 5\frac{1}{2} + 5\frac{1}{2} + 5\frac{1}{2} + 5\frac{1}{2} + 5\frac{1}{2} + 5\frac{1}{2} + 5\frac{1}{2} + 5\frac{1}{2}$

Example 1

Of the 2,400 seats in an auditorium, $\frac{4}{5}$ are on the main floor. Of the main floor seats, $\frac{2}{3}$ are in the center section. These are the most expensive seats. What fraction of the total number of seats are the most expensive?

Solution $\frac{4}{5}$ of 2,400 seats are on the main floor: $\frac{4}{5} \cdot 2{,}400 =$ 1,920 seats. The center section contains $\frac{2}{3}$ of these 1,920 seats: $\frac{2}{3} \cdot 1{,}920 = 1{,}280$ seats. Compare 1,280 to 2,400 to find the fraction of seats that are the most expensive. $\frac{1{,}280}{2{,}400} = \frac{8}{15}$; Of the 2,400 seats, $\frac{8}{15}$ are the most expensive.

QY1

Suppose there were 900 seats in the auditorium.

a. How many seats would be considered the most expensive?

b. What fraction of the total number of seats is this?

What if there were n seats in the auditorium? The most expensive seats would be $\frac{2}{3}$ of $\frac{4}{5}$ of n seats: $\frac{2}{3} \cdot \frac{4}{5} n$. You would expect this to be $\frac{8}{15}$ of n seats, as in Example 1. The product of the two fractions $\frac{2}{3}$ and $\frac{4}{5}$ gives you the fraction of the total seats that are the most expensive.

One way to compute $\frac{2}{3} \cdot \frac{4}{5}$ is to draw an array. The denominators of the fractions are 3 and 5, so think of an array with 3 rows and 5 columns. For $\frac{2}{3}$, circle two of the three rows and for $\frac{4}{5}$, circle four of the five columns. Eight dots are in both circled areas. So the product is 8 of 15 dots or $\frac{8}{15}$ of the array.

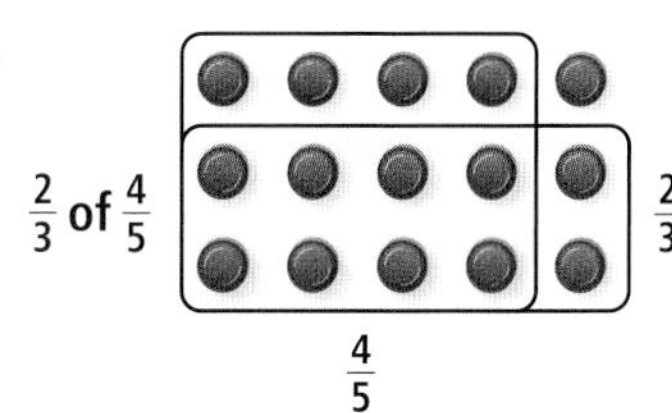

Notice the pattern that connects $\frac{2}{3}$, $\frac{4}{5}$, and the answer $\frac{8}{15}$: The numerator, 8, is $2 \cdot 4$, the product of the numerators of the factors, and the denominator, 15, is $3 \cdot 5$, the product of the denominators of the factors.

Example 2

In 2000, about $\frac{1}{8}$ of the people in the United States were of Hispanic origin. Of these Hispanics, $\frac{2}{3}$ traced their origins to Mexico. What fraction of the U.S. population had ancestors from Mexico?

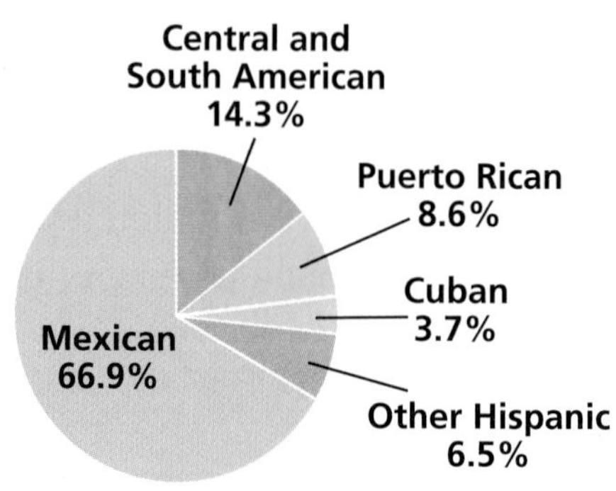

Solution You want to find $\frac{2}{3}$ of $\frac{1}{8}$ or $\frac{2}{3} \cdot \frac{1}{8}$. Because the denominators of the fractions are 3 and 8, you can picture the multiplication with a rectangular array of 3 rows and 8 columns.

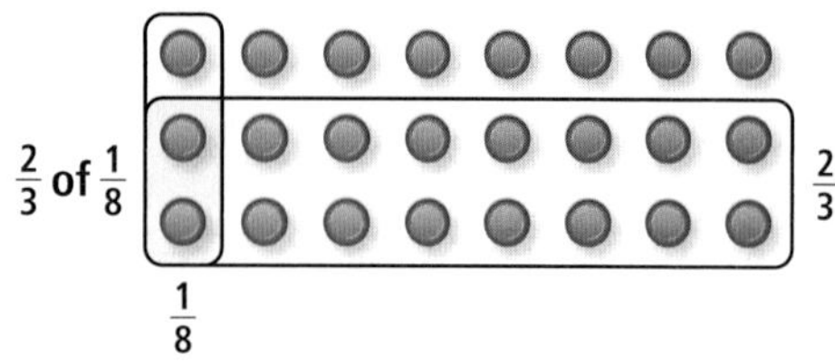

Two rows and one column give a total of 2 dots out of 24. So $\frac{2}{24}$ of the people in the U.S. were Hispanics of Mexican origin.

$\frac{2}{3} \cdot \frac{1}{8} = \frac{2}{24} = \frac{1}{12}$

Note also that $\frac{2}{3} \cdot \frac{1}{8} = \frac{2 \cdot 1}{3 \cdot 8} = \frac{2}{24}$. This pattern, seen in Examples 1 and 2, indicates how to multiply fractions.

Multiplication of Fractions Property

For all numbers a and c, and all nonzero numbers b and d,

$\frac{a}{b} \cdot \frac{c}{d} = \frac{ac}{bd}$.

QY2

Consider $\frac{2}{5} \cdot \frac{4}{7}$.

a. Multiply, using the Multiplication of Fractions Property.

b. Check your answer by drawing an array.

The Multiplication of Fractions Property works even when a factor is a whole number.

Example 3

The rangers said that $\frac{3}{5}$ of the 2,200 acres in the state park are burning. How many acres are burning?

Solution $\frac{3}{5}$ of the 2,200 acres are burning. So multiply $\frac{3}{5} \cdot 2{,}200$. To use the Multiplication of Fractions Property, write 2,200 as the fraction $\frac{2{,}200}{1}$.

$\frac{3}{5} \cdot 2{,}200 = \frac{3}{5} \cdot \frac{2{,}200}{1}$ Substitution

$= \frac{3 \cdot 2{,}200}{5 \cdot 1}$ Multiplication of Fractions Property

$= \frac{6{,}600}{5}$ Multiply.

$= 1{,}320$ Meaning of fraction as division

1,320 acres are burning.

When a numerator and a denominator have common factors, you can simplify before you multiply.

About 800 square miles of land burned during the 2007 Southern California wildfires.

Source: Associated Press

Example 4

Compute $\frac{7}{9} \cdot \frac{18}{21}$ and put the product in lowest terms.

Solution 1 Multiply. Then put the product in lowest terms.

$\frac{7}{9} \cdot \frac{18}{21} = \frac{7 \cdot 18}{9 \cdot 21} = \frac{126}{189}$ Multiplication of Fractions Property

$= \frac{\cancel{3}^{1} \cdot 42}{\cancel{3}_{1} \cdot 63}$ Equal Fractions Property (common factor is 3)

$= \frac{42}{63}$

$= \frac{\cancel{7}^{1} \cdot 6}{\cancel{7}_{1} \cdot 9}$ Equal Fractions Property (common factor is 7)

$= \frac{6}{9}$

$= \frac{3 \cdot 2}{3 \cdot 3}$ Equal Fractions Property (common factor is 3)

$= \frac{2}{3}$

Solution 2 Show (but do not do) the multiplication. Then simplify using common factors in the numerator and denominator before multiplying.

$\frac{7}{9} \cdot \frac{18}{21} = \frac{7 \cdot 18}{9 \cdot 21}$ Multiplication of Fractions Property

$= \frac{\cancel{7}^{1} \cdot 2 \cdot \cancel{9}^{1}}{\cancel{9}_{1} \cdot 3 \cdot \cancel{7}_{1}}$ Equal Fractions Property (common factors 7 and 9)

$= \frac{1 \cdot 2}{1 \cdot 3}$

$= \frac{2}{3}$

Using a Calculator to Multiply Fractions

Some calculators can multiply fractions directly.

Activity

MATERIALS calculator with fraction capabilities

Consider the multiplication $\frac{9}{13} \cdot \frac{7}{11} = \frac{63}{143}$.

Step 1 Experiment with your calculator to determine a key sequence for multiplying fractions. Some calculators may require you to use a [F↔D] key to change a decimal answer to a fraction.

Step 2 Write a successful key sequence for multiplying these two fractions on your calculator.

Now you can play *Top-It: Fraction Multiplication*. The directions for this game are on page G20 at the back of your book.

Questions

COVERING THE IDEAS

1. a. Draw an array to represent $\frac{7}{8}$ of $\frac{2}{3}$.
   b. Verify your answer by multiplying the fractions.

2. Write a fraction multiplication expression shown by the array below.

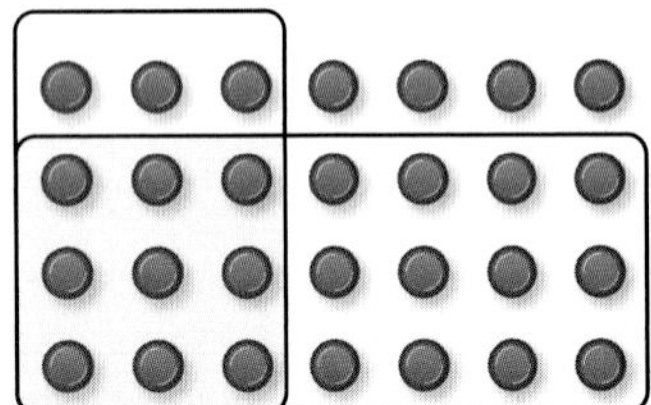

In 3–6, write each expression as a single fraction in lowest terms.

3. $\frac{2}{3} \cdot \frac{2}{5}$
4. $\frac{7}{9} \cdot 3$
5. $400 \cdot \frac{3}{20}$
6. $\frac{24}{25} \cdot \frac{5}{16}$

7. Patty planted petunias. $\frac{17}{20}$ of the petunia seeds sprouted. $\frac{4}{5}$ of these plants produced flowers. What fraction of the seeds resulted in flowers?

Petunias grow quickly to a height of 10 to 16 inches.

Source: www.gardenguides.com

In 8 and 9, use a calculator to find the product.

8. $\frac{9}{14} \cdot \frac{13}{23}$

9. $\frac{4}{17} \cdot \frac{19}{33}$

10. Solve the following to add a word to the quote for this chapter. Save this word for Question 24 in Lesson 6-10 on page 389.

$\frac{3}{5} \cdot \frac{2}{4} = \text{i}$ $\frac{3}{7} \cdot \frac{5}{9} = \text{l}$ $5 \cdot \frac{3}{8} = \text{e}$ $\frac{1}{3} \cdot \frac{4}{12} = \text{p}$

$\frac{11}{12} \cdot \frac{1}{4} = \text{m}$ $\frac{5}{6} \cdot \frac{7}{8} = \text{r}$ $\frac{3}{10} \cdot \frac{7}{10} = \text{s}$

?	?	?	?	?	?	?
$\frac{21}{100}$	$\frac{3}{10}$	$\frac{11}{48}$	$\frac{1}{9}$	$\frac{5}{21}$	$1\frac{7}{8}$	$\frac{35}{48}$

APPLYING THE MATHEMATICS

In 11–15, write each expression as a single fraction in lowest terms. Here *x* and *y* are not equal to zero.

11. $8 \cdot \frac{2}{5} \cdot \frac{3}{4}$

12. $5 \cdot \frac{1}{x}$

13. $\frac{x}{7} \cdot \frac{7}{x}$

14. $\frac{2x}{5} \cdot \frac{1}{y}$

15. $\frac{\left(\frac{1}{3} \cdot 900\right)}{\left(\frac{2}{3} \cdot 450\right)}$

16. Here is a product of seven fractions: $\frac{2}{5} \cdot \frac{3}{4} \cdot \frac{6}{7} \cdot \frac{9}{2} \cdot \frac{7}{8} \cdot \frac{5}{3} \cdot \frac{8}{9}$.
    a. Multiply these fractions by multiplying all the numerators and multiplying all the denominators.
    b. Describe an easier way to multiply the fractions.

17. Multiply $0.75 \cdot 0.5 \cdot 0.1\overline{6}$ by changing the decimals to fractions, multiplying the fractions, and then changing your answer back to a decimal.

18. Find two simple fractions whose product is $\frac{14}{15}$.

19. In 1958, the astronomer Harlow Shapley estimated that 1 star in a thousand might have planets, 1 in a thousand planets might be able to harbor life, and 1 in a thousand of those would actually have life. What fraction of stars would then have planets with life?

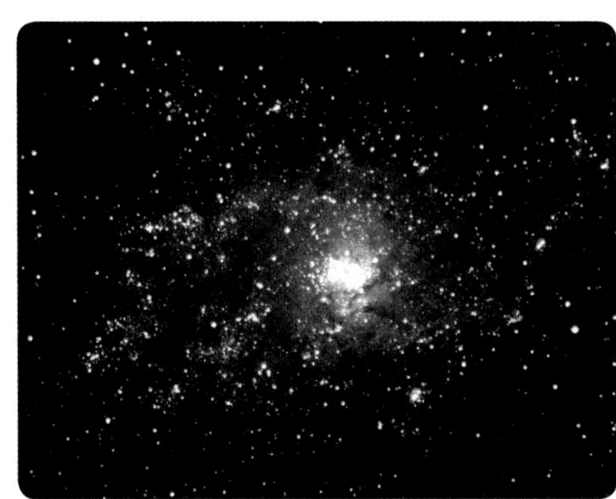
a star cluster

20. Carl ate $\frac{1}{3}$ of a hero sandwich at lunch. Later in the day he ate $\frac{1}{2}$ of what was left. How much of the original sandwich did he eat?

21. A box of battery-powered clocks fell out of a truck. $\frac{3}{5}$ of the clocks had cracked cases. $\frac{2}{7}$ of the remaining clocks would not start when a battery was put in. What fraction of clocks was undamaged and working?

REVIEW

22. **True or False** The product of two numbers is always greater than at least one of the numbers. **(Lesson 6-1)**

23. Without multiplying, tell whether the product is greater or less than 22. **(Lesson 6-1)**
    a. $\frac{5}{6} \cdot 22$ b. $22 \cdot 2.8$ c. $0.0679 \cdot 22$ d. $1.01 \cdot 22$

24. The bar graph below shows the number of goal-scoring players with different numbers of goals scored for the New York Red Bulls Major League Soccer team in a recent season. **(Lesson 5-4)**
    a. What is the mode number of goals?
    b. What is the mode frequency of goals?

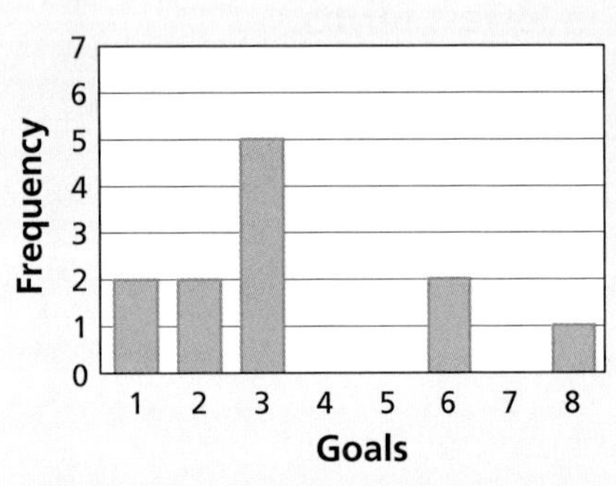

Marvell Wynne of New York dribbles past Andy Williams of Real Salt Lake in a match won by New York in 2006.

25. Give a set of 10 different numbers that have the same mean and median. **(Lesson 5-1)**

26. Add $5.023 + 3.98$ without using a calculator. **(Lesson 3-1)**

EXPLORATION

27. a. A *nanosecond* is one thousandth of one millionth of a second. What single fraction of a second is one nanosecond?
    b. A *microgram* is one thousandth of one thousandth of a gram. What single fraction of a gram is one microgram?

QY ANSWERS

1a. 480

1b. $\frac{8}{15}$

2a. $\frac{8}{35}$

2b.

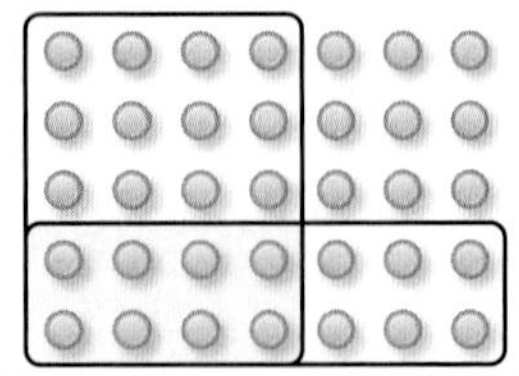

Lesson

6-3 Multiplication and Area

Vocabulary

dimensions

▸ **BIG IDEA** The product of any two positive numbers can be pictured as the area of a rectangle whose dimensions are those numbers.

How is Area Measured?

Mental Math

Find the median.

a. 6.8, 6.08, 6.18, 6.099, 6.28

b. 20%, $\frac{2}{5}$, 0.5, $\frac{1}{3}+\frac{1}{5}$, 1

c. 54, 34, 23, 33

The area of a figure is the amount of a surface it encloses or covers. Regardless of a figure's shape, it is customary to measure its area in square units. In the United States, areas are measured in customary square units (in^2, ft^2, yd^2, or mi^2). For example, the area of Lake Michigan is about 22,300 mi^2.

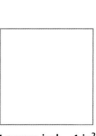

1 square inch = 1 in^2

4 square inches = 4 in^2

In most other parts of the world, area is measured in metric square units (mm^2, cm^2, m^2, km^2, and so on).

1 square millimeter = 1 mm^2

100 mm^2
or 1 square centimeter = 1 cm^2

The area of a pixel on a typical computer display is about 0.055 mm^2.

The area of many postage stamps is about 5 cm^2.

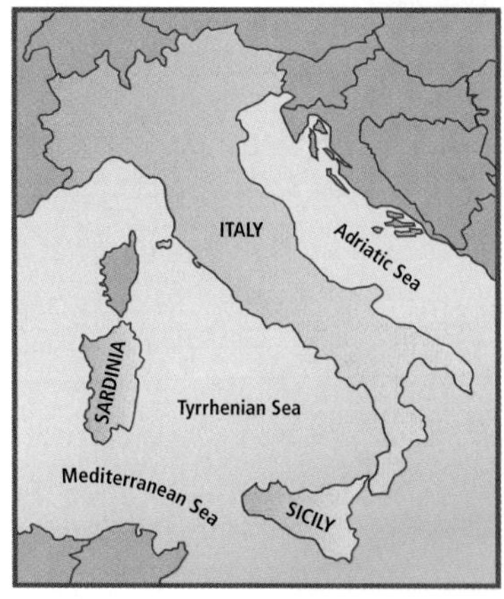

The area of Italy is about 301,230 km^2.

The area swept by Saturn's orbit around the sun is about 6,400,000 square gigameters (Gm^2).

Activity

MATERIALS regular dot paper

Step 1 Draw each of the figures below on a sheet of dot paper. Think of each little square on the dot paper as one square unit of area.

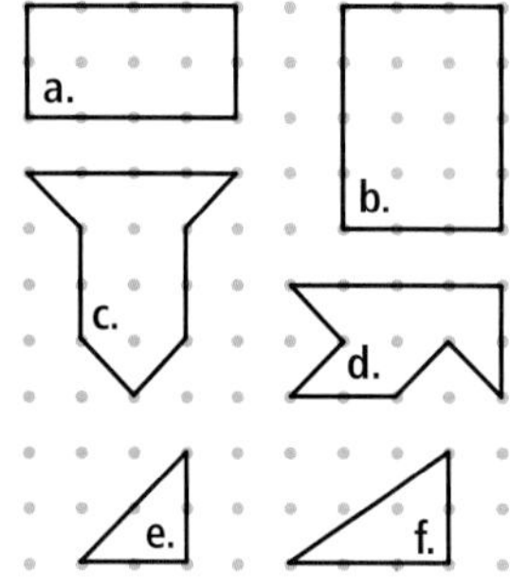

Step 2 Working with a partner, find the area of each figure.

Step 3 See if you and your partner can discover another way to find the area of any of the figures.

There are many ways to find the areas of figures.

1. *Count:* In the figure at the right, each square is 1 square centimeter. By counting squares, you can see that rectangle *ABCD* has an area of 6 cm^2.

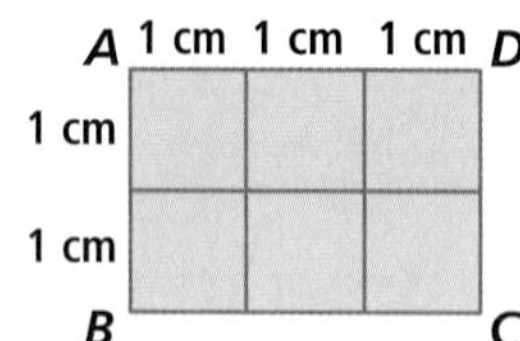

2. *Rearrange:* You can cut and rearrange the parts of a figure to find its area. When the figure at the left is rearranged into the rectangle at the right, you can see that its area is 6 cm^2.

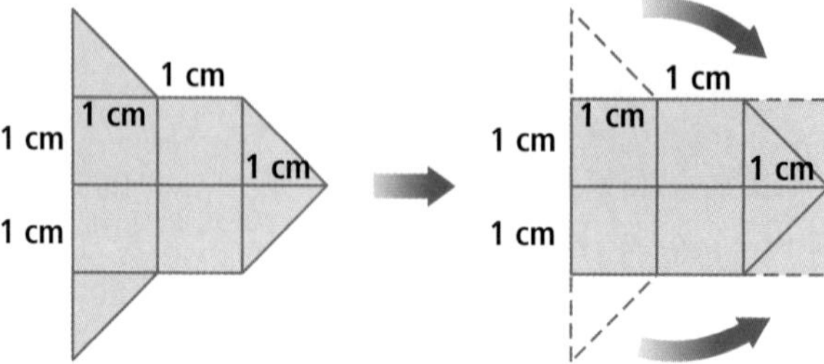

3. *Use a formula:* For a rectangle, multiply its dimensions. In the figure at the right, one dimension is 3 cm and the other is 2 cm, and 3 cm • 2 cm gives the area of 6 cm^2.

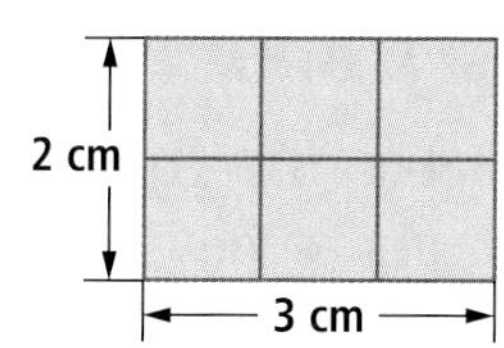

The rectangle at the right pictures the multiplication 2 • 3. Any multiplication of positive numbers can be pictured by the area of a rectangle. This is a basic use of multiplication.

The Area Model for Multiplication

The area of a rectangle with length ℓ units and width w units is $\ell \cdot w$ (or ℓw) square units.

As a formula, if A is the area of a rectangle with length ℓ and width w, then $A = \ell w$. The length and width are the **dimensions** of a rectangle. The area of a rectangle is the product of its dimensions.

QY

A volleyball court is a rectangle with dimensions 18 meters and 9 meters. What is its area?

GUIDED

Example 1

The rectangle below has ruler markings along each side so that you can see its length and its width in inches. What is its area?

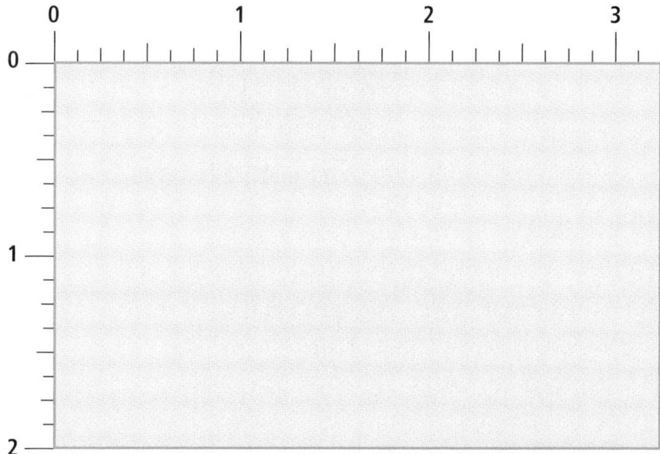

Solution First, find the length L and width W of the rectangle.

$L = 3 + \frac{?}{4} = \frac{?}{?}$ inches as an improper fraction.

$W =$ _?_ inches

Now using multiplication, find the area of the rectangle.

Area $= L \cdot W = \frac{?}{?} \cdot$ _?_ $=$ _?_ in^2 as a mixed number.

The Commutative Property of Multiplication

A rectangular room that is 9 feet by 15 feet has area $9 \cdot 15 = 135$ square feet. At the right are two possible diagrams. Comparing the rectangles, you could say the length and width have been switched. You could also think that one of the rectangles has been rotated 90°. Because the two rectangles have the same area, $9 \cdot 15 = 15 \cdot 9$.

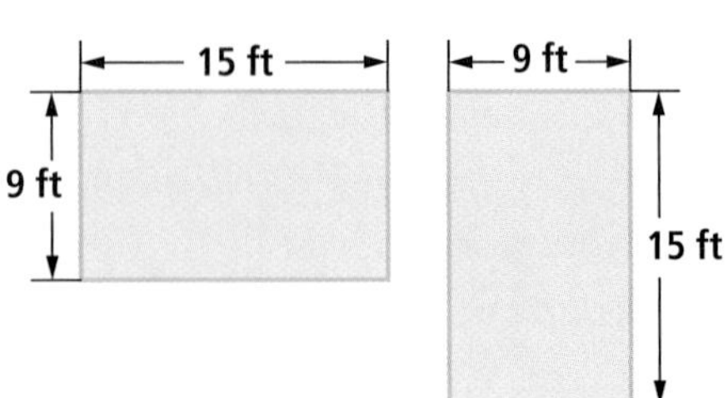

The area will be the same regardless of the order of the dimensions. In this way, the area of a rectangle pictures a basic property of multiplication.

The Commutative Property of Multiplication

For any numbers a and b, $ab = ba$.

The Commutative Property of Multiplication applies to all numbers, positive, negative, or zero.

Example 2

Ten ceiling panels were used in a drop ceiling in a hallway. Each panel is 3 feet by 2 feet. What is area of the ceiling?

Solution 1 You can picture the panels laid out in a row. Multiply the number of panels times the area of one panel.

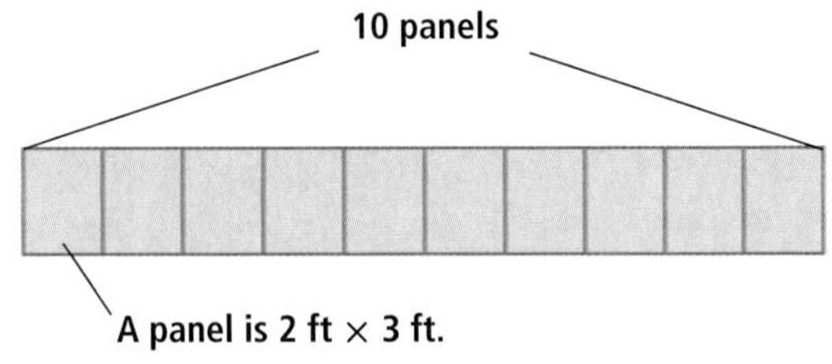

$$\begin{aligned}\text{Total area} &= 10 \cdot (2 \cdot 3)\\ &= 10 \cdot 6\\ &= 60 \text{ square feet}\end{aligned}$$

Solution 2 The panels laid in a row make a long rectangle. It has length $10 \cdot 2$ feet and width 3 feet.

$$\begin{aligned}\text{Area} &= 10 \cdot (2 \cdot 3)\\ &= (10 \cdot 2) \cdot 3\\ &= 20 \cdot 3\\ &= 60 \text{ square feet}\end{aligned}$$

The order of multiplications in the two solutions is different, but both give the same area: $10 \cdot (2 \cdot 3) = (10 \cdot 2) \cdot 3$. This is an example of the *Associative Property of Multiplication.*

The Associative Property of Multiplication

For any numbers a, b and c, $a(bc) = (ab)c$.

Questions

COVERING THE IDEAS

Matching **In 1–6, choose the unit in which the area would most likely be measured.**

1. the area of the floor of a hotel room
2. the area swept by Earth's orbit around the Sun
3. the surface area of Lake Lucerne on the border of Switzerland and Germany
4. the amount of wrapping paper needed to wrap a book
5. the area of the surface of a calculator key
6. the area of the city of Memphis, Tennessee

a. square feet

b. square centimeters

c. square miles

d. square kilometers

e. square millimeters

f. square gigameters

Lake Lucerne has an area of 44 square miles or 114 square kilometers.

Source: *Encyclopedia Britannica*

7. State the Area Model for Multiplication.
8. What is meant by the *dimensions* of a rectangle?
9. In the diagram below, the distance between neighboring dots is one unit. What is the area of the figure?

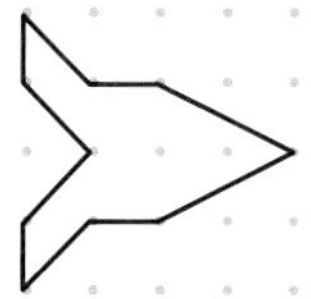

10. The base of a rectangular building is t feet by s feet. George says the area is ts square feet. Gina says the area is st square feet. Who is right? Explain why.
11. Rectangle $NICE$ represents the floor of a room. If each small square represents a 1 ft-by-1 ft tile, estimate the area of the room.

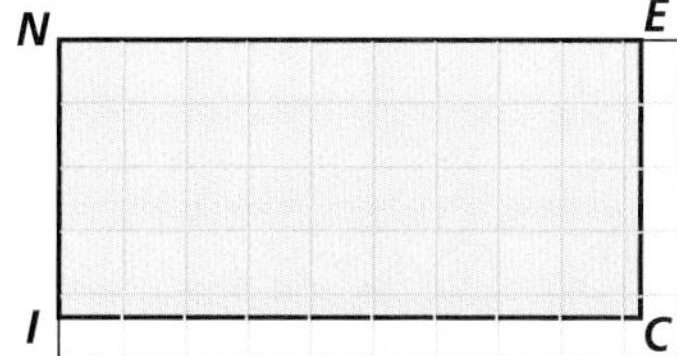

12. A rectangle has dimensions $\frac{3}{4}$ ft and $\frac{3}{8}$ ft. Find the area of this rectangle using appropriate units.

13. a. Show that these two multiplication problems give the same product: $\left(30 \cdot \frac{2}{3}\right) \cdot 11$ and $30 \cdot \left(\frac{2}{3} \cdot 11\right)$.

    b. What property is shown by Part a?

14. Tonisha's bedroom has a length of 12' and a width of 8'. Her cousin's bedroom has a length of 8' and a width of 12'.

    a. Tonisha claims that her bedroom is bigger than her cousin's. Is she correct? If she is correct, give the areas of the two rooms. If she is not correct, explain why she is wrong.

    b. What basic property of multiplication can help Tonisha compare the area of the two rooms?

15. A desktop is 5' long and $2\frac{1}{2}$' deep. Find its area.

APPLYING THE MATHEMATICS

16. A square has a side length of 18 centimeters. Is this enough information to find the area of the square? If so, find it. If not, explain what additional information you would need.

17. The rents for stores on New York's Fifth Avenue in Manhattan make it the world's most expensive shopping location. In 2005, the average annual rent on Fifth Avenue was about $1,300 per square foot. If a company wants space for a store with dimensions 50 feet by 200 feet, how much would the annual rent be?

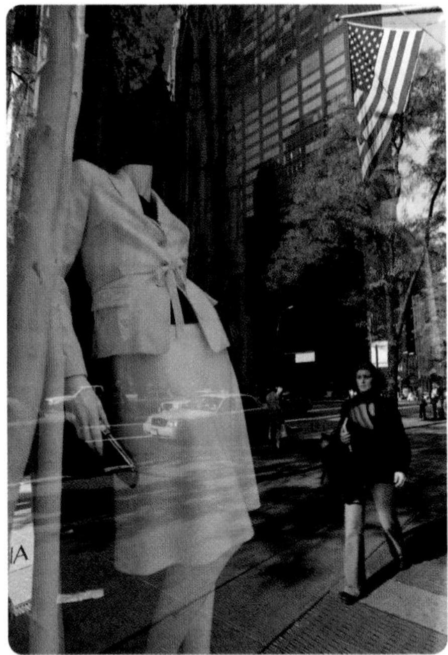

This is a storefront in Midtown Manhattan.

18. a. Measure the dimensions of rectangle *RECT* to the nearest eighth inch.

    b. What is the area of rectangle *RECT*?

    c. What is the perimeter of rectangle *RECT*?

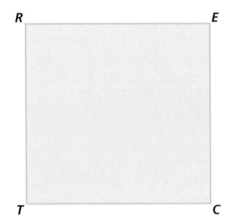

19. Suppose each little square at the right is 1 square inch. What is the area of the shaded region?

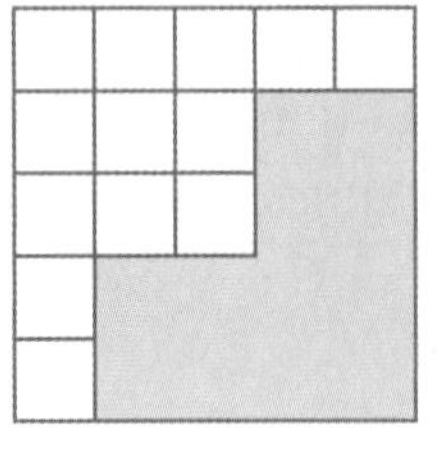

20. In the hexagon below, all of the angles are right angles. Find the area of the hexagon.

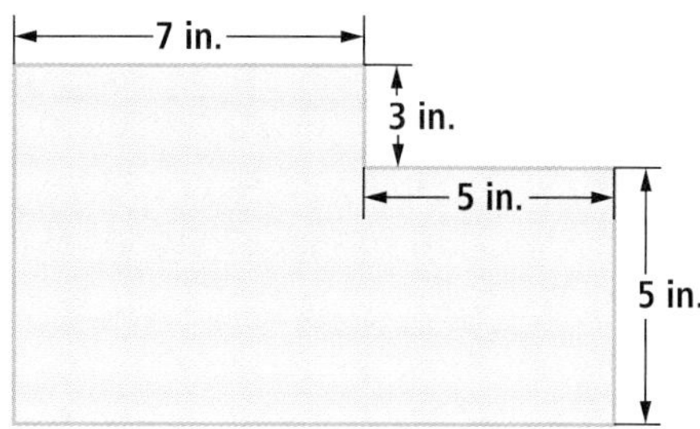

21. Eduardo and Pablo are planning to wallpaper the wall illustrated at the right. They will not cover the window or the door. One roll of paper will cover 40 square feet.
    a. Find the area that will be covered.
    b. How many rolls of paper will they need?

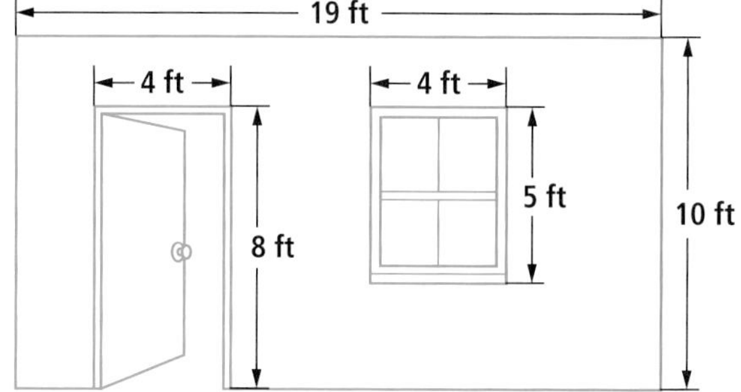

22. Find the area of the figure below.

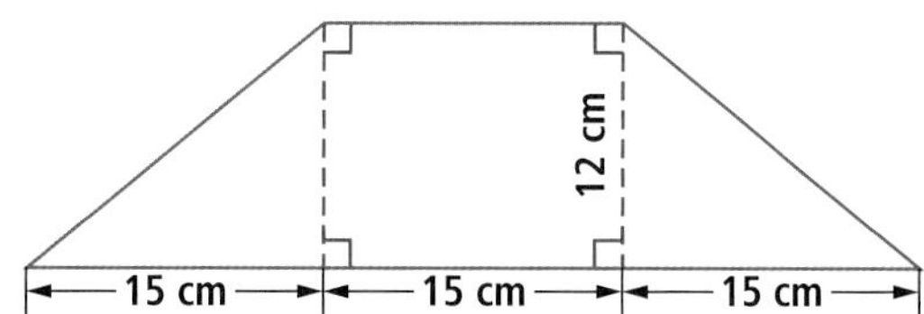

23. A rectangle has an area of 1 square unit. Its length is 4 units. What is its width?

REVIEW

24. **Fill in the Blanks**
    a. When $a = \frac{1}{2}$ and $t = \frac{2}{3}$, then $at =$ _?_.
    b. When $i = \frac{3}{4}$ and $s = \frac{2}{3}$, then $is =$ _?_.
    c. When $b = 4$ and $e = \frac{1}{6}$, then $be =$ _?_.
    d. In Parts a–c, the variable expressions are the two-letter words *at, is,* and *be*. The word whose value is $\frac{2}{3}$ is a code word. Save this word for the quote in Question 24 in Lesson 6-10 on page 389. **(Lesson 6-2)**

25. Of the girls in a class, $\frac{3}{4}$ play a musical instrument. If $\frac{2}{5}$ of the students in the class are girls, what fraction of the class are girls that do *not* play an instrument? **(Lesson 6-2)**

The clarinet is a musical instrument in the woodwind family.

26. Find two numbers whose product is less than either number. **(Lesson 6-1)**

27. Draw an array to find $\frac{1}{5}$ of $\frac{1}{4}$ of 40. **(Lesson 6-1)**

In 28 and 29, calculate. (Lessons 4-1, 3-1)

28. $7.6 - 2.95$

29. $10.7 + 13.26 + 4$

30. Draw an acute angle. Label your angle with its degree measure. **(Lesson 3-5)**

31. Measure the angle below to the nearest degree. **(Lesson 3-5)**

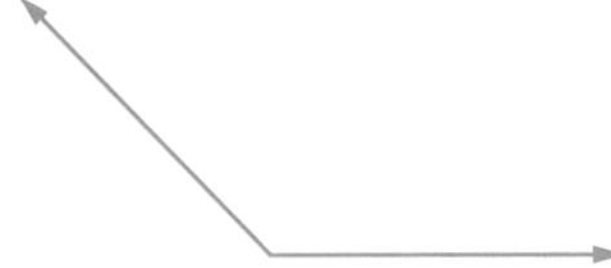

32. A school has 600 students. **(Lesson 2-3)**
    a. What is $\frac{1}{10}$ of the school's population?
    b. Use your answer to find $\frac{3}{10}$, $\frac{7}{10}$, and $\frac{4}{5}$ of the school's population.

33. Find the product: $3 \cdot 3 \cdot 3 \cdot 3 \cdot 3$. **(Previous Course)**

EXPLORATION

34. Each square below is drawn by connecting the midpoints of the sides of the next larger square. The area of the largest square is how many times the area of the smallest square?

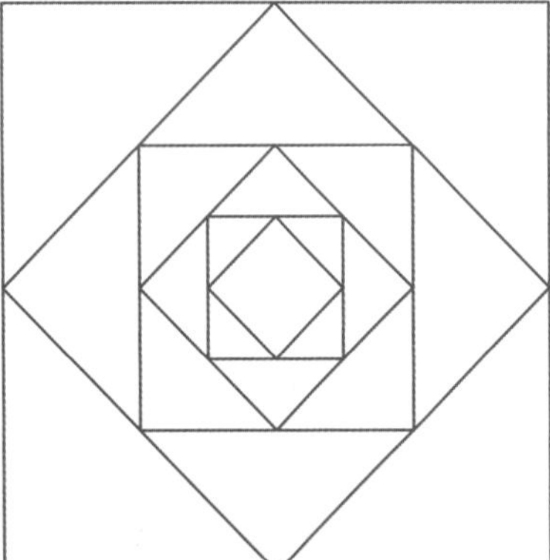

QY ANSWER

162 square meters

Lesson 6-4 Powers

Vocabulary

base
exponent
exponential form
squared
cubed
expanded notation

▶ **BIG IDEA** The product of n factors of x can be written as x^n.

In the year 1500, there were about 500 million people on Earth. According to United Nations estimates, the population doubled by 1804. There were then

$2 \cdot 500$ million, or 1,000 million, or 1 billion people on Earth.

The population doubled again by 1927. Then there were

$2 \cdot 2 \cdot 500$ million, or 2,000 million, or 2 billion people on Earth.

The population doubled again by 1974. There were then about

$2 \cdot 2 \cdot 2 \cdot 500$ million, or 4,000 million, or 4 billion people on Earth.

One estimate is that the world population will double again by 2025. The population will then be about

$2 \cdot 2 \cdot 2 \cdot 2 \cdot 500$ million, or 8,000 million, or 8 billion people.

Multiplication situations in which the same factor is repeated occur so often that there is a shorthand way of writing this. The shorthand uses a small raised number called an *exponent.*

$$x \cdot x = x^2$$
$$x \cdot x \cdot x = x^3$$
$$x \cdot x \cdot x \cdot x = x^4$$

Mental Math

Last Monday, my dog Rex had 5 fleas. Each day he had twice as many fleas as the previous day. How many fleas did Rex have

a. on Tuesday?

b. on Wednesday?

c. on Thursday?

d. today, which is Sunday?

Repeated Multiplication Model for Powers

When n is a whole number greater than 1, then the nth power of x,
$x^n = \underbrace{x \cdot x \cdot \ldots \cdot x}_{n \text{ factors}}.$

For example, $2 \cdot 2 \cdot 2 \cdot 2 \cdot 500 = 2^4 \cdot 500$ and $6^3 = 6 \cdot 6 \cdot 6 = 216$. The expression 6^3 is read "six to the third power." 6 is the **base** and 3 is the **exponent.** We say that 216 is the third power of 6.

Exponential Form

When a number is written as a power, it is said to be in **exponential form.**

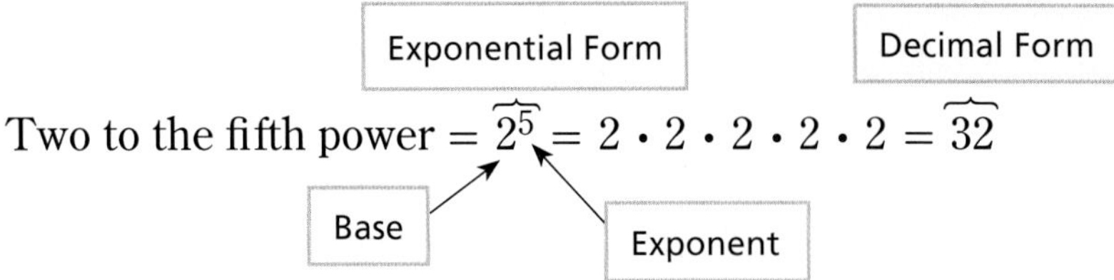

Two to the fifth power = $2^5 = 2 \cdot 2 \cdot 2 \cdot 2 \cdot 2 = 32$

Activity 1

Complete the table.

Exponential Form	Words	Repeated Multiplication	Decimal Form
10^2	= ten to the second power	$= 10 \cdot 10$	= 100
8^3	= eight to the ? power	= ?	= 512
?	= two to the sixth power	= ?	= ?
0^5	= ?	= ?	= ?
$\left(\frac{1}{3}\right)^4$	= ? to the ? power	$= \frac{1}{3} \cdot \frac{1}{3} \cdot \frac{1}{3} \cdot \frac{1}{3}$	= ?

Activity 2

Complete this table of powers. Write each power in base 10.

Base	2nd Power	3rd Power	4th Power	5th Power	6th Power
2	?	?	?	?	?
3	?	?	?	?	?
4	?	?	?	?	?
5	?	?	?	?	?
6	?	216	?	?	
7	?	?	?	?	
8	?	512			
9	?	?			
10	100	?	?	?	?

There are special ways to read second and third powers: 10^2 can also be read as "ten **squared,**" and 8^3 can be read as "eight **cubed.**"

QY1

a. What number equals nine squared?

b. What number equals twenty cubed?

Example 1

Write $3 \cdot 5 \cdot 5 \cdot x \cdot x \cdot x \cdot 3 \cdot x \cdot 5 \cdot x$ with exponents.

Solution Use the Commutative and Associative Properties of Multiplication to group the same factors.

$$3 \cdot 3 \cdot 5 \cdot 5 \cdot 5 \cdot x \cdot x \cdot x \cdot x \cdot x$$

There are 2 factors of 3, 3 factors of 5, and 5 factors of x.

$$3^2 \cdot 5^3 \cdot x^5$$

When a number does not have an exponent, it is understood that the exponent is one: $3 = 3^1$. This makes sense in terms of the Repeated Multiplication Model for Powers—the 3 appears as a factor once. For all numbers x, $x^1 = x$.

Powers of Ten

Place values in the decimal system are powers of 10.

Activity 3

Step 1 Copy and complete the table at the right.

Step 2 What is the relationship between the number of zeros in the decimal following the 1 and the exponent of the power?

Step 3 Fill in the powers of ten in the place-value chart below.

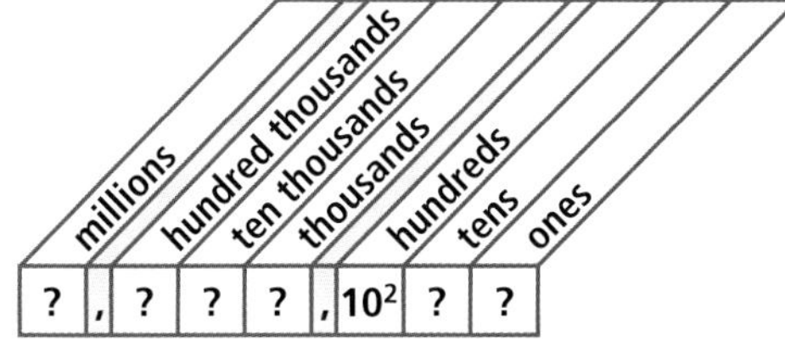

Word Name	Decimal	Power of 10
ten	10	10^1
hundred	?	?
thousand	?	?
ten-thousand	10,000	10^4
hundred-thousand	?	?
million	?	?
billion	1,000,000,000	?

Step 4 What can you say about place value and powers of ten?

Notice the pattern: $1{,}000 = 10^3$, $100 = 10^2$, and $10 = 10^1$. Dividing by 10 reduces the exponent by 1. So it makes sense that $1 = 10^0$. In general, $x^0 = 1$, as long as x is not zero.

STOP **See QY2 at the right.**

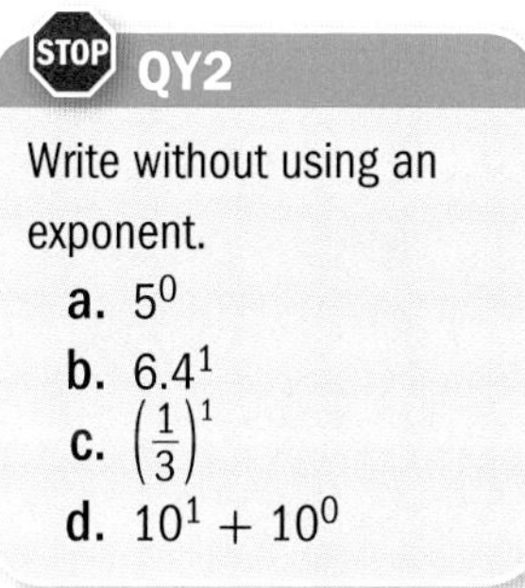

STOP **QY2**

Write without using an exponent.

a. 5^0

b. 6.4^1

c. $\left(\frac{1}{3}\right)^1$

d. $10^1 + 10^0$

Powers explain why we call our usual way of writing numbers *base 10.* **Expanded notation** shows the powers of ten that are added to give the value of a decimal.

Example 2

Write the decimal 4,508 in expanded notation.

Solution 4,508 is four thousand, five hundred eight, or

$4 \cdot 1{,}000 + 5 \cdot 100 + 0 \cdot 10 + 8 \cdot 1 =$

$4 \cdot 10^3 + 5 \cdot 10^2 + 0 \cdot 10^1 + 8 \cdot 10^0$

Typical keys for computing powers on a calculator are y^x or ^. Use $3^4 = 81$ to experiment to see how your calculator does this computation.

 See QY3 at the right.

STOP **QY3**

Evaluate 5^6 on your calculator.

Questions

COVERING THE IDEAS

1. a. Write 7^6 in words. b. Write 7^6 in base 10.
2. **Evaluate.**
   a. 3^5 b. 5^3
3. Write an expression with 100 as the exponent and 2.9 as the base.

In 4 and 5, write the power in exponential form and in decimal form.

4. twelve to the second power
5. eight to the fourth power
6. Write two-thirds cubed as a fraction.
7. Write the area of the square at the right in exponential form.

In 8–11, write without an exponent.

8. $1{,}000^0$ 9. $(0.1541)^1$
10. m^1 11. q^0
12. Write 72,946 in expanded notation.
13. Write 8,050,403 in expanded notation.
14. Write each of these estimates of the world population as a number times a power of 10.
    a. 1927 estimate: $2 \cdot 2 \cdot 500$ million
    b. 1974 estimate: $2 \cdot 2 \cdot 2 \cdot 500$ million
    c. 2025 estimate: $2 \cdot 2 \cdot 2 \cdot 2 \cdot 500$ million

15. Write ten million as a decimal and in exponential form.

16. Write $2^5 \cdot 3^2$ as a decimal.

APPLYING THE MATHEMATICS

17. a. Write $(2y)^3$ as a multiplication problem.

 b. Write $(2y)^3$ as a product of a power of 2 and a power of y.

18. Bernoulli School parents have organized a "calling tree" to notify families when the school is closed because of bad weather. The principal calls the president of the parent organization. The president calls four parents. Each of these calls four other parents, each of those calls four parents, so on.

Level on Calling Tree	Number of Parents Called at this Level
1 (President calls four parents)	4
2	$4 \cdot 4 = 16$
3	?
4	?
5	?

 a. Copy the table above and fill in the values.

 b. By level 2, twenty parents have been contacted. Why is this number different from the 16 shown on row 2?

 c. If there are 590 parents to be contacted, how many levels must the calling tree have so that all parents are called?

In 19–22, write <, >, or = to make a true sentence.

19. a. 7^3 __?__ 3^7 b. 2^3 __?__ 3^2

20. a. 3^{50} __?__ 3^{49} b. 0^{50} __?__ 0^{49}

21. a. 1^{10} __?__ 2^4 b. $\left(\frac{3}{4}\right)^{10}$ __?__ $\left(\frac{3}{4}\right)^{11}$

22. a. 2^1 __?__ 6^0 b. x^0 __?__ y^0

23. When a species of beetle called the ash borer reached the town of Ash Grove, trees started to die. A yearly tree survey showed only 90% of the ash trees survived each year.

The larvae of the Emerald Ash Borer feed on the inner bark of ash trees, disrupting the trees' ability to transport water and nutrients throughout the tree.

Source: www.emeraldashborer.info

Years After First Ash Borer	Percent of Original Trees Left
1	90%
2	$90\% \cdot 90\% = (90\%)^2 = ?$
3	$90\% \cdot 90\% \cdot 90\% = (90\%)^3 = ?$
4	?
5	?

 a. Copy and complete the table above.

 b. After how many years will fewer than 50% of the original trees be alive?

 c. After how many years will fewer than 25% of the original trees be alive?

24. Order from least to greatest to form a word: $Y = 10^2$, $N = 2^{10}$, $H = 3^5$, $T = 5^3$, $G = 3^{10}$, $I = 10^3$, $E = 0^{100}$, $R = 1^{101}$, $V = \left(\frac{1}{2}\right)^4$, $E = \left(\frac{1}{2}\right)^2$. Save this word for the quote in Question 24 in Lesson 6-10 on page 389.

25. What number of the small cubes is needed to make each of the large cubes? Write your answers using exponents.

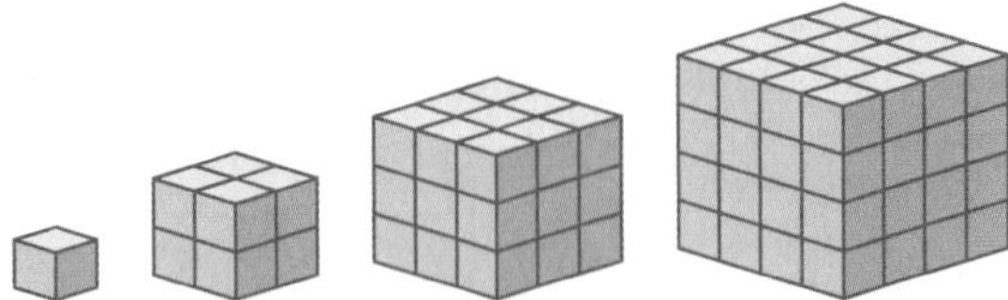

26. Use your calculator to help you write 1,679,616 in exponential form using 6 as the base.

REVIEW

27. a. What is the area of a soccer field that is 120 yards long and 75 yards wide?
    b. If you wanted to cover this field with 1-foot squares of sod, how many squares would you need? **(Lesson 6-3)**

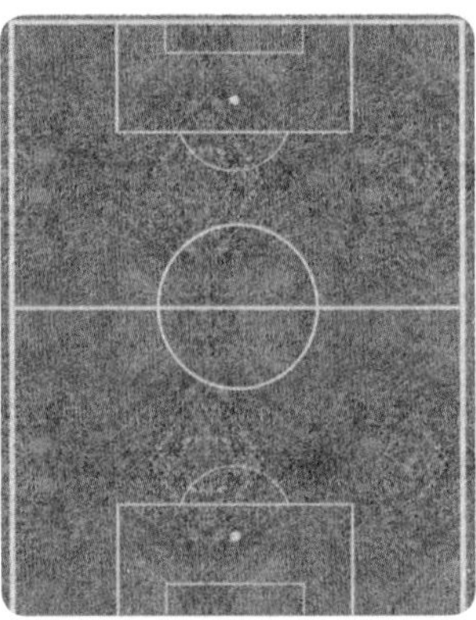

The 11 players on a soccer team are made up of forwards, halfbacks, fullbacks, and the goalie.

In 28 and 29, find the product. (Lesson 6-2)

28. $\frac{2}{3} \cdot \frac{5}{2}$

29. $\frac{1}{8} \cdot \frac{3}{7}$

30. What can you say about the measure of an angle if the angle is
    a. acute?
    b. obtuse?
    c. a right angle?
    d. formed by two perpendicular rays?
    e. an angle in an equilateral triangle? **(Lessons 3-5, 3-7)**

EXPLORATION

31. a. Write 64 in exponential form in three different ways.
    b. Find two other whole numbers that can be written in exponential form in three different ways.
    c. Find a whole number that can be written in exponential form in 10 different ways.

QY ANSWERS

1a. 81

1b. 8,000

2a. 1

2b. 6.4

2c. $\frac{1}{3}$

2d. 11

3. 15,625

Lesson 6-5 Multiplying Decimals

▸ **BIG IDEA** Decimals can be multiplied just as whole numbers are, with the decimal point in the appropriate location in the answer.

Marcos was multiplying decimals. Unfortunately, the decimal point on his calculator was sticking. When he keyed 15.3, the calculator showed 153. So the calculator only multiplied whole numbers.

Mental Math

Compute.

a. $\frac{1}{2} \cdot \frac{3}{4}$

b. $4 \cdot \frac{3}{4}$

c. $3 \cdot \frac{3}{4}$

d. $\frac{4}{3} \cdot \frac{3}{4}$

Activity 1

Step 1 Copy the table below. Use estimation to help Marcos put the decimal points in the correct place in the products.

Multiplication	Product
15.3 • 10.07	154071
6.82 • 1.8	12276
2.54 • 6.5	16510
0.869 • 3	2607
9.009 • 4.04	3639636
0.5 • 0.2	10

Step 2 Copy the table at the right. Use what you know about multiplication by powers of 10 and powers of $\frac{1}{10}$ to find the products. Do not use a calculator.

Multiplication	Product
1 • 0.6	?
\$59.95 • 1000	?
0.01 • 2.5	?
0.01 • 0.01	?
\$0.78 • 10	?

Step 3 Compare your answers to those of other students. See if you can all agree on the correct answers.

Using Estimation to Place the Decimal Point

In Step 1 of Activity 1, you used your estimation skills to place the decimal point. For example, in Part a, you can think "15 • 10 = 150, so the answer is close to 150." For many multiplication situations, this is a good strategy.

Example 1

Marcos wants to find the area of a rectangular garden with side lengths of 12.3 m and 5.76 m. He multiplies length times width as 12.3 • 5.76, but his calculator shows 70848. Use estimation to help him place the decimal point.

A gardener uses a compass to measure a garden.

Solution 1 Round 12.3 and 5.76 to the nearest whole numbers 12 and 6. Estimate by multiplying 12 • 6 = 72. The area should be close to 72. The area of the garden is 70.848 m^2.

Solution 2 Round 12.3 and 5.76 down to the nearest whole numbers, 12 and 5. A 12 m-by-5 m rectangle will be smaller than Marcos's rectangle. Rounding 12.3 and 5.76 up to the next whole number gives a 13 m-by-6 m rectangle. This will be larger than Marcos's rectangle. So the area of Marcos' garden is between 12 m × 5 m = 60 m^2 and 13 m × 6 m = 78 m^2. The area of the garden must be 70.848 m^2.

Solution 3 Draw the rectangle on grid paper where each square represents 1 square meter. Estimate area by counting squares. There are 5 • 12 or 60 full squares and 18 partial squares. 70.848 m^2 is correct.

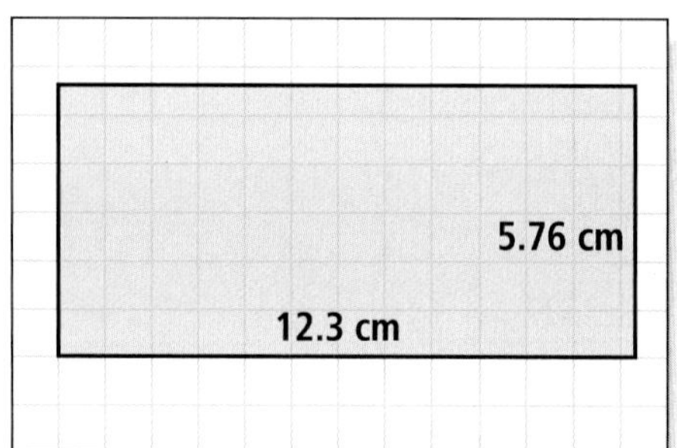

GUIDED

Example 2

Calculate 0.82 • 0.4 without a calculator.

Solution Multiply the factors as if they were whole numbers to get _?_. Because 0.82 is close to 1, 0.82 • 0.4 ≈ _?_ • _?_ = _?_. The product should be close to 0.4. The product is _?_.

See QY1 at the right.

QY1

Use the fact that 4 • 38 = 152 to find the following products:

a. 0.4 • 38

b. 4 • 0.38

c. 0.4 • 0.38

d. 0.04 • 0.0038

Using Fractions to Place the Decimal Point

Marcos multiplies 0.075 • 0.04 with his "point-less" calculator and gets 300. How can he tell that 0.075 • 0.04 is 0.003? The numbers do not round to whole numbers that will help him place the decimal point. One way is to change the decimals to fractions.

Example 3

Multiply 0.075 by 0.04 by changing the decimals to fractions.

Solution

$$0.075 \cdot 0.04 = \frac{75}{1{,}000} \cdot \frac{4}{100}$$

$$= \frac{300}{100{,}000} \quad \text{Multiplication of Fractions}$$

$$= \frac{3}{1{,}000} \quad \text{Divide numerator and denominator by 100.}$$

$$= 0.003$$

STOP QY2

Multiply 0.16 • 0.025 by changing the decimals to fractions.

Multiplying by Powers of Ten

In Chapter 2, you multiplied by 10, 100, 1000, and so on, by moving the decimal point a certain number of places to the right. Since these numbers equal 10^1, 10^2, 10^3, and so on, you can use the same idea to multiply by powers of 10.

Activity 2

Step 1 Copy and complete this table.

Step 2 Write a rule for multiplying by 10^n.

Multiplication	Factors Written as Decimals	Product
$3.5 \cdot 10^2$	$3.5 \cdot 100$	350
$10^4 \cdot 1.46$	?	14,600
$10^1 \cdot 0.8$	?	?
$72.53 \cdot 10^3$	?	?
$10^6 \cdot 0.53$	?	?
$8.25 \cdot 10^5$	?	?
$10^0 \cdot 0.475$	?	?

Now you can play *Decimal Dash.* The directions for this game are on page G21 at the back of your book.

Questions

COVERING THE IDEAS

In 1–3, use estimation to place the decimal point in the product.

1. $8 \cdot 2.6 = 208$
2. $6.82 \cdot 1.8 = 12276$
3. $14.2 \cdot 9.07 = 128794$

In 4–6, use estimation to place the decimal point in the product. You may have to insert some zeros.

4. $0.8 \cdot 0.73 = 584$
5. $0.59 \cdot 0.529 = 31211$
6. $0.0025 \cdot 0.04 = 1$

7. Find the area of the rectangle below.

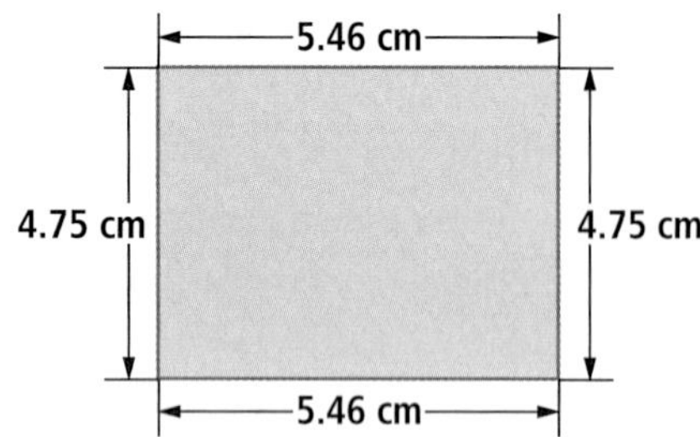

8. Central Park in New York City is rectangular. It is about 0.5 mile wide and 2.55 miles long. What is its area in square miles?

9. Use fractions to multiply 0.34 by 0.05.

In 10–12, multiply without using a calculator.

10. $10^3 \cdot 52.7$
11. $0.038 \cdot 10^5$
12. $10^2 \cdot 0.00274$

Central Park covers 843 acres. This is 6% of the area of Manhattan.

Source: centralpark.com

APPLYING THE MATHEMATICS

13. FICA tax is paid by most employed people in the United States as part of the social security system. Instructions on one tax form say, "To compute FICA tax, multiply your gross income by .0765." Mr. Torres has a gross income of $37,481. What is his FICA tax?

14. Taylor and Andrew disagree on where to put the decimal point in this product: $1.95 \cdot 6.6 = 1287$. Taylor says, "Because 1.95 is close to 2 and 6.6 is close to 7, the product should be close to $2 \cdot 7$, or 14. So the answer is 12.87." Andrew says, "Since there are two decimal places to the right of the decimal point in the first factor, and one decimal place in the second factor, there should be three decimal places in the product. The answer is 1.287."
    a. Who is right? Explain your reasoning.
    b. What mistake did the other person make?

In 15 and 16, one of the numbers in the equation is missing a decimal point. Place the decimal point in the number to make a true equation.

15. $5803 \cdot 6.114 = 354.79542$

16. $0.03 \cdot 455 = 0.001365$

17. I multiplied two numbers and the product was 2.25. Neither number was a whole number. What numbers might I have multiplied?

18. Rebecca's bedroom measures 12 feet by 15 feet. She is deciding between two types of carpet for her room. Shag carpet is \$18.45 per square yard. Berber carpet is \$13.89 per square yard. The cost to install either carpet is \$5.40 per square yard.
   a. How many square yards of carpet does she need?
   b. Calculate the total cost of purchasing and installing shag carpet in Rebecca's bedroom.
   c. Calculate the total cost of purchasing and installing Berber carpet in Rebecca's bedroom.
   d. What is the difference in the total costs?

Carpeting can be manufactured by three processes: weaving, tafting, and needlefelting.

Source: buycarpetinfo.com

19. I multiplied three numbers and got the product 12.06. Exactly one of the numbers was a whole number. What is a possible set of three numbers I might have multiplied?

20. Fill in the blank with the letter corresponding to the correct value for x to get the next code word. Save this word for Question 24 in Lesson 6-10 on page 389. Use T = 10, N = 100, and O = 1000.

?	?	?
$0.035x = 3.5$	$5.2x = 5200$	$0.004 = 0.0004x$

REVIEW

21. Write $2 \cdot 5 \cdot 4 \cdot 2 \cdot 4 \cdot 5 \cdot n \cdot 4 \cdot n$ using exponents. **(Lesson 6-4)**

22. In the figure below, all angles are right angles. Find its area. **(Lesson 6-3)**

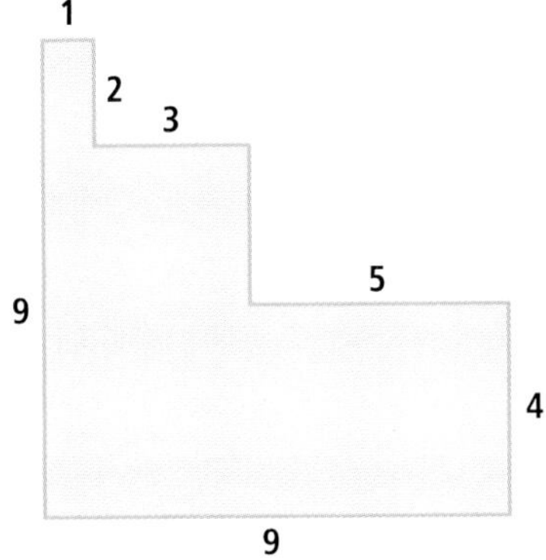

23. Copy and complete the table below. **(Lesson 6-2)**

n	$\frac{2}{3}n$
18	?
10	?
75	?
$\frac{3}{4}$	?
4	?

24. The table below shows percents of the world population on various continents. Make a circle graph of this information. **(Lesson 5-4)**

Continent	Percent of World Population
Asia	60.5%
Europe	11%
Africa	14%
North America	8%
South America	6%
Australia/Oceania	0.5%

Source: U.S. Census Bureau

In 25–28, compute the difference by rewriting each subtraction problem as an addition problem. (Lesson 4-3)

25. $7 - 5$

26. $-10 - 6$

27. $8.5 - -5$

28. $-1.3 - -1.3$

29. A rectangular window is $36\frac{1}{4}$" by $23\frac{7}{8}$". What is its perimeter? **(Lessons 3-9, 3-2)**

EXPLORATION

30. Find at least three ways to place decimal points in the factors below so that the product is correct.

$$1234 \cdot 5678 = 700.6652$$

QY ANSWERS

1a. 15.2

1b. 1.52

1c. 0.152

1d. 0.000152

2. 0.004

Lesson 6-6 Calculating Percents in Your Head

BIG IDEA If you know 10% of a number, which you can compute in your head, you can also calculate 1%, 5%, 20%, and many other percents of that number.

You often hear people say things like:

20% of the students in the school went to the basketball game.

You must score at least 90% on the test to get an A.

40% of the adults surveyed favor a longer school day.

30% of the farm is left unplanted each year.

In this lesson, you will practice calculating with these percents in your head.

10% of a Quantity

Recall that $10\% = \frac{1}{10} = 0.1$. So 10% of $40 = \frac{1}{10} \cdot 40$, or $0.1 \cdot 40 = 4$. In general, you can find 10% of a number in your head by moving the decimal point one place to the left.

QY1

Calculate the following in your head.

a. 10% of 80 b. 10% of 5 c. 10% of $35.50

Other Percents of a Quantity

You can use 10% of a number to find 5%, 20%, 30%, and other percents of that number.

Example 1

20% of 70 students went to the game. How many students is this?

Solution 1 Use 10% of 70 = 7.

20% of 70 will be twice as much. 20% of 70 = 14

14 of the 70 students went to the game.

(continued on next page)

Mental Math

All the small rectangles have the same area. What fraction of the large rectangle is shaded?

a.

b.

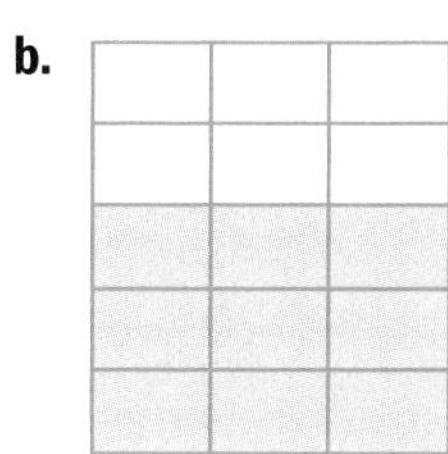

c.

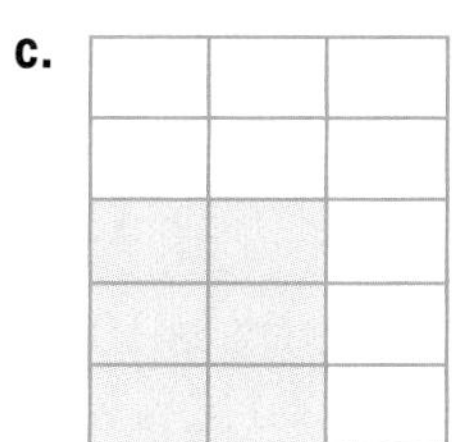

Solution 2 Use substitution.

$20\% = \frac{2}{10}$, or $\frac{1}{5}$. Substitute $\frac{1}{5}$ for 20% and multiply.

20% of 70 $= \frac{1}{5} \cdot 70 = 14$

14 of the 70 students went to the game.

Example 1 gives two methods for finding 20% of 70. You may have other shortcuts for calculating percents of numbers in your head.

QY2

Calculate the following in your head.

a. 30% of 70 b. 40% of 70 c. 50% of 70

Example 2

Use the fact that 10% of 78 = 7.8 to find the following without a calculator.

a. 5% of 78 **b. 20% of 78** **c. 30% of 78**

d. 90% of 78 **e. 110% of 78**

Solution

a. 5% is half of 10%. So 5% of 78 is half of 10% of 78.
So 5% of 78 $= \frac{1}{2} \cdot 10\% \cdot 78 = \frac{1}{2} \cdot 7.8 = 3.9$.

b. 20% is twice as much as 10%. So 20% of 78 is twice as much as 10% of 78.
So 20% of 78 $= 2 \cdot 10\% \cdot 78 = 2 \cdot 7.8 = 15.6$.

c. 30% is three times as much as 10%. So 30% of 78 is three times as much as 10% of 78.
So 30% of 78 $= 3 \cdot 7.8 = 23.4$.

d. 100% of 78 is 78. 90% is 10% less than 100%.
90% of 78 $= 78 - 7.8 = 70.2$.

e. 110% is 10% more than 100%.
So 110% of 78 is $78 + 7.8 = 85.8$.

You can use the fact that $50\% = \frac{1}{2}$, $25\% = \frac{1}{4}$, and $75\% = \frac{3}{4}$ to calculate percents of quantities by using fractions.

GUIDED

Example 3

Find 75% of 32.

Solution 1 75% equals the fraction ___?___.
So 75% of 32 = ___?___ • 32 = ___?___.

Solution 2 $25\% = \frac{1}{4}$. So 25% of 32 = ___?___ • 32 = ___?___.
75% of 32 = (3 • 25%) of 32 = 3 • (25% of 32) = 3 • ___?___ = ___?___

Since $1\% = \frac{1}{100}$, you can find 1% of a number by moving the decimal point two places to the left. For instance, 1% of 50.6 is 0.506.

GUIDED

Example 4

Find 21% of 800.

Solution 21% of 800 is the sum of 20% of 800 and 1% of 800.

10% of 800 is __?__, so 20% of 800 is __?__.

1% of 800 is __?__.

So 21% of 800 is __?__ + __?__ = __?__.

Questions

COVERING THE IDEAS

1. a. Calculate 30% of 1,500 by changing 30% to a fraction.
   b. A television that originally cost $1,500 is on sale for 30% off. What is the sale price?
2. Do each calculation in your head.
   a. 10% of 120
   b. 5% of 120
   c. 30% of 120
   d. 25% of 120
   e. 75% of 120
   f. 130% of 120
3. According to the U.S. Census Bureau, in July 2007, the U.S. population was estimated to be 301,139,947. Use the estimate 300 million for the U.S. population. In your head, determine 1% of this estimate. Use this result to estimate each percent of the population.
   a. 2%
   b. 3%
   c. 4%
   d. 5%

In 4–6, calculate in your head. (*Hint:* Your answer to Part a may help you find the answers to the other parts.)

4. a. 50% of 6,000 b. 25% of 6,000 c. 25% of 600
5. a. 10% of 8 b. 20% of 8 c. 40% of 8
6. a. 50% of 2 million b. 150% of 2 million c. 250% of 2 million

In 7–14, calculate in your head.

7. 5% of 20
8. 30% of 30
9. 90% of 60
10. 5% of 25
11. 20% of $242
12. 25% of 28
13. 50% of 9
14. 75% of 12

APPLYING THE MATHEMATICS

15. How is multiplying by $\frac{1}{10}$ related to multiplying by 10?
16. 40% of the 55 students in an orchestra are girls.
    a. How many girls are in the orchestra?
    b. How many boys are in the orchestra?

In 17 and 18, explain what each remark means.

17. "We are with you 100%!"
18. "Let's split it 50-50."

In 19–22, tell whether the statement is *true* or *false*.

19. You can substitute $\frac{3}{5}$ for 60% in *any* computation and the answer will not be affected.
20. 60% of 120 will give the same result as $\frac{3}{5}$ of 120.
21. $60\% + 30\% = \frac{3}{5} + \frac{3}{10}$
22. $30\% \cdot \$6{,}000 = \frac{3}{10} \cdot \$6{,}000$
23. The jacket you have wanted has gone on sale for 30% off the original price of $79.95. Use rounding to estimate in your head
    a. the amount you will save buying it on sale.
    b. the sale price of the jacket. (Do not consider sales tax.)
24. Chenoa wants to calculate 15% of 60. Explain how she could do this in her head.

In 25–27, use this information. Customers in restaurants often tip servers about 15% to 25% of the total bill. Round the amount of the bill to the nearest dollar and estimate the tip.

25. 15% of $30.43
26. 20% of $23.81
27. 25% of $15.05

One way a server can increase the amount of a tip is to personalize his/her appearance; wear a funny tie, hat, or flower to make him/her stand out.

REVIEW

28. Maricela wants to buy three grapefruits for \$1.29 each. How much must she pay in total? **(Lesson 6-5)**

29. **Matching** Find the letter for each ordered pair in the list below to form another word for the quote in Question 24 in Lesson 6-10 on page 389. **(Lesson 5-7)**

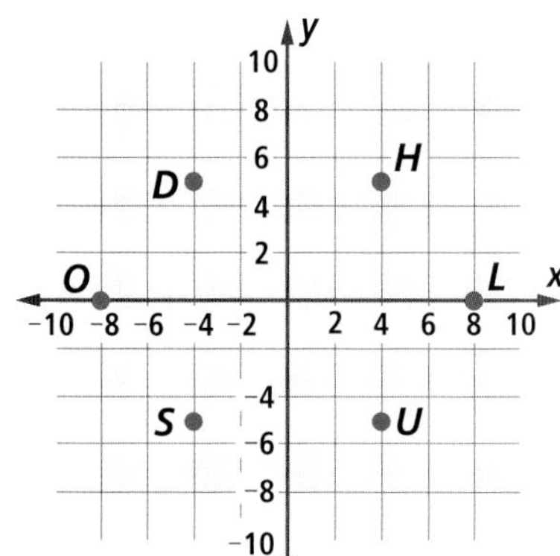

(-4, -5) = ___?___
(4, 5) = ___?___
(-8, 0) = ___?___
(4, -5) = ___?___
(8, 0) = ___?___
(-4, 5) = ___?___

30. Add 13.4 + 2.68 without using a calculator. **(Lesson 3-1)**

31. a. Write $\frac{36}{100}$ as a fraction in lowest terms.
    b. Write $\frac{36}{100}$ as a decimal.
    c. Write $\frac{36}{100}$ as a percent. **(Lessons 2-7, 1-6)**

32. The peak of the volcano Popocatépetl near Mexico City is about 5,426 meters above sea level. **(Lessons 2-5, 1-7)**
    a. Should you call its height 5,426 meters, or -5,426 meters?
    b. Round its height to the nearest 10 meters.
    c. Round its height to the nearest 100 meters.
    d. Round its height to the nearest 1,000 meters.

Popocatépetl near Mexico City, one of the highest volcanoes in the world, erupted in 2004.

Source: *The World Almanac*

33. Multiply 9720.6104 by each number. **(Lesson 2-3)**
   a. 1
   b. 0.1
   c. 0.01
   d. 0.001

34. Reduce $\frac{560}{720}$ to lowest terms. Is this fraction proper, improper, or neither? **(Lesson 1-5)**

In 35 and 36, use the ruler below (marked in inches) and the line segment above it.

35. Determine the length of the line segment. **(Lesson 1-3)**

36. Trace the segment. Use lined paper to divide the segment into 6 equal parts. **(Lesson 1-2)**

EXPLORATION

37. a. Find a use of percent in a newspaper or magazine.
   b. Make up a question about the information you have found.
   c. Answer the question you have made up.

QY ANSWERS

1a. 8

1b. 0.5

1c. $3.55

2a. 21

2b. 28

2c. 35

Lesson 6-7 Using the Percent of a Quantity

▶ **BIG IDEA** Multiplication with percents has numerous uses, including the calculation of discounts, taxes, parts of wholes, and percents of increase and decrease.

Both estimates and exact answers are important in percent situations. Suppose a store advertises a \$29.50 swimming suit "marked down 20%." Think "20% of \$29.50 is close to 20% of \$30, which is about \$6. The suit will cost about \$6 less than the price on the tag." If you buy the suit, then the salesperson will compute the exact cost (\$23.60).

Mental Math

Compute.

a. 50% of 50?

b. 20% of 20?

c. 10% of 10?

d. 10% of 20?

Example 1

Suppose 48% of the 650 students at Park Junior High are boys. How many students is this?

Solution First estimate the answer. 48% is a little less than 50% or $\frac{1}{2}$. One-half of 650 is 325, so 48% of 650 students should be a little less than 325. Now find the exact answer by multiplying.

$48\% \text{ of } 650 = 48\% \cdot 650 = 0.48 \cdot 650 = 312$

312 of the 650 students at Park Junior High are boys.

Check The exact answer agrees with the estimate.

Percents are often used when items are put on sale.

Example 2

A sofa normally sells for \$789.95. It is on sale at 20% off.

a. How much will a person save by buying the sofa during the sale?

b. What will the sale price be?

Solution First estimate. The price of the sofa is about \$800. To compute 20% of 800, first take 10% of 800, which is \$80. Doubling this gives \$160 for the estimate for Part a. For Part b, estimate the sale price by computing $\$800 - \$160 = \$640$. Now find the exact values.

(continued on next page)

a. A person will save 20% of $789.95.

20% of $\$789.95 = .2 \cdot \$789.95 = \$157.99$

b. Subtraction gives the sale price.

$789.95	original price
−157.99	amount saved
$631.96	sale price

Check The values in both parts are close to the estimated values, so they seem reasonable.

Alaska, Delaware, Montana, New Hampshire, and Oregon are the only states with no sales tax.

Source: Federation of Tax Administrators

Percents and Taxes

Most states and some cities in the United States add sales tax to an amount you pay for goods. (Sometimes there are exceptions for some items, such as food.) The sales tax rate ranges from 0% (where no sales tax is charged) in five states to 7% or more in a few states.

Example 3

Suppose you are in Kansas, where the sales tax rate is 5.3%. You buy some clothes that cost $119.43. How much tax will you pay?

Solution The amount of the tax is 5.3% of $119.43.

5.3% of $\$119.43 = 5.3\% \cdot 119.43$

$= 0.053 \cdot 119.43$ Change 5.3% to a decimal.

$= 6.32979$

Now round the amount of tax up to the nearest penny. You will likely have to pay $6.33 in tax. (To find the total price, add $119.43 + $6.33 for a total price of $125.76.)

Percents of a Whole

In Chapter 2, you made circle graphs using percents of a whole. This is a common use of percents. In this use, the percents add to 100% (the whole).

GUIDED

Example 4

The United States can be split into four regions as shown in the table at right. If the total U.S population in July 2007 was about 301,000,000, round (to the nearest million) how many people lived in each region.

Region	Percent of U.S. Population in 2005
Northeast	19%
Midwest	22%
South	36%
West	23%

Source: U.S. Census Bureau

Solution

Northeast region

19% • 301,000,000 = ___?___ (exactly)

= ___?___ (to the nearest million)

Midwest region

___?___ • 301,000,000 = ___?___ (exactly)

= ___?___ (to the nearest million)

Work out exact populations for the South and West regions.

South region: ___?___ West region: ___?___

Round to the nearest million.

South region: ___?___ West region: ___?___

Check The four exact answers should add to ___?___, which they do.

Questions

COVERING THE IDEAS

In 1–3, calculate.

1. 36% of 50
2. 24% of 90
3. 148% of 24

In 4 and 5, find

a. the amount the item is marked down.

b. the final cost of the sale item, not including sales tax.

4. a $1,148 item marked down 20%
5. a $295.95 item marked down 35%

In 6 and 7, find

a. the amount of sales tax.

b. the total cost of the item with tax.

6. a $1.23 item with 6% sales tax
7. a $51.99 item with 4.75% sales tax

8. In the 1860 U.S. presidential election, there were four major candidates. A total of 4,676,853 people voted for these four candidates.

   39.9% voted for Abraham Lincoln

   29.4% voted for Stephen Douglas

   18.1% voted for John Breckinridge

   a. What percent of people voted for John Bell, the 4th major candidate?

   b. To the nearest ten thousand, how many people voted for each candidate?

The front of the Lincoln Memorial extends from the reflecting pool up 98 stairs to a statue of the seated 16th President of the United States.

Source: National Park Service

9. a. Refer to Example 3. Compute the sales tax in Kansas on a \$29.95 pair of shorts.
   b. What is the total cost of the shorts?

APPLYING THE MATHEMATICS

10. According to Nielsen Media Research, in September 2005, 110.2 million U.S. households owned at least one TV set, and 84% of these households had a DVD player. About how many households in the U.S. owned a DVD player at this time?

11. Suppose a sound system normally sells for \$197.75 but is on sale for 20% off. Answer Parts a–e without using a calculator.
    a. To estimate the sale price of the sound system, what value can you use in place of \$197.75?
    b. Estimate the amount of money you would save.
    c. Estimate the sale price.
    d. If there is a 5% tax, estimate the amount of tax.
    e. Estimate the total price of the sound system with sales tax.
    f. Find exact answers for Parts b–e.

12. In July, 2007, the U.S. population was 301,139,947. Use the estimate 300 million for the U.S. population. The U.S. population is now increasing at the rate of about 0.92% a year. How many people is this per year?

13. The population of San Jose, California, was about 95,000 in 1950 and increased about 840% from 1950 to 2000.
    a. How many additional people is this?
    b. What was the approximate population of San Jose in 2000?

San Jose Museum of Art

14. An interest penalty is charged on credit card purchases if the bill is overdue. Suppose a person has \$1,000 in overdue bills. If the penalty is 1.5% per month, how much interest will the person have to pay the first month?

15. In Store A, you see a stereo on sale at 25% off its list price. In Store B, the same stereo at the same price is on sale at 20% off. Which store has the lower sale price for this stereo?

16. a. A large-screen TV normally sells for \$1,395. What would be the price during a 20% off sale?
 b. Find 80% of \$1,395.00.
 c. How are the answers to Parts a and b related?

REVIEW

17. One number in each equation is missing a decimal point. Place the decimal point in that number. (Lesson 6-5)
 a. $5.311 \cdot 847.0 = 44984170$
 b. $23.59 \cdot 5612 = 1.3238708$

18. In the expression x^n identify (Lesson 6-4)
 a. the base.
 b. the exponent.
 c. the power.

19. List the letters for the sectors of the circle below in order from smallest sector to largest sector to form the next word for the quote in Question 24 in Lesson 6-10 on page 389. (Lesson 5-5)

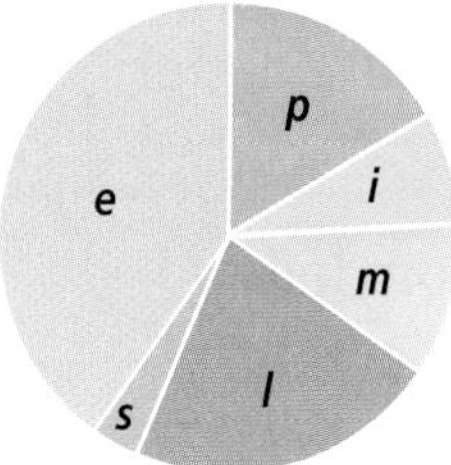

In 20–22, calculate. (Lessons 4-1, 3-1)

20. \$20.00 – \$8.43
21. 4.65 – 2.83 – 0.5
22. 72.803 – .041 + 2.769

23. The Sniff City Bloodhounds win 53% of their games. Do they win or lose more often? Justify your answer. (Lesson 2-10)

EXPLORATION

24. Use the Internet or another source to locate the current state sales tax rates. One website is www.taxadmin.org. Using the rate for your state or a neighboring state, calculate the tax and the total price for an automobile purchase of \$17,400.

Lesson 6-8 Order of Operations

Vocabulary

numerical expression

value

evaluating the expression

BIG IDEA When an expression has more than one operation, there is a specified order in which the operations should be performed so that everyone will interpret the expression in the same way.

Mental Math

Compute.

a. 5 minus the product of 3 and 4

b. The product of 5 minus 3 and 4

c. 8 multiplied by 10, divided by 2

d. 8 multiplied by 2, divided by 10

Ashley and Odell were asked to calculate $20 - 8 - 7$.
Ashley did the left subtraction first: $20 - 8 - 7 = 12 - 7 = 5$.
Odell did the right (easier) subtraction first: $20 - 8 - 7 = 20 - 1 = 19$.

As you can see, they got different answers. This lesson is about the order in which calculations should be performed.

The Importance of Order of Operations

Odell's and Ashley's calculation involves only subtraction. Things get more complicated when there is more than one operation.

Mr. and Mrs. Johnson were buying tile for the room diagrammed at the right. Mr. Johnson found the area of the square $(3 \cdot 3)$ plus the area of the rectangle $(7 \cdot 10.5)$. He wrote $3 \cdot 3 + 7 \cdot 10.5$.

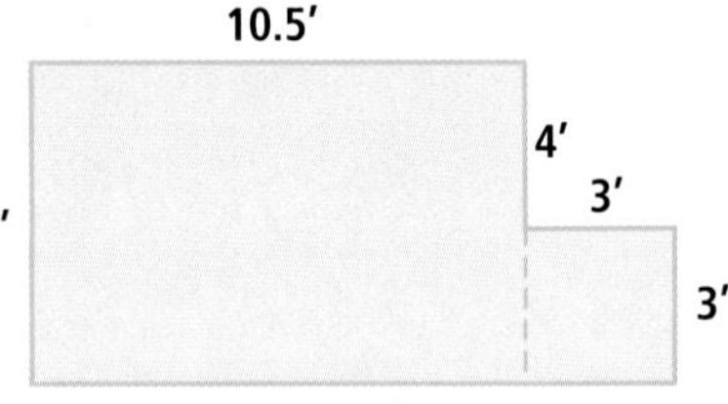

Mrs. Johnson then did the calculation. She worked from left to right.

$$\begin{aligned} 3 \cdot 3 + 7 \cdot 10.5 &= 9 + 7 \cdot 10.5 \\ &= 16 \cdot 10.5 \\ &= 168 \text{ square feet} \end{aligned}$$

Mr. Johnson was puzzled at the result his wife got. He said, "The entire room is smaller than a 7-by-14 foot rectangle, which has an area of 98 square feet. You've made a mistake in your calculations." While Mrs. Johnson's calculations are correct, she did the operations in a different order than Mr. Johnson intended. He intended to do the two multiplications first, computing the area of each smaller rectangle.

$$\begin{aligned} 3 \cdot 3 + 7 \cdot 10.5 &= 9 + 73.5 \\ &= 82.5 \text{ square feet} \end{aligned}$$

Mr. Johnson said to his wife, "If we had used your calculation, we would have bought twice as much tile as we needed."

Mr. Johnson had written down a *numerical expression*. A **numerical expression** is made up of numbers and operation symbols. For example, $20 - 8 - 7$ and $3 \cdot 3 + 7 \cdot 10.5$ are numerical expressions. The **value** of a numerical expression is the answer found by completing the operations. Finding the value is called **evaluating the expression.** Rules have been developed to standardize the order in which operations are performed.

Rules for Order of Operations

1. Work in parentheses, from inside to outside.
2. Evaluate all powers in order from left to right.
3. Multiply or divide in order from left to right.
4. Add or subtract in order from left to right.

If Mrs. Johnson had used the rules for order of operations, she would have gotten the same answer as Mr. Johnson.

QY1

Using the correct order of operations, who was right, Ashley or Odell?

Example 1

Evaluate $2 \cdot 3 - 9 \cdot 4$.

Solution There are no powers, so do the two multiplications before the subtraction. To avoid mistakes, write each step on a new line.

$$2 \cdot 3 - 9 \cdot 4 = 6 - 36$$
$$= -30$$

GUIDED

Example 2

Evaluate $15 \div 3 \cdot 6 - 4^2$.

Solution

$15 \div 3 \cdot 6 - 4^2$

$= 15 \div 3 \cdot 6 -$ _?_   Calculate the power first.

$=$ _?_ $\cdot$ _?_ $-$ _?_   Next multiply or divide from left to right. Here divide first, then multiply.

$=$ _?_ $-$ _?_   Finally, subtract.

$= 14$

Using Parentheses

Suppose in Example 2, you really wanted to do the subtraction $6 - 4$ first. Then you need to write parentheses around the subtraction because expressions in parentheses are evaluated first. By writing $15 \div 3 \cdot (6 - 4)^2$, you change the order of operations.

STOP See QY2 at the right.

The fraction bar in a fraction acts as parentheses. So, if you see an operation in the numerator or denominator of a fraction, it must be done first. For example, to evaluate $\frac{18 + 12}{18 - 3}$, think $\frac{(18 + 12)}{(18 - 3)}$. The parentheses indicate that you must add in the numerator and subtract in the denominator before you can do the division indicated by the fraction. So $\frac{18 + 12}{18 - 3} = \frac{30}{15} = 2$. However, the fraction slash does *not* indicate parentheses. So $18 + 12/18 - 3 = 18 + \frac{2}{3} - 3 = 15\frac{2}{3}$.

STOP QY2

Evaluate $15 \div 3 \cdot (6 - 4)^2$.

Order of Operations on a Calculator

Scientific and graphing calculators follow the order of operations. If you want to do an addition before a multiplication, you will need to use parentheses keys.

STOP See QY3 at the right.

STOP QY3

What does your calculator show for each of the key sequences 3 [+] 5 [×] 8 and [(] 3 [+] 5 [)] [×] 8?

Activity

MATERIALS calculator

Evaluate each numerical expression. Use Examples 1 and 2 as a guide in writing out your steps. Compare your answers with a partner's. Check your work with a calculator.

1. $10 - 8 + 3 - 12$
2. $8 + 9 \cdot (2 + 3)$
3. $-200 + 200 \cdot (2 \cdot 3)^2$
4. $2 \cdot 5^4$
5. $10 + 20 \div (2 + 3 \cdot 6)$
6. $4 - \frac{3 + 5}{1 + 2} \cdot 6$

GAME Now you can play *Scrambling: Order of Operations*. The directions for this game are on page G22 at the back of your book.

Questions

COVERING THE IDEAS

1. What can be in a numerical expression?
2. Getting a single value for an expression is called __?__.

In 3–6, suppose both operations appear in the same numerical expression. In evaluating the expression, which should you do first?

3. powering and division
4. multiplication and subtraction
5. addition and multiplication
6. subtraction and addition

7. Suppose you want to add before multiplying in the expression $6 \cdot 3 + 4$. How should you indicate this?

In 8–13, evaluate each expression. Do not use a calculator.

8. $80 + 3 \cdot 10$
9. $15 - 1.4 \cdot 10$
10. $50 \div 10 \div 5$
11. $2^2 + 3^2$
12. $(2 + 3)^2$
13. $20 - 4 \cdot 3^2 + 5 \cdot 2^3$

APPLYING THE MATHEMATICS

14. Write the key sequence for entering $\frac{19}{4 - 3}$ on your calculator. (*Hint:* You will need to use parentheses.)

15. Write a numerical expression for the words and evaluate the expression. You may need to use parentheses.
    a. The sum of 3 and 4 is multiplied by 10.
    b. the sum of 3 and the product of 4 and 10

In 16 and 17, evaluate each expression. Write a separate line for each level of computation.

16. $3\frac{1}{2} + 2\frac{3}{4} \cdot 1\frac{1}{3}$
17. $2 \cdot (3.9 + 4.6)^2$

In 18–21, evaluate each expression when $x = 5$, $y = 10$, and $z = 2$.

18. a. $x - 4y - 5z$ b. $(x - 4) \cdot (y - 5z)$
19. a. $z - xy$ b. $(z - x) \cdot y$
20. a. $(2y)z$ b. $2yx$
21. a. $z + \frac{y}{z}$ b. $\frac{z + y}{z}$

In 22–24, a false equation is given.

a. Evaluate the left side of the equation to show it does not equal the right side.

b. Insert parentheses on the left to make the equation true.

22. $25 - 10 - 5 = 20$
23. $16 - 8 - 4 - 2 = 10$
24. $3 \cdot 5 - 2 \cdot 4 = 36$

25. An item costs $39.95. Add 7% to the price for tax. Then add $5 for shipping and handling.
   a. Write an expression using these numbers that indicates the total cost.
   b. Evaluate your expression.

26. **Fill in the Blank** Fill in the blanks with a letter from the box below to form a word. Save this word for the quote in Question 24 in Lesson 6-10 on page 389.

   $2 \cdot (2 - 2\frac{3}{4}) = \underline{\ ?\ }$ $\qquad$ $(4 - 2 - 1 - .5)^2 = \underline{\ ?\ }$

$Q = 3\frac{2}{3}$	$T = 5\frac{1}{3}$
$A = -1\frac{1}{2}$	$S = \frac{1}{4}$
$I = -\frac{3}{4}$	$N = -2\frac{5}{6}$

REVIEW

In 27 and 28, a group goes to dinner. The total bill comes to $304.17. (Lessons 6-7, 6-6)

27. If they tip 18% to the server, what amount do they leave as a tip?
28. If they give an extra 10% tip to the hostess, how much money does the hostess receive?

In 29–31, write in base-10 notation. (Lesson 6-4)

29. $5 \cdot 10^3 + 7 \cdot 10^2 + 5 \cdot 10^1 + 8 \cdot 10^0$
30. $9 \cdot 10^5 + 4 \cdot 10^2$
31. $6 \cdot 10^8 + 5 \cdot 10^6 + 3 \cdot 10^7 + 2 \cdot 10^5 + 4 \cdot 10^4$

EXPLORATION

32. *Nested parentheses* are parentheses inside parentheses. To evaluate an expression with nested parentheses, start inside the innermost parentheses and work to the outside. Evaluate each expression.
   a. $(5000 - (500 - (50 - 5)))$
   b. $((3^2)^2)^2$
   c. $425 - (120 + 0.6(200 - 50))$

QY ANSWERS

1. Ashley
2. 20
3. Answers vary. Sample: 43; 64

Lesson

6-9 Multiplying Mixed Numbers

BIG IDEA To multiply two mixed numbers you can use the Distributive Property.

Mental Math

Calculate the area of each region.

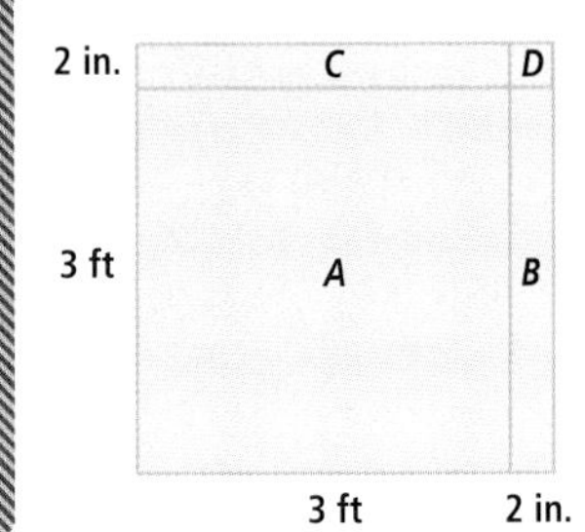

In this lesson, you will see a way to multiply two mixed numbers. The idea is based on a fundamental property connecting multiplication and addition.

The Distributive Property

Suppose you buy 6 cans of frozen orange juice for \$1.99 each and then another 3 cans of frozen lemonade for \$1.99 each. You have two ways to calculate the total cost.

Add the number of cans and multiply by the price.	Add the total cost of the orange juice to the total cost of the lemonade.
$(6 + 3) \cdot \$1.99$	$6 \cdot \$1.99 + 3 \cdot \$1.99$

These two numerical expressions have the same value. Follow the order of operations.

$(6 + 3) \cdot \$1.99$	$6 \cdot \$1.99 + 3 \cdot \$1.99$
$= 9 \cdot \$1.99$	$= \$11.94 + \$5.97$
$= \$17.91$	$= \$17.91$

The example above illustrates the *Distributive Property of Multiplication over Addition.*

The Distributive Property of Multiplication over Addition

For any numbers a, b, and c, $a \cdot (b + c) = a \cdot b + a \cdot c$. That is, $a(b + c) = ab + ac$.

The name of this property comes from the fact that the multiplication of a by $b + c$ is distributed over b and c. We call it the Distributive Property for short.

Picturing the Distributive Property Using Area

The Kims have a driveway next to their house that is 30 feet long and 7 feet wide, as shown at the right.

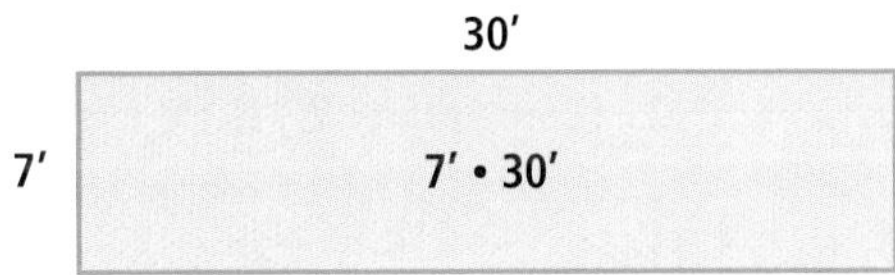

QY1

What is the area of the Kims' driveway on the previous page?

Example 1

Sam Kim built a shed for his jet ski at one end of the driveway. The shed is 8 feet long and 7 feet wide. Show two ways to find the total area of the shed and driveway.

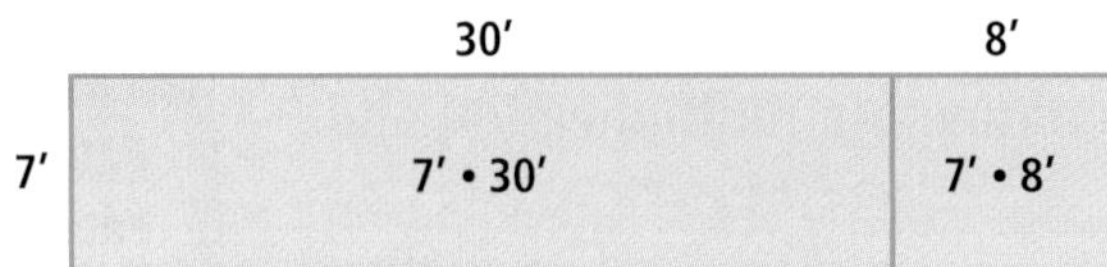

Jet skis represent about 10% of all boats.

Source: U.S. Coast Guard

Solution 1 Find the area of each section and then add. The area of the driveway is $7 \cdot 30 = 210$ ft^2. The area of the shed is $7 \cdot 8 = 56$ ft^2. The total area is $7 \cdot 30 + 7 \cdot 8$ ft^2.

Solution 2 Notice that the driveway and shed form a rectangle with dimensions 7 ft and (30 + 8) ft. So the total area is $7 \cdot (30 + 8)$ ft^2.

These two ways of computing the area illustrate the Distributive Property:

$$7 \cdot (30 + 8) = 7 \cdot 30 + 7 \cdot 8$$

QY2

Evaluate the expressions $7 \cdot 30 + 7 \cdot 8$ and $7 \cdot (30 + 8)$ following the order of operations to show that they have the same value.

Multiplications with One Mixed Number

Another application of the Distributive Property is in multiplying by a mixed number.

Example 2

A carpenter needs 4 strips of wood, each $2\frac{1}{3}$ feet long. How many feet of wood are needed in all?

Solution 1 Draw a picture.

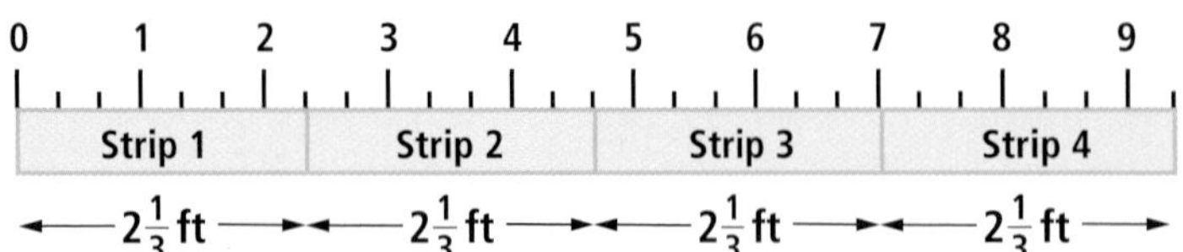

The total length is $9\frac{1}{3}$ feet.

Solution 2 Use the Distributive Property. Write $2\frac{1}{3}$ as a sum: $2\frac{1}{3} = 2 + \frac{1}{3}$.

$$\begin{aligned} 4 \cdot 2\tfrac{1}{3} &= 4 \cdot (2 + \tfrac{1}{3}) \\ &= 4 \cdot 2 + 4 \cdot \tfrac{1}{3} \\ &= 8 + \tfrac{4}{3} \\ &= 8 + 1\tfrac{1}{3} \\ &= 9\tfrac{1}{3} \text{ feet} \end{aligned}$$

Check Each of the 4 strips can be thought of as joining a piece of wood 2 feet long with a piece $\frac{1}{3}$ foot long. So the carpenter needs $4 \cdot 2$ feet and $4 \cdot \frac{1}{3}$ feet. Multiplying gives $4 \cdot 2 = 8$ and $4 \cdot \frac{1}{3} = \frac{4}{3} = 1\frac{1}{3}$. The total length is $8 + 1\frac{1}{3} = 9\frac{1}{3}$ feet.

Multiplying Two Mixed Numbers

You can use the Distributive Property to multiply two mixed numbers. However, since each mixed number is a sum, you need to use the property twice.

Example 3

Multiply $4\frac{2}{3}$ by $5\frac{6}{7}$.

Solution 1 Use the Distributive Property. Think of one of the mixed numbers as a sum. We choose $5\frac{6}{7} = 5 + \frac{6}{7}$.

$$\begin{aligned} 4\tfrac{2}{3} \cdot 5\tfrac{6}{7} &= 4\tfrac{2}{3} \cdot \left(5 + \tfrac{6}{7}\right) \\ &= 4\tfrac{2}{3} \cdot 5 + 4\tfrac{2}{3} \cdot \tfrac{6}{7} && \text{Use the Distributive Property.} \\ &= \left(4 + \tfrac{2}{3}\right) \cdot 5 + \left(4 + \tfrac{2}{3}\right) \cdot \tfrac{6}{7} && \text{Rewrite the other number, } 4\tfrac{2}{3}\text{, as a sum.} \\ &= 4 \cdot 5 + \tfrac{2}{3} \cdot 5 + 4 \cdot \tfrac{6}{7} + \tfrac{2}{3} \cdot \tfrac{6}{7} && \text{Apply the Distributive Property twice.} \\ &= 20 + \tfrac{10}{3} + \tfrac{24}{7} + \tfrac{12}{21} \\ &= 20 + \tfrac{70}{21} + \tfrac{72}{21} + \tfrac{12}{21} \\ &= 20 + \tfrac{154}{21} && \text{Add the fractions.} \\ &= 20 + 7\tfrac{7}{21} \\ &= 27\tfrac{7}{21} \\ &= 27\tfrac{1}{3} \end{aligned}$$

(continued on next page)

 Convert both mixed numbers to improper fractions.

$$4\tfrac{2}{3} \cdot 5\tfrac{6}{7} = \left(4 + \tfrac{2}{3}\right) \cdot \left(5 + \tfrac{6}{7}\right)$$

$$= \left(\tfrac{12}{3} + \tfrac{2}{3}\right) \cdot \left(\tfrac{35}{7} + \tfrac{6}{7}\right)$$

$$= \tfrac{14}{3} \cdot \tfrac{41}{7}$$ Work first inside the parentheses.

$$= \tfrac{14 \cdot 41}{3 \cdot 7}$$ Multiply the fractions.

$$= \tfrac{82}{3} = 27\tfrac{1}{3}$$

STOP **QY3**

Before multiplying in Example 3, how do you know that the answer will be between 20 and 30?

Questions

COVERING THE IDEAS

1. Justice pays \$14.95 a month for Internet service. She started the service 7 months ago. If she continues the service for another 17 months, she wants to know how much she will have paid in all at the end of that time.
   a. Find how much she will have paid by using one addition and one multiplication. Show the expression.
   b. Find how much she will have paid by using two multiplications and one addition. Show the expression.

2. a. State the Distributive Property in words.
   b. State the Distributive Property in symbols.

3. A farm is shaped like a rectangle 2 miles long and $3\frac{3}{4}$ miles wide. Determine the area of the farm by picturing it as a sum of areas of rectangles.

The number of farms in the United States decreased from 6.35 million in 1940 to 2.11 million in 2004.

Source: U.S. Department of Agriculture

4. Rachel said that she knew the answer to Question 3 was between 6 and 8 square miles before she did any calculations with fractions. How did she know that?

In 5 and 6, calculate the product.

5. $2\frac{2}{3} \cdot 15$

6. $3 \cdot 7\frac{2}{5}$

7. Multiply $5\frac{5}{6}$ by $4\frac{2}{7}$
   a. by using the Distributive Property.
   b. by converting each number to an improper fraction.

In 8–10, multiply the mixed numbers. Write your answer in lowest terms.

8. $52\frac{2}{3} \cdot 6\frac{1}{2}$

9. $5\frac{3}{5} \cdot 2\frac{1}{7}$

10. $1\frac{7}{8} \cdot 9\frac{3}{4}$

APPLYING THE MATHEMATICS

11. An area picture of the multiplication $1\frac{3}{8} \cdot 3\frac{1}{3}$ is shown below with a letter inside each of the four regions. Put the letter above the correct area to get a code word.

?	?	?	?
$\frac{1}{8}$	$\frac{1}{3}$	$1\frac{1}{8}$	3

Save the word for the quote in Question 24 in Lesson 6-10 on page 389.

	3	$\frac{1}{3}$
1	*e*	*a*
$\frac{3}{8}$	*d*	*m*

12. A study found that 11-year-olds, on average, sleep $9\frac{3}{5}$ hours a night (the recommended amount is 10 hours). According to these findings, how many hours does the average 11-year-old sleep in one year?

13. Multiply $38 \cdot 97$ by writing 38 as $30 + 8$ and 97 as $90 + 7$ and using the Distributive Property.

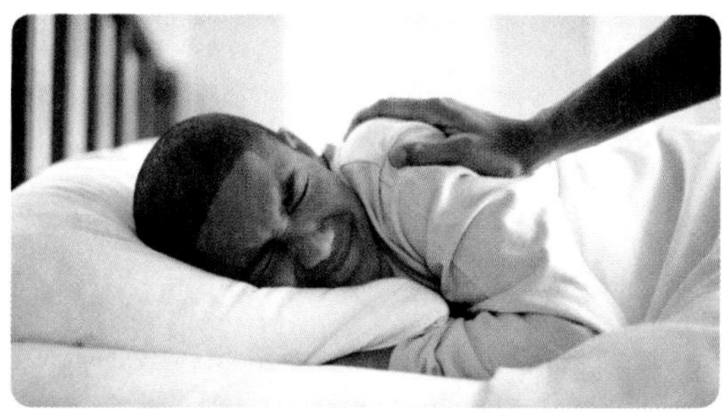

For a better night's sleep, finish eating at least 2 to 3 hours before your regular bedtime.

Source: National Sleep Foundation

In 14–16, Rex Reck is converting a room that measures 13'10" by 9'3" into a media area. Use the diagram below to help answer the questions.

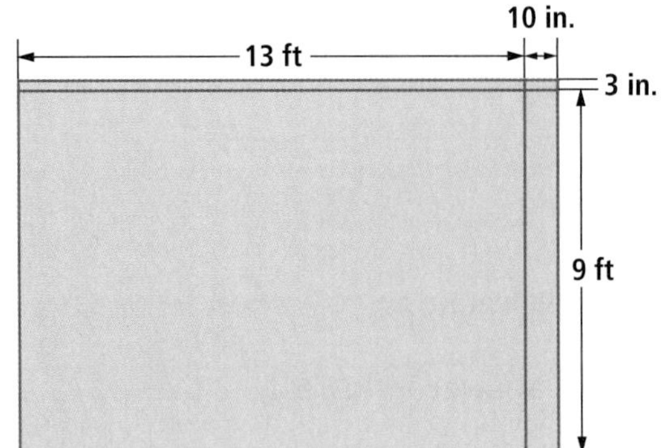

14. Rex wants to paint the ceiling.

a. What multiplication does he need to do to determine the area of the ceiling?

b. How can you write 10" and 3" to make the units all feet?

c. What is the area that needs painting?

15. Rex wants to tile the floor with square tiles that are 1 foot on a side. To save money, he wants to use as few tiles as possible.

a. How many tiles can he put on the floor without cutting any?

b. What is the smallest number of tiles he can use to cover the floor?

16. Rex wants to put wallpaper on the largest wall. The ceiling is 8'2" high.

a. What are the dimensions of the largest wall?

b. What is the area of that wall?

Paper was first used as a wall covering in the 1400s in England.

Source: *History Magazine*

17. A strip of wallpaper is 30 inches wide and 50 feet long. What is its area in square feet?

REVIEW

18. Calculate $5 + 4 \cdot 3 \div 2 - (7 + 4)$ using the correct order of operations. **(Lesson 6-8)**

19. Insert parentheses to make each equation true. **(Lesson 6-8)**

   a. $4 + 3 \cdot 2 \cdot 6 + 1 = 98$

   b. $4 + 3 \cdot 2 \cdot 6 + 1 = 46$

   c. $4 + 3 \cdot 2 \cdot 6 + 1 = 41$

20. Shoes that normally sell for $109.99 are 40% off. You have a gift certificate for $60. Will it fully cover the cost of the shoes? Explain your reasoning. **(Lessons 6-6, 6-5)**

21. Calculate $\left(1\frac{2}{5}\right)^2$. **(Lesson 6-4)**

22. Compute. **(Lessons 6-2, 4-7, 3-8)**

   a. $\frac{5}{8} + \frac{4}{9}$ b. $\frac{5}{8} - \frac{4}{9}$ c. $\frac{5}{8} \cdot \frac{4}{9}$

23. Suppose a person volunteers one day per week at a soup kitchen. During the first week, she has a choice of 5 days to volunteer. During the second week, there is a choice of 4 days to volunteer. How many combinations of two days can the person choose? **(Lesson 6-1)**

24. a. Draw a line that passes through exactly three quadrants on a coordinate grid. **(Lesson 5-6)**

   b. Draw a line that passes through exactly two quadrants.

   c. Is it possible to draw a line that passes through only one quadrant? Explain your reasoning.

   d. Is it possible to draw a line that passes through all four quadrants? If so, provide an example.

25. a. Rewrite $2 - 5 - {}^{-}4 - 8$ as an addition problem.

   b. Compute the sum. **(Lesson 3-4)**

EXPLORATION

26. A student did the following computation: $3\frac{1}{5} \cdot 5\frac{2}{3} = 15\frac{2}{15}$. Without calculating the correct answer, explain how you know this student's answer is wrong. (You may want to use pictures.)

QY ANSWERS

1. 210 ft^2

2. $7 \cdot 30 + 7 \cdot 8 = 210 + 56 = 266$; $7 \cdot (30 + 8) = 7 \cdot 38 = 266$

3. Rounding down, $4\frac{2}{3} \cdot 5\frac{6}{7}$ is larger than $4 \cdot 5$, which is 20. Rounding up, the product is smaller than $5 \cdot 6$ or 30.

Lesson 6-10 Multiplying Positive and Negative Numbers

▸ **BIG IDEA** If a number is multiplied by a positive number, it keeps its direction; if it is multiplied by a negative number, its direction changes.

When thinking about multiplication of positive and negative numbers, it helps to consider situations involving opposites. One familiar situation is the change in water level when you run water into or drain water from a sink.

Mental Math

Answer *always, sometimes but not always,* or *never*.

a. When two different negative numbers are added, the sum is negative.

b. When two positive numbers are added, the sum is positive.

c. When a positive number and a negative number are added, the sum is negative.

d. When a negative number is added to itself, the sum is zero.

The Product of Two Positive Numbers

You have been multiplying positive numbers for many years. The product of two positive numbers is always positive. Example 1 shows a situation like this.

Example 1

The water level in a sink goes up 3 cm every minute. How much will the water have risen 5 minutes from now?

Solution (3 cm per minute) • (5 minutes) = 15 cm higher than now. All of these numbers are positive. Five minutes from now the water will be 15 cm higher than now.

The Product of a Positive Number and a Negative Number

Think of going back in time as negative. Five minutes ago can be written as -5 minutes.

Example 2

Suppose the water level in a sink goes up 3 cm every minute. What would the water level have been 5 minutes ago?

Solution 1

(3 cm per minute) • (5 minutes ago) = 15 cm lower than now

$3 \cdot -5 = -15$

So five minutes ago, the water level was 15 cm lower.

Another way to interpret $3 \cdot -5$ is with repeated addition:

$$3 \cdot -5 = -5 + -5 + -5 = -15$$

Because multiplication is commutative, $3 \cdot -5 = -5 \cdot 3$. So $-5 \cdot 3 = -15$. The product of any negative number and any positive number is negative, and the product of any positive number and any negative number is negative.

QY1

Calculate.

a. $-2 \cdot 8$ **b.** $8 \cdot -2$ **c.** $-8 \cdot 2$ **d.** $2 \cdot -8$

The Product of Two Negative Numbers

By thinking of water draining out of a sink, we have a multiplication situation with two negative numbers. Example 3 illustrates that the product of a negative number and a negative number is positive.

Example 3

Suppose water drains out of a sink at 3 cm per minute. What would the water level have been 5 minutes ago?

Solution Because the water level is going down, the rate of change in the water level is represented by –3 cm per minute. The time is represented by –5.

(draining 3 cm per min) • (5 min ago) = 15 cm higher than now

$$-3 \cdot -5 = 15$$

The water level would have been 15 cm higher five minutes ago.

QY2

Calculate.

a. $5 \cdot 7$ **b.** $-5 \cdot 7$ **c.** $5 \cdot -7$ **d.** $-5 \cdot -7$

Examples 1, 2, and 3 illustrate the following properties of the products of positive and negative numbers.

Multiplying Positive and Negative Numbers

The product of two positive numbers, or of two negative numbers, is positive.

The product of one positive and one negative number is negative.

See QY3 at the right.

QY3

Determine which of the following products are positive and which are negative. Then calculate.

a. $-35 \cdot 12$

b. $-\frac{4}{7} \cdot -\frac{2}{3}$

c. $18.0683 \cdot 0.02$

d. $629 \cdot -17$

GUIDED

Example 4

LeAnn has been taking \$12.50 a week from her savings to pay for her piano lessons.

a. What will be the change in LeAnn's savings in 9 weeks?

b. How did LeAnn's savings 6 weeks ago compare to her savings today?

The piano has 88 keys and of these, 36 are black keys.

Source: www.pianoworld.com

Solution

a. The \$12.50 that LeAnn takes each week is represented by ?. LeAnn takes money for ? weeks. Find the product of the amount per week (a negative number) and the number of weeks: ? • ?. LeAnn's savings will be ? less in 9 weeks.

b. The money LeAnn takes each week is represented by ?. 6 weeks ago is represented by ?. Multiply two negative numbers: ? • ?. LeAnn's savings 6 weeks ago were ? more than her savings today.

Activity

MATERIALS calculator, spreadsheet (optional)

Copy the following table. Use a spreadsheet if one is available. Fill in each cell with the product of the numbers in its row and column.

	−5	−4	−3	−2	−1	0	1	2	3	4	5
5	?	?	−15	−10	−5	0	5	10	15	20	25
4	?	?	?	?	?	?	?	?	?	?	20
3	?	?	?	?	?	?	?	?	?	?	15
2	?	?	?	?	?	?	?	?	?	?	10
1	?	?	?	?	?	?	?	?	?	?	5
0	?	?	?	?	?	?	?	?	?	?	0
−1	?	?	?	?	?	?	?	?	?	?	−5
−2	?	?	?	?	?	?	?	?	?	?	−10
−3	?	?	?	?	?	?	?	?	?	?	?
−4	?	?	?	?	?	?	?	?	?	?	?
−5	?	?	?	?	?	?	?	?	?	?	?

Questions

COVERING THE IDEAS

1. a. A watch has been losing time at a rate of 3 seconds per day since the first day of the month. If today is the 27th day of the month, how does the time on the watch compare to the actual time?

   b. Write a multiplication involving at least one negative number that gives the answer to Part a.

2. a. The temperature has been decreasing by 1.5°F per hour for the last 5 hours. How does the temperature now compare to the temperature 4 hours ago?

   b. Write a multiplication involving at least one negative number that gives the answer to Part a.

3. a. If the floodwaters in a delta are receding by $\frac{1}{4}$ inch per hour, how will the water level have changed 2 days from now?

   b. Write a multiplication involving at least one negative number that gives the answer to Part a.

4. Use repeated addition to explain why 4 • -37 = -148.

In 5–8, find the product.

5. 5 • -2.5
6. -15 • -4
7. -9.23 • -4.11
8. $-\frac{8}{11} \cdot 2\frac{3}{4}$

9. Which of the statements below about multiplying positive and negative numbers are correct? Use the letters of the correct statements to form a word, and put the word in the table in Question 24 on page 389.

O	negative • negative = negative
B	negative • negative = positive
R	positive • negative = positive
U	positive • negative = negative
F	negative • positive = positive
T	negative • positive = negative

APPLYING THE MATHEMATICS

10. Calculate the products in Parts a–c.

    a. -2 • -3 • -4

    b. -2 • -3 • -4 • -5

    c. -2 • -3 • -4 • -5 • -6

    d. Explain why the product of three negative numbers must be negative.

    e. Explain why the product of four negative numbers must be positive.

    f. Generalize the results of Parts a–e.

11. Calculate the products in Parts a–f.

    a. -1 • 1

    b. -1 • -1

    c. -1 • -4

    d. -1 • 4

    e. -1 • -76.22

    f. -1 • 76.22

    g. Generalize the results of Parts a–f.

12. Which is greater, the sum of -2.4 and -3.7 or the product of -2.4 and -3.7? How can you tell without doing any computing?

13. Which is greater, the sum of 40 and -50 or the product of 40 and -50? How can you tell without doing any computing?

14. Find a positive number and a negative number such that the product of the two numbers is greater than the sum of the two numbers.

15. Ty and Terrell are buying each other's belongings. Ty pays Terrell \$18.37 apiece for three DVDs. Terrell pays Ty \$14.32 apiece for four CDs.

a. Write the amounts of money spent and taken in from Ty's perspective.

b. Write the amounts of money spent and taken in Terrell's perspective.

REVIEW

16. Mary is farming a flower patch that is 30 feet long. She is also farming a tomato patch that is 13 feet long. The patches are side by side on an 18 foot-wide piece of land. What is the total area of her two patches? **(Lessons 6-9, 6-3)**

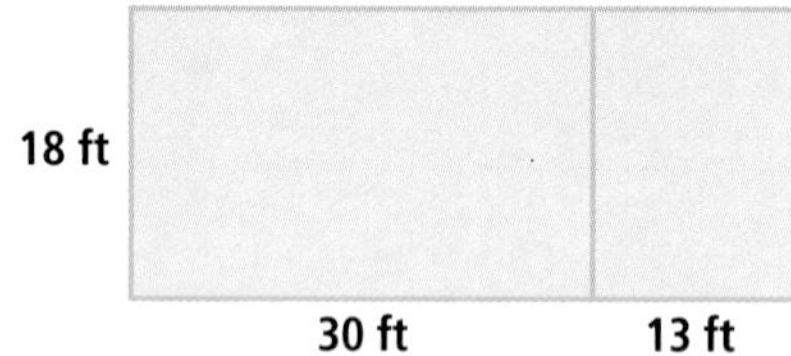

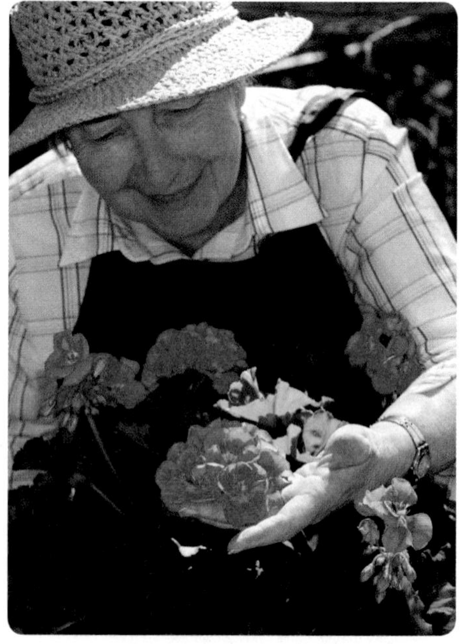

a woman tending to her geraniums

In 17 and 18, calculate. (Lesson 6-8)

17. $2 + 4 \cdot \frac{15}{7} - 5^2$

18. $(1 + 3) \cdot 6^2 - 8$

19. The sixth graders at Entrepreneur Middle School are raising money by selling slices of pizza. They order 10 large pizzas at \$9.69 apiece. They have to pay 25% more for delivery and tip. If each pizza is cut into 12 slices and each slice is sold for \$1.50, how much will they make if they sell all the slices? **(Lessons 6-6, 6-5)**

In 20 and 21, place the decimal point in the product by estimating the answer. (Lesson 6-5)

20. $3.2 \cdot 2 \cdot 2.5 = 16$

21. $0.008 \cdot 0.0070 = 56$

22. In a class of 24 students, $\frac{2}{3}$ are girls, and $\frac{1}{2}$ of the girls play basketball. How many girls play basketball? **(Lesson 6-2)**

EXPLORATION

23. a. Write a problem about a situation not discussed in this lesson where you would need to multiply a positive number times a negative number. Then write the answer.

b. Write a problem about a situation not discussed in this lesson where you would need to multiply two negative numbers. Then write the answer.

24. a. In the table below, place the words you decoded from this chapter.

Lesson	Word
6-1	?
6-2	?
6-3	?
6-4	?
6-5	?
6-6	?
6-7	?
6-8 (Use twice.)	?
6-9	?
6-10	?

b. Rearrange the words to form a quote from Albert Einstein, the famous 20th century physicist who discovered the relationship $E = mc^2$ (the energy available from an atom equals the product of its mass and the square of the speed of light). (*Hint:* One word is used twice.)

Albert Einstein

QY ANSWERS

1a. −16

1b. −16

1c. −16

1d. −16

2a. 35

2b. −35

2c. −35

2d. 35

3a. negative; −420

3b. positive; $\frac{8}{21}$

3c. positive; 0.361366

3d. negative; −10,693

Chapter 6 Projects

1 Scientific Notation

Scientific notation is a way of writing large numbers using powers of ten. $4.5 \cdot 10^5$ is in scientific notation because it has a number between 1 and 10 being multiplied by an integer power of ten.

- Write these scientific-notation numbers in decimal form: $8.9 \cdot 10^4$, $2.3 \cdot 10^5$, $1.7 \cdot 10^8$.
- Write 320,000 in scientific notation.
- Why is $35.8 \cdot 10^5$ not in scientific notation? Rewrite it in scientific notation.
- Find two examples from a book, magazine, or website where scientific notation is used to represent a number.

The moon's mass is 7.3483×10^{22} kg.

Source: NASA

2 Multiplying Fractions Versus Multiplying Decimals or Percents

Instead of multiplying 2.5 by 3.75, you could multiply $\frac{5}{2}$ by $\frac{15}{4}$. Instead of taking 20% of some quantity, you could take $\frac{1}{5}$ of that quantity. When is it easier to multiply fractions? When is it easier to multiply with decimals or percents? Write an essay giving examples to support your opinions.

3 Russian Peasant Multiplication

How would you like to be able to do multiplication problems using only doubling and halving numbers and addition? A method called the *Russian peasant method* does just that. Find out how to multiply two whole numbers using this method. Tell why it works. Write a report on your findings, including at least two examples.

4 Last digits of powers

This table shows the last digits of the first 8 powers of two:

Powers of 2	Value	Last Digit
2^1	2	2
2^2	4	4
2^3	8	8
2^4	16	6
2^5	32	2
2^6	64	4
2^7	128	8
2^8	256	6

There seems to be a repeating pattern (2, 4, 8, 6, ...) in the last digits of powers of two. What is the pattern for powers of 3? Make a table and note the pattern. What about powers of 4? Check other powers. What about powers for numbers like 32? Report on your findings.

Powers of 3	Value	Last Digit
3^1	?	?
3^2	?	?
3^3	?	?
3^4	?	?
3^5	?	?
3^6	?	?
3^7	?	?
3^8	?	?

5 Four Fours

Using exactly four 4s, parentheses, and any operation symbols you want, write numerical expressions for as many integers from 0 to 50 as you can, following the order of operations. For example, $36 = (4 + 4) \cdot 4 + 4$. You can also use numbers like 4.4 and 44.

6 The King's Chessboard

Read *The King's Chessboard* by David Birch. Write a summary of the story, including a detailed description of its use of exponents. Justify the calculations made in the book using paper and pencil, calculator, or a spreadsheet. Explain why the outcome of the request to the king is unexpectedly impossible.

Chapter 6 Summary and Vocabulary

- **Multiplication** gives answers to a wide variety of problems. The number of elements in a **rectangular array** is the product of the number of rows and the number of columns in the array. The **area** of a rectangle is the product of its length and width. Using an integer **exponent *n*** with a number is a shortcut indicating multiplication of the number times itself n times. To find a **percent of a number,** rewrite the percent as a fraction or decimal and calculate the product.

- You can use an **array** to represent multiplication. For example, to multiply $\frac{2}{3}$ by $\frac{4}{5}$, you can use the 3×5 array below. In general, for all numbers a, b, c, and d with $b \neq 0$ and $d \neq 0$, $\frac{a}{b} \cdot \frac{c}{d} = \frac{ac}{bd}$.

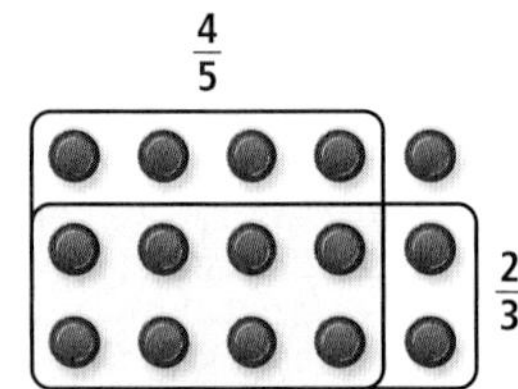

- The product of a number, a, and a sum, $b + c$, can be pictured by the total area of two rectangles, as shown at the right.

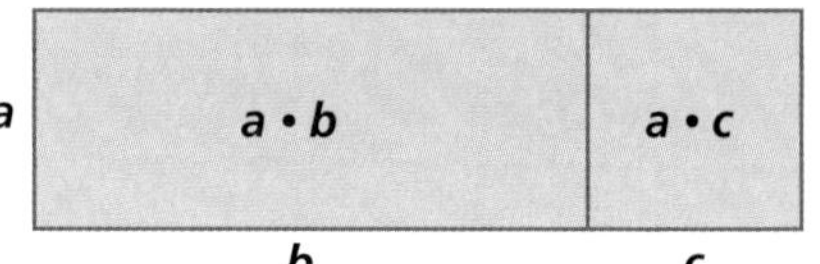

- The sum is $ab + ac$. These rectangles picture the **Distributive Property** and help to explain how to multiply a number a by a mixed number with whole number part b and fraction part c.

- There is a set of rules that standardize the **order of operations:** parentheses first, then powers, then multiplications or divisions from left to right, then additions or subtractions from left to right.

- The product of two positive numbers, or of two negative numbers, is positive. The product of one positive and one negative number is negative.

Vocabulary

6-1
rectangular array

6-3
dimensions

6-4
exponent
base
exponential form
squared
cubed
expanded notation

6-8
numerical expression
value
evaluating the expression

Theorems and Properties

Array Model for Multiplication (p. 329)
Multiplication of Fractions Property (p. 336)
Area Model for Multiplication (p. 343)
Commutative Property of Multiplication (p. 344)
Associative Property of Multiplication (p. 344)
Repeated Multiplication Model for Powers (p. 349)
Distributive Property of Multiplication over Addition (p. 377)

Chapter 6 Self-Test

Take this test as you would take a test in class. You will need a calculator. Then use the Selected Answers section in the back of the book to check your work.

1. A farmer has 8 rows of raspberries, and each row has 16 bushes. If the farmer harvests half of the raspberry bushes, and uses $\frac{1}{4}$ of those bushes to make jam, how many total raspberry bushes will be used to make jam?

2. One of the sides of a rectangular cutting board is three times as long as the other. If the shorter side is 4 inches long, what is the area of the cutting board?

In 3–10, calculate without using a calculator. Write fraction answers in lowest terms.

3. $300 \cdot \frac{3}{8}$
4. $\frac{9}{10} \cdot \frac{5}{12}$
5. $3.4 \cdot 2.5$
6. $0.9 \cdot 10.16$
7. $3\frac{1}{5} \cdot 6$
8. $1\frac{7}{8} \cdot 1\frac{2}{3}$
9. $-\frac{1}{5} \cdot -\frac{5}{7}$
10. $9.45 \cdot -5.12$

11. Explain how to find the result without a calculator.
    a. 10% of 427
    b. 20% of 427

12. If 47% of the 1,175 students at Nye High School are female, how many male students are there?

13. Devon's kitchen has a length of 23 feet and a width of 13 feet. His living room has a length of 13 feet and a width of 23 feet.
    a. Devon says his kitchen is bigger than his living room. Is he correct? Explain.
    b. What basic property of multiplication would have helped Devon compare the areas of the two rooms?

14. Alexus and Pedro bought a gallon of water for $5.52. Alexus drank $\frac{3}{4}$ of the gallon and paid for his share.
    a. How much did Alexus pay?
    b. How much did Pedro pay?

15. A rectangular city playground is $\frac{3}{5}$ mile by $\frac{2}{3}$ mile.
    a. Draw a picture of the playground as a part of a square mile.
    b. Find the area of the playground.

In 16–22, calculate.

16. $20 \cdot 18.5 + 3.5 \cdot 10$
17. $10 - 6 \cdot 5^2$
18. $\frac{100 + 14}{10 + 7}$
19. 4^3
20. $-(6)^2$
21. $(-3)^4$
22. $\left(\frac{2}{5}\right)^3$

23. Sonia is spending $560 more per month than she earns.
    a. Write an expression using integers to show the change in the amount of money she has after 4 months.
    b. Compared to today, how much money will she have in four months?
    c. Write an expression using integers to show how much more money she had 2 months ago.
    d. Compared to today, how much money did Sonia have 2 months ago?

24. Mikayla wants to buy a pair of tennis shoes with a 12.5% discount. The regular cost of the tennis shoes is $45.65.
   a. How much is the discount?
   b. How much will Mikayla pay?

In 25 and 26, write each expression using exponents.

25. $g \cdot g \cdot g \cdot g \cdot g \cdot g$
26. $0.5 \cdot 0.5 \cdot 0.3 \cdot 0.5 \cdot 0.3$

27. Noel has a wall that needs painting. The wall is a rectangle 12 feet, 4 inches by 7 feet, 8 inches. What is the area of the wall in square feet?

28. Write 32,000 using expanded notation.

Chapter 6 Chapter Review

SKILLS
PROPERTIES
USES
REPRESENTATIONS

SKILLS Procedures used to get answers

OBJECTIVE A Multiply fractions and mixed numbers. (Lessons 6-2, 6-9)

In 1–12, calculate.

1. $\frac{1}{5}$ of 20
2. $\frac{9}{11}$ of 66
3. $\frac{1}{2} \cdot \frac{1}{3}$
4. $\frac{1}{3} \cdot \frac{3}{4}$
5. $\frac{5}{6} \cdot \frac{8}{9} \cdot \frac{9}{5}$
6. $4 \cdot 7\frac{1}{2}$
7. $\frac{1}{2} + \frac{1}{3} \cdot \frac{1}{4}$
8. $2 - \frac{3}{5} \cdot 5$
9. $5\frac{3}{4} \cdot 6\frac{1}{2}$
10. $18\frac{2}{3} \cdot 2\frac{1}{5}$
11. $1\frac{5}{6} \cdot 5\frac{5}{11}$
12. $3\frac{1}{2} \cdot \frac{2}{7}$

OBJECTIVE B Evaluate numerical expressions using the correct order of operations. (Lesson 6-8)

In 13–16, calculate.

13. $2 + 3 - (5 \cdot 2)$
14. $8^2 \cdot 5^3 - 1$
15. $17.8 \cdot (5.4 - 6) + 2.19$
16. $47 + (2^3 - 3)^2 \div 5$

OBJECTIVE C Multiply decimals. (Lesson 6-5)

In 17 and 18, calculate.

17. $5.4 \cdot 3.9$
18. $31.4 \cdot 27.8$

In 19 and 20, place the decimal point in the product to make the equation true.

19. $4.7 \cdot 5.3 = 2491$
20. $3.54 \cdot 9.82 = 347628$

In 21 and 22, convert the decimals to fractions to calculate.

21. $0.25 \cdot 0.75$
22. $1.5 \cdot 0.5 \cdot 3.5$

OBJECTIVE D Find the percent of a quantity. (Lessons 6-6, 6-7)

In 23–26, calculate the percent in your head.

23. 20% of 70
24. 5% of 90
25. 50% of 400
26. 10% of 45.7

In 27–30, calculate.

27. 15% of 79
28. 72% of 140
29. 4.6% of 20
30. 5% of 17.2

OBJECTIVE E Multiply positive and negative numbers. (Lesson 6-10)

In 31–34:

a. Decide whether the product will be positive or negative.
b. Find the product.

31. $-4 \cdot -5$
32. $-3 \cdot 7.4 \cdot 8.6$
33. $\frac{1}{2} \cdot -\frac{2}{3} \cdot -5$
34. $-\frac{3}{4} \cdot -\frac{4}{5} \cdot \frac{5}{8}$

OBJECTIVE F **Calculate the values of and simplify expressions with exponents. (Lesson 6-4)**

In 35–38, calculate.

35. 8^5

36. 1^{17}

37. 0.3^4

38. $\left(3\frac{1}{2}\right)^2$

In 39–42:

a. Rewrite the expression in exponential form.

b. Calculate.

39. $7 \cdot 7 \cdot 7$

40. $4 \cdot 4 \cdot 5 \cdot 4 \cdot 4 \cdot 5$

41. $2.1 \cdot 2.1 \cdot 2.1 \cdot 2.1 \cdot 2.1 \cdot 2.1 \cdot 2.1 \cdot 2.1$

42. $0.8 \cdot 0.8 \cdot 0.08 \cdot 0.8 \cdot 0.08$

In 43 and 44, write in exponential form.

43. sixteen to the eighth power

44. three hundred cubed

PROPERTIES The principles behind the mathematics

OBJECTIVE G **Rewrite numbers in base 10 using expanded notation. (Lesson 6-4)**

In 45–48, write the base-10 number in expanded notation.

45. 4,552

46. 75

47. 10,800

48. 9,876,543

OBJECTIVE H **Identify the Commutative and Associative Properties of Multiplication. (Lesson 6-3)**

In 49–52, name the property that is being used.

49. $60 \cdot \frac{3}{4} = \frac{3}{4} \cdot 60$

50. $7.32 \cdot (8.25 \cdot -3.75) = (7.32 \cdot 8.25) \cdot -3.75$

51. The area of a room with dimensions 9 feet by 12 feet is the same as the area of a room with dimensions 12 feet by 9 feet.

52. The product of three numbers is always the same, regardless of the order of multiplication.

USES Applications of mathematics in real-world situations

OBJECTIVE I **Find areas in real-world situations. (Lesson 6-3)**

53. What is the area of the football field pictured below?

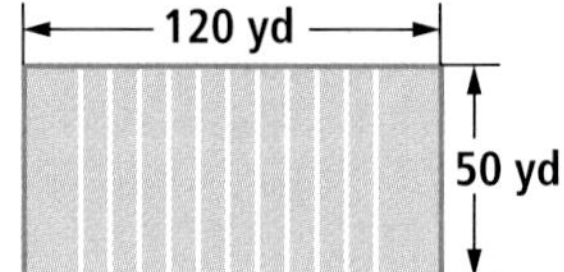

54. Benito wants to tile his floor with square tiles that measure 2 feet on each side. If Benito's floor has dimensions 12 feet by 17 feet, how many tiles does he need to tile his floor? (If necessary, parts of tiles may be used.)

55. What is the area of a tablecloth needed to cover a picnic table that is 1 yard wide and 8 feet long?

56. Omar is looking at apartments. The first apartment has a bedroom that measures 20 feet by 12 feet. The second apartment has a bedroom that measures 15 feet by 18 feet.

a. Which apartment has the larger bedroom?

b. How much larger is it?

OBJECTIVE J **Use the Array Model for Multiplication in real-world situations. (Lesson 6-1)**

57. How many outfits can you make with 7 pairs of shorts and 4 blouses?

58. How many outfits can you make with 4 pairs of shoes, 3 hats, and 5 shirts?

59. There are 80 seats in an auditorium. Half of the seats have someone sitting in them, and $\frac{1}{8}$ of those seats have backpacks underneath them. How many seats have backpacks underneath them?

OBJECTIVE K **Multiply fractions and decimals in real-world situations. (Lessons 6-2, 6-5)**

60. It is 9 kilometers from Allen's school to home and Allen has already traveled $\frac{3}{10}$ of the way.

a. How many kilometers has he traveled?

b. How many kilometers does Allen have left to travel?

61. Sukie is purchasing school supplies for the Homework Club. Pencils come in packs of 8, and erasers in packs of 6. She needs to purchase a minimum of 60 pencils and erasers, and she wants to have exactly one eraser for every pencil. How many packages of pencils and erasers should Sukie purchase?

62. There were five half-gallon containers of orange juice in Aisha's refrigerator before she and her friends drank $\frac{1}{4}$ of it. How many gallons of juice did they drink?

63. Plaxico is running the marathon, which is 26.2 miles long. If he is $\frac{3}{4}$ of the way through the race, how many miles has he run?

OBJECTIVE L **Find the percent of a quantity in real-world situations. (Lesson 6-7)**

64. 80% of the 60 members of a professional basketball league are over six-feet tall. How many players is this?

65. Lindsay earns $65,200 and pays 17% of her income in state and federal taxes. How much does she pay in taxes?

66. Of the $15 list price of a novel, an author receives a royalty of 12%. How much would an author receive from the sale of 25 books?

67. A car weighs 3,150 lb with one passenger. If an empty car represents 95% of this weight, how much does the passenger weigh?

OBJECTIVE M **Multiply positive and negative numbers in real-world situations. (Lesson 6-10)**

68. a. Claudia pays $950 per month on rent and $400 per month on groceries. Her salary is $45,000 per year after taxes. How much money does she have left each month after budgeting for rent and groceries?

b. Write an expression involving at least one negative number that gives the answer to Part a.

69. a. Every year, the houses in a neighborhood sink about $\frac{1}{4}$ of an inch. How much will they sink in 54 months?

b. Write a multiplication involving at least one negative number that gives the answer to Part a.

REPRESENTATIONS Pictures, graphs, or objects that illustrate concepts

OBJECTIVE N **Represent the Distributive Property by areas of rectangles. (Lesson 6-9)**

In 70–73, picture the product as a sum of areas of rectangles.

70. $5\frac{1}{4} \cdot 16$

71. $30(25 + 5)$

72. $12 \cdot 3\frac{1}{2}$

73. $8(11 + 19)$

Chapter

7 Using Division

Contents

Division is the fourth of what are often called the "four fundamental operations of arithmetic." (Addition, subtraction, and multiplication are the other three.) A division such as 100 ÷ 6 can answer a wide variety of questions, including those in the following seven situations:

Question 1: If 6 stamp collectors share a package of 100 stamps, how many will each person get?

Question 2: Megan rode her bike 100 kilometers in 6 hours. What was her average speed?

Question 3: On a school trip, 100 sixth graders will be transported by vans seating 6 passengers each. How many vans will the school need?

Question 4: One salted nut contains 6 mg of sodium (salt). If Manuel likes to snack on nuts, but he needs to keep his maximum intake of sodium from snacks to 0.1 g or less, how many nuts can he eat?

Question 5: The six Kwan children decide to share the cost of repaying a $100 debt. How much will each sibling's savings change?

Question 6: Is $\frac{100}{6}$ a terminating or repeating decimal?

Question 7: If $6x = 100$, what is x?

To answer each question, you need to find $100 \div 6$. However, the answers are different!

Answer 1: Two collectors get 16 stamps and four get 17 stamps.

Answer 2: $\frac{100\text{ km}}{6\text{ hr}}$ is $16\frac{2}{3}$ km/hr.

Answer 3: The school will need 17 vans (otherwise, some students will be left at school).

Answer 4: Sixteen nuts will keep his sodium intake under 0.1 g, but seventeen would have slightly more than 0.1 g of sodium.

Answer 5: Two children will have their savings changed by –$16.66, and four children will have their savings changed by –$16.67.

Answer 6: Since $\frac{100}{6} = 16.\overline{6}$, it is a repeating decimal.

Answer 7: $x = \frac{100}{6}$ or $16\frac{4}{6}$ or $16\frac{2}{3}$ or $16.\overline{6}$.

This is the first of two chapters on division. In this chapter, you will work with situations leading to division of fractions, decimals, and positive and negative numbers.

Lesson

7-1 The Rate Model for Division

Vocabulary

dividend
divisor
quotient
rate
rate unit

▶ **BIG IDEA** Rates are calculated by division.

The first division problems in history, like QY1 below, involved splitting things up.

QY1

A coin collector left 48 silver dollars to be split evenly among his four children. How many coins would each child get?

Mental Math

Name a number between

a. $\frac{1}{2}$ and $\frac{1}{3}$.

b. $\frac{1}{3}$ and $\frac{1}{4}$.

c. $\frac{11}{4}$ and $\frac{11}{5}$.

The Words of Division

The words "divide" and "division" come from Latin. The prefixes "di-" and "dis-" mean to split apart. A *di*ameter splits apart a circle. Something is *dis*tinct if you can separate it from other things. The roots "vid" and "vis" also mean to separate.

In QY1, 48 coins is the quantity that is going to be split. It is called the **dividend,** just as a number to be added is called an *addend* and the number that is subtracted is called the *subtrahend*. The number 4 is doing the dividing. It is called the **divisor.** The answer, 12 silver coins, is called the **quotient.**

$$\frac{\text{dividend}}{\text{divisor}} = \text{quotient} \quad \rightarrow \quad \frac{48 \text{ coins}}{4 \text{ children}} = 12 \text{ coins per child}$$

The denominator of the fraction is the divisor. The numerator of the fraction is the dividend. The value of the fraction is the quotient.

The Symbols of Division

There are three common symbols for division. One is the sign ÷, read "divided by." The symbol ÷ was first used in 1659 by the Swiss mathematician Johann Rann. The fraction bar (–) and the slash (/) also indicate division. The fraction bar was first used by the Arab mathematician al-Hassar in the late 1100s. The fraction bar, the slash, and the ÷ all mean the same thing. Below are divisions written with these symbols.

$$48 \div 4 = \frac{48}{4} = 48/4 = 12$$

$$\text{dividend} \div \text{divisor} = \frac{\text{dividend}}{\text{divisor}} = \text{dividend/divisor} = \text{quotient}$$

QY2

Five hero sandwiches are to be split evenly among 10 people. How much of a sandwich will each person get?

a. Express this division problem using each of the three symbols for division.

b. What is the answer to this problem—that is, what is the quotient?

Fact Triangles for Multiplication and Division

The numbers in QY1 and QY2 can be put into fact triangles for multiplication and division.

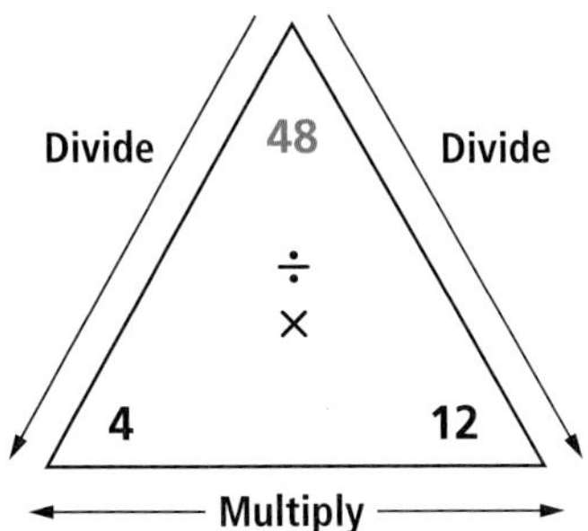

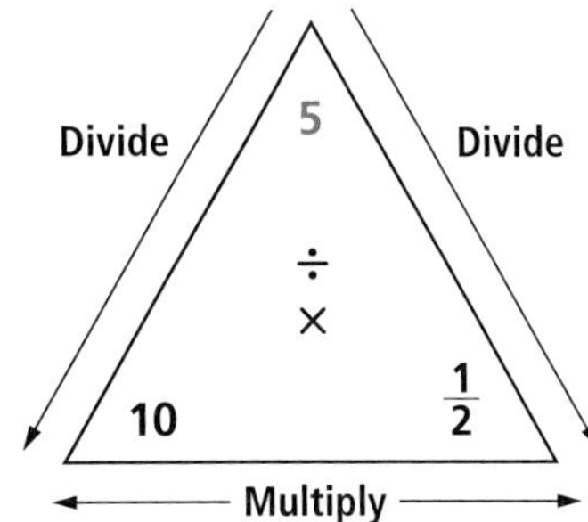

Each fact triangle gives four related facts.

$4 \cdot 12 = 48$ | $10 \cdot \frac{1}{2} = 5$

$12 \cdot 4 = 48$ | $\frac{1}{2} \cdot 10 = 5$

$48 \div 4 = 12$ | $5 \div 10 = \frac{1}{2}$

$48 \div 12 = 4$ | $5 \div \frac{1}{2} = 10$

The Rate Model for Division

In QY1, the quotient is 12 coins per child. In QY2, the quotient is $\frac{5}{10}$, or $\frac{1}{2}$, sandwich per person. The quantity "12 coins per child" is an example of a *rate*. A **rate** is a division involving quantities with different units. The unit "coins per child," "coins/child," or "$\frac{\text{coins}}{\text{child}}$" is a **rate unit.** In a rate unit, the slash (/) or the fraction bar is read as "per."

 **See QY3 at the right.**

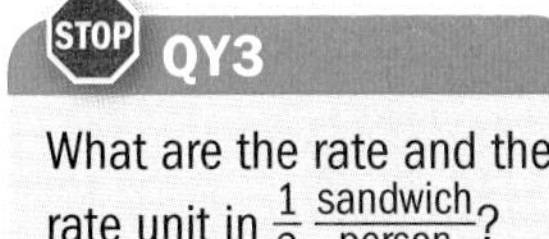

QY3

What are the rate and the rate unit in $\frac{1}{2}\,\frac{\text{sandwich}}{\text{person}}$?

The Rate Model for Division

When two quantities with different kinds of units are divided, the quotient is a rate.

Rates are useful in many situations.

Example 1

If you buy 3 cans of frozen orange juice for \$2.79, what is the cost per can?

Solution The phrase "cost per can" means that the total cost will be divided by the number of cans.

$$\text{cost per can} = \frac{\$2.79}{3 \text{ cans}} = 0.93 \frac{\text{dollars}}{\text{can}} = \$0.93 \text{ per can}$$

Check $3 \cdot \$0.93 = \$2.79$. It checks.

 **See QY4 at the right.**

One serving of orange juice provides over 100% of your daily value for vitamin C.

Source: USDA

QY4

A 22-pound bag of rice costs \$19.95. Five families share this rice and its cost evenly.

a. How many pounds of rice does each family receive?

b. How much does each family need to pay?

GUIDED

Example 2

According to the National Center of Health Statistics, there were 4,112,052 babies born in the United States in 2004. On average, how many babies was this per day?

Solution "Babies per day" is the total number of babies divided by the number of days. Since 2004 was a leap year, it had 366 __?__.

$$\frac{4{,}112{,}052 \text{ babies}}{1 \text{ year}} = \frac{4{,}112{,}052 \text{ babies}}{? \text{ days}} = \frac{4{,}112{,}052}{?} \frac{\text{babies}}{\text{day}}$$

Use a calculator to divide and round to the nearest integer.

$$\underline{\ ?\ } \frac{\text{babies}}{\text{day}} \text{ were born in 2004.}$$

Check Multiply $\underline{\ ?\ } \frac{\text{babies}}{\text{day}}$ by $366 \frac{\text{days}}{\text{year}}$, working with the units just as if they were fractions.

$$\underline{\ ?\ } \frac{\text{babies}}{\text{day}} \times 366 \frac{\text{days}}{\text{year}} = \underline{\ ?\ } \frac{\text{babies}}{\text{year}}$$

This is close to 4,112,052 babies. It is only off by __?__, which is due to rounding the rate to the nearest baby per day.

Questions

COVERING THE IDEAS

1. Identify the divisor, the dividend, and the quotient in the following: Seven is equal to forty-two divided by six.

2. In $\frac{\$3.00}{2} = \$1.50$, identify the divisor, the dividend, and the quotient.

3. **Multiple Choice** Suppose $x \div y = z$. Which of the following is true?

   A $\frac{y}{x} = z$ B $\frac{y}{z} = x$ C $\frac{x}{y} = z$ D $\frac{z}{y} = x$

4. There are 13 large vans available to take 104 team members, parents, and coaches to the state basketball tournament. How many people per van are there?
   a. What division problem is represented by this situation?
   b. What is the answer to the problem?
   c. What is the rate unit in this problem?
5. Draw a multiplication-and-division fact triangle for the numbers 200, 900, and 4.5.
6. If there are 240 seats in 12 rows in an auditorium, how many seats are there per row?
7. Draw a multiplication and division fact triangle for Example 1.
8. The longest nonstop flight in aviation history was 26,389 miles and took place in February, 2006. It was completed in about 76 hours. What was the average speed (in miles per hour)?

APPLYING THE MATHEMATICS

9. A charity collected $24,385 from the gifts of 178 people.
   a. What was the mean gift per person to the nearest penny?
   b. One person gave $10,000 and another gave $4,000. Other than these two people, what was the mean gift amount per person?
10. In 1997, the University of Michigan reported that more than 17 million phone calls were handled at the university per month. About how many phone calls is this per minute in a 30-day month?
11. What rate unit is used to compare fuel economy for cars?
12. The USS Independence is a 1,070-foot-long aircraft carrier with 4.1 acres of flight deck and a crew of 2,300. At its top speed of 25 knots, this ship consumes 150,000 gallons of fuel a day. What is the rate of fuel consumption per hour?

The USS Independence leaves its home port of Yokusuka, Japan.

In 13 and 14, write the four multiplication and division facts that relate the numbers or quantities.

13. $\frac{1}{2}, \frac{1}{8}, \frac{1}{4}$
14. 45 miles, 22.5 miles per hour, 2 hours
15. A park is a square 200 yards on a side. The officials of the park want to split it into four squares of equal size.
    a. What will be the area of each part?
    b. A fence needs to be put around each part. What will be the perimeter of the fence around one part?
    c. How much total fencing is needed? (*Hint:* Be careful!)

16. Suppose a person reads 300 words per minute.
    a. At this rate, how many words does the person read in 20 minutes?
    b. Use your answer to Part a to write two division facts related to this situation.

17. Henry traveled 27.25 miles in 30 minutes. What is his speed in miles per hour?

18. Replace the question mark in the fact triangle at the right with the correct number. Write the two division facts that the fact triangle displays.

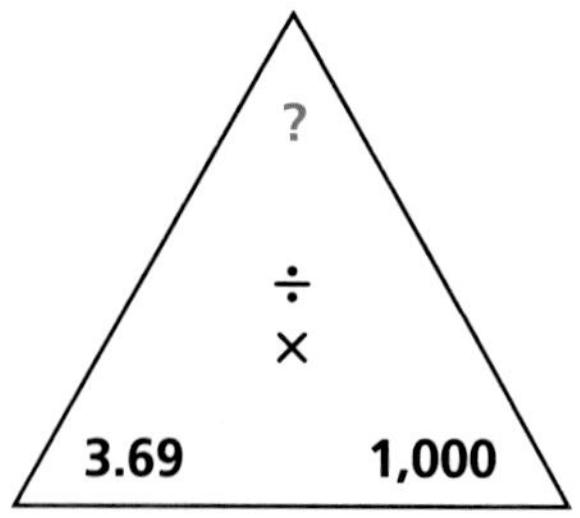

REVIEW

19. Which is greater, the sum of $-\frac{1}{2}$ and $\frac{1}{4}$ or the product of $-\frac{1}{2}$ and $\frac{1}{4}$? **(Lessons 6-10, 3-3)**

20. a. Picture $33\frac{1}{3} \cdot 12$ as a sum of areas of rectangles.
    b. Calculate the product. **(Lesson 6-9)**

21. What is the area of a wall 12 feet, 2 inches tall and 20 feet long? **(Lesson 6-3)**

22. If $g = -2$, is g^7 positive or negative? **(Lesson 6-4)**

23. a. Plot the points (3, 4), (-2, -1), (7, 8), and (5, 4) on a coordinate grid.
    b. Which point in Part a does not lie on the same line as the other three? **(Lesson 5-7)**

24. Find the value of x in the figure below. **(Lesson 3-7)**

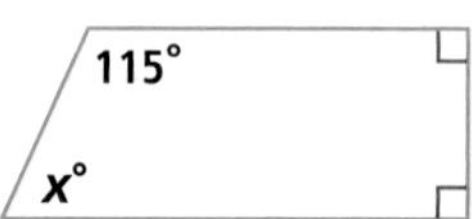

EXPLORATION

25. An old Persian puzzle goes like this.

> A man with three sons had 17 camels. He died and left $\frac{1}{2}$ of his camels to his eldest son, $\frac{1}{3}$ of his camels to his second son, and $\frac{1}{9}$ of his camels to his third son. Since 17 is not divisible by 2, 3, or 9, the sons did not know what to do. They consulted a sage. The sage said, "Imagine an 18th camel."

How does this sage's advice solve their problem?

QY ANSWERS

1. 12 coins each

2a. $5 \div 10$, 5/10, and $\frac{5}{10}$

2b. $\frac{1}{2}$ of a sandwich

3. rate: $\frac{1}{2}$ sandwich/person; rate unit: sandwich per person.

4a. 4.4 pounds per family

4b. $3.99 per family

Lesson 7-2 Arrays and Divisibility

Vocabulary

remainder

▸ **BIG IDEA** You can tell if a whole number n is divisible by another whole number d by drawing an array with n dots split into d rows.

Mental Math

If gas costs $3.20 per gallon, what is the cost of

a. 2 gallons?

b. 4 gallons?

c. 10 gallons?

d. 20 gallons?

The operation of division differs from addition, subtraction, and multiplication in a basic way: you can divide whole numbers and get an answer that is not a whole number.

QY1

Each of the 210 sixth graders at Jefferson Middle School is to receive a patch with the school logo. If the patches come in packages of 30, how many packages does the principal need to buy?

The principal from QY1 started writing down the *multiples* of thirty: 30, 60, 90, 120, 150, 180, 210, … . In doing this, she realized that 210 is *evenly divisible by* 30: $210 \div 30 = 7$. If the principal orders 7 packages, every student will get a patch.

QY2

The patches also come in packages of 50. If she orders these packages, how many does the principal need?

In the situation in QY2, the principal wrote down multiples of fifty: 50, 100, 150, 200, 250, … . She saw that 210 is *not* evenly divisible by 50. Four packages have 200 patches, so if she were to order four, she would be 10 patches short. The number left over is the **remainder.**

Notice the difference between the situations for the two package sizes.

Packages of 30	Packages of 50
$210 = 30 \cdot x$ $210 = 30 \cdot 7$ $210 \div 30 = 7$	$210 = 50 \cdot y$ No integer value of y works. $210 \div 50 = 4$ remainder 10
210 students will use all the patches in 7 packages.	210 students will use all the patches in 4 packages, but 10 students will not get a patch.

Division of 210 by 30 has no remainder and division of 210 by 50 has a remainder. Here are some ways to say that division of 210 by 30 has no remainder.

30 is a *factor* of 210.
30 *divides evenly* into 210.
210 is *divisible by* 30.
210 is a *multiple* of 30.

Definition of Factor

d is a **factor** of n if and only if $\frac{n}{d}$ is an integer. In other words, d is a factor of n if and only if there is no remainder when n is divided by d.

Arrays and Divisibility

Because $15 \div 3 = 5$, 15 is divisible by 3. On the other hand, 16 is not divisible by 3. These two situations can be pictured using arrays. Notice that 15 dots $\div$ 3 rows $= 5\ \frac{\text{dots}}{\text{row}}$, which is a rate. Also, 3 rows $\cdot\ 5\ \frac{\text{dots}}{\text{row}} = 15$ dots.

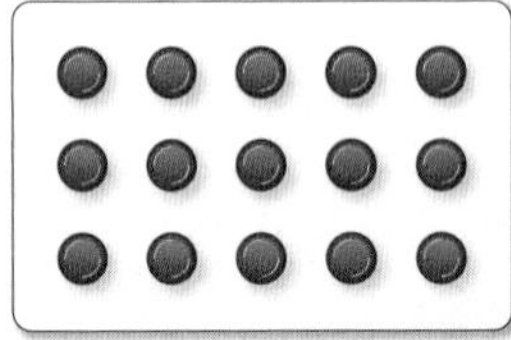

$15 = 3 \cdot 5$

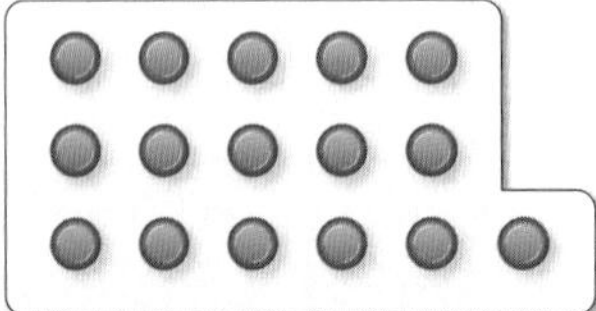

$16 = 3 \cdot 5 + 1$

If n is divisible by d, then n dots can be arranged in a rectangular array with d rows.

QY3

True or False Answer these in your head.

a. $(3 \cdot 2)$ is divisible by 3.
b. $(4 \cdot 3)$ is divisible by 4.
c. 7 is divisible by 3.
d. 32 is divisible by 16.
e. 52 is divisible by 4.
f. 100 is divisible by 3.

Example 1

Is 384,597 divisible by 3?

Solution Divide to determine divisibility.

$384{,}597 \div 3 = 128{,}199$. 384,597 is divisible by 3.

Once you have found one number that is divisible by a number *d*, it is easy to find other numbers that are divisible by *d*. Just add *d* to or subtract *d* from the number. From Example 1, you can add 3 to 384,597 to determine that 384,600; 384,603; 384,606, and so on, are all divisible by 3. You can also subtract 3: 384,594; 384,591; 384,588, and so on, are all divisible by 3.

Activity

MATERIALS calculator

Consider the number 129,550. Complete the following statements.

129,550 (is/is not) divisible by 2 because __?__ ÷ 2 = __?__.

129,550 (is/is not) divisible by 3 because __?__ ÷ __?__ = __?__.

129,550 (is/is not) divisible by 5 because __?__ ÷ __?__ = __?__.

129,550 (is/is not) divisible by 8 because __?__ ÷ __?__ = __?__.

129,550 (is/is not) divisible by 10 because __?__ ÷ __?__ = __?__.

129,550 (is/is not) divisible by 2,590 because __?__ ÷ __?__ = __?__.

129,550 (is/is not) divisible by 2,591 because __?__ ÷ __?__ = __?__.

GUIDED

Example 2

Which numbers of days between 100 and 150 divide evenly into 7-day weeks?

Solution First divide the numbers between 100 and 150 by 7, in order, until you find a multiple.

100 ÷ 7	100 = 7 • 14 + 2
101 ÷ 7	101 = __?__ • __?__ + __?__
102 ÷ 7	102 = __?__ • __?__ + __?__
103 ÷ 7	103 = __?__ • __?__ + __?__
104 ÷ 7	104 = __?__ • __?__ + __?__
105 ÷ 7	105 = __?__ • __?__

Every multiple of 7 is 7 greater than the previous multiple. So the next multiple will be __?__. Continue adding 7 until you reach or go past 150. The multiples of 7 between 100 and 150 are 105, __?__, __?__, __?__, __?__, __?__, and __?__. These numbers of days divide evenly into 7-day weeks.

QY4

Use your answer to Example 2 to find the multiples of 7 between 50 and 100.

Example 3

When n is an integer, is $3n + 2$ ever divisible by 3?

Solution Try some values of n.

When $n = 4$, $3n + 2 = 3 \cdot 4 + 2 = 14$. Is 14 divisible by 3?

When $n = 5$, $3n + 2 = 3 \cdot 5 + 2 = 17$. Is 17 divisible by 3?

When $n = 6$, $3n + 2 = 3 \cdot 6 + 2 = 20$. Is 20 divisible by 3?

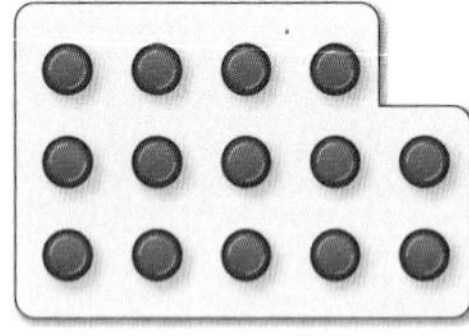

$3 \cdot 4 + 2 = 14$

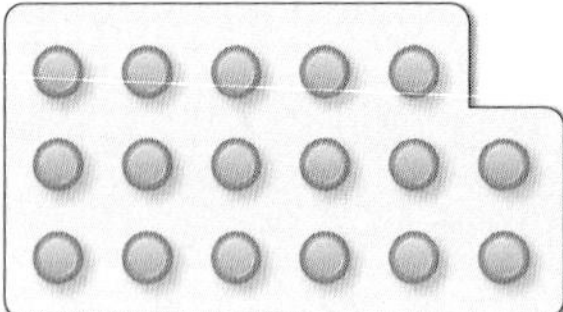

$3 \cdot 5 + 2 = 17$

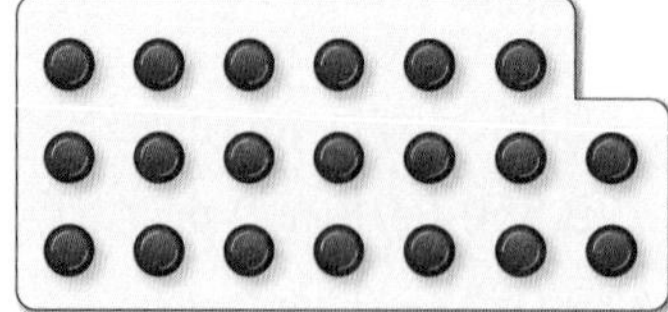

$3 \cdot 6 + 2 = 20$

It seems as if $3n + 2$ is never divisible by 3. A general picture of $3n + 2$ is at the right. The shading is used to indicate missing columns of dots.

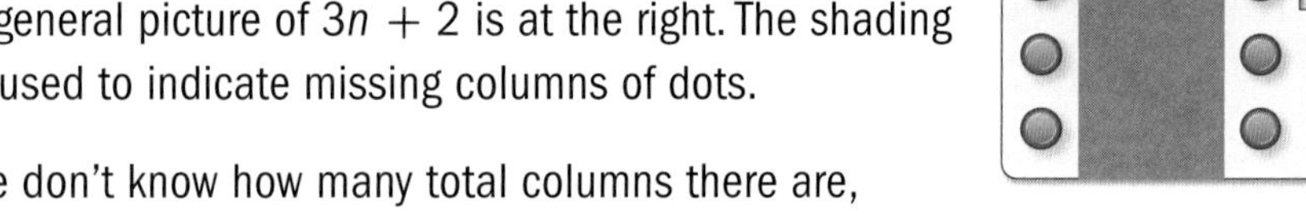

We don't know how many total columns there are, but the last one is always incomplete. $3n + 2$ is never divisible by 3 when n is an integer.

Questions

COVERING THE IDEAS

1. There are 24 students in a class. Brand A pencils come in boxes of eight and Brand B pencils come in boxes of ten. The teacher wants to supply each student with a pencil.
   a. If the teacher buys only Brand A, how many boxes will she have to buy? What if she buys only Brand B?
   b. For which brand will she have extra pencils?
2. What are the four smallest positive multiples of 35?
3. Use an array to show that 20 is a multiple of 4.
4. Use an array to show that 23 is not a multiple of 4.
5. Give two other ways of saying, "11 divides evenly into 121."
6. Give three other ways of saying, "38 is not a factor of 338."

In 7–9, tell whether the statement is true or false.

7. 50 is a factor of 2.
8. 60 is divisible by 8.
9. 7 divides evenly into 63.

10. If an array contains A dots and 5 rows, how many dots per row are there?

11. **Multiple Choice** Without counting, in which drawing is the number of dots divisible by 3?

A 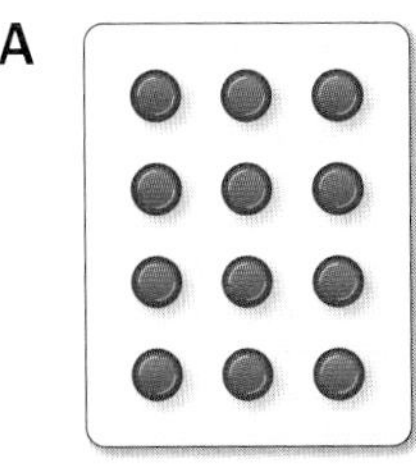 B C 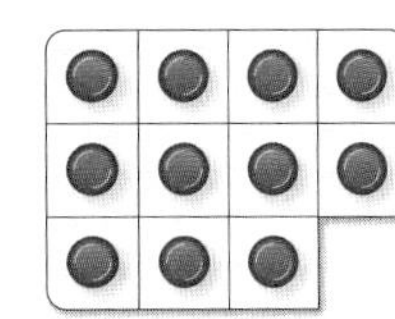

12. Write down the positive whole numbers less than 100 that are divisible by 13.

13. 17,000 is a multiple of 17.
    a. What are the next two greater multiples of 17?
    b. What are the next two lower multiples of 17?

14. Forty-two students are going on a picnic. Hot dogs come in packages of 10 and hot dog buns come in packages of 8. Each student will get one hot dog on a bun.
    a. How many packages of hot dogs are needed? How many extra hot dogs will there be?
    b. How many packages of buns are needed? How many extra buns will there be?

Every year, an American eats on average 60 hot dogs.

Source: whatscookingamerica.net

15. If n is an integer, explain why $4n + 3$ is never divisible by 4.

APPLYING THE MATHEMATICS

16. Use arrays to explain why 1 is a divisor of every positive integer.

17. a. Is 4^3 divisible by 3?
    b. Is 3^4 divisible by 3?

18. My whole number is 4 times your whole number. Is my number a multiple of 2?

19. If a number can be divided evenly by both 2 and 3, what is another divisor of the number?

20. Explain why 0 cannot be a factor of any number other than 0.

REVIEW

21. If six cans of frozen juice cost \$4.56, what is the cost per can? **(Lesson 7-1)**

22. Some experts have predicted that the population of Italy could decrease by an average of about 400,000 people per year from 2007 until 2050. The 2007 population of Italy is about 58,150,000. **(Lesson 6-7)**

 a. If this happens, what would be the total change in Italy's population from 2007 until 2050?

 b. **Multiple Choice** If this happens, what would be the percent of change in Italy's population over that time period?

 A 0.59% B 29.58% C 0.2958% D 59%

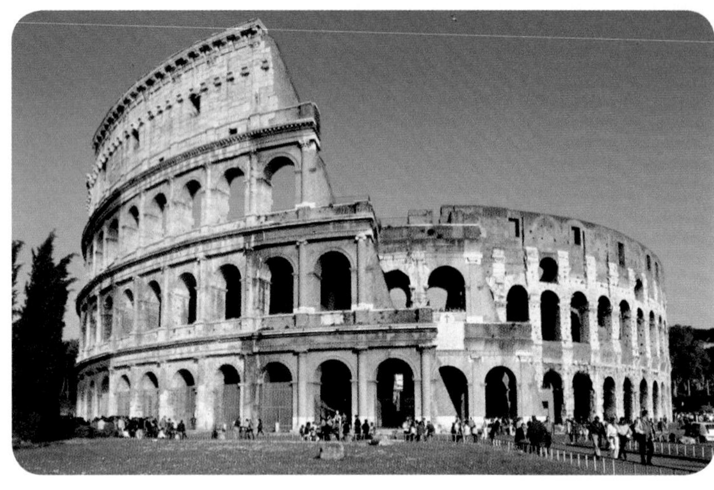

Colosseum, Rome, Italy

23. Kiara and Ashlee were both asked to determine the value of four squared. Kiara wrote $2^4 = 2 \times 2 \times 2 \times 2 = 16$. Ashlee wrote $4^2 = 4 \times 4 = 16$. Their answers are both right, but who just got lucky? **(Lesson 6-4)**

24. Identify the base and exponent in the expression 67^{89}. **(Lesson 6-4)**

25. Find two possible pairs of dimensions for a rectangle with an area of 12 square feet. **(Lesson 6-3)**

26. Find the area of the figure at the right. **(Lesson 6-3)**

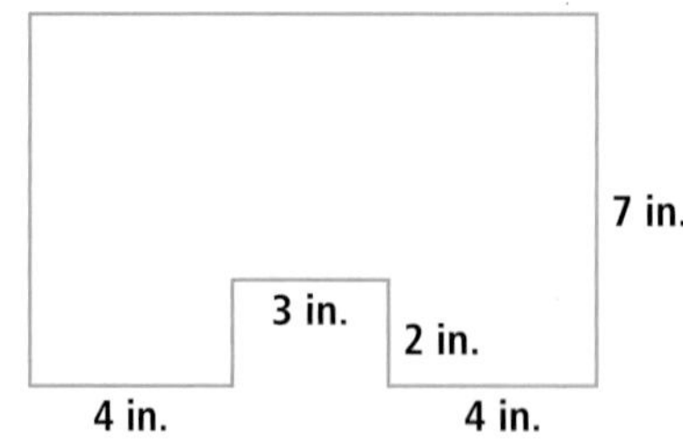

EXPLORATION

27. a. Among any three consecutive integers, is one integer always divisible by 3? Explain your answer using arrays.

 b. Among any three consecutive integers, is one integer always divisible by 4? Explain why or why not.

QY ANSWERS

1. 7 packages

2. 5 packages

3a. true

3b. true

3c. false

3d. true

3e. true

3f. false

4. 98, 91, 84, 77, 70, 63, 56

Lesson 7-3 Using Factorization to Make Division Easier

Vocabulary

prime number
composite number
prime factorization
factor tree

BIG IDEA Finding the prime factorization of a number can make it easier to do some division problems.

Mental Math

Calculate.

a. $360 \div 36 \div 2$

b. $15 \div 5 \times 3$

c. $5 \times 3 \div 15$

d. $100 \div 10 + 10 \div 5$

You can use factorizations of numbers to make it easier to find quotients. Of all factorizations, prime factorizations are the most useful.

Prime Numbers

Recall that a positive integer that has exactly two factors, itself and 1, is called a **prime number.** The smallest prime number is 2. Factors can be thought of as divisors, so a prime number is *divisible* only by itself and 1.

Showing that a number is prime requires showing that it has no factors other than itself and 1. We know 23 is prime because it is not evenly divisible by 2, 3, 4, 5, or any other number between 1 and 23. So one way to show that a number is prime is to do many divisions and show that they do not come out even.

QY1

a. What is the smallest 2-digit prime number? **b.** Why isn't 26 a prime number?

A positive integer that has more than two factors, like 26, is called a **composite number.** The number 1 is neither prime nor composite.

See QY2 at the right.

QY2

Explain why 72 is a composite number.

Every composite number can be written as a product of prime numbers. For example, $26 = 2 \cdot 13$, $8 = 2 \cdot 2 \cdot 2$, and $385 = 5 \cdot 7 \cdot 11$. You can simplify some division problems by writing the dividend and divisor in this way.

Systematically Finding which Numbers are Prime

Eratosthenes was a Greek mathematician who lived from about 276–194 BCE. By looking at the height of the Sun from two different places on Earth on the same day of the year, he correctly estimated that the circumference of Earth was about 25,000 miles. He is also known for the method he used to determine whether numbers are prime. His method filters out composite numbers and, for this reason, is called a *sieve.*

Activity 1

MATERIALS table of integers from 1 to 200

The goal of this activity is to find all the prime numbers less than 200. You may find it helpful to work with a partner.

Step 1 In your table of numbers, cross out 1. It is not prime.

Step 2 Do not cross out 2. It is prime. Starting from 2, cross out every 2nd number. These are the multiples of 2.

Step 3 The next smallest number that has not been crossed out is 3. Do not cross out 3, but, starting from 3, cross out every 3rd number. These are the multiples of 3. (Some of these numbers have already been crossed out.)

Step 4 The next smallest number that has not been crossed out is 5. Do not cross out 5, but, starting from 5, cross out every 5th number. These are the multiples of 5.

Step 5 Continue this process until you come to an uncrossed-out number for which every multiple has already been crossed out. Now answer the following questions.

a. What is the first number you came to for which every multiple was crossed out?

b. How many numbers between 1 and 100 are prime?

c. How many numbers between 100 and 200 are prime?

d. Identify all the prime numbers between 100 and 110.

e. Which columns of your table have no primes? Why don't they have any primes?

f. Which columns of your table have only one prime?

g. What is the longest group of consecutive numbers in the table that are composite numbers?

h. **Fill in the Blanks** Make predictions about the primes from 200 to 300: There will be __?__ primes in all. There will be no primes that end in the digits ___?___.

▸ READING MATH

Many Greek mathematicians were fascinated by prime numbers. The mathematician Euclid, who is known for his geometry book, *The Elements*, proved that there is an infinite number of prime numbers.

Prime Factorizations

Expressing a number as the product of its prime factors is called writing the **prime factorization** of the number. One method of identifying all of the prime factors of a composite number is to use a **factor tree.**

Activity 2

Use a factor tree to find the prime factorization of 232.

Step 1 Write the number to be factored. Underneath the number, write one of its factor pairs. As you work, draw a rectangle around composite numbers and a circle around prime numbers. Connect each number to its factors with segments as shown and include a multiplication symbol between factors.

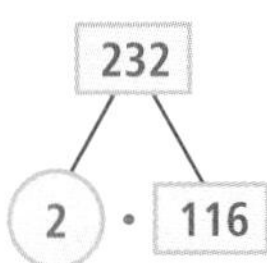

Step 2 Continue the process of Step 1 with any factors that are not prime numbers. If a factor is prime, simply write it again in the next row.

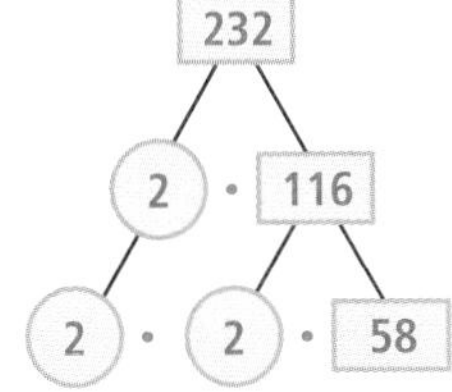

Step 3 When all factors in a row are prime numbers, you are done. The prime factorization of 232 is $2 \cdot 2 \cdot 2 \cdot 29$, as shown at the right.

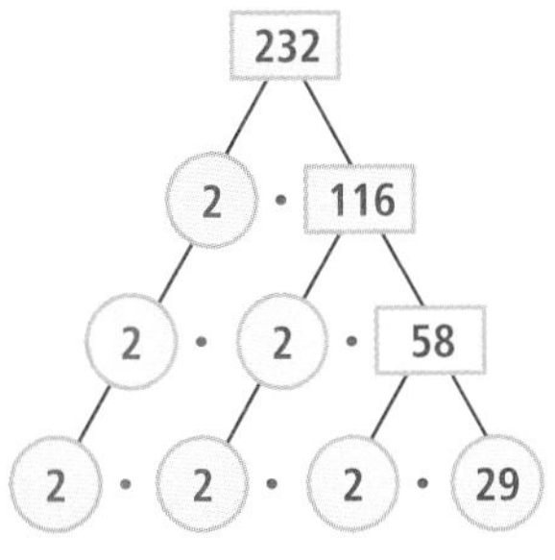

Step 4 Make another factor tree for 232 by starting with a different factor pair.

Step 5 Make factor trees for the following numbers.

a. 66 b. 98 c. 280

The same number may have different factor trees, but the prime factorization in each will be the same, except for the order in which the prime factors appear.

Prime factorizations can help you put fractions into lowest terms.

Example

Write $\frac{864}{81}$ in lowest terms.

Solution

$$\begin{aligned} 864 &= 8 \cdot 108 \\ &= 2 \cdot 4 \cdot 2 \cdot 54 \\ &= 2 \cdot 2 \cdot 2 \cdot 2 \cdot 6 \cdot 9 \\ &= 2 \cdot 2 \cdot 2 \cdot 2 \cdot 2 \cdot 3 \cdot 3 \cdot 3 \end{aligned}$$

$$\begin{aligned} 81 &= 9 \cdot 9 \\ &= 3 \cdot 3 \cdot 3 \cdot 3 \end{aligned}$$

So, $\frac{864}{81} = \frac{2 \cdot 2 \cdot 2 \cdot 2 \cdot 2 \cdot \overset{1}{\cancel{3}} \cdot \overset{1}{\cancel{3}} \cdot \overset{1}{\cancel{3}}}{3 \cdot \underset{1}{\cancel{3}} \cdot \underset{1}{\cancel{3}} \cdot \underset{1}{\cancel{3}}} = \frac{32}{3}$.

Check Use a calculator. $\frac{864}{81} = 10.6666...$ and $\frac{32}{3} = 10.666...$.

Notice in the Example that $\frac{864}{81} = 864 \div 81$. So by looking at this fraction as a division, we see that $\frac{864}{81} = 10\frac{2}{3}$.

Writing Prime Factorizations with Exponents

As you have seen, the prime factorization of a number can include many factors. For example,

$$\begin{aligned}\text{one billion} &= 1{,}000{,}000{,}000\\ &= 10^9\\ &= 10 \cdot 10 \cdot 10 \cdot 10 \cdot 10 \cdot 10 \cdot 10 \cdot 10 \cdot 10\\ &= 2 \cdot 5 \cdot 2 \cdot 5 \cdot 2 \cdot 5 \cdot 2 \cdot 5 \cdot 2 \cdot 5 \cdot 2 \cdot 5 \cdot 2 \cdot 5 \cdot 2 \cdot 5 \cdot 2 \cdot 5\\ &= 2^9 \cdot 5^9\end{aligned}$$

Using exponents makes the prime factorization clearer to read and understand.

QY3

Write the prime factorization of 232 using exponents.

Now you can play *Factor Captor*. You will find the directions on page G23 in the back of the book.

Questions

COVERING THE IDEAS

1. Of the whole numbers 20, 21, 22, 23, 24, 25, 26, 27, 28, 29, and 30, which are prime and which are composite?
2. Explain why 6 is a composite number.
3. What does it mean to say that 101 is a prime number?
4. Is 323,323 prime or composite?
5. James stated that the prime factorization of 900 is $3 \cdot 2 \cdot 3 \cdot 5$. He made the factor tree below to support his statement. Explain why you think James's factor tree is or is not correct.

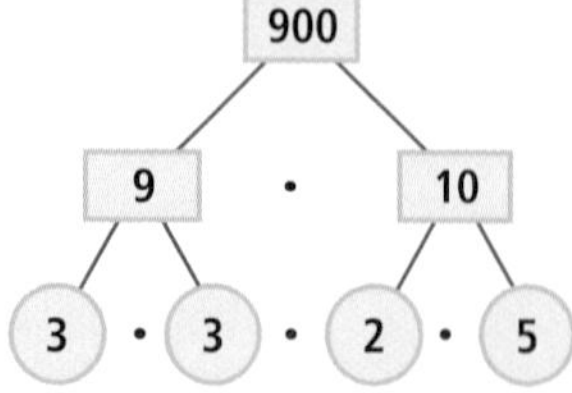

In 6–9, find the prime factorization.

6. 27
7. 318
8. 87
9. 840

Matching In 10–13, match the integer with its prime factorization. Then, write the prime factorization using exponents.

i. $2 \cdot 2 \cdot 3 \cdot 3 \cdot 7$ ii. $3 \cdot 5 \cdot 11 \cdot 11$

iii. $2 \cdot 13 \cdot 13 \cdot 13 \cdot 17$ iv. $3 \cdot 3 \cdot 3 \cdot 3 \cdot 2 \cdot 5 \cdot 2 \cdot 5$

10. 1,815 11. 74,698 12. 252 13. 8,100

In 14–19, find the prime factorizations of the divisor and dividend. Then write the quotient in lowest terms.

14. $243 \div 9$ 15. $\frac{3240}{16}$ 16. $\frac{287}{77}$

17. $15 \div 415$ 18. $5{,}454 \div 60$ 19. $\frac{236}{244}$

APPLYING THE MATHEMATICS

20. The nine members of a baseball team went out to eat. The bill came to $107.53. How much does each team member owe if they split the bill evenly?

21. **True or False** 139 is a prime number. Explain how you know.

22. The prime factorization of 1,001 is $7 \cdot 11 \cdot 13$. Use this information to rewrite the fraction $\frac{182}{1001}$ in lowest terms.

23. a. What is the smallest number that is the product of 7 prime numbers, allowing for a prime to be repeated as many times as you wish?
    b. What is the smallest number that is the product of 7 different prime numbers?

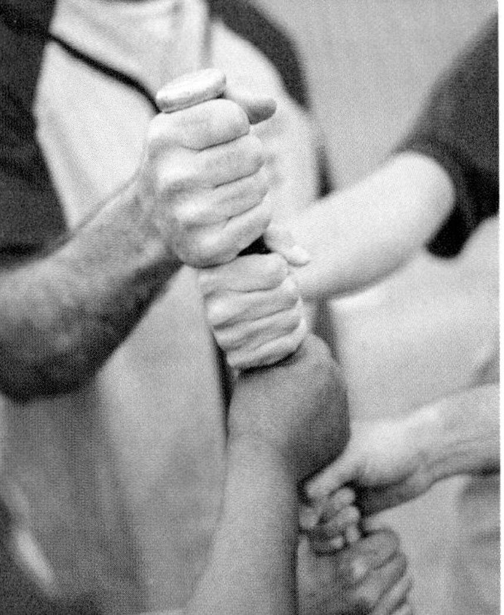

The first professional baseball league was formed in 1876 with 8 teams playing a 70-game schedule.

Source: www.baseball-almanac.com

REVIEW

24. There are 50 stars on the flag of the United States.
    a. Can these stars be evenly arranged in rows of 8?
    b. Can they be evenly arranged in rows of 10? **(Lesson 7-1)**

25. **Multiple Choice** Which statement is described by the array below? **(Lesson 7-1)**

A 7 is not divisible by 18. B 18 is not divisible by 3.

C 18 is not divisible by 7. D 7 is not divisible by 3.

26. In 1974, inside the tomb of the first emperor of the Qin Dynasty near Xian, China, local farmers discovered the first of over 8,000 life-sized terracotta figures of soldiers, chariots, and horses. Some of the soldiers are marching in an array 4 soldiers across and 38 rows deep. How many of the soldiers are in this array? **(Lesson 6-1)**

Terracotta statues in Qin Shi Huangdi Tomb

27. $\angle A$ and $\angle B$ are supplementary angles. $\angle A$ and $\angle C$ are complementary angles. If $m\angle C = 57°$, find $m\angle A$ and $m\angle B$. **(Lessons 4-6, 4-5)**

28. Write the related facts that correspond to the fact triangle shown below. **(Lesson 4-4)**

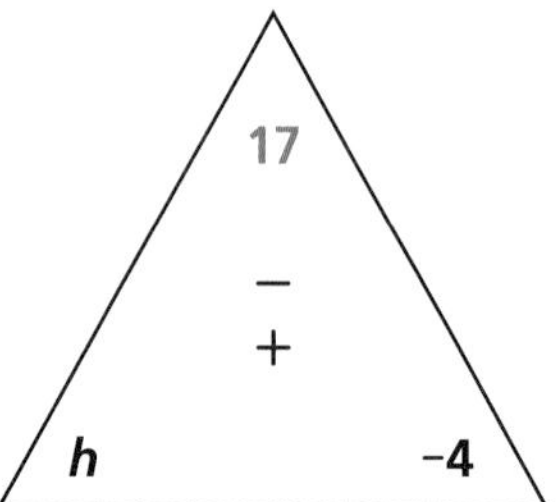

EXPLORATION

29. Use the Internet to find the largest known prime number. Write the number using exponents. In base 10, how many digits does the number have?

QY ANSWERS

1a. 11

1b. 26 is not prime because it is evenly divisible by 2 and 13.

2. 72 is evenly divisible by 8 and 9, as well as several other numbers.

3. $2^3 \cdot 29$

Lesson 7-4 Integer Division

Vocabulary

integer division

BIG IDEA In some situations, the answer to a division problem is a quotient together with a remainder of how many are left over.

Mental Math

Four friends are dividing 50 DVDs evenly.

a. How many DVDs does each person get?

b. How many extra DVDs are there?

c. If five friends, instead of four, divide the DVDs, how many does each person get?

d. How many extra DVDs will there be?

Mrs. Jackson's 6 grandchildren are coming to visit her in Florida. Mrs. Jackson is buying juice boxes to take to the beach. They come in packages of 8. She would like to have the same number of boxes for each grandchild with no extra boxes.

If Mrs. Jackson purchases one package, there will be 8 boxes. Each grandchild will get 1 box and there will be 2 left over.

$$8 = 6 \cdot 1 + 2 \quad \text{or} \quad 8 \div 6 = 1 \text{ R2}$$

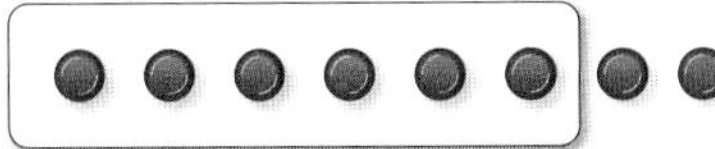

The equation $8 \div 6 = 1$ R2 is read: "8 divided by 6 equals 1 with remainder 2." If Mrs. Jackson buys 2 packages, she will have 16 boxes. Each grandchild will get 2, and there will be 4 left over.

$$16 = 6 \cdot 2 + 4 \quad \text{or} \quad 16 \div 6 = 2 \text{ R4}.$$

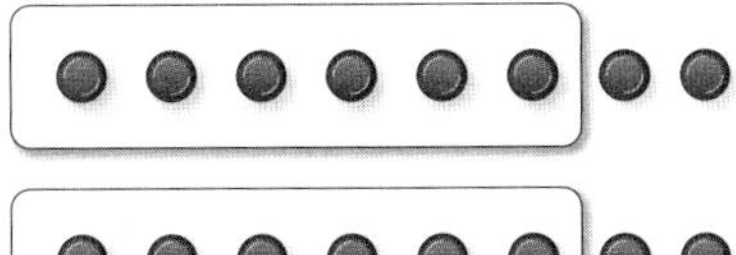

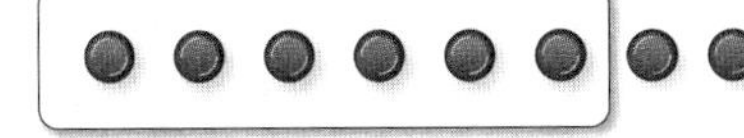

STOP QY1

a. Fill in the blanks if Mrs. Jackson purchases three packages.

___?___ ÷ 6 = ___?___ R ___?___

(number of juice boxes) ÷ 6 = (juice boxes per child) R ?

b. Use the array below to show dividing three packages among the 6 grandchildren.

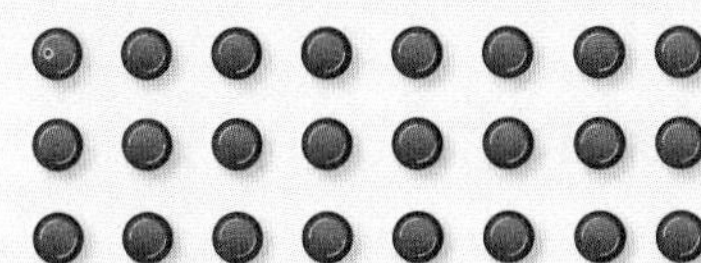

What Is Integer Division?

The juice-box situation involves **integer division** because the numbers in the problem and in the answer are integers. We use the capital letter R to indicate the remainder. For example $36 \div 7 = 5$ R1. In general, dividend ÷ divisor = quotient R remainder. This can also be written as:

$$\text{divisor}\overline{)\text{dividend}}^{\text{quotient R remainder}} \quad \text{or} \quad 7\overline{)36}^{\text{5 R1}}$$

Given $36 \div 7 = 5$ R1, you can also write $36 = 7 \cdot 5 + 1$. This last equation shows how the divisor, dividend, quotient, and remainder are related using multiplication and addition. This is called the *Quotient-Remainder Formula*.

Quotient-Remainder Formula

Let d = divisor, n = dividend, q = integer quotient, and r = remainder.

Then, when $n \div d = q$ Rr, it is also the case that $n = d \cdot q + r$.

When you do integer division in this book, you will either see the ÷ sign or the $\overline{)\quad}$ symbol.

Activity

MATERIALS calculator

Use the Quotient-Remainder Formula to complete this table. Work with a partner or group if needed.

Integer Division Problem	Integer Division Answer	Quotient-Remainder Formula
$100 \div 15$	6 R10	$100 = 15 \cdot 6 + 10$
$83 \div$?	? R ?	$83 = 12 \cdot 6 + 11$
$10\overline{)93}$	9 R ?	? = ? • ? + ?
? ÷ ?	4 R8	56 = ? • ? + ?
? ÷ ?	? R ?	? $= 7 \cdot 5 + 2$
$29 \div$?	3 R5	? = ? • ? + ?
? $\overline{)}$?	13 R2	? $= 11 \cdot 13 +$?

Using Repeated Subtraction to Obtain the Quotient

Just as multiplication of integers can be thought of as repeated addition, answers to an integer division can be calculated using repeated subtraction.

GUIDED

Example 1

Kayla is putting stickers into bags as gifts for 8 friends coming to her Valentine's Day Party. She has 101 stickers. How many stickers can Kayla put in each bag so all her friends get the same number of stickers?

Solution Think of dividing a pile of 101 stickers among 8 people. This is integer division where the number of stickers each person gets is the quotient and the number of stickers left over is the remainder. Use repeated subtraction. Each time a sticker is put into each of the 8 bags, subtract 8 from the remaining stickers and add 1 to the quotient.

```
 101
 - 8
 ---
  93   The quotient is 1.
 - ?
 ---
   ?   The quotient is _?_.
```

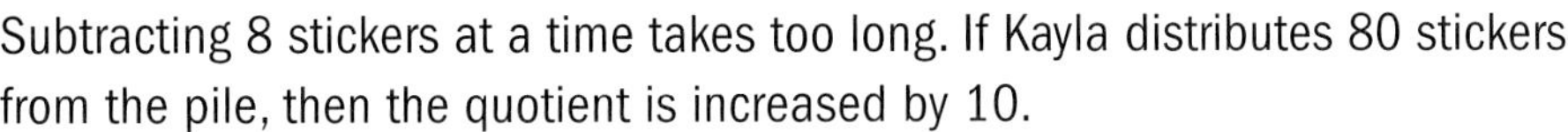

Subtracting 8 stickers at a time takes too long. If Kayla distributes 80 stickers from the pile, then the quotient is increased by 10.

```
  85
- 80
----
   ?   The quotient is _?_.
```

Because 5 is less than 8, Kayla is finished distributing the stickers. Kayla can put _?_ stickers in each bag, and she'll have _?_ stickers left over.

Stickers are popular gifts at children's parties.

You can use the answer to an integer division problem to obtain the answers to other integer division problems.

Example 2

What is $102 \div 8$?

Solution From Example 1, $101 \div 8 = 12$ R5. Think: If you add one sticker, you will have one more left over. Thus, by adding 1 to the dividend, you add 1 to the remainder. So, $102 \div 8 = 12$ R6.

Check $12 \cdot 8 + 6 = 102$

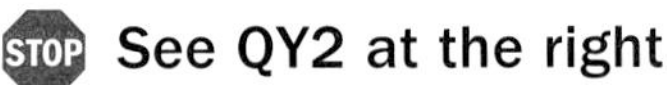

See QY2 at the right.

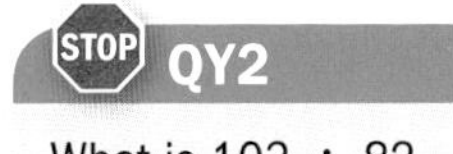

QY2

What is $103 \div 8$?

Using a Calculator for Integer Division

Some calculators have an INT÷ key. INT stands for integer and gives the answer in quotient-remainder form instead of as a decimal. See if your calculator does integer division. If it does, experiment to find the key sequence for calculating integer division.

QY3

Use the INT÷ or similar key to find the following quotients.

a. $104 \div 6$ b. $63\overline{)2{,}016}$

Questions

COVERING THE IDEAS

1. Mr. Jackson is freezing lemonade ice cubes for his 6 grandchildren and one of their friends. His ice cube trays will each freeze 12 cubes at a time. How many cubes will each of the 7 children get and how many will remain if
   a. he uses 1 ice cube tray?
   b. he uses 2 ice cube trays?
   c. he uses 5 ice cube trays?
   d. he uses 14 ice cube trays?

Ice cubes melt more slowly than crushed ice.

2. a. Find the integer quotient and remainder to $46 \div 13$ by using repeated subtraction.
   b. Use your answer to Part a to find $47 \div 13$.

In 3 and 4, perform the integer division without a calculator.

3. $100 \div 7$
4. $91 \div 6$

In 5 and 6, use paper and pencil or the INT÷ key on a calculator to perform the integer division.

5. $61 \div 4$
6. $186 \div 23$

7. Five people are enjoying a picnic. They have 11 nectarines to share.
   a. How many whole nectarines can each person have? How many will be left?
   b. There is a knife and cutting board to divide the 11 nectarines evenly. Exactly how many nectarines does each person get?
   c. Express the answer to Part b as a rate.

APPLYING THE MATHEMATICS

8. $1{,}200 \div 19 = 63$ R3. From this information, find $1{,}202 \div 19$.

9. Use the fact that $476 \div 65 = 7$ R21 to find
   a. $477 \div 65$. b. $480 \div 65$. c. $550 \div 65$.

10. A board is 179 inches long. How long is this in feet and inches?

11. Do the integer division $5^3 \div 2^3$.

12. Mrs. Campos asked her class to help her with the following problem: She has printed 80 special envelopes for 14 people who are raising money for a charity. She wants each helper to get the same number of envelopes.

    a. Eric and Jacquelyn both divided 80 by 14. Eric said, "Each helper gets 5 envelopes and there are some left over." Jacquelyn said, "My answer is closer to 6, so the helpers should get 6 envelopes each." Which student is correct? Why?

    b. After the envelopes are distributed, how many are left over?

In 13 and 14, there are 288 students at Fiddle Middle School.

13. The principal wants to divide the students into 20 homerooms.

    a. Describe a set of 20 class sizes that will distribute the students as evenly as possible.

    b. When given this problem, Sara responded "Each homeroom should have 14 remainder 8 students." Is this a reasonable solution? Explain why or why not.

14. The students will be divided into teams of 14 children each for a soccer tournament.

    a. How many soccer teams can be made?

    b. How many students will be left over?

15. A college has 1,634 graduates who are going to get framed diplomas. Frames must be ordered in boxes of 48 frames each.

    a. How many boxes are needed?

    b. How many frames will be unused?

During the 2002–2003 academic year, women earned 60 percent of all Associate's Degrees, 58 percent of all Bachelor's Degrees, and 59 percent of all Master's Degrees.

Source: National Center for Education Statistics

16. Binder clips come in packs of 10 for \$1.00. Economy size packages of 24 cost \$2.00. There are 141 students who each need exactly one binder clip.

    a. What is the cheapest way to purchase 141 binder clips?

    b. How many clips will be left over?

    c. Find the total cost.

17. If $772 \div x = 17$ R7, what is x?

REVIEW

18. Find the prime factorization of 2,100. **(Lesson 7-3)**

19. There are four tellers at Equality Bank available to help customers, and a crowd of 17 people waiting to enter the bank. If the customers line up as evenly as possible in four lines, how many people will the longest line have? **(Lesson 7-2)**

20. One-half divided by one-fourth equals two. Identify the dividend, the divisor, and the quotient. **(Lesson 7-2)**

21. Is there a commutative property for division? Use an example to justify your answer. **(Lessons 7-2, 5-1)**

22. Draw a fact triangle for the equation $\frac{0.72}{0.4} = 1.8$. **(Lesson 7-1)**

23. At the local farmers' market, Casey bought 4.5 pounds of peaches for \$6.75. What was the price per pound? **(Lesson 7-1)**

One peach contains 87% water.

Source: Georgia Department of Agriculture

24. Antonio bought 4 pounds of turkey to make sandwiches for a picnic. The turkey cost \$4.25 per pound.
    a. How much did he pay in all? **(Lesson 6-5)**
    b. If there is a 4% sales tax, how much tax did he pay? **(Lesson 6-6)**

25. Your friend claims that a given rectangular poster has an area of 553 square inches. The poster has dimensions 36 inches by 15 inches. **(Lesson 6-3)**
    a. How can you determine that 553 square inches is an incorrect area without performing any calculations?
    b. Find the correct area of the poster.

26. A number n is less than 40 and has 2 and 7 as factors. Its digits add to 10. What is n? **(Lesson 6-2)**

EXPLORATION

27. What is the smallest number that satisfies all of the following:
    - When divided by 5, it leaves a remainder of 2.
    - When divided by 6, it leaves a remainder of 3.
    - When divided by 7, it leaves a remainder of 4.
    - When divided by 8, it leaves a remainder of 5.
    - When divided by 9, it leaves a remainder of 6.

QY ANSWERS

1a. $24 \div 6 = 4$ R0

1b.

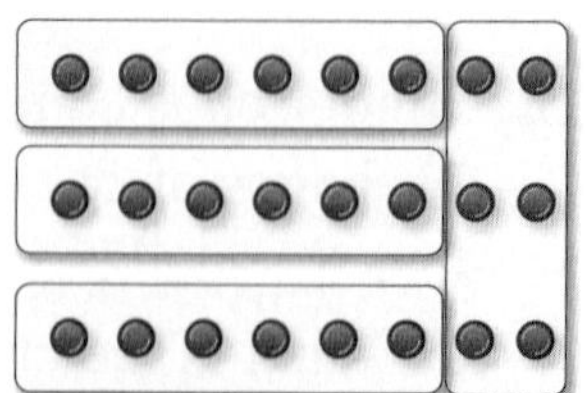

2. 12 R7

3a. 17 R2

3b. 32 R0

Lesson 7-5 Short Division

▶ **BIG IDEA** Short division is a process for determining the quotient when a small whole number is the divisor.

Marquis wanted to know how many yards are in a mile. He remembered that there are 5,280 feet in a mile. He knew there are 3 feet in a yard. So he had to divide 5,280 by 3 to find the answer.

When the divisor is a single digit, you can use a process called *short division* to determine quotients and remainders in integer division. Here is how the process works on the division problem 5,280 ÷ 3. In the QY and steps below, q stands for quotient and r for remainder.

 **See QY at the right.**

Mental Math

Multiple Choice Suppose a secret number x is multiplied by 3. The result is another secret number y. What can you do to y to get back to x?

A Divide y by 3.

B Subtract 3 from y.

C Subtract y from 3.

D Divide 3 by y.

 **QY**

If $15 = 2 \cdot 6 + 3$, find the q and r for $15 \div 6$.

The Steps in Short Division

Step 1 Set up the division problem as $\text{divisor}\overline{)\text{dividend}}$ with the quotient above.

Substitute for the divisor and dividend. Leave room for the quotient at the top.

$3\overline{)5280}$

Step 2 Ask yourself: What are the q and r when 5 (the left digit) is divided by 3? The answers are $q = 1$, $r = 2$.

Write "1" above the 5 and write a small 2 in front of the 2 in 5280. Note that this 2 looks like an exponent but is not an exponent.

$$\begin{array}{r} 1 \\ 3\overline{)5^{2}280} \end{array}$$

The 1 in the quotient stands for 1000. In this step you have subtracted 1000 times 3 from 5280 and are now left with 2280.

Step 3 Move to the next digit, remembering that you still have the small 2. Ask yourself: What are the q and r when 22 is divided by 3? The answer is $q = 7$, $r = 1$. Write "7" above the 2. Write a small 1 to the left of the 8.

$$\begin{array}{r} 1\;7 \\ 3\overline{)5^{2}2^{1}80} \end{array}$$

The 17 in the quotient stands for 1700. You have now subtracted 1700 times 3 from 5280 and are left with 180.

Step 4 Move to the next digit, 8, remembering that you still have the small 1. Ask yourself: What are the q and r when 18 is divided by 3? The answer is $q = 6$, $r = 0$. Write "6" above the 8. Since r is 0, you don't need to write a small number next to the 0 in 5280.

$$\begin{array}{r} 1\ 7\ 6\ \ \\ 3\overline{)5^22^180} \end{array}$$

You have now subtracted 1,760 times 3 from 5280 and are left with 0. The written work does not show this, so there is one more step.

Step 5 Move to the final digit, 0. Ask yourself: What are the q and r when 0 is divided by 3? The answer is $q = 0$, $r = 0$. So put 0 in the quotient above the 0.

$$\begin{array}{r} 1760 \\ 3\overline{)5^22^180} \end{array}$$

The short division shows that $5{,}280 \div 3 = 1{,}760$, so there are 1,760 yards in one mile.

Check by multiplication: $1{,}760 \cdot 3 = 5280$.

Here is an example of short division with a remainder at the end.

Example 1

Suppose 1,000 balloons are to be divided evenly among seven classrooms. How many will each classroom receive?

One of the very first types of balloons were made from animal bladders and intestines.

Source: www.balloonhq.com

Solution The problem is $1{,}000 \div 7$ or $7\overline{)1000}$.

Step 1 Ask yourself: What are the q and r when 10 is divided by 7? The answer is $q = 1$, $r = 3$. Write the q above the 10, and remember the r.

$$\begin{array}{r} 1\ \ \ \ \\ 7\overline{)10^300} \end{array}$$

Step 2 Ask yourself: What are the q and r when 30 is divided by 7? The answer is $q = 4$, $r = 2$. Write the q above the 0 of 30, and remember the r.

$$\begin{array}{r} 14\ \ \\ 7\overline{)10^30^20} \end{array}$$

Step 3 Ask yourself: What are the q and r when 20 is divided by 7? Here $q = 2$ and $r = 6$. Write the q above the 0 of 20, and remember the r.

$$\begin{array}{r} 142 \\ 7\overline{)10^30^20^6} \end{array}$$

Step 4 The 6 is the final remainder. So $1{,}000 \div 7 = 142$ R6.
Each classroom receives 142 balloons and there will be 6 left over.

Check $7 \cdot 142 + 6 = 994 + 6 = 1{,}000$; It checks.

GUIDED

Example 2

Find the quotient and remainder for 9,354 ÷ 8.

Solution

Step 1 Write the problem as $8\overline{)9354}$.

Step 2 Ask how many 8s are in 9. Find the *quotient* and *remainder*. Fill in the numbers shown at the right.

$$\begin{array}{r} ? \\ 8\overline{)9^{?}354} \end{array}$$

Step 3

$$\begin{array}{r} ?\ ? \\ 8\overline{)9^{?}3^{?}54} \end{array}$$

Step 4

$$\begin{array}{r} ?\ ?\ ? \\ 8\overline{)9^{?}3^{?}5^{?}4} \end{array}$$

Step 5

$$\begin{array}{r} ?\ ?\ ?\ ? \\ 8\overline{)9^{?}3^{?}5^{?}4^{?}} \end{array}$$

Step 6 The quotient is _?_ and the remainder is _?_.

Check Multiply the quotient by the divisor and add the remainder. You should get the dividend.

Does _?_ • _?_ + _?_ = _?_?

Questions

COVERING THE IDEAS

In 1–3, do short division to find the quotient. Show your work.

1. 3,186 ÷ 9
2. 12,472 ÷ 8
3. A profit of $6,512 is to be divided equally among four owners of a construction company. How much does each receive?

In 4–6, do short division to find the quotient and remainder. Show your work.

4. 214 ÷ 9
5. 8,182 ÷ 7
6. 127 students are being divided into teams of 8 students each. How many teams are there?

APPLYING THE MATHEMATICS

7. Eight parents are stuffing 5,457 envelopes with the district schedule for the next school year. How would you divide the envelopes as evenly as possible among the eight parents?

In 8–11, use short division to help in answering the question. Show your work.

8. How many weeks and days are in a leap year?
9. How many minutes and seconds are in 2,120 seconds?

10. An army platoon has 30 members. How many platoons can 1,000 soldiers fill?

11. In January 2000, nine people shared a 30,500,000 pound lottery prize in the United Kingdom's National Lottery. How much was each winner's share?

REVIEW

12. *J* is a number between 25 and 50. When *J* is divided by 13, it has a remainder of 11. What is *J*? **(Lesson 7-4)**

13. Use repeated subtraction to perform integer division of 24 by 7. Show your work. **(Lesson 7-4)**

14. Dog biscuits come 25 in a box. Hoshi gives each of her two basset hounds three biscuits a day. How many whole days worth of biscuits are in a box? How many biscuits remain after that many days? **(Lesson 7-4)**

The basset hound thrived for centuries in Europe and was primarily used to hunt rabbits, hare, and deer.

Source: American Kennel Club

15. 2 and 3 are consecutive prime numbers. Explain why there are no other consecutive prime numbers. **(Lesson 7-3)**

16. In the equation $24 \div 12 = 2$, identify the quotient, divisor, and dividend. **(Lesson 7-2)**

17. Draw a fact triangle and find the related facts for the equation $10 \div 4 = 2.5$. **(Lesson 7-1)**

In 18–20, identify the property or rule that the equation demonstrates. (Lessons 6-3, 6-2, 6-1)

18. $6 \cdot 4 = 4 \cdot 6$ 19. $\frac{3}{2} \cdot \frac{4}{5} = \frac{3 \cdot 4}{2 \cdot 5}$ 20. $-4 \cdot 3 = -(4 \cdot 3)$

21. Alfalfa, an African elephant, eats $\frac{2}{7}$ of his weight in one week. If he weighs 14,000 pounds, about how much food does he eat on average
    a. in one week?
    b. in one day?
    c. in one hour? **(Lesson 6-2)**

EXPLORATION

22. How many days, hours, minutes, and seconds are in one million seconds?

23. Some people do short division with two-digit divisors when multiples of those divisors are easy to calculate. Try short division on these division problems.
    a. $20\overline{)4{,}315}$ b. $50\overline{)26{,}143}$ c. $11\overline{)81{,}422}$

QY ANSWER

q is 2 and *r* is 3.

Lesson 7-6 Flexibility Using Division

Vocabulary

rational number division

BIG IDEA Depending on the situation, the answer to a division problem may be written as an integer, decimal, mixed number, or quotient with a remainder.

Example 1 in Lesson 7-5 uses the division problem 1,000 ÷ 7. Here are two other questions that lead to this same division problem:

Question A: How many weeks are in 1000 days?

Question B: If a small plane traveled 1000 miles in 7 hours, what was its average speed?

You have seen three methods of division.

Method 1: Short division: $7\overline{)10^{3}0^{2}0^{6}}$ with quotient 1 4 2

Method 2: Integer division on a calculator:

1000 [INT÷] 7 [ENTER].

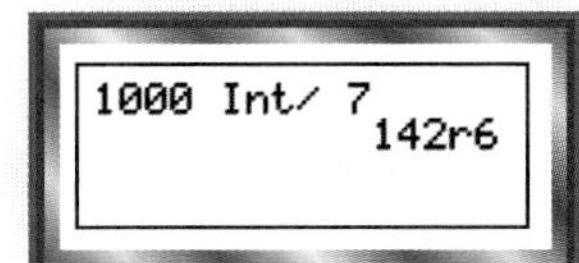

Method 3: Decimal division on a calculator:

1000 [÷] 7 [ENTER].

1000/7
142.8571429

You can use either the first or second method to answer Question A: 142 weeks with 6 days left over. To answer Question B, you would use the third method because 6 miles left over is not meaningful when the answer is in miles per hour. The plane averaged about 142.86 miles per hour.

Mental Math

In intergalactic money, 8 yarbs equal 3 narbs.

a. How many narbs are in 1 yarb?

b. How many yarbs are in 1 narb?

c. Which is more valuable, 1 yarb or 1 narb?

Turning Remainders into Fractions

In the short division of 1000 ÷ 7, the small 6 at the right remains to be divided by 7. Since $6 \div 7 = \frac{6}{7}$, the quotient is $142\frac{6}{7}$. Notice what has happened. The remainder in the integer division was changed to a fraction. This changes the quotient to a mixed number. The exact answer to Question B above can also be written as $142\frac{6}{7}$ miles per hour.

You are using **rational number division** when you express the remainder in a division problem as a fraction or a decimal. Notice the difference between integer division and rational number division.

integer division of 1,000 ÷ 7: quotient 142, remainder 6
rational number division of 1,000 ÷ 7: quotient $142\frac{6}{7}$ or 142.8571...

To change integer division to rational number division, the whole number part of the quotient is the same. The fraction part of the mixed number is the remainder divided by the divisor.

QY

In integer division, 6,528 ÷ 23 = 283 R19. What is the quotient in rational number division?

Example 1

The 8 members of a club have collected 573 cans in a charity food drive. What is the mean number of cans each member collected?

Solution Divide 573 by 8. Short division shows that the quotient is 71 and the remainder is 5. This means each person, on average, collected $71\frac{5}{8}$ cans.

$$8\overline{)57^{1}3^{5}} \quad \text{quotient } 71$$

Many food drives take place in the fall to help stock foodbanks for the winter months.

Turning Remainders into Decimals

One way to find the decimal equal to $71\frac{5}{8}$ is to recall that the decimal for $\frac{5}{8}$ is 0.625. So $71\frac{5}{8} = 71.625$. A second way is to use a calculator. The key sequence 573 [÷] 8 [ENTER] gives the answer 71.625. A third way is to do short division, adding zeros after a decimal point, as shown at the right.

$$8\overline{)57^{1}3^{5}.0^{2}0^{4}0} \quad \text{quotient } 71.625$$

Activity 1

Work with a partner. Fill in the chart for the three different forms for the answer to a division problem.

Problem	Integer-Division Answer	Mixed-Number Answer	Decimal Answer
1,000 ÷ 7	142 R6	$142\frac{6}{7}$	142.857142...
65 ÷ 4	? R ?	?	?
? ÷ 3	? R ?	$15\frac{2}{3}$	?
113 ÷ ?	? R ?	?	22.6
? ÷ 6	51 R3	?	?

GUIDED

Example 2

Three people want to share a $29.57 bill evenly. How much should each person pay?

Solution 1 Use short division. $? \overline{)29^?.5^?7^?}$ with quotient ? .? ?

The answer means that if each person pays $_?_, the group will still owe $_?_.

Solution 2 Use a calculator. A key sequence is _?_ _?_ _?_ [ENTER].

The display is _?_. This means that if each person pays $_?_, there will be $_?_ left over.

Both solutions to Example 2 require you to interpret the answer to the division problem to answer the question.

Questions

COVERING THE IDEAS

1. How do the quotients in integer division differ from quotients in rational number division?

For each situation in 2–4, tell which of the three division methods you would use.

2. Ten friends are dividing up 15 bottles of iced tea. How many bottles will each get?
3. 42 stickers are being divided among 4 friends. How many should each get?
4. Three siblings have been asked to take turns babysitting their cousin for a total of 4 hours. How long should each turn be?

5. $100 \div 14 = 7$ R2; What is the quotient $100 \div 14$ in rational number division?

In 6 and 7, tell whether the question is better answered by integer division or by rational number division. Then answer the question.

6. a. A box holds 8 books. How many boxes are needed for 100 books?
   b. An artist can decorate 8 eggs in an hour. How much time is needed to decorate 100 eggs?

Every spring, each state sends a decorated egg representing their state to the White House to put on display.

Source: www.whitehouse.gov

7. a. Twenty-five sheets of paper are split among four students. How many sheets does each student get?
   b. A ribbon 25 feet long is cut into 4 equal pieces. How long is each piece?

In 8–10, do not use a calculator. Give the results of the division
   a. with a remainder.
   b. with the quotient as a mixed number.
   c. with the quotient as a decimal.

8. $50 \div 4$ 9. $1{,}783 \div 5$ 10. $12{,}016 \div 10$

In 11–14, a fraction is given.
   a. Convert the fraction to a mixed number.
   b. Convert the fraction to a decimal.

11. $\frac{701}{2}$ 12. $\frac{65}{8}$ 13. $\frac{5{,}104}{11}$ 14. $\frac{5}{6}$

15. A neighbor gives you and two friends \$25 for cleaning some rooms. How much should each person receive?

16. A bill for \$42.96 is to be split evenly among 6 people. What will each person pay?

APPLYING THE MATHEMATICS

17. In Question 15, suppose you worked twice as long as each of your friends. If you receive twice as much money as each of your friends, how much will you receive?

18. A 4-person 400-meter relay team wishes to run the race in under 50.5 seconds. On average, what time will each person have to run?

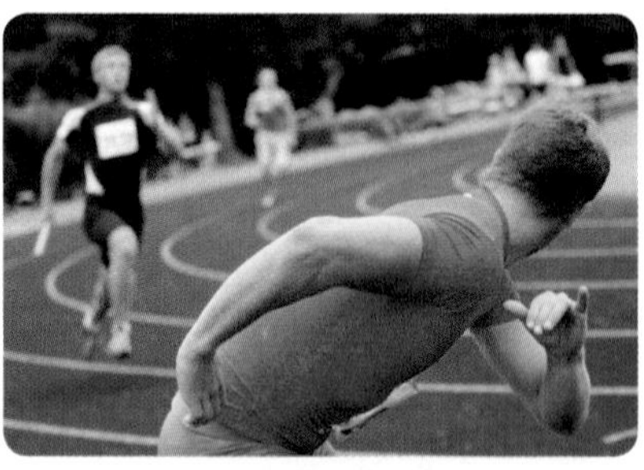

The men's Olympic record for the four-person 400-meter is 37.40 seconds by the United States in the 1992 Olympics.

Source: *The World Almanac*

19. Eight friends order 3 foot-long sandwiches that cost \$8.95 each. Is it possible for each person to pay exactly the same amount of money? How much should each pay?

20. A rectangle has an area of 42.6 square centimeters. It is 3 inches wide. What is its length?

21. A deep-dish pizza has about 2,270 calories. A 12-year-old boy uses about 250 calories per hour walking. Answer one of these questions with a calculator and one without. Give your answer in what you think is the most sensible form: with a remainder, as a mixed number, or as a decimal.
   a. How long would the boy have to walk to burn the calories in the whole pizza?
   b. Four friends ate equal portions of the deep-dish pizza. How many calories did each friend consume?

REVIEW

In 22–24, perform short division to find the quotient and the remainder. (Lesson 7-5)

22. $1{,}234 \div 4$ **23.** $1{,}357 \div 9$ **24.** $4^5 \div 2^3$

25. How many square yards are in a house with area 2431 square feet? (*Hint:* How many square feet are in 1 square yard?) **(Lesson 7-2)**

26. Lauren is dividing walnuts into packages of 35. If she has 200 walnuts, how many packages will she make, and how many walnuts will be left over? **(Lesson 7-2)**

27. $g \cdot -8 = -23.88$. Is g positive or negative? **(Lesson 6-10)**

28. Find the area of the large rectangle below. **(Lesson 6-7)**

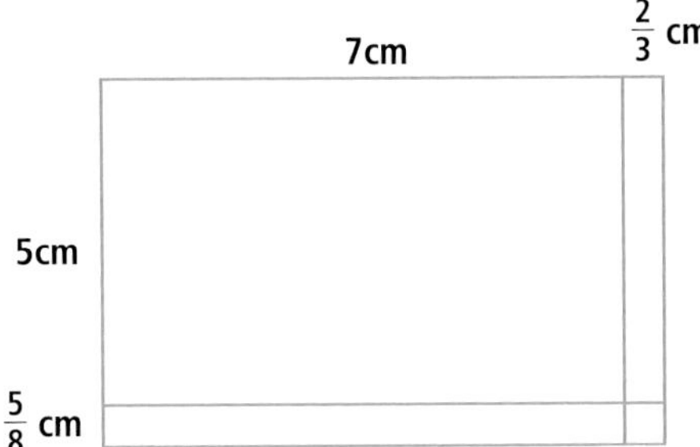

29. A planning committee is trying to decide how many pizzas to buy for a school-wide party. They assume that only $\frac{2}{3}$ of the school's 300 students will attend and on average each will consume 1.5 slices of pizza. **(Lessons 6-5, 6-2, 6-1)**

a. About how many slices of pizza will be consumed?

b. If each pizza has 8 slices, how many pizzas do they need to buy?

30. a. Evaluate $\left(\frac{1}{2}\right)^2$.

b. Evaluate $\left(\frac{1}{2}\right)^5$.

c. Fill in the Blank Compare using < or >: $\left(\frac{1}{2}\right)^5$ _?_ $\left(\frac{1}{2}\right)^2$

(Lessons 6-4, 6-2, 2-10)

EXPLORATION

31. If M, A, and D stand for different digits in short division, what could they be?

$$M\overline{)A\ D^A\ D^A}\quad \text{quotient: } A\ A$$

QY ANSWER

$283\frac{19}{23}$

Lesson 7-7 Deciding whether a Decimal Terminates or Repeats

Vocabulary

unit fraction

BIG IDEA When a fraction is in lowest terms, the denominator determines whether its decimal will terminate or repeat forever.

In the previous lesson, you saw that $\frac{573}{8} = 573 \div 8 = 71\frac{5}{8} = 71.625$. So the decimal 71.625 is a terminating decimal. It terminates after three decimal places. However, some decimals do not terminate. Look at this short division for $\frac{32}{9}$ or $32 \div 9$:

$$9\overline{)32}\ \text{gives}\ 3\ \text{R}5 \quad \text{extended to a decimal is} \quad 9\overline{)32.{}^{5}0{}^{5}0{}^{5}0{}^{5}0\ldots}\ \text{gives}\ 3.5\,5\,5\,5\ldots$$

Every time the 5 in the quotient is multiplied by 9, the product 45 is 5 less than 50, so a small 5 appears. The 5s go on forever. 3.555... is an infinite repeating decimal.

The decimal for $\frac{8}{11}$ repeats after two decimal places.

$$11\overline{)8}\ \text{gives}\ 0\ \text{R}8 \quad \text{extended to a decimal is} \quad 11\overline{)8.0{}^{3}0{}^{8}0{}^{3}0{}^{8}0\ldots}\ \text{gives}\ .7\,2\,7\,2\,7\ldots$$

The two digits 7 and 2 repeat forever. So $\frac{8}{11} = .72727272727272\ldots$.

The digits that repeat, in this case 72, are the repetend of the decimal. Recall that we draw a bar over the repetend to signal that it repeats. So, for $\frac{8}{11}$, you can write either $0.\overline{72}$ or 0.727272... .

Cautions:

(1) Some decimals seem to be repeating, but are not. For example, 91.888888 terminates after six decimal places. On the other hand, $91.\overline{8}$ and 91.888888... do repeat.

(2) A decimal may be rounded in a calculator display to look like it is not repeating. One calculator shows .7272727273 for $\frac{8}{11}$. Because it is impossible to show all digits for $0.\overline{72}$, the calculator rounded to the 10th decimal place.

Mental Math

Find the decimal equivalent of the fraction.

a. $\frac{3}{4}$

b. $\frac{7}{4}$

c. $2\frac{3}{4}$

d. $-2\frac{3}{4}$

STOP QY1

a. Write the decimal equal to $\frac{32}{9}$ using a repetend bar.

b. Write the first 10 digits of $0.\overline{45}$ and $0.61\overline{6}$.

Activity 1

MATERIALS calculator

In 1–5, complete Parts a–c.

a. Write a key sequence for determining the decimal equal to the fraction.

b. Write the exact number displayed on the screen.

c. What do you think is the decimal equivalent for the number?

1. $\frac{4}{15}$ 2. $\frac{533}{20}$ 3. $\frac{64}{33}$ 4. $\frac{189}{125}$ 5. $\frac{937}{64}$

6. Which of these fractions equal terminating decimals? Which equal repeating decimals?

Predicting Which Fractions Equal Terminating Decimals

Why do three of the fractions in Activity 1 equal terminating decimals? Could you predict those without dividing? To help look for a pattern, look at *unit fractions*. A **unit fraction** is a simple fraction with 1 in the numerator. The table below lists the unit fractions $\frac{1}{2}$ through $\frac{1}{20}$ and their equivalent decimal forms. Terminating decimals are shown in red.

$\frac{1}{2} = 0.5$	$\frac{1}{9} = 0.\overline{1}$	$\frac{1}{15} = 0.0\overline{6}$
$\frac{1}{3} = 0.\overline{3}$	$\frac{1}{10} = 0.1$	$\frac{1}{16} = 0.0625$
$\frac{1}{4} = 0.25$	$\frac{1}{11} = 0.\overline{09}$	$\frac{1}{17} = 0.\overline{0588235294117647}$
$\frac{1}{5} = 0.2$	$\frac{1}{12} = 0.08\overline{3}$	$\frac{1}{18} = 0.0\overline{5}$
$\frac{1}{6} = 0.1\overline{6}$	$\frac{1}{13} = 0.\overline{076928}$	$\frac{1}{19} = 0.\overline{052631578947368421}$
$\frac{1}{7} = 0.\overline{142857}$	$\frac{1}{14} = 0.0\overline{714285}$	$\frac{1}{20} = 0.05$
$\frac{1}{8} = 0.125$		

Activity 2

Step 1 List the denominators from 2 to 20 of the unit fractions with terminating decimals.

Step 2 Find the prime factorizations of the numbers from Step 1.

Step 3 What do all the factorizations in Step 2 have in common?

Think of the prime factorization of 10, 100, 1000, and so on: $10 = 2 \cdot 5$, $100 = 2 \cdot 5 \cdot 2 \cdot 5$, $1000 = 2 \cdot 5 \cdot 2 \cdot 5 \cdot 2 \cdot 5$, and so on. Because the prime factors of the denominators in Activity 2 are only 2s and 5s, these denominators are factors of some power of 10. This is the key to knowing when a simple fraction equals a terminating decimal.

What about the decimals for fractions with numerators other than 1? Consider the fraction $\frac{3}{8}$. Because $\frac{3}{8} = 3 \cdot \frac{1}{8}$, multiply 0.125 by 3 to get 0.375. In general, if the decimal for $\frac{1}{n}$ terminates, so does the decimal for any other simple fraction $\frac{m}{n}$.

Putting this information together, you can determine whether a simple fraction equals a terminating decimal.

Fractions as Terminating Decimals

If a simple fraction is in lowest terms and its denominator can be written using only factors of 2 or 5, then the fraction equals a terminating decimal.

For example, since $20 = 2 \cdot 2 \cdot 5$, the decimals for the fractions $\frac{1}{20}$, $\frac{3}{20}$, $\frac{9}{20}$, ... all terminate.

All other simple fractions in lowest terms equal infinite repeating decimals.

Fractions as Infinite Repeating Decimals

If a simple fraction is in lowest terms and its denominator has a prime factor other than 2 and 5, then the fraction equals an infinite repeating decimal.

For example, since $15 = 3 \cdot 5$ has a factor other than 2 and 5, the decimals for $\frac{1}{15}$, $\frac{2}{15}$, $\frac{4}{15}$, $\frac{7}{15}$, ... are infinite repeating decimals.

When simple fractions are not in lowest terms, the denominator does not determine whether they equal terminating or infinite repeating decimals.

QY2

Which fraction, $\frac{5}{15}$ or $\frac{6}{15}$, equals a terminating decimal? Which equals a repeating decimal?

Activity 3

Copy and complete the following table.

Unit Fraction	Decimal	Other Fraction	Decimal
$\frac{1}{2}$	0.5	$\frac{3}{2}$	?
$\frac{1}{4}$	0.25	$\frac{15}{4}$	?
$\frac{1}{5}$	?	$\frac{4}{5}$	?
$\frac{1}{8}$	?	$4\frac{1}{8}$	?
?	0.1	$\frac{17}{10}$	?
?	0.0625	$2\frac{1}{16}$	?
?	0.05	$-6\frac{9}{20}$	?

Questions

COVERING THE IDEAS

In 1 and 2, a fraction is given.

a. Tell whether its decimal is terminating or repeating.

b. Use short division to determine the decimal.

1. $\frac{10}{11}$

2. $\frac{971}{8}$

In 3–5, tell whether the fraction equals a terminating or repeating decimal. Make your predictions without dividing numerator by denominator.

3. $\frac{3}{20}$

4. $\frac{21}{40}$

5. $\frac{43}{60}$

6. Tell whether the quotient or mixed number equals a terminating or repeating decimal. Check your answer with a calculator.
   a. $13 \div 16$ b. $16 \div 13$ c. $2\frac{13}{16}$ d. $5\frac{16}{13}$

7. a. Consider $\frac{1}{6}$, $\frac{2}{6}$, $\frac{3}{6}$, $\frac{4}{6}$, and $\frac{5}{6}$. Write each in lowest terms.
   b. Which of these fractions equal repeating decimals?
   c. Give the decimal for each fraction. Use short division to calculate any you do not know already.

8. Repeat Question 7 for the simple fractions with denominator 11.

9. A store is selling oranges at 3 for \$1.00. What should you expect to pay for
   a. 1 orange? b. 2 oranges? c. 8 oranges?

The majority of oranges sold in the United States come from California, Florida, and Texas.

10. A store is selling boxes of frozen dinners at 7 for $20.00. What should you pay for

a. 1 box? **b.** 2 boxes? **c.** 5 boxes?

11. When Dakota looks at his calculator display for $7 \div 22$, he sees .3181818182. He claims $\frac{7}{22}$ is a terminating decimal. Is he correct? Why or why not?

APPLYING THE MATHEMATICS

12. Use the decimal 0.2 for $\frac{1}{5}$ to obtain the decimal for $\frac{1}{25}$ without dividing.

13. a. If you divide the decimal for $\frac{1}{4}$ by 2, you will get the decimal for what fraction?

b. If you divide the decimal for $\frac{1}{8}$ by 2, you will get the decimal for what fraction?

c. Find the decimal for $\frac{1}{32}$ without dividing 1 by 32.

d. Find the decimal for $\frac{1}{64}$ without dividing 1 by 64.

14. Let p be a prime number greater than 5. Is the decimal equivalent for $\frac{1}{p}$ terminating or repeating? Why?

15. Find five unit fractions with denominators greater than 100 that equal terminating decimals.

16. a. Use your calculator to find the decimal equivalents for $\frac{1}{7}$, $\frac{2}{7}$, $\frac{3}{7}$, $\frac{4}{7}$, $\frac{5}{7}$, and $\frac{6}{7}$.

b. Study your answers in Part a. What pattern do you see?

REVIEW

In 17 and 18, a division problem is given. (Lesson 7-5)

a. Write the quotient as a mixed number.

b. Write the quotient as a decimal.

17. $52{,}001 \div 7$ **18.** $4{,}897 \div 6$

19. Use short division to help you find how many weeks and days are in 332 days. **(Lesson 7-5)**

20. Write a question about a real situation that can be represented by the equation $64 \div 9 = 7$ R1. **(Lessons 7-4, 7-2)**

21. a. Evaluate $\left(-\frac{2}{3}\right)^3$.

b. Evaluate $\left(-\frac{2}{3}\right)^4$.

c. Fill in the Blank Compare using < or > :

$\left(-\frac{2}{3}\right)^4$ ___?___ $\left(-\frac{2}{3}\right)^3$ **(Lessons 6-10, 6-4, 6-2, 2-10)**

22. Calculate $-8 + 4 \cdot -3 - 2 \div 2$. **(Lesson 6-8)**

23. The largest open urban square in the world is Tiananmen Square in Beijing, China. It is not a square, but a rectangle. It measures 880 meters on one side and 500 meters on another. What is its area? **(Lesson 6-3)**

Tiananmen Square

24. Find the perimeter of the figure at the right. **(Lesson 3-2)**

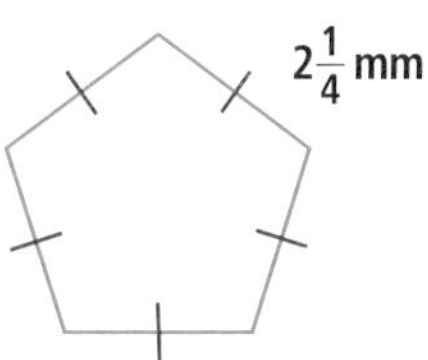

EXPLORATION

25. a. Copy and complete this table.

Unit Fraction	Decimal Equivalent	Prime Factorization of Denominator	Number of Places to Terminate
$\frac{1}{8}$	0.125	$8 = 2 \cdot 2 \cdot 2$	3
$\frac{1}{125}$	?	?	?
$\frac{1}{200}$	?	?	?
$\frac{1}{625}$	?	?	?
$\frac{1}{800}$	?	?	?
$\frac{1}{5{,}000}$	?	?	?
$\frac{1}{125{,}000}$	?	?	?

b. How can you predict how many places it will take for a decimal equivalent to terminate?

QY ANSWERS

1a. $3.\overline{5}$

1b. 0.4545454545 and 0.6166666666

2. $\frac{5}{15} = \frac{1}{3}$, repeating; $\frac{6}{15} = \frac{2}{5}$, terminating

Lesson

7-8 Division of Decimals

▸ **BIG IDEA** Decimals are divided just like whole numbers, except that the decimal point must be placed in the appropriate position in the quotient.

Stores often display a single price for more than one item. For example, lemons might be advertised as "5 for $1.29" or CDs might be on sale "3 for $40." Computing the cost per item often involves division of decimals.

Mental Math

Multiple Choice
Which does not equal $584 \div 7$?

A $\frac{584}{7}$
B $83\frac{3}{7}$
C 83.428571
D $70\frac{94}{7}$

Rewriting Division of Fractions as Division of Integers

One way to divide decimals is to convert the division of decimals into a division of integers. Just multiply both the divisor and dividend by a power of 10 large enough to eliminate the decimals.

Example 1

A bakery announces that, until closing, bagels will be on sale for 55¢ each. Bridget buys all of the remaining bagels. The total cost before tax is $17.60. How many bagels does she buy?

Solution The idea is to compare $17.60 to 55¢. You need to determine how many times 55¢ goes into $17.60, that is, to compute $\frac{\$17.60}{55¢}$. The unit in the numerator is dollars, but the unit in the denominator is cents. To make the units consistent, change the cents to dollars: $\frac{\$17.60}{\$0.55}$.

Multiplying both the numerator and denominator by 100 (using the Equal Fractions Property) changes the division to integer division of whole numbers: $\frac{\$17.60}{\$0.55} \cdot \frac{100}{100} = \frac{1{,}760}{55}$. Now you can use any method to find the quotient.

 See QY1 at the right.

 **QY1**

Finish Example 1 to find out how many bagels Bridget bought.

Example 2

Write the quotient $0.038 \div 1.9$ as a decimal.

Solution Ask yourself: By what power of 10 can I multiply both 0.038 and 1.9 to eliminate the decimal points from both? Since 0.038 has 3 decimal places and 1.9 has 1 decimal place, multiplying both numbers by 10^3, or 1000, will yield two integer products.

$$0.038 \div 1.9 = \frac{0.038}{1.9} = \frac{0.038 \cdot 1000}{1.9 \cdot 1000} = \frac{38}{1,900}$$

Notice that 19 is a factor of both the numerator and the denominator.

$$\frac{38}{1900} = \frac{19 \cdot 2}{19 \cdot 100} = \frac{2}{100} = 0.02$$

Thus, $0.038 \div 1.9 = 0.02$.

Check Use related facts. Does $1.9 \cdot 0.02 = 0.038$? Yes, it checks.

 **See QY2 at the right.**

 **QY2**

In Example 2, why is it possible to multiply by $\frac{1000}{1000}$ without changing the value of the quotient?

GUIDED

Example 3

Nickel donations to a local food bank were collected in a meter-long "nickel tube," a plastic pipe capped on one end that could be stacked with nickels. At the end of the drive, the food bank had 13.5 meters of nickels. One nickel is 2 millimeters, or 0.002 meters, thick. About how many nickels had the food bank collected?

Solution The number of nickels is the total length of the stack of nickels divided by the thickness of a single nickel, or __?__ meters ÷ __?__ meters.

This can be changed to a division of whole numbers by multiplying the numerator and denominator by __?__, which results in the whole number division $\frac{13,500}{2}$.

Using short division, the quotient is __?__. The food bank collected __?__ nickels.

GUIDED

Example 4

A particular bacterium is about 0.00000173 meters long. Estimate how many of these bacteria, if laid end to end, would fit in an inch, which is 0.0254 meters.

Solution 1 Determine which number should be divided by the other and write the division as a fraction: $\frac{?}{?}$

Multiply both the numerator and denominator by __?__ to eliminate the decimal places.

The quotient is __?__ divided by 173, or about 14,682. About 14,700 bacteria will fit in an inch.

Check Use related facts. Multiply 14,682 by __?__ and you should get a number close to __?__.

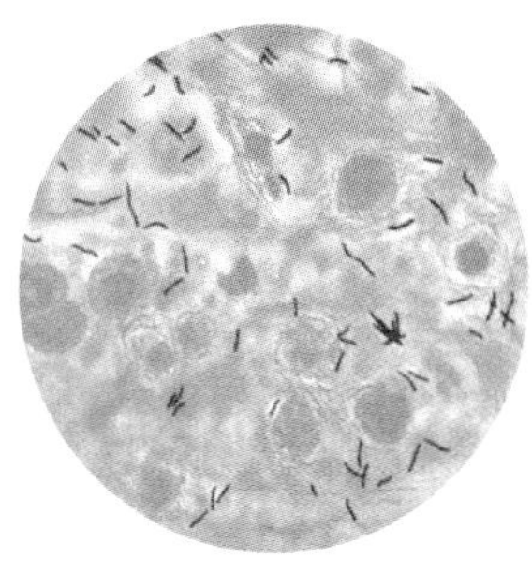

This is the bacteria that causes tuberculosis.

Now you can play *Decimal Dash: Division Variation*. You will find the directions on page G21 in the back of this book.

Questions

COVERING THE IDEAS

In 1 and 2, write each quotient as a decimal.

1. a. $\frac{7}{14}$ b. $\frac{0.7}{14}$ c. $\frac{0.07}{14}$ d. $\frac{0.007}{14}$
2. a. $\frac{90}{15}$ b. $\frac{90}{1.5}$ c. $\frac{90}{0.15}$ d. $\frac{90}{0.015}$

In 3–6, a division situation is given. Determine the quotient without a calculator.

3. Hikers covered 28.8 miles in 4 days. How many miles per day did they cover?
4. $40 \div 0.2$ 5. $23 \div 0.023$ 6. $\frac{4.38}{0.005}$
7. **Multiple Choice** $326.86 \div 5.9 =$
   A 5540 B 554 C 55.4 D 5.54
8. How many 39¢ pens can you buy with $25?
9. A pixel on a 17" monitor with a resolution of 1024 pixels × 768 pixels has a length of about 0.34 mm. About how many pixels placed end-to-end are there in 10 mm, which is 1 cm?

APPLYING THE MATHEMATICS

10. In the 2004 Olympics in Athens, Greece, Tonique Williams-Darling of the Bahamas ran the 400-meter race in 49.41 seconds and won the gold medal. To the nearest hundredth, what was her speed in meters per second?

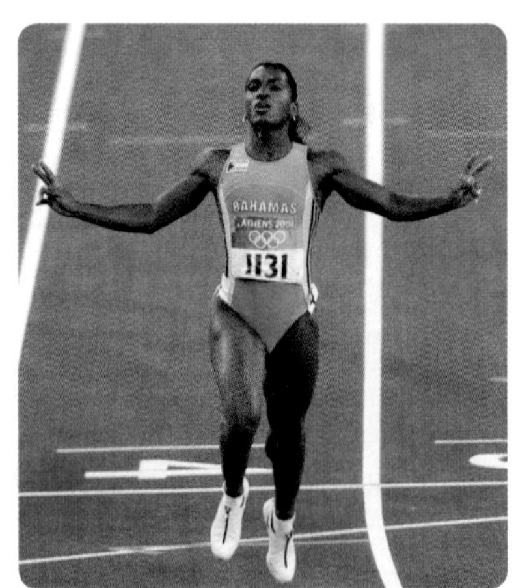

Tonique Williams-Darling crosses the finish line as the gold medalist in the 2004 Olympics.

11. It takes Pluto about 247.69 Earth years to orbit the Sun. It takes Jupiter about 11.86 Earth years to orbit the Sun. About how many times as long does it take Pluto to orbit the Sun than Jupiter?
12. a. By eliminating decimals, convert $8.64 \div 0.0009$ to a short division problem.
    b. Find the quotient by doing this short division.
13. Suppose a bag of apples weighs about 3.6 pounds.
    a. How many bags of apples would weigh a total of about 100 pounds?
    b. How many pounds would 100 bags weigh?
14. Terrance earns $8.75/week for walking a dog after school. How many weeks will he need to walk the dog to earn $159 to buy an MP3 player?

15. In Example 4, suppose the length of the bacterium was off by 0.00000002 meter. How much would that error affect the number of bacteria that would fit in 0.0254 meter?

16. The gas tank in Martha's car holds 14.8 gallons. After filling the tank, Martha noted that the mileage on the odometer was 31,289.3 miles. By the time she ran out of gas, the odometer read 31,610.7 miles. How many miles per gallon did she drive her car since she filled up?

REVIEW

17. Express $\frac{3}{7}$ as a decimal. **(Lesson 7-8)**

18. Consider the fraction $\frac{5322}{3}$. **(Lessons 7-8, 7-7)**
    a. Does it equal a terminating or repeating decimal?
    b. Use short division to find its decimal equivalent.

19. Suppose five buses are used to transport 158 tourists on a trip along the Skyline Drive in Virginia. What is the average number of people on each bus? Express your answer as a mixed number. **(Lesson 7-5)**

20. In Parts a–f, find the remainder using integer division.
    a. $32 \div 14$ b. $32 \div 7$ c. $26 \div 14$
    d. $26 \div 7$ e. $543 \div 14$ f. $543 \div 7$
    g. When x is divided by 14, there is a remainder of 10. What is the remainder when x is divided by 7? **(Lesson 7-4)**

21. Earth covers about 300,000 miles in $4\frac{1}{2}$ hours as it travels through space in orbit around the sun. **(Lesson 7-1)**
    a. What is its approximate speed in miles per hour?
    b. What is its approximate speed in miles per second?

22. Find the product of 1.6 and –0.4. **(Lessons 6-10, 6-5)**

EXPLORATION

23. **Fill in the Blanks** Fill the first three spaces below with any three digits, and then repeat the same digits again for the next three spaces to form a terminating decimal. For example, a possible decimal could be 0.123123.

    0._?_ _?_ _?_ _?_ _?_ _?_

    Now use your calculator to divide the number by 0.07. Then divide the quotient by 0.11. Then, divide this second quotient by 0.13. Repeat the same steps, starting with other three-digit sequences. What happens with the final quotients? Why do you think this happens?

QY ANSWERS

1. 32
2. Multiplying by $\frac{1000}{1000}$ does not change the value because $\frac{1000}{1000} = 1$.

Lesson

7-9 Division with Negative Numbers

▸ **BIG IDEA** Division of positive and negative numbers follows the same rules of signs as multiplication.

As you know, negative numbers can express ideas such as a decrease in a bank account balance, a loss in weight, or a drop in temperature. Division with negative numbers occurs in many situations. One kind of situation involves rates.

Mental Math

Decide whether the result will be positive or negative.

a. the product of two negative numbers

b. the sum of two negative numbers

c. the product of three negative numbers

d. the sum of three negative numbers

Rates with Negative Numbers

The numbers in a rate can be negative.

Example 1

Miranda is going on a 7-day Alaskan cruise that costs \$2,369. What is the cost per day?

Solution 1 Ignore negative numbers. The cost per day is $\frac{\$2369}{7 \text{ days}}$. Divide 2,369 by 7. \$338.43 is the cost per day.

Solution 2 Use negative numbers. A cost of \$2,369 can be written as -\$2,369. So the cost per day is $\frac{-\$2369}{7 \text{ days}}$. From Solution 1 we know this is about -\$338.43 per day.

$\frac{-\$2369}{7 \text{ days}} \approx -338.43 \frac{\text{dollars}}{\text{day}}$

Passengers on a cruise ship float past the John Hopkins Glacier along Glacier Bay, Alaska.

Example 1 illustrates two important principles. First, you can divide negative numbers just like you divide positive numbers, but you have to decide whether the answer is positive or negative. Second, when a negative number is divided by a positive number, the quotient is negative.

GUIDED

Example 2

Miranda pays the $2,369 cost of the cruise by having installments deducted from her checking account. She chooses the 12-month payment plan, meaning the $2,369 is divided evenly over 12-months. How much will her monthly payment be?

Solution Use division, with cost as a negative number and months as a positive number. The answer should be a cost per month, which would be negative.

$$\underline{\ ?\ } \div \underline{\ ?\ } = \underline{\ ?\ }$$

Miranda's monthly payment is ___?___.

Is the Answer Positive or Negative?

Example 3

How fast is the temperature changing (in degrees per hour) if it was 10° warmer two hours ago?

Solution 1 Ignore negative numbers. If it was 10° warmer two hours ago, then the temperature has been going down 5° per hour.

Solution 2 Use negative numbers. Warmer is positive. 2 hours ago is -2 hours.

$$\frac{10° \text{ warmer}}{2 \text{ hours ago}} = \frac{10°}{-2 \text{ hours}} = -5° \text{ per hour}$$

Example 3 suggests that when a positive number is divided by a negative number, the quotient is negative. You can use 10 ÷ -2 = -5 to create a fact triangle. From this fact triangle you can find the related facts: 10 ÷ -5 = -2, -2 • -5 = 10, and -5 • -2 = 10.

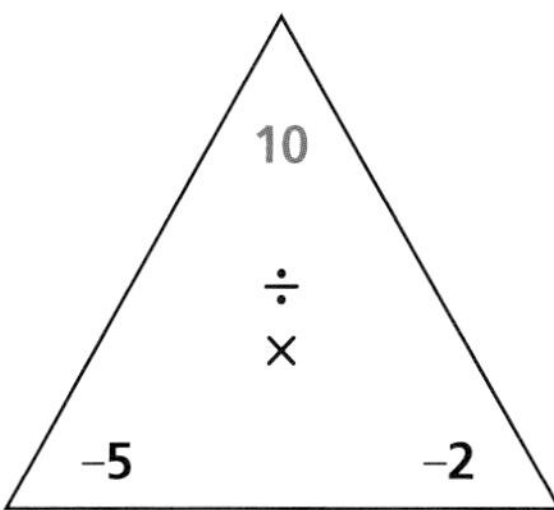

Notice that the multiplications follow the rules for multiplying two negative numbers from Lesson 6-10. Division has the same rules for positive and negative numbers as does multiplication.

Example 4

How fast is the temperature changing (in degrees per hour) if it was 12° colder three hours ago?

Solution 1 Ignore negative numbers. If it was 12° colder three hours ago, then the temperature has been rising. It rose 12° in 3 hours, or $\frac{12°}{3 \text{ hr}} = 4°$ hr.

Solution 2 Use negative numbers. Colder is negative. So is three hours ago. $\frac{12° \text{ lower}}{3 \text{ hr ago}} = \frac{-12°}{-3 \text{ hr}}$. This change is $\frac{4°}{\text{hr}}$.

Solution 2 demonstrates that $\frac{-12}{-3} = 4$. The quotient of two negative numbers is positive.

 **See QY1 at the right.**

 **QY1**

Create a fact triangle using the situation in Example 4.

Examples 1–4 show all possible combinations of dividing positive and negative numbers. You could put any numbers in place of the numbers that are in these examples. The general properties are the same as the properties for multiplying positive and negative numbers you learned in Lesson 6-10.

Dividing Positive and Negative Numbers

The quotient of two positive numbers or of two negative numbers is positive.

The quotient of one positive number and one negative number is negative.

 **QY2**

A zoo is keeping track of the weight of its animals. Calculate the change in weight per week. Assume the statements below involve positive and negative numbers.

a. A bear lost 40 pounds in 5 weeks during the winter.
b. A fox gained 2 pounds in a half a month.
c. An elephant lost 75 pounds in 60 weeks.

The National School Lunch Act was created in 1946 to provide to students low cost or free school lunch meals.

Source: USDA

Questions

COVERING THE IDEAS

1. Last week Miranda bought five lunches and spent a total of \$15.65.
   a. Calculate the cost per lunch using negative numbers.
   b. Express your answer to Part a as a rate.

In 2–5, give the quotient.

2. $-16 \div 8$ 3. $54 \div -3$ 4. $\frac{-9}{72}$ 5. $\frac{-30}{-18}$

Fill in the Blanks **In 6–8, use the given information to complete this sentence: "The change in temperature is _?_ ° per hour." Use negative numbers when appropriate.**

6. Four and a half hours ago, it was 9 degrees colder.
7. In 10 hours, we expect the temperature to fall 5 degrees.
8. 48 hours ago, the temperature was 17° warmer than the temperature now.

In 9 and 10, are the rates in Situations A and B equal or *not* equal?

9. **Situation A:** The price of a gallon of gas went up 20¢ in 2 weeks.
   Situation B: The price of a gallon of gas was 20¢ higher 2 weeks ago.
10. **Situation A:** There were 300 fewer students in the school 6 years ago.
    Situation B: We expect 100 more students in the school 2 years from now.

In 11 and 12, a fact is given. State the other three related facts.

11. $-2 \cdot -3 = 6$ 12. $\frac{-25.42}{6.2} = -4.1$

In 13 and 14, write the answer to the division as a terminating or repeating decimal.

13. $-7 \div -9$ 14. $-\frac{3,100}{800}$

APPLYING THE MATHEMATICS

In 15 and 16,

a. **express the rate in the situation as a division problem involving negative numbers.**
b. **answer the question or calculate the rate.**

15. If you spend an average of \$150 a day, how long will it take you to spend \$6000?
16. The thickness of the Arctic sea ice has decreased from a mean of 10 feet forty years ago to a mean of 6 feet in recent years.
17. Separate these six numbers into two groups of equal numbers.

a. $\frac{-12,345}{-54,321}$ b. $-\frac{-12,345}{54,321}$

c. $-\frac{-12,345}{-54,321}$ d. $\frac{12,345}{54,321}$

e. $\frac{12,345}{-54,321}$ f. $-\frac{12,345}{54,321}$

18. Suppose p is a positive number and n is a negative number. Tell whether the result is positive or negative.

a. $\frac{p}{n}$ b. $\frac{n}{p}$ c. $\frac{n}{n}$ d. $\frac{3p}{-4n}$

19. A male black bear that weighs 880 lb will lose about a third of his body weight during his 100 days of hibernation.

a. What will be his total weight loss during hibernation?

b. What will be his average weight loss per day?

The black bear species also come in the colors white, brown, cinnamon, and blue.

Source: Alaska Department of Fish and Game

In 20–23, compute.

20. $\frac{-2}{-8} + \frac{-8}{-2} + (-8)(-2)$

21. $\frac{7{,}188}{-3{,}592} + \frac{-7{,}188}{-3{,}592}$

22. $\left(-\frac{1}{2}\right)\left(-\frac{1}{3}\right) - \frac{1}{2} \cdot \frac{1}{3}$

23. $\frac{ab}{c}$ if $a = -8$, $b = -7$, and $c = -2$

REVIEW

24. Calculate $4500 \div 0.075$. Round your result to the nearest whole number, if necessary. **(Lesson 7-8)**

In 25–27, state whether the product is a terminating or a repeating decimal. (Lesson 7-7)

25. $\frac{7}{10} \cdot \frac{1}{4}$ 26. $\frac{2}{7} \cdot \frac{4}{5}$ 27. $\frac{3}{5} \cdot \frac{2}{3} \cdot \frac{1}{3}$

28. a. Use short division to show that a 365-day year cannot be divided evenly into weeks.

b. Is the same true for a leap year of 366 days? Explain how you can answer this question using your answer from Part a. **(Lesson 7-5)**

In 29 and 30, consider the circle graph below, which shows the country of birth for players who batted on the 2007 Baltimore Orioles baseball team. (Lessons 6-7, 6-5)

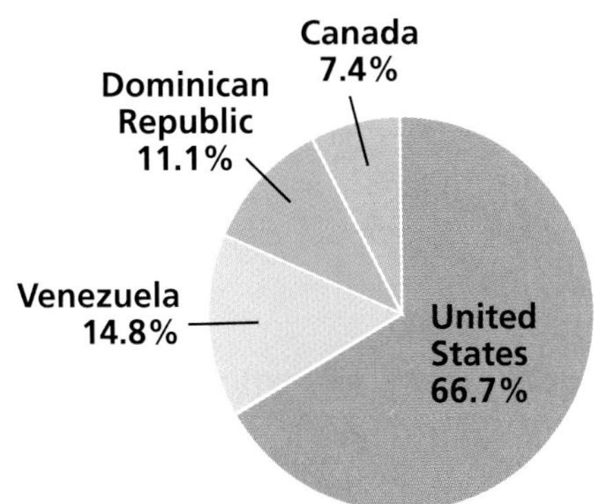

29. To the nearest degree, what angle is formed by the sector of the circle graph that represents Venezuela?

30. The information in the circle graph is based on a survey of 27 baseball players. How many players are in each category?

EXPLORATION

31. a. Is $\frac{-(-(-(-(-(-(-(-80)))))))}{-(-(-(-200)))}$ positive or negative?

b. Explain how you determined your answer to Part a.

c. What strategy can you use to solve any problem like the one in Part a?

QY ANSWERS

1.

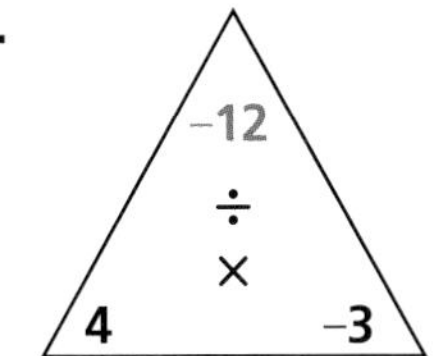

2a. –8 lb/wk

2b. 4 lb/month

2c. –1.25 lb/wk

Lesson 7-10 Solving Multiplication and Division Equations Using Fact Triangles

▸ **BIG IDEA** Simple equations involving only multiplication and division can be solved using fact triangles.

In Chapter 4, you used fact triangles relating addition and subtraction to help solve algebraic equations. You can also use fact triangles to solve equations involving multiplication or division.

Mental Math

Use the array below.

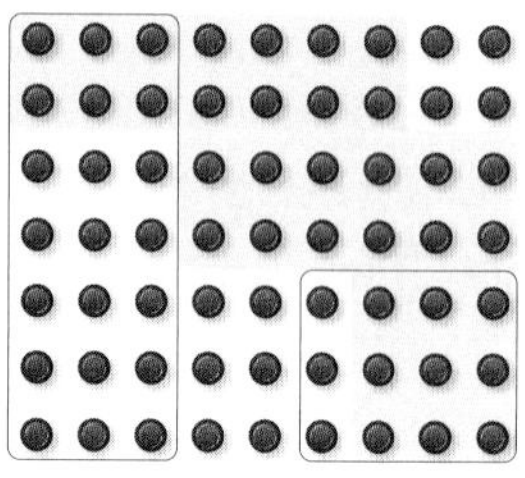

a. How many dots are in the array?

b. What fraction are shaded?

c. What fraction are circled?

d. What fraction are both circled and shaded?

Example 1

Twenty students are trying out for a part in a play. If there is a total of 3 hours for auditions, how many minutes should an average audition last?

Solution 1 Think multiplication. It takes m minutes for each audition. Then it will take $20m$ minutes for 20 auditions.

3 hours $= 3 \cdot 60$ minutes $= 180$ minutes; So you want to find m when $20m = 180$.

Draw a fact triangle for $20m = 180$ and list the related facts.

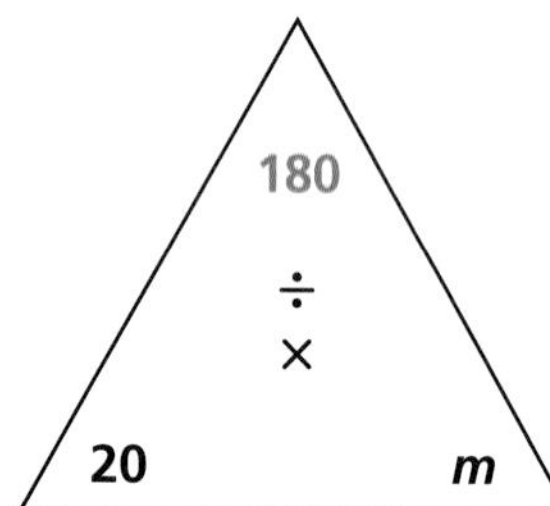

$20 \cdot m = 180$

$m \cdot 20 = 180$

$180 \div m = 20$

$180 \div 20 = m$

The related fact with m isolated on one side is $180 \div 20 = m$. So, $m = 9$.

Solution 2 Think rate division.

$$\frac{3 \text{ hours}}{20 \text{ auditions}} = \frac{3 \cdot 60 \text{ minutes}}{20 \text{ auditions}} = \frac{180}{20} \frac{\text{minutes}}{\text{audition}} = 9 \frac{\text{minutes}}{\text{audition}}$$

Solution 1 used a multiplication and division fact triangle to solve the equation. There were two multiplication facts: $20 \cdot m = 180$ and $m \cdot 20 = 180$. However, you only need to use one of these facts because the Commutative Property of Multiplication shows that they are equivalent.

Example 2 shows how to find an unknown in a fraction using related facts.

Example 2

Solve the equation $\frac{400}{d} = 1600$.

Solution

Step 1 Write the fact triangle, as shown at the right.

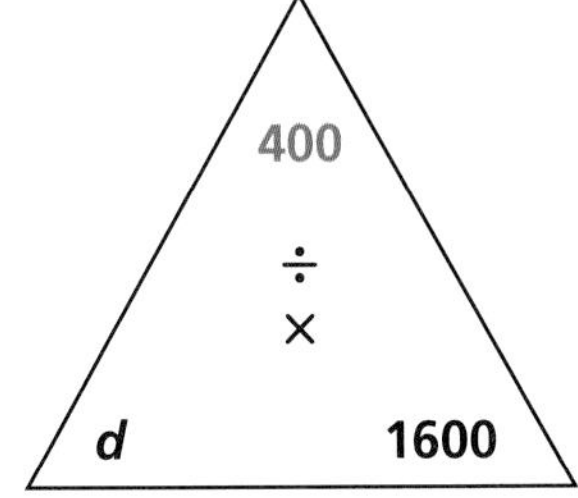

Step 2 Use the triangle to list the related facts.

$\frac{400}{d} = 1600$, $\frac{400}{1600} = d$, $1600d = 400$, $d \cdot 1600 = 400$

Step 3 Pick the fact that has d alone on one side and do the computation.

$\frac{400}{1600} = \text{d}$ means $\text{d} = \frac{1}{4} = 0.25$.

Check 1 Substitute 0.25 for d. Does $\frac{400}{0.25} = 1600$? Yes, it does.

Check 2 $\frac{1}{4}$ goes 1600 times into 400.

Here is an example with negative numbers.

GUIDED

Example 3

Solve $10 = -2.5x$.

Solution

Step 1 Complete the fact triangle.

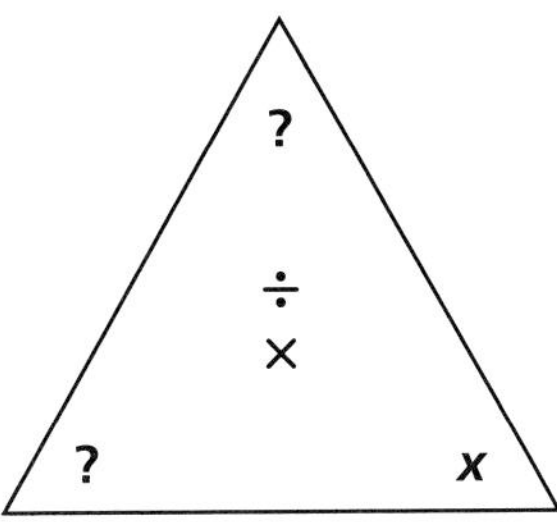

Step 2 Write the related facts.

$-2.5x = 10$? • ? = ?

? ÷ ? = ?   ? ÷ ? = ?

Step 3 Pick the related fact with x alone on one side and do the computation. $x =$?

Questions

COVERING THE IDEAS

In 1–4,

a. Draw a fact triangle for the equations.
b. Using the triangle, write the related facts.
c. Use one of the facts to find the value of the variable.
d. Check your answer by substituting it for the variable in the original equation.

1. $-8x = 32$
2. $\frac{630}{y} = 4.5$
3. $3 = 60m$
4. $1{,}000{,}000d = 26{,}500{,}000$

Multiple Choice In 5–8, identify all the solutions to the equation

5. $-45 = -9x$

   A -5 B $\frac{1}{5}$ C 5 D $-\frac{1}{5}$

6. $1\frac{1}{2} \div y = 3$

   A $\frac{1}{2}$ B $4\frac{1}{2}$ C $1\frac{1}{2}$ D 2

7. $0 = 0 \cdot q$

   A 98 B $-6\frac{2}{3}$ C 0 D 14.8

8. $15 = \frac{-315}{x}$

   A -21 B 21 C $-4{,}815$ D $-\frac{5}{7}$

APPLYING THE MATHEMATICS

9. Jasmin and Janelle are driving to Cincinnati. They think they can average 60 miles per hour for the 310 miles. At this rate, how long will it take them to get to Cincinnati?
   a. Let t be the time (in hours) it will take them. Write an equation involving t that can answer the question.
   b. Solve your equation. Check the solution in the original equation.
   c. Answer the question with a sentence.

In 10 and 11, use the formula $C = \pi d$, where C represents the circumference of a circle, d represents the diameter of the circle, and $\pi \approx 3.14159$.

10. It takes about 10 minutes to walk around a circular museum building. At this rate, how long would it take to walk through the museum along a diameter, if it were possible?

This is a circular walkway at the Guggenheim Museum in New York City.

11. Mike's bike wheels are about 27 inches in diameter. What is the circumference of one of the wheels?

In 12–14, use this information taken from a catering menu.

Item	Price per person
Breakfast	
Fresh bagel with cream cheese	\$3.50
With Salmon	\$4.50
Fresh Fruit Platter	\$4.00
Coffee	\$1.50
Lunch	
Choice of sandwiches on freshly baked bread served with roasted potatoes	\$8.00
Caesar Salad	\$5.50
With roasted chicken	\$6.00
With grilled shrimp	\$6.50
With grilled salmon fillet	\$7.00
Desserts	
Cookie Tray	\$3.95
Mini Pastries and Tarts	\$4.95

a. **Write an equation that describes the situation.**

b. **Solve the equation using a fact triangle.**

c. **Check the answer by substituting it for the variable in the original equation.**

d. **In a sentence, answer the question.**

12. Kyle plans to order a platter of sandwiches for the reunion planning committee. The food budget allows \$60 for lunch. How many sandwiches can Kyle order?

13. Gerardo ordered desserts for 45 people, and the total came to \$222.75. All the desserts were the same. Which dessert did Gerardo choose?

14. Caroline ordered a bagel with salmon, the fruit plate, and coffee for each attendee of a meeting. If the total came to \$370, how many people attended the meeting?

15. Victor was solving the equation $t \div 80 = 3.5$. He changed it to $80 \div t = 3.5$. Why are the two equations *not* equivalent?

REVIEW

16. After a flash flood, the water level in the Geyser family's basement receded 14 inches in 3 hours and 30 minutes. What was the rate of change in the water level in inches per hour? **(Lessons 7-9, 7-1)**

17. **Skill Sequence** Calculate each expression. **(Lessons 7-9, 7-8)**
    a. $79.5 \div 53$ b. $-79.5 \div 53$ c. $-79.5 \div -53$

18. Calculate $\frac{123.5104}{38.112^0}$. **(Lessons 7-8, 6-4)**

19. a. Give the equivalent decimals for the following fractions: $\frac{1}{9}, \frac{2}{9}, \ldots, \frac{8}{9}$
    b. Describe the pattern you find in Part a. **(Lesson 7-7)**

20. Find the values of T, H, O, R, and N in the division below. **(Lesson 7-5)**

$$\begin{array}{r} T\ O\ N \\ 4\overline{)7^H\ 5^R\ 7^1} \end{array}$$

21. If there are 53,400 people watching a football game in a stadium that has 18 sections, how many people, on average, are there per section? **(Lesson 7-1)**

EXPLORATION

22. Consider Mike's bike wheel in Question 11.
    a. Suppose you rode Mike's bike home from your school. How far would you travel? How many revolutions would the bike wheel make?
    b. Suppose Mike was to bike across the United States from Seattle, Washington, to Miami, Florida, a distance of 3,424 miles. To the nearest hundred thousand, how many revolutions would Mike's bike wheel make during the trip?

About 27.3% of people 16 and over rode a bicycle at least once during the summer of 2002. This is about 57 million Americans.

Source: National Survey of Pedestrian and Bicyclist Attitudes and Behaviors, 2002

Chapter 7 Projects

1 Divisibility Tests

Make up or find tests that can tell you when a number in base 10 is divisible by 7, 8, 12, 15, and 25. Demonstrate each test either on a poster or in a class presentation.

2 Integer Arithmetic with Negative Divisors

Extend the idea of a quotient and remainder to cover division by -2, -3, and other negative integers. Assume that the remainder will always be positive. For example, calculate the quotient and remainder when 382 is divided by -7 and when -200 is divided by -3. Explain how you obtained your results and why you believe they are correct.

3 Rate Units

Miles per gallon and kilometers per hour are two common rate units. Look through newspapers and magazines to find at least ten other rate units. Write a report on your findings describing the units, their meaning, and how they are used in the articles.

All cars produced for the United States contain a speedometer that shows miles per hour and kilometers per hour.

Michael Phelps celebrates after winning the gold medal in the 400-meter individual medley during the 2004 Olympic Games.

4 World Record Rates

Look in an almanac or other reference book for the world records in an event in running or swimming from 1972 to the present. Calculate the average speed of each record holder. Graph the ordered pairs (year, average speed) and describe what you find. A spreadsheet is helpful in organizing your data and calculating the speed.

5 Twin Primes

Two prime numbers that differ by 2, such as 5 and 7, or 41 and 43, are called *twin primes*. Find some information about twin primes. What is the largest known pair of twin primes? Are there infinitely many twin primes? The primes 3, 5, and 7 are three consecutive odd numbers that are prime. Are there any other *prime triplets*?

Chapter 7 Summary and Vocabulary

- The division $a \div b$, read "a divided by b" arises directly from situations in the real world, such as rates (the rate of a per b).

- In whole number division, there is a whole number quotient q and a whole number remainder r that is less than b with $a = b \cdot q + r$. For example, if 22 people are going to a party in taxicabs that seat 4 people each, then the division $22 \div 4 = 5$ R2 means that $22 = 4 \cdot 5 + 2$ and that 5 full taxicabs are needed with 2 people left over for a 6th taxi.

- In rational number division, there is simply a quotient q with $a = b \cdot q$. For example, if a wall 22 feet long is to be cleaned by 4 people, then the division $22 \div 4 = 5\frac{2}{4} = 5\frac{1}{2} = 5.5$ determines how much wall each person cleans. So each person must clean 5.5 feet of the wall.

- Any numbers may be divided, except that the divisor cannot be zero. Prime factorization can be used to simplify numbers used in division. Division with small whole number divisors can be done using short division. In this algorithm, $b\overline{)a}$ with q above and the remainders are put in between the digits of a. If decimal accuracy is wanted, zeros can be put to the right of the digits of a and the short division extended. This method can be used to determine whether the decimal for a simple fraction will terminate or repeat forever. More complicated division problems can be done on a calculator, though the displayed answer may not be the final answer. The process you use to divide and the form of the answer (quotient/remainder, fraction, mixed number, or decimal, exact or rounded) depends on the situation.

- Division with negative numbers follows rules similar to those for multiplication: If the divisor and dividend are both positive or both negative, then the quotient is positive. If the divisor and dividend do not have the same sign, then the quotient is negative. Fact triangles can help solve equations involving multiplication or division.

Theorems and Properties

Rate Model for Division (p. 401)
Quotient Remainder Formula (p. 418)

Vocabulary

7-1
dividend
divisor
quotient
rate
rate unit

7-2
remainder

7-3
prime number
composite number
prime factorization
factor tree

7-4
integer division

7-6
rational number division

7-7
unit fraction

Chapter 7 Self-Test

Take this test as you would take a test in class. You will need a calculator. Then use the Selected Answers section in the back of the book to check your work.

1. Perform integer division on 135 ÷ 11 to find the quotient and remainder.

2. Use short division to find how many minutes and seconds are in 1,000 seconds. Show your work.

3. Express 17,049 ÷ 9 as a mixed number.

4. How many weeks and days are 432 days?

In 5 and 6, divide and express the quotient as a decimal.

5. 17 ÷ 0.25

6. 29.96 ÷ 10.7

7. Find the quotient of $\frac{-92}{-8}$.

8. It took Cheyenne and Mark just under 4 hours and 40 minutes to drive from Washington D.C. to Roanoke, Virginia. They drove the distance of 241 miles at an average speed of 52 miles per hour.
   a. Put the numbers into a division equation.
   b. Identify the divisor.
   c. Identify the dividend.
   d. Identify the quotient.

9. Does $\frac{83}{7}$ equal a terminating decimal or an infinite repeating decimal? Explain.

10. Write the prime factorization of 72 using exponents.

11. Marco is putting his baseball cards into 7 stacks. If he has 1,240 cards, how many cards will go in each stack. How many cards will be left over?

12. Is 149 prime or composite? Explain how you know.

13. Suppose we changed our calendar so that a 365-day year had 9 months with each month having the same number of days. How many days would be in each month and how many days would be left over?

14. A grocery store says that 1 half-gallon of orange juice costs $2.54, but 3 half-gallons cost $6.99. How much cheaper is 1 half-gallon if it is bought in a group of 3?

15. Tania is reimbursed 41.5¢ per mile for her traveling expenses to and from work. Tania commuted to and from work Monday through Friday for 4 weeks, missing two days of work. She received a reimbursement check for $283.86. How many miles does Tania live from her workplace?

16. On Sunday, Whelan pool was filled to the brim and had a depth of 4 feet. By Thursday, the pool had lost 1.5 inches due to evaporation and splashing. What is the average loss in depth per day?
   a. Express as a division problem using negative numbers.
   b. Solve and answer the question using a sentence.

17. Using an array, show that when n is a whole number, no number of the form $4n + 1$ is divisible by 2.

18. Create a multiplication and division fact triangle to show the relationship between the numbers -1.5, 0.375, -4.

In 19 and 20,

a. Draw a fact triangle for the equation.

b. Using the triangle, write the related facts.

c. Use one of your facts to find a value for the variable.

d. Check your solution by substituting it back into the original equation.

19. $\frac{10}{x} = 16.\overline{6}$

20. $120 = -0.75y$

Chapter 7 Chapter Review

SKILLS
PROPERTIES
USES
REPRESENTATIONS

SKILLS Procedures used to get answers

OBJECTIVE A Write the prime factorization of a number. (Lesson 7-3)

In 1–4, write the prime factorization of the number. Use exponents when the same prime factor is repeated.

1. 500
2. 512
3. 513
4. 511

OBJECTIVE B Find answers to integer divisions. (Lesson 7-4)

In 5–8, perform integer division to find the quotient and the remainder.

5. $48 \div 7$
6. $17 \div 5$
7. $617 \div 8$
8. $109 \div 9$

OBJECTIVE C Divide by small whole numbers using short division. (Lesson 7-5)

In 9–12, use short division to find the quotient and remainder. Show your work.

9. $4{,}587 \div 8$
10. $5{,}674 \div 3$
11. $22{,}140 \div 4$
12. $16{,}001 \div 7$

OBJECTIVE D Find quotients in rational number divisions. (Lessons 7-6, 7-8)

In 13–16, express the quotient in mixed number form.

13. $8{,}001 \div 2$
14. $8{,}045 \div 5$
15. $9{,}876 \div 7$
16. $9{,}875 \div 6$

In 17–20, divide. Round answers to the nearest hundredth.

17. $36.2 \div 54.01$
18. $1{,}345.83 \div 0.96$
19. $7.3 \div 1.87$
20. $24.6 \div 0.015$

OBJECTIVE E Divide positive and negative numbers. (Lesson 7-9)

In 21–28, find the quotient.

21. $6 \div -6$
22. $0 \div -8$
23. $-11 \div -22$
24. $-80 \div -8$
25. $58 \div -6$
26. $-49 \div -9$
27. $-5.47 \div 3.61$
28. $-62.31 \div -7.5$

PROPERTIES The principles behind the mathematics

OBJECTIVE F Convert between the language of fractions and the language of division. (Lesson 7-1)

In 29–32, change the statement about fractions to the equivalent statement about division.

29. $\frac{60}{20} = 3$
30. $\frac{-\frac{1}{2}}{\frac{1}{4}} = -2$
31. One fourth of sixteen is four.
32. If a numerator is multiplied by 5, then the value of the fraction is multiplied by 5.

In 33 and 34, identify the dividend, divisor, and quotient.

33. $45 \div 5 = 9$
34. $m \div n = x$

OBJECTIVE G Tell whether a number is prime or composite. (Lesson 7-3)

In 35–37, indicate whether the number is prime or composite.

35. 682

36. 793

37. 1,013

38. Explain why 411 is a composite number.

OBJECTIVE H Tell whether a simple fraction equals a terminating or repeating decimal. (Lesson 7-7)

In 39–42, without using a calculator, determine whether the fraction equals a repeating or terminating decimal. Give a reason for your answer.

39. $\frac{1}{40}$

40. $\frac{7}{30}$

41. $\frac{547}{16}$

42. $\frac{548}{18}$

43. One fraction equals a terminating decimal. Another equals an infinite repeating decimal. Can their product be a terminating decimal? Justify your answer.

44. a. If you divide the decimal for $\frac{1}{5}$ by 3, you will have the decimal for what fraction?

b. Find the decimal.

USES Applications of mathematics in real-world situations

OBJECTIVE I Use integer division in real situations. (Lesson 7-4)

45. There are 57 children who want to play basketball. If they divide into teams of 5, how many teams can they make, and how many children will be left over?

In 46 and 47, suppose a baker makes 182 muffins.

46. How many dozen muffins can the baker package? How many muffins will be left over?

47. In a "baker's dozen," there are 13 muffins per package. How many baker's dozens can the baker package? How many muffins will be left over?

48. In the Iditarod sled race, teams of dogs race 1,150 miles across the frozen tundra of Alaska. If there are a total of 144 dogs,

a. how many 12-dog teams can there be?

b. how many 16-dog teams can there be?

OBJECTIVE J Use the rate model for division. (Lesson 7-1)

49. Within 2 hours of the end of a TV popularity contest, 7,100,000 ballots were cast. How many ballots is this per minute, rounded to the nearest ten thousand?

50. Mr. and Mrs. Staubach have 5 children and 32 grandchildren. How many grandchildren is this per child on average? (Answer as a decimal.)

51. The temperature at 9:00 A.M. was 10°F. At 3:00 P.M., the temperature was 33°F. To the nearest degree, what was the rate of change in temperature per hour?

52. If 37 volunteers pick up 2,340 cans in a highway clean-up, how many cans were picked up per volunteer?

OBJECTIVE K Use decimal division in real situations. (Lesson 7-8)

In 53–55, round your answer to the nearest hundredth.

53. Kelvin bought 2.2 pounds of raw oats that cost him a total of $1.97. How much would 1 pound of oats cost?

54. One inch equals 2.54 centimeters. How many centimeters are there in $\frac{1}{16}$ inch?

55. If a six-pack of soda costs $2.58, what is the cost per can?

OBJECTIVE L Use division with positive and negative numbers in real situations. (Lesson 7-9)

In 56–57,

a. write the calculation as a division involving negative numbers.

b. answer the question(s) with a sentence.

56. A glacier has melted 20 inches in 11 years. How many inches per year change is this?

57. Angelica earned \$210 dollars for taking care of her friend's cat Shady Lady. If she uses \$13 per week to go out to lunch, how many weeks can Angelica go out to lunch with the money she earned? How much money will she have left over?

58. The record low temperature in the United States was recorded in Prospect Creek, Alaska at -62 degrees Celsius. To convert this to degrees Fahrenheit, you can use the formula $F = \frac{9}{5}C + 32$, where C is the temperature in degrees Celsius. Calculate the record low temperature in degrees Fahrenheit.

REPRESENTATIONS Pictures, graphs, or objects that illustrate concepts

OBJECTIVE M Use arrays to picture divisibility. (Lesson 7-2)

In 59–62, draw an array to show that the number is composite. Variables represent whole numbers.

59. 36

60. 24

61. $7q$

62. $3p$

OBJECTIVE N Use fact triangles to solve equations and show relationships involving multiplication and division. (Lessons 7-1, 7-10)

In 63 and 64, construct a multiplication-and-division fact triangle using the given numbers.

63. -2.8, 5.5, -15.4

64. 0.11, 6.16, 56

In 65 and 66,

a. write the related facts, and

b. find the value of the variable.

65.

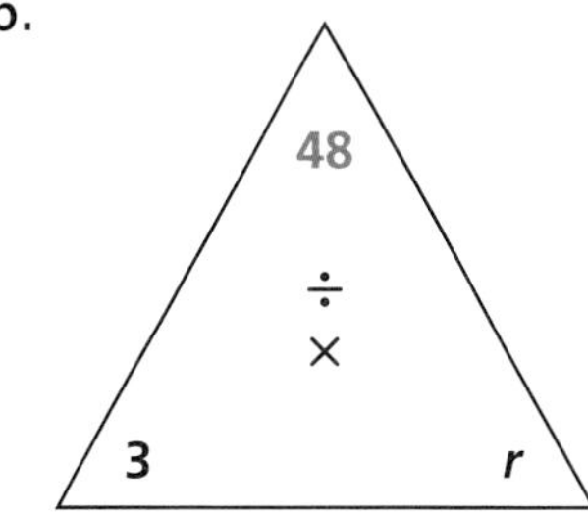

66.

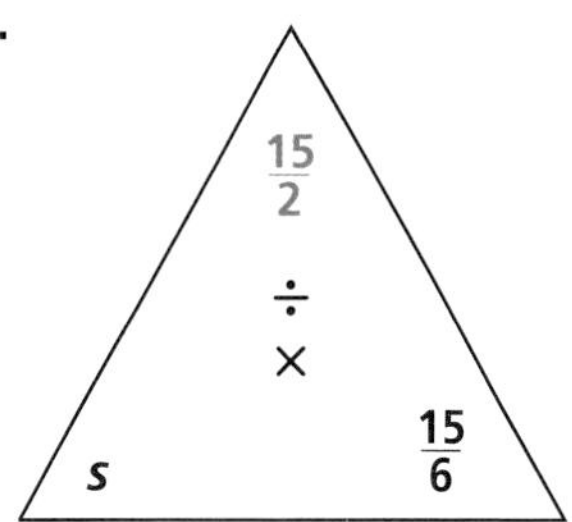

In 67 and 68, draw a fact triangle for the equation and use it to solve the equation.

67. $5a = 53$

68. $\frac{4}{f} = 7.5$

Chapter

8 Ratio and Proportion

Contents

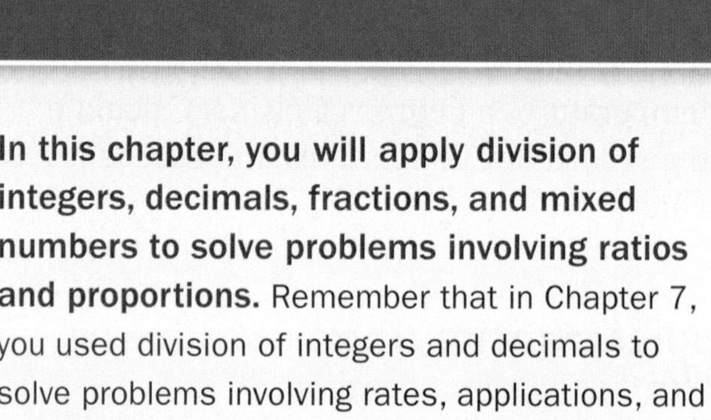

In this chapter, you will apply division of integers, decimals, fractions, and mixed numbers to solve problems involving ratios and proportions. Remember that in Chapter 7, you used division of integers and decimals to solve problems involving rates, applications, and equations.

An example of the kind of situation you will see in this chapter is pictured above. The photograph is of the dome of Santa Maria del Fiore, a cathedral in Florence, Italy. The construction of this dome, from 1420 to 1436 CE, was one of the great engineering accomplishments of its era. The finished dome weighs 37,000 tons and contains more than 4 million bricks.

You can use ratios and proportions to estimate the dome's height. Notice the people in the photo standing just above the colored bricks at the top of the dome. In the photograph, the height of a person is quite small, about 2 mm. The height of the dome in the photograph is about 113 mm. So, the ratio of the height of the dome to the height of a person is $\frac{113 \text{ mm}}{2 \text{ mm}} = 56.5$. This means the dome is 56.5 times the height of a person.

Assume the actual height of a person is 1.75 meters. If the dome is h meters high, then $h = 56.5 \cdot 1.75 \approx 98.875$ meters.

Notice how the numbers are related.

$$\frac{\text{height of dome in photo}}{\text{height of person in photo}} = \frac{\text{height of actual dome}}{\text{height of actual person}}$$

$$= 56.5$$

That is, $\frac{113 \text{ mm}}{2 \text{ mm}} = \frac{h \text{ meters}}{1.75 \text{ meters}}$.

We found that $h \approx 98.875$, so $\frac{113}{2} \approx \frac{98.875}{1.75}$.

The equations $\frac{113}{2} = \frac{h}{1.75}$ and $\frac{113}{2} \approx \frac{98.875}{1.75}$ are both *proportions*.

Finding unknown heights and distances is just one of the many applications of ratios and proportions. In this chapter, you will use reciprocals, algebra, and the Equal Fractions Property to solve a wide variety of problems involving ratios and proportions.

Lesson

8-1 The Ratio Comparison Model for Division

Vocabulary

ratio

ratio comparison

▸ **BIG IDEA** Ratios are computed by division.

You can compare two numbers by subtracting one from the other. You can also compare two numbers by dividing one number by the other.

When comparing two quantities with the same unit by division, the division is called a **ratio.** For instance, suppose you sleep for about 9 hours. To compare the number of sleeping hours with the number of hours in a day, you can divide 9 by 24.

$$9 \div 24 = \frac{9}{24} = \frac{3}{8}$$

In other words, you spend $\frac{3}{8}$ of your day sleeping. The ratio of hours sleeping to hours in a day is 3 to 8. This ratio can be written as the fraction $\frac{3}{8}$ or with a colon as 3:8 (read "3 *to* 8").

The order in which quantities are compared determines how to write the ratio. To compare the number of hours in a day with the number of hours asleep, you would write the division $\frac{24}{9}$, simplified to $\frac{8}{3}$. So, the ratio of hours in a day to sleeping hours is 8:3.

Mental Math

Which is greater?

a. $\frac{2}{3}$ or $\frac{3}{4}$

b. $\frac{5}{8}$ or $\frac{5}{9}$

c. $\frac{12}{7}$ or $\frac{12}{5}$

d. $\frac{5}{13}$ or $\frac{3}{7}$

Ratio Comparison Model for Division

If a and b are quantities with the same unit, then $\frac{a}{b}$ compares a to b.

Although a ratio is a comparison between quantities with the same or like units, a ratio itself does not have a unit. This use of division is called **ratio comparison.** Ratio comparison uses of division are different from rate uses. Rates are measures that result from dividing quantities with different units. Rates have units like miles per hour or students per class. Ratios have no units.

$$\frac{180 \text{ students}}{7 \text{ classes}} \approx \underbrace{26 \frac{\text{students}}{\text{class}}}_{\text{a rate}}$$

$$\frac{180 \text{ students (in a grade)}}{30 \text{ students (in your class)}} = 6$$

↑ a ratio

GUIDED

Example 1

Hakeem completed 24 questions on a 32-question test.

a. What is the ratio of completed questions to questions on the test?

b. Write this ratio in lowest terms.

Solution

a. The ratio is $\frac{\text{number of completed questions}}{\text{number of questions on the test}}$. Using substitution, this ratio is $\frac{24}{?}$.

b. In lowest terms, $\frac{24}{?} = \frac{?}{?}$.

In Example 1, you could say that Hakeem completed $\frac{3}{4}$ of the questions on the test. You could also say that Hakeem completed 75% of the questions. Both $\frac{3}{4}$ and 75% are ratios.

Percents as Ratios

Because percents result from comparing two quantities with the same units, percents can be considered ratios.

Example 2

When Jack and Jill ate at a restaurant, they left a \$3.00 tip for a \$16.39 check. What percent tip did they leave?

Solution Compare \$3.00 to \$16.39. Use the Ratio Comparison Model and divide \$3.00 by \$16.39.

$\frac{\$3.00}{\$16.39} = \frac{3}{16.39}$

The calculator shows that $\frac{3}{16.39} \approx .18308$.

As a percent, .183038 = 18.3038%.

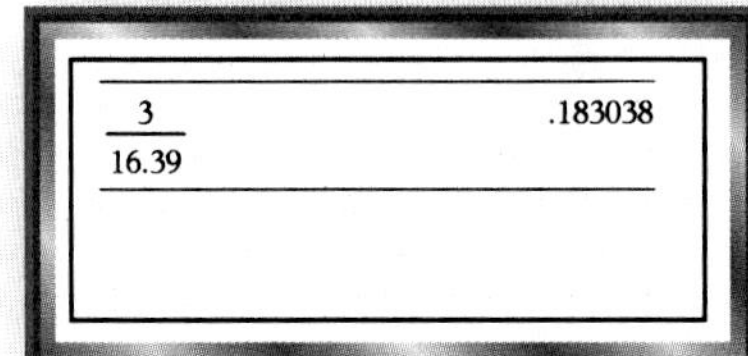

The tip is slightly more than 18%.

When a positive number is compared to a smaller positive number, the ratio is greater than 1.

Example 3

The Perez family is looking at two stereo systems. One system costs \$285. The other costs \$500. The higher cost is how many times the lower cost?

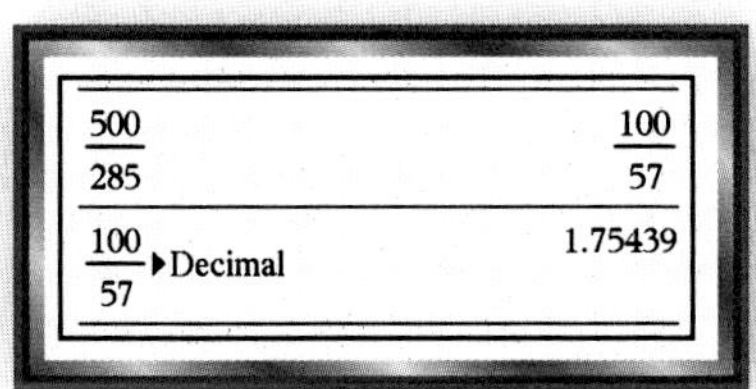

Solution Divide 500 by 285. The quotient $\frac{500}{285}$ is about 1.75.

The more expensive stereo system costs about 1.75 times, or 175% of, the cost of the less expensive system.

Examples 2 and 3 show that to find what percent one number is of another, you can divide the first number by the second.

 **See QY at the right.**

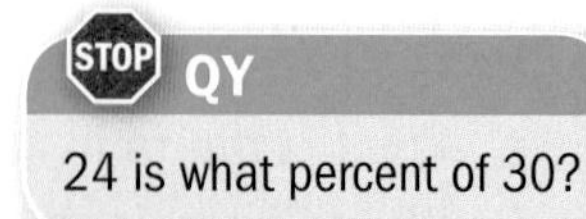
QY

24 is what percent of 30?

Activity

Step 1 Describe three comparison situations. For instance, the number of students in your class who walk to school compared to the number who do not.

Step 2 Work with a partner to estimate a ratio that would be reasonable for each situation.

Less than 15% of school children use active modes of transportation to get to school.

Source: cdc.gov

Questions

COVERING THE IDEAS

1. What is the difference between a rate and a ratio?
2. Refer to Example 1.
   a. What is the ratio of the number of questions Hakeem did *not* complete to the number of questions on the test?
   b. Write the ratio in Part a as a fraction in lowest terms.
   c. Write the ratio in Part a as a percent.
   d. **Fill in the Blank** Hakeem completed __?__ times as many questions as he didn't complete.

In 3–5, write each ratio as a fraction and as a percent.

3. the ratio of the cost of a dozen apples, \$3.69, to the cost of a dozen oranges, \$2.59
4. the ratio of the width of a rectangle, 4.5 cm, to its length, 8.5 cm
5. the ratio of 15 red markers in a bag to 20 blue markers in the bag

6. a. If you leave a \$2 tip for a meal that cost \$10, have you left at least 15%?
   b. What if you leave a \$2 tip for a meal that cost \$15?

In 7–10, give your answer to the nearest percent.

7. 60 is what percent of 6?
8. 0.08 is what percent of 0.24?
9. 12 is what percent of 20?
10. 40 is what percent of 25?

11. Use your answers for Questions 7–10 and the box below to identify a four-letter word. Save this word for the table in Question 22 in Lesson 8-8 on page 503.

Your answer is equivalent to:		
P $\frac{1}{4}$	C $\frac{3}{5}$	I $\frac{1}{3}$
S $\frac{2}{8}$	H $1\frac{3}{5}$	R $\frac{1}{10}$ of 10,000

Question	7	8	9	10
Letter	?	?	?	?

APPLYING THE MATHEMATICS

In 12–15, use this table of costs for computer storage devices.

Year	Capacity	Price	Cost per Megabyte
1981	18 megabytes	$4,200	$233
1985	10 megabytes	$710	?
1989	40 megabytes	$1,200	$30
1995	1 gigabyte (=1,024 megabytes)	$850	$0.83
2000	20 gigabytes	$260	$0.013
2004	250 gigabytes	$250	$0.00098
2007	500 gigabytes	$118	?

12. Compute the missing value in the second line of the table and tell what it means.
13. Complete the missing value in the last line of the table and tell what it means.
14. a. What is the ratio of the capacity of computer storage devices available in 2000 to those available in 1995?
    b. What is the ratio of cost per megabyte of computer storage devices available in 2000 to those in 1995?
15. a. What is the ratio of the capacity of computer storage devices available in 2007 to those in 2000?
    b. What is the ratio of cost per megabyte of computer storage devices available in 2007 to those in 2000?

REVIEW

16. Draw a fact triangle and write the related equations for the equation $\frac{7}{3}y = -4.8$. **(Lesson 7-10)**
17. **True or False** If a and b are positive, $-a \div -b$ is positive. **(Lesson 7-9)**

18. Trisha bought 16 gallons of gas for \$43.18. To the nearest cent, how much did she pay per gallon? **(Lessons 7-1, 2-6)**

In January of 2000, the average national cost for a gallon of gasoline was \$1.29. In September of 2007, the average cost was \$2.80 per gallon.

Source: U.S. Department of Energy

19. a. Find the area of a 4 ft-by-3 ft rectangle in square feet.
    b. Find the area of the rectangle in Part a in square inches.
    c. Explain how you can use your answers to Parts a and b to determine the number of square inches in a square foot. **(Lesson 6-3)**

20. Use the table below, which displays distances traveled in a car over a certain period of time. **(Lesson 5-7)**

Minutes	0	10	20	30	40
Miles traveled	0	6	12	18	24

a. Plot these data on a coordinate grid, with minutes on the horizontal axis.
b. Predict how far the car will travel in 60 minutes at this rate. Explain your reasoning.

21. Find w if $4.9 + w = 2.8$. **(Lesson 4-9)**

EXPLORATION

22. Refer to the table in Questions 12–15. Use the Internet to find the current cost of 500 gigabytes of computer storage. What is the ratio of the cost you find to the cost in the table, written as a percent?

QY ANSWER

80%

Lesson 8-2 Reciprocals

Vocabulary

multiplicative inverse

reciprocal

▸ **BIG IDEA** If you divide two numbers in the two possible orders, the quotients are reciprocals.

When two quantities have the same unit, they can be compared as a ratio in two ways.

Mental Math

Calculate.

a. $(-1) \cdot (-1)$

b. $2 \cdot \frac{1}{2}$

c. $3 \cdot \frac{1}{3}$

d. $25\% \cdot 4$

Example 1

Ruby is 42. Her daughter Jeanette is 18.

a. Use a ratio to compare Ruby's age to Jeanette's age.

b. Use a ratio to compare Jeanette's age to Ruby's age.

Solution

a. $\frac{42}{18} = \frac{7}{3} = 2\frac{1}{3}$ so, Ruby is $2\frac{1}{3}$ times as old as Jeanette.

b. $\frac{18}{42} = \frac{3}{7}$ so, Jeanette is $\frac{3}{7}$ times as old as Ruby.

 **See QY1 at the right.**

QY1

Multiply the ratios from Parts a and b of Example 1. What is their product?

Example 2

Use ratios to compare the world population in 1900, about 1,650,000,000 people, to the world population in 2000, about 6,070,000,000 people.

Solution The units (people) are the same.

The ratio of the smaller population to the greater population is

$\frac{1,650,000,000}{6,070,000,000} \approx 0.2718 = 27.18\%$. This means the world population in 1900 was about 27% of the world population in 2000.

The ratio of the greater population to the smaller population is

$\frac{6,070,000,000}{1,650,000,000} \approx 3.679 \approx 368\%$. This means the world population in 2000 was about 3.7 times, or about 370% of the population in 1900.

In both examples, the product of the two ratios is 1. In Example 1, $\frac{42}{18} \cdot \frac{18}{42} = 1$. In Example 2, $\frac{1,650,000,000}{6,070,000,000} \cdot \frac{6,070,000,000}{1,650,000,000} = 1$. By the Multiplication of Fractions Property, $\frac{a}{b} \cdot \frac{b}{a} = \frac{ab}{ab} = 1$.

Property of Reciprocals

When the product of two numbers is 1, the numbers are called **multiplicative inverses** or **reciprocals.**

Property of Reciprocals

1. For any nonzero number a, a and $\frac{1}{a}$ are reciprocals.
2. For any nonzero numbers a and b, $\frac{a}{b}$ and $\frac{b}{a}$ are reciprocals.

To find the reciprocal of a number on a calculator, enter the number, then press the $\boxed{\frac{1}{x}}$ or the $\boxed{x^{-1}}$ key. If your calculator does not have a reciprocal key, you can divide 1 by x to calculate the reciprocal of x.

QY2

a. What is the reciprocal of $\frac{3}{20}$?
b. What is the reciprocal of –2?
c. What number has no reciprocal?

Different Forms of Reciprocals

Since $\frac{5}{8} \cdot \frac{8}{5} = 1$, $\frac{5}{8}$ and $\frac{8}{5}$ are reciprocals. Because $\frac{5}{8}$ can be written as a fraction, decimal, or percent $\left(\frac{5}{8}, 0.625, \text{ or } 62.5\%\right)$, so can its reciprocal.

$$\frac{8}{5} = \frac{1}{\frac{5}{8}} = 1\frac{3}{5} = 1.6 = 160\%$$

It is easy to write the reciprocal of a number if it is a whole number or simple fraction. But you may need to use a calculator if you need to write the reciprocal as a decimal or percent.

Example 3

The number of adult tickets sold for a movie was 2.4 times the number of children's tickets sold. The number of children's tickets sold was how many times the number of adult tickets sold?

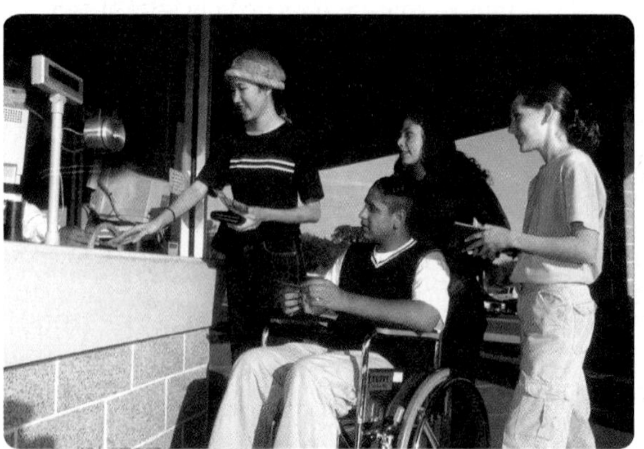

The average movie ticket price in 2006 was $6.55.

Source: National Association of Theatre Owners

Solution The information given is that

$$\frac{\text{number of adult tickets sold}}{\text{number of children's tickets sold}} = 2.4.$$

Take the reciprocal of each side of the equation.

$$\frac{\text{number of children's tickets sold}}{\text{number of adult tickets sold}} = \frac{1}{2.4}$$

Rewrite the result as a simple fraction, as a decimal, and as a percent: $\frac{1}{2.4} = \frac{10}{24} = \frac{5}{12} = 0.41\overline{6} = 41.\overline{6}\%$.

The number of children's tickets sold was $\frac{5}{12}$, or about 41.6%, of the number of adult tickets sold.

Check Multiply 2.4 by 41.6%. The product is about 1.

The product of a number and its reciprocal can be pictured with a multiplication-division fact triangle with the number 1 at the top. The other two numbers will be reciprocals.

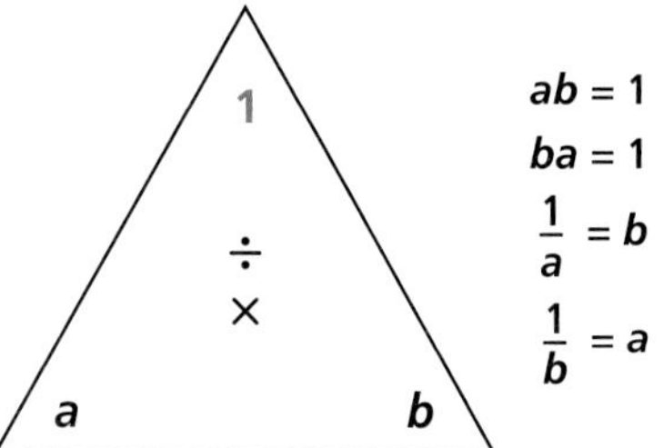

Questions

COVERING THE IDEAS

1. If the ratio of boys to girls in a class is $\frac{8}{7}$, what is the ratio of girls to boys?

2. **Fill in the Blank** Another name for reciprocal is __?__ inverse.

In 3–7, find the reciprocal. Write your answer as a simple fraction.

3. 100 4. $\frac{1}{3}$ 5. $-\frac{9}{5}$ 6. $\frac{13}{0.2}$ 7. $3\frac{2}{5}$

8. $\frac{a}{b}$, where $a \neq 0$ and $b \neq 0$

9. **Multiple Choice** Which is *not* the reciprocal of 3.5?
   A $\frac{1}{3.5}$ B $\frac{7}{2}$ C $\frac{2}{7}$ D $\frac{10}{35}$

10. In 1900, the population of the United States was about 76,094,000. By 2000, it was about 272,700,000. Compare using ratios and interpret these two populations in two ways.

11. a. Write a decimal equal to $\frac{1}{0.8}$.
    b. Multiply your answer in Part a by 0.8. Does it check?

12. a. Use a calculator to find the reciprocal of 0.3125.
    b. Write the key sequence you used to compute the reciprocal.

APPLYING THE MATHEMATICS

13. Solve the equation $8x = 1$.

14. Solve for a: $1.25a = 1$.

15. Write and solve a multiplication equation shown by the fact triangle below.

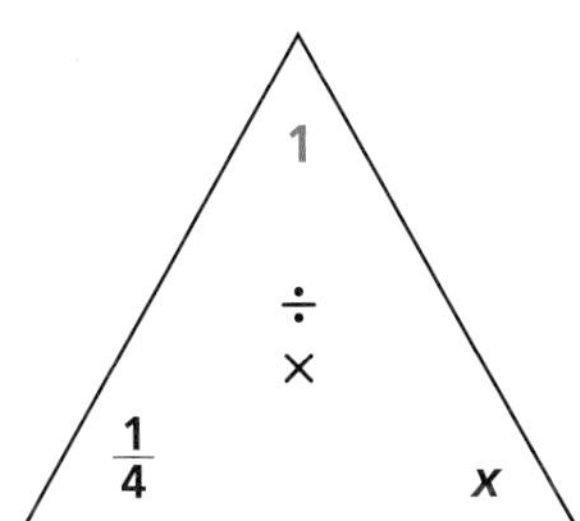

16. In 2002, the United States produced 8.97 billion bushels of corn. In 2003, production increased to 10.1 billion bushels. Compare these two quantities using ratios in two ways. Write a statement interpreting each comparison.

17. In 2005, 22.5 million digital audio players were sold. In 2004, 4.4 million were sold. Compare these two sales figures in two ways. Write a statement interpreting each comparison.

Do you own a digital audio player?

18. What is the reciprocal of each number?

a. 1 **b.** -1 **c.** 0.01 **d.** 10%

19. In Parts a and b, round your answer to the nearest hundredth of a percent.

a. 30 is what percent of 70?

b. 70 is what percent of 30?

c. **True or False** The answers to Parts a and b are reciprocals.

20. Find the reciprocal of each number below. Put the reciprocals in order from greatest to least. Save this word for the quote in Question 22 in Lesson 8-8 on page 503.

$\frac{42}{18} = \text{O}$ $-\frac{5}{3} = \text{E}$ $0.25 = \text{A}$ $34\% = \text{L}$ $2.6 = \text{N}$

REVIEW

21. The ratio of the age of Dominique's mother to Dominique's age is 3 to 1. In 11 years, the ratio of these ages will be 2 to 1. By trial and error, find the current age of Dominique and of her mother. **(Lesson 8-1)**

22. A brother or sister is a *sibling.* Suppose you have an older sibling. As you and your older sibling get older,

a. does the ratio of your age to that of your sibling increase, stay the same, or decrease?

b. does the ratio of your sibling's age to your age increase, stay the same, or decrease? **(Lesson 8-1)**

23. If you leave a total of \$33 for a meal that cost \$28.87, have you left at least a 15% tip? **(Lesson 8-1)**

24. Give the two division facts related to $-4.5 \cdot 2.8 = -12.6$. **(Lesson 7-10)**

25. Use an array to show that 25 is not divisible by 3. **(Lesson 7-2)**

26. A group of five students worked together to complete 100 math problems. A circle graph was created from the following table. The table shows the number of math problems each student finished. However, the students forgot to label the circle graph. Indicate which sector of the circle graph represents each student's work. **(Lesson 5-5)**

Student	Number of Problems
Gabriela	30
Jorge	10
Todd	20
Kameron	25
Pam	15

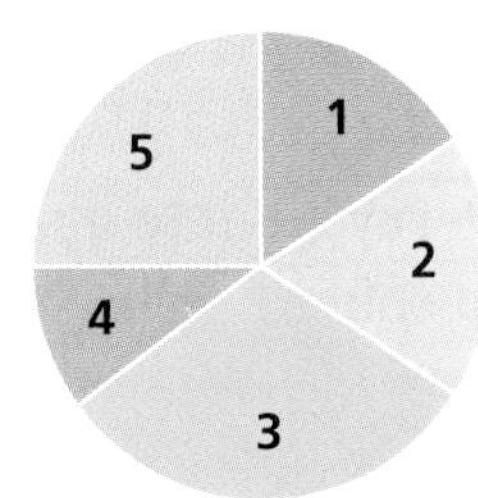

EXPLORATION

27. Some calculators use exponential notation, x^{-1}, for reciprocals. Explore why.

a. Complete all but the last row of the table below.

Exponential Notation	Decimal Form
10^3	1000
10^2	?
10^1	?
10^0	?
$10^?$	?

b. Look at the pattern in the second column. What would you predict for the number in the last row? What is its reciprocal?

c. Look at the pattern of exponents in the first column. What would you predict as the exponent in the last row?

d. Build a new table with powers of 2 instead of 10. Do the same patterns hold?

28. Look back at the table for Questions 12–15 in Lesson 8-1. When the cost per megabyte of computer storage became low, people started calculating megabytes per dollar. For the years 1995, 2000, 2004, and 2007, calculate the megabytes per dollar. How are these numbers related to the ideas in this lesson?

QY ANSWERS

1. 1

2a. $\frac{20}{3}$

2b. $\frac{1}{-2}$ or $-\frac{1}{2}$

2c. 0

Lesson 8-3 Division of Fractions

▸ **BIG IDEA** The property, $\frac{a}{b} = a \cdot \frac{1}{b}$ connects fractions to division and can be used to divide one fraction by another.

Jerry, Kerri, Larry, Mary, Barry, and Perry went to a restaurant. The bill totaled \$40.80. They decided to split the bill evenly. They knew that to find $\frac{1}{6}$ of \$40.80 they could divide \$40.80 by 6. That is, $\frac{\$40.80}{6} = \$40.80 \cdot \frac{1}{6}$.

Notice that the division problem $40.80 \div 6$ has been converted to the multiplication problem $40.80 \cdot \frac{1}{6}$. Instead of dividing by 6, you can multiply by $\frac{1}{6}$. Dividing by a number is the same as multiplying by its reciprocal.

Letting a stand for the restaurant bill, \$40.80 and b the 6 people, the equation $\frac{\$40.80}{6} = \$40.80 \cdot \frac{1}{6}$ becomes $\frac{a}{b} = a \cdot \frac{1}{b}$. This formula is the *Mult-Rec Property,* an abbreviation of "Multiply by the Reciprocal Property."

Mental Math

a. How many fifths are in 1?

b. How many fifths are in 5?

c. How many fifths are in 10?

d. How many fifths are in 3?

Algebraic Definition of Division (Mult-Rec Property)

For any numbers a and b, $b \neq 0$, a divided by b equals a times the reciprocal of b: $\frac{a}{b} = a \cdot \frac{1}{b}$.

QY1

In Lesson 8-2, you saw that $41.\overline{6}\%$ and 2.4 are reciprocals. Verify that dividing 50 by 2.4 gives the same answer as multiplying 50 by 41.6%.

The reciprocal of $\frac{1}{2}$ is 2, so the Mult-Rec Property says that dividing by $\frac{1}{2}$ is the same as multiplying by 2. You will explore this idea in the next activity.

Activity 1

Step 1 What is $6 \div \frac{1}{2}$? To answer this question, look at the ruler on the next page to see how many $\frac{1}{2}$-inch segments are in 6 inches.
$6 \div \frac{1}{2} =$ __?__

Step 2 Use the ruler to help you determine the answer.

a. $6 \div \frac{1}{4} = \underline{\ ?\ }$ b. $6 \div \frac{1}{8} = \underline{\ ?\ }$ c. $6 \div \frac{1}{16} = \underline{\ ?\ }$

Step 3 Generalize your results: $6 \div \frac{1}{n} = 6 \cdot \underline{\ ?\ }$.

Division of Fractions Using the Mult-Rec Property

You can divide any number by a fraction if you use the Mult-Rec Property.

Example 1

Use the Mult-Rec Property to calculate $\frac{5}{8} \div \frac{1}{4}$.

Solution Rewrite $\frac{5}{8} \div \frac{1}{4}$ as a multiplication using the Mult-Rec Property. $\frac{5}{8} \div \frac{1}{4} = \frac{5}{8} \cdot \frac{4}{1}$. Now, multiply the fractions: $\frac{5}{8} \cdot \frac{4}{1} = \frac{20}{8} = \frac{5}{2}$ or $2\frac{1}{2}$.

Check 1 Use estimation: $\frac{5}{8}$ is greater than $\frac{1}{2}$. Since there are two fourths in $\frac{1}{2}$, the answer should be a little more than 2. It is.

Check 2 Use a fact triangle for $\frac{5}{8} \div \frac{1}{4} = 2\frac{1}{2}$.

The fact triangle at the right shows that $2\frac{1}{2} \cdot \frac{1}{4} = \frac{5}{8}$. Checking this fact, we see that it checks.

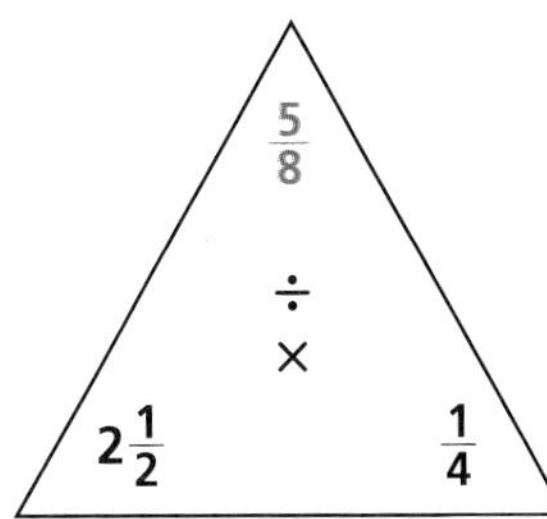

Example 2

A recipe for chicken-pecan salad calls for 3 tablespoons of spicy mustard. Carla wants to use all of the $\frac{2}{3}$ cup of mustard she has. She knows there are 16 tablespoons in a cup. How many times the recipe can Carla make?

Solution Since 1 tablespoon is $\frac{1}{16}$ cup, 3 tablespoons is $\frac{3}{16}$ cups. Carla needs to compare the $\frac{2}{3}$ cup mustard she has to the $\frac{3}{16}$ cup needed in the recipe. This division gives this ratio: $\frac{\frac{2}{3}\text{ cup}}{\frac{3}{16}\text{ cup}}$.

Use the Mult-Rec Property. The reciprocal of $\frac{3}{16}$ is $\frac{16}{3}$.

(continued on next page)

Pecans are a great source of dietary fiber!

$$\frac{2}{3} \div \frac{3}{16} = \frac{2}{3} \cdot \frac{16}{3}$$ Mult-Rec Property of Division

$$= \frac{32}{9}$$ Multiplication of Fractions Property

$$= 3\frac{5}{9}$$ Change to a mixed number.

Carla can make a little more than $3\frac{1}{2}$ times the recipe.

Check Use related facts. (Use $3\frac{5}{9} = \frac{32}{9}$.)

$\frac{3}{16}$ cups per recipe $\cdot \frac{32}{9}$ recipes $= \frac{96}{144}$ cup $= \frac{2}{3}$ cup

GUIDED

Example 3

Write $\frac{\frac{4}{5}}{\frac{3}{10}}$ as a simple fraction and as a mixed number.

Solution

$$\frac{\frac{4}{5}}{\frac{3}{10}} = \frac{4}{5} \div \frac{3}{10}$$ Rewrite as a division problem.

$$= \frac{4}{5} \cdot \frac{?}{?}$$ Apply the Mult-Rec Property and write your answer as a mixed number.

$$= \underline{\ ?\ }$$

$$= \underline{\ ?\ }$$

Check Rewrite $\frac{4}{5}$ and $\frac{3}{10}$ as decimals.

$$\frac{\frac{4}{5}}{\frac{3}{10}} = \frac{?}{?} = 2.7.$$

This is the decimal equivalent of your simple fraction.

QY2

Rewrite each division as a multiplication.

a. $\frac{1}{2} \div \frac{1}{4}$

b. $\frac{4}{5} \div \frac{2}{5}$

c. $\frac{\frac{7}{9}}{\frac{9}{10}}$

STOP **See QY2 at the right.**

Questions

COVERING THE IDEAS

1. **Fill in the Blanks** You and six friends decide to split a restaurant bill evenly. To figure out what your share is, you can divide the total bill by __?__ or multiply the total bill by __?__.

2. a. Write the reciprocal of 4 as a decimal.
   b. Multiply 37 by 4.
   c. Divide 37 by the reciprocal of 4.
   d. How do your answers to Parts b and c compare?

3. To divide 6,000 by 50, you can multiply 6,000 by what number?

Many restaurants automatically add a gratuity for large parties. "Gratuity" is a synonym for "tip."

4. To divide 8 by 7, Ciara multiplied $\frac{1}{8}$ by 7. She got the answer 0.875.
   a. What did Ciara do wrong?
   b. Give the correct decimal answer to the nearest hundredth.

5. To divide 12 by 15, Tia multiplied $\frac{1}{12}$ by $\frac{1}{15}$.
   a. What did Tia did do wrong?
   b. Write the correct answer as a decimal.

6. How many segments of each length need to be put together to make an 8-inch segment?
   a. 2 inches b. $\frac{1}{2}$ inch c. $\frac{1}{4}$ inch

7. José used 4 yards of twine to bundle the newspapers he delivers. If each bundle required $\frac{2}{3}$ of a yard of twine, how many bundles did he make?

8. State the Algebraic Definition of Division.

9. Divide $3\frac{1}{2}$ yards
   a. by $\frac{1}{2}$. b. in half. c. by 2.

In 10–14, write the quotient as a simple fraction.

10. $\frac{5}{3} \div \frac{1}{4}$ 11. $\frac{3}{4} \div 5$ 12. $\frac{\frac{1}{4}}{\frac{1}{2}}$

13. $\frac{\frac{7}{8}}{\frac{3}{4}}$ 14. $\frac{\frac{3}{4}}{\frac{7}{8}}$

Newspaper boys were a product of the Great Depression, born of the need to boost revenues and increase readership.

Source: *Oxford Journals*

APPLYING THE MATHEMATICS

15. Phil and Gil are twins. They always get the same-size helpings of food at dinner. Gil ate $\frac{1}{3}$ of the helping of peas given to him, while Phil ate $\frac{2}{3}$ of his helping of peas.
    a. Compare the amount of peas Phil ate to the amount of peas Gil ate.
    b. Compare the amount of peas Gil ate to the amount of peas Phil ate.

16. How can you use the fact that $8 \div \frac{1}{3} = 24$ to compute $8 \div \frac{2}{3}$?

17. Calculate the division problems below. On the line under each problem, write the letter corresponding to the value of the quotient in the box at the right. Save this word for the quote in Question 22 in Lesson 8-8 on page 503.

$\frac{5}{\frac{1}{2}}$	$\frac{5}{\frac{1}{4}}$	$\frac{4}{\frac{1}{5}}$	$\frac{12}{\frac{1}{3}}$	$\frac{\frac{1}{5}}{\frac{1}{10}}$	$\frac{\frac{3}{17}}{\frac{1}{17}}$
?	?	?	?	?	?

F = 20	A = 10
D = 3	O = 36
R = 2	

18. a. Copy and complete the table at the right.
    b. Which division problems in the table have a quotient less than 20, the dividend?
    c. Which problems have a quotient equal to the dividend?
    d. Which problems have a quotient greater than the dividend?
    e. Write a sentence that describes the pattern you see in Parts b–d.

Division	Quotient
$20 \div 10$	2
$20 \div 5$	?
$20 \div 4$	?
$20 \div 2$	?
$20 \div 1$	?
$20 \div \frac{1}{2}$	?
$20 \div \frac{1}{4}$	80
$20 \div \frac{1}{5}$	?
$20 \div \frac{1}{10}$	?

19. **Multiple Choice** Which of the following *cannot* be performed?
    A $\frac{2}{3} \div \frac{4}{5}$ B $\frac{0}{4} \div \frac{5}{6}$ C $\frac{4}{3} \div \frac{0}{2}$ D $\frac{3}{2} \div \frac{6}{5}$

20. Without doing the division, determine whether $1\frac{1}{2} \div \frac{5}{6}$ is greater than or less than 1. How do you know?

21. Divide $0.625 \div \frac{3}{4}$ in two ways. First use fractions, and then use decimals. Check that your two answers are equal.

REVIEW

In 22–27, give the reciprocal of the number. (Lesson 8-2)

22. $\frac{3}{7}$ 23. $\frac{6}{5}$ 24. $\frac{13}{4}$

25. 9 26. 2.3 27. 75%

28. **True or False** If a is the reciprocal of b, then b is the reciprocal of a. (Lesson 8-2)

29. Mozart wrote 27 piano concertos, only 2 of which were written in a minor key. To the nearest whole number percent, what percent of Mozart's piano concertos were written in a major key (that is, not in a minor key)? (Lesson 8-1)

Mozart began composing music at the age of five!

Source: *Encyclopedia Britannica*

30. Freida's Fruit Punch is sold in 1.5 liter bottles. If you want to fill up an 8.75-liter punch bowl, how many bottles should you buy? (Lesson 8-1)

31. Write three-fourths to the fourth power as a simple fraction. (Lesson 6-4)

EXPLORATION

32. A water-balloon toss is scheduled for a picnic. To prepare, volunteers have filled balloons with water and stored them in large utility buckets.
    a. The water balloons each hold about 18 fluid ounces. Water weighs approximately $\frac{13}{200}$ pound per fluid ounce. In lowest terms, about how much does each water balloon weigh? (Balloons weigh very little and their weight can be ignored.)
    b. The utility buckets are designed to hold up to 60 pounds. What is the maximum number of balloons the volunteers should put into each bucket?

QY ANSWERS

1. $50 \div 2.4 \approx 20.8$; $50 \cdot 41.6\% = 50 \cdot 0.416 = 20.8$

2a. $\frac{1}{2} \cdot 4$

2b. $\frac{4}{5} \cdot \frac{5}{2}$

2c. $\frac{7}{9} \cdot \frac{10}{9}$

Lesson 8-4 Division of Mixed Numbers

Vocabulary

complex fraction

▶ **BIG IDEA** One way to divide with mixed numbers is by changing them to improper fractions.

What do you do when you are presented with a new type of problem? One strategy is to turn it into an equivalent problem you already know how to solve. In this lesson, you will see that you can divide mixed numbers by rewriting them as improper fractions. Then you can divide, using the same procedure you used for simple fractions.

Mental Math

Find the area of the given region or regions.

	10	4
5	D	C
8	A	B

a. A

b. B

c. C

d. A, B, C, and D together

Complex fractions

You have seen fractions in which the numerator or denominator or both are fractions. When a fraction has a fraction in its numerator or denominator, it is called a **complex fraction.** For instance, in Example 3 of Lesson 8-3, $\frac{\frac{4}{5}}{\frac{3}{10}}$ is a complex fraction. Using division, you can rewrite a complex fraction as a simple fraction, even when there are mixed numbers.

GUIDED

Example 1

Write $\frac{6\frac{1}{2}}{3\frac{5}{7}}$ as a simple fraction.

Solution

$\frac{6\frac{1}{2}}{3\frac{5}{7}} = \underline{\ ?\ } \div \underline{\ ?\ }$ Rewrite the fraction as a division.

$= \frac{13}{2} \div \frac{?}{?}$ Rename the mixed numbers as improper fractions.

$= \frac{13}{2} \cdot \frac{?}{?}$ Use the Mult-Rec Property.

$= \frac{?}{?}$ Multiply the fractions.

$= \frac{?}{4}$ Divide the numerator and denominator by any common factors.

$= \underline{\ ?\ }$ If necessary, change the improper fraction to a mixed number.

Check Does $3\frac{5}{7} \cdot$ your answer $= 6\frac{1}{2}$?

In Guided Example 1, you could have predicted that the answer would be between 1 and 2. This is because $3\frac{5}{7}$ is less than $6\frac{1}{2}$ (so the quotient is greater than 1) and $2 \cdot 3\frac{5}{7}$ is greater than $6\frac{1}{2}$ (so the quotient is less than 2). It is always a good idea to estimate the answer to a division problem before you divide.

Activity

Step 1 Discuss the first row of the table below with a partner. How could you find an estimate? How could you check your answer?

Step 2 Work with a partner to complete the table.

Computation	Estimated Answer	Rewritten Problem	Answer (in lowest terms, as mixed number if possible)
1. $1\frac{3}{4} \div \frac{1}{8}$	between 8 and 16	$\frac{7}{4} \div \frac{1}{8} = \frac{7}{4} \cdot \frac{8}{1}$	$\frac{56}{4} = 14$
2. $38\frac{1}{2} \div 1\frac{2}{3}$	?	?	?
3. $70\frac{4}{5} \div 89\frac{19}{20}$	?	?	?
4. $10\frac{5}{61} \div 2\frac{2}{5}$	?	?	?
5. $1 \div 4\frac{1}{8}$	?	?	?

Step 3 Compare your answers with those of another pair of students. Discuss any solutions you do not understand.

Order of Operations and Division

Remember that under the order of operations, the fraction bar acts like parentheses. This means you do the operations in the numerator and denominator first, before doing any division.

Example 2

Molly rode her bike $3\frac{1}{2}$ miles to her friend Tara's house in 30 minutes. Then the two of them rode $4\frac{2}{5}$ miles to Sandy's house in 45 minutes. On average, how fast was Molly biking in miles per hour?

Most historians believe that the first bicycle with foot pedals was invented by Baron Karl von Drais de Sauerbrun of Germany in 1817.

Source: *Encyclopedia Britannica*

Solution 1 To find Molly's rate in miles per hour, find the total number of miles and divide by the total number of hours: $\dfrac{3\frac{1}{2} + 4\frac{2}{5}}{\frac{1}{2} + \frac{3}{4}}$.

(Note: 30 minutes $= \frac{1}{2}$ hour, 45 minutes $= \frac{3}{4}$ hour.)

$$\frac{3\frac{1}{2} + 4\frac{2}{5}}{\frac{1}{2} + \frac{3}{4}} = \frac{3\frac{5}{10} + 4\frac{4}{10}}{\frac{2}{4} + \frac{3}{4}} = \frac{7\frac{9}{10}}{\frac{5}{4}} = \frac{7\frac{9}{10}}{1\frac{1}{4}}$$

This is now a division of mixed numbers. It can be done using the process in Guided Example 1.

$$\frac{7\frac{9}{10}}{1\frac{1}{4}} = 7\frac{9}{10} \div 1\frac{1}{4} = \frac{79}{10} \div \frac{5}{4} = \frac{79}{10} \cdot \frac{4}{5} = \frac{316}{50} = 6\frac{16}{50} = 6\frac{8}{25}$$

Molly averaged $6\frac{8}{25}$ miles per hour, or 6.32 $\frac{\text{mi}}{\text{hr}}$.

Solution 2 Enter the calculation into a calculator. Be careful to use parentheses for each numerator and denominator:

$\left(3\frac{1}{2} + 4\frac{2}{5}\right) \div \left(\frac{1}{2} + \frac{3}{4}\right) = 6.32\ \frac{\text{mi}}{\text{hr}}$.

$\dfrac{3+\frac{1}{2}+4+\frac{2}{5}}{\frac{1}{2}+\frac{3}{4}}$ $\qquad \dfrac{158}{25}$

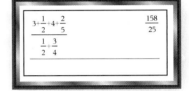

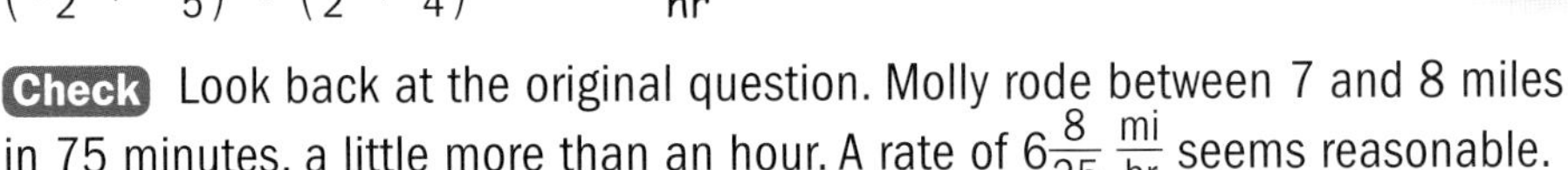

Check Look back at the original question. Molly rode between 7 and 8 miles in 75 minutes, a little more than an hour. A rate of $6\frac{8}{25}\ \frac{\text{mi}}{\text{hr}}$ seems reasonable.

Now you can play *Match-It: Fraction Division*. The directions for this game are on page G24 at the back of your book.

Questions

COVERING THE IDEAS

1. Abby's punch bowl holds 16 cups of punch. She plans to serve $\frac{3}{4}$-cup servings to her guests.
   a. Write a division problem that would find how many servings the punch bowl holds.
   b. Find the answer to your division problem.
   c. Check your answer by using multiplication.

2. A builder is planning a patio that will be $16\frac{2}{3}$ feet long. The stones he will use to pave it are $1\frac{2}{3}$ feet long. How many stones will be placed along the length of the patio?

The word "punch" comes from the Hindi word *panch* meaning "five".

Source: *Pittsburgh Post Gazette*

In 3–7, divide the fractions by multiplying by the reciprocal.

3. $2\frac{2}{3} \div \frac{3}{5}$

4. $\dfrac{\frac{11}{12}}{2\frac{1}{16}}$

5. $6\frac{1}{4} \div 2\frac{1}{4}$

6. $14\frac{2}{7} \div \frac{7}{10}$

7. $\dfrac{4\frac{2}{3}}{2\frac{3}{6}}$

8. **Fill in the Blank** The expressions in Questions 4 and 7 are called __?__.

9. Destinee ran $5\frac{1}{3}$ miles in $\frac{3}{4}$ of an hour. When she arrived home, she wanted to know her speed in miles per hour. Destinee's husband Jerome said "Easy, just divide $\frac{3}{4}$ by $5\frac{1}{3}$." Destinee was not so sure. She thinks she should divide $5\frac{1}{3}$ by $\frac{3}{4}$.
   a. Who is correct? Explain how you know.
   b. Find Destinee's speed in miles per hour.

10. Will drove 10 miles in 20 minutes and then drove 6 miles in 15 minutes. What was his average speed, in miles per hour?

In 11 and 12, simplify the expression.

11. $\dfrac{15\frac{3}{4} + 2\frac{7}{8}}{6\frac{1}{8} + 4\frac{1}{2}}$

12. $\dfrac{3\frac{3}{4} + 1}{3\frac{3}{4} - 1}$

13. Write the key sequence for evaluating the expression in Question 11 on your calculator.

APPLYING THE MATHEMATICS

14. a. Divide $3\frac{1}{2} \div \frac{3}{4}$.
   b. Your answer to Part a should be greater than 1. How could you have known this before you divided?

15. a. Divide $3\frac{1}{2} \div 4\frac{4}{5}$.
   b. Your answer to Part a should be less than 1. How could you have known this before you divided?

16. Mona made a dozen of her famous peanut butter roll-ups for her soccer team. She used a total of $1\frac{1}{2}$ cups of peanut butter.
   a. Set up and solve a division problem to determine the amount of peanut butter in each roll-up.
   b. There are 16 tablespoons in 1 cup. How many tablespoons of peanut butter are in each roll-up?

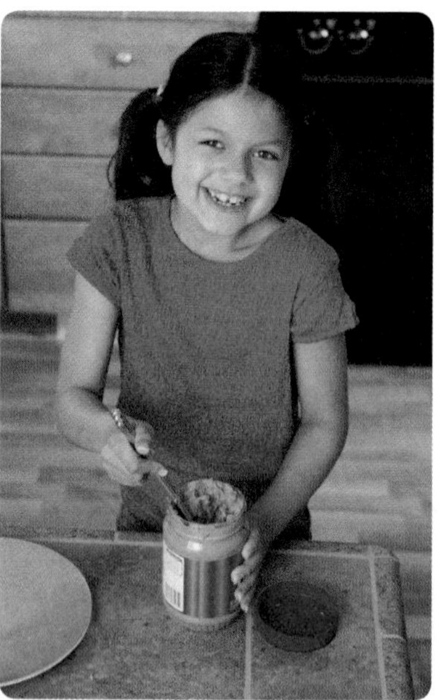

George Washington Carver is widely considered the inventor of peanut butter, but in fact, it was likely only popularized by him.

Source: *Encyclopedia Britannica*

In 17 and 18, rewrite each expression as a simple fraction.

17. $\left(2\frac{1}{2} + \frac{1}{3}\right)^2$

18. $\dfrac{1}{\frac{3}{4} + \frac{7}{10}}$

19. a. Put these values in order from least to greatest. Save the word for the quote in Question 22 in Lesson 8-8 on page 503.

$A = \dfrac{2\frac{3}{4}}{1\frac{1}{2}}$ $\quad N = \dfrac{2\frac{3}{4}}{1\frac{1}{10}}$ $\quad M = \dfrac{2\frac{3}{4}}{4\frac{1}{2}}$

b. Describe the pattern shown by the ordered divisions.

REVIEW

20. Li decided to study for $\frac{3}{4}$ of an hour for each of his classes. He has 5 hours total that he can dedicate to studying. How many classes will he have time to fully study for? **(Lesson 8-3)**

In 21 and 22, the local grocery store donated 40 pounds of grapes for the sixth-grade picnic. Student helpers are dividing the grapes into portion-sized bags. (Lesson 8-3)

21. How many full bags of grapes can they make if they use the indicated portion size?

a. $\frac{1}{4}$ lb b. $\frac{1}{5}$ lb c. $\frac{1}{8}$ lb

22. Suppose the student helpers divide the grapes so that each of the 124 sixth graders and their five teachers gets a bag. Express the weight of each bag as a fraction in lowest terms.

23. The tallest giraffe on record was about 5.5 m tall, while the average human height is about 1.75 m. **(Lesson 8-3)**

a. Convert these heights into simple fractions.

b. Tell how many times as tall as the average human the giraffe was.

c. Check your answer by dividing the decimals.

24. **Fill in the Blank** A reciprocal is a number whose __?__ with the original number is 1. **(Lesson 8-2)**

25. An apple orchard has trees planted in small plots of land that are 6 feet wide by 6 feet long. If there are 25 trees in the orchard, what is the area of the orchard? **(Lesson 6-3)**

In 26 and 27, fill in the blanks. (Lesson 6-2)

26. $1\frac{2}{5}$ of 20 is __?__.

27. $\frac{2}{3}$ of $\frac{3}{4}$ is __?__.

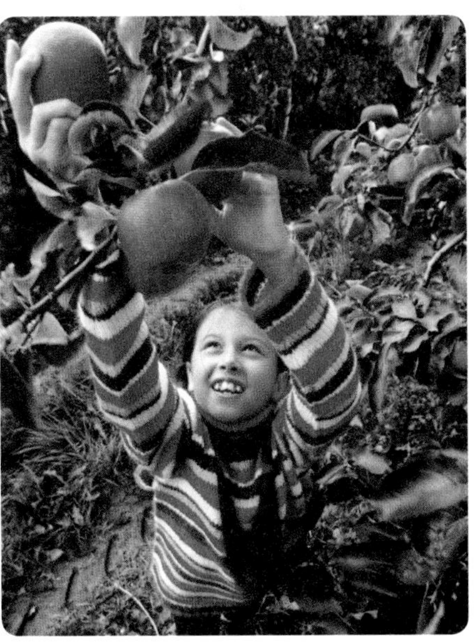

Red apples tend to taste sweeter, while green apples tend to taste more tart.

28. Tell whether each statement is *always, sometimes but not always,* or *never* true. (Lesson 4-6)
   a. If two angles of a triangle are acute, the third is obtuse.
   b. If three angles of a quadrilateral are acute, the fourth is obtuse.

EXPLORATION

29. Juan runs a full lap around a circular track in 60 seconds. Su-Lin runs the opposite direction, and meets Juan every 40 seconds.
   a. How long does it take Su-Lin to run around the track?
   b. Wayne is running in the same direction as Juan and passes him every 120 seconds. How frequently do Wayne and Su-Lin pass each other?

Lesson 8-5 Solving Equations of the Form $ax = b$

BIG IDEA You can solve equations of the form $ax = b$ by using the Multiplication Property of Equality.

You have used pan balances and fact triangles to solve equations of the form $ax = b$. Consider the equation $3x = 6$. Imagine a balance. On one side are three identical bags of unknown weight x. On the other side are six 1-pound weights. The sides are balanced.

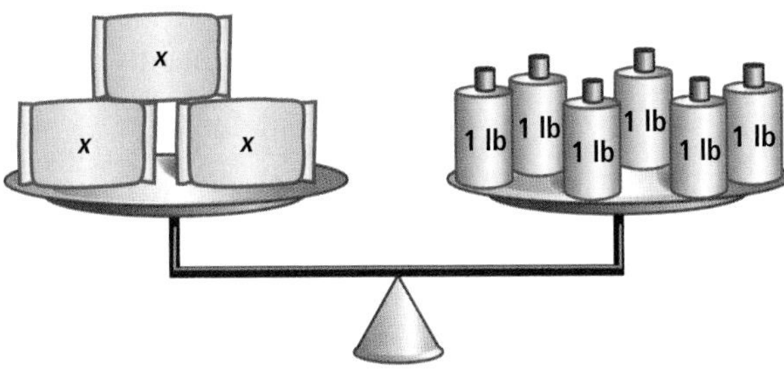

By grouping the six 1-pound weights into three pairs, you can see that each bag balances with 2 pounds. So x equals 2 pounds.

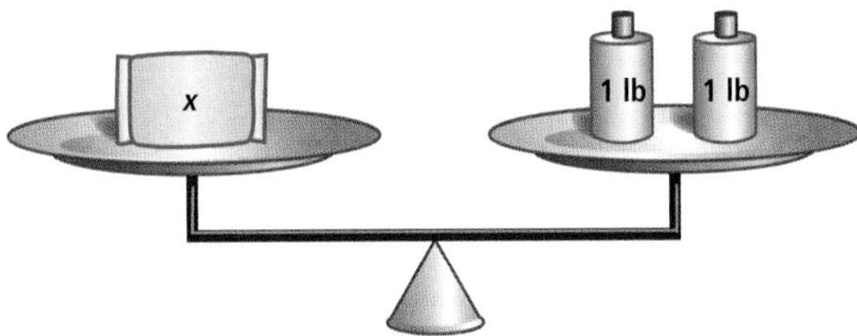

You can also solve the equation $3x = 6$ by using a fact triangle and related facts.

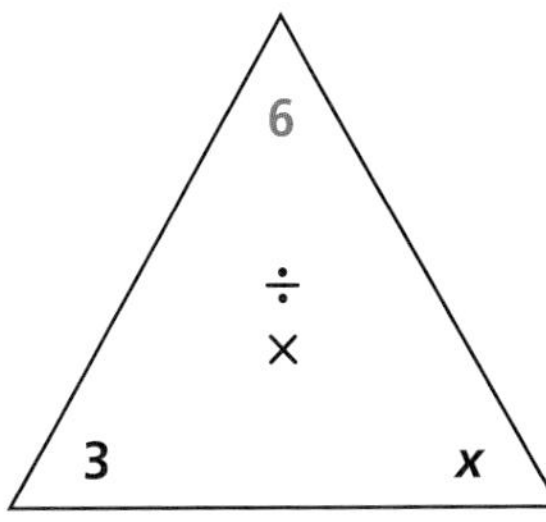

$$3x = 6$$
$$x \cdot 3 = 6$$
$$6 \div x = 3$$
$$6 \div 3 = x$$

The last related fact leads to $x = 2$.

In Chapter 4, you used the Addition Property of Equality to solve equations of the form $a + x = b$. You can use the *Multiplication Property of Equality* to solve equations of the form $ax = b$.

Mental Math

There are 8 ounces in 1 cup, and there are 16 tablespoons in 1 cup.

a. How many ounces are in a tablespoon?

b. How many tablespoons are in an ounce?

c. How many ounces are in $1\frac{1}{2}$ cups?

d. How many tablespoons are in $1\frac{1}{2}$ cups?

The Multiplication Property of Equality

If $x = y$, then $ax = ay$.

▸ **READING MATH**

Algebra is a language of numbers, operations, and variables. The word *algebra* comes from the Arabic word for restoration, *al-jabru*.

To solve $3x = 6$ using algebra, the goal is to have x by itself on one side of the equation. To undo the multiplication by 3, multiply both sides by its reciprocal, $\frac{1}{3}$.

$3x = 6$	Original Equation
$\frac{1}{3} \cdot 3x = \frac{1}{3} \cdot 6$	Multiplication Property of Equality
$1 \cdot x = \frac{6}{3}$	Property of Reciprocals
$x = 2$	Multiplication Property of One and arithmetic

You should learn to use the Multiplication Property of Equality for two reasons. First, when numbers get difficult, it may be the easiest way to solve an equation. Second, it is a basic property that you will use to solve more complicated equations throughout your study of algebra.

GUIDED

Example 1

Solve $\frac{8}{15}x = \frac{2}{3}$.

Solution Multiply both sides of the equation by the reciprocal of $\frac{8}{15}$.

$\underline{\ ?\ } \cdot \frac{8}{15}x = \underline{\ ?\ } \cdot \frac{2}{3}$	Multiplication Property of Equality
$1 \cdot x = \underline{\ ?\ }$	Property of Reciprocals and arithmetic
$x = \underline{\ ?\ }$	Multiplication Property of One

Check Substitute your value for x in the original equation. Does $\frac{8}{15} \cdot \underline{\ ?\ } = \frac{2}{3}$? Do the multiplication. Does it check?

Equations of the Form $\frac{x}{a} = b$

The Multiplication Property of Equality can also be used to solve equations of the form $\frac{x}{a} = b$.

GUIDED

Example 2

Solve $\frac{m}{9} = 1.13$.

Solution Dividing by 9 is the same as multiplying by $\frac{1}{9}$, so rewrite the equation as $\frac{1}{9}m = 1.13$ and solve using the Multiplication Property of Equality.

$\frac{1}{9}m = 1.13$

$\underline{\ ?\ } \cdot \frac{1}{9}m = \underline{\ ?\ } \cdot 1.13$

$m = \underline{\ ?\ }$

Check Does $\frac{1}{9}m = \frac{1}{9} \cdot \underline{\ ?\ } = 1.13$?

STOP See QY at the right.

QY

Solve $\frac{p}{-0.3} = 2.7$ using the Multiplication Property of Equality.

GAME Now you can play *X-Tac-Toe: ax = b*. The directions for this game are on page G25 at the back of your book.

Questions

COVERING THE IDEAS

1. The pan balance shows 4 cans of tennis balls on the left and two 3-lb weights at the right.
   a. What equation does this balance picture?
   b. Determine x.

In 2 and 3, the scale is balanced.

a. **Write the equation pictured by the balance.**

b. **Solve the equation.**

2.

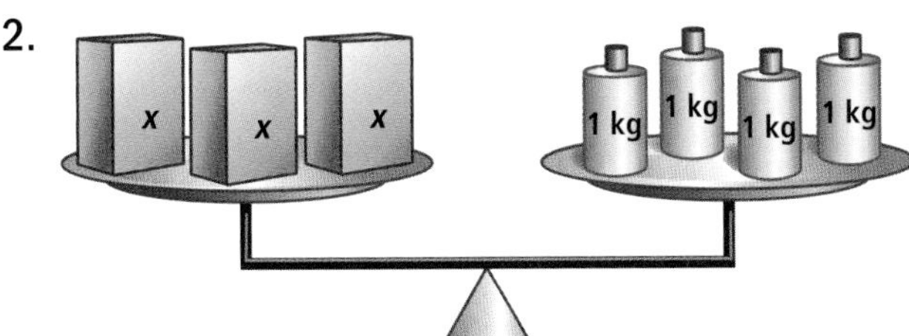

3.

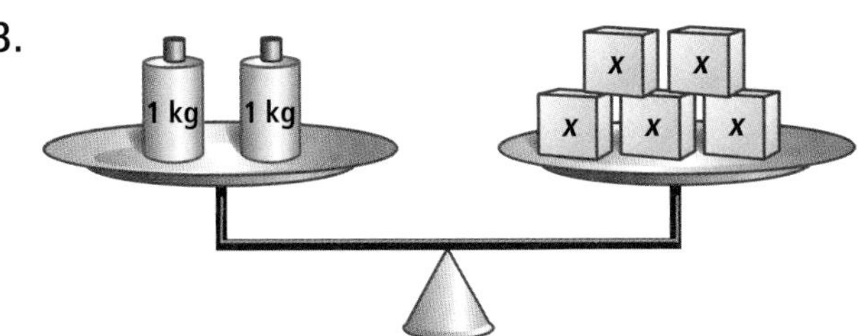

4. Marquise purchased b bottles of juice for the soccer team. They were \$0.75 each, and she spent \$18.00 total. How many bottles did she buy?

In 5 and 6, rewrite the division equation as a multiplication equation of the form $ax = b$.

5. $\frac{s}{81} = 2.65$
6. $93 = \frac{w}{56.4}$
7. **Fill in the Blank** If $20x = 50$, then $8 \cdot 20x = \underline{\ ?\ }$.
8. State the Multiplication Property of Equality.

In 9 and 10, tell whether the statement is *true* or *false*.

9. 9 is a solution to the equation $4 = 36x$.
10. -6 is a solution to the equation $\frac{54}{y} = -9$.

Multiple Choice In 11 and 12, tell which number is a solution to the equation.

11. $5y = 6$

A $\frac{6}{5}$ B 1 C 30 D $\frac{5}{6}$

12. $\frac{p}{8} = -3$

A $\frac{3}{8}$ B -3.8 C -24 D 24

In 13–17, solve the equation and check your solution.

13. $20x = -2$
14. $65 = 3.9y$
15. $\frac{7}{8}z = \frac{3}{4}$
16. $\frac{m}{7} = 10$
17. $-6\frac{2}{3} = 13\frac{1}{3}c$

In 18–21, a situation is given and a variable is identified.

a. Write an equation of the form $ax = b$ or $\frac{x}{a} = b$ using the variable that is named.

b. Solve your equation using the Multiplication Property of Equality.

c. Check the solution.

d. Write a sentence answering the question.

18. A flight from New York City to Sacramento, California, covers 2,475 miles and takes 5.8 hours. What is the average speed s of the plane?

19. Yesterday Katy's commute home from work took 1.5 times as long as normal. If it took 45 minutes for Katy to get home, how many minutes n does it normally take her to get home?

20. Cesar drinks 3 quarts of vanilla soymilk a week. Yesterday, he went to the wholesale club and purchased 32 quarts of soymilk. How many weeks w before Cesar will need to stock up again?

Some jumbo jets can weigh about 800,000 pounds!

Source: Boeing

21. Mr. Prince and his wife and daughter went to dinner with 8 other people. His family's share of the dinner cost was \$58.50. If everyone's share was equal, what was the total bill B for everyone at the dinner?

APPLYING THE MATHEMATICS

22. The scale below is balanced. Which of the boxes, A or B, is heavier? Why?

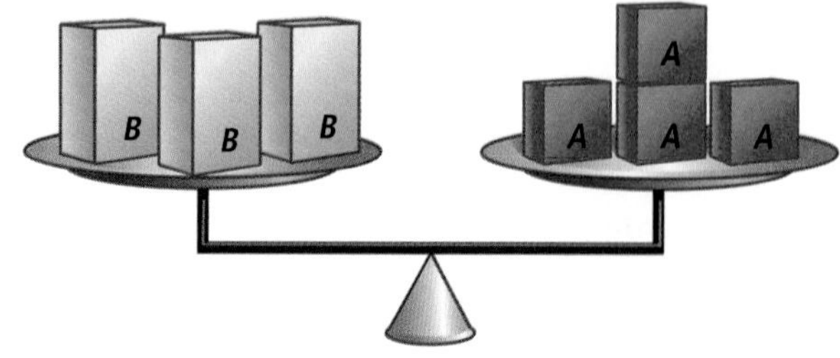

REVIEW

In 23–26, a division is given.

a. Without dividing, determine if the quotient is greater than or less than 1.

b. Calculate the quotient. (Lessons 8-4, 8-3)

23. $\frac{7}{\frac{1}{2}}$ 24. $\frac{3}{4} \div \frac{9}{10}$ 25. $1\frac{7}{8} \div \frac{3}{4}$ 26. $\frac{\frac{2}{5}}{\frac{3}{7}}$

27. a. 9 is what percent of 30?
    b. 9 is what percent of 60?
    c. 9 is what percent of 120?
    d. 9 is what percent of $4\frac{1}{2}$? **(Lesson 8-1)**

28. Find the value of x in the triangle below. **(Lesson 4-5)**

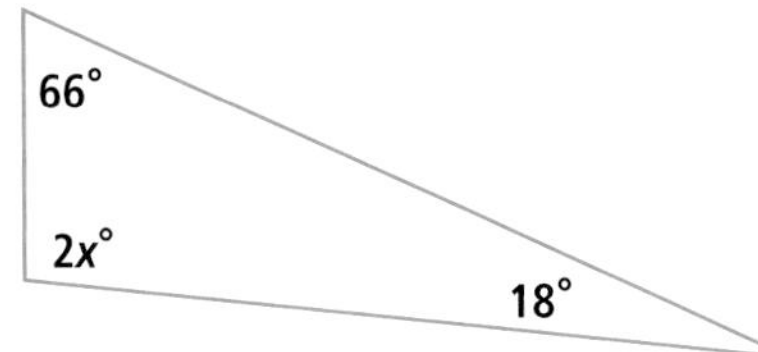

29. Put the numbers in order from least to greatest. Save the word for the quote in Question 22 in Lesson 8-8 on page 503. **(Lesson 2-10)**

N = 100% H = 0.1 T = 5%

S = $1\frac{1}{2}$ G = $\frac{4}{3}$ I = $\frac{3}{4}$

EXPLORATION

30. Dominick is participating in a bike-a-thon. Donors pledge based on the number of miles m a participant bikes. Uncle Tyson offered Dominick four choices of donation plans. For each plan, d represents Uncle Tyson's donation in dollars and m represents the number of miles that Dominick bikes.

    i. $d = \frac{m}{4}$ ii. $d = m - 10$

    iii. $d = 0.25m$ iv. $d = \frac{m}{0.8}$

    a. For each plan, describe in words how Dominick would calculate the donation.
    b. Do all the plans result in a different donation for a given number of miles? Explain.
    c. If you were Dominick, which plan would you choose?

Always wear a helmet when riding a bike. It could save your life!

QY ANSWER

$p = -0.81$

Lesson 8-6 Proportions

Vocabulary

proportion
terms of a proportion
proportional terms
true proportion
solve a proportion
geometric mean

▸ **BIG IDEA** Proportions arise from situations that involve equal rates or equal ratios.

A car is advertised as getting 30 miles per gallon of gas. From this information, you can tell how far the car should go on any number of gallons of gas.

Mental Math

If 2 pizzas can feed 7 people, how many people can be fed by

a. 6 pizzas?

b. 1 pizza?

c. 20 pizzas?

d. 5 pizzas?

Activity

MATERIALS graph paper, calculator

A car gets 30 miles per gallon of gas.

Step 1 Copy and complete this table.

Gallons	$\frac{1}{2}$	1	2	3	4	5	10
Miles	?	30	?	?	?	?	?

Step 2 a. How many miles should the car go on a full tank of 17.5 gallons?
b. How many gallons of gas are needed for the car to go 105 miles?

Step 3 Graph the first six pairs (gallons, miles) from your table. The pair (1, 30) is graphed already. It means you can get 30 miles on 1 gallon of gas. All your points should lie on the same line. Draw the line.

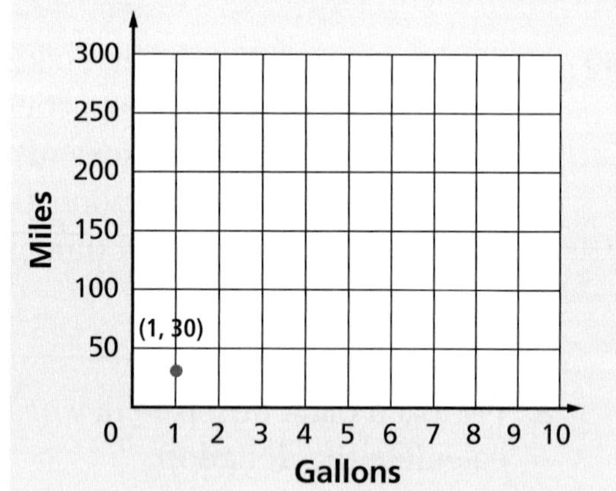

Step 4 Pick any two points along the line. Show that the rate in miles per gallon is equal for both points.

Step 5 Pick two other points along the line. Show that the rate in gallons per mile is equal for both points.

It is not difficult to fill in the table in the Activity because you are told how far the car goes on 1 gallon of gas. The example on the next page shows a problem that is a little more complicated.

Example

Henry is reading a story that is 32 pages long. He read the first 8 pages in 13 minutes. At this rate, how long will it take him to read the entire story?

Solution 1 Find the rate at which Henry is reading. It is $\frac{13 \text{ minutes}}{8 \text{ pages}}$. If he reads the entire story in t minutes, then the rate for the entire story is $\frac{t \text{ minutes}}{32 \text{ pages}}$.

Since his reading rate is assumed to stay the same,

$\frac{13 \text{ minutes}}{8 \text{ pages}} = \frac{t \text{ minutes}}{32 \text{ pages}}$.

Now, drop the units: $\frac{13}{8} = \frac{t}{32}$.

Think: If these are equal fractions, what must t be? Since 8 is multiplied by 4 to get 32, 13 must be multiplied by 4 to get t. So $t = 13 \cdot 4 = 52$.

At this rate, it will take Henry 52 minutes to read the story.

Solution 2 If Henry reads 8 pages in 13 minutes, then he can read 16 pages in 26 minutes. If he can read 16 pages in 26 minutes, then he can read 32 pages in 52 minutes.

The average reading speed of an adult is 230 words per minute.

Source: www.speedreading.com

The equation $\frac{13}{8} = \frac{t}{32}$ is a *proportion.* A **proportion** is a statement that two fractions are equal. The numbers 13, 8, t, and 32 are the **terms of the proportion.** Every proportion has exactly four terms. In this proportion, 13 is the first term, 8 is the second term, t is the third term, and 32 is the fourth term.

QY1

Explain why $\frac{1}{2} + \frac{1}{3} = \frac{5}{6}$ is not a proportion.

There are two common ways to read the proportion $\frac{13}{8} = \frac{t}{32}$. Some people read it as "13 over 8 equals t over 32. Others read it as "13 is to 8 as t is to 32." Notice that the terms are always read in order.

QY2

$\frac{36}{54} = \frac{10}{15}$ can be read: __?__ is to __?__ as __?__ is to __?__.

A proportion may be *true,* as in $\frac{150}{300} = \frac{50}{100}$. A proportion may also be *false*, as in $\frac{50}{100} = \frac{150}{200}$. When a proportion is true, we say that its four terms are called **proportional terms.**

QY3

Explain why $\frac{36}{54} = \frac{10}{15}$ is a true proportion.

Where Do Proportions Come From?

Equal rates lead to proportions. Consider the ordered pairs $\left(\frac{1}{2}, 15\right)$ and (4, 120), which are in the table and on the graph in the Activity. The numbers can be used to form several **true proportions.**

With gasoline prices on the rise, consumers look for cars with good fuel economy.

Both rates equal 30 miles per gallon:

$$\frac{15 \text{ miles}}{\frac{1}{2} \text{ gallon}} = \frac{120 \text{ miles}}{4 \text{ gallons}}$$

Both rates equal $\frac{1}{30}$ gallon per mile:

$$\frac{\frac{1}{2} \text{ gallon}}{15 \text{ miles}} = \frac{4 \text{ gallons}}{120 \text{ miles}}$$

Proportions can also come from equal ratios. The numerators and denominators of the above fractions also form true proportions. For example:

$$\frac{\frac{1}{2} \text{ gallon}}{4 \text{ gallons}} = \frac{15 \text{ miles}}{120 \text{ miles}}$$

Proportions can be used to solve a wide variety of problems. If two rates or two ratios are equal, and you know the values of three of the four terms, a proportion will help you find the unknown value. To **solve a proportion** means to find the value of the variable that makes the equation true. You solved the proportion $\frac{13}{8} = \frac{t}{32}$ in the first solution in the Example.

In the Question section, you are asked to solve proportions. You should use what you know about equal fractions or arithmetic. In Lesson 8-7, you will see a strategy that works when you cannot solve a proportion in your head.

Questions

COVERING THE IDEAS

1. What is a proportion?
2. Give an example of a proportion.
3. A car gets 20 miles per gallon of gas.
   a. Complete the table below.
   b. Graph the four ordered pairs from the table.
   c. Write two proportions using this information.

Gallons	1	2	3	4
Miles	20	?	?	?

4. Suppose you have read 40 pages of a book in 75 minutes. At this rate, how long will it take you to read the remaining 80 pages?

5. **Fill in the Blanks** You can read $\frac{5}{8} = \frac{10}{16}$ as 5 __?__ __?__ 8 as 10 __?__ __?__ 16.

6. Roberta says that $\frac{10}{2} = \frac{6}{1}$ is a proportion. Is Roberta right? Why or why not?

7. Ismael is dreaming of a time when he will be able to drive 110 miles on a gallon of gas.
   a. How many gallons would Ismael use in driving the 2,640 miles from Boise, Idaho, to Orlando, Florida?
   b. **Multiple Choice** Which of the following proportions represents this information?

   A $\frac{110 \text{ miles}}{1 \text{ gallon}} = \frac{g \text{ gallons}}{2640 \text{ miles}}$
   B $\frac{110 \text{ miles}}{1 \text{ gallon}} = \frac{2640 \text{ miles}}{g \text{ gallons}}$
   C $\frac{1 \text{ gallon}}{110 \text{ miles}} = \frac{2640 \text{ miles}}{g \text{ gallons}}$
   D $\frac{g \text{ gallons}}{1 \text{ gallon}} = \frac{110 \text{ miles}}{2640 \text{ miles}}$

In 8–11, tell whether the equation is a proportion. If it is a proportion, tell whether it is true or not. If it is not a proportion, explain why it is not.

8. $\frac{3}{4} = \frac{6}{8}$
9. $\frac{3}{4} = \frac{12}{n}$
10. $\frac{12}{6} - \frac{5}{6} = \frac{7}{6}$
11. $\frac{3}{5} = \frac{3}{4}$

In 12–14, solve the proportion.

12. $\frac{3}{5} = \frac{12}{m}$
13. $\frac{15}{n} = \frac{30}{52}$
14. $\frac{5}{8} = \frac{x}{96}$

APPLYING THE MATHEMATICS

15. Lucas earns 45 dollars for 5 hours of work, and y dollars for 90 hours of work.
   a. Write a proportion that describes this situation.
   b. Solve and check your proportion.

16. Amanda can type 7 words in 6 seconds. If she continues working at this rate, how many words can she type in 3 minutes?

17. While traveling in Italy in July 2006, Enrique bought a soccer jersey for 35 Euros. If one Euro cost about \$1.25 the day he bought the jersey, how much did he pay in dollars?

18. Rene and Keanu have the same birthday. Rene is 15. Keanu is 5. How old will Keanu be when Rene is 30?

In 2006, Italy won the FIFA World Cup hosted in Germany.

REVIEW

19. A marathon is a race that is 26.2 miles long. Selena ran a marathon in 3 hours, 24 minutes. **(Lesson 8-5)**
    a. Write Selena's time in fraction or decimal form.
    b. Write an equation in the form $ax = b$ for Selena's average speed x.
    c. Solve your equation from Part b.

In 20–22, solve and check. (Lesson 8-5)

20. $4x = 3$
21. $-5y = 2$
22. $\frac{1}{2}z = 4.5$

In 23 and 24, divide. (Lessons 8-4, 8-3)

23. $\frac{3}{4} \div \frac{2}{7}$
24. $8\frac{1}{2} \div 2\frac{1}{3}$

25. According to one source, the largest millipede in the world is *Graphidostreptus gigas* of Africa, which reaches a length of 11 inches and a width of $\frac{3}{4}$ inch. **(Lessons 8-3, 8-1)**
    a. Write a division problem to find how many times as long the millipede is as it is wide.
    b. Find the quotient.

Despite their name, millipedes have no more than 300 legs, depending on the species.

Source: Woodland Park Zoo

26. Below are ratios of men's to women's earnings in the United States for different amounts of education, according to the U.S. Census Bureau in 2002. Estimate the quotients to the nearest hundredth and write the corresponding letter in the appropriate blank below. Save the word for the quote in Question 22 in Lesson 8-8 on page 503. **(Lesson 8-1)**

High School graduate:	$\frac{\text{men's earnings}}{\text{women's earnings}} = \frac{32{,}024}{19{,}156}$	R
Some college:	$\frac{\text{men's earnings}}{\text{women's earnings}} = \frac{39{,}031}{23{,}015}$	O
Associate's Degree (2 yr):	$\frac{\text{men's earnings}}{\text{women's earnings}} = \frac{40{,}608}{26{,}104}$	P
Bachelor's Degree (4 yr):	$\frac{\text{men's earnings}}{\text{women's earnings}} = \frac{56{,}779}{32{,}816}$	N
Master's Degree:	$\frac{\text{men's earnings}}{\text{women's earnings}} = \frac{67{,}202}{41{,}270}$	I
Doctorate:	$\frac{\text{men's earnings}}{\text{women's earnings}} = \frac{91{,}982}{56{,}807}$	T

?	?	?	?	?	?	?	?	?	?
1.56	1.67	1.70	1.60	1.70	1.67	1.62	1.63	1.70	1.73

27. Suppose today is Monday, and your birthday is in 100 days. Use integer division to determine how many weeks until the week of your birthday and what day of the week your birthday falls on. (Lesson 7-3)

28. Give the coordinates of a point that is
   a. in Quadrant II.
   b. in Quadrant III.
   c. not in any quadrant. (Lesson 5-6)

EXPLORATION

29. When the second and third terms of a true proportion are equal, the repeated number is the **geometric mean** of the other two numbers. For the proportion $\frac{2}{8} = \frac{8}{32}$, 8 is the geometric mean of 2 and 32.
   a. Find another pair of numbers whose geometric mean is 8.
   b. Find another proportion showing a geometric mean of a different pair of numbers.

QY ANSWERS

1. The left side is not a single fraction.
2. 36; 54; 10; 15
3. In lowest terms, both fractions equal $\frac{2}{3}$.

Lesson 8-7 Solving Proportions

▸ **BIG IDEA** You can use the Multiplication Property of Equality and properties of reciprocals to solve proportions.

Since every proportion is an equation, you can solve proportions just as you solve other equations. You now have many tools and skills you can use to do this with success.

When the variable is in a numerator of a proportion, you can use the Multiplication Property of Equality to solve the proportion.

Mental Math

A muffin costs \$1.50. How many muffins can you buy with

a. \$10?

b. \$20?

c. \$5?

Example 1

A trucker has driven 187 miles in 2 hours, 45 minutes. He plans to drive 8 hours today. How far will he drive if he continues to drive at the same speed?

Solution Set up a proportion using equal rates. 2 hours, 45 minutes is $2\frac{45}{60}$, or 2.75, hours. One rate is 187 miles per 2.75 hours. The other is the unknown distance *d* in 8 hours: $\frac{187 \text{ miles}}{2.75 \text{ hours}} = \frac{d \text{ miles}}{8 \text{ hours}}$.

Now ignore the units: $\frac{187}{2.75} = \frac{d}{8}$.

You can solve this exactly the way you solved equations in Lesson 8-5.

$8 \cdot \frac{187}{2.75} = 8 \cdot \frac{d}{8}$ Multiply both sides by 8.

$\frac{1{,}496}{2.75} = d$ Divide.

$544 = d$

At this rate, the trucker will go 544 miles in 8 hours.

Check Going 544 miles in 8 hours is a rate of $\frac{544}{8}$, or 68, miles per hour. Going 187 miles in 2.75 hours is a rate of $\frac{187}{2.75}$, which is also 68 miles per hour.

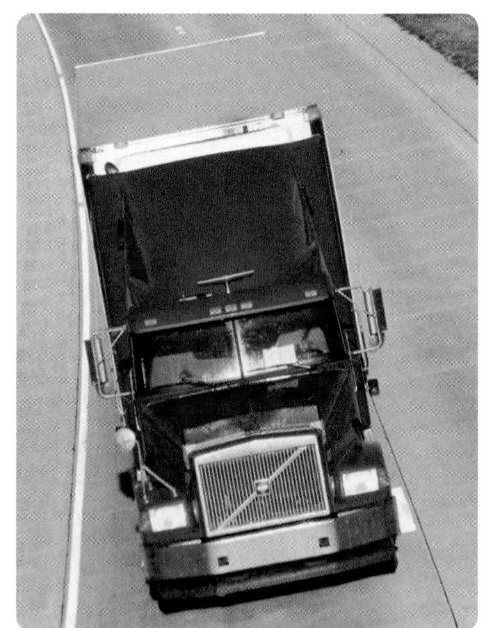

Semi-trailer trucks deliver everything from canned goods to livestock to automobiles.

You can use the idea of Example 1 to solve any proportion in which the variable is in the numerator. Only one more step is needed if the variable is in the denominator. The idea is to take the reciprocal of both sides of the equation.

GUIDED

Example 2

Solve the proportion $\frac{3}{4} = \frac{28}{n}$.

Solution If two numbers are equal, so are their reciprocals.

$$\frac{4}{3} = \frac{n}{28}$$

Now the equation is like the one in Example 1 with the variable in the numerator. Multiply both sides by 28.

$$28 \cdot \frac{?}{?} = 28 \cdot \frac{?}{?}$$

$$\frac{?}{?} = n$$

So, n = __?__.

Check Substitute $37\frac{1}{3}$ for n in the original equation: $\frac{3}{4} = \frac{?}{?}$.

Evaluate the right side by performing the division: 28 ÷ __?__ = 0.75.

Both sides equal $\frac{3}{4}$, so the solution is correct.

Questions

COVERING THE IDEAS

In 1–4, solve the proportion.

1. $\frac{3}{4} = \frac{6}{n}$
2. $\frac{p}{4.8} = \frac{12.8}{3.2}$
3. $\frac{5.6}{2.24} = \frac{q}{4.8}$
4. $\frac{3}{g} = \frac{5\frac{1}{3}}{16}$

In 5 and 6, solve using a proportion.

5. David can solve two math problems in 3 minutes. At this rate, how long will it take him to finish a math test with 15 problems?
6. Karen has a summer job painting fences. She charges \$25 to paint a 20-foot-long fence. If her rate is proportional to the length of the fence, how much should she charge to paint a 30-foot fence?

Painting fences is hard work!

7. Marlene rode her bike $10\frac{1}{2}$ miles in $1\frac{1}{4}$ hours. If she keeps up the same pace for 25 miles, how long will her entire trip take?
   a. Write a proportion with a variable that will help answer the question. Include the units.
   b. Solve and check.
   c. Write a statement that answers the question in the problem.

APPLYING THE MATHEMATICS

8. On a trip to Europe, Evita exchanged $600 for 475.33 euros. When she returned to the United States, she exchanged the 25 Euros she had left for U.S. dollars. If the exchange rate was the same, how many dollars did she get?

The Eurozone (countries that have adopted the euro) had 13 members.

9. Martin's slow printer printed 9 pages in 2 minutes, 15 seconds. At this rate, how long will it take a 48-page report to print?
10. On a backpacking trip, Jade has walked $1\frac{1}{2}$ miles in 2 hours. She must walk another $2\frac{1}{4}$ miles.
    a. How long will it take her to walk those $2\frac{1}{4}$ miles if she continues at the same pace?
    b. What is the total time she will have spent walking?
11. Kara has a book report due in two days. She is reading a book that is 124 pages long. After reading for 2 hours, 30 minutes, she has finished 55 pages. She always reads at the same rate.
    a. How long will it take her to read the entire book?
    b. How long will it take her to finish the pages she has not read?

In 12–15, tell whether it would make sense to use proportions to solve the problem. Explain your answer.

12. If Alfred runs 100 meters in 18 seconds, how long will it take him to run 1 kilometer?
13. Carl makes punch from white-grape juice concentrate and sparkling water. He adds $1\frac{1}{3}$ cups of concentrate to 4 cups of sparkling water. Carl would like to make enough punch for a party, so he decides to use 10 cups of concentrate. How much water should he add? How much punch will he have?
14. Maria has a hybrid car that gets 60 miles per gallon of gas. How many miles can she go on 90 gallons?
15. If a shop sells 400 Christmas cards in December, about how many cards do you think this shop will sell in 12 months?

16. Solve the proportions and order the variables from greatest to least value to form a word. Save the word for the quote in Question 22 in Lesson 8-8, on page 503.

$\frac{7}{9} = \frac{28}{m}$	$\frac{13}{b} = \frac{104}{36}$	$\frac{29}{51} = \frac{u}{255}$	$\frac{311}{e} = \frac{1244}{16}$	$\frac{r}{82} = \frac{1}{1886}$	$\frac{77}{105} = \frac{693}{n}$
?	?	?	?	?	?

REVIEW

17. A car is traveling 60 miles per hour. **(Lesson 8-6)**
   a. Create a table of time and distance values for this situation.
   b. Create a graph to represent this situation.

In 18–20, write as a simple fraction. (Lesson 8-4)

18. $1\frac{1}{5} \div 2$
19. $3\frac{2}{3} \div \frac{5}{3}$
20. $\frac{4}{9} \div 3\frac{2}{7}$

21. Five people ate at a restaurant, and the bill was \$48.53. If they want to add a tip of about 15% and then split the total evenly, about how much should each person pay? **(Lessons 8-1, 7-5)**

EXPLORATION

22. In a scale drawing, all the actual lengths are multiplied by the same factor to get the lengths in the drawing. In architectural drawings, it is typical for 1 foot in a room to be represented by $\frac{1}{4}$ inch on the drawing.
   a. What does the ratio $\frac{1 \text{ foot}}{\frac{1}{4} \text{ inch}}$ equal?
   b. Choose a room in your home, school, or another place and make a scale drawing of the room with this scale.

23. Using eight matches, Elu made a ladder with two steps, like the one at the right. How many matches would he need to make a ladder with 20 steps?

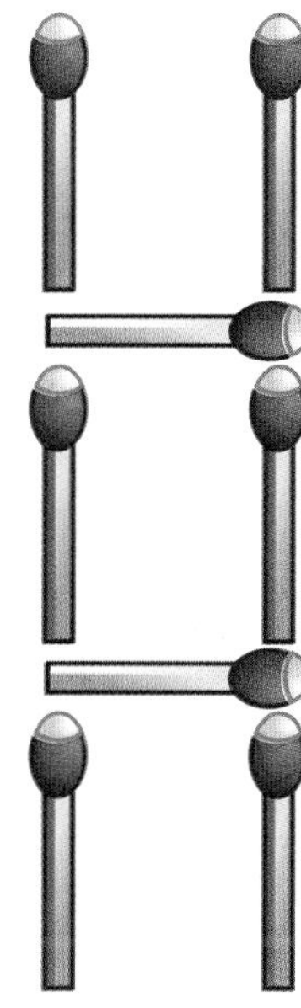

Lesson

8-8 Proportions in Pictures and Maps

Vocabulary

scale

▶ **BIG IDEA** A common application of proportions is to find unknown lengths or distances.

Judging actual size from a photograph can be tricky. This is why a ruler or an object with known size is often placed next to objects photographed by crime scene investigators as shown below. You can find the actual length of an object in a photograph like the footprint below by solving a proportion.

Mental Math

If $x = 3$ and $y = 4$, tell which expression has the lesser value.

a. $x - y$ or $y - x$

b. $\frac{y}{x}$ or $\frac{x}{y}$

c. x^y or y^x

d. $y \cdot x$ or $x \cdot y$

Activity 1

MATERIALS ruler, calculator, penny

Follow these steps to find the diameter and width of the footprint in the police-evidence photograph above.

Step 1 Measure and record the length of the penny in the photo to the nearest millimeter.

Step 2 Measure and record the length of the footprint in the photo to the nearest millimeter.

Step 3 Measure and record the diameter of an actual penny to the nearest millimeter.

Step 4 You can set up a proportion of this form:

$$\frac{\text{diameter of pictured penny}}{\text{length of pictured footprint}} = \frac{\text{diameter of actual penny}}{\text{length of actual footprint}}$$

$$\frac{?}{?} = \frac{?}{?}$$

Substitute the measures you know. Let *f* represent the length of the actual footprint.

Step 5 Solve your proportion. Make sure your answer is reasonable for the length of a footprint.

Step 6 Compare your answer to those of other students. Did you have exactly the same answer as others? If not, why do you think the answers are different?

Step 7 Repeat Steps 1–5 to find the width of the footprint.

STOP **See QY at the right.**

QY

The actual footprint is how many times the length of the footprint in the photo?

Maps are like photographs. Both show images of actual objects. In the case of maps, the objects are portions of Earth's surface. The **scale** of a map is the ratio of a distance on the map to the true distance. On the map of Mexico and Central America below, a distance equal to 600 km is shown in the lower left corner. You use this distance to determine actual distances between locations on the map.

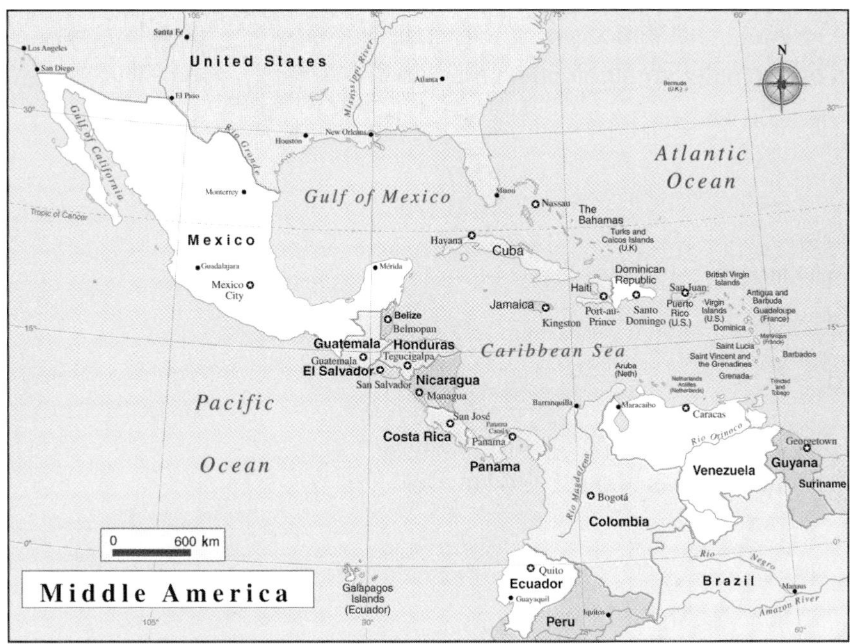

Example 1

What is the scale of this map of Mexico and Central America?

Solution Measure the segment that is 600 km long in centimeters. You should find that it is 1.05 cm long. Write the ratio of the map length to the actual length. Convert both lengths to meters so the units are the same.

$$\text{scale} = \frac{1.05 \text{ cm}}{600 \text{ km}} = \frac{1.05 \cdot 0.01 \text{ m}}{600 \cdot 1000 \text{ m}} = \frac{0.0105}{600{,}000}$$

Most people prefer to write a scale with 1 in the numerator, so solve the proportion $\frac{0.0105}{600{,}000} = \frac{1}{x}$.

(continued on next page)

Take the reciprocal of each side.

$$\frac{600{,}000}{0.0105} = \frac{x}{1}$$

$$57{,}000{,}000 \approx x$$

The approximate scale of the map is the ratio $\frac{1}{57{,}000{,}000}$.
This means that the actual distances are 57,000,000 times the distances on the map.

Fortunately, you do not need to know the scale to find the distance between cities on the map.

Example 2

Use the map on the previous page to estimate the distance between Havana, Cuba and Mexico City.

Solution The distance between Havana and Mexico City is 3.1 cm on the map. The actual distance *d* can be estimated by solving the proportion.

$$\frac{1.05 \text{ cm}}{600 \text{ km}} = \frac{3.1 \text{ cm}}{d}$$

Rewrite, using the reciprocals.

$$\frac{600 \text{ km}}{1.05 \text{ cm}} = \frac{d}{3.1 \text{ cm}}$$

$$3.1 \text{ cm} \bullet \frac{600 \text{ km}}{1.05 \text{ cm}} = d$$

$$1771 \text{ km} \approx d$$

Check The distance between Havana, Cuba and Mexico City is about 1771 km. A reference book says the distance is about 1784 km. Our estimate is not far off!

Activity 2

MATERIALS map (with a scale), ruler, calculator

Step 1 Identify two points on a map.

Step 2 Measure the distance between the points on the map.

Step 3 Use the scale and set up a proportion to determine the actual distance between the points.

Step 4 Solve the proportion to find the actual distance.

Step 5 If possible, check your work with a mileage table or by finding the distance on the Internet.

Questions

COVERING THE IDEAS

1. Mrs. Washington has a picture of her four-year old son Quincy holding a stuffed plush soccer ball. The actual ball has a diameter of 8 inches. In the picture, the ball is 1 inch high and Quincy is $4\frac{1}{2}$ inches high. Use a proportion to find Quincy's height.
2. The Statue of Liberty is about 46.5 m high from the base to the torch. Carrie and Jenna plan to make a 1.5 m high model of the statue for their school's History Fest.
   a. Below are the lengths of some parts of the actual statue. Use proportions to find out how long each of these parts should be on their model. Show your work.
      hand: 5.00 m   right arm: 12.80 m   nose: 1.48 m
   b. There are 25 windows in the crown of the Statue of Liberty. How many windows should the crown of the model have?
3. Use the map on page 499 to estimate the distance between Santa Fe, New Mexico, and San Jose, Costa Rica.

APPLYING THE MATHEMATICS

4. In many dollhouses, 1 inch represents 12 inches in a real house.
   a. The length of a room in a dollhouse is 15 inches. How many inches would this be in a real house? How many feet?
   b. A dollhouse room is $13\frac{1}{2}$ inches wide. How wide would the real room be in inches? How wide in feet?
   c. Find the perimeter of the dollhouse room in inches.
   d. Use your answer from Part c to find the perimeter of the actual room in inches.
   e. What is the ratio of the dollhouse room perimeter to the actual room perimeter?

Dollhouses date back 400 years and originated in Europe.

In 5–7, a copy machine was used to enlarge a polygon, as shown below. Use proportions to find the missing length.

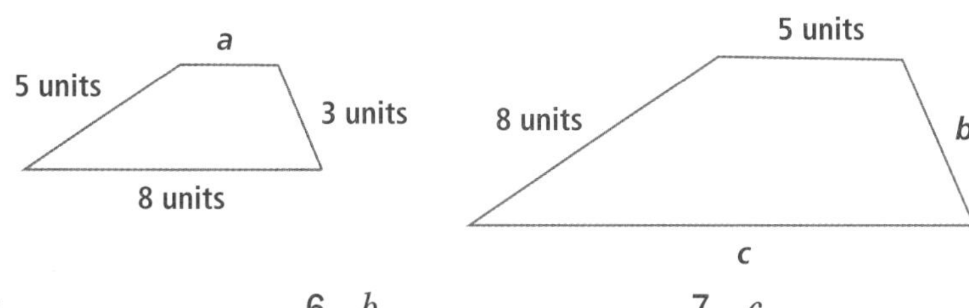

5. a 6. b 7. c

In 8 and 9, Mrs. Ling is remodeling her kitchen. She has laid out the design on a piece of $\frac{1}{4}$-inch grid paper. Each $\frac{1}{4}$-inch on the grid paper represents 1 foot of the real kitchen. (This is a standard scale used by designers.) Use proportions to solve the following questions.

8. The cabinet for the sink measures 30 inches. How long will it be on the grid paper?

9. The grid paper shows the island in the kitchen to be 1 inch long. How long will it be in the real kitchen?

10. The photograph at the right shows the Temple of Heaven in Beijing, China. You can see people at the top of the steps approaching the temple.
    a. Assume the actual heights of the people to be about 1.75 m. Approximate the height of the temple in meters by using a proportion.
    b. What might cause your approximation to differ from the actual height?

During the Ming and Qing dynasties, emperors prayed to the Temple of Heaven for good harvests.

Source: Beijing International

REVIEW

11. A college has an 8:1 student-faculty ratio. (For every eight students, there is one faculty member.) If there are 5,200 students in this college, how many faculty members are there? **(Lesson 8-7)**

In 12–14, determine whether the two fractions are equal. (Lesson 8-6)

12. $\frac{32}{21}, \frac{11}{7}$
13. $\frac{36}{45}, \frac{18}{22.5}$
14. $\frac{8.1}{16.9}, \frac{9}{13}$

15. Using a calculator to calculate the value of the fraction $\frac{8.4 + 14.7}{3.5 + 0.7}$ is tricky. Three attempts are shown below. **(Lesson 8-4)**

```
8.4+14.7/3.5+0.7
8.4+14.7/(3.5+0.7)
(8.4+14.7)/(3.5+0.7)
```

    a. Find the value that results from each attempt and replace it with the corresponding letter below. (*Note:* One letter is not used.)

       M = 12.7   E = 11.9   L = 13.3   T = 5.5

    b. Use the three letters as the final code word for this chapter's quote. Enter the word in the table in Question 22 on page 503.
    c. Which value is the correct value of the fraction?

In 16–19, evaluate. (Lesson 8-3)

16. $\frac{4}{5} \div \frac{2}{3}$

17. $\frac{11}{4} \div \frac{21}{2}$

18. $\left(4 + \frac{3}{5}\right) \div \left(\frac{2}{7} - 3\right)$

19. $2 \cdot 3 + \frac{1}{4} \div \frac{5}{7} \cdot \frac{9}{8}$

20. In 2001, a solar-powered airplane called the Helios reached an altitude of 96,500 feet. Express this altitude in miles and feet. **(Lesson 7-4)**

EXPLORATION

21. One way to enlarge a picture is to use a ruler to draw a grid with $\frac{1}{2}$-inch squares on top of the picture. Then make a larger grid with 1 or 2 inch squares. Try to reproduce the figure on the larger grid. Focus on where the grid lines intersect the character. Find a comic strip character and use grids to enlarge it.

22. a. Copy the table at the right and place the word you decoded in each lesson of this chapter.

b. Rearrange the words and put one in each blank below to form a saying by Henry David Thoreau.

A __?__ is __?__ in __?__ to the __?__ of __?__ which he can __?__ to __?__ __?__.

Table to Record Decoded Puzzle Words

Lesson	Word
8-1	?
8-2	?
8-3	?
8-4	?
8-5	?
8-6	?
8-7	?
8-8	?

QY ANSWER

about 3 times

Chapter 8 Projects

1 Copies of All Sizes

Most copy machines enlarge and reduce. Choose an interesting original picture and make copies of various sizes. Then make copies of copies to obtain other sizes. Put all the copies together in a display explaining what you have done, and give the percents of the size changes from the original picture.

2 Half-Size You

Measure the length and width of your legs, toes, arms, hands, fingers, face, nose, mouth, eyes, and so on. Make a 2-D model of yourself that is half your real size. Record some dimensions of you and your half-size model in a table.

3 Proportional Thinking

Invent ten real-world problems that can be solved with proportions and that are different from those given in this chapter. Include your solutions.

4 Scale Drawing

Make an accurate map of one floor of the place where you live using the scale $\frac{1}{4}$ inch to 1 foot.

5 A Different Way to Divide Fractions

A student divided fractions in the following way. First, the student renamed the two fractions with a common denominator. Then the student ignored the denominators and just divided the numerators to obtain the answer. Does this method work? Try it on enough examples to form a conclusion about whether it works *always*, *sometimes but not always*, or *never*.

6 Finding Sizes of Monuments

Use family photographs or pictures you find on the Internet and proportions to estimate the size of at least three well-known, large monuments or natural sites. Possible choices might include the Great Pyramid, the Washington Monument, St. Peter's Basilica, the Taj Mahal, Angkor Wat, a skyscraper, a waterfall, or a redwood tree. Try to find the actual sizes. How close was your calculation? If it was not very accurate, how do you account for your error?

Between the years of 1998–2004, the Petronas Towers in Malaysia were the world's tallest buildings.

Source: PBS

Chapter 8 Summary and Vocabulary

- When two quantities with the same unit are divided, the quotient is a **ratio.** Ratios compare quantities and have no units. Percents also compare quantities with the same units, so they can be considered ratios.

- The algebraic definition of division (dividing by n is the same as multiplying by the **reciprocal** of n) can be used to divide fractions. Since the reciprocal of $\frac{c}{d}$ is $\frac{d}{c}$, $\frac{a}{b} \div \frac{c}{d} = \frac{a}{b} \cdot \frac{d}{c} = \frac{ad}{bc}$. This algorithm can also be used to divide mixed numbers if they are first changed to **improper fractions.**

- To solve an equation of the form $ax = b$, you can use the **Multiplication Property of Equality** and multiply both sides of the equation by $\frac{1}{a}$, the reciprocal of a. If the equation is of the form $\frac{x}{a} = b$, you can think of it as $\frac{1}{a}x = b$ and multiply both sides of the equation by a, the reciprocal of $\frac{1}{a}$.

- A **proportion** is a statement that two fractions are equal. A proportion has the form $\frac{a}{b} = \frac{c}{d}$. Proportions are very common in problems and arise from equal rates or equal ratios. Often you know three of the four parts of a proportion; **solving the proportion** means finding the missing part. You can solve some proportions using equal fractions, while proportions with more complicated numbers can be solved using the Multiplication Property of Equality.

Vocabulary

8-1
ratio
ratio comparison

8-2
multiplicative inverse
reciprocal

8-4
complex fraction

8-6
proportion
terms of a proportion
proportional terms
true proportion
solve a proportion
geometric mean

8-8
scale

Theorems and Properties

Property of Reciprocals (p. 468)
Algebraic Definition of Division (Mult-Rec Property) (p. 472)
Multiplication Property of Equality (p. 484)

Chapter 8 Self-Test

Take this test as you would take a test in class. You will need a calculator. Then use the Selected Answers section in the back of the book to check your work.

1. September had 5 rainy days and 25 non-rainy days.
   a. Find the ratio of the number of rainy days to the number of non-rainy days to the nearest tenth.
   b. Find the ratio of the number of non-rainy days to the number of rainy days to the nearest tenth.

2. Of the 125 students in Tim's middle school, 85 are in the band. What percent of the students are in band?

3. a. Change $\frac{a}{b} \div \frac{c}{d}$ to a multiplication problem.
   b. Find the product of your answer to Part a.

4. Determine the reciprocal of $2\frac{2}{3}$. Check your work by finding the product of the original number and its reciprocal.

5. **Multiple Choice** Which of the following is the reciprocal of 0.3? (There may be more than one correct answer.)
   A $\frac{1}{0.3}$
   B 3
   C $3\frac{1}{3}$
   D $\frac{10}{3}$

In 6–9, divide without using a calculator.

6. $\frac{7}{8} \div \frac{2}{7}$

7. $6\frac{3}{4} \div 1\frac{1}{5}$

8. $40\frac{1}{5} \div 2\frac{2}{5}$

9. $\dfrac{2\frac{1}{2} + 1\frac{1}{3}}{\frac{1}{2} + \frac{1}{3}}$

10. Solve each equation using the Multiplication Property of Equality. Show your work. Check the solution in the original equation.
    a. $12A = 20$
    b. $-1.4B = 56$

11. Leticia has made 4 gallons of orange juice for a large brunch reception. She plans to serve $\frac{3}{4}$ of a cup to each guest. How many $\frac{3}{4}$-cup servings does she have?
    a. Represent this situation with a division problem.
    b. Use the division problem to answer the question.

12. Nigel has five cans that each contains $2\frac{1}{2}$ cups of tomatoes. He needs $3\frac{1}{2}$ cups of tomatoes for each batch of his spaghetti sauce. How many batches can he make?
    a. Represent this situation with a division problem.
    b. Use the division problem to answer the question.

In 13 and 14, a situation is given.
a. Represent the situation by an equation of the form $ax = b$.
b. Solve the equation using the Multiplication Property of Equality.
c. Check the solution in the original equation.
d. Answer the question in a complete sentence.

13. Susan can type 75 words per minute. She needs to type a 1,530-word paper. To the nearest minute, how long will it take her to type the document?

14. Manuel has only 30% as much money now as he had 4 months ago. He now has $1,830. How much money did he have 4 months ago?

15. Virginia is at the fitness club. In order to determine her heart rate, she counts the number of beats in 10 seconds. She counts 18 beats.

a. Complete the table below, assuming her heart beats at a constant rate.

Beats	?	18	27	?	135	?
Time (sec)	5	10	?	60	?	90

b. Graph the six points on a coordinate grid.

In 16–18, solve the proportion.

16. $\frac{2.5}{3} = \frac{25}{x}$

17. $\frac{36}{4} = \frac{y}{0.5}$

18. $\frac{4.2}{3.6} = \frac{z}{2.7}$

In 19 and 20, a situation is given.

a. Write a proportion to represent the situation.

b. Solve your proportion and check the answer.

c. Write a sentence to answer the question.

19. It takes Eric's dad 2 hours, 20 minutes to get to Grand Rapids, Michigan, which is 140 miles away from his home on Higgins Lake, Michigan. At that rate, how long (in hours and minutes) would it take him to travel the 390 miles from his home to Indianapolis, Indiana?

20. Veronica is an amateur filmmaker. She is sketching a plan for a movie set on grid paper. In her sketch, $\frac{1}{4}$ inch represents 1 foot. A portion of the set will be 18 feet long. How long will it be on the plan?

Chapter 8 Chapter Review

SKILLS
PROPERTIES
USES
REPRESENTATIONS

SKILLS Procedures used to get answers

OBJECTIVE A Divide fractions and mixed numbers. **(Lessons 8-3, 8-4)**

In 1–4, evaluate the expression.

1. $\frac{4}{5} \div \frac{5}{2}$
2. $\frac{3}{8} \div \frac{7}{9}$
3. $6\frac{1}{3} \div \frac{2}{9}$
4. $11\frac{5}{7} \div 5\frac{1}{8}$
5. Which is greater, $6\frac{1}{3} \div \frac{2}{3}$ or $6\frac{1}{3} \div \frac{2}{7}$? Explain how you know.
6. Which is greater, $6\frac{1}{3} \div \frac{2}{9}$ or $6\frac{1}{5} \div \frac{2}{9}$? Explain how you know.

OBJECTIVE B Evaluate expressions containing fractions. **(Lesson 8-4)**

In 7–10, evaluate the expression.

7. $\frac{\frac{1}{2}}{\frac{2}{3} + \frac{4}{5}}$
8. $8 - \frac{6}{2} + 2^3$
9. $3 \cdot \frac{5+1}{5-1} - \frac{1}{12 - 2.5}$
10. $\frac{4+5}{-2+5} + \frac{7-9}{-4+5}$

OBJECTIVE C Solve equations of the form $ax = b$ using the Multiplication Property of Equality. **(Lesson 8-5)**

In 11–16, find the value of the variable.

11. $3x = 4$
12. $2.7m = \frac{3}{4}$
13. $\frac{8}{7}p = \frac{6}{5}$
14. $2\frac{1}{4}j = 8\frac{5}{7}$
15. $6u = 4.8$
16. $145 = 51q$

OBJECTIVE D Solve proportions. **(Lessons 8-6, 8-7)**

In 17–20, solve the proportion.

17. $\frac{45}{k} = \frac{4.5}{8}$
18. $\frac{63}{l} = \frac{9}{15}$
19. $\frac{81}{13} = \frac{0.81}{p}$
20. $\frac{1.3}{3.5} = \frac{g}{7}$

PROPERTIES The principles behind the mathematics

OBJECTIVE E Know and apply the Property of Reciprocals. **(Lesson 8-2)**

In 21–24, find the reciprocal.

21. $\frac{4}{7}$
22. $-\frac{32}{5}$
23. 7
24. 83
25. **True or False** The product of any number and its reciprocal is 1.
26. **True or False** Every integer has a reciprocal.

OBJECTIVE F Apply the Mult-Rec Property of Division. **(Lesson 8-3)**

27. **Fill in the Blank** $15 \div 7 = 15 \cdot$ _?_
28. Explain why $\frac{10}{\frac{1}{n}}$ is a whole number whenever n is a whole number.
29. **Fill in the Blanks** $\frac{1}{5} \div \frac{a}{b} =$ _?_ $\cdot$ _?_
30. **Fill in the Blanks** $\frac{x}{y} \div 6 =$ _?_ $\cdot$ _?_

USES Applications of mathematics in real-world situations

OBJECTIVE G Understand and use the Ratio Comparison Model for Division. (Lesson 8-1)

31. At Hopscotch University, 543 freshmen participate in at least one sport, while 142 freshmen do not participate in a sport. To the nearest tenth, what is the ratio of the number of freshmen who participate in sports to the number who do not?

32. At Topnotch University, 732 freshmen play at least one musical instrument, while 84 freshmen do not play an instrument. To the nearest tenth, what is the ratio of the number of freshmen who play an instrument to the number who do not?

33. On the 2006 Arsenal soccer team roster, there were 9 defenders, 3 goalies, 10 midfielders, and 7 strikers. What is the ratio of defenders to other team members?

34. The ratio of the number of dog owners to the number of non-owners in a classroom is 2:1. If there are 30 students in the class, how many own dogs?

35. Minnesota, known as the Land of 10,000 Lakes, has an area of 86,943 square miles. 79,617 square miles are land, while the remaining 7,326 square miles are water. What percent of Minnesota's total area is water?

36. In one survey, it was found that out of 500 children aged 4 to 14, 205 owned a video game system. What percent of children did not own a video game system?

37. A recipe for chiles rellenos calls for 19 tablespoons of oil, 3 tablespoons of which are for the sauce. What percent of the oil is used for the sauce?

38. Express the ratio of the number of rhyming words to total number of words in the following sentence as a percent: *The band Strand and Land can't stand sand.*

OBJECTIVE H Use division of fractions and mixed numbers in real-world situations. (Lessons 8-3, 8-4)

39. Tino is making a batch of chili for a chili cook-off competition. He is making 5 times the amount he makes for his regular recipe. If he uses $6\frac{1}{4}$ pounds of beef, how many pounds of beef are in his regular recipe?

40. Tallulah ran $7\frac{1}{2}$ miles around a $\frac{1}{4}$-mile track. How many laps did she run?

41. If your history class is $\frac{2}{3}$ of an hour long, and the school day lasts for $6\frac{1}{2}$ hours, for what fraction of the school day are you in history class?

42. While running the 100-meter dash, Tiffany covers the first $6\frac{3}{4}$ meters in 1 second. If she continues at this rate, how many seconds will it take her to finish the race?

OBJECTIVE I Use equations of the form $ax = b$ to solve problems in real-world situations. (Lesson 8-5)

In 43–46, a situation is given.

a. Represent the situation by an equation of the form $ax = b$.

b. Solve the equation using the Multiplication Property of Equality.

c. Check the solution in the original equation.

d. Answer the question in a complete sentence.

43. A bag of bagels costs \$3.25. If there are 6 bagels in a bag, how much would you expect to pay for one bagel?

44. Jackson can eat a foot-long tuna sandwich in 5 minutes, 15 seconds. If he is eating at a constant rate, how long does it take for him to eat two inches of the sandwich?

45. When Lawanda went to bed at 10 P.M., there were 3 inches of snow on the ground. When she woke up the next day at 6 A.M., there were $9\frac{1}{2}$ inches of snow on the ground. If the snow fell at a constant rate all night, how many inches of snow fell in one hour?

46. The ai, a three-toed sloth in Central and South America named for its shrill cry "ai-ai," climbs at a rate of 6 to 8 feet per minute. If an ai wants to climb a 60-foot tree, what is the minimum time it will take to get to the top?

OBJECTIVE J Use proportions in real-world situations. **(Lessons 8-6, 8-7, 8-8)**

47. Logan took a trip to Scotland. During the first eight days of his trip, he spent $480 on lodging and food. Assuming that these expenses remain constant, how much money m will he spend in fourteen days?

48. A 36-ounce container of cottage cheese contains 18 grams of fat. If one serving is 8 ounces, how many grams of fat are in one serving?

49. Alicia is making guacamole. For a single recipe, she uses one avocado, three tablespoons of salsa, and two tablespoons of lime juice. If she uses four avocados, how much salsa and lime juice should she use?

50. The ratio of television sets to homes for one class is 3:2. If there are 24 students in the class, none of whom live together, how many television sets would you expect there to be?

51. Ten miles is represented by 2 inches on a map of Kansas City. If two parks are 1.5 inches apart on the map, how far apart are they in the city?

52. A survey done in a certain town showed that the average family consists of 3.7 people and owns 1.2 cars. If there are about 2000 people in the town, about how many cars are there?

53. Last week, Chantel and her friends studied for $2\frac{1}{2}$ hours, and went through $2\frac{1}{4}$ bottles of orange juice. If she plans for the next study session to last at least four hours, what is the minimum amount of orange juice she should she have on hand?

54. The type of stainless steel that is most widely used in construction is called Grade 304 Stainless Steel. The two main elements that make up this steel are iron and chrome. For every 0.02 kilograms of iron in this steel, there are between 0.008 to 0.011 grams of chrome. Suppose that in creating stainless steel for a building, 70 metric tons of iron were used. How much chrome, at most, was needed?

REPRESENTATIONS Pictures, graphs, or objects that illustrate concepts

OBJECTIVE K Graph pairs of numbers from equal ratios or rates. **(Lesson 8-6)**

55. Kendrick took a road trip in his car. The table below shows how far he traveled in the first four hours of the trip.

Time (hr)	1	2	3	4
Distance Traveled (mi)	55	110	165	220

a. Plot these data on a coordinate grid.

b. On the graph you drew in Part a, draw the distance Kendrick traveled for a fifth hour, if he travels at the same rate.

56. Josephine collected data on the number of boys and girls in her college's dorms.

Year	2004	2005	2006	2007	2008
Boys	400	450	440	420	500
Girls	600	675	660	620	750

a. Plot these data on a coordinate grid whose two axes are number of boys and number of girls.

b. What seems to be Josephine's dorm's policy about the ratio of the number of boys to the number of girls?

57. An archeologist created a table detailing all of the cases in which sacks of grain were traded for bolts of wool in an ancient Babylonian market. Part of that table is shown below. Each column shows one such trade, and tells how many bolts of wool were traded for how many sacks of grain.

Bolts of wool	$3\frac{1}{2}$	2	$1\frac{1}{3}$	4
Sacks of grain	$5\frac{1}{4}$	3	2	6

a. Plot these data on a graph.

b. How many sacks of grain was each bolt of wool worth?

Chapter

9 Area and Volume

Contents

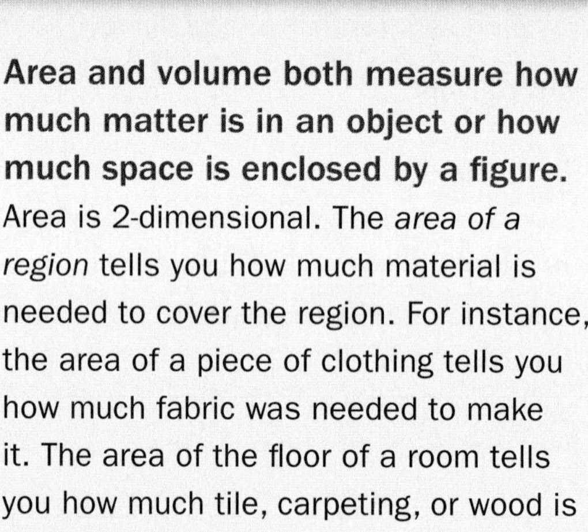

Area and volume both measure how much matter is in an object or how much space is enclosed by a figure. Area is 2-dimensional. The *area of a region* tells you how much material is needed to cover the region. For instance, the area of a piece of clothing tells you how much fabric was needed to make it. The area of the floor of a room tells you how much tile, carpeting, or wood is necessary to cover it.

The *area of a closed figure*, like a polygon or a circle, tells you how much 2-dimensional space the figure contains. For instance, the area of a garden tells you how much room there is for planting flowers. The area of the central circle on a dartboard tells you how much room you have to hit a bull's-eye.

Volume is 3-dimensional. The *volume of a solid* tells you how much material is in the solid, like the amount of clay used to make a brick. The *volume of a closed surface* like a box, cube, or sphere tells you how much space is enclosed by the surface, like the amount of helium in a balloon.

In this chapter, you will study formulas for calculating the area or volume of simple figures. You will also see how to estimate the area or volume of more complicated figures.

Lesson

9-1 Area and Operations of Arithmetic

Vocabulary

semicircle

▶ **BIG IDEA** Calculating the areas of figures may involve the operations of addition, subtraction, multiplication, division, and squaring.

All four of the basic arithmetic operations may be used in calculating areas.

Multiplication and Area

Areas of rectangles can be calculated by using the Area Model for Multiplication.

QY1

What are the areas of the figures below?

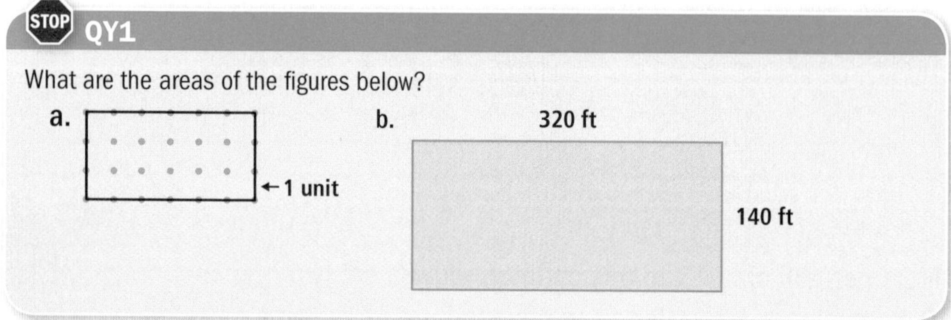

Mental Math

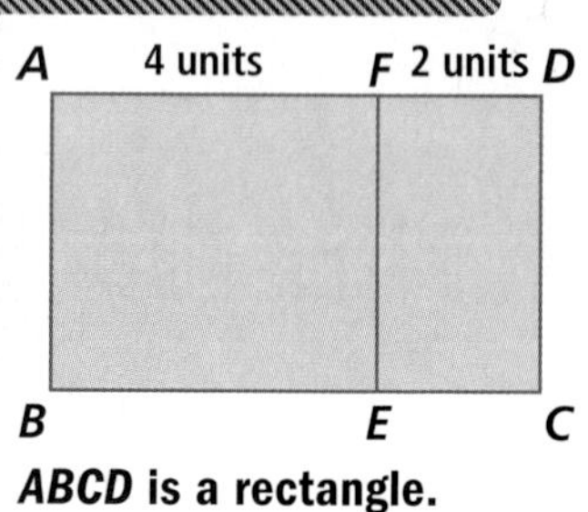

***ABCD* is a rectangle.**
***ABEF* is a square.**

a. What is the area of *ABCD*?

b. What is the perimeter of *ABCD*?

c. What is the area of *ABEF*?

d. What is the perimeter of *ABEF*?

Addition of Areas

Some areas can be found by adding other areas. Example 1 below uses the Putting-Together Model for Addition. In this example, the unit is the *acre*, which is a common unit used for measuring land area. A small lot for a house might have an area of about $\frac{1}{5}$ acre.

Example 1

A city is combining three parcels of land to form a park. The area of each of the parcels (lots) is shown in the diagram. What will be the total acreage of the park?

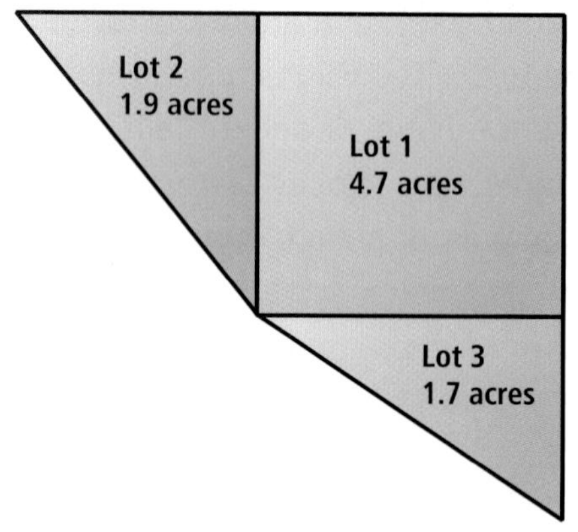

Solution Add the areas of the three lots.

The total acreage is 1.9 + 4.7 + 1.7 acres, or 8.3 acres.

Subtraction of Areas

Some areas can be calculated by using the Take-Away Model for Subtraction.

STOP QY2

The plans for the park in Example 1 call for a 2.3-acre lake, with the rest of the park planted in grass. How many acres of grass will be in the park?

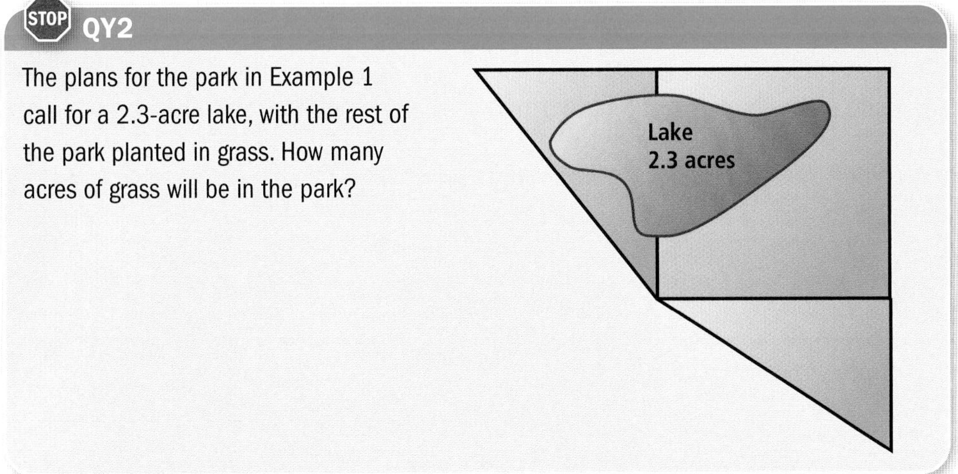

Division and Area

Consider the following situation. A bathroom floor is covered with triangular tiles. Four tiles make up a square. Because each square area is 1 square unit, each tile has an area of $\frac{1}{4}$ square unit.

Area = 1 unit^2

Area = $\frac{1}{4}$ unit^2

By splitting a rectangle, you can find the area of a right triangle.

Activity 1

MATERIALS ruler, scissors, tape, grid paper

Step 1 Make a 3 unit-by-2 unit rectangle by cutting a sheet of paper. The unit can be any size you wish.

Step 2 Draw grid lines, or use grid paper, to show that the area of the rectangle is 6 square units.

Step 3 Draw a diagonal of the rectangle. Shade one of the triangular regions as shown at the right. Cut the rectangle along its diagonal into two equal pieces.

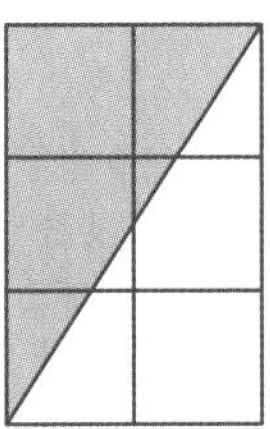

Step 4 By cutting and taping parts of the shaded region, show that its area is 3 square units.

Area and the Squares of Numbers

There is a fundamental connection between area and squares of numbers.

Activity 2

The drawing at the right shows squares with sides of length 1 unit to 9 units.

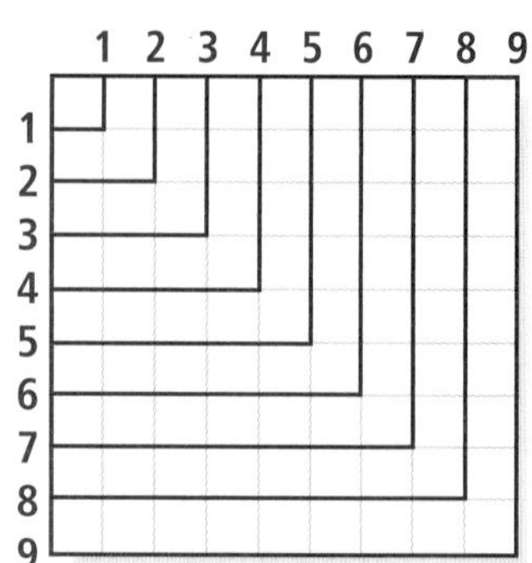

Step 1 Complete the following table.

Side Length of Square (units)	1	2	3	4	5	6	7	8	9
Area of Square (square units)	1	4	?	?	?	?	?	?	?

Step 2 Predict the area of a square with side length 10 units.

Step 3 Predict the area of a square with side length 11 units.

In Activity 2, you should have found that the area of a square with side length s units is s^2 square units. This is why we often read s^2 as "s squared."

Different units of area are often related by squares of numbers. The diagram at the right shows why 1 square yard = 9 square feet.

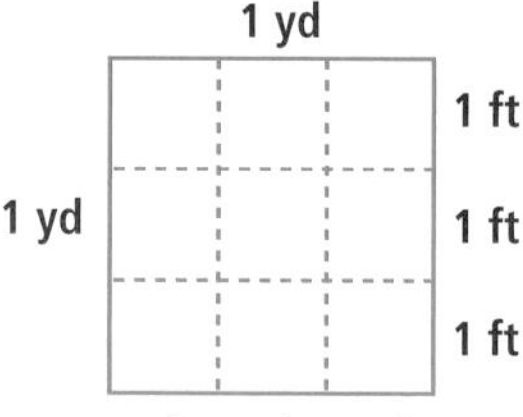

GUIDED

Example 2

A square room is 45 feet on a side.

a. What is the area of the room in square feet?

b. What is the area of the room in square yards?

Solution

a. The area of the room is 45 ft • 45 ft = __?__ ft^2

b. Since 3 ft = 1 yd, 45 ft = __?__ yd. So Area = 45 ft • 45 ft = __?__ yd • __?__ yd = __?__ yd^2.

Questions

COVERING THE IDEAS

1. The apartment where Marisol lives is made up of four rectangular rooms. There is a large 18 ft-by-13 ft room separated into a living room and kitchen, two bedrooms which are 10 ft-by-12 ft each, and a 7 ft-by-9 ft bathroom. What is the total area of the apartment?

2. Suppose that a rectangular sheet cake has dimensions 24" by 18". If this cake is split into 2"-by-3" pieces, how many pieces are formed?

In 3–8, use octagon *ADEFGHIJ* at the right. Each angle in the octagon is a right angle.

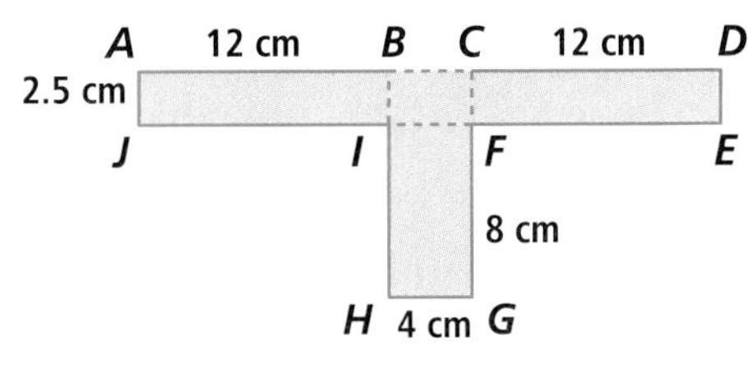

3. Find the dimensions, perimeter, and area of rectangle *ABIJ*.
4. Find the area of rectangle *ADEJ* by splitting it into three rectangles.
5. Explain why you cannot find the perimeter of rectangle *ADEJ* by splitting it into three rectangles.
6. Find the area enclosed by the octagon.
7. Imagine that $\overline{CH}$ is drawn. Find the area of $\triangle BCH$.
8. If $\overline{BF}$ and $\overline{CI}$ are drawn, they will split the region *BCFI* into four triangular regions of equal area. What is the area of one of those regions?

9. A 9 foot-by-12 foot bedroom is to be carpeted.
   a. How many square feet of carpeting are needed?
   b. How many square yards of carpeting are needed?
   c. If one store advertises a particular carpeting at $4.95 a square foot, and another advertises the same carpeting at $40 a square yard, which store has the lower price?

10. What is the area of a square with four sides of length 13 meters?

APPLYING THE MATHEMATICS

11. The numbers 1, 4, 9, 16, and 25 are examples of *perfect squares*. Explain why they have this name and why 24 is not a perfect square.

12. Explain why there are 144 square inches in a square foot.

13. There are 10 millimeters in a centimeter. How many square millimeters are in a square centimeter?

14. Half a circle is called a **semicircle.** In the figure at the right, a semicircular region with diameter $\overline{BC}$ has been cut off rectangle *ABCD* and attached to side $\overline{AD}$.

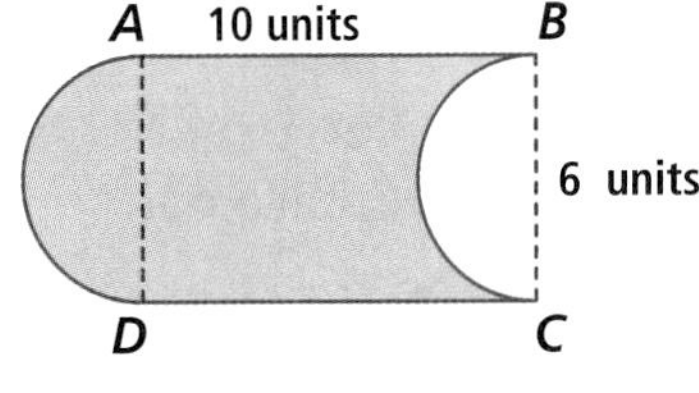

   a. What is the area of the shaded region?
   b. Explain how the Area Model for Multiplication, the Putting-Together Model for Addition, and the Take-Away Model for Subtraction justify your answer to Part a.

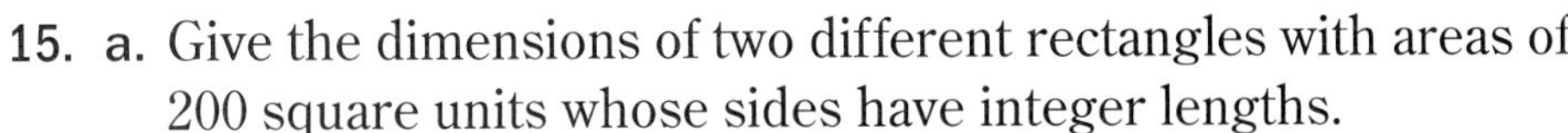

15. a. Give the dimensions of two different rectangles with areas of 200 square units whose sides have integer lengths.
    b. Attach these rectangles to each other with no overlap. Show that the perimeter of the combined region is not equal to the sum of the perimeters of the two rectangles you started with.
    c. Is the area of the combined region equal to the sum of the areas of the two rectangles you started with?

16. You see a sign that says, "New 30,000 square-foot store to be built here." Give two possible dimensions of the store, assuming it is rectangular.

17. Draw a 6 unit-by-6 unit square. Connect the midpoints of the sides of the square to form a tilted square in the middle. What is the area of the tilted square?

18. How many 3 in.-by-3 in. square tiles are needed to replace a single 1 ft-by-1 ft square tile?

19. Use a fact triangle to find the length of a rectangle that has a width of 8 feet and an area of 384 ft^2.

REVIEW

20. In a 4" × 5" photograph, Dana's dachshund is 5.4 centimeters long. Dana wants to enlarge the portrait of her pooch to a poster measuring 20" by 25". Write and solve a proportion to find how long the dog will be in the new picture. **(Lesson 8-8)**

21. 2.3 pounds of apples cost $4.33. At this rate, how much would 5 pounds of apples cost? **(Lesson 8-7)**

22. Edward has $3\frac{1}{4}$ hours of talk time left on his cellular phone plan for the remaining 10 days of the month. On average, how many hours per day can he talk? **(Lesson 8-4)**

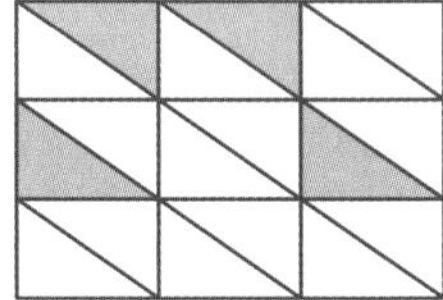

23. If the area of the large rectangle at the right is $15\frac{3}{8}$ in^2, what is the total area of the shaded regions of the rectangle? **(Lessons 8-4, 4-1)**

24. Find the perimeter of the isosceles triangle at the right. **(Lesson 3-2)**

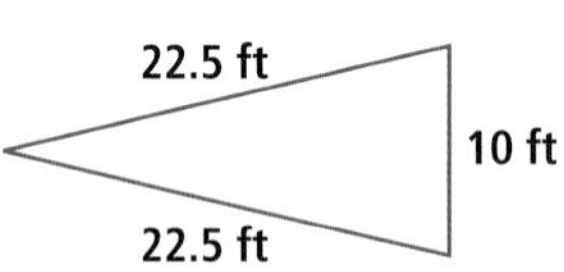

25. Draw a line segment $2\frac{3}{8}$ in. long. **(Lesson 1-3)**

EXPLORATION

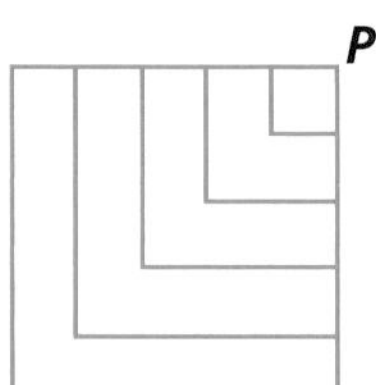

26. The 5-by-5 square region shown at the right has been split into a single square and four L-shaped regions.
    a. Find the area of each of the five regions.
    b. Find the area of each of the five squares that has P as one of its vertices.
    c. Use your answers to Parts a and b to find five different odd numbers whose sum is 25.
    d. Use your answers to Parts a and b to find eight different odd numbers whose sum is 64.
    e. Use your answers to the previous parts to find the sum of the odd numbers from 1 to 99.

QY ANSWERS

1a. 18 units^2

1b. 44,800 ft^2

2. 6 acres

Lesson 9-2 The Area of a Triangle

Vocabulary

legs of a right triangle
hypotenuse
base of a triangle
altitude of a triangle
height of a triangle

▸ **BIG IDEA** The area of any triangle can be found either by adding the areas of two right triangles or by taking half the area of a rectangle.

Mental Math

Calculate.

a. $7 \cdot 8 \cdot 10$

b. $7 \cdot 4 \cdot 10$

c. $7 \cdot 8 \cdot \frac{1}{2} \cdot 10$

d. $14 \cdot 8 \cdot \frac{1}{2} \cdot \frac{1}{2} \cdot 10$

Triangles are found everywhere. At the right is a picture of Fountain Place, a building in Dallas, Texas, in which you can see a number of triangles.

Triangles are important in calculating the areas of figures because many figures cannot easily be split into rectangles.

The irregular figure below can be approximated by a polygon. The polygonal region can be split into triangles.

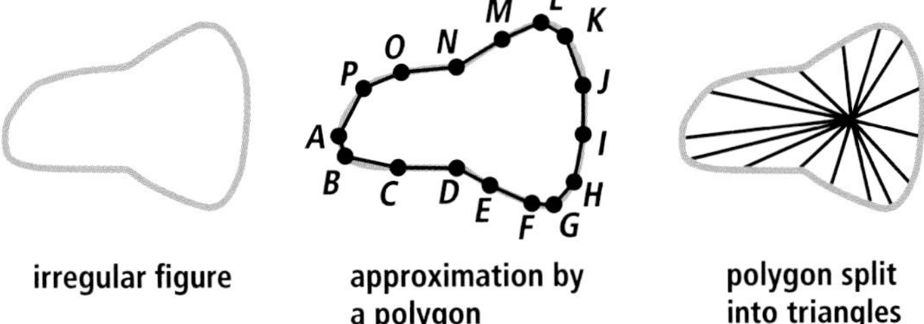

Each triangular region can be further split into two right triangles as shown below. Recall that a right triangle has a 90° angle. The two sides that form the 90° angle are the **legs.** The side opposite the 90° angle is the **hypotenuse.** The hypotenuse is always the longest side of a right triangle.

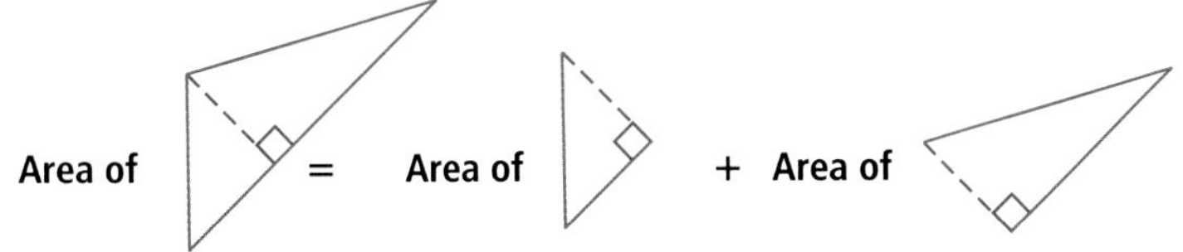

So, if you can find the area of a right triangle, then you can find the area of all sorts of polygons. Also, you can estimate the area of an irregular figure.

Fountain Place is internationally recognized as a superior architectural achievement.

Area of a Right Triangle

Two copies of any right triangle can be used to make a rectangle, with the legs of the triangles as its sides. Here are two examples.

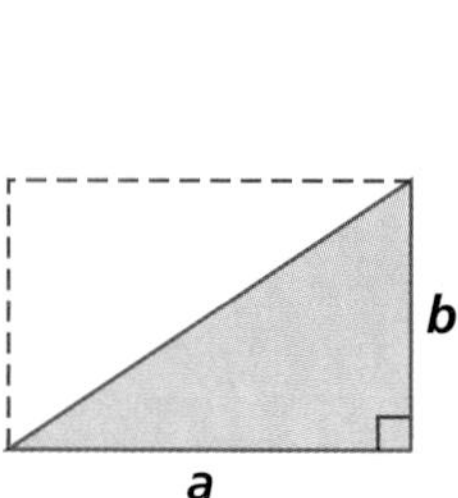

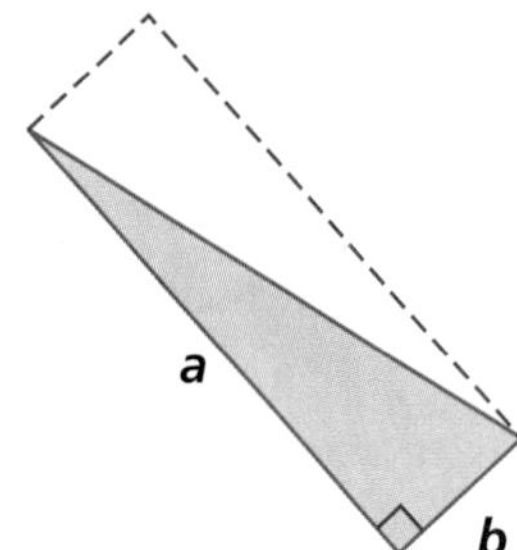

Example 1

Washington, Kennedy, and Lincoln Streets form the border of a piece of land. Kennedy runs north and south, and Washington runs east and west. So these two streets form a 90° angle. If the legs of the right triangle formed by the three streets are 300 and 450 feet long, what is the area of the piece of land they border?

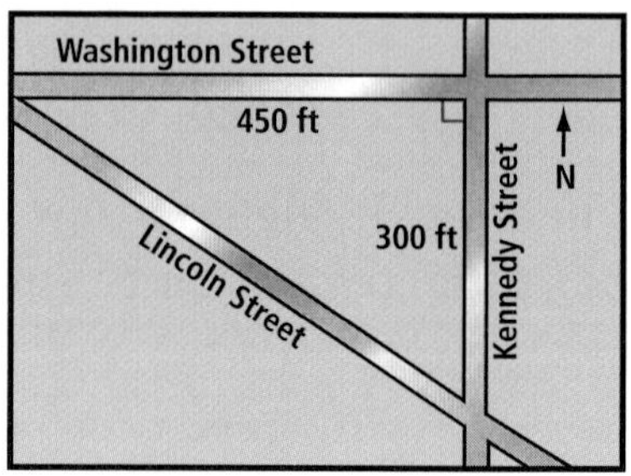

Solution Think of the right triangle as half a rectangle with dimensions 300 feet and 450 feet. The area of this rectangle is 300 feet • 450 feet, or 13,500 square feet. So the area of the piece of land is $\frac{1}{2} \cdot 13{,}500 =$ 6,750 square feet.

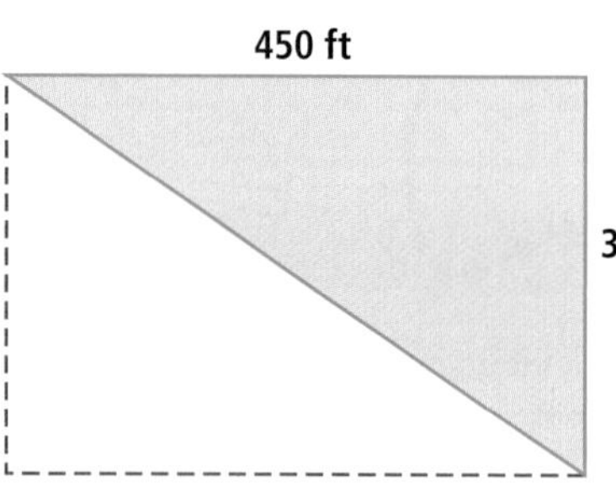

QY

Is the perimeter of the right triangle in Example 1 half of the perimeter of the rectangle? Why or why not?

The method used in Example 1 works with any right triangle.

Area Formula for a Right Triangle

The area A of a right triangle is one half the product of the lengths of its legs a and b: $A = \frac{1}{2}ab$.

Area of Any Triangle

The area of any triangle can be found by adding or subtracting areas of right triangles.

GUIDED

Example 2

Find the area of $\triangle ABC$ at the right.

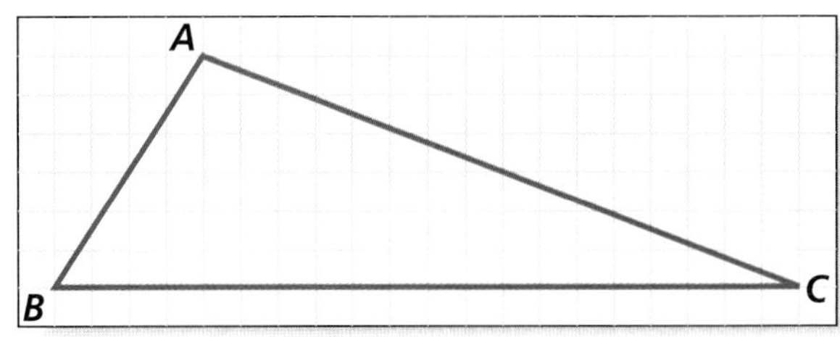

Solution Split the triangle into two right triangles *ADB* and *ADC* as shown below.

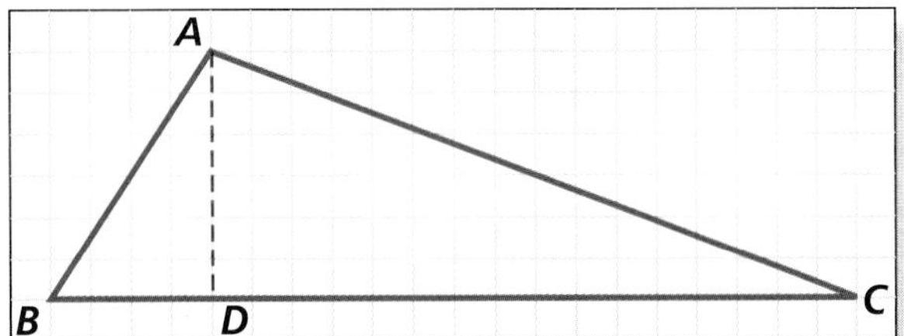

Now count to find the lengths of the legs of these right triangles:

AD = __?__ units, BD = __?__ units, and DC = __?__ units

The area of $\triangle$ADB is $\frac{1}{2}$ • __?__ • __?__ square units. The area of $\triangle$ADC is $\frac{1}{2}$ • __?__ • __?__ square units. So the area of $\triangle$ABC is __?__ square units.

Example 3

Find the area of $\triangle EFG$ on the grid at the right. Each square is 1 square centimeter.

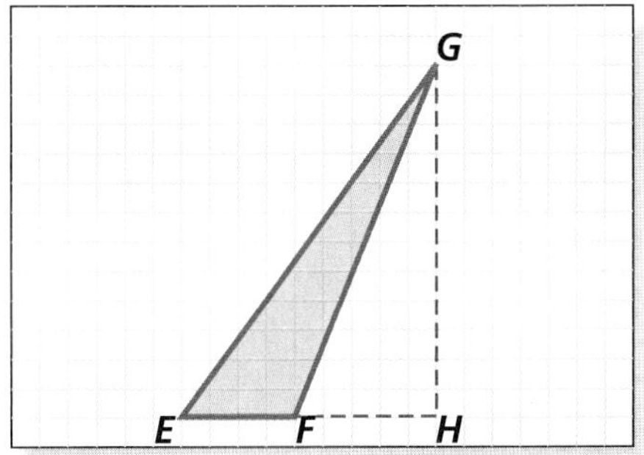

Solution Notice that $EF = 4$ cm. Extend $\overline{EF}$ and draw $\overline{GH}$ to form a right triangle *EGH*. You can count to see that $GH = 12$ and $FH = 5$. The area of $\triangle EFG$ can be found by calculating the area of right triangle *EGH* and subtracting the area of right triangle *FGH* from it.

Use the formula for the area of a right triangle.

Area of $\triangle$EGH $= \frac{1}{2} \cdot EH \cdot GH = \frac{1}{2} \cdot 9 \cdot 12 = 54 \text{ cm}^2$

Area of $\triangle$FGH $= \frac{1}{2} \cdot FH \cdot GH = \frac{1}{2} \cdot 5 \cdot 12 = 30 \text{ cm}^2$

So the area of $\triangle$EFG $= 54 - 30 = 24 \text{ cm}^2$.

Recall that the sides of a 90° angle lie on *perpendicular lines*. In Example 3, $\overline{GH}$ and $\overline{EF}$ lie on perpendicular lines. $\overline{EF}$ is a **base** of the triangle and $\overline{GH}$ is the **altitude,** or **height,** of the triangle to that base. Notice that the area of $\triangle EFG$ equals one-half of the product of the lengths of the base and the height.

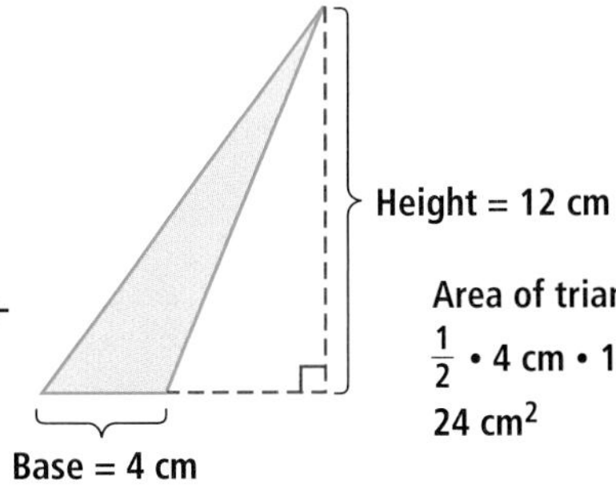

This is true for any triangle.

Area Formula for Any Triangle

The area A of any triangle is one half the product of the lengths of its base b and its height h: $A = \frac{1}{2}bh$.

Caution: The base and the height must be perpendicular. As in Example 3, sometimes the drawing of the segment for the height is outside the triangle.

In Example 3, the side with length 4 cm was the base. However, you can use any of the sides as the base. In the Activity, you are asked to find the area of the same triangle in two ways, using different bases.

Activity

MATERIALS ruler, tracing paper

Step 1 Trace the triangle at the right.

Step 2 Use the 36 mm side as the base of the triangle. Use a ruler to draw and measure the height to this base to the nearest millimeter.

Step 3 Use the formula to find the area of the triangle.

Step 4 Now, use the 30 mm side as the base. You may rotate the triangle until this side is horizontal if needed. Draw and measure the height to the 30 mm base.

Step 5 Use the formula to find the area of the triangle.

Step 6 Are your areas from Step 3 and Step 5 the same? Why or why not?

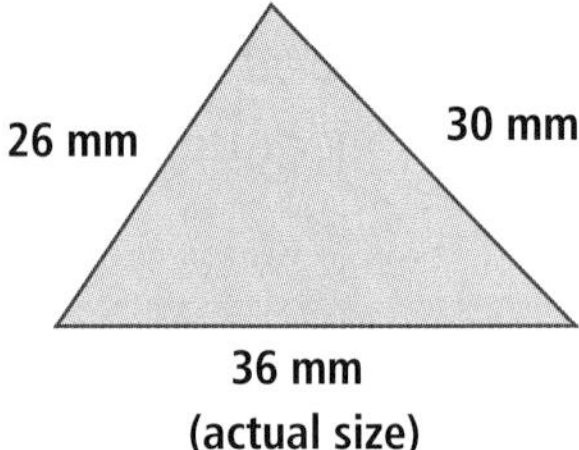

(actual size)

Questions

COVERING THE IDEAS

In 1 and 2, a right triangle is shown. Find its area by

a. drawing a rectangle whose area is twice the area of the triangle.

b. using the formula for the area of a right triangle.

1.

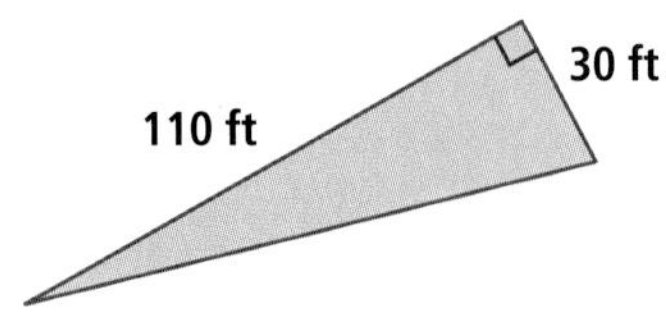

2.

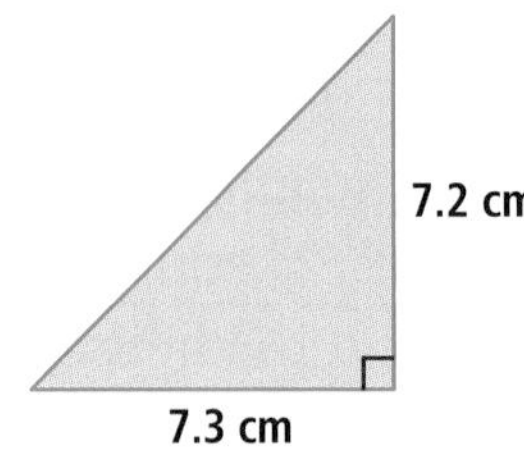

3. Identify the legs and the hypotenuse of triangle RGT at the right.

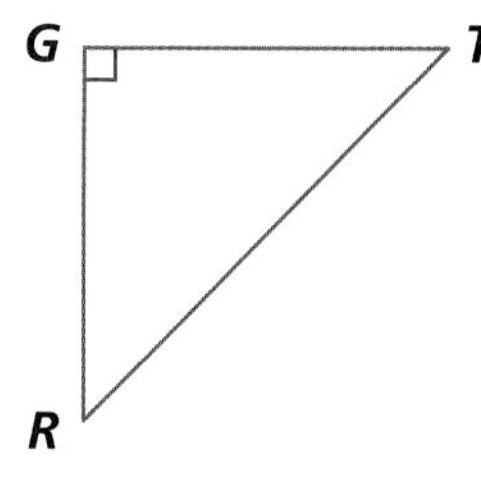

4. a. Find the area of the triangle at the right by splitting it into two right triangles and adding their areas.
   b. Find the area of the triangle by using the Area Formula for Any Triangle.

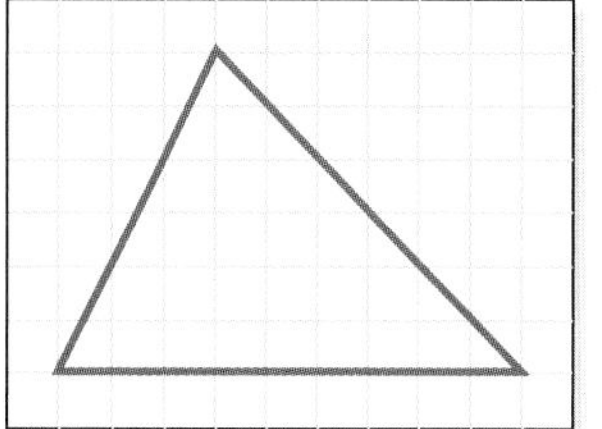

In 5 and 6, find the area of the triangle.

5.

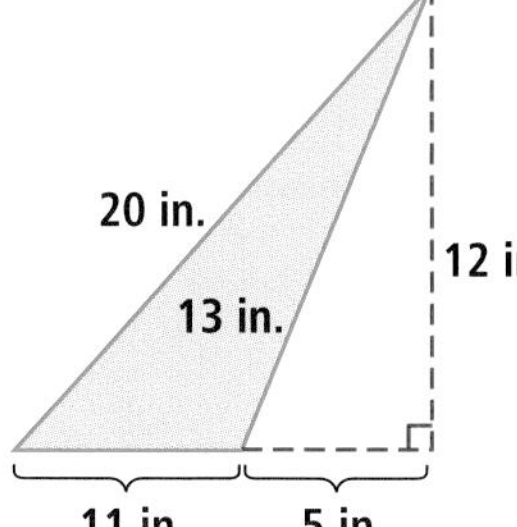

6.

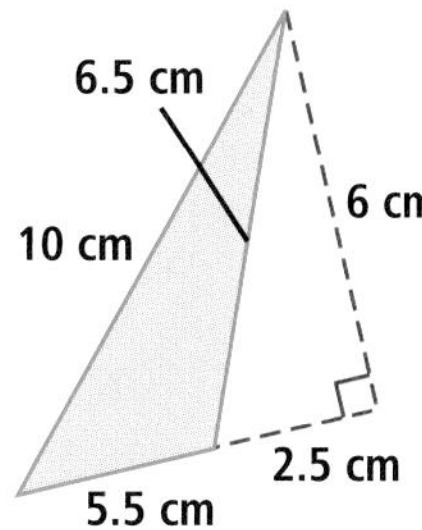

In 7 and 8, use the red side of the triangle as the base. Trace the triangle and draw the height for that base. If you want, use grid paper to help. Then measure the base and height and find the area of the triangle in square centimeters.

7.

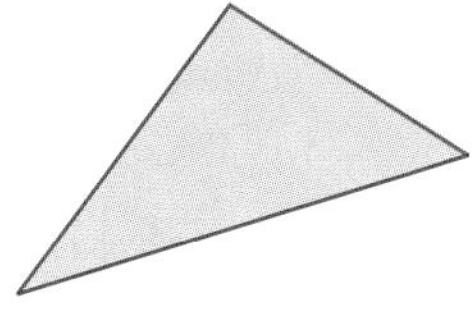

8.

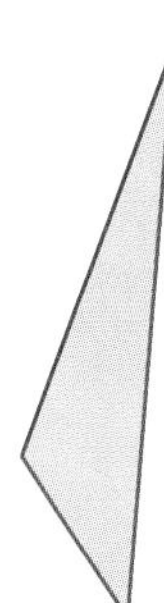

9. Look at the irregular figure and polygon $ABCDEFGHIJKLMNOP$ on page 519.
   a. Which has the greater area, the irregular figure or the polygon?
   b. Into how many triangles is the polygon divided in order to find its area?

APPLYING THE MATHEMATICS

10. Make three copies of the triangle at the right.
    a. In each copy, draw the height to a different side.
    b. Measure each base and height to the nearest millimeter.
    c. Find the area of each copy.
    d. Compare the three areas. How could you account for any differences in the areas?

11. A painter needs to calculate the amount of paint needed for the roof of a house. A gallon of paint can cover about 325 square feet. The roof has four sections. Each is a triangle 30 feet wide at the base and 25 feet high.
    a. What is the total area he must paint?
    b. How many gallons are needed for one coat of paint?

12. Draw a rectangle whose area is twice that of $\triangle ABC$ in Example 2. Find the area of $\triangle ABC$ by calculating half the area of the rectangle.

13. The triangle at the right is a right triangle.
    a. Calculate its area.
    b. Calculate its perimeter.
    c. Are the area and perimeter equal? Why or why not?

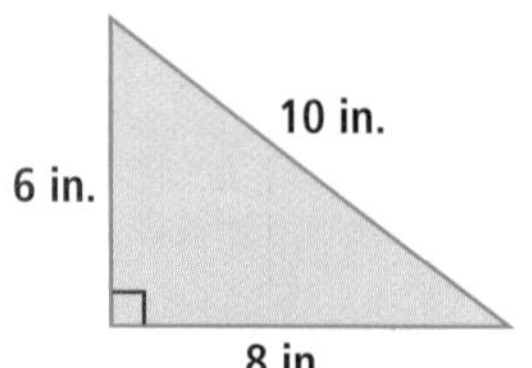

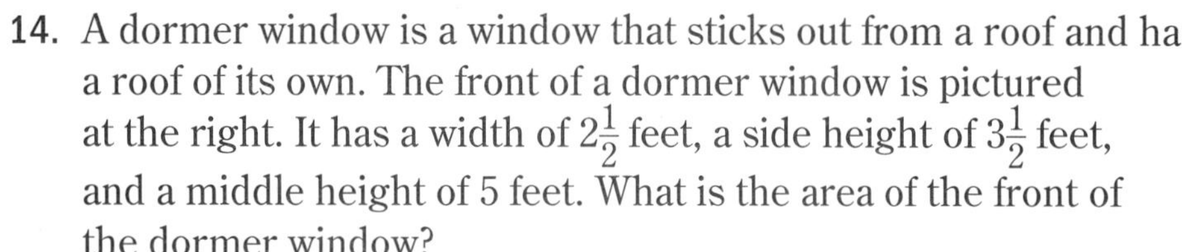

14. A dormer window is a window that sticks out from a roof and has a roof of its own. The front of a dormer window is pictured at the right. It has a width of $2\frac{1}{2}$ feet, a side height of $3\frac{1}{2}$ feet, and a middle height of 5 feet. What is the area of the front of the dormer window?

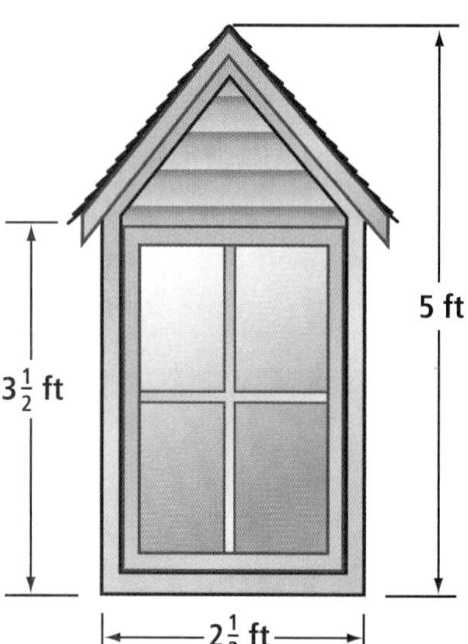

REVIEW

In 15 and 16, determine which figure has the greater area, and tell how much greater it is. All angles are right angles. (Lessons 9-1, 4-2)

15. i.

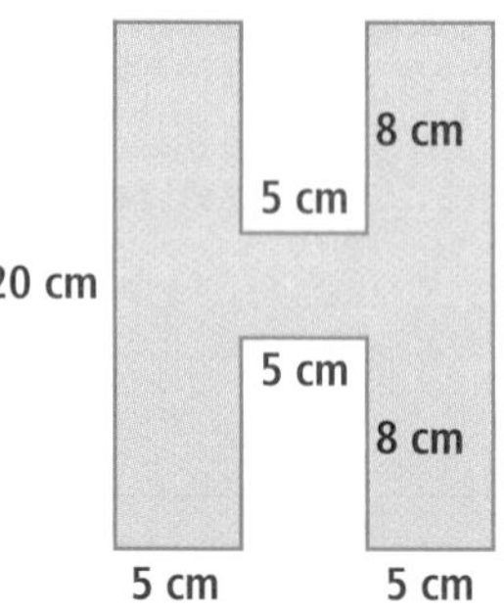

ii.

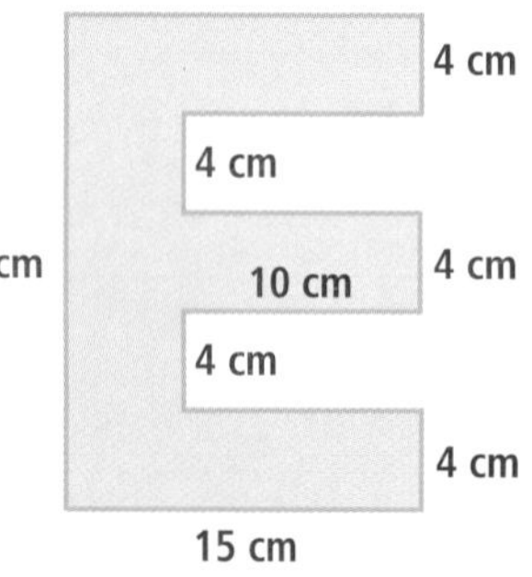

16. i.

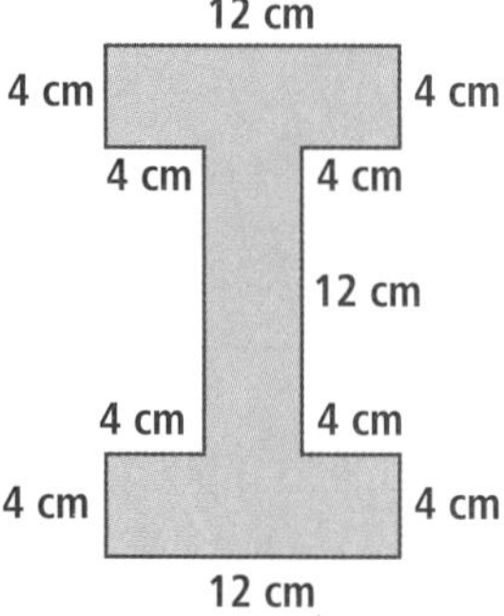

ii.

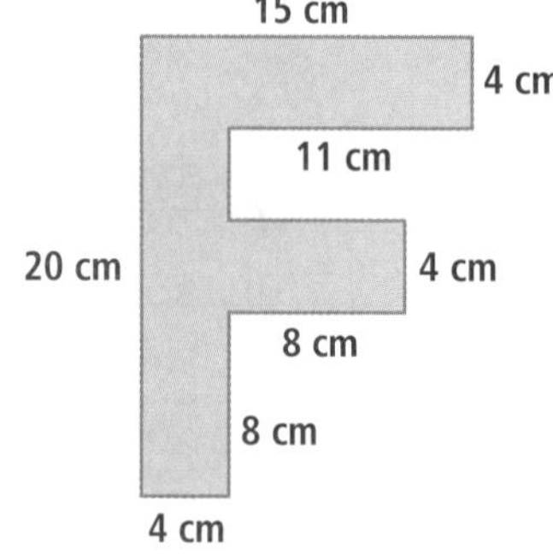

17. The first two chapters of a 27-chapter book contain a total of 8,943 words. At this rate, how many words would you expect there to be in the entire book? **(Lesson 8-7)**

18. Solve $\frac{5.6}{p} = \frac{112}{15}$. **(Lesson 8-6)**

19. **Multiple Choice** On which balance is *X* heavier than *Y*? **(Lesson 8-5)**

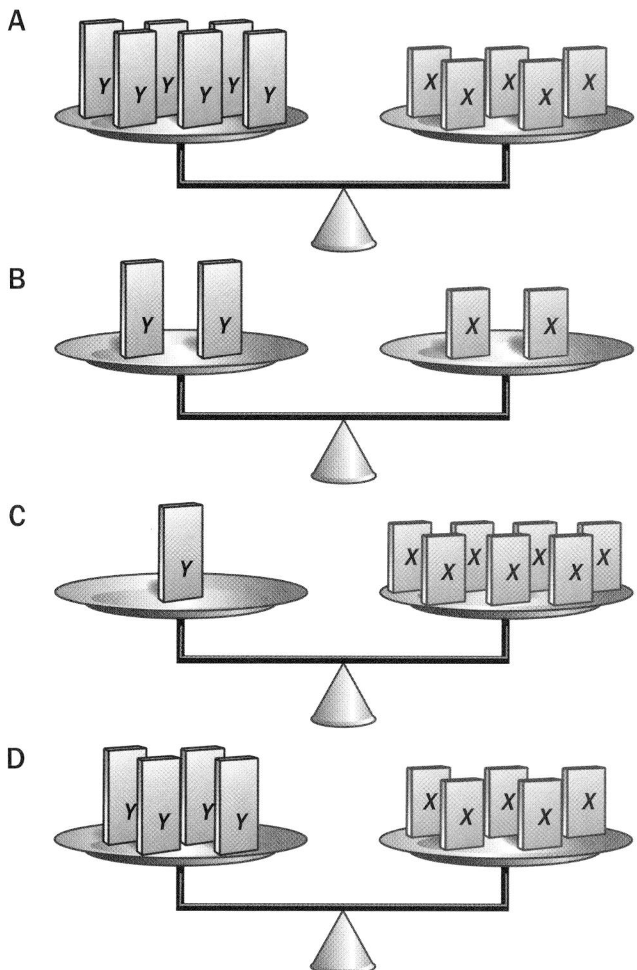

20. In a survey asking 34 students where they learned the most about current events, 14 read news on the Internet, 12 watch news coverage on television, and 8 read newspapers or magazines. Make a circle graph of these data. Indicate the measure of each of the central angles. **(Lessons 5-4, 2-8)**

21. Draw a parallelogram consisting of two line segments measuring 1.2 cm and two line segments measuring 3.4 cm. **(Lesson 2-4)**

EXPLORATION

22. Look in your school, home, or other places, and find a triangle-shaped object with an area you can calculate. Calculate that area by measuring and using a formula.

QY ANSWER

Answers vary. Sample: No, the length of the two legs is equal to half the perimeter of the rectangle. The perimeter of the right triangle includes the length of the hypotenuse.

Lesson

9-3 The Area of a Parallelogram

Vocabulary

parallel lines
parallelogram
base of a parallelogram
altitude of a parallelogram
height of a parallelogram

BIG IDEA The area of any parallelogram is equal to the area of a rectangle with the same base and same height to that base.

Mental Math

True or False

a. All linear pairs of angles are supplementary.

b. All supplementary angles are linear pairs.

c. If ∠1 and ∠2 are supplementary, and ∠2 and ∠3 are supplementary, then ∠1 and ∠3 are supplementary.

d. If ∠1 is a supplement to ∠2, and ∠2 has the same measure as ∠3, then ∠1 is a supplement of ∠3.

When two different lines in the same plane have no points in common, they are **parallel lines.** A **parallelogram** is a quadrilateral with two pairs of parallel sides. In the parallelogram *PLAY* below, $\overline{PL}$ and $\overline{YA}$ are opposite sides and are parallel to each other. Angles *P* and *A* are opposite angles. In a parallelogram, opposite sides have the same length and opposite angles have the same measure.

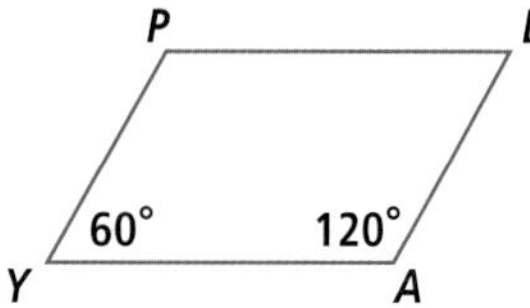

QY

Name the other pair of opposite sides and the other pair of opposite angles in parallelogram *PLAY* above.

Area of a Parallelogram

You can find the area of a parallelogram by forming a rectangle with the same area.

Example 1

Find the area of parallelogram *LOGR* below.

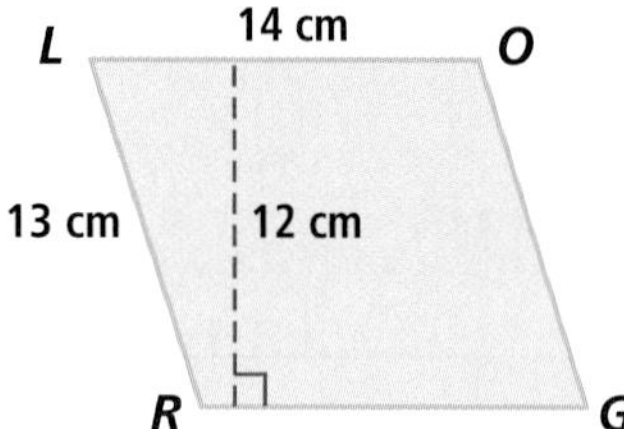

Solution On the next page, we show the parallelogram on a centimeter grid. Each square on the grid has an area of 1 cm^2.

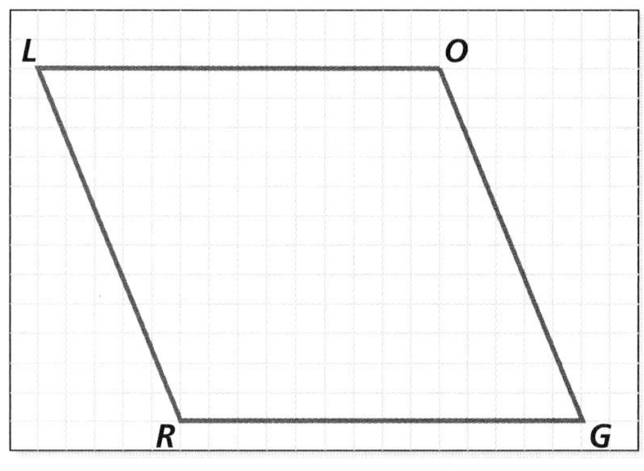

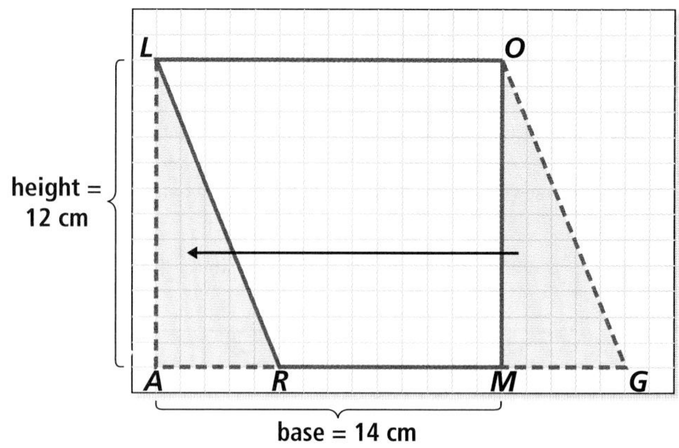

You could try to count the squares to find the area of *LOGR*, but that would be rather difficult. Instead, cut off a right triangle from parallelogram *LOGR* and move it to the opposite side to form a rectangle *LOMA* as shown above at the right. Rectangle *LOMA* and parallelogram *LOGR* have the same area.

The area of rectangle *LOMA* can be found by multiplying its dimensions: $12 \text{ cm} \cdot 14 \text{ cm} = 168 \text{ cm}^2$. So the area of the parallelogram is 168 cm^2.

You can find the area of any parallelogram by using the method of Example 1. However, there is a shortcut. As with a triangle, you can choose any side of a parallelogram to be the **base of the parallelogram.** The side opposite that base has the same length as the base. The **altitude,** or **height, of the parallelogram** to that base is the perpendicular distance between the bases.

GUIDED

Example 2

a. Show that the perimeters of the parallelograms *ABCD* and *EFCD* at the right are not equal.

b. Show that the areas of these parallelograms are equal.

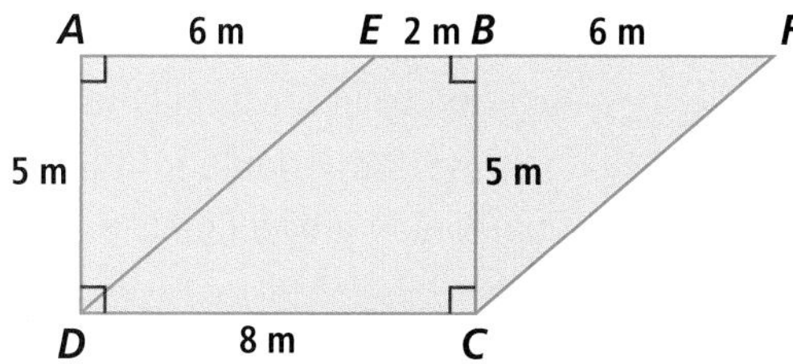

Solution

a. Perimeter of ABCD = AD + DC + CB + BA

Perimeter of EFCD = _?_ + _?_ + _?_ + _?_

Since $\overline{ED}$ is the hypotenuse of $\triangle ADE$, it is the longest side. So, $ED > AD$. Since $\overline{CF}$ is the hypotenuse of _?_, $CF >$ _?_.

Thus, two of the numbers added to get the perimeter of EFCD are greater than the numbers added to get the perimeter of ABCD. The remaining two lengths are the same in both figures. So the perimeter of EFCD is _?_ than the perimeter of ABCD.

b. The area of rectangle ABCD is _?_.

(continued on next page)

The area of EBCD is the area of rectangle ABCD minus the area of △AED. The area of △AED is ? .

So, the area of EBCD is ? .

The area of △CBF is ? .

So, the area of parallelogram EFCD is ? + ? , or ? .

Thus, the areas of ABCD and EFCD are equal.

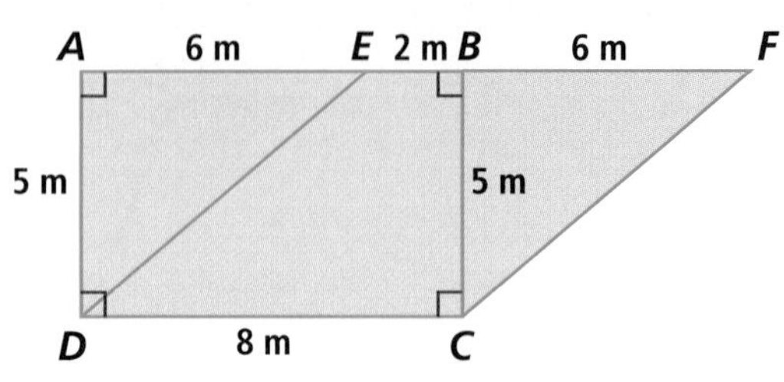

In Example 2, notice that the base of rectangle *ABCD* is the same as the base of the parallelogram *EFCD*. You can find the area of a parallelogram by multiplying its base by its height.

Area Formula for a Parallelogram

The area A of a parallelogram is the product of the lengths of a base b and of the height to that base h: $A = bh$.

Caution: The base and the height *are perpendicular*. The height is not the same as the length of a side, except when the parallelogram is a rectangle.

Activity

MATERIALS ruler, centimeter grid paper

Find the area of the parallelogram at the right in square millimeters.

Step 1 Measure the base and the height to that base to the nearest millimeter, using a ruler. Then use the formula for the area of a parallelogram to find the area.

Step 2 Trace the parallelogram onto centimeter grid paper. Use areas of triangles and rectangles to find the area of the parallelogram.

Step 3 Compare your two answers. Are they exactly the same? Compare your answers with those of other students. How do they compare? Why might answers be different?

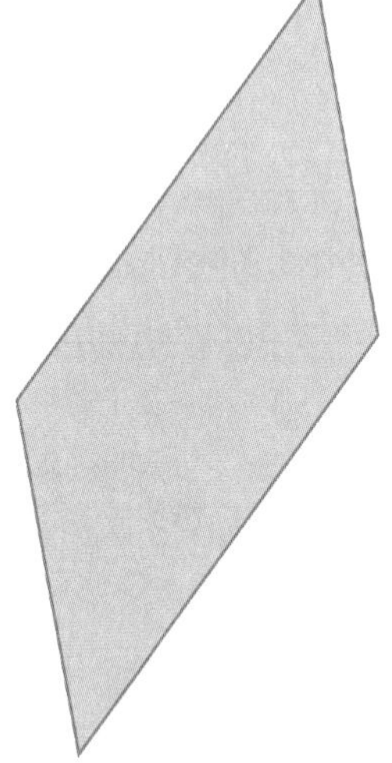

Knowing how to find the area of a parallelogram enables you to obtain the areas of many other figures.

Questions

COVERING THE IDEAS

1. Find the area of parallelogram *FINE* below in *three* ways.

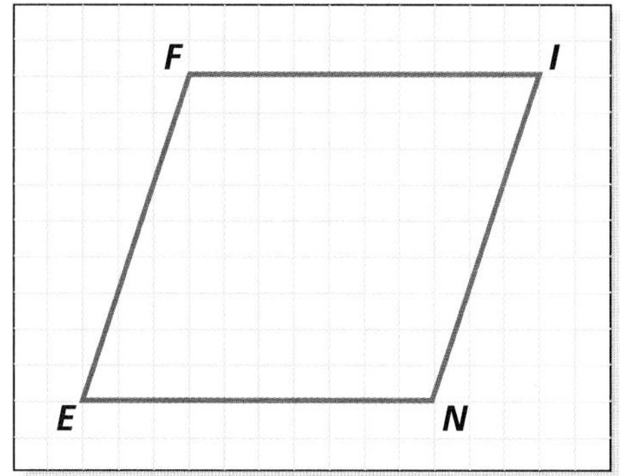

a. Split it into two right triangles and a rectangle, and add the areas of these three shapes.

b. Find a rectangle that has the same area and use the area of that rectangle.

c. Use the formula for the area of a parallelogram.

In 2 and 3, find the area of the largest parallelogram.

2.

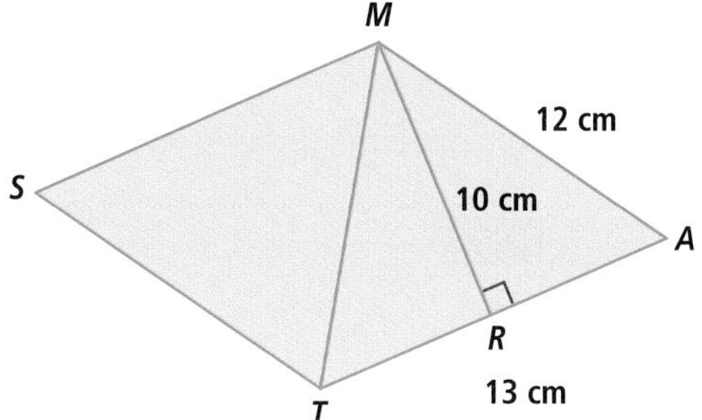

3.

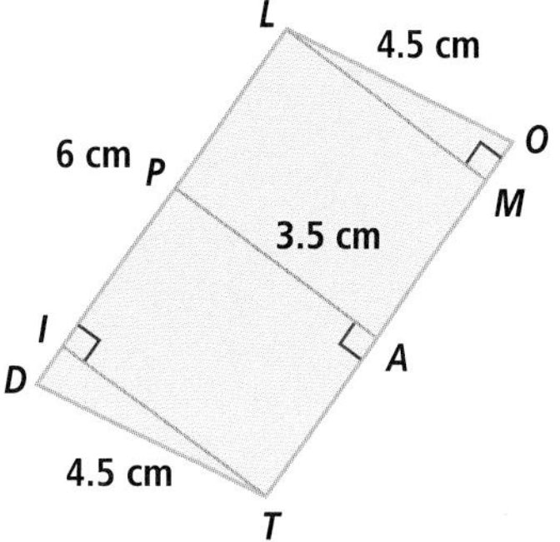

4. a. Copy $\triangle NOW$ at the right onto grid paper. Show how you can add a copy of the triangle to this grid to make a parallelogram.

b. Find the area of the parallelogram. Use that area to find the area of $\triangle NOW$.

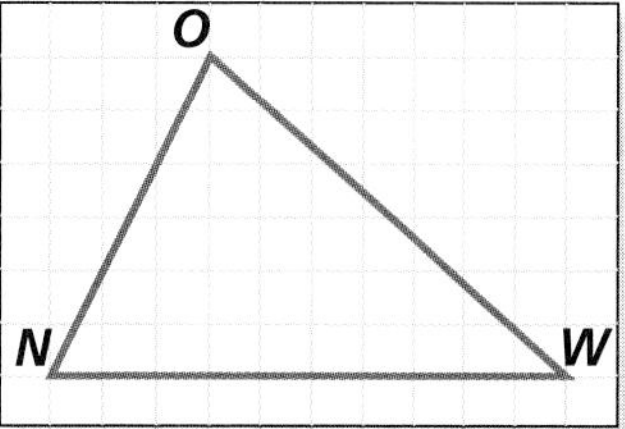

5. Explain why the perimeter of parallelogram *MARS* is greater than the perimeter of rectangle *ARTS*.

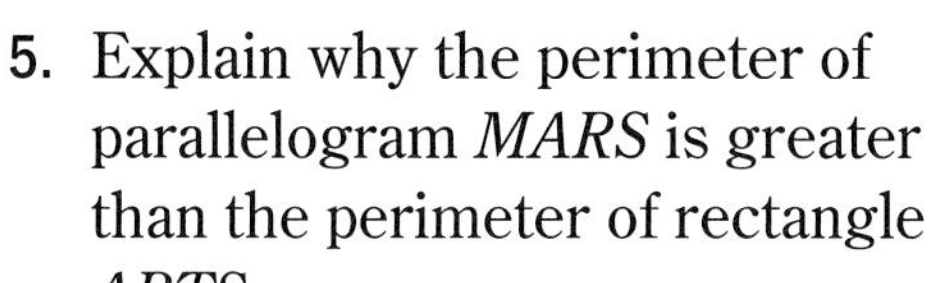

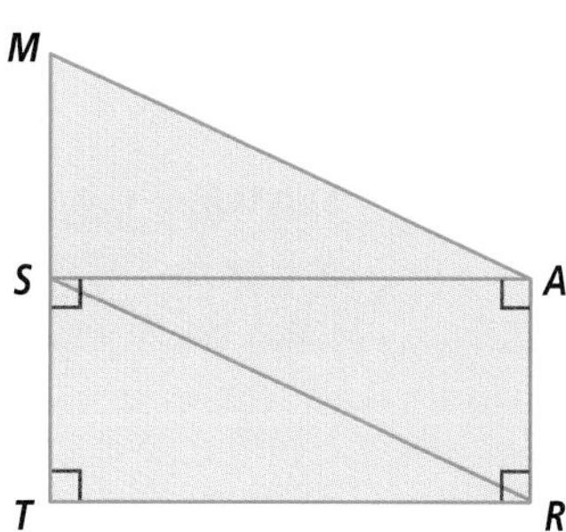

In 6–8, use the red side of the parallogram as the base. Trace the parallelogram and draw the height for that base. If you want, use grid paper to help. Then measure the base and height and find the area of the parallelogram in square centimeters.

6.

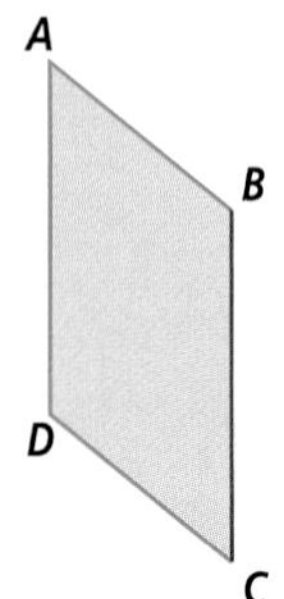

7.

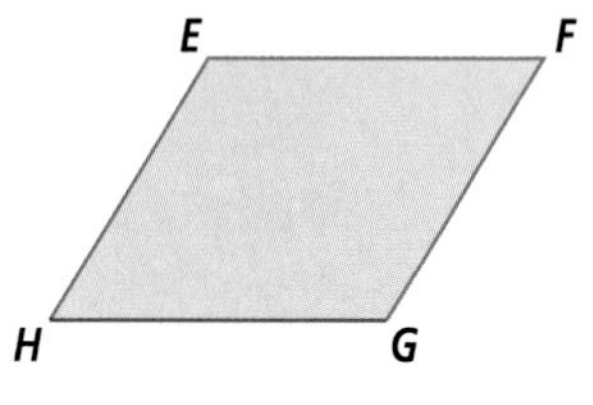

8.

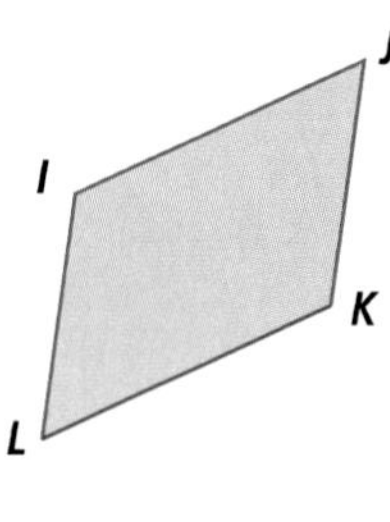

9. Find the area of parallelogram *MNPQ* below.

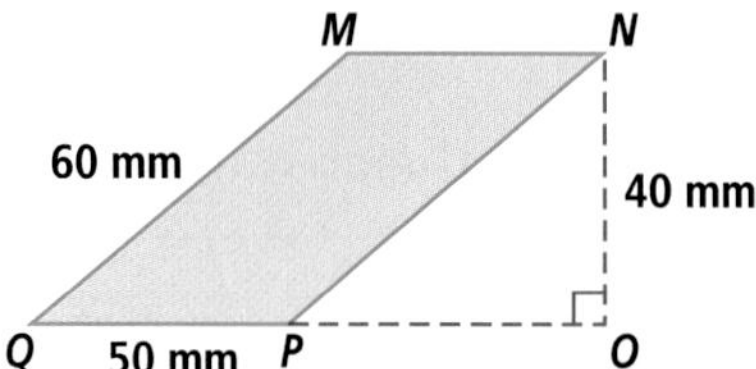

10. a. Find the area of quadrilateral *RSTW*.

b. Can you do the problem more than one way?

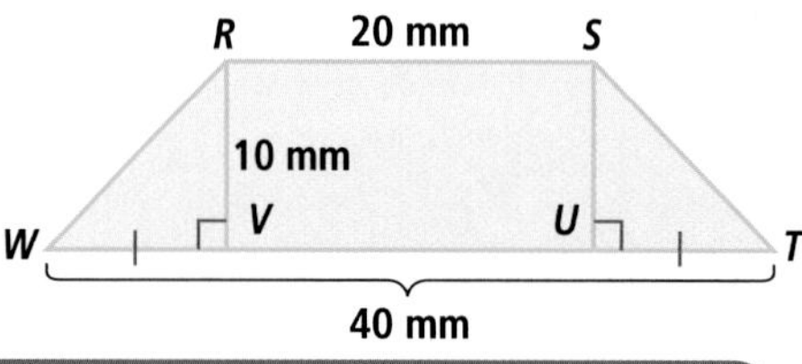

APPLYING THE MATHEMATICS

11. Find the area of polygon *CXYZAB* below.

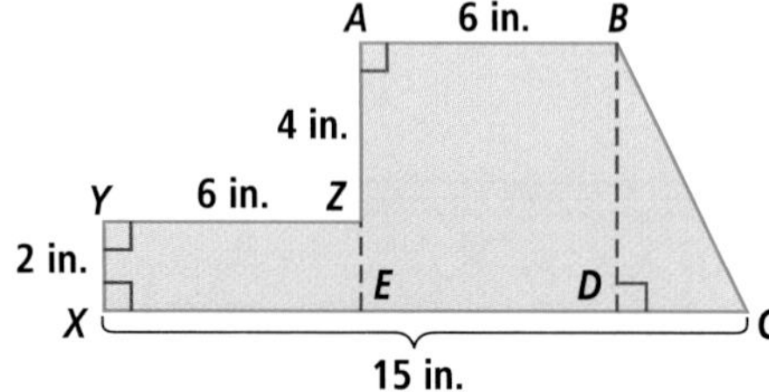

12. The parallelogram below has sides of lengths 13 units and 14 units. The height to the 13-unit side is 12 units. What is the perimeter of the parallelogram?

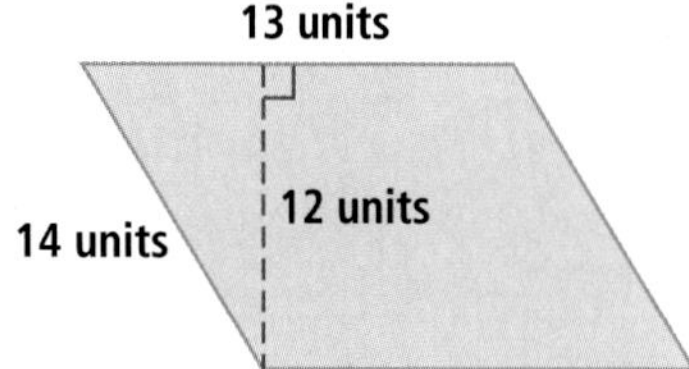

13. Mrs. Franklin is calculating the number of bricks she needs for her patio, shown in the diagram at the right.

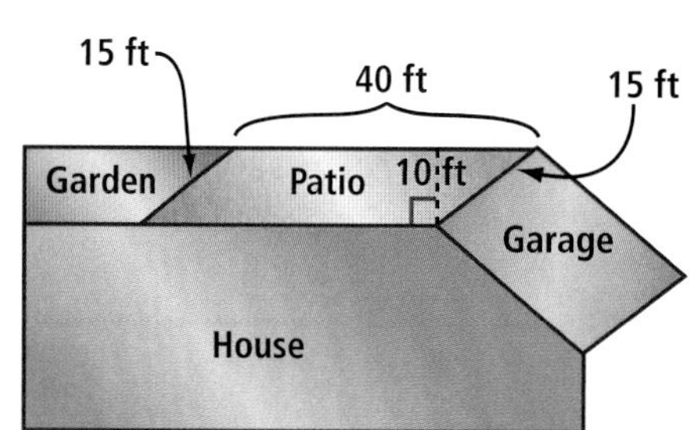

   a. Find the area of the patio.
   b. She will need 45 bricks for 10 square feet. Use a proportion to find how many bricks in all Mrs. Franklin will need.
   c. She wants to order an extra 10% in case of breakage or other problems. How many bricks is this?
   d. How many bricks should Mrs. Franklin order?

REVIEW

14. A *tricorne* is a three-cornered hat. The front of the hat is a corner and the back is a side of a triangle. The tricorne shown at the right is 14" along the back side, and 10" long from front to back. What is the approximate area of the triangle covered by the hat? **(Lesson 9-2)**

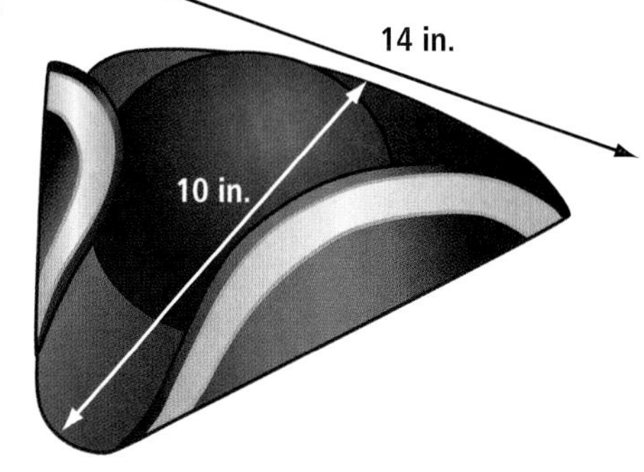

15. Below is a scale drawing for the floor plan for the first floor of a house. How many square feet are on the first floor? **(Lesson 9-1)**

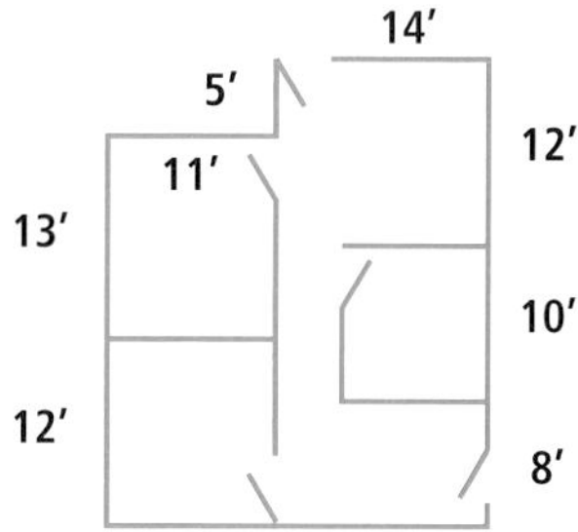

16. Cierra is baking a chocolate cake. The recipe makes enough to serve 6 people, but Cierra needs enough for 15. Tell whether each quantity below from the recipe should be adjusted using a proportion. If so, determine the adjusted quantity. If not, explain why not. **(Lesson 8-7)**

   a. $2\frac{1}{2}$ cups of flour
   b. $\frac{1}{2}$ teaspoon of nutmeg
   c. oven temperature 350 degrees
   d. 3 eggs
   e. bake for 40 minutes

In 17–19, give the sum of the angle measures. (Lesson 3-7)

17.

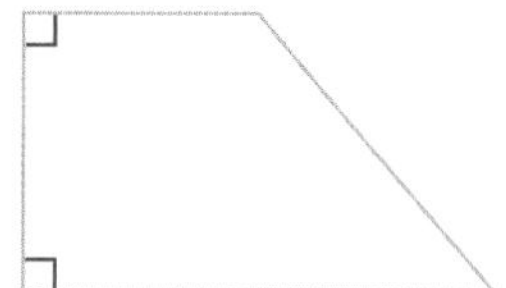

18.

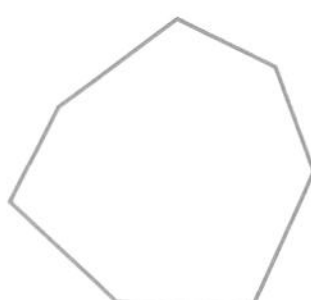

19. a regular decagon (10-sided polygon)

20. Find the values of x, y, and z in the figure below. **(Lessons 4-6, 3-7)**

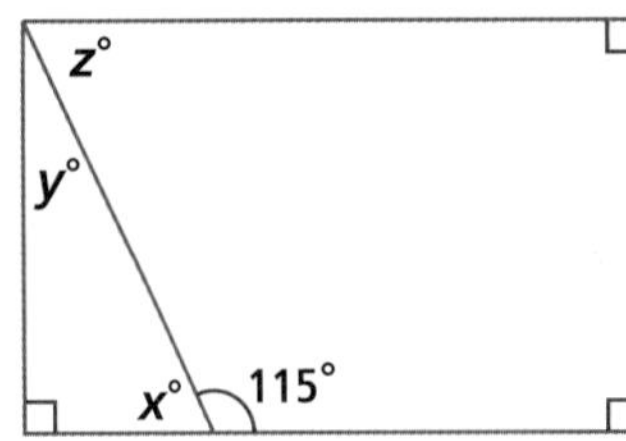

21. The circle at the right is divided into eight sectors by angles of equal measure at its center. What is the measure of each of the eight angles? **(Lesson 3-6)**

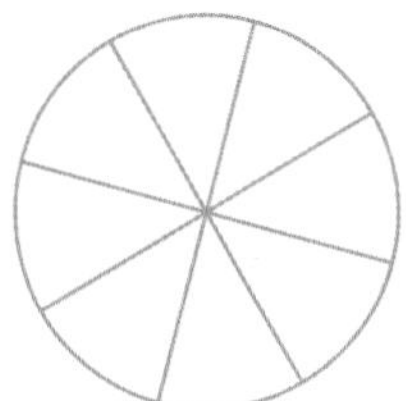

22. Estimate the area of the circle below by counting squares. **(Previous Course)**

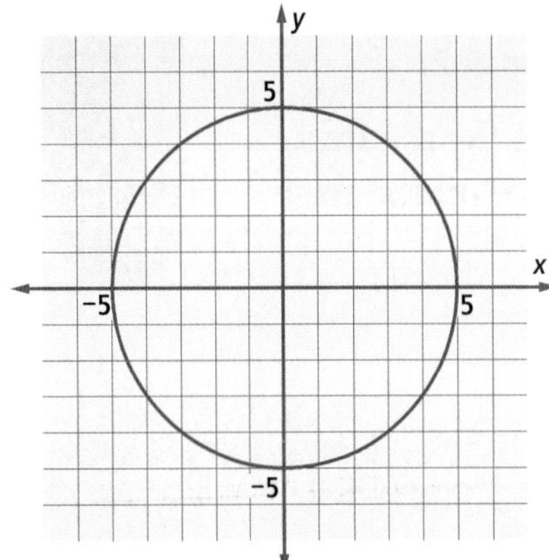

EXPLORATION

23. In the figure below, $\overline{TP}$ and $\overline{RA}$ are parallel.

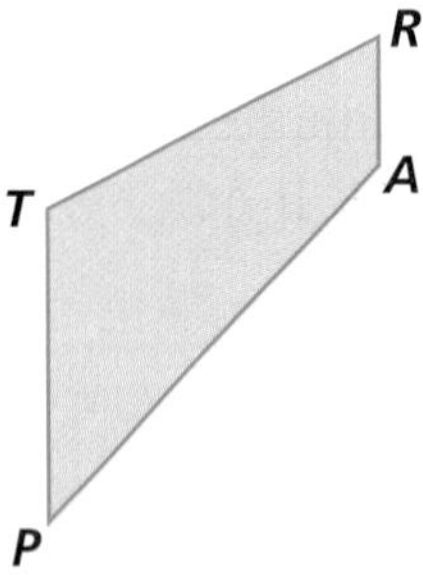

a. Find the area of quadrilateral *TRAP*. Describe how you found the area.

b. Use a second way to find the area of *TRAP*. Describe the method you used.

QY ANSWER

sides $\overline{PY}$ and $\overline{LA}$, angles Y and L

Lesson 9-4 The Circumference and Area of a Circle

Vocabulary

pi

circumference

radius

▸ **BIG IDEA** By rearranging sectors of a circle, the area of a circle with radius r can be shown to equal πr^2.

Unlike polygons, all circles look alike. Circles differ only in their size. The size of a circle can be measured by its radius, diameter, perimeter, or area.

Thousands of years ago, mathematicians discovered that when a wheel was rolled one revolution, a point on the wheel would travel horizontally a little over 3 times the diameter of the circle. Below, the point A travels to A^* as the wheel turns half way, and then to A'.

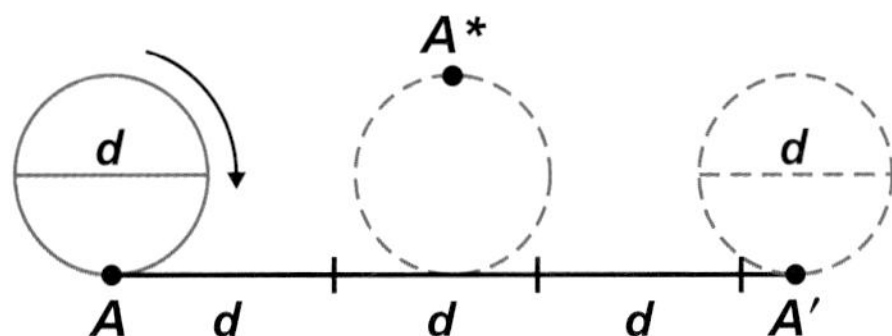

The Greeks named this multiple of the diameter by the letter π, called **pi.** Today we know that, as a decimal, $\pi = 3.14159265\ldots$, and we know that the decimal digits keep going and do not repeat in a pattern.

Activity 1

MATERIALS large wheel (as on a bicycle) or an aluminum can

Step 1 Measure the diameter d of the wheel, from edge to edge, as accurately as you can.

Step 2 Stand the wheel upright on the floor. Identify the point where the wheel touches the floor. Mark both the wheel and the floor at that point. Call that place on the floor point A.

Step 3 Roll the wheel exactly one revolution, until the mark on the wheel again touches the floor. Call that place on the floor point A'.

Step 4 Measure AA'. This length is equal to the perimeter of the circle. A circle's perimeter is called its **circumference** C.

Step 5 Calculate $C \div d$.

Step 6 Compare the value you found for $C \div d$ with the values found by other students in your group or class. What do you notice?

Mental Math

Four teams raced in a series of bike races. Each team won the number of times shown in the circle graph.

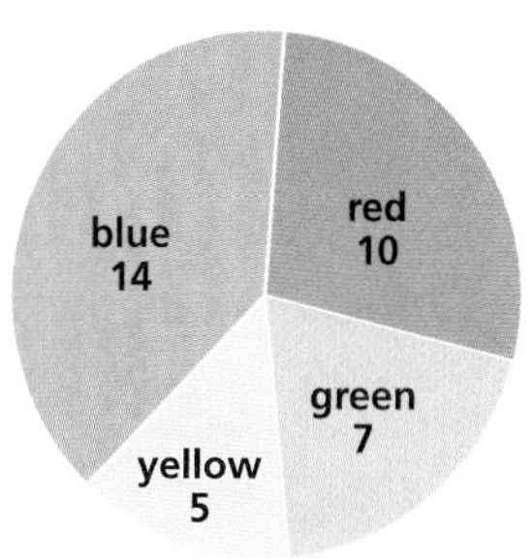

a. How many races were there?

b. What fraction of the races did the blue or red teams win?

c. What percent of the races did the yellow or green teams win?

Circumference of a Circle

The relationship between π, a circle's diameter, and its circumference is expressed in a formula for calculating circumference.

Formula for Circumference of a Circle

In every circle with diameter d and circumference C, $C = \pi d$.

The two most common values used to approximate π are the decimal 3.14 and the fraction $\frac{22}{7}$, which equals the decimal $3.\overline{142857}$. Both of these approximations differ from 3.14159… . The decimal is less than π and the fraction is greater than π. The difference can be significant. Calculators give a more accurate value.

 **See QY1 at the right.**

 **QY1**

Find the π key on your calculator and see what it displays for π.

Example 1

The equator of Earth, shown by the line drawn around the middle of the globe, is very nearly a circle. The diameter of Earth at its equator is about 7926 miles. What is the distance around Earth at the equator?

Solution Using the formula $C = \pi d$, the equator is about 7926π miles. To get a decimal or fraction answer, use an approximation for π.

$$7926 \cdot 3.14 = 24{,}887.64$$

$$7926 \cdot \frac{22}{7} \approx 24{,}910.29$$

The distance around Earth at the equator is about 24,900 miles.

 **See QY2 at the right.**

Have you ever viewed a globe from a previous decade? How does it compare to a globe of today?

The Area of a Circle from the Area of a Parallelogram

You can approximate the area of a circle by the area of a parallelogram.

Activity 2

MATERIALS compass, ruler, protractor, scissors

Step 1 Draw a circle. Draw a diameter. Draw a second diameter perpendicular to the first. Now draw two more diameters making eight sectors of equal area as shown at the right.

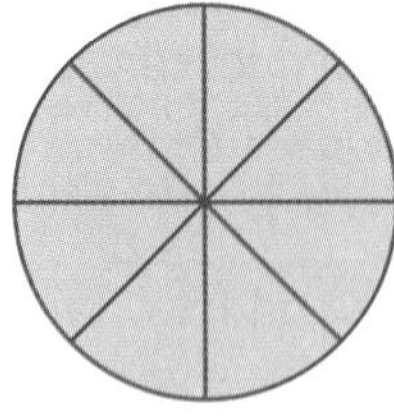

 **QY2**

Use the value of π on your calculator to obtain a more accurate distance around Earth at the equator.

Step 2 Cut apart the eight sectors and arrange them to form a "parallelogram" with four pieces pointing up and four pointing down.

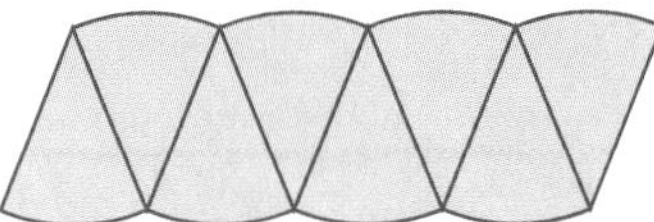

The circle has been rearranged so that it looks like a parallelogram. Assume that it is a parallelogram. How can you find its area?

Step 3 In your cut-out figure, darken the "base" of the parallelogram. What is the "height"?

 **See QY3 at the right.**

 **QY3**

How would the parallelogram be different if you had cut out and arranged 16 sectors of equal area?

The **radius** of a circle is the length of a segment from the center to the circle. So a radius is half a diameter. The "height" of the parallelogram in Activity 2 is a radius r. The "base" is made up of 4 of the 8 equal arcs of the circle.

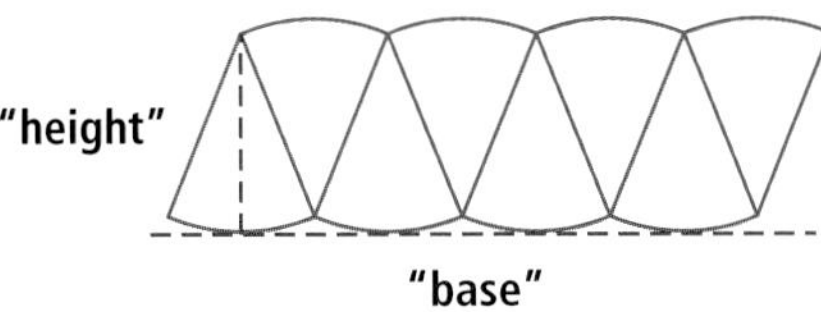

So the "length" of the base is $\frac{1}{2}$ the circumference, or $\frac{1}{2}\pi d$. Since $\frac{1}{2}d$ is the same as a radius, $\frac{1}{2}\pi d$ is the same as πr. The area of the "parallelogram," height times base, is $r \cdot \pi r$, πrr, or πr^2. This is also the area of the circle.

Area Formula for a Circle

The area A of a circle with radius r is given by the formula $A = \pi r^2$.

Example 2

A pizzeria sells pizza in two sizes. A small pizza has a 10-inch diameter and a large has a 14-inch diameter. A small pizza costs \$8, and a large costs \$14. Which is the better buy?

Solution To answer this question, find the price per square inch.

Find the area of each pizza. To use the formula, you need the radius of each pizza. The small pizza has a radius of 5 inches. The large has a radius of 7 inches.

(continued on next page)

Small: $\pi \cdot 5^2 = 25\pi \approx 78.54 \text{ in}^2$ Large: $\pi \cdot 7^2 = 49\pi \approx 153.94 \text{ in}^2$

To find the price per square inch, divide the cost by the area.

Small: $\frac{\$8}{78.54} \text{ in}^2 \approx \frac{\$0.102}{1} \text{ in}^2$, or about $10 \frac{\text{cents}}{\text{in}^2}$

Large: $\frac{\$14}{153.94} \text{ in}^2 \approx \frac{\$0.091}{1} \text{ in}^2$, or about $9 \frac{\text{cents}}{\text{in}^2}$

The large pizza is the better buy because it costs less per square inch.

Questions

COVERING THE IDEAS

1. In a circle with diameter d and radius r, $d = \underline{\ ?\ }\ r$.
2. What is another name for the perimeter of a circle?
3. Explain how one revolution of a wheel or other circular object can be used to approximate the circumference of a circle.
4. A calculator shows π to be 3.141592654.
   a. Is this an exact value or an estimate?
   b. Round this number to the nearest ten-thousandth.
5. What simple fraction is often used to approximate π?

In 6 and 7, find the circumference of the circle to the nearest tenth.

6. circle with diameter 13.8 m
7. circle with radius 12 in.
8. Write a formula for the area of a circle.
9. a. Draw a "parallelogram" to represent the area of a circle with radius 5 feet.
   b. What is the area of this circle to the nearest tenth?

In 10 and 11, find the area of each circle to the nearest tenth.

10. circle with radius 6.8 m
11. circle with diameter 24 in.
12. A French bakery sells its famous chocolate cake in three sizes: 15 cm, 20 cm, and 25 cm in diameter. The cakes are the same height and cost \$8, \$16, and \$20, respectively.
    a. Which size gives the most cake per dollar?
    b. Which size gives the least cake per dollar?

The French are well known for creating delectable baked goods!

APPLYING THE MATHEMATICS

13. According to CNN, the world's biggest cookie was baked in Hendersonville, North Carolina to raise money to build a folk art museum. The all-natural chocolate chip cookie had a diameter of about 100 feet. Suppose a 1 square foot piece of the cookie sold for $14.98.

  a. How many pieces could be sold?

  b. How much money would the sale of the entire cookie earn?

14. Brooklyn has a piece of square cloth that measures 1 meter on a side.

  a. What is the length of a side of the cloth in centimeters?

  b. How many square centimeters of cloth does she have?

  c. What are the diameter and radius of the largest circular tablecloth she can make from this material?

  d. How many square centimeters of material would she have left after making the tablecloth?

15. One mountain cruiser bicycle has a wheel diameter of 24 inches.

  a. What is the circumference of the wheel, to the nearest 0.1 in.?

  b. How many inches are in a mile?

  c. How many complete turns will the wheel make in a mile-long ride?

16. What is the diameter of a circle with a circumference of $94\frac{1}{4}$ inches?

17. The Arch of Constantine shown below was erected in Rome around 315 BCE. It commemorates Constantine's rise to power following his defeat of his main rival, Maxentius, at the Battle of the Milvian Bridge. The middle arch is made up of a 8.25 m-by-6.5 m rectangle and half a circle, or semicircle. The height of the middle arch at its highest point is 11.5 m. What is the area of the opening of the middle arch?

Arch of Constantine

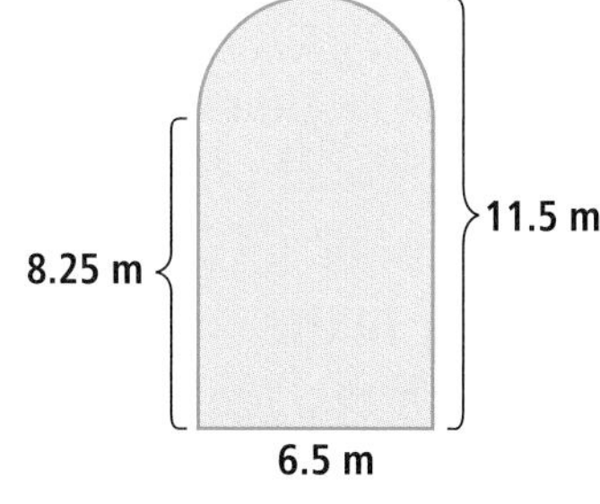

In 18 and 19, find the area of the figure. The arcs are semicircles.

18.

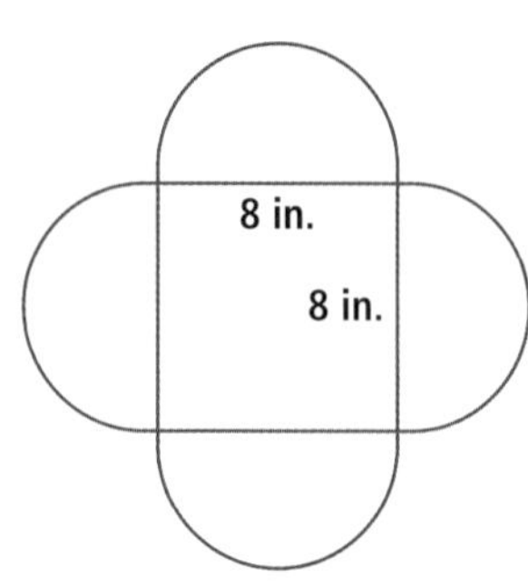

19.

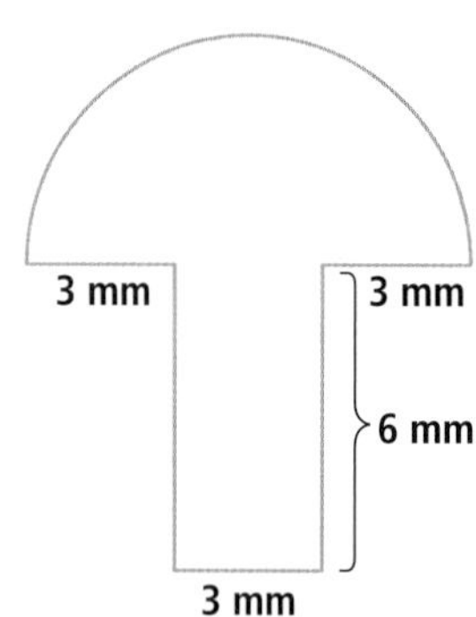

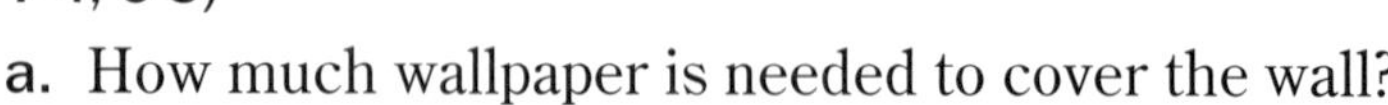

REVIEW

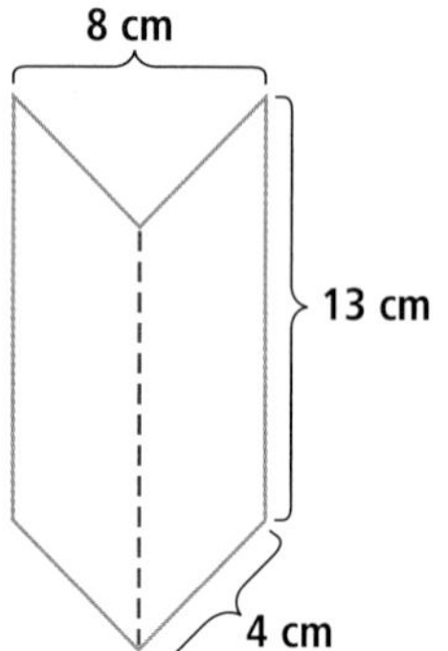

20. The shapes of some military insignia are *chevrons*, which are made up of two parallelograms that are reflection images of each other. What is the area of the chevron at the right? **(Lessons 9-3, 9-1)**

21. The windmill at the right has four identical sails. What is the total surface area (back and front) of all four sails? **(Lesson 9-2)**

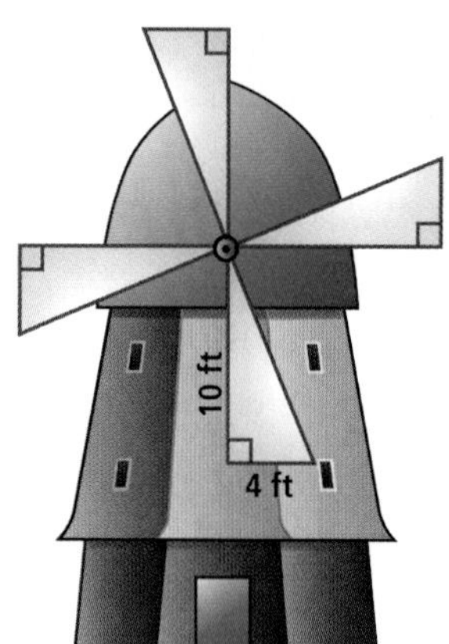

In 22 and 23, solve the equation. (Lesson 8-5)

22. $-16j = 96$

23. $\frac{1}{6}y = -78$

24. One wall of a room is going to be covered by wallpaper. The wall, shown at the right, has two windows and a door. Wallpaper is sold in rolls of 60 square feet. **(Lessons 7-4, 6-3)**
    a. How much wallpaper is needed to cover the wall?
    b. How many rolls will be needed?
    c. How much wallpaper will be leftover?

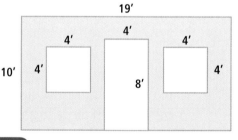

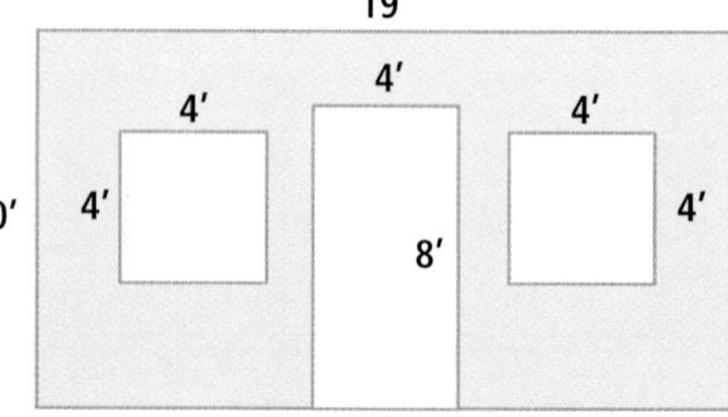

EXPLORATION

25. The shaded region at the right is the overlap of two quarter-circular regions. The quarter circles have their centers at opposite corners of the square.
    a. Find the perimeter of the shaded region to the nearest tenth of a foot.
    b. Find the area of the shaded region to the nearest tenth of a square foot.

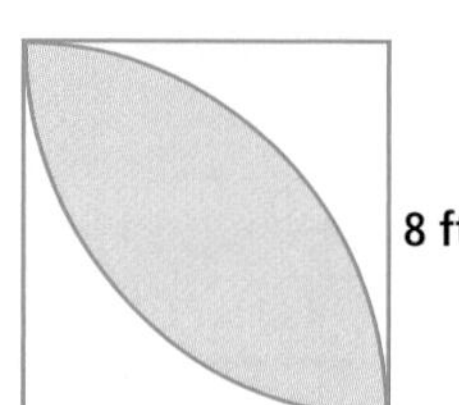

QY ANSWERS

1. Answers vary. Sample: 3.141592654.
2. Answers vary. Sample: $7926\pi \approx 24900.3$
3. Answers vary. Sample: The base would more closely resemble a line segment.

Lesson 9-5 Areas of Frames and Rings

Vocabulary

concentric circles

ring

▸ **BIG IDEA** The areas of frames, rings, and other thick borders of common figures can be found by subtracting two areas.

In the last two lessons, you added areas of regions to find areas of larger regions. In this lesson, you will use subtraction to find the areas of frames, rings, and other shapes.

Frames

To find the area of a frame, use an indirect strategy. Find the area of the object with the frame and then subtract the area of the object.

Activity

MATERIALS ruler

Suppose a 5"-by-7" photo is surrounded by a 2"-wide frame. What is the area of the frame?

Step 1 Sketch the photo. Label its dimensions.

Step 2 Sketch the frame around the photo. Label the thickness of the frame.

Step 3 Determine the length and width of the frame.

Step 4 What is the area of just the frame in square inches?

Step 5 Compare your answer with those of your classmates. If you do not all agree, try to find out why.

A pathway around a building or other region can be considered to be like a picture frame.

GUIDED

Example 1

Wildwood Park has a swimming pool that is a 75 foot-by-25 foot rectangle. The pool is surrounded by an indoor-outdoor carpet that is 12 feet wide. How many square feet of carpet surround the pool?

carpet
pool
12 ft
12 ft

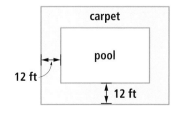

(continued on next page)

Mental Math

A tomato patch is enclosed by *x* feet of fence.

a. If the patch is a square, what is the length of one side?

b. If the patch is an equilateral triangle, what is the length of one side?

c. If the patch is a circle, what is its diameter?

d. Which of the three lengths in Parts a–c is greatest?

Solution Copy the diagram, adding the dimensions of the pool.

The length of the pool and carpet together is ___?___.
The width of the pool and carpet together is ___?___.
The area of the pool and carpet together is ___?___.
The area of the pool is ___?___. So the area of the carpet is ___?___ − ___?___ = ___?___ square feet.

Rings

Two circles with the same center are **concentric circles**. A **ring** is the region between two concentric circles, sometimes including one or both of the circles. If a region is circular, then a frame around it is a ring.

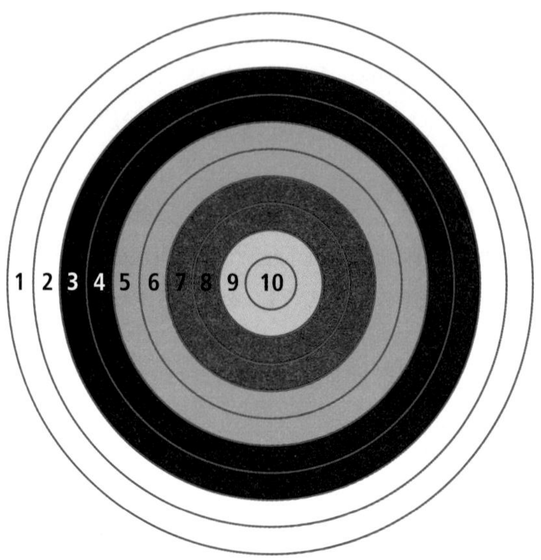

In archery, the archer uses a bow to shoot an arrow at a target that consists of concentric circles. The rings are white, black, blue, and red, with a yellow (or gold) center. Each colored ring is split into two parts by a circle. These circles form nine rings and a center disk, called the *bull's-eye*, as shown at the right. Shooting an arrow into the bull's-eye is worth 10 points, into the ring surrounding it 9 points, into the next larger ring 8 points, and so on. An arrow landing in the outermost ring earns 1 point.

Example 2

The target pictured above has a diameter of 60 cm. The smallest circle in the center has a diameter of 6 cm. The diameter of the next circle is 12 cm. The diameters increase by 6 cm with each larger circle. What is the area of the ring that is colored red, to the nearest square centimeter?

Solution The outer circle of the red ring has a diameter of 24 cm. So its radius is 12 cm. Using $A = \pi r^2$, the area of the outer circle of the red ring is $\pi \cdot 12^2$, or 144π cm^2.

The inner circle of the red ring has a diameter of 12 cm. So its radius is 6 cm. So the area of this inner circle is $\pi \cdot 6^2$, or 36π cm^2.

The area between these circles is the area of the red ring:

$$144\pi - 36\pi = 108\pi \approx 339.29 \text{ cm}^2$$

To the nearest square centimeter, the area of the red ring is 339 cm^2.

Notice that we waited until the end to calculate with π. This simplified the computation.

QY1

a. Which color covers the greatest area?
b. Which color covers the least area?

One reason to calculate area is to determine what fraction or percent of the target is a certain color. You can also determine what fraction or percent of the target will get you a certain number of points.

Example 3

What percent of the target in Example 2 yields a score of 4 points or less?

Solution To score 4 points or less, the arrow has to land in the black or white regions.

Find the area of the entire target. Since the target's diameter is 60 cm, its radius is 30 cm.

$$\text{Area of entire target} = \pi \cdot 30^2 = 900\pi \text{ cm}^2$$

Find the area of the part of the target that is not black or white. That part is inside a circle with diameter 36 cm. So the radius of this circle is 18 cm.

$$\text{Area of parts worth more than 4 point} = \pi \cdot 18^2 = 324\pi \text{ cm}^2$$

Subtract to find the area of the white and black ring.

$$\begin{aligned}&\text{Area of target} - \text{area of parts worth more than 4 points}\\ &= 900\pi \text{ cm}^2 - 324\pi \text{ cm}^2\\ &= 576\pi \text{ cm}^2\end{aligned}$$

Find the ratio of the area of the ring to the area of the entire target.

$$\begin{aligned}\frac{\text{area of 4-points or less ring}}{\text{area of target}} &= \frac{576\pi}{900\pi}\\ &= \frac{576}{900}\\ &\approx 0.64 = 64\%\end{aligned}$$

64% of the target yields a score of 4 points or less.

By not estimating π, we were able to simplify the fraction and never see decimals. The answer is exact.

 **See QY2 at the right.**

QY2

What percent of the target yields a score of more than 4 points?

Questions

COVERING THE IDEAS

1. What are *concentric circles*?

2. Determine the area of the shaded region.

a. 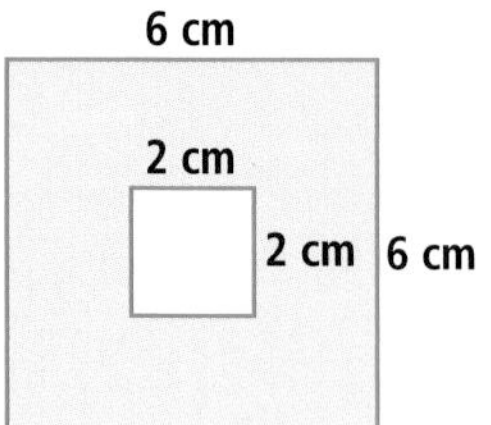

b. 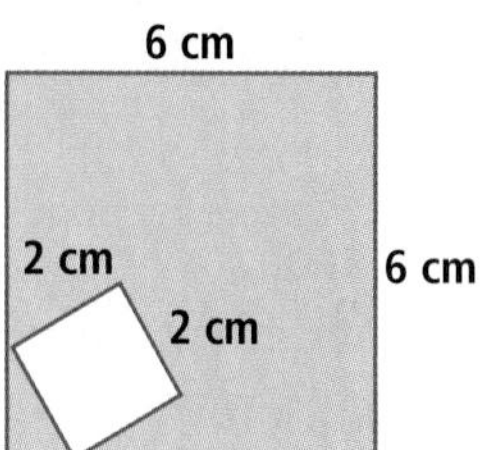

c. 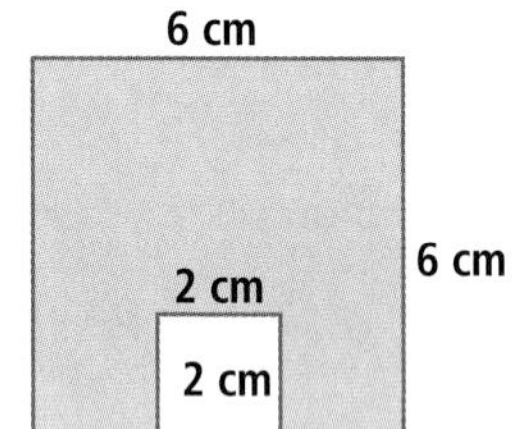

d. 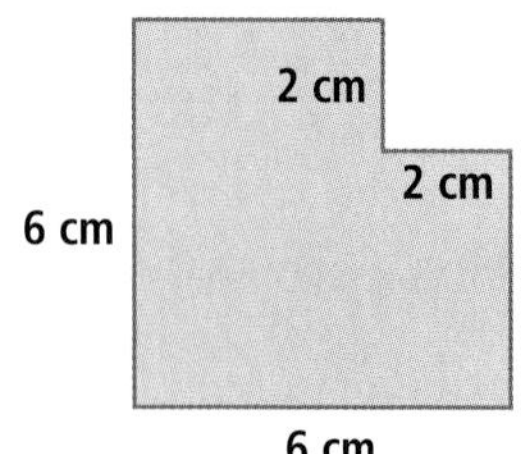

3. A photo is 6" × 8" and its frame is 1" wide.
   a. Sketch the photo.
   b. Sketch the frame around the photo.
   c. Find the dimensions of the frame.
   d. Find the area of the photo alone and the area of the photo with its frame.
   e. Subtract the areas found in Part d to find the area of the frame.
4. Refer to Examples 2 and 3. Consider the part of the archery target that yields a score of 1 or 2 points.
   a. Which region(s) is this?
   b. Find the area of the ring that yields a score of 1 or 2 points.
   c. What percent of the target is this ring?
5. Use the archery target pictured on page 540.
   a. What percent of the target yields a score of 10?
   b. What percent yields a score of 9?
   c. What is the ratio of the 10-point area to the 9-point area?
6. The Loopers are installing a sidewalk around their 25 meter-by-15 meter rectangular pool. The dimensions of the rectangle formed by the pool and the sidewalk are 31 meters by 21 meters.
   a. Draw a picture and label it with the given dimensions.
   b. Find the width of the sidewalk surrounding the pool.
   c. Find the area of the sidewalk.
   d. The cost of installing the sidewalk is $11.10 per square meter. What is the total cost of installing the sidewalk?

APPLYING THE MATHEMATICS

7. A *washer* is a small, flat metal or rubber ring. If the diameter of the hole of a washer is 10.5 mm and the outer diameter is 20 mm, what is the area of the washer?

8. The frame pictured at the right has matting cut out for several photographs. If the frame is one inch wide, find the area of the remaining matting.

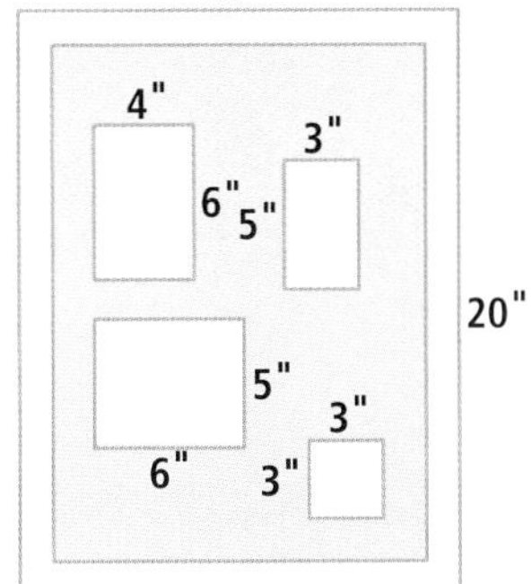

9. Anne's backyard is made up of a 10 foot-by-10 foot square brick patio, surrounded on three sides by a garden border 1 yard wide.
   a. Sketch the patio and its border, labeling all dimensions.
   b. Find the perimeter of the outside of the border.
   c. Find the area of the garden border.
   d. What percent of the backyard is the patio?

10. A standard piece of copy paper measures 8.5" × 11". Byron is working on a document and has the margins set at 1" all around. What is the area of the working surface of each page?

8.5 in.
1 in. 1 in. 1 in.
11 in.
1 in.

11. Regina is making Linzer cookies. Linzer cookies are sandwich cookies with a full circle on the bottom, a middle layer of jam, and another circle on the top that has a design cut out of the center. Regina's cookies are 5 cm in diameter, with a circular hole on the top cookie that has a diameter of 1.5 cm.
    a. Find the area of the top of a Linzer cookie made by Regina.
    b. Regina has a rectangle of dough that measures 30 cm by 40 cm. Sketch a diagram that represents what the rectangle of dough looks like after the 6 tops and 6 bottoms are cut out.
    c. Find the area of the remaining dough.

Linzer cookies are said to have originated from Linz, Austria, hence the name "Linzer."

REVIEW

12. **Multiple Choice** The circumference of a circle is 12 cm. Which value is nearest to its area? **(Lesson 9-4)**

    A 11.5 cm^2 B 18.8 cm^2
    C 37.7 cm^2 D 452.4 cm^2

In 13–16, calculate the area of the figure. (Lessons 9-3, 9-2)

13.

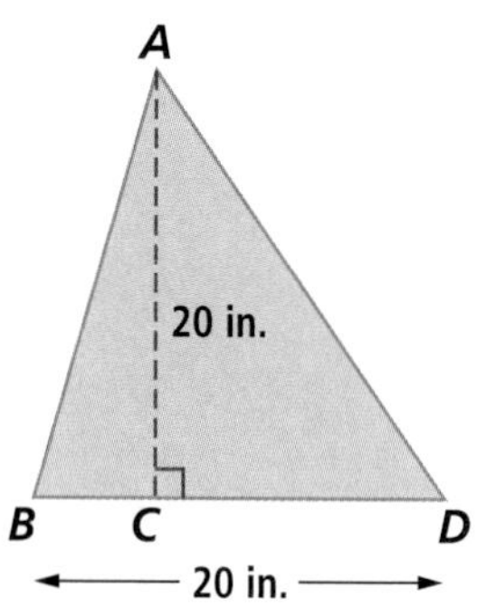

14.

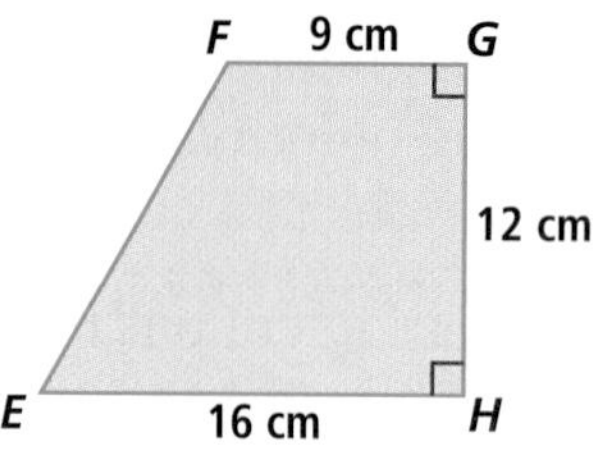

15.

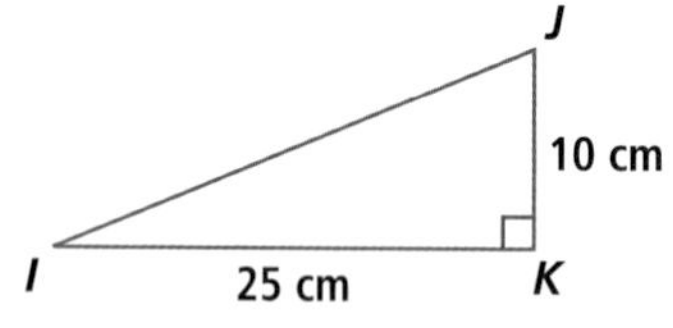

16.

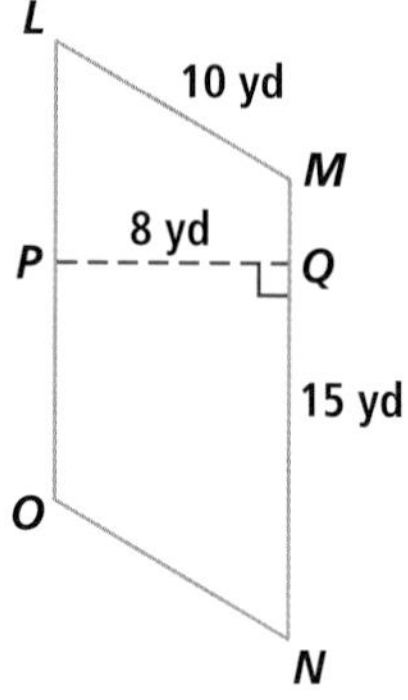

17. A soccer field has a maximum length of 120 yards and a maximum width of 75 yards. Find the maximum area of a soccer field. (Lesson 5-1)

18. A 5"-by-7" picture is cut into two parts of the same size. (Lesson 5-1)
    a. Find the area of each half. Does it make a difference how you cut the picture?
    b. Consider the perimeters of the resulting halves. Does it make a difference how you cut the picture?

19. Solve for p: $4.8 + p = 3.05 + 2$. (Lesson 4-9)

20. In 2007, a nationwide restaurant chain advertised three-course dinners with 5 choices for an appetizer, 12 choices for an entreé, and 4 choices for dessert. How many different dinners are possible? (Lesson 3-1)

EXPLORATION

21. To *inscribe* a circle in a polygon means to draw a circle within the polygon so that each side of the polygon touches the circle in exactly one point. At the right, a circle is inscribed in a square that has an area of 16 cm^2. To the nearest hundredth of a square centimeter, find the area of the shaded part of the figure.

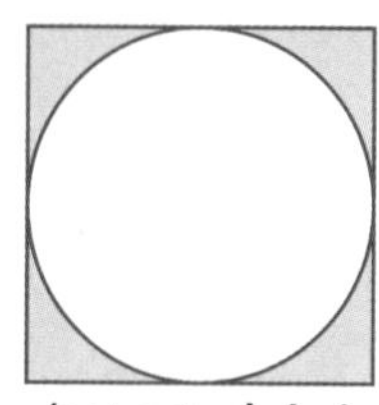

(not actual size)

QY ANSWERS

1a. white

1b. gold

2. 36%

Lesson 9-6 Drawing Boxes

Vocabulary

box
face
edges of a box
vertex, vertices of a box
rectangular solid
dimensions
length, width, height, depth of a box
cube

▶ **BIG IDEA** The six faces of a box are rectangular regions, but in a typical drawing, four of the six faces look like parallelograms.

When you think of a box, what shape comes to mind? There are many kinds and shapes of boxes: hat boxes, shoeboxes, boxes for tissues, and so on. However, in mathematics, the word "box" has a specific meaning.

A **box** is a 3-dimensional figure with 6 **faces** that are all rectangles. When you see a box pictured, like the one at the right, you can identify the faces as top, bottom, left, right, front, and back. The top face is the rectangle *ABCD*. The left face is the rectangle *ADHE*.

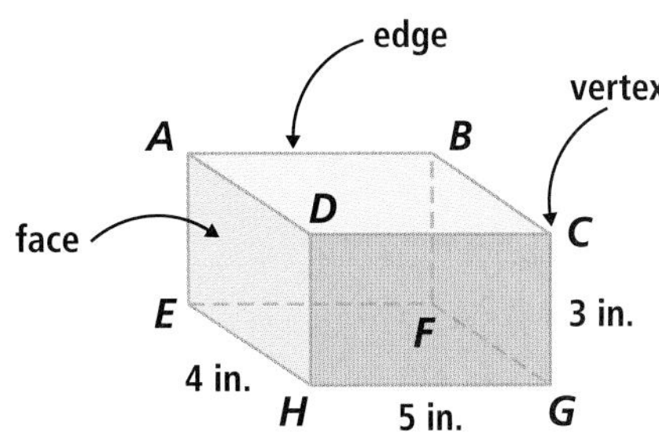

QY1

Name the front, back, and right faces of the box pictured above.

The sides of the faces are called **edges.** Above, for example, $\overline{FG}$ is an edge. Any vertex of a face is a **vertex** of the box. The plural of vertex is **vertices.** *G* and *C* are two of the vertices of this box.

A box is like an empty carton. It does not include the points inside of it. When you include the points inside, then the figure is called a **rectangular solid.** Bricks and dice are rectangular solids.

Mental Math

20% of the interior of a parallelogram is shaded and 58% is striped. The rest is plain.

a. What percent of the parallelogram is neither shaded nor striped?

b. What percent is not shaded?

c. What percent is striped or plain?

d. What percent is striped and plain?

Activity 1

Consider the box pictured at the right. Copy and complete the following chart.

Part of Box	How Many?	Names of All
Faces	?	*ABCD*, ?
Vertices	?	*A*, ?
Edges	?	$\overline{AB}$, ?

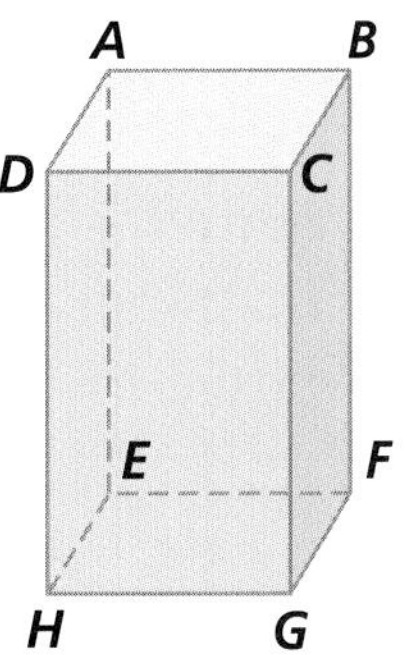

Because the opposite sides of a rectangle have the same length, many edges of a box have the same length.

GUIDED

Example

Which edges of the box at the right have length 5"?

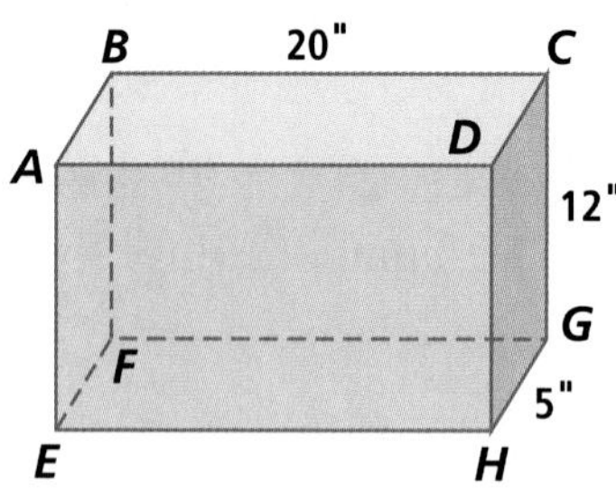

Solution $\overline{GH}$ is an edge of the bottom face, *EFGH,* and $\overline{GH}$ and $\overline{EF}$ are opposite sides of *EFGH,* so EF = 5". $\overline{GH}$ is also an edge of the right face __?__, and that face is a rectangle, so __?__ = 5". Last, *ABEF* is a rectangle, and since *EF* = 5", so also __?__ = 5".

See QY2 at the right.

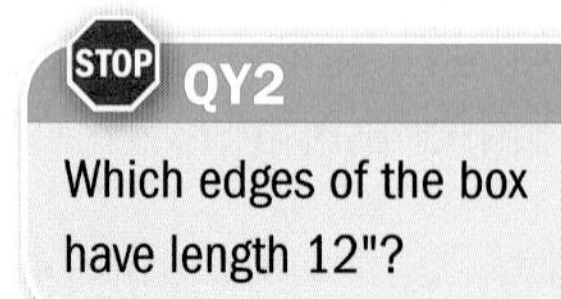

QY2

Which edges of the box have length 12"?

The lengths of the edges of a box are called its **dimensions: length, width,** and **height.** The dimensions of the box in Example 1 are 5 in., 12 in., and 20 in. Sometimes one dimension is called the **depth.** Without being told, you cannot know which dimension is length, width, height, or depth. For instance, in the box in Example 1, either 5 in. or 12 in. might be the depth. Any dimension might be the width, length, or height.

Drawing Boxes

It is useful to be able to draw a picture of a box with paper and pencil. Look closely at the boxes that are pictured. Some of the faces look like rectangles and some do not. This is because boxes are 3-dimensional but a drawing of a box can have only two dimensions. These steps will help you draw a box.

Step 1 Draw the rectangle that will be the front face of your box.

Step 2 Draw a rectangle of the same size slightly above and to one side of your first face.

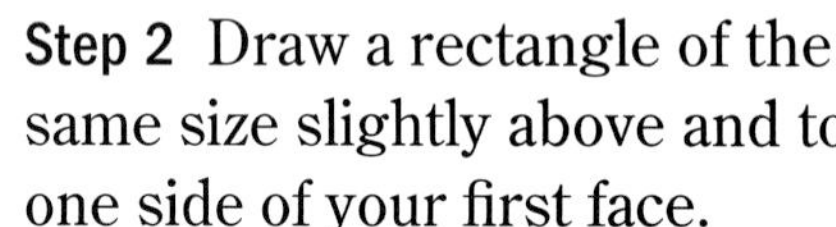

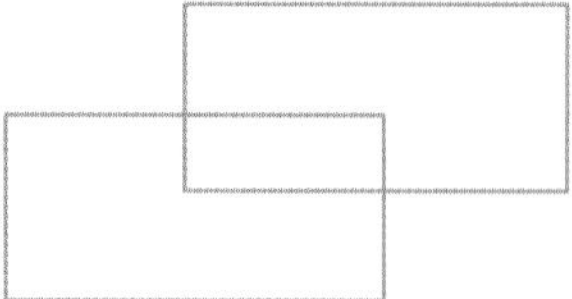

Step 3 Connect the vertices, as shown in the figure below.

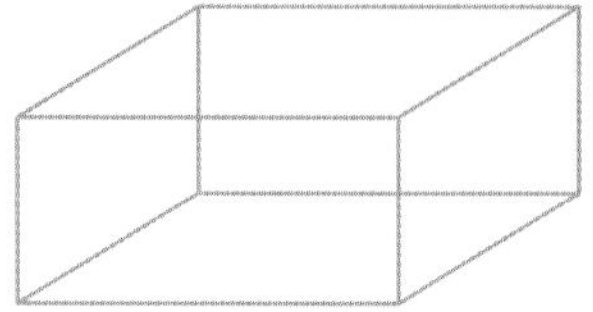

Step 4 To make your box look more realistic, dash the edges that would not be visible in a real box.

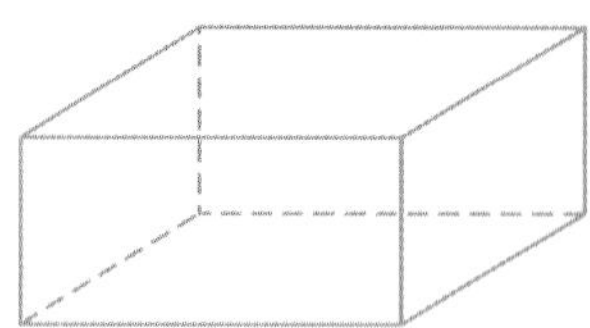

Activity 2

Trace the rectangle *NICE* at the right. Follow the above steps to draw a box with this rectangle as the front face.

When all the faces of a box are squares, the box is a **cube.** A *die* (the singular of *dice*) is a solid cube.

QY3

Give the dimensions of a cube that measures 4" on each edge.

Questions

COVERING THE IDEAS

In 1–6, use the box at the right.

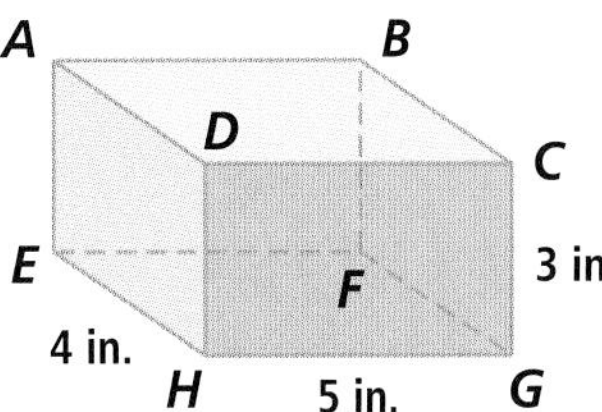

1. Name the top and bottom faces of this box.
2. Name the vertices of the left face.
3. Name the edges of the back face.
4. Why is $\overline{EF}$ drawn with a dashed line?
5. Name all the edges with length 5".
6. Name all the edges with length 4".

In 7–9, copy the table. Give the dimensions of all the faces for each box shown.

Box	Front	Back	Top	Bottom	Right	Left
7. (7 mm, 4 mm, 5 mm)	?	?	?	?	?	?
8. (10 m, 10 m, 10 m)	?	?	?	?	?	?
9. (6 ft, 1.5 ft, 3 ft)	?	?	?	?	?	?

10. a. How many faces does a box have?
    b. How many edges does a box have?
    c. How many vertices does a box have?

11. Draw a box with dimensions 7 cm, 3 cm, and 8 cm. Your drawing does not have to be actual size.

APPLYING THE MATHEMATICS

12. Imagine a box with its top taken off. How many faces, edges, and vertices does such a box have?

13. At the right is a picture of the right face of a box. Draw a possible box with this face.

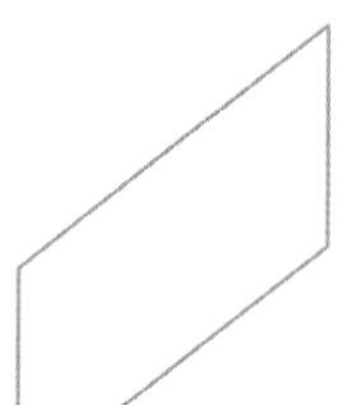

In 14–16, the rectangular solid that is pictured is made from centimeter cubes.

a. Give the dimensions of each solid.

b. How many cubes make up the solid?

14. 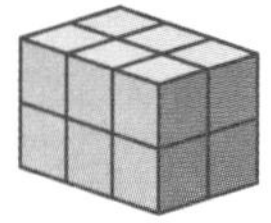

15. 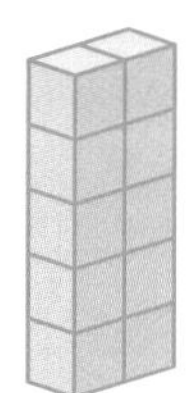

16. 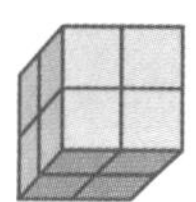

17. A box has the following characteristics. Its length is twice its width. Its width is one-third its height.
    a. Find two sets of possible dimensions for this box.
    b. Sketch both boxes you found for Part a.

REVIEW

In 18 and 19, one playing card has an area of about 56 cm^2.

18. Sixty cards are dealt on a table. If no cards overlap, what area of the table is covered by cards? **(Lesson 9-1)**

19. A hole-puncher cuts a hole with an area of about 0.5 cm^2. If you were to punch 15 non-overlapping holes in a card, what would be the remaining area of the card? **(Lessons 9-5, 9-1)**

20. The radius of a circular pie is 6 inches. If 35% of the pie has been eaten, what is the area of the remaining pie to the nearest tenth of a square inch? **(Lessons 9-4, 6-6, 4-4)**

21. A photo developer will print a 16" × 20" photograph for $14.89 and a 20" × 30" photograph for $19.99. **(Lessons 8-1, 7-1, 6-3)**
   a. What is the price per square inch of each photo?
   b. Per square inch, how many times more expensive is one size than the other?

22. Use the histogram below. **(Lessons 6-3, 5-4)**

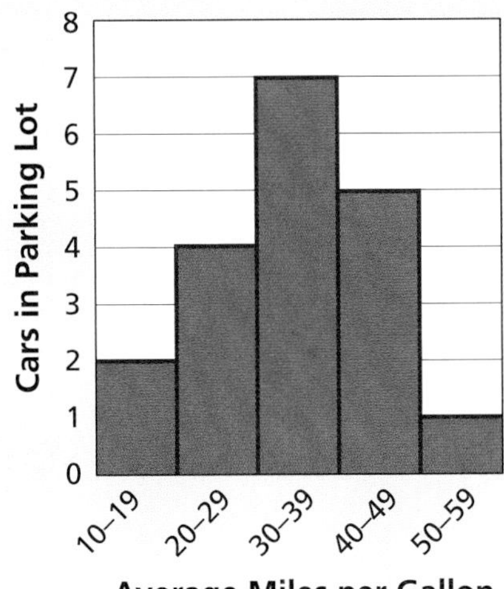

   a. How many cars are in the parking lot?
   b. Suppose the width of each interval on the graph is 2 cm and the interval for each car is 1 cm high. What is the area of the shaded region of the histogram?
   c. Explain how the result in Part a is related to the result in Part b.

EXPLORATION

23. A *sphere* is a ball-shaped object. Baseballs and other spherical objects are typically packaged in boxes shaped like cubes. Why?

24. Which typically melts faster: a single block of ice or the same size block of ice cut into two cubes? Why?

QY ANSWERS

1. *DCGH, ABFE, BCGF*
2. $\overline{AE}$, $\overline{BF}$, $\overline{DH}$, $\overline{CG}$
3. 4 in. by 4 in. by 4 in.

Lesson 9-7 Building Boxes

Vocabulary

net

▶ BIG IDEA A 3-dimensional box can be built by folding a 2-dimensional net.

Mental Math

8 blasters are worth 3 thrashers.

a. How many thrashers are worth 1 blaster?

b. How many blasters are worth 1 thrasher?

c. What is the least integer number of thrashers worth the same as an integer number of blasters?

While it looks like you could paste together six rectangles to make a box, most boxes are not made in this way. They are made by folding a pattern called a *net*. A **net** is a 2-dimensional pattern that, when folded, will create a box or other 3-dimensional figure. A single box has many possible nets.

Activity 1

MATERIALS centimeter grid paper, scissors, ruler

Each net below is made up of 6 squares.

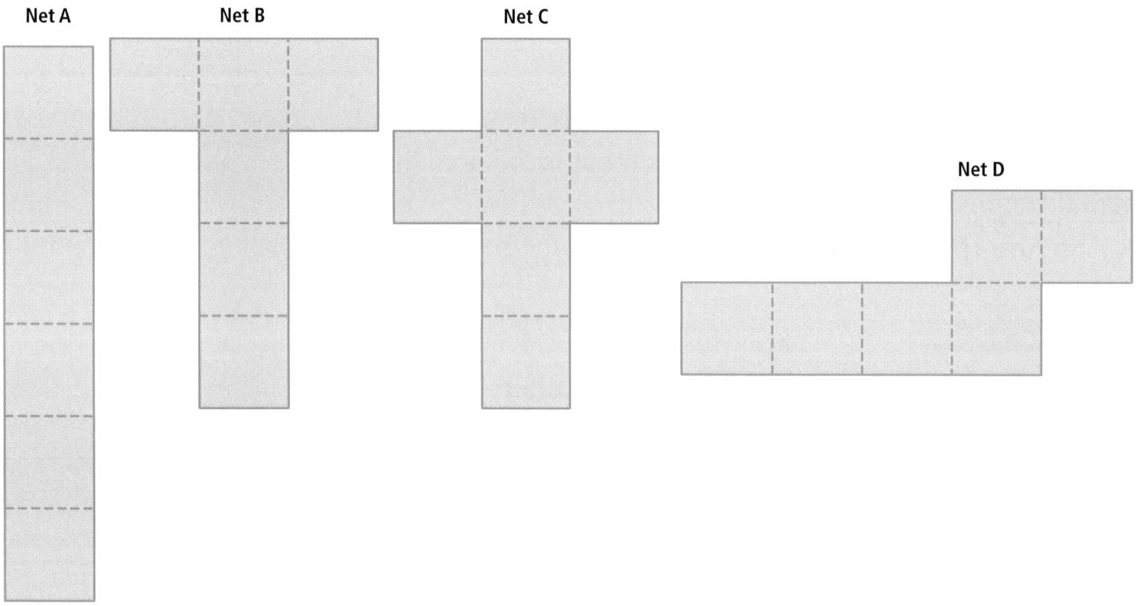

Net A

Net B

Net C

Net D

Step 1 Look at each net carefully. Some of them can be folded along the dotted segments into cubes and some cannot. Which ones are nets for a cube?

Step 2 Copy each net onto grid paper, cut it out, and try folding it into a cube.

Step 3 Draw a net that is not like any of the above nets and that folds into a cube. Cut it out and show that it folds into a cube.

Nets can also be drawn for boxes that are not cubes. Examine the box shown below. Its six faces are drawn beside it.

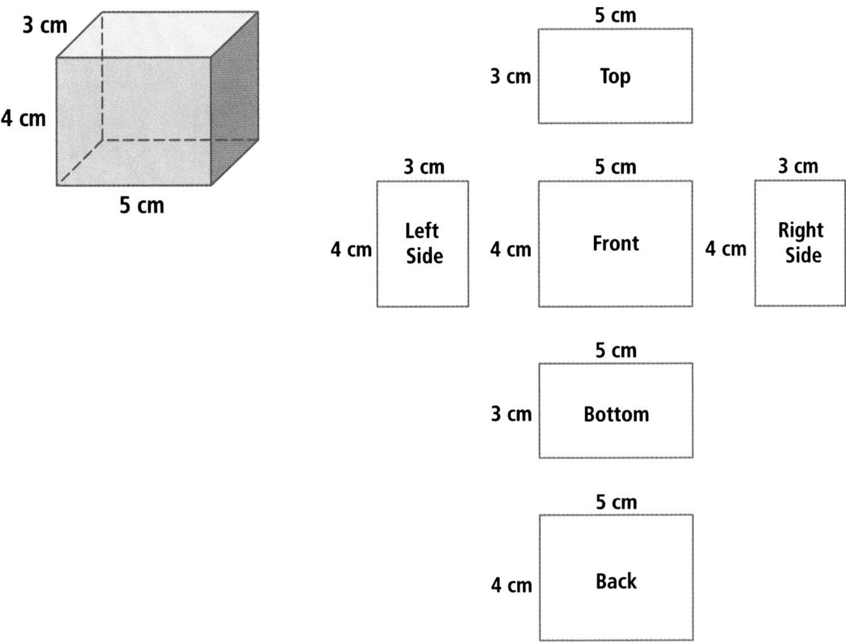

These 6 faces can be arranged into nets for the box in different ways. Two of the easiest look like the letters T and t.

Activity 2

MATERIALS centimeter grid paper, scissors, ruler

Draw the two nets below on centimeter grid paper, cut them out, and fold them into boxes.

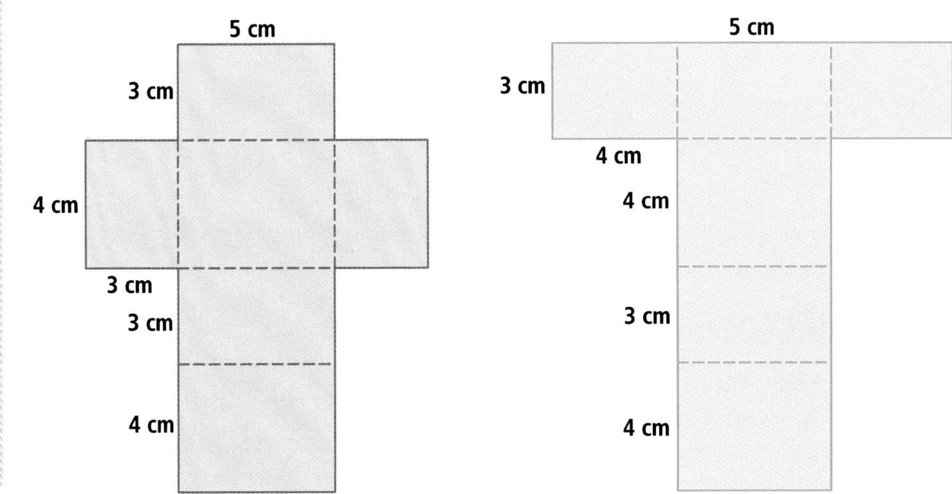

Activity 3

MATERIALS ruler, centimeter grid paper

Using centimeter grid paper, draw a net for the box at the right. Make it look like a T or a t, or experiment with another net that you think will work.

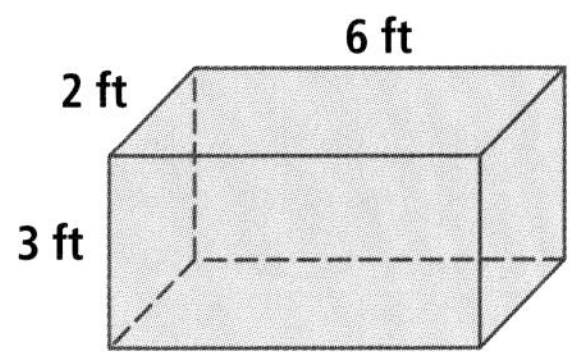

Questions

COVERING THE IDEAS

1. What is a *net* for a 3-dimensional shape?
2. a. How many squares does it take to make a net for a cube?
   b. How do you know your answer to Part a is correct?

In 3–5, complete Parts a and b.

a. Determine whether the shape can be folded into a cube.

b. If the shape can be folded into a cube, indicate (by letter) which faces are opposite each other.

3. 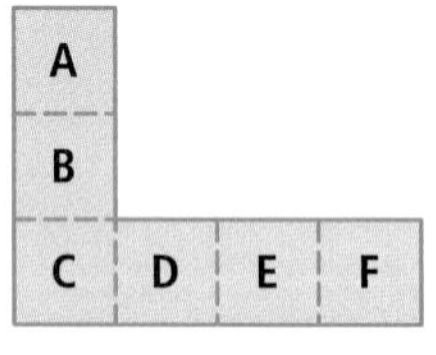

4. 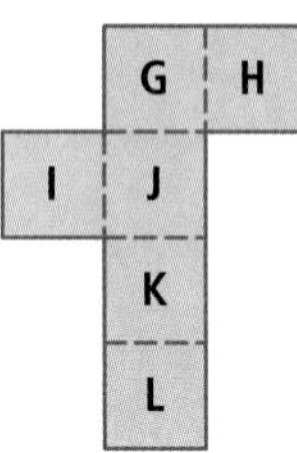

5. 

6. **Fill in the Blank** Each face of a box is a __?__.

In 7–9, make an actual-size net for the box.

7. a box with dimensions 6 cm, 3.5 cm, and 5 cm
8. 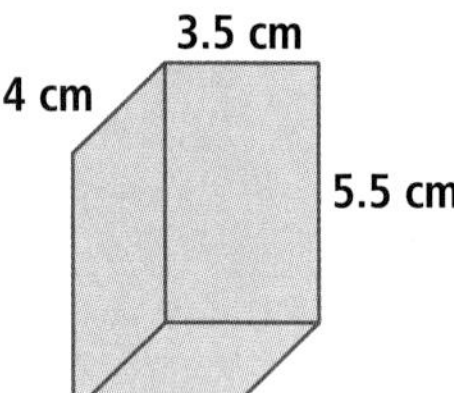

9. 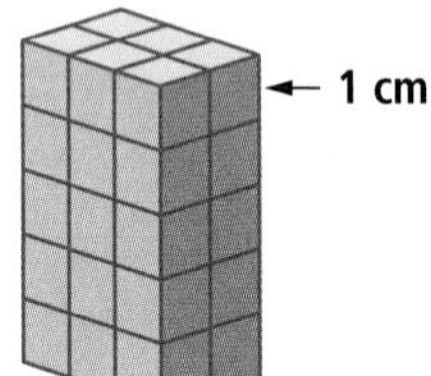

APPLYING THE MATHEMATICS

10. Below are three views of the same cube with the names of the faces labeled. Make a net for this cube. Label the faces with their names in their paper positions so that the cube has these views when the net is folded.

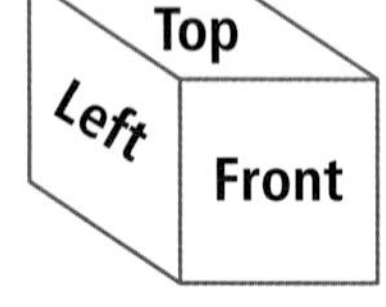

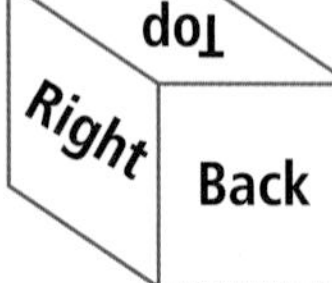

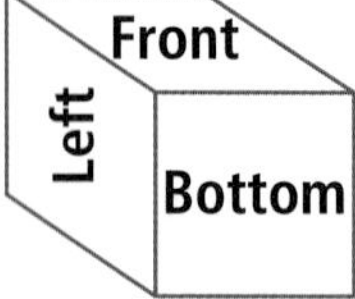

In 11–13, the outline of a net for a box is shown. Copy the net onto centimeter grid paper. Draw dashed segments to show where the net would be folded. Examine each net and find the dimensions (length, width, and height) of the box that the net will make. Show that your answer is correct by identifying each face of the box on the net.

11. 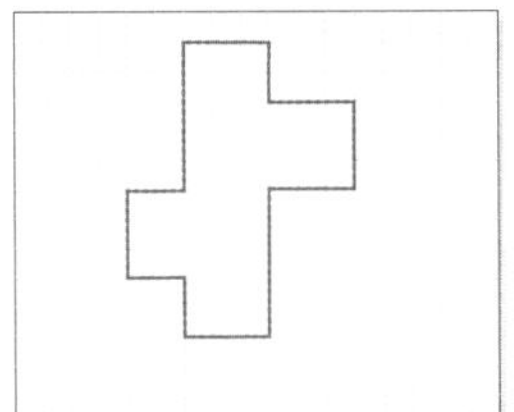

12. 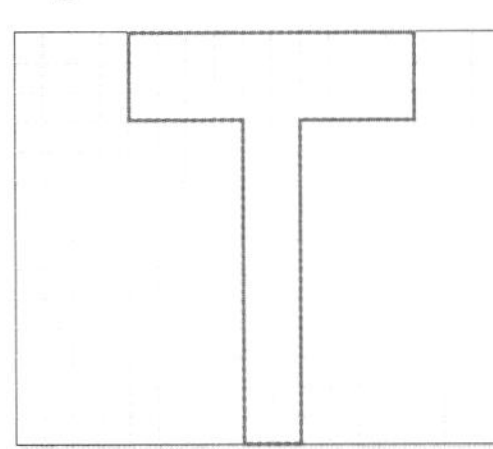

13. 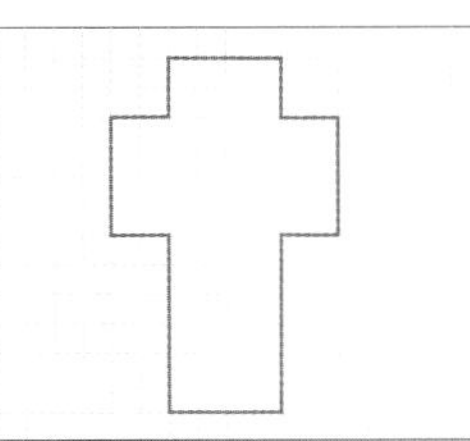

REVIEW

In 14 and 15, use the following information. Lance's family is redecorating his bedroom. The floor of Lance's bedroom is 10 feet long and 14 feet wide. The room has a height of 8 feet.

14. Draw a picture of Lance's bedroom. **(Lesson 9-6)**

15. a. One of the long walls has a door that is 7 feet high and 3.5 feet wide. What is the area of this wall (not including the door)?
    b. The opposite wall has a window that is 4 feet high and 6 feet wide. What is the area of this wall (not including the window)? **(Lesson 9-5)**

16. Find the area of the shaded part of the parallelogram below, to the nearest tenth of a square unit. **(Lesson 9-5, 9-4, 9-3)**

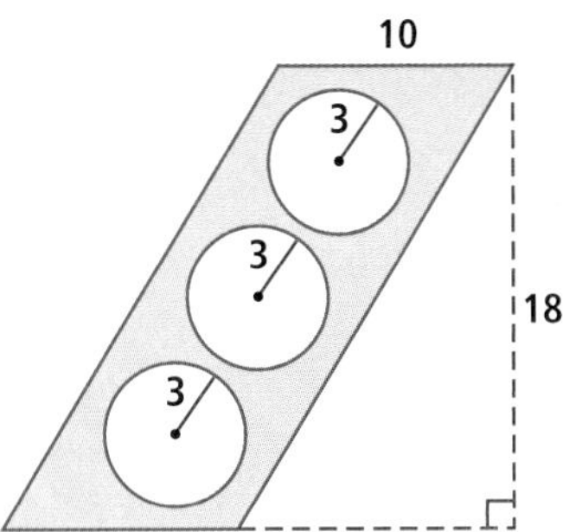

17. An article in *Asian Economic News* reported that, in 1982, New Zealand's sheep population was at an all-time high of 70.3 million sheep. New Zealand's total land area is 268,021 square kilometers. On average, how many sheep were there per square kilometer? Round your answer to the nearest whole number. **(Lesson 7-1)**

Estimates put New Zealand's sheep population in 2003 at around 40 million.

Source: Asian Economic News

18. Use a coordinate grid labeled like the one below.

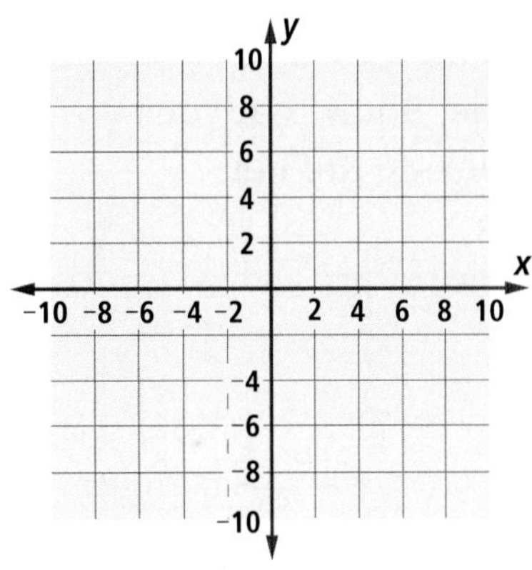

a. Draw a graph of the line $y = x - 5$ on the grid. **(Lesson 5-8)**

b. The x-axis, y-axis, and the line $y = x - 5$ enclose a triangle. What is its area? **(Lesson 9-2)**

EXPLORATION

19. Draw a net for a piece of clothing such as a skirt, dress, or a pair of pants. Be sure to indicate where the seams of your piece of clothing will be.

Lesson 9-8 Surface Area and Volume of a Cube

Vocabulary

surface area
volume
capacity

▸ **BIG IDEA** The surface area of a cube is the area of its net; the volume is a measure of the amount of space enclosed by the surface.

The sum of the areas of all the faces of a cube is its **surface area.** To find the surface area of a cube, start with its net. For example, suppose the edge length of a cube is 2 cm. Then one face has an area equal to 2 cm • 2 cm = 4 cm^2. The six faces together have an area of 6 • 4 cm^2, or 24 cm^2. So, the surface area of the cube is 24 cm^2.

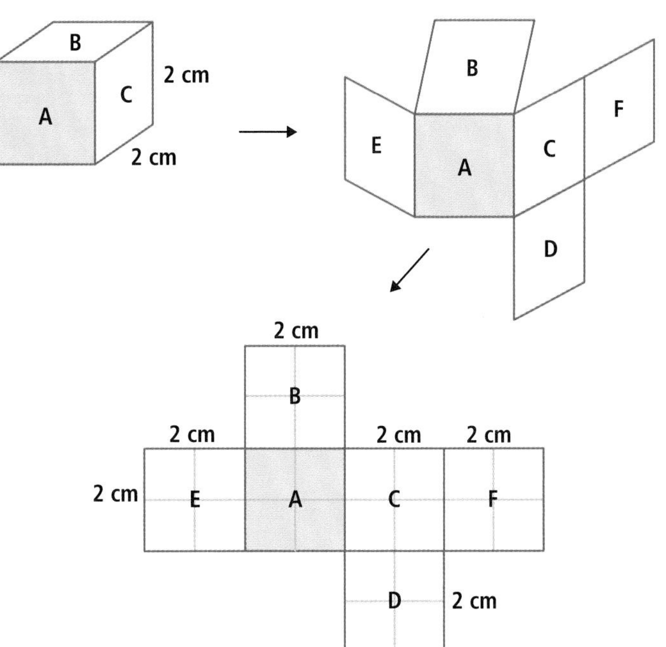

Mental Math

If a dozen roses cost $30, how much would you expect to pay for each number of roses?

a. 2 dozen

b. 6

c. 3

d. 9

GUIDED

Example 1

What is the surface area of a cube whose edges measure *s* cm?

Solution

1. The area of one of the faces of the cube is __?__ cm^2.
2. Multiply the area of one face by the number of faces of the cube.

   The surface area of a cube whose edges measure s cm is equal to __?__. (Remember to use appropriate units.)

Surface Area Formula for a Cube

The surface area *S.A.* of a cube with edge length s units is $6s^2$ square units: $S.A. = 6 \cdot s^2$.

 See QY1 at the right.

QY1

What is the surface area of a cube in which the length of each edge is $\frac{1}{2}$ inch?

What is Volume?

Volume is the amount of space inside a 3-dimensional figure. It is easy to understand that objects such as a fish tank and a suitcase have volume, because we put things inside of them. You can think of volume as a measure of what a box, jar, or other container can hold. This is sometimes called a container's **capacity.** With solid objects like a pencil, a brick, or a baseball, you can think of volume as how much material is in them.

Whatever the shape of the figure, its volume is measured in cubic units. A cubic inch and a cubic centimeter are common units of volume.

In a cubic inch, the length of each edge is 1 inch. The area of each of the six faces of the cube is 1 square inch, so the surface area is 6 square inches, or 6 in^2. The volume is 1 cubic inch, written as 1 in^3.

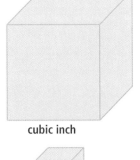

cubic inch

In a cubic centimeter, the length of each edge is 1 centimeter. The area of each face is 1 square centimeter, so the surface area is 6 square centimeters, or 6 cm^2. The volume is 1 cubic centimeter, written as 1 cm^3. In some applications, like medicine, this volume is written 1 cc (read "one cc").

cubic centimeter

Just as area and perimeter measure different characteristics in 2-dimensional figures, volume and surface area measure different characteristics in 3-dimensional figures. A long thin box, such as one for a fishing rod or skis, has a large surface area compared to its volume. On the other hand, a sphere, such as a globe or baseball, has a large volume for its surface area. You may find this table useful.

What is Measured?	2-Dimensional Regions	3-Dimensional Solids
Boundary	perimeter (units)	surface area (square units)
Inside	area (square units)	volume (cubic units)

Finding Volume

When the edge length of a cube is a small whole number of units, then you can find the volume of the cube by counting.

Example 2

What is the volume of a cube whose edges have length 5 cm?

Solution You can break the cube into unit cubes because the length of each edge is a whole number. The volume of the large cube is the number of unit cubes.

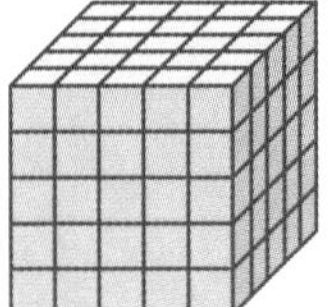

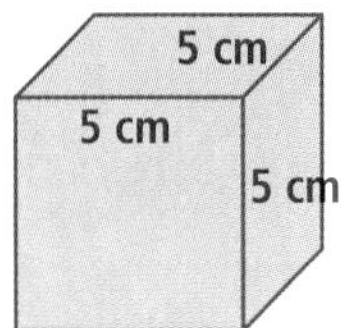

To count the unit cubes, begin with the bottom layer. There are 5 rows with 5 cubes in each row. So there are 25 cubes in the layer. Since there are 5 layers, there will be 5 • 25, or 125 cubes in all. The volume of the original cube is 125 cm^3.

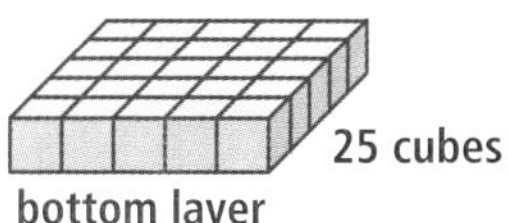

In Example 2, notice that the volume is 5 cm • 5 cm • 5 cm, or $(5\text{ cm})^3$. It is the product of the three dimensions of the cube. This is why, when a number is raised to the third power, we sometimes say it is "cubed."

The example is an instance of the volume formula for a cube.

Volume Formula for a Cube

The volume V of a cube with edges of length s units is $s \cdot s \cdot s$ or s^3 cubic units: $V = s^3$.

 **See QY2 at the right.**

 **QY2**

What is the volume of a cube in which each edge is $\frac{1}{2}$ inch long?

Activity

How does multiplying the lengths of the edges of a cube by some number change the volume and surface area of the cube?

Step 1 Fill in the table below.

Edge Length (cm)	1	2	3	4	5	6
Surface Area (cm^2)	6	?	?	?	?	?
Volume (cm^3)	?	?	?	?	?	?

(continued on next page)

Step 2 Use the information in the table to write the following ratios:

a. The surface area for a cube with edge length 2 cm to the surface area of a cube with edge length 1 cm.

b. The surface area for a cube with edge length 4 cm to the surface area of a cube with edge length 2 cm.

c. The surface area for a cube with edge length 6 cm to the surface area of a cube with edge length 3 cm.

d. The surface area for a cube with edge length 8 cm to the surface area of a cube with edge length 4 cm.

e. Study your answers to Parts a–d. If the edge length of a cube is multiplied by 2, its surface area is multiplied by __?__.

Step 3 Use the information in the table to write the following ratios:

a. The volume for a cube with edge length 2 cm to the volume of a cube with edge length 1 cm.

b. The volume for a cube with edge length 4 cm to the volume of a cube with edge length 2 cm.

c. The volume for a cube with edge length 6 cm to the volume of a cube with edge length 3 cm.

d. The volume for a cube with edge length 8 cm to the volume of a cube with edge length 4 cm.

e. Study your answers to Parts a–d. If the edge length of a cube is multiplied by 2, its volume is multiplied by __?__.

Questions

COVERING THE IDEAS

1. **a.** Draw the net for a cube with edges of length 3 cm.
   b. What is the surface area of the cube? (Include the unit.)
2. What is the volume of a cube whose edges measure 3 cm? (Include the unit.) Make a sketch like the one in Example 2.

In 3–5, the length of an edge of a cube is given.

a. Give the surface area of the cube.

b. Give its volume. (Use appropriate units in both parts.)

3. $1\frac{1}{2}$ in. 4. 4.2 mm 5. x units

6. Suppose a cube has edges of length 12 inches.
   a. What is its volume in cubic inches?
   b. What is its volume in cubic feet?
7. A sugar cube is 1 cm long, 1 cm wide, and 1 cm high.
   a. What is the volume of the sugar cube?
   b. What is the surface area of the sugar cube?

In 2004, 2.4 million acres of U.S. soil were devoted to the production of sugar. Talk about a sweet tooth!

Source: American Sugar Alliance

In 8 and 9, the lengths of the edges of a cube are doubled, from 20 cm to 40 cm.

8. How many times as large is the surface area of the enlarged cube than the surface area of the original cube?
9. How many times as large is the volume of the enlarged cube than the volume of the original cube?

APPLYING THE MATHEMATICS

10. The country estate Wilton House in England has two particularly famous rooms: the Single Cube Room and the Double Cube Room.
    a. The Single Cube Room is 30 ft long, 30 ft wide, and 30 ft high. What is the volume of the room?
    b. The Double Cube Room is twice as long as the Single Cube Room, but has the same width and height. What is the volume of this room?
    c. The power of an air conditioner is often measured in British Thermal Units (BTUs). If 18,000 BTUs will cool a room with volume 8,000 cubic feet, about how many BTUs would be needed to cool the Single Cube Room?
11. Give the length of an edge of a cube whose volume is 27 cubic units.
12. Suppose a cube has a surface area of 600 cm^2. What is its volume?

In 13 and 14, use this information. A cubic inch of water weighs about 0.036 pounds.

13. a. About how much does a cubic foot of water weigh?
    b. About how much does a cubic yard of water weigh?
14. One gallon of water has a volume of 231 cubic inches.
    a. Estimate the weight of a gallon of water.
    b. Estimate the weight of a fish tank filled with 10 gallons of water if the tank weighs 30 pounds when empty.

REVIEW

In 15 and 16, tell whether the shape can be folded into a cube. If it can, use the letters to indicate which faces are opposite each other. (Lesson 9-7)

15.

		A
B	C	D
		E
		F

16.

	G	
H	I	
	J	K
	L	

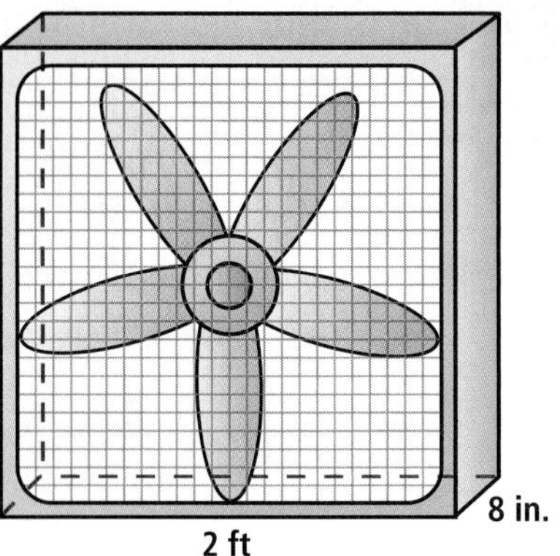

17. A box fan consists of a fan spinning inside a box that can fit into a window. A typical box fan has a face 2' square and is 8" deep. **(Lesson 9-6)**
    a. Draw a box enclosing the fan.
    b. How many edges are there of each length?

18. a. What is the area of the top surface of the table below?
    b. If two leaves, each 2 feet wide, are added to extend the length of the table, what is the resulting area of the table?
    c. What is the ratio of the area of the table with leaves to the area of the table without leaves? **(Lessons 9-1, 8-1)**

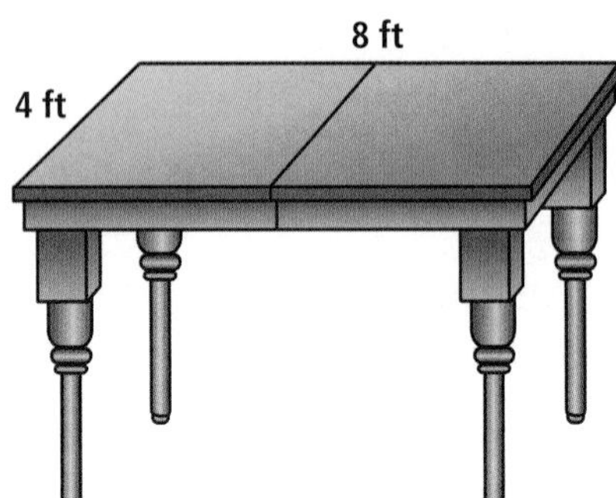

19. A square washcloth is folded in half to form a rectangle with a perimeter of 36 inches. What is the area of the original washcloth? **(Lessons 6-3, 3-2)**

20. Below is a picture of a cube made up of smaller cubes.

    a. How many smaller cubes are in the bigger cube?
    b. If the bigger cube were dipped into paint, how many smaller cubes would have paint on
        i. exactly one face?
        ii. exactly two faces?
        iii. exactly three faces?
        iv. more than three faces?
        v. no faces?

QY ANSWERS

1. $1\frac{1}{2}$ in^2
2. $\frac{1}{8}$ in^3

Lesson 9-9 Surface Area and Volume of a Box

Vocabulary

base of a box

height of a box

▸ **BIG IDEA** The surface area of a box is the area of its net; its volume is the product of its dimensions.

Finding the surface area of a box is similar to finding the surface area of a cube. You need to find the total area of the faces. The difference is that in a box, the dimensions of the faces do not have to be the same.

Activity

MATERIALS ruler, grid paper

Step 1 Draw a net for the box at the right. Label the dimensions and name each face "front," "back," "left," and so on.

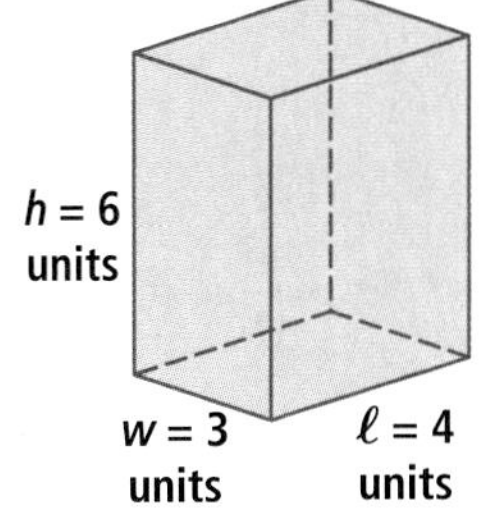

Step 2 Copy the following table. Fill in all the rows but the bottom row.

Face Name	Area in Numbers	Area in Variables
Front	24 square units	$\ell \cdot h$
Back	?	?
Left	?	?
Right	?	?
Top	?	?
Bottom	?	?
Surface Area	?	?

Step 3 Look at the first six values in the Area in Numbers column. What do you notice?

Step 4 Fill in the bottom row to find the total surface area.

Step 5 Use the entry in the bottom row and right column of the table to write a formula for the surface area of a box.

STOP QY

What is the least amount of wrapping paper needed to cover a box that is 18" long, 15" wide, and 4" high?

Mental Math

The cube below has 6" edges. *A* and *B* are midpoints for two edges as shown. What is the shortest distance from *A* to *B*?

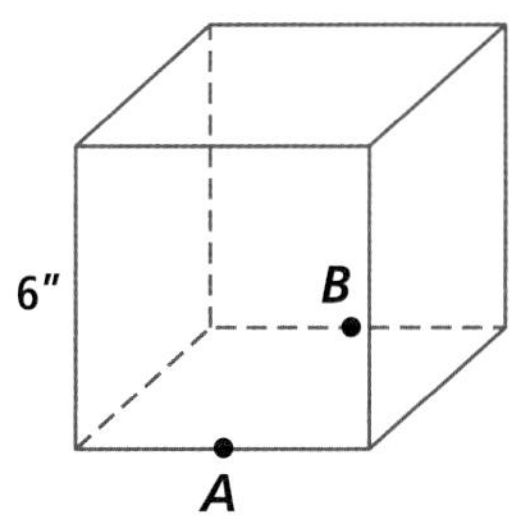

a. through the cube?

b. around the cube along its edges?

c. over the top of the cube?

Volume of a Box

To find the volume of a cube, you multiply its three dimensions. The same is true if you want to find the volume of a box.

Example 1

Find the volume of the box in the Activity, with length 4 units, width 3 units, and height 6 units.

Solution Since the bottom face of the box has dimensions 3 units by 4 units, you can fit a layer of 12 cubic units in the bottom of the box, as shown below. And, since the height of the box is 6 units, you can fit 6 such layers in the box. This indicates that $6 \cdot 12$, or $6 \cdot 3 \cdot 4$, or 72 unit cubes can fit in the box. The volume of the box is 72 cubic units, or 72 units^3.

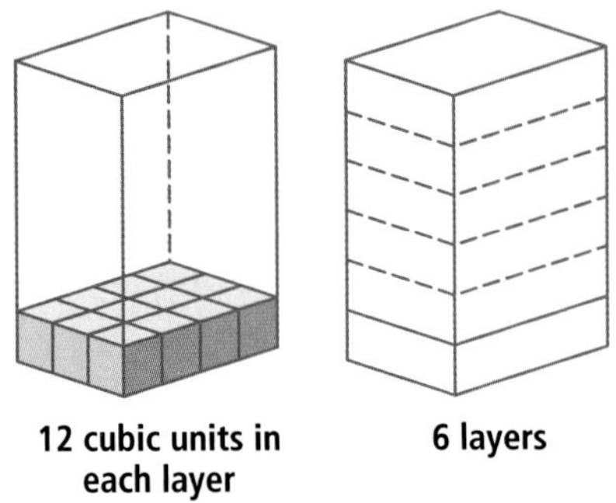

GUIDED

Example 2

Suppose the box of Example 1 was tipped over so that its left side was on the bottom. What is the volume of the box?

Solution 1 Use the same process as in Example 1. When tipped over, the bottom of the box is a 3-by-6 rectangle. So there would be __?__ cubes in the bottom layer. The height of the box is now __?__ units, so there are __?__ layers. The volume of the box is __?__ • __?__ • __?__, or __?__ cubic units.

Solution 2 Tilting or tipping the box does not change its volume. Its volume is 72 cubic units, the volume found in Example 1.

Examples 1 and 2 show that to find the volume of a box, you can consider any face to be the bottom, or **base.** The number of cubes in the bottom layer is the area B of the base, which is the product of two of the box's dimensions. The third dimension is the **height** h of the box with that base. To find the volume, you multiply the area of the base by the height. In symbols, $V = B \cdot h$.

If the dimensions of the base are ℓ and w, then $B = \ell \cdot w$. So another formula for the volume of a box is $V = \ell \cdot w \cdot h$.

Two Formulas for the Volume of a Box

The volume V of a box is the area B of a base times the height h to that base: $V = Bh$.

The volume V of a box with dimensions ℓ, w, and h is the product of these dimensions: $V = \ell wh$.

GUIDED

Example 3

Brittany Freestyle has a small pool. The floor of the pool is a rectangle that is $9\frac{1}{2}$ feet by $12\frac{1}{2}$ feet, and the pool is $6\frac{1}{2}$ feet deep. How many square tiles, measuring 3 inches on a side, will Brittany need to line the pool sides and floor?

Solution The question requires the surface area of the pool, without the top. Draw a picture of the pool when empty. Label the dimensions and face names.

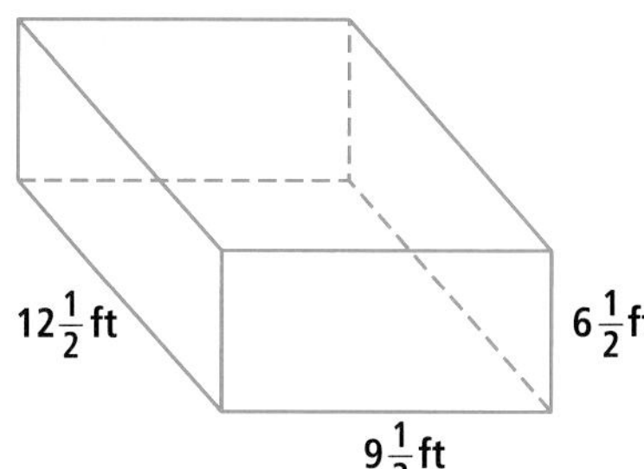

Find the area of each face:

Front: ___?___ Back: ___?___

Left: ___?___ Right: ___?___ Bottom: ___?___

Total surface area (without the top): ___?___

The square tiles have 3-inch sides, so there are ___?___ tiles in a square foot.

Number of tiles needed = $\underset{\text{surface area (in ft}^2\text{)}}{\underline{\quad ? \quad}} \cdot \underset{\text{number of tiles per square foot}}{\underline{\quad ? \quad}}$

Brittany will need ___?___ tiles.

GUIDED

Example 4

There are about $7\frac{1}{2}$ gallons of water in a cubic foot. How many gallons of water would it take to fill the pool from Example 3? Round your answer up to the nearest hundred gallons.

Solution The volume of the pool is the product of the three dimensions.

Volume = ___?___ • ___?___ • ___?___

= ___?___

(continued on next page)

Since each cubic foot contains 7.5 gallons of water, multiply __?__ by 7.5 to determine the number of gallons that will fill the pool.

Number of gallons needed $= 7\frac{1}{2}\,\frac{\text{gal}}{\text{ft}^3} \bullet \underline{\ ?\ }\ \text{ft}^3 \approx 5789.1$ gal

Rounded up to the nearest hundred gallons, __?__ will fill the pool.

Questions

COVERING THE IDEAS

In 1 and 2, use the box at the right.

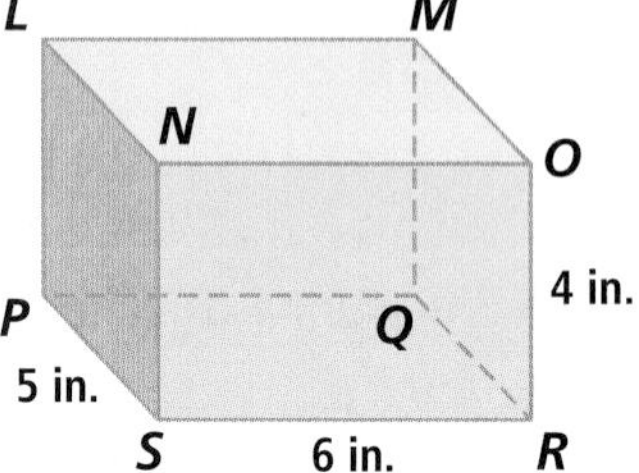

1. a. How many 1-inch cubes would fit in the bottom layer?
   b. How many layers of cubes would fit in the box?
   c. What is the volume of this box?
2. Consider *LNSP* as the base of the box.
   a. What, then, is the height of the box?
   b. What is the volume of the box?

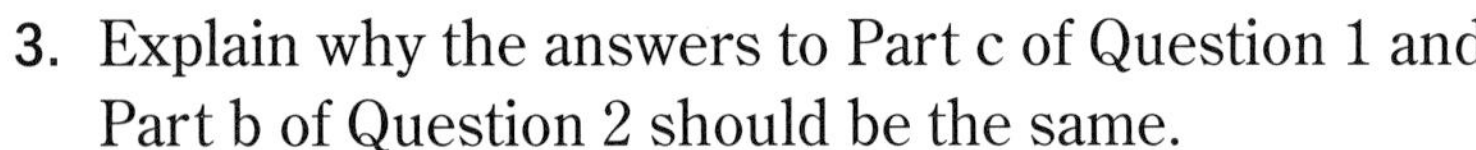

3. Explain why the answers to Part c of Question 1 and Part b of Question 2 should be the same.

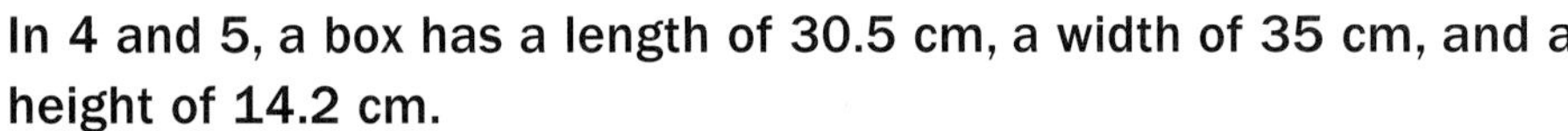

In 4 and 5, a box has a length of 30.5 cm, a width of 35 cm, and a height of 14.2 cm.

4. What is its volume?
5. What is its surface area?

In 6–8, find the volume of the rectangular solid.

6. The area of a base is 40 square centimeters, and the height to that base is 4.3 centimeters.
7. The base measures 10 inches by 2 feet, and the height to that base is 3 inches.
8. The base has area *A* square units, and the height to that base is 50 units.

In 9 and 10, find the surface area of the solid.

9. a standard building brick in Australia, with dimensions 76 mm, 210 mm, and 130 mm
10. a standard building brick in the United States, with dimensions $2\frac{1}{4}''$, 8", and $3\frac{1}{2}''$.

APPLYING THE MATHEMATICS

11. Find a formula for the surface area of a box with length ℓ, width w, height h, and no top.

In 12 and 13, a plastic box has inside dimensions of 20 centimeters by 25 centimeters by 12 centimeters. The box is made of material that is 0.3 cm thick.

12. How many liters of fluid can the box hold? Use the fact that 1 liter = 1000 cubic centimeters.
13. What is the outside surface area of the box?
14. A 3" cube is placed on top of a 10" cube as shown below.

   a. What is the volume of the resulting solid?
   b. What is the surface area of the resulting solid?

15. Frederick made a 3-by-3-by-3 cube out of centimeters cubes and then removed the column of 3 cubes in the middle as shown at the right.

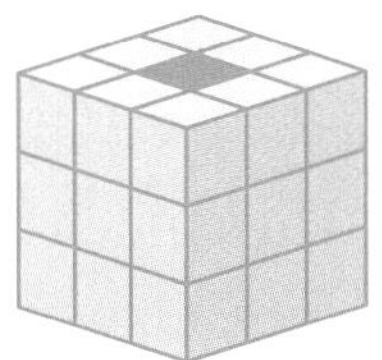

   a. What is the volume of the resulting solid?
   b. What is the surface area of the resulting solid?

16. Suppose the floor of a rectangular storage area has dimensions 11.75 feet by 10.25 feet and the ceiling is 8.5 feet high. How much storage space is in this room?
17. Give two possible sets of dimensions for a rectangular solid whose volume is 144 cubic units.
18. You are designing a trial size of an individual-serving-size cereal box. Each box is to hold 100 cm^3 of cereal.
   a. If each dimension is no smaller than 2 cm or no greater than 10 cm, there are only two possible sets of whole number dimensions for the box. What are they?
   b. Which of the two boxes in Part a uses less cardboard?
   c. If the cardboard costs \$0.00125 per cm^2, how much would it cost to make 50 boxes for each set of dimensions?

REVIEW

In 19–22, convert measurements. (Lessons 9-8, 9-1)

19. How many square centimeters are in 5 square meters?
20. How many square inches are in 1.5 square feet?
21. How many cubic inches are in a cubic foot?
22. How many cubic centimeters are in $\frac{1}{4}$ of a cubic meter?

23. **Multiple Choice** A cube has a surface area of 96 cm^2. What is its volume? **(Lesson 9-8)**

A 4 cm^3 B 16 cm^3 C 64 cm^3 D 256 cm^3

24. Find the dimensions of the box with the net at the right. Each small square measures 1 unit on a side. **(Lesson 9-7)**

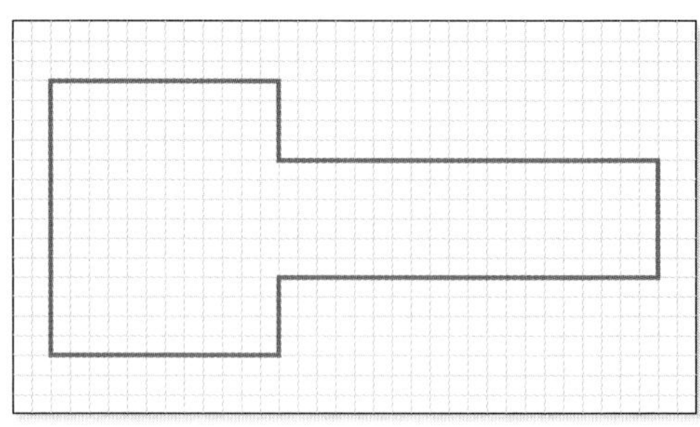

In 25 and 26, use this information. In some parts of the United States, a square plot of land is watered by a long arm that rotates in a circle. This yields plots that consist of circles inscribed in squares like those shown at the right.

25. Suppose the length of the side of one square is $\frac{1}{2}$ mile. **(Lessons 9-5, 9-4)**
    a. What is the area of the square?
    b. What is the area of the circle?
    c. What percent of the land in each square is being watered?

26. The circle graph at the right shows how a circular plot with diameter $\frac{1}{2}$ mile is divided among three crops. **(Lessons 6-6, 5-4)**
    a. How much land area is allocated to each crop?
    b. Explain why a circle graph is a useful way to describe this situation.

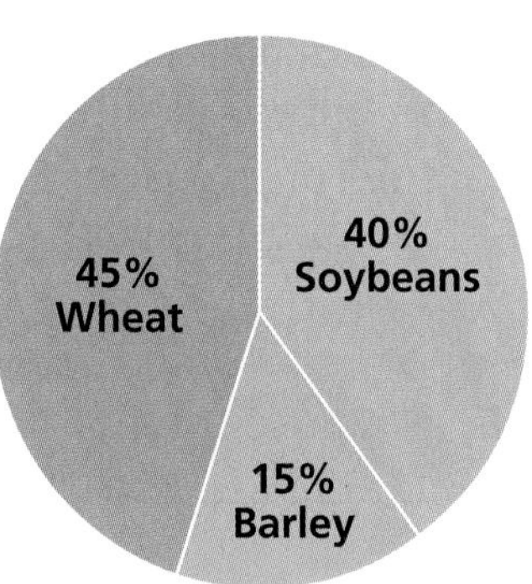

EXPLORATION

27. Find a room that is shaped like a box. Estimate its surface area and volume. Then find its dimensions, and calculate its surface area and volume. Ignore windows and doors.

28. In the box shown at the left below, there are six paths that start at vertex A and end at vertex H and pass through all 8 vertices without retracing an edge. One such path, A to B to C to D to A to E to F to G to H, is shown at the right. Find the other five paths. Do not visit any one vertex more than twice. Describe each path by identifying the vertices and edges included in the path.

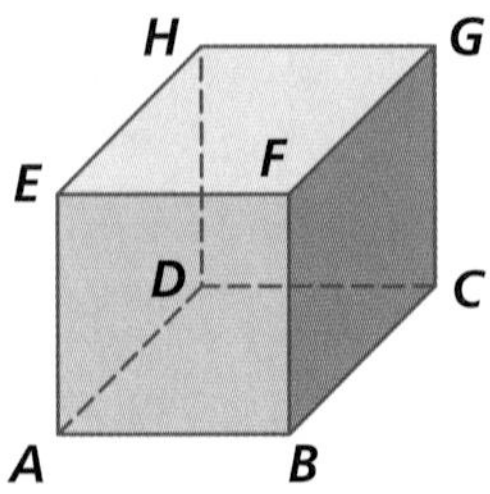

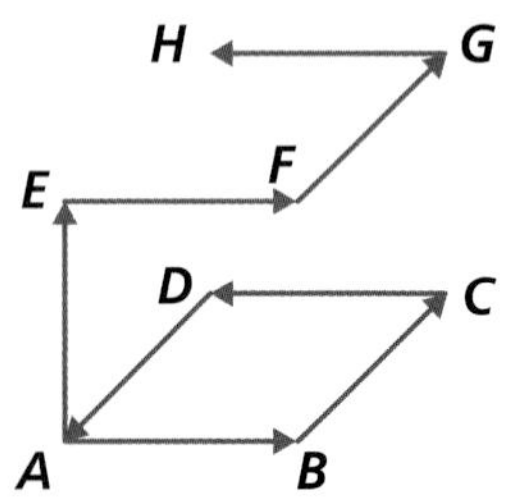

QY ANSWER

804 square inches

Lesson 9-10 Surface Area and Volume of Prisms and Cylinders

Vocabulary

right prism

cylinder

▶ **BIG IDEA** The surface area of a prism or cylinder is the sum of the areas of its bases and the area of its side or sides. The volume of a right prism or right cylinder is the product of the area of its base and its height.

Mental Math

a. How many seconds are in 3 minutes?

b. How many minutes are in 3 hours?

c. How many hours are in 3 days?

d. How many days are in 3 weeks?

A **right prism** is a three-dimensional figure with two bases that are polygons of the same size and shape and have rectangular faces. Below are three examples: one with hexagons as bases, one with triangles as bases, and one with quadrilaterals as bases.

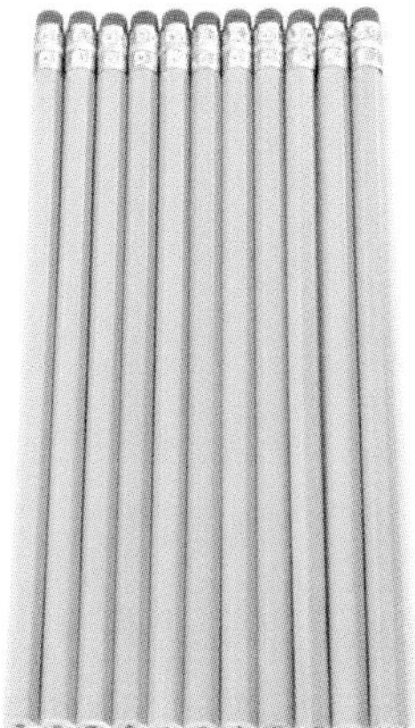

Hexagonal Prisms

Triangular Prism

Quadrilateral Prism

A **cylinder** is like a prism, but it has circular bases and a curved side, like the can and middle part of the rolling pin pictured below.

Can

Rolling Pin

A box is a right prism whose base is a rectangle. Finding the volume of a prism or a cylinder is like finding the volume of a box.

Volume Formula for a Prism or a Cylinder

The volume V of a prism or cylinder equals the product of the area B of a base and the height h to that base: $V = Bh$.

Because the base of a cylinder is a circle, calculating the surface area or volume of a cylinder will involve π. Notice in Example 1 that we wait until the very end before using an approximation for π.

GUIDED

Example 1

A typical soda can has a base that is about 6.5 cm in diameter. The can is 12.5 cm high. About how much soda, to the nearest cubic centimeter, does it hold?

Solution The can's capacity is its volume, so use $V = Bh$. The base is a circle, so the area of the base is $A = \pi r^2$.

The diameter of the circle is 6.5 cm, so its radius is __?__.
Area of base $= \pi r^2 = \pi \cdot (\underline{\ \ ?\ \ })^2 \approx \underline{\ \ ?\ \ }$
Volume of can $= Bh = \underline{\ \ ?\ \ } \cdot \underline{\ \ ?\ \ } \approx 414.58 \text{ cm}^3$
To the nearest cubic centimeter, the can holds __?__ cm^3.

GUIDED

Example 2

A prism that disperses light is solid and triangular with dimensions shown at the right. How much glass was used to make the prism?

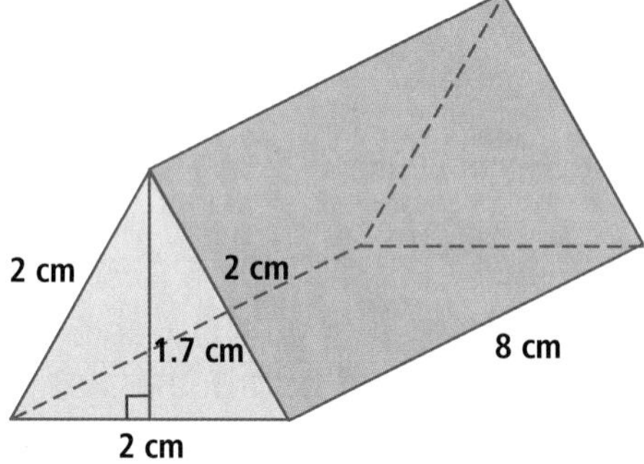

Solution The triangle is the base, so first find the area of the triangle.

Area of base $= B = \frac{1}{2}bh = \frac{1}{2} \cdot \underline{\ \ ?\ \ } \cdot \underline{\ \ ?\ \ } = \underline{\ \ ?\ \ } \text{ cm}^2$
$V = Bh = \underline{\ \ ?\ \ } \cdot \underline{\ \ ?\ \ } = 13.6 \text{ cm}^3$

Surface Area

To find the surface area of any solid, find the area of each face and add. The surface area of a right prism is the sum of the areas of its bases and the areas of the rectangular faces.

Activity 1

MATERIALS ruler, grid paper (optional)

Step 1 Draw a net of the prism in Guided Example 2. Label the dimensions and label each face with one of the names given in the table on the next page.

Step 2 Fill in this table.

Face Name	Area (cm^2)
Front base	?
Back base	?
Rectangle 1	?
Rectangle 2	?
Rectangle 3	?

Step 3 Use the data in the table to calculate the surface area of the prism.

Step 4 The rectangular faces on your net form a single, larger rectangle when placed together. What are the dimensions of this larger rectangle?

The surface area of a cylinder is the sum of the areas of its two circular bases plus the area of the "side" of the cylinder.

Activity 2

Step 1 At the right is a can of tomatoes and its net. What is the area of one base? What is the sum of the areas of both bases?

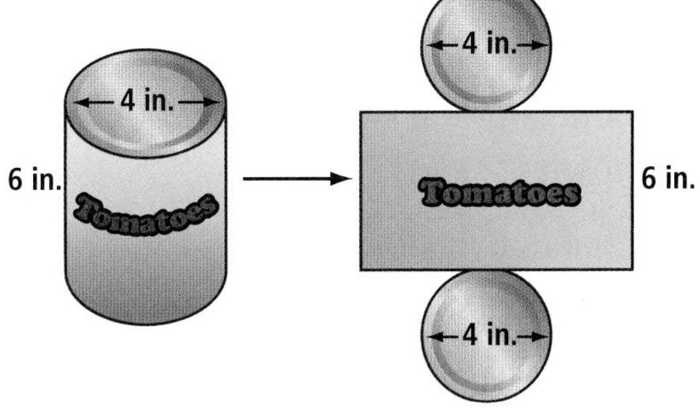

Step 2 What part of the can forms the shorter dimension of the rectangle in the net? What is the length of this dimension?

Step 3 What part of the can forms the longer dimension of the rectangle in the net? What is the length of this dimension?

Step 4 Find the area of the side of the can.

Step 5 What is the surface area of the can?

Surface Area for a Right Prism or Cylinder

The surface area of a right prism or cylinder is the sum of the areas of its two bases and the area of its sides. The area of its sides is the product of the perimeter of the base and the height.

Example 3

Find the surface area of the light prism in Guided Example 2.

Solution Each base is a triangle. As was shown in Example 2, the area of each triangle is 1.7 cm^2. The total area of the sides of the prism is the perimeter of the base times its height. The perimeter of the triangle is 2 cm + 2 cm + 2 cm = 6 cm. Because the height is 8 cm, the area of the sides is 8 cm • 6 cm = 48 cm^2.

So the surface area is 1.7 cm^2 + 1.7 cm^2 + 48 cm^2 = 51.4 cm^2.

Questions

COVERING THE IDEAS

In 1–3, name the solid pictured.

1.

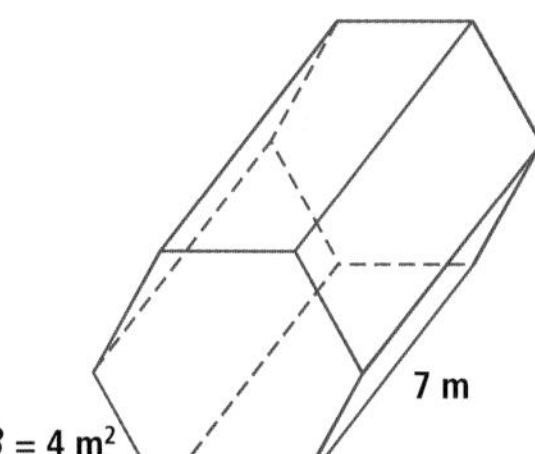

2.

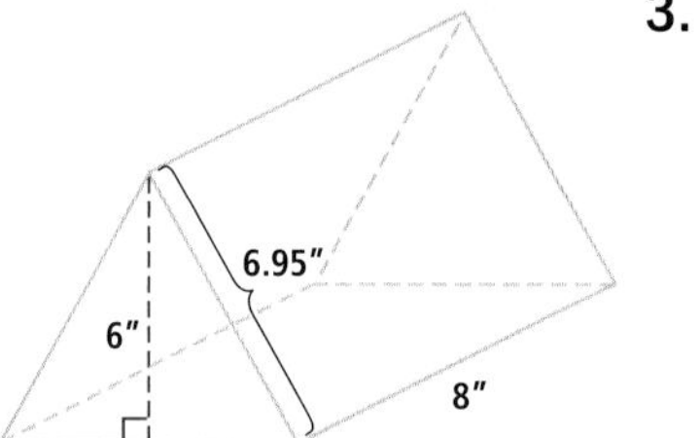

3.

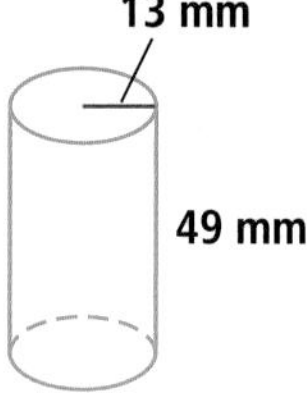

4. Name a prism with bases that are a different polygon than those shown in Questions 1 and 2.

5. What is a formula for the volume of a prism or a cylinder?

In 6–11, copy and fill in the table. Remember to include units.

	Solid from	Area of the Base	Height	Volume
6.	Question 1	?	?	?
7.	Question 2	?	?	?
8.	Question 3	?	?	?

	Solid from	Area of each Base	Area of Each Side	Surface Area
9.	Question 1	?	?	?
10.	Question 2	?	?	?
11.	Question 3	?	?	?

12. Each base of a right pentagonal prism has a perimeter of 27.6 cm and an area of 102.16 cm^2. The height of the prism is 6.5 cm. What is the prism's surface area?

13. Tiana had a food can with a diameter of 8.5 cm and a height of 12.5 cm. She calculated the surface area of the can using the equation $(8.5\pi \cdot 12.5) + (4.25^2\pi) = 390.54 \text{ cm}^2$. Is this correct? Explain why or why not.

APPLYING THE MATHEMATICS

14. At the right is a sketch of a horse trough that is a right quadrilateral prism.

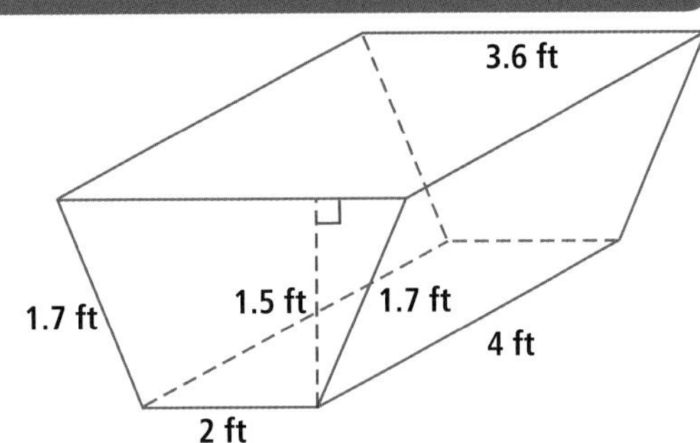

   a. Ignoring overlap, how much material was required to make it?
   b. How much water will it hold?

15. The William J. Campbell Courthouse Annex in Chicago, shown at the right, is shaped like a right triangular prism. It is about 290 feet tall, and the triangular bases measure about 120 feet by 120 feet by 170 feet. Assume the side faces of the building are to be covered with limestone tile. How much tile is required?

In 1977, the William J. Campbell Courthouse Annex received an honor award for excellence from the American Institute of Architects.

Source: The American Institute of Architects

16. A certain wading pool is a cylinder with a diameter of 14 feet and a height of 12 inches.
   a. When the pool is filled to the top, how many gallons of water does it hold? (*Note*: 231 cubic inches = 1 gallon)
   b. When the water in the pool has a height of only 9 inches, how many gallons are in the pool?

17. One chocolate bar is in the shape of a triangular prism. It is $8\frac{1}{4}$ inches long, and the triangular bases have sides about 1.6 inches long and a height of $1\frac{3}{8}$ inches. Another chocolate bar is in the shape of a box 7 inches long, $3\frac{1}{2}$ inches wide, and $\frac{1}{4}$ inch thick. Both bars cost \$2.99.
   a. What is the cost of each bar per cubic inch? (*Hint:* you may want to convert the dimensions to decimals.)
   b. Which is the better buy?

REVIEW

18. Jorge and Fujita are packing containers of macaroni for their school's food drive. Each macaroni container is a 4"-by-6"-by-2" box. The box they are packing the containers in has dimensions 28.2"-by-42.2"-by-14.2". (Lesson 9-9)
   a. How many containers of macaroni will fit in the packing box?
   b. What is the total volume (in cubic inches) of macaroni that will be packed in the box?

19. The faces of a box are squares with sides of length 6 cm and rectangles with dimensions 8 cm by 6 cm. **(Lesson 9-9)**
   a. What is the surface area of the box?
   b. What is the volume of the box?

20. Find the area of parallelogram *ABCD* below in square units. **(Lesson 9-3)**

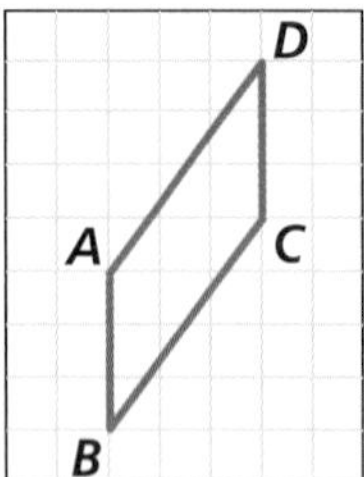

21. What is the reciprocal of 50%? **(Lesson 8-2)**

22. If the population of an ant colony doubles every week, how many times as big as today's population will the population be six weeks from today? **(Lesson 6-4)**

Have you ever owned an ant farm?

EXPLORATION

23. Copy and complete the following table.

Type of Prism	Number of Edges
Triangular Prism	?
Rectangular Prism	?
Pentagonal Prism	?
Hexagonal Prism	?
n-sided Prism	?

Chapter 9 Projects

1 Large Buildings and Monuments

Over the ages, people have built many large buildings and monuments, including the pyramids of the Maya, the Babylonians, and the Egyptians; the temples of Angkor Wat in Cambodia and Machu Picchu in Peru; the Pentagon building in Washington D.C.; and the Kremlin in Russia. Pick one of these or choose some other famous large building or monument. Draw an accurate picture, labeling important points. Describe its area and volume, or areas and volumes related to it. Write a paragraph describing how and when the structure was built and what its use was or is.

At different times in its history, Angkor Wat has served as a religious center for both Hindus and Buddhists.

2 Area of Your Residence

The floor area of an apartment or house is the area enclosed by the outer walls of the residence. Sketch the shape of the place where you live and, by measuring, calculate this area for your residence.

3 Surface Areas and Volumes of Boxes

Find at least six boxes of various sizes and calculate their surface areas and volumes. Explain why a box that has greater volume might not have greater surface area.

Cardboard boxes are recyclable.

4 Approximations of π

The number π (pi) has a long history. People from many cultures, including the Chinese, Hindus, Egyptians, and Greeks used approximations for π, beginning over 2,500 years ago. Find out what these approximations of π were. Describe how at least one of the approximations was determined.

5 Borders and Land Area

The length of a border of a country is its perimeter. Using the *CIA World Factbook* at www.cia.gov, pick ten countries with a range of sizes. Divide the border length of each country by its area, and make a display of your data. Is there any trend to this relationship as the area of the country grows?

6 Circles and Equilateral Triangles

A polygon is *inscribed in* a circle if all of its vertices lie on the circle. A polygon is *circumscribed about* a circle if each of its sides intersects the circle in exactly one point that is not a vertex. Make a careful drawing of a circle. Inscribe an equilateral triangle in the circle and then circumscribe a second equilateral triangle about the circle. Measure a side and height of each triangle, and use these measures to find the areas of both triangles. Find the ratio of the area of the larger triangle to the area of the smaller triangle. Can you show why this ratio has the value it has?

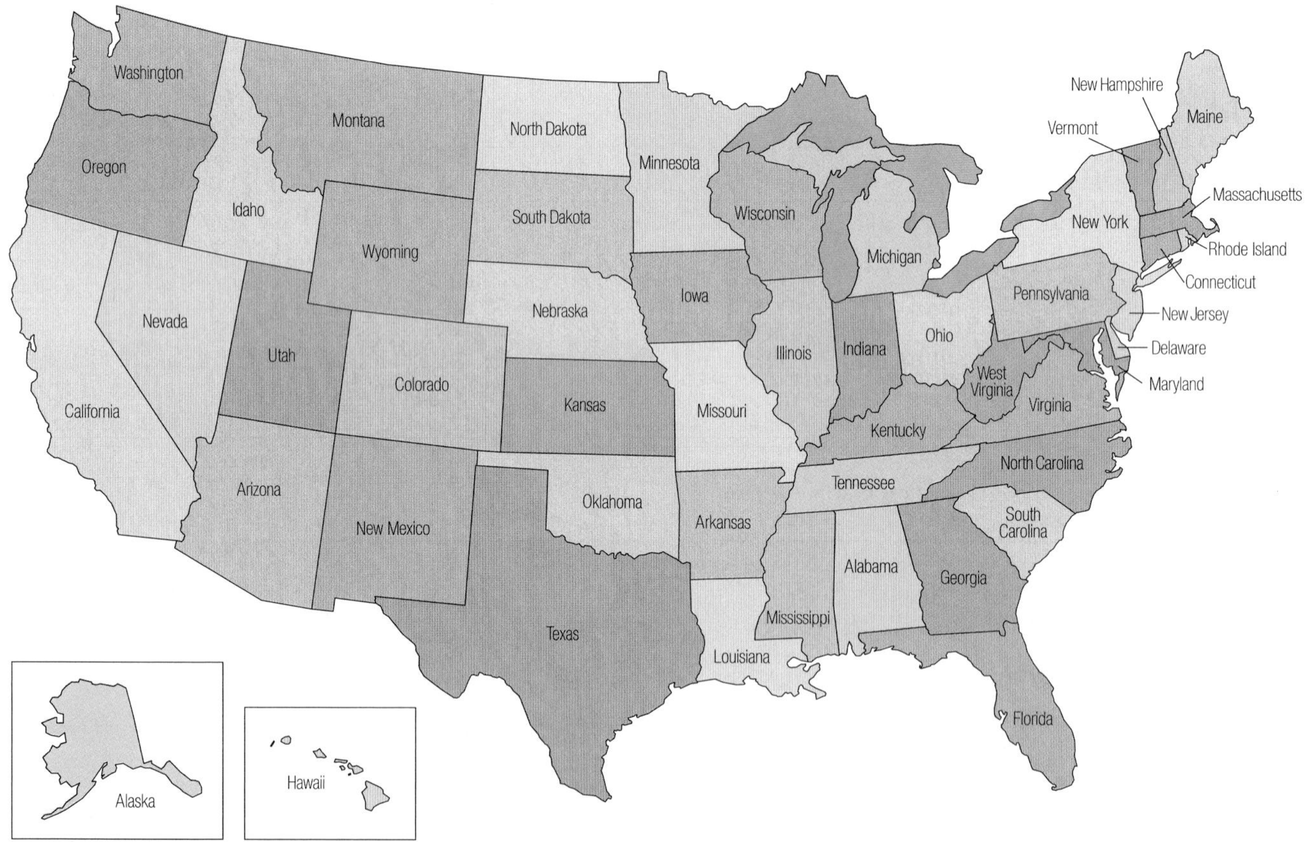

In 2000, the total U.S. land area was 3,537,438.44 square miles.

Source: U.S. Census Bureau

Chapter 9 Summary and Vocabulary

- Area measures the space inside or amount of material in a 2-dimensional figure and is measured in square units, such as square centimeters or square feet. Volume measures the space inside or amount of material in a 3-dimensional figure and is measured in cubic units, such as cubic centimeters or cubic feet. The operations of arithmetic are often applied to lengths, areas, and volumes.

- There are three ways to find area: counting square units, rearranging the figure to form a more convenient shape and finding that shape's area, or using an appropriate formula. A formula for the area of a parallelogram is $A = bh$. A formula for the area of a triangle is $A = \frac{1}{2}bh$. A formula for the area of a circle is $A = \pi r^2$. The formula for the circumference of a circle, $C = \pi d$, also involves the number π. Areas formed by combinations of geometric figures often appear, for example, in architecture, frames, or target rings.

- A common 3-dimensional figure is a box or rectangular solid. A net is a 2-dimensional pattern that can be folded to create a 3-dimensional figure. Looking at a net for a box can help in determining its surface area *S.A.*, the sum of the areas of its six faces. You can also use the formula $S.A. = 2lw + 2lh + 2wh$. The volume V of a box can be found by either $V = lwh$ or $V = Bh$. If the box is a cube with edges of length s, then these formulas can be simplified to $S.A. = 6s^2$ and $V = s^3$. For a right prism or a cylinder, the area of the rectangular faces or the side is found by multiplying the perimeter of a base times the height of the prism or cylinder. To find total surface area, add the area of the two bases to the area of the sides. Volume, like the volume of a box, is given by $V = Bh$.

Theorems and Properties

Area Formula for a Right Triangle (p. 520)
Area Formula for Any Triangle (p. 522)
Area Formula for a Parallelogram (p. 528)
Formula for Circumference of a Circle (p. 534)
Area Formula for a Circle (p. 535)
Surface Area Formula for a Cube (p. 556)
Volume Formula for a Cube (p. 557)
Two Formulas for the Volume of a Box (p. 563)
Volume Formula for a Prism or a Cylinder (p. 568)
Surface Area for a Right Prism or a Cylinder (p. 569)

Vocabulary

Lesson 9-1
semicircle

Lesson 9-2
legs of a right triangle
hypotenuse
base of a triangle
altitude of a triangle
height of a triangle

Lesson 9-3
parallel lines
parallelogram
base of a parallelogram
altitude of a parallelogram
height of a parallelogram

Lesson 9-4
pi, circumference
radius

Lesson 9-5
concentric circles, ring

Lesson 9-6
box, face, edges of a box
vertex, vertices of a box
rectangular solid
dimensions
length, width
height, depth of a box
cube

Lesson 9-7
net

Lesson 9-8
surface area
volume, capacity

Lesson 9-9
base of a box
height of a box

Lesson 9-10
right prism
cylinder

Chapter 9 Self-Test

Take this test as you would take a test in class. You will need a calculator. Then use the Selected Answers section in the back of the book to check your work.

In 1 and 2, find the area of the shape.

1\.

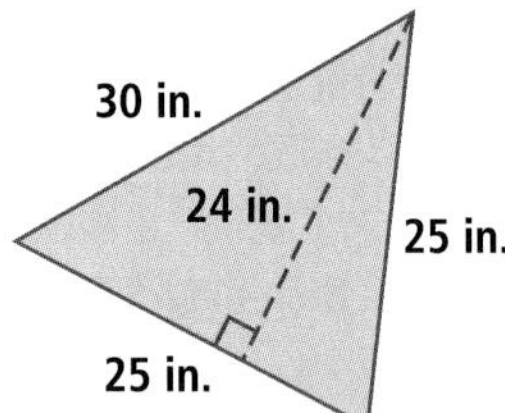

2\.

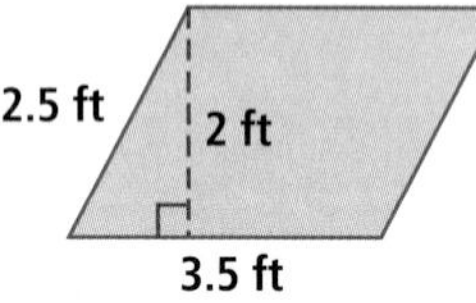

3\. a. What is the area of the circle at the right?

b. What is its circumference?

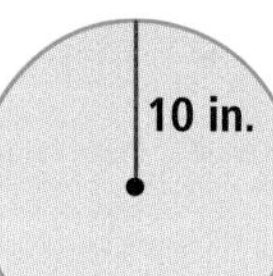

4\. Find the area of the shaded part of the figure below. Round your answer to the nearest tenth of an inch.

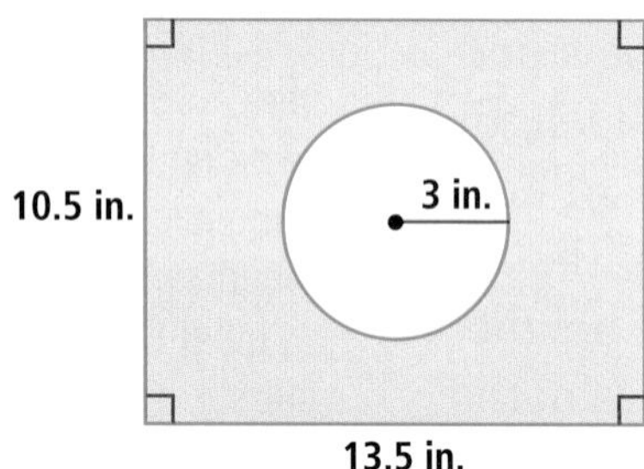

5\. Find the area of the polygon below. All angles are right angles.

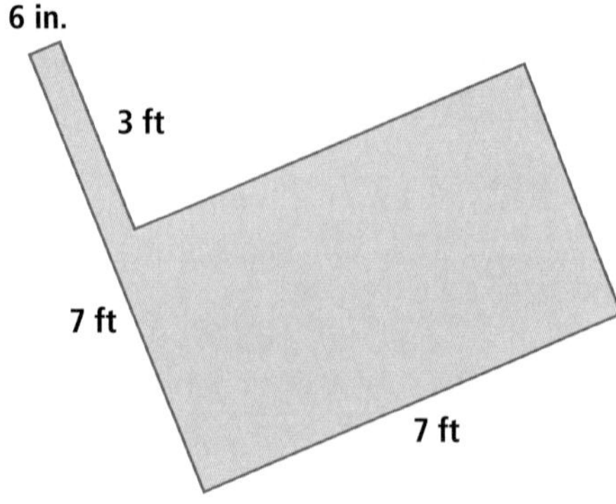

6\. Jazmine is putting decorative edging around three circular gardens in her yard. The first garden has a radius of 3 m, the second has a radius of 4.5 m, and the third has a radius of 5 m.

a. How much edging does Jazmine need? (Round your answer to the nearest tenth of a meter.)

b. What is the total area of Jazmine's gardens?

7\. Kendall is painting a wall in his living room, which has a cathedral ceiling, as shown below. The wall is 18 feet long. At its highest point, the ceiling is 15 feet above the floor. At its lowest point, the ceiling is 9 feet above the floor. There is a rectangular window measuring 10 feet by 5 feet in the wall. How many square feet must Kendall paint?

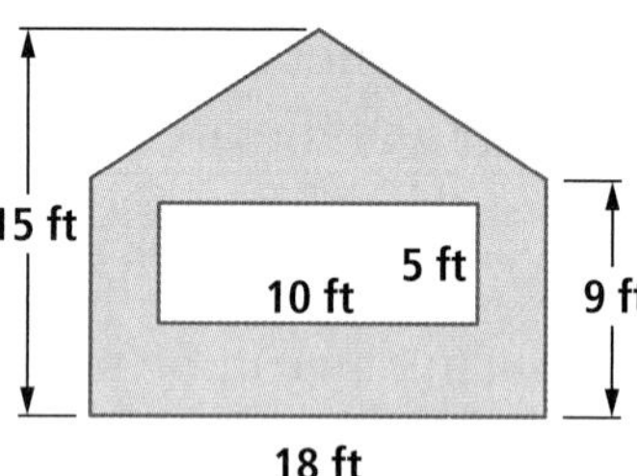

8\. Di Vere has a rectangular swimming pool that measures 18 feet by 30 feet. It is surrounded on all four sides by a deck that is 6 feet wide.

a. Draw and label a picture of the pool and the deck.

b. Find the area of the deck.

In 9–12, use the box at the right.

9\. Name the blue edge.

10\. Name two vertices on the shaded face.

11\. Name the shaded face.

12\. Draw the six faces and label their dimensions.

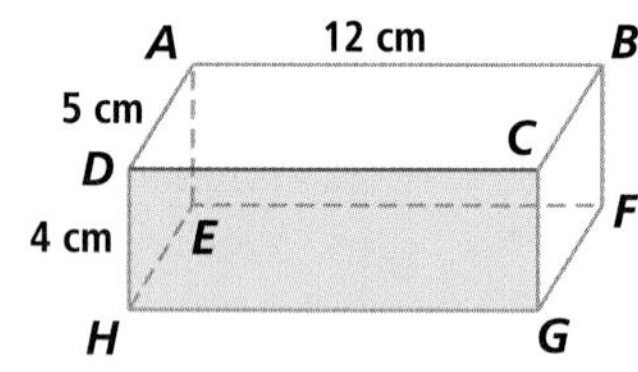

In 13–15, a cube has an edge 3 cm long.

13. Draw and label a net for the cube.
14. Find the surface area of the cube.
15 Find the volume of the cube.

In 16–18, use the box below.

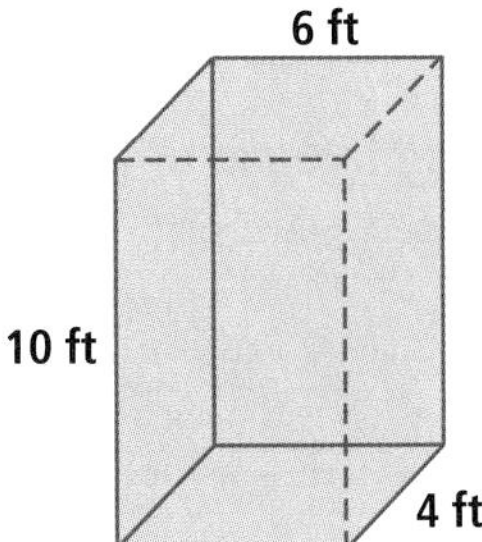

16. Draw and label a net for the box.
17. How much cardboard would it take to make the box?
18. How much would the box hold?
19. Find the surface area and volume of the right prism below.

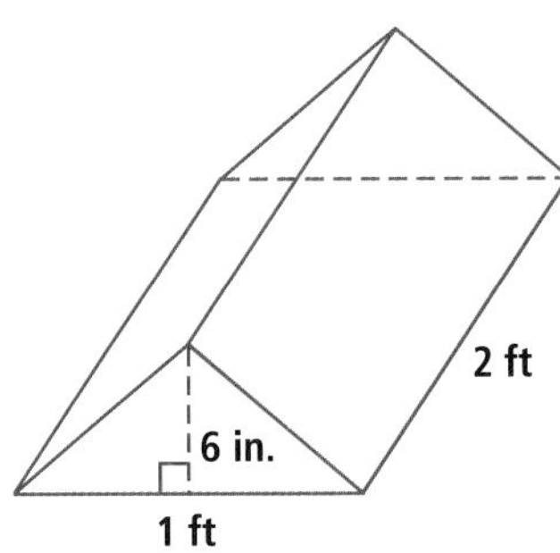

In 20 and 21, use the cylindrical can below.

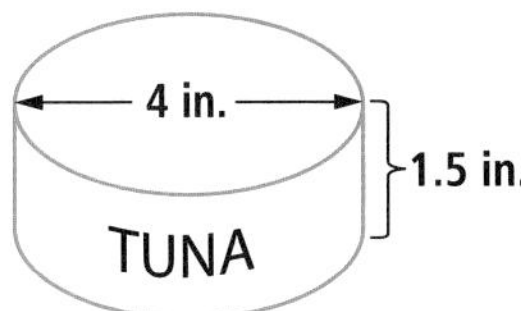

20. How much metal is needed to make the can? (Assume there is no overlap.)
21. How much tuna can it hold?
22. Use the diagram below. Explain why the area of $\triangle DEC$ is half the area of rectangle $ABCD$.

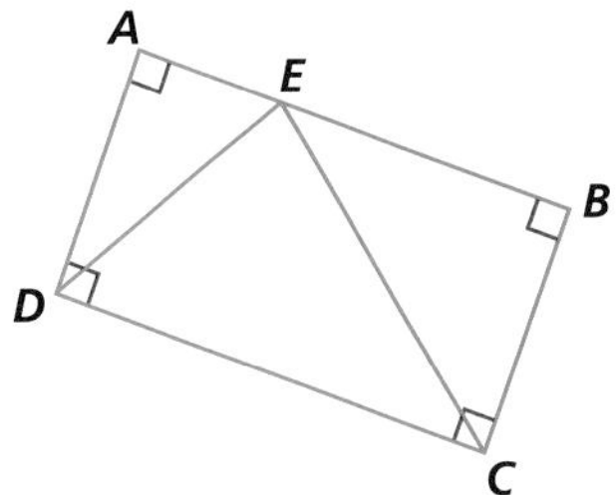

Chapter 9 Chapter Review

SKILLS
PROPERTIES
USES
REPRESENTATIONS

SKILLS Procedures used to get answers

OBJECTIVE A Find the areas of parallelograms, triangles, and circles. (Lessons 9-2, 9-3, 9-4)

In 1–4, find the area of the figure.

1. 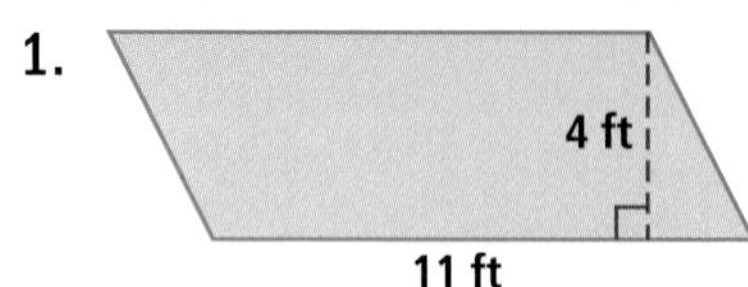

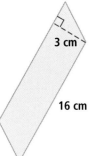

2. 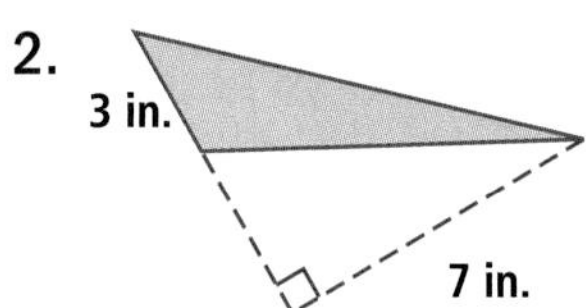

3.

4. 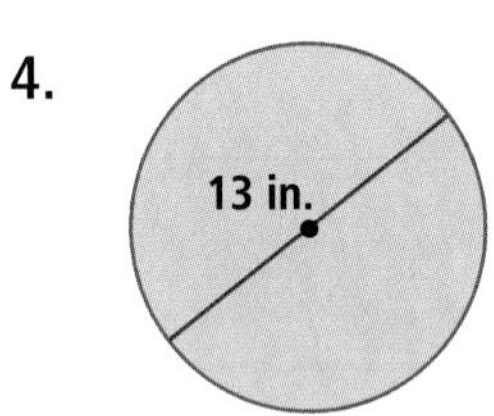

5. Find the area of a right triangle with legs of length 4" and 6".

6. Find the area of a circle with radius 8 mm.

OBJECTIVE B Find the circumference of a circle. (Lesson 9-4)

In 7–10, find the circumference of the circle to the nearest tenth of the given unit.

7. 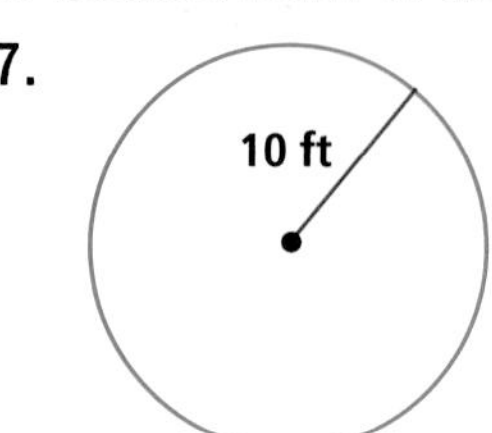

8. 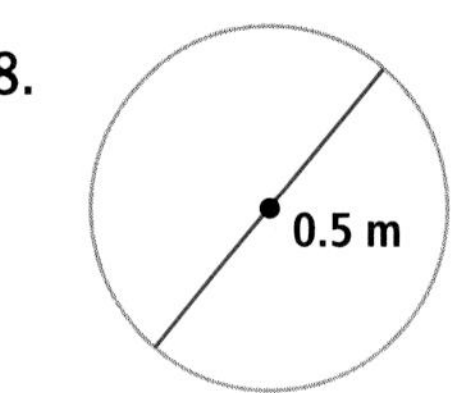

9. a circle with radius 5 cm

10. a circle with diameter 11"

OBJECTIVE C Use addition and subtraction to calculate the areas of geometric figures formed from combinations of parallelograms, triangles, and circles. (Lessons 9-1, 9-4, 9-5)

In 11–14, find the area of the shaded region.

11. 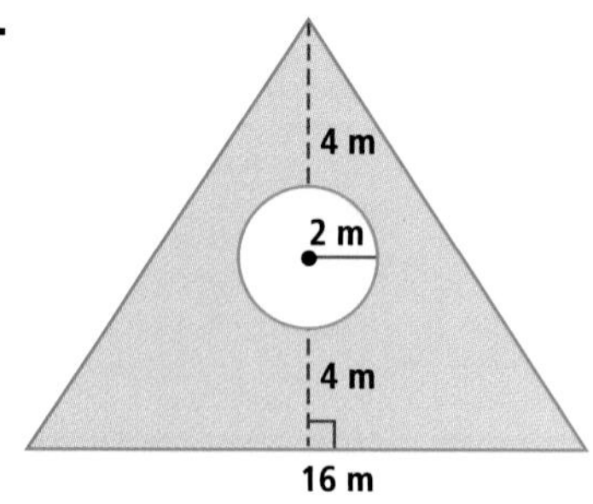

12. 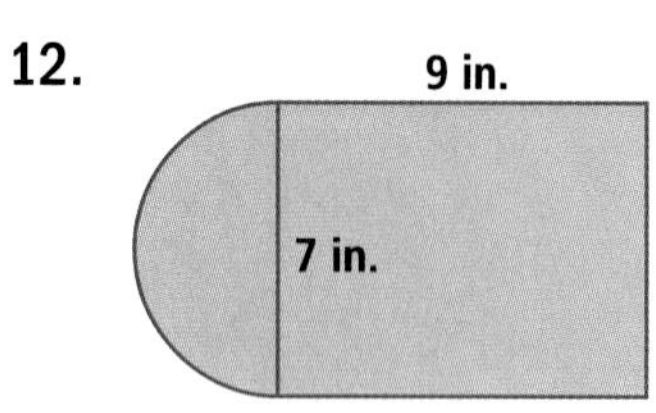

13.

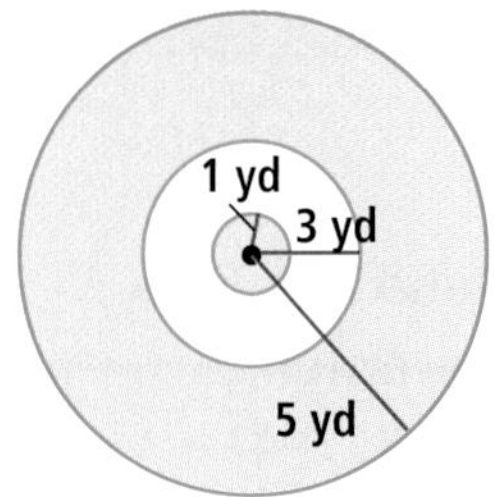

14. *ABCD* is a parallelogram.

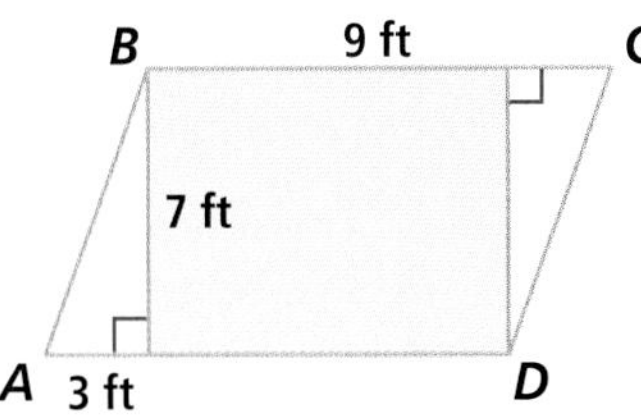

In 15 and 16, determine the area of the polygon. All angles of the polygon are right angles. The dimensions are in meters.

15.

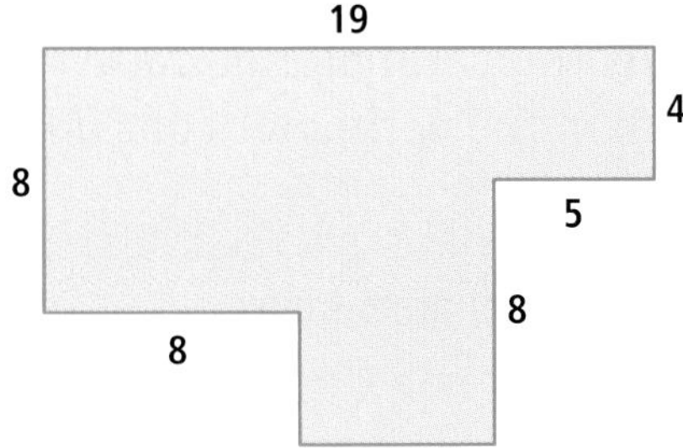

16.

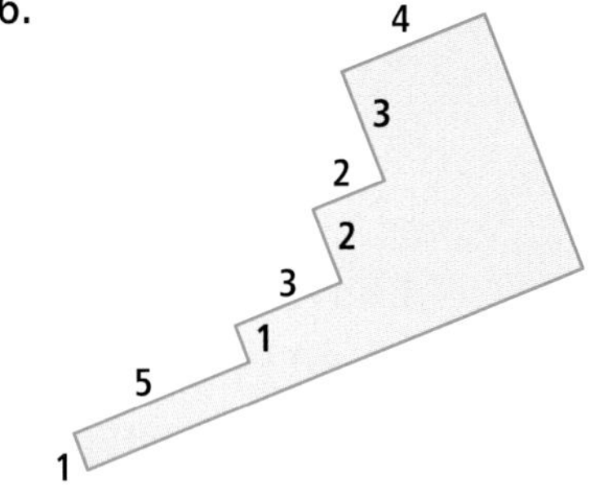

OBJECTIVE D Find the surface area of a box. **(Lessons 9-8, 9-9)**

In 17 and 18, find the surface area of the box.

17.

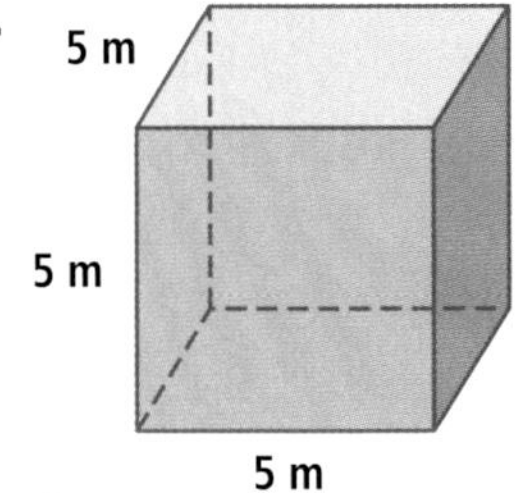

18.

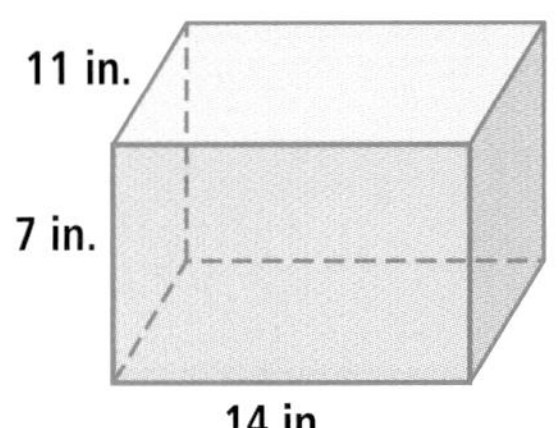

In 19 and 20, find the surface area of the box. Notice that one face is missing.

19.

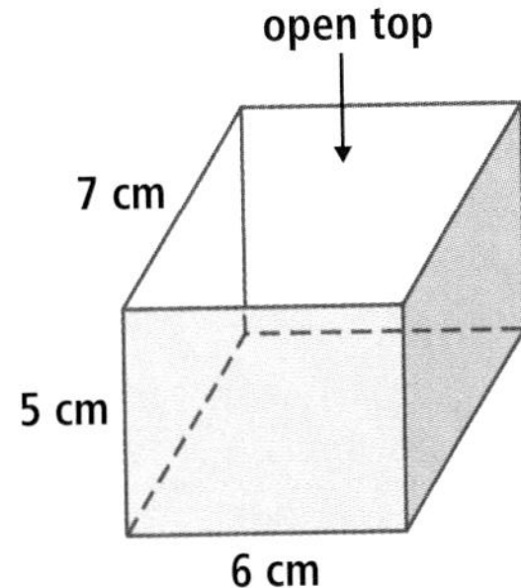

20.

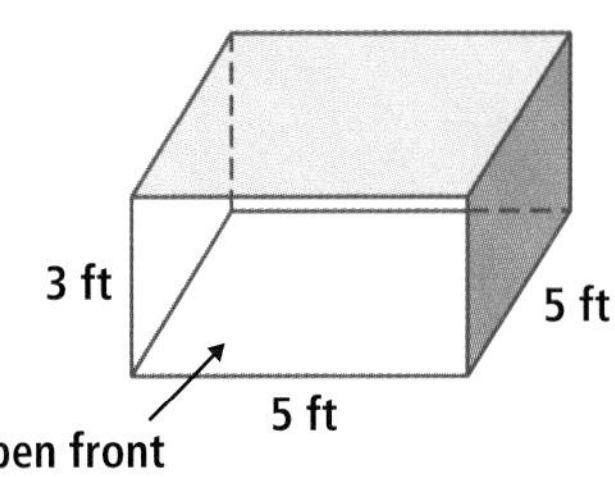

OBJECTIVE E Find the volume of a box. **(Lessons 9-8, 9-9)**

In 21–24, find the volume of the box.

21.

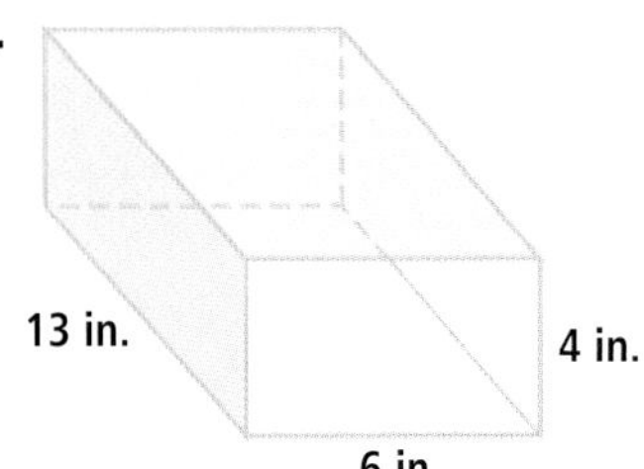

22.

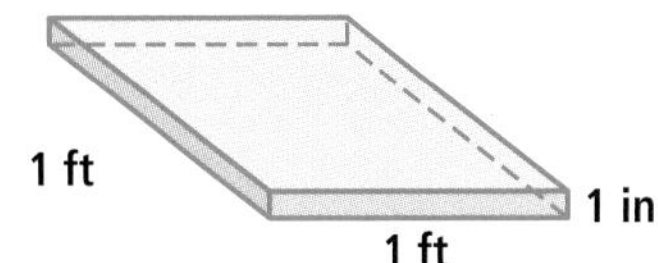

23.

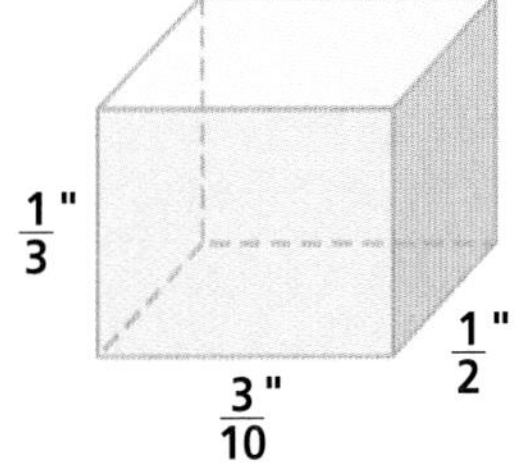

24.

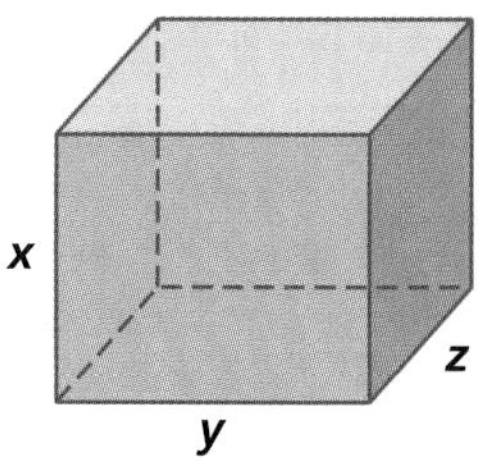

OBJECTIVE F **Find the surface area and volume of prisms and cylinders. (Lesson 9-10)**

In 25 and 26, find the surface area and volume of the prism.

25. triangular prism

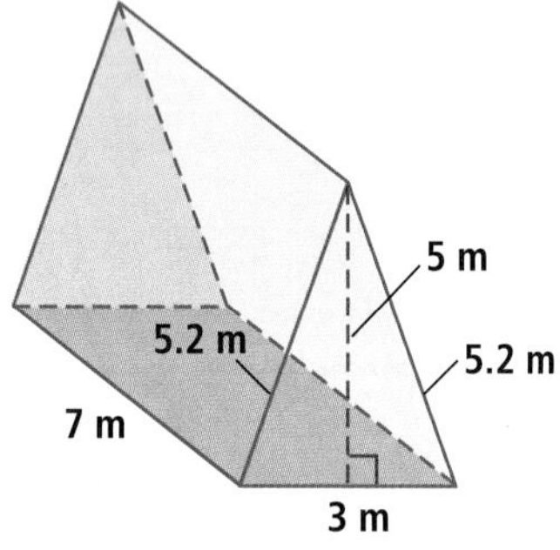

26. hexagonal prism with base perimeter 7.0 in.

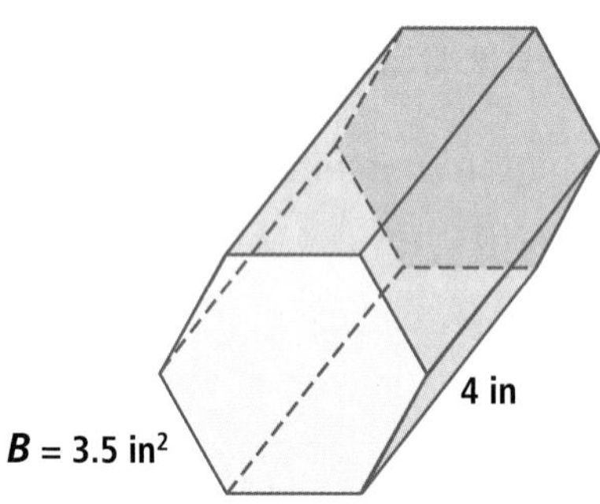

In 27 and 28, find the surface area and volume of the cylinder.

27. **28.**

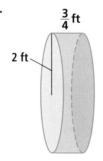

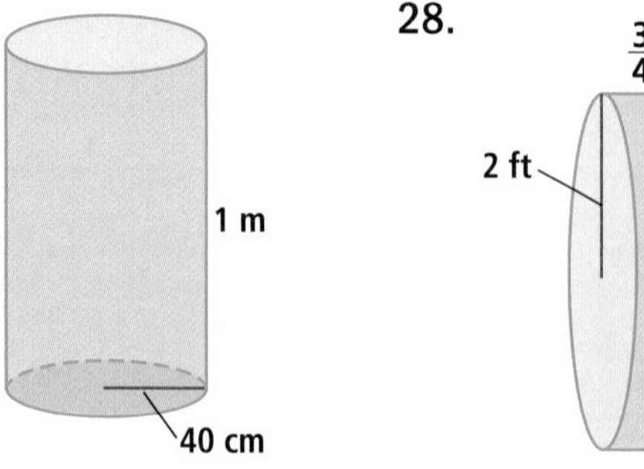

PROPERTIES The principles behind the mathematics

OBJECTIVE G **Understand the area and length relationships among figures. (Lessons 9-1, 9-3, 9-4)**

In 29 and 30, use the triangle below.

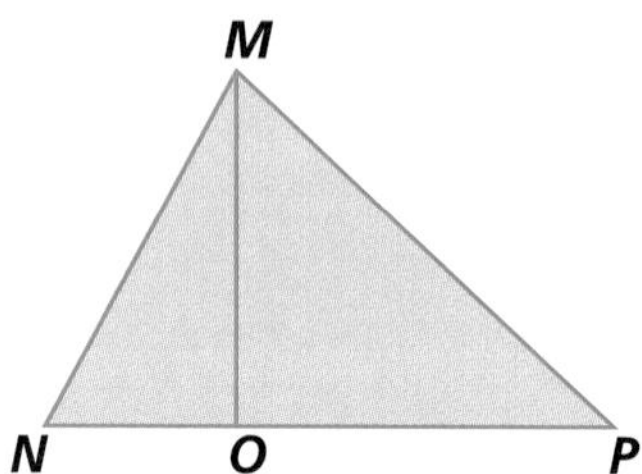

29. How is the area of $\triangle MNO$ related to the areas of $\triangle MNP$ and $\triangle MOP$?

30. Explain why the perimeter of $\triangle MNP$ is *not* the sum of the perimeters of $\triangle MNO$ and $\triangle MOP$.

In 31 and 32, use the diagram below.

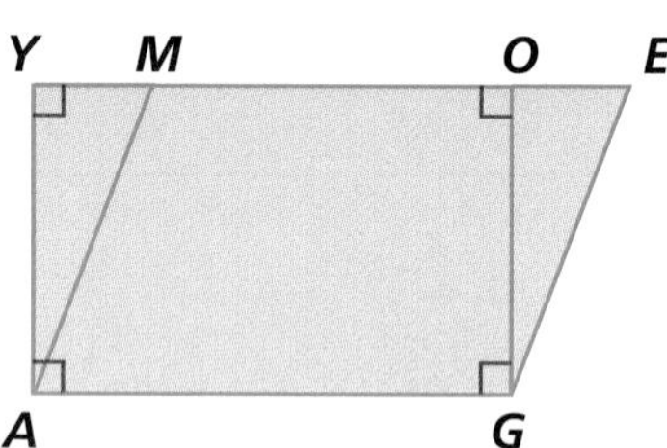

31. Does rectangle *YOGA* have the same perimeter as parallelogram *GAME*?

32. Does rectangle *YOGA* have the same area as parallelogram *GAME*?

33. **Multiple Choice** If the radius of a circle is doubled from 5 cm to 10 cm, then

A its circumference is doubled and its area is quadrupled.

B its circumference is quadrupled and its area is doubled.

C its circumference and its area are both doubled.

D its circumference and its area are both quadrupled.

OBJECTIVE H **Name the faces, edges, and vertices of a box and give the dimensions for each face of a given box. (Lesson 9-6)**

In 34–37, use the box shown below.

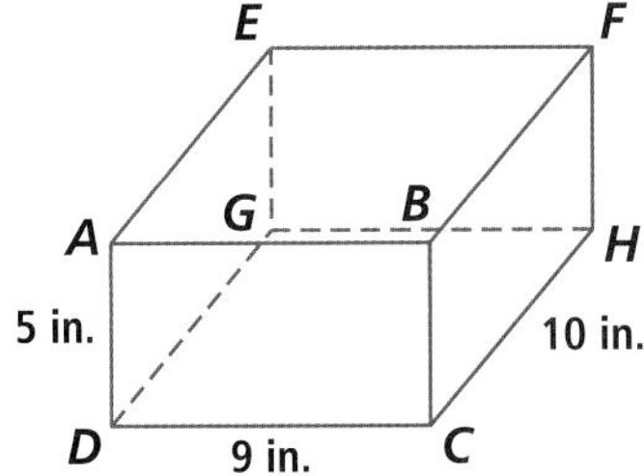

34. List the edges of the box.
35. List the vertices of the box.
36. List the faces of the box.
37. Give the dimensions of each face of the box.

USES Applications of mathematics in real-world situations

OBJECTIVE I **Use the formula for the circumference of a circle in real situations. (Lesson 9-4)**

38. A dartboard has a diameter of 45 centimeters. What is its circumference, to the nearest tenth of a centimeter?
39. Wade is making a clock with a face that has a circumference of 60 inches. One of the hands he wants to use for the clock is 10 inches long. Can Wade put this hand on the clock so that it does not run over the edge of the clock face?
40. A crop circle in Colorado has a diameter of 2,500 feet. To the nearest ten feet, what is the circumference of this crop circle?
41. If a bike travels 17.5 meters when its wheels rotate 5 times, what is the radius of a wheel, to the nearest centimeter?

OBJECTIVE J **Use the formulas for areas of parallelograms, triangles, and circles in real situations. (Lesson 9-2, 9-3, 9-4)**

42. Cherokee is painting his deck. The deck is in the shape of a right triangle with leg lengths 51 feet and 25 feet. If one can of paint covers 350 square feet, how many cans of paint does Cherokee need to paint the entire deck?
43. The Shapleigh Fountain in St. Louis is a circular fountain 50 feet in diameter. Find the area of the base of this fountain to the nearest square foot.
44. The total area of the football field shown below is 57,600 ft^2. Find the width w of the field.

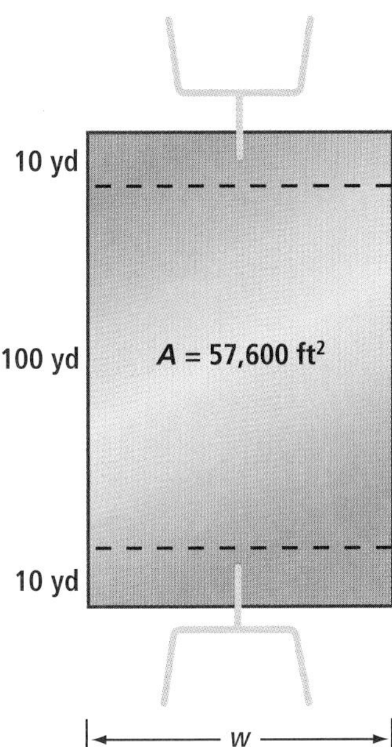

45. Paul is building a chair. For one part, he must cut a piece of wood into the parallelogram shown below. What is the area of this piece?

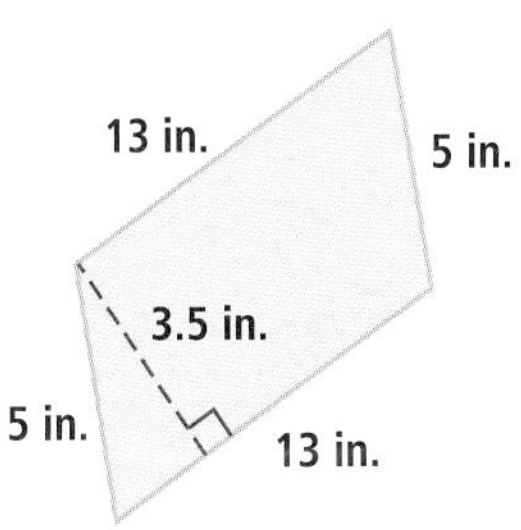

OBJECTIVE K **Use addition and subtraction to calculate areas of regions formed by combining figures in real situations. (Lessons 9-4, 9-5)**

46. A roof is to be made using two identical parallelograms and two identical triangles. The triangles have a height of 8 feet and a base length of 15 feet, while the parallelograms have a height of 10 feet and a base length of 20 feet. Find the combined area of the material used for the roof.

47. Find the amount of glass (to the nearest square inch) needed for the window below. Ignore the wood between the wood panes.

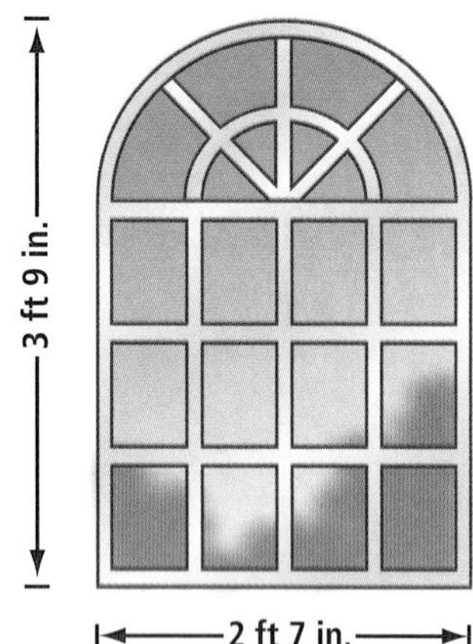

48. A circular dartboard has a bull's eye with radius 13 mm and other circles with radii as labeled below.

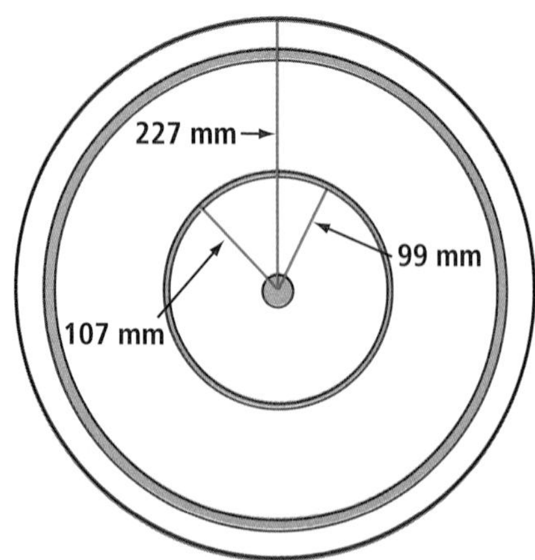

a. Find the area of the bull's-eye, the area of the inner shaded ring, and the area of the entire dartboard to the nearest mm^2.

b. What percent of the total area is in the bull's-eye?

c. What percent of the total area is in the inner shaded region?

49. Find the area of the shaded portion of the North African tile pattern shown below.

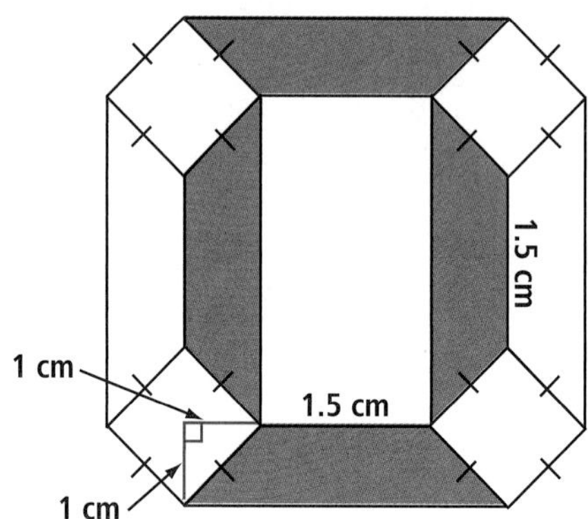

OBJECTIVE L **Use volume and surface area formulas for boxes, prisms, and cylinders in real situations. (Lessons 9-9, 9-10)**

50. A Rubik's Cube® is made up of smaller cubes. If the edges of 3 smaller cubes cover an edge of the larger cube, how many smaller cubes make up a Rubik's cube?

51. A soccer ball has a volume of just under 400 in^3. Alejandro says if they find a box with a volume of over 400 in^3, the ball will fit completely inside. Karla disagrees. Who is right? Explain your answer.

52. How much grain can a silo hold if it is a cylinder with a height of 12.4 m and circular base of diameter 7.2 m?

53. If someone is painting the outside of the silo in Question 52, what area must be covered by paint? (The bottom will not be painted.)

54. A building is shaped like a triangular prism. Its base has an area of 75 m^2 and it will be 12 m tall. Each floor is to be 3 m tall.
    a. What is the volume of one floor?
    b. What is the volume of the entire building?

55. Find the area of wallpaper needed to cover the walls of a rectangular room of length 5 m, width 4 m, and height 2.5 m.

REPRESENTATIONS Pictures, graphs, or objects that illustrate concepts

OBJECTIVE M Draw and label a net for a given box. (Lesson 9-7)

In 56 and 57, draw and label a net for the given box.

56.

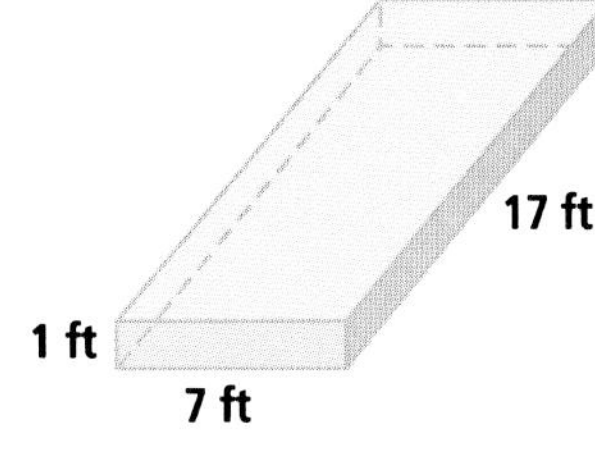

57.

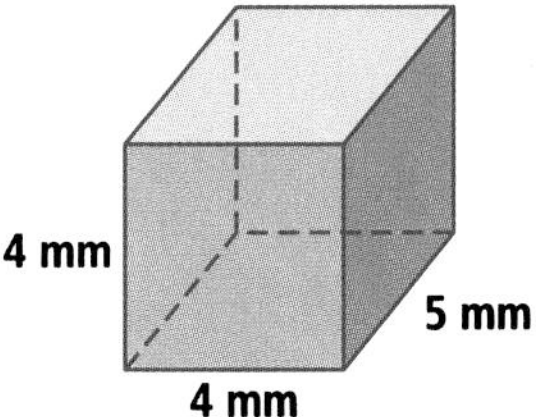

In 58 and 59, draw and label a net for the given box. Notice that one face is missing.

58.

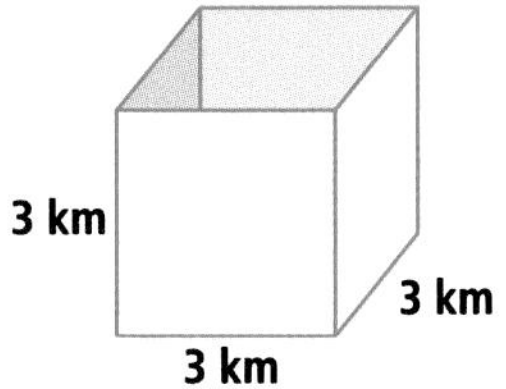

59.

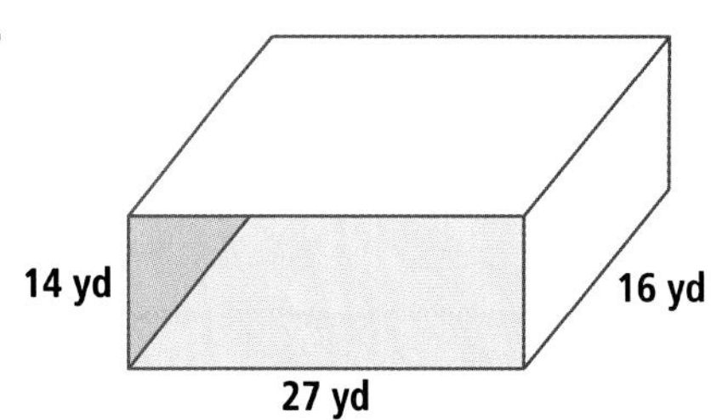

60. **Multiple Choice** Which cannot be a net for a box?

A

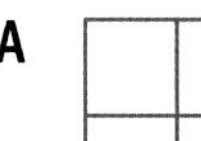

B

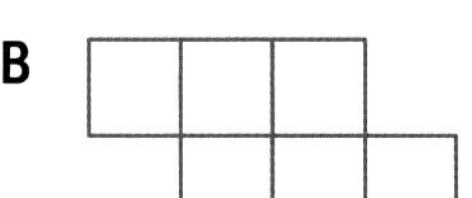

C

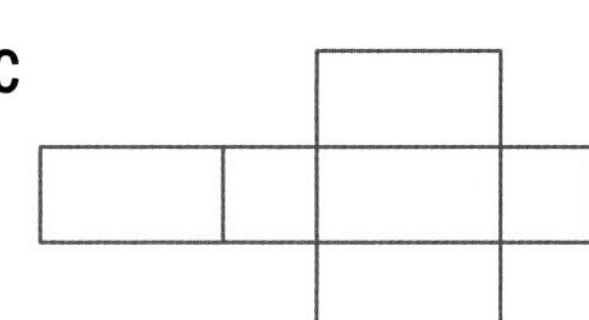

D

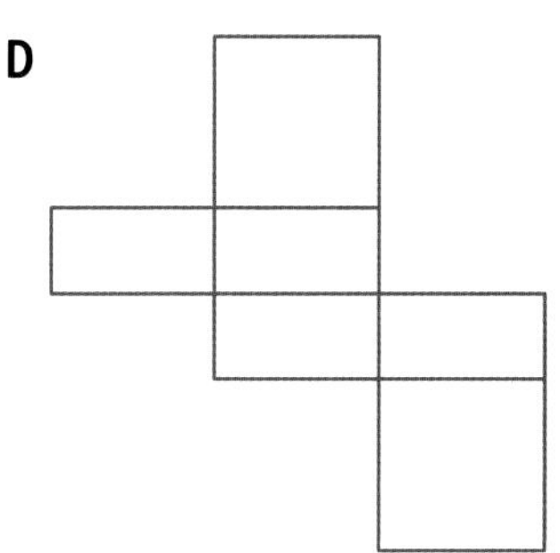

Chapter

10 Probability

Contents

The *probability* of an event is a number from 0 to 1 that indicates how likely the event is. If you know an event's probability, you can tell whether the event is to be expected or whether it is a surprise.

Here are some typical questions that involve probability.

Is this unusual? You are riding in a car and see that the car in front of you has a license plate with five odd digits and no even digits.

How lucky is this? You are at a party that has a haunted-house maze. After walking through the maze, you hope to end up in the goblin room with all the party favors. You are successful on your first trip through the maze.

Is this game fair? A friend describes a game involving three playing cards in a bag: two kings and one queen. Without looking, you pick two cards from the bag. Your friend says he wins if the cards you pick are different. If the cards you pick are the same, you win.

Can he miss four free throws in a row? Rick Barry led the National Basketball Association in free-throw shooting percentage six times, more than any other player. His career percentage was .900, or 90%.

Is the coin biased? You toss a coin 20 times and 13 heads occur. You wonder if the coin is biased. What if you toss a coin 2,000 times and 1,300 heads occur?

In this chapter, you will study the ideas needed to answer these questions along with many others related to probability.

Lesson 10-1 The Multiplication Counting Principle

Vocabulary

tree diagram

BIG IDEA Some counting problems can be solved by multiplying key numbers in the problem.

How many toes do you have? How many students are in your class today? Counting by ones will answer these questions.

How many license plates are possible in your state? How many different phone numbers are possible in the United States? Ordinary counting will not work here. There are too many possibilities. In situations like these, you can use multiplication to find counts.

Mental Math

Calculate.

a. $2 \cdot 3$

b. $2 \cdot 3 \cdot 4$

c. $2 \cdot 3 \cdot 4 \cdot 5$

d. $2 \cdot 3 \cdot 4 \cdot 5 \cdot 6$

Example 1

Sixth graders at Lincoln Middle School have choices in three areas. They must choose Spanish or French for foreign language; band, orchestra, or choir for music; and tutoring or recycling for community service. How many different course selections are possible among these areas?

The first recycling center in the United States officially opened its doors in 1896.

Solution 1 List all the possible course selections. To save time, use only the first letters. So Spanish-Band-Tutoring becomes S-B-T. Arrange your work systematically.

S-B-T S-O-T S-C-T F-B-T F-O-T F-C-T

S-B-R S-O-R S-C-R F-B-R F-O-R F-C-R

There are 12 different course selections possible.

Solution 2 Make a *tree diagram*. Begin by connecting a point to the 2 language choices: Spanish and French. Each of these choices is then connected to each of the 3 possible music choices, creating a second layer of the "tree." Each of the branches in this second layer is then connected to each of the 2 community service choices.

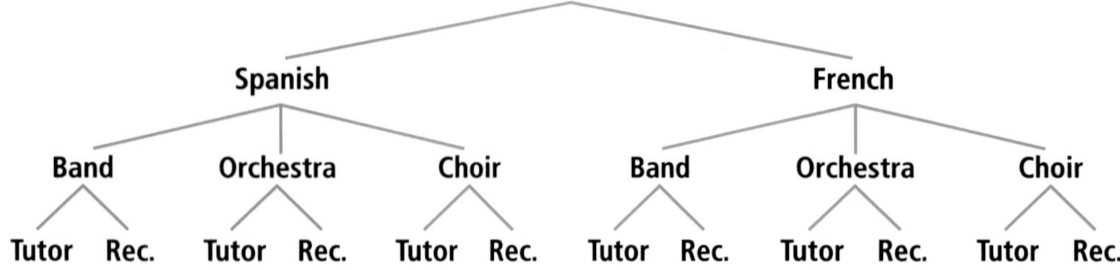

Following the branches at the far left, you see the outcome S-B-T because Spanish is connected to Band, which is connected to Tutoring. The tree diagram gives the same possible outcomes as in Solution 1.

The diagram in Solution 2 is called a **tree diagram** because if you turn the diagram 180° it looks like a tree with branches.

 **See QY at the right.**

 **QY**

How many different course selections include Orchestra?

Solution 2 shows that the number of course selections can be found by multiplication. In this case, there are 2 language choices, 3 music choices, and 2 community-service choices. Multiplying these numbers gives $2 \cdot 3 \cdot 2 = 12$ course selections. The general idea is called the *Multiplication Counting Principle.*

Multiplication Counting Principle

If one choice can be made in m ways, and a second choice can then always be made in n ways, then there are mn ways of making the first choice followed by the second choice.

The Multiplication Counting Principle can be applied to any number of choices.

Example 2

How many four-digit numbers are even?

Solution Use the Multiplication Counting Principle. Think of four spaces to be filled, one for each digit of a four-digit number.

$\underline{?} \quad \underline{?} \quad \underline{?} \quad \underline{?}$

The leftmost digit is the thousands digit. Any digit from 1 to 9 can be that digit, so there are 9 choices for that digit. Put 9 in that space.

$\underline{9} \quad \underline{?} \quad \underline{?} \quad \underline{?}$

There are 10 choices (0, 1, 2, 3, 4, 5, 6, 7, 8, 9) each for the hundreds and tens digits, so put 10 in each of those spaces.

$\underline{9} \quad \underline{10} \quad \underline{10} \quad \underline{?}$

Since the number is even, there are 5 choices for the ones digit: 0, 2, 4, 6, and 8. Put 5 in the rightmost space.

$\underline{9} \quad \underline{10} \quad \underline{10} \quad \underline{5}$

There are $9 \cdot 10 \cdot 10 \cdot 5 = 4{,}500$ even four-digit numbers.

GUIDED

Example 3

In California, many license plates have three letters followed by three digits. For instance, MIL 677 is a possible license plate. In 2006, California had about 18.5 million registered passenger cars. Were there enough different license plates of this type for these cars?

Solution There are six spaces to be filled.

? ? ? ? ? ?

There are ? choices for each letter space, and there are ? choices for each digit space. (0 is allowed to be a digit.)

To determine how many different license plates there are, multiply.

? • ? • ? • ? • ? • ? = ?

Since ? < 18.5 million, there were not enough license plates of this type for all the registered passenger cars in California in 2006.

Questions

COVERING THE IDEAS

1. Suppose you have a red shirt, a white shirt, and a light blue shirt, and you have five pair of slacks: brown, black, blue, tan, and grey.
   a. Make a tree diagram to show all the possible outfits you could wear.
   b. How many outfits are possible?
2. a. How many possible license plates have two digits followed by four letters? (Assume that 0 is allowed for either digit.)
   b. How many possible license plates have four digits followed by two letters?
   c. Why are the answers to Parts a and b different?

License plates are also referred to as vehicle registration plates, number plates, and vehicle tags.

3. A pizzeria advertises that because you can choose from 2 kinds of crust, 3 kinds of cheese, and 12 different toppings, over 100 different kinds of pizza are possible. Is the advertisement true?
4. How many three-digit numbers end in a 3?
5. How many five-digit numbers start and end with even digits and have odd digits in the other three places?
6. A teacher says that every student must read a short story and a poem this week from a list of S short stories and six poems. How many different pairs of short stories and poems could students read?

7. Every day students choose from the same choices for lunch: 6 entrees, 4 side dishes, 5 drinks, and 3 desserts.
   a. If you eat in the cafeteria every school day, how many days could you go without repeating the same meal?
   b. If you choose coleslaw as your side dish, how many different meals are possible?
   c. If you have the same side dish and drink every day, how many different meals are possible?

In recent years, school cafeterias have made a concentrated effort to offer healthier items.

8. Suppose you roll a die three times. One possible outcome is 3-6-1. How many different outcomes are there?

9. The tree diagram below describes some 3-digit area codes. Find all the possible area codes represented by this tree diagram.

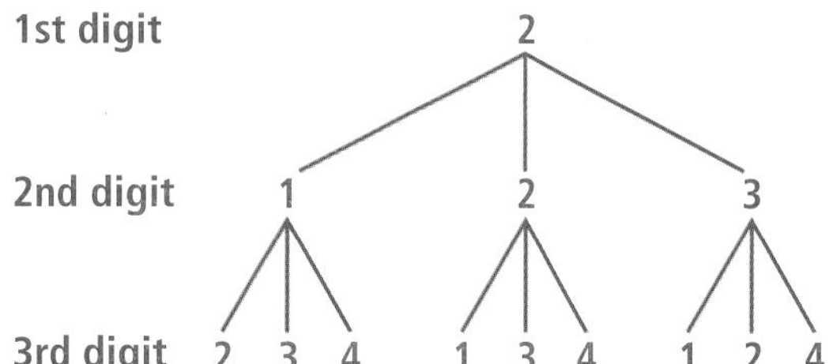

APPLYING THE MATHEMATICS

10. The following is a list of all the possible 3-letter words beginning with B or P and ending with D or T with a vowel A, E, I, O, or U in between. Make a tree diagram of these 20 words. BAD, BAT, BED, BET, BID, BIT, BOD, BOT, BUD, BUT, PAD, PAT, PED, PET, PID, PIT, POD, POT, PUD, PUT.

11. Suppose you toss a coin four times. One possible outcome is HTTH, which means you get heads on the first and last tosses and tails on the other two tosses.
    a. Make a tree diagram to show all the possible outcomes if a coin is tossed four times.
    b. How many outcomes are there?
    c. Use the Multiplication Counting Principle to check Part b.
    d. How many outcomes other than HTTH have exactly 2 heads?
    e. What percent of the outcomes have exactly two heads?

12. a. How many four-digit numbers have only even digits?
    b. How many four-digit numbers have only odd digits?
    c. Why are the answers to Parts a and b not equal?
    d. Is it unusual to find a five-digit license plate with all odd digits?

13. a. Use the Multiplication Counting Principle to find the number of two-letter ordered pairs that can be made with the vowels a, e, i, o, and u. For example, one possible pair is (a, e).
    b. List all the two-letter ordered pairs *with different letters* that can be made with the vowels a, e, i, o, and u.
    c. Use the Multiplication Counting Principle to find the number of pairs in your list for Part b.

REVIEW

In 14 and 15, suppose a cardboard shipping container is a cube measuring 21 inches on one edge. (Lesson 9-8)

14. What is its surface area? **15.** What is its volume?

16. a. Write a division statement described by the array at the right.

b. If the same number of dots were placed in an array with ten dots in each row, how many rows would be filled? How many dots would be left over? (Lesson 7-2)

In 17 and 18, calculate. (Lesson 6-2)

17. $\frac{2}{3} \cdot \frac{4}{5}$ **18.** $\frac{1}{4} \cdot \frac{3}{7}$

19. If $\frac{1}{3}$ of 630 students are on an athletic team, and $\frac{1}{7}$ of these students are sixth graders, how many sixth graders are on the athletic team? (Lesson 6-2)

EXPLORATION

20. How many ways can books be arranged on a shelf? Arrangements of the kind explored in this problem are called *permutations*. For just one book *A*, there is only one way to put it on a shelf. With two books, *A* and *B*, there are two ways, which can be represented by *AB* and *BA*.

a. Suppose that you have three books, *A*, *B*, and *C*. *BCA* represents one way to arrange the three books on a shelf. Make a list showing all the ways the three books can be arranged on a shelf. How many ways are possible?

b. The Multiplication Counting Principle can also be used to answer Part a. For the first position, there are three books to choose from. For the second position there are only two books left to choose. For the last position there is only one book left. The number of ways is $3 \cdot 2 \cdot 1 = 6$. The table above lists the ways to arrange books. Copy and complete the table.

c. List the ways that four books, *A*, *B*, *C* and *D*, can be arranged on a shelf. Does your count agree with the number you wrote in the table?

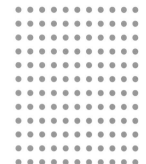

Ways to Arrange Books

Number of Books	Ways to Place	Counting Principle
1	1	1
2	2	$2 \cdot 1$
3	6	$3 \cdot 2 \cdot 1$
4	?	?
5	?	?
6	?	?

QY ANSWER

4

Lesson

10-2 Sample Spaces and Probability

Vocabulary

sample space
event
probability
fair (unbiased)

▶ **BIG IDEA** When the outcomes of a situation are equally likely, the probability of an event is the ratio of the number of outcomes in the event to the number of possible outcomes of the situation.

People often wonder how likely it is for an event to happen. How likely is it that you will roll doubles when playing a board game? How likely is it that a tornado will occur? How likely is it that a person will get the flu?

Mental Math

Calculate.

a. 4^2

b. 2^4

c. $\left(\frac{1}{2}\right)^4$

d. $\left(\frac{1}{4}\right)^2$

Probability

A *probability* is a number from 0 to 1 that expresses how likely it is that an event will occur. A probability can be written as a fraction, decimal, or percent. If an event is impossible, like the sun rising in the west, the probability is 0. If an event is certain, like the sun rising in the east, the probability is 1. The closer an event's probability is to 1, the more likely it is to happen. At the right is a "probability meter," which you may be familiar with from earlier courses.

100%	Certain	1
	Extremely Likely	
90%		0.90
	Very Likely	
80%		0.80
75%		0.75
70%	Likely	0.70
60%		0.60
50%	50-50 Chance	0.50, $\frac{1}{2}$, $\frac{2}{4}$
40%		0.40, $\frac{2}{5}$, $\frac{4}{10}$
30%	Unlikely	0.30, $\frac{3}{10}$
25%		0.25, $\frac{1}{4}$, $\frac{2}{8}$
20%		0.20, $\frac{1}{5}$
	Very Unlikely	
10%		0.10, $\frac{1}{10}$
	Extremely Unlikely	
0%	Impossible	0, $\frac{0}{100}$

See QY1 at the right.

QY1

What is wrong with the statement, "I am 110% certain our team will win the baseball game today."

A **sample space** S is the set of all possible outcomes of a situation. An **event** is any set of outcomes from the sample space.

Definition of Probability (for equally likely outcomes)

Let E be an event that consists of some of the outcomes of a sample space S. If the outcomes are equally likely, then the **probability** of E, denoted $P(E)$, is defined as follows:

$$P(E) = \frac{\text{number of outcomes in } E}{\text{number of outcomes in } S}$$

QY2

Suppose a hat contains cards labeled *A, A, A, A, A, A, B, B, B, C, C*, and *D*. You draw one card without looking.

a. What is the number of outcomes in the sample space *S*?

b. What is P(*B*), the probability you will draw a *B*?

When the outcomes of a situation are equally likely, the situation is called **fair,** or **unbiased.** Similarly, a coin or die is fair if the possible outcomes of a toss are equally likely.

Using a List to Find a Sample Space

Because of the definition of probability, identifying the number of outcomes in the sample space is an important part of determining a probability. One way to determine the sample space is to list all of its outcomes.

GUIDED

Example 1

Three fair coins—a penny, a nickel, and a dime—are tossed together. What is the probability that 1 head and 2 tails appear?

Solution Make a list of the outcomes in the sample space. First, list all the outcomes with the penny showing heads. List the penny first, then the nickel, and then the dime. Use H for heads, T for tails.

HHH HHT HTH ___?___

Next, list the outcomes where the penny lands tails up.

___?___ ___?___ ___?___ ___?___

The sample space has ___?___ outcomes. Of these outcomes, ___?___ have 1 head and 2 tails.

Since the coins are fair, the probability of getting 1 head and 2 tails is ___?___.

Using the Multiplication Counting Principle to Find the Size of a Sample Space

Consider this situation from the first pages of this chapter: "You are riding in a car and see that the car in front of you has a license plate with five odd digits and no even digits. Is this unusual?" Example 2 uses the Multiplication Counting Principle to answer this question.

GUIDED

Example 2

What is the probability that a five-digit license plate has all odd digits?

Solution The sample space is the set of possible five-digit plates. Let *E* be the set of license plates with all odd digits. Then:

$$P(E) = \frac{\text{number of all-odd-digit license-plate numbers}}{\text{number of 5-digit license-plate numbers}}$$

If 0 is allowed to be the first digit, then there are ten possibilities for each place: 0, 1, 2, 3, 4, 5, 6, 7, 8, and 9. Using the Multiplication Counting Principle, there are

_?_ • _?_ • _?_ • _?_ • _?_ = _?_ possible 5-digit license plates

Now find the number of plates with all odd digits. First, list the odd digits: _?_. Again, using the Multiplication Counting Principle, there are _?_ • _?_ • _?_ • _?_ • _?_ = _?_ possible license plates with all odd digits.

Thus, the probability that a five-digit license plate will have all odd digits is, $\frac{3{,}125}{100{,}000}$, which in lowest terms is _?_, or as a decimal = _?_, and as a percent = _?_.

Looking at the result of Example 2, someone might say, "You picked the wrong sample space! It should include all the license plates with 5 *letters or numbers,* including license plates such as AB123 and XLNCF." Then the sample space would be larger, so the probability would be smaller.

GUIDED

Example 3

What is the probability that a license plate with five *digits or letters* has five odd digits? Do not allow the letters O and I because they get confused with the digits 0 and 1.

Solution The sample space *S* is the set of all five-symbol license plates, where the symbols are digits or letters except O and I. There are _?_ digits and _?_ letters possible for each space, so there are _?_ symbols possible for each space.

There are 5 spaces, so by the Multiplication Counting Principle, there are _?_ • _?_ • _?_ • _?_ • _?_, outcomes in S.

Let *E* be the set of all license plates with five odd digits. From Guided Example 2, there are _?_ outcomes in *E*.

$$P(E) = \frac{\text{number of outcomes in E}}{\text{number of outcomes in S}} = \frac{?}{?} \approx 0.00006878$$

With the sample space used in Guided Example 3, you can see why seeing a license plate with five odd digits might be so unusual. Out of all license plates, fewer than 7 in 100,000 have that property.

Questions

COVERING THE IDEAS

1. What is the *sample space* of a situation?

2. Refer to the situation in Guided Example 1. What is the probability that all three coins land tails up?

3. a. Make a list of the sample space if a fair nickel and a fair dime are tossed together.
   b. What is the probability of two heads?
   c. What is the probability of two tails?
   d. What is the probability of one head and one tail?

4. Refer to Guided Example 2. Do you think a license plate with all odd digits is unusual? Explain your answer.

5. Suppose you see a license plate with four digits that are all even, such as 0484.
   a. If a license plate has four digits, what is the probability that they are all even digits?
   b. If a license plate has four symbols that are either digits or letters (not including I or O), what is the probability that all four symbols are even digits?
   c. What is different about Parts a and b, the sample space or the event?

6. a. Find the probability that a seven-digit number has all 8s or 9s if you allow the first digit to be 0.
   b. Find the probability that a seven-digit number has all 8s or 9s if you do *not* allow the first digit to be 0.
   c. Which sample space is bigger, the one in Part a or the one in Part b?

7. Five blue chips, three red chips, and two yellow chips are placed in a box, and one chip is drawn at random.
   a. How many outcomes are in the sample space?
   b. What is the probability the drawn chip is blue?
   c. What is the probability the drawn chip is red?
   d. What is the probability the drawn chip is green?

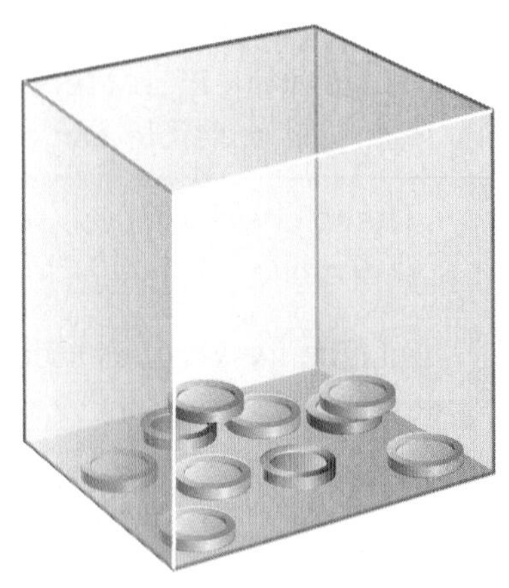

APPLYING THE MATHEMATICS

8. In Guided Example 2, what is the probability all digits will be odd if the first digit cannot be 0? Write your answer as a decimal approximation.

In 9 and 10, consider an event to be unusual if its probability is less than 1%.

9. You can write a date by writing the numbers for the month, the day of the month, and the year, separated by slashes. For example, February 9, 2009, can be written 2/9/2009.
   a. Calculate the probability that a date in the year 2009 will have only the digits 2, 0, or 9.
   b. Is the event in Part a unusual?
10. You toss a fair coin seven times.
    a. What is the probability of the event "heads occurs every time"?
    b. What is the probability of the event "the coin lands the same side up every time"?
    c. Is either the event in Part a or the event in Part b unusual?

11. Lakita puts cards with letters of the alphabet in a hat. There is exactly one card for each letter. Then she draws a card at random.
    a. Describe the sample space.
    b. What is the probability she draws a vowel?
    c. What is the probability she draws a letter in the word *math*?
    d. What is the probability she draws a letter between h and p (not including h and p) in the alphabet?

12. In the situation of Question 11, if Lakita puts the card back and then draws a card at random, what is the probability that the second card is the same card as the first card she drew? Explain your answer.

13. The words *capacity*, *candle*, and *napkin* are written on pieces of paper, cut up into individual letters, and placed in a box. One letter is drawn out of the box. The three letters that have the greatest probability of being drawn form a word for the quote in Question 18 of Lesson 10-6 on page 622.

The first known existence of a necktie was in China in 210 BCE.

Source: infoplease.com

REVIEW

14. The total number of suits and ties that each of the Dapper brothers has is 14. Ned has 4 suits and 10 ties. Ted has 8 suits and 6 ties. Zed has 7 suits and 7 ties. **(Lesson 10-1)**
    a. Who can form the greatest number of different outfits with one suit and one tie?
    b. Who can form the least number of different outfits?

15. Find the area of a circle with diameter 7 inches. **(Lesson 9-4)**

16. The *resistance* of an electrical circuit (in ohms) is a measure of how much a circuit opposes, or resists the passage of electric current. The *conductance* (in mhos) measures how easily current flows through the circuit. The conductance is the reciprocal of the resistance. Copy and complete the table below, showing the value of these quantities in commercially available resistors. **(Lesson 8-2)**

Resistance (ohms)	Conductance (mhos)
0.0001	?
0.005	?
0.3	?
1	?
15	?
750	?
10,000	?

In a circuit, electricity must flow from a power source to a switch, then to an electrical appliance, and then back to the power source to power the appliance.

Source: Southern Polytechnic State University

17. Write the prime factorization of one trillion. **(Lesson 7-3)**

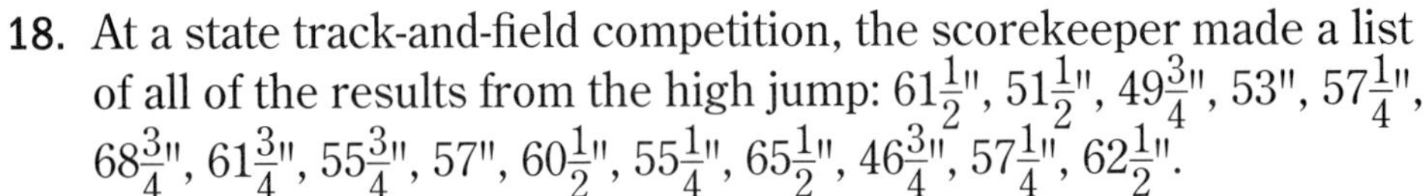

18. At a state track-and-field competition, the scorekeeper made a list of all of the results from the high jump: $61\frac{1}{2}''$, $51\frac{1}{2}''$, $49\frac{3}{4}''$, $53''$, $57\frac{1}{4}''$, $68\frac{3}{4}''$, $61\frac{3}{4}''$, $55\frac{3}{4}''$, $57''$, $60\frac{1}{2}''$, $55\frac{1}{4}''$, $65\frac{1}{2}''$, $46\frac{3}{4}''$, $57\frac{1}{4}''$, $62\frac{1}{2}''$.
    a. Round each height to the nearest whole number of inches. (Round halves up.) Then create a stem-and-leaf plot of these data.
    b. Did more people jump between 5 feet and 5 feet, 6 inches or between 4 feet, 6 inches and 5 feet? **(Lesson 5-3)**

EXPLORATION

19. Find at least one probability reference in a newspaper or magazine article or on the Internet. What event is being described? What is the sample space? Is it likely or unlikely?

QY ANSWERS

1. It is impossible to have a probability greater than 100%.

2a. 12

2b. $\frac{1}{4}$

Lesson 10-3 Probability Tree Diagrams

BIG IDEA Tree diagrams are useful for calculating probabilities in situations that involve one choice after another.

Writing a tree diagram can be a lot of work. Why would you want to create such a diagram? One reason is that by putting the probabilities of various outcomes on a tree diagram, you can answer some questions about probabilities of events that are not equally likely.

Example 1

Three workers in an office take turns bringing breakfast for each other on Fridays. This Friday's theme is "Bagel Grab Bag." Ms. Blackwell has put a sesame bagel, a whole wheat bagel, and an onion bagel in one bag. In another bag, she has put two servings of plain cream cheese and two servings of veggie cream cheese. Each worker randomly grabs a bagel out of one bag and a serving of cream cheese out of the other bag. What is the probability that Ms. Blackwell will grab a whole wheat bagel and plain cream cheese if she is the first to pick?

Solution Make a tree diagram of the possible outcomes.

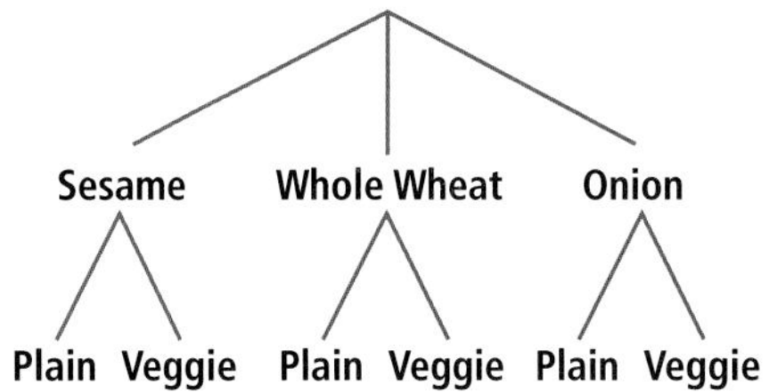

When Ms. Blackwell grabs a bagel, there is a 1 out of 3, or $\frac{1}{3}$ probability she will grab each one of the three bagels. So put $\frac{1}{3}$ by each branch, as shown below. The probability of choosing each flavor of cream cheese is $\frac{2}{4}$, or $\frac{1}{2}$. Add this information to the tree diagram. To find the probability for a combination (for example, a sesame bagel with plain cream cheese), multiply the probabilities leading to it. Ms. Blackwell has a $\frac{1}{3} \cdot \frac{1}{2}$, or $\frac{1}{6}$, chance of choosing a whole wheat bagel with plain cream cheese.

$\frac{1}{3}$ $\frac{1}{3}$ $\frac{1}{3}$

Sesame Whole Wheat Onion

$\frac{1}{2}$ $\frac{1}{2}$ $\frac{1}{2}$ $\frac{1}{2}$ $\frac{1}{2}$ $\frac{1}{2}$

Plain Veggie Plain Veggie Plain Veggie

$\frac{1}{6}$ $\frac{1}{6}$ $\frac{1}{6}$ $\frac{1}{6}$ $\frac{1}{6}$ $\frac{1}{6}$

Check The probabilities for the final outcomes should add to 1:
$\frac{1}{6} + \frac{1}{6} + \frac{1}{6} + \frac{1}{6} + \frac{1}{6} + \frac{1}{6} = 1.$

Mental Math

a. What is the area of a rectangle with side lengths of 1 unit and 3 units?

b. What is the area of a square with perimeter 8 units?

c. True or False A rectangle with perimeter 8 units that is not a square will have an area smaller than the square in Part b.

In the next example, the situation does not have equally likely outcomes.

Example 2

The maze at the right shows part of a haunted house. Suppose a person enters the maze at the top and makes a decision randomly whenever a path branches. Rewrite the maze as a tree diagram and insert the probabilities.

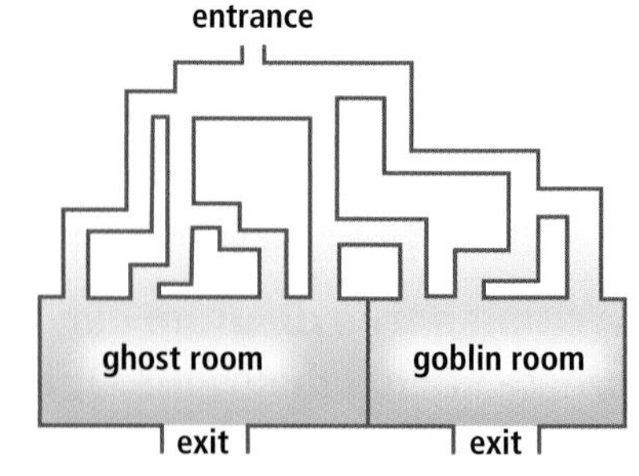

Solution Write probabilities at each branch point of the maze. There are four choices of paths at the beginning, each with probability $\frac{1}{4}$. Label each path.

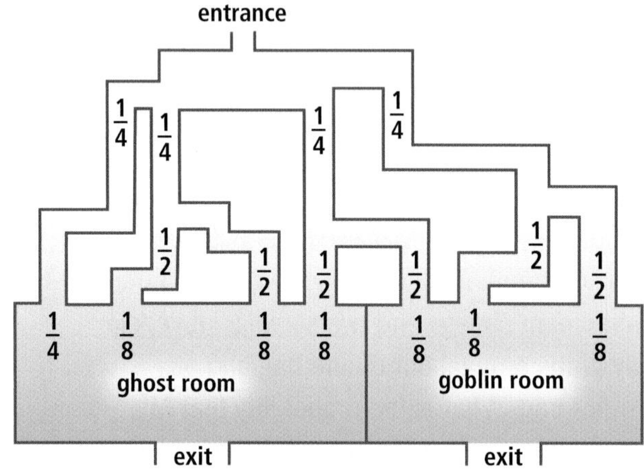

Now look at each new branch. The left branch goes directly to the ghost room. The other branches each have one place where the path branches into two. In those places, write $\frac{1}{2}$ by each part. Multiply the probabilities for each path to find the probability of entering the ghost room and goblin room by each door.

Here is the same maze, represented as a tree diagram. Compare this diagram with the maze.

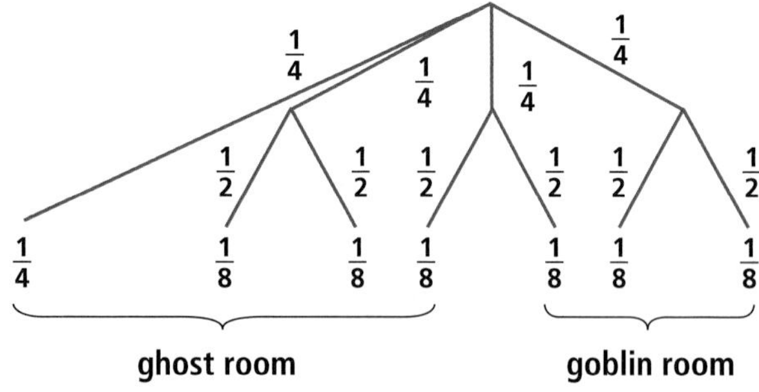

QY1

Check that the probabilities in the bottom row of the tree diagram at the left sum to 1.

GUIDED

Example 3

Using the probability tree from Example 2, calculate the probability that a person will end up in the Ghost Room.

Solution There are four paths that will lead a person to the Ghost Room, and their probabilities are _?_, _?_, _?_, and _?_. Add these probabilities. The probability that the person will arrive in the Ghost Room is $\frac{5}{8}$.

QY2

What is the probability that the person will arrive in the Goblin Room?

Activity

The spinner at the right has an equal probability of landing in each of the four regions. Suppose the spinner is spun twice.

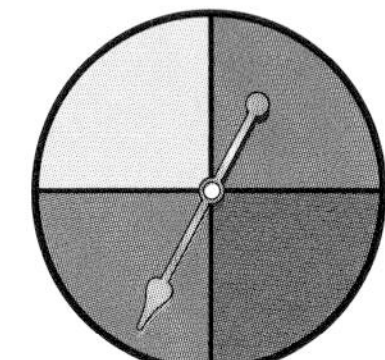

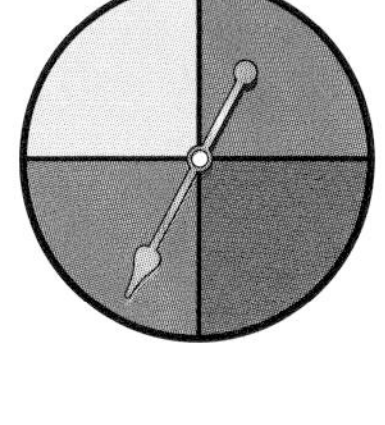

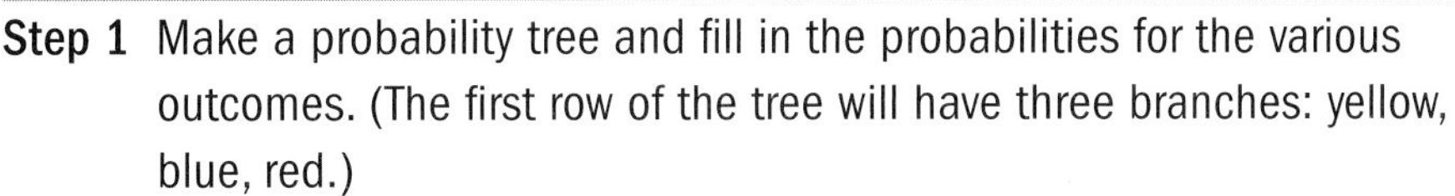

Step 1 Make a probability tree and fill in the probabilities for the various outcomes. (The first row of the tree will have three branches: yellow, blue, red.)

Step 2 What is the probability of landing in a blue region both times?

Step 3 What is the probability of landing in a red region and then a yellow region in the two spins?

Questions

COVERING THE IDEAS

1. Refer to Example 1.
   a. What is the probability that Ms. Blackwell will grab an onion bagel and plain cream cheese?
   b. What is the probability that Ms. Blackwell will pick a bagel that is not sesame?
2. The maze at the right shows another part of the haunted house from Example 2. Again assume a person makes decisions randomly when faced with a choice.
   a. Create a probability tree from this maze.
   b. What is the probability of entering the trick room?
   c. What is the probability of entering the treat room?
   d. What is the sum of the answers to Parts b and c?

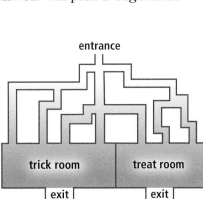

3. Alyssa has a few decisions to make this morning. She can wear her hair in braids or a ponytail. For breakfast she can eat bran flakes, oatmeal, or yogurt. To get to school, she can walk with friends or ride her bike.
   a. Create a tree diagram showing all the possible outcomes of Alyssa's choices.
   b. If Alyssa decides to pull her choices out of a hat without looking, what is the probability of each outcome?

In 4–6, refer to the Activity on page 599.

4. What is the probability that, spun once, the spinner will land on red?
5. What is the probability that, spun twice, the spinner will land on red both times?
6. Add the probabilities of all the possible outcomes if the spinner is spun twice. What is the sum of the probabilities?
7. Consider the two spinners below. Each circle is divided into equal sectors.

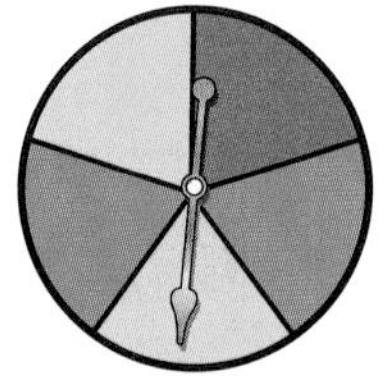

Spinner I

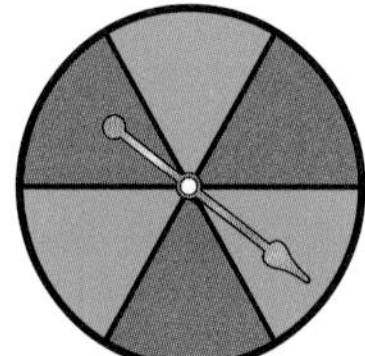

Spinner II

   a. Create a probability tree showing the possible pairs of colors and their probabilities when a person spins Spinner I first, followed by Spinner II.
   b. Check that your probabilities sum to 1.
   c. What is the probability of landing on red both times?
   d. What is the probability of landing on blue, then green?
   e. What is the probability of landing on blue, then yellow?

APPLYING THE MATHEMATICS

8. A student in a new school is looking for the north gym. He begins at the entrance at the left and makes decisions randomly as to which direction to go.
   a. What is the probability the student will enter the north gym?
   b. What is the probability the student will enter the cafeteria first, then walk back, and then enter the north gym?

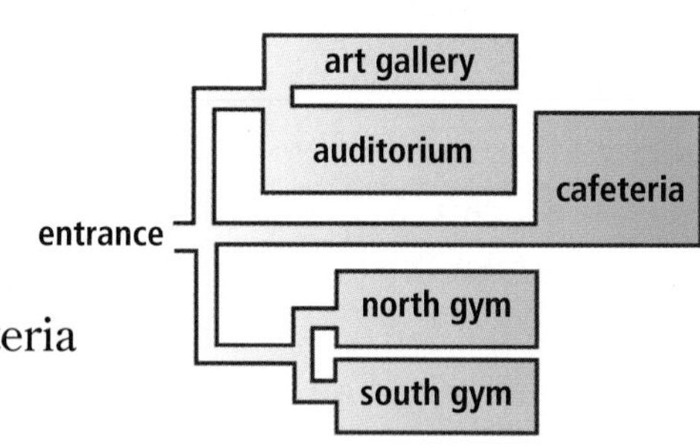

9. Think about Alyssa's breakfast choices in Question 3. Imagine Alyssa determines her breakfast the following way:

   Step 1 Flip a coin. If heads, eat bran flakes. If tails, eliminate bran flakes and go to Step 2.

   Step 2 Flip a coin. If heads, eat oatmeal. If tails, eat yogurt.

   a. Make a probability tree for this situation.

   b. Does each breakfast food have an equal chance of being eaten by Alyssa? Explain why or why not.

10. Raheem is picking his clothes from the following choices: blue jeans, sweat pants, khakis; yellow T-shirt, grey T-shirt; jean jacket, hooded sweatshirt, and red fleece. He will randomly pick one item from each category, with one exception: if he picks the blue jeans, he won't choose the jean jacket because he doesn't like to wear jeans with a jean jacket.

    a. Represent this situation with a tree diagram.

    b. What is the probability that Raheem will wear sweat pants, a yellow T-shirt, and a red fleece?

    c. What is the probability that Raheem will wear blue jeans, a yellow T-shirt, and a jean jacket?

In 11 and 12, use the following information. Once a week, Julio travels from New York City to Chicago for a meeting. He has four choices of morning flights out of LaGuardia Airport (LGA) in New York City and three choices for evening flights out of O'Hare Airport (ORD) in Chicago.

Flights from LGA to ORD	Flights from ORD to LGA
6:00 A.M.	6:00 P.M.
7:00 A.M.	7:00 P.M.
8:00 A.M.	8:30 P.M.
9:00 A.M.	

11. Show all the possible pairs of flights on a tree diagram.

12. If Julio randomly selects departing and returning flights, calculate the probability of each of the following:

    a. Julio takes the 9:00 A.M. flight to Chicago.

    b. Julio returns on the 7:00 P.M. flight to New York.

    c. Julio takes the 9:00 A.M. flight and returns on the 7:00 P.M. flight.

    d. Julio leaves for Chicago before 8:00 A.M.

    e. Julio does not return on the 6:00 P.M. flight.

    f. Julio boards a return flight 12 hours after boarding a morning flight.

13. A paper bag holds three eggs. One is cooked and two are raw. An egg is randomly selected and then returned to the bag three times.
   a. Show the possible outcomes from the three selections. For instance, if you pick a raw egg first, and then the cooked egg the other two times, the outcome is RCC.
   b. What is the probability the egg will be raw each time?
   c. What is the probability the egg will be cooked each time?
   d. What is the probability you will pick a cooked egg once and a raw egg twice?

REVIEW

14. An unabridged English dictionary contains about 1,000 three-letter words. If the three letters are each chosen at random from the alphabet, what is the probability that they form a word? **(Lesson 10-2)**

15. A salad bar has three types of lettuce: iceberg, romaine, and mixed greens; and five kinds of salad dressing: Italian, Russian, Thousand Island, French, and oil and vinegar. The salads come with one of two types of bread: white and whole wheat. Draw a tree diagram to determine how many different salads are possible. **(Lesson 10-1)**

A salad is a good way to meet the USDA's recommended guideline of daily vegetable intake.

16. How many positive 3-digit even numbers are there? **(Lesson 10-1)**

17. If 15 out of 24 students in a class do *not* bike to school, what percent of the students do bike to school? **(Lesson 6-6)**

18. Find each statistic below for the following data set: 23, 8, 5, 14, 5, 22, 5, 18. Arrange the statistics from least to greatest. Save the corresponding word for the quote in Question 18 in Lesson 10-6 on page 622 at the end of the chapter. **(Lesson 5-2)**

E	Mean = ?	**R**	Sum of data = ?
N	Median = ?	**E**	Number of pieces of data = ?
W	Mode = ?	**H**	Minimum = ?
E	Maximum = ?	**V**	Range = ?

19. **True or False** -23 is a solution of $15 - x = -8$ **(Lesson 4-9)**

EXPLORATION

20. Each day Belinda has a choice of three ways to walk home. She makes her decision by looking at the first car that drives by and using the last digit in its license plate. If the digit is a 1, 2, or 3, she takes the route by the library. If the digit is a 4, 5, 6, or 7, she takes the route past the convenience store. If the digit is an 8, 9, or 0, she takes the route through the park. Assume the digits occur randomly. What is the probability that she will take the same route all five days next week?

QY ANSWERS

1. Yes; $\frac{3}{8} + \frac{5}{8} = 1$
2. $\frac{3}{8}$

Lesson 10-4 Fair Games

Vocabulary

fair game

unfair game

▸ **BIG IDEA** You can use probability to determine whether a game is fair or unfair.

Luis and Miranda were arguing about who would stay home to baby-sit their younger sister. Luis grabbed three playing cards—two kings and one queen. He told Miranda to choose a card, look at it, and then choose another card. If her two cards matched, then she would win. If they did not match, he would win. Miranda was suspicious. She wasn't sure whether this was fair or not.

Mental Math

The probability that an event occurs is given. What is the probability that the event will not occur?

a. $\frac{1}{2}$

b. $\frac{2}{13}$

c. 61%

d. 0.3%

e. 0.995

f. 0.0007

Example 1

For the game described above, find P(Miranda wins) and P(Luis wins).

Solution 1 Make a tree diagram to analyze the game. The first set of branches shows the three choices for the first pick. Given the choice of the first card, the second set of branches shows the two remaining choices for the second pick.

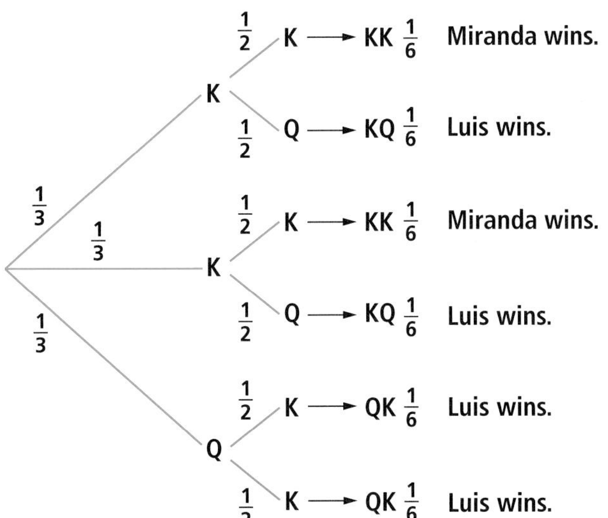

Miranda wins with 2 of the 6 possible outcomes, each of which has a probability of $\frac{1}{6}$. Therefore P(Miranda wins) $= \frac{2}{6}$, or $\frac{1}{3}$. Luis has 4 different ways to win, so P(Luis wins) $= \frac{4}{6}$, or $\frac{2}{3}$.

(continued on next page)

Solution 2 You can combine the two branches that show Miranda picking a king on her first draw as shown below.

$\frac{2}{3}$ K, then $\frac{1}{2}$ K → KK $\frac{2}{3} \cdot \frac{1}{2} = \frac{2}{6}$ **Miranda wins.**

$\frac{2}{3}$ K, then $\frac{1}{2}$ Q → KQ $\frac{2}{3} \cdot \frac{1}{2} = \frac{2}{6}$ **Luis wins.**

$\frac{1}{3}$ Q, then $\frac{2}{2}$ K → QK $\frac{1}{3} \cdot \frac{2}{2} = \frac{1}{3}$ **Luis wins.**

P(Miranda wins) $= \frac{2}{6}$, or $\frac{1}{3}$. P(Luis wins) $= \frac{2}{6} + \frac{1}{3}$, or $\frac{2}{3}$.

QY

Explain the meaning of "$\frac{2}{2}$" along the bottom branch of the tree diagram above.

Check Always make sure that the sum of the final probabilities on the tree is 1. In Solution 2, $\frac{2}{6} + \frac{2}{6} + \frac{1}{3} = 1$. This does not *guarantee* that the answer is correct. But, if the probabilities do not add to 1, the answer is definitely *not* correct.

A game is a **fair game** if each player has the same chance of winning; otherwise, it is an **unfair game.** The game in Example 1 is an unfair game because the probability that Luis wins is $\frac{2}{3}$, and the probability that Miranda wins is $\frac{1}{3}$.

A Fair Game

An example of a fair game with two players is *Rock, Paper, Scissors.* In this game, there are three hand positions: a fist indicates "rock," a flat palm down indicates "paper," and two fingers extended indicates "scissors." Each player chooses one of the hand positions, and both players display their choices at the same time. The rules of the game are as follows: rock breaks scissors (rock wins), scissors cut paper (scissors win), and paper covers rock (paper wins). If both players display the same hand position, there is a tie and they go again.

Rock

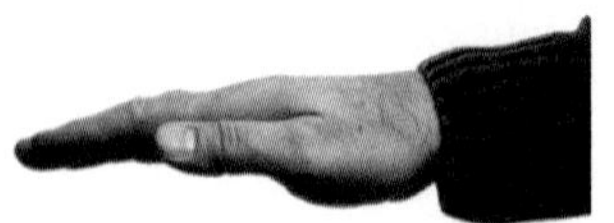
Paper

Scissors

GUIDED

Example 2

Use the tree diagram to help you analyze the outcomes *of Rock, Paper, Scissors.* Complete the table at the right. Is the game fair?

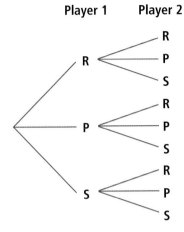

Outcome	Who wins?
RR	tie
RP	Player 2
?	?
?	?
?	?
?	?
?	?
?	?
?	?

Solution The tree diagram and table show that for each player P(winning) = _?_ and P(tie) = _?_. The sum of the probabilities equals _?_. Rock, Paper, Scissors is a fair game because __?__.

GUIDED

Example 3

Miranda complained that the game in Example 1 was unfair. So Luis changed the game so that Miranda would pick two cards from 3 kings and 1 queen. If her cards matched, she would win. If not, Luis would win. Is this game fair?

Solution Make a probability tree diagram.

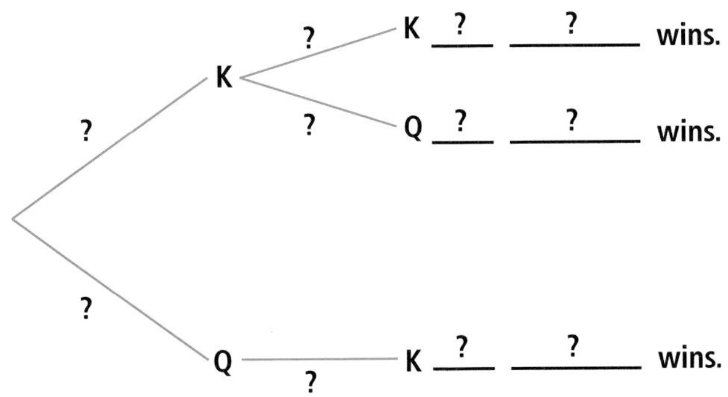

P(Miranda wins) = _?_ P(Luis wins) = _?_

Since the probabilities are _?_, this _?_ a fair game.

Check Is the sum of the final probabilities equal to 1?

Example 4

Suppose you toss two fair pennies. You win if one penny lands heads up and one penny lands tails up. You lose otherwise. Is this a fair game?

Solution 1 Examine the probability tree diagram below.

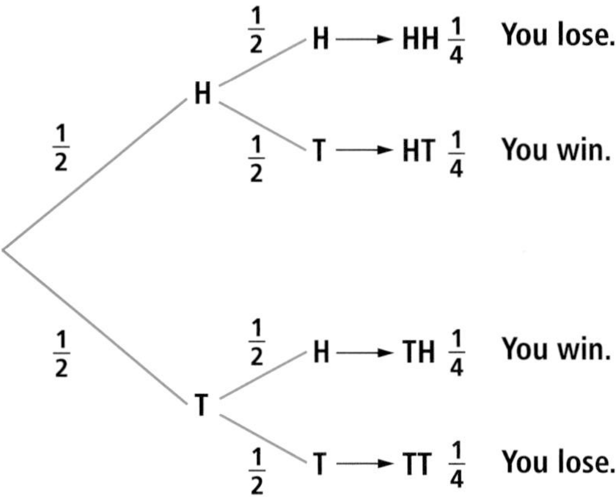

P(you win) is found by adding the probabilities of HT and TH.

$P(\text{you win}) = \frac{1}{4} + \frac{1}{4} = \frac{1}{2}$

P(you lose) is found by adding the probabilities of HH and TT.

$P(\text{you lose}) = \frac{1}{4} + \frac{1}{4} = \frac{1}{2}$

Since P(you win) = P(you lose), the game is fair.

Solution 2 Write all the possibilities: HH, HT, TH, and TT. They all have equal probability since the coin is fair. Since you win on two of the four possibilities, P(you win) $= \frac{2}{4}$, or $\frac{1}{2}$. Since you lose on the other two possibilities, P(you lose) $= \frac{2}{4}$, or $\frac{1}{2}$. The game is fair.

Questions

COVERING THE IDEAS

1. What is meant by a fair game?

2. a. Suppose Luis changes the game in Example 1 so that Miranda chooses from two kings and two queens. Make a probability tree diagram for this game.
   b. Calculate P(cards match).
   c. Calculate P(cards don't match).
   d. Is this game fair?

3. Two white marbles, one red marble, and one blue marble are placed in a jar. Suppose two marbles are drawn randomly at the same time. Copy and complete the probability tree at the right to find P(both are the same color) and P(one red and one blue).

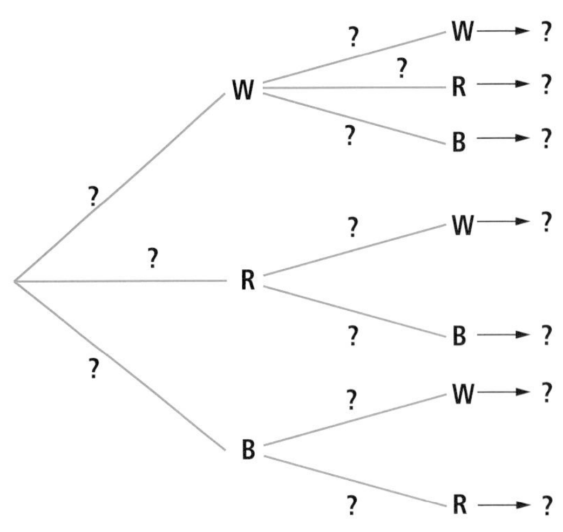

4. Three white marbles, one blue marble, and one red marble are placed in a jar. Two marbles are drawn at random. Find P(two whites) and P(one white and one red).

5. Amber wasn't sure how to check the probabilities for the game in Example 4. She had two answers for the sum of the probabilities from the tree diagram. Which of the two answers below is correct?

   i. $\frac{1}{2} + \frac{1}{2} = 1$ ii. $\frac{1}{2} + \frac{1}{2} = \frac{1}{4}$

   If i. is correct, use the word *count*. If ii. is correct, use the word *read*. Save the word for Question 18 in Lesson 10-6 on page 622.

APPLYING THE MATHEMATICS

6. Suppose you write the letters B, A, N, A, N, A on cards (one letter per card) and put the cards in a hat. You draw one card, look at it and do not replace it, then draw another card. Using a probability tree diagram
   a. find P(one A and one N, in either order).
   b. find P(an A on the first card and an N on the second card).

7. Suppose you have the same situation as in Question 6, but after you look at the first card, you put it back into the hat. Then you draw the second card.
   a. Find P(one A and one N in either order).
   b. Find P(an A on the first card and an N on the second card).

8. Myron has four black socks and four striped socks loose in his drawer. One morning, he pulls out two socks without looking. What is the probability the socks match?

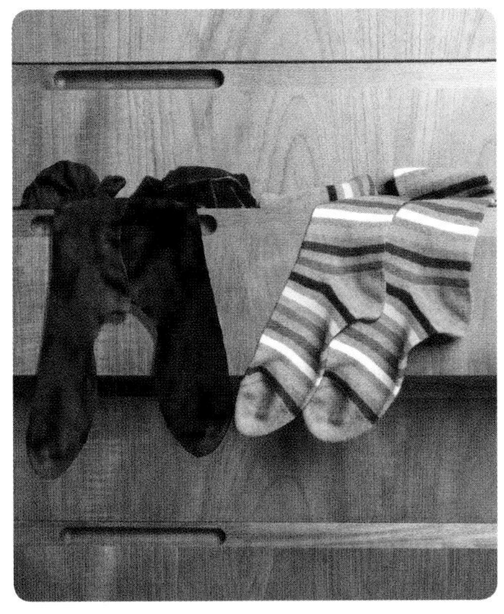

The first real knit socks were discovered in Egyptian tombs from the 3rd to 6th centuries.

Source: about.com

9. The next morning, after Myron's mother has done the wash, he has six loose black socks and six loose blue socks in his drawer. He picks two socks randomly.
   a. What is the probability he picks a blue pair?
   b. What is the probability he picks a black pair?
   c. What is the probability he picks one blue sock and one black sock?
   d. If Myron has 20 socks of each color, does his probability of getting a match increase or decrease? (Answer without making a tree diagram.) Give reasons for your answer.

10. Lulu is shooting free-throws. She normally makes 30% of her shots and misses 70%. However, if she misses her first shot, she makes the second shot only 20% of the time. If Lulu shoots two times, find the probability that
    a. she makes both shots.
    b. she makes exactly one shot.
    c. she misses both shots.

The distance from the basket to the free throw line is 15 feet.

Source: nba.com

REVIEW

In 11 and 12, use the following table.

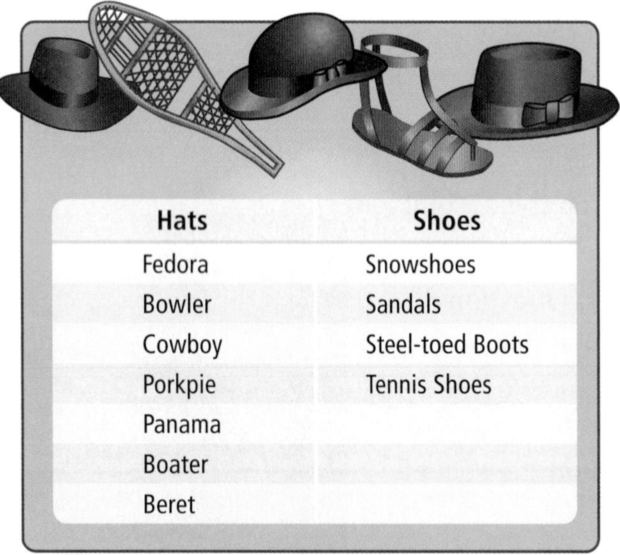

Hats	Shoes
Fedora	Snowshoes
Bowler	Sandals
Cowboy	Steel-toed Boots
Porkpie	Tennis Shoes
Panama	
Boater	
Beret	

11. List all of the possible hat-shoe pairs you can make from the hats and shoes listed in the table. **(Lesson 10-1)**
12. If types of hats and shoes are picked at random, what is the probability of picking a pair with snowshoes? **(Lesson 10-3)**

13. a. How many four-symbol passwords can you make, using letters from the English alphabet? **(Lesson 10-1)**
    b. Answer Part a if you can use all ten digits as well for each symbol.

14. Anwar kept track of how many miles he had driven, starting with a full tank of gas. He kept the results in a table. (Lesson 5-5)

Fraction of Tank Remaining	Miles Traveled
1	0
$\frac{7}{8}$	38
$\frac{3}{4}$	70
$\frac{1}{2}$	151
$\frac{3}{8}$	177
$\frac{1}{4}$	200

a. Draw a line graph of these data. Place Miles Traveled on the x-axis.

b. Estimate how many miles Anwar's car can go before running out of gas.

EXPLORATION

15. Play the game in Example 1 thirty times.

a. How many times did the cards match?

b. If you played the game sixty times, would you expect the number of matches to double? Why or why not?

QY ANSWER

Answers vary. Sample: If the queen is drawn first, there are 2 ways of drawing a king out of a sample space of 2.

Lesson 10-5 Relative Frequency and the Law of Large Numbers

Vocabulary

experiment

trial

▸ **BIG IDEA** As an experiment is repeated more and more times, the relative frequency of an event should get closer to the probability of that event.

In the last lesson, you evaluated games by calculating the probability that each person would win. If each person playing has the same probability of winning, then the game is fair. What actually happens when you play a game a large number of times?

Mental Math

Billy has 40 nickels, Betty has 20 dimes, and Bobby has 10 quarters.

a. Who has the most money?

b. How much money does that person have?

c. How much money do they have in all?

Frequency and Relative Frequency

When a situation is repeated again and again, we call the situation an **experiment.** Each repetition of an experiment is a **trial.**

Recall that the number of times an event (such as winning a game) occurs is the frequency of the event.

You can think of each time a game is played as a trial. Obviously, the more trials, the more times you are likely to win. Remember that the *relative frequency* of an event compares the number of times an event occurred to the number of times it *could* have occurred. So, the relative frequency of an event is

$$\frac{\text{number of times the event occurred}}{\text{number of trials}}.$$

Like a probability, a relative frequency is a number from 0 to 1 and may be expressed as a fraction, decimal, or percent. But relative frequency is based on *actual data,* while probability is based on logic and assumptions.

Activity 1

MATERIALS calculator

You will need a partner.

Step 1 Copy the table at the right. Play *Rock, Paper, Scissors* 30 times. After each round, tally whether you won, lost, or tied.

Partner Results

Event	Win	Loss	Tie
Tallies	?	?	?
Frequencies	?	?	?
Relative Frequencies	?	?	?

Step 2 Examine the tallies and record the frequencies of wins, losses, and ties. The frequencies should total 30 since you played the game 30 times.

Step 3 Divide each frequency by 30 (the total number of times the event could possibly have occurred) and record this number in the relative frequency cell.

Step 4 In Lesson 10-4, you saw that the probability of winning in *Rock, Paper, Scissors* is $\frac{1}{3}$. The probability of losing is also $\frac{1}{3}$. The probability of a tie is also $\frac{1}{3}$. How do your relative frequencies compare to these probabilities?

In the Activity, you may have had relative frequencies near 0. A relative frequency of 0 means that a particular event has not occurred. It does not mean the event will never happen. Below, relative frequency is compared to probability. A relative frequency close to 1 means the event occurred often. A relative frequency of 1 means the event occurred every time it could. However, unlike a probability of 1, it does not mean the event will always occur.

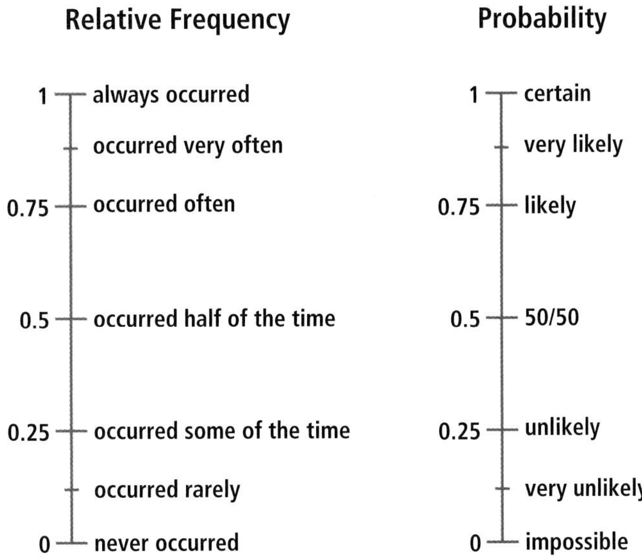

The Law of Large Numbers

Most of the time, the more trials of an experiment, the closer the relative frequency of an event is to the probability of the event. This principle is known as *The Law of Large Numbers.*

▸ READING MATH

The Law of Large Numbers was proved by Swiss mathematician Jacob Bernoulli. Bernoulli died in 1705, but the proof was not published until 1713.

The Law of Large Numbers

In general, the more trials of an experiment, the closer the relative frequency of an event will be to the event's probability.

Activity 2

MATERIALS calculator

To get more trials, pool the Activity 1 data from all pairs of students. Pick one partner from each pair to report to the class.

Step 1 On a table on the board or on poster paper, have each reporter record his or her pair's frequencies of wins, losses, and ties.

Event	win	loss	tie
Tally			
Frequency			
Relative Frequency			

Step 2 Find the total numbers of wins, losses, ties, and trials for the whole class.

Step 3 Calculate the relative frequencies for all the games played by the class.

Step 4 Compare the relative frequencies for individual pairs in Activity 1 with those for the entire class. Did the Law of Large Numbers "work" here?

Now you can play *Spinner Sums*. The directions for this game are on page G26 at the back of your book.

Questions

COVERING THE IDEAS

1. Many students in your class complain that their pencils do not have good erasers. You survey the class and find that there are 49 pencils in your class and 16 have good erasers.
   a. What is the frequency of pencils with good erasers?
   b. What is the relative frequency of pencils with good erasers?
   c. What is the relative frequency of pencils that do not have good erasers?

2. Nadia spun a spinner with orange, red, and blue sectors. The spinner landed on orange 10 times, red 4 times, and blue 6 times.
   a. Copy and complete the table at the right. Give the relative frequencies as percents.
   b. Based on the relative frequencies, which color do you think has the largest sector on the spinner? The smallest?

Color	Orange	Red	Blue
Frequency	?	?	?
Relative Frequency	?	?	?

3. Consider the game *Rock, Paper, Scissors.*
   a. If you show "rock," what is the probability you will win?
   b. If you show "rock," what is the probability you will lose?
   c. If you show "rock," what is the probability you will tie?

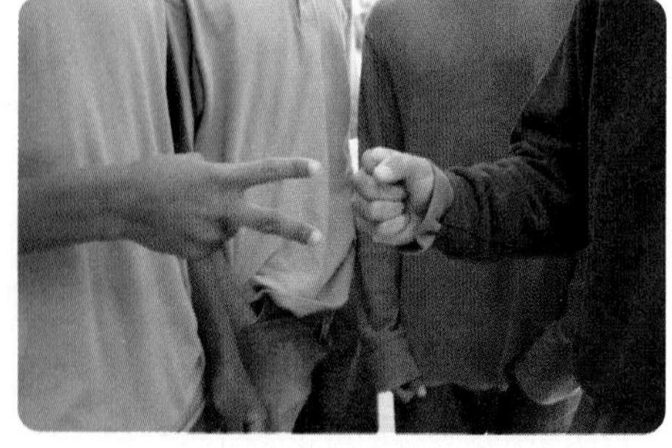

Who wins this round?

4. How are relative frequencies different from probabilities?

5. What is the Law of Large Numbers?

In 6–9, fill in the blanks.

6. An event that must occur has a probability of ___?___.

7. An event that occurred as often as it didn't occur has a ___?___ of ___?___.

8. An event that has never occurred has a ___?___ of 0.

9. An event that cannot occur has a ___?___ of ___?___.

10. Spike spun a spinner five times. Below is a table showing his results. Tevin looked at Spike's table without looking at the spinner and concluded that it was impossible to land on yellow. Is Tevin's conclusion justified? Why or why not?

Color	Purple	Green	Yellow
Frequency	3	2	0
Relative Frequency	$\frac{3}{5}$	$\frac{2}{5}$	0

11. Use relative frequency to answer the question on page 585. Rick Barry led the National Basketball Association in free throw shooting percentage six times, more than any other player. His lifetime percentage was .900 or 90%. Could he miss four free throws in a row?

Rick Barry

APPLYING THE MATHEMATICS

12. Consider the game in Example 1 of Lesson 10-4. Make three cards of the same size, two of them kings and one a queen. Pick two of the cards blindly. You win if the cards are the same. Play this game 20 times replacing and shuffling the cards after each turn. Keep track of the results.
    a. How many times did you win?
    b. What was your relative frequency of winning?
    c. Compare your relative frequency of winning with the probability of winning found in Lesson 10-4. What is the difference?

13. Make 10 slips of paper. Write the digits 0, 1, 2, 3, 4, 5, 6, 7, 8, 9 on the slips. Use the slips to play a game. Pick a slip of paper without looking. Then pick a second slip. You win if the number on the second slip is greater than the number on the first slip.
    a. Play this game 25 times. Record the relative frequencies of winning and losing.
    b. This game is fair if you have the same chance of winning as you do of losing. Is this game fair?
    c. What could you do to better evaluate whether or not the game is fair?

14. Here is another game. You write the digits 1, 2, and 3 in some order on a piece of paper. Your opponent also writes the digits 1, 2, and 3 in some order. You win if at least one of your digits is in the same position in your number as it is in your opponent's. For instance, you win if you write 132 and your opponent writes 231, because 3 is in the same position in both numbers. Otherwise you lose.
    a. Try this game at least 10 times. Record the results.
    b. Is this a fair game?
    c. What could you do to better evaluate whether or not the game is fair?

15. Suppose each of the 50,000 people in a football stadium flip a penny ten times.
    a. If the coin is fair, what is the probability of getting all heads?
    b. If someone in the stadium got all heads, would you think there was something "unfair" about his coin? Why or why not?

REVIEW

16. a. Redraw the maze at the right as a tree diagram and insert the probabilities.
    b. Sheryl has entered the maze. What is the probability of her finding the treasure room? **(Lesson 10-3)**

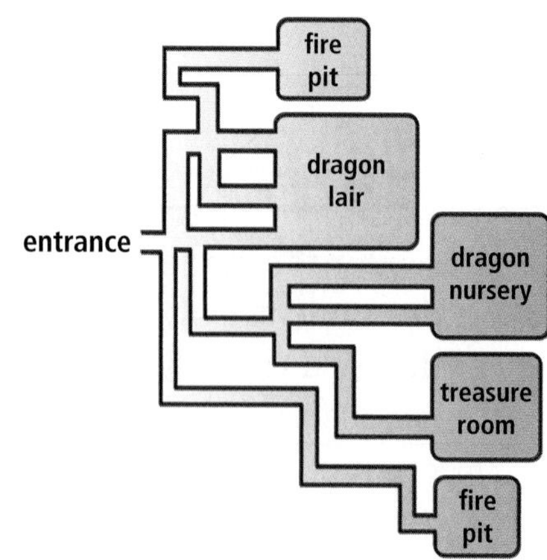

17. Make a tree diagram to find the next word for the quote in Question 18 in Lesson 10-6 on page 622. For the first branch, the choices are W or Y. For the second branch: A or O. For the third branch: L, U, or T. The probability of choosing W is $\frac{2}{3}$. The probability of choosing A is $\frac{2}{5}$. The probability of choosing L is $\frac{1}{7}$, and the probability of choosing U is $\frac{5}{7}$. Make a word by choosing the three-letter string with a probability of $\frac{1}{7}$. **(Lesson 10-3)**

18. At the right is a scale drawing of a building. A length of $\frac{1}{2}$ cm on the drawing corresponds to an actual length of 1 meter on the building. Use a ruler to measure the lengths on the drawing.

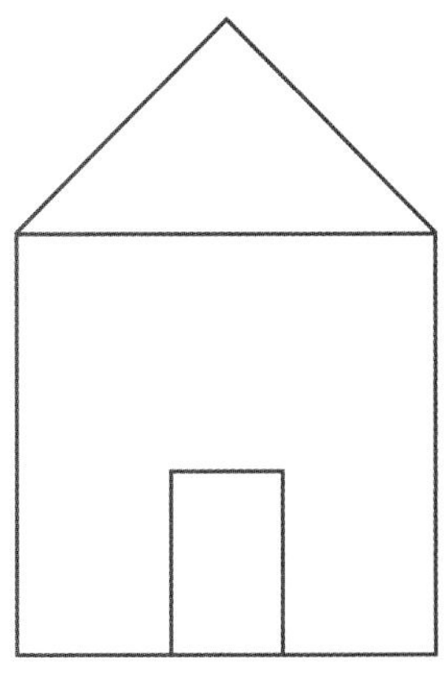

  a. What is the door's actual height?
  b. What is the door's actual width?
  c. What is the area of the front wall of the building, including the door?
  d. What is the area of the wall of the building, not including the door? **(Lessons 9-1, 8-8, 6-3, 1-3)**

19. The circle graph below shows the political party of the first 42 Presidents of the United States. Use the circle graph to estimate how many of the 42 were of each party. **(Lesson 5-5)**
  a. Democrats
  b. Republicans
  c. Democratic-Republicans
  d. Whigs

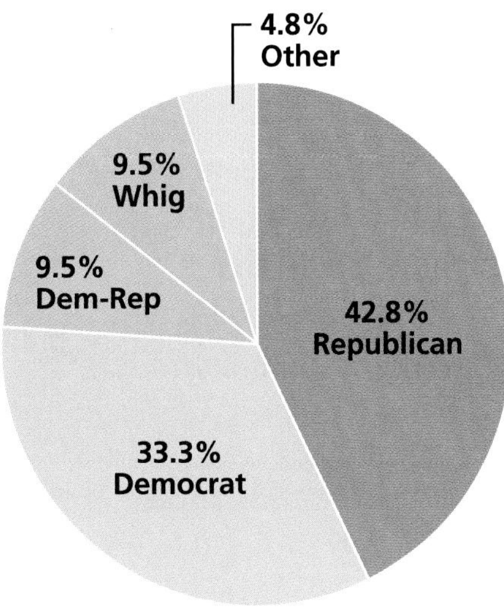

Source: *www.mapsofworld.com*

EXPLORATION

20. Find out something about how your local weather service makes predictions. Are these predictions probabilities or relative frequencies? Support your answer.

Lesson 10-6 Randomness and Random Numbers

Vocabulary

random
at random
random number
simulation

▸ **BIG IDEA** You can sometimes estimate an event's probability by using random numbers to simulate the experiment.

Courtney told her teacher that when she plays *Rock, Paper, Scissors* with her 4-year-old brother she wins almost all the time! "Why is that?" her teacher asked. "Because my brother almost always shows 'rock.'" replied Courtney. "I have learned to show 'paper' and so I win."

In this case, P(winning) for Courtney is not $\frac{1}{3}$ because her brother is not acting randomly. He is acting predictably.

Mental Math

Multiple Choice Sheila has more than Greg and less than Nicole. Nicole has less than Bill and more than Charlie. Which of the following must be true?

A Greg has more than Sheila.

B Bill has more than Greg.

C Charlie has more than Greg.

Randomness and Probability

Outcomes of a situation are **random,** or occur **at random,** when each has the same probability of occurring. Often we assume that events occur randomly. When a coin is *fair,* then its outcomes heads (H) and tails (T) occur randomly because P(heads) = P(tails) = $\frac{1}{2}$. If you pick a card at random from a deck of 52 cards, then the probability of picking any particular card is $\frac{1}{52}$.

QY1

Suppose you roll a fair six-sided die. What is the probability you will roll a 4?

In Example 1 of Lesson 10-4, when finding probabilities for the game that involved picking two cards from two kings and one queen, we assumed the cards were picked at random. That is why the probability of picking a king is $\frac{2}{3}$ and of picking a queen is $\frac{1}{3}$.

These examples show how closely randomness and probability are related.

Randomness and Probability Property

If an event has n outcomes that occur randomly, then the probability that any one of them will occur is $\frac{1}{n}$. The probability that one of m of the outcomes will occur is $\frac{m}{n}$.

Can You Tell if a Real Coin is Fair?

A person shows you a coin and says it is fair. Can you tell if it is? Try this activity to find out.

Activity 1

MATERIALS coin, calculator, graph paper

Step 1 Toss a coin 20 times. Record the number of heads.

Step 2 Combine your result with the results of other students in your class. Graph the frequency of each number of heads in a bar graph. (For instance, if 3 students toss 11 heads, then the bar over the number 11 will be three units high.)

Step 3 Determine the total number of tosses and the total number of heads for your class. Calculate the relative frequency of heads for the entire class.

Even though you might think a coin is fair, Step 2 shows that you will not always get 10 heads in 20 tosses.

If a coin is fair, according to the Law of Large Numbers, the relative frequency of heads will get closer and closer to $\frac{1}{2}$ *in the long run*. But the Law of Large Numbers does not say that the frequency will equal exactly $\frac{1}{2}$. Also, "in the long run" may be a long time. If the coin is fair, your relative frequency may not be close to $\frac{1}{2}$ after 20 trials or even after 200 trials. It could take much longer.

How then, can you know that a coin is fair? You cannot be absolutely sure. It is only possible to determine the *probability* that a coin is fair if you know the relative frequency of heads in a number of tosses. You will learn how to do this in your future study of statistics. For now, you should just recognize that even a fair coin will give you a variety of results when it is tossed.

Random Numbers

Ramon shuffles a deck of ten number cards, one card for each of the integers 1–10 and fans them out, face down. Gustavo picks one card without looking, and then places the card back in the deck. There are ten possible outcomes: 1, 2, 3, 4, 5, 6, 7, 8, 9, or 10. Assuming that the cards are unmarked, this deck of cards is said to be fair, or unbiased, because there is no pattern and the next number to appear is unpredictable.

See QY2 at the right.

Since the outcomes have the same probability, each single pick generates a **random number** from 1 through 10.

QY2

If Ramon and Gustavo repeat their card-picking activity many times, what percent of the time would you expect Gustavo to pick the number 6?

Activity 2

MATERIALS calculator

In this activity, you will use a calculator and work with a partner to generate 50 random numbers.

Step 1 Copy this table.

Outcome	Tally Mark	Frequency	Percent
1	?	?	?
2	?	?	?
3	?	?	?
4	?	?	?
5	?	?	?
6	?	?	?
7	?	?	?
8	?	?	?
9	?	?	?
10	?	?	?
Total Number of Random Numbers		50	100%

Step 2 Determine the key sequence to generate random integers, displayed one number at a time, on your calculator.

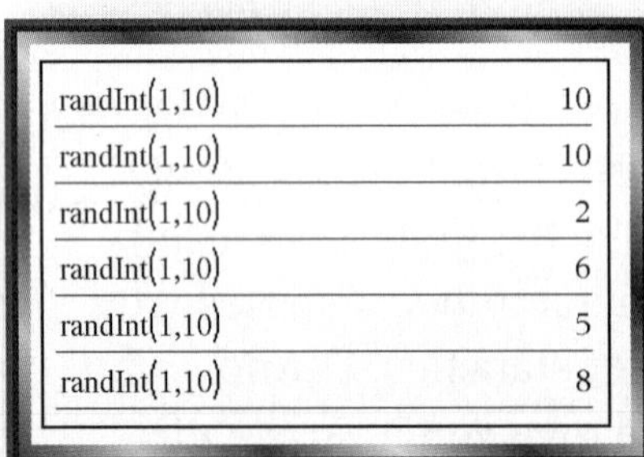

Step 3 Have one partner generate 25 random integers from 1 to 10 on the calculator, while the other partner records each number as a tally mark in your table.

Step 4 Switch places with your partner. Continue to generate and record numbers in the table until you have 50 random numbers.

Step 5 Count the number of 1s, 2s, 3s, and so on, and record those frequencies in the table. Then determine and record the relative frequencies as a percent.

Step 6 Do your results appear random? Why or why not?

Using Random Numbers to Simulate an Experiment

A **simulation** is a process by which you examine a problem by using materials that are different from those in the actual problem. Random numbers are often used to simulate problems for which you want to assume fairness.

Activity 3

MATERIALS calculator

Use your calculator to simulate Activity 1, that is, tossing a fair coin 20 times.

Step 1 Write the command to make your calculator generate the numbers 0 and 1 randomly. What percent of your outcomes do you expect to be 0s?

Step 2 Copy this table.

Outcomes	Tally Marks	Frequency	Percent
0	?	?	?
1	?	?	?
Total Number of Random Numbers		20	100%

Step 3 Generate 20 random zeros and ones on your calculator and tally the results in the table. Fill in the frequencies and percents.

Step 4 Let 0 stand for heads and 1 for tails. How do your results compare with what you found in Activity 1?

Step 5 Combine your results with those of others in your class. How close is the class's relative frequency of heads to $\frac{1}{2}$?

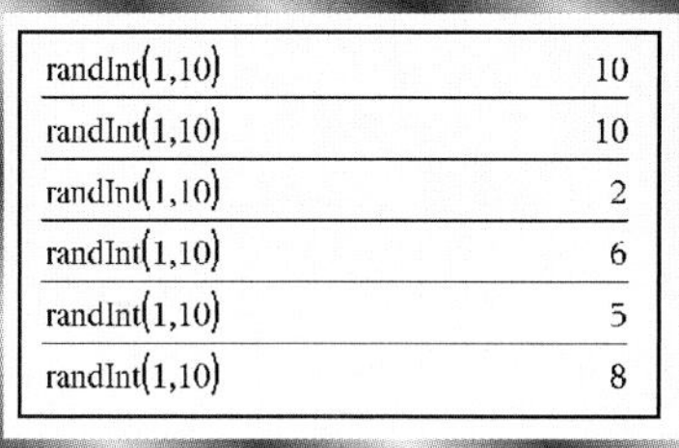

Questions

COVERING THE IDEAS

1. If you roll a fair six-sided die with the numbers 1, 2, 3, 4, 5, 6, on its faces, what is the probability you will roll a number that is greater than 4?
2. In Question 1, why is the word "fair" an important word?
3. If you roll a fair six-sided die, will you roll a 1 exactly $\frac{1}{6}$ of the time? Why or why not?
4. If you have to simulate a situation that has two possible randomly selected outcomes, which would you prefer to use, a lima bean or a coin. Why?

Like most beans, lima beans are a great source of protein.

5. a. Generate random integers from 1 to 6 on a calculator to simulate tossing a die 30 times. Record the 30 integers you obtained.
   b. Make a bar graph to show the frequency of each integer.

APPLYING THE MATHEMATICS

6. Ramon and Gustavo decided to use the numbers 21–30 instead of 1–10 for Activity 2. If they follow the same steps to select 50 random numbers, should they get very different frequencies for these new numbers? Why or why not?

7. Ramon and Gustavo now decide to use 5 number cards (instead of 10) with the numbers 1–5 for Activity 2. If they randomly select 50 numbers, in the long run, how many times should the number 3 be selected?

8. A restaurant serves a "soup of the day" as part of its menu. Chef Lentil randomly selects one out of six soups each day. How can you simulate this situation with a spinner?

9. Mia randomly selects a type of salad each day for lunch. She has three choices. How can you simulate Mia's selection process using random numbers?

Lentil soup is high in dietary fiber.

REVIEW

10. Suppose three coins are tossed together. Make a table showing the outcomes, and then determine the probability of
    a. at least two heads.
    b. all three coins showing the same side.
    c. either at least two heads *or* all three coins showing the same side. **(Lesson 10-5)**

11. **Multiple Choice** A bag has an unknown number of colored marbles. Destiny picks one marble from the bag, records the color and replaces it. Her results are below.

White	Green	Blue	Red
127	48	73	0

Based on these data, which of the following is a good estimate of the probability of obtaining each color from the bag? **(Lesson 10-5)**

A White: 127% Green: 48% Blue: 73% Red: 0%
B White: 51% Green: 19% Blue: 30% Red: 0%
C White: 25% Green: 25% Blue: 25% Red: 25%
D White: $33\frac{1}{3}\%$ Green: $33\frac{1}{3}\%$ Blue: $33\frac{1}{3}\%$ Red: 0%

12. **Multiple Choice** Which of the following could be an appropriate estimate for how much wallpaper is needed to cover a wall? (Lesson 9-6)

A 35
B 35 yards
C 35 square yards
D 35 cubic yards

In 1960, there were about 350,000 licensed barbers in the U.S. In 2005, there were about 168,000.

In 13 and 14, 500 tickets for a charity raffle are being sold. A group of seven friends has bought 150 of the tickets.

13. What percent of the total number of tickets did the group buy? (Lesson 8-1)

14. If the seven people try to divide their tickets evenly, how many will each person get? How many tickets will be left over? (Lesson 7-4)

15. Ali cut 17 people's hair at his barbershop in 6 hours, working steadily, but with 3 minutes between haircuts. Determine how long, on average, each haircut took. (Lesson 7-10)

16. Refer to the figure at the right. $m\angle ABC = 62°$, and $\angle ABC$ and $\angle ABD$ form a linear pair. Find $m\angle ABD$. (Lesson 4-5)

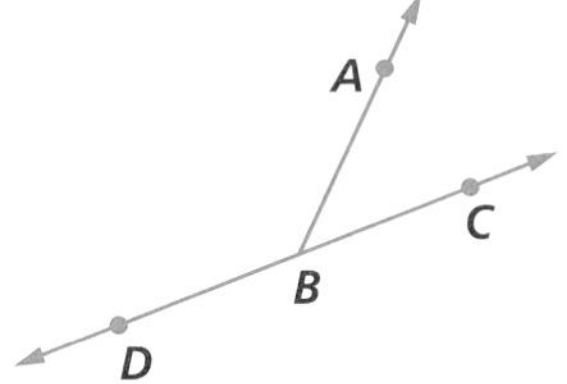

EXPLORATION

17. For the following activities, use three dice with the numbers shown on the nets below.

Die A

	4	
1	5	1
	5	
	4	

Die B

	3	
3	3	3
	3	
	3	

Die C

	2	
2	6	2
	6	
	2	

In this game, two players each roll one of the dice once. The player who rolls the higher number wins the game. The problem is to determine which die allows you to win most often. Do the following experiment to see which die is the best. Work with a partner.

a. Copy the table on the following page to record your findings. To start, one of you should roll or simulate rolling Die A and the other Die B. Simulate 30 to 100 trials. For each trial, make a check mark for the die that wins. You will need from 30 to 100 rolls to see a clear pattern of which die is winning most of the time.

Die ? vs Die ?																			
Wins for Die ?										Wins for Die ?									

b. Repeat Part a for Die A and Die C.

c. Repeat Part b for Die B and Die C.

d. Answer the following questions.

- **i.** Did Die A win more times than Die B?
- **ii.** Did Die B win more times than Die C?
- **iii.** Did Die A win more times than Die C?

18. a. In the table below, place the words you decoded from the rest of the chapter.

Lesson	Word
10-2	?
10-3	?
10-4	?
10-5	?

b. Place the words from the table in the blanks to form a quote from Sir Francis Galton, a 19th century statistician.

__?__ __?__ __?__, __?__!

QY ANSWERS

1. $\frac{1}{6}$

2. 10% of the time

Chapter 10 Projects

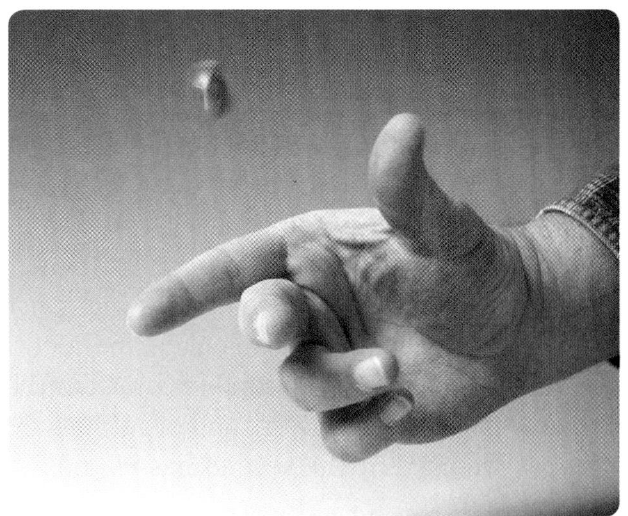

1 A Probability Experiment

Use a computer or calculator to generate 200 random integers from 1 to 8. Assign these numbers to the eight outcomes possible when tossing three coins: HHH, HHT, HTH, HTT, THH, THT, TTH, and TTT. For example, the number 1 might represent HHH, the outcome of getting all heads. Compare the relative frequencies you find for obtaining 0, 1, 2, and 3 heads with the probabilities of these events. Then expand your experiment by generating 200 more trials and recalculating the relative frequencies with all 400 trials. Compare the relative frequencies with the probabilities again. Compare your results for both experiments.

2 Probability or Relative Frequency?

Find at least five references to the idea of chance in a newspaper, magazine, or on the Internet. Describe each reference and decide whether you think it is a probability or a relative frequency. Support your decision. Make a poster illustrating your results.

3 Fair Game?

Invent a two-person game like one of those in Lesson 10-4. Determine the probability of each person winning your game. Play or simulate the game at least 50 times to see if the relative frequencies of winning come close to the probabilities of winning. Is your game fair? Why or why not?

4 Streaks

Toss a coin at least 250 times, recording heads or tails for every toss. You can toss an actual coin or use a random number generator to simulate tossing a coin.

a. What is the relative frequency of heads for your tosses?

b. After each head, what is the relative frequency that the next toss is heads?

c. After each pair of heads, what is the relative frequency that the third toss is heads?

d. After each set of three heads in a row, what is the relative frequency that the fourth toss is heads?

e. Judging from what you find in Parts a–d, do you think that getting heads on one toss affects what happens on the next toss? Explain why or why not.

5 Random Numbers

There are several methods for generating numbers. Research some methods and describe them in an essay.

Chapter 10 Summary and Vocabulary

- An **experiment,** like tossing a coin, has a set of possible **outcomes** that makes up the **sample space** for the experiment. With a small number of outcomes, it is possible to make a **tree diagram** or a list to show them. For some experiments, the sample space can be quite large, such as in determining how many license plates are possible. It is sometimes possible to calculate the total number of possible outcomes using the **Multiplication Counting Principle:** if one event has m outcomes and a second event has n outcomes, then the first event followed by the second has mn possible outcomes.

- A **probability** is a number from 0 to 1 that tells how likely an **event** is to happen. A probability of 0 means an event is impossible; a probability of 1 means it is a certainty. A probability can be expressed as a fraction, a decimal, or a percent. To calculate the probability of an event, divide the number of outcomes in the event by the total number of possible outcomes. Probability tree diagrams can help determine probabilities when outcomes are not **equally likely.**

- A **simulation** is an experiment using **random numbers** or other objects like number cards or spinners, to represent items or people in a situation. You can use a simulation to investigate how relative frequencies compare with calculated probabilities. Either way, **the Law of Large Numbers** states that, the more trials performed, the closer the relative frequency gets to the actual value. Many calculators have a way to generate random numbers. Computer simulations can be used to perform a very large number of trials quickly.

Theorems and Properties

Multiplication Counting Principle (p. 587)
Law of Large Numbers (p. 611)
Randomness and Probability Property (p. 616)

Vocabulary

10-1
tree diagram

10-2
sample space
event
probability
fair (unbiased)

10-4
fair game
unfair game

10-5
experiment
trial

10-6
random
at random
random number
simulation

Chapter 10 Self-Test

Take this test as you would take a test in class. You will need a ruler. Then use the Selected Answers section in the back of the book to check your work.

In 1–4, use the table below. A bag holds 30 colored marbles. In an experiment, each student in a class chose a marble, recorded its color, and put it back into the bag. The table shows the results of this experiment.

1. Find the relative frequency of each color.

Color	Frequency	Relative Frequency
Red	7	?
Yellow	3	?
Blue	2	?
White	2	?
Purple	5	?
Orange	1	?

2. How many purple marbles would you predict are in the bag? Explain how you got your answer.

3. Predict the probability of getting a purple marble. Explain how you got your answer.

4. Without looking in the bag, what could you do to increase the accuracy of your prediction in Question 3?

5. Carly drew 5 shapes out of a bag. The relative frequency of circles was 1. She concluded that the probability of drawing a circle was 1. Was Carly justified in her conclusion? Explain.

6. Isabel drew 5 shapes out of a bag. The relative frequency of squares was 0. She concluded that the probability of drawing a square was 0. Was Isabel justified in her conclusion? Explain.

7. **Matching** Match the statement with its most appropriate probability,
   a. The sun will rise in the west tomorrow.
   b. The sun will rise in the east tomorrow.
   c. Tomorrow will be sunny.
   i. 0 ii. 0.7 iii. 1

8. The spinner below is spun twice and lands randomly in the circle. The three sectors are of equal size.

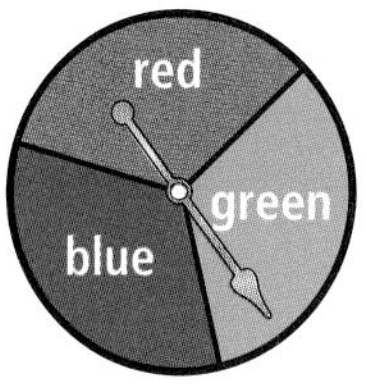

   a. Using an organized list, write the sample space.
   b. Use your list to find the probability that the spinner lands on the same color both times.
   c. Use your list to find the probability that the spinner lands on red at least once.

9. The spinner below is spun twice and lands randomly in the circle. The four sectors are of equal size. Make a probability tree diagram to find

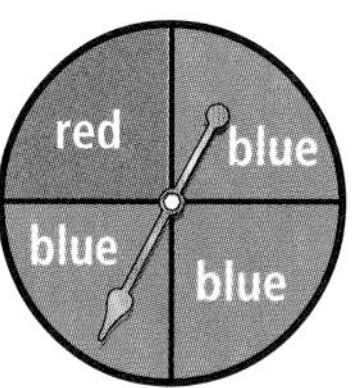

   a. both spins are red.
   b. both spins are blue.
   c. one spin is red and one spin is blue.

10. Make a tree diagram that shows how many outfits you can make from two pairs of pants (blue or khaki), three shirts (red, green, or yellow), and two pairs of shoes (black or white).

11. Two fair, six-sided dice are rolled, and the numbers shown are multiplied.
    a. Make a table showing all possible outcomes.
    b. Use your table to find P(15).
    c. Use your table to find P(21).
    d. Use your table to find P(a number greater than 20).

12. How many 3-number combinations can be made on a lock numbered from 0 to 29?

13. A teacher is grading papers. In his bag, he has five red pens and three green pens. Without looking, he takes out one pen, lays it down, and then takes out a second pen. Use a probability tree diagram to find the probability that he has taken one red pen and one green pen.

14. Imagine tossing a fair coin four times. What is the probability of getting
    a. no heads?
    b. three heads?

15. Explain one way to generate a random whole number between 1 and 6.

16. Alfredo, Raven, and Yoshi were playing *Rock, Paper, Scissors.* Alfredo said that to decide the champion, Raven and Yoshi should play, and the winner of that should play Alfredo for the title. Does everyone have an equal chance of winning? Why or why not?

Chapter 10 Chapter Review

SKILLS
PROPERTIES
USES
REPRESENTATIONS

SKILLS Procedures used to get answers

OBJECTIVE A Find the probability of an event as a percent, fraction, or decimal. (Lesson 10-2)

1. When a fair coin is tossed, what is the probability of heads?
2. Find the probability that the next integer a random number generator produces will be odd.
3. What is the probability of rolling a number less than 3 on a die?
4. What is the probability of rolling two dice and getting a sum over 12?

OBJECTIVE B Generate random numbers. (Lesson 10-6)

5. Roll a die 10 times to generate random numbers.
6. From a set of 10 cards labeled 1–10, draw a card six times, replacing the card after each draw, to generate random numbers.
7. Use your calculator to generate 30 random integers from 50 to 70.

PROPERTIES The principles behind the mathematics

OBJECTIVE C Relate probability to the likelihood of an event. (Lesson 10-2)

8. An event that is certain to occur has what probability?
9. An event that is impossible has what probability?
10. If the probability of an event is 0.8, how likely is it to occur?
11. If the probability of an event is 0.08, how likely is it to occur?

OBJECTIVE D Understand the Law of Large Numbers. (Lesson 10-5)

12. When flipping a fair coin, would you expect the ratio of heads to tails to be closer to 1 or further from 1 as the number of flips increases? Explain your answer.
13. A weatherman says that in each of the next two days, there is a 50% chance of rain. Another weatherman says there is a 50% chance of rain every day for the next two weeks. During which of the two time periods (the two days or the two weeks) would you expect the ratio of rainy days to total days to be closer to $\frac{1}{2}$?
14. When rolling a fair die six times, Mingmei rolled three 2s. Would you expect this trend to continue if she rolled the die 100 times?
15. Jordan reached into a bag filled with 1,000 marbles of five different colors. She pulled out 10 marbles: 2 blues, 2 yellows, 3 greens, 1 orange, and 2 reds. She then put them back. Jane pulled out 100 marbles: 13 blues, 23 yellows, 20 greens, 15 oranges, and 25 reds. If you had to guess what fraction of the marbles were of each color, whose results would you use? Why?

USES Applications of mathematics in real-world situations

OBJECTIVE E Use the Multiplication Counting Principle. (Lesson 10-1)

16. How many outfits can be made from 3 pairs of pants, 3 shirts, and 3 hats?

17. How many ten-digit numbers are there using only the digits 1, 2, 3, 4, or 5?

18. If you get three books for your birthday, in how many orders can you read the books?

19. A restaurant offers 3 appetizers, 2 salads, 5 entrees, and 2 desserts. How many different four-course meals can you make?

OBJECTIVE F Find the size of a sample space. (Lesson 10-2)

In 20–23, find the size of the sample space.

20. Hailey wants to know the probability of correctly guessing the page her friend is on in a 1000-page novel.

21. Devonté wants to find the probability that the pitcher is not going to throw a fastball on his next pitch if he always throws either fastballs, curveballs, or change-ups during a game.

22. Marina wants to find the probability of having a five-digit license plate with all odd digits.

23. Erin wants to find the probability of getting three 1s in three rolls of a die.

OBJECTIVE G Find the probability of an event in a real-world situation. (Lessons 10-4, 10-5)

24. Players are using the spinner below for a board game. Find the probability of going forward.

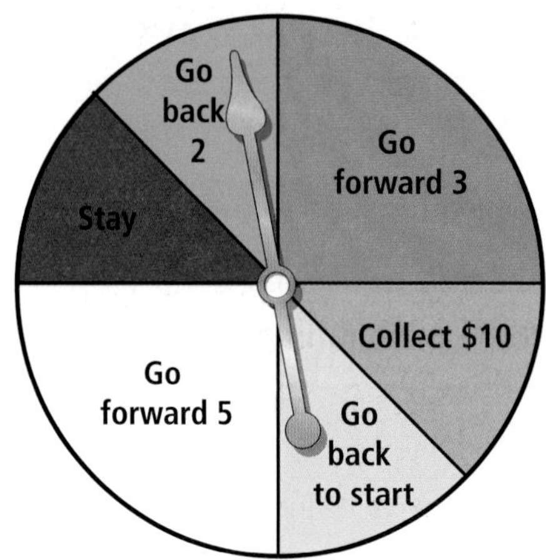

25. Maggie is picking her chore for the day out of a hat. If the chores are cleaning the bathroom, dusting the house, vacuuming the carpet, washing the windows, sweeping the porch, fixing dinner, and walking the dog, what is the probability that she will have to clean something?

26. Justin has 3 blue socks and 2 red socks in his drawer. If he reaches in and grabs two socks at random, what is the probability that his socks will match?

27. If the boys' soccer team wins 60 percent of its games, and the girls' soccer team wins 80 percent of its games, what is the probability that both the boys' and girls' soccer teams will win their next game?

OBJECTIVE H Determine whether a game is fair or not fair. **(Lesson 10-4)**

28. Rico has 5 black cards and 2 red cards. He tells James to choose one card at random, and then choose another. If the cards match, James wins. If they don't, Rico wins. Is this game fair? If not, who has the advantage?

29. Lawanda tells Vanessa to guess whether the whole number from 1 to 9 she has written down is odd or even. If Vanessa guesses right, she wins. Is this game fair? Why or why not?

OBJECTIVE I Calculate the relative frequency for an event as a percent or fraction. **(Lesson 10-5)**

In 30–33, calculate the relative frequency for the event.

30. A coin is flipped 50 times, and it lands tails up 29 times.
31. Mark draws 13 cards from a deck, and 3 of them are face cards.
32. On average, the temperature in Minneapolis drops below freezing 156 days per year.
33. Laura counted the number of days in the week that end in the letter "y".

REPRESENTATIONS Pictures, graphs, or objects that illustrate concepts

OBJECTIVE J Represent counting situations using lists and tree diagrams. **(Lessons 10-1)**

34. List all the possible two-letter strings that contain one vowel and one of the letters b, d, and f.

35. List every possible string of three consecutive days of the week. (For example, list Monday, Tuesday, Wednesday, but *not* Monday, Tuesday, Thursday.)

36. Draw a tree diagram representing the following situation: Emma draws one card from a group of 4 cards that includes a King, two Jacks, and a Queen. She then draws a second card without replacing the first one.

37. Deja and Grace are going to an art museum, to shop, and to sightsee but they can't decide in what order. Draw a tree diagram showing all the possible orders of these activities.

OBJECTIVE K Represent probability situations using probability tree diagrams. **(Lessons 10-3, 10-4)**

In 38–41, draw a probability tree diagram to calculate the probability.

38. Find the probability that a two-letter combination of the letters A, B, and C has a first letter of A. Letters can be repeated.
39. Find the probability that a two-letter combination of the letters A, B, and C has a first letter of A. Letters *cannot* be repeated.
40. Before getting dressed, Alonzo can choose from a pair of white pants and a pair of black pants. He can choose from a white shirt, a gray shirt, and a blue shirt. If he picks his outfit at random, what is the probability that he will have an outfit that has at least one white item of clothing?
41. Packing a lunch, Georgia grabs a piece of fruit and a yogurt at random out of the fridge. If there is a plum, a peach, and an apple, and strawberry yogurt, boysenberry yogurt, and peach yogurt, what is the probability that she ends up with a peach and a peach yogurt?

Chapter

11 Constructing and Drawing Figures

Contents

In this chapter, you will use pencils, rulers, compasses, protractors, and technology to picture various geometric figures and their images under certain transformations.

We distinguish among *rough sketches*, *drawings*, and *constructions*.

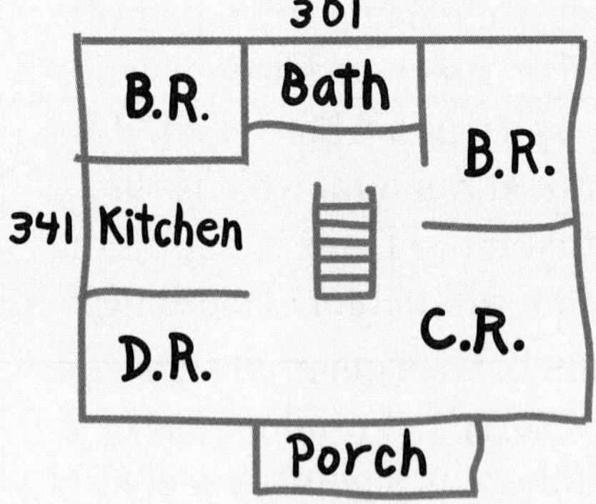

A *rough sketch* is a quickly made picture. It can be used as a starting point for a complicated accurate drawing. Rough sketches may have some lengths and angle measures marked, but these are not usually accurately represented. At the left is a rough sketch of a 2-bedroom apartment. The lengths on this sketch are not to scale, and you cannot determine the dimensions of the rooms.

A *drawing* is more carefully done than a rough sketch. In a drawing, you make measurements and use a variety of equipment: stencils, graph paper, rulers, paper folding, protractors, and tracing paper. At the right, a triangle has been drawn with angles of 35° and 100° and an included side of length 2 centimeters.

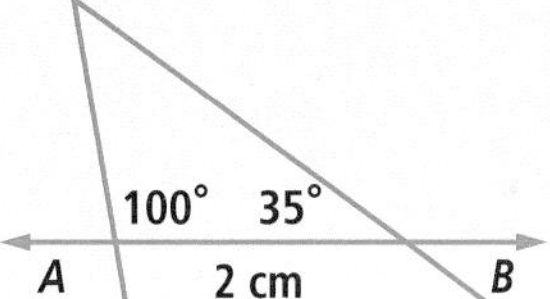

A *construction* in mathematics is a very special kind of picture. It is a figure made using only two pieces of equipment: something to draw lines (a straightedge) and something to draw circles (a compass). At the right, from two points *A* and *B*, an equilateral triangle has been constructed.

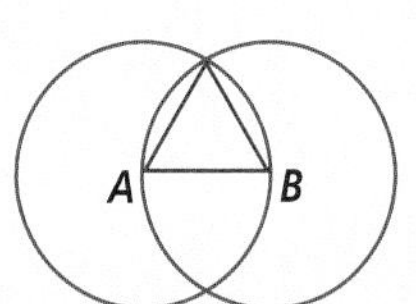

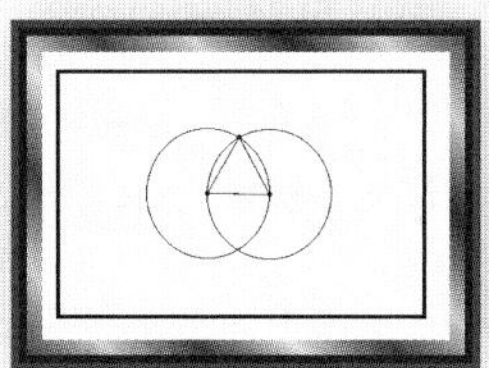

Some calculators and computer software allow you to draw or construct. You need to know how to describe constructions in order to get the technology to operate at your command.

In this chapter, you will draw and construct geometric figures and their images under three kinds of transformations: reflections, rotations, and translations. By working with these pictures, you will learn much about these figures and these transformations.

Lesson 11-1 Geometry Tools for Making Drawings and Constructions

Vocabulary

angle bisector
straightedge
compass
Euclidean construction
Dynamic Geometry System (DGS)

BIG IDEA A variety of tools are available to make geometric drawings. The oldest of these are the straightedge and the compass.

Making drawings of geometric figures is an important part of geometry. This lesson includes four different methods for making figures.

Mental Math

a. What is the perimeter of a square with area 49 cm^2?

b. What is the circumference of a circle with area 36π ft^2?

c. Give two possible perimeters of a rectangle with area 15 cm^2.

Drawing with Ruler and Protractor

You used a ruler and protractor to draw shapes in earlier lessons.

QY

Using a ruler and a protractor, make an accurate drawing of a rectangle with side lengths of $2\frac{1}{2}$ inches and 4 inches.

Paper Folding

Paper folding is another technique for drawing figures. Thin tracing paper works particularly well. For some activities, you may need a pencil or a ruler.

Activity 1

MATERIALS tracing paper, ruler

Step 1 With heavy lines, use a ruler to draw an angle on tracing paper. Label the vertex *A*, as shown at the right.

Step 2 Carefully fold and crease the paper so that the crease goes through point *A* and one side of the angle lands on top of the other.

Step 3 Unfold the paper and draw a dashed line over the crease. You have drawn an *angle bisector*. The **angle bisector** (the dashed line) cuts the angle into two equal angles.

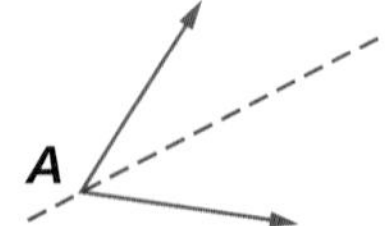

Constructions with Straightedge and Compass

Greek geometers studied figures they could draw using only a *straightedge* and a *compass*. A straightedge is used for drawing lines and line segments. A **straightedge** is like a ruler but it has no markings on it. A **compass** is a tool for drawing circles. It also can be used for copying and marking off lengths.

Making a figure using only a straightedge and compass is called a **Euclidean construction,** after the Greek geometer Euclid. Numeric measurements are not used in Euclidean constructions. When doing constructions, you may draw lines with a ruler, but you may not measure or use the markings on the ruler in any way.

▸ READING MATH

Another type of construction uses only a compass. This compass-only construction is called a *Mascheroni construction* after the Italian geometer Lorenzo Mascheroni.

Activity 2

MATERIALS straightedge, compass, plain paper

Follow the steps to construct a hexagon within a six-petaled rose as shown at the right.

Step 1 Use your compass to draw a circle in the middle of a sheet of paper. All the circles in this activity will have the same radius as this circle, so keep the compass opening the same.

Step 2 Placing the point of the compass anywhere on the circle, draw a second circle.

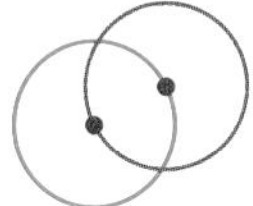

Step 3 Place the point of the compass at one of the two points where the two circles intersect. Then draw a third circle. Explain why the centers of these circles are vertices of an equilateral triangle.

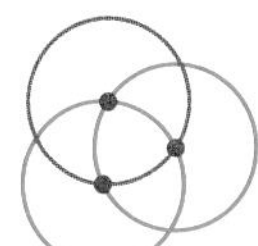

Step 4 Construct four more circles around the edge of the first circle by placing the point of the compass where the last circle intersects the first circle. The outside six circles form the rose in the original circle.

Step 5 With a straightedge, connect the centers of the outside six circles to form a hexagon like the one seen above. Explain why the sides of the hexagon are all the same length.

A compass can also be used to construct a copy of a line segment.

Activity 3

MATERIALS straightedge, compass

Step 1 Use your straightedge to draw a line segment that is clearly longer than $\overline{AB}$ shown at the right. Remember, when doing constructions, measurement is not permitted.

Step 2 Mark a point toward one end of your line segment and label it C.

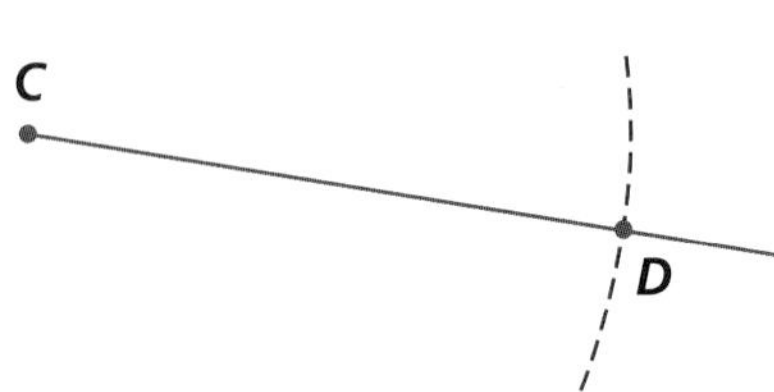

Step 3 Open the compass to the length of $\overline{AB}$ by putting the point on A and the pencil on B. Keep the opening fixed.

Step 4 Now place the compass point on C and swing an arc of a circle (with the opening from Step 3) that intersects the line segment. Label the point D where the arc intersects the segment. Explain why $\overline{CD}$ is the same length as $\overline{AB}$.

Drawings by Computer Using a Dynamic Geometry System

Construction software, running on computers or handheld calculators, adds a dynamic twist to making geometric figures. This kind of software, called a **Dynamic Geometry System,** or **DGS,** enables you to make discoveries about a construction by manipulating the result after it has been completed.

If you have access to a DGS, you should explore it to learn how it works. Because becoming familiar with DGS software takes time and patience, work closely with your teacher and other students.

Activity 4

MATERIALS DGS software

Step 1 Construct two points on the screen. In this construction, these points will be two vertices of an equilateral triangle.

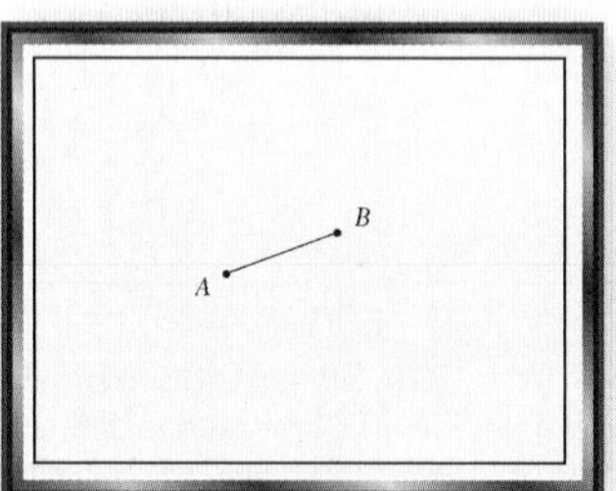

Steps 1-3

Step 2 Name the points A and B.

Step 3 Construct the line segment $\overline{AB}$, joining A and B.

Step 4 Construct the circle with center A that contains point B.

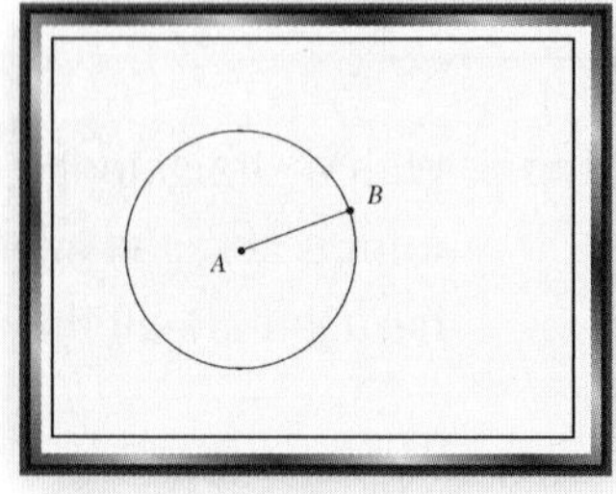

Step 4

Step 5 Construct the circle with center *B* that contains point *A*.

Step 6 Name one of the two points of intersection of the circles point *C*.

Step 7 Construct $\overline{AC}$ and $\overline{BC}$. Explain why $\triangle ABC$ is equilateral.

Step 8 Using the mouse or the pointer, drag point *A*. Does $\triangle ABC$ remain equilateral?

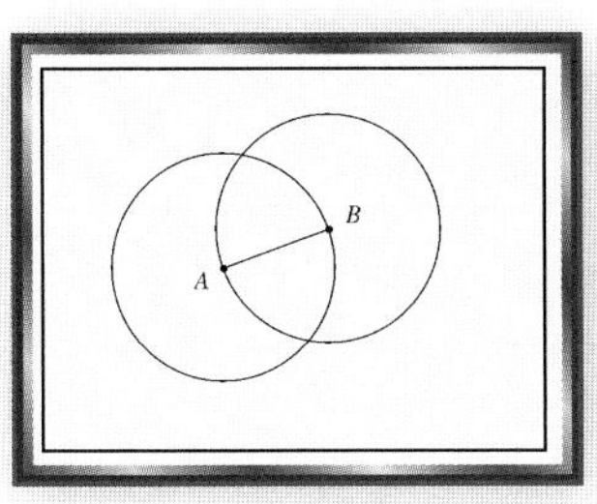

Step 5

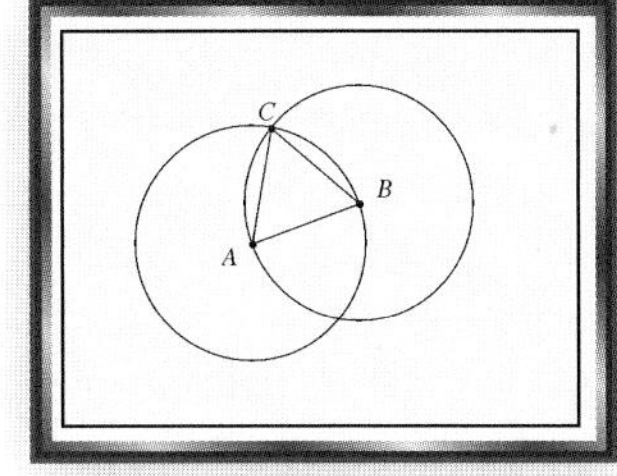

Steps 6 and 7

Questions

COVERING THE IDEAS

1. Using a ruler and protractor, draw a square with side length 5 cm.

2. Draw a circle with radius $2\frac{1}{2}''$.

3. With heavy lines, draw a triangle on tracing paper with vertices labeled *A*, *B*, and *C* as shown at the right. Follow these steps for a surprise ending.

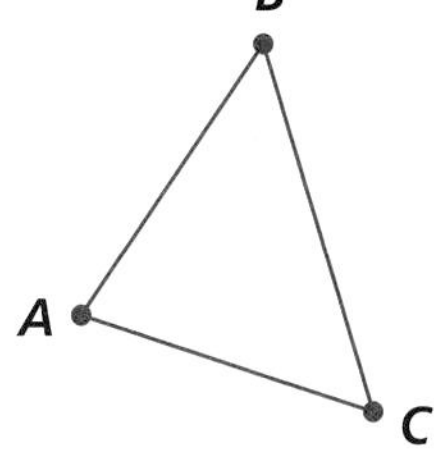

   Step 1 Fold point *A* onto point *B* and crease.
   Step 2 Fold point *B* onto point *C* and crease.
   Step 3 Label the point where the two creases meet *X*.
   Step 4 Construct the circle with center *X* containing *A*. What is the surprise ending?

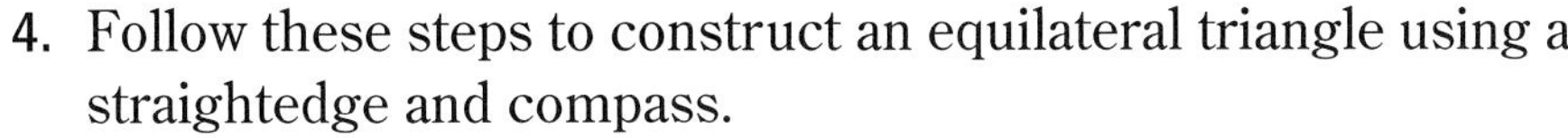

4. Follow these steps to construct an equilateral triangle using a straightedge and compass.
   Step 1 Place two points on your paper roughly 3 inches apart. Label these points *P* and *Q* and connect them.
   Step 2 Construct the circle with center *P* containing *Q*.
   Step 3 Construct the circle with center *Q* containing *P*.
   Step 4 Label one of the two intersection points *X*.
   Step 5 Construct the two segments $\overline{PX}$ and $\overline{QX}$.
   Step 6 Explain why $\triangle PQX$ has three sides of equal length.

5. Using a straightedge and compass, construct a line segment whose length is the sum of the lengths of the two segments at the right.

6. Using a DGS, draw the rose figure from Activity 2.

APPLYING THE MATHEMATICS

7. At right is a rough sketch of Nina's bedroom, closet, and window alcove. The room is a 14'-by-12' rectangle. The closet is a 3'-by-6' rectangle, and the window alcove is a semicircle with a diameter of 6'. Using a scale of 1 in. = 4 ft, draw an accurate diagram of Nina's room.

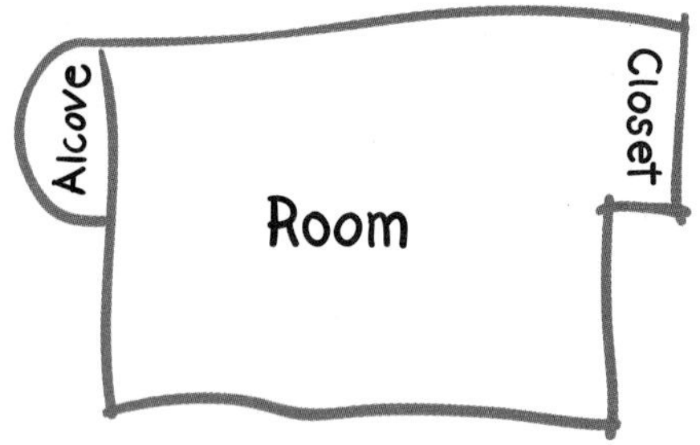

8. Suppose a city park consists of a rectangle and a semicircle. The rectangle is 200' wide and 75' long. The semicircle has diameter 200' and its diameter is one side of the rectangle. Using a scale of 1 in. = 50 ft, accurately draw a diagram of the park. Be sure to include the scale on your drawing.

9. Draw a sector so that the two sides are 4.5 in. long and the angle between them has measure 52°.

10. Segment $\overline{AB}$ has length 2". A point is located $3\frac{15}{16}$" from one endpoint of $\overline{AB}$ and $2\frac{1}{8}$" from the other.
    a. Draw $\overline{AB}$ and construct the four possible locations of that point. Call the four locations W, X, Y and Z.
    b. Draw $\triangle ABW$, $\triangle ABX$, $\triangle ABY$ and $\triangle ABZ$.
    c. What four-sided figure is formed by connecting W, X, Y and Z?

In 11–13, use the line segments below.

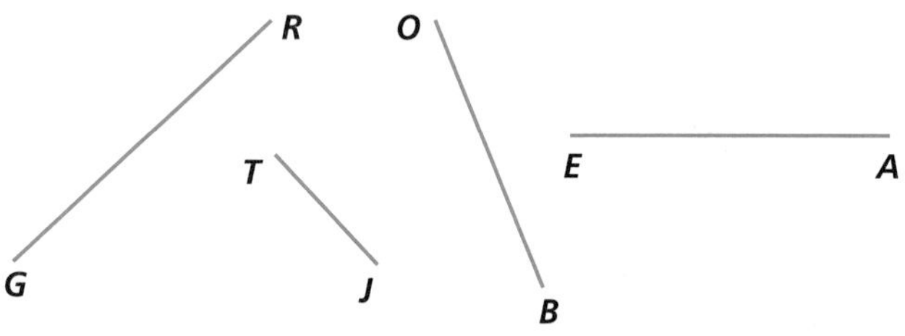

11. Construct a segment $\overline{ZY}$ whose length is $GR + EA$.
12. Construct a segment $\overline{XW}$ that is three times as long as $\overline{TJ}$.
13. Construct a segment whose length is $OB - GR$.

14. Using a DGS or a straightedge and compass, construct any $\triangle ABC$. Then, construct the circle with center A that contains B, the circle with center B that contains C, and the circle with center C that contains A.

REVIEW

15. Suppose that every person applying for a particular job is randomly assigned a two-letter code from the 26 letters of the alphabet.
    a. What is the probability that a person's code has two vowels?
    b. What is the probability that a person's code has two consonants?
    c. What is the probability that a person's code has one vowel and one consonant? **(Lessons 10-6, 10-2)**

16. Mikayla surveyed 25 of the 210 people in her school and found that 17 of them owned a pet.
    a. Use a proportion to estimate the number of students in Mikayla's school who own pets.
    b. If a student is picked at random, what would you estimate is the probability that he or she owns a pet? **(Lessons 10-5, 8-6)**

17. In 32 at-bats, Clay Foote hit 6 singles, 1 double, 0 triples, and 2 home runs. The other times he made an out.
    a. What is the relative frequency of his getting a hit?
    b. Do you think the probability of his hitting a triple is zero? Explain why or why not. **(Lesson 10-5)**

18. **Multiple Choice** An airline has a restriction on baggage, which states that the sum of the length, width, and depth of a bag cannot exceed 62 inches. Which of the following suitcase dimensions meet this limit *and* has the greatest volume? **(Lesson 9-9)**
    A length: 25 inches; width: 16 inches; depth: 10 inches
    B length: 34 inches; width: 12 inches; depth: 8 inches
    C length: 24 inches; width: 15 inches; depth: 12 inches
    D length: 32 inches; width: 20 inches; depth: 12 inches

EXPLORATION

19. Repeat Question 3 but start with a different triangle each time. First do the problem with a right triangle. Then do it with an obtuse triangle as shown below. What have you discovered?

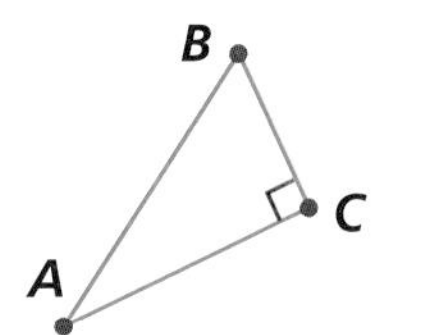

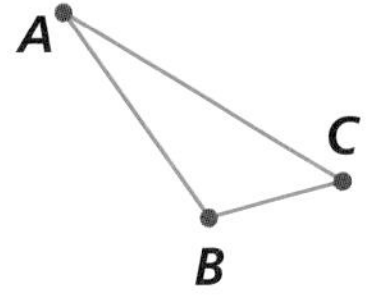

QY ANSWER

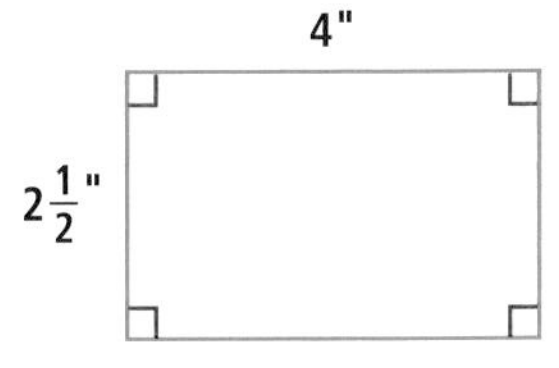

Lesson 11-2 Perpendicular Segments and Bisectors

Vocabulary

bisector of a segment
perpendicular bisector of a segment

▸ **BIG IDEA** Using a straightedge and compass, you can construct the perpendicular bisector of a segment, which also gives the midpoint.

Recall that lines, rays, or line segments that meet to form a 90° angle are called *perpendicular*. Perpendicular segments can be found in many places. Below are two examples.

Mental Math

Decide whether the equation is true, false, or whether it is impossible to determine based on the information given.

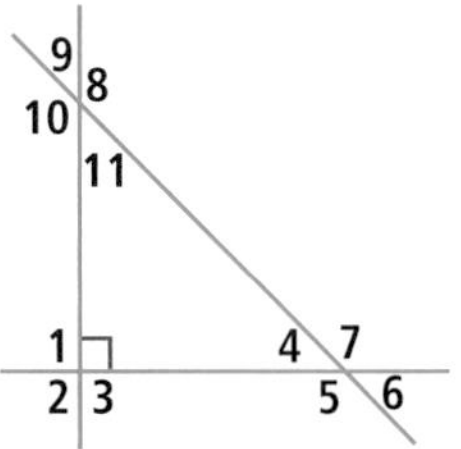

a. $m\angle 1 = m\angle 4$

b. $m\angle 1 = m\angle 11$

c. $m\angle 4 + m\angle 11 = m\angle 5$

d. $m\angle 6 = m\angle 8 - m\angle 1$

Activity 1

MATERIALS tracing paper, straightedge

Step 1 Draw a segment $\overline{AB}$ on a sheet of tracing paper.

Step 2 Fold the paper so that point *A* is on top of point *B*.

Step 3 Open the paper and draw a dashed line along the fold. What do you notice about the relationship between the line on the fold and $\overline{AB}$?

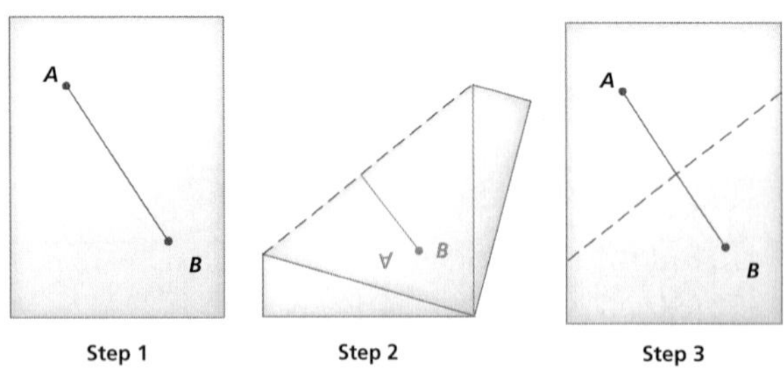

Perpendicular Bisectors

The line on the fold in Activity 1 is the *perpendicular bisector* of $\overline{AB}$. A **bisector of a segment** is any line, ray, or segment that intersects the segment at its midpoint, dividing the segment into two equal parts. The **perpendicular bisector of a segment** is the line that both bisects the segment and is perpendicular to it. A segment has many bisectors but only one perpendicular bisector. In the drawings below, M is the midpoint of $\overline{CD}$. The symbol $\perp$ means "is perpendicular to."

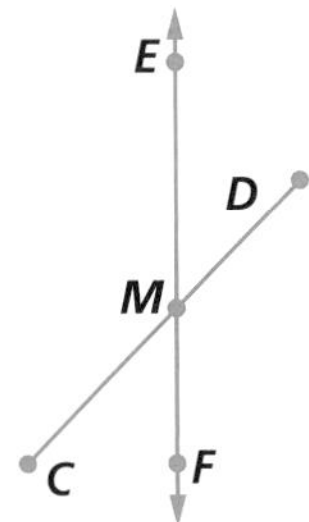

$\overleftrightarrow{EF}$ is a bisector of $\overline{CD}$.
$\overleftrightarrow{EF}$ is not perpendicular to $\overline{CD}$.

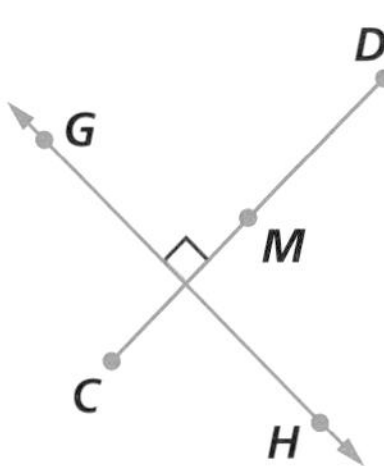

$\overleftrightarrow{GH} \perp \overline{CD}$.
$\overleftrightarrow{GH}$ is not a bisector of $\overline{CD}$.

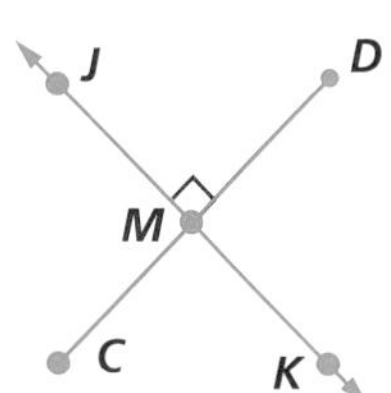

$\overleftrightarrow{JK}$ is the perpendicular bisector of $\overline{CD}$.

 See QY at the right.

 **QY**

Trace $\overline{AB}$ of Activity 1 and use a straightedge to draw a different line WZ that is perpendicular to $\overline{AB}$ but does not bisect $\overline{AB}$.

Construction of the Perpendicular Bisector of a Segment

Constructing the perpendicular bisector of a segment is one of the most basic of all constructions. It is used in many other constructions.

Activity 2

MATERIALS compass, straightedge

Step 1 Start with points A and B at least 1" apart on a sheet of paper. Construct $\overline{AB}$ by connecting points A and B using a straightedge.

Step 2 Construct the circle with center A containing point B.

Step 3 Construct the circle with center B containing point A.

Step 4 Name the two intersection points of the circles C and D.

Step 5 Construct $\overleftrightarrow{CD}$. $\overleftrightarrow{CD}$ is the perpendicular bisector of $\overline{AB}$.

Step 6 $\overleftrightarrow{CD}$ intersects $\overline{AB}$. Name the point of intersection M. M is the midpoint of $\overline{AB}$. Your figure should look like the one at the right.

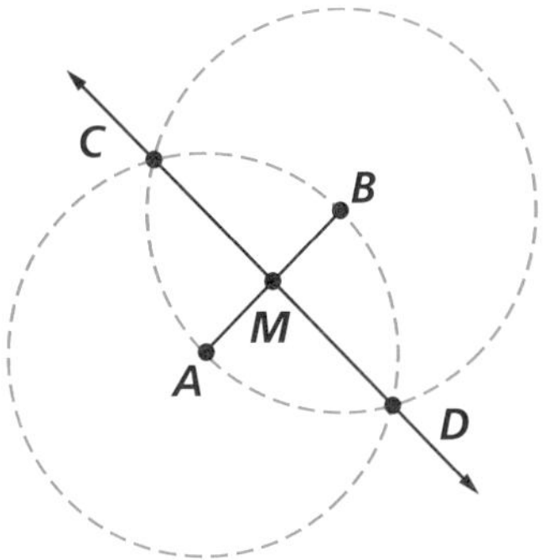

Step 6 shows that, when you construct the perpendicular bisector of a segment, you have also constructed the midpoint of the segment.

Constructing Perpendicular Lines Through a Point

Exactly one line is perpendicular to a line through a given point. In Activity 3, you are asked to draw this line. In Activity 4, you are asked to construct this line.

Activity 3

MATERIALS protractor, straightedge

Step 1 Trace $\overleftrightarrow{ME}$ and point *C* at the right. Draw the line that is perpendicular to $\overleftrightarrow{ME}$ and contains *M*.

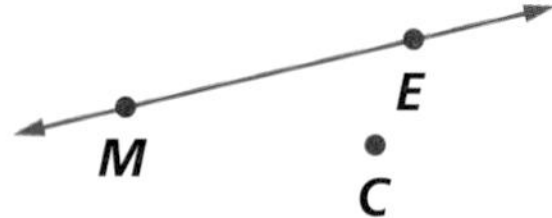

Step 2 On the same sheet as Step 1, draw the line that is perpendicular to $\overleftrightarrow{ME}$ and contains *C*.

Step 3 Trace $\overleftrightarrow{YZ}$ and point *A* at the right. Draw the line that is perpendicular to $\overleftrightarrow{YZ}$ and contains *Z*.

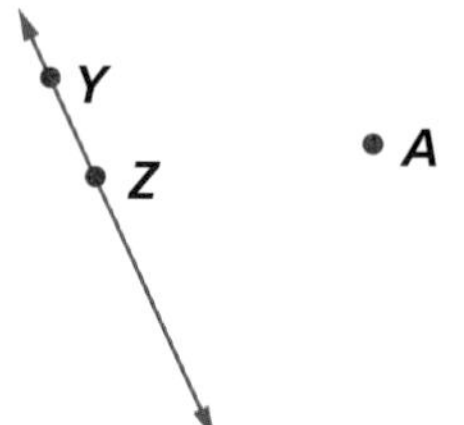

Step 4 Draw the line that is perpendicular to $\overleftrightarrow{YZ}$ and contains *A*.

Activity 4

MATERIALS compass, straightedge

Step 1 Trace $\overleftrightarrow{AB}$ and point *C*.

Step 2 Construct the circle with center *A* containing *C*.

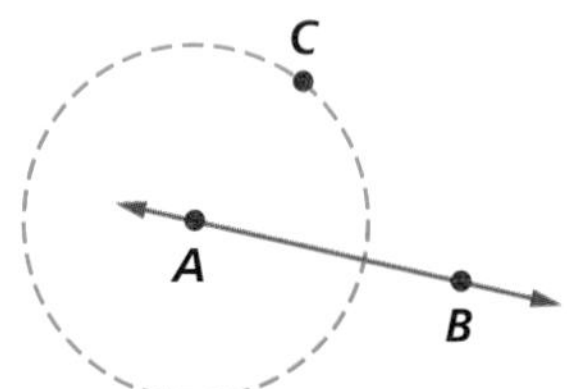

Step 3 Construct the circle with center *B* containing *C*. Name the second point of intersection *D*.

Step 4 Construct $\overleftrightarrow{CD}$.

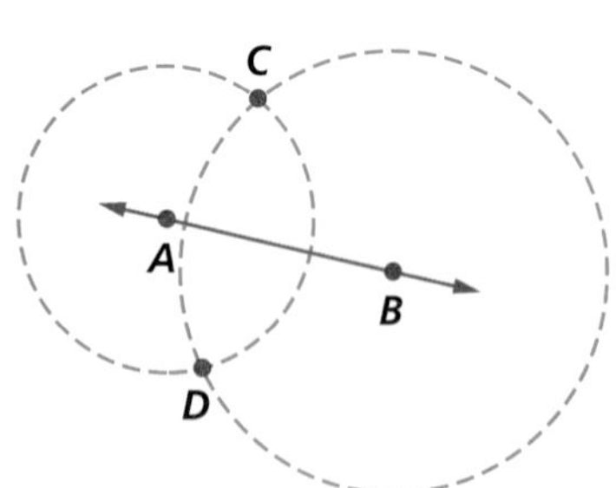

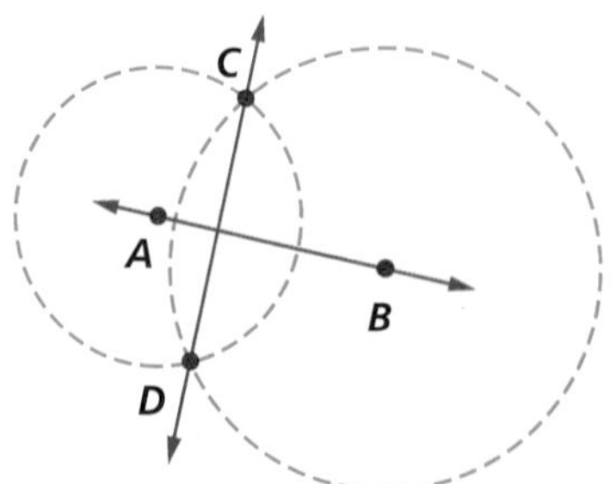

Questions

COVERING THE IDEAS

1. Name three examples of perpendicular lines, rays, or segments in things you see every day.

In 2–4, refer to the letters of the alphabet as written below.

A B C D E F G H I J K L M
N O P Q R S T U V W X Y Z

2. Which letters include perpendicular segments?
3. Which letters include segments that bisect each other?
4. Which letters have a segment that lies on the perpendicular bisector of another segment?

In 5 and 6, trace the segment before doing the construction. You do not need to write down the steps of the construction.

5. Construct the midpoint of $\overline{ER}$.

6. Construct the perpendicular bisector of $\overline{DW}$.

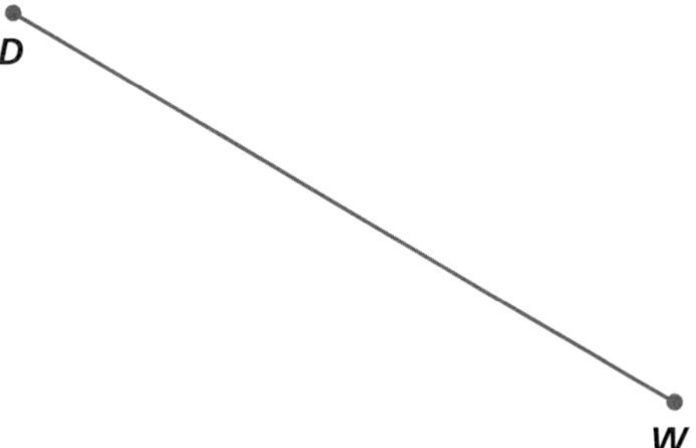

7. Start with three points E, F, and G.
   a. Construct $\overleftrightarrow{EF}$.
   b. Construct the perpendicular from G to $\overleftrightarrow{EF}$.

APPLYING THE MATHEMATICS

8. Why can there be no bisector of a line?
9. Is it possible for $\overline{AB}$ to be a bisector of $\overline{CD}$ but not perpendicular to $\overline{CD}$ and, at the same time, for $\overline{CD}$ to be a bisector of $\overline{AB}$? If so, draw an example. If not, explain why not.

10. a. Perform the following construction.

 Step 1 Start with $\overleftrightarrow{OP}$.

 Step 2 Construct the circle with center O containing P.

 Step 3 Name Q the second point of intersection of $\overleftrightarrow{OP}$ and circle O.

 Step 4 Construct the circle with center P containing Q.

 Step 5 Circle P intersects $\overleftrightarrow{OP}$ at two points. One point is Q. Name the second point of intersection R.

 b. How does the radius of circle O compare to the radius of circle P?

 c. How does the area of circle P compare to the area of circle O?

11. a. Perform the following construction. (*Note:* Step 2 requires many smaller steps.)

 Step 1 Start with points P and Q on circle C. P and Q should not be endpoints of the same diameter.

 Step 2 Construct the perpendicular bisector of $\overline{PQ}$.

 b. Describe the relationships you see in this construction.

12. Sun was using the map below to design a flight plan for a trip from Charleston, West Virginia to Cheyenne, Wyoming. Although she did not have mileage figures, she wanted to mark the midpoint of this flight on the map. Explain how making a construction might help her.

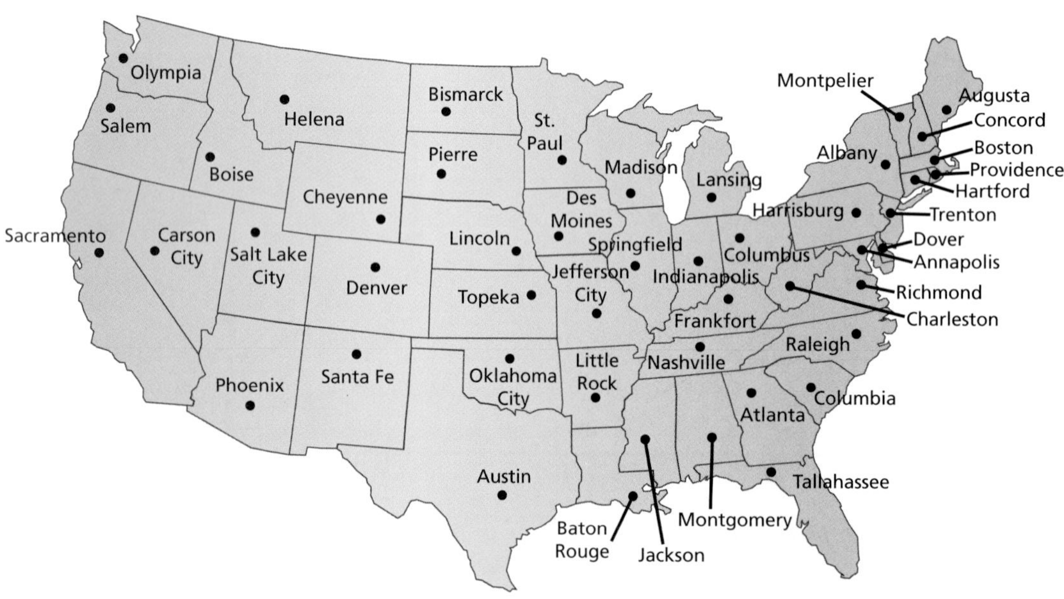

REVIEW

13. The lengths of the segments at the right are a and b. Draw a segment with length $b - a$. **(Lesson 11-1)**

a

b

14. Using the following lengths for your radii, construct three concentric circles (circles with the same center). **(Lesson 11-1)**

2 cm　　　5 cm　　　6 cm

15. In archery, Guadalupe hits the bulls-eye 90 percent of the time. She wants to hit one bulls-eye before she leaves. **(Lesson 10-2)**
   a. What is the probability that she will leave after the first shot?
   b. What is the probability that she will have to take a second shot?

16. **Multiple Choice** If p and q are positive integers, then $\frac{2}{3} \div \frac{p}{q}$ is greatest when **(Lesson 8-3)**
   A p is greater than q.　　B $p = q$.　　C p is less than q.

17. Use a ruler and protractor to draw an angle of measure 168°. **(Lesson 3-5)**

18. Use a protractor to measure the angle below. **(Lesson 3-5)**

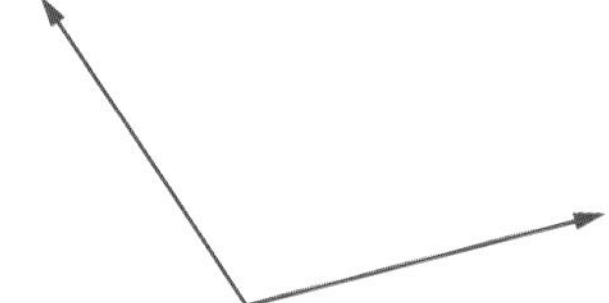

EXPLORATION

19. Most DGS technology has a menu item or button that constructs a perpendicular bisector. If you have a calculator or computer with DGS software, find out how to construct the perpendicular bisector of a segment.

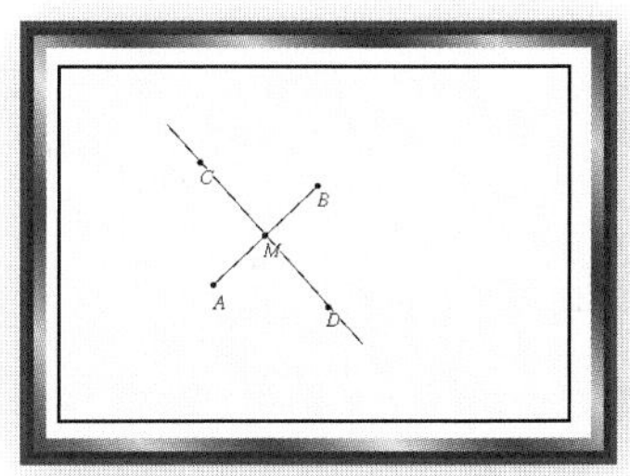

20. If you have a calculator or computer with DGS software, find out how to construct a perpendicular to $\overleftrightarrow{AB}$ from a point C not on the line.

21. Trace $\triangle ABC$ below. Construct the perpendicular to $\overline{AB}$ from point C. Name the point of intersection E. Measure AB and CE. Find the area of $\triangle ABC$.

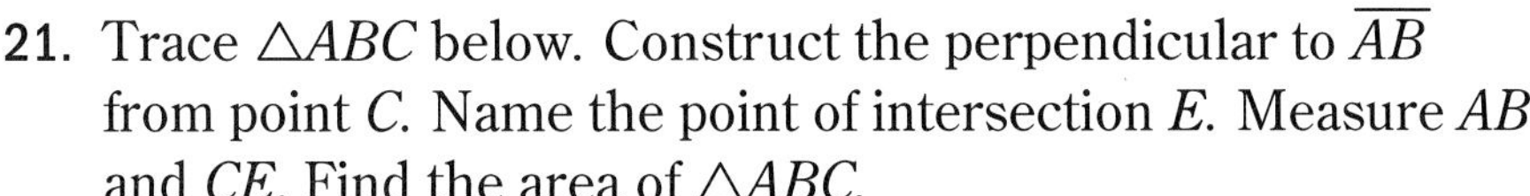

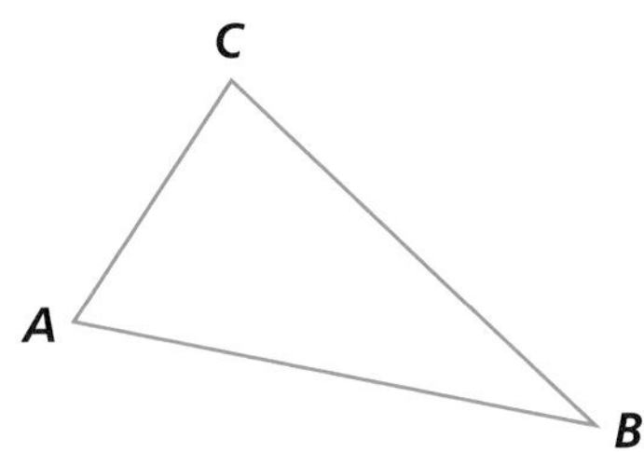

QY ANSWER

Answers vary. Sample:

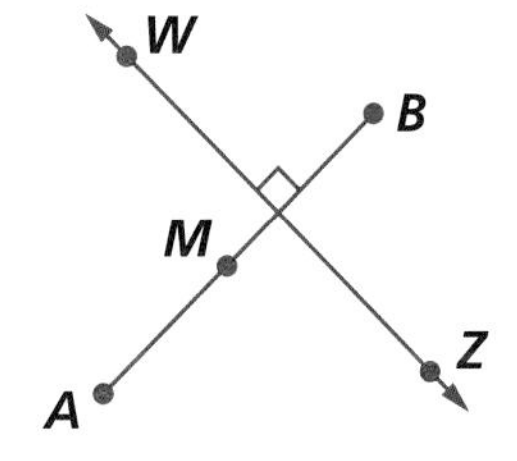

Lesson 11-3 Reflections

Vocabulary

reflection image of *A* over the line *m*

reflecting line, line of reflection, mirror

▶ **BIG IDEA** The reflection image of a point over a line can be described using the idea of perpendicular bisector.

Mental Math

Identify the additive inverse of the expression.

a. –4

b. 5.7

c. $(-8)^2$

d. $a + b$

In the rest of this chapter, you will study three ways geometric figures can be changed or transformed: by reflection, by translation, and by rotation. This lesson is about the type of transformation called a *reflection.*

Even if you have never studied reflections before, you already have experience with them. When you look in a mirror, you see the reflection image of your face. Images of the trees in the picture above are found in the water. Geometry shows how reflections work.

The word *image* suggests a mirror. Below are two triangles, $\triangle BIT$ and $\triangle CAP$. $\triangle CAP$ is the *reflection image of* $\triangle BIT$ *over the line (or mirror) m.*

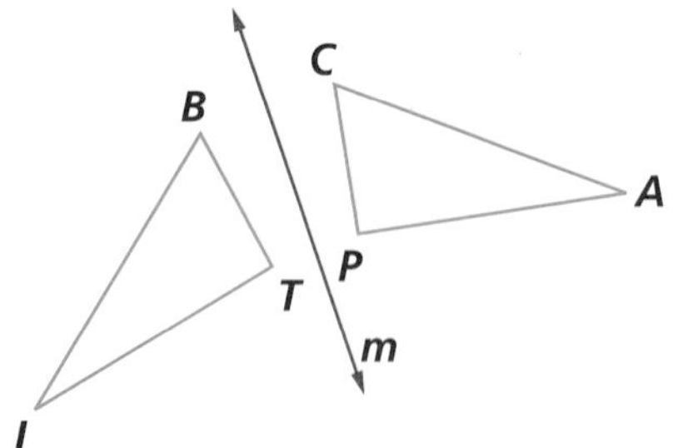

Notice that if you connect B and C, m is the perpendicular bisector of $\overline{BC}$. The mirror m is also the perpendicular bisector of $\overline{PT}$ and $\overline{AI}$. This tells us how to locate the reflection image of a point.

Suppose a point A is not on line m. Point B is the **reflection image of A over line m** if and only if m is the perpendicular bisector of $\overline{AB}$. If A is on line m, then A is its own reflection image. Line m is called the **reflecting line**, or **line of reflection**, or **mirror.**

You can construct a reflection image using what you know about perpendicular bisectors. Here is a two-step process for reflecting a point A over a line m. (*Note:* Step 2 combines a few steps.)

Activity 1

MATERIALS compass, straightedge

Step 1 Begin with a point A not on line m.

Step 2 Construct the perpendicular to line m through A. Label the point of intersection M.

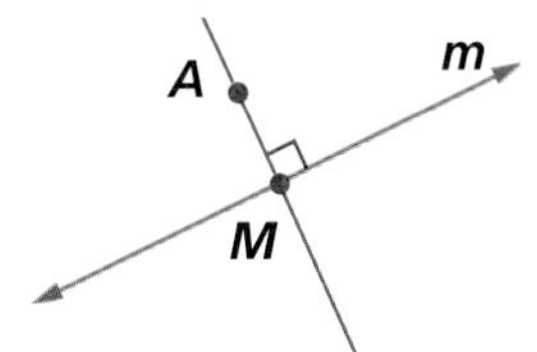

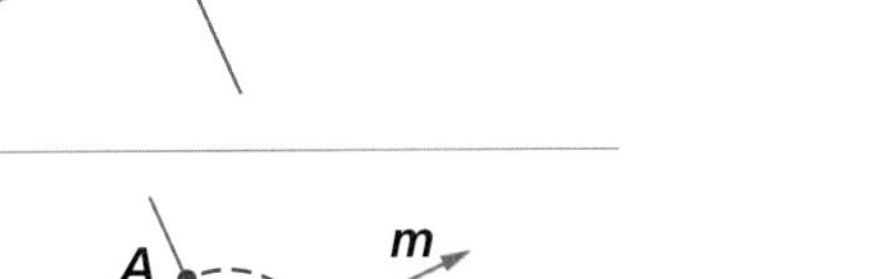

Step 3 Construct the circle with center M containing A. Let A' be the second point of intersection of $\overleftrightarrow{AM}$ and the circle. Then, $AM = A'M$.

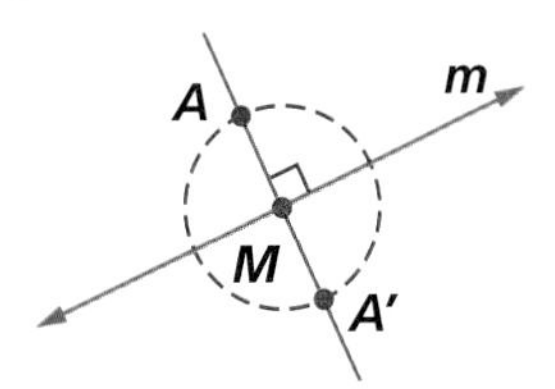

The image of a point is denoted by using the symbol ′, read "prime." So A', read "A prime" is understood to be the image of A, and so on.

Drawing the Reflection Image of a Figure

To find the reflection image of a figure, reflect important points, such as vertices. Then connect the images of these points to get the sides of the image. Three ways to create a reflection image are paper folding, a construction, and technology.

Activity 2

MATERIALS compass, straightedge

Follow these steps to construct the reflection image of pentagon *HOUSE* over line *m*.

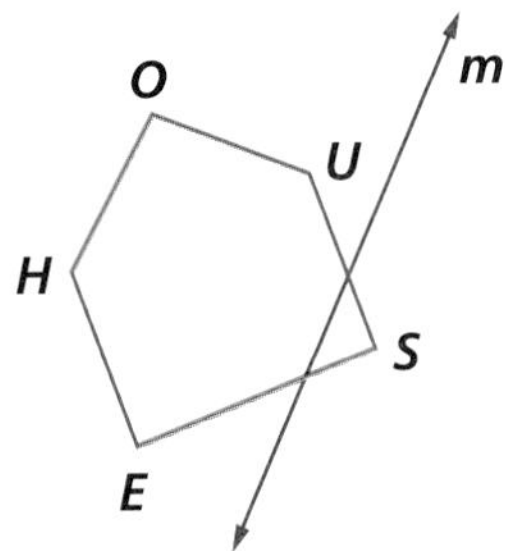

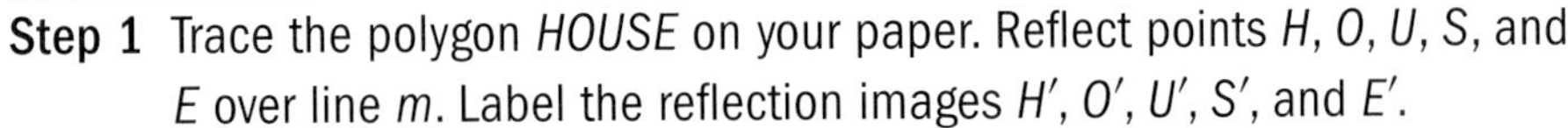

Step 1 Trace the polygon *HOUSE* on your paper. Reflect points H, O, U, S, and E over line m. Label the reflection images H', O', U', S', and E'.

Step 2 Connect the image points to get the sides of the reflection image.

Step 3 Check your work by folding the paper along the line of reflection.

Activity 3

MATERIALS three sheets of tracing paper, three colored pencils

Follow these steps for each figure below. Use a separate sheet of paper for each figure.

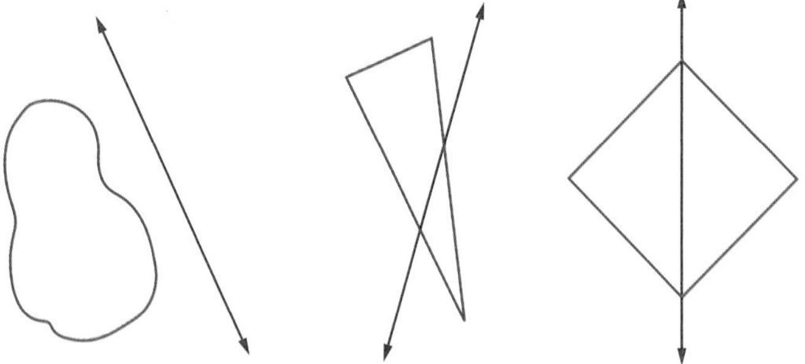

Step 1 Trace the figure and the reflecting line.

Step 2 Using a second color, sketch what you think is the reflection image.

Step 3 Fold the paper along the line of reflection.

Step 4 Find the reflection image of the figure and draw it in a third color.

Step 5 How close was your predicted image to the actual image?

Questions

COVERING THE IDEAS

1. Give a real-world example of a reflection.
2. Name three types of transformations.
3. Trace the figure at the right. Label the reflection images of the vertices of *NICELY* with the letters N', I', C', E', L', and Y'.

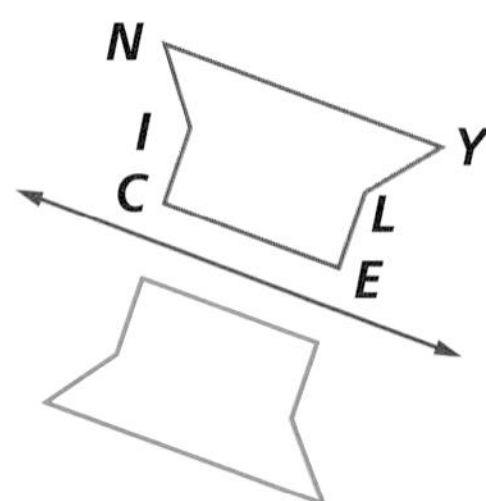

In 4 and 5, trace the figure and construct the reflection image of the triangle over the line.

4. 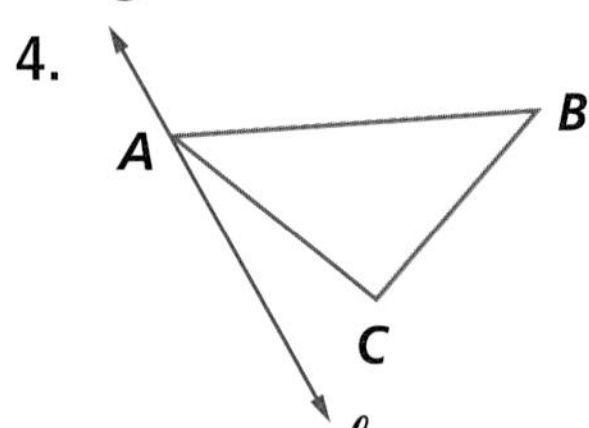

5. 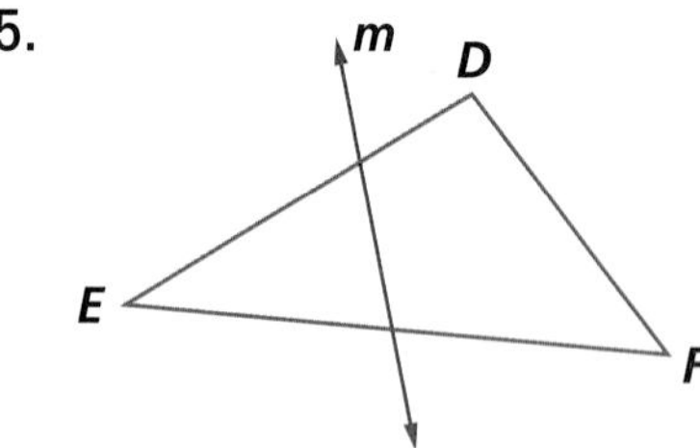

In 6 and 7, trace the figure and use paper folding to find the reflection image.

6. 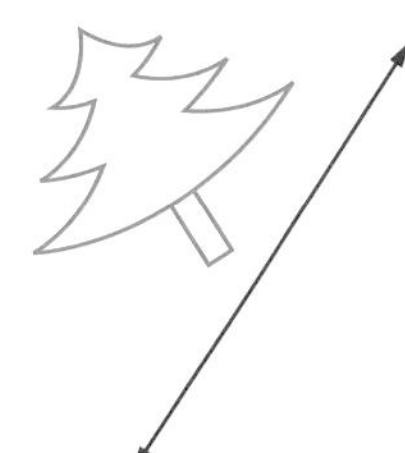

7. 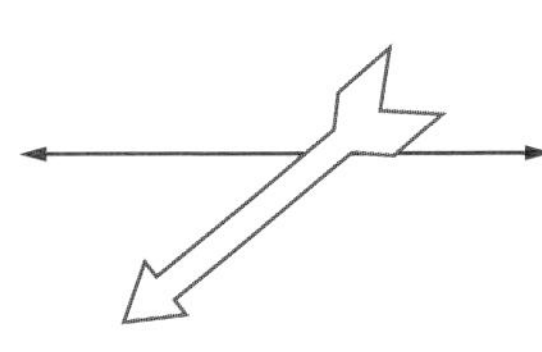

8. Trace this figure and construct the reflection image of *MOUNT* over line ℓ.

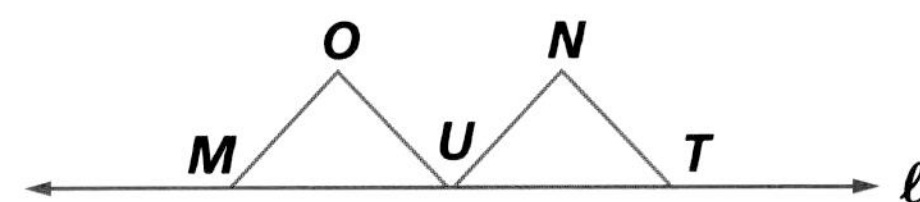

APPLYING THE MATHEMATICS

9. Trace the figures at the right. Construct a line so that rectangle G is the image of rectangle F over the line.

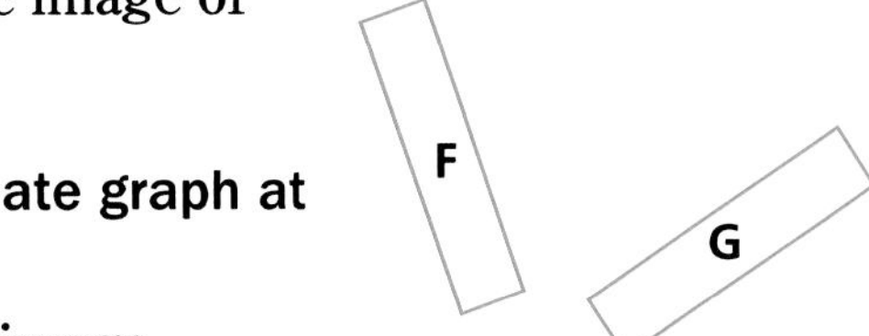

In 10 and 11, consider the coordinate graph at the right.

10. a. Give the coordinates of the image points B', R', A', V', and E' when B, R, A, V, and E are reflected over the x-axis.

    b. When a point (x, y) is reflected over the x-axis, what are the coordinates of its image?

11. a. Give the coordinates of the image points B'', R'', A'', V'', and E'' (read "double prime") when B, R, A, V, and E are reflected over the y-axis.

    b. When a point (x, y) is reflected over the y-axis, what are the coordinates of its image?

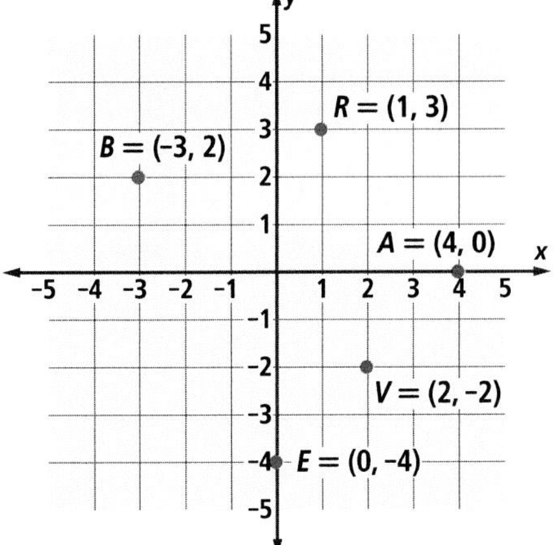

In 12–14, what figure results if you combine the original figure with its reflection image?

12. 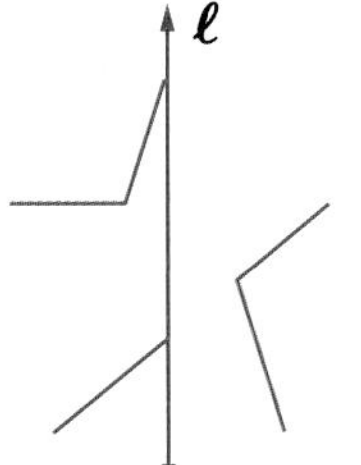

13. 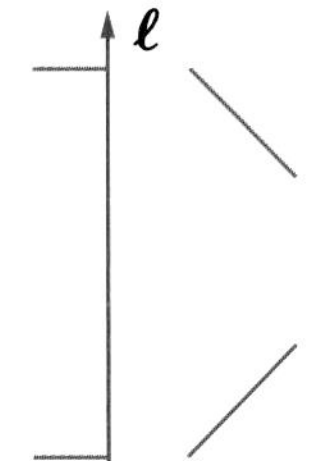

14. 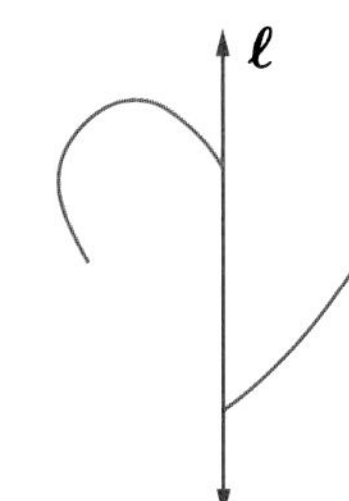

REVIEW

15. Trace $\overline{AB}$ at the right. Construct the perpendicular bisector of $\overline{AB}$. Label the intersection of $\overline{AB}$ with its perpendicular bisector D. Label a point C on the perpendicular bisector but not on $\overline{AB}$. **(Lesson 11-2)**

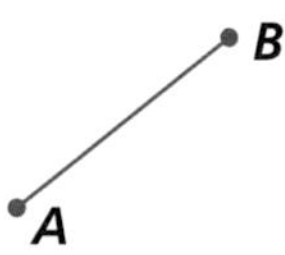

16. Consider all the figures constructed by all the people who do Question 15. Answer *always, sometimes but not always,* or *never.* **(Lesson 11-1)**
    a. $AB > CD$
    b. area of $\triangle ABC$ = area of $\triangle ACD$
    c. $BC > AD$

17. The distance between two stores on a map is 3 cm. If the map has a scale of 1:75,000, what is the actual distance in kilometers between the stores? **(Lesson 8-8)**

18. Draw two supplementary angles that are not a linear pair. **(Lesson 4-5)**

EXPLORATION

19. Explore a DGS to find out how to draw a figure and its reflection image, such as the one shown below.

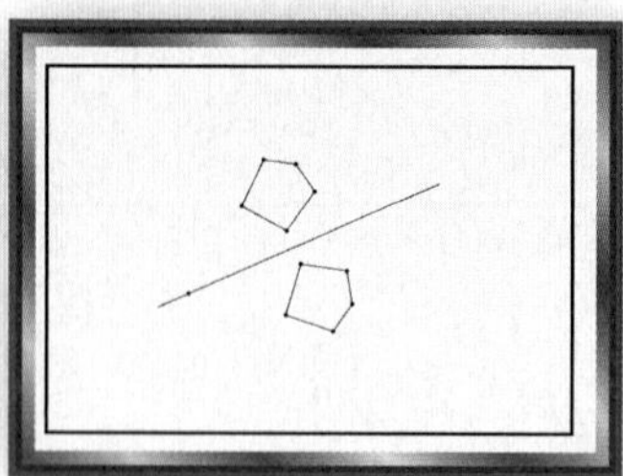

Lesson

11-4 Angles and Rotations

Vocabulary

duplicating an angle

rotation

▸ **BIG IDEA** A rotation is a turn of a certain magnitude around a fixed point.

In earlier lessons, you drew angles of a given measure. In this lesson you will draw triangles given some side lengths and angle measures, construct a copy of a given angle, and use angles to rotate figures.

Mental Math

Identify the point on the coordinate grid with the coordinates.

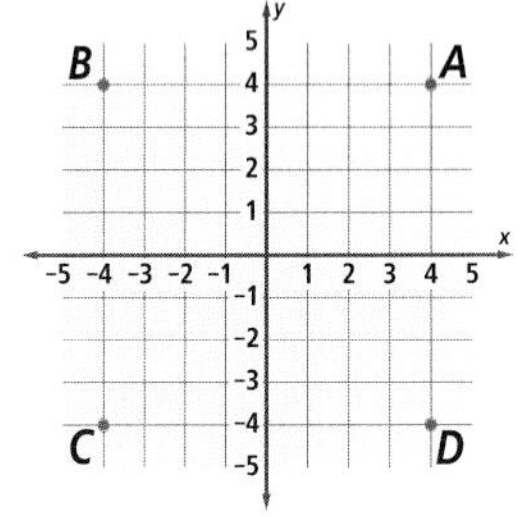

a. (–4, –4)

b. (4, 4)

c. (4, –4)

d. (–4, 4)

Drawing a Triangle with Sides and Angles of Given Lengths

There are many triangles with a side of length 2 inches. There are even many triangles with a side of length 2 inches and a 50° angle. But if you are given the length of one side and the measure of two angles, then the triangle's other sides and other angle measure are determined. You can draw a triangle with that given information using a ruler and protractor.

MATERIALS ruler, protractor

Step 1 Draw a line segment that is 2 inches long. Label its endpoints S and A.

Step 2 Draw a right angle at S. Name point B so that this is $\angle ASB$.

Step 3 Use your protractor to make a 50° angle with vertex A and one side $\overline{AS}$. Name point C so that this is $\angle SAC$.

Step 4 Let T be the intersection of $\overrightarrow{SB}$ and $\overrightarrow{AC}$. Then $\triangle SAT$ is the desired triangle.

Step 5 Calculate the measure of the third angle. What should it be? Check it with your protractor.

Duplicating an Angle

Suppose you want to draw an angle that has the same measure as an angle drawn on a piece of paper. However, you have no protractor and you cannot trace the angle. For this situation, you can use a construction called *duplicating an angle.* **Duplicating an angle** means creating a new angle with the same measure as a given angle.

In Activity 2, you will duplicate an angle of the same measure as $\angle B$ at the right .

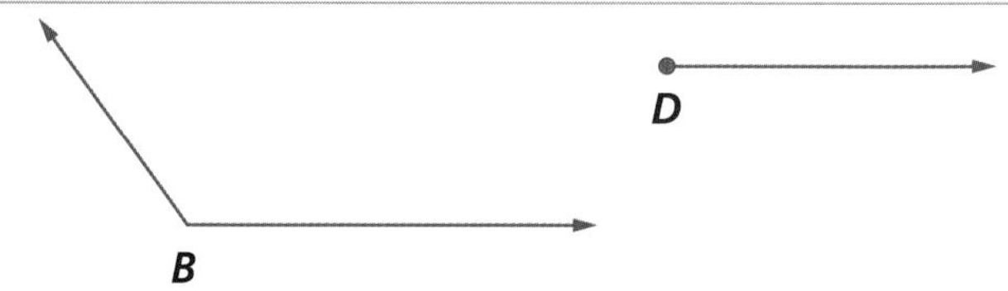

Activity 2

MATERIALS straightedge, compass

Step 1 Trace $\angle B$. above. Then draw a ray with end point D.

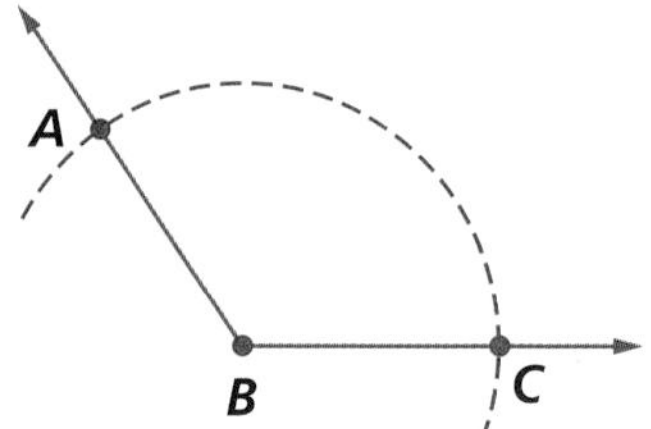

Step 2 Draw an arc of a circle with center B that crosses both sides of $\angle B$. Label the intersectopm points A and C.

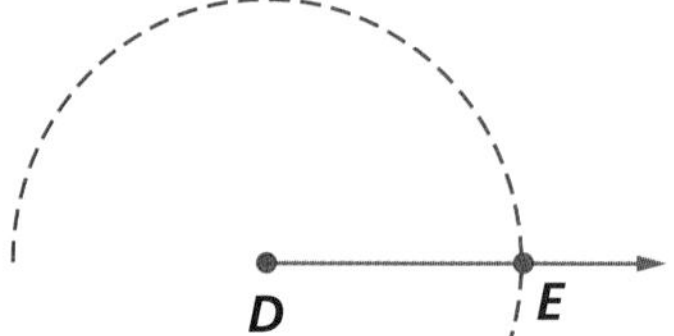

Step 3 Using the same radius as in Step 2, draw a large arc of a circle with center D from the ray in Step 1. Label the point of intersection E.

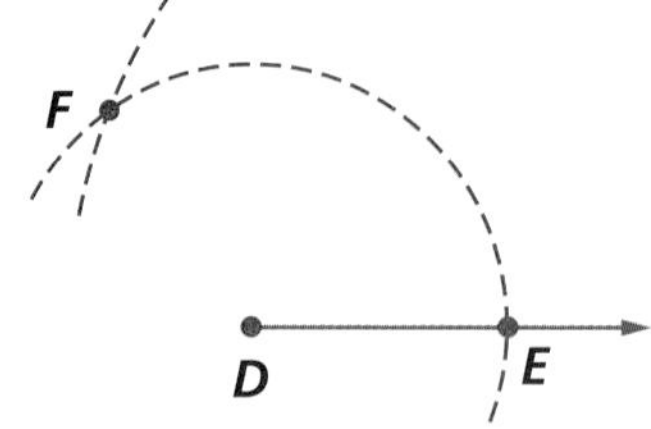

Step 4 Go back to $\angle B$ and adjust your compass to create opening AC. Then draw an arc with center E. Label a point of intersection of the two arcs F.

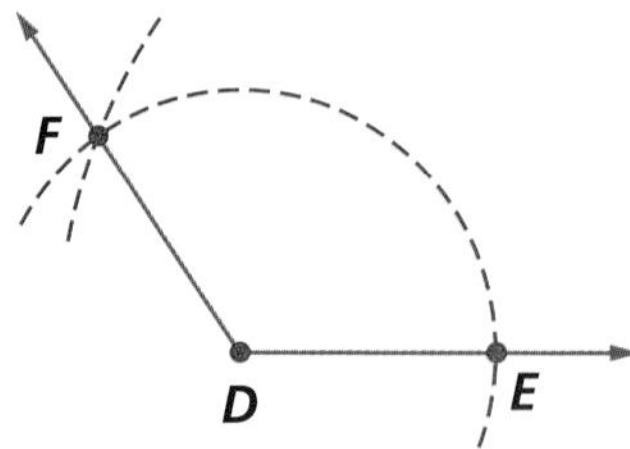

Step 5 Draw $\overrightarrow{DF}$. Measure $\angle B$ and $\angle D$. They should have the same measure.

Rotation of a Figure

A **rotation** is a turn around a fixed point. You can describe a rotation by giving the number of degrees in the rotation and its direction, clockwise (negative) or counterclockwise (positive). For instance, think of the second hand of a watch or a clock. In 60 seconds, the second hand rotates one revolution clockwise or -360°. So in 5 seconds, the hand rotates -30°. The measure of the angle between the second hand at one instant and the same hand 5 seconds later is 30°.

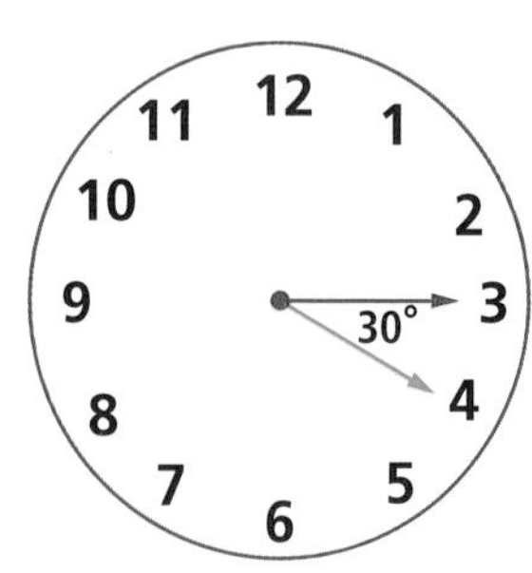

Geometric figures can be rotated about points by using angles. In the drawing below, figure I is rotated 110° about point *C* to create the image II.

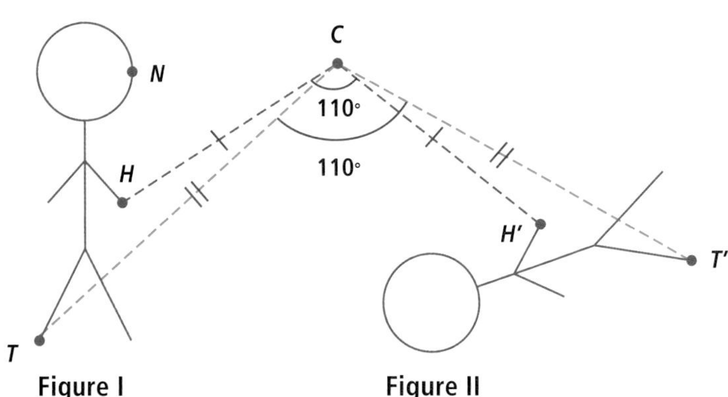

Activity 3

MATERIALS ruler, protractor

Step 1 Trace figure I, its rotation image figure II, and points *A* and *C* above. On your drawing, locate the image of point *N*. Call the image *N′*.

Step 2 Measure $\angle NCN'$. How close is the measure to 110°?

Step 3 Draw the circle *C* with radius *CA*.

Step 4 Find the image of *A* under the 110° rotation with center *C*.

In Activity 4, you are asked to rotate the arrow below 120° counterclockwise about point *K*.

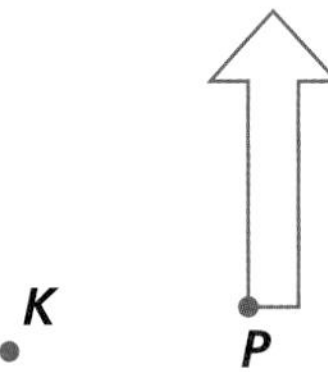

Activity 4

MATERIALS two sheets of tracing paper, ruler, protractor

Step 1 On both sheets of tracing paper, trace the arrow and points *K* and *P*. Since 120° is $\frac{1}{3}$ of the way around a circle, the image of the arrow should be $\frac{1}{3}$ of the way counterclockwise around point *K*. Draw a rough sketch on one of the sheets of paper where you think the image should be.

(continued on next page)

Step 2 On the second sheet of paper, draw a 120° angle *PKU* as shown at the right.

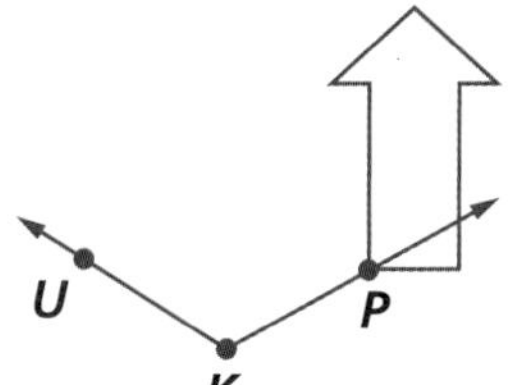

Step 3 Place the second sheet of paper on the top of the one with your estimate so that one point *K* is on top of the other point *K*. Holding the tip of your pencil firmly on point *K*, turn the bottom sheet of tracing paper until point *P* is on side $\overline{KU}$. Then trace the image of the arrow onto the top sheet of tracing paper.

Step 4 Using a protractor compare your rough sketch with the final image. How close were you?

Step 5 Do the construction using technology. Below is an arrow and its image as constructed by a DGS. If you have access to a calculator or computer with DGS software, draw an arrow and a point *K*, and instruct your technology to do the rotation.

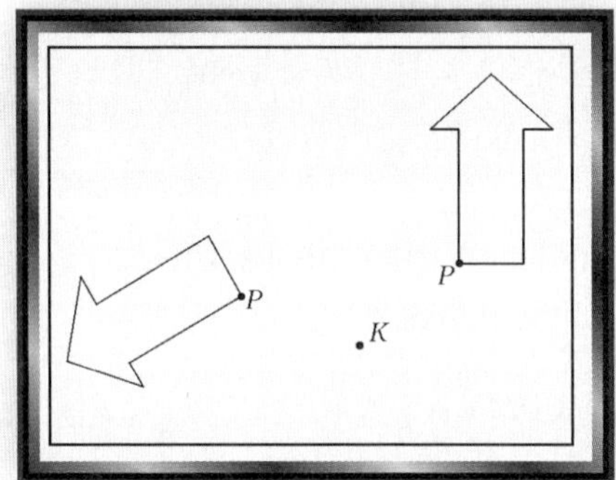

Questions

COVERING THE IDEAS

In 1 and 2, draw a triangle that meets the given conditions.

1. The lengths of sides $\overline{DO}$ and $\overline{OG}$ are 4 cm, and $m\angle O = 40°$.

2. The length of side $\overline{CA}$ is $3\frac{1}{2}$ inches, $m\angle TCA = 45°$, and $m\angle TAC = 60°$.

In 3 and 4, duplicate the angle using a compass and a straightedge.

3.

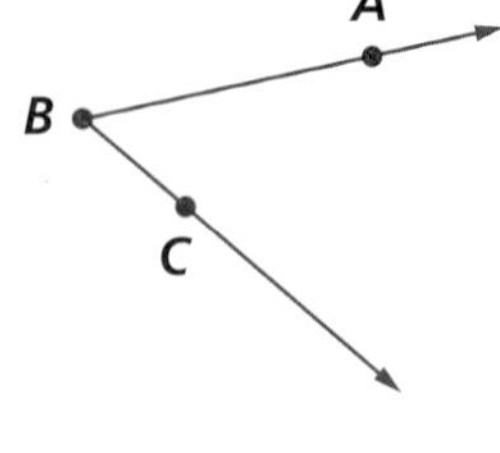

4.

5. **Fill in the blank** Another word for *rotation* is __?__?
6. What information is sufficient to describe a rotation?
7. In a rotation of -75°, what point is the same as its rotation image?
8. How many degrees does the second hand of a watch rotate in 25 seconds?
9. How many degrees does the hour hand of a watch rotate in 15 minutes?
10. Trace $\triangle ABC$ and point P at the right. Consider rotating the triangle 70° in a clockwise direction around point P.
    a. Draw a rough sketch of the image where you think it should be.
    b. Make a more accurate drawing of the image.

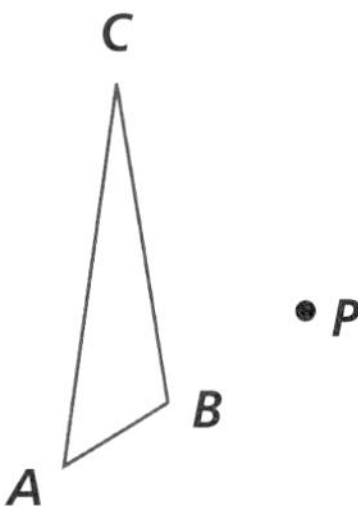

APPLYING THE MATHEMATICS

11. Draw a pentagon with all sides the same length and all angles of equal measure. Make each side 5 cm long.
12. Use a straightedge and compass to construct an angle with a measure twice the measure of $\angle BIG$ below.

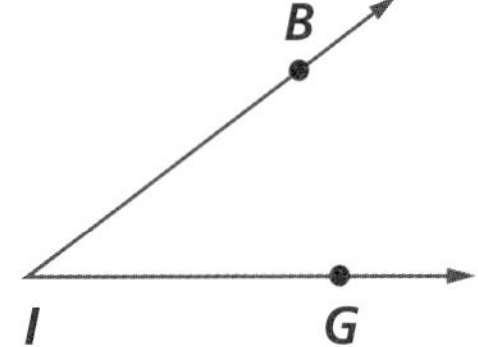

For 13–16 use rectangle *READ* below.

13. Trace *READ,* and draw its image under a rotation of 180° with center D.
14. Trace *READ,* and draw its image under a rotation with center D and measure -90°.
15. Trace *READ*. Find a center of rotation P on *READ* so that under a rotation of 180° about P, *READ* and its rotation image together form a new rectangle with twice the length of *READ*.
16. Trace *READ*. Find a center of rotation Q on *READ* so that under a rotation of 180° about Q, *READ* and its rotation image together form a new rectangle with twice the width of *READ*.

17. $\triangle A'E'P'$ at the right is the image of $\triangle AEP$ under a rotation.

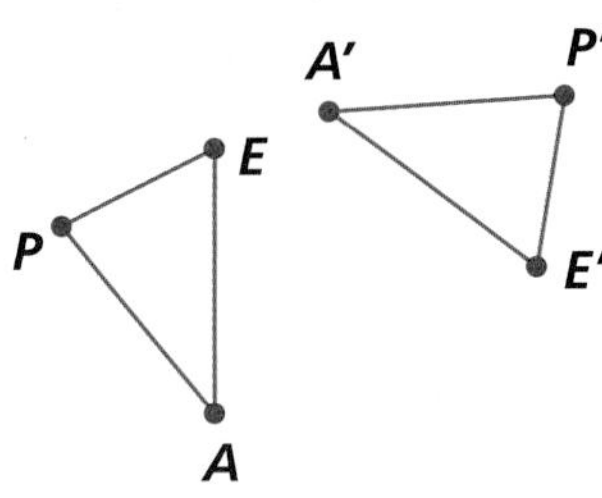

Step 1 Trace both triangles in the center of a large sheet of paper.

Step 2 Connect $\overline{AA'}$ and $\overline{PP'}$.

Step 3 Construct the perpendicular bisectors of $\overline{AA'}$ and $\overline{PP'}$. The intersection of these perpendicular bisectors is the center of the rotation. Label it C.

Step 4 Check the center of the rotation by tracing.

18. **a.** Use a protractor and ruler to draw a triangle with sides 1.5 cm and 2.4 cm and a 115° angle between those sides.

    b. Estimate the length of the third side of the triangle.

REVIEW

19. Consider the two line segments and the semicircle at the right as one figure. **(Lesson 11-3)**

    a. Reflect the figure over of the y-axis.

    b. Reflect the figure over the x-axis.

20. Suppose you are a contestant on a game show.

    a. In one room, a bike sits behind one of five doors. If you are given one choice, what is the probability you will choose the door that has the bike behind it?

    b. In another room, a bike sits behind ten out of fifty doors. If you are given one choice, what is the probability you will choose a door that has a bike behind it?

    c. If you are given three choices instead of one, in which room would you rather make your choices? Why? **(Lessons 10-5, 10-2)**

EXPLORATION

21. Under a rotation of 100° with center C, A' is the image of A.

    a. Explain why $\triangle A'AC$ has two sides of the same length.

    b. What would the measure of $\angle A'CA$ have to be in order for $\triangle A'AC$ to be equilateral?

Lesson 11-5 Angles and Parallel Lines

Vocabulary

transversal

corresponding angles

BIG IDEA When parallel lines are intersected by a transversal, many pairs of supplementary angles and many angles of equal measure are created.

Recall from Lesson 9-3 that two different lines in the same plane either intersect or are parallel. Straight train tracks lie on parallel lines, as do the opposite edges of a piece of notebook paper. When lines a and b are parallel, we write $a \parallel b$, read "a is parallel to b."

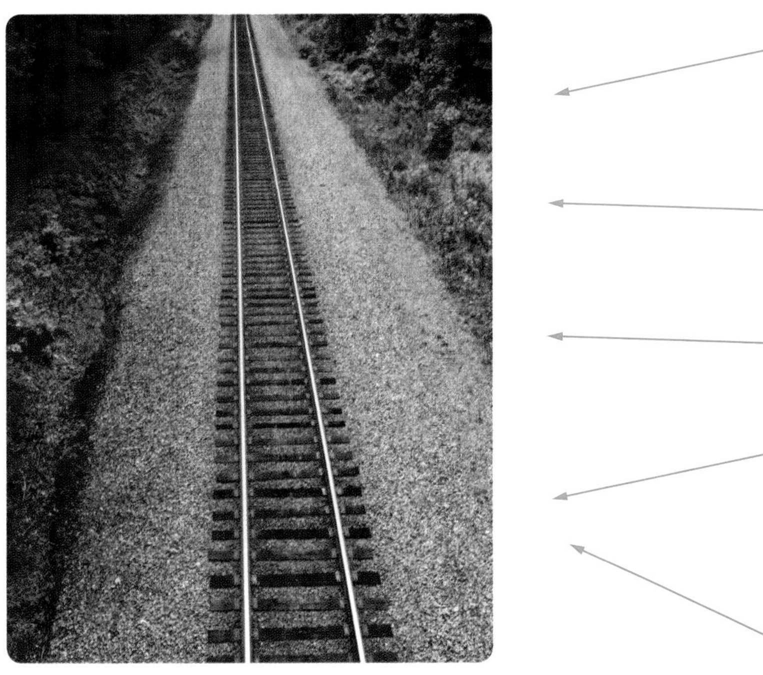

Mental Math

Refer to the pan balance.

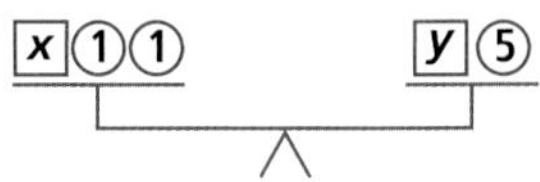

a. If $x = 3$, find y.

b. If $y = 7$, find x.

c. $y = \underline{\ ?\ } + x$

QY1

Which of the five lines above seem to be parallel to each other?

Corresponding Angles

A **transversal** is a line that intersects two or more lines. For instance, line c at the right is a transversal to lines a and b. **Corresponding angles** are pairs of angles in similar locations in relation to a transversal. Angles 1 and 5 are corresponding angles because they are both in the upper left position at the intersection with the transversal c.

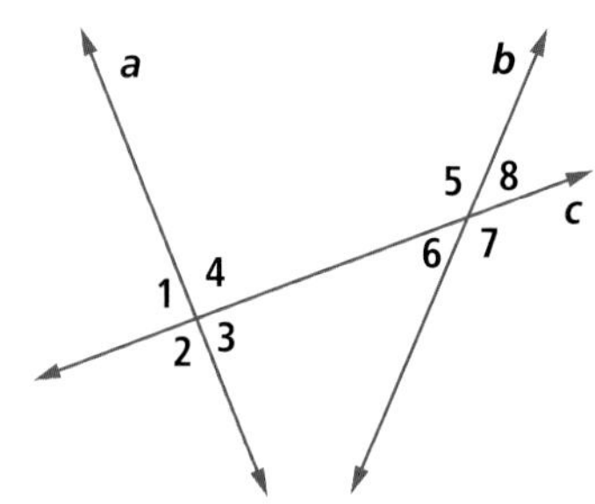

Activity 1

MATERIALS protractor

Step 1 Name the other three pairs of corresponding angles formed by lines *a*, *b*, and transversal *c* on the previous page.

Step 2 Using a protractor, find the measures of the eight numbered angles.

Step 3 Fill in the table at the right. Describe at least two patterns in the angle measures.

Angle	Angle Measure	Pair of Corresponding Angles
∠1	87°	∠1 and ∠5

Lines intersected by a transversal do not have to be parallel. But when they are parallel as in the figure at the right, the corresponding angles have the same measure. Likewise, when corresponding angles have the same measure, the lines are parallel. This important property is called the *Corresponding Angles Property*.

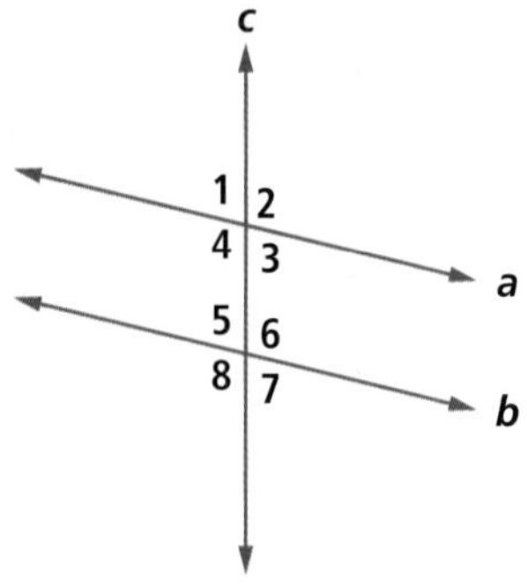

Corresponding Angles Property

When two lines are intersected by a transversal, corresponding angles have the same measure if and only if the lines are parallel.

Activity 2

MATERIALS protractor

In the figure at the right above, *a* || *b* and *c* is a transversal.

Step 1 Using a protractor, find the measures of the eight numbered angles.

Step 2 Fill in the table. Describe the patterns in the angle measures.

Angle	Angle Measure	Pair of Corresponding Angles
∠1	75°	∠1 and ∠5

STOP QY2

When two parallel lines are intersected by a transversal, eight angles are formed. At most, how many different measures do these angles have?

Drawing Parallel Lines

In Lesson 11-2, you constructed a line perpendicular to a given line through a point not on that line. Here is a way to draw a line *parallel* to a given line through a point not on that line.

Activity 3

MATERIALS unlined paper, protractor

Step 1 Draw a line across the center of your paper. Do not make it parallel to any side of the paper.

Step 2 Place two points P and Q on your line. Using a protractor, draw a line t that forms a 40° angle APQ with your line.

Step 3 Using a protractor, make a corresponding angle of 40°, with A as the vertex.

Step 4 Extend one side of the angle to show more of the parallel line.

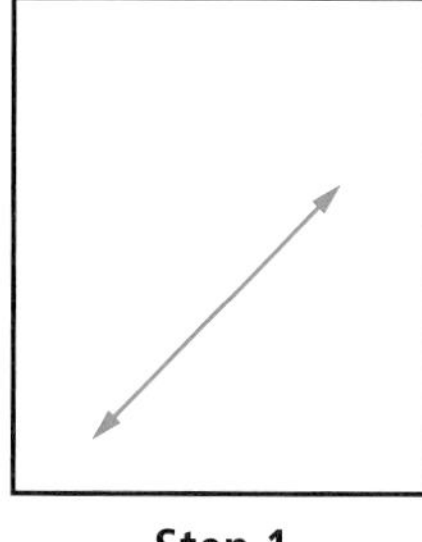
Step 1

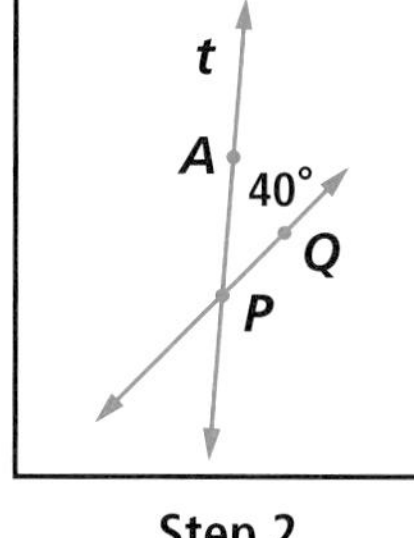

Step 2

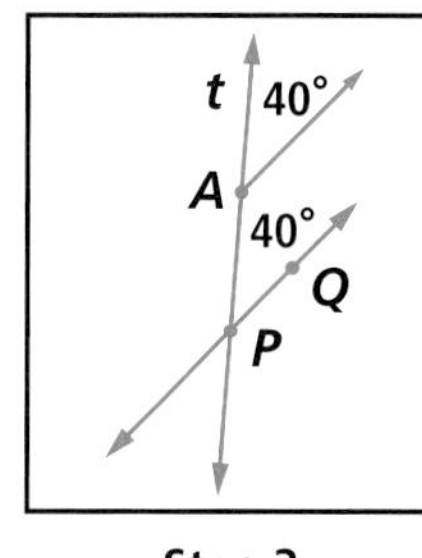

Step 3

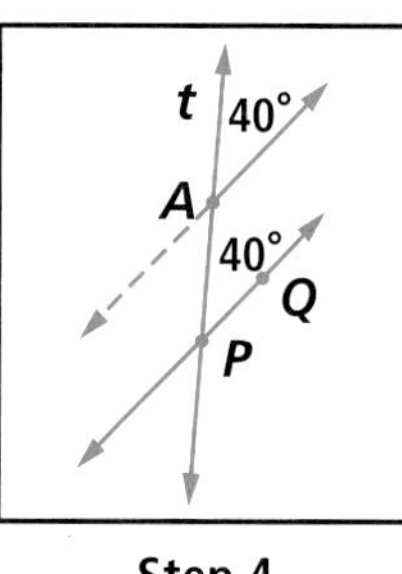

Step 4

On the diagram in the Guided Example below, the arrows drawn in the middle of lines a and c indicate that the lines are parallel.

GUIDED

Example

In the figure at the right, $a \parallel c$ and $m\angle 1 = 43°$. Find the measures of the other numbered angles.

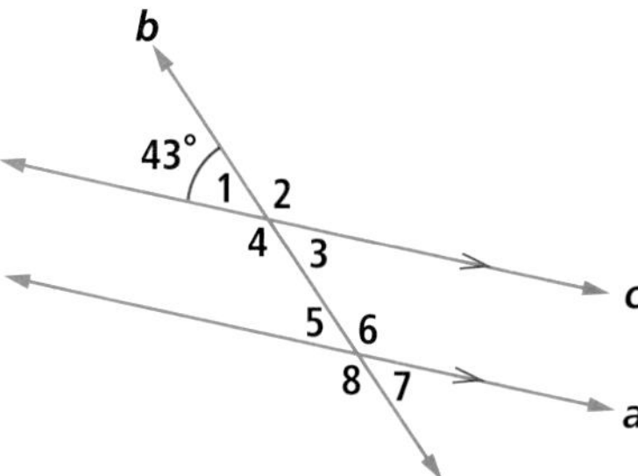

Solution Since $m\angle 1 = 43°$ and $\angle 4$ and $\angle 1$ form a linear pair, $m\angle 4 =$ _?_. $\angle 2$ and $\angle 1$ also form a linear pair, so $m\angle 2 =$ _?_. Since $\angle 3$ and $\angle 1$ are vertical angles, $m\angle 3 =$ _?_.

At the intersection of a and b, because $\angle 1$ and _?_ are corresponding angles, m _?_ $= 43°$. $m\angle 6 =$ _?_ because $\angle 6$ and $\angle 5$ form a _?_. Because $\angle 7$ and _?_ are corresponding angles, m_?_ = _?_, and because $\angle 8$ and _?_ are corresponding angles, $m\angle 8 =$ _?_.

Questions

COVERING THE IDEAS

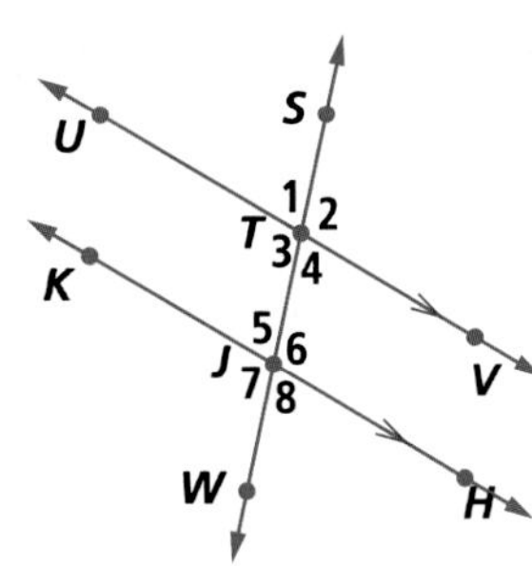

1. In the drawing at the right, which angles are corresponding angles?
2. State the Corresponding Angles Property.
3. Are lines *x* and *y* at the right parallel? Why or why not?

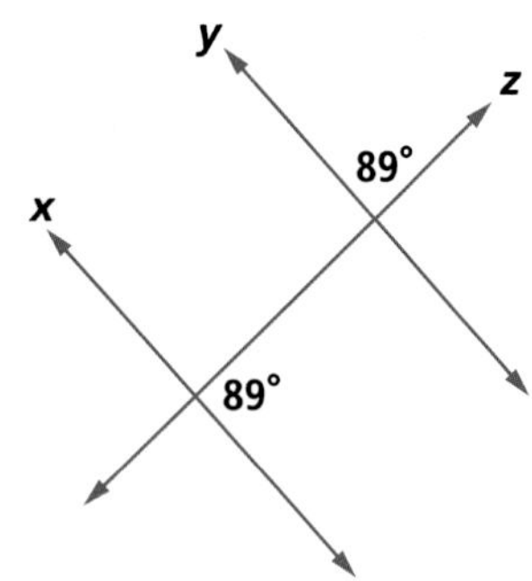

In 4 and 5, trace the drawing below.

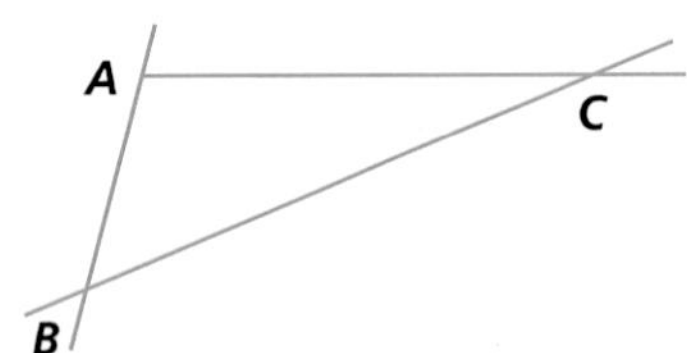

4. Measure angles to draw the line parallel to $\overline{AC}$ through *B*.
5. Measure angles to draw the line parallel to $\overline{BC}$ through *A*.

In 6 and 7, use the diagram at the right.

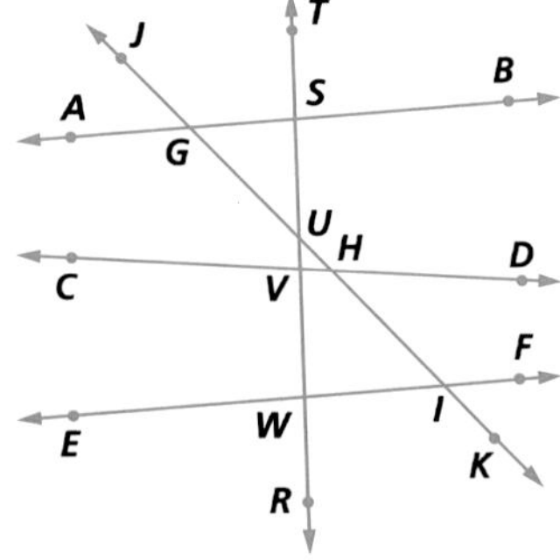

6. Suppose $m\angle RSA = 97.6°$ and $\overline{AB} \parallel \overline{EF}$. Find the measures of as many angles as possible from this information.
7. Suppose $\overline{AB} \parallel \overline{EF}$, $m\angle SGU = 50°$, and $m\angle VUH = 30°$. Find the measures of as many angles as possible from this information.

APPLYING THE MATHEMATICS

In 8 and 9, find the measures of the numbered angles. You may want to trace the figure and extend some lines.

8.

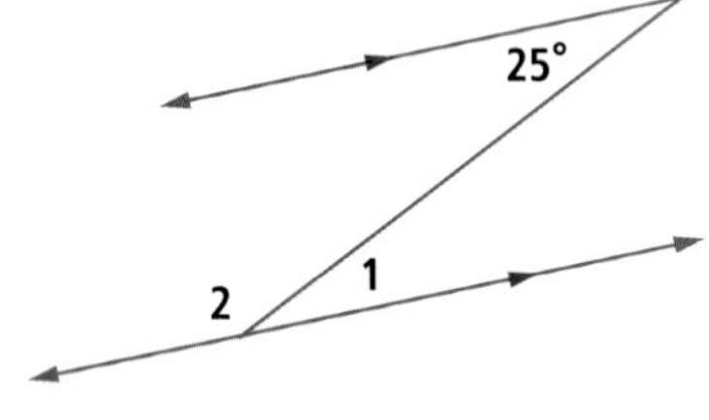

9.

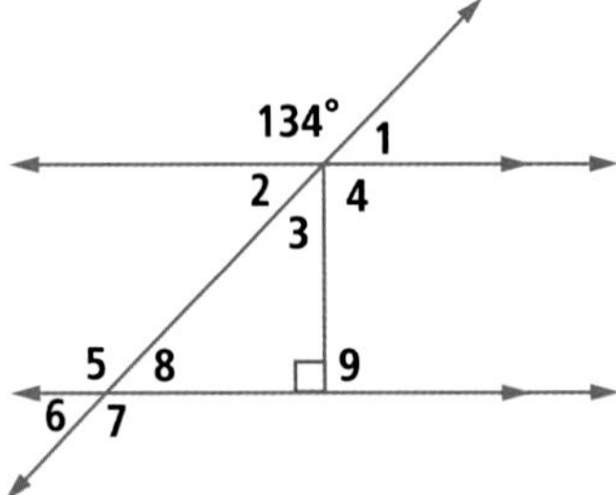

10. Suppose $\overline{TR} \perp \overline{EF}$ and $\overline{EF} \parallel \overline{AB}$. Explain why $\overline{TR} \perp \overline{AB}$.
11. **Multiple Choice** Suppose *P*, *Q*, and *R* are three different points in order on the same line. Line *m* is the perpendicular bisector of $\overline{PQ}$, and line *n* is the perpendicular bisector of $\overline{PR}$. Which is always true?

    A *m* and *n* are parallel.

    B *m* and *n* are perpendicular.

    C *m* and *n* have a point in common but they are not necessarily perpendicular.

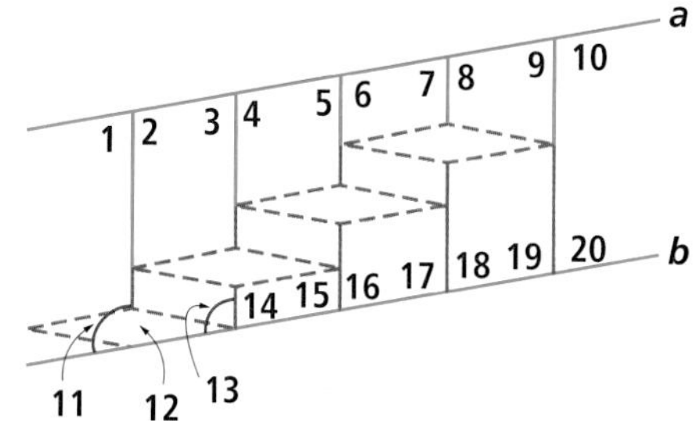

12. One angle of a parallelogram has measure 10°. What are the measures of the other three angles of the parallelogram?

13. In the picture of a staircase at the right, if $a \parallel b$ and the other segments are vertical, which angles have the same measure as $\angle 1$?

REVIEW

14. An object is rotated 48° clockwise and then 75° counterclockwise.
    a. How many degrees clockwise can the object be rotated to return to its original position?
    b. How many degrees counterclockwise can the object be rotated to return to its original position? **(Lesson 11-4)**

15. Copy $\overline{MJ}$ at the right and construct its perpendicular bisector. **(Lesson 11-2)**

16. **Multiple Choice** The formula for the area of a rectangle is $A = \ell w$, where ℓ represents the length and w represents the width. Which of the following will double the area of a rectangle? **(Lesson 6-3)**
    A doubling its length
    B halving its width
    C adding 2 to the length and width
    D multiplying the length and width by 2

17. If $\frac{1}{2} + x = \frac{2}{3}$, what is x? **(Lesson 4-8)**

EXPLORATION

18. In this lesson, you were shown how to draw parallel lines using corresponding angles. Here is a way to construct the line parallel to a given line $\overleftrightarrow{AB}$ through a point P not on $\overleftrightarrow{AB}$. Follow the directions and show the construction.

    Step 1 Draw a line $\overleftrightarrow{AB}$ and a point P not on $\overleftrightarrow{AB}$.

    Step 2 Construct $\overleftrightarrow{AP}$.

    Step 3 Construct the circle with center P and radius AB.

    Step 4 Construct the circle with center B and radius AP.

    Step 5 There is one point of intersection of the circles on the same side of $\overleftrightarrow{AB}$ that P is on. Label this point Q.

    Step 6 Construct $\overleftrightarrow{PQ}$. This line is the desired parallel line.

QY ANSWERS

1. $b \parallel c$ and $a \parallel d$

2. at most 2

Lesson 11-6 Translations

Vocabulary

translation/slide

vector

▸ **BIG IDEA** A translation is a slide of a figure (without changing its tilt) a certain distance in a certain direction.

Mental Math

Multiple Choice If $a < b$ and $c < d$, which of the following must be true?

A $a + b < c + d$

B $d < a + c$

C $a + c < b + d$

D $a < d$

A reflection produces a mirror image of a figure. A rotation produces the image of a figure after a turn. A third type of transformation produces an image of a figure after a slide. The horse head at the left below is the image of the horse head at the right. The transformation is called a **translation**, or slide.

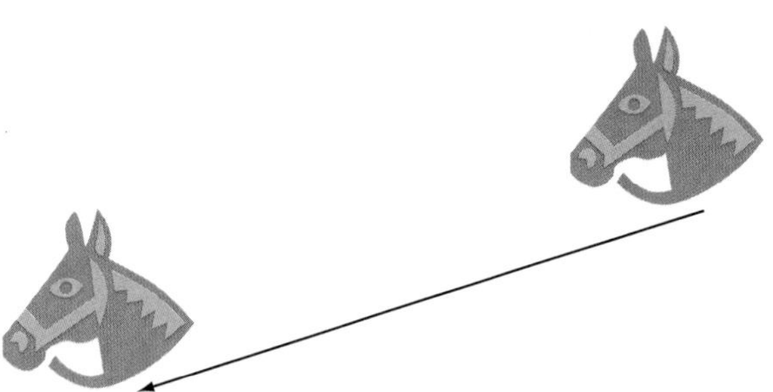

Because a translation is determined by its direction and its length, it is possible to describe a translation with an arrow, as above. The arrow points in the direction of the translation. The length of the arrow (from the start to the tip of the arrowhead) is the distance between a point and its translation image. A translation arrow is sometimes called a **vector.** No matter which two corresponding points you choose on a figure and its translation image, the vector will have the same direction and the same length.

QY

Trace the horse heads above and draw three segments connecting points and their translation images.

See QY at the right.

Once you know the image of one point under a translation, you can find the images of all other points.

Activity 1

MATERIALS tracing paper, ruler

In this activity, you will draw the translation image of $\triangle TRI$ given that R' is the translation image of R.

Step 1 Copy $\triangle TRI$ and point R'.

Step 2 Put tracing paper over your copy and draw an arrow from R to R'.

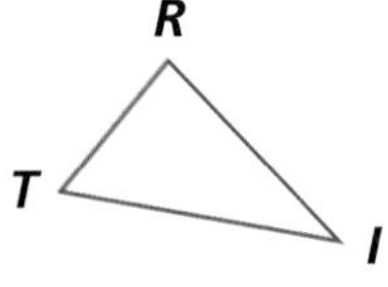

Step 3 Now put the tracing paper with the arrow on it underneath in the paper with the triangle. Without turning the tracing paper, slide the top paper so the start of the arrow is on point *T*. Use the arrow to determine *T′*, the translation image of *T*.

Step 4 Repeat Step 2 to find *I′*, the translation image of *I*.

Step 5 Connect the image points to draw the image triangle.

If you have dot paper or graph paper, you can translate figures by seeing how far horizontally and how far vertically a point is from its image.

Activity 2

MATERIALS dot paper (or graph paper)

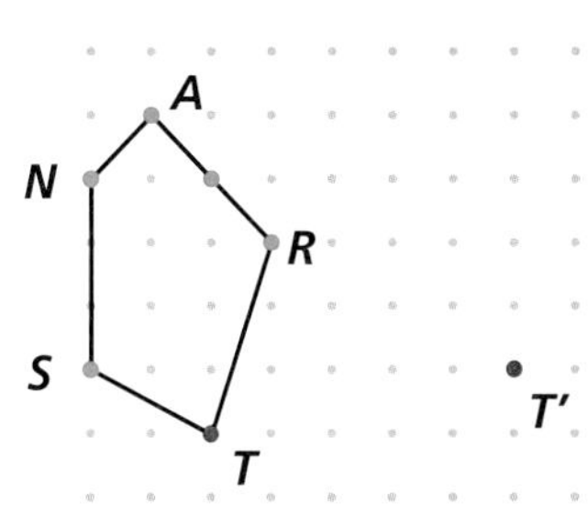

Step 1 Copy this figure onto dot paper.

Step 2 How far to the right or left is *T′* from *T*? How far up or down is *T′* from *T*?

Step 3 Find the image *S′* of *S* by moving *S* in the same direction and distance *T* moved to get *T′*.

Step 4 Find *R′*, *A′*, and *N′*.

Step 5 Draw polygon *T′R′A′N′S′*.

Step 6 Draw $\overline{TT'}$, $\overline{RR'}$, $\overline{AA'}$, $\overline{NN'}$, and $\overline{SS'}$.

Step 7 What two things do you notice about the line segments in Step 6?

Translations and Addition

Remember when you used arrows to add positive and negative numbers? The Slide Model of Addition relates addition to translating points on the number line. Adding numbers to one or both coordinates of a point applies a translation to that point.

GUIDED

Example

In a transformation of *ABCD* at the right, 5 is added to the first coordinate of each point and −15 is added to the second coordinate. Describe the transformation.

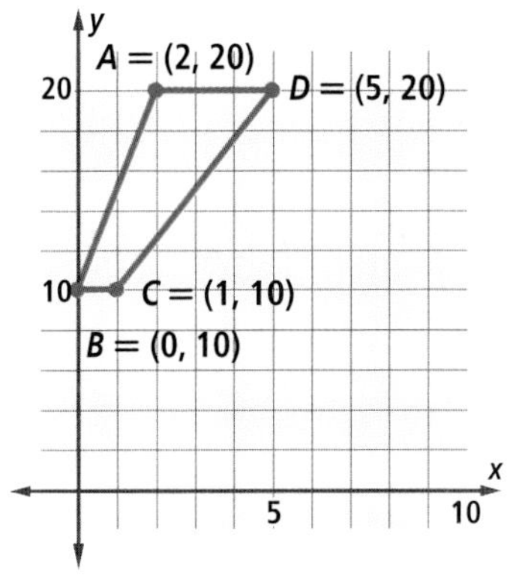

(continued on next page)

Solution

Add 5 to the first coordinate of A and add –15 to the second coordinate. Call the image A'.

$A' = (2 + 5, 20 + -15) = (\underline{\ ?\ }, \underline{\ ?\ })$

Do the same for B, C, and D.

$B' = (0 + \underline{\ ?\ }, 10 + \underline{\ ?\ }) = (\underline{\ ?\ }, \underline{\ ?\ })$

$C' = (\underline{\ ?\ } + 5, \underline{\ ?\ } + -15) = (\underline{\ ?\ }, \underline{\ ?\ })$

$D' = (\underline{\ ?\ } + \underline{\ ?\ }, \underline{\ ?\ } + \underline{\ ?\ }) = (\underline{\ ?\ }, \underline{\ ?\ })$

Graph quadrilateral $A'B'C'D'$.

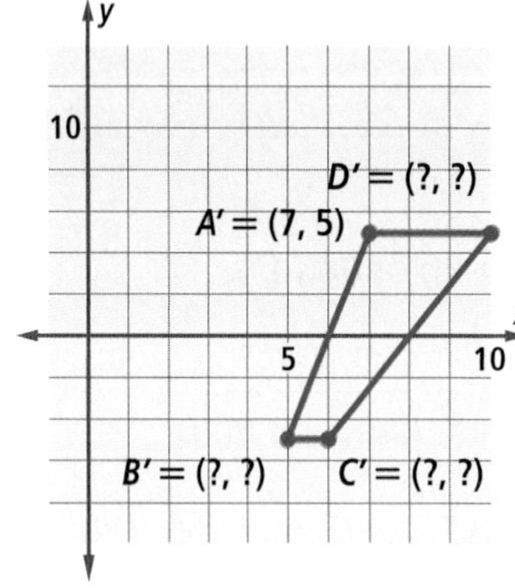

The transformation is a translation __?__ units to the right and __?__ units down.

Questions

COVERING THE IDEAS

1. What is another word for *translation*?
2. How does an arrow help in describing a translation?

In 3 and 4, use the diagram at the right.

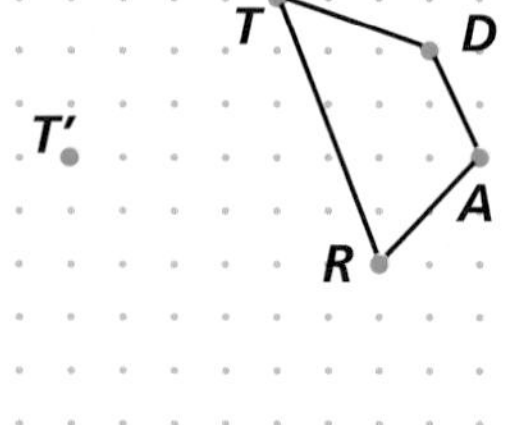

3. Find the translation image of *DART* given that *T′* is the image of *T*.
4. Name two things that are true about $\overline{AA'}$ and $\overline{RR'}$.
5. Trace this diagram and construct the translation image of $\triangle ART$ given that *T′* is the image of *T*.

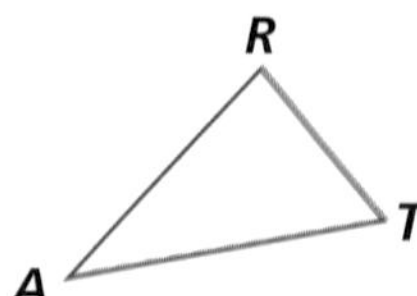

•T′

In 6–8, use the coordinate axes and *PENTA* at the right.

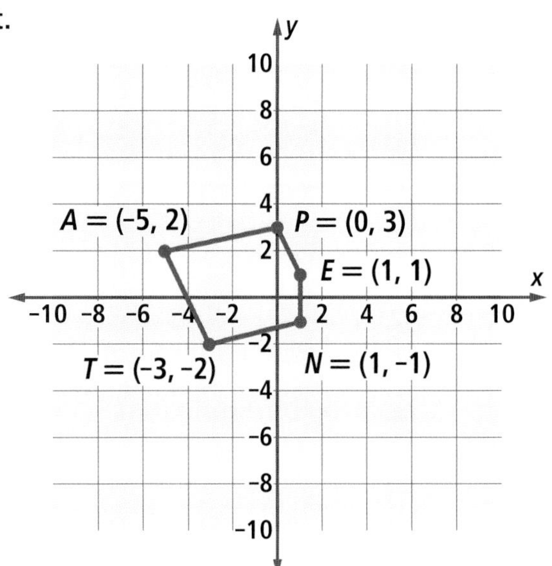

6. a. Translate *PENTA* 5 units to the right. Label the image $P'E'N'T'A'$.
   b. What are the coordinates of P', E', N', T', and A'?
   c. If the point (x, y) is translated a units horizontally, what are the coordinates of its image?

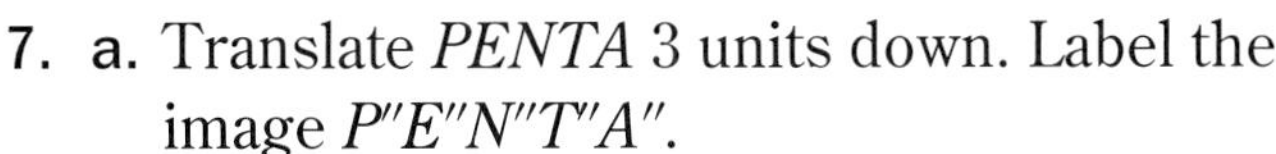

7. a. Translate *PENTA* 3 units down. Label the image $P''E''N''T''A''$.
   b. What are the coordinates of P'', E'', N'', T'', and A''?
   c. If the point (x, y) is translated b units vertically, what are the coordinates of its image?

8. a. Translate *PENTA* 2 units to the left and 3 units up. Label the image $P_1E_1N_1T_1A_1$.
   b. What are the coordinates of P_1, E_1, N_1, T_1, and A_1?
   c. If the point (x, y) is translated a units horizontally and b units vertically, what are the coordinates of its image?

APPLYING THE MATHEMATICS

In 9 and 10, use quadrilateral *ABCD* from the Guided Example.

9. Change the first coordinate of each point to its opposite and keep the second coordinate the same.
   a. Graph *ABCD* and its image $A'B'C'D'$ under this transformation.
   b. Describe the transformation.

10. Change the first coordinate of each point to the opposite of the second coordinate, and change the second coordinate to the first coordinate.
    a. Graph *ABCD* and its image $A^*B^*C^*D^*$ under this transformation.
    b. Describe the transformation.

11. Reflect the letter R over the line ℓ. Then apply the translation described by the arrow v to its image.

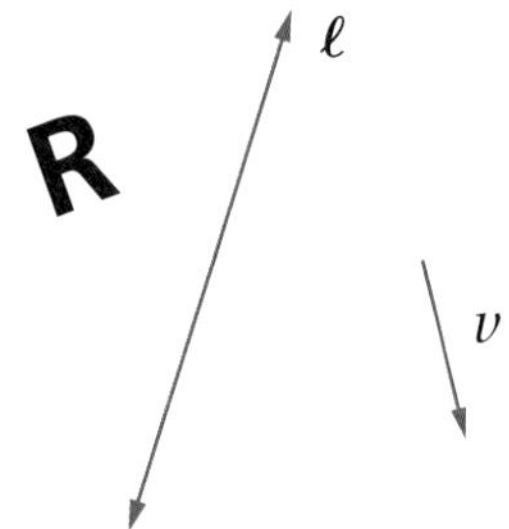

REVIEW

12. **True or False** If two lines are intersected by a transversal and corresponding angles are not congruent, then the two lines are not parallel. **(Lesson 11-5)**

13. Draw the reflection image of the figure at the right over the line. **(Lesson 11-3)**

14. a. Graph the line with equation $y = x - 2$ on a coordinate grid.
    b. Draw its image under a reflection over the x-axis.
    c. What is an equation for the image line? **(Lessons 11-3, 5-8)**

15. Karissa wants to make $3\frac{1}{2}$ dozen cupcakes. Each cupcake uses $1\frac{1}{2}$ teaspoons of icing.
    a. How many teaspoons of icing does she need?
    b. A teaspoon is $\frac{1}{3}$ of a tablespoon. How many tablespoons of icing does she need?
    c. A tablespoon is $\frac{1}{16}$ of a cup. Melanie has a 1 cup container of icing. Does she have enough? **(Lesson 6-9)**

16. As of 2006, the largest land vehicle in the world is an earthmoving machine in Germany manufactured by Man Takraf. It extracts coal from open-pit mines. It can move about $8\frac{1}{2}$ million tons of earth per day.
    a. How many tons can the machine extract in one week, assuming that it is used every day without a break?
    b. How many million tons of earth can it extract during the month of June? **(Lesson 6-9)**

EXPLORATION

17. The square at the right pictures a floor tile with one corner, a quarter of the tile, shaded. Sixteen of these tiles are to be arranged to make a large 4 tile-by-4 tile square.
    a. Create a 4 tile-by-4 tile pattern using only translation images of the figure at the right.
    b. Create a 4 tile-by-4 tile pattern using translation and rotation images of this tile.

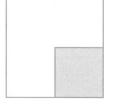

18. Below is a figure and a translation image of it constructed by a DGS. If you have access to a DGS package, explore to find out how to make a translation.

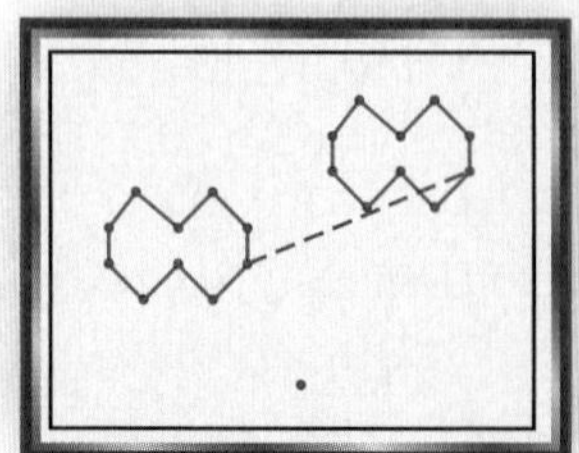

QY ANSWERS

Answers vary.

Chapter 11 Projects

1 Diagonals of Regular Polygons

A *regular polygon* is one in which all sides have the same length and all angles have the same measure. In a regular polygon, many of the diagonals have the same length. For instance, the nine diagonals of a regular hexagon have only two different lengths. Explore the diagonals of regular polygons with various numbers of sides. How many different lengths are there in the diagonals of a regular heptagon? What about a regular octagon? Try to find patterns and predict the number of different lengths for diagonals in a regular 25-gon and a regular 50-gon.

2 Constructing Angle Bisectors

In Lesson 11-2, you saw how to create an angle bisector of a segment by folding. Find out how to construct an angle bisector using only a compass and a straightedge. Start with a line and construct another line perpendicular to it. Then use angle bisector and other constructions you know to construct angles with measures 45°, $22\frac{1}{2}°$, $56\frac{1}{4}°$, and $7\frac{1}{2}°$.

3 Euclid's *Elements*

Euclid's *Elements* is one of the most influential books ever written. Its importance lies in its logical development of geometry and other branches of mathematics. It has influenced the development of science as well as mathematics. Write a report about this famous work, including when and how it was written, a description of its contents, and how it has been used.

4 A Man, a Plan, a Canal, Panama

Some alphabet letters can be bisected in such a way so as to be a mirror image of themselves, such as the uppercase letters A and T. A *palindrome* is a word, phrase, or sentence that reads the same backward and forward, such as RACECAR and HANNAH. Give examples of word palindromes that can be bisected into two mirror images. Can you generalize about when a palindrome has this property? Try to find examples of sentence palindromes with this property.

5 Transform This

Find out how to compose two reflections to result in a translation, and how to compose two reflections to result in a rotation. Use an object and two mirrors to demonstrate these compositions.

6 Spirograph Constructions

A Spirograph is a geometric drawing toy that produces various mathematical curves. Use the internet to find a spirograph applet that allows you to draw examples of these curves. Use the various options to display six different drawings, and present these on a poster. Write a couple of sentences about how the spirograph works.

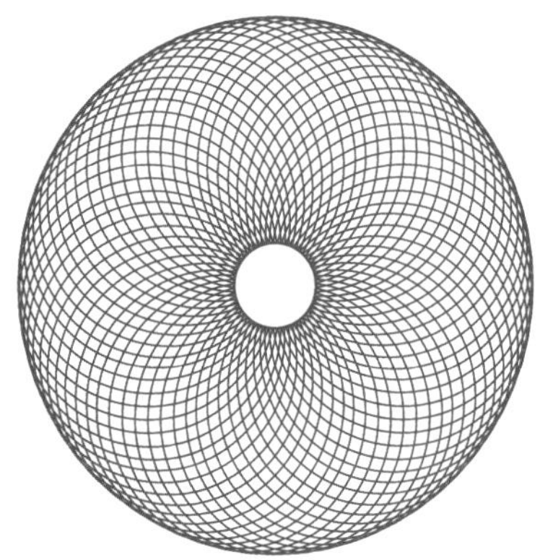

Chapter 11 Summary and Vocabulary

- Many tools and techniques have been developed for drawing geometric figures. A **Euclidean construction** is created using only a **straightedge** and **compass.** Other careful and accurate drawings make use of all sorts of tools, such as a ruler, protractor, and tracing paper. Paper folding, dot paper, and a Dynamic Geometry System are other ways to draw, copy, or find transformation images of figures.

- Three **transformations** were introduced in this chapter. **Reflections** produce mirror images of a figure, **rotations** produce the image of a figure after a turn around a fixed point, and **translations** produce a slide image. Paper folding, measuring, coordinate graphing, constructions, and technology are all used to find images.

- A number of constructions with straightedge and compass are in this chapter, including the **duplication of line segments and angles** and the construction of the **perpendicular bisector of a segment,** the perpendicular to a line through a point on the line, and the perpendicular to a line through a point not on the line. Using these constructions, it is possible to make other constructions, such as parallel lines and triangles with given information.

- **Parallel lines** lie in the same **plane** and go in the same direction. If a **transversal** intersects one of a set of parallels, it must intersect all the others. Sets of equal angles are formed when parallel lines are cut by a transversal. Angles in the same position are called **corresponding angles** and have equal measures. Given information about parallel lines and equal angles in a figure, it is possible to find the measures of some or all of the other angles.

Theorems and Properties

Corresponding Angles Property (p. 656)

Vocabulary

11-1
angle bisector
straightedge
compass
Euclidean construction
Dynamic Geometry System (DGS)

11-2
bisector of a segment
perpendicular bisector of a segment

11-3
reflection image of *A* over the line *m*
reflecting line, line of reflection, mirror

11-4
rotation
duplicating an angle

11-5
transversal
corresponding angles

11-6
translation/slide
vector

Chapter 11 Self-Test

Take this test as you would take a test in class. You will need a straightedge, a compass, a ruler, a protractor, and tracing paper. Then use the Selected Answers section in the back of the book to check your work.

In 1 and 2, copy $\overline{PQ}$ below on your paper.

1. a. Construct the perpendicular bisector of $\overline{PQ}$ with a straightedge and compass.
   b. Label the midpoint of $\overline{PQ}$.
2. Construct the line perpendicular to $\overline{PQ}$ through Q.
3. Using a ruler and protractor, draw a right triangle with one leg 3 inches long and a 35° angle.
4. Given that lines ℓ and m below are parallel, find the measures of angles 1–5.

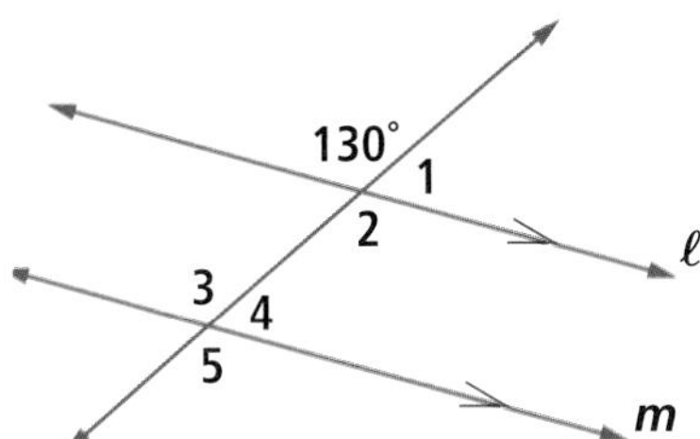

5. Copy the angle below using a straightedge and compass.

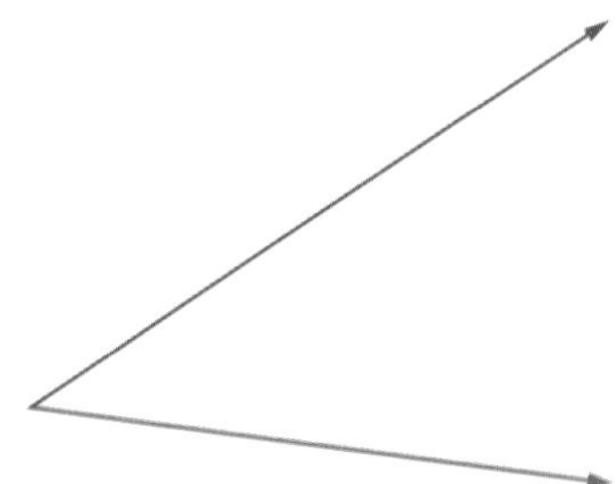

6. Draw a line on a sheet of paper. Name a point on the line point A. Use a protractor to measure and draw an angle with measure 55° as shown below. Place a point C on the other side of the angle. Then measure and draw another 55° angle at this second point so that parallel lines are formed.

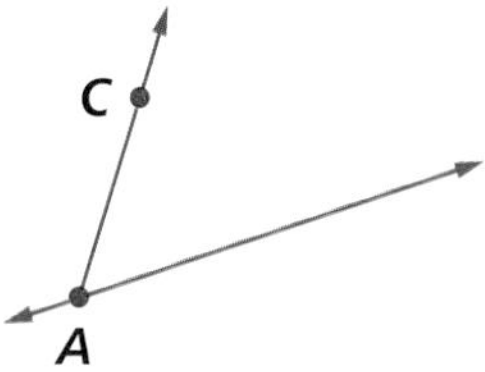

In 7 and 8, use the figure below. Name the transformation under which

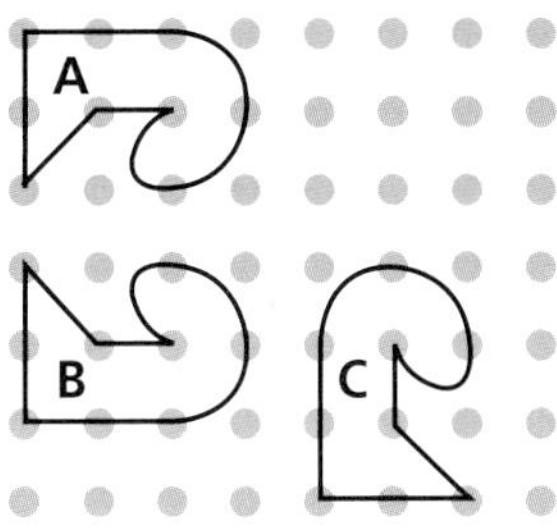

7. B is the image of A.
8. C is the image of A.
9. What are the coordinates of the image of the point (–18, 42) translated 19 units to the left and 37 units down?
10. Under what transformation is triangle 2 the image of triangle 1?

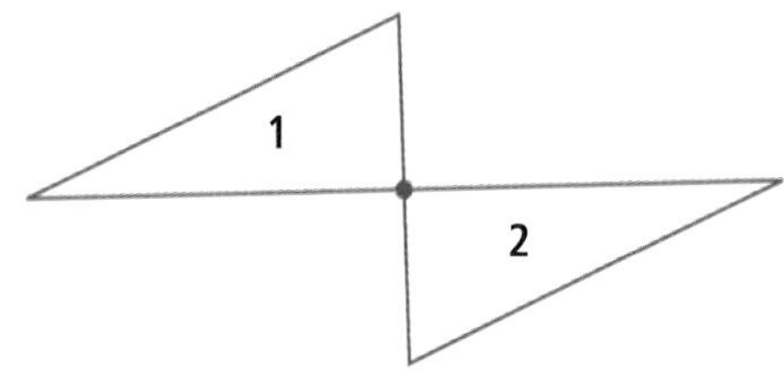

11. List all pairs of corresponding angles in the diagram below.

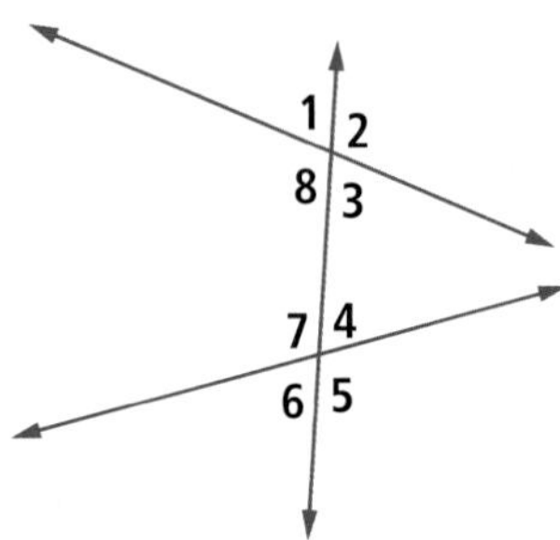

12. Draw a line and segment $\overline{PI}$ off the line as shown below. Construct the reflection image of $\overline{PI}$ over the line.

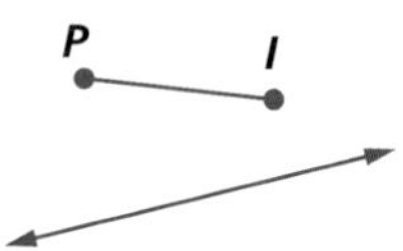

13. A running track is shaped like a rectangle with semicircles on each end. Each straightaway is 100 meters long, and the semicircular ends each have a radius of 25 meters. Using a ruler, protractor, and compass, draw a scale diagram of this track using a scale of 1 cm = 10 m.

14. Use the pattern below.

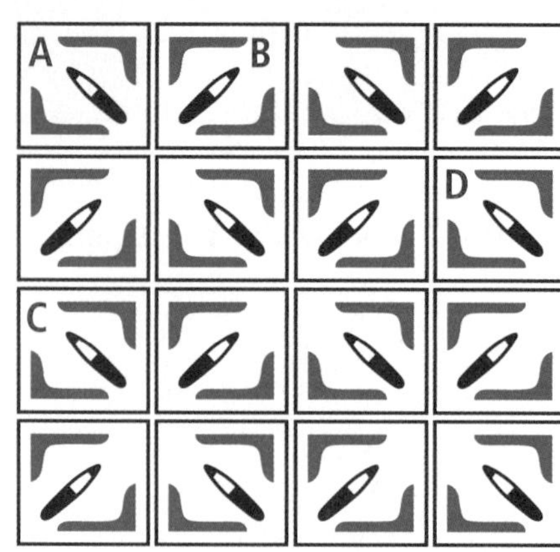

a. Which of the lettered tiles, B, C, or D, could be a translation image of tile A?

b. Which of the lettered tiles could be a rotation image of tile A?

c. Which of the lettered tiles could be a reflection image of tile A?

15. Trace the figure below on tracing paper and then draw its reflection image over the line.

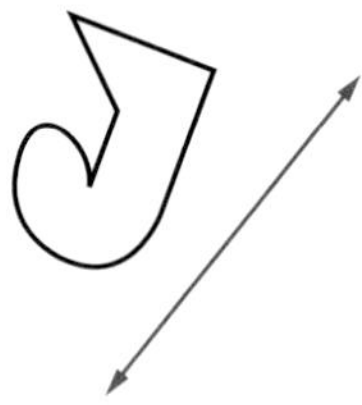

Chapter 11 Chapter Review

SKILLS
PROPERTIES
USES
REPRESENTATIONS

SKILLS Procedures used to get answers

OBJECTIVE A Copy and draw geometric figures using various geometry tools. **(Lessons 11-1, 11-4)**

1. Construct an equilateral triangle.
2. Construct a right triangle with a 60° angle.
3. Use a ruler and protractor to draw a rectangle with side lengths 4 inches and 3 centimeters.
4. Use tracing paper, a protractor, and a ruler to draw the angle bisector of a 37° angle.
5. Use tracing paper and a protractor to draw the angle bisector of a 165° angle.
6. Use a ruler and compass to construct a circle of radius 2.5 cm and a circle with the same center of radius 3 cm.
7. Use a DGS to make a triangle with two sides of length 4.5 units and one side of length 8 units.
8. Use a DGS to construct the perpendicular bisector of a segment.

In 9 and 10, construct a copy of the angle.

9. 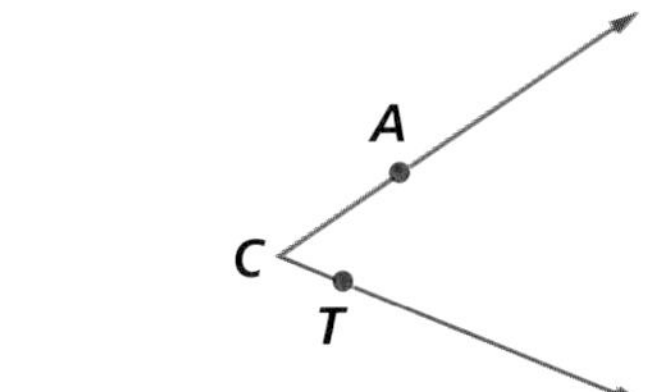

10. 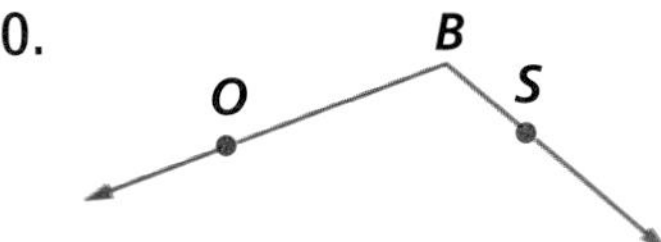

11. Draw an angle measuring 123°.

12. Draw an angle measuring 23°.

OBJECTIVE B Construct the perpendicular bisector of a segment. **(Lesson 11-2)**

In 13–16, construct the perpendicular bisector of the segment.

13. 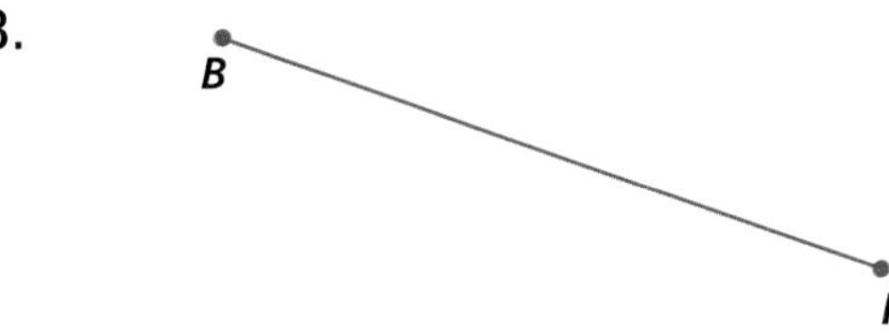

14. O F

15. 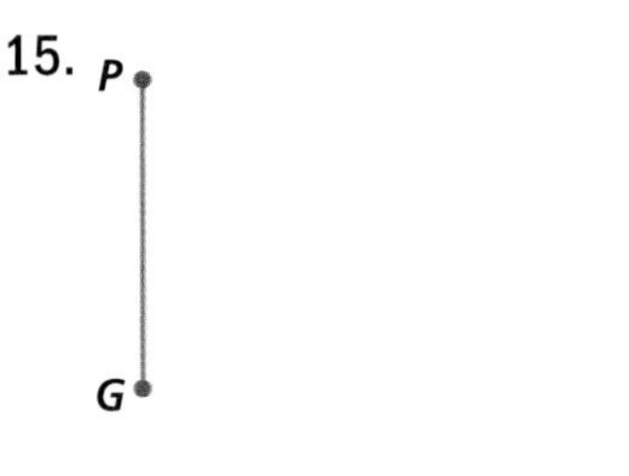

16. M E

OBJECTIVE C Construct the perpendicular to a line through a point. **(Lesson 11-2)**

In 17–20, trace the triangle below and construct the appropriate line.

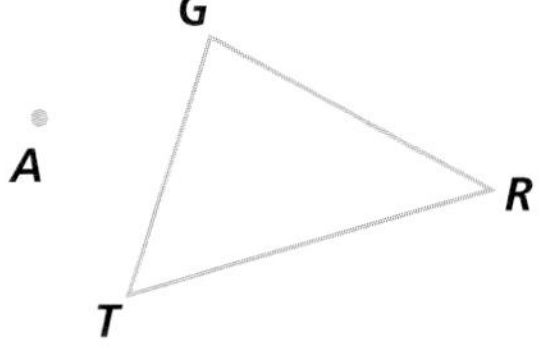

17. the perpendicular to $\overline{RT}$ through G
18. the perpendicular to $\overline{GT}$ through R
19. the perpendicular to $\overline{GR}$ through G
20. the perpendicular to $\overline{GT}$ through A

OBJECTIVE D **Find the measures of angles created by parallel lines intersected by a transversal. (Lesson 11-5)**

21. In the figure below, $\overleftrightarrow{HJ} \parallel \overleftrightarrow{GM}$ and $m\angle 2 = 55°$. Determine the following angle measures.

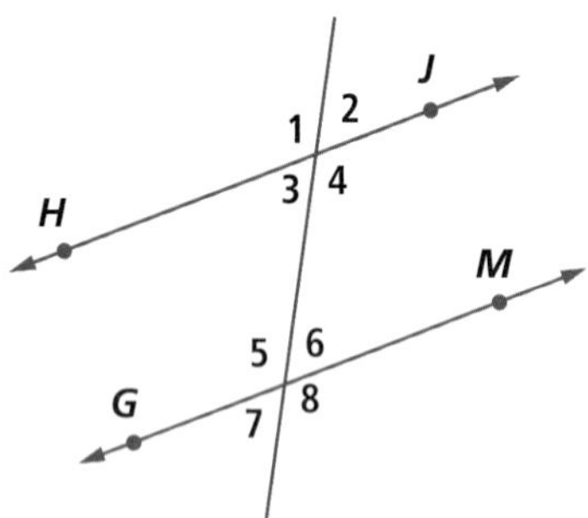

a. $m\angle 1$ b. $m\angle 6$

c. $m\angle 8$ d. $m\angle 5$

22. In the figure below, $\overleftrightarrow{AB} \parallel \overleftrightarrow{CD} \parallel \overleftrightarrow{EF}$.

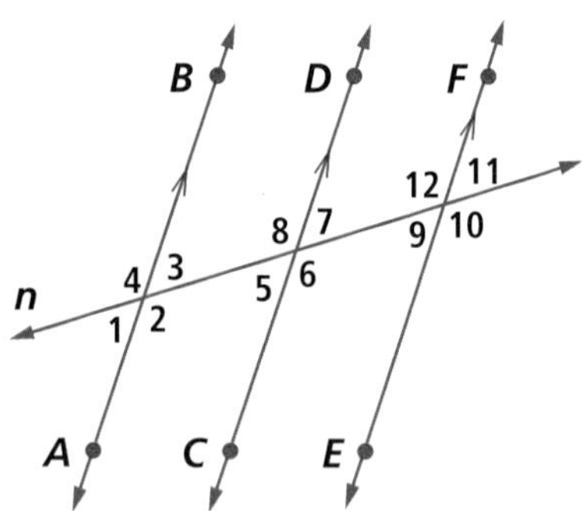

a. Identify all the corresponding angles.

b. **True or False** If line *n* is rotated, the corresponding angles will remain congruent.

OBJECTIVE E **Draw lines parallel to a line. (Lessons 11-5)**

In 23–26, construct a line parallel to the given line through the given point.

23.

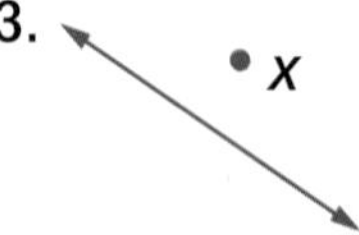

24.

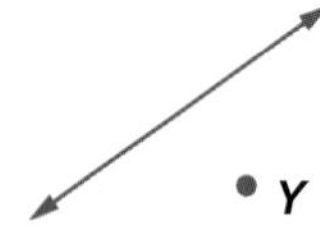

25.

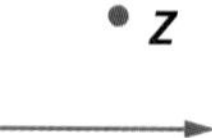

26.

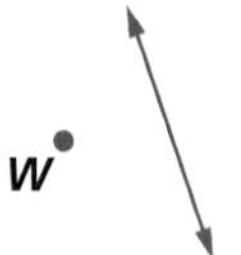

OBJECTIVE F **Recognize, draw, and construct reflection images of figures. (Lessons 11-3)**

27. **Multiple Choice** Which shows the reflection image of the figure below over line *m*?

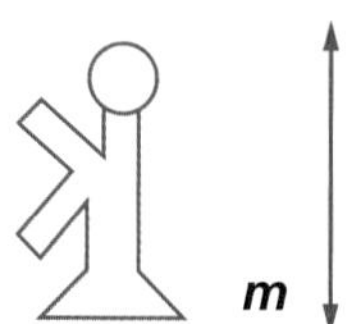

A

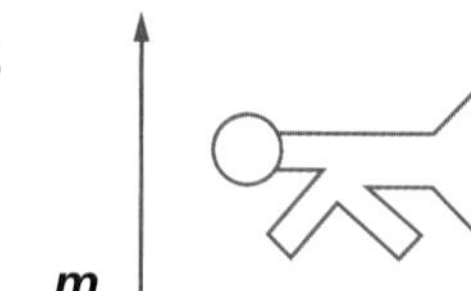

B

C

D

28. **Multiple Choice** Which shows the reflection image of the figure below over line m?

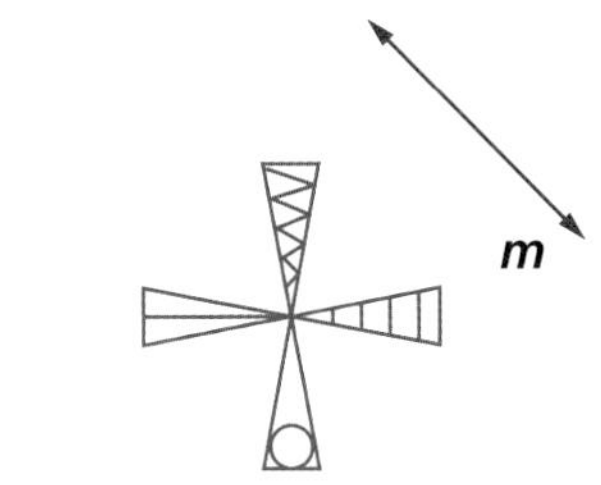

A

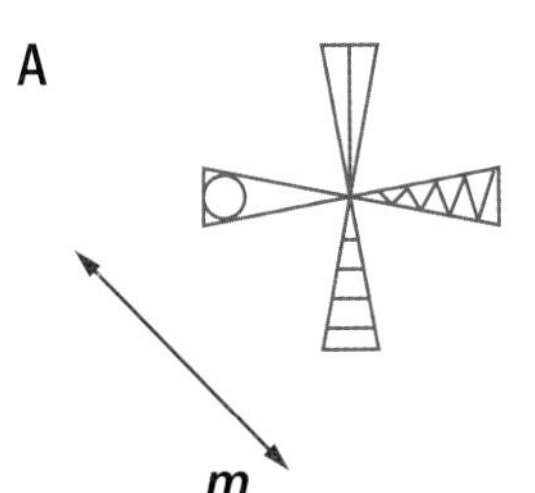

B

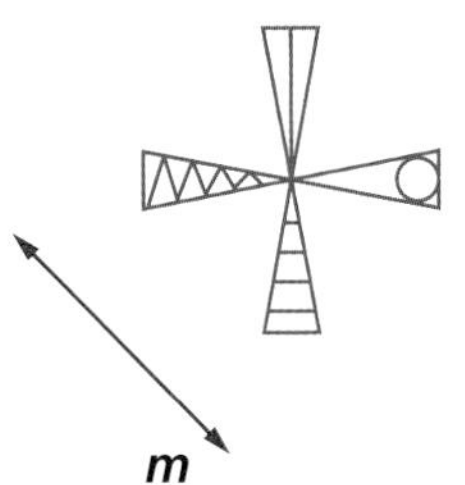

C

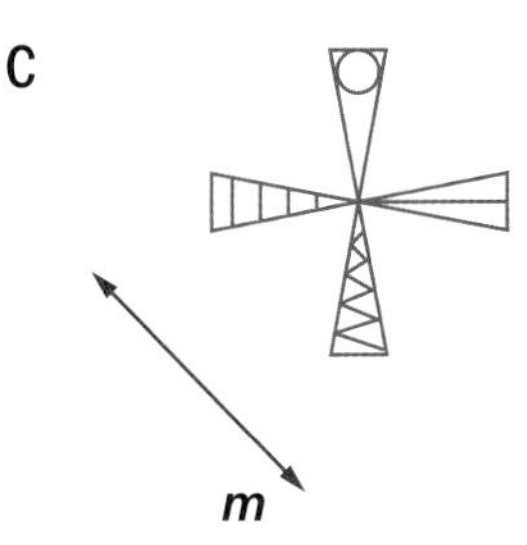

D

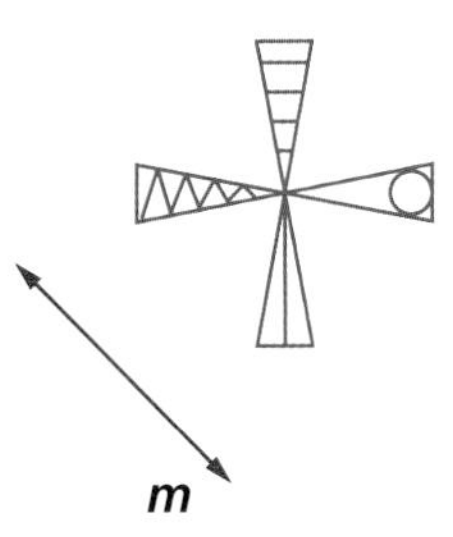

In 29–32, trace the figure and draw its reflection image over line m.

29.

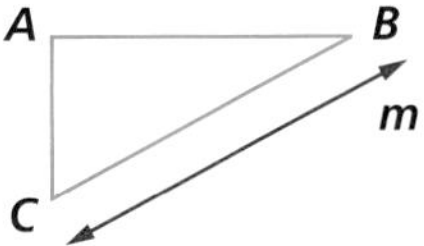

30.

31.

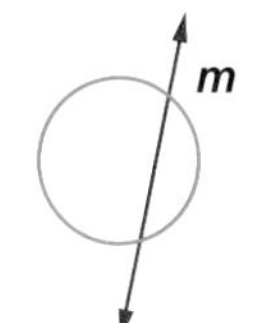

32.

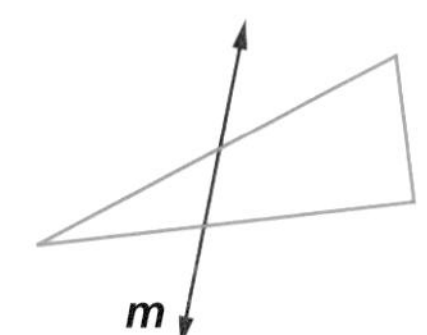

In 33 and 34, trace the figure and draw its reflection image over the line.

33.

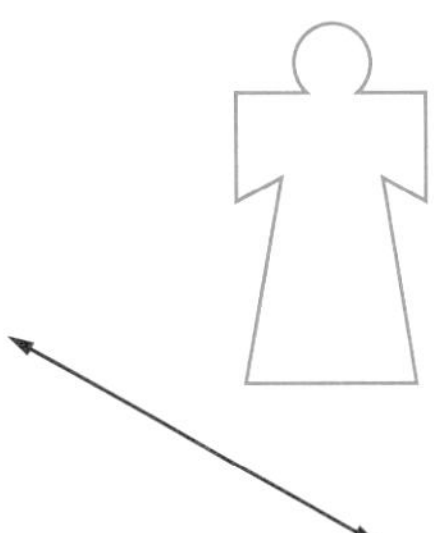

34.

OBJECTIVE G Recognize, draw, and construct rotation images of figures. **(Lessons 11-4)**

In 35 and 36, rotate the figure 135° about point O.

35.

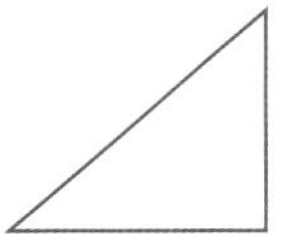

36.

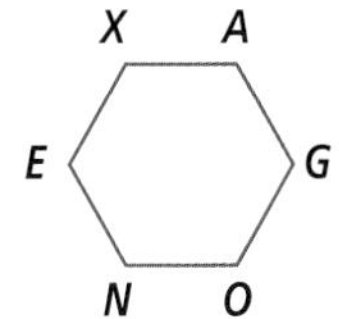

37. Explain why rotating a figure 90° is the same as rotating it -270°.

38. **Multiple Choice** If (3, 4) is rotated 150° about (0, 0), in which quadrant will the image be?

A I B II

C III D IV

In 39 and 40, rotate the figure about the point using tracing paper.

39. 160° counterclockwise

40. 35° clockwise

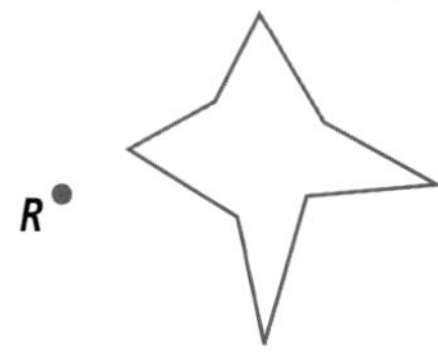

PROPERTIES The principles behind the mathematics

OBJECTIVE H Apply properties of corresponding angles for lines cut by a transversal. **(Lesson 11-5)**

In 41–44, use the diagram below. Lines *m* and *n* are parallel.

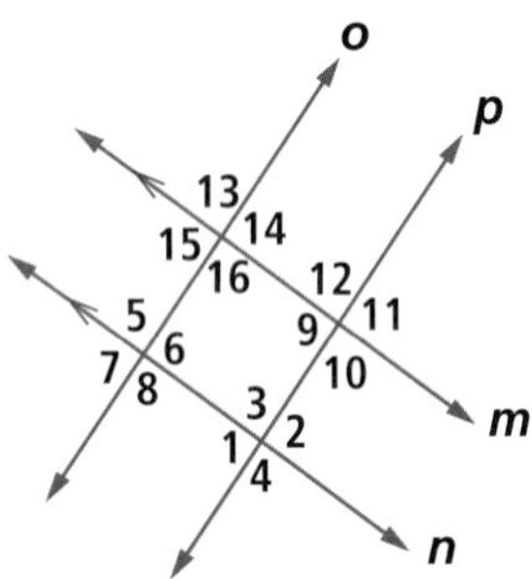

41. List all pairs of corresponding angles.
42. List all angles congruent to angle 3.
43. List all the angles congruent to angle 7.
44. **True or False** If $m\angle 4 = m\angle 5$, then lines *o* and *p* are parallel.

USES Applications of mathematics in real-world situations

There are no objectives in Uses for this chapter.

REPRESENTATIONS Pictures, graphs, or objects that illustrate concepts

OBJECTIVE I Recognize rotation, reflection, and translation images of figures in designs. **(Lessons 11-3, 11-4, 11-6)**

In 45–47, use the designs below.

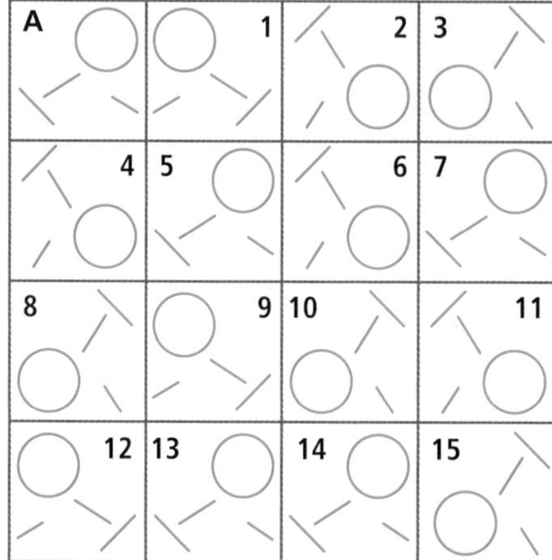

45. Which of the designs are translation images of design A?
46. Which of the designs are rotation images of design A?
47. Which of the designs are reflections of design A?
48. If the picture below is rotated 180° about its center, what will the number in the image read?

18018

OBJECTIVE J **Recognize, draw, or construct translation images of figures in the coordinate plane or described by vectors. (Lesson 11-6)**

49. Graph the translation image of $\triangle ABC$ 3 units up and 2 units to the left.

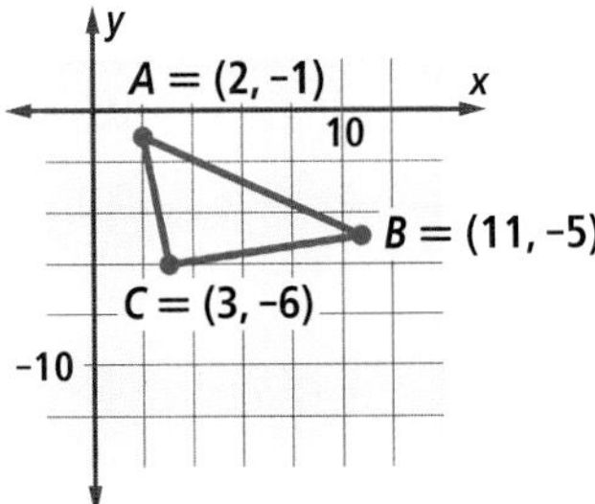

50. Draw *DEFG* and its image under the translation described by the vector.

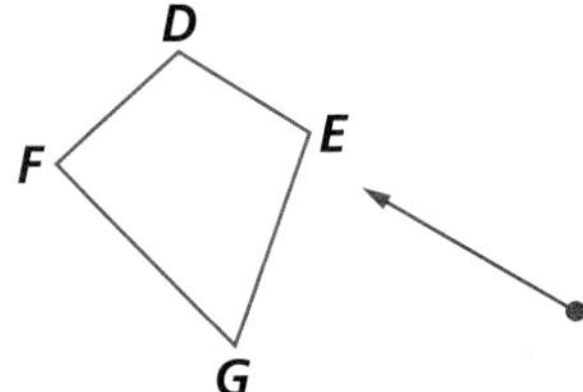

In 51 and 52, give the coordinates of the translation image of the point.

51. (4.5, 7) translated 3 units to the left and 4 units down.

52. $\left(\frac{1}{2}, \frac{3}{4}\right)$ translated 2 units right and $\frac{5}{2}$ units up.

Chapter

12 Exploring Triangles and Quadrilaterals

Contents

Triangles and quadrilaterals occur in famous structures all around the world.

Four triangles form the faces of the pyramid in the courtyard of the Musée du Louvre in Paris, France pictured above.

The Smurfit-Stone building in Chicago has a slanting rhombus-shaped roof and long, thin rectangles on its lateral faces as seen in the picture at the left.

Four-square is a game played on a square court made up of smaller squares.

The Kuwaiti flag pictured at the right and many Mexican pyramids all make use of trapezoids.

In this chapter, you will investigate properties of triangles and quadrilaterals. Learning about the properties of these shapes can help you to see why they are so useful and aesthetically appealing.

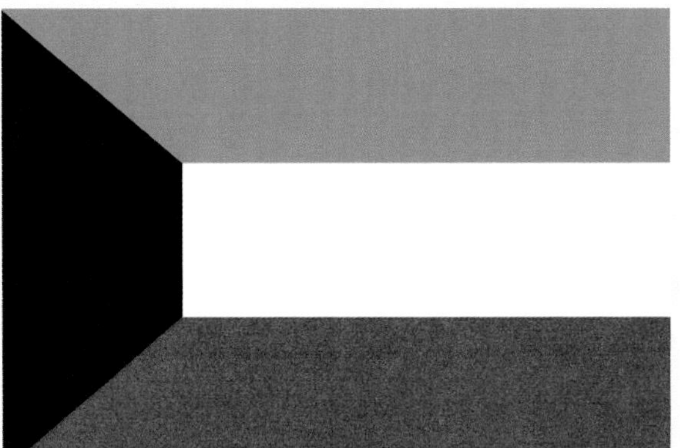

Lesson 12-1 Congruent Figures

Vocabulary

congruent figures
corresponding parts

▸ **BIG IDEA** When two figures are congruent, the angles and segments on one figure have the same measures as their corresponding parts on the other figure.

Mental Math

$\overline{AB}$ is 3 feet, 5 inches long. How long is a segment that is

a. double the length of $\overline{AB}$?

b. double the length of the segment in Part a?

c. three times the length of $\overline{AB}$?

On the Chase Manhattan Bank Building in New York City shown at the right, there are hundreds of rectangles with the same dimensions. Such rectangles are *congruent*. When two figures are congruent, you can use slides, turns, or reflections on one of the figures to the position of the other figure. In general, two figures F and G are **congruent figures** if and only if G is the image of F under a translation, rotation, reflection, or some combination of these transformations.

When two figures F and G are congruent, we write F ≅ G, read "F is congruent to G."

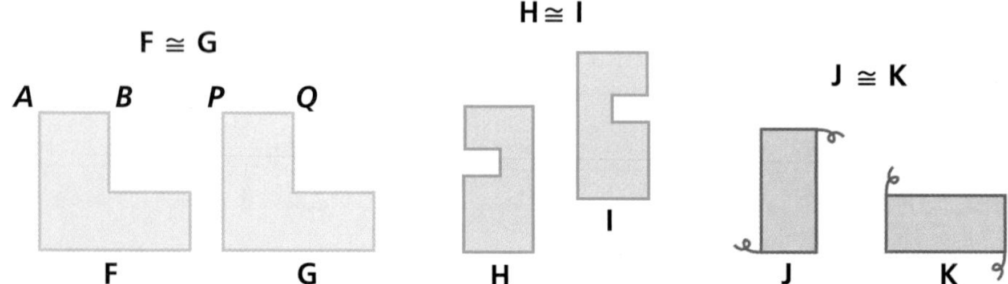

When you see two congruent figures, like the three pairs of congruent figures above, you can usually see how one figure could be translated, rotated, or reflected so that its image is the other figure. For instance, figure J is the image of figure K under a rotation of 90° about a point somewhere between them. (In Question 25, you are asked to locate that point.)

 **See QY at the right.**

 **QY**

Refer to the figures on this page.

a. Under what kind of transformation is G the image of F?

b. Under what combination of transformations is I the image of H?

If figures are congruent, then **corresponding parts** of the figures are also congruent. For instance, in figures F and G above, $\overline{AB}$ and $\overline{PQ}$ are corresponding sides so $\overline{AB} \cong \overline{PQ}$.

The Importance of Congruent Objects

It is useful to be able to recognize congruent objects. For example, when a AA battery loses its charge, you need to replace it with a congruent battery, that will fit exactly where the old battery was. Keys that fit in the same lock are congruent. Left and right shoes of the same size and style are congruent. Congruent objects can be mass-produced.

If two segments have different lengths, then no translation, rotation, or reflection can send one to the other. So they cannot be congruent.

If two segments have the same length, then you can always describe a combination of transformations so that one segment is the image of the other. For instance, $\overline{AB}$ and $\overline{CD}$ at the right are the same length.

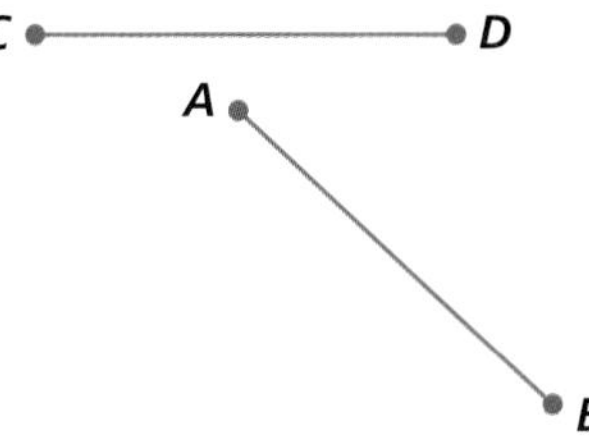

You can translate $\overline{AB}$ so that the image of A is C. Then you can rotate the image of the segment about point C. This shows that $\overline{AB} \cong \overline{CD}$.

This is the first of four important properties of congruence.

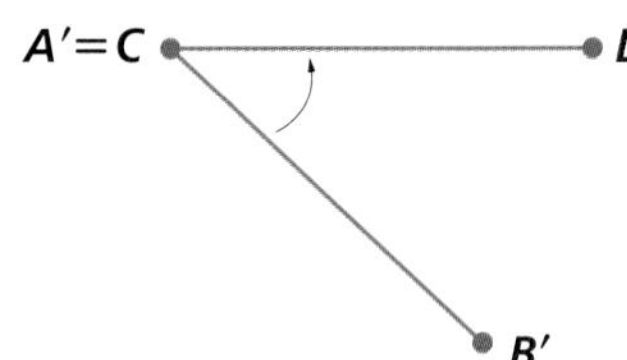

Congruence Property 1

Two segments with the same length are congruent.

Congruent Triangles

In the activity, you will see that lengths of segments can determine whether triangles are congruent.

Activity

MATERIALS ruler, scissors, 2 sheets of plain paper

Step 1 On one piece of paper, measure and cut out three very thin strips of length 7 cm, 11 cm, and 14 cm.

Step 2 Place your strips on another clean sheet of paper, and use your strips to make a triangle.

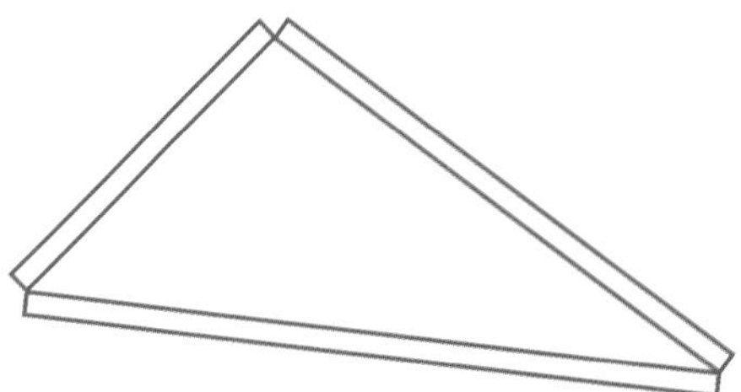

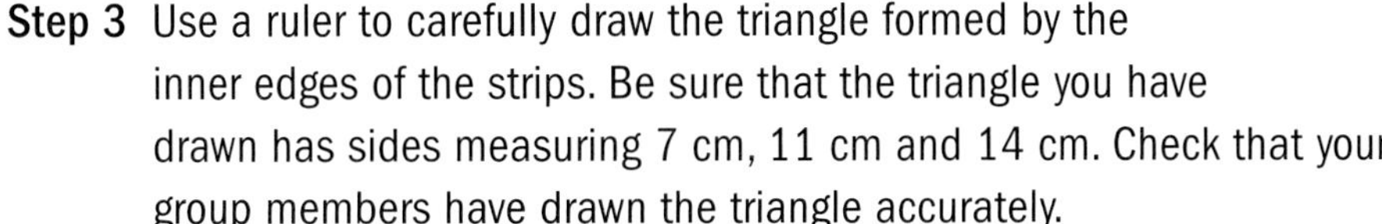

Step 3 Use a ruler to carefully draw the triangle formed by the inner edges of the strips. Be sure that the triangle you have drawn has sides measuring 7 cm, 11 cm and 14 cm. Check that your group members have drawn the triangle accurately.

Step 4 Cut out the triangle you drew in Step 3.

Step 5 Compare your triangle with those of other students. What can you conclude?

What you found in Step 7 on the previous page illustrates the second congruence property.

Congruence Property 2

Two triangles with sides of the same three lengths are congruent.

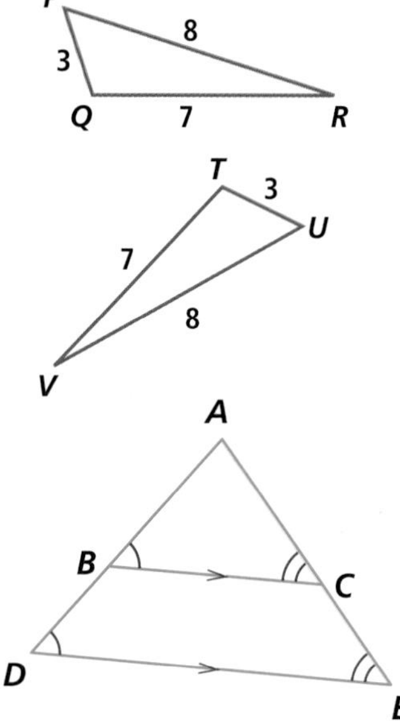

Having the same angle measures is not enough to determine congruence. For instance, because $\overline{BC} \parallel \overline{DE}$, triangles *ABC* and *ADE* at the right have angles of the same measure, but their sides have different lengths, so they are not congruent.

It is more difficult to determine when polygons are congruent. Quadrilaterals *EFGH* and *JIGH* at the right have sides of the same length, but they are not congruent because their angles have different measures. Except for Congruence Property 2, to tell whether polygons are congruent, you must know both their side lengths and their angle measures.

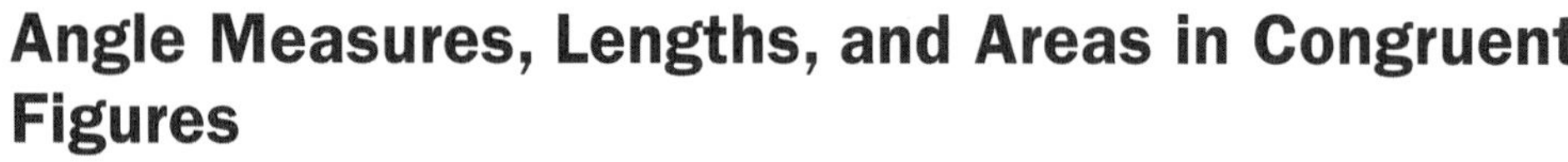

Angle Measures, Lengths, and Areas in Congruent Figures

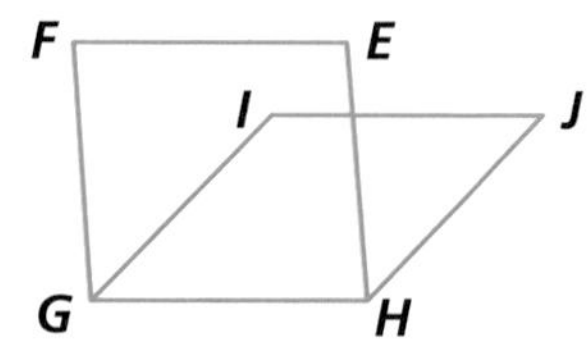

Not only are the sides of congruent triangles equal in length, but so are their corresponding altitudes. As a result, the perimeters and areas and corresponding angles of congruent triangles are equal. For instance, in the triangles above, $m\angle QRP = m\angle TVU$. This is true of all congruent figures.

Congruence Property 3

If figures are congruent, then their perimeters, areas, and corresponding angles are equal in measure.

Example 1

One closet has a rectangular floor with dimensions 3' by 8'. Another closet has a floor with dimensions 4' by 6'. Even though the areas of these floors are equal, explain why these floors are not congruent.

(continued on next page)

Solution The perimeter of the floor of the first closet is 22 feet. The perimeter of the floor of the second closet is 20 feet. If the floors were congruent, they would have the same perimeter. But they don't. So they are not congruent.

Example 1 shows that two figures can have the same area, but not be congruent. Two figures can also have the same perimeter and not be congruent, but if two angles have the same measure, then they are congruent.

Congruence Property 4

Two angles with the same measure are congruent.

You can use the properties of congruence to determine angle measures.

GUIDED

Example 2

Consider the figure at the right of four congruent right triangles, formed by constructing the perpendicular bisector of $\overline{AB}$. Find the measures of the angles of $\triangle AMC$.

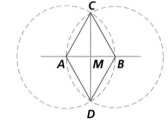

Solution $\triangle ABC$ is equilateral (all of its sides have the same length as $\overline{AB}$), so its angles are congruent. Since the sum of the measures of the angles of a triangle is __?__, each angle of $\triangle ABC$ has measure __?__. Thus, $m\angle CAM =$ __?__. Because $\overline{CD} \perp \overline{AB}$, $m\angle CMA =$ __?__. Since $\triangle ACM$ and $\triangle BCM$ are congruent, $\angle ACM$ and $\angle BCM$ are congruent. Since $m\angle ACB = 60°$, $m\angle ACM =$ __?__.

Questions

COVERING THE IDEAS

In 1–3, the figure is an image of the figure at the right. Tell which transformation was applied to the original figure to get the image.

1. 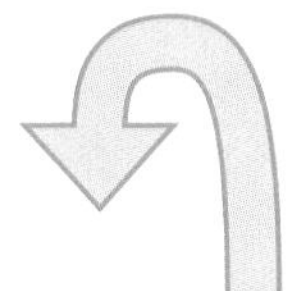

2. 

3. 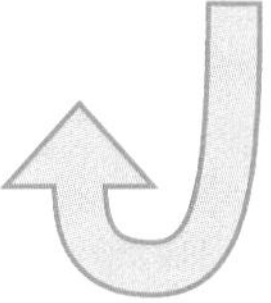

original

4. What is a definition of *congruent figures*?

5. Draw two parallelograms *ABCD* and *EFGH* that have parallel corresponding sides but that are not congruent.

In 6 and 7, suppose you draw a rectangle with dimensions 3 centimeters and 4 centimeters.

6. A classmate draws a rectangle with dimensions 3 inches and 4 inches. Are your rectangles congruent?
7. Another classmate draws a rectangle with dimensions 4 centimeters and 3 centimeters. Are your rectangles congruent?
8. You draw a triangle with sides measuring 3 cm, 4 cm, and 5 cm, with the longest side horizontal. Your friend draws a triangle with sides measuring 3 cm, 4 cm, and 5 cm, with the shortest side horizontal. Are the triangles congruent? Why or why not?

In 9 and 10, use the figure of Example 2.

9. Name all triangles congruent to $\triangle ABC$.
10. Name all triangles congruent to $\triangle ACM$.

APPLYING THE MATHEMATICS

11. Suppose $m\angle A = 4°$.
    a. If $\angle A$ and $\angle B$ are congruent, what is $m\angle B$?
    b. If $\angle A$ and $\angle C$ are complementary, what is $m\angle C$?
    c. If $\angle A$ and $\angle D$ are supplementary, what is $m\angle D$?
12. Two segments $\overline{MP}$ and $\overline{NT}$ satisfy the following conditions: $\overline{MP} \cong \overline{NT}$, A is on $\overline{MP}$, O is on $\overline{NT}$, and $AP = OT$.
    a. Draw a diagram to illustrate this situation.
    b. **Fill in the Blank** $MA =$ _?_.
    c. Save your answer to Part b for the quote in Question 12 in Lesson 12-6 on page 708 at the end of this chapter.
13. a. Give the side lengths of two triangles with perimeter 20 units that are not congruent.
    b. Construct the triangles of Part a to show that they are not congruent.
14. Draw two triangles that have the same area but that are not congruent.
15. Line m is the perpendicular bisector of $\overline{AA'}$, $\overline{BB'}$, and $\overline{CC'}$.
    a. Name a segment congruent to $\overline{AN}$.
    b. Name a segment congruent to $\overline{B'C}$.
    c. Name an angle congruent to $\angle CAB$.
    d. Name a triangle congruent to $\triangle C'NB$.

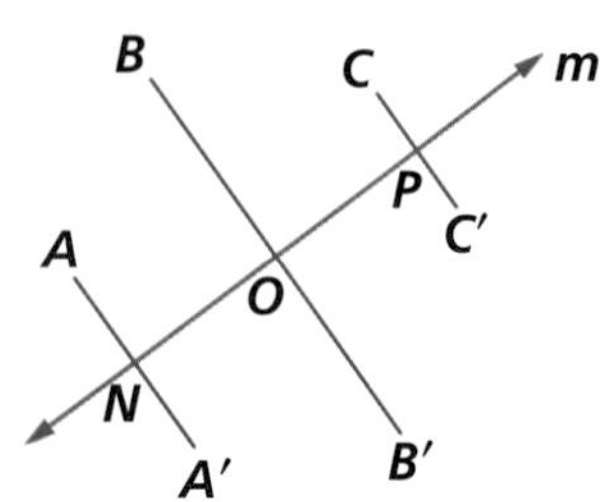

16. Here are two buildings as seen from the top. All angles are right angles, $\overline{AB} = \overline{A'B'} = 100$ feet, and all sides have lengths that are multiples of 50 feet.

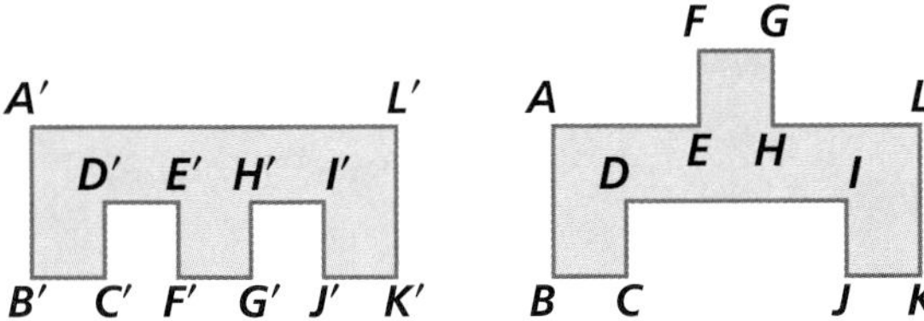

a. How many sides does each building have?

b. What is the perimeter of each building?

c. What is the area of each building?

d. Are the buildings congruent?

REVIEW

17. What is a transversal? **(Lesson 11-5)**

18. **True or False** If line ℓ is parallel to segment s, and ray r is parallel to segment s, then ray r is parallel to line ℓ. **(Lesson 11-5)**

19. Use the Law of Large Numbers to explain why a fair coin can land heads up six times in a row. **(Lesson 10-5)**

In 20–22, find the reciprocal. (Lesson 8-2)

20. $\frac{1.7}{5}$ 21. 5.2 22. 2^5

23. a. Explain why a triangle cannot have two obtuse angles.

b. Can a triangle have one obtuse angle? If so, draw such a triangle. **(Lesson 4-6)**

24. **Multiple Choice** If one angle of a triangle is a right angle, then the other two angles must be **(Lessons 4-6, 3-7)**

A acute. B right. C obtuse. D neither A, B, or C.

EXPLORATION

25. Trace figures J and K at the beginning of this lesson. Find the center of the rotation for which K is the image of J.

26. The two 12-gons (*dodecagons*) in Question 16 have the same number of sides, the same perimeter, and the same area, yet they are not congruent. Draw two polygons with fewer sides with the same characteristics.

QY ANSWER

a. translation

b. reflection and translation

Lesson 12-2 Congruent Triangles

Vocabulary

acute triangle
right triangle
obtuse triangle
isosceles triangle
scalene triangle
included side

▶ **BIG IDEA** When two or more triangles have certain combinations of three corresponding side lengths or angle measures that ore equal, then the triangles are congruent.

Mental Math

Identify the expression whose value does not equal the others.

a. 5^2, 25, -5^2, $(-5)^2$

b. 15 + 32, 7^2, 23 + 26, −9 + 58

c. 3 − 14, −15 + 4, −6 − −5, $3^2 - 5 \cdot 4$

d. 147 • 52, 81 • 95, 1911 • 4, 26 • 294

Triangles can be classified by their angle measures. Recall that an *acute angle* measures between 0° and 90°, a *right angle* measures 90°, and an *obtuse angle* measures between 90° and 180°. A triangle is called *acute, right,* or *obtuse,* depending on the measure of its largest angle.

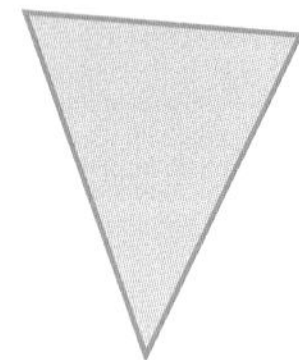

acute triangle
largest angle is acute

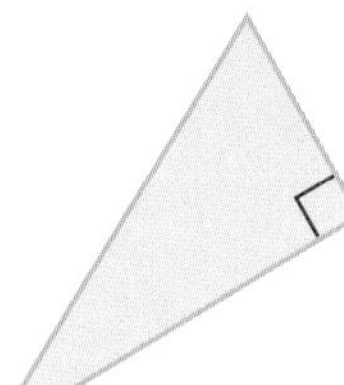

right triangle
largest angle is right

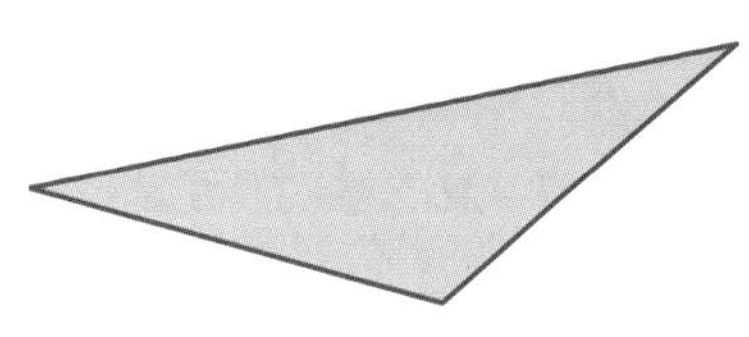

obtuse triangle
largest angle is obtuse

Triangles can also be classified according to the lengths of their sides. Triangles with at least two sides of the same length are called **isosceles triangles.** As you know, triangles with all three sides the same length are called *equilateral triangles.* Triangles with all sides of different lengths are called **scalene triangles.** The right triangle above is a scalene triangle. The other two triangles are isosceles.

See QY1 at the right.

QY1

Draw a scalene obtuse triangle.

Constructing Triangles

If two triangles are congruent, all three pairs of corresponding sides have the same length, and all three pairs of corresponding angles have the same measure. This means there are six pairs of congruent parts. Fortunately, to know that two triangles are congruent, you don't have to compare all six pairs. In the following activities, you will explore the conditions that guarantee two triangles are congruent even if you know of only *three* pairs of congruent parts.

Activity 1

MATERIALS compass, protractor, ruler, straightedge

Construct a triangle given two angles and the included side, the side which is on a side of both of the angles: $\angle P$, $\angle Q$, and $\overline{PQ}$.

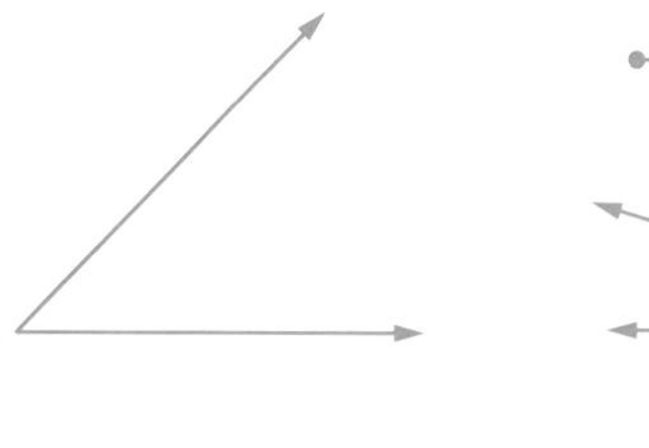

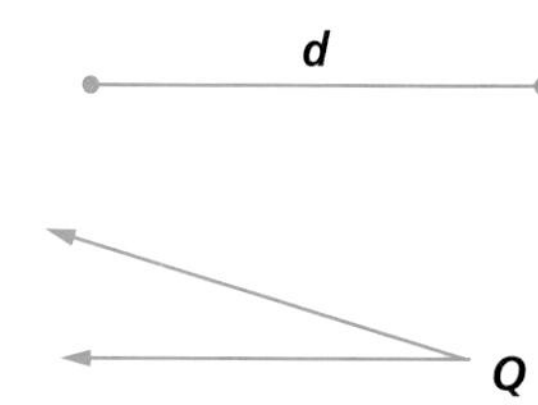

Step 1 Using a compass and straightedge, draw a line. Copy the segment of length d on it. Label your segment $\overline{P'Q'}$.

Step 2 Copy $\angle P$ so that the vertex of your angle is P' and one side of your angle contains $\overline{P'Q'}$.

Step 3 Copy $\angle Q$ so that the vertex of your angle is Q' and one side of your angle contains $\overline{P'Q'}$.

Step 4 Label the point of intersection of the other sides of $\angle P'$ and $\angle Q'$ as R'.

Step 5 Use a ruler and protractor to make sure your $\triangle P'Q'R'$ has angles congruent to $\angle P$ and $\angle Q$ and a side with length d.

Step 6 Compare your triangle to those of your classmates. Are they all congruent?

Activity 1 is an instance of the property that all triangles with two angles and the included side of the same measures are congruent. In Activity 2, you will construct $\triangle CUB$ with two given sides and a non-included angle.

 **See QY2 at the right.**

 **QY2**

Refer to Activity 1.

a. Is $\triangle P'Q'R'$ isosceles or scalene?

b. Is $\triangle P'Q'R'$ acute, right, or obtuse?

Activity 2

MATERIALS compass, straightedge

Follow the steps to draw $\triangle CUB$ with the given sides and angle measure.

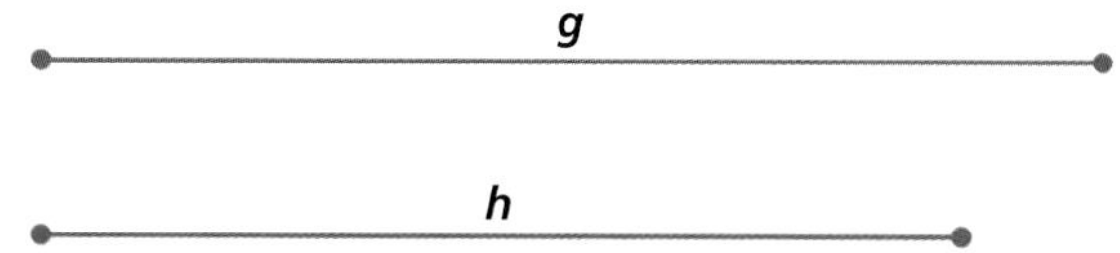

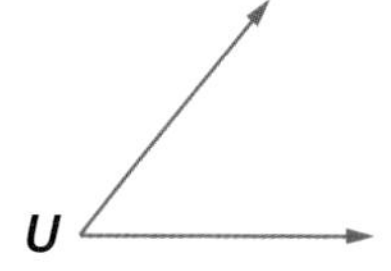

Step 1 Using compass and straightedge, draw a line. Copy a segment with length g, and label your segment $\overline{C'U'}$.

Step 2 Copy $\angle U$ so that the vertex of your angle is U' and one side contains $\overline{C'U'}$. Extend the new ray several inches.

(continued on next page)

Step 3 Construct the circle with center C' and radius h.

Step 4 Your circle should intersect the other side of your angle U' in two points. Name the point closest to $U'B'$ and the other point B^*.

Step 5 Draw $\overline{C'B'}$ and $\overline{C'B^*}$.

Step 6 One of $\triangle C'U'B'$ and $\triangle C'U'B^*$ is acute and one is obtuse. Which is which?

Because $m\angle U'B'C' \neq m\angle U'B^*C'$, the triangles $C'U'B'$ and $C'U'B^*$ are not congruent. Thus, Activity 2 shows that knowing that the lengths of two sides and the measure of a non-included angle are equal in two different triangles is not sufficient to guarantee that the two triangles are congruent.

By drawing two triangles with three pairs of corresponding angles of the same measure, you can test whether this condition leads to congruent triangles.

Activity 3

MATERIALS protractor, ruler

Step 1 Using ruler and protractor, draw $\triangle BAT$ with $m\angle B = 40°$, $m\angle A = 60°$, and $m\angle T = 80°$.

Step 2 Compare your triangle to those of your classmates.

Step 3 If three angles of one triangle have the same measures as the three angles of another triangle, must the two triangles be congruent? Explain your answer.

Questions

COVERING THE IDEAS

1. Two sides of a triangle have lengths 20 cm and 24 cm. The perimeter of the triangle is 68 cm. Is the triangle scalene, isosceles, or equilateral?
2. Explain why every equilateral triangle is isosceles.
3. **Multiple Choice** Which is a correct definition of *acute triangle?*
   A An acute triangle is a triangle with at least two acute angles.
   B An acute triangle is a triangle with at most one acute angle.
   C An acute triangle is a triangle whose smallest angle is acute.
   D An acute triangle is a triangle whose largest angle is acute.

4. Sketch an obtuse isosceles triangle.

5. Sketch an acute scalene triangle.

6. Construct a triangle with angles congruent to $\angle A$ and $\angle B$ below and the included side congruent to $\overline{AB}$.

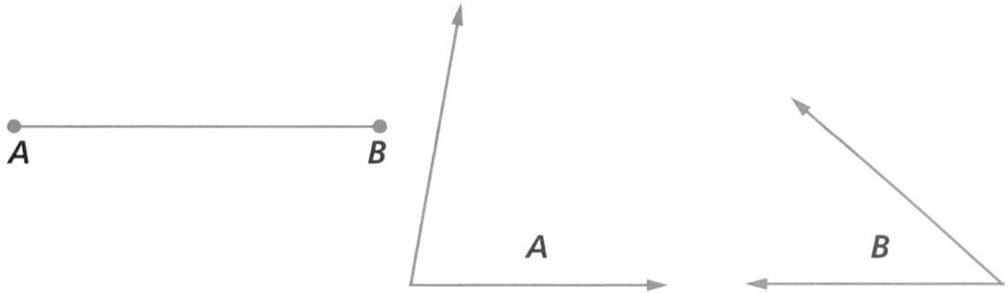

7. a. Draw two different triangles with angles of measure 30°, 30°, and 120°.
   b. What do you notice about the triangles?

8. Draw $\triangle WIN$ with $IN = 8$ cm, $m\angle I = 110°$, and $m\angle N = 40°$. If all the students in your class do this problem correctly, will all the triangles drawn be congruent?

In 9–11, is the given information enough to guarantee that all triangles drawn will be congruent?

9. the measures of the three angles of the triangle

10. the measures of the two angles of the triangle and the length of a non-included side

11. the lengths of three sides of the triangle

12. a. Draw $\triangle TRY$ with $TR = 2\frac{1}{4}$ inches, $RY = 2\frac{1}{4}$ inches, and $m\angle R = 70°$.
    b. Will all triangles with the measures from Part a be congruent?
    c. Is $\triangle TRY$ obtuse, acute, or right?
    d. Is $\triangle TRY$ scalene, isosceles, or equilateral?

APPLYING THE MATHEMATICS

13. One angle of a right triangle has measure 71°. What can you conclude about the measures of the other angles?

14. Two angles of a triangle have measures 37° and 57°. Is the triangle acute, right, or obtuse?

15. Draw $\triangle NOW$ with a right angle at vertex O, $NO = 3$ cm, and $NW = 5$ cm. Will all triangles drawn with this information be congruent?

16. Three ships A, B, and C are at sea. From ship A, ship B is 50° north of east and ship C is 70° north of east. The captain of ship A knows that ships B and C are 12 miles apart. Is this enough information for the captain to know exactly where ships B and C are? Why or why not?

The USS Cole is 505 feet long and 148 feet high at its highest point.

Source: U.S. Navy

17. In the figure at the right, $\triangle HIS \cong \triangle HER$.

  a. Which length is equal to *ER*?

  b. Use the word in Part a for the quote in Question 12 in Lesson 12-6 on page 708 at the end of this chapter.

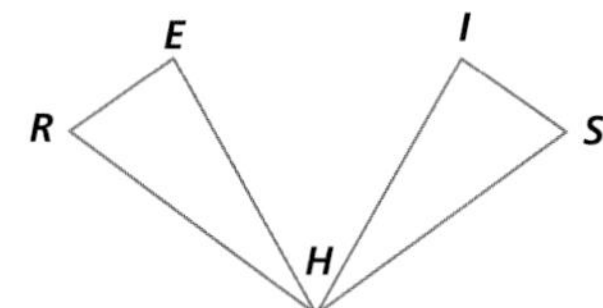

REVIEW

18. **True or False** If two triangles have the same perimeter and area, then they must be congruent. **(Lesson 12-1)**

19. If lines *a* and *b* at the right are parallel, name all the angles congruent to $\angle 2$. **(Lesson 11-5)**

20. Can a parallelogram have two neighboring obtuse angles? Justify your answer. **(Lesson 11-4)**

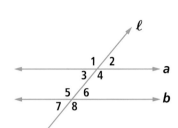

21. a. Use segment $\overline{GO}$ at the right to construct the following.

  Step 1 Copy segment $\overline{GO}$.

  Step 2 Construct the circle with center *G* and radius $\overline{GO}$.

  Step 3 Construct the circle with center *O* and radius $\overline{GO}$.

  Step 4 Name the points of intersection of the two circles *L* and *F*.

  b. **True or False** $\overline{LF}$ lies on the perpendicular bisector of $\overline{GO}$. **(Lesson 11-2)**

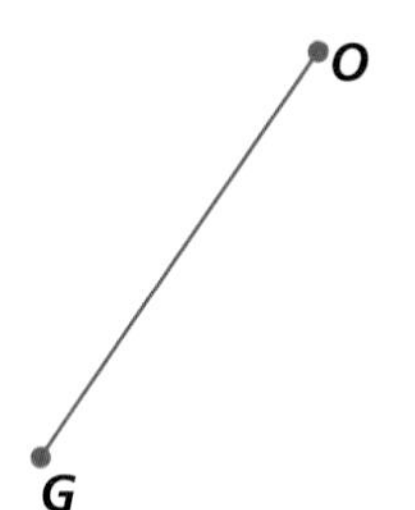

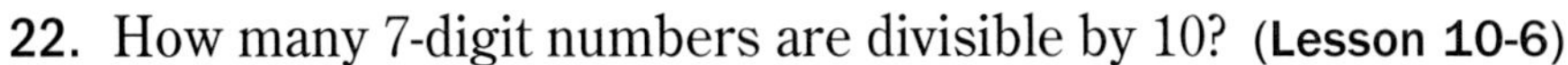

22. How many 7-digit numbers are divisible by 10? **(Lesson 10-6)**

23. In the drawing below, each of the small angles has the same measure. If $\widehat{BF} = 120°$, what is the measure of $\angle CAE$? **(Lesson 3-6)**

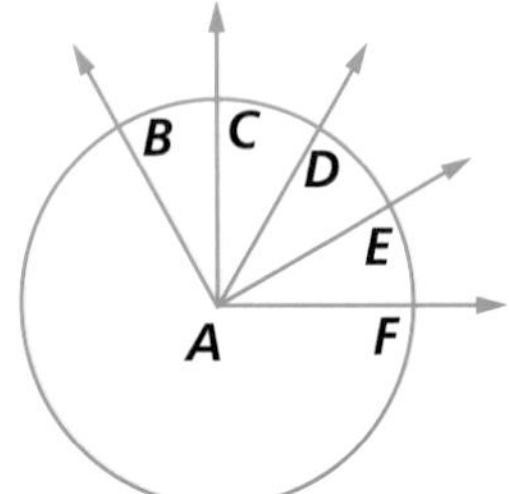

EXPLORATION

24. The sides of a triangle have integer lengths, and the perimeter of the triangle is *p* inches.

  a. If $p = 6$, explain why the triangle must be equilateral.

  b. If $p = 7$, explain why the triangle must be isosceles.

  c. If $p = 9$, must the triangle be isosceles? Why or why not?

  d. If $p = 10$, must the triangle be isosceles? Why or why not?

QY ANSWERS

1. Answers vary. Sample:

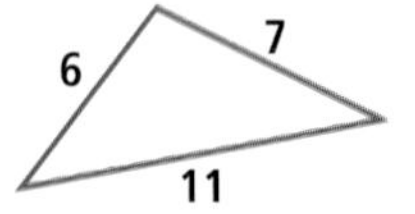

2a. scalene

2b. obtuse

Lesson 12-3 Symmetry and Congruence

Vocabulary

symmetric

reflection-symmetric

symmetry line

rotation-symmetric (rotation symmetry)

center of symmetry

▶ **BIG IDEA** Many figures and objects in our world possess reflection or rotation symmetry. When they do, corresponding parts have the same measure.

You can translate, reflect, or rotate the face at the left below. For instance, rotating it 180° about the point P gives you the upside-down image in the middle. Reflecting the face over the line m gives you the face at the right.

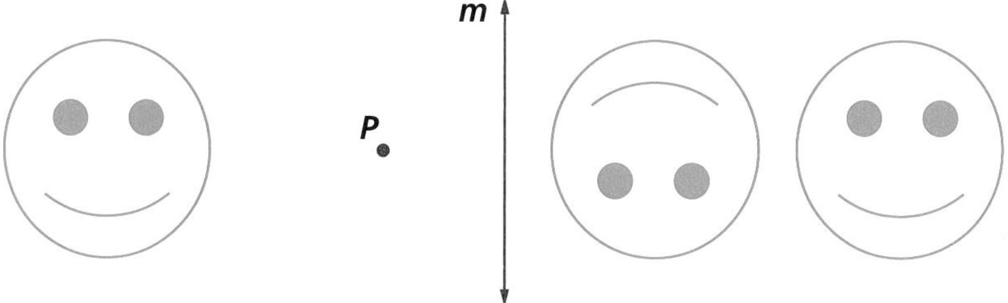

But notice what happens if you reflect the face over the line n through its center, as shown at the right. Then you cannot tell the image from the preimage. This is because the face is *symmetric*.

A figure is **symmetric** if it is unchanged after a transformation that does move some points. If the transformation is a reflection, as above, then we say that the figure is **reflection-symmetric.** The line n is a **symmetry line** for the figure.

Many of the most common figures are reflection-symmetric. Every angle has a line of symmetry. Every segment has two lines of symmetry. Every isosceles triangle has at least one line of symmetry. Lines of symmetry do not have to be horizontal or vertical.

Mental Math

Suppose two angles of a triangle have the same measure.

a. The two equal angles must be acute.

b. The third angle must be acute.

c. The third angle must be obtuse.

d. Two of the sides of the triangle must have the same length.

STOP QY

Trace the figure and draw all lines of symmetry.

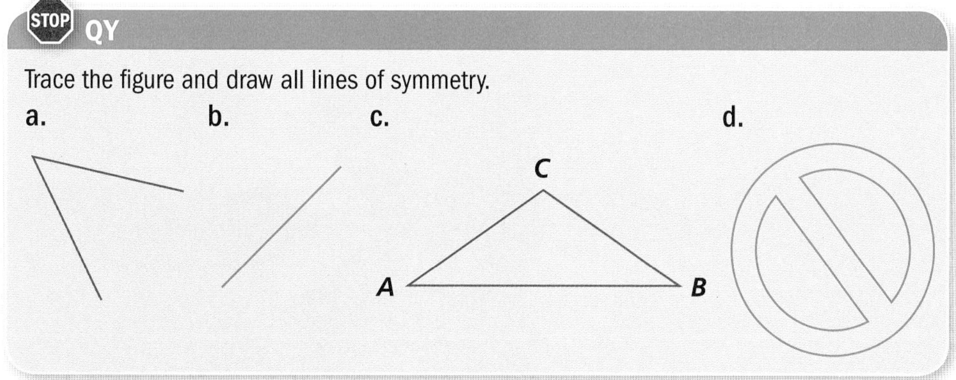

The Advantage of Knowing that a Figure is Symmetric

Knowing that a figure is symmetric is helpful because any part of a figure will have the same measure as its image. Look at Part c of the QY. Angles A and B in the isosceles triangle must have the same measure because each is the image of the other under a reflection. For the same reason, segments $\overline{CA}$ and $\overline{CB}$ have the same length.

GUIDED

Example

Quadrilateral *QUAD* at the right has two symmetry lines. Trace the figure and draw the symmetry lines. Name all angles with the same measure as $\angle UAD$. Name all segments with the same length as $\overline{QD}$.

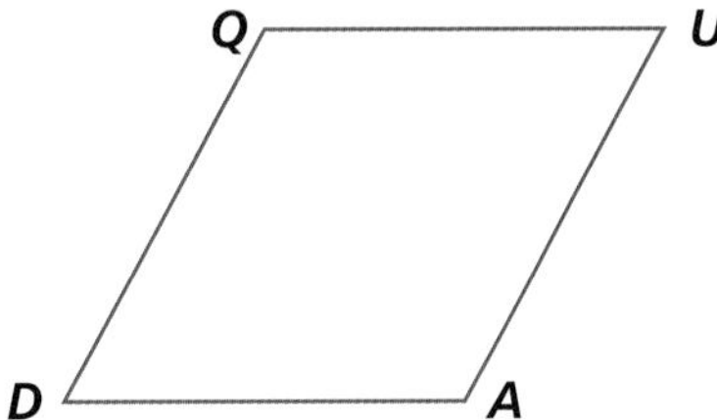

Solution First, notice that there is not a vertical symmetry line. Nor is there a horizontal symmetry line. One symmetry line is $\overleftrightarrow{UD}$. The other is ___?___.

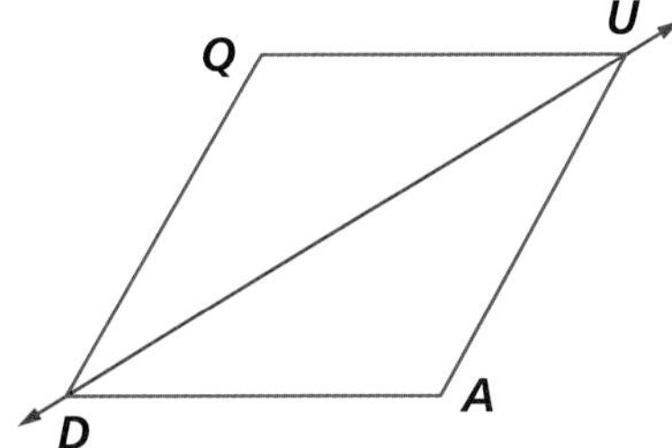

The reflection image of $\angle UAD$ over the symmetry line $\overleftrightarrow{UD}$ is $\angle UQD$. So $\angle UQD$ has the same measure as $\angle UAD$. The reflection image of $\angle UAD$ over the other symmetry line ___?___ is itself. So, no other angle of equal measure is found.

The reflection image of $\overline{QD}$ over line $\overleftrightarrow{UD}$ is $\overline{AD}$. So $QD = AD$. The reflection image of $\overline{QD}$ over the other symmetry line is $\overline{QU}$. So $QD =$ ___?___. Also, the reflection image of $\overline{AD}$ over that other symmetry line is ___?___. So, $AD =$ ___?___. This means that all four sides of *QUAD* have the same length.

Rotation Symmetry

The red flag at the right is the flag of the Isle of Man, a self-governing Crown dependency of England located in the Irish Sea. The figure on the flag is called a *triskelion*. The triskelion has *rotation symmetry*.

A figure is **rotation-symmetric,** or has **rotation symmetry,** if and only if there is a point about which the figure can be rotated between 0° and 360° so that the image coincides with the original figure. That point is the **center of symmetry.** In the triskelion, the center of symmetry is the intersection of the three yellow segments in the middle of the figure.

Activity

MATERIALS tracing paper

Step 1 Trace the triskelion onto your tracing paper.

Step 2 Place your tracing directly over the triskelion in your book. Put your pencil point at the center of rotation and turn the tracing paper counterclockwise. How many degrees do you have to turn your tracing paper until the traced image first coincides with the preimage?

Step 3 Turn the paper once again the same number of degrees. What happens?

When a figure has rotation symmetry, there will be congruent segments and angles because figures and their images have the same lengths and angle measures. In the triskelion on the previous page, the three feet have the same length. In the next few lessons, you will see how reflection and rotation symmetry can help you find and remember properties of quadrilaterals.

Questions

COVERING THE IDEAS

In 1–5, trace the figure and draw all lines of symmetry.

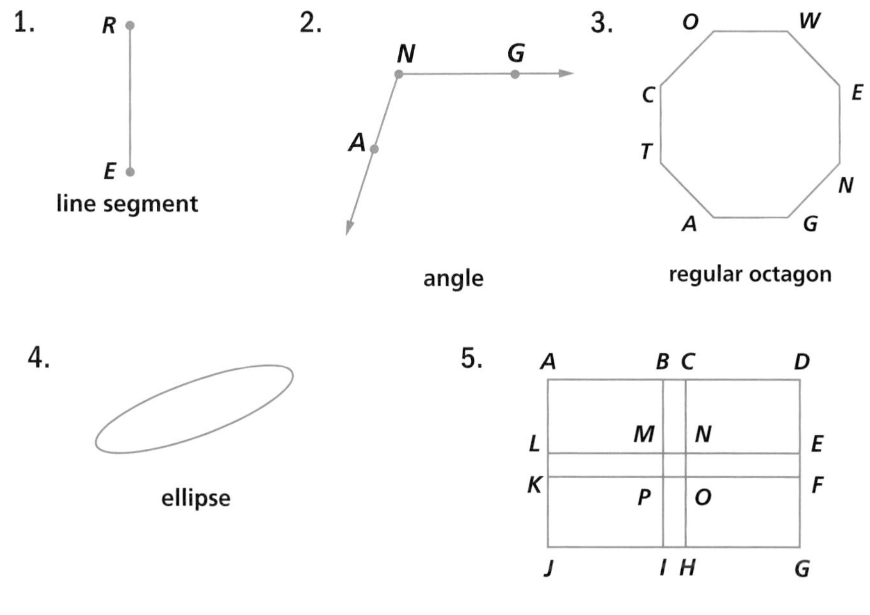

In 6 and 7, trace the figure. Identify on it any center of symmetry. Then, determine the measure of the smallest counterclockwise rotation that will turn the figure onto itself.

6. 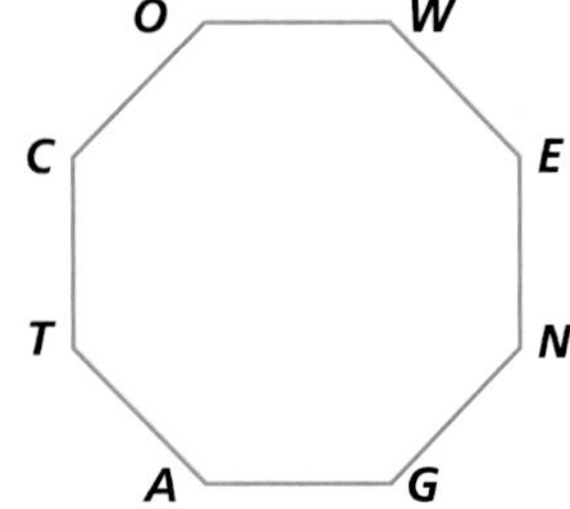

7. A B C D L M N E K F P O J I H G

8. In Question 7, due to the symmetry, which segments have the same length as $\overline{OH}$?

9. In Question 7, due to the symmetry, which angles have the same measure as $\angle NED$?

APPLYING THE MATHEMATICS

In 10 and 11, trace the figure and identify on it any center of symmetry. Then determine the magnitude of the smallest counterclockwise rotation that will turn the figure into itself.

10. 

11. 

12. a. Draw an 8×8 checkerboard.
    b. How many lines of symmetry does this figure have?
    c. How many centers of symmetry does the figure have?

13. Draw a figure that can be rotated onto itself with a rotation of $72°$.

14. Draw a figure that has six lines of symmetry.

REVIEW

15. If a triangle has one angle measuring $32°$ and is obtuse, what does this tell you about the other two angles? **(Lesson 12-2)**

16. Draw a triangle with side lengths 10 mm, 24 mm, and 26 mm. **(Lesson 12-1)**

17. Find the area of the triangle in Question 16. **(Lesson 9-2)**

In 18 and 19, solve for *m*. (Lessons 8-5, 4-8)

18. $8m = 27$

19. $342 + m = 169$

EXPLORATION

20. **a.** Among the letters of the English alphabet, 16 capital letters have reflection symmetry. Find these letters and show their lines of symmetry.

    b. Are there any capital letters that have rotation symmetry? Find these letters and show their centers of symmetry.

    c. One of the words below has exactly three different letters with at least one type of symmetry. Save this word for Question 12 in Lesson 12-6, page 708.

    FATHER   CASTLE   ROYAL   FROG

QY ANSWERS

a.

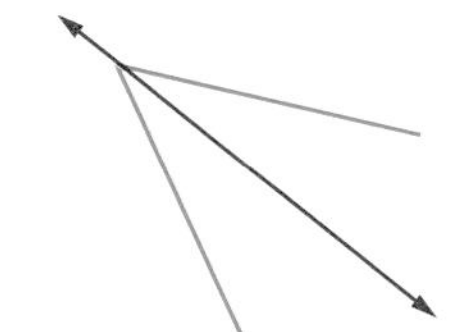

b.

c.

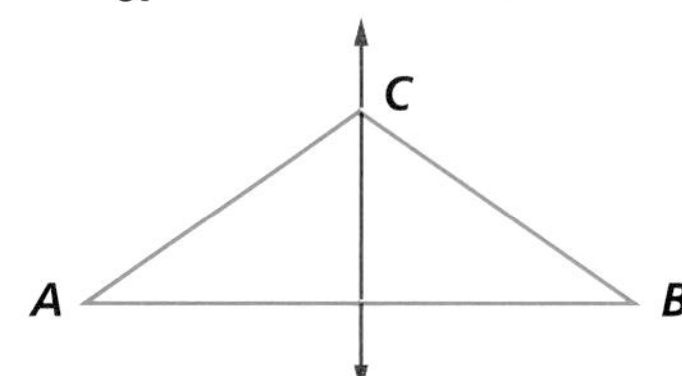

d.

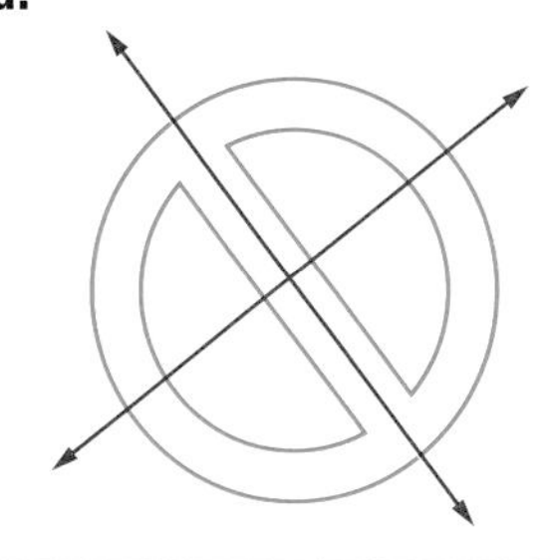

Lesson

12-4 The Parallelogram Family

Vocabulary

opposite sides of a quadrilateral

opposite angles of a quadrilateral

Venn diagram

rhombus

BIG IDEA The parallelogram family includes parallelograms, rectangles, rhombuses, and squares.

Remember that a *quadrilateral* is a four-sided polygon. At the right is quadrilateral *ABCD*. The sides $\overline{AB}$ and $\overline{CD}$ are **opposite sides.** The angles *A* and *C* are **opposite angles.**

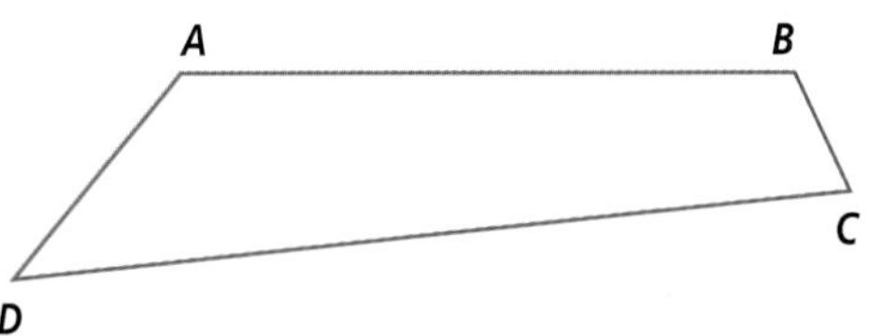

QY1

Refer to the above figure.

a. Name the other pair of opposite sides of *ABCD*.

b. Name the other pair of opposite angles of *ABCD*.

Mental Math

Use the figure below.

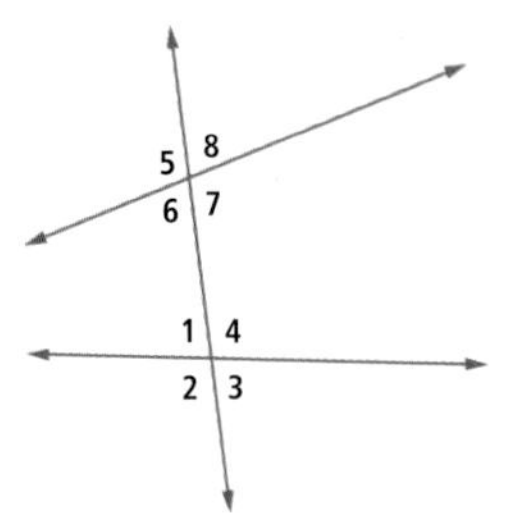

a. Identify the corresponding angles.

b. Identify the linear pairs.

c. Identify all angles with measure equal to the measure of ∠2.

Quadrilaterals come in all sizes and many shapes. A *parallelogram* is a quadrilateral in which both pairs of opposite sides are parallel. The five figures below each have two pairs of parallel sides, so they are all parallelograms.

The third figure above is a rectangle, and the fourth figure is a square. Because squares and rectangles have two pairs of parallel sides, they are parallelograms.

QY2

Which of figures A–H appear to be parallelograms?

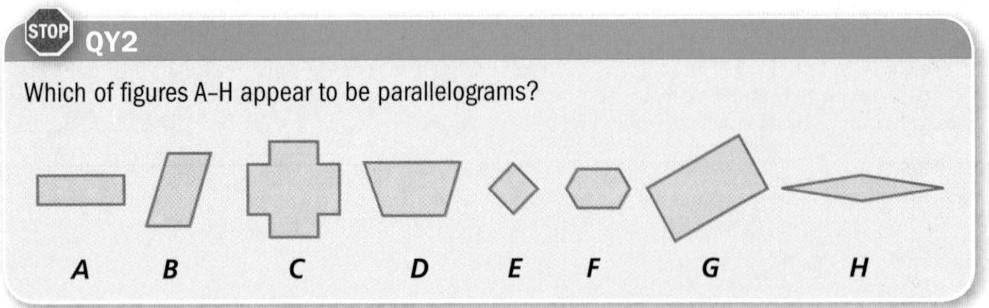

Properties of Parallelograms

Other than the parallel sides, parallelograms have many properties. Some of the properties can be seen easily. Others are not so obvious.

Activity 1

MATERIALS DGS software

If you have access to a pre-constructed sketch of a parallelogram *ABCD*, then skip to Step 6.

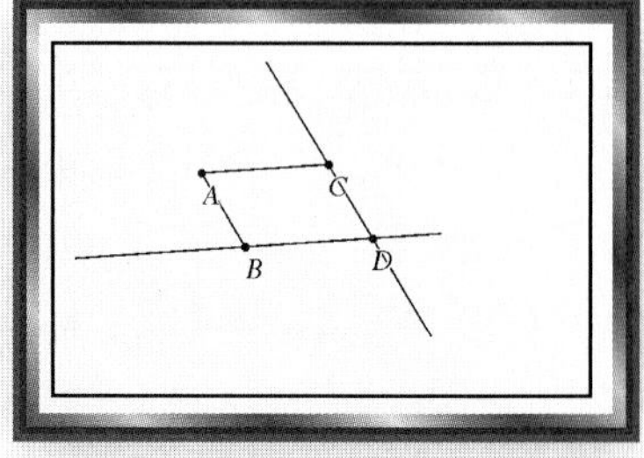

Step 1 Construct two points and label them A and B. Construct $\overline{AB}$.

Step 2 Construct a point C not on $\overline{AB}$. Draw $\overline{AC}$.

Step 3 Construct the line through C that is parallel to $\overline{AB}$.

Step 4 Construct the line through B that is parallel to $\overline{AC}$.

Step 5 The lines in Steps 3 and 4 intersect at a point. Call the point D. (Your figure should look somewhat like the one at the right, but with different angle and side measures.) Explain why $ABDC$ is a parallelogram.

Step 6 Use the DGS to measure the opposite sides $\overline{AC}$ and $\overline{BD}$. Also, measure the opposite angles A and D.

Step 7 Measure $\overline{AB}$ and $\overline{CD}$. Are they congruent? Do they have the same length as either $\overline{AC}$ and $\overline{BD}$?

Step 8 Drag points A, B, and C. What happens to the measures of opposite sides and angles?

Do not clear the screen. You will do more with $ABDC$ in Activity 2.

Activity 1 illustrates two properties of all parallelograms.

1. Opposite sides of a parallelogram have the same length.
2. Opposite angles of a parallelogram have the same measure.

STOP **See QY3 at the right.**

Activity 2

MATERIALS DGS software

Use parallelogram *ABDC* from Activity 1.

Step 1 Construct $\overline{AD}$ and $\overline{BC}$, the diagonals of the parallelogram.

Step 2 Let M be the point of intersection of $\overline{AD}$ and $\overline{BC}$. Measure to find AM, BM, CM, and DM.

(continued on next page)

STOP **QY3**

The drawing of quadrilateral $ABCD$ shows the measures of some sides and angles.

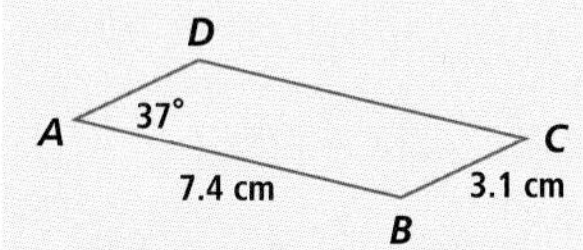

a. What is the length of $\overline{DC}$?

b. What is $m\angle C$?

c. What is $m\angle D$?

Step 3 Determine which, if any, of these statements are true.

a. M is the midpoint of $\overline{BC}$.

b. M is the midpoint of $\overline{AD}$.

c. $\overline{AD}$ bisects $\overline{BC}$.

d. $\overline{BC}$ bisects $\overline{AD}$.

In Activity 2, you should have found that the diagonals of the parallelogram have the same midpoint. For this reason, if you rotate parallelogram $ABDC$ 180° about this midpoint, the parallelogram will coincide with its image. This means that the parallelogram is rotation-symmetric.

QY4

Which of figures A–H on the first page of the lesson are rotation-symmetric?

Rectangles and Parallelograms

Since a rectangle has four right angles, its opposite sides form corresponding angles with measure 90°, and so opposite sides are parallel. Therefore, any rectangle is also a parallelogram. But not all parallelograms are rectangles.

A **Venn diagram** uses circles or ovals to show relationships among sets of objects. Below is a Venn diagram relating rectangles and parallelograms.

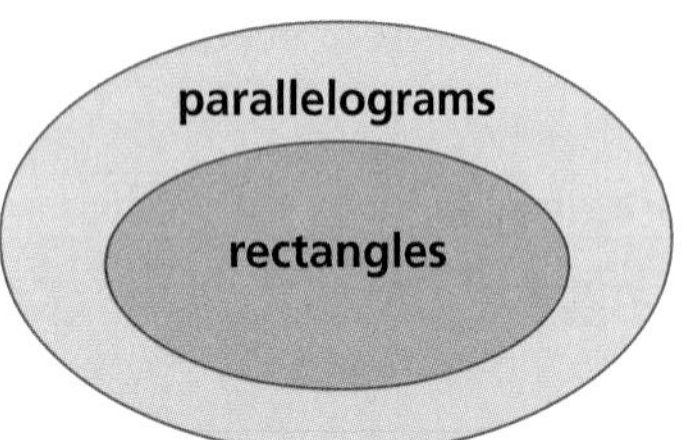

Rhombuses and Parallelograms

A **rhombus** is a quadrilateral with all four sides of the same length. Notice that, in all the rhombuses on the dot grid at the right, opposite sides seem to be parallel.

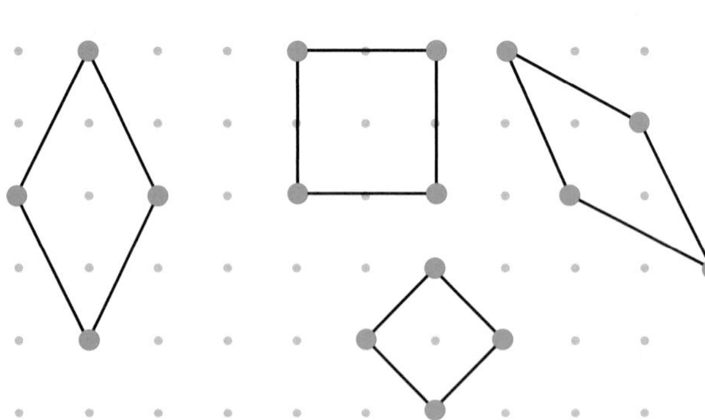

QY5

Which of figures A–H at the beginning of this lesson appear to be rhombuses? Do all of the rhombuses appear to be parallelograms?

Activity 3

MATERIALS DGS software (or straightedge and compass)

Step 1 Construct a point *A*. Then construct a circle with center *A*.

Step 2 Place two points *B* and *C* on the circle, as at the right.

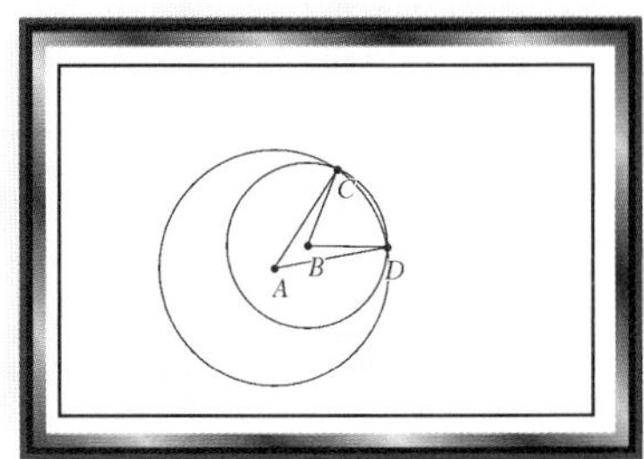

Step 3 Construct the circle with center *B* and containing *A*. Then construct the circle with center *C* and containing *A*.

Step 4 The two circles constructed in Step 3 intersect at *A* and at a second point *D*. Draw $\overleftrightarrow{AB}$, $\overleftrightarrow{AC}$, $\overleftrightarrow{DB}$, and $\overleftrightarrow{DC}$ to outline the quadrilateral *ABDC*.

Step 5 Why is it always true that *ABDC* is a rhombus?

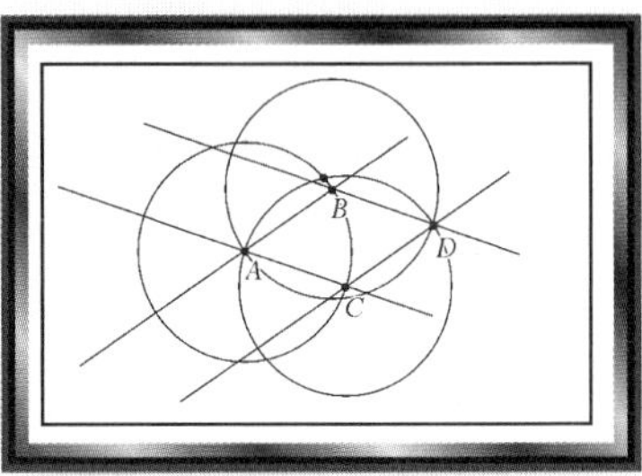

Step 6 Construct the diagonal $\overleftrightarrow{AD}$. Measure two corresponding angles to test whether sides $\overleftrightarrow{AB}$ and $\overleftrightarrow{DC}$ are parallel.

Step 7 If you are using a DGS, drag the points *B* and *C* around to see a variety of rhombuses. What happens to the measures of your corresponding angles?

You should find that your corresponding angles are always of the same measure. For this reason, every rhombus is a parallelogram. But not all parallelograms are rhombuses.

We again show this with a Venn diagram.

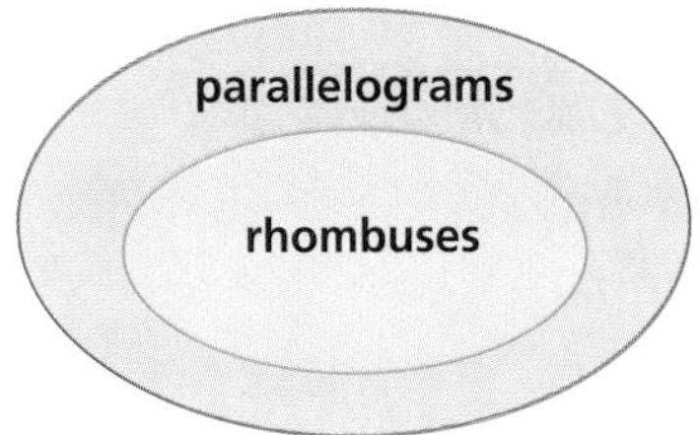

Since a square is a quadrilateral with four sides of the same length and four right angles, every square is both a rhombus and a rectangle, and so every square is also a parallelogram.

QY6

Which of figures A–H at the beginning of this lesson appear to be squares?

Parallelograms, rectangles, rhombuses, and squares make up the parallelogram family of quadrilaterals. The Venn diagram at the right shows how these figures are related.

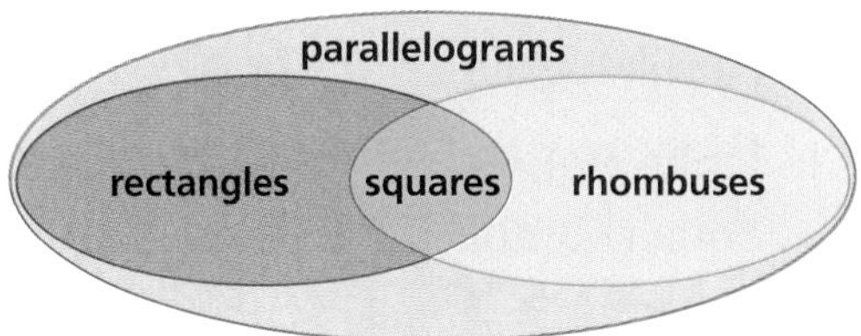

Questions

COVERING THE IDEAS

In 1–4, use a ruler and protractor to make an accurate drawing of the figure, and label each side length and angle measure. Then, tell whether everyone's drawings will be congruent to yours.

1. a parallelogram with sides of 5 cm and 3 cm, and one angle of 60°
2. a rectangle with length 95 mm and width 20 mm
3. a rhombus with sides of 3 inches and one angle of 165°
4. a square with one side of length 6 cm

In 5–8, choose the true statement.

5. i. All squares are rectangles.
   ii. All rectangles are squares.
6. i. Some but not all rhombuses are squares.
   ii. Some but not all squares are rhombuses.
7. i. If a figure is a parallelogram, then it is a quadrilateral.
   ii. If a figure is a quadrilateral, then it is a parallelogram.
8. i. Every quadrilateral is a rectangle.
   ii. Every rectangle is a quadrilateral.
9. a. Draw a square *SQUA*. On your figure, show the center of rotation symmetry *C* of the square.
   b. What is the smallest magnitude of a positive rotation about the point *C* under which the square is its own image?

APPLYING THE MATHEMATICS

10. a. Using a straightedge and compass, do the following construction.
    Step 1 Draw two points *P* and *Q* on your sheet.
    Step 2 Construct the circle with center *P* that contains *Q*.
    Step 3 Construct the circle with center *Q* that contains *P*.
    Step 4 Label the two points where the circles intersect *R* and *S*.
    Step 5 Form the quadrilateral *PRQS*.
    b. Being most specific, what kind of quadrilateral is *PRQS*?
11. Draw a quadrilateral with two right angles that is not a rectangle.
12. Draw a quadrilateral with a pair of parallel sides that is not a parallelogram.
13. Draw a quadrilateral with three sides of the same length that is not a rhombus.

In 14 and 15, sketch the figure. Then label the measure of each side and angle.

14. Figure *HELP* below is a parallelogram.

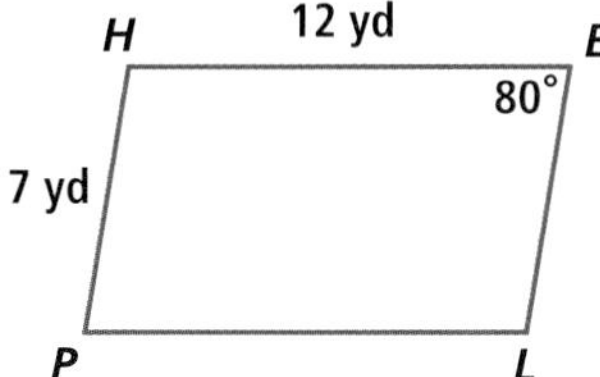

15. Figure *RHOM* below is a rhombus.

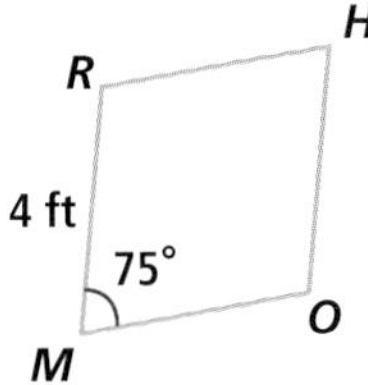

16. The midpoints of the sides of the rectangle below have been connected and form a rhombus. Without using a protractor, find the measures of the angles identified as *R, E, H, S,* and *T*. Then, on each of the spaces below, write the letter that corresponds to the degree measure given. Save this word for the quote in Question 12 in Lesson 12-6 on page 708 at the end of the chapter.

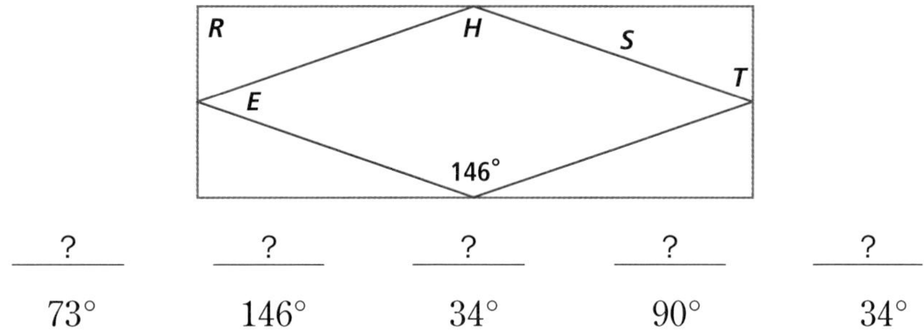

?	?	?	?	?
73°	146°	34°	90°	34°

In 17–19, choose the types of figures that meet the criterion from this list: parallelogram, rhombus, rectangle, or square.

17. quadrilateral with four angles of equal measure

18. quadrilateral with four sides of equal length

19. quadrilateral with two pairs of opposite angles of equal measure

In 20–23, is the statement *always, sometimes but not always,* or *never* true?

20. A rhombus has reflection symmetry.

21. A parallelogram has rotation symmetry.

22. A diagonal of a rectangle is a symmetry line for the rectangle.

23. A parallelogram is reflection-symmetric.

REVIEW

24. a. Construct a triangle with side lengths 21 mm, 22 mm, and 4 cm.
    b. Is your triangle acute, obtuse, or right? **(Lesson 12-2)**

25. Is it possible for a triangle to be both scalene and right? Why or why not? **(Lesson 12-2)**

26. **Multiple Choice** Which of the following must be congruent?
    A two triangles with equal area
    B two triangles with equal perimeter
    C two triangles with three pairs of corresponding angles with the same measure
    D two triangles with three pairs of corresponding sides of the same length **(Lesson 12-2)**

27. At the market, Anton bought three dozen eggs for $2.14 per dozen and two variety packs of cereal for $5.43 each. Now, he wants to buy a magazine that costs $3.59. If he had $20 before going to the market, does he have enough money to buy the magazine? **(Lesson 3-1)**

EXPLORATION

28. Draw some squares, rectangles, and rhombuses. Draw both diagonals of each figure. You should find that the diagonals of each type of figure have special properties involving bisectors, angles, or lengths. What special properties do the diagonals of each member of the parallelogram family have?

QY ANSWERS

1a. $\overline{BC}$ and $\overline{AD}$

1b. B and D

2. A, B, E, G, H

3a. 7.4 cm

3b. 37°

3c. 143°

4. A, B, C, E, F, G, H

5. E, H; yes

6. E

Lesson 12-5 The Kite Family

Vocabulary

convex
nonconvex
adjacent sides
kite

▸ **BIG IDEA** The kite family includes rhombuses and squares.

All of the quadrilaterals you have studied so far are *convex*. Closed figures are **convex** if they do not bend in.

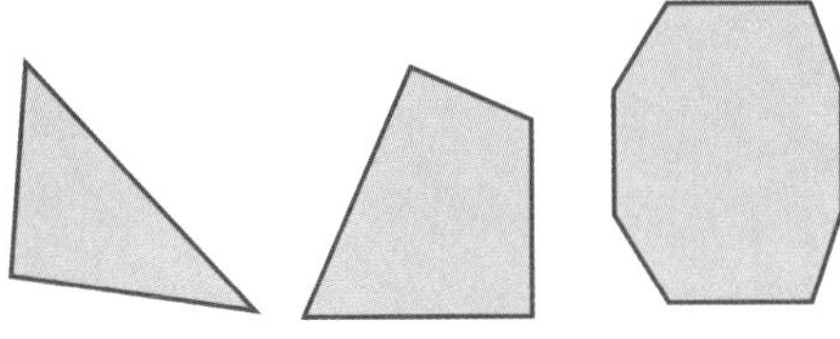

convex polygons

When a figure is **nonconvex**, there is a segment connecting two points in the figure that has points outside the figure.

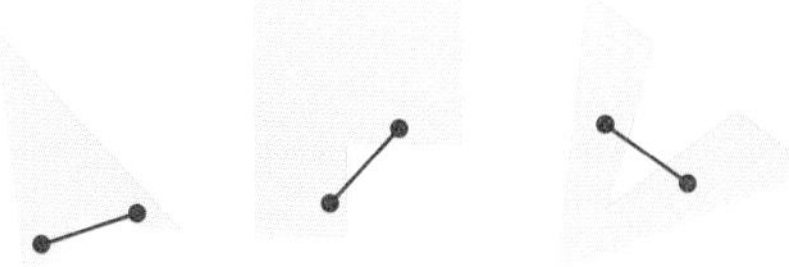

Kites are a special kind of quadrilateral that includes some convex figures and some nonconvex figures.

What Is a Kite?

Suppose you have four pieces of wood with lengths 2', 5', 2', and 5'. You can make many quadrilaterals from these pieces. If you put the congruent pieces across from each other, you will get a parallelogram. If you put the congruent pieces next to each other, you will get a kite.

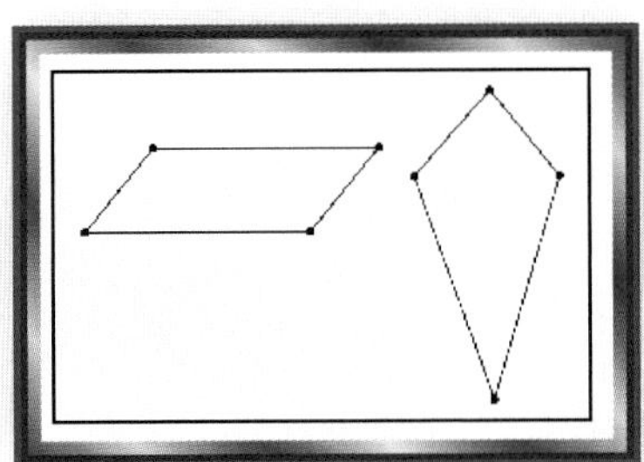

Mental Math

Bananas cost 50¢ per pound, pears cost 25¢ per pound, and apples cost 75¢ per pound. You have $6.

a. How many pounds of bananas can you buy?

b. How many pounds of pears can you buy?

c. How many pounds of apples can you buy?

d. If you buy an equal weight of each fruit, how much of each can you buy?

Adjacent sides of a polygon are sides that are next to each other. A **kite** is defined as a quadrilateral that has two pairs of adjacent sides of equal length. These figures are called "kites" because convex kites resemble a typical kite you might fly in the air. Nonconvex kites resemble arrowheads. All kites (both convex and nonconvex) have reflection symmetry.

convex kite

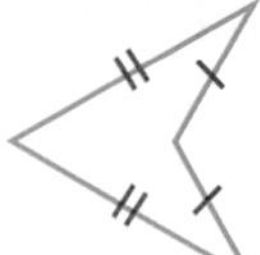

nonconvex kite

When two circles with centers A and B intersect at points C and D, a quadrilateral $ACBD$ can be formed. This quadrilateral is a kite. Activity 1 will help you construct and explore this idea with your DGS.

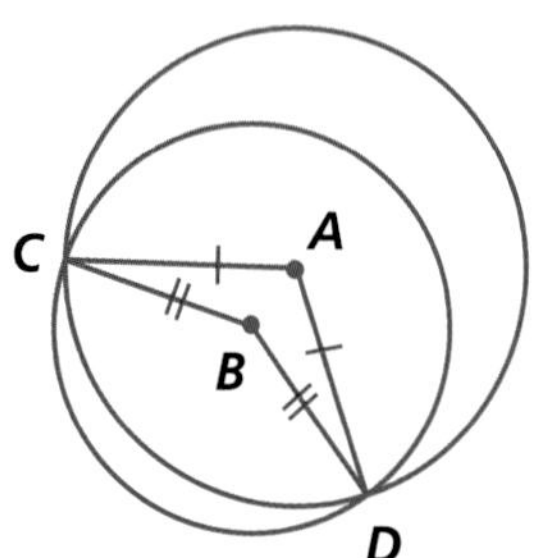

▸ READING MATH

The arrowheads used by North American Indians were made of stone, copper, wood, bone, and other materials. In addition to being tips of arrows for hunting or war, they were used as knives and scrapers.

Activity 1

MATERIALS DGS software

Step 1 Draw two circles *A* and *B* with different radii. Move the circles until they intersect in two points *C* and *D*.

Step 2 Connect *A*, *C*, *B*, and *D* to form kite *ACBD*. Draw that kite on your paper.

Step 3 Move one of the circles so that the overlap of the circles is small and draw the kite that results.

Step 4 Move one of the circles so that the overlap of the circles is large and draw the kite that results.

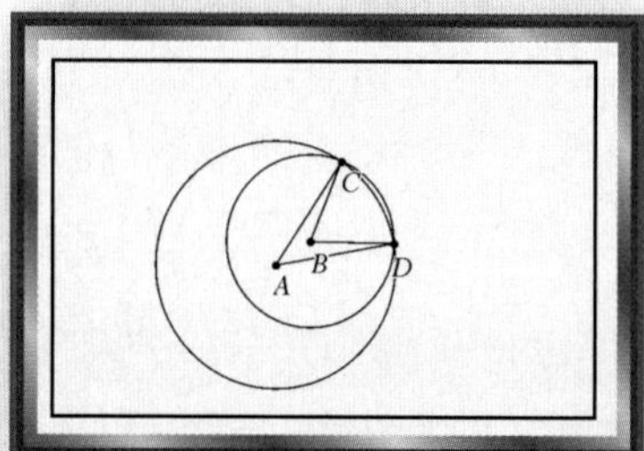

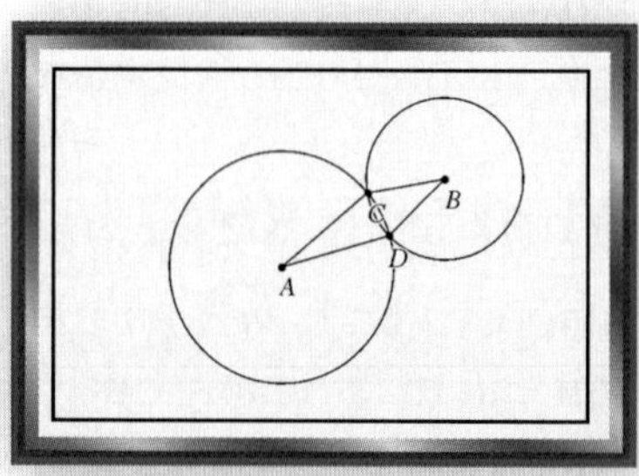

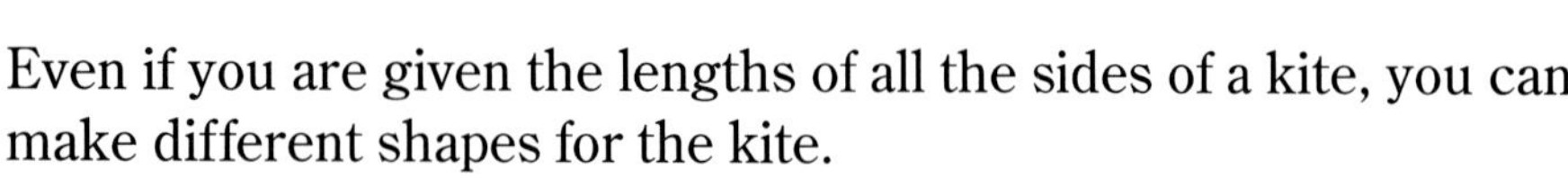

Even if you are given the lengths of all the sides of a kite, you can make different shapes for the kite.

Activity 2

MATERIALS two straws, scissors, ruler

Step 1 Using two straws, cut two pieces that are 2 inches long and two pieces that are 5 inches long.

Step 2 Arrange the straw pieces into a parallelogram. Is your parallelogram congruent to the parallelograms of other students? If not, how are they different?

Step 3 Keep your straw pieces in the same order, but change the angles the pieces make. Draw two of the many different parallelograms you can make with these side lengths.

Step 4 Change the order of the pieces and arrange them into a convex kite. Is your kite congruent to the kites of other students? If not, how are they different?

Step 5 Keep your straw pieces in the same order, but change the angles that the pieces make. Draw two of the many different convex kites you can make with these side lengths.

Step 6 Arrange the pieces into a nonconvex kite. Is your nonconvex kite congruent to the nonconvex kites of other students? If not, how are they different?

Step 7 Again keep your straw pieces in the same order, but change the angles that the pieces make. Draw two of the many different nonconvex kites you can make with these side lengths.

Notice that whatever shape you have for a kite, it has a symmetry line. Every kite is reflection-symmetric.

If you have four segments, two with one length and two with another, you can always create both convex and nonconvex kites as in Activity 2. However, if the four segments are the same length, then only convex kites are possible. These kites are rhombuses.

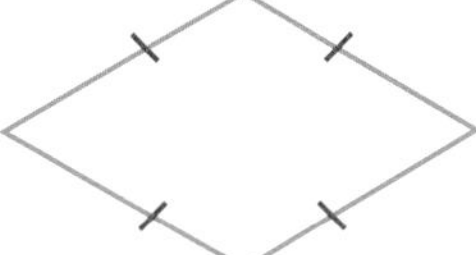

Every rhombus is a kite.

 **See QY1 at the right.**

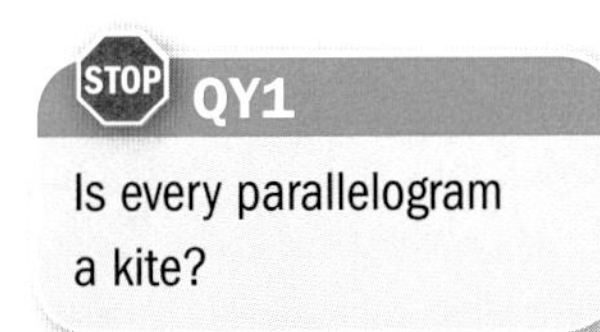

Picturing the Kite Family

Since every square is a rhombus, every square is a kite. Kites, rhombuses, and squares make up the kite family of quadrilaterals. The Venn diagram below shows how they are related.

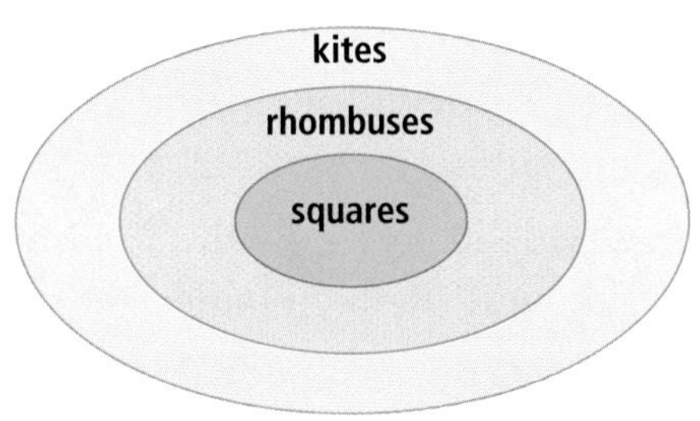

Parallelograms, Kites, and Rhombuses

Parallelograms have two pairs of opposite sides of the same length. Kites have two pairs of adjacent sides of the same length. Rhombuses have *all* sides of the same length. The Venn diagram below shows how parallelograms and kites are related.

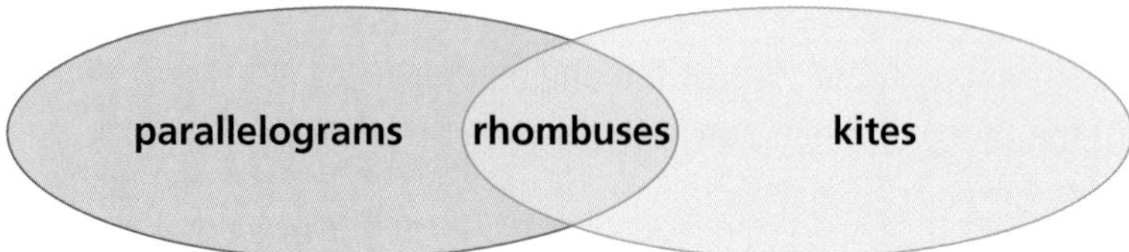

 **See QY2 at the right.**

 **QY2**

Where should squares be placed in the Venn diagram at the left above?

Since parallelograms have rotation symmetry and kites have reflection symmetry, every rhombus has both kinds of symmetry.

Questions

COVERING THE IDEAS

1. Label each shape *convex kite, nonconvex kite,* or *not a kite.*

a.

7 in.
5 in. 5 in.
7 in.

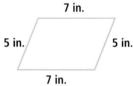

b.

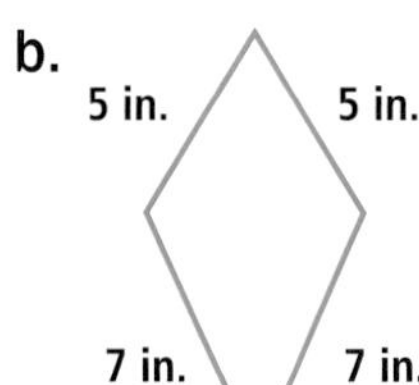

c.

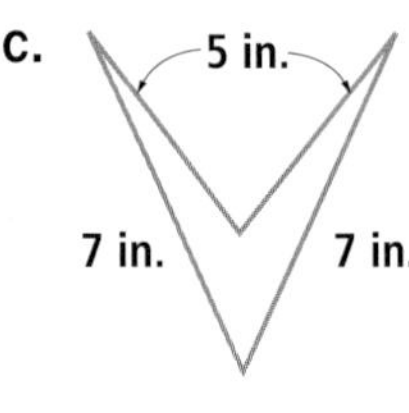

2. Draw two noncongruent parallelograms with side lengths of 4 cm and 6 cm.

3. Draw two noncongruent convex kites with side lengths of 4 cm and 6 cm.

4. Draw two noncongruent nonconvex kites with side lengths of 4 cm and 6 cm.

5. Explain why every rhombus is a kite.

APPLYING THE MATHEMATICS

6. a. Draw a kite with two sides of length 5 cm, two sides of length 3 cm, and a 45° angle between the two 5-cm sides.
   b. Draw a kite with two sides of length 5 cm, two sides of length 3 cm, and a 45° angle between the two 3-cm sides.
   c. Draw a kite with two sides of length 5 cm, two sides of length 3 cm, and a 45° angle between the 3-cm side and the 5-cm side.
   d. Will all other correctly-drawn kites in Parts a–c be congruent to yours? If not, draw one that is not congruent to yours.

7. One diagonal of a kite connects the vertices where the sides of equal length intersect, and divides the kite into two triangles.
   a. Draw a picture of this situation.
   b. Explain why the two triangles are congruent.

8. a. Trace kite *KITE* at the right.
   b. Draw $\overline{KT}$ and $\overline{IE}$.
   c. Identify the line of symmetry.
   d. Which angles of *KITE*, if any, have the same measure?

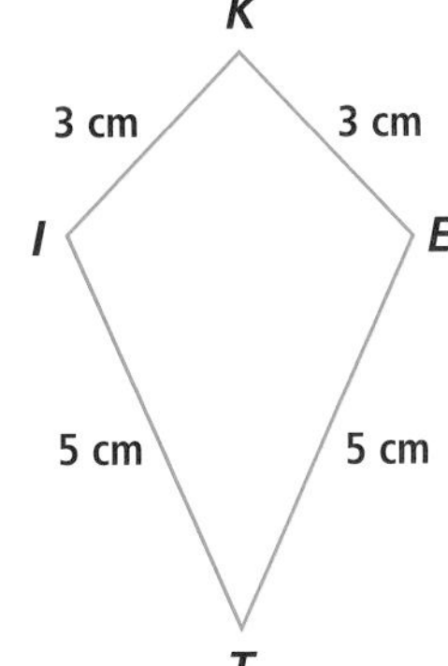

9. a. Draw a kite with four sides of length 5 cm and a 90° angle.
   b. What more specific name can be used to describe the shape you drew in Part a?

10. The Venn diagram below is marked a–f. Copy the diagram and fill in the correct name for each oval from this list: *kites, parallelograms, quadrilaterals, rectangles, rhombuses,* and *squares.*

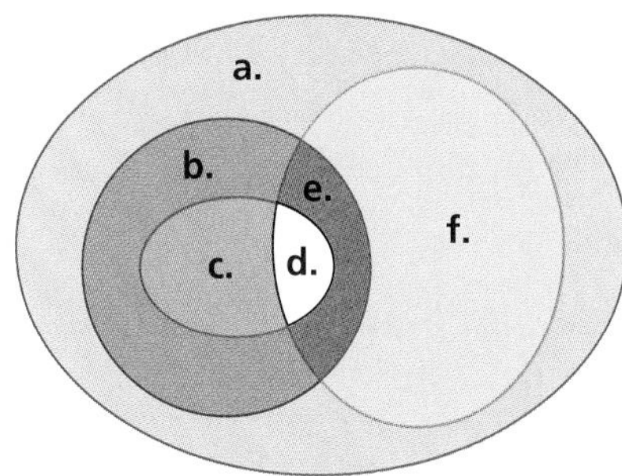

In 11–15, using only the symbols on the figure, determine whether the figure is a kite, parallelogram, rectangle, rhombus, or square. (Figures can fall into more than one category.)

11. 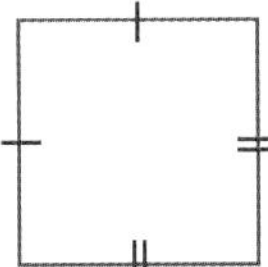

12. 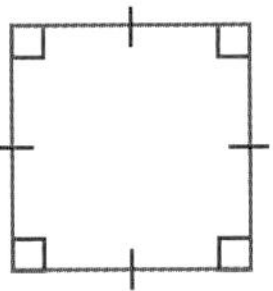

13. 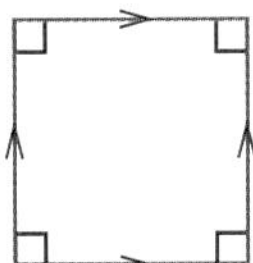

14. 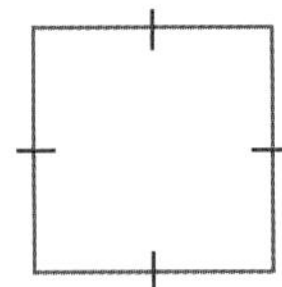

15. 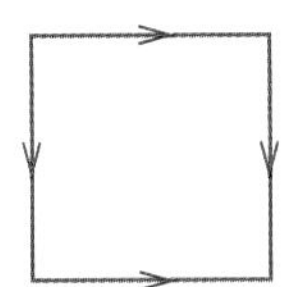

REVIEW

16. Define *parallelogram.* **(Lesson 12-4)**

17. Construct a triangle with sides of length 4 cm, 5 cm, and 8 cm. **(Lesson 12-3)**

In 18–20, find the area of the shaded region. (Lessons 9-4, 9-3, 9-2)

18.

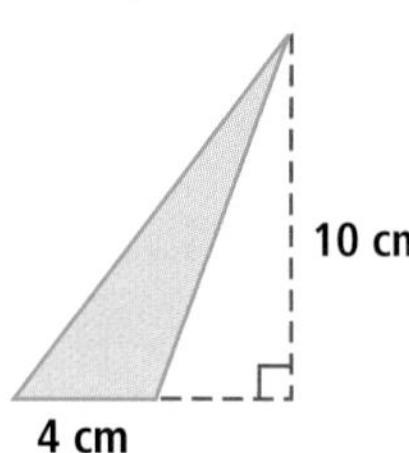

19.

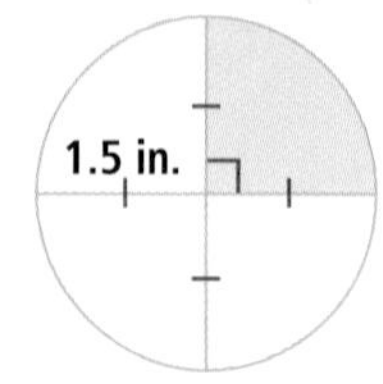

20.

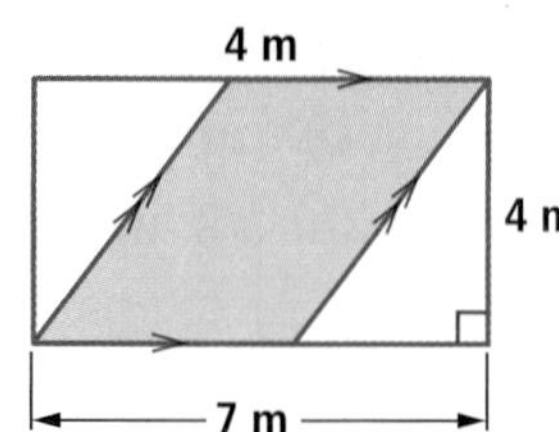

21. Write each power below in base-10 notation. Then order the numbers from least to greatest. The corresponding letters will spell the word to save for the quote in Question 12 in Lesson 12-6 on page 708 at the end of this chapter. (Lesson 6-4)

$9^3 = \underline{\ ?\ }$ M $7^5 = \underline{\ ?\ }$ Y $5^4 = \underline{\ ?\ }$ O

$8^4 = \underline{\ ?\ }$ E $5^6 = \underline{\ ?\ }$ R $4^4 = \underline{\ ?\ }$ E

$3^5 = \underline{\ ?\ }$ G $6^5 = \underline{\ ?\ }$ T

EXPLORATION

22. In Activity 2, you made parallelograms from straws with lengths 2 inches and 5 inches. In Parts a–c, consider all such parallelograms. If it is helpful, use straws or a DGS to help you.
    a. Consider the angle between a 2-inch side and 5-inch side. Which angle measure seems to form the parallelogram with the greatest area?
    b. What is the greatest area that can be formed?
    c. What seems to be the smallest area that can be formed?
    d. What is the greatest and least perimeter that can be formed?

QY ANSWERS

1. no
2. inside rhombuses

Lesson 12-6 The Trapezoid Family

Vocabulary

trapezoid
bases of a trapezoid
nonbases of a trapezoid
isosceles trapezoid

▶ **BIG IDEA** The trapezoid family includes the parallelogram family as well as isosceles trapezoids.

You have seen five special types of quadrilaterals so far in this chapter: parallelograms, rectangles, rhombuses, squares, and kites. This lesson covers two other special types: the *trapezoid* and the *isosceles trapezoid*.

Mental Math

Which has the greater area?

a. a square 1000 m on a side or a rectangle with dimensions 4000 m and 500 m

b. a triangle with height 60 m and base 30 m or a triangle with height 180 m and base 9 m

c. a square with perimeter 36 units or a rectangle with dimensions 7 by 8 units

A **trapezoid** is a quadrilateral with at least one pair of parallel sides, called its **bases.** The top of the desk and the faces of the guitar pictured above are trapezoids. All of the following figures are trapezoids.

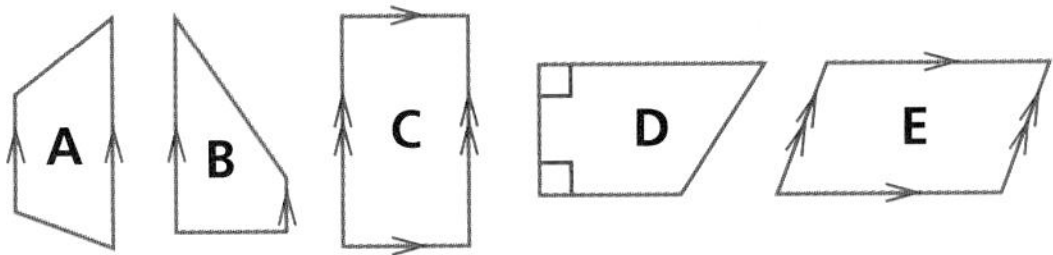

QY1

Why is figure D a trapezoid?

When both pairs of opposite sides of a trapezoid are parallel, then the trapezoid is a parallelogram. This is the case with figures C and E above. So parallelograms and trapezoids are related as follows.

1. Every parallelogram is a trapezoid.
2. Some but not all trapezoids are parallelograms.

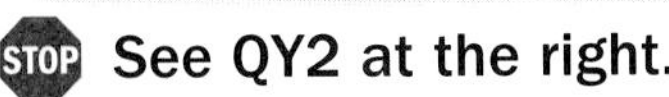
See QY2 at the right.

QY2

Draw a trapezoid that is different from the figures above and that is not a parallelogram.

Trapezoids are often used to estimate areas of regions that have curved boundaries. In the figure at the right, the area of the ellipse can be approximated by the sum of the areas of three trapezoids.

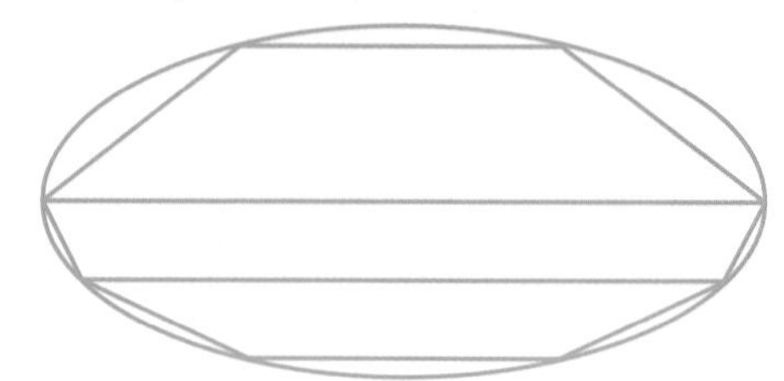

Isosceles Trapezoids

We call the sides of a trapezoid that are not bases its **nonbases.** A trapezoid with a line of symmetry, such as the three trapezoids in the ellipse above, is called an *isosceles trapezoid.* Due to this symmetry, each isosceles trapezoid has congruent nonbases and two pairs of angles with the same measure. By definition, an **isosceles trapezoid** is a trapezoid in which the two angles that contain a base are equal in measure.

The name "isosceles trapezoid" comes from the fact that an isosceles trapezoid can be formed by slicing an isosceles triangle with a line parallel to its base. At the right, $\triangle ABC$ is an isosceles triangle, and $\overleftrightarrow{DE}$ is parallel to its base $\overleftrightarrow{BC}$. This forms an isosceles trapezoid *BDEC* with the same symmetry line as $\triangle ABC$.

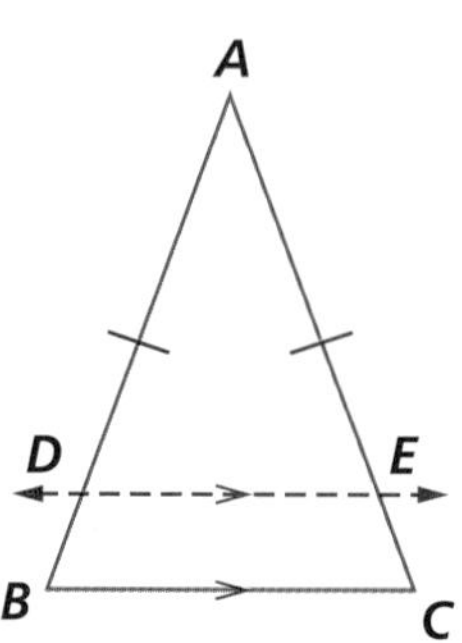

GUIDED

Example

How many pairs of angles of equal measure does an isosceles trapezoid have?

Solution 1 Work with a specific isosceles trapezoid. Use a protractor to measure each angle of isosceles trapezoid *BDEC* above.

$m\angle B =$ _?_ $m\angle C =$ _?_ $m\angle BDE =$ _?_ $m\angle CED =$ _?_

An isosceles trapezoid has _?_ pair(s) of angles that are equal in measure.

Solution 2 Use symmetry. The reflection image of $\angle BDE$ over the line of symmetry is _?_, so $m\angle BDE =$ _?_. The reflection image of $\angle B$ over the line of symmetry is _?_. So $m\angle B =$ _?_.

Activity

MATERIALS compass, straightedge

Step 1 Draw a line. Label two points *A* and *B*, about 4 cm apart on the line.

Step 2 Construct the circle with center *A* and radius *AB*.

Step 3 Construct the circle with center *B* and radius *AB*.

Step 4 $\overleftrightarrow{AB}$ and circle *B* intersect at point *A* and at a second point. Label the second point of intersection *C*.

Step 5 Construct the circle with center *C* and radius *BC*.

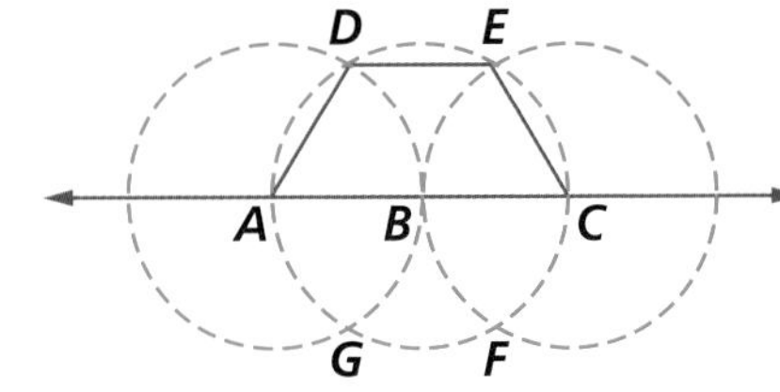

Step 6 The circles with centers A and B intersect in two points. Label the points of intersection as D and G.

Step 7 The circles with centers B and C also intersect in two points. Label these points E and F so that D and E are on the same side of line $\overline{AB}$.

Step 8 With your straightedge, form quadrilateral $ADEC$.

Step 9 Explain why $EC = AD$.

Step 10 What kind of figure is $ADEC$?

Isosceles Trapezoids and Rectangles

In an isosceles trapezoid, when the angles that contain a base are right angles, then the isosceles trapezoid is a rectangle. So isosceles trapezoids and rectangles are related as follows.

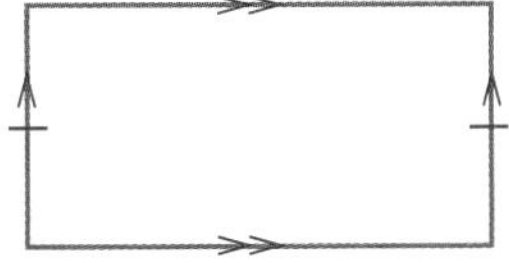

1. Every rectangle is an isosceles trapezoid.
2. Some but not all isosceles trapezoids are rectangles.

Using these definitions, the following Venn Diagram shows the trapezoid family, whose members include trapezoids, isosceles trapezoids, parallelograms, rectangles, and squares.

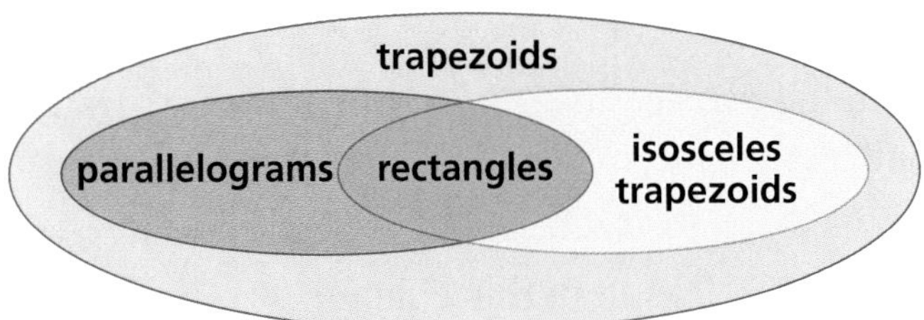

 **See QY3 at the right.**

 **QY3**

Where would squares go in this diagram?

Questions

COVERING THE IDEAS

1. Explain why every parallelogram is a trapezoid.
2. Trace the closed curve at the right. Show how its area can be approximated by the areas of trapezoids.

3. Draw a trapezoid in which one base has length 3 times the other base.

4. a. Draw an isosceles trapezoid with a right angle.
   b. What kind of quadrilateral is this?

5. Draw a Venn diagram to indicate the relationships among isosceles trapezoids, parallelograms, and rectangles.

6. Explain why any square is also an isosceles trapezoid.

APPLYING THE MATHEMATICS

7. a. Draw a trapezoid that is not an isosceles trapezoid. Add any lines of symmetry.
   b. Draw an isosceles trapezoid. Add any lines of symmetry.

8. a. Explain why the points $A = (0, 0)$, $B = (10, 0)$, $C = (7, 15)$, and $D = (1, 15)$ are vertices of a trapezoid $ABCD$.
   b. To what location can you move vertex D so that $ABCD$ will be an isosceles trapezoid?

9. a. Draw a trapezoid with a 70° angle and a 40° angle.
   b. What are the measures of the two other angles of the trapezoid? (*Hint:* Extend sides to create corresponding angles.)

10. In the diagram at the right, more general types of figures are connected down to more specific kinds of figures. The most specific quadrilateral, the square, is at the bottom. Put the terms *isosceles trapezoids, kites, parallelograms, rectangles, rhombuses,* and *trapezoids* in Parts a–f.

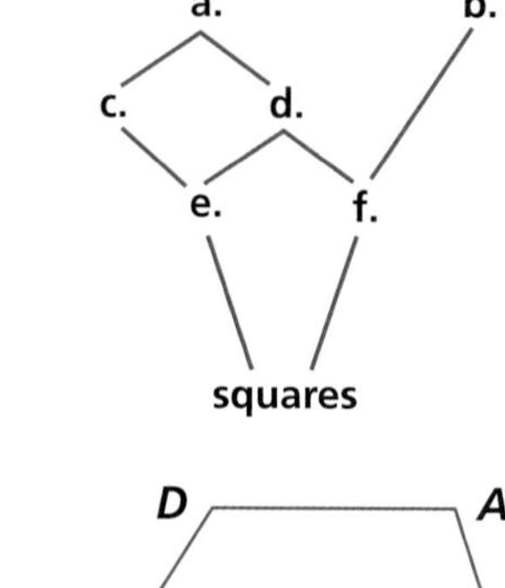

11. Find the measures of each angle in the trapezoid at the right. Put the letters in order from smallest measure to largest measure to get the last word for the quote in Question 12 below.

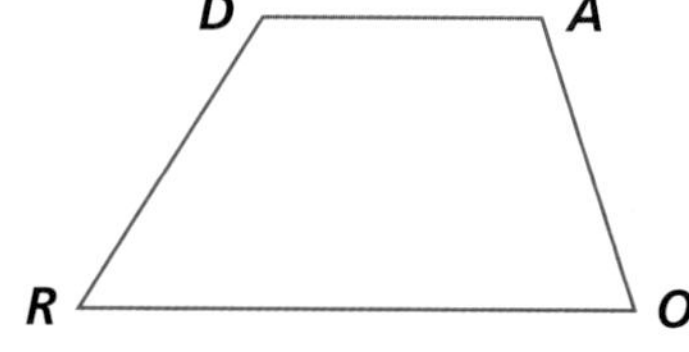

12. Fill in the table with the words from each lesson in this chapter. Then unscramble them to complete what Euclid is reported to have said to Ptolemy I, the ruler of Egypt, when Ptolemy wanted a quick way to learn mathematics.

Lesson	Word
12-1	?
12-2	?
12-3	?
12-4	?
12-5	?
12-6	road

_?_ _?_ _?_ _?_ _?_ to _?_.

REVIEW

In 13 and 14, the following segments show the lengths of the sides of a quadrilateral. (Lessons 12-5, 12-4)

13. Tell whether the four segments can be put together to form the indicated figure.
    a. parallelogram　　b. rhombus　　c. kite
    d. rectangle　　e. square
14. Put the segments together to form two different kinds of quadrilaterals.

In 15–19, examine the kites, parallelograms, rectangles, rhombuses, and squares that have been drawn in this chapter. Determine which types of figures have the following properties. (Lessons 12-5, 12-4)

15. Their opposite sides are congruent.
16. Their opposite angles have the same measure.
17. Their diagonals have the same midpoint.
18. Their diagonals are the same length.
19. Their diagonals lie on perpendicular lines.
20. Using the drawing at the right, identify each angle by its number. (Lesson 3-5)
    a. $\angle ABC = \underline{\ ?\ }$　　b. $\angle ABD = \underline{\ ?\ }$
    c. $\angle BGE = \underline{\ ?\ }$　　d. $\angle BDG = \underline{\ ?\ }$
    e. $\angle BGD = \underline{\ ?\ }$　　f. $\angle DGF = \underline{\ ?\ }$
    g. $\angle FGH = \underline{\ ?\ }$

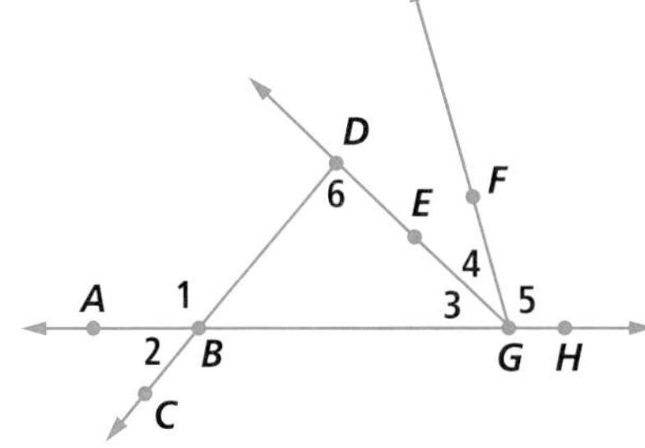

EXPLORATION

21. Copy the figure from the Activity in this lesson.
    a. Connect some of the named points to show six equilateral triangles. Name these triangles.
    b. How many rhombuses are now in your figure?
    c. Explain why $m\angle ADE = 120°$.
    d. Explain why E, B, and G are on the same line.
    e. Connect more named points to show three rectangles. Name these rectangles.
    f. How many equilateral triangles are now in your figure?
    g. What is the name of the shape that you have made?

QY ANSWERS

1. because corresponding angles are equal, so two of its sides are parallel
2. Answers vary. Sample:

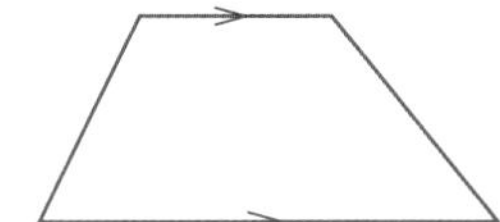

3. completely within the region of rectangles

Chapter 12 Projects

1 Symmetry

Find an example of a figure or object with rotation symmetry but no reflection symmetry. Find an example of a figure or object with reflection symmetry but no rotation symmetry. Lastly, find an example of a figure or object with both reflection and rotation symmetry. In all cases, use examples that are not found in this chapter. Photocopy or trace each example, and identify all lines of symmetry and centers of rotation symmetry.

2 Inscribed Polygons

A polygon is said to be *inscribed* in a circle if each vertex of the polygon touches the circle. Research how to inscribe the following polygons: equilateral triangle, square, regular hexagon, regular octagon, and regular pentagon. Make a careful construction of each of these inscribed figures with straightedge and compass.

3 The Area of a Quadrilateral with Perpendicular Diagonals

The diagonals of a quadrilateral $ABCD$ are the segments $\overline{AC}$ and $\overline{BD}$, as pictured below. If the diagonals of a quadrilateral are perpendicular, there is a formula for the area of the quadrilateral in terms of the lengths of the diagonals. Find this formula and give examples of its use with a kite, a convex quadrilateral that is not a kite, and with a nonconvex quadrilateral.

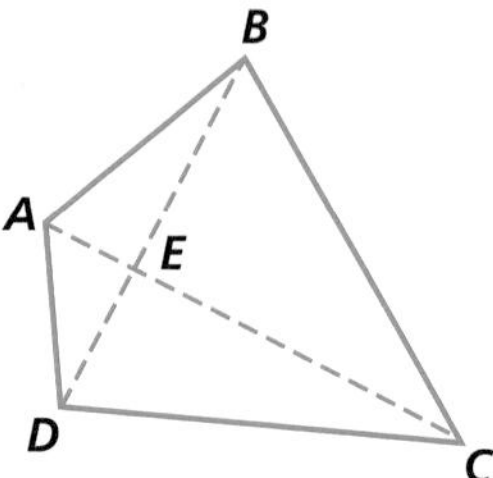

4 Penrose Tiles

Roger Penrose is a mathematician born in Essex, England in 1931. While he was a student at Cambridge University, he began working on a question about tilings. His work resulted in tiles that are now called *Penrose tiles*. Find out what Penrose tiles are and why they are important. Then create your own Penrose tiling.

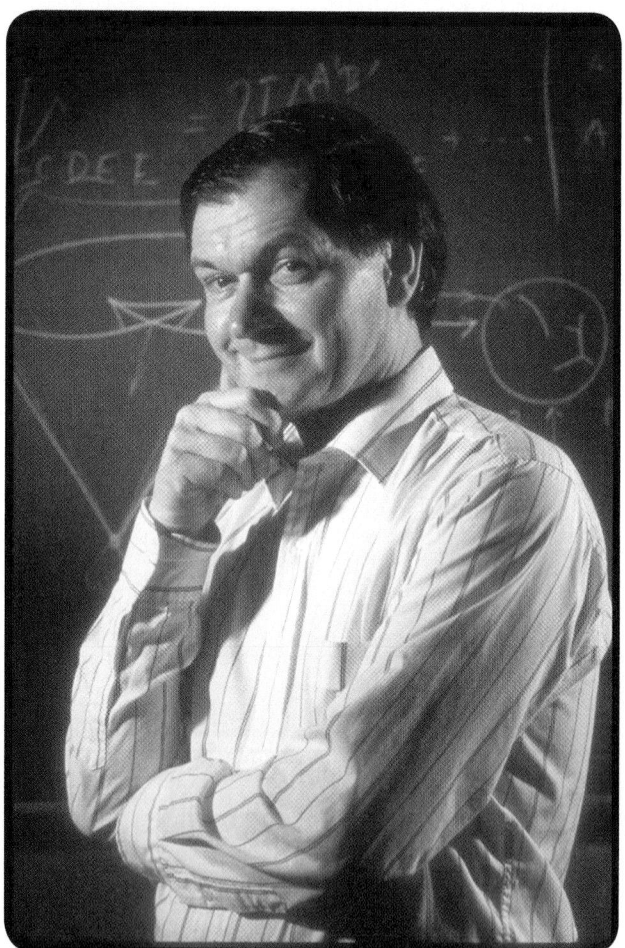

5 Circumcenter, Incenter, and Centroid of a Triangle

What is the *circumcenter* of a triangle? What is the *centroid* of a triangle? What is the *incenter* of a triangle? Make a poster with a description and a careful construction of each.

Chapter 12 Summary and Vocabulary

- A figure is **reflection-symmetric** if it coincides with its image under a reflection. The **reflecting line** is a **line of symmetry** for the figure. Reflection-symmetric figures studied in this chapter include **isosceles triangles, rhombuses, rectangles, kites, isosceles trapezoids**, and **squares.** A figure is **rotation-symmetric** is it coincides with its image under a rotation. The **center of rotation** is a **center of symmetry.** The rotation-symmetric figures studied in this chapter are **parallelograms,** rectangles, rhombuses, and squares.

- Figures are **congruent** if one is the image of the other under a reflection, rotation, **translation,** or some combination of these **transformations.** In congruent figures, **corresponding sides** have the same length and **corresponding angles** have the same measure.

- Triangles can be classified by their sides (**scalene, isosceles,** or **equilateral**) or by their angles (**acute, right,** or **obtuse**). Sometimes, only three lengths or angle measures need to be given to draw a unique triangle.

- Quadrilaterals are related to each other as shown in the following diagram.

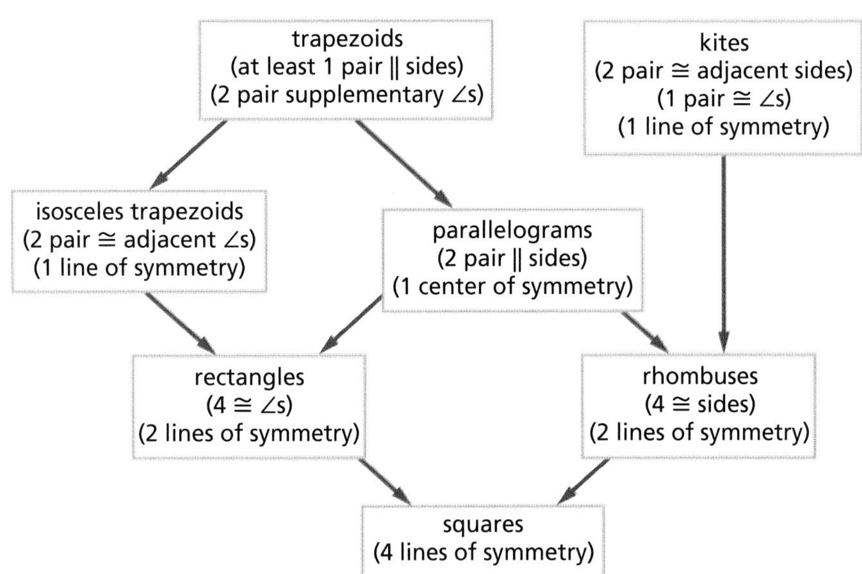

Vocabulary

12-1
congruent figures
corresponding parts

12-2
acute triangle
right triangle
obtuse triangle
isosceles triangle
scalene triangle
included side

12-3
symmetric figure
reflection-symmetric figure
rotation-symmetric figure
line of symmetry
center of symmetry

12-4
opposite sides of a quadrilateral
opposite angles of a quadrilateral
Venn diagram
rhombus

12-5
convex
nonconvex
adjacent sides
kite

12-6
trapezoid
bases of a trapezoid
nonbases of a trapezoid
isosceles trapezoid

Chapter 12 Self-Test

Take this test as you would take a test in class. You will need a compass, a straightedge, and a protractor. Then use the Selected Answers section in the back of the book to check your work.

1. Draw a pentagon with exactly one line of symmetry that is horizontal.
2. What is the measure of the smallest angle through which the figure can be rotated to coincide with its image?

a.

b.

c.

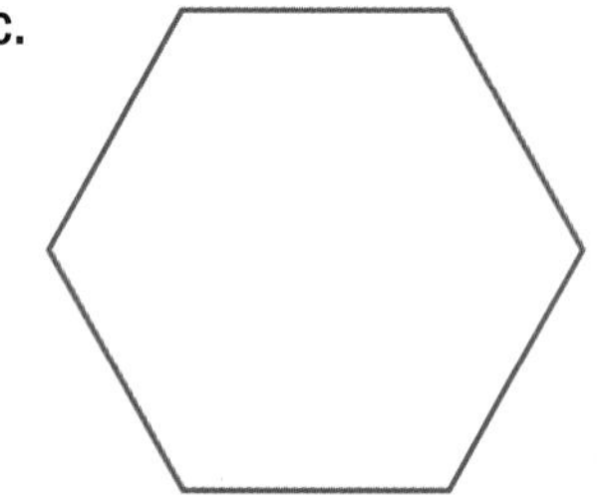

In 3–5, tell whether it is possible to create a triangle with the given measures. If so, draw such a triangle and tell whether it is the only triangle with those measures.

3. side lengths of 2", 5", and 6"
4. angle measures of 75°, 91°, and 14°
5. side lengths of 4 cm and 4 cm, and an angle of 70°

6. Classify each quadrilateral as a kite, trapezoid, isosceles trapezoid, parallelogram, rhombus, square, or rectangle. (*Note:* Figures can fall into more than one category.)

a.

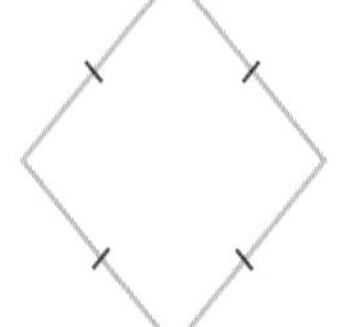

b.

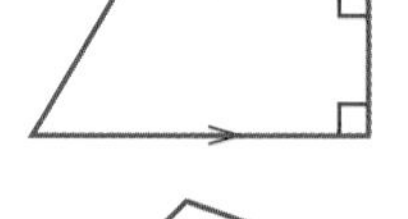

c.

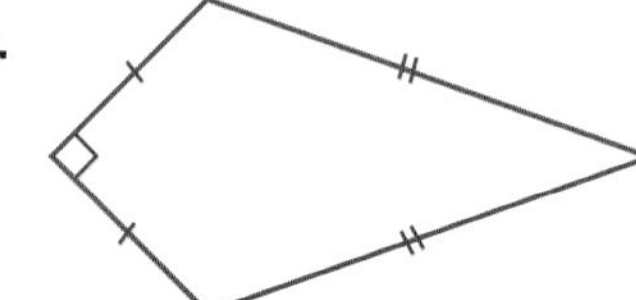

7. **Multiple Choice** Which is *not* a characteristic of a rhombus?
   - A Diagonals are perpendicular.
   - B Opposite sides are parallel.
   - C Diagonals are of equal length.
   - D Adjacent sides are of equal length.
8. I am a quadrilateral. My diagonals meet at right angles, have equal length, and have the same midpoint. What am I?
9. Complete the information about parallelogram $ABCD$ below.

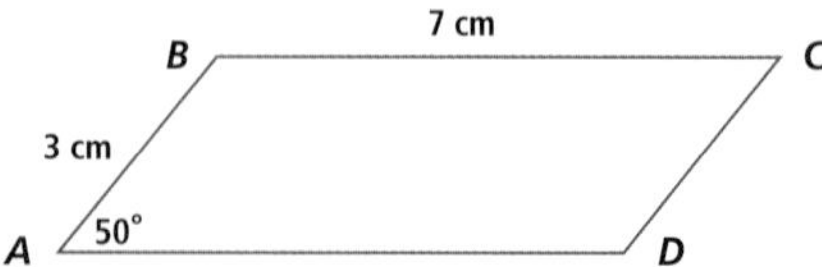

a. $m\angle C = \underline{\ ?\ }$

b. $m\angle B = \underline{\ ?\ }$

c. $CD = \underline{\ ?\ }$

10. An isosceles trapezoid has side lengths 1" and 0.5" and a base angle of 30°. Determine the measures of the other three angles.

11. Draw a quadrilateral with diagonals of lengths 3.5" and 3" that share the same midpoint. What kind of quadrilateral is this?

12. a. Plot points $M = (-1, -1)$, $N = (-3, -1)$, and $P = (4, -3)$ on a coordinate grid.

b. Identify a point Q such that $MNQP$ is a parallelogram.

13. Paul's mother Pauline makes pasta shaped like perfect parallelograms, with side lengths 1" and 2.5". She forgot what angles she must use in her pasta parallelograms, but they can't be rectangles, and they must fit inside a rectangle that is 1.5" by 3".

a. Draw a parallelogram with the proper properties.

b. Does this figure have reflection symmetry?

c. Does this figure have rotation symmetry?

In 14 and 15, determine whether all quadrilaterals with the given measures are congruent.

14. isosceles trapezoid with angle measures 60°, 60°, 120°, 120°; sides with lengths 3.5 cm, 2 cm

15. a kite with side lengths $\frac{1}{2}$ in. and 2 in.

16. True or False If a figure has reflection symmetry, it has rotation symmetry.

Chapter 12 Chapter Review

SKILLS
PROPERTIES
USES
REPRESENTATIONS

SKILLS Procedures used to get answers

OBJECTIVE A Recognize reflection symmetry in a figure. **(Lesson 12-3)**

In 1 and 2, trace the figure and draw all lines of symmetry.

1.

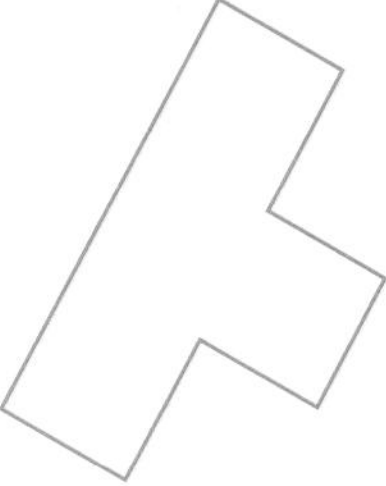

2.

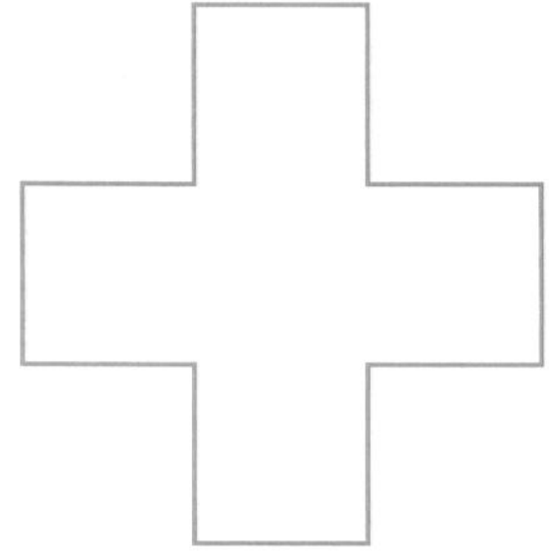

3. Draw a figure with exactly three symmetry lines.
4. Draw a figure that has reflection symmetry but does not have rotation symmetry.

OBJECTIVE B Recognize rotation symmetry in a figure. **(Lesson 12-3)**

5. Consider the letters H, I, J, K. Copy each letter with rotation symmetry and identify the center of rotation.
6. Repeat Question 5 for the letters L, M, N, O.

In 7 and 8, what is the measure of the smallest angle through which the figure can be rotated to coincide with its image?

7.

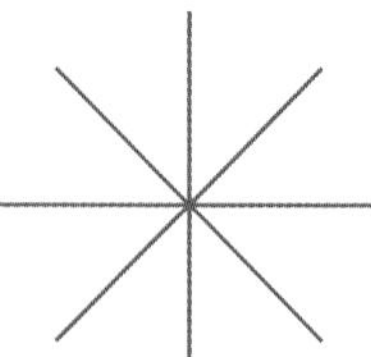

8.

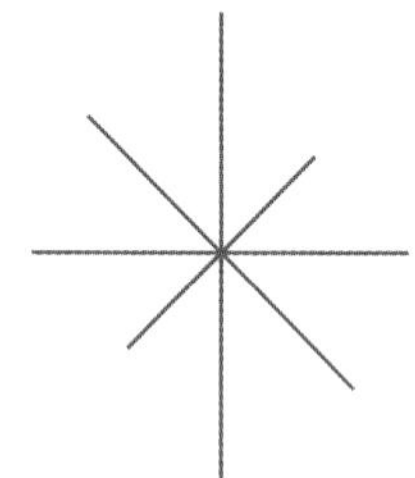

OBJECTIVE C Given some side lengths and/or angle measures, draw a quadrilateral or triangle. **(Lessons 12-1, 12-2)**

In 9 and 10, draw the triangle with the given measurements.

9. sides with lengths 2 cm, 4 cm, and 5 cm
10. sides with lengths 1.5 in. and 2.5 in. and an included angle of 35°

In 11 and 12, construct a triangle with the given parts.

11.

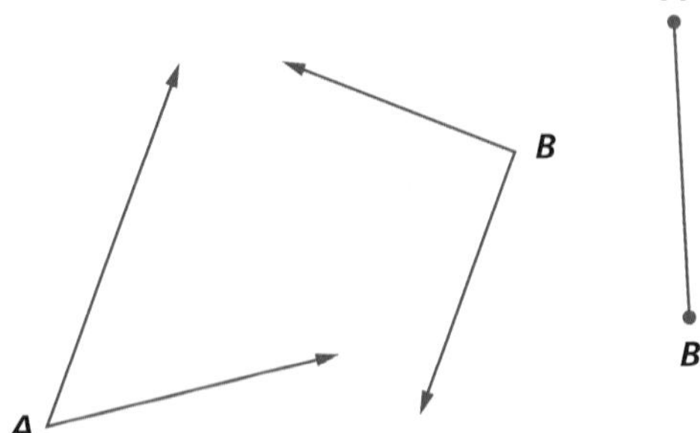

12.

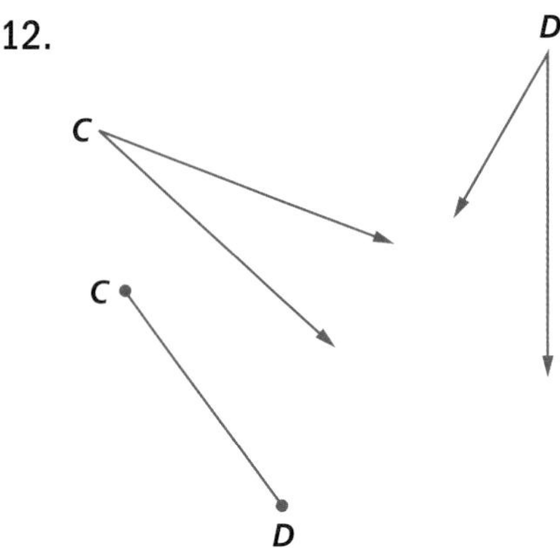

PROPERTIES The principles behind the mathematics

OBJECTIVE D **Know the symmetry properties of types of figures. (Lesson 12-3)**

13. **True or False** Every trapezoid has at least one symmetry line.

14. **True or False** If a figure has more than two lines of symmetry, it is *not* a rectangle.

15. Every parallelogram has rotation symmetry. Trace the parallelogram and accurately locate its center of rotation.

16. Does every rhombus have rotation symmetry? Explain your answer.

OBJECTIVE E **Use properties of parallelograms to find measures of angles and lengths of sides. (Lessons 12-4)**

17. If one angle of a parallelogram has a measure of 35°, find the measures of the other three angles.

18. In parallelogram $ABCD$, $m\angle A = 110°$ and $AB = 7$. Find the measures of as many other sides and angles as you can.

19. In rhombus $ABCD$, $m\angle A = 110°$ and $AB = 7$. Find the measures of as many other sides and angles that you can.

20. In parallelogram $PQRS$, $PQ \perp RQ$ and $RS = 15$. Find the measures of as many other sides and angles that you can.

OBJECTIVE F **Given information about side lengths and angle measures, determine if all polygons drawn would be congruent. (Lessons 12-1, 12-2)**

In 21–24, determine whether all triangles with the given characteristics are congruent.

21. sides with lengths 5 in., 4 in., and 7 in.
22. sides with lengths 3 cm, 4 cm, and a 30° angle between them
23. angles with measures 70° and 50° and one side with length 11 mm
24. angles with measures 45°, 50°, and 85°

In 25–28, determine whether all quadrilaterals with the given characteristics are congruent.

25. rectangle with sides of length 10 m and 12 m
26. parallelogram with sides of length 10 m and 12 m
27. kite with two sides of length 10 m and two sides of length 12 m
28. isosceles trapezoid with two sides of length 10 m and two sides of length 12 m

OBJECTIVE G **Use definitions and properties of quadrilaterals to indicate relationships among isosceles trapezoids, kites, parallelograms, rectangles, rhombuses, squares, and trapezoids. (Lessons 12-4, 12-5, 12-6)**

In 29–32, tell which of the following quadrilaterals have the given property: isosceles trapezoids, kites, parallelograms, rectangles, rhombuses, squares, trapezoids. There may be more than one right answer.

29. three right angles

30. two pairs of parallel sides
31. diagonals of the same length that bisect each other
32. perpendicular diagonals
33. Explain why every rectangle is a parallelogram.
34. Explain why every rectangle is an isosceles trapezoid.

USES Applications of mathematics in real-world situations

OBJECTIVE H Recognize reflection and rotation symmetry in everyday figures. **(Lessons 12-3)**

In 35–38, trace the figure.

a. Tell whether the figure has reflection symmetry. If so, draw all its symmetry lines on your tracing.
b. Tell whether the figure has rotation symmetry. If so, locate any centers of rotation and the measure of the smallest angle through which the figure can be rotated to coincide with its image.

35.

36.

37.

38.

REPRESENTATIONS Pictures, graphs, or objects that illustrate concepts

OBJECTIVE I Draw and interpret diagrams relating the various kinds of quadrilaterals. **(Lessons 12-4, 12-5, 12-6)**

39. Draw a rectangle $ABCD$ and its diagonals, which intersect at point E. Name at least three right triangles and at least three isosceles triangles in your drawing.

In 40–42, from *only* the markings on the figure, classify the figure as a kite, trapezoid, isosceles trapezoid, parallelogram, rhombus, square, or rectangle. (Figures can fall into more than one category.)

40.

41. 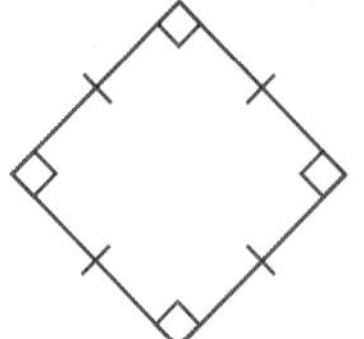

42. 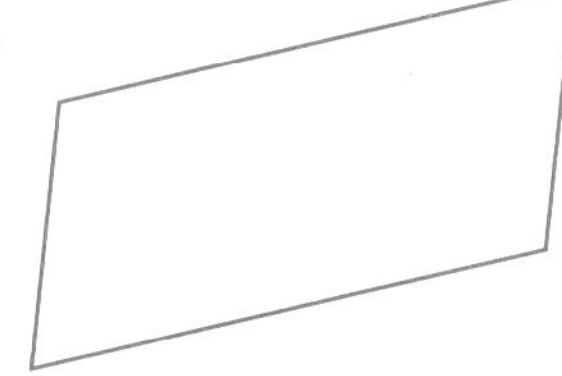

43. a. Plot the points (–4, 1), (4, 1), (–2, 4), (2, 4) and connect them with line segments.

b. What type of quadrilateral have you formed? Explain.

Chapter

13 Collecting and Comparing Data

Contents

Statistics are collected for many reasons. For instance, statistics are used to help people make wise decisions. What is the best treatment for a disease? Is there global warming and, if so, what are its effects? Are certain species of fish in danger of extinction because too many are being caught? These questions are about issues that affect everyone.

Some questions involving statistics apply directly to you. How are you performing in a particular sport or game? Are you improving over time? How does your performance compare to that of other players?

To answer these and thousands of other questions, people collect data. They then organize and summarize the data using tables, graphs, and statistics. These displays are used to compare the collected data with other data, or with what might be expected to occur.

Data are collected and used for many purposes. Weather balloons, like the one shown in the photo, are used for collecting data about the weather. The collected data include information about temperature, relative humidity, pressure, and wind and may be used for preparing weather forecasts.

An important example from history, the draft for the Vietnam War, caused people to use statistics to compare data. In 1969, during the Vietnam War, the U.S. armed forces needed troops. Since not everyone aged 18–26 was needed, the government held a drawing to determine which young men would be drafted into the armed forces. This war was not popular in many places. So this drawing was important to many people.

The idea was to randomly pick men aged 18–26 by their birthdays. Capsules containing slips of paper with the days of the year were put into a glass cylinder. They were then mixed up and pulled out one at a time. The first day pulled out was read out loud and given the number 1. Men aged 18–26 with that birthday (September 14) were to be drafted first. Then, additional capsules were pulled out, until the last capsule (with the date June 8) was pulled out and given number 366. The table in Lesson 13-3 gives all the dates with their numbers.

Almost immediately after the drawing, there was controversy. In this chapter, you will learn the reasons for this controversy. You will also collect data to help you make decisions, and you will learn about the largest collection of data conducted in the United States, the U.S. census.

Lesson 13-1 Paper Folding and Geometry

▶ **BIG IDEA** Perpendicular bisectors and angle bisectors are basic ideas in the geometry of paper folding.

Traditional Origami

Paper folding began in China centuries ago and spread to the nearby countries of Korea and Japan, as well as to Muslim countries further west. The word *origami* is Japanese and literally means "paper folding." The object of origami is to create a figure out of a single sheet of paper without cutting or pasting. As the dinosaurs at the right show, it is possible to create quite complicated figures. In recent years, origami has become more than just a hobby or an art form. Ideas from origami suggested how to blow up an air bag or a parachute from a flat arrangement to a 3-dimensional cushion capable of withstanding a strong force.

Doing origami is like doing a geometric construction. There is a mathematical theory behind origami as there is in straightedge-and-compass constructions. You need to be precise in your work in origami just as you do when you use a straightedge and compass.

In traditional origami, you begin with a thin square piece of paper. "Origami paper" has one color on one side and a different color on the other.

Three traditional origami folds are described in Activity 1. You will use these folds to make a tool for gathering data in Lesson 13-2.

Mental Math

Find the measure of each part if a right angle is

a. bisected.

b. trisected.

c. divided into 6 equal parts.

d. divided into 12 equal parts.

Acrocanthosaurus by Jerry Harris

Triceratops by Jerry Harris

Activity 1

MATERIALS origami paper or a square sheet of paper

Step 1 Draw two points P and Q lightly on the sheet of paper so that $\overleftrightarrow{PQ}$ is not parallel to any side of the paper. Do not draw $\overleftrightarrow{PQ}$, but fold the paper on $\overleftrightarrow{PQ}$. Let $\ell = \overleftrightarrow{PQ}$.

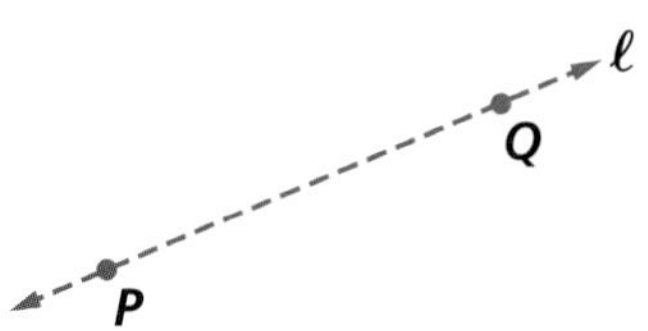

Step 2 Unfold the paper back to its original form. Now fold the paper so that *P* falls on *Q*. Call this fold *m*.

a. How is *m* related to *P* and *Q*?

b. There are now two folds on your paper. How are ℓ and *m* related?

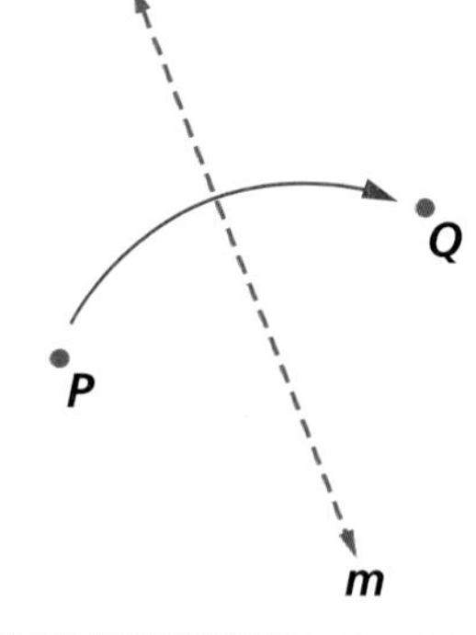

Step 3 Fold ℓ onto *m*. How is the fold you created in this step related to the two other folds?

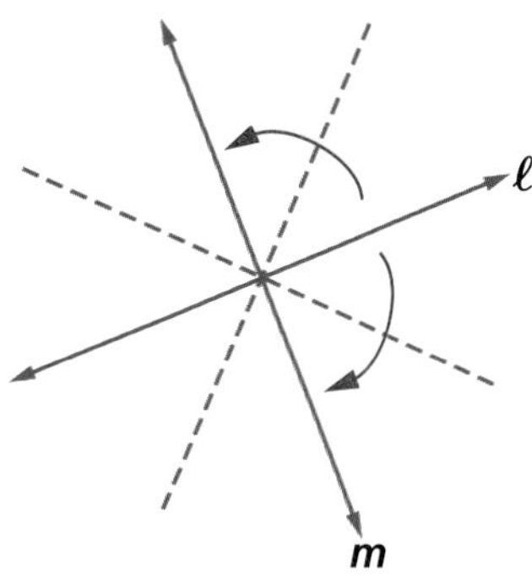

The steps of Activity 1 use three common folds allowed in origami.

- Given two points *P* and *Q*, you can make a fold on $\overleftrightarrow{PQ}$.
- Given two points *P* and *Q*, you can make a fold on the perpendicular bisector of $\overline{PQ}$.
- Given two lines ℓ and m: If ℓ intersects m, you can make a fold on the bisector of either angle determined by ℓ and m. If $\ell || m$, you can make a fold on the line halfway between the two lines.

A Boat Made of Paper

Folds allowed in origami can be done on any thin paper. By combining the above folds you can make many figures out of paper. In Activity 2, you will make a boat. Along the way, you will make a hat.

Activity 2

MATERIALS rectangular sheet of paper

Step 1 Name the sheet *ABCD*, with $\overline{AB}$ one of the shorter sides. Fold $\overline{AD}$ onto $\overline{BC}$. Call the fold line ℓ. Unfold and fold $\overline{AB}$ onto $\overline{CD}$. Call this fold line *m*.

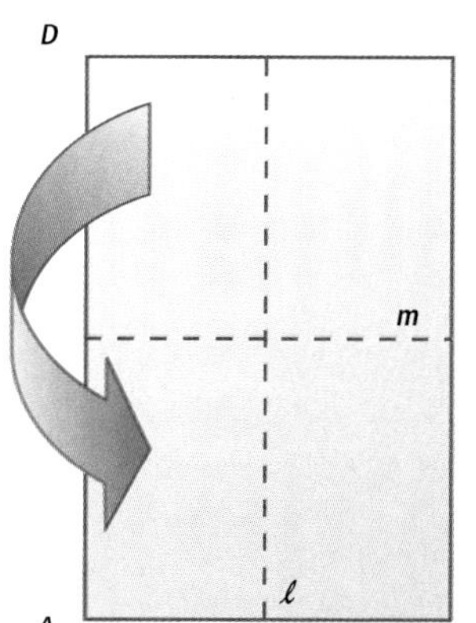

(continued on next page)

Step 2 After folding at line *m*, fold parts of *m* onto ℓ, folding down each side to make triangles. The rectangle at the bottom has two layers.

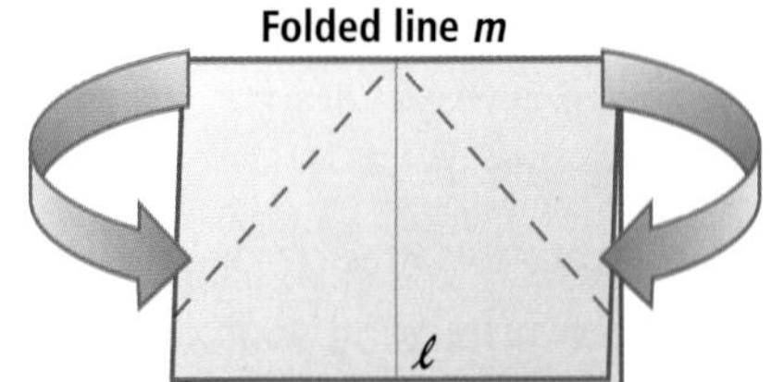

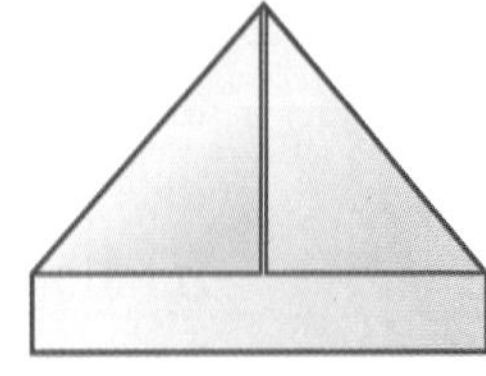

Step 3 Fold the rectangle in the top layer over its top side. There will be two small triangles that overlap the hypotenuses of the right triangles. Fold them backwards to make them disappear.

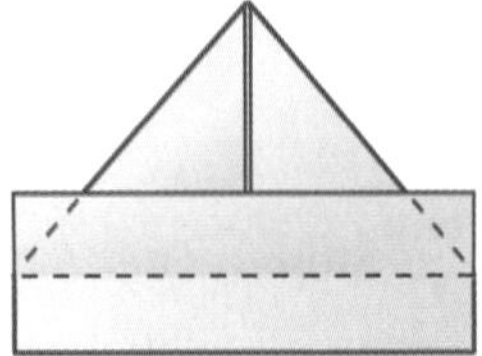

Step 4 Turn the paper over and fold the rectangle in what was the bottom layer over its top side. You have formed a paper hat.

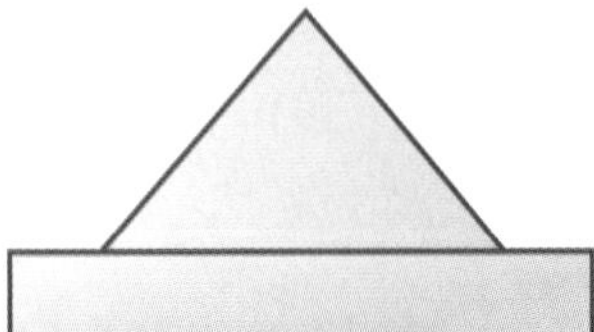

Step 5 Open the hat so you are looking inside the part you would wear on your head. Place your thumbs inside and lightly pinch each side, as shown at the left below. Slowly pull your thumbs away from each other. This will cause the upper and the lower parts to fall on each other so you obtain a flattened square as seen at the right below.

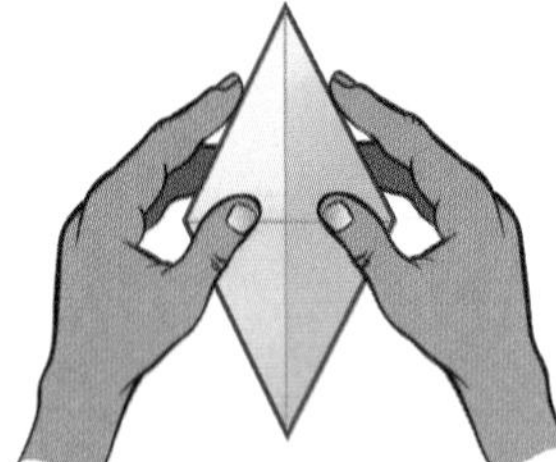

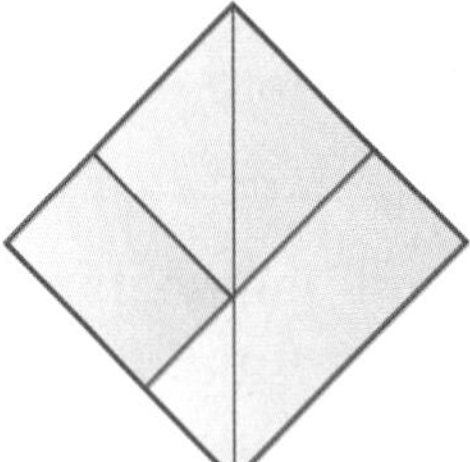

Step 6 Fold the upper layer of the lower front triangle upward on the dashed red line as shown in the drawing at the left below. You should have a figure like the one at the right below.

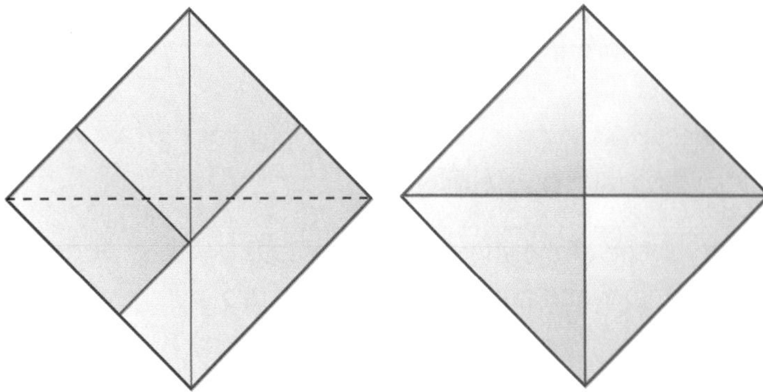

Step 7 Turn the paper over and fold the other triangle up. Your paper should look like a hat, without the brim this time, as shown at the right.

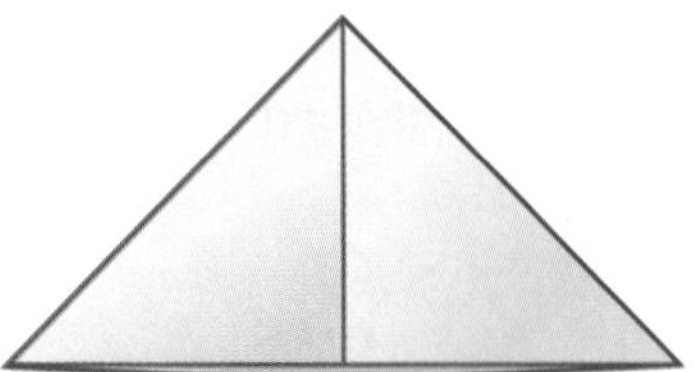

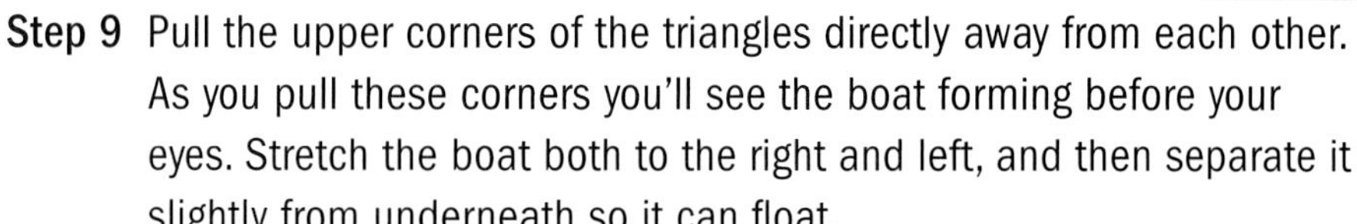

Step 8 Open the new hat, pinch the sides, and pull your thumbs away from each other to flatten it and make a new square shape.

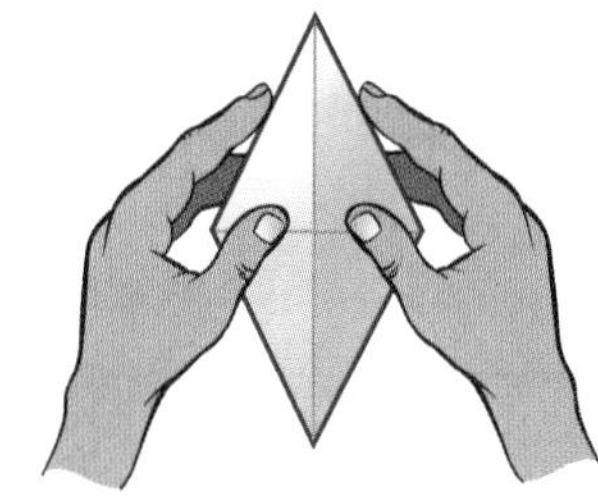

Step 9 Pull the upper corners of the triangles directly away from each other. As you pull these corners you'll see the boat forming before your eyes. Stretch the boat both to the right and left, and then separate it slightly from underneath so it can float.

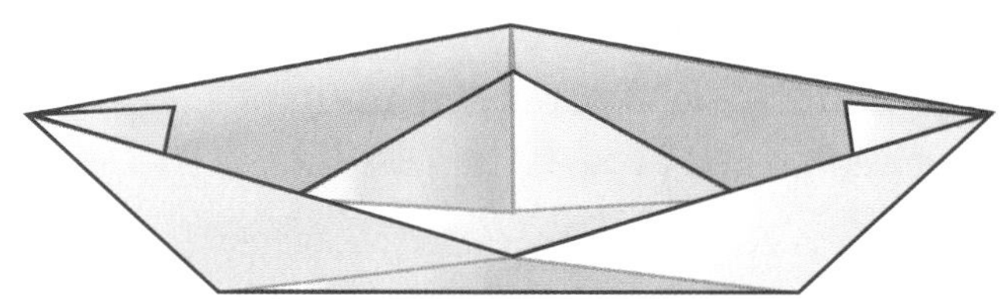

If you can, test to see that your boat floats. Even though the boat is made of paper, it should float until the paper becomes waterlogged.

Questions

COVERING THE IDEAS

1. **Fill in the Blanks** *Origami* comes from the __?__ language and means __?__.
2. In what country did origami originate?
3. On a sheet of paper, draw a segment $\overline{OR}$ about 2 inches long.
   a. Make a fold on the paper so that point O falls on point R.
   b. How is the fold related to the segment $\overline{OR}$?
4. On a sheet of paper, trace the angle at the right.
   a. Make a fold so that one side of the angle falls on the other side. (You may want to extend what is shown of the shorter side.)
   b. How is the fold related to the angle?

5. On a sheet of paper, trace the figure below.

   a. Make a paper fold so that the figure falls on itself.
   b. **Fill in the Blank** The fold is a __?__ for the figure.
6. Trace the regular hexagon at the right and create folds over all of its symmetry lines.

7. Trace the equilateral triangle at the right and create folds over all of its symmetry lines.

APPLYING THE MATHEMATICS

8. Corinne has a 15cm-by-13 cm sheet of paper.
   a. She folds a longer side onto its opposite side. What are the perimeter and area of the resulting rectangle?
   b. Corinne unfolds the paper and then folds a shorter side onto its opposite side. What are the perimeter and area of the resulting rectangle?

9. Follow these steps to make a paper equilateral triangle.

   Step 1 Fold the longer side of a rectangular sheet of paper onto its opposite side, and then unfold it. Call the fold line m.

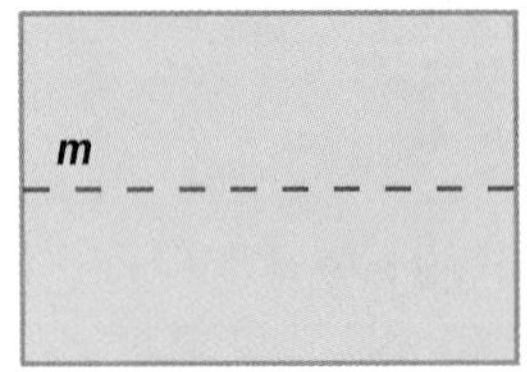

Step 1

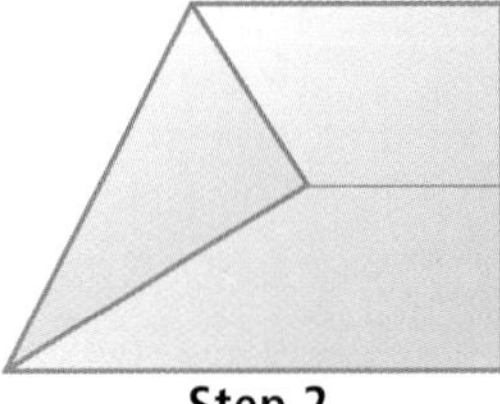
Step 2

   Step 2 Fold the top left corner onto m so that the fold passes through the bottom left corner and the top left corner lies on m.

   Step 3 Fold the top right corner down so that the top edge of the paper lies on the fold line created in Step 2.

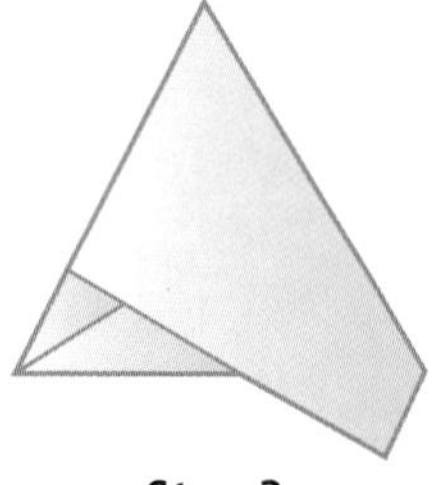
Step 3

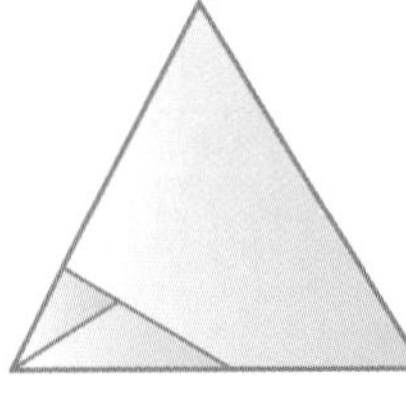
Step 4

   Step 4 Fold the extra flap at the bottom of the triangle underneath the original bottom side of the rectangle.

10. Name a sheet of 8.5" by 11" paper $ABCD$, with $AB = 8.5''$. Fold the paper so $\overline{AB}$ falls on segment $\overline{BC}$.
   a. What type of quadrilateral results from this fold?
   b. Find the lengths of three sides of the quadrilateral without measuring. Then, measure to find the length of the fourth side.
   c. What is the perimeter of this quadrilateral?
   d. What is the area of this quadrilateral?
   e. Without using a protractor, give the angle measure of each angle in the folded quadrilateral.

REVIEW

11. The pentagon at the right consists of a square attached to an isosceles right triangle. Draw the pentagon using a ruler and protractor.**(Lessons 12-3, 11-1)**

In 12 and 13, use the graph at the right which shows the number of males per 100 females in the United States based on U.S. Census data. (Lesson 5-4)

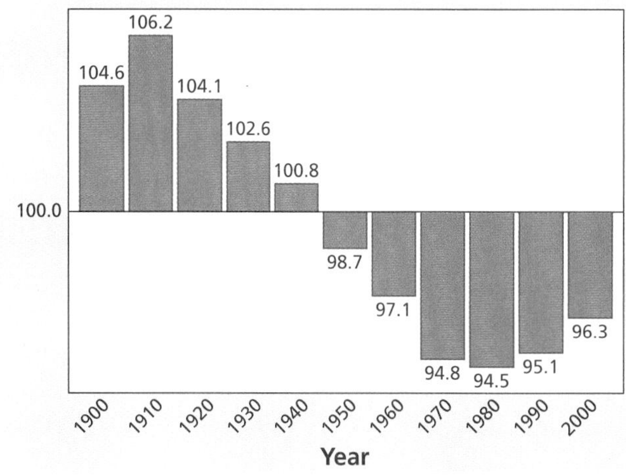

12. In which year
    a. was the percent of men in the U.S. population highest?
    b. was the percent of women in the U.S. population highest?
    c. What does it mean when a bar extends below the 100.0 line?
13. In 2000, the number of females in the U.S. was 143.4 million. How many males were there?

In 14 and 15, use the table at the right, which shows the population of the six New England states according to the 2000 U.S. Census. (Lesson 5-1, Previous course)

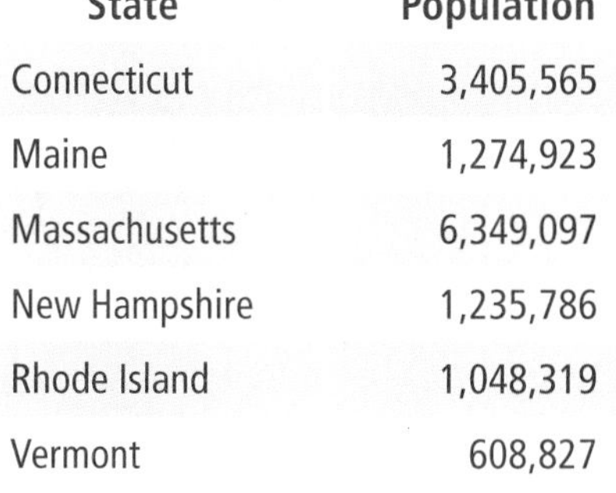

State	Population
Connecticut	3,405,565
Maine	1,274,923
Massachusetts	6,349,097
New Hampshire	1,235,786
Rhode Island	1,048,319
Vermont	608,827

14. a. Rank the states in order from least to greatest population.
    b. **True or False** More people lived in Massachusetts in 2000 than in the rest of New England combined.
15. In 2000, according to the U.S. Census, the total U.S. population was 281,421,906. What percent of the population was made up of people from these six New England states?

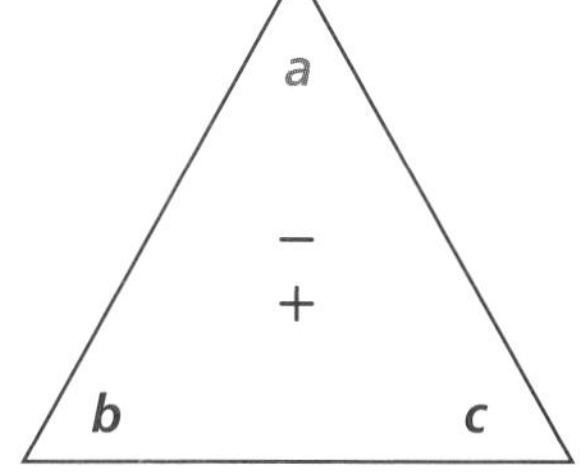

16. The fact triangle at the right relates three quantities a, b, and c, where a = the number of degrees in a right angle, and c = the number that, when followed by a percent sign, is equal to $\frac{3}{4}$. What is b? **(Lessons 4-6, 4-4, 2-10)**

EXPLORATION

17. There is a Japanese saying that if you make a thousand origami paper cranes, then your wish will be granted. It is not easy to make a crane, but directions for making a crane can be found on many web sites and in many books on origami. Go to one of them and follow the directions to make a crane.

Lesson 13-2 Statistics from an Experiment: Jumping Frogs

▸ **BIG IDEA** Data are often collected and analyzed from experiments.

Recall that an experiment is a situation that can be repeated. Some data come from experiments. In this lesson, the data will come from experiments with origami frogs.

It may surprise you that you can make origami figures that can be made to jump. In Activity 1, you make an origami frog. Then you will gather data to see how far and how high your frog can jump.

Mental Math

Find the mean of the data set.

a. 2, 4, 6, 8, 10

b. 2, 4, 6, 8, 15

c. 2, 4, 6, 8, 25

d. 2, 4, 6, 8, 110

Activity 1

MATERIALS origami paper or a square sheet of paper

Step 1 Make folds over both diagonals of the square. Then unfold.

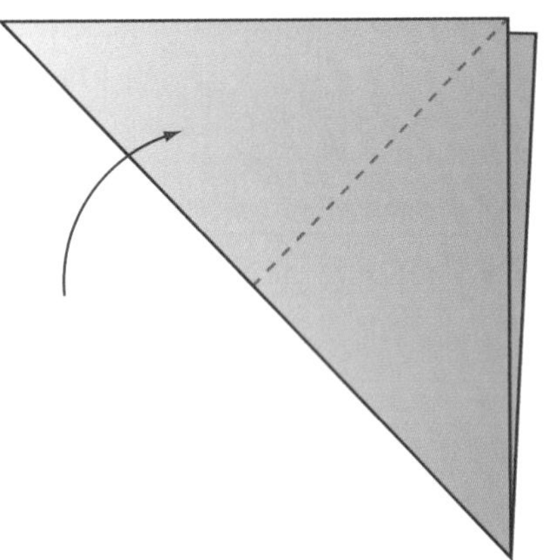

Step 2 Fold one side of the square onto its opposite side.

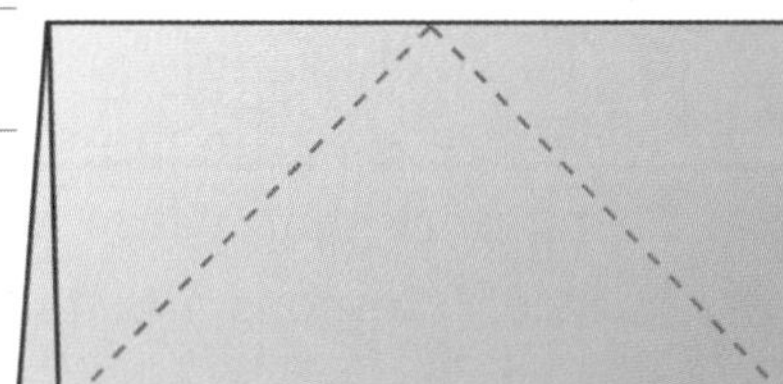

Step 3 Reverse the folds at the two ends and then push them inward.

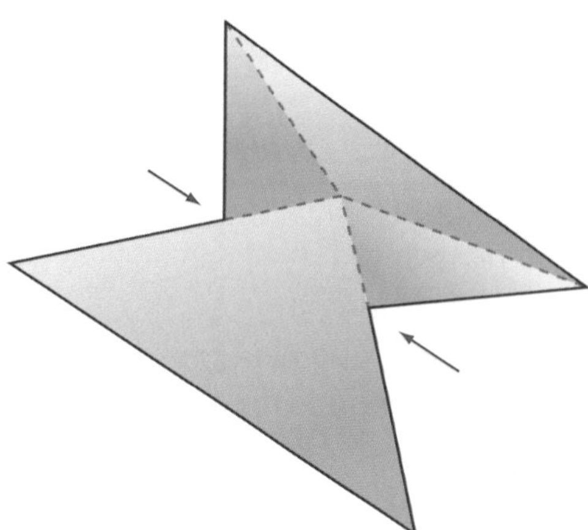

Step 4 Your paper should look like isosceles $\triangle ABC$ below with three layers. Make a pencil mark at the midpoint of $\overline{BC}$. Name this point M.

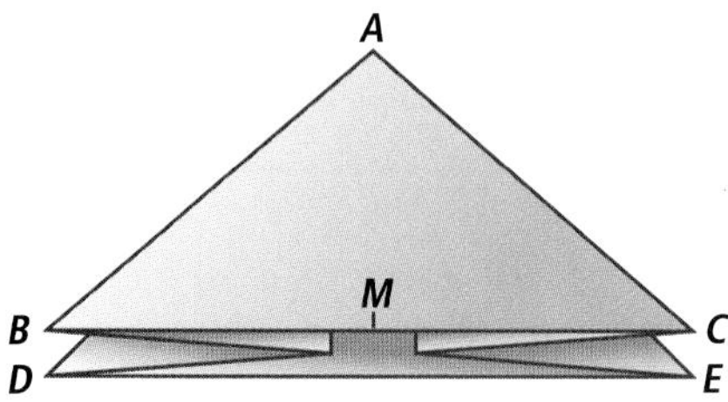

Step 5 Fold $\overline{AC}$ onto $\overline{AM}$, then fold $\overline{AB}$ onto $\overline{AM}$.

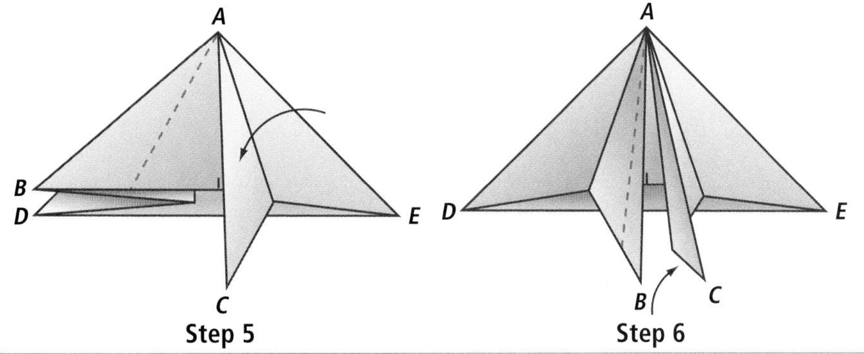

Step 6 Fold $\overline{AC}$ and $\overline{AB}$ back out about $\frac{1}{3}$ of the way.

Step 7 Turn over what you have constructed. Fold corners D and E up to A. These flaps will be the front legs of your frog.

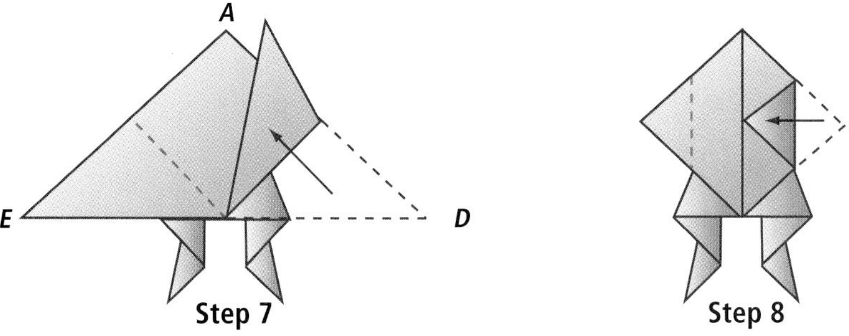

Step 8 Fold the left and right corners on the square to the center. Your figure should begin to look like a frog. This side will be the bottom of your frog.

Step 9 Turn the frog over to its top side. Draw a line x on your frog along the middle of its body as shown below.

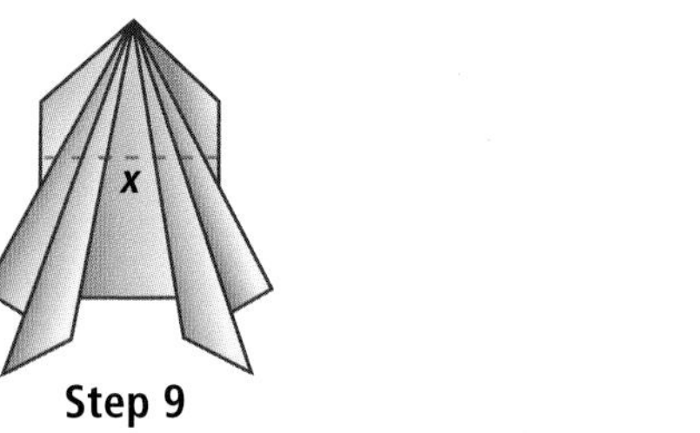

Step 10

Step 10 Fold down on line x and crease tightly.

(continued on next page)

Step 11 Draw a line *y* on your frog along the middle of its lower body (the end with the legs sticking out).

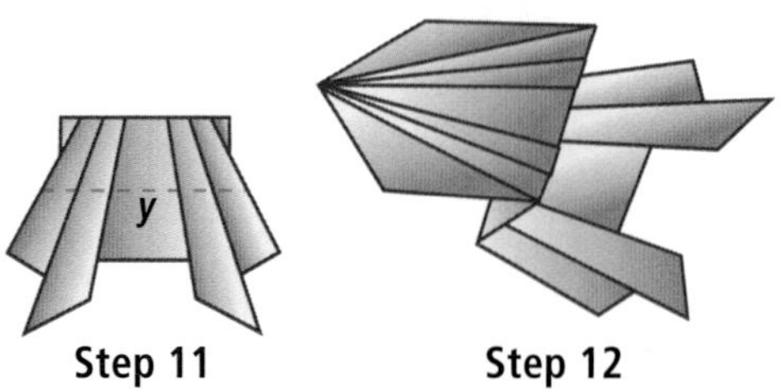

Step 11 Step 12

Step 12 Fold up line *y* (in the opposite direction of line *x*) and crease tightly.

Step 13 With the frog bottom-side up, fold back the front two legs as shown in the diagram.

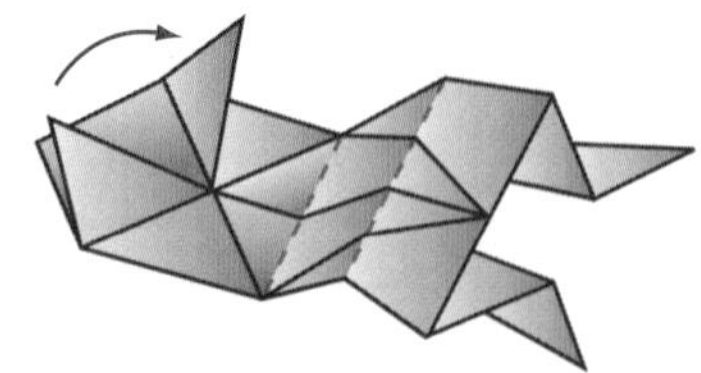

Step 14 Test your frog to make sure it will jump. Put it on a flat surface. Push down on its back and let go.

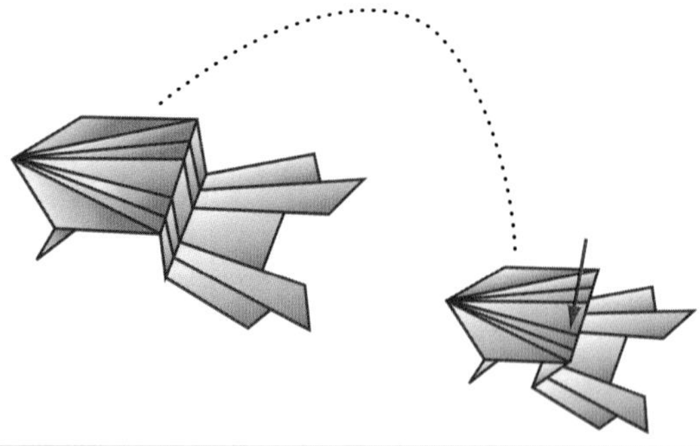

You are now ready to collect some data about how well your frog can jump. But first you are asked for some data about the size of your frog.

Activity 2

MATERIALS origami frog, ruler

Step 1 Copy the table at the right. Make your frog jump five times, and record the length of each jump. You can also put your data in a spreadsheet and share it with your classmates.

Step 2 What is the mean length of the five jumps?

Step 3 What is the median length of the five jumps?

Step 4 What is the range of the five jumps?

Jump	Length (cm)
1	
2	
3	
4	
5	

Now that you have practiced, it is time to see how far you can make your frog jump.

Activity 3

MATERIALS origami frog, ruler, rod or pencil

Event 1: Long Jump

Step 1 Put your frog on the floor or a flat surface such as a table. Draw a line on the table and place your frog behind the line.

Step 2 Make your frog jump six times. Each time, measure the distance in centimeters from the line to the part of the frog that is farthest forward. Record the six distances.

Step 3 What is the length of your longest jump?

Event 2: High Jump

Step 1 Place your frog on a flat surface. Have someone hold a pencil horizontally so that its top is 2 cm above the surface.

Step 2 You have three tries to get the frog to jump over the pencil. If you are successful, then the person should raise the pencil to 3 cm above the surface.

Step 3 Again, you have three tries to get your frog to jump over the pencil. Keep going, raising the pencil 1 cm each time your frog is successful, until you have three misses in a row.

Step 4 Record the last height your frog jumped.

Your teacher may collect the results from Step 3 of Event 1 and Step 4 of Event 2 so that you have data for Questions 3–6 and 8 in the following pages. Take your data and jump into your homework assignment!

To review how to find the mean, median, mode, and range of a data set, you can play *Let's Data Deal*. The directions for this game are on pages G18 and G19 at the back of your book.

Questions

COVERING THE IDEAS

In 1 and 2, refer to your six long-jump distances from Activity 3.

1. a. What is the mean of these distances?
   b. What is the median of these distances?
   c. What is the range of these distances?
2. Which do you think would best tell how far an origami frog jumps: the maximum distance, the mean distance, or the median distance? Why?

In 3 and 4, use the best long jumps from your classmates from Activity 3.

3. a. What is the mean of those distances?
   b. What is the median of those distances?
   c. What is the range of those distances?
4. Create a histogram of the data.

In 5 and 6, use the best high jumps from your classmates from Activity 3.

5. a. What is the mean of those heights?
   b. What is the median of those heights?
   c. What is the range of those heights?
6. Create a histogram of the data.

7. What do you think is the best way to compare one frog's ability to jump to another frog's ability? Write a few sentences defending your answer.

APPLYING THE MATHEMATICS

8. Use the information from Questions 1–3 of Activity 2, and the best long jumps and high jumps from your classmates from Activity 3.
   a. For each student in your class, create the ordered pair (maximum long jump of frog, maximum high jump of frog). Graph these ordered pairs on the same grid. For instance, if your frog long jumps 40 cm and high jumps 30.4 cm, you would graph the ordered pair (40, 30.4).
   b. From your data, does it seem that frogs that jump higher tend to jump farther?
9. Follow Steps 1–9 below to make a simpler frog than the one in the lesson.

   Step 1 Start with a square sheet of paper. Fold over the perpendicular bisectors of the sides and unfold.

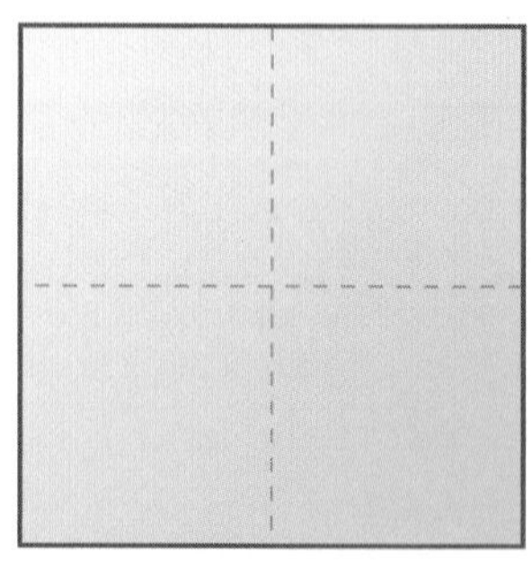

Step 2 Fold each vertex of the square onto the center of the square. This gives you a new square with half the area of the original square.

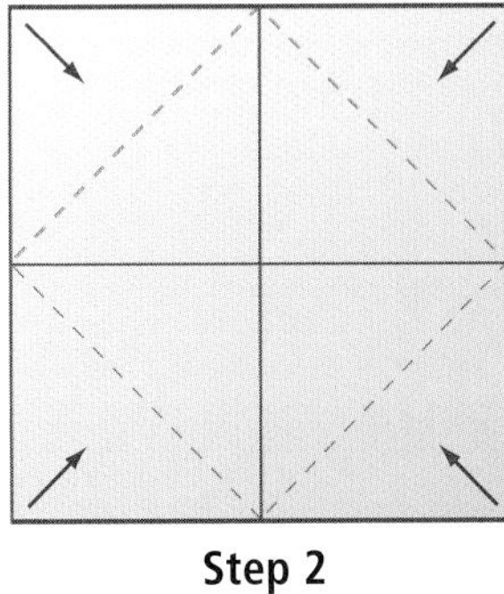
Step 2

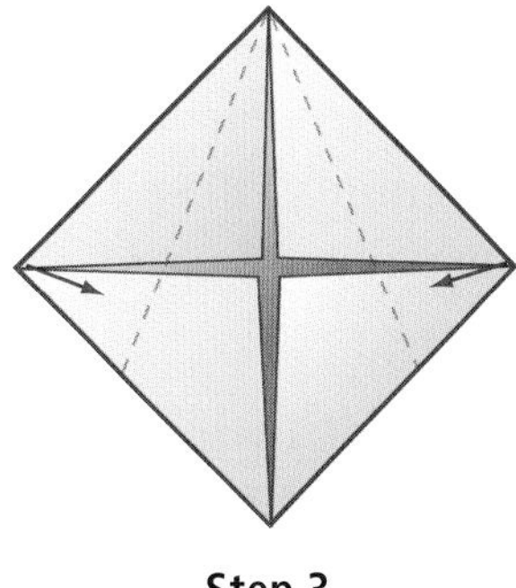
Step 3

Step 3 Fold each of the top sides of the new square onto its vertical diagonal to create a kite.

Step 4 Fold the triangle at the bottom of the kite upward to create an isosceles triangle.

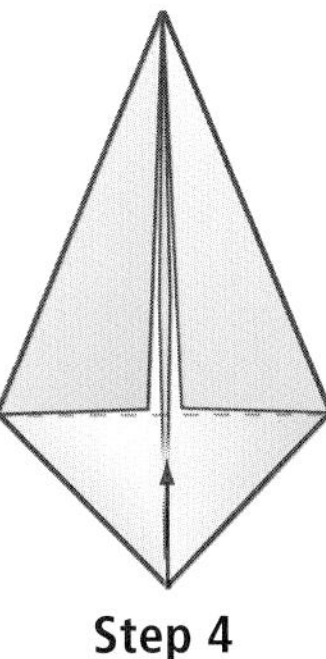
Step 4

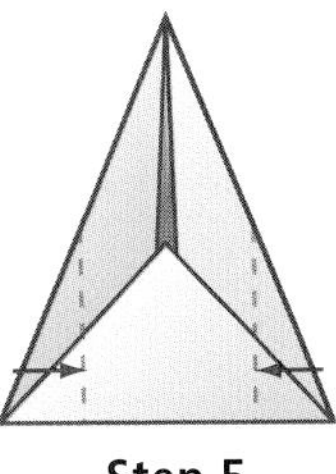
Step 5

Step 5 Fold each of the bottom two vertices of the triangle to the midpoint of the bottom edge.

Step 6 Draw a horizontal line across the middle of the bottom. Fold the bottom portion upward along the horizontal line.

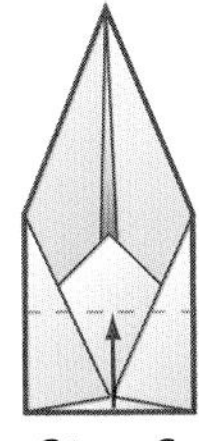
Step 6

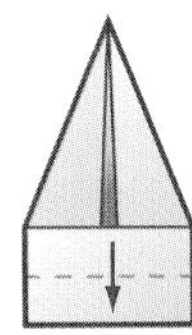
Step 7

Step 7 Draw another horizontal line across the newly formed rectangle. Fold the rectangle downward across the line and toward yourself. This forms the frog's legs.

Step 8 Flip your frog over, then give your frog a head by folding a small part of the triangle downward. Draw two eyes, and your frog is done.

Step 9 To make your frog jump, push a finger down at the spot marked X while sliding that finger away from the frog.

Step 10 Repeat Activity Steps 1–4 of Activity 2 for the lengths of the jumps.

REVIEW

10. On Wednesday, Maizie ate corn-on-the-cob for dinner, so she had to brush her teeth 2.5 times as long as usual. If she brushed her teeth for 2 minutes, 40 seconds on Wednesday, how long does it usually take for her to brush her teeth? **(Lesson 8-5)**

11. The driving distance from New York City to San Francisco is about 2,900 miles. The driving distance from Oslo, Norway to Stockholm, Sweden is about 520 km. About how many times farther is it to drive from New York to San Francisco than to drive from Oslo to Stockholm? **(Lesson 7-5)**

Oslo, Norway

12. Calculate. **(Lesson 6-6)**
    a. 10% of 306
    b. 15% of 40
    c. 20% of 82
    d. 12% of 965

13. Use arrays to show $\frac{5}{7} \cdot \frac{2}{3}$. **(Lesson 6-1)**

14. Give the coordinates of two other points on the line that contains the points (2, 3) and (–7, –5). **(Lesson 5-7)**

EXPLORATION

15. Perhaps you have made paper airplanes out of one piece of paper. If not, explore how to make paper airplanes.
    a. Make a paper airplane.
    b. Repeat Steps 1–4 of Activity 2 of this lesson for your paper airplane to describe how far it can fly.

16. Read Mark Twain's short story *The Jumping Frog of Calaveras County.* Write a paragraph or two describing the story and what you thought of it.

Lesson 13-3 Comparing Distributions of Data

Vocabulary

distribution

double histogram

▶ **BIG IDEA** In many situations, distributions of data are compared using displays and statistics.

Mental Math

If 9 cans of tuna cost \$6, how much would you expect to pay for

a. 27 cans?

b. 3 cans?

c. 1 can?

d. 11 cans?

In Lesson 13-2, you compared how well origami frogs jumped by collecting data and finding means, medians, or ranges. This is a very common way of comparing *distributions* of data.w

Comparing Distributions Using Tables

A **distribution** is the set of all frequencies or relative frequencies of all possible outcomes of an experiment. In this book, you have seen distributions pictured in tables, bar graphs, circle graphs, line graphs, histograms, and stem-and-leaf diagrams.

Activity 1 refers to the Vietnam War draft birthday numbers discussed on the first pages of this chapter and shown on the following page. It turned out that men with birthday numbers from 1 to 195 were drafted. In Activity 1, the 366 draft numbers are summarized in two distributions that you can compare.

Activity 1

Here is a table with the number of birthday numbers in each month that were from 001 to 195 (drafted) and from 196 to 366 (not drafted).

Month	Jan	Feb	Mar	Apr	May	Jun	Jul	Aug	Sep	Oct	Nov	Dec
≤195	14	13	10	12	14	14	18	19	19	14	22	26
>195	17	16	21	18	17	16	13	12	11	17	8	5

Here is a true statement about these data:

The sum of the two numbers in the April column is the same as the number of days in April.

Step 1 Discuss this statement with two or three classmates.

Step 2 Decide whether the statement is the result of (i) something unusual or peculiar, (ii) something not guaranteed but also not unusual, or (iii) something that must happen because of the way the experiment was carried out.

(continued on next page)

Step 3 Give reasons for your choice in Step 2.

Step 4 Repeat Steps 1–3 for each of the following statements.

a. *November and December have many more birthday numbers less than or equal to 195 than other months do.*

b. *The sum of the 12 numbers in the top row of numbers is 195, which is the number in the left column.*

c. *Three months have exactly the same numbers in both rows.*

Vietnam War Draft Lottery

	Jan	Feb	Mar	Apr	May	Jun	Jul	Aug	Sep	Oct	Nov	Dec
1	305	086	108	032	330	249	093	111	225	359	019	129
2	159	144	029	271	298	228	350	045	161	125	034	328
3	251	297	267	083	040	301	115	261	049	244	348	157
4	215	210	275	081	276	020	279	145	232	202	266	165
5	101	214	293	269	364	028	188	054	082	024	310	056
6	224	347	139	253	155	110	327	114	006	087	076	010
7	306	091	122	147	035	085	050	168	008	234	051	012
8	199	181	213	312	321	366	013	048	184	283	097	105
9	194	338	317	219	197	335	277	106	263	342	080	043
10	325	216	323	218	065	206	284	021	071	220	282	041
11	329	150	136	014	037	134	248	324	158	237	046	039
12	221	068	300	346	133	272	015	142	242	072	066	314
13	318	152	259	124	295	069	042	307	175	138	126	163
14	238	004	354	231	178	356	331	198	001	294	127	026
15	017	089	169	273	130	180	322	102	113	171	131	320
16	121	212	166	148	055	274	120	044	207	254	107	096
17	235	189	033	260	112	073	098	154	255	288	143	304
18	140	292	332	090	278	341	190	141	246	005	146	128
19	058	025	200	336	075	104	227	311	177	241	203	240
20	280	302	239	345	183	360	187	344	063	192	185	135
21	186	363	334	062	250	060	027	291	204	243	156	070
22	337	290	265	316	326	247	153	339	160	117	009	053
23	118	057	256	252	319	109	172	116	119	201	182	162
24	059	236	258	002	031	358	023	036	195	196	230	095
25	052	179	343	351	361	137	067	286	149	176	132	084
26	092	365	170	340	357	022	303	245	018	007	309	173
27	355	205	268	074	296	064	289	352	233	264	047	078
28	077	299	223	262	308	222	088	167	257	094	281	123
29	349	285	362	191	226	353	270	061	151	229	099	016
30	164	--	217	208	103	209	287	333	315	038	174	003
31	211	--	030	--	313	--	193	011	--	079	--	100

QY1

a. What was the draft number for October 24th?

b. Would a person whose birthday was October 24th have been drafted?

When people studied the draft numbers for the 366 days of a year, they realized that the draft numbers for dates in November and December were lower on average than the draft numbers for other months. It turned out that the January capsules were put into the cylinder first, then February, then March, and so on. So the November and December capsules were at the top. The capsules were not mixed up enough, making the November and December capsules more likely to be selected first. Draft lotteries were carried out for three more years, and efforts were made in those years to mix up the days better.

▸ READING MATH

Many states have lotteries with numbers selected by machines specifically designed to mix numbers. These machines are tested regularly to ensure the numbers selected are random.

Comparing Distributions Using Histograms

Activity 1 compared distributions using two rows in a table. Activity 2 uses two histograms to compare the heights of people in two groups.

Activity 2

MATERIALS calculator, graph paper, measuring tape

For this activity, you need the heights of each person in your class rounded to the nearest inch. These heights should be separated into two data sets: one for girls and one for boys. If your class is all boys or all girls, then you will need height data for your class and for another class.

Step 1 Organize the heights of the boys (or of one class) into a histogram with the scale below.

47–49 in. | 50–52 in. | 53–55 in. | 56–58 in. | 59–61 in. | 62–64 in.

Step 2 Organize the heights of the girls (or the other class) into a histogram with the same scale as in Step 1.

Step 3 Create a *double histogram*. A **double histogram** consists of two histograms with the same scale but going in opposite directions from the scale line. Your scale line should be vertical as shown at the right. Make two bars, one to the left and one to the right, showing the number of boys and girls in each height interval.

Boys	Inches	Girls
	47–49	
	50–52	
	53–55	
	56–58	
	59–61	
	62–64	

Step 4 Look at the double histogram. Which of the following do you think is true for your class?

A In general, the girls are taller.

B In general, the boys are taller.

C In general, the heights of the girls and boys are about the same.

(continued on next page)

Step 5 Determine the median height for the girls and the median height for the boys. Do the medians support your choice in Step 4?

Step 6 Calculate the mean height for the girls and the mean height for the boys. Do the means support your choice in Step 4?

Step 7 Give the shortest and tallest heights for the girls and the shortest and tallest heights for the boys. Do the ranges support your choice in Step 4?

In Activity 2, you created two frequency distributions, one for boys' heights and one for girls' heights. To people who build houses or furniture, or who manage clothing stores, knowing the distribution of heights is important. They need to be able to answer questions such as: How high off the ground should a drinking fountain be? How large a bed is needed? What inseam lengths for jeans need to be in stock?

Comparing Data Using Line Graphs

Of course, children's heights change with age. In most kindergarten classrooms, chairs and desks and shelves are lower than in later grades. Some rides in theme parks require that riders be a certain height. Because knowing heights is so important, the government collects data about heights.

The two grids on the following page display multiple line graphs. They show the distribution of heights (called "stature") from age 2 to age 20 for boys and girls in the United States. Heights are scaled in centimeters and inches.

Each multiple line graph has three curves. Each curve is a line graph. The numbers 10, 50, and 90 appear at the right ends of the curves. We call the curves the 10-curve, 50-curve, and 90-curve. These numbers represent the percent of boys or girls whose height is less than or equal to that height.

Each vertical line has information regarding heights at a particular age. For instance, suppose you want to find the distribution of heights for boys at age 20. Look for 20 along the horizontal (bottom) axis of the left grid. The number 20 is at the far right. Read up from 20. Because 168 cm and 66 in. are where the 10-curve crosses 20, 10% of 20-year-old boys have heights less than or equal to 168 cm or 66 in.

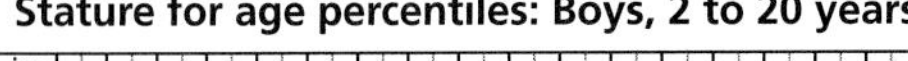

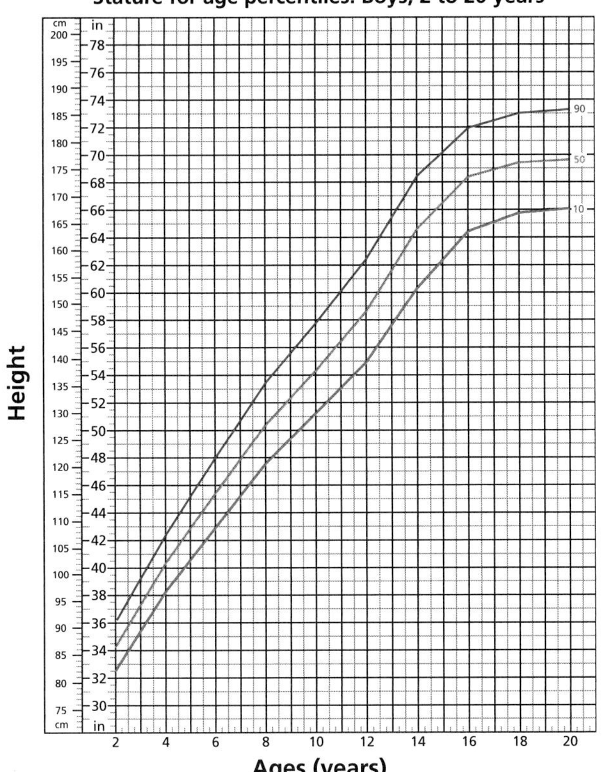

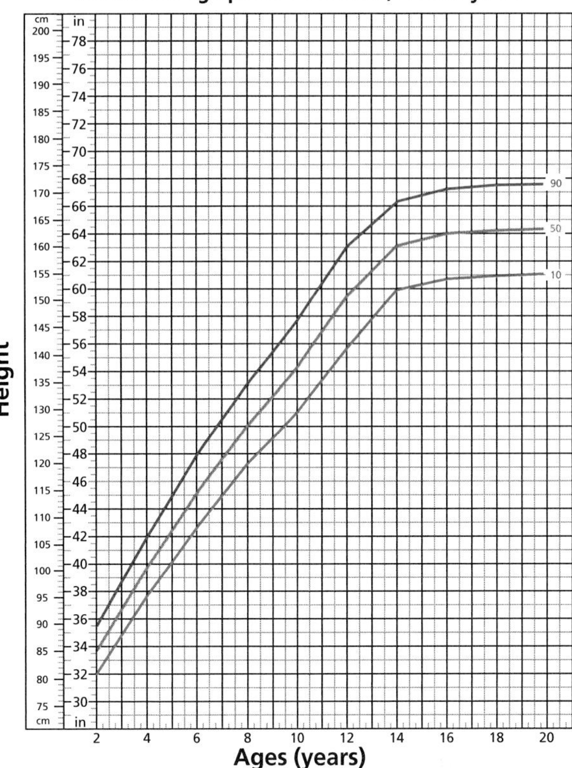

Source: Center for Disease Control

 See QY2 at the right.

Remember that about half of the values in a data set are less than its median and half are greater than its median. Thus the 50-curve on these graphs gives the median height from age 2 to 20.

Example

Refer to the two grids giving heights at ages 2–20.

a. What is the median height in inches for a 19-year-old girl?

b. What is the median height in centimeters for a 19-year-old girl?

c. What percent of 11-year-old boys are taller than 4'6"?

Solution

a. Using the Girls' grid, find age 19 on the horizontal axis. Read up vertically to the 50-curve. The median height for 19-year-old girls is a little over 64 inches.

b. The median height for 19-year-old girls is about 163 centimeters.

c. Change 4'6" to inches. 4'6" $= 4 \bullet 12 + 6 = 54$ inches. Look at the vertical line above 11 on the Boys' grid. The 54-inch line intersects the age 11 line just above the 25-curve. This means that 25% of 11-year-old boys are shorter than 4'6", so 75% of 11-year-old boys are taller than 4'6".

STOP QY2

Fill in the Blanks

Refer to the graphs above.

a. 10% of 20-year-old girls have heights less than or equal to __?__ inches.

b. 50% of 20-year-old boys have heights less than or equal to __?__ centimeters.

Notice that the heights of boys and girls are about the same until a certain year. After that time, on average, boys are taller.

Activity 3

Determine how your class's height data compares with the national data.

Step 1 Determine the mode age for boys and the mode age for girls in your class.

Step 2 Find the median height of boys and the median height of girls for this age on the height grids.

Step 3 In general, are the boys and girls in your class taller than, shorter that, or about the same height as the same age group in the United States as a whole?

Questions

COVERING THE IDEAS

In 1–6, use the double histogram at the right. It shows the age distribution of males and females in the 2000 U.S. population. So, for example, the bottom bar on the right tells you there were between 9 and 10 million girls whose age was from 0 (birth) to 4.

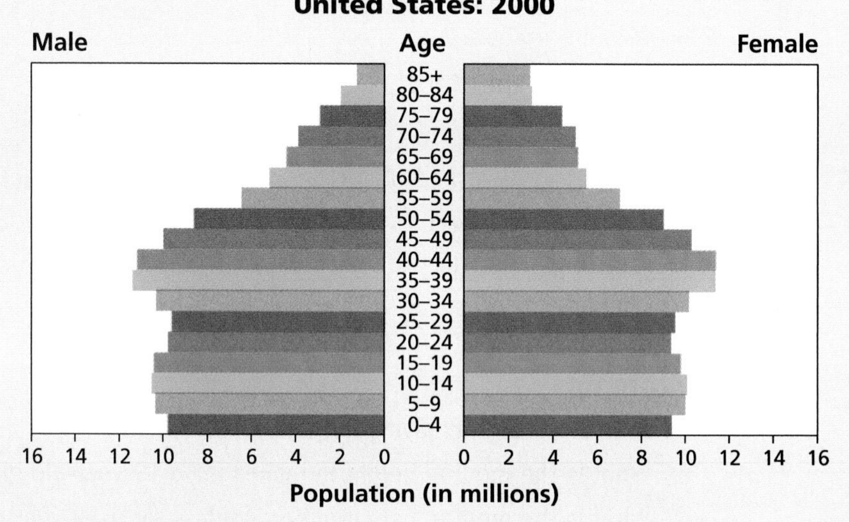

Source: U.S. Census Bureau

1. About how many U.S. boys in 2000 were from 10 to 14 years old?
2. About how many U.S. women in 2000 were from 55 to 59 years old?
3. Which 5-year age span had the most males?
4. Between the top bars in this double histogram is "85+". What does "85+" mean?
5. Were there more men or more women between the ages of 50 and 54 in 2000?
6. Why are the top bars shorter than the bottom bars?
7. Give two reasons why people might be interested in the distribution of heights in their community.

8. A survey yielded the following average weekly allowance given to children by their parents, depending on age and gender.

Age	Boys	Girls
11	$6.80	$9.07
12	$9.38	$9.85
13	$9.95	$9.10
14	$13.50	$13.51
15	$16.65	$14.38
16	$15.79	$19.62
17	$27.65	$35.61

Create a double line graph of the information in the table. If you get an allowance, is it close to the value in the double line graph corresponding to your age and gender?

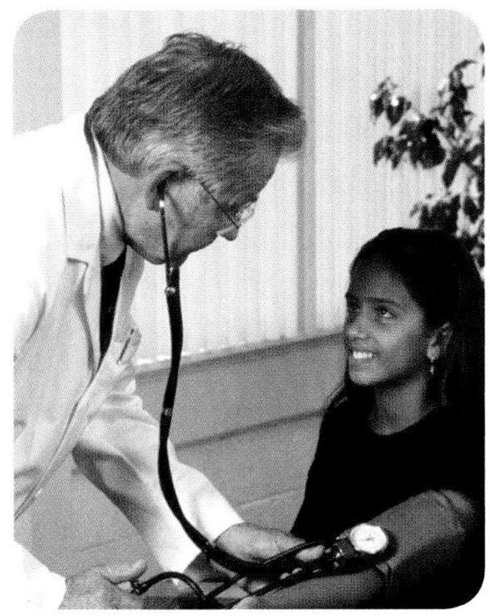

7.5% of all primary care physicians are pediatricians.

Source: U.S. Dept. of Labor

In 9–12, refer to the height grids in the lesson.

9. 90% of 8-year-old girls are no taller than what height?
10. Find the median height for 7-year-old boys.
11. Find the median height for $17\frac{1}{2}$-year-old girls.
12. Francesca's doctor told her that she is at the 10th percentile in height for girls her age. If Francesca is 12 years old, how tall is she?

APPLYING THE MATHEMATICS

In 13–18, refer to the double histograms showing age distributions for the 2000 populations of Canada and Mexico. (The histogram for Mexico is on the next page.)

13. In 2000, about how many males in Mexico were between the ages of 40 and 44? How many females?
14. In 2000, about how many males in Canada were between the ages of 25 and 29? How many females?
15. What might it mean that the top bar for females in Canada is so much longer than the top bar for males?

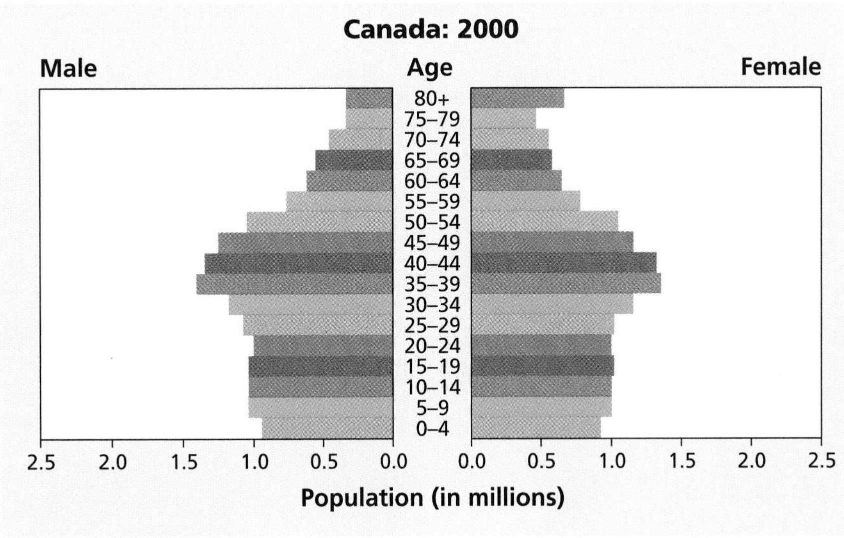

Source: U.S. Census Bureau

16. The double histogram for Mexico shows why this double histogram is sometimes called a *population pyramid*. Why does the double histogram for Canada *not* have the shape of a pyramid?

17. Which country has the lower median age? How can you tell?

18. In which of these two countries does it appear that the birth rate is going down?

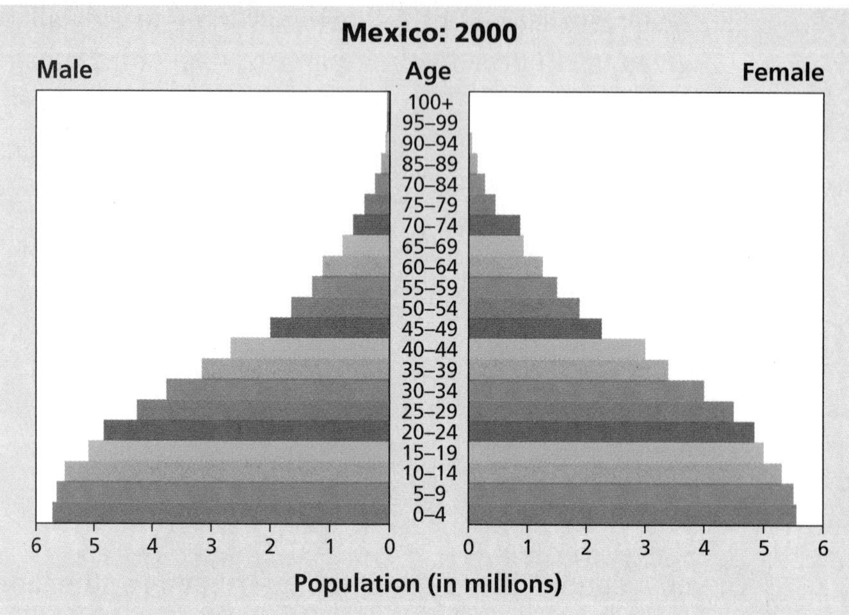

Source: U.S. Census Bureau

In 19–22, refer to the height grids in the lesson.

19. Terrence is 15 years old and is 5 feet, 9 inches tall. Is he taller than the median height for his age?

20. How much difference in height is there between the 10-curve and the 90-curve for a 12-year-old girl? Answer in inches and in centimeters.

21. The Hematics have a $2\frac{1}{2}$-year-old boy, Matt. Only about 10% of boys his age are taller than he. What is Matt's height? Answer in inches and centimeters.

22. According to these multiple line graphs, at what age do boys start to become taller than girls?

REVIEW

23. In a long-jump competition, each competitor is allowed six jumps. The competitor with the longest jump wins. Here are the lengths of the jumps of two women, Jane and Kate, in meters. **(Lesson 13-2)**

Jump	1	2	3	4	5	6
Jane	5.65	foul	5.42	5.74	foul	foul
Kate	5.70	5.65	5.63	5.66	5.71	5.48

a. Who won the competition?
b. Who had the higher mean length of jump?
c. Who had the higher median length of jump?
d. Do you think the better jumper won? Why or why not?

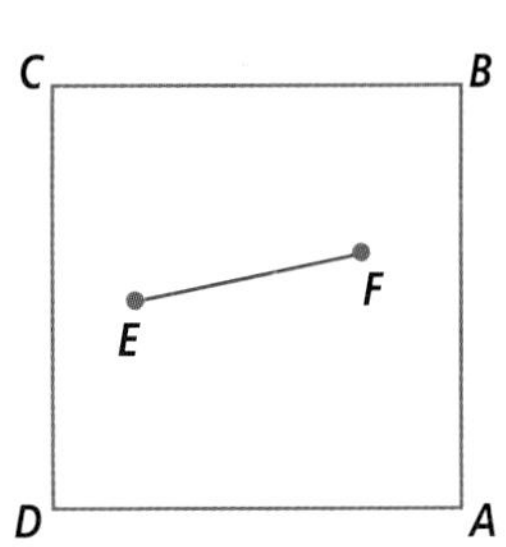

24. **Multiple Choice** Pictured at the right is a square piece of paper *ABCD* with line segment $\overline{EF}$ drawn on it. If you fold the paper so that *A* lands on *F*, what describes the fold line? (Lesson 13-1)
    A the bisector of $\angle EFA$
    B the bisector of $\angle FAE$
    C the perpendicular bisector of $\overline{EA}$
    D the perpendicular bisector of $\overline{FA}$

25. This lesson includes distributions of draft numbers and of heights for your class and for the U.S. population. Which of these is a frequency distribution? Which is a relative frequency distribution? (Lesson 10-5)

26. If you roll a fair 20-sided die numbered 1–20, what is the probability that you will roll a number less than 5? (Lesson 10-2)

27. a. Arrange the data from Activity 2 of this lesson into two stem-and-leaf plots, one for boys and one for girls.
    b. Which display method do you prefer, the stem-and-leaf plot or the double histogram? Explain. (Lesson 5-3)

28. Refer to the 366 draft birthday numbers in the table on page 734. Find the medians of the numbers for January, March, May, August, and December. Do these medians bear out the claim that a person who was born in December is more likely to be drafted? (Lesson 5-1)

EXPLORATION

29. In a group of six sixth-graders, one student is 148 cm and another is 160 cm tall.
    a. Find possible heights of the other four students if the mean height of the students is 150 cm.
    b. Find possible heights of the other four students if the mean height of the students is 150 cm and the median height is 152 cm.
    c. Find possible heights of the other four students if the mean height is 150 cm, the median height is 152 cm, and the mode height is 154 cm.
    d. Find possible heights of the other four students if the mean height is 150 cm, the median height is 152 cm, the mode height is 154 cm, and the range is 26 cm.

QY ANSWERS

1a. 196 **2a.** 60

1b. no **2b.** 176

Lesson 13-4 Statistics from a Survey: The U.S. Census

Vocabulary

census

survey

▸ **BIG IDEA** Every ten years since 1790, a census has collected a large amount of data about the population of the United States.

The United States declared independence from Great Britain in 1776. Eleven years later, in 1787, the Constitution of the United States was approved by enough states that its provisions became law. Section 2 of Article 1 of the Constitution included the following statement:

> "[An] Enumeration shall be made within three Years after the first Meeting of the Congress of the United States, and within every subsequent Term of ten Years, in such Manner as they shall by Law direct."

The word "enumeration" means a count. A **survey** uses questions to collect data. A **census** is a survey that attempts to count or question every member of a population. The United States census is the most comprehensive survey in the world.

Mental Math

Insert parentheses in the expression $5 + 2 \cdot 3^2 - 7$ to get the result shown.

a. 114

b. 34

c. 14

d. 16

The 1790 Census

Congress first met in 1789, and the first national census was conducted in 1790. Every ten years since then, there has been a national census.

The table on the next page shows the 1790, 1990, and 2000 census population totals for the areas counted in the 1790 census. Note that three areas were *territories* in 1790, but since have become states.

STOP See "QY" at the right.

STOP QY

According to the table on the following page, in 1790, which three states had the largest populations? Where did these states rank in 2000?

Comparing Historical Apportionments

A major reason to know population totals is that the U.S. Constitution requires that the number of representatives each state has in Congress depend on the state's population. Over time, as populations increase, the census and the methods used to calculate the number of representatives, called *apportionment,* has grown in complexity.

To determine the number of representatives in the first Congress of 1789, the U.S. Constitution established a minimum ratio of 1 representative to every 30,000 persons. After the first census in 1790, this ratio was changed to 1 representative to every 34,436 persons.

Resident Population of the United States

Area	1790	1990	2000	Change from 1990 to 2000	State Rank		
					1790	1990	2000
Connecticut	237,655	3,287,116	3,405,565	118,449	6	27	29
Delaware	59,096	666,168	783,600	117,432	16	46	45
Georgia	82,638	6,478,216	8,186,453	1,708,237	15	11	10
Kentucky	*73,677	3,685,296	4,041,769	356,473	14	23	25
Maine	*96,643	1,227,928	1,274,923	46,995	11	38	40
Maryland	319,728	4,781,468	5,296,486	515,018	7	19	19
Massachusetts	378,556	6,016,425	6,349,097	332,672	3	13	13
New Hampshire	141,899	1,109,252	1,235,786	126,534	9	40	41
New Jersey	184,139	7,730,188	8,414,350	684,162	8	9	9
New York	340,241	17,990,455	18,976,457	986,002	4	2	3
North Carolina	395,005	6,628,637	8,049,313	1,420,676	5	10	11
Pennsylvania	433,611	11,881,643	12,281,054	399,411	2	5	6
Rhode Island	69,112	1,003,464	1,048,319	44,855	13	43	43
South Carolina	249,073	3,486,703	4,012,012	525,309	10	25	26
Vermont	*85,341	562,758	608,827	46,069	12	48	49
Virginia	747,610	6,187,358	7,078,515	891,157	1	12	12

*Territories

Source: U.S. Census Bureau

It is rare that apportionment ratios result in integer quotients. Since 1790, there have been five basic methods for handling remainders in the division of apportionment ratios. In 1792, the *Jefferson method* was used. This method rejected fractional remainders.

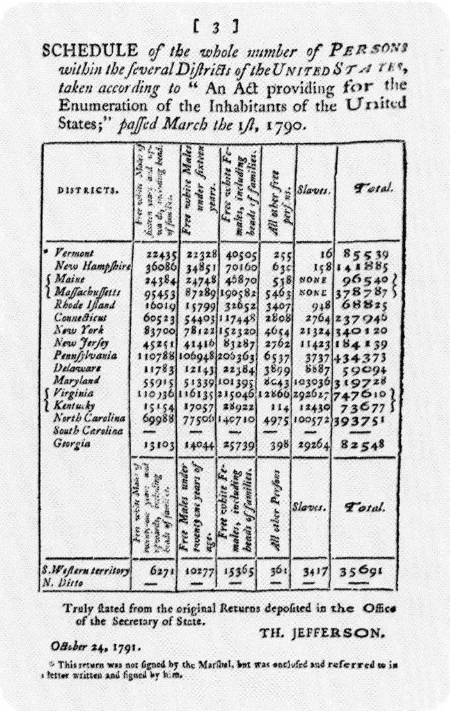

[3]

SCHEDULE *of the whole number of* PERSONS *within the several Districts of the* UNITED STATES, *taken according to* " An Act providing for the Enumeration of the Inhabitants of the United States;" *passed March the 1st*, 1790.

DISTRICTS.	Free white Males of sixteen years and upwards, including heads of families.	Free white Males under sixteen years.	Free white Females, including heads of families.	All other free persons.	Slaves.	Total.
* Vermont	22435	22328	40505	255	16	85539
New Hampshire	36086	34851	70160	630	158	141885
Maine	24384	24748	46870	538	NONE	96540
Massachusetts	95453	87289	190582	5463	NONE	378787
Rhode Island	16019	15799	32652	3407	948	68825
Connecticut	60523	54403	117448	2808	2764	237946
New York	83700	78122	152320	4654	21324	340120
New Jersey	45251	41416	83287	2762	11423	184139
Pennsylvania	110788	106948	206363	6537	3737	434373
Delaware	11783	12143	22384	3899	8887	59094
Maryland	55915	51339	101395	8043	103036	319728
Virginia	110936	116135	215046	12866	292627	747610
Kentucky	15154	17057	28922	114	12430	73677
North Carolina	69988	77506	140710	4975	100572	393751
South Carolina	—	—	—	—	—	—
Georgia	13103	14044	25739	398	29264	82548
	Free white Males of twenty-one years and upwards, including heads of families.	Free Males under twenty-one years of age.	Free white Females, including heads of families.	All other Persons	Slaves.	Total.
S. Western territory	6271	10277	15365	361	3417	35691
N. Ditto	—	—	—	—	—	—

Truly stated from the original Returns deposited in the Office of the Secretary of State.

TH. JEFFERSON.

October 24, 1791.

* This return was not signed by the Marshal, but was enclosed and referred to in a letter written and signed by him.

U.S. Census results from 1790

Activity

MATERIALS calculator

Step 1 Copy the table at the right. For each state or territory, determine the number of representatives for the second congress in 1792 by dividing the 1790 census population by 34,436. Discard the remainders.

Step 2 Check to make sure that the total number of Representatives in 1792 adds up to 105.

Step 3 Which areas had changes in the number of representatives from the first congress to the second?

Area	Number of Representatives	
	1789	1792
Connecticut	5	
Delaware	1	
Georgia	3	
Kentucky		
Maine		
Maryland	6	
Massachusetts	8	
New Hampshire	3	
New Jersey	4	
New York	6	
North Carolina	5	
Pennsylvania	8	
Rhode Island	1	
South Carolina	5	
Vermont		
Virginia	10	
Total	65	105

Source: U.S. Census Bureau

The U.S. Census involves mathematics and statistics in a variety of ways. Mathematicians and others continue to explore apportionment calculation methods that will fulfill the promise of fairness intended in the Constitution.

Current Census Information

As the years have gone by, more and more people have realized the importance of good census information. Today, virtually every country in the world conducts censuses, often every ten years, following the U.S. model.

Census information is used by governments to help determine where to build roads and schools and other improvements. It is used by businesses to help figure out who is buying their products and where they should advertise. It is used by people who are trying to trace their ancestors and relatives. And of course, it is used by people interested in the history of our country.

As censuses have become more important, more information has been collected. Often different information is collected in one census than in the next. While information on states and communities are announced as soon as possible, detailed information about families, including names, ages, and ethnicities, is kept private for 72 years. This means that detailed information from the 1930 Census became available in 2002.

For the 2000 Census, everyone was counted, but more detailed information was obtained from only a sample of people. In 2000, the total U.S. population was 281,421,906, according to the Census.

The circle graph at the right displays estimates (in millions) of the 2006 population split by ethnicity. Because many people fall into more than one of the categories, the reported totals may be inaccurate. This illustrates the importance of analyzing census or other survey data carefully.

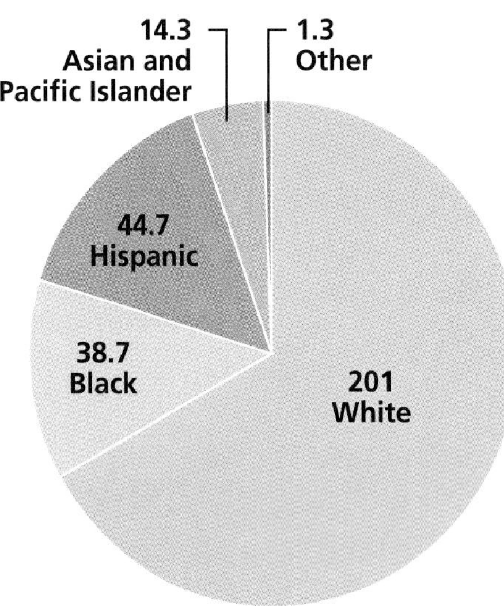

Source: Pew Hispanic Center

Questions

COVERING THE IDEAS

In 1–4, refer to the table on page 743.

1. What three U.S. states or territories had the smallest populations in 1790?
2. In the 1790 census, what was the population of the territory now occupied by the state of Kentucky?
3. Examine the numeric changes in population for the states shown from 1990 to 2000.
   a. Which three states had the largest change in population?
   b. Which three states had the smallest change in population?
4. a. Which states had a lower state rank in 2000 than they did in 1990?
   b. If a state did not have a negative numeric change in population, what would cause the state to have a lower state rank?
5. If the results of the apportionment calculations ratio always rounded up, how would the assignment of the number of representatives in the 1792 congress have changed?
6. According to the circle graph above, about what percent of the people in the United States in 2006 were of Asian or Pacific Islander origin?

The Pacific Islands are divided into three divisions: Melanesia, Micronesia, and Polynesia.

APPLYING THE MATHEMATICS

In 7–12, consider only the original 13 states. Do not consider the territories.

7. What was the mean population of these states in 1790?
8. What was the median population of these states in 1790?
9. What was the mean population of these states in 2000?
10. What was the median population of these states in 2000?

11. a. Which state had the greatest population increase from 1790 to 2000?
    b. If you divide each state's 2000 population by its 1790 population, for which state will you the get the greatest quotient? What is that quotient?

12. a. Rank the 13 states in 1790 from greatest to least in population. Rank the 13 states in 2000 the same way.
    b. Which state's rank fell the most from 1790 to 2000?
    c. Which state's rank climbed the most from 1790 to 2000?

13. In 1790, of the 3,929,214 total U.S. population, 201,655 people lived in urban areas, and the rest lived in rural areas. In 1990, 187,053,487 of the people in the census population of 248,709,873 lived in urban areas, and the rest lived in rural areas.
    a. What percent of people lived in urban areas in 1790?
    b. What percent of people lived in urban areas in 1990?
    c. Construct two circle graphs that show where people lived in 1790 and where people lived in 1990.

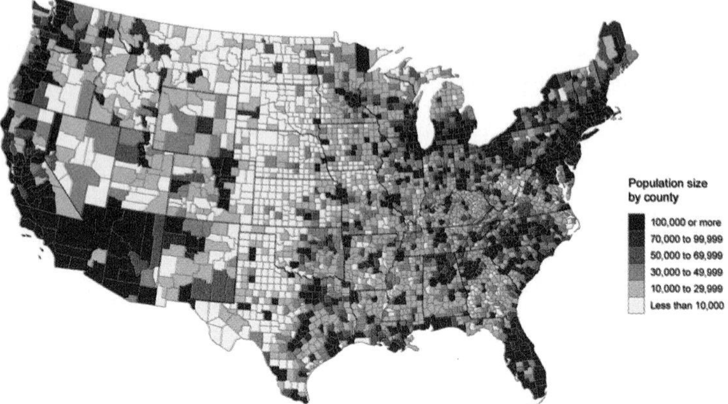

The east coast of the U.S. from Boston, MA to Washington, D.C. is considered a megapolis.

REVIEW

14. Refer to the U.S. 2000 population pyramid on page 738. **(Lesson 13-3)**
    a. In what age group is the ratio of females to males the highest?
    b. Estimate the ratio from Part a.

15. Tell whether each statement is true or false. Draw examples or use properties of the quadrilaterals to support your claims. **(Lessons 12-6, 12-5, 12-4)**
    a. Every isosceles trapezoid is a rectangle.
    b. Every rectangle is a parallelogram.
    c. Some kites are rectangles.
    d. All squares are trapezoids.
    e. Some rectangles are not parallelograms.

16. **True or False** An angle bisector lies on a line of symmetry for that angle. **(Lessons 12-3, 11-2)**

17. What percent of the square at the right is shaded? **(Lessons 9-5, 8-1)**

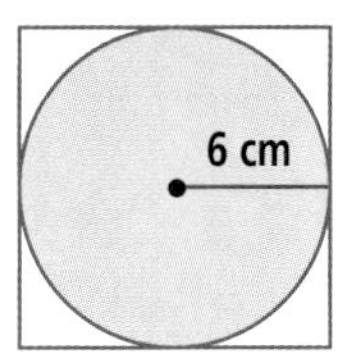

18. What is the remainder when 9,816,489,437,772,103 is divided by 5? Explain how you can tell without doing the division. **(Lesson 7-3)**

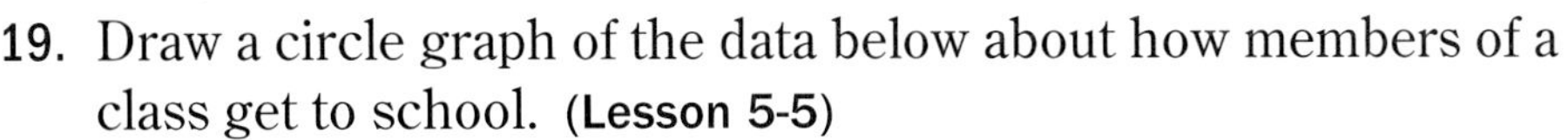

19. Draw a circle graph of the data below about how members of a class get to school. **(Lesson 5-5)**

Walk: 5 Take a bus: 17 Are driven by car: 3

20. Solve for m: $3 + m = -5$. **(Lesson 4-8)**

EXPLORATION

21. In the 2000 census, some of the questions asked in each household were the following:
    (1) How many people were living or staying in this house, apartment, or mobile home on April 1, 2000?
    (2) What is the name of each person in the household? What is their age and date of birth? How are they related to the head of the household?
    (3) For each person, is the person Spanish/Hispanic/Latino? If so, is the person Puerto Rican, Mexican or Chicano, Cuban, or other (indicate the group)?
    (4) For each person, what is the person's race? You may indicate more than one race for each person.
    white;
    black, African American, or Negro;
    American Indian or Alaska Native (give name of principal tribe);
    Asian (choose between Asian Indian, Chinese, Filipino, Japanese, Korean, Vietnamese, other Asian (give race), Native Hawaiian, Guamanian or Chamorro, Samoan, or other Pacific Islander (give race); some other race.
    a. Discuss the above questions with people in your household. How would people in your household have answered the questions? How easy is it to answer these questions? Are there questions people in your household were not able to answer because they didn't know? (You do not have to write the answers on your homework paper if you want to keep the information private.)
    b. Why might people not want to make the information on the census form public? Do you think 72 years is about the right amount of time before that information becomes public, or should the information be available before then, or much after then?

QY ANSWER

Virginia, Pennsylvania, and North Carolina; 12th, 6th, and 11th

Lesson 13-5 Writing Survey Questions

Vocabulary

open-ended item

BIG IDEA It takes great care to write a good survey question because so many things can make the responses difficult to analyze.

In Lesson 13-3, you saw the results of surveys of the heights of boys and girls and of the age distribution of people in various countries. There is usually no question what a person's age is. You can measure a person's height. Few decisions are involved in gathering survey data like these. However, some data are not so objective. Consider this example.

Mental Math

Use the diagram below.

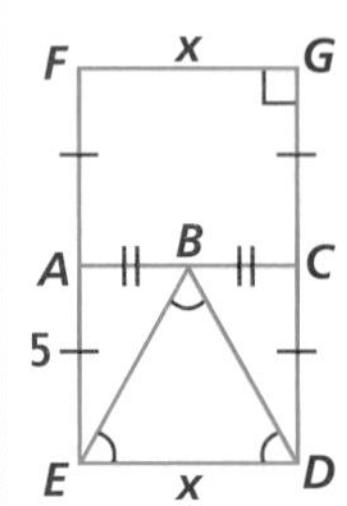

a. Find the area of *ACDE*.

b. Find the area of *EBD*.

c. Find the area of *ABE*.

d. Find the area of *EFGD*.

Example 1

A cell phone company considered letting people talk free to members of their family. To help decide, the company wanted to know the size of a typical family. So they randomly chose 500 people and asked: *How big is your family?* When they got the results, they found they could not interpret them. What happened?

Solution The difficulty is with the wording of the question. It is not clear what "family" means.

Activity

Assume you are answering the question asked by the cell phone company in Example 1. Which people would you consider to be in your family? Discuss your answers with other students in your class.

A a cousin living with you
B a cousin living next door
C a married brother or sister not living with you
D a grandparent living with you
E a very close friend with whom you talk every day
F an exchange student living in your house

Opinion Polls

An opinion poll is a very common type of survey. Many TV and radio programs ask listeners to call or use the internet to respond to a question about something that has happened that day. Before elections, there are polls indicating which candidate voters prefer. You may have answered a survey about what kind of clothes or type of entertainment you prefer.

In all surveys and opinion polls, the data collected are only as good as the survey questions. Here are some helpful hints for writing good questions for an opinion poll.

Suggestions for Good Opinion-Survey Items

1. Make certain the words you use are clear and easily understood.
2. Try to determine the possible opinions in advance.
3. Decide whether you wish to present choices or not.
4. Do not lead the person answering the survey to one opinion over another.
5. Keep the items as short as you can.

Example 2

a. Evaluate this survey question using the suggestions above.

A part of the park is being wasted. Many people would like to see a baseball field there. Do you agree?

Yes ____ No ____

b. Improve the survey question.

Solution

a. Suggestion 1 was not followed. Some words do not have a clear meaning. Which part of what park is meant? How big of a baseball field is desired?

Suggestion 2 may not have been followed. How should a person respond if the person has no opinion?

Suggestion 3 was followed. Two choices were given: Yes and No.

Suggestion 4 was not followed. The question says many people would like to see a baseball field there. But, it is possible that many people would not like to see a baseball field there. The use of the word "wasted" suggests that the surveyor wants the baseball field.

Suggestion 5 was followed.

b. Here is a possible improvement.

The northeast corner of Calhoun Park is currently used on occasion for picnics, and part of it contains many trees. There is a proposal to put a baseball diamond there. Do you agree with the proposal? Yes ____ No ____ Not sure ____

See QY at the right.

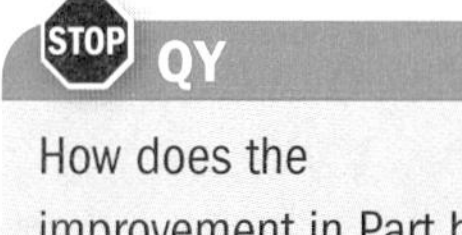

How does the improvement in Part b follow Suggestion 2?

Determining Good Choices for an Item

Some survey questions have a list of choices, while others do not. Suppose you want to know what people's favorite sports team is. You cannot list every team. So you might want to allow any response. This kind of item is called **open-ended.** However, if you are surveying people in a large city with a few local professional teams, then you might want to list teams. Or, you might want to list some teams and then have a choice of "other."

To determine possible choices, some people do a preliminary survey of just a few people to try to learn the most likely answers in advance. The choices should include the most likely answers, but they should also be clearly different. For instance, if asking about someone's favorite color, then you would not want to list both "blue" and "navy blue" because they overlap.

Suggestions for Good Choices for Survey Items

1. Choices should include all the most likely answers.
2. Choices should not overlap.

Questions

COVERING THE IDEAS

In 1–4, indicate a word or phrase that would cause the survey results to be hard to interpret. You do not have to answer the question.

1. What is your favorite activity outside of school?
2. Do you understand multiplication of fractions?
3. How many good friends do you have?
4. Did you like what you ate for dinner last night?

In 5 and 6, a survey item is given. Name at least one reasonable choice that is missing. You do not have to answer the survey question.

5. What is your favorite kind of weather?
   A sunny B rainy C snowy
6. What is your age?
   A under 12 B over 12

In 7 and 8, read survey questions (i) and (ii).

a. **Which one would be better as an open-ended item?**

b. **What would you list as the choices for the other item?**

7. (i) What is your favorite color of the rainbow?
   (ii) What is your favorite color?

Syracuse, New York receives an average of 115.6 inches of snowfall a year.

8. (i) What do you think the world population is now, to the nearest billion?
   (ii) What do you think the world population will be in 2050, to the nearest billion?

In 9 and 10, a survey question and some choices are given. How could you improve the choices?

9. What is the most recent sport you watched on television?
   A baseball **B** basketball **C** football **D** auto racing
10. How often do you have a glass of water at a meal?
    A almost always **B** often
    C a lot **D** sometimes
    E rarely **F** never

APPLYING THE MATHEMATICS

In 11–14, decide if the survey question is well-written. If the question is not well-written, try to make it better.

11. Do you usually get enough sleep?
    A yes **B** no
12. Teachers are usually impressed with students who spend lots of time doing their homework. How much time did you spend doing homework last night?
13. Where was the TV that you watch most often manufactured?
    A Asia **B** Europe **C** North America
14. During a typical week, how many times do you drink beverages sweetened with sugar (soda, sports drinks, fruit punch, lemonade, and so on)?

The National Education Assosociation recommends 30 to 60 minutes of homework a day for the average sixth grader.

In 15 and 16, the two groups of people are to be asked a survey question.

a. Write a question that would likely get very different responses from the two groups, so it would be easy to tell which set of data matched which group.

b. Write a question that would likely get similar responses from the two groups, so it would be difficult to tell which set of data matched which group.

15. a class of sixth graders and their parents
16. a group of vegetarians and a group of people eating at a hot dog/hamburger stand

REVIEW

17. Copy points F and D at the right.

D

F

    a. Construct a fold along $\overline{FD}$.
    b. Construct a fold along the perpendicular bisector of $\overline{FD}$.
    c. Construct a fold along the angle bisector of the folds in Parts a and b. **(Lesson 13-1)**

18. **True or False** If a triangle has two acute angles, it is acute. **(Lesson 12-2)**

19. **True or False** If a triangle has one obtuse angle, it is obtuse. **(Lesson 12-2)**

20. Supat is stacking boxes in a truck. All of the boxes are the same size. He can fit 7 boxes across the width of the truck, 4 boxes up the side of the truck, and 5 boxes deep into the truck. How many boxes can he fit into the truck in all? **(Lesson 9-9)**

When fuel cost increases one penny, the cost of mailing packages increases over 8 million annually.

21. In the following problem, which step uses the Associative Property of Addition, and which step uses the Commutative Property of Addition?

    $a + (b + a) + b$

    Step 1 $a + (a + b) + b$
    Step 2 $(a + a) + (b + b)$
    Step 3 $2a + 2b$ **(Lessons 3-2, 3-1)**

22. There are exactly 2.54 centimeters in 1 inch. **(Lessons 2-6, 2-5)**
    a. Round this measurement up to the next tenth of a centimeter.
    b. Round this measurement down to the previous whole centimeter.
    c. Round this measurement to the nearest ten centimeters.

EXPLORATION

23. Look in a book or on the internet to find at least two of the questions that were asked in the most recent U.S. Census. Do the questions follow the suggestions outlined in this lesson?

QY ANSWER

A third choice, "not sure," was added to cover all possibilities.

Lesson 13-6 Creating Your Own Survey

▸ **BIG IDEA** There are four parts to conducting a survey: designing the survey, collecting the data, displaying the results, and drawing conclusions.

Mental Math

Calculate.

a. $\frac{1}{3} + \frac{5}{3}$

b. $\frac{2}{3} + \frac{4}{6}$

c. $\frac{3}{8} - \frac{1}{2}$

d. $-\frac{15}{17} + \frac{15}{34}$

The results of a good survey can tell you what people think or give you information about what is around you. In this lesson, you are asked to conduct a survey. You should apply what you have learned throughout this book. To guide you, we have made up a story about a survey that was constructed and conducted by Holly Wood.

Holly was chosen to pick the movie for eighth-grade movie night. She decides to survey her classmates about their movie preferences.

Designing the Survey

Holly gets permission to have all the sixth graders in her school fill out a short questionnaire in math class. She decides to have two questions, one with a list of choices and one open-ended. Her questionnaire is shown at the right.

1. What's your favorite type of movie? Please circle one.
   Action
   Animation
   Comedy
   Documentary
   Drama
   Horror
   Musical
   Mystery
   Science Fiction/Fantasy
2. What is your favorite movie or movie series?
   ____

Activity

Imagine Holly is asking your class to fill out this survey.

Step 1 Take Holly Wood's survey.

Step 2 Collect and tabulate the results on the board as a class.

Step 3 Decide which movie or movie series your class would choose based on the survey.

Step 4 Do you think this is a good survey for determining which movie would make the most people happy on movie night? What would you do, if anything, to improve Holly Wood's survey?

Conducting the Survey and Tabulating the Results

Holly gives one questionnaire to each student. In examining the responses, Holly was surprised by how many different answers she saw for Question 2. She decided to create a category called "Other" where she placed all favorite movies that were listed by fewer than three students. Her tallies are on the following page.

1. What's your favorite type of movie? Please circle one.
   - Action 卌 卌 卌 卌 卌 卌
   - Animation 卌 卌 ||
   - Comedy 卌 卌 卌
   - Documentary ||
   - Drama 卌 |||
   - Horror 卌 |
   - Musical |||
   - Mystery 卌 ||
   - Science Fiction/Fantasy 卌 卌 卌 卌 卌 卌 卌

2. What's your favorite movie or movie series?
   - Harry Potter 卌 卌 卌 卌 ||||
   - Shrek 卌 卌 |||
   - Pirates of the Caribbean 卌 卌
   - X-Men 卌
   - Spiderman 卌 ||||
   - Star Wars 卌 卌 卌 卌
   - Napoleon Dynamite 卌 |||
   - Other 卌 卌 卌 卌 卌 ||||

QY1

There are 121 sixth grade students at Holly's School. Did Holly get a response from all the students?

Displaying the Results

You have seen several types of displays in this book: tables, bar graphs, histograms, line graphs, circle graphs, and stem-and-leaf plots. Holly needs to decide on the best type of display for her two sets of data.

QY2

a. What display would you use for the data from Question 1? Why?

b. What display would you use for the data from Question 2? Why?

Holly decides on a bar graph for Question 1 and a circle graph for Question 2. She uses a spreadsheet to construct her graphs.

	A	B
1	Favorite Type of Movie	
2	Action	30
3	Animation	12
4	Comedy	15
5	Documentary	2
6	Drama	8
7	Horror	6
8	Musical	3
9	Mystery	7
10	Science Fiction/Fantasy	35

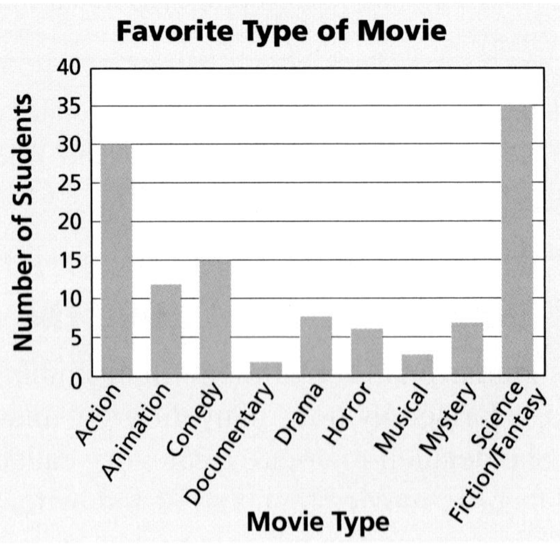

	A	B
1	Favorite Movie or Movie Series	
2	Harry Potter	24
3	Shrek	13
4	Pirates of the Caribbean	10
5	X-Men	5
6	Spiderman	9
7	Star Wars	20
8	Napoleon Dynamite	8
9	Other	29

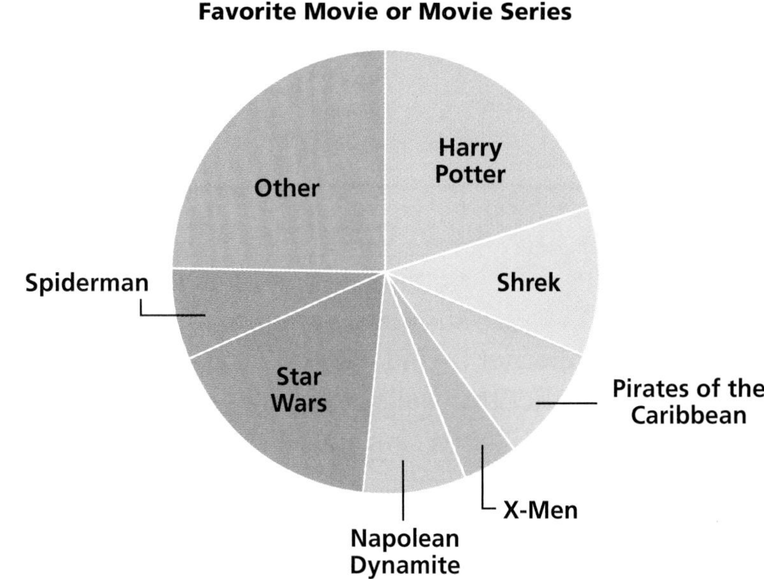

Drawing Conclusions

Based on her survey results, Holly Wood concluded that the most popular movie or movie series was Harry Potter. She noted that this choice was consistent with the movie category preferences assessed in Question 1. Since the most popular movie category was Science Fiction/Fantasy and Harry Potter can be classified as Fantasy, Holly decided to select a Harry Potter film for the sixth-grade movie night.

If she were to do this survey again, Holly decided she would try to make sure everyone's vote counted because the preferences of those in the "Other" category were ignored, and the "Other" category was the largest. She determined that she could use her initial survey as a preliminary survey and then give another survey that limits the movie choices to the seven most popular films generated from Question 2 of the first survey. That way, those in the "Other" category of the first survey could have a voice in the final decision.

Finally, Holly wondered whether a person's favorite movie was also the movie that person wished to see on movie night. She thought it might help if she was clear about the purpose of the survey so that students would know how their responses would be used.

Question

APPLYING THE MATHEMATICS

Choose a topic other than favorite movie, and complete your own survey. Use the four steps described in this lesson: design the survey, conduct the survey and tabulate the results, display the results, and draw conclusions. Present your survey and results in a report or on a poster. Include an evaluation of your work. Did you like your topic? Were your questions good? Were you able to draw a conclusion? If you were to repeat your survey, what would you do the same and what would you do differently?

QY ANSWERS

1. No; she has 118 responses, so 3 students did not participate.

2a. Answers vary. Sample: a bar graph because it shows categories and is easy to compare frequencies.

2b. Answers may vary. Sample: a circle graph because it shows size compared to the whole.

Chapter 13 Projects

1 What is Allowed in Origami?

There are six allowable folds in origami. Three of the folds are shown in Lesson 13-1. Use the internet to find a source that discusses the other three allowable folds. Describe them with diagrams and by folding paper.

2 Unit Origami

Research *unit origami* and how to make a single unit. You might find this information on the internet or in a book by Tomoko Fuse. Use six units to make a cube. Then make one other 3-dimensional shape of your choice.

Tomoko Fuse is a master of unit origami.

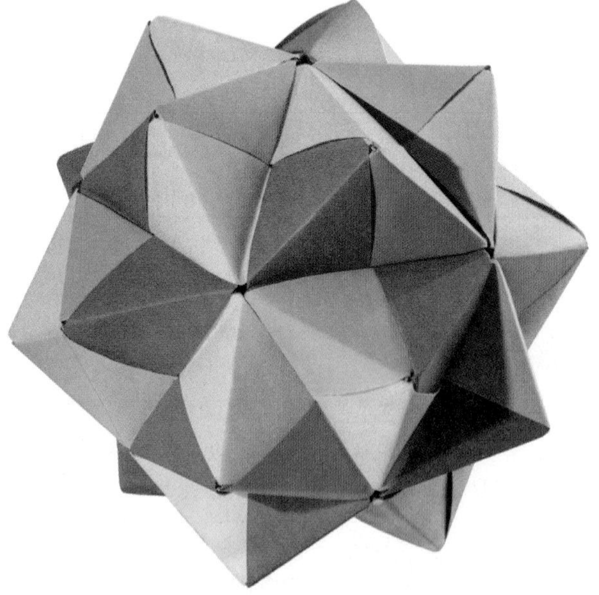

Unit origami

3 A Survey of Electricity

Pick 10 light bulbs in different locations in your home. Estimate how many hours each week each bulb is on. Then estimate how many hours each week each bulb is actually used. Describe how each bulb is used and how you made your estimates. Compare the two sets of numbers in some way and estimate how much electricity might be saved if people always turned off lights when they were not in use.

4 Population Changes

Obtain population information from the last two censuses for at least 10 towns and communities in your geographic area. Make a double bar graph to display your data. Identify the places that have had the greatest percent of growth and the least percent of growth. Identify the places whose populations have grown by the greatest amount and those whose populations have declined the most (or grown the least).

In recent years, Phoenix, Arizona has experienced significant growth in its population.

5 Advertising Choices

Companies who advertise on television carefully consider the types of shows on which their commercials appear. Pick a daily half-hour children's show and a daily half-hour news program. Watch both every day for one week. Record the number of commercials that occur during the half-hour time slot of each program. Record the products that are advertised each day and classify them into one of eight categories: junk food, other food, children's toys, automobiles, medicines, clothing, household products, or other. At the end of the week, calculate the percent of commercials in each category for each of the two programs. Construct a double bar graph to show the results. Describe the similarities and differences in the data for the two programs. Do the differences make sense? Explain your answers.

Times Square in New York City is a prime target for advertisers because of the significant amount of pedestrians that pass through it every day.

Chapter 13 Summary and Vocabulary

- Two sources of data are experiments and surveys. In both experiments and surveys, it is useful to compare data from one place with data from another. Data can be compared statistically by calculating means, medians, and ranges. Data can be visually compared in double bar graphs, double histograms, or multiple line graphs.

- A person doing an experiment usually has some goal in mind. To see if that goal is reached, data are collected. In this chapter, a jumping frog was created by folding a single sheet of paper. The same frog will jump different heights and distances. Gathering data on many frogs gives a clearer picture of how high and how far a typical origami frog jumps and whether a particular frog is typical or unusual.

- Origami is the process of making a figure out of a single sheet of paper by folding and without cutting or pasting. Several origami techniques were used in this chapter. The folds used include the line through two points, the perpendicular bisector of a segment, and the bisector of an angle. From even these simple folds, a wide variety of figures, including boats, birds, frogs, dinosaurs, and geometric shapes, can be constructed.

- **Surveys** involve questions that are asked to learn about a topic of interest. The largest survey in the United States is the Census which is conducted every 10 years. The U.S. Constitution requires each census to determine the population of every place in the United States. Also collected from each person is other information, such as age and racial background. More detailed information is collected from a sample of the population. Census information is used by the government to determine how many representatives a state has in Congress and how much government money should be given to communities for various projects.

- Survey items need to be carefully written. Items need to use words that are clearly understood. They should not lead a person to a particular response. They should be as short as possible. If there are choices, the choices should not overlap and should include all the most likely responses. When conducting a survey, you need to pay careful attention to its four steps: designing the survey, collecting the data, displaying the results, and drawing conclusions. It is important to keep in mind that the results of a survey can only be as good as the questions that are asked.

Vocabulary

13-3
distribution
double histogram

13-4
census
survey

13-5
open-ended item

Chapter 13 Self-Test

Take this test as you would take a test in class. You will need rectangular paper, graph paper, and calculator. Then use the Selected Answers section in the back of the book to check your work.

1. The table below shows the approval ratings of nine presidents at the ends of their presidencies and the results of the following election. The political party of Democrat (D) or Republican (R) is indicated in parentheses.

End-of-Presidency Job Approval Ratings

President	Rating (%)	Following Election Results
Dwight Eisenhower (2 terms, R, 1961)	59	Kennedy (D) defeats Nixon (R)
John F. Kennedy (partial term, D, 1963)	63	VP Johnson (D) defeats Goldwater (R)
Lyndon Johnson (1+ terms, D, 1969)	49	Nixon (R) defeats Humphrey (D)
Richard Nixon (partial term, R, 1974)	24	Carter (D) defeats VP Ford (R)
Gerald Ford (partial term, R, 1977)	53	Carter (D) defeats Ford (R)
Jimmy Carter (1 term, D, 1981)	34	Reagan (R) defeats Carter (D)
Ronald Reagan (2 terms, R, 1989)	64	VP Bush (R) defeats Dukakis (D)
George Bush (1 term, R, 1993)	56	Clinton (D) defeats Bush (R)
Bill Clinton (2 terms, D, 2001)	65	VP Gore (D) wins popular vote, but Bush (R) wins electoral college vote

a. Create a bar graph from these data. If the next president elected is of a different political party, shade the bar.

b. What trends do you notice in your graph? Explain why you think these trends exist.

(continued on next page)

2. Follow the steps to create a paper airplane.

Step 1 Fold the longer side of a rectangular sheet of paper onto the opposite side of the rectangle and then unfold it.

Step 2 Fold the two endpoints of a shorter side to meet at the same point on the first fold. This will create a pentagon shape.

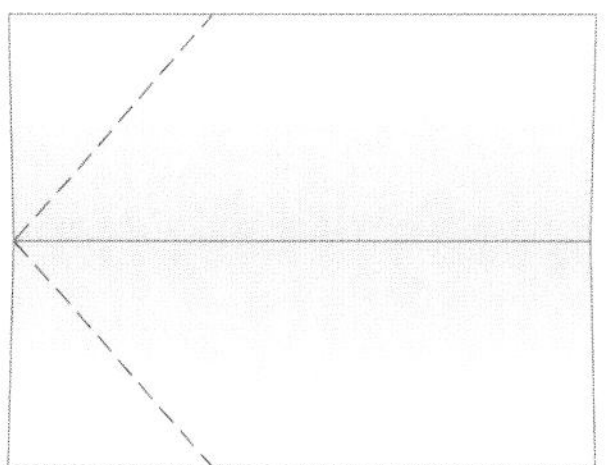

Step 3 Turn the paper over, and fold the top of the pentagon back about $\frac{1}{2}''$ below the triangular portion.

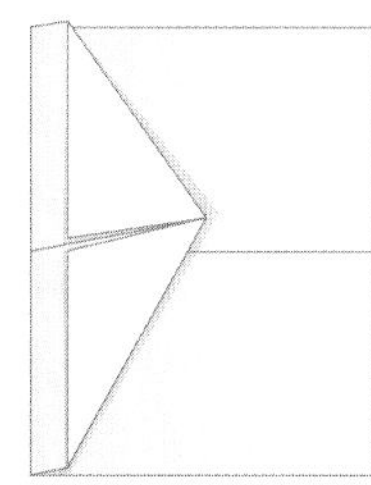

Step 4 Fold down the top endpoints of the shorter side to meet at the center fold, creating another pentagon.

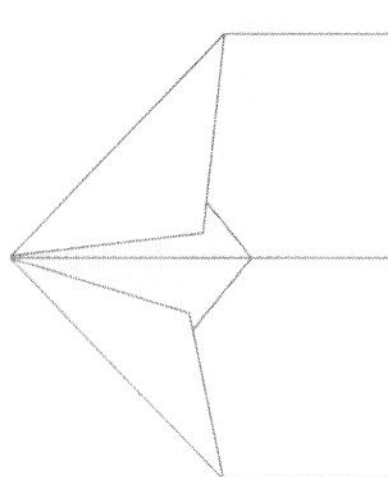

Step 5 Fold the small triangle over so it is pointing in the same direction as the larger triangle.

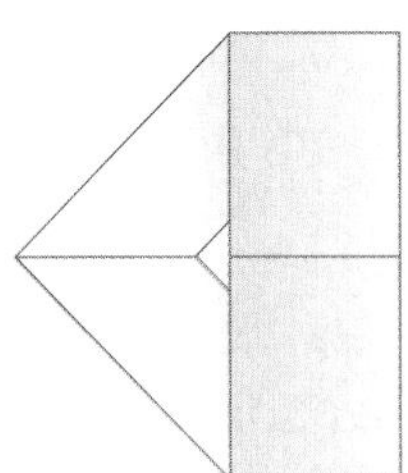

Step 6 Fold the figure in half so that all of the previous folds are on the outside of the plane.

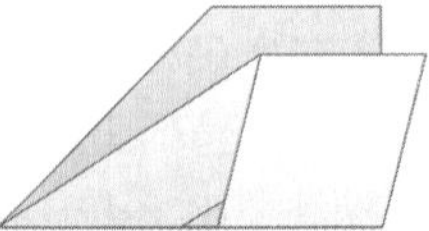

Step 7 Fold down the wings and align them with the base. Your airplane is ready.

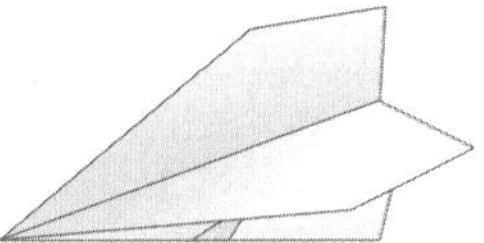

In 3 and 4, use the following: From 1990 to 2001, Greg Maddux, a Major League Baseball pitcher, allowed the following number of earned runs per nine innings each season: 3.35, 2.18, 2.36, 1.56, 1.63, 2.72, 2.20, 2.22, 3.57, 3.00, and 3.05.

3. What is the median of this data set?
4. What is the mean of this data set?
5. Two lines on a sheet of paper intersect at a 40° angle. Describe how to make a fold that creates a 70° angle.
6. Explain what is wrong with the following survey question and rewrite it to make it better: *Which is your favorite color in the world—purple or blue?*
7. In 2006, based on the race and ethnicity graph on page 745, what percent of people were classified as "other"?

In 8 and 9, use the following table, which lists the highest and lowest temperatures recorded in the 14 U.S. states that border the Atlantic Ocean.

State	Low (°F)	High (°F)
Connecticut	−32	106
Delaware	−17	110
Florida	−2	109
Georgia	−17	112
Maine	−48	105
Maryland	−40	109
Massachusetts	−35	107
New Hampshire	−47	106
New Jersey	−34	110
New York	−52	108
North Carolina	−34	110
Rhode Island	−25	104
South Carolina	−19	111
Virginia	−30	110

8. Create a double bar graph of the data, with the low temperatures on the left and a scale of 0°F to −60°F. Put the high temperatures on the right with a scale of 100°F to 120°F. Place the names of the states alphabetically down the middle of the chart.
9. Which state(s) has the greatest range of temperatures?

In 10 and 11, use the table below, which gives the amount earned by the leading money-winner on the men's and women's Professional Golf Association tours from 1995 through 2005.

Year	Women	Men
1997	$1.2 million	$2.1 million
1998	$1.1 million	$2.6 million
1999	$1.6 million	$6.6 million
2000	$1.9 million	$9.2 million
2001	$2.1 million	$5.7 million
2002	$2.9 million	$6.9 million
2003	$2.0 million	$7.6 million
2004	$2.5 million	$10.9 million
2005	$2.6 million	$10.6 million
2006	$2.6 million	$9.9 million
2007	$4.4 million	$10.9 million

10. a. Create a double line graph of these data. Remember to label the axes and give a title for your graph.

b. What trends do you notice in this graph?

11. How much money would you expect the leading men's and women's money-winner to make in 2015?

In 12 and 13, use the population data on page 743.

12. What was the percent of change in population for the state of New York from 1990 to 2000?

13. Find the state with the least amount of change in population from 1790 to 1990.

Chapter 13 Chapter Review

SKILLS
PROPERTIES
USES
REPRESENTATIONS

SKILLS Procedures used to get answers

OBJECTIVE A From data, compare means, medians, ranges, and distributions. (Lessons 13-2, 13-3)

In 1–4 use these data from the National Basketball Association.

City	Wins (2006–2007)	Losses (2006–2007)	Championships (1982–2006)	City Population in millions (2000)
Philadelphia	35	47	1	1.5
Chicago	49	33	6	2.8
Los Angeles	42	40	7	3.8
New York	33	49	0	8.1
Boston	24	58	2	0.6
Houston	52	30	2	2.0
Seattle	31	51	0	0.6
Miami	44	38	1	0.4
San Antonio	58	24	3	1.3
Detroit	53	29	3	0.9

1. Identify the team with the greatest number of wins and the team with the greatest number of losses.
2. What is the median number of championships for the teams on this list?
3. Describe the distribution of the number of championships.
4. What is the range of city populations on this list?

In 5–8, use the table below and decide whether the statement is definitely true, somewhat true, or not true. Defend your answer.

Animal	Adult Weight	Adult Length	Weight at Birth
Cheetah	143 lb	4.4'	10 oz
Giant Panda	330 lb	5'	4 oz
Chimpanzees	120 lb	3'	4 lb
Elephant	15,000 lb	13'	330 lb
Hyena	121 lb	3.9'	25 oz

5. Animals that weigh more at birth also weigh more as adults.
6. Animals that weigh less at birth are not as long as adults.
7. Adult animals that are longer also weigh more.
8. The ratio of weights of animals at birth has a wider range than the ratios of weights of adult animals.

OBJECTIVE B Given steps with diagrams, create a figure by paper-folding. (Lessons 13-1, 13-2)

9. Carefully follow the steps below to build a cube out of a square sheet of paper.

Step 1 Fold back and forth along both diagonals, and then fold back and forth along a line through midpoints of opposite sides.

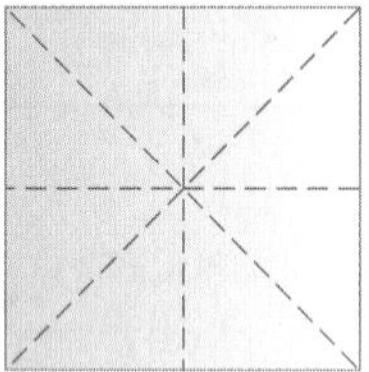

Step 2 Collapse by pressing in as shown at the left, resulting in the diagram at the right.

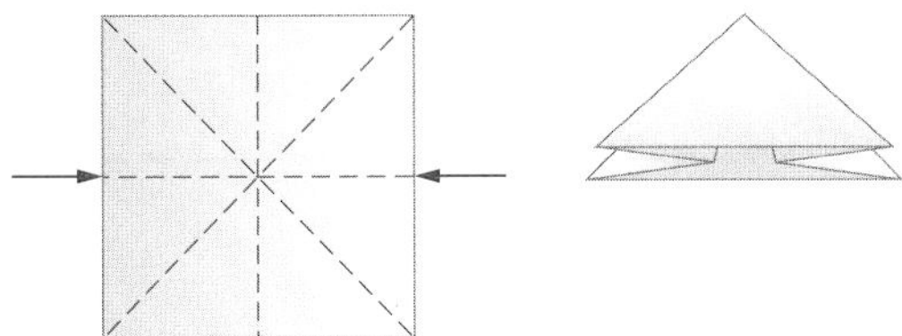

Step 3 Fold the top layer upward on the dotted lines as shown at the left, resulting in the diagram at the right.

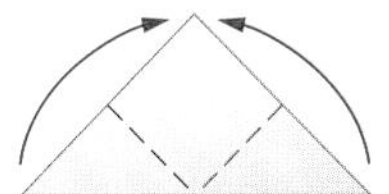
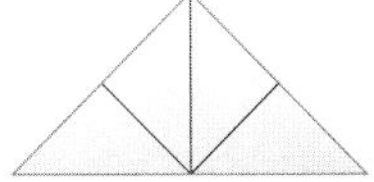

Step 4 Fold over the dotted lines as shown at the left to get the figure at the right.

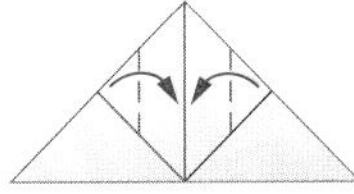
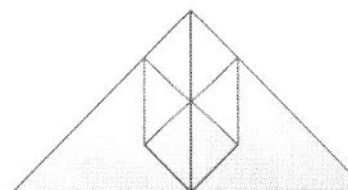

Step 5 Fold the two small triangles down (top layer only) on the dotted line as shown.

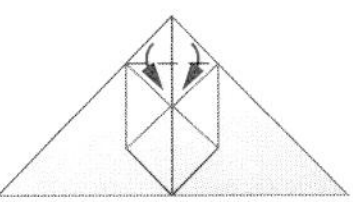

Step 6 Fold and unfold to create a crease. Stick each small corner at the top into the triangle pockets on each side to end up with the figure at the far right. (This move requires a little maneuvering.)

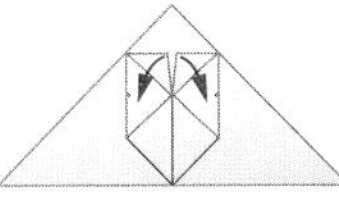
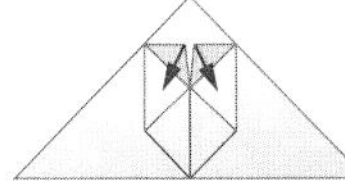
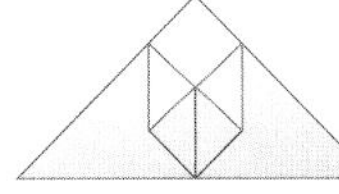

Step 7 Turn the whole triangle over and repeat Steps 3–6 on this side. You should be left with a figure like the one at the right.

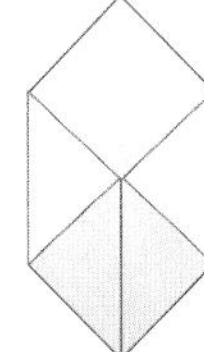

Step 8 Fold and unfold along the dotted lines to make creases. Blow into the hole at the bottom. The cube should unfold in your hands!

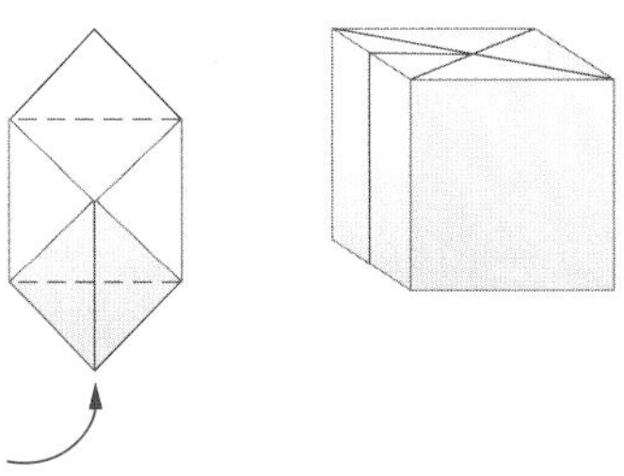

10. **a.** Copy points P and T below.

b. Fold along $\overline{PT}$

c. Fold along the perpendicular bisector of $\overline{PT}$.

d. Describe how to make a 45° angle using only folds.

PROPERTIES The principles behind the mathematics

OBJECTIVE C Relate simple paper folds to geometric figures. (Lesson 13-1)

11. **Multiple Choice** Which of the following is *not possible* by folding paper in one step?

A Given two points, you can make a fold on the perpendicular bisector of the segment connecting the two points.

B Given two intersecting lines, you can make a fold on a line parallel to one of the given lines.

C Given two points, you can make a fold on the line containing the two points.

D Given two intersecting lines, you can make a fold on the bisector of an angle formed by the lines.

12. Explain how to make a fold on the perpendicular bisector of a segment $\overline{AB}$.

13. Given two parallel lines, where is the fold when one line is placed on top of the other?

14. Suppose ℓ and m are parallel lines. Explain how to make a fold on the line that is three times closer to line m than line ℓ. You may make more than one fold, but you may not use a ruler. Fold ℓ on top of m. Then fold that fold on top of m.

USES Applications of mathematics in real-world situations

OBJECTIVE D Be able to identify strengths and weaknesses in opinion-survey questions. (Lesson 13-5)

In 15–18, explain what is wrong with the given survey question. Then rewrite the question to make it better.

15. Why are the New York Yankees the best baseball team ever?

16. What is your favorite time of day?

17. **Multiple Choice** From this list, what is your favorite animal?

A monkey B ape

C chimpanzee D tiger

18. How many people are in your school?

OBJECTIVE E Make observations from census and other large-survey data. (Lesson 13-4)

In 19–22, refer to the data on pages 743 and 744.

19. In what year was the first U.S. Census held?

20. Which state was the most populous according to the 1790 Census?

21. How much has the population of Pennsylvania increased from 1790 to 2000?

22. Which states moved up in population rank from 1790 to 2000?

In 23–26, use the graph below.

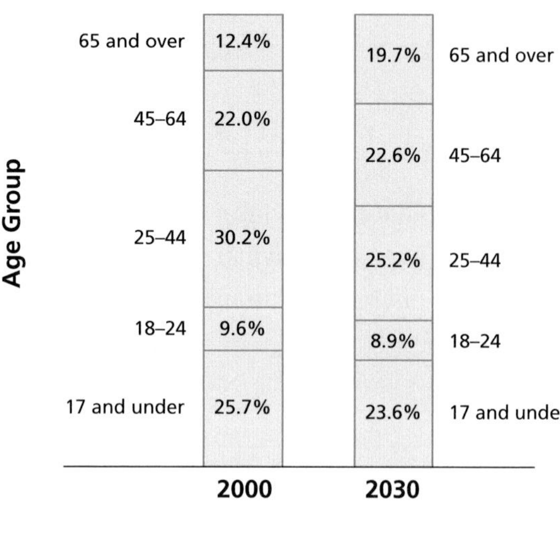

23. In 2000, which age group had the greatest percent of the population?

24. Which age group has the smallest range?

25. Which age group is projected to have the greatest increase in percent by 2030?

26. How might the 2030 data have been predicted?

REPRESENTATIONS Pictures, graphs, or objects that illustrate concepts

OBJECTIVE F Create and interpret a double bar graph or double histogram. (Lesson 13-3)

27. a. Using the data from Questions 1–4, create a double bar graph of the data for each team, with wins on the right and losses on the left.

b. What do you notice about the double bar graphs for each team? Explain why this is so.

28. Do you notice any relationship between the size of a city and the number of wins or losses its basketball team has? What do you conclude from this?

29. What can you conclude about the relationship between the number of championships a team has won over the past 25 years and its record for the 2006–2007 season?

OBJECTIVE G Create and interpret a line graph with multiple lines. (Lesson 13-3)

In 30-34, use the data below showing the average daily minimum temperature in degrees Celsius for Minneapolis, Minnesota, and Ushuaia, Argentina, the southernmost city in the world.

Month	Minneapolis	Ushuaia
Jan	−16.2	5.7
Feb	−12.7	5.2
Mar	−5.2	3.5
Apr	2.3	2.1
May	8.7	0.1
Jun	14.2	−1.3
Jul	17.3	−1.4
Aug	15.7	−1.0
Sep	10.2	0.5
Oct	3.8	2.3
Nov	−3.8	3.9
Dec	−12.1	4.9

Source: National Weather Service

30. Make a double line graph of this data, with the month on the horizontal axis.
31. What is the warmest month in Ushuaia?
32. During which months is the average daily minimum temperature lower in Ushuaia?
33. During which month are the average daily minimum temperatures of the two cities the farthest apart?
34. From these data alone, which city would you say has a warmer climate? Explain your answer.

OBJECTIVE H Create bar, line, and circle graphs from survey data or experimental data. (Lessons 13-2, 13-6)

In 35 and 36, a survey was conducted of 8,500 people who had uninstalled their web browsers. The reasons given were (number of respondents in parentheses): Temporary, will reinstall browser soon (2520); some web pages wouldn't work (1320); some features didn't work (1310); delayed performance (1260); incompatibility (770); missing features (540); poor security (360); hard to use (300); printing errors (120).

35. a. Create a bar graph of these data, with the percent for each response on the vertical axis.
    b. Why should the percents on your bar graph add to 100%?
36. For what percent of the respondents was the removal of the browser *not* temporary?

37. Create a circle graph of the data in Questions 35 and 36, replacing the frequencies by relative frequencies written as percents.

In 38–41, use this data which shows one archer's results in a contest. On an archery target, there are 10 scoring areas, with the closest to center (area 1) worth 10 points, and the farthest from center (area 10) worth 1 point.

Scoring Area	Number of Hits
10	7
9	12
8	6
7	8
6	5
5	0
4	3
3	4
2	2
1	1

38. a. Create a circle graph of the data.
    b. How many sectors are in your graph? Explain why there are not 10.
39. a. Create a line graph of these data, with the scoring area on the horizontal axis.
    b. Describe any trends you notice in this graph. Does the archer seem to hit some areas more than others?
40. How many of the arrows hit the target?
41. What is the total score for the archer, based on these data?

A Guide to Games

Games

Throughout the year, you will play games that help you practice important math skills in a way that is different and enjoyable. We hope that you will play often and have fun!

In this Appendix, you will find the directions for each game. The numbers in most games are generated randomly, so that the games can be played over and over without repeating the same problems.

Many students have created their own variations to these games to make them more interesting. We encourage you to do this too.

Materials

You will need a deck of number cards for many of the games. You can use the red UCSMP Math Deck, a deck of regular playing cards, or make your own deck out of index cards.

A UCSMP Math Deck includes 54 cards. There are four cards each for the numbers 0–12, and there are two WILD cards.

You can also use a deck of regular playing cards after making a few changes. A deck of playing cards includes 54 cards (52 regular cards, plus 2 jokers). To create a deck of number cards, use a permanent marker to mark the cards in the following ways:

- Mark each of the four aces with the number 1.
- Mark each of the four jacks with the number 11.
- Mark each of the four queens with the number 12.
- Mark each of the four kings with the number 0.
- Mark each of the two jokers as WILD cards.

For some games, you will have to make a gameboard, a score sheet, or a set of cards that are not number cards. The instructions for doing these things are included with the game directions. More complicated gameboards and card decks are available from your teacher.

Number Top-It

Materials	Place-Value Mat (Game Master 1, p. GM2) or Decimal Place-Value Mat (Game Master 2, p. GM3)
	number cards 0–9
Players	2 to 5
Skill	Practicing place value for whole numbers
Objective	To make the largest seven-digit number

millions	hundred-thousands	ten-thousands	thousands	hundreds	tens	ones

Place-Value Mat

Advance Preparation

Assemble the Place-Value Mat. Each player should cut the master along the dotted line, fold one piece along its fold line, and align the crease with the fold line on the other piece. Then tape the two pieces together.

Directions

1. Shuffle the cards and place them number-side down on the table.
2. Each round, players take seven turns. Each turn, a player takes the top card from the deck and places it number-side down on any empty slot on his or her mat. Players may look at the cards before placing them, but should not show them to their opponent(s).
3. After each round, players flip their cards over and compare their numbers. The player with the smallest number earns 1 point; the player with the next smallest number earns 2 points; and so on. Record each player's score on a piece of paper.
4. Play five rounds for a game. Shuffle the deck between each round. The player with the highest total number of points wins.

Example

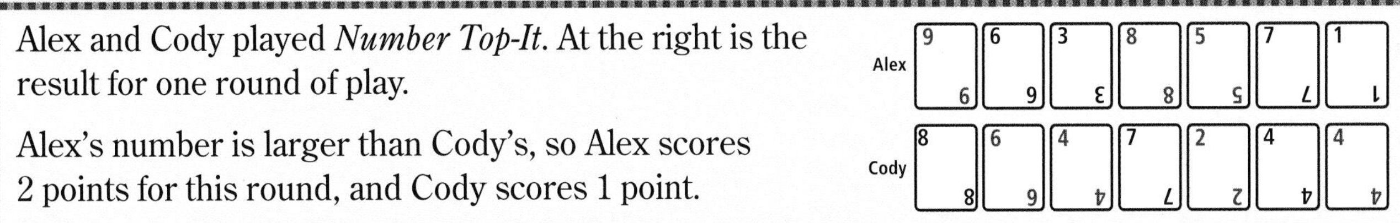

Alex and Cody played *Number Top-It.* At the right is the result for one round of play.

Alex's number is larger than Cody's, so Alex scores 2 points for this round, and Cody scores 1 point.

Decimal Variation

Play the game using the Decimal Place-Value Mat to practice reading and comparing decimal numbers.

Build-It: Positive Fractions
Build-It: Negative Fractions

Materials	*Build-It* Gameboards (Game Master 3, p. GM4)
	Build-It: Positive Fractions Cards (Game Master 4, p. GM5) or *Build-It: Negative Fractions* Cards (Game Master 5, p. GM6)
	calculator (optional)
Players	2
Skill	Comparing and ordering fractions
Objective	To be the first player to arrange five fraction cards in order from least to greatest

Build-It **Gameboard**

Directions

The directions for these two *Build-It* games are the same. Use the *Build-It: Positive Fractions* Cards to play *Build-It: Positive Fractions* and use the *Build-It: Negative Fractions* Cards to play *Build-It: Negative Fractions.*

1. Shuffle the fraction cards. Deal one card number-side down on each of the five spaces on the two *Build-It* gameboards in the order in which the cards are drawn.
2. Put the remaining cards number-side down for a draw pile.
3. Each player turns over the five cards on his or her gameboard. Players do not change the order of the cards at any time during the game.
4. Take turns. When it is your turn:
   - Take the top card from the draw pile or the top card from the discard pile (the player who goes first has to take a card from the draw pile because there will not yet be any cards in the discard pile).
   - Use the card to replace one of the five cards on your *Build-It* gameboard. Put the replaced card on a discard pile. Your turn is over.
5. If all the cards in the draw pile are used, shuffle the cards in the discard pile. Place them number-side down in a draw pile.
6. The winner is the first player to have all five cards on his or her gameboard in order from least to greatest. If players disagree about whether the fractions are in order, a calculator may be used to check.

***Build-It Positive Fractions* Cards**

***Build-It Negative Fractions* Cards**

Example 1

Valeria is playing *Build-It: Positive Fractions.* This is what her gameboard looks like:

She draws the $\frac{3}{4}$ card. She knows that $\frac{3}{4}$ is greater than $\frac{2}{3}$ but $\frac{1}{6}$ is not greater than $\frac{2}{3}$, so she uses the $\frac{3}{4}$ card to replace the $\frac{1}{6}$ card on her gameboard. She places the $\frac{1}{6}$ card on the discard pile and her turn is over.

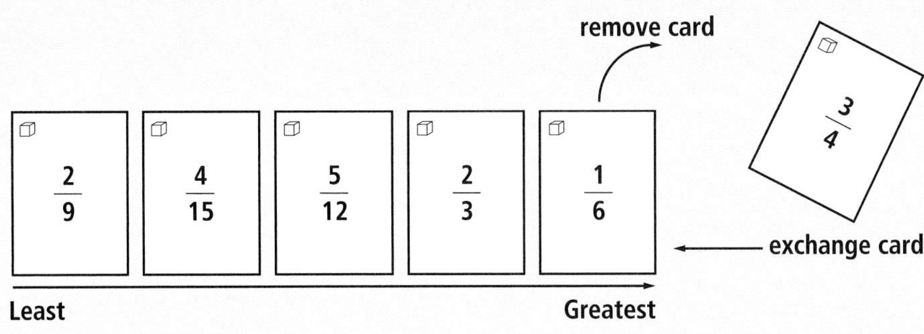

Example 2

Seamus is playing *Build-It: Negative Fractions.* This is what his gameboard looks like:

He draws the $-\frac{2}{5}$ card. He knows that $-\frac{2}{5}$ is greater than $-\frac{2}{3}$ but $-\frac{5}{6}$ is not greater than $-\frac{2}{3}$, so he uses the $-\frac{2}{5}$ card to replace the $-\frac{5}{6}$ card on his gameboard. He places the $-\frac{5}{6}$ card on the discard pile and his turn is over.

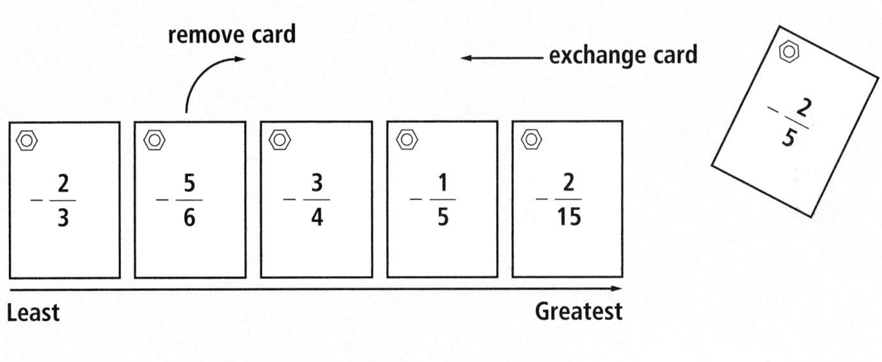

Tens-Tac-Toe

Materials	*Tens-Tac-Toe* Gameboard (Game Master 6, p. GM7)
	Times-Ten Cards (Game Master 7, p. GM8)
	Decimal Place-Value Mat (Game Master 2, p. GM3)
	number cards 0–9
	counters (two colors) or pennies
Players	2
Skill	Ordering decimals, estimating, multiplying by powers of 10
Objective	To cover three squares in a row by manipulating decimals and powers of ten

Advance Preparation

See *Number Top-It* on page G3 for directions on how to assemble the Decimal Place-Value Mat.

Decimal Place-Value Mat

thousands	,	hundreds	tens	ones	.	tenths	hundreths	thousandths

Directions

1. Shuffle the number cards and Times-Ten cards separately and set them number-side down in two different piles.
2. Take turns. When it is your turn:
   - Draw three number cards, and arrange them face-up on the Decimal Place-Value Mat. They must be placed consecutively and remain in the same order that you draw them, but you can choose which unit to begin with. Your first card may be in the tens place, the ones place, or the tenths place.
   - Flip over a Times-Ten card, and multiply the number on the Decimal Place-Value Mat by the number on the Times-Ten card. Move the cards on the mat to the right or to the left to show the product.
   - There are two WILD cards. If you draw a WILD card, you may perform any power-of-ten multiplication you like, as long as you are moving the cards within a range of three decimal places to the right or to the left.
   - After multiplying, your cards may be moved off the mat, so make sure you keep your place values straight.
   - Match the product to a square on the *Tens-Tac-Toe* gameboard, and place a counter of your color on the square. Your turn is over. If no match is found, your turn is over.

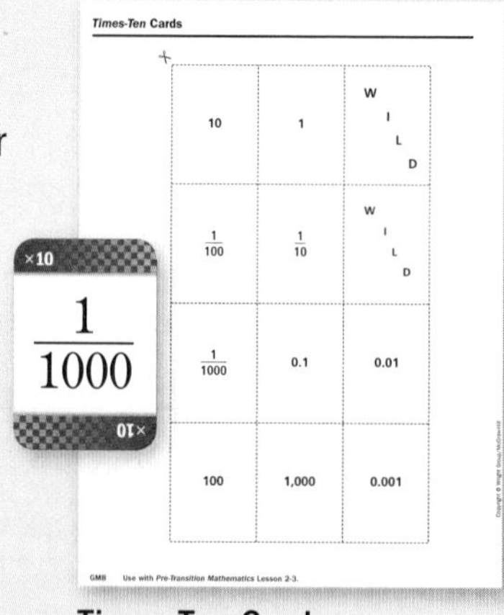

Times-Ten Cards

3. After each turn, place the number cards in one discard pile and the Times-Ten card in another discard pile. When all the number cards or all the Times-Ten cards have been drawn, shuffle the corresponding discard pile and turn it number-side down to form a draw pile.

4. The first player to cover three squares in a row in any direction (horizontally, vertically, or diagonally) is the winner of the game.

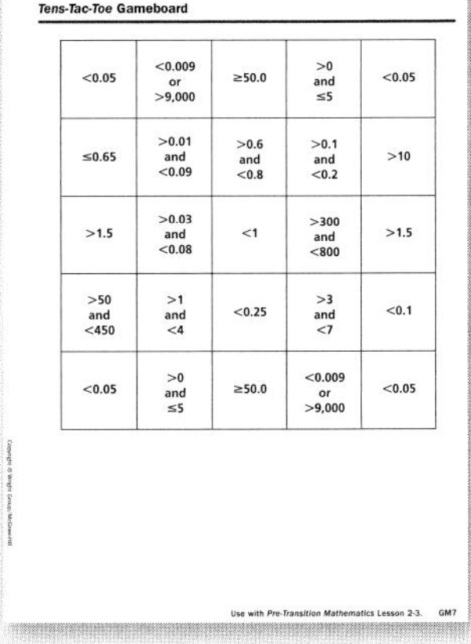

Tens-Tac-Toe Gameboard

<0.05	<0.009 or >9,000	≥50.0	>0 and ≤5	<0.05
≤0.65	>0.01 and <0.09	>0.6 and <0.8	>0.1 and <0.2	>10
>1.5	>0.03 and <0.08	<1	>300 and <800	>1.5
>50 and <450	>1 and <4	<0.25	>3 and <7	<0.1
<0.05	>0 and ≤5	≥50.0	<0.009 or >9,000	<0.05

Use with Pre-Transition Mathematics Lesson 2-3. GM7

Tens-Tac-Toe Gameboard

Example

Cedric is playing *Tens-Tac-Toe*. He draws a 6, a 4, and a 2 from the number card pile. He chooses to start at the ones place and forms 6.42 on the Decimal Place-Value Mat.

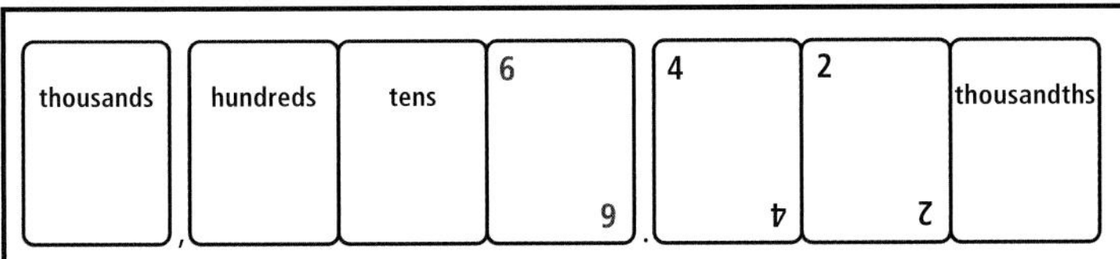

Then he draws the $\frac{1}{100}$ card from the Times-Ten pile, so he moves his number cards two slots to the right on the Decimal Place-Value Mat to form 0.0642. (*Note:* The number 2 has moved off the mat.)

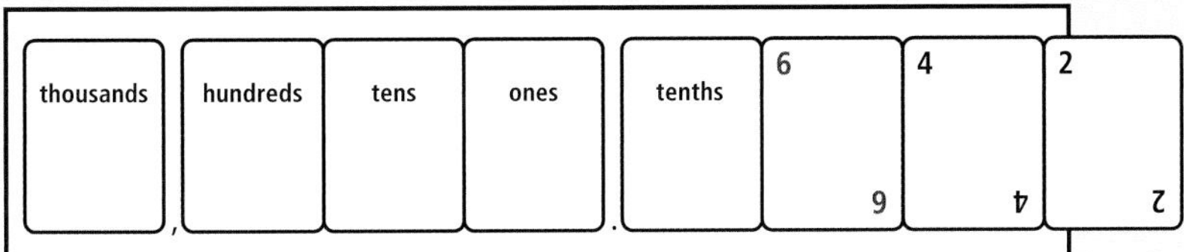

He covers the "> 0.03 and < 0.08" square on the gameboard, discards his cards, and his turn is over.

Frac-Tac-Toe

Materials	*Frac-Tac-Toe* Gameboard (Game Master 8, p. GM9)
	Frac-Tac-Toe Number-Card Board (Game Master 9, p. GM10)
	number cards 0–10
	counters (two colors) or pennies
	calculator (optional)
Players	2
Skill	Finding fraction and decimal equivalents
Objective	To cover three squares in a row by recognizing fraction-decimal equivalents

Numerator Pile
Place cards number-side down.
When all cards are used, shuffle and replace.

Numerator Pile
Place cards number-side up.

Denominator Pile
Place cards number-side down.
When all cards are used, just replace. Do not shuffle!

Denominator Pile
Place cards number-side up.

Frac-Tac-Toe Number-Card Board

Advance Preparation

Separate the cards into two piles on the number-card board: a numerator pile and a denominator pile. Place two each of the 2, 3, 4, 5, 6, 8, and 10 cards in the denominator pile. All other cards are placed in the numerator pile.

Shuffle the cards in each pile. Place the piles number-side down in the left-hand spaces on the number-card board.

Directions

1. Take turns. When it is your turn:
   - Turn over the top card from each pile and place it on the right-hand space on the number-card board to form a fraction (numerator card above denominator card).
   - Try to match the fraction shown with one of the squares on the gameboard. If a match is found, cover that square with one of your counters, and your turn is over. If no match is found, your turn is over.
2. To change the fraction shown by the cards to a decimal, players may use either a calculator or the table of decimal equivalents for fractions on page 110.
3. When all the cards in the numerator pile have been used, reshuffle that pile, and place it number-side down on the left-hand space. When all the cards in the denominator pile have been used, turn the pile over and place it number-side down in the left-hand space without reshuffling it.
4. The first player to cover three squares in a row in any direction (horizontally, vertically, or diagonally) is the winner of the game.

Frac-Tac-Toe Gameboard

>1.0	2.0 or $0.\overline{2}$	>2.0	0 or 1	<1
0.1 or 0.9	0.2 or 0.125	0.25 or $0.\overline{3}$	0.3 or 0.375	0.4 or $1.\overline{6}$
≥ 1.5	0.5 or $0.1\overline{6}$	>2.5	0.5 or $0.8\overline{3}$	≥ 1.5
0.6 or $1.\overline{3}$	0.7 or 0.625	0.75 or $0.\overline{6}$	0.8 or 0.875	0.1 or 0.9
<1	0 or 1	>2	$0.\overline{3}$ or 1.125	>1.0

Use with *Pre-Transition Mathematics* Lesson 2-8. GM9

Frac-Tac-Toe Gameboard

Example 1

The cards show the fraction $\frac{4}{5}$, which is equivalent to the decimal 0.8. The player may cover the square labeled "0.8 or 0.875" or either of the squares labeled "< 1," unless those squares have all already been covered.

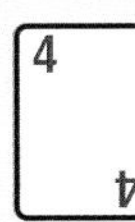

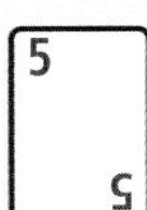

Example 2

The cards show the fraction $\frac{0}{5}$. The player may cover any one of the four squares labeled "0 or 1" or "< 1" that has not already been covered.

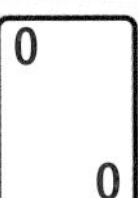

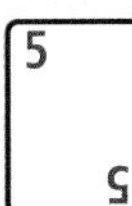

Example 3

The cards show the fraction $\frac{4}{2}$. The player may cover any one of the five squares labeled "> 1.0," "2.0 or $0.\overline{2}$," or "≥ 1.5" that has not already been covered. The player may not cover a square labeled "> 2.0" or "> 2" because $\frac{4}{2}$ is equal to but not greater than 2.

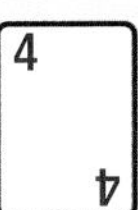

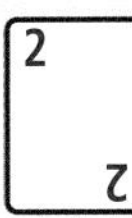

Match-It: Four-Way Conversion

Materials	*Match-It: Four-Way Conversion* Level 1 Cards (Game Master 10, p. GM11) or *Match-It: Four-Way Conversion* Level 2 Cards (Game Master 11, p. GM12)
Players	2
Skill	Converting between decimals, fractions, percents, and graphic representations
Objective	To collect the most sets of equal-valued cards

Directions

1. Shuffle the *Match-It: Four-Way Conversion* Level 1 Cards.
2. Place the cards face down on the table in a rectangular array in any order.
3. Take turns. When it is your turn:
   - Turn over two cards so that they are visible to both players.
   - If the cards "match," that is, if the two cards represent equal values, then take the two cards. Your turn is over.
   - If there is no match, turn the cards face down. Your turn is over.
4. Continue playing until all the cards have been matched.
5. Check all of your matches to see if you have collected any sets of four cards that all have the same value. For every set of four matching cards, you score 5 points. For each pair that is not part of a set of four, you score 2 points. Record your scores on a piece of paper. The player with more points wins.

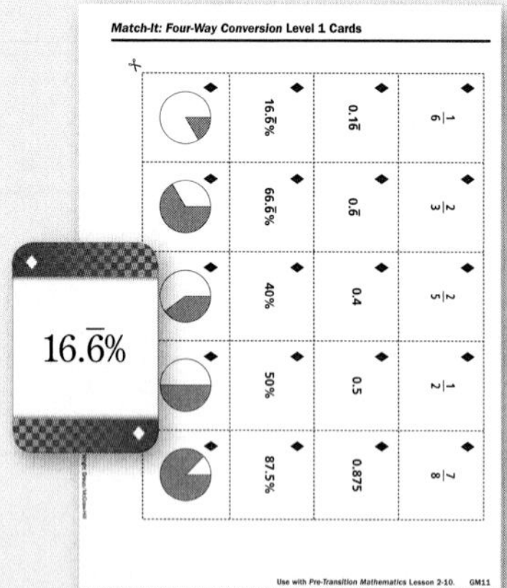

Match It: Four-Way Conversion Level 1 Cards

Example

Amy and Brenda played *Match-It: Four-Way Conversion.* Here are the cards each player collected and the points they earned.

Amy		Brenda	
Cards	Points	Cards	Points
$\frac{2}{3}$, $0.\overline{6}$	2	$66.\overline{6}\%$, [circle graph]	2
$0.1\overline{6}$, $16.\overline{6}\%$	2	[circle graph], $\frac{1}{2}$	2
0.875, [circle graph]	2	$\frac{7}{8}$, 87.5%	2
0.5, 50%	2	[circle graph], $\frac{1}{6}$	2
$\frac{2}{5}$, 0.4, 40%, [circle graph]	5		
Total	13	Total	8

Variation

Use the *Match-It: Four-Way Conversion* Level 2 Cards. These conversions will be more difficult.

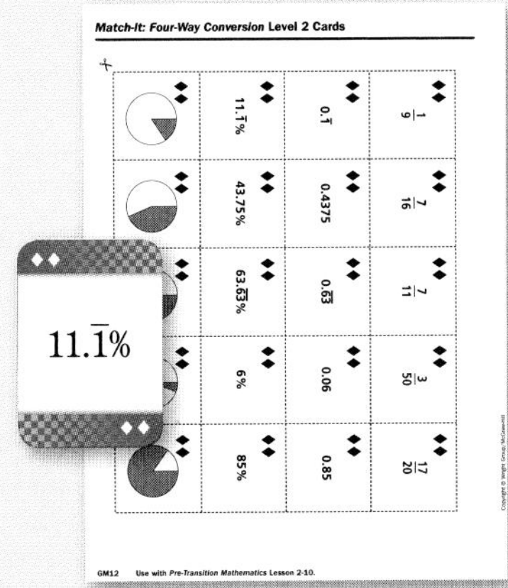

Match It: Four-Way Conversion Level 2 Cards

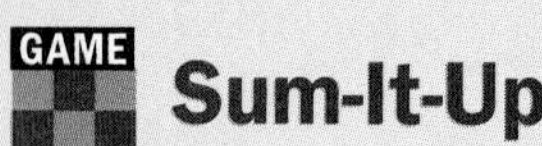

Sum-It-Up

Materials	*Sum-It-Up* Gameboard (Game Master 12, p. GM13)
Players	2
Skill	Adding integers
Objective	To get the highest number of points by adding lists of positive and negative integers

Directions

1. Player 1 uses the even numbers from 2 to 20 {2, 4, 6, 8, 10, 12, 14, 16, 18, 20}. Player 2 uses the opposites of these numbers {-2, -4, -6, -8, -10, -12, -14, -16, -18, -20}.
2. Player 1 begins the game. Players take turns writing one of their numbers in a cell in the 4-by-5 region of shaded cells in the center of the *Sum-It-Up* Gameboard. Once a player has written a number, it cannot be used again. Only one number can be written in each cell. Players continue to take turns until all the numbers are used and all the shaded cells are filled.

   Here is what a *Sum-It-Up* Gameboard might look like after this step:

						Total
	16	-16	18	-12	2	
	-2	6	-10	-14	-8	
	6	4	12	-20	8	
	-18	10	20	14	-4	
Total						

3. Player 1 fills in the column at the far right of the gameboard by adding the integers in each row. Player 2 fills in the bottom row by adding the integers in each column.
4. Players check each other's addition. The sum of the column totals and the sum of the row totals should both be 0.
5. Now look at each of the row and column totals. Player 1 scores a point for any positive total. Player 2 scores a point for any negative total. Neither player gets a point for a 0.
6. The player with more points wins. Try playing best 2 out of 3.

Angle Tangle

Materials	protractor
	straightedge
Players	2
Skill	Estimating and measuring angle sizes
Objective	To get the lowest number of points by estimating angle sizes accurately

Directions

1. Player 1 draws an angle on a sheet of paper with a straightedge.
2. Player 2 estimates the degree measure of the angle and records his or her estimate on a different sheet of paper.
3. Players agree on the measure of the angle by using a protractor. Player 2 records the actual measure next to his or her estimate.
4. Player 2 finds the positive difference between the actual measure and his or her estimate and records it. This difference is Player 2's score for the round.
5. Players trade roles and repeat Steps 1–4 to complete a round.
6. Players add their scores at the end of five rounds. The player with the lower total score wins.

Example

Ayana and Francisco played *Angle Tangle*. Here are their scores.

	Ayana			Francisco		
	Estimate	Actual	Score	Estimate	Actual	Score
Round 1	115°	109°	6	45°	38°	7
Round 2	75°	72°	3	12°	14°	2
Round 3	43°	38°	5	50°	50°	0
Round 4	25°	24°	1	26°	22°	4
Round 5	27°	30°	3	79°	81°	2
Total Score			18			15

Francisco has the lower total score, so he wins the game.

Scrambling: Fraction Addition

Materials	*Scrambling: Fraction Addition* Gameboard (Game Masters 13 and 14, pp. GM14 and GM15)
	number cards 1–12
	2 WILD cards
	calculator (optional)
Players	2 to 4 teams of 1 to 3 players
Skill	Adding fractions
Objective	To get the highest number of points by creating sums of fractions from a set of number cards

Advance Preparation

To assemble the gameboard, fold Game Master 13 along its fold line. Then align the crease along the fold line of Game Master 14 and tape the pages in place. The assembled gameboard should look like the picture at the right.

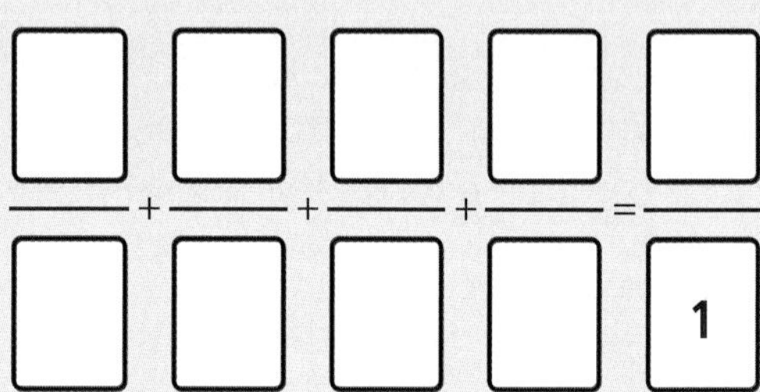

Scrambling: Fraction Addition Gameboard

Directions

1. Shuffle the cards, and deal ten cards facedown to each player or team.
2. Teams take turns. When it is your team's turn:
   - Place as many of your ten cards on the gameboard as you can to form a true number sentence involving the sum of at least two fractions. For the sum, you may use one card or two cards. If you use one card, it will represent a whole number. Place that card in the numerator space of the sum and leave the "1" in the denominator space showing. If you use two cards, they will represent a fraction. Cover the "1" with the card you are using as the denominator and place the numerator card in the space above it.
   - You earn one point for each card that you use correctly in a fraction. For the sum, if you only use one card to represent a whole number, you do not earn any points for that card. If you use two cards to represent a fraction for your final sum, you earn one point for each of those cards.
   - You must add at least two fractions in a round to score points. Equations showing equivalent fractions do not count. For example, you cannot use $\frac{2}{4} = \frac{3}{6}$ as your play for the round. If you are unable to find any sum, you get zero points for that round.

- You might not be able to use all of your cards in one round. The more cards you use correctly, the more points you earn, but you are not required to use all of your cards.
- There may be many possible correct combinations that can be played during a given round, but you may select only one combination for that round.

3. If you pick a WILD card, you can use it to represent any of the numbers 1–12, but you do not get a point for that card. If you use two WILD cards in one round, you must use both of them to represent the same number in that specific round. You may change the value of the WILD in other rounds.
4. You may use a calculator to find solutions and check answers.
5. After the first round, determine your score and record it on a sheet of paper. Place your cards on a discard pile. Play continues with the next player or team. The round is over when every player or team has had a turn. Reshuffle the number cards and deal again to start a new round.
6. The player or team with the most points at the end of three rounds wins.

Example

Mariko and Jeff are playing *Scrambling: Fraction Addition.* Mariko is dealt the cards 1, 2, 2, 3, 4, 5, 6, 6, 7, and 11. She uses her 1, 2, 3, 5, 6, and 6 cards to form $\frac{2}{3} + \frac{1}{6} = \frac{5}{6}$. She earns 6 points for that round.

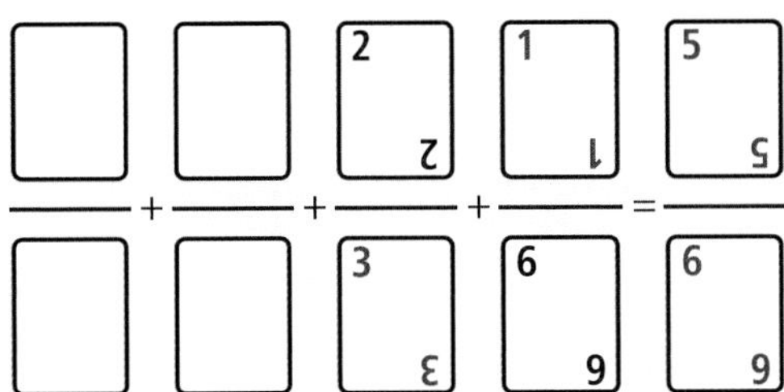

Jeff is dealt the cards 1, 2, 2, 2, 3, 3, 4, 5, 5, and 9. He uses his 1, 2, 2, 3, 3, 4, and 6 cards to form $\frac{2}{1} + \frac{2}{4} + \frac{3}{6} = 3$. He does not get a point for the whole-number sum, so he also earns 6 points for that round.

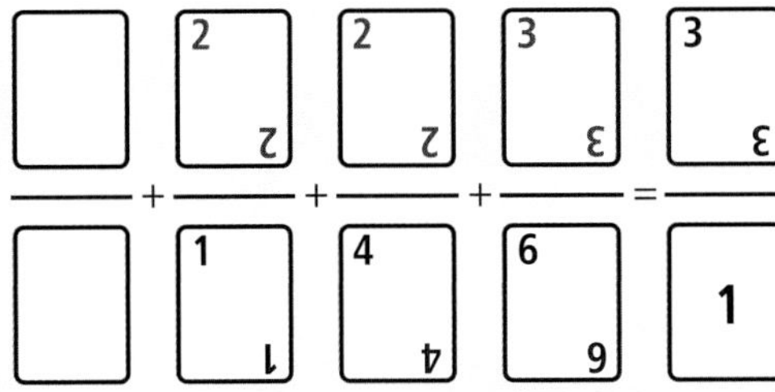

Top-It: Integer Subtraction

Materials	number cards 0–12
	calculator (optional)
Players	2 to 4
Skill	Subtracting integers
Objective	To collect the most cards

Directions

The color of each card tells if the number is positive or negative.

- Black cards (spades and clubs) are *positive numbers.*
- Red cards (hearts and diamonds) are *negative numbers.*

1. Shuffle the deck and place it number-side down.
2. Each player turns over two cards, one at a time, and subtracts the second number from the first number. The player with the largest answer takes all of the cards.
3. In case of a tie, each tied player turns over two more cards and finds the difference. The player with the largest answer takes all cards from both plays. Check answers with a calculator if needed.
4. The game ends when there are not enough cards left for each player to have another turn. The player with the most cards wins.

Example

Erica turns over a black 2 first, then a red 3.

$$+2 - (-3) = 5$$

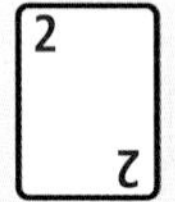

Deion turns over a red 5 first, then a black 8.

$$-5 - (+8) = -13$$

$$5 > -13$$

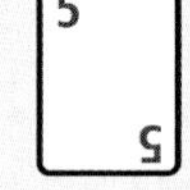

Erica takes all four cards because 5 is greater than -13.

Variation (Subtraction with Three Cards)

Each player turns over three cards, subtracts the second number from the first number, and then subtracts the third number from the result. The player with the largest final answer takes all the cards.

GAME X-Tac-Toe: $x + a = b$

Materials	*X-Tac-Toe* Gameboard (Game Master 15, p. GM16)
	X-Tac-Toe Number-Card Board (Game Master 16, p. GM17)
	number cards 1–10
	counters (two colors) or pennies
	calculator (optional)
Players	2
Skill	Solving equations of the form $x + a = b$
Objective	To cover three squares in a row in any direction (horizontally, vertically, or diagonally)

$x + a = b$

$x +$ [1st card drawn] $=$ [2nd card drawn]

X-Tac-Toe: x + a = b
Number-Card Board

Directions

Black cards (spades and clubs) are *positive numbers*. Red cards (hearts and diamonds) are *negative numbers.*

1. Shuffle the number cards and place the deck face down in a draw pile on the table.
2. Take turns. When it is your turn:
   - Draw two cards from the deck and place them face up on the Number-Card Board in the order they were drawn. The numbers on these cards are the values a and b, respectively, in $x + a = b$.
   - Solve the equation shown on the Number-Card Board.
   - Try to match the solution with an interval that contains it on the gameboard. If a match is found, cover that square with a counter. Your turn is over. If no match is found, your turn is over. Each square may be covered only once. Place the used cards into a discard pile.
   - If a player puts a counter on an incorrect square, the other player may place his or her color counter on a correct square. The counter on the incorrect square should then be removed.
3. When there are no cards left in the draw pile, shuffle the cards in the discard pile to make a new draw pile.
4. The first player to cover three squares in a row in any direction (horizontally, vertically, or diagonally) wins the game.

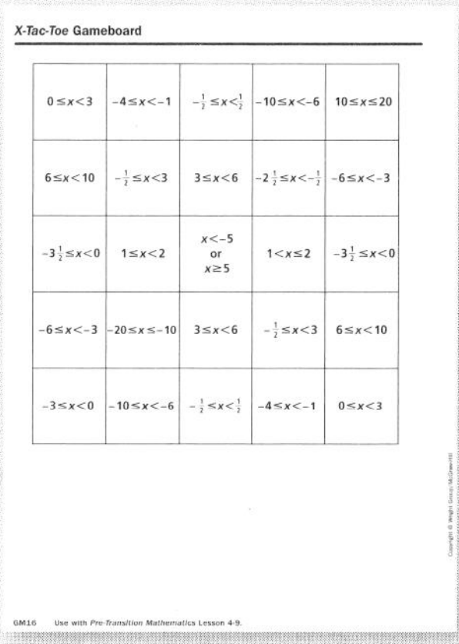

X-Tac-Toe Gameboard

$0 \le x < 3$	$-4 \le x < -1$	$-\frac{1}{2} \le x < \frac{1}{2}$	$-10 \le x < -6$	$10 \le x \le 20$
$6 \le x < 10$	$-\frac{1}{2} \le x < 3$	$3 \le x < 6$	$-2\frac{1}{2} \le x < -\frac{1}{2}$	$-6 \le x < -3$
$-3\frac{1}{2} \le x < 0$	$1 \le x < 2$	$x < -5$ or $x \ge 5$	$1 < x \le 2$	$-3\frac{1}{2} \le x < 0$
$-6 \le x < -3$	$-20 \le x \le -10$	$3 \le x < 6$	$-\frac{1}{2} \le x < 3$	$6 \le x < 10$
$-3 \le x < 0$	$-10 \le x < -6$	$-\frac{1}{2} \le x < \frac{1}{2}$	$-4 \le x < -1$	$0 \le x < 3$

X-Tac-Toe Gameboard

Example

Angelo turns over a red 5 and then a black 4. His equation is $x + -5 = 4$. He gets a solution of 9. He can place his counter on any one of the three squares labeled "$6 \le x < 10$" or "$x < -5$ or $x \ge 5$" that is not already covered.

Let's Data Deal

Materials	*Let's Data Deal* Cards (Game Master 17, p. GM18)
	Let's Data Deal Score Sheet (Game Master 18, p. GM19)
	number cards 0–12
Players	2 to 4
Skill	Finding the range, mode, median, and mean
Objective	To score the most points by finding data measures

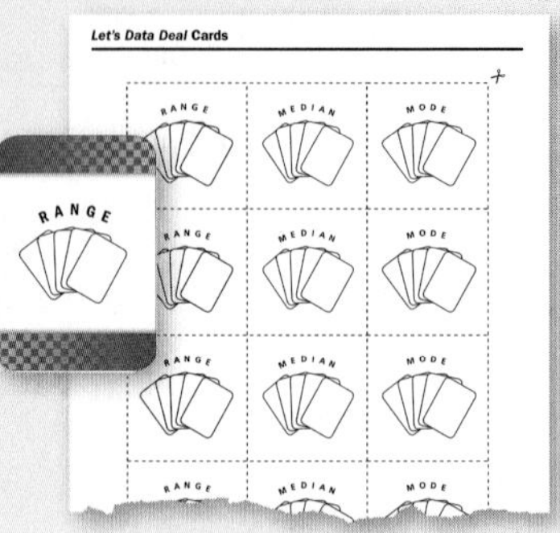

Let's Data Deal Cards

Directions

1. Shuffle the number cards and deal five to each player number-side down. Players order their cards from least to greatest without revealing them.
2. There are three ways a player may score points using their cards.

Example

- *Range*: The player's score is the range of the five numbers.

Tanisha's hand:

Range = 12 – 1 = 11

Points scored = 11

Example

- *Median:* The player's score is the median of the five numbers.

Kylie's hand:

Median = 9

Points scored = 9

Example

- *Mode:* The player must have at least two cards with the same number. The player's score is found by multiplying the mode of the five numbers by the number of modal cards. If there is more than one mode, the player uses the mode that will produce the most points.

Jerome's hand:

Mode = 8

Points scored = 2 • 8 = 16

3. Each player decides which data measure to use and calculates his or her score for the round. Players indicate their choices by placing one of the three *Let's Data Deal* Cards on the table.

4. Players lay down their cards and record their points on the score sheet.

5. **Bonus Points:** Each player calculates the *mean* of his or her card numbers to the nearest tenth, and records it on the second row of the score sheet. Each player's score for the round is the sum of their points scored, plus any bonus points.

6. Repeat Steps 1–5 for each round. The winner is the player with the most points after five rounds.

Let's Data Deal Score Sheet

Discard Variation

After Step 3, players may try to improve their scores by exchanging up to three cards for new cards, keeping in mind that the mean is added as bonus points. The initial choice of data measure must remain the same. After exchanging cards, players continue with Step 4.

Examples

Tanisha's hand:

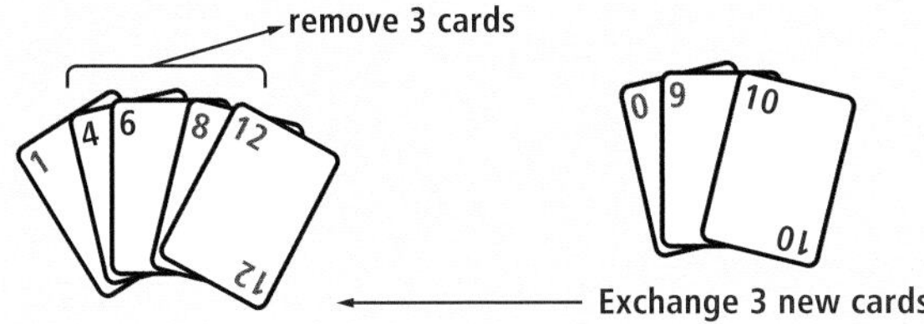

1st Range = 12 – 1 = 11 New Range = 12 – 0 = 12 **New points scored** = 12

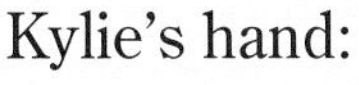

Kylie's hand:

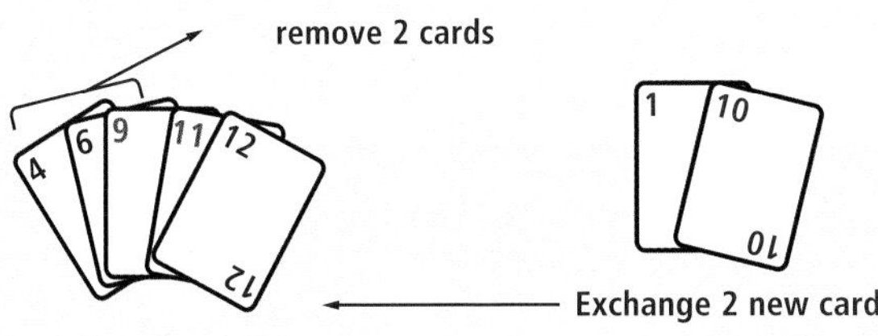

1st Median = 9 New Median = 10 **New points scored** = 10

Jerome's hand:

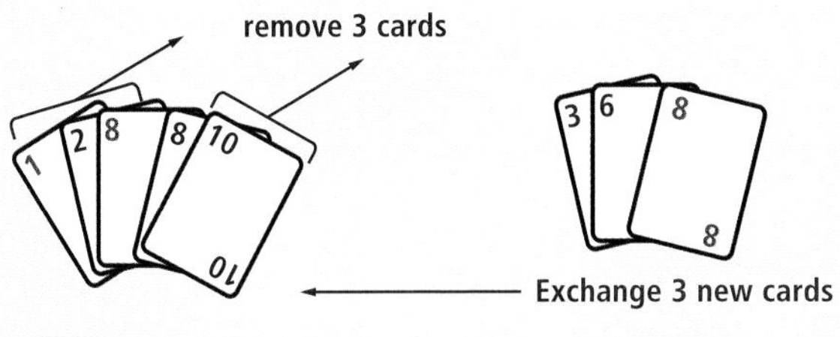

1st Mode = 8 New Mode = 8 **New points scored** = 3 • 8 = 24

Top-It: Fraction Multiplication

Materials	number cards 1–12
	calculator (optional)
Players	2
Skill	Multiplying and comparing fractions
Objective	To collect the most cards

Directions

1. Shuffle the cards and place them number-side down on the table.
2. Each player turns over four cards. The card numbers are used to form two fractions.
   - The first card drawn is placed number-side up on the table. This card is the numerator of the first fraction.
   - The second card drawn is placed number-side up below the first card. This card is the denominator of the first fraction.
   - The third and the fourth cards drawn form the numerator and denominator, respectively, of the second fraction.
3. Each player calculates the product of their fractions and calls it out. The player with the largest product takes all the cards. Players may use a calculator to compare their products.
4. In case of a tie for the largest product, players repeat Steps 2 and 3. The player with the largest product takes all the cards from both plays.
5. The game ends when there are not enough cards left for each player to have another turn. The player with the most cards wins.

Example

Austin turns over a 1, a 2, a 4, and an 8, in that order.

Clara turns over a 2, a 3, a 5, and a 5, in that order.

Austin's product is $\frac{1}{2} \cdot \frac{4}{8} = \frac{4}{16} = \frac{1}{4}$.

Clara's product is $\frac{2}{3} \cdot \frac{5}{5} = \frac{10}{15} = \frac{2}{3}$.

$\frac{1}{4} < \frac{2}{3}$

Clara's product is greater, so she takes all of the cards.

Austin		Clara	
1	4	2	5
2	8	3	5

Decimal Dash

Materials	2 Decimal Place-Value Mats (Game Master 2, p. GM3)
	number cards 0–9
	calculator
Players	2
Skill	Multiplying decimals and rounding to the nearest
Objective	To force your opponent over the limit by estimating and calculating products of decimal numbers

Directions

1. Both players agree on a limit. This can be any positive number.
2. Take turns. When it is your turn, draw four cards and arrange them into 2 two-digit decimal numbers by placing them on the Decimal Place-Value Mats. You must have at least one digit to the right of the decimal point in each number. For example, Jacob draws the cards 4, 9, 2, and 1 and arranges them into the numbers 1.2 and 9.4.
3. Calculate the product of the two numbers. (You may use a calculator to help.) Report your answer in one of three ways:
   - Exactly (Jacob gets 11.28)
   - Rounded to the nearest whole number (Jacob gets 11)
   - Rounded to the nearest tenth (Jacob gets 11.3)
4. Record your answer. Discard your cards. Your turn is over.
5. Now your opponent draws four new cards, forms two numbers, calculates a product in the same way, and adds that product to yours. If the sum is less than the limit number, you take another turn.
6. If all of the number cards have been drawn, reshuffle the discard pile and place the cards number-side down to form a draw pile.
7. Continue to take turns calculating products and sums until one player adds a number that pushes the sum over the limit that you set in Step 1. The last player to add a number without pushing the sum over the limit wins. If a player hits the limit number exactly, that player wins.

Division Variation

Play the game again, but this time divide the two decimal numbers instead of multiplying them. You may choose which number to use as the dividend and which to use as the divisor.

Scrambling: Order of Operations

Materials	*Scrambling: Order of Operations* Cards (Game Master 19, p. GM20)
	number cards 0–9
	calculator
Players	2 to 3
Skill	Using the order of operations
Objective	To get the lowest number of points by creating expressions with the largest value

Directions

Black cards (spades and clubs) are *positive numbers*. Red cards (hearts and diamonds) are *negative numbers*.

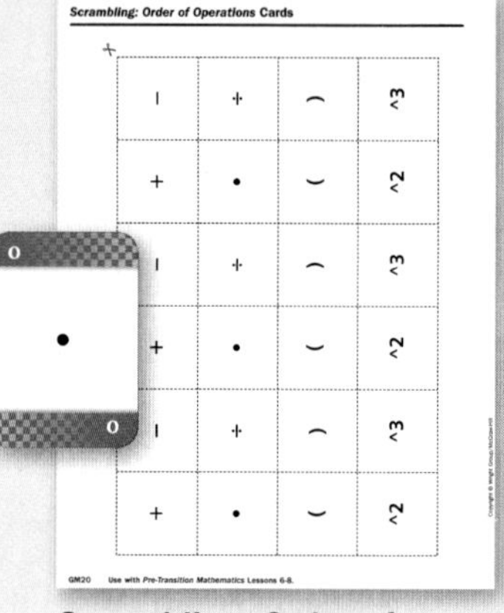

Scrambling: Order of Operations Cards

1. Deal the operation cards so that each player has a full set of operations. Deal five number cards to each player, number-side down.
2. Use the operation cards to arrange all five number cards into an expression with the largest possible value.
   - Number cards cannot be used to create multi-digit numbers.
   - Use all number cards and all operation cards in each round.
3. Use a calculator to find the value of your expression. The player with the expression that has the largest value wins the round, and gets 0 points; the next largest value gets 1 point, and so on.
4. Deal out a new set of number cards to start a new round. If all number cards have been used, shuffle the discard pile and deal from that deck.
5. You may play as many rounds as you want. The player with the least number of points at the end of the game wins.

Example

Beth is dealt the cards –7, 4, 1, 5, and –4. She creates this expression:

5 ^3 • (7 + 4) ^2 − 4 ÷ 1

Aiden is dealt the cards 1, –7, 9, 2, and 4. He creates this expression:

9 ^2 • (4 − 7) ^3 + 2 ÷ 1

The value of Beth's expression is 15,121. The value of Aiden's expression is 107,813. Aiden gets 0 points, and Beth gets 1 point.

Factor Captor

Materials	*Factor Captor* Grid (Game Master 20, p. GM22)
	color pencils
	calculator (optional)
Players	2
Skill	Finding factors of numbers
Objective	To get the higher score by finding factors

Factor Captor Grid

1	1	2	2	2	2	2	3	3	3
3	3	4	4	4	4	5	5	5	5
6	6	6	7	7	7	8	8	9	9
10	10	11	12	13	14	15	16	17	18
19	20	21	22	23	24	25	26	27	28
29	30	31	32	33	34	35	36	37	38
39	40	42	43	44	45	46	48	49	50
51	52	53	54	55	56	58	60	61	62
63	64	65	66	67	68	70	71	72	73
75	76	77	78	79	80	81	82	84	85
86	88	90	91	92	93	94	95	98	100

GM22 Use with *Pre-Transition Mathematics* Lesson 7-3.

Factor Captor Grid

Directions

1. To play a round:
   - Player 1 chooses a number from 10–100 on the *Factor Captor* Grid, crosses it out with his or her color pencil, and records the number on a piece of paper. This is Player 1's score for the round.
   - Player 2 uses his or her color pencil to cross out all of the factors of Player 1's number. Player 2 finds the sum of the factors and records it on paper. This is Player 2's score for the round. **A factor may only be crossed out once during a round.** For example, if 5 is a factor, only one square with a 5 in it may be crossed out in that round.
   - If Player 2 missed any factors, Player 1 can cross them out and add them to his or her score.
2. Any number that is crossed out is no longer available and may not be used again.
3. In the next round, players switch roles.
4. The first player in any round may not choose a number that is less than 10, unless no other numbers are available.
5. Play continues with players trading roles after each round until all numbers on the grid have been crossed out. Players may then use their calculators to find their total scores. The player with the higher score wins the game.

Example

Jacqueline and Tyrell are playing *Factor Captor*. Jacqueline crosses out the number 55. Tyrell knows that $55 = 1 \cdot 5 \cdot 11$, so he crosses out one of the 1s, one of the 5s and the 11 on the *Factor Captor* Grid. Jacqueline's score for the round is 55, and Tyrell's score is $1 + 5 + 11 = 17$.

Match-It: Fraction Division

Materials	*Match-It: Fraction Division* Level 1 Cards (Game Master 22, p. GM24) or *Match-It: Fraction Division* Level 2 Cards (Game Master 23, p. GM25)
	calculator (optional)
Players	2
Skill	Dividing fractions
Objective	To collect the most cards by matching division problems to their quotients

Match-It: Fraction Division
Level 1 Cards

Directions

1. Shuffle the *Match-It: Fraction Division* Level 1 Cards.
2. Place the cards face down in a rectangular array in any order.
3. Take turns. When it is your turn:
   - Turn over two cards.
   - If the cards "match," that is, if one card is a division and the other card is the solution to that division, then take the two cards. Your turn is over.
   - If there is no match, turn the cards face down. Your turn is over.
4. You may check your answers using a calculator if you wish.
5. The game ends when all the cards have been matched. The player with more cards wins.

Example

Carina turns over two cards as shown at the right. Because $\frac{13}{14} \div \frac{1}{7} = \frac{3}{2}$, the cards match, and Carina takes the two cards.

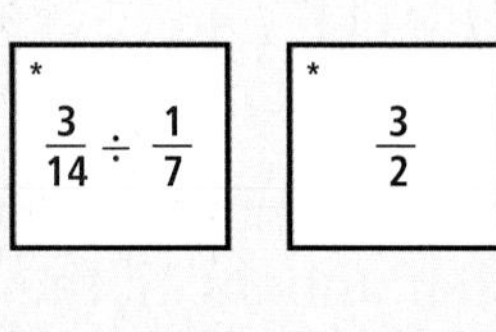

Santiago turns over two cards as shown at the right. Because $\frac{100}{9} \neq \frac{9}{4}$, he turns the cards face down.

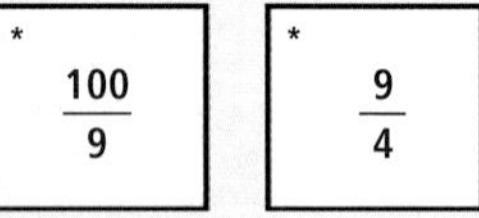

Variation

Use the *Match-It: Fraction Division* Level 2 Cards. With these cards, you must match a division to another division with the same answer.

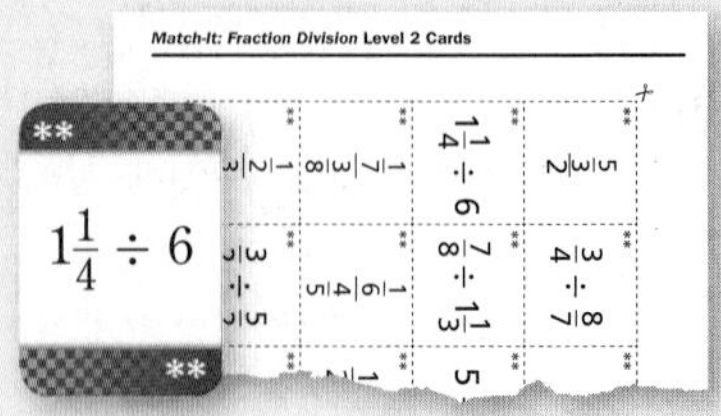

Match-It: Fraction Division
Level 2 Cards

X-Tac-Toe: $ax = b$

Materials	*X-Tac-Toe* Gameboard (Game Master 24, p. GM26)
	X-Tac-Toe Number-Card Board (Game Master 25, p. GM27)
	number cards 1–10
	counters (2 colors) or pennies
	calculator (optional)
Players	2
Skill	Solving equations of the form $ax = b$
Objective	To cover three squares in a row in any direction (horizontally, vertically, or diagonally)

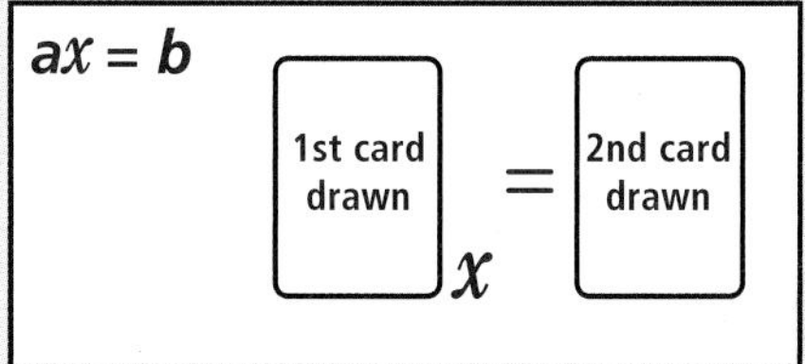

X-Tac-Toe: ax = b
Number-Card Board

Directions

Black cards (spades and clubs) are *positive numbers*. Red cards (hearts and diamonds) are *negative numbers*.

1. Shuffle the number cards and place the deck face down in a draw pile on the table.
2. Take turns. When it is your turn:
   - Draw two cards from the deck and place them face up on the Number-Card Board in the order they were drawn. The numbers on these cards are the values a and b, respectively, in $ax = b$.
   - Solve the equation shown on the Number-Card Board.
   - Try to match the solution with an interval that contains it on the gameboard. If a match is found, cover that square with a counter. Your turn is over. If no match is found, your turn is over. Each square can be covered only once. Place the used cards into a discard pile.
   - If a player puts a counter on an incorrect square, the other player may place his or her color counter on a correct square. The counter on the incorrect square should then be removed.
3. When there are no cards left in the draw pile, shuffle the cards in the discard pile to make a new draw pile.
4. The first player to cover three squares in a row in any direction (horizontally, vertically, or diagonally) wins the game.

X-Tac-Toe Gameboard

$0 \le x < 3$	$-4 \le x < -1$	$-\frac{1}{2} \le x < \frac{1}{2}$	$-10 \le x < -6$	$10 \le x \le 20$
$6 \le x < 10$	$-\frac{1}{2} \le x < 3$	$3 \le x < 6$	$-2\frac{1}{2} \le x < -\frac{1}{2}$	$-6 \le x < -3$
$-3\frac{1}{2} \le x < 0$	$1 \le x < 2$	$x < -5$ or $x \ge 5$	$1 < x \le 2$	$-3\frac{1}{2} \le x < 0$
$-6 \le x < -3$	$-20 \le x \le -10$	$3 \le x < 6$	$-\frac{1}{2} \le x < 3$	$6 \le x < 10$
$-3 \le x < 0$	$-10 \le x < -6$	$-\frac{1}{2} \le x < \frac{1}{2}$	$-4 \le x < -1$	$0 \le x < 3$

X-Tac-Toe Gameboard

Example

Tracy turns over a red 3 and a black 1. Her equation is $-3x = 1$. She gets a solution of $-\frac{1}{3}$. She can place her counter on any one of the seven squares labeled "$-\frac{1}{2} \le x < \frac{1}{2}$," "$-3\frac{1}{2} \le x < 0$", "$-\frac{1}{2} \le x < 3$", or "$-3 \le x < 0$".

Spinner Sums

Materials	*Spinner Sums* Spinners and Outcome Bar (Game Master 26, p. GM28)
	2 large paper clips
	counters
Players	2
Skill	Using probabilities to make predictions
Objective	To gather the most counters by using probabilities to make predictions

Directions

1. Player 1 writes 0, 1, or 2 in each section of the two spinners. He or she may repeat any of the numbers as often as he or she wishes. In each trial, Player 1 will spin each spinner once and add the two resulting numbers to get a single outcome.
2. Based on the numbers that Player 1 wrote in the spinners, Player 2 predicts what the outcomes of five trials will be. Player 2 places counters above the Outcome Bar to indicate his or her predictions for all five trials. For example, if Player 2 believes the outcome will be 3 in two of the trials, he or she would place two counters above the 3 on the Outcome Bar.
3. Player 1 spins the spinners and sums the results. If Player 2 placed a counter above that sum on the Outcome Bar, he or she takes the counter. This process repeats four more times.
4. After five trials, any remaining counters are discarded. Player 1 erases the numbers in the spinners, and the round is over.
5. In the next round, players switch roles. Player 2 writes numbers in the spinners and Player 1 makes predictions.
6. The player with more counters after four rounds wins the game.

Example

Caleb and Yuan are playing *Spinner Sums*. Caleb wrote the numbers in the spinners and Yuan placed his counters above the Outcome Bar. Caleb spins the two spinners, and the paper clips land on 2 and 1, for an outcome of 3. Yuan takes one of the counters he placed above the 3 and Caleb spins again.

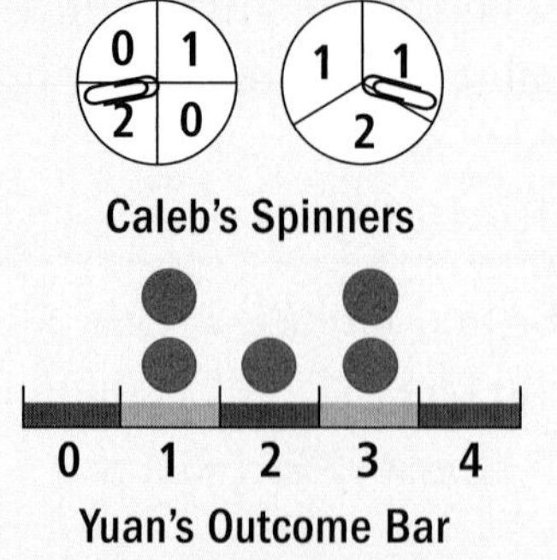

Selected Answers

Chapter 1

Lesson 1-1 (pp. 6-11)

Questions: **1.** 10 **3.** Answers vary. Sample: You can write very large numbers in a smaller space. **5.** false **7.** 10,046,908 **9.** 9,700; species **11.** 10 quintillion; insects **13.** fifty-six million **15. a.** 9,999 **b.** 99,999 **c.** 9,999,999,999 **17. a.** 1,023,456,789 **b.** one billion, twenty-three million, four hundred fifty-six thousand, seven hundred eighty-nine **19. a.** 24 **b.** 16 **c.** 5 **d.** 63 **e.** 4 **f.** 20

Lesson 1-2 (pp. 12-18)

Questions:

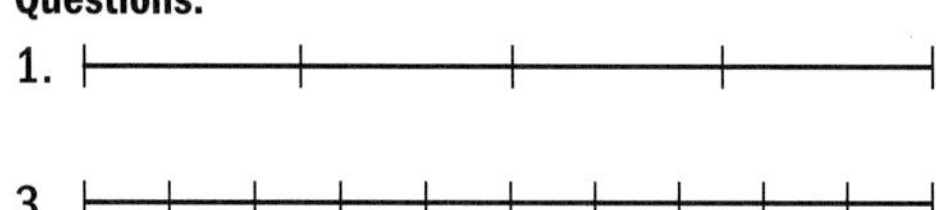

5. 5 ft **7. a.** $\frac{50}{200}$ **b.** $\frac{130}{200}$ **c.** $\frac{0}{200}$ **d.** $\frac{200}{200}$ **9. a.** Desiree **b.** Answers vary. Sample: If the track is divided into 3 parts, one part is longer than if the track is divided into 4 parts. So the part of the track that Desiree has run is longer than what Alicia has run. **11. a.** $\frac{1}{8}$ **b.** $\frac{7}{8}$ **13. a.** China, India, United States, Indonesia, Brazil, Pakistan, Bangladesh, Russia, Nigeria, Japan **b.** one hundred ninety million, ten thousand, six hundred forty-seven people

Lesson 1-3 (pp. 19-25)

Guided Example 4: 12; 5; 12; 60; 60; 4; 64
Questions: **1. a.** 3 in. **b.** $2\frac{1}{2}$ in. **c.** $2\frac{3}{4}$ in. **d.** $2\frac{6}{8}$ in. **e.** $2\frac{11}{16}$ in. **3.** 1 and 2 **5.** Answers vary. Sample: feet, inches, miles **7.** $\frac{1}{1,760}$ **9. a.** 1 in. **b.** $1\frac{1}{8}$ in. **11.** Check students' work. They should draw a segment $1\frac{3}{8}$ in. long. **13. a.** Answers vary. Sample: 78 in. **b.** Answers vary. Sample: 6 ft, 6 in. **15.** Answers vary. Sample: $7\frac{3}{4}$ in. **17.** 333 yd, 1 ft **19.** 2; 3 **21.** 8 ft, 11 in. **23.** $\frac{1}{2}$ **25.** nine

Lesson 1-4 (pp. 26-31)

Guided Example 2: **a.** 4; 4; $12\frac{1}{2}$ **b.** $\frac{1}{4}$, $\frac{1}{2}$; 2; 12; 2 **c.** 4; 4; 200
Questions: **1.** 8 **3. a.** 3 gal, 3 qt **b.** $3\frac{3}{4}$ gal **c.** 60 servings **5. a.** 165 min **b.** $2\frac{3}{4}$ hr **7. a.** 4 hr, 15 min **b.** $4\frac{1}{4}$ hr **9.** $\frac{1}{4}$ pt **11.** Clem should clam up. A min is $\frac{1}{60}$ hr, and a second is $\frac{1}{60}$ min. So, a second is $\frac{1}{3,600}$ hr. **13. a.** $26\frac{7}{32}$ mi **b.** 138,435 ft **15.** 5 mi; 5 mi is equal to 26,400 ft. **17.** tons **19.** seconds **21.** teaspoons **23.** $3\frac{3}{4}$ in. **25. a.** Check students' drawings. The segment should be $3\frac{7}{16}$ in. long with left endpoint L and right endpoint R. **b.** $3\frac{2}{4}$ in. **27.** 509,067,312

Lesson 1-5 (pp. 32-37)

Guided Example 1: 6; 6; 11; 55; 1,000; 1,400; 55; 1,000; 1,400 **Guided Example 2:** 10; 10; 25; 25; 50; 50; 10; 6
Questions:

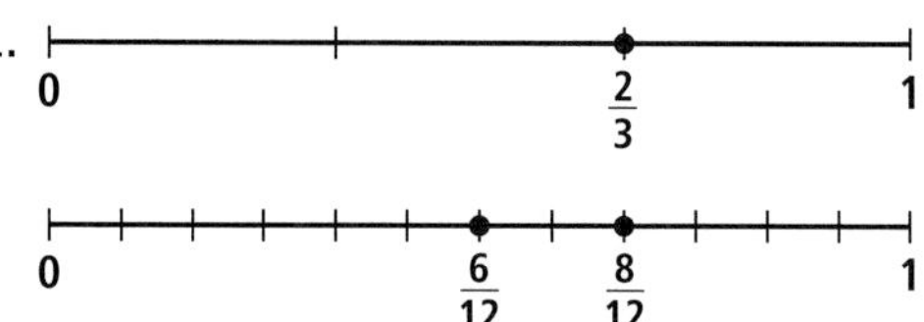

3. Answers vary. Sample: $\frac{2}{14}, \frac{4}{28}, \frac{6}{42}$ **5.** $\frac{15 \div 3}{18 \div 3} = \frac{5}{6}$ **7.** $\frac{75 \div 25}{125 \div 25} = \frac{3}{5}$ **9.** Answers vary. Sample: Neither reduced the fraction to lowest terms. However, Derrick's answer is an equivalent fraction, which he could reduce to lowest terms, whereas Nat's answer is incorrect. **11. a.** $\frac{2}{3}$ **b.** $\frac{3}{2}$ **c.** Answers vary. Sample: The answers are similar because the fractions are upside-down versions of each other. They are different because they represent different values.
13.

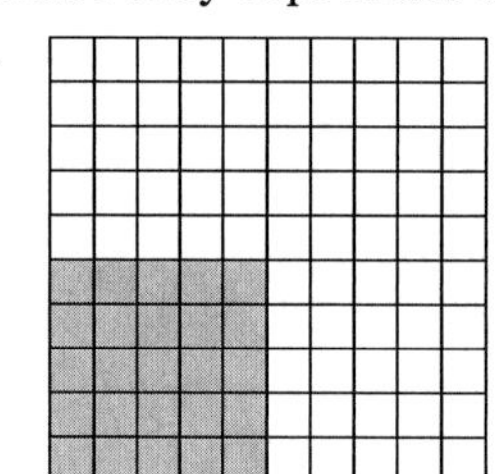

15. $\frac{12}{1}$; 12 **17.** Answers vary. Sample: $\frac{14}{1}, \frac{28}{2}, \frac{42}{3}$ **19.** 60; Answers vary. Sample: The product of the divisors in each step is the number that would complete this problem in one step, so $10 \times 2 \times 3 = 60$. **21. a.** 5 and 6 **b.** 6 **23. a.** Answers vary. Sample: 5 in. **b.** Answers vary. Sample: 5 in. **c.** Answers vary. Sample: $5\frac{1}{4}$ in.

Lesson 1-6 (pp. 38-44)

Questions: **1. a.** $90 \div 4$ **b.** $\frac{90}{4}$ min per drawer **c.** $22\frac{1}{2}$ min per drawer **3.** $\frac{8}{3}$ hr or $2\frac{2}{3}$ hr **5. a.** 20 **b.** 10 **c.** $\frac{1}{20}$ **d.** $\frac{1}{10}$ **7.** $\frac{20}{16}$ oz; $1\frac{1}{4}$ oz **9.** $\frac{3}{8}$ oz **11.** $1,154\frac{1}{4}$ pesos **b.** 7,200 pieces of eight **c.** 450 pieces of eight **13. a.** on pace **b.** ahead of pace **c.** ahead of pace **d.** ahead of pace **e.** ahead of pace **f.** on pace **g.** ahead of pace **h.** on pace **15.** $\frac{5}{6}$ **17. a.** $\frac{6}{8} = \frac{3}{4}$ shaded **b.** $\frac{2}{8} = \frac{1}{4}$ unshaded **19. a.** $\frac{4}{6}$ or $\frac{2}{3}$ of the wall **b.** 72 in.

Lesson 1-7 (pp. 45-49)

Questions: **1.** negative eight, opposite of eight **3.** left **5.** Answers vary. Sample: 9 **7.** Answers vary. Sample: -3 **9.** zero; positive; negative

11. a.

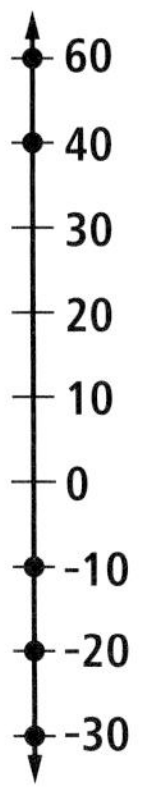

b. Answers vary. Sample: -30 to 60 **13.** 0 **15.** Answers vary. Sample: -5 **17. a.** -7 **b.** -44 **c.** 53 **21. a.** improper **b.** $\frac{9}{4}$ **23. a.** neither **b.** $\frac{1}{1}$ **25. a.** $\frac{3}{5}$ of a dollar **b.** \$3.43 **27.** Check students' work. They should draw a segment $\frac{9}{16}$ in. long. **29.** three million, seven hundred ninety-four thousand, eighty-five square miles

Lesson 1-8 (pp. 50-54)

Guided Example 1: 3; 4; 6; 5; first; 4; 5; 10; 9; seventh

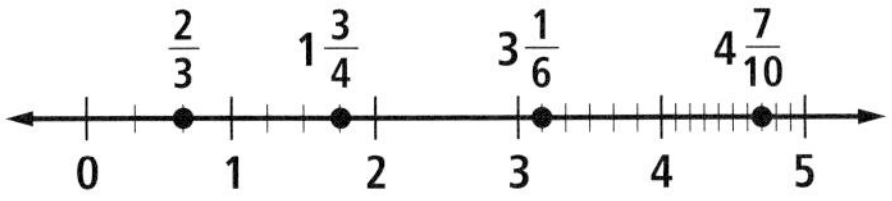

Guided Example 2: 6; $-8\frac{8}{14}$; $-8\frac{6}{14}$; $-8\frac{8}{14}$; $-8\frac{7}{14}$

Questions:

1. a.

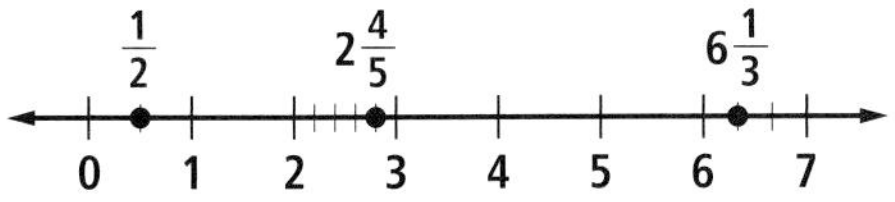

b.

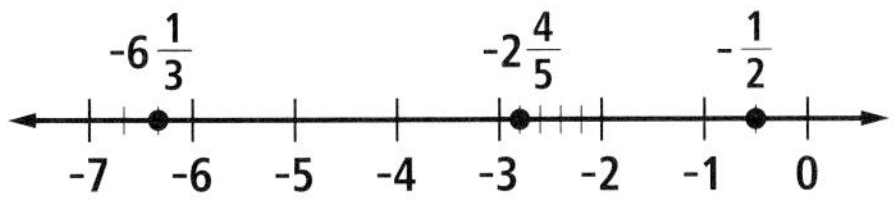

3.

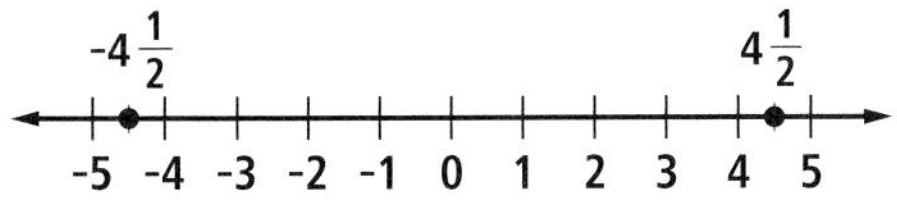

5. $5\frac{1}{2}$, 0, $-1\frac{4}{5}$, $-2\frac{1}{3}$, -3 **7.** A **9.** $-3\frac{1}{2}$ **11.** Answers vary. Sample: $-9\frac{3}{4}$ **13.** Answers vary. Sample: $-1\frac{11}{18}$ **15. a.** $\frac{1}{24}$ **b.** $-\frac{5}{24}$ **c.** $\frac{12}{24}$ or $\frac{1}{2}$ **d.** $\frac{36}{24}$ or $-1\frac{1}{2}$ **17.** *J* **19.** none

21.

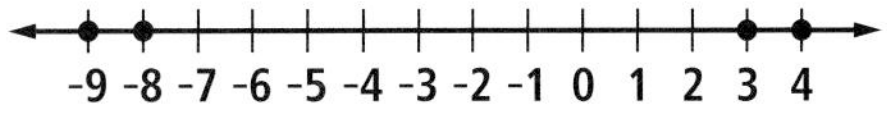

23. They can't croak. **25.** Answers vary. Sample: $\frac{8}{1}$, $\frac{24}{3}$, $\frac{64}{8}$, $\frac{160}{20}$

Self-Test (p. 58)

1. 508,027,412 **2.** nine million, one hundred twenty-three thousand, eighty-three **3.** $2\frac{2}{4}$ in.

4.

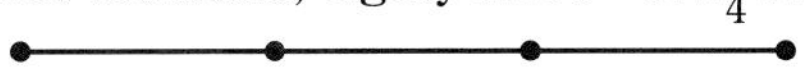

5. Check students' work. They should draw a segment $2\frac{3}{8}$ in. long.

6. a.

b. $\frac{16 \div 4}{20 \div 4} = \frac{4}{5}$ **7.** $-2\frac{5}{6}$, $-2\frac{2}{3}$, $-\frac{2}{3}$, 0, $1\frac{5}{8}$, $1\frac{3}{4}$ **8.** $6 \times 12 + 5 = 77$ in. **9.** Answers vary. Sample: $\frac{9 \times 4}{20 \times 4} = \frac{36}{80}$, $\frac{9 \times 7}{20 \times 7} = \frac{63}{140}$, $\frac{9 \times 5}{20 \times 5} = \frac{45}{100}$ **10.** Answers vary. Sample: $\frac{5 \times 6}{9 \times 6} = \frac{30}{54}$, $\frac{5 \times 2}{9 \times 2} = \frac{10}{18}$, $\frac{5 \times 3}{9 \times 3} = \frac{15}{27}$ **11.** False; it is equal to $7 \div 13$. **12.** $3 \times 6 = 18$, so $2 \times 6 = 12$ **13. a.** $800 \div 12 = \frac{800}{12} = 66\frac{8}{12} = 66\frac{2}{3}$ in. **b.** $800 \div 144 = \frac{800}{144} = 5\frac{80}{144} = 5\frac{5}{9}$ ft **14.** $\frac{1{,}280}{50} = 25\frac{30}{50} = 25\frac{3}{5}$ **15.** $\frac{416}{35} = 11\frac{31}{35}$ **16.** $\frac{66 \div 3}{15 \div 3} = \frac{22}{5}$

17.

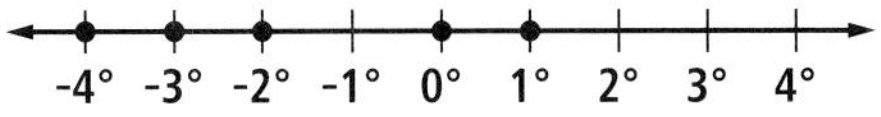

18. a. *V* **b.** *Z* **c.** *T* **d.** *Y* **e.** *X* **19.** 29,035 **20.** 0 **21.** Answers vary. Sample: By the Equal Fractions Property, $\frac{100}{80} = \frac{100 \div 20}{80 \div 20} = \frac{5}{4}$.

Chapter Review (pp. 59-61)

1. ninety-one million, four hundred two thousand, seven hundred twenty-five **3.** 5 **5.** 7,053,196

The chart below keys the **Self-Test** questions to the objectives in the **Chapter Review** at the end of the chapter. This will enable you to locate those **Chapter Review** questions that correspond to questions missed on the **Self-Test.** The lesson where the material is covered is also indicated on the chart.

Question	**1**	**2**	**3**	**4**	**5**	**6**	**7**	**8**	**9**	**10**
Objective(s)	A	A	F	L	K	L	E	H	B	B
Lesson(s)	1-1	1-1	1-3	1-2	1-3	1-2	1-7, 1-8	1-4	1-5	1-5
Question	**11**	**12**	**13**	**14**	**15**	**16**	**17**	**18**	**19**	**20**
Objective(s)	G	G	D	D	C	B	J	J	I	I
Lesson(s)	1-5, 1-6	1-5, 1-6	1-6	1-6	1-6	1-5	1-7, 1-8	1-7, 1-8	1-7	1-7
Question	**21**									
Objective(s)	G									
Lesson(s)	1-5, 1-6									

7. $\frac{2}{3}$ **9.** $\frac{11}{7}$ **11.** Answers vary. Sample: $\frac{134}{8}, \frac{201}{12}, \frac{268}{16}$ **13.** Answers vary. Sample: $-\frac{51}{4}, -\frac{153}{12}, -\frac{102}{8}$ **15.** $12\frac{1}{2}$ **17.** $1\frac{173}{200}$ **19.** Answers vary. Sample: $4 = \frac{12}{3}$, so $4 + \frac{2}{3} = \frac{12}{3} + \frac{2}{3} = \frac{14}{3}$ **21.** $1\frac{4}{5}$ **23.** $37\frac{1}{2}$ **25.** $\frac{1}{8}, \frac{1}{6}, \frac{2}{9}, \frac{2}{7}$ **27.** $-5\frac{5}{3}, -\frac{19}{3}, -\frac{11}{3}, -2\frac{1}{3}$ **29.** $2\frac{5}{8}$ in. **31.** Equal Fractions Property **33.** Multiply $\frac{1}{2}$ by $\frac{25}{25}$. **35. a.** 125 oz **b.** $7\frac{13}{16}$ lb **37.** 51 in. **39. a.** $26\frac{7}{32}$ mi **b.** 46,145 yd **41.** -$25 **43.** $0

45.

15

-30 -20 -10 0 10 20 30

47. *B* **49.** Check students' work. They should draw a segment $2\frac{1}{4}$ in. long. **51.** Check students' work. They should draw a segment $3\frac{5}{16}$ in. long. **53.** 12 tick marks

55. a.

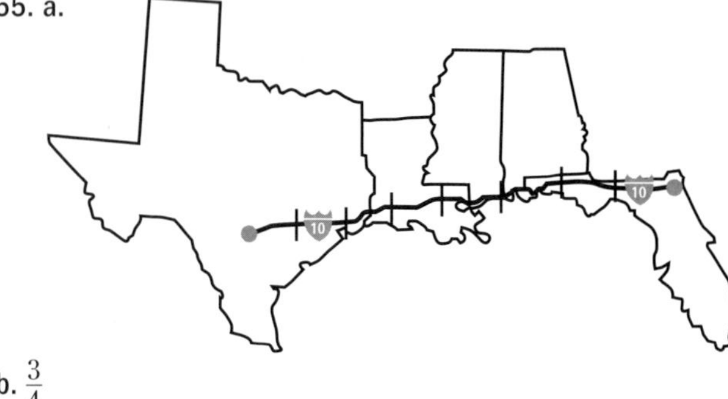

b. $\frac{3}{4}$

Chapter 2

Lesson 2-1 (pp. 64-70)

Guided Example 2: 5; 7; 0.005312; 0.00579; 0.005312; 0.00579

Questions: 1. a. 31 and 32 **b.** 6 **c.** 6 **3.** 3 **5.** Answers vary. Sample: Decimals are often easier to order and compare. **7.** 3.8, 4.321, 5.289 **9.** 0.34, 0.3445, 0.345 **11. a.** $81\frac{3}{10}$; 81.3 **b.** $81\frac{9}{10}$; 81.9 **c.** $82\frac{4}{5}$; 82.8 **d.** $81\frac{1}{2}$; 81.5 **13. a.** $\frac{1}{16}$ **b.** six hundred twenty-five ten thousandths **15.** Answers vary. Sample: 45.82

17. a., c.

9.67 9.77

9.65 9.70 9.75 9.80

b. 9.67 sec **19.** twenty-one thousandths, twenty-one, twenty-one thousand **21.** 10 trains **23 a.** iii. **b.** i. **c.** iv. **d.** ii. **e.** v.

Lesson 2-2 (pp. 71-76)

Guided Example 1: b. 3; 100; 3; 100; 93; 100; 9,300 **c.** 4; 10; 25; 4; 10; 100; 10; 1,000

Guided Example 2: 1,000,000,000; 2,340,000,000

Questions: 1. a. 40 **b.** 8,000 **c.** 10,000 **d.** 0.06 **e.** 0.002 **3.** 6,480 **5.** 0.7 **7.** 69,700 **9.** 125,220 **11. a.** When you multiply a decimal by 10, move the decimal point one place to the right. **b.** When you multiply a decimal by 10,000,000, move the decimal point seven places to the right. **13.** 82,000 **15.** one million **17.** one trillion **19.** one quintillion **21.** 7,242,300,000,000; 257,664,400,000 **23.** $23,518,760,000.00 **25.** 290 million people **27.** 26.5 trillion miles to the nearest star **29. a.** 0.6 **b.** 0.9 **c.** E **31. a.** $4\frac{1}{10}$ **b.** $4\frac{1}{100}$ **c.** $4\frac{1}{1,000}$

Lesson 2-3 (pp. 77-82)

Guided Example 1: 3; 1.16; 0.1; 0.1; 0.00116; 0.00116

Guided Example 2: b. 0.01; 0.01; 4; 0.01; 0.084 **c.** 0.001; 3; 0.001; 3; 150; 0.001; 450; 0.450

Questions: 1. 0.1 **3.** Move the decimal point one place to the left. **5.** $7,500.00 **7.** 9.2 **9.** 0.2764946 **11.** 0.01 **13.** 0.00001 **15.** 0.015 **17.** 0.0000000024 sec **19.** 0.0011 oz **21. a.** $\frac{1}{10}$ **b.** 1,000 **c.** one million **23.** 0.0012 **25.** 0.0000000056 **27.** 1,000 **29.** 100,000 **31. a.** -17, -1.7, 0.17

b.

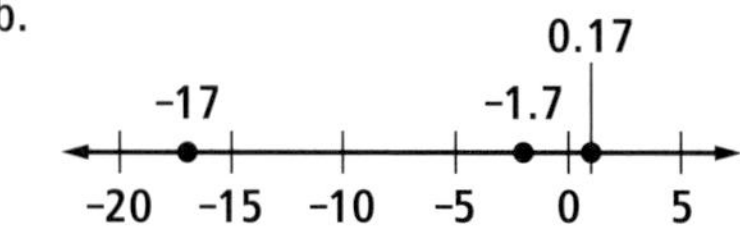

33. 513,561; guests **35. a.** $\frac{1}{2}$ **b.** 50%

Lesson 2-4 (pp. 83-89)

Guided Example 2: 10 mm; $\frac{1}{1000}$ m; 1000; 1000

Guided Example 3: 0.001; 0.412

Questions: 1. a. 100 **b.** 1,000 **c.** 10 **3.** 1 L = 1,000 mL; 1 mL = 0.001 L **5.** Answers vary. Sample: length of a pencil eraser **7.** Answers vary. Sample: thickness of a paper clip **9.** C **11.** 5,000 m **13.** 5 g **15.** 10 kg **17.** 0.4; 0.004 **19. a.** yes **b.** 25.4 **c.** 0.0254 **21. a.** $0.03 **b.** 13,567¢ **c.** 319.9¢ per gallon **23.** five; left

25.

$-\frac{2}{3}$ $\frac{1}{6}$ $\frac{3}{4}$

-1 0 1

27. 4 in.; $4\frac{1}{2}$ in.; $4\frac{2}{4}$ in.; $4\frac{3}{8}$ in.

Lesson 2-5 (pp. 90-96)

Questions: 1. hundreds **3.** 40 pencils **5. a.** 5 cars **b.** 50 scouts and leaders **7.** 55¢ **9. a.** -6,500 **b.** -6,400 **11. a.** $23,300 **b.** $23,300 **c.** $24,000

13. a. 460 km b. 450 km

c. 

15. a. 46% b. 50% c. 40% 17. –38° 19. a. 77% a. 80% b. 70% 21. 0.03 sec 23. 0.0001 25. a. Q b. R c. Y

Lesson 2-6 (pp. 97–103)

Guided Example 2: a. 2; 3; 3; 3 b. 2.7; 2.8; 2.7; 2.7
Guided Example 3: **Solution 1.** –509; –508; –508
Solution 2.

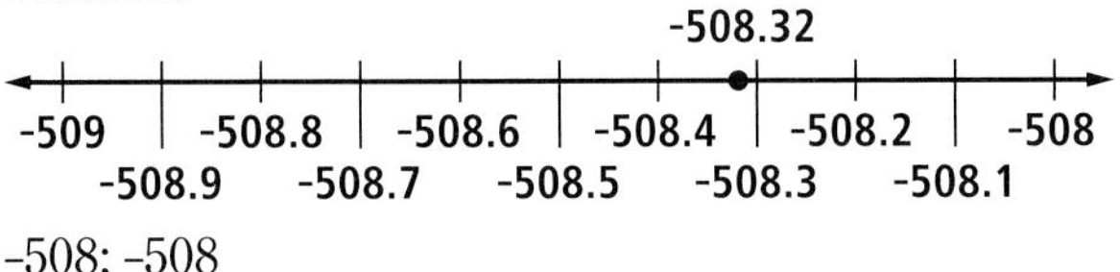

–508; –508

Questions: 1. a. –70 b. –40 c. –40 3. 300 5. a. 290,000 b. 285,000 c. 285,200 or 285,100 7. a. 274 b. 270 c. 300 d. 273.8 or 273.9 9. a. 6,000 b. 6,000 c. 6,000 d. 6,000 e. 10,000 11. $48 13. 442 15. nearest hundred pounds 17. nearest whole number 19. a. Answers vary. Sample: 70% b. 73% c. 70% d. rounded value 21. a. 75 b. 84 23. a. high b. low c. high d. high 25. a. $7\frac{3}{4}$ hr b. $7\frac{75}{100}$ 27. $14\frac{7}{50}$

Lesson 2-7 (pp. 104–109)

Guided Example 2: 1. 65; 6 **Guided Example 3:** a. 0.5625; 0.75; $\frac{3}{4}$; $\frac{3}{4}$ b. 0.75; 0.5625; 0.1875; 0.1875 in.
Questions: 1. Answers vary. Sample: Decimals may be easier to order, round, add, and subtract than fractions. 3. $\frac{3}{4}$ in. 5. $\frac{934}{1265} = 0.73834$, $\frac{7390}{9999} = 0.73907$, $\frac{17}{23} = 0.73913$ 7. a. 9 b. 0.2699999999 c. 0 and 1 9. $\frac{184}{365}$; 0.5041 11. a. 0.077 b. 20.077 c. –20.077 13. a. = b. ≈ c. ≈ d. = 15. a. $\frac{39}{50}$ b. 0.78 17. 108,700,000 19. You should round up, to make sure you have enough batter for the batch. 21. 99.8°F

Lesson 2-8 (pp. 110–113)

Guided Example 1: 8; 12; $\frac{12}{96}$; 0.125; 24; $\frac{24}{96}$; $\frac{1}{4}$; 0.25; The sum should add up to 1. The answers check.
Questions: 1. a. 0.1 b. 0.2 c. 0.3 d. 0.4 e. 0.5 f. 0.2 g. 0.4 h. 0.6 i. 0.5 j. 0.25 k. 0.75 l. 0.6 m. 0.7 n. 0.8 o. 0.9 p. 0.8 q. 0.375 r. 0.625 s. 0.875 t. $0.\overline{3}$ u. $0.\overline{6}$ v. $0.\overline{6}$ w. $0.1\overline{6}$ x. $0.8\overline{3}$ 3. a. $\frac{3}{8}$; 0.375 b. $\frac{5}{8}$; 0.625 5. 0.08; 0.12; 0.16 7. 1.98; 16.98 9. a. $\frac{1}{9}, \frac{2}{9}, \frac{4}{9}, \frac{5}{9}, \frac{7}{9}, \frac{8}{9}$ b. $0.\overline{1}$, $0.\overline{2}$, $0.\overline{4}$, $0.\overline{5}$, $0.\overline{7}$, $0.\overline{8}$ c. Answers vary. Sample: For ninths, the decimal is a repetend, and that repetend is the same number as the numerator. 11. Answers vary. Sample: Because $\frac{7}{15} < \frac{1}{2}$ (which equals 0.5), the decimal must be less than 0.5, which is not true for 0.715. 13. 0.875 + 0.75 + 1.5 = 3.125 15. 999,500 17. 862.000861

Lesson 2-9 (pp. 114–120)

Guided Example 1:

	Percent	As a Fraction	As a Decimal
a.	50%	$50 \times \frac{1}{100} = \frac{50}{100} = \frac{1}{2}$	$50 \times 0.01 = 0.5$
b.	63.1%	$63.1 \times \frac{1}{100} = \frac{63.1}{100} \times \frac{10}{10} = \frac{631}{1000}$	$63.1 \times 0.01 = 0.631$
c.	4%	$4 \times \frac{1}{100} = \frac{4}{100} = \frac{1}{25}$	$4 \times 0.01 = 0.04$
d.	12.5%	$12.5 \times \frac{1}{100} = \frac{12.5}{100} \times \frac{10}{10} = \frac{125}{1000}$	$12.5 \times 0.01 = 0.125$
e.	100%	$100 \times \frac{1}{100} = \frac{100}{100} = 1$	$100 \times 0.01 = 1$
f.	125%	$125 \times \frac{1}{100} = \frac{125}{100} = 1\frac{1}{4}$	$125 \times 0.01 = 1.25$

Questions: 1. percent; multiply by one-hundredth 3. Multiply the decimal by 100%. 5. 0.35; $\frac{7}{20}$ 7. 1.5 9. 325% 11. 0.119 13. a. 50% b. 25% c. 12.5% d. 37.5%

15. **Leah's Spending**

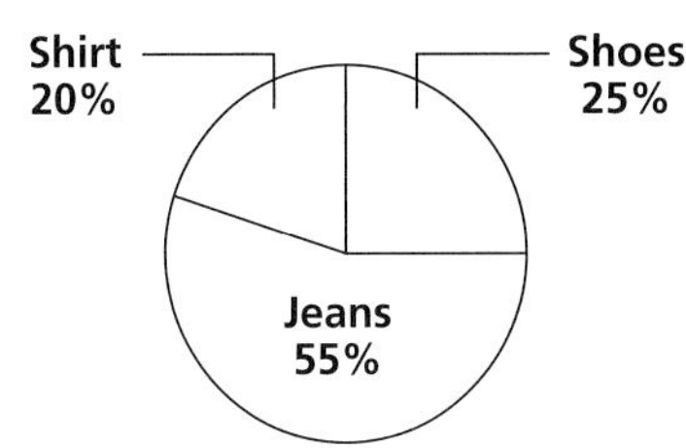

17. 

19. **Sunscreen Use**

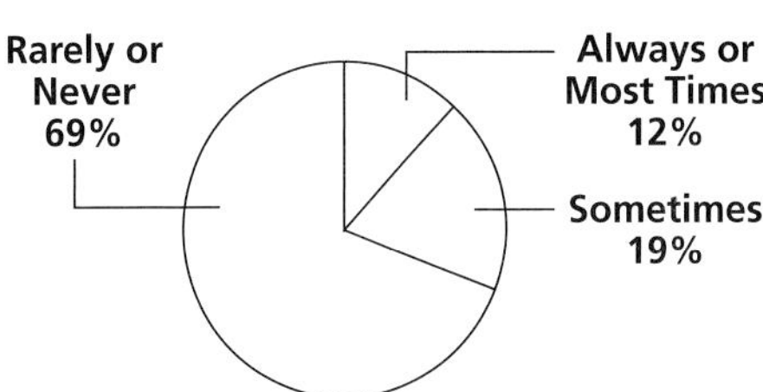

21. a. E b. B c. C d. 0% 23. 0.142857 25. a. 10,000,000 b. 10,111,213.141516 c. 10,111,213.14152 d. 10,110,000 27. a. about 220 lb b. about 116.6 lb c. 2.5 kg d. about 5.5 lb

Lesson 2-10 (pp. 121–126)

Questions: 1. a. > b. < 3. 25 mm < 3 cm 5. > 7. > 9. <; < 11. Chloe 13. a. $\frac{22}{100}$, 0.222, $\frac{2}{9}$ b. $-\frac{2}{9}$, –0.222, $-\frac{22}{100}$ 15. less than 17. a. $\frac{3}{60}$ or $\frac{1}{20}$ b. 5% c. $\frac{3}{24}$ or $\frac{1}{8}$ d. 12.5% e. $\frac{1}{100}$ f. 1% 19. a. 456,000 mg b. 0.456 kg

Self-Test (pp. 130–131)

1. nine ten-thousandths 2. 3,400,000,000,000 3. a. hundred-thousandths b. hundredths 4. Answers vary. Sample: 27.8951, 27.8952312327, and 27.895698

5. 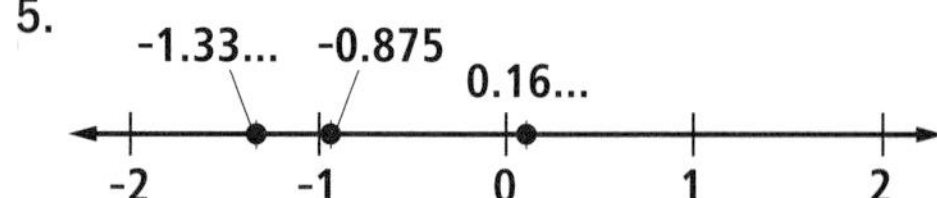

6. a. $\frac{50}{75} = \frac{2}{3}$, so $0.\bar{6}$ or $66.\bar{6}\%$ **b.** $\frac{33}{18} = \frac{11}{6}$, so $1.8\bar{3}$, or $183.\bar{3}\%$ **7. a.** $12 + 15 + 2 + 9 = 38$ lb **b.** Yes, this is less than 40 lb, but you should also consider the weight of the bag. You might come very close. **8. a.** rounds up to 46.0 **b.** rounds down to 45.97 **c.** Because the digit in the ten-thousandths place is a 5, you can round to either 45.973 or 45.972. **9.** to the right two places **10.** to the left six places **11. a.** $\frac{1}{20} = 0.05$, so $0.005 < \frac{1}{20}$ **b.** $1\frac{6}{8} = 1.75$, so $1.78 > 1\frac{6}{8}$ **c.** < **12.** $0.\overline{05}$ **13.** $2.\bar{6}$ **14.** 0.8; 80% **15.** 04; 5; 4; 50 **16.** Check students' work. They should draw a segment 8.7 cm long. **17.** 71 mm **18. a.** 3 kg + 576 g = 3,000 g + 576 g = 3,576 g **b.** 50 cm = 0.5 m **19. a.** University of Arizona: 33, $\frac{27}{33}$; University of Illinois: 33, $\frac{32}{33}$ Louisiana State University: 29, $\frac{20}{29}$; University of Nevada: 30, $\frac{24}{30}$; University of Texas: 30, $\frac{20}{30}$; University of Wisconsin-Milwaukee: 29, $\frac{24}{29}$ **b.** 1. University of Illinois: $\frac{32}{33} \approx 97.0\%$; 2. University of Wisconsin-Milwaukee: $\frac{24}{29} \approx 82.8\%$; 3. University of Arizona: $\frac{27}{33} \approx 81.8\%$; 4. University of Nevada: $\frac{24}{30} = 80.0\%$; 5. Louisiana State University: $\frac{20}{29} \approx 69.0\%$; 6. University of Texas: $\frac{20}{30} \approx 66.7\%$. **c.** The University of Illinois had the highest winning percentage, winning 97.0% of its games.

20. 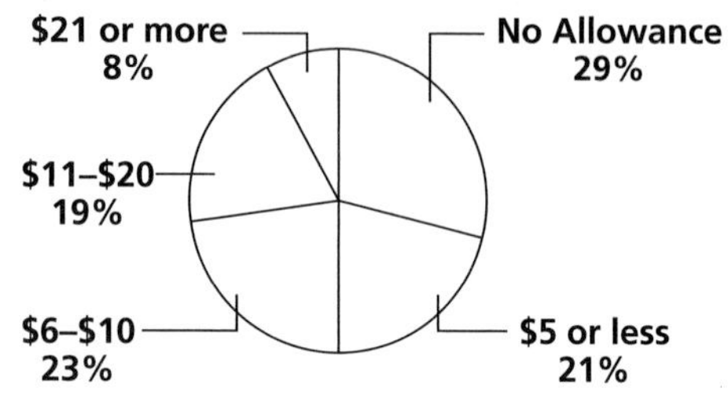

Self-Test Correlation Chart

Question	1	2	3	4	5	6	7	8	9	10
Objective(s)	B	B	A	C	L	F	D	D	C, G	G
Lesson(s)	2-1, 2-2	2-1, 2-2	2-1, 2-2	2-1, 2-10	2-1	2-7, 2-8, 2-9, 2-10	2-5, 2-6	2-5, 2-6	2-1, 2-2, 2-3, 2-10	2-2, 2-3

Question	11	12	13	14	15	16	17	18	19	20
Objective(s)	C	H	H	I	I	E	E	K	J	M
Lesson(s)	2-1, 2-10	2-7	2-7	2-2, 2-9	2-2, 2-9	2-4	2-4	2-4	2-9	2-9

Chapter Review (pp. 134–135)

1. 0 **3.** 3 **5.** ten-thousandths **7.** 0.0093 **9.** 4,700,000 **11.** forty and eight hundred sixty-seven thousandths **13.** 0.00523, 0.0523, 0.523 **15.** 11.2764, 11.2774, 11.2779 **17.** 4%, 30%, 0.35 **19.** Answers vary. Sample: 79.1231 and 79.1237 **21.** > **23.** = **25.** 5,000 **27.** 4,983 **29. a.** \$5, \$7, \$8 **b.** \$20 **31.** 7.2 cm **33. a.** 202 **b.** 20.2 **35.** Check students' work. They should draw a segment 62 mm long. **37.** Check students' work. They should draw a segment $4\frac{1}{2}$ cm long. **39.** 0.875 **41.** $0.\bar{6}$ **43.** 0.0144 **45.** $3.\overline{12}$ **47.** $\frac{1}{6}$ **49.** $\frac{8}{3}$ **51.** $166.\bar{6}\%$ **53.** 1.9% **55.** $\frac{1}{1{,}000}$; multiplying by $\frac{1}{1{,}000}$ moves the decimal point three places to the left **57. a.** 367.42 **b.** 3.6742 **c.** 0.36742 **d.** 0.0036742 **59.** $0.8\bar{3}$ **61.** $1.\overline{631}$ **63.** 2.34; $2\frac{17}{50}$ **65.** 0.4 **67.** 71% **69.** 8 mi **71.** 0.98 L **73.** 165,000 m **75.** *K, D, A, B* **77.** ≈33%

Chapter 3

Lesson 3-1 (pp. 138–143)

Questions: 1. 114.72 sec **3.** 250 in. **5.** Commutative Property of Addition **7.** $100\frac{5}{8}$ **9.** No, the total height when Joy stands on Harry's shoulders is $5\frac{5}{12} + 5\frac{8}{12} = 10\frac{10}{12} = 10\frac{5}{6}$ ft, which is more than $10\frac{1}{2}$ ft, so Joy's head will not fit under the bottom of the banner. **11.** $b + g + 1$ **13.** 19 lb, 14 oz

15.

Employee Height (in.)	Height in Clown Uniform (in.)
60	108
65	113
70	118
75	123
h	$h + 48$

17. \$34.90 **19.** \$3.20

21. a. Check students' work. They should draw a segment $4\frac{1}{2}$ in. long. **b.** Check students' work. They should draw a segment $4\frac{7}{8}$ in. long. **c.** $4\frac{7}{8}$ in.

Lesson 3-2 (pp. 144-152)

Guided Example 1: 14.23; 14.53; 1; 14.53

Guided Example 4: s; s; s; 4; 24 cm

Questions:

1. a.

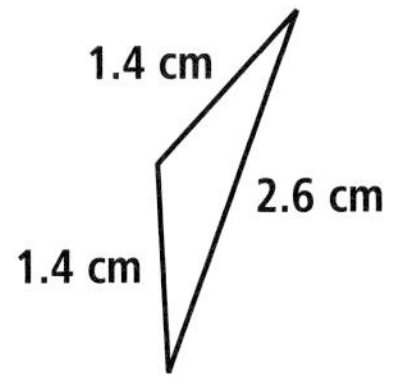

b. $p = (1.4 + 1.4) + 2.6 = 5.4$; $p = 1.4 + (1.4 + 2.6) = 5.4$; The perimeter is 5.4 cm. **3.** 16.75 mi **5. a.** $7639.7 + \left(\frac{3}{7} + \frac{4}{7}\right) = 7639.7 + 1 = 7640.7$ **b.** Associative Property of Addition

7. a.

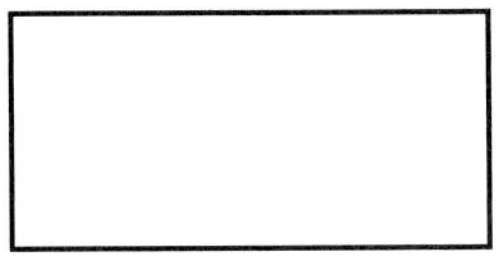

b. $p = 2L + 2W = 2 \cdot 6.5 + 2 \cdot 3.2$ $p = 19.4$; The perimeter of the rectangle is 19.4 cm, or 194 mm. **9. a.** C **b.** $p = 37.2$ cm

11. a.

b. yes; $p = 10.8$ cm **13. a.** They represent the distance between a city and itself. **b.** 0 **15. a.** Yes, the information in the bottom row is contained in the last column. **b.** Yes, the information in the nth column is contained in the nth row. **c.** 12

17. a. 4,608 ft

b.

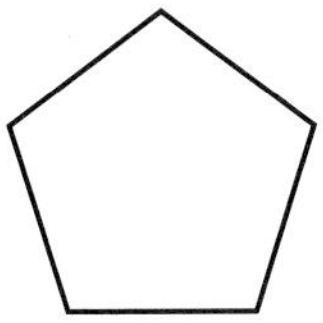

c. $5L$ **19.** packages 1, 2, 3, and 5 **21.** 6:25 P.M. **23. a.** 0.2, 20% **b.** 0.4, 40% **c.** 0.6, 60% **d.** 0.8, 80% **e.** 1, 100%

Lesson 3-3 (pp. 153-158)

Guided Example 3: 432; 581; 432; 581; -149; $149; 432; [(-)]; 432; -581; -149

Guided Example 4: –1; –5; –7; 14; 18; 6; 38; 25

Questions: 1. $4 + 5 = 9$; Margaret has $9. **3.** $18 + -5 = 13$; Brooklyn has $13. **5.** Melvin lost 2 pounds. **7. a.** negative **b.** positive **c.** negative **9.** 0 **11.** -3 **13.** The plot from after a month of training is the plot from before training slid one minute down (to the left). **15.** never **17. a.** iv **b.** Diagram iv shows an arrow pointing right that is one unit long starting at 0, followed by an arrow four units long pointing left starting at 1 and ending at -3. **c.** In diagram i, the arrow pointing right starts at 1 instead of 0. In diagram ii, both arrows start at 0. In iii, both arrows point to the left. **19.** $-143 + 38$; -105 m **21. a.** $-5 + -8 + -7 + 11$ **b.** -9 **c.** -9.15 **d.** The estimate was 0.15 too low. **23.** 34.25 ft **25.** -13°F is warmer **27.** neither

Lesson 3-4 (pp. 159-164)

Questions: 1. $66 + 0 = 66$; 66 in. **3.** $0 + 0.75 = 0.75$; 0.75 m **5.** The sum of any number and zero is the original number. **7.** $3\frac{3}{4} + -3\frac{3}{4} = 0$; 0 ft **9.** $10 + -10 = 0$; 0 yd **11.** opposite **13.** $-\frac{5}{8}$ in. **15.** $-m = 3.5$

17.

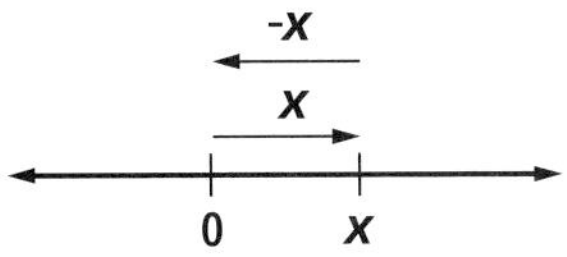

19. $\frac{4}{9}$ **21.** 1 **23.** $\frac{5}{6}$ **25. a.** -1, 1, -1 **b.** $\frac{4}{9}$; If there are an even number of negative signs, the answer is positive; if there are an odd number of negative signs, the answer is negative. Fifty is an even number, so the answer is positive. **27. a.** negative **b.** positive **c.** negative **29.** 7 weeks

Lesson 3-5 (pp. 165-171)

Questions: 1. $\overrightarrow{ZX}$, $\overrightarrow{ZY}$ **3.** $\angle XZY$, $\angle YZX$, $\angle Z$ **5.** Because $m\angle APB$ represents the measure of the angle for the shorter arc $\overset{\frown}{AB}$, he should have written $m\angle APB = 120°$. **7.** $m\angle HAT = 75°$ **9.** $m\angle A = 50°$ **11.** $m\angle A = 165°$

13.

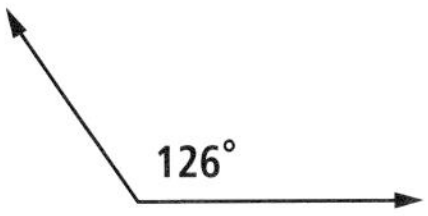

15.

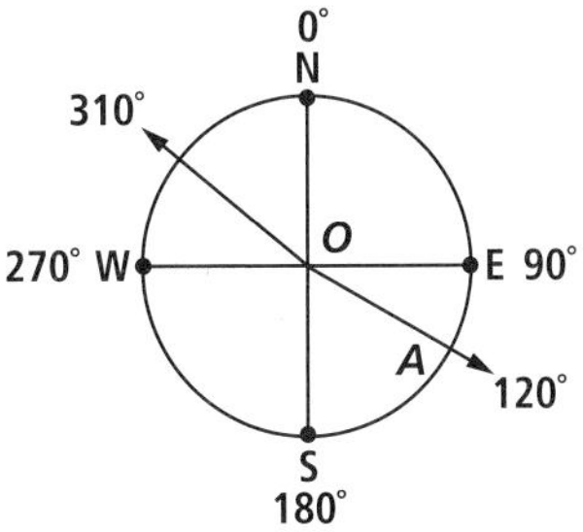

17. a. 3.6° **b.** 36° **c.** 90° **19.** 0¢; Additive Property of Opposites **21.** Selena's mom told her that if she ate her vegetables, she would be happy. **23. a.** 140 students **b.** 69 sixth graders **c.** 49.3% **d.** 69 students **e.** 49.3% **f.** Marcus **25.** $5\frac{1}{9}$

Lesson 3-6 (pp. 172-177)

Guided Example 2: a. $\frac{360}{5}$; 72° **b.** 2; 2; 72; 144°

Questions: 1. $\overset{\frown}{ED}$ **3.** Answers vary. Sample: $\angle ACE$ and $\angle ECB$ **5.** 110° **7.** 90° **9.** 45° **11.** 45° **13.** 180° **15.** 180° **17.** 180° **19.** 45° **21.** 180°

23. a.

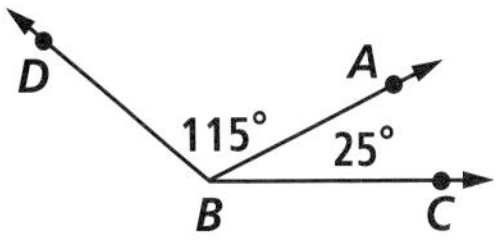

b. The angles do not add up to 180°. **25. a.** 18° **b.** 144° **c.** 54° **27.** 0° **29. a.** Liddle Middle School **b.** 6th graders **c.** 110 students **d.** 44%

Lesson 3-7 (pp. 178-183)

Questions: 1. $35.9 + 65.3 + a = 180$ **3.** 94°

5.

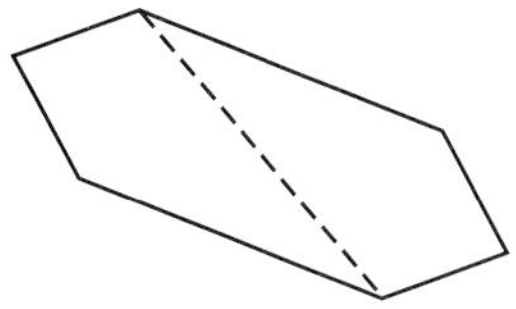

$2 \times 360° = 720°$ **7.** $m\angle A = 108°$ **9.** impossible, because then the third angle would be 0° **11.** possible, because three acute angles can add up to 180°

13. possible, because even if all angles are 90°, the angles add to 360° **15.** possible, because the fourth angle can be small enough that the angles still add up to 360° **17.** 137° **19.** 20° **21.** 83 ft

Lesson 3-8 (pp. 184–190)

Guided Example 2: Solution 1 18; 30; 36; 42; 54; 32; 40; 48; 56; 24; 48; $\frac{4}{4}$; $\frac{4}{24}$; $\frac{3}{3}$; $\frac{9}{24}$ **Solution 2** $\frac{8}{8}$; $\frac{8}{48}$; $\frac{6}{6}$; $\frac{18}{48}$; $\frac{26}{48}$; $\frac{13}{24}$

Guided Example 3: 48; 48; 96; 144; 192; 72; 144; 216; 188; 144; $\frac{3}{3}$; $\frac{39}{144}$; $\frac{2}{2}$; $\frac{38}{144}$; $\frac{77}{144}$

Questions: 1. $\frac{11}{4}$ mi **3.** $\frac{3}{4}$ in. + $\frac{5}{8}$ in. = $\frac{11}{8}$ in.

$\frac{3}{4}$" $\frac{5}{8}$"

5. $\frac{887}{2,000}$ **7.** 150 **9.** $\frac{21}{y}$; Let $y = 3$. $\frac{14}{3} + \frac{3}{3} + \frac{4}{3} = \frac{21}{3} = 7$ **11.** $\frac{9}{8}$; $0.625 + 0.5 = 1.125 = \frac{9}{8}$ **13.** $\frac{59}{60}$; $0.0167 + 0.9667 \approx 0.9834 = \frac{59}{60}$ **15. a.** $\frac{1}{4} + \frac{5}{10}$ **b.** $\frac{3}{4}$ **17. a.** Answers vary. Sample:

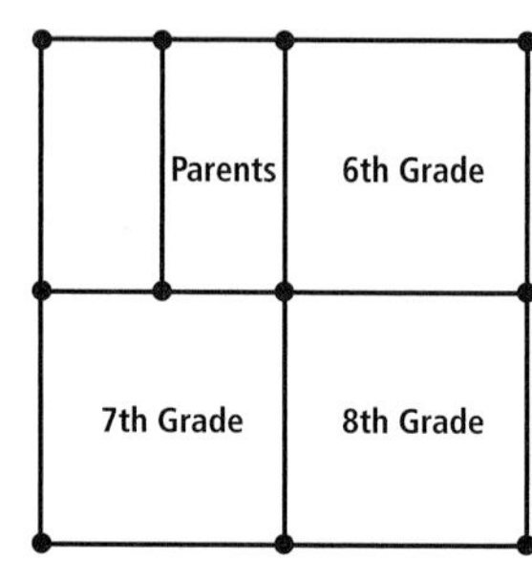

b. 12.5% **c.** $\frac{1}{16}$ **19.** $-\frac{5}{6}$; $-\frac{5}{6} \approx -0.833 \approx -\frac{10}{12}$ **21. a.** $\frac{21}{k}$ **b.** Answers vary. Sample: $k = 54$ **c.** Answers vary. Sample: $k = 4$ **d.** $k = 21$ **23.** 1,080° **25.** 18 in. **27.** Answers vary. Sample: -2 + 3 + -2 = -1; one stroke under par

Lesson 3-9 (pp. 191–195)

Guided Example 2: $8\frac{1}{2}$; $1\frac{3}{8}$; $1\frac{3}{8}$; $8\frac{4}{8}$; $1\frac{3}{8}$; $1\frac{3}{8}$; 10; $\frac{10}{8}$; 10; $1\frac{2}{8}$; $11\frac{2}{8}$; $11\frac{1}{4}$; Answers vary. Sample: The height of the completed picture is $11\frac{1}{4}$ inches.

Questions: 1. $9\frac{3}{4}$" × 13" **3.** $2\frac{11}{12}$ c **5.** $5\frac{4}{5} + 1\frac{5}{6} = 5\frac{24}{30} + 1\frac{25}{30} = 6\frac{49}{30} = 7\frac{19}{30}$ **7.** $32\frac{8}{45} + 18\frac{8}{9} = 32\frac{8}{45} + 18\frac{40}{45} = 50\frac{48}{45} = 51\frac{1}{15}$ **9.** $\frac{26}{9}$ **11. a.** 9' 8" **b.** $5\frac{9}{12} - \frac{11}{12} + 4\frac{10}{12} = 9\frac{8}{12}$ **13.** $1.625 + 13.24 + 9.265625 = 24.130625 = 24\frac{209}{1600}$ **15.** longer **17.** false **19.** 270° **21.** greater than **23.** 1,000,000,000

Self-Test (pp. 199–200)

1. $P = 2(l + w) = 2(30.5 + 15.6) = 2(46.1) = 92.2$ meters **2.** 20' = 240"; F = 2(30") + 240" = 300" = 25' **3.** 543 + (-4,210) = 543 – 4,210 = -3,667 **4.** $\left(-\frac{3}{5} + \frac{3}{5}\right) + \frac{7}{5} = 0 + \frac{7}{5} = \frac{7}{5}$ **5.** $3\frac{2}{3} + 3\frac{2}{3} = \frac{11 + 11}{3} = \frac{22}{3} = 7\frac{1}{3}$ miles **6.** m∠SOX = 360° – m∠TOX – m∠BOT – m∠BOS = 360° – 110° – 80° – 75° = 95° **7.** $\frac{5 + 3 + 6}{7} = \frac{14}{7} = 2$ **8.** $2\frac{7}{10} - \frac{3}{5} = \frac{27}{10} - \frac{6}{10} = \frac{21}{10}$ **9.** $-3\frac{3}{4} + -2 + \frac{3}{4} = -3 - 2 = -5$ **10.** Opposite of Opposites Property **11.** Additive Property of Opposites **12.** Commutative Property of Addition **13.**

-7
13
-5 0 5 10 15

14. ∠O, ∠NOT, ∠TON **15.** 130° **16.** 4' 7" + 2' 6" = 7' 1"

17.

-110
-36
-150 -100 -50 0

18. $p = 6 + 7 + 13 + 8 + 2 + 6 + 5 = 47$ cm

19. $p = 4 \cdot 7.6 = 30.4$ cm **20.** $4\frac{3}{4} + 7\frac{1}{2} = (4 + 7) + (\frac{3}{4} + \frac{7}{4}) = 12\frac{1}{4}$ lb **21.** $31\frac{41}{60} - 2\frac{18}{60} = 29\frac{23}{60}$ min

22. D; m∠LIT + m∠TIP = 50° + 130° = 180°

23. m∠E = 360° – 88° – 55° – 77° = 140°

24. m∠S = 180° – 49.2° – 38.7° = 92.1°

Self-Test Correlation Chart

Question	**1**	**2**	**3**	**4**	**5**	**6**	**7**	**8**	**9**	**10**
Objective(s)	I	I	B	B	J	F	D	D	D	E
Lesson(s)	3-1	3-1	3-3	3-3	3-2	3-6	3-8, 3-9	3-8, 3-9	3-8, 3-9	3-1, 3-2, 3-4
Question	**11**	**12**	**13**	**14**	**15**	**16**	**17**	**18**	**19**	**20**
Objective	E	E	L	C	C	H	L	A	A	H
Lesson(s)	3-1, 3-2, 3-4	3-1, 3-2, 3-4	3-3	3-5	3-5	3-1, 3-9	3-3	3-2	3-2	3-1, 3-9
Question	**21**	**22**	**23**	**24**						
Objective	K	F	G	G						
Lesson(s)	3-3	3-6	3-7	3-7						

Chapter Review (pp. 201-205)

1. 32 cm **3.** 25.4 m **5.** 10.84 yd **7.** 2.3 **9.** 83 **11.** $y + z$ **13.** 95° **15.** 45° **17.** $\angle AEB$ **19.** $\frac{8}{19}$ **21.** $-\frac{1}{6}$ **23.** 6 **25.** $7\frac{2}{9}$ **27.** 50; Additive Identity Property of Zero **29.** 0; Additive Property of Opposites **31.** 17 **33.** $m\angle OCT = 116°$ **35.** $m\widehat{AC} = 120$ **37.** $m\angle AHB = 60°$ **39.** $m\angle A = 100°$ **41.** 9 mi **43.** $5\frac{1}{6}$ mi **45.** 5,298 feet above sea level **47.** 25.75 km **49.** 2.36 m **51.** 6.5 mi **53.** 123 yd **55.** 5 ft back

57.

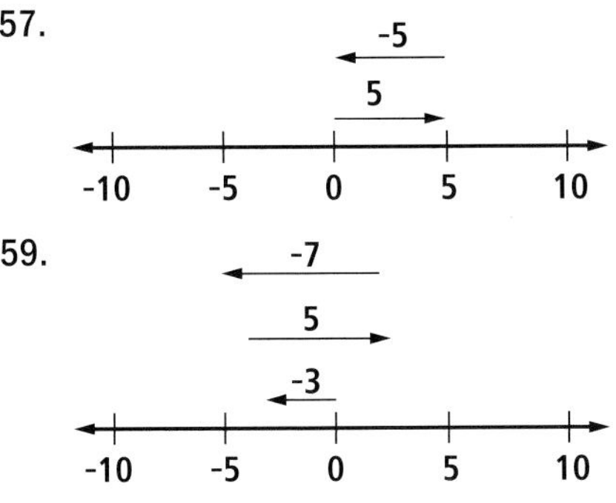

59.

61. -40 feet

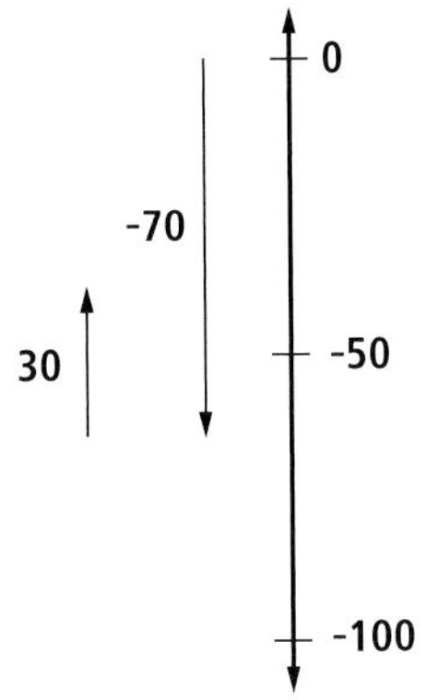

Chapter 4

Lesson 4-1 (pp. 208-213)

Guided Example 1: 7.6; 110; 110; 7.6; 102.4; 70; 7.6; 62.4; 102.4 cm; 62.4 cm

Questions: **1.** \$7.74 **3.** 52 cm by 32 cm **5.** 42 in. **7. a.** $107\frac{3}{4}$ lb **b.** $106\frac{3}{4}$ lb **c.** 111.7 lb **d.** 108 lb **e.** $108 - n$ lb **9. a.** 37 **b.** 43 **c.** 37 **11. a.** false **b.** $2 = 4 - 2 \neq 2 - 4 = -2$ **13. a.** deficit **b.** \$248,100,000,000 **15. a.** $LP = 1{,}190 - 174 = 1{,}016$ mi **b.** $SW = 808$ mi; $SP = 634$ mi **17. a.** 66 games **b.** $162 - W - L$ games **19.** $\frac{131}{225}$ **21.** 75° **23.**

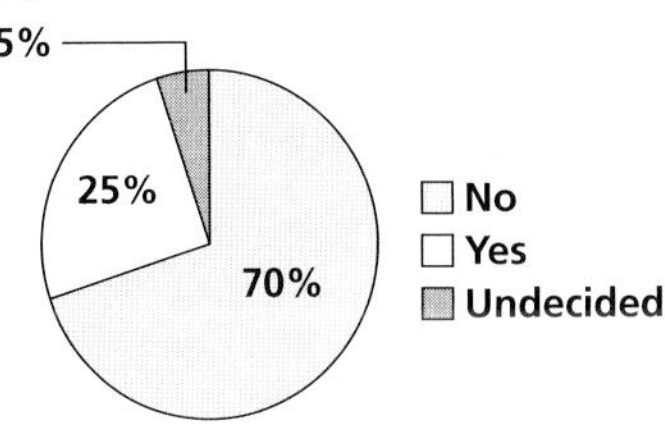

Lesson 4-2 (pp. 214-219)

Questions: **1.** Yolanda held her breath 45 seconds (or $\frac{3}{4}$ minute) longer. **3.** Mia was 8 points too low. Jacqueline was 4 points too high. Nina was 3 points too low. Russell was 16 points too low. **5.** 50.628 sec **7.** The Mountain Lion cabin campers ate more by 4 ounces. **9.** 20% **11.** Answers vary. Sample: 519 pages **13.** 285 days old **15.** $5\frac{3}{4}$ hr **17.** 1,186 peanuts **19.** \$53 **21.** Answers vary. Sample: $\frac{2}{5}$, $\frac{4}{10}$, $\frac{56}{140}$, $\frac{28}{70}$

Lesson 4-3 (pp. 220-225)

Guided Example 2: -11°C; 8°C; -19°C; -11°C; -8°C; -19°C; -19°C **Guided Example 4:** -18; 5; -8; 1; -18; -8; -18; -8; 5; 25; 1; -33; 31; -2

Questions: **1.**

-4 -3 -2 -1 0 1 2 3 4 5 6 7

3. a. $44 - 7$ **b.** $44 + -7$ **c.** 38°F **5.** 17

7. a. -28°C

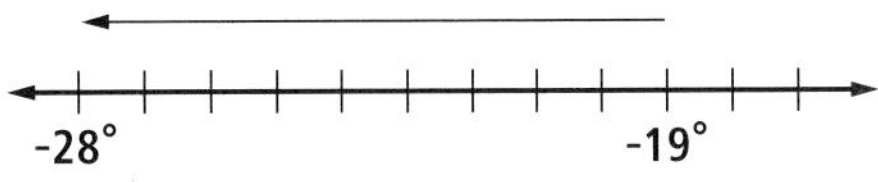

b. -10°C

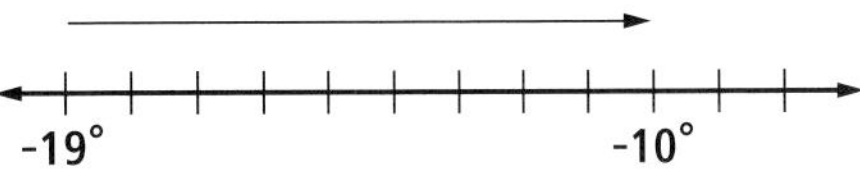

9. 9.5 **11.** -486 **13.** $-\frac{7}{12}$ **15. a.** She is not doing the problems correctly. She should not switch the sign of the minuend. **b.** $-4 - 8 = -4 + -8$; $-13 - -12\frac{1}{2} = -13 + 12\frac{1}{2}$; $47 - -20.5 = 47 + 20.5$ **17. a.** \$145 **b.** $m - 5$

19. a.

Kelvin	Celsius	Letter
0	-273°	G
273	0°	I
373	100°	H
383	110°	T
100	-173°	N
300	27°	S
d	$(d - 273)°$	

b. THINGS **21.** $B - R$ magazines **23. a.** 11 lb, 2 oz **b.** 178 oz **25.** 3,000 **27.** B

Lesson 4-4 (pp. 226-229)

Guided Example 2: **a.** -418; 9,266; 9,266 **b.** 9,266; -418; 8,848; -418; 9,266; 8,848; 8,848; -418; 9,266; 8,848; 9,266; -418

Questions: **1.** $-8 - -5 = -3$; $-8 - -3 = -5$; $-3 + -5 = -8$; $-5 + -3 = -8$

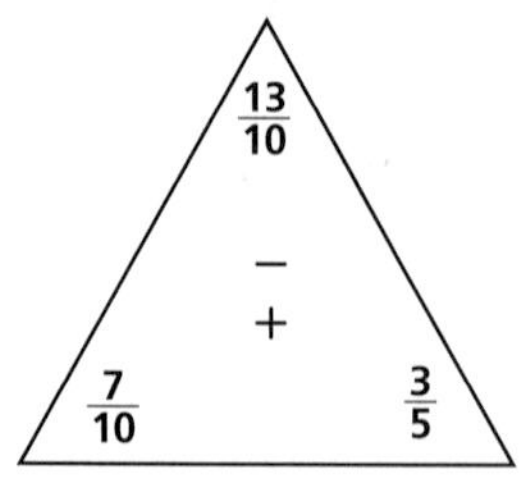

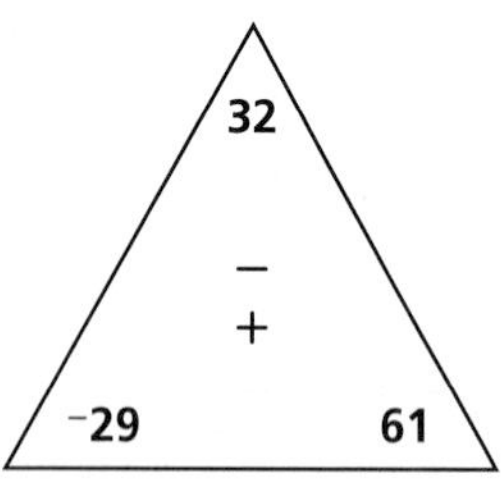

3. $\frac{13}{10} - \frac{7}{10} = \frac{3}{5}; \frac{13}{10} - \frac{3}{5} = \frac{7}{10}; \frac{7}{10} + \frac{3}{5} = \frac{13}{10}; \frac{3}{5} + \frac{7}{10} = \frac{13}{10}$ **5.** $32 - -29 = 61$; $32 - 61 = -29$; $-29 + 61 = 32$; $61 + -29 = 32$ **7.** $\frac{1}{6}$ of the box of cereal

9. a. The 1 should be at the top. What she currently has is $1 + -2 = 3$, which is not true. **b.**

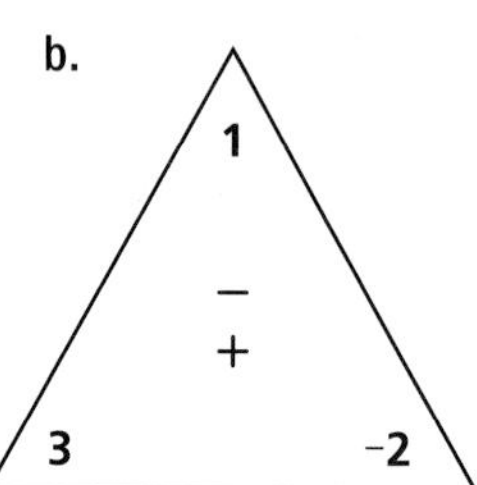

11. incorrect; Answers vary. Sample: 0.420 should be 6.18. The student used 0.64 as the minuend instead of 6.4. **13.** correct; $-57 + 11 = -46$

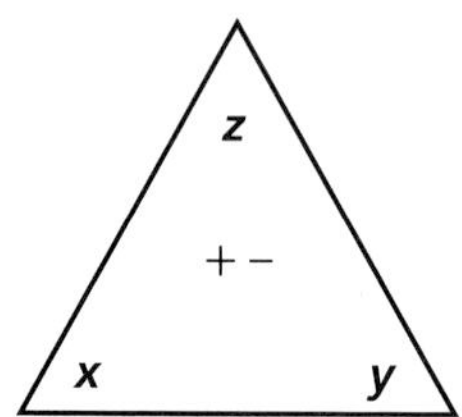

15. B, C, G **17.** 2 **19. a.** about 13 ft^2 **b.** about 41 ft^2

Lesson 4-5 (pp. 230-236)

Guided Example 2: 73°; supplementary; 41; 180°
Questions: 1. $136\frac{19°}{30}$ **3.** supplementary **5.** $\overleftrightarrow{XZ}$ intersects $\overrightarrow{WY}$ at its endpoint. **7.** 135° **9.** 179.5° **11.** 30° **13.** 120° **15.** $180° - x$ **17. a.** $49° + x° = 87°$ **b.** 38° **19.** 14° **21. a.** No, ∠1 is not part of a linear pair, nor is it a vertical angle with a known angle. **b.** No, ∠2 is not part of a linear pair, nor is it a vertical angle with a known angle. **c.** yes; m∠1 + m∠2 + m∠3 = 235° **23.** 67.46° **25.** 1,378,220

Lesson 4-6 (pp. 237-242)

Questions: 1. obtuse **3.** acute **5.** straight **7.** Answers vary. Sample: Webster Ave. **9.** Answers vary. Sample: Bristol Street **11.** 90°, 42° **13. a.** ∠*BCA* and ∠*ACE* **b.** ∠*BAC* and ∠*ACB* **15.** m∠1 = 90°, m∠2 = m∠3 = 135° **17.** $a = 90°$, $b = c = d = 30°$ **19.** Answers vary. Sample: Because Willow Street and Berkshire Street are parallel to each other, then angles 11 and 12 are supplementary.

21.

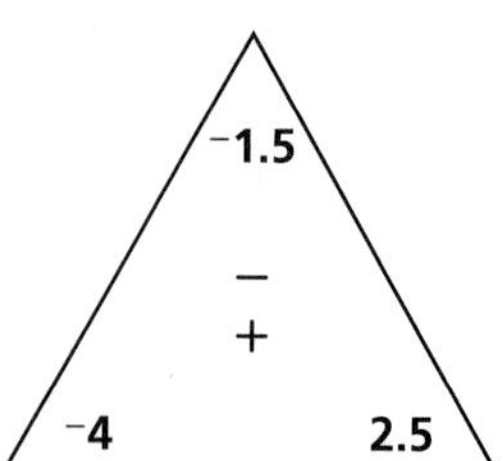

23. $\frac{1}{4}$ **25.** $-\frac{13}{12}$ **27.** Answers vary. Sample: "Half of the people are carrying umbrellas." or "One in two people are carrying umbrellas."

Lesson 4-7 (pp. 243-248)

Guided Example 2: Solution 1. $\frac{17}{5}; \frac{9}{5}; \frac{8}{5}; \frac{3}{5}$ **Solution 2.** $3; 1; \frac{2}{5}; \frac{4}{5}; 1\frac{3}{5}$ **Guided Example 3:** 2; 3; 8; 3
Questions: 1. 1.75 mi **3. a.** Answers vary. Sample: 30, 60, 90 **b.** 30 **c.** $\frac{101}{30}$ **5. a.** $10\frac{3}{5}$ **b.** $\frac{53}{5}$ **7.** $-\frac{6}{z}$ **9.** $1\frac{11}{12}$ **11.** $5\frac{17}{20}$ **13. a.** Jessica, Pearl, Yuma **b.** $\frac{2}{15}$ **c.** more than **15.** Stephanie; 30 min **17. a.** 55° **b.** 35° **19.** $-52 - -31 = -21$; $-52 - -21 = -31$; $-31 + -21 = -52$; $-21 + -31 = -52$ **21.** The program rounded up, because flour costs \$3.62192, and it is rounded to \$3.63.

Lesson 4-8 (pp. 249-254)

Guided Example 2: $-3\frac{2}{5}$; $9 - A = -3\frac{2}{5}$; $9 - -3\frac{2}{5} = A$; $A + -3\frac{2}{5} = 9$; $-3\frac{2}{5} + A = 9$; 9; $-3\frac{2}{5}$; 9; $3\frac{2}{5}$; $12\frac{2}{5}$
Guided Example 3: a. *c*
b.

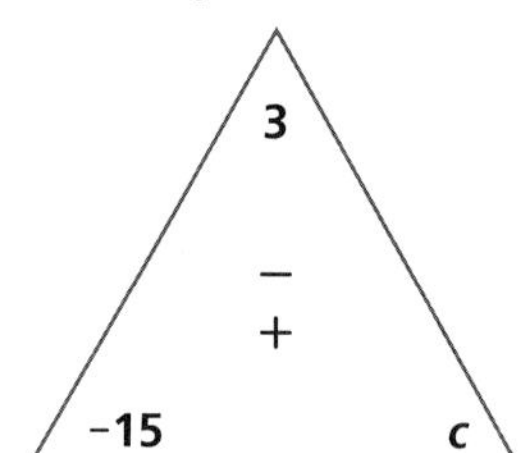

$c + -15 = 3$; $-15 + c = 3$; $3 - c = -15$; $3 - -15 = c$; $c = 3 - -15$; 18 **c.** -15; 18; 3 **d.** 18

Questions: 1. a. Yes, it is a mathematical sentence with an equal sign. **b.** No, it does not have an equal sign. **c.** Yes, it is a mathematical sentence with an equal sign. **d.** Yes, it is a mathematical sentence with an equal sign. **3.** B
5. a.

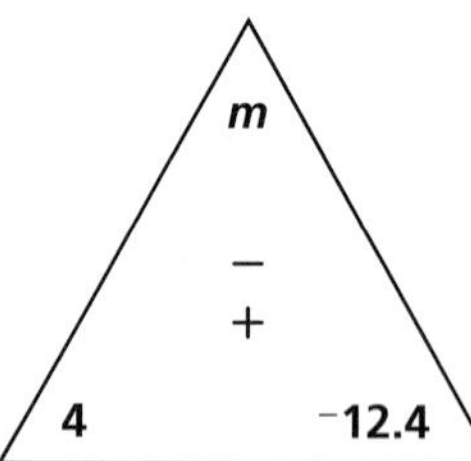

b. $m - -12.4 = 4$; $m - 4 = -12.4$; $4 + -12.4 = m$; $-12.4 + 4 = m$ **c.** $4 + -12.4 = m$; $m = -8.4$ **d.** $-8.4 - 4 = -12.4$ **7. a.** Answers vary. Sample: $90° - b° = 23°$

b.

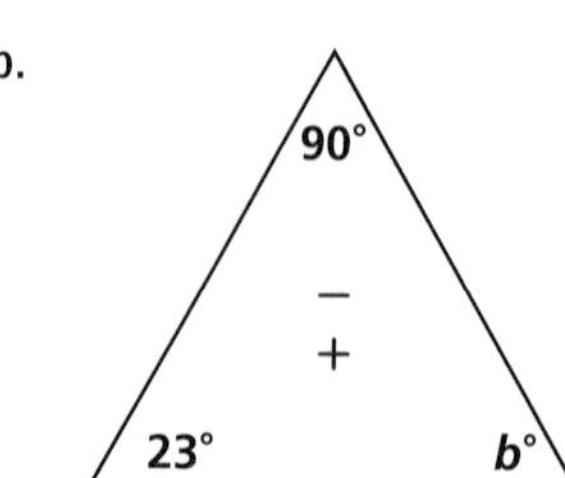

c. $90° - 23° = b°$; $67° = b°$ **9.** Answers vary. Sample: $a = 70$, $b = 110$; $a = -25$, $b = 205$; $a = 132$, $b = 48$ **11. a.** $80 - 12.60 - h = 52.90$ **b.** $h = 14.50$

c. Josh paid \$14.50 for his haircut. **13.** Answers vary. Sample: Darius multiplied the left side of the equation by -1 but not the right side. He needs to multiply both sides of the equation by the same number to maintain equality. **15. a.** 42 **b.** -28 **c.** -49 **d.** 32.7 **e.** -2.2 **f.** 17 CANNOT **17. a.** ∠1, ∠3 **b.** ∠2 **c.** ∠4 **d.** none

Lesson 4-9 (pp. 255–260)

Guided Example 2: 25.75; 41.34; 67.09: -67.09; -67.09; -67.09; 0; 12.91; 12.91: 25.75 + 41.34 + 12.91 = 80; They will need \$12.91 more to buy Rodney's present.
Questions: **1.** true **3. a.** $x + 500 = 18{,}000$ **b.** $x = 17{,}500$ grams **5.** C **7.** D **9. a.** $-\frac{1}{3}$ **b.** $x = -1$ **11. a.** 46.3 **b.** $m = 129.2$ **13. a.** $w - 105 = 175$ **b.** $w - 105 + 105 = 175 + 105$; $w + 0 = 280$; $w = 180$ **c.** 280 – 105 = 175 **d.** Governor Huckabee weighed 280 pounds before dieting. **15.** *known* **17.** 990 g **19.** \$6.08 **21.** 4 **23.** 1 **25. a.** 0.5428 **b.** 5.428 **c.** 54.28 **d.** 5,428 **e.** 54,280

Self-Test (p. 264–265)

1. 15 – 42 – -5 = 15 + -42 + 5 = -42 + (15 + 5) = -42 + 20 = -22 **2.** -4.15 – -3.9 + 4.85 = -4.15 + 3.9 + 4.85 = -4.15 + (3.9 + 4.85) = -4.15 + 8.75 = 4.6 **3.** $\frac{4}{7}$ **4.** $-1\frac{1}{24}$ **5.** $1\frac{19}{20}$ **6.** \$3.94 **7.** 65.82 points **8.** 59° + m∠*DOA* = 180°; 59° + -59° + m∠*DOA* = 180° + -59°; m∠*DOA* = 121° **9.** 59° **10.** ∠2 and ∠3 **11.** Answers vary. Sample: ∠4 is acute and ∠1 is obtuse **12.** $x - -25 = -73$; $x + 25 = -73$; $x + 25 + -25 = -73 + -25$; $x = -98$; -98 – -25 = -98 + 25 = -73 **13. a.** $x + 3.7 = 5.7$ **b.** $x + 3.7 + -3.7 = 5.7 + -3.7$; $x = 2$ **c.** 2 + 3.7 = 5.7 **d.** Moses needs to save \$2.00 more. **14.** $h + 3.7 = 5$ ft, 3 in. = 63 in.; $h + 3.7 = 63$; $h + 3.7 + -3.7 = 63 + -3.7$; $h = 59.3 = 4$ ft, 11.3 in. **15.** $3\frac{1}{2}$ **16.** 1.7 – 1.3 = 1.7 + -1.3 = 0.4

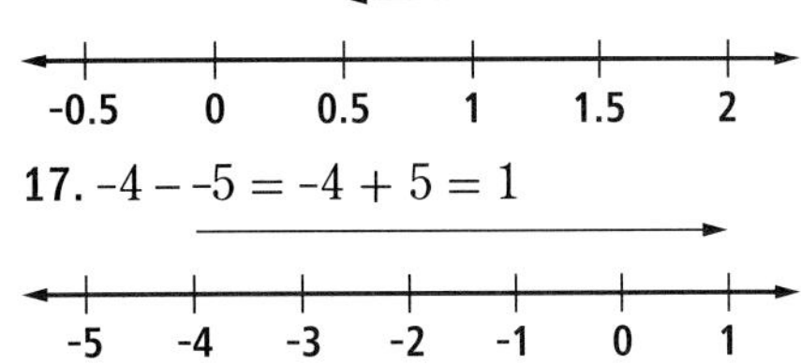

17. -4 – -5 = -4 + 5 = 1

-5 -4 -3 -2 -1 0 1

18. 8.8 – 13.2 = -4.4; 8.8 – -4.4 = 13.2; -4.4 + 13.2 = 8.8; 13.2 + -4.4 = 8.8
19. a.

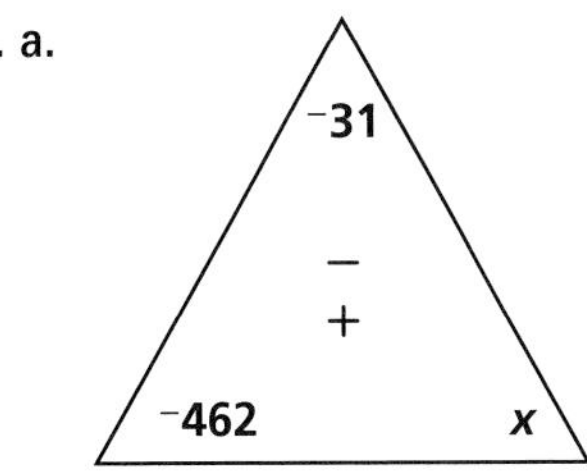

b. $-462 + x = -31$; $x + -462 = -31$; $-31 - x = -462$; $-31 - -462 = x$ **c.** $x = -31 - -462$; $x = -31 + 462$; $x = 431$ **20.** $w + 0.8$ kg = 2 kg + 7 kg + 8 kg + 3 kg + 8 kg; $w + 0.8$ kg + -0.8 kg = 28 kg + -0.8 kg; $w = 27.2$ kg **21.** -5 **22.** $-m$; s; r **23.** $12 - t = 92$; $12 + -t + t = 92 + t$; $12 + -92 = 92 + t + -92$; $-80 = t$; -80°F **24.** $45 + 30 + x = 180$; $75 + x = 180$; $75 + -75 + x = 180 + -75$; $x = 105$; 105° **25.** $2.7 - n = -5.3$; $2.7 + -n + n = -5.3 + n$; $2.7 + 5.3 = -5.3 + 5.3 + n$; $n = 8$

Self-Test Correlation Chart

Question	1	2	3	4	5	6	7	8	9	10
Objective(s)	A	A	A	A	A	H	I	D	D	E
Lesson(s)	4-3, 4-7	4-3, 4-7	4-3, 4-7	4-3, 4-7	4-3, 4-7	4-1	4-2	4-5	4-5	4-5, 4-6
Question	**11**	**12**	**13**	**14**	**15**	**16**	**17**	**18**	**19**	**20**
Objective(s)	E	G	K	J	I	L	L	M	M	N
Lesson(s)	4-5, 4-6	4-9	4-8, 4-9	4-3	4-2	4-3	4-3	4-4, 4-8	4-4, 4-8	4-9
Question	**21**	**22**	**23**	**24**	**25**					
Objective(s)	C	C	J	F	B					
Lesson(s)	4-3	4-3	4-3	4-5, 4-6	4-8					

Chapter Review (pp. 266–269)

Questions: **1.** 39 **3.** -74 **5.** $-\frac{23}{26}$ **7.** $3\frac{5}{8}$ **9.** $m = 18$ **11.** $x = 10.76$ **13.** -3 + 9 + -5 = 1 **15.** 3.5 + 2.45 + -1.28 = 4.67 **17.** $m + -n$ **19.** ∠*BOD*, ∠*BOA*, ∠*DOC* **21.** 88° **23.** Answers vary. Sample: Two angles are complementary when they add up to 90°. **25.** obtuse **27.** acute **29.** 90°; right **31.** $a = 140°$; $b = 50°$; $c = 90°$; $d = 90°$ **33.** -23; $x = -8$; 23 + -8 = 15 **35.** $-3\frac{3}{4}$; $a = -2\frac{1}{4}$; $1\frac{1}{2} = -2\frac{1}{4} + 3\frac{3}{4}$ **37.** -3.2; $c = -1.4$; -1.4 – -3.2 = 1.8 **39.** $\frac{17}{20}$ **41.** 336 **43.** 0.035 **45.** -54,269 **47.** 6° **49.** $w + \frac{5}{8} = 3\frac{1}{2}$; $w = 2\frac{2}{3}$ lb

51.

-14 -12 -10 -8 -6 -4 -2 0

53.

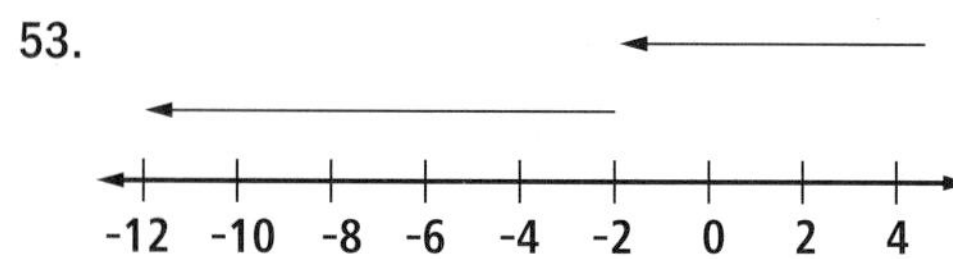

55.

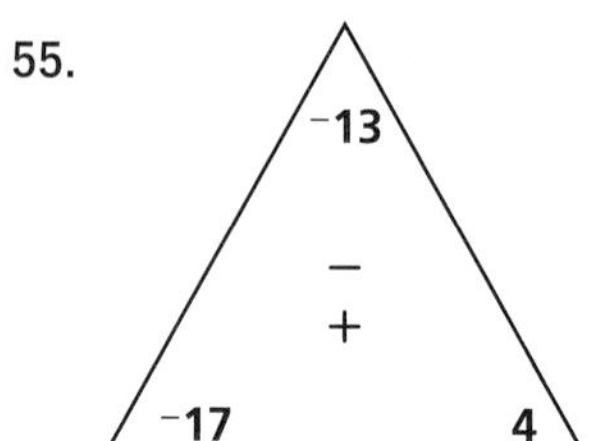

57.

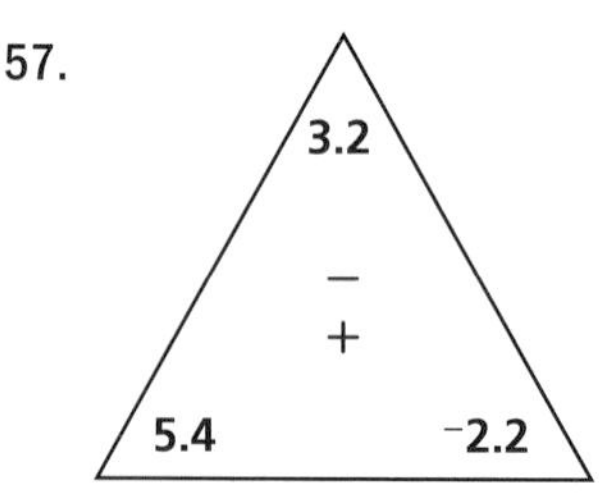

59. 5.7 + -5.5 = 0.2; -5.5 + 5.7 = 0.2; 0.2 – 5.7 = -5.5; 0.2 – -5.5 = 5.7

61. $x = 2.85 - 0.25 = 2.6$

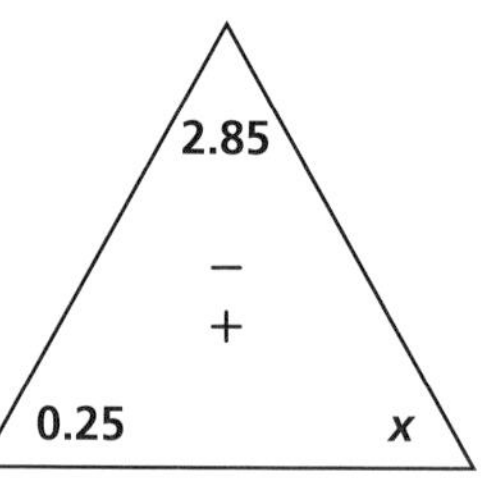

63. 13.76 – 10.4 = d; 13.76 – d = 10.4; 10.4 + d = 13.76; d + 10.4 = 13.76; d = 3.36 65. 32,500 g 66. 32,500 g

67. $m = 270$ g

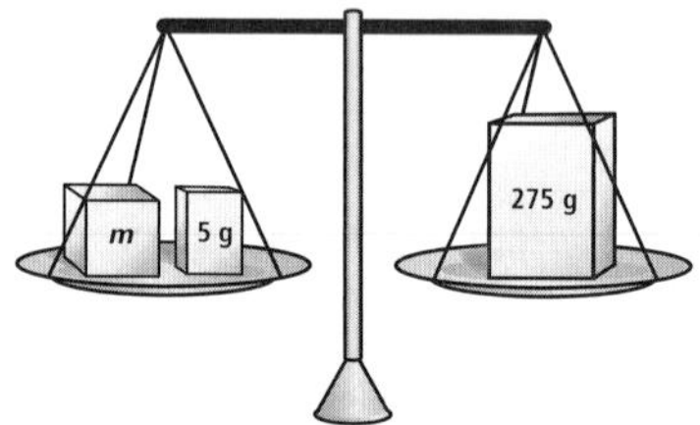

Chapter 5

Lesson 5-1 (pp. 272-277)

Questions: 1. One meaning of the word statistics is that it is a field of study—the science of the collection, organization, and interpretation of data. The second meaning is a single number used to describe a set of numbers. 3. 774,250 5. true 7. mean 9. mode 11. a. 2 b. 1 and 2 c. 1.9 d. 5 e. Answers vary. Sample: The easiest value to find was the mode because each frequency of each age is already displayed in the table. The mean was the most difficult to find because it required adding all of the data and dividing by the total number of students. 13. a. mean, median b. none c. minimum, maximum, mode 15. Answers vary. Sample:

Number	Frequency
5	1
6	0
7	1
8	1
9	6
10	1
11	1
12	6
13	4

17. mode 19. Addition Property of Equality 21. false 23. a. from left to right: Hong Kong, Honolulu, London, Los Angeles b. Chicago, Washington, D.C., New York, Honolulu, London, Paris, Hong Kong c. This number appears twice because there are two cells in the table that give the distance between Los Angeles and Hong Kong, namely 7,195 miles.

Lesson 5-2 (pp. 278-283)

Questions: 1a. subtract 1,623 from the current year b. Germany 3. Answers vary. Sample: [STAT] 2: Sort A [2nd] [L1] [ENTER] 5. 580 7. 2,149 9. a. 0, 10, 20, 25, 30, 40, 45, 75, 128, 180 b. max: 180; min: 0; range: 180; median: 35 c. 55.3 d. 553 min 11. a. 95 b. 90 13. a. max: 7.82; min: 2.65; range: 5.17; mode: 7.82; median: 7.12; mean: 6.32 b. yes; 2.65, 4.19, 5.61, 5.72, 7.49, 7.64, 7.82, 7.82 c. yes; 4.19, 5.61, 5.72, 7.11, 7.13, 7.49, 7.64, 7.82 d. no e. yes; 2.65, 4.19, 5.61, 5.72, 7.11, 7.13, 7.49, 7.64 15. 90 17. a. \$20.67 b. min: 33 oranges; max: 45 oranges c. min: \$0.46; max: \$0.63 19. ten

Lesson 5-3 (pp. 284-288)

Guided Example 1: 2, 9, 3, 4, 5, 0, 1, 1, 1, 2, 4, 3, 6, 7, 2, 5, 3; 62; 12th; 13th; 100; 101; 100.5; 133; 101; 71

Guided Example 2:

Stem	Leaves										
1	2										
0											
–0	2										
–1	5	6	7	7	9	9					
–2	7	3	5	7	9						
–3	0	2	2	4	4	5	6	6	7	7	9
–4	0	0	0	0	2	5	7	7	7	8	8
–5	0	0	0	1	2	4	5	8			
–6	0	0	0	1	6	9					
–7	0										
–8	0										

Questions: **1.** The record low temperature of two states is -17. **3.** 1 **5.** The 0 stem is for numbers between 0 and 10, and the -0 stem is for numbers between 0 and -10. **7.** Answers vary. Sample: A stem-and-leaf plot is like a histogram on its side, so you can visually see the distribution of the statistics, which you cannot do with a table. Also, the data on a stem-and-leaf plot can be ordered, making it easier to determine values like the median, mode, and range. **9.** -80 **11.** -39.9

13. a.

Stem	Leaves
0	7
1	3 3 4 4 5 6 6 7 7 7 8 8 9 9 9
2	0 1 1 1 3 4 4 4 4 5 6 6 7 8
3	1 1

b. max: 31; min: 7; range: 24; median: 19.5; mode: 24 **c.** Answers vary. Sample: It would be easier to find the mean from a calculator list because the calculator can find all single-variable statistics for this set. **d.** 20.25 **e.** Answers vary. Sample: The average NFL team threw 20 touchdown passes in 2006. However, there were some that threw as many as 31 touchdowns. **15.** true **17.** Answers vary. Sample: 5, 7, 8, 12, 13 **19.** $m = 2.9$ **21.** $k = 98.3°$

Lesson 5-4 (pp. 289–294)

Guided Example 1:

Weight Interval (pounds)	Frequency	Relative Frequency
60-69	3	$\frac{3}{24} = 12.5\%$
70-79	1	$\frac{1}{24} \approx 4.17\%$
80-89	3	$\frac{3}{24} = 12.5\%$
90-99	4	$\frac{4}{24} \approx 16.7\%$
100-109	7	$\frac{7}{24} \approx 29.2\%$
110-119	3	$\frac{3}{24} = 12.5\%$
120-129	2	$\frac{2}{24} \approx 8.33\%$
130-139	1	$\frac{1}{24} \approx 4.17\%$

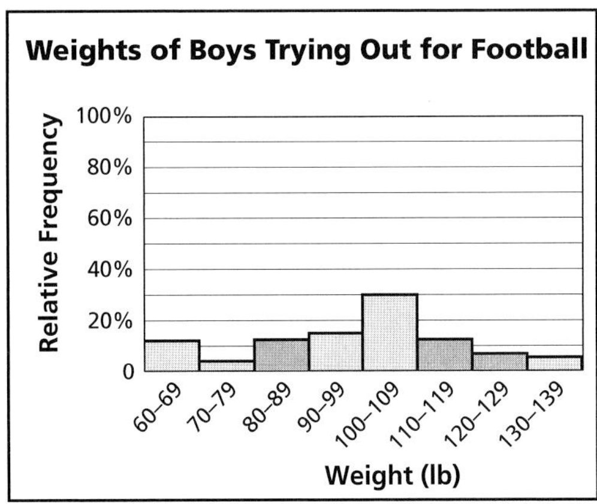

Questions: **1. a.** min: 65; max: 100; median: 88

b.

Exam Scores	Frequency	Relative Frequency
61-70	1	3.33%
71-80	4	13.3%
81-90	15	50.0%
91-100	10	33.3%

c.

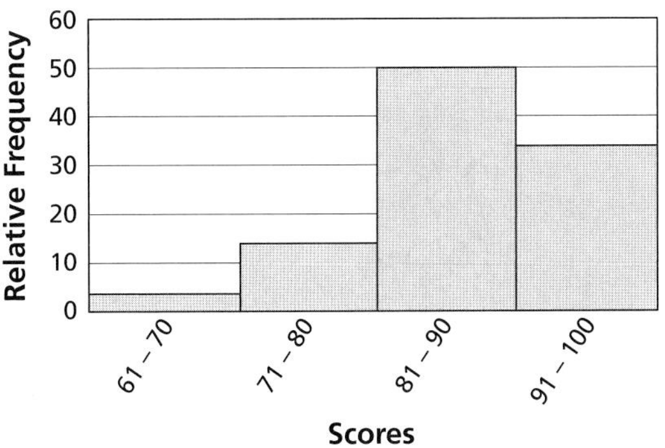

3. Answers vary. Sample: The histogram of Example 1 records the same data as the stem-and-leaf plot of Lesson 5-3. We can imagine a fraction of each bar as a representation of a respective stem-and-leaf plot entry. **5. a.** Version 2 **b.** Version 1 has a *y*-scale that does not start from zero. Version 3 has a *y*-scale that does not have uniform intervals. Version 4 has bars that do not have uniform width. **7.** Graph A is a bar graph that gives the mean salaries of workers 18 years and older in 2002 given the amount of education the workers have received. **9.** about \$9,000 **11.** about 22 million **13.** Graph B **15.** $a = -\frac{5}{6}$ **17.** $1\frac{1}{10}$ cups

Lesson 5-5 (pp. 295-300)

Guided Example 1:

Step 1		Step 2	Step 3	
Activity	Amount of Time (hr)	Fraction of Total	Calculation	Degrees
Sleeping	9	$\frac{9}{24}$	$\frac{9}{24} \cdot 360°$	135°
School	7	$\frac{7}{24}$	$\frac{7}{24} \cdot 360°$	105°
Soccer	2	$\frac{2}{24}$	$\frac{2}{24} \cdot 360°$	30°
Homework	1	$\frac{1}{24}$	$\frac{1}{24} \cdot 360°$	15°
Other	5	$\frac{5}{24}$	$\frac{5}{24} \cdot 360°$	75°
Total	24	$\frac{24}{24}$	$1 \cdot 360°$	360°

Step 5 and 6

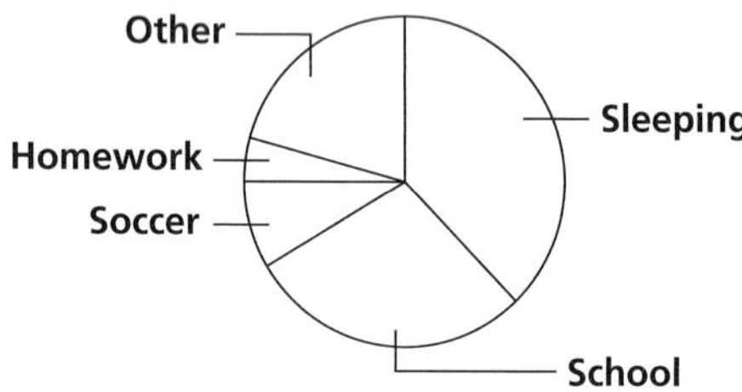

Questions: **1. a.** 3 **b.** rode the bus: 225°; walked: 60°; rode in a car: 75°

c.

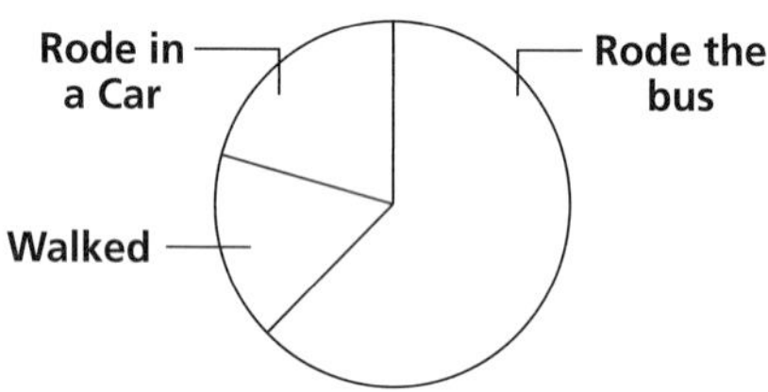

3. bar graphs, circle graphs **5. a.** Kahoolawe

b.

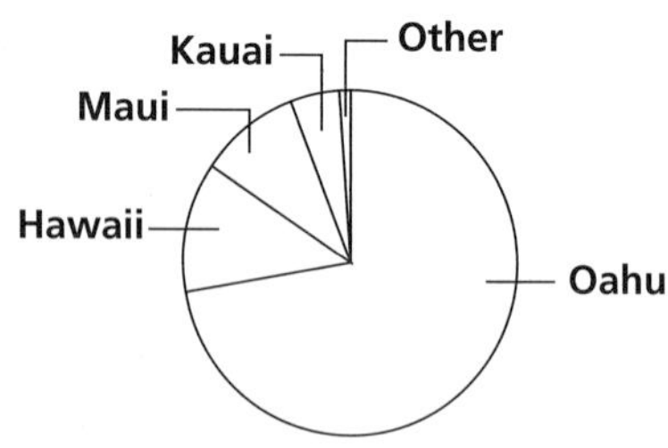

c. Answers vary. Sample: The island with the greatest area, Hawaii (Big Island), does not have the greatest population. Oahu has the greatest population yet it is rather small in area. **7. a.** categorical **b.** numerical **9. a.** poultry and eggs: 82.8°; cattle and calves: 147.6°; dairy: 68.4°; hogs and pigs: 43.2°; all other livestock: 14.4° **b.** cattle and calves **c.** False

11. a. 1900: Graph 1; 2000: Graph 2 **b.** B **c.** Answers vary. Sample: I estimated that the hogs and pigs sector was between $\frac{1}{4}$ and $\frac{1}{3}$ of the circle graph, and that amount is within the 21–40% range. **d.** Answers vary. Sample: The biggest change occurred in the amount of cattle. In 1900, a little over 33% of livestock was cattle, and in 2000, the amount of cattle nearly doubled.

13. a.

6	0 1 1 3 3 3 4 5 7 8
7	0 2 2 3

b.

Temperature (°F)	Frequency
60-63	6
64-67	3
68-71	2
72-75	3

c.

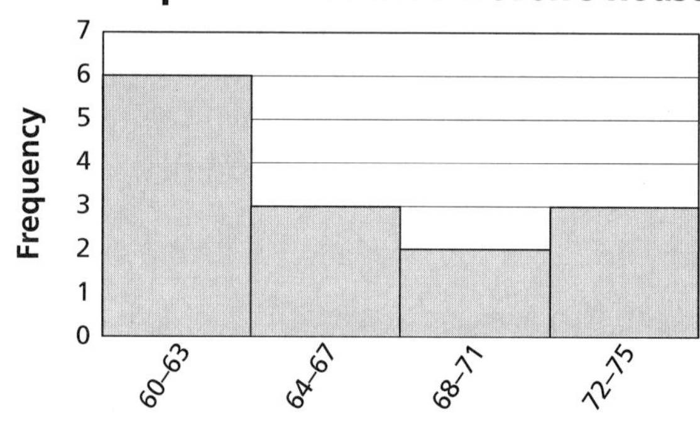

15. a.

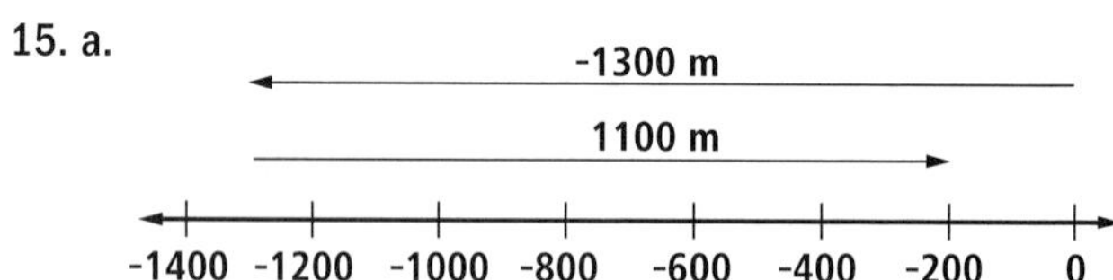

b. –200 m

Lesson 5-6 (pp. 301-306)

Questions: **1.** Answers vary. Sample: Graphs and other displays make it easier for an audience to understand the data presented. They also often help highlight certain information such as trends and distributions. **3.** a graph of ordered pairs of numbers connected by segments from left to right **5.** The line showing male data moves downward over this period. **7.** The point showing male data is higher in 1900 than the women's point in 1968. **9.** 1990 **11.** Answers vary. Sample: whole milk: 60 lbs; lowfat: 60 lbs; skim: 75 lbs

13. a.

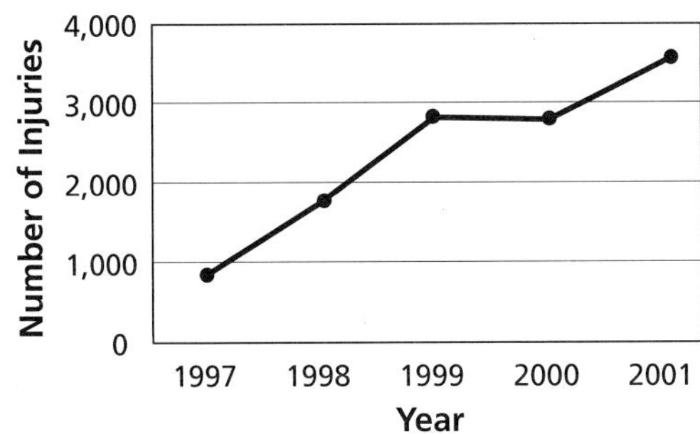

b. Answers vary. Sample: More people may have played paintball with each passing year, so while the number of injuries increased, the percent of people being injured may have stayed the same or decreased.
15. Bar graph; it is good for comparing the popularity of the magazines. 17. Histogram, because it can show frequency on the vertical axis and intervals of heights of 8th graders on the horizontal axis.
19. a. $\frac{1}{4}$ b. $\frac{1}{8}$ c. $\frac{1}{16}$ 21. a. $\frac{3}{4}$ b. $\frac{7}{8}$ c. $\frac{15}{16}$

Lesson 5-7 (pp. 307-312)

Questions:

1. Answers vary. Sample: Coordinate graphs aid in visualizing lists of data. 3. a. iii b. v c. i d. ii e. vi f. iv 5. (30, -10) 7. (40, 30) 9. (10, 0)
11. a. (negative, positive) b. (negative, negative) c. (positive, negative) d. (positive, 0) e. (0, negative)
13. a. S_1 = (-3, -1), W_1 = (5, 2), I_1 = (-5, 5), T_1 = (2, -3), C_1 = (0, 1), H_1 = (-6, 0)

b.

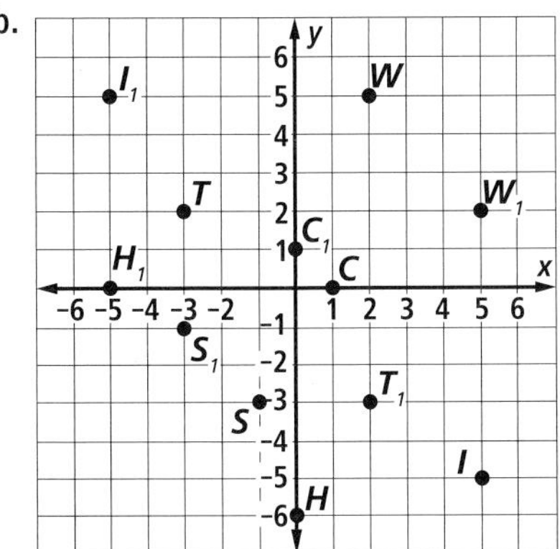

c. Each member of a pair is a reflection of the other across a diagonal line. 15. a. the point from which displacement is measured b. how far (in inches) the North Pole has moved c. about (11.5, -12) on Nov. 1, 2005; (9, -2.5) on Dec. 1, 2005; (-7, 3.5) on Jan. 1, 2006; (-8.5, 4) on Feb. 1, 2006; (-1.5, 3) on Feb. 14; 2006
17. B 19. C 21. 25 days

Lesson 5-8 (pp. 313-317)

Questions:

1. a.

Day (x)	Earnings (y)
0	\$0
3	\$7.50
5	\$12.50
9	\$22.50
10	\$25

b.

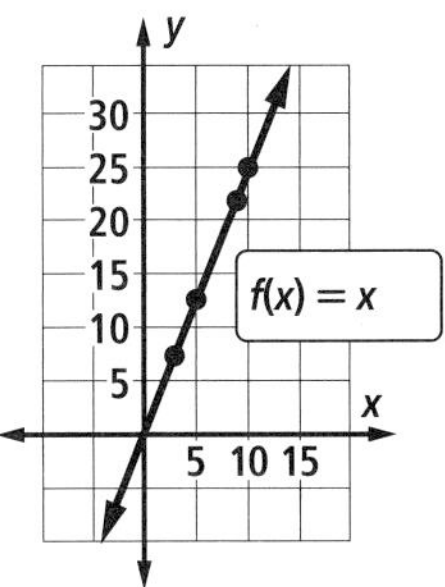

c. 8 days
3. a. Answers vary. Sample: [Y=] [X,T,Θ,n] [−] 8 [GRAPH] b.

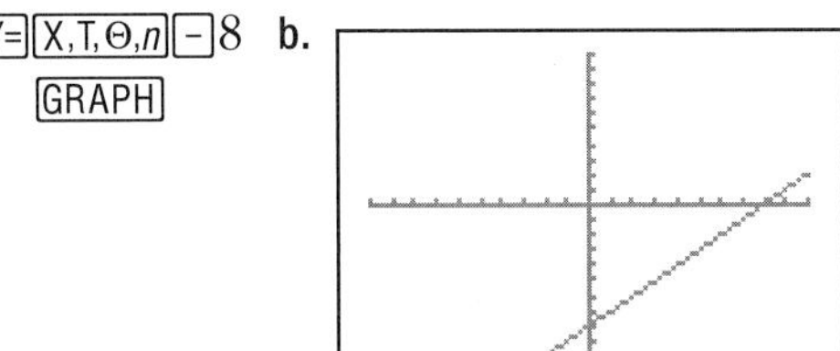

5. $y = x + 4$ 7. a. i b. ii c. iv d. iii 9. a. A: (45, 45); B: (15, 75) b. Answers vary. Sample: x and y should sum to 90.

11.

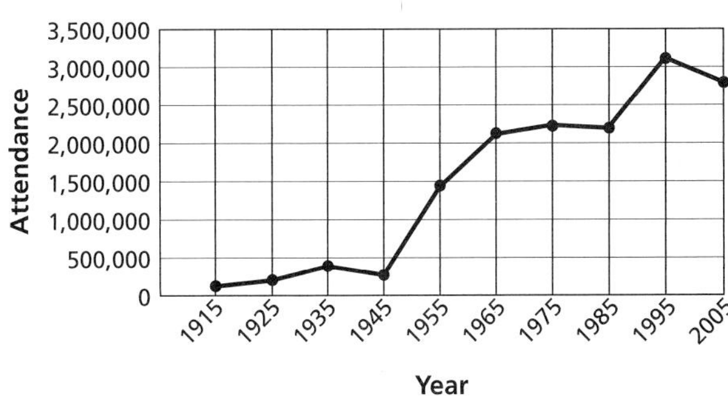

13. a. 2 b. 1 c. 1; right; 10

Self-Test (pp. 320-321)

1.

Stem	Leaf
0	7
1	8
2	2 5 6 8 9
3	0 1 6 8
4	2 3 7 7 8
5	2 2 4 8 9
6	1
7	
8	6

2. 42 3. 42.5 4. The intervals are not of uniform length on the horizontal axis, some intervals are omitted, and there is no title.
5. 0–15, 15–30, 30–45, 45–60, 60–75 6. a. Answers vary. Sample: A circle graph because it shows the values for each category.
b. Answers vary. Sample: A line graph because both of the axes represent data numerically. 7. There were a total of 5 + 15 + 12 + 9 + 5 + 3 + 1 = 50 students in the survey. 8. 5 + 3 + 1 = 9 students have more than 3 pets

9.

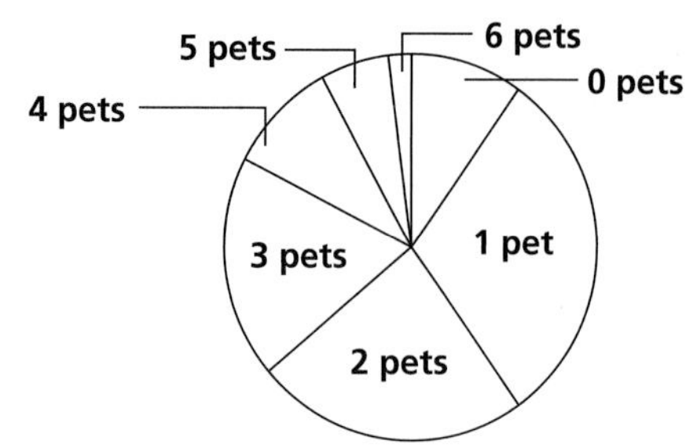

10. $\frac{9}{50} = \frac{x}{360}$; $50 \cdot x = 9 \cdot 360$; $x = \frac{9 \cdot 360}{50}$; $x = 64.8°$

11.

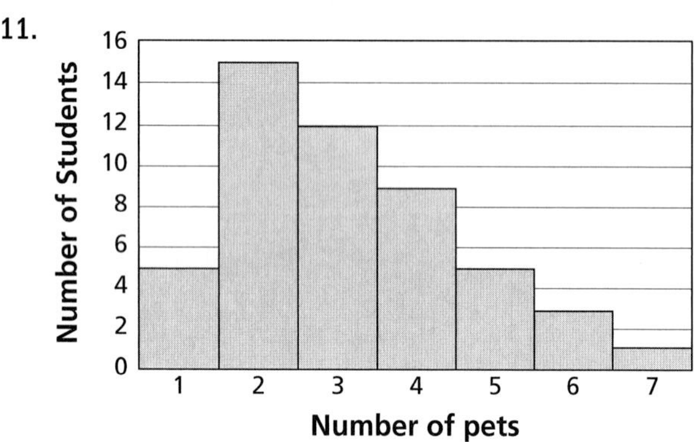

12. a. Answers vary. Sample: When $x = 0$, $y = 7 - 0 = 7$. So (0, 7) is one coordinate. When $y = 0$, $0 = 7 - x$. So $x = 7$. Thus, (7, 0) is another coordinate.

b.

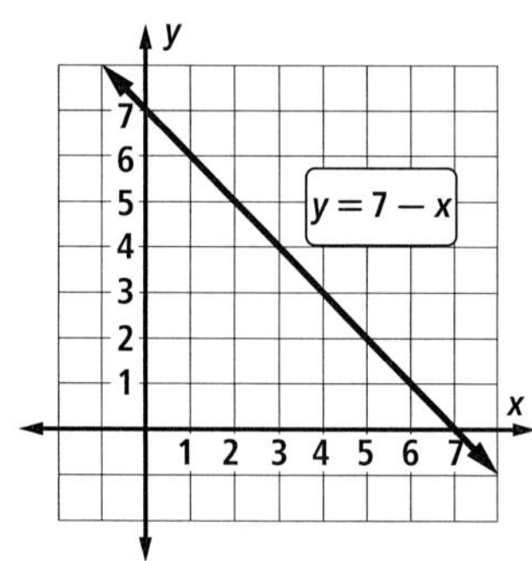

13. IV

14.

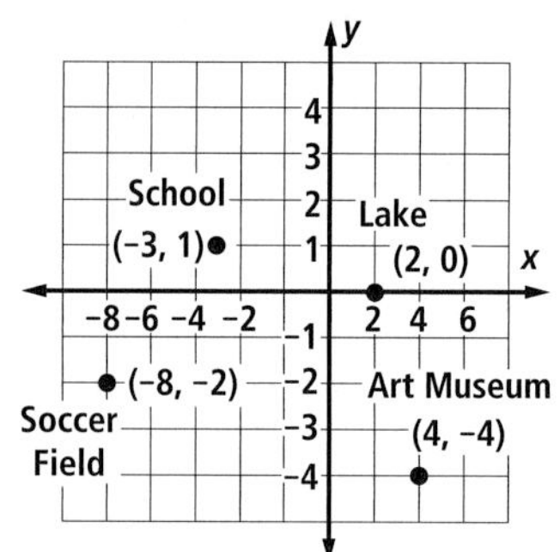

15.

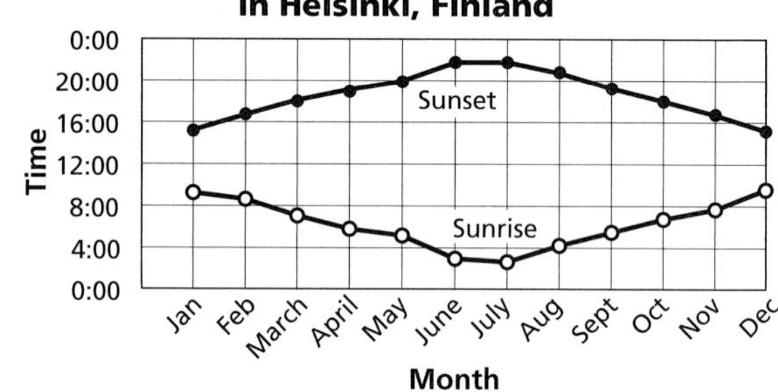

16. The line for sunrise and the line for sunset are reflections of each other over a horizontal axis. The line for sunrise decreases as the line for sunset increases and vice versa.

Chapter Review (pp. 322-325)

1. 2.64 3. 42,847 mi 5. 1.06 7. yes 9. 0.974 11. III 13. line 15. numerical 17. numerical 19. categorical 21. Jupiter, Saturn, Uranus, Neptune 23. a. 446.99 b. 128.99 25. 158–165 lb; 7 wrestlers 27. 64 million 29. black 31. 57.6° 33. Answers vary. Sample: about 255 35. increase: 2000–2002, 2003–2006; decrease: 2002–2003 37. Answers vary. Sample: below 60, 60–70, 70–80, 80–90, 90–100

Self-Test Correlation Chart

Question	1	2	3	4	5	6	7	8	9	10
Objective(s)	H	A	A	E	E	C	D	D	I	F
Lesson(s)	5-3, 5-4	5-1, 5-2	5-1, 5-2	5-3, 5-4	5-3, 5-4	5-5	5-1	5-1	5-5	5-5
Question	**11**	**12**	**13**	**14**	**15**	**16**				
Objective(s)	H	L	B, K	K	J	G				
Lesson(s)	5-3, 5-4	5-8	5-7	5-7	5-6	5-6				

39.

4	3
5	
6	1 8
7	0 3 5 6 8 9
8	0 1 2 2 4 5 7 8 8
9	0 1 1 4 5 8

41.

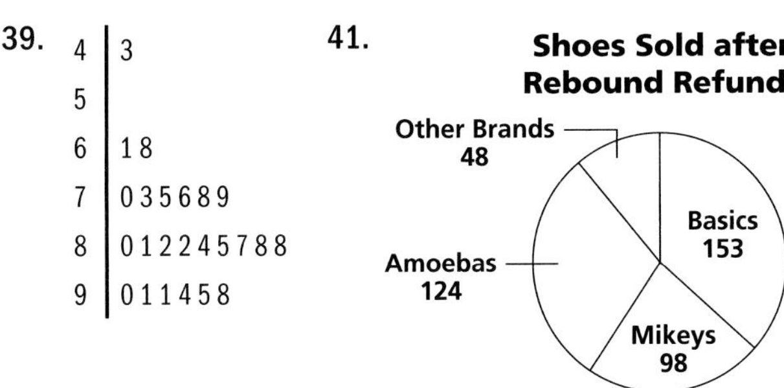

43.

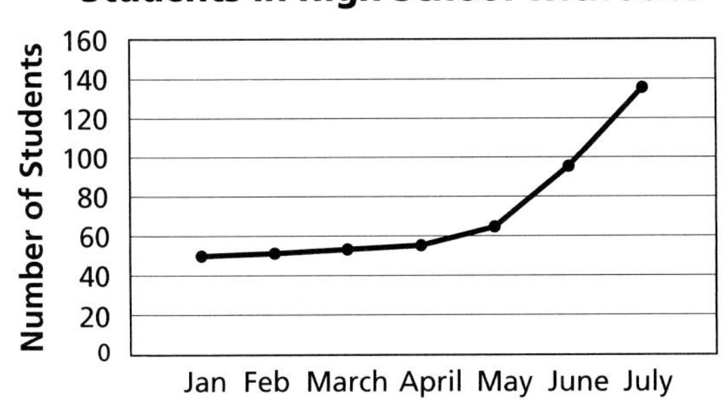

45. Answers vary. Sample: You can trace a particular line graph or set the two graphs to have different appearances. **47.** Answers vary. Sample: The low temperatures move in a general upward trend over the course of the week. **49.** Friday **51. a.** (7, 2) **b.** (-1, 5) **c.** (-8, 4) **d.** (-5, -6) **e.** (3, -4)

53.

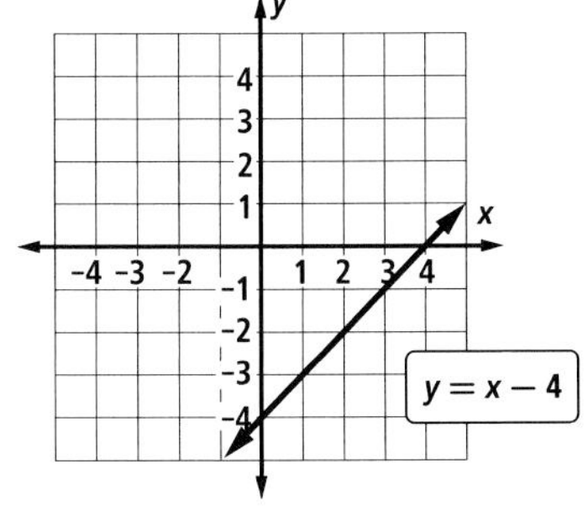

Answers vary. Sample: (0, -4), (1, -3), (2, -2)

55.

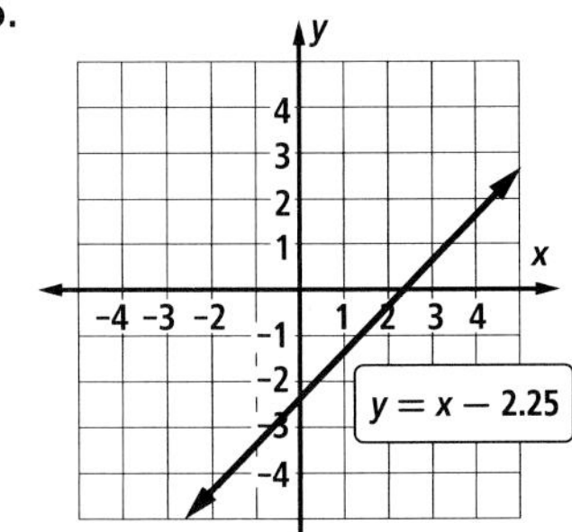

Answers vary. Sample: (0, -2.25), (1, -1.25), (2, -0.25)

Chapter 6

Lesson 6-1 (pp. 328-334)

Questions:

1. a.

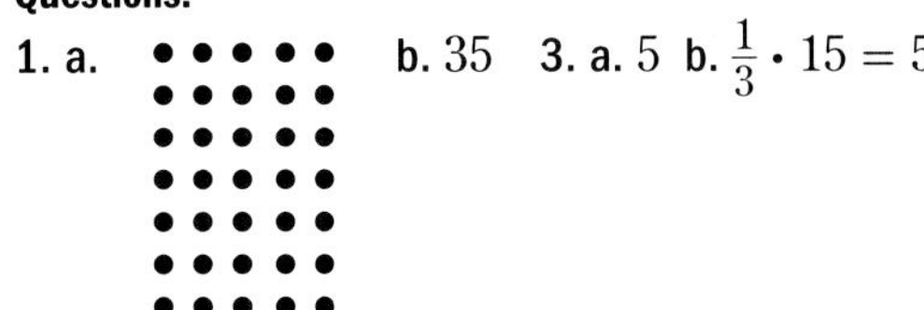

b. 35 **3. a.** 5 **b.** $\frac{1}{3} \cdot 15 = 5$

5. 12

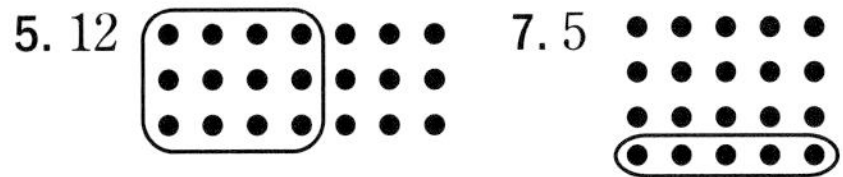

7. 5

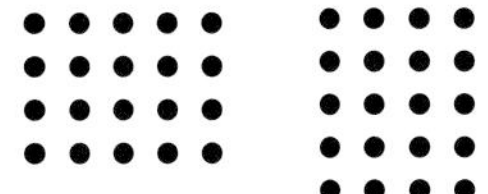

9. \$77 **11.** There are 20 items in both arrays.

13. 48 **15.** 28 **17.** 4 megapixels **19.** 60 **21. a.** median: 92; mean: 95 **b.** median: 95; mean: $96.\overline{09}$ **c.** No, the loser of the World Series from 1996–2006 tended to win more in the regular season than the winner. **23.** \$0.40, \$2.75, \$0.63, \$0.67, \$0.33, \$0.70, \$1.50 **25.** $\frac{80}{100}$ m

Lesson 6-2 (pp. 335-340)

Questions: 1. a.

b. $\frac{7}{8} \times \frac{2}{3} = \frac{14}{24} = \frac{7}{12}$ **3.** $\frac{4}{15}$ **5.** $\frac{60}{1}$ **7.** $\frac{17}{25}$ **9.** $\frac{76}{561}$ **11.** $\frac{12}{5}$ **13.** 1 **15.** 1 **17.** 0.0625 **19.** 1 in a billion stars **21.** $\frac{2}{7}$ **23. a.** less than **b.** greater than **c.** less than **d.** greater than **25.** Answers vary. Sample: 1, 2, 3, 4, 5, 6, 7, 8, 9, 10

Lesson 6-3 (pp. 341-348)

Guided Example 1: $L = 3 + \frac{1}{4}$ inches $= \frac{13}{4}$ inches. $W =$ 2 inches. Area $= L \cdot W = \frac{13}{4} \cdot 2$ in^2 $= 6\frac{1}{2}$ as a mixed number.

Questions:

1. a. **3.** d. **5.** e. **7.** The area of a rectangle with length l units and width w units is $l \cdot w$ square units. **9.** 6 units^2 **11.** 40 ft^2 **13. a.** $\left(30 \cdot \frac{2}{3}\right) \cdot 11 = 20 \cdot 11 = 220$ and $30 \cdot \left(\frac{2}{3} \cdot 11\right) = 30 \cdot \frac{22}{3} = 220$ **b.** Associative Property of Multiplication **15.** 12.5 ft^2 **17.** \$13,000,000 **19.** 12 in^2 **21. a.** 138 ft^2 **b.** 4 **23.** 0.25 unit **25.** $\frac{1}{10}$

27. 2

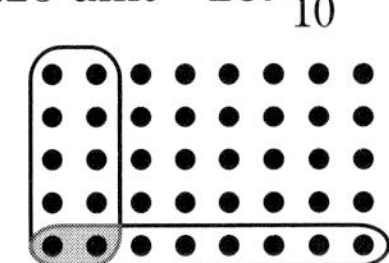

29. 27.96 **31.** 135° **b.** 180, 420, 480 **33.** 243

Lesson 6-4 (pp. 349-354)

Questions: **1. a.** seven to the sixth power **b.** 117,649 **3.** 2.9^{100} **5.** 8^4; 4,096 **7.** s^2 **9.** 0.1541 **11.** 1 **13.** $8 \cdot 10^6 + 0 \cdot 10^5 + 5 \cdot 10^4 + 0 \cdot 10^3 + 4 \cdot 10^2 + 0 \cdot 10^1 + 3 \cdot 10^0$ **15.** 10,000,000; 10^7 **17. a.** $2y \cdot 2y \cdot 2y$ **b.** $2^3 \cdot y^3$ **19. a.** < **b.** < **21. a.** < **b.** >

23. a.

Years After First Ash Borer	Percent of Original Trees Left
1	90%
2	$90\% \cdot 90\% = (90\%)^2 = 81\%$
3	$90\% \cdot 90\% \cdot 90\% = (90\%)^3 = 72.9\%$
4	$90\% \cdot 90\% \cdot 90\% \cdot 90\% = (90\%)^4 = 65.61\%$
5	$90\% \cdot 90\% \cdot 90\% \cdot 90\% \cdot 90\% = (90\%)^5 = 59.05\%$

b. 7 years after the first ash borer **c.** 14 years after the first ash borer **25.** 1^3; 2^3; 3^3; 4^3 **27. a.** 9,000 yd^2 **b.** 81,000 one foot squares **29.** $\frac{3}{56}$

Lesson 6-5 (pp. 355-360)

Guided Example 2: 328; 1; 0.4; 0.4; 0.328

Questions: **1.** 20.8 **3.** 128.794 **5.** 0.31211 **7.** 25.935 cm^2 **9.** $\frac{34}{100} \cdot \frac{5}{100} = \frac{17}{1{,}000}$ **11.** 3,800 **13.** \$2,867.30 **15.** 58.03 **17.** Answers vary. Sample: 1.5, 1.5 **19.** Answers vary. Sample: 1, 8.04, 1.5 **21.** $2^2 \cdot 4^3 \cdot 5^2 \cdot n^2$

23.

n	$\frac{2}{3}n$
18	12
10	$\frac{20}{3}$
75	50
$\frac{3}{4}$	$\frac{1}{2}$
4	$\frac{8}{3}$

25. $7 + -5 = 2$ **27.** $8.5 + 5 = 13.5$ **29.** $120\frac{1}{4}$"

Lesson 6-6 (pp. 361-366)

Guided Example 3: $\frac{3}{4}$; $\frac{3}{4}$; 24; $\frac{1}{4}$; 8; 8; 24 **Guided Example 4:** 80; 160; 8; 160; 8; 168

Questions: **1. a.** $\frac{3}{10} \cdot 1{,}500 = \frac{4{,}500}{10} = 450$ **b.** \$1,050 **3. a.** 6 million **b.** 9 million **c.** 12 million **d.** 15 million **5. a.** 0.8 **b.** 1.6 **c.** 3.2 **7.** 1 **9.** 54 **11.** \$48.40 **13.** 4.5 **15.** Answers vary. Sample: The decimal point is moved one place, but in the opposite direction. **17.** Answers vary. Sample: The speakers are giving their complete support. **19.** true **21.** true **23. a.** about \$24 **b.** about \$56 **25.** about \$4.50 **27.** about \$3.75 **29.** SHOULD **31. a.** $\frac{9}{25}$ **b.** 0.36 **c.** 36% **33. a.** 9,720.6104 **b.** 972.06104 **c.** 97.206104 **d.** 9.7206104 **35.** $2\frac{11}{16}$ in.

Lesson 6-7 (pp. 367-371)

Guided Example 4: **1.** 57,190,000; 57,000,000 **2.** 22%; 66,220,000; 66,000,000 **3.** South: 108,360,000; West: 69,230,000 **4.** 301,000,000

Questions: **1.** 18 **3.** 35.52 **5. a.** \$103.58 **b.** \$192.37 **7. a.** \$2.47 **b.** \$54.46 **9. a.** \$1.59 **b.** \$31.54 **11. a.** \$200 **b.** \$40 **c.** \$160 **d.** \$8 **e.** \$168 **f.** \$39.55; \$158.20; \$7.91; \$166.11 **13. a.** 798,000 **b.** 893,000 **15.** Store A **17. a.** 4,498.4170 **b.** 0.05612 **19.** simple **21.** 1.32 **23.** They win more often because 53% is greater than 50%.

Lesson 6-8 (pp. 372-376)

Guided Example 2: 16; 5; 6; 16; 30; 16

Questions: **1.** numbers and operation symbols **3.** powering **5.** multiplication **7.** $6 \cdot (3 + 4)$ **9.** 1 **11.** 13 **13.** 24 **15. a.** $(3 + 4) \cdot 10$; 70 **b.** $3 + 4 \cdot 10$; 43 **17.** 144.5 **19. a.** -48 **b.** -30 **21. a.** 7 **b.** 6 **23. a.** 2 **b.** $16 - (8 - (4 - 2))$ **25. a.** Answers vary. Sample: $(39.95 \cdot 0.07) + 39.95 + 5$ **b.** \$47.75 **27.** \$54.75 **29.** 5,758 **31.** 635,240,000

Lesson 6-9 (pp. 377-383)

Questions: **1. a.** $14.95 \cdot (7 + 17) = \$358.80$ **b.** $(14.95 \cdot 7) + (14.95 \cdot 17) = \$358.80$ **3.** $7\frac{1}{2}$ mi^2 **5.** 40 **7. a.** $(5 \cdot 4) + \left(5 \cdot \frac{2}{7}\right) + \left(\frac{5}{6} \cdot 4\right) + \left(\frac{5}{6} \cdot \frac{2}{7}\right) = 25$ **b.** $\frac{35}{6} \cdot \frac{30}{7} = \frac{1{,}050}{42} = 25$ **9.** 12 **11.** made **13.** $(30 + 8) \cdot (90 + 7) = 30 \cdot 90 + 30 \cdot 7 + 8 \cdot 90 + 8 \cdot 7 = 3{,}686$ **15. a.** 117 **b.** 128 **17.** 125 ft^2 **19. a.** $(4 + 3) \cdot 2 \cdot (6 + 1)$ **b.** $4 + 3 \cdot 2 \cdot (6 + 1)$ **c.** $4 + 3 \cdot 2 \cdot 6 + 1$ **21.** $1\frac{24}{25}$ **23.** 20 **25. a.** $2 + -5 + 4 + -8$ **b.** -7

Lesson 6-10 (pp. 384-389)

Guided Example 4: **a.** -12.5; 9; -12.5; 9; \$112.50 **b.** -12.5; -6; -12.5; -6; \$75

Questions: **1. a.** 1 min 21 seconds behind **b.** Answers vary. Sample: $-3 \cdot 27$ **3. a.** It will have receded 12 in. **b.** $-\frac{1}{4} \cdot 2 \cdot 24$ **5.** -12.5 **7.** 37.9353 **9.** BUT **11. a.** -1 **b.** 1 **c.** 4 **d.** -4 **e.** 76.22 **f.** -76.22 **g.** $-1 \cdot x = -x$ **13.** The sum; the product is negative and the multiplication involves large numbers. **15. a.** $14.32 \cdot 4 + 3 \cdot (-18.37)$ **b.** $(-14.32) \cdot 4 + 3 \cdot 18.37$ **17.** $-14\frac{3}{7}$ **19.** \$58.87 **21.** 0.000056

Self-Test (pp. 393-394)

1.

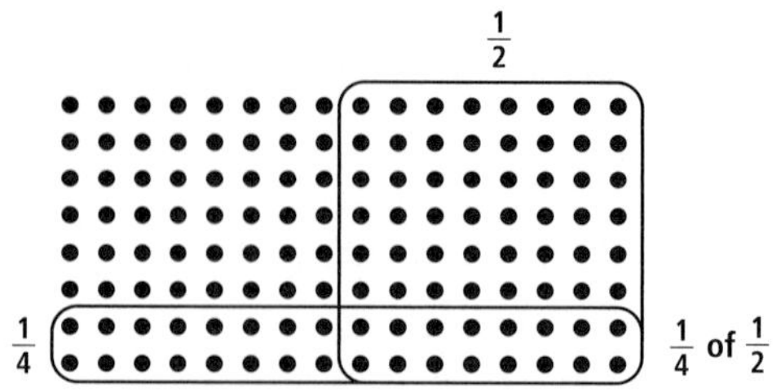

$\frac{1}{2}$

$\frac{1}{4}$ $\frac{1}{4}$ of $\frac{1}{2}$

The farmer will use $\frac{1}{4}$ of $\frac{1}{2}$ of 128, or 16 bushes to make jam. **2.** $4 \cdot (3 \cdot 4) = 4 \cdot 12 = 48$ in^2 **3.** $300 \cdot \frac{3}{8} = \frac{300}{1} \cdot \frac{3}{8} = \frac{900}{8} = 112\frac{1}{2}$ **4.** $\frac{9}{10} \cdot \frac{5}{12} = \frac{9 \cdot 5}{10 \cdot 12} = \frac{45}{120} = \frac{3}{8}$ **5.** $3.4 \cdot 2.5 = 3.4 \cdot \frac{5}{2} = 1.7 \cdot 5 = 8.5$ **6.** $0.9 \cdot 10.16 = \frac{9}{10} \cdot 10.16 = 9.144$ **7.** $3\frac{1}{5} \cdot 6 = \frac{16}{5} \cdot \frac{6}{1} = \frac{96}{5} = 19\frac{1}{5}$ **8.** $1\frac{7}{8} \cdot 1\frac{2}{3} = \frac{15}{8} \cdot \frac{5}{3} = \frac{75}{24} = 3\frac{1}{8}$ **9.** $-\frac{1}{5} \cdot -\frac{5}{7} = \frac{1}{7}$ **10.** $9.45 \cdot -5.12 = \frac{189}{20} \cdot -\frac{128}{25} = -\frac{6{,}048}{125} = -48.384$ **11. a.** Move the decimal one place to the left, which is 4.27. **b.** 10% of 427 is 42.7; 2 times 42.7 is 85.4. **12.** $0.53 \cdot 1{,}175 \approx 623$ **13. a.** no; their areas are equal: 299 ft^2 **b.** Commutative Property of Multiplication **14a.** $0.75 \cdot 5.52 = \$4.14$ **b.** $5.52 - 4.14 = \$1.38$

15. a.

1 mi

$\frac{3}{5}$ mi

1 mi

$\frac{2}{3}$ mi

b. $\frac{3}{5} \cdot \frac{2}{3} = \frac{6}{15} = \frac{2}{5}$ mi^2 **16.** $20 \cdot 18.5 + 3.5 \cdot 10 = 370 + 35 = 405$ **17.** $10 - 6 \cdot 5^2 = 10 - 6 \cdot 25 = 10 - 150 = -140$

18. $\frac{100 + 14}{10 + 7} = \frac{114}{17} = 6\frac{12}{17}$ **19.** $4 \cdot 4 \cdot 4 = 64$ **20.** $-(6 \cdot -6) = -36$ **21.** $-3 \cdot -3 \cdot -3 \cdot -3 = 81$ **22.** $\frac{2}{5} \cdot \frac{2}{5} \cdot \frac{2}{5} = \frac{8}{125}$ **23. a.** $-560 \cdot 4$ **b.** \$2,240 less **c.** $-560 \cdot -2$ **d.** \$1,120 more **24. a.** $0.125 \cdot 45.65 = \$5.71$ **b.** $45.65 - 5.71 = \$39.94$ **25.** g^6 **26.** $0.5^3 \cdot 0.3^2$ **27.** $12\frac{4}{12} \cdot 7\frac{8}{12} = 94\frac{5}{9}$ft^2 **28.** $32{,}000 = 3 \cdot 10^4 + 2 \cdot 10^3 + 0 \cdot 10^2 + 0 \cdot 10^1 + 0 \cdot 10^0$

Self-Test Correlation Chart

Question	1	2	3	4	5	6	7	8	9	10
Objective(s)	J	I	A	A	C	C	A	A	E	E
Lesson(s)	6-1	6-3	6-2, 6-9	6-2, 6-9	6-5	6-5	6-2, 6-9	6-2, 6-9	6-10	6-10
Question	**11**	**12**	**13**	**14**	**15**	**16**	**17**	**18**	**19**	**20**
Objective(s)	D	L	H, I	K	I, K	B	B	B	F	F
Lesson(s)	6-6, 6-7	6-7	6-3	6-2	6-2, 6-3, 6-5	6-8	6-8	6-8	6-4	6-4
Question	**21**	**22**	**23**	**24**	**25**	**26**	**27**	**28**		
Objective(s)	F	F	M	L	F	F	I, N	G		
Lesson(s)	6-4	6-4	6-10	6-7	6-4	6-4	6-3, 6-9	6-4		

Chapter Review (pp. 395–397)

1. 4 **3.** $\frac{1}{6}$ **5.** $1\frac{1}{3}$ **7.** $\frac{7}{12}$ **9.** $37\frac{3}{8}$ **11.** 10 **13.** -5 **15.** -8.49 **17.** 21.06 **19.** 24.91 **21.** $\frac{3}{16}$ **23.** 14 **25.** 200 **27.** 11.85 **29.** 0.92 **31. a.** positive **b.** 20 **33. a.** positive **b.** $1\frac{2}{3}$ **35.** 32,768 **37.** 0.0081 **39. a.** 7^3 **b.** 343 **41. a** 2.1^8 **b.** 378.23 **43.** 16^8 **45.** $4 \cdot 10^3 + 5 \cdot 10^2 + 5 \cdot 10^1 + 2 \cdot 10^0$ **47.** $1 \cdot 10^4 + 0 \cdot 10^3 + 8 \cdot 10^2 + 0 \cdot 10^1 + 0 \cdot 10^0$ **49.** Commutative Property of Multiplication **51.** Commutative Property of Multiplication **53.** 6,000 yd^2 **55.** 24 ft^2 **57.** 28

59. 5 **61.** 9 packs of pencils and 12 packs of erasers **63.** 19.65 mi **65.** \$11,084 **67.** 157.5 lb **69. a.** $1\frac{1}{8}$ in. **b.** $\left(\frac{54}{12}\right) \cdot \left(-\frac{1}{4}\right)$

71.

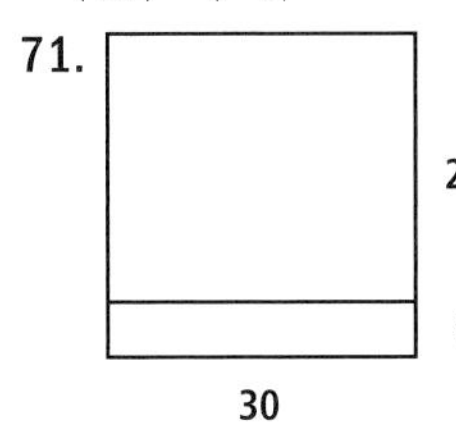

73.

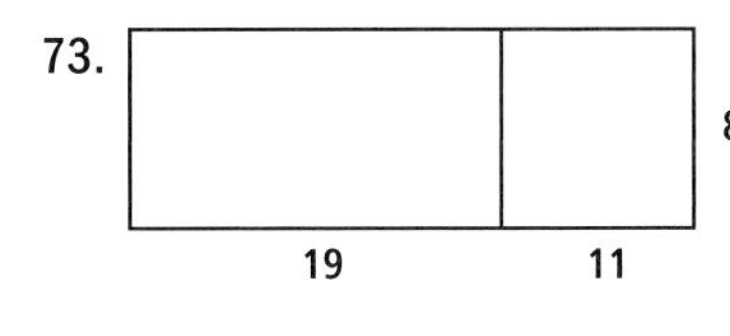

Selected Answers

Chapter 7

Lesson 7-1 (pp. 400–404)

Guided Example 2: days; 366; 366; 11,235; 11,235; 11,235; 4,112,010; 42

Questions: **1.** divisor: 6; dividend: 42; quotient: 7 **3.** C

5.

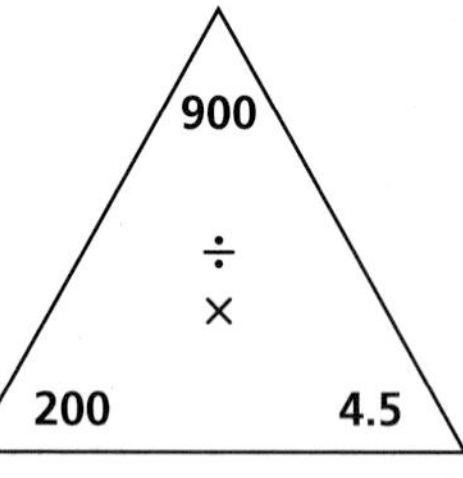

7.

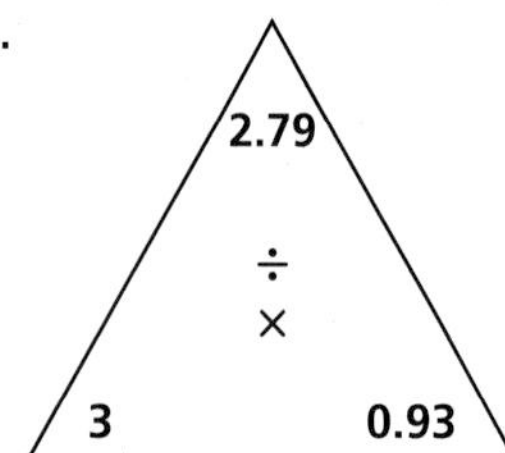

9. a. \$136.99 **b.** \$59.01 **11.** miles per gallon
13. $\frac{1}{2} \cdot \frac{1}{4} = \frac{1}{8}$; $\frac{1}{8} \div \frac{1}{2} = \frac{1}{4}$; $\frac{1}{8} \div \frac{1}{4} = \frac{1}{2}$; $\frac{1}{4} \cdot \frac{1}{2} = \frac{1}{8}$
15. a. 10,000 yd^2 **b.** 400 yd **c.** 1,200 yd **17.** 54.5 mi/hr
19. the product of $-\frac{1}{4}$ and $\frac{1}{2}$ **21.** $243\frac{1}{3}$ ft^2

23. a.

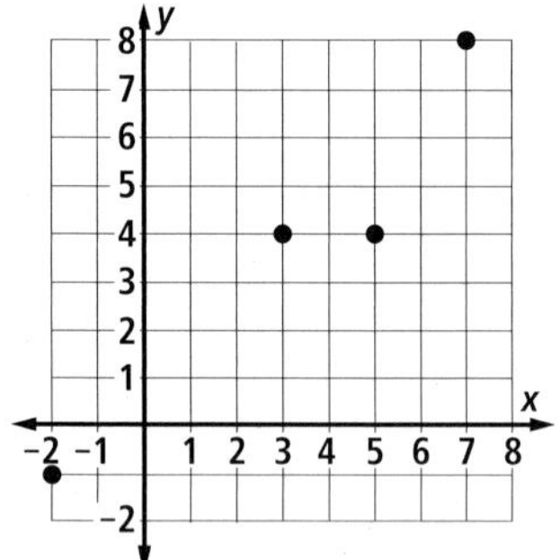

b. (5, 4)

Lesson 7-2 (pp. 405–410)

Guided Example 2: 7; 14; 3; 7; 14; 4; 7; 14; 5; 7; 14; 6; 7; 15; 112, 112, 119, 126, 133, 140, 147

Questions: **1. a.** 3 boxes of Brand A or 3 boxes of Brand B **b.** Brand B will leave her with extra pencils.

3.
• • • • •
• • • • •
• • • • •
• • • • •

5. Answers vary. Sample: 11 is a factor of 121. 121 is a multiple of 11. **7.** false **9.** true **11.** A
13. a. 17,017, 17,034 **b.** 16,983, 16,966 **15.** An array of $4n + 3$ dots always contains $n + 1$ columns such that n columns contain 4 dots and the last column is incomplete; therefore, $4n + 3$ is never divisible by 4.
17. a. no **b.** yes **19.** 6 **21.** \$0.76 **23.** Kiara
25. Answers vary. Sample: 2' by 6'; 3' by 4'

Lesson 7-3 (pp. 411–416)

Questions: **1.** prime: 23, 29; composite: 20, 21, 22, 24, 25, 26, 27, 28, 30 **3.** 101 is only divisible by 1 and itself. **5.** His factor tree is incorrect. $9 \cdot 10 = 90 \neq 900$. The factors in the second row should be 9 and 100 (or any other two numbers that multiply to 900).
7. $2 \cdot 3 \cdot 53$ **9.** $2^3 \cdot 3 \cdot 5 \cdot 7$ **11.** iii; $2 \cdot 13^3 \cdot 17$
13. iv; $2^2 \cdot 3^4 \cdot 5^2$ **15.** $\frac{3240}{16} = \frac{2^3\, 3^4 \cdot 5}{2^4} = \frac{405}{2} = 202\frac{1}{2}$
17. $15 \div 415 = (5 \cdot 3) \div (5 \cdot 83) = \frac{3}{83}$
19. $\frac{236}{244} = \frac{2 \cdot 2 \cdot 59}{2 \cdot 2 \cdot 61} = \frac{59}{61}$ **21.** True; 139 is not divisible by any positive integer other than 1 and itself. **23. a.** 128 **b.** 510,510 **25.** C **27.** $m\angle A = 33°$, $m\angle B = 147°$

Lesson 7-4 (pp. 417–422)

Guided Example 1: 8; 85; 2; 5; 12; 12; 5

Questions: **1. a.** 1; 5 **b.** 3; 3 **c.** 8; 4 **d.** 24; 0 **3.** 14 R2
5. 15 R1 **7. a.** 2; 1 **b.** $2\frac{1}{5}$ **c.** $2\frac{1}{5}\ \frac{\text{nectarines}}{\text{person}}$ **9. a.** 7 R22 **b.** 7 R25 **c.** 8 R30 **11.** 15 R5 **13. a.** 12 classes of 14 students, 8 classes of 15 students **b.** No, because the remaining students would not have a homeroom.
15. a. 35 **b.** 46 **17.** 45 **19.** 5 **21.** No. Answers vary. Sample: $4 \div 2 = 2$ but $2 \div 4 = \frac{1}{2}$. **23.** \$1.50
25. a. Answers vary. Sample: 553 is an odd number, yet the dimensions indicate an even area. **b.** 540 in^2

Lesson 7-5 (pp. 423–426)

Guided Example 2: $8\overline{)9^1\,354}$ (quotient 1); $8\overline{)9^1\,3^5\,54}$ (quotient 1 1); $8\overline{)9^1\,3^5\,5^7\,4}$ (quotient 1 1 6); $8\overline{)9^1\,3^5\,5^7\,4^2}$ (quotient 1 1 6 9); 1,169; 2; 1,169; 8; 2; 9,354

Questions: **1.** 354 **3.** \$1,628 **5.** 1,168 R6 **7.** 7 parents stuff 682 envelopes and 1 parent stuffs 683 envelopes.
9. 35 min and 20 sec **11.** 3,388,888.89 pounds
13. 3 R3 **15.** In any other pair of consecutive integers, one must be even (and thus divisible by 2).

17.
10
÷
×
2.5
4

$2.5 \cdot 4 = 10$; $4 \cdot 2.5 = 10$; $10 \div 2.5 = 4$; $10 \div 4 = 2.5$
19. Multiplying Fractions Property
21. a. 4,000 lb **b.** 571.4 lb **c.** 23.8 lb

Lesson 7-6 (pp. 427–431)

Guided Example 2: Solution 1. $3\overline{)29.^2\,5^1\,7^2}$ (quotient 9 . 8 5); 9.85; 0.02
Solution 2. 29.57; ÷; 3; 9.856666667; 9.86; 0.01

Questions: **1.** Answers vary. Sample: Integer division leaves the remainder as a whole number while rational number division expresses it as a fraction or decimal. **3.** integer division **5.** $7\frac{1}{7} \approx 7.143$
7. a. integer division; 6 sheets each with 1 left over **b.** rational number division; 6.25 ft **9. a.** 356 R3 **b.** $356\frac{3}{5}$ **c.** 356.6 **11. a.** $350\frac{1}{2}$ **b.** 350.5 **13. a.** 464 **b.** 464 **15.** \$8.33 **17.** \$12.50

19. No; 5 people should pay \$3.36 and 3 pay \$3.35. **21. a.** 9.08 hr **b.** $567\frac{1}{2}$ calories **23.** 150 R7 **25.** 270.11 yd^2 **27.** positive **29. a.** 300 slices **b.** 38 pizzas

Lesson 7-7 (pp. 432–437)

Questions: 1. a. repeating **b.** $0.\overline{90}$ **3.** terminating **5.** repeating **7. a.** $\frac{1}{6}, \frac{1}{3}, \frac{1}{2}, \frac{2}{3}, \frac{5}{6}$ **b.** $\frac{1}{6}, \frac{1}{3}, \frac{2}{3}, \frac{5}{6}$ **c.** $0.1\overline{6}$, $0.\overline{3}$, 0.5, $0.\overline{6}$, $0.8\overline{3}$ **9. a.** \$0.33 **b.** \$0.67 **c.** \$2.67 **11.** No; the prime factorization of the fraction's denominator is 2 • 11, thus the decimal is repeating. The calculator rounded the result to the 10th decimal. **13. a.** $\frac{1}{8}$ **b.** $\frac{1}{16}$ **c.** 0.03125 **d.** 0.015625 **15.** Answers vary. Sample: $\frac{1}{125}, \frac{1}{400}, \frac{1}{200}, \frac{1}{500}, \frac{1}{1{,}000}$ **17. a.** $7{,}428\frac{5}{7}$ **b.** $7{,}428.\overline{714285}$ **19.** 47 weeks, 3 days **21. a.** $-\frac{8}{27}$ **b.** $\frac{16}{81}$ **c.** > **23.** 440,000 m^2

Lesson 7-8 (pp. 438–441)

Guided Example 3: 13.5; 0.002; 1,000; 6,750; 6,750
Guided Example 4: $\frac{0.0254}{0.00000173}$; 100,000,000; 2,540,000; 173; 2,540,000
Questions: 1. a. 0.5 **b.** 0.05 **c.** 0.005 **d.** 0.0005 **3.** 7.2 **5.** 1,000 **7.** C **9.** about 29 **11.** about 20.9 times **13. a.** 28 **b.** 360 lb **15.** by about 170 bacteria **17.** $0.\overline{428571}$ **19.** $31\frac{3}{5}$ **21. a.** about 66,666.7 mi/hr **b.** about 18.5 mi/sec

Lesson 7-9 (pp. 442–447)

Guided Example 2: -2,369; 12; -197.4167; \$197.42
Questions: 1. a. -\$3.13 **b.** -\$3.13 per lunch **3.** -18 **5.** $\frac{5}{3}$ **7.** -0.5 **9.** not equal **11.** -3 • -2 = 6, 6 ÷ -3 = -2, 6 ÷ -2 = -3 **13.** $0.\overline{7}$ **15. a.** $\frac{-6000}{-150}$ **b.** 40 days **17. a.** a, b, and d are equal; c, e, and f. are equal. **19. a.** 293.3 lb **b.** 2.93 lb per day **21.** 0 **23.** -28 **25.** terminating **27.** repeating **29.** 53°

Lesson 7-10 (pp. 448–452)

Guided Example 3:

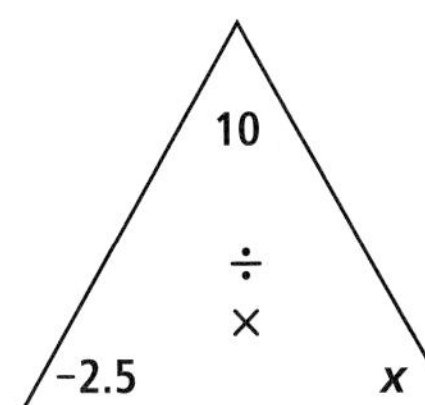

$x \cdot -2.5 = 10$; $10 \div -2.5 = x$; $10 \div x = -2.5$;
$x = 10 \div -2.5 = -4$

Questions:

1. a.

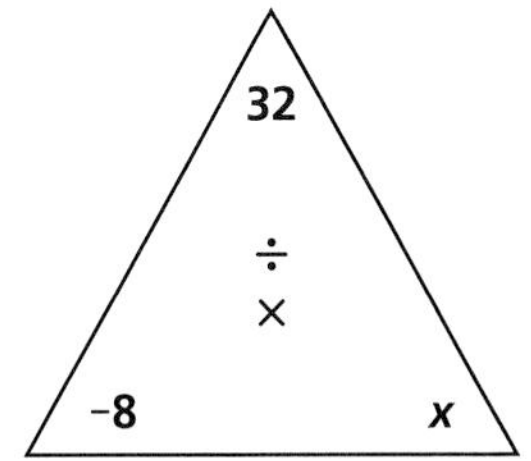

b. $x \cdot -8 = 32$; $32 \div -8 = x$; $32 \div x = -8$ **c.** $x = -4$ **d.** $-8 \cdot -4 = 32$

3. a.

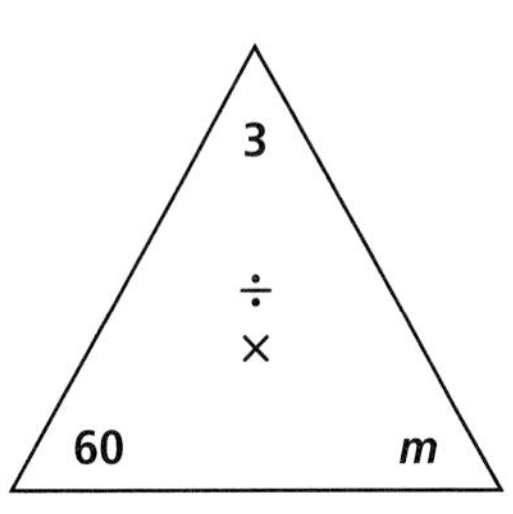

b. $\frac{3}{60} = m$; $\frac{3}{m} = 60$ **c.** $m = \frac{1}{20}$ **d.** $3 = 60 \cdot \frac{1}{20}$ **5.** C **7.** A, B, C, and D **9. a.** Answers vary. Sample: $60t = 310$ **b.** 5 hr and 10 min, $60 \cdot 5\frac{1}{6} = 310$ **c.** It will take them 5 hours and 10 minutes to get to Cincinnati. **11.** about 84.82 in. **13. a.** Let d be the price of the dessert Gerardo ordered. Then $45d = 222.75$. **b.** $d = 4.95$ **c.** 45 • 4.95 = 222.75 **d.** Gerardo ordered the mini pastries and tarts. **15.** Answers vary. Sample: Division is not commutative. **17. a.** 1.5 **b.** -1.5 **c.** 1.5 **19. a.** $0.\overline{1}$, $0.\overline{2}$, $0.\overline{3}$, $0.\overline{4}$, $0.\overline{5}$, $0.\overline{6}$, $0.\overline{7}$, $0.\overline{8}$ **b.** Each equivalent decimal is $0.\overline{1}$ times the numerator. **21.** about 2,967 people

Self-Test (pp. 455–456)

1. $\begin{array}{r} 1\ 2 \\ 11\overline{)13^{2}5^{3}} \end{array}$; the quotient is 12 and the remainder is 3.
2. $\begin{array}{r} 1\ 6 \\ 60\overline{)100^{40}0^{40}} \end{array}$; there are 16 min and 40 sec in 1,000 sec.
3. $\begin{array}{r} 1\ 8\ 9\ 4 \\ 9\overline{)17^{8}0^{8}4^{3}9^{3}} \end{array}$, so $\frac{17{,}049}{9} = 1{,}894\frac{1}{3}$. **4.** $\begin{array}{r} 6\ 1 \\ 7\overline{)43^{1}2^{5}} \end{array}$; there are 61 weeks and 5 days in 432 days. **5.** First, multiply both numbers by 100 so that they are both whole numbers. $\begin{array}{r} 6\ 8 \\ 25\overline{)170^{20}0} \end{array}$; $17 \div 0.25 = 68$
6. First, multiply both numbers by 100 so that they are both whole. $\begin{array}{r} 2 \\ 1070\overline{)2996^{856}} \end{array}$, and $\frac{856}{1{,}070} = \frac{8}{10} = 0.8$, so $\frac{29.96}{10.7} = 2.8$. **7.** There is a negative number on both the top and bottom, so the negative signs cancel each other out. Thus, the answer is $\frac{92}{8} = \frac{2 \cdot 2 \cdot 23}{2 \cdot 2 \cdot 2} = \frac{23}{2} = 11\frac{1}{2}$. **8. a.** $52 = \frac{241}{4\frac{2}{3}}$ **b.** $4\frac{2}{3}$ **c.** 241 **d.** 52 **9.** It is a repeating decimal because 7 is a prime factor other than 2 or 5. **10.** $3^2 \cdot 2^3$ **11.** 1,240 ÷ 7 = 177 R1; therefore, 177 cards will go in each stack, with one card left over. **12.** 149 is prime because it is only divisible by 1 and itself.

13. $365 \div 9 = 40$ R5, so there will be 40 days in each month with 5 days left over (not counting the $\frac{1}{4}$ day that is accounted for in leap years). **14.** $3 \cdot \$2.54 = \$7.62$, and $\$7.62 - \$6.99 = \$0.63$, so a total of 63¢ is saved. Then $\$0.63 \div 3 = \$0.21$, so you save 21¢ on each half-gallon. **15.** Tania worked $4 \cdot 5 - 2 = 18$ days during those 4 weeks, and made $18 \cdot 2 = 36$ total trips. If m is the number of miles from her house to work, then $0.415 \cdot 36 \cdot m = 283.86$, so $m = 19$. Emily lives 19 mi from work. **16. a.** $-1.5 \div 4$ **b.** -0.375; On average, the pool lost 0.375 inches per day.
17. The last column always has one dot, which shows that the number $4n + 1$ will have a remainder of 1 when divided by 2, meaning that $4n + 1$ is not divisible by 2.

18.

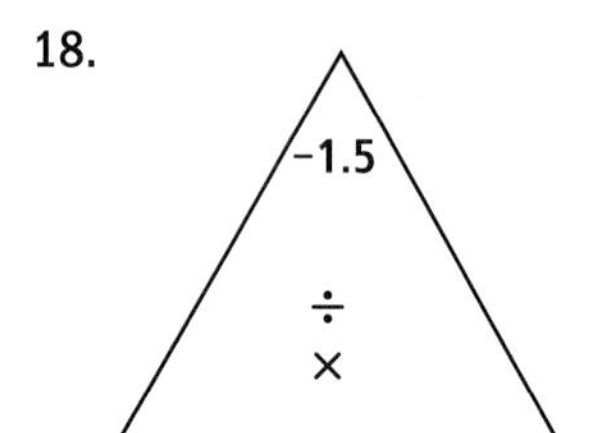

19. a.

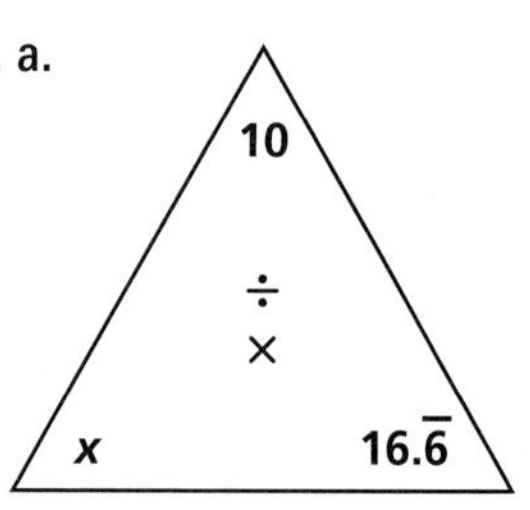

b. $10 \div x = 16.\overline{6}$, $16.\overline{6} \cdot x = 10$, $10 \div 16.\overline{6} = x$, $x \cdot 16.\overline{6} = 10$ **c.** $x = 0.6$ **d.** $\frac{10}{0.6} = 16.\overline{6}$

20. a.

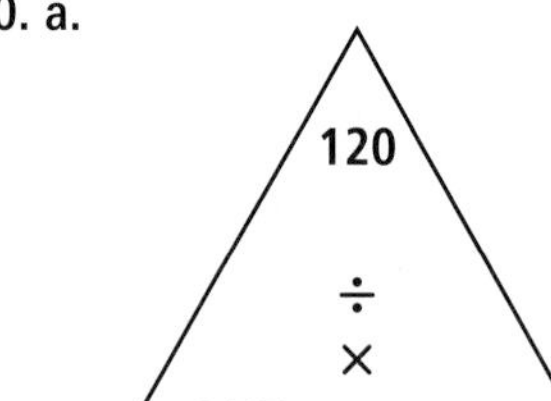

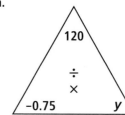

b. $120 \div -0.75 = y$, $120 \div y = -0.75$, $y \cdot -0.75 = 120$, $-0.75y = 120$ **c.** $y = -160$ **d.** $120 = -0.75 \cdot -160$

Self-Test Correlation Chart

Question	1	2	3	4	5	6	7	8	9	10
Objective(s)	B	I	C, D	I	D	D	E	F	H	A
Lesson(s)	7-4	7-4	7-5, 7-6, 7-8	7-4	7-6, 7-8	7-6, 7-8	7-9	7-1	7-7	7-3
Question	**11**	**12**	**13**	**14**	**15**	**16**	**17**	**18**	**19**	**20**
Objective(s)	I	G	I	J	K	L	M	N	N	N
Lesson(s)	7-4	7-3	7-4	7-1	7-8	7-9	7-2	7-1, 7-10	7-1, 7-10	7-1, 7-10

Chapter Review (pp. 457–459)

1. $2^2 \cdot 5^3$ **3.** $3^3 \cdot 19$ **5.** 6 R6 **7.** 77 R1 **9.** $\begin{array}{r} 5\;7\;3 \\ 8\overline{)45^5\,8^2\,7^3} \end{array}$; 573 R3 **11.** $\begin{array}{r} 5\,5\;3\;5 \\ 4\overline{)22^2 1^1 4^2 0} \end{array}$; 5,535 R0 **13.** $4{,}000\frac{1}{2}$ **15.** $1{,}410\frac{6}{7}$ **17.** 0.67 **19.** 3.90 **21.** -1 **23.** $\frac{1}{2}$ **25.** $-\frac{29}{3}$ **27.** $-\frac{547}{361} \approx 1.515$ **29.** $60 \div 20 = 3$ **31.** 16 divided by 4 is 4. **33.** dividend: 45, divisor: 5, quotient: 9
35. composite **37.** prime **39.** terminating; 40 can be written as a product of 2s and 5s, $40 = 2 \cdot 2 \cdot 5$.
41. terminating; 16 can be written as a product of 2s: $16 = 2 \cdot 2 \cdot 2 \cdot 2$. **43.** No, because the denominator of the infinite repeating decimal cannot be written as a product of only 2 and 5, and so the product of this denominator and the denominator of the terminating decimal cannot be written as the product of only 2 and 5. **45.** They can make 11 teams and 2 children will be left over. **47.** The baker can package 14 baker's dozens and 0 donuts will be left over.
49. 60,000 **51.** 4° per hr **53.** \$0.90 **55.** \$0.43 per can
57. $210 \div -13$; 16 weeks; \$2 left

59. Answers vary. Sample:

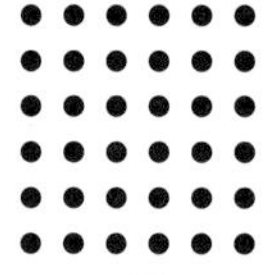

61. Answers vary. Sample:

63.

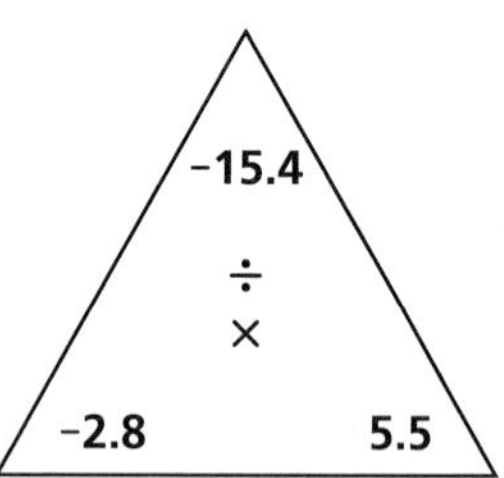

65. a. $48 \div 3 = r$, $3 \cdot r = 48$, $r \cdot 3 = 48$, $48 \div r = 3$ **b.** $r = 16$

67. $a = 10.6$

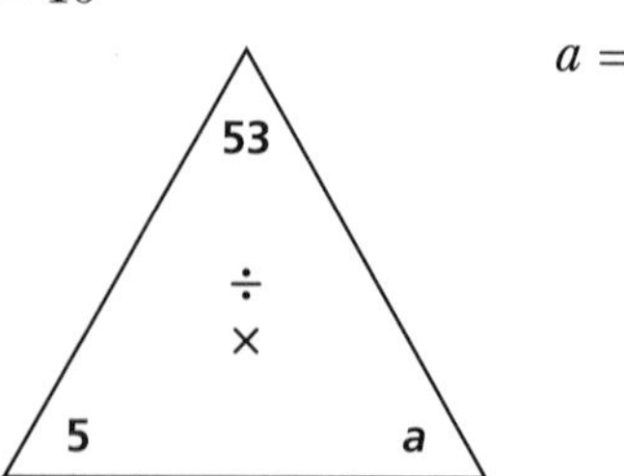

Chapter 8

Lesson 8-1 (pp. 462–466)

Guided Example 1: **a.** $\frac{24}{32}$ **b.** $\frac{24}{32} = \frac{3}{4}$

Questions: **1.** Rates have units, ratios do not. **3.** $\frac{3.69}{2.59}$; 143% **5.** $\frac{3}{4}$; 75% **7.** 1000% **9.** 60% **11.** RICH **13.** \$0.0002305; It is the rate of dollars per megabyte of memory in 2007. **15. a.** 25 **b.** 0.01773 **17.** true **19. a.** 12 ft^2 **b.** 1,728 in^2 **c.** Divide 1,728 in^2 by 12 ft^2 to get 144 in^2 per square foot. **21.** $w = -2.1$

Lesson 8-2 (pp. 467–471)

Questions: **1.** $\frac{7}{8}$ **3.** $\frac{1}{100}$ **5.** $-\frac{5}{9}$ **7.** $\frac{5}{17}$ **9.** B **11. a.** 1.25 **b.** $1.25 \cdot 0.8 = 1$; yes, it checks. **13.** $x = \frac{1}{8}$ **15.** Answers vary. Sample: $\frac{1}{4}x = 1$; $x = 4$ **17.** The digital audio players sold in 2005 were $\frac{22.5}{4.4} = 511.4\%$ of the digital audio players sold in 2004. The digital audio players sold in 2004 were $\frac{4.4}{22.5} = 19.6\%$ of the digital audio players sold in 2005. **19. a.** 42.86% **b.** 233.33% **c.** true **21.** Dominique's mother is 33 and Dominique is 11. **23.** no **25.** The array indicates that when 25 is divided by 3, there is a remainder; thus, 25 is not divisible by 3.

● ● ● ● ● ● ● ●
● ● ● ● ● ● ● ●
● ● ● ● ● ● ● ● ●

Lesson 8-3 (pp. 472–476)

Guided Example 3: $\frac{10}{3}$; $\frac{8}{3}$; $2\frac{2}{3}$; $\frac{0.8}{0.3}$

Questions: **1.** 7; $\frac{1}{7}$ **3.** $\frac{1}{50}$ **5. a.** Tia should have taken the reciprocal of 15 only, and not of 12. **b.** 0.8 **7.** 6 bundles **9. a.** 7 yd **b.** $1\frac{3}{4}$ yd **c.** $1\frac{3}{4}$ yd **11.** $\frac{3}{20}$ **13.** $\frac{7}{6}$ **15. a.** $\frac{2}{3} \div \frac{1}{3} = 2$; Phil ate twice the amount of peas that Gil ate. **b.** $\frac{1}{3} \div \frac{2}{3} = \frac{1}{2}$; Gil ate half the amount of peas that Phil ate. **17.** AFFORD **19.** C **21.** $\frac{625}{1000} \div \frac{3}{4} = \frac{625}{1000} \cdot \frac{4}{3} = \frac{2500}{3000} = \frac{5}{6} = 0.83\overline{3}$; $0.625 \div 0.75 = 0.83\overline{3}$ **23.** $\frac{5}{6}$ **25.** $\frac{1}{9}$ **27.** $\frac{4}{3}$ **29.** 93% **31.** $\left(\frac{3}{4}\right)^4 = \frac{81}{256}$

Lesson 8-4 (pp. 477–482)

Guided Example: $6\frac{1}{2}$; $3\frac{5}{7}$; $\frac{26}{7}$; $\frac{7}{26}$; $\frac{91}{52}$; 7; $1\frac{3}{4}$

Questions: **1. a.** $16 \div \frac{3}{4}$ **b.** about 21.3 servings **c.** $21.3 \cdot \frac{3}{4} = 16$ **3.** $\frac{40}{9}$ **5.** $\frac{25}{9}$ **7.** $\frac{28}{15}$ **9. a.** Destinee; you need to have units in miles divided by hours. **b.** about 7.1 mph **11.** $\frac{149}{85}$ **13.** Answers vary. Sample:

[(] 15 [+] 3 [÷] 4 [+] 2 [+] 7 [÷] 8 [)] [÷] [(] 6 [+] 1 [÷] 8 [+] 4 [+] 1 [÷] 2 [)] [ENTER] **15. a.** $\frac{35}{48}$ **b.** The divisor is greater than the dividend.

17. $\frac{289}{36}$ **19. a.** MAN **b.** If the numerators are the same, the greater the denominator, the smaller the quotient. **21. a.** 160 bags **b.** 200 bags **c.** 320 bags **23. a.** Giraffe: $\frac{11}{2}$ m, Human: $\frac{7}{4}$ m **b.** The giraffe is about 3 times taller than the average human. **c.** 3.14 times **25.** 900 ft^2 **27.** $\frac{1}{2}$

Lesson 8-5 (pp. 483–487)

Guided Example 1: $\frac{15}{8}$, $\frac{15}{8}$, $\frac{5}{4}$, $\frac{5}{4}$, $\frac{5}{4}$; yes

Guided Example 2: 9; 9; 10.17; 10.17; yes

Questions: **1. a.** $4x = 6$ **b.** $x = \frac{3}{2}$ lb **3. a.** $2 = 5x$ **b.** $x = \frac{2}{5}$ kg **5.** $\frac{1}{81}s = 2.65$ **7.** 400 **9.** false **11.** A **13.** $x = -\frac{1}{10}$; $20 \cdot -\frac{1}{10} = -2$ **15.** $x = \frac{6}{7}$; $\frac{7}{8} \cdot \frac{6}{7} = \frac{3}{4}$ **17.** $c = -\frac{1}{2}$; $13\frac{1}{3} \cdot -\frac{1}{2} = -6\frac{2}{3}$ **19. a.** $1.5n = 45$ **b.** $n = 30$ **c.** $1.5 \cdot 30 = 45$ **d.** Answers vary. Sample: It normally takes Katy 30 minutes to commute to work. **21. a.** $\frac{3}{11}B = 58.50$ **b.** $B = 214.5$ **c.** $\frac{3}{11} \cdot 214.5 = 58.5$ **d.** Answers vary. Sample: The total bill for everyone was \$214.50. **23. a.** greater than **b.** 14 **25. a.** greater than **b.** $\frac{5}{2}$ **27. a.** 30% **b.** 15% **c.** 7.5% **d.** 200% **29.** THINGS

Lesson 8-6 (pp. 488–493)

Questions: **1.** a statement that two fractions are equal

3. a.

Gallons	1	2	3	4
Miles	20	40	60	80

b.

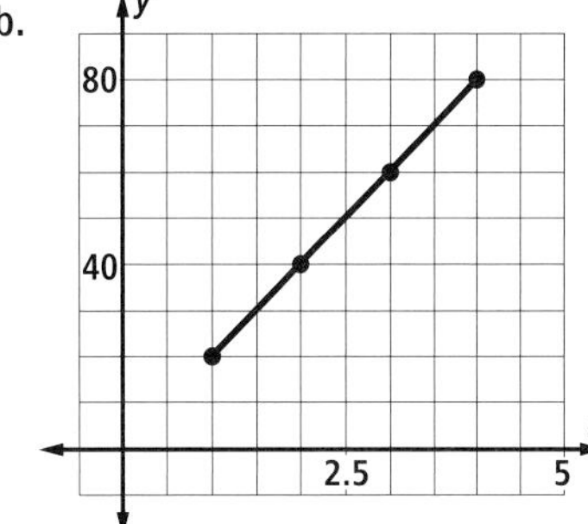

c. Answers vary. Sample: $\frac{20 \text{ miles}}{1 \text{ gallon}} = \frac{60 \text{ miles}}{3 \text{ gallons}}$ **5.** 5 is to 8 as 10 is to 16 **7. a.** 24 gal **b.** B **9.** Yes; true for some values of n. **11.** yes; false **13.** $n = 26$ **15. a.** $\frac{45}{5} = \frac{y}{90}$ **b.** $y = 810$; $\frac{45}{5} = \frac{810}{90}$ **17.** \$43.75 **19. a.** 3.4 or $\frac{17}{5}$ **b.** $3.4x = 26.2$ **c.** $x = 7.71$ mph **21.** $y = -\frac{2}{5}$; $-5 \cdot -\frac{2}{5} = 2$ **23.** $\frac{21}{8}$ **25. a.** $11 \div \frac{3}{4} = x$ **b.** $14\frac{2}{3}$ **27.** 14 weeks; Wednesday

Lesson 8-7 (pp. 494–497)

Guided Example 2: $\frac{4}{3}$; $\frac{n}{28}$; $\frac{112}{3}$; $\frac{112}{3}$; $\frac{28}{37\frac{1}{3}}$; $\frac{112}{3}$

Questions: **1.** $n = 8$ **3.** $q = 12$ **5.** 22.5 min **7. a.** $\frac{10.5 \text{ mi}}{1.25 \text{ hr}} = \frac{25 \text{ mi}}{l \text{ hr}}$ **b.** $l = 2.98$; $\frac{10.5}{1.25} = \frac{25}{2.98}$ **c.** Answers vary. Sample: Marlene rode her bike 25 miles in 2.98 hours. **9.** 12 min **11. a.** 5 hr, 38 min

b. 3 hr, 8 min **13.** Answers vary. Sample: Yes; the drink should have the same proportion of ingredients. **15.** Answers vary. Sample: No, the shop probably sells more Christmas cards in December than it sells any type of card in any other month.

17. a.

Hours	1	2	3	10
Miles	60	120	180	600

b.

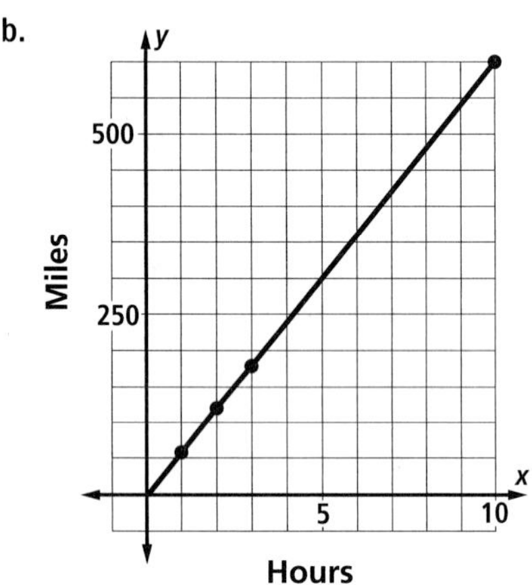

19. $2\frac{1}{5}$

21. $11.16

Lesson 8-8 (pp. 498–503)

Questions: 1. 36 in. **3.** about 3,543 km **5.** $\frac{5}{8} = \frac{a}{5}$, $a = 3.125$ **7.** $\frac{8}{c} = \frac{5}{8}$, $c = 12.8$ **9.** 48 in. **11.** 650 faculty members **13.** yes **15. a.** 13.3, 11.9, 5.5 **b.** LET **c.** 5.5 **17.** $\frac{11}{42}$ **19.** $\frac{1023}{160}$

Self-Test (pp. 506–507)

1. a. $5 \div 25 = 0.2$ **b.** $25 \div 5 = 5$ **2.** $(85 \div 125) \cdot 100 = 68\%$ **3. a.** $\frac{a}{b} \div \frac{c}{d} = \frac{a}{b} \cdot \frac{d}{c}$ **b.** $\frac{ad}{bc}$ **4.** $2\frac{2}{3} = \frac{8}{3}$, $\frac{8}{3} \cdot \frac{3}{8} = \frac{24}{24} = 1$ **5.** A, C, D **6.** $\frac{7}{8} \div \frac{2}{7} = \frac{7}{8} \cdot \frac{7}{2} = \frac{49}{16}$ **7.** $6\frac{3}{4} \div 1\frac{1}{5} = \frac{27}{4} \div \frac{6}{5} = \frac{27}{4} \cdot \frac{5}{6} = \frac{45}{8}$ **8.** $40\frac{1}{5} \div 2\frac{2}{5} = \frac{201}{5} \div \frac{12}{5} = \frac{201}{5} \cdot \frac{5}{12} = \frac{201}{12} = \frac{67}{4}$ **9.** $\frac{2\frac{1}{2} + 1\frac{1}{3}}{\frac{1}{2} + \frac{1}{3}} = \frac{\frac{5}{2} + \frac{4}{3}}{\frac{1}{2} + \frac{1}{3}} = \frac{\frac{15}{6} + \frac{8}{6}}{\frac{3}{6} + \frac{2}{6}} = \frac{\frac{23}{6}}{\frac{5}{6}} = \frac{23}{6} \cdot \frac{6}{5} = \frac{23}{5}$ **10. a.** A = $1\frac{2}{3}$; $12 \cdot \frac{5}{3} = 20$ **b.** B = -40; -1.4(-40) = 56 **11. a.** $16 \cdot 4 = 64$, $64 \div \frac{3}{4}$ **b.** $64 \div \frac{3}{4} = 64 \cdot \frac{4}{3} \approx 85.33$ servings **12. a.** $12\frac{1}{2} \div 3\frac{1}{2}$ **b.** $12\frac{1}{2} \div 3\frac{1}{2} = \frac{25}{2} \cdot \frac{2}{7} \approx 3.57$ batches **13. a.** $75x = 1{,}530$ **b.** $\frac{1}{75} \cdot 75x = \frac{1}{75} \cdot 1530$; $x = 20.4$ **c.** $75(20.4) = 1{,}530$ **d.** It will take Susan 20.4 minutes to enter the document. **14. a.** $0.30x = 1{,}830$ **b.** $\frac{1}{0.30} \cdot 0.30x = 1830 \cdot \frac{1}{0.30}$; $x = 6{,}100$ **c.** $0.30(6100) = 1{,}830$ **d.** Martin had $6,100 four months ago.

15. a.

Beats	9	18	27	108	135	162
Time(sec)	5	10	15	60	75	90

b.

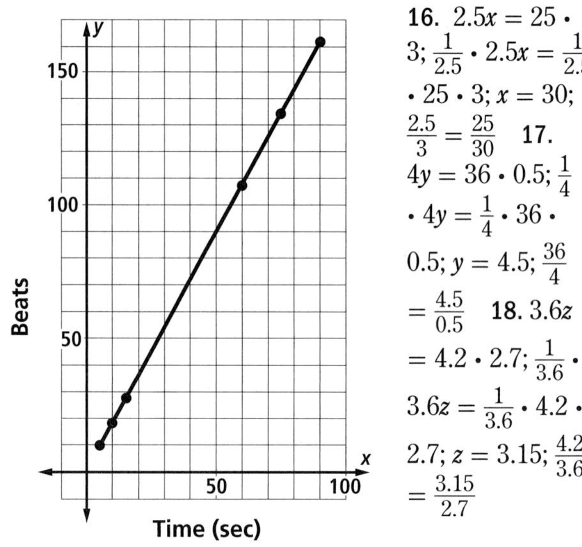

16. $2.5x = 25 \cdot 3$; $\frac{1}{2.5} \cdot 2.5x = \frac{1}{2.5} \cdot 25 \cdot 3$; $x = 30$; $\frac{2.5}{3} = \frac{25}{30}$ **17.** $4y = 36 \cdot 0.5$; $\frac{1}{4} \cdot 4y = \frac{1}{4} \cdot 36 \cdot 0.5$; $y = 4.5$; $\frac{36}{4} = \frac{4.5}{0.5}$ **18.** $3.6z = 4.2 \cdot 2.7$; $\frac{1}{3.6} \cdot 3.6z = \frac{1}{3.6} \cdot 4.2 \cdot 2.7$; $z = 3.15$; $\frac{4.2}{3.6} = \frac{3.15}{2.7}$

19. a. $\frac{2\frac{1}{3}}{140} = \frac{x}{390}$ **b.** $140x = 2\frac{1}{3} \cdot 390$; $\frac{1}{140} \cdot 140x = \frac{1}{140} \cdot 2\frac{1}{3} \cdot 390$; $x = 6.5$ **c.** If Eric's dad travels at the speed at which he gets to Grand Rapids, Michigan, he can get to Indianapolis, Indiana in 6 hours, 30 minutes. **20. a.** $\frac{18}{1} = \frac{x}{\frac{1}{4}}$ **b.** $x = 18 \cdot \frac{1}{4}$; $x = 4\frac{1}{2}$; $\frac{18}{1} = \frac{4\frac{1}{2}}{\frac{1}{4}}$ **c.** If on Veronica's plan $\frac{1}{4}$-inch paper represents 1 ft, then a portion of the set that is 18 ft long will be $4\frac{1}{2}$ in. on the plans.

Chapter Review (pp. 508–511)

1. $\frac{8}{25}$ **3.** $\frac{57}{2}$ **5.** $6\frac{1}{3} \div \frac{2}{9}$ is larger; $\frac{2}{9}$ is smaller than $\frac{2}{7}$, so $\frac{2}{9}$ will divide more times into $6\frac{1}{3}$.

Self-Test Correlation Chart

Question	1	2	3	4	5	6	7	8	9	10
Objective(s)	G	G	F	E	E	A	A	A	B	C
Lesson(s)	8-1	8-1	8-3	8-2	8-2	8-3, 8-4	8-3, 8-4	8-3, 8-4	8-4	8-5
Question	**11**	**12**	**13**	**14**	**15**	**16**	**17**	**18**	**19**	**20**
Objective(s)	H	H	I	I	K	D	D	D	J	J
Lesson(s)	8-3, 8-4	8-3, 8-4	8-5	8-5	8-6	8-6, 8-7	8-6, 8-7	8-6, 8-7	8-6, 8-7	8-6, 8-7

7. $\frac{15}{44}$ **9.** $\frac{167}{38}$ **11.** $x = \frac{4}{3}$ **13.** $p = \frac{21}{20}$ **15.** $u = 0.8$ **17.** $k = 80$ **19.** $p = 0.13$ **21.** $\frac{7}{4}$ **23.** $\frac{1}{7}$ **25.** true **27.** $\frac{1}{7}$ **29.** $\frac{1}{5} \cdot \frac{b}{a}$ **31.** 3.8 **33.** 0.3 **35.** 8.43% **37.** 15.79% **39.** $1\frac{1}{4}$ lb of beef **41.** $\frac{4}{39}$ of the day **43. a.** $6x = 3.25$ **b.** $x = \frac{3.25}{6}$; $x \approx 0.54$ **c.** $6(0.54) \approx 3.25$ **d.** Answers vary. Sample: One bagel would cost about \$0.54. **45. a.** $8x = 9\frac{1}{2}$ **b.** $x = \frac{9\frac{1}{2}}{8}$; $x = \frac{29}{2} \cdot \frac{1}{8}$; $x = 1\frac{3}{16}$ **c.** $8\left(1\frac{3}{16}\right) = 9\frac{1}{2}$ **d.** Answers vary. Sample: $1\frac{3}{16}$ inches of snow fell per hour. **47.** \$840 **49.** 12 tbs of salsa, 8 tbs of lime juice **51.** 7.5 mi apart **53.** 4 bottles of orange juice

55. a–b.

Distance Traveled (mi) vs. Time (hr): (1, 55), (2, 110), (3, 165), (4, 220), (5, 275)

57. a.

Sacks of Grain vs. Bolts of Wool

b. about $1\frac{1}{2}$ sacks of grain

Chapter 9

Lesson 9-1 (pp. 514–518)

Guided Example 2: **a.** 2,025 **b.** 15; 15; 15; 225

Questions: **1.** 537 ft^2 **3.** 12 cm × 2.5 cm; 29 cm; and 30 cm^2 **5.** Answers vary. Sample: Some of the sides of the rectangles are shared and would be counted twice if the perimeter was found by breaking it up into three rectangles. **7.** 21 cm^2 **9. a.** 108 ft^2 **b.** 12 yd^2 **c.** the store with the carpeting at \$40/yd^2 **11.** Answers vary. Sample: They have this name because they are each the square of a whole number. 24 is not a perfect square because there are no whole numbers that equal 24 when squared. **13.** 100 mm^2

15. a. Answers vary. Sample: 50 × 4; 25 × 8

b.

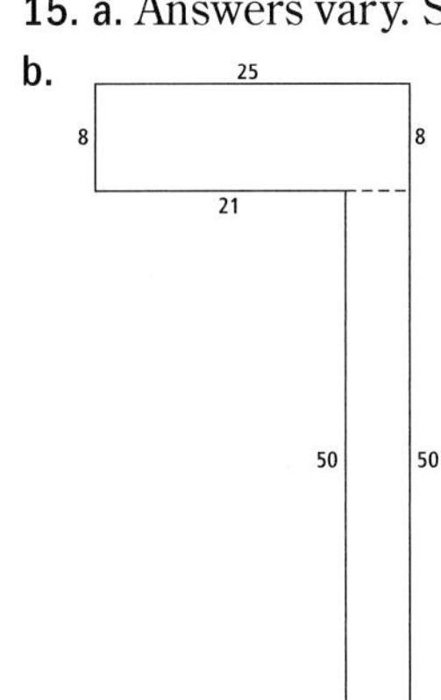

The perimeter of combined region = 166; The perimeter of the 25 × 8 rectangle = 66; The perimeter of 50 × 4 rectangle = 108

c. The area of combined region = 400; The area of the 25 × 8 rectangle = 200; The area of the 50 × 4 rectangle = 200; Yes, the area of the combined region is equal to the sum of the areas of the two rectangles you started with.

17.

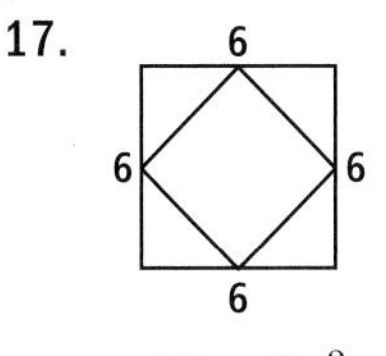

18 units^2

19.

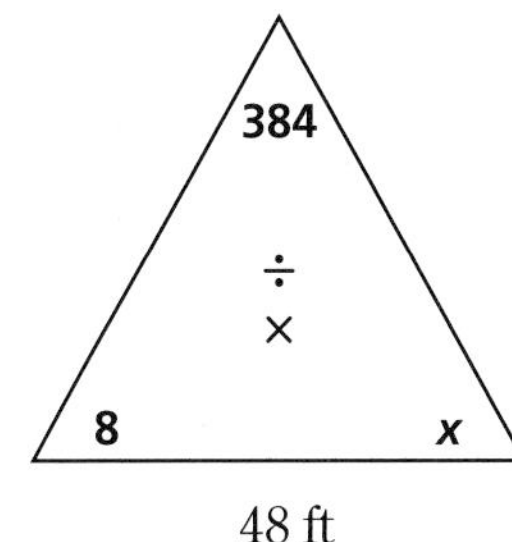

48 ft

21. \$9.41 **23.** $3\frac{5}{12}$ in^2 **25.** Check students' drawings.

Lesson 9-2 (pp. 519–525)

Guided Example 2: 6; 4; 16; 6; 4; 6; 16; 60

Questions: **1. a.** 1,650 ft^2 **b.** $\frac{1}{2}(110)(30) = 1{,}650$ ft^2

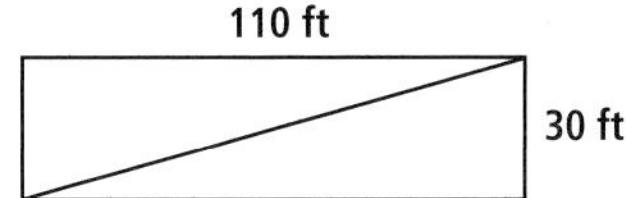

3. legs: $\overline{GR}, \overline{GT}$; hypotenuse: $\overline{RT}$ **5.** 66 in^2

7. Answers vary. Sample: $\frac{1}{2}(3)(1.25) = 1.875$ cm^2

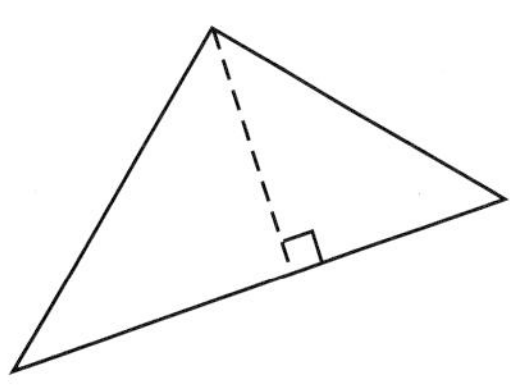

9. a. The irregular figure has a larger area. **b.** 16 **11. a.** 1,500 ft^2 **b.** 5 gal **13. a.** 24 in^2 **b.** 24 in. **c.** No, square inches are a different unit of measure than inches. **15.** The figures have the same area. **17.** 120,731 words **19.** A

21. Answers vary. Sample:

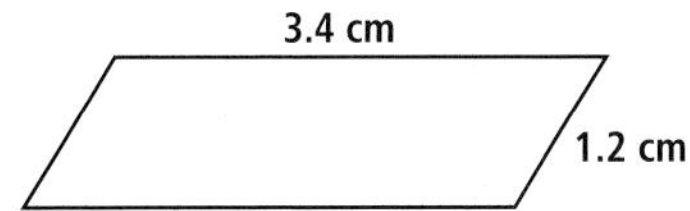

Lesson 9-3 (pp. 526–532)

Guided Example: a. EF; FC; CD; DE; $\triangle BCF$; BC; greater b. 40m^2; 15m^2; 25m^2; 15m^2; 15m^2; 25m^2; 40m^2

Questions: 1. a. $2[\frac{1}{2}(3)(9)] + (7)(9) = 90$

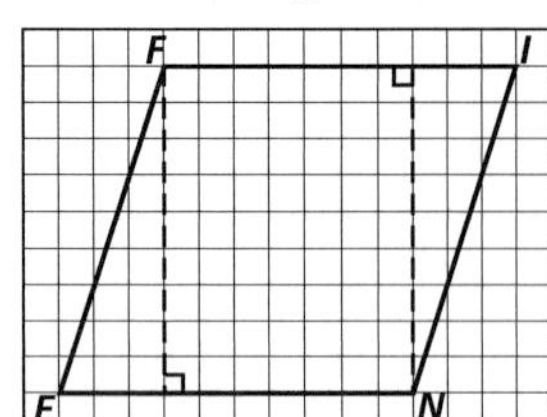

b. 10×9 rectangle; $A = 90$ c. $A = 10 \cdot 9 = 90$ 3. 21 cm^2

5. $\overline{MA}$ is the hypotenuse of $\triangle MAS$, so $MA > AS$. Similarly, the case with RS and $\triangle RST$, so $RS > RT$.

7. $2.6 \cdot 1.7 = 3.91$ cm

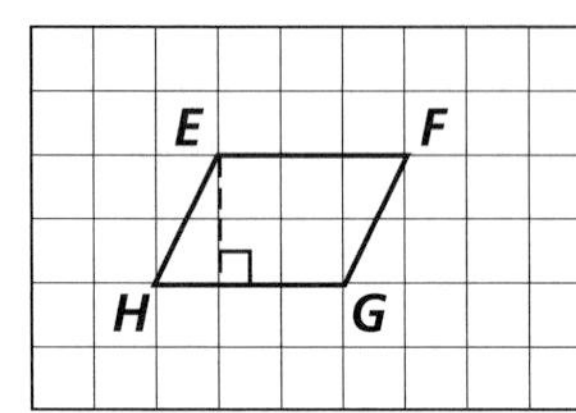

9. 2,000 mm^2 11. 57 in^2 13. a. 400 ft^2 b. $\frac{45}{10} = \frac{x}{400}$; $x = 1{,}800$ bricks c. 180 bricks d. 1,980 bricks

15. 695 ft^2 17. 360° 19. 1440° 21. 45°

Lesson 9-4 (pp. 533–538)

Questions: 1. 2 3. Answers vary. Sample: The distance traveled by a point on a wheel in one revolution is about equal to π times the diameter. 5. $\frac{22}{7}$ 7. 73.4 in.

9. a.

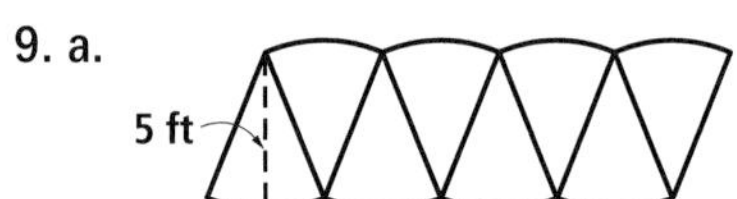

b. 78.5 ft^2 11. 452.4 in^2

13. a. 7,854 pieces b. $117,637.94 15. a. 75.4 in. b. 63,360 in. c. 840 turns 17. 70.2 m^2 19. 49.8 mm^2 21. 160 ft^2 23. $y = -468$

Lesson 9-5 (pp. 539–544)

Guided Example 1: 99 ft; 49 ft; 4,851 ft^2; 1,875 ft^2; 4,851 ft^2; 1,875 ft^2; 2,976 ft^2

Questions: 1. circles with the same center

3. a.

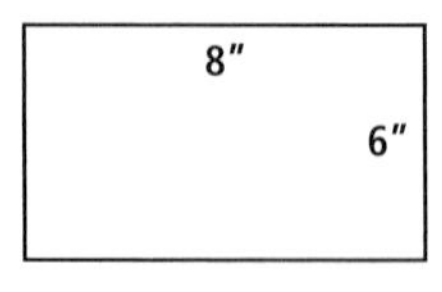

b.

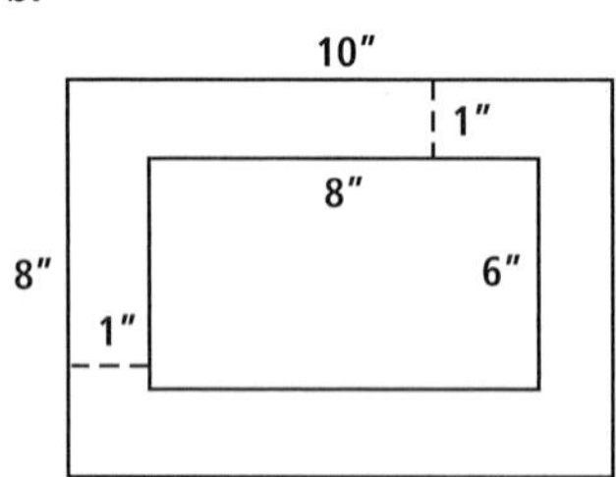

c. 8″ × 11″ d. Area of photo: 48 in^2; Area of framed photo: 80 in^2 e. Area of frame: 32 in^2 5. a. 1% b. 3% c. $\frac{1}{3}$ 7. 227.6 mm^2

9. a.

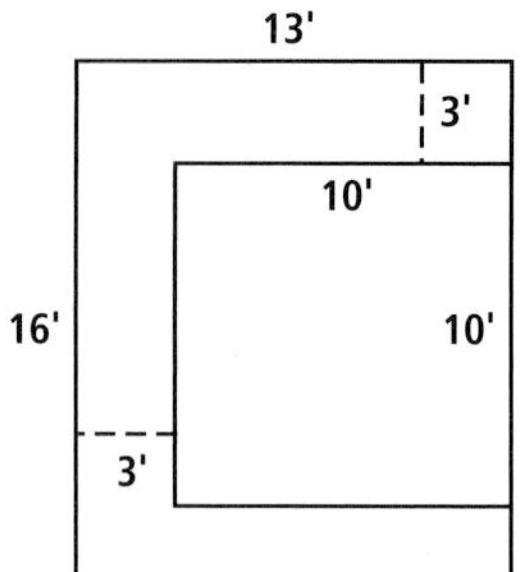

b. 58 ft c. 108 ft^2 d. 48.1%

11. a. 17.9 cm^2 b.

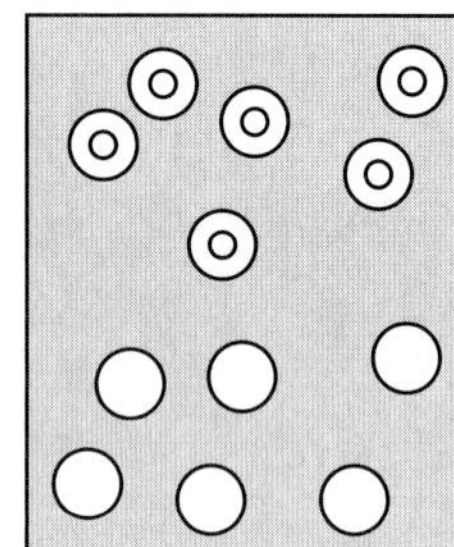

c. 975.0 cm^2 13. 200 in^2 15. 125 in^2 17. 9,000 yd^2 19. $p = 0.25$

Lesson 9-6 (pp. 545–549)

Guided Example 1: $GHDC$; CD; AB

Questions: 1. $ABCD$ and $EFGH$ 3. $\overline{AB}$, $\overline{BF}$, $\overline{FE}$, $\overline{EA}$ 5. $\overline{HG}$, $\overline{DC}$, $\overline{AB}$, $\overline{EF}$

box	front	back	top	bottom	right	left
7.	5 mm × 4 mm	5 mm × 4 mm	7 mm × 5 mm	7 mm × 5 mm	4 mm × 7 mm	4 mm × 7 mm
9.	3 ft × 1.5 ft	3 ft × 1.5 ft	3 ft × 6 ft	3 ft × 6 ft	6 ft × 1.5 ft	6 ft × 1.5 ft

11.

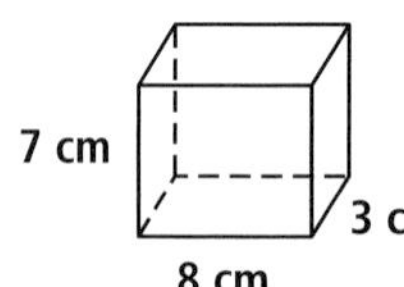

13.

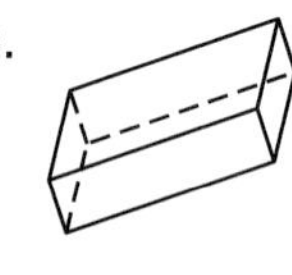

15. a. $1 \times 2 \times 5$ b. 10 17. a. $2 \times 1 \times 3$ and $6 \times 3 \times 9$

b.

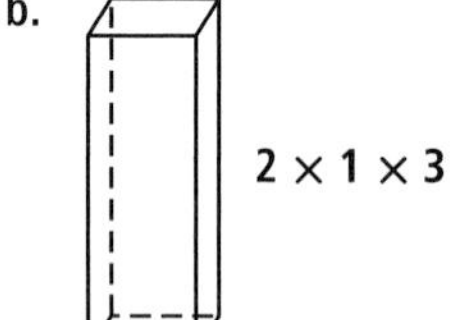

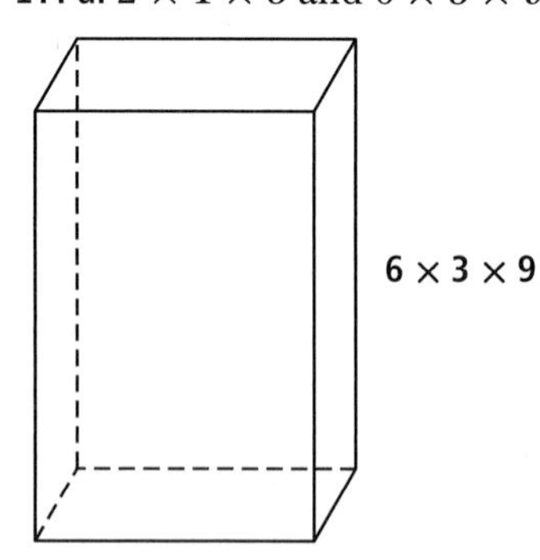

19. 48.5 cm^2 21. a. The 16 × 20 photograph is about $0.0465 per square inch and the 20 × 30 photograph is about $0.0333 per square inch. b. The smaller photograph is about 1.4 times more expensive per square inch.

Lesson 9-7 (pp. 550–554)

Questions: **1.** A 2-D pattern that will create the 3-D shape when folded. **3.** no **5.** Answers vary. Sample: yes; M and P, N and R, O and Q
7. Answers vary. Sample:

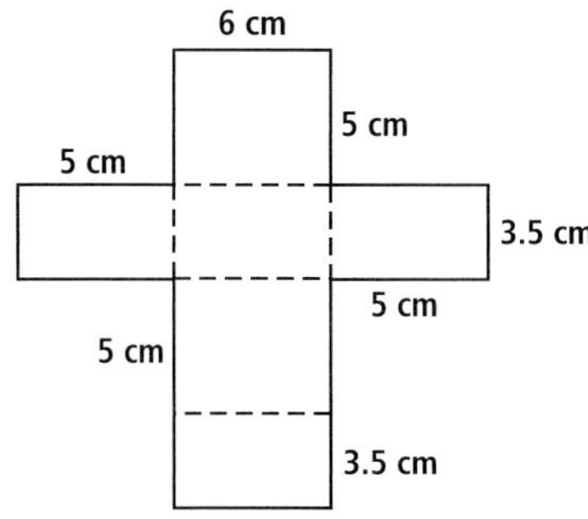

9. Answers vary. Sample:

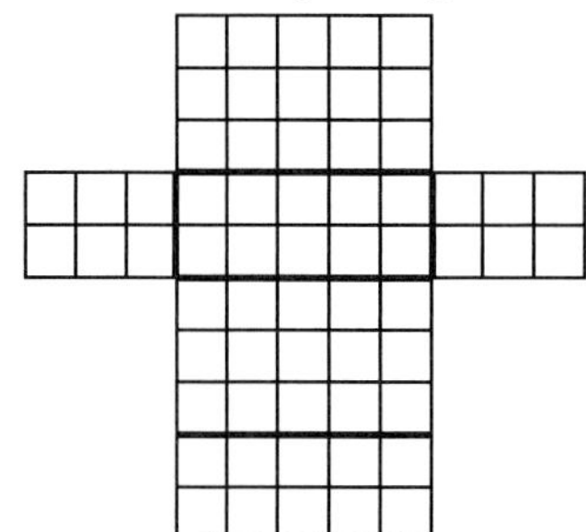

11. $3 \times 3 \times 2$ **13.** $4 \times 4 \times 2$

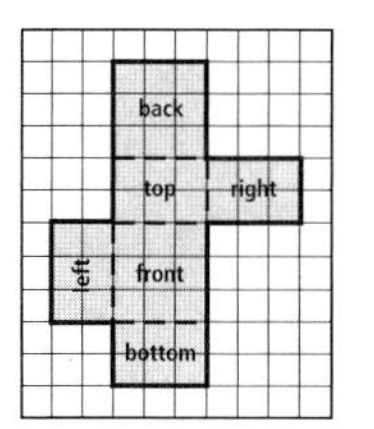

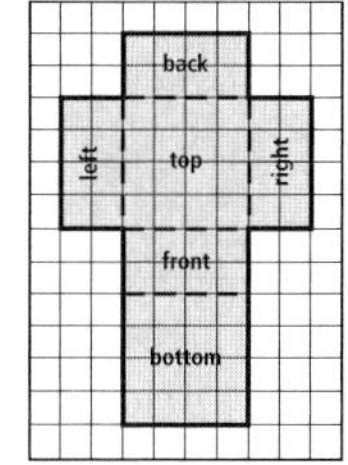

15. a. 87.5 ft^2 **b.** 88 ft^2 **17.** 262 sheep per km^2

Lesson 9-8 (pp. 555–560)

Guided Example 1: s; $6s^2$ cm^2
Questions: **1. a.** Answers vary. Sample:

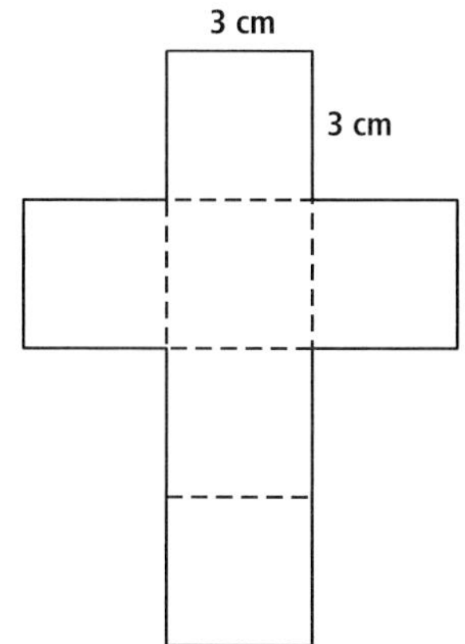

b. 54 cm^2

3. a. 13.5 in^2 **b.** 3.375 in^3 **5. a.** $6x^2$ square units **b.** x^3 cubic units **7. a.** 1 cm^3 **b.** 6 cm^2 **9.** 8 times as large **11.** 3 units **13. a.** 62.2 lb **b.** 1,679.6 lb **15.** no
17. a.

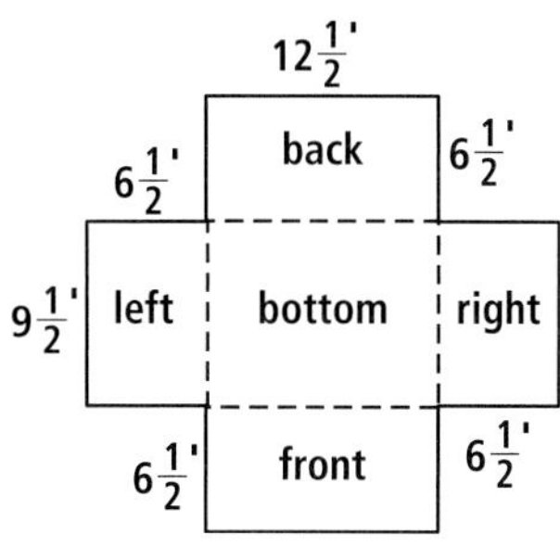

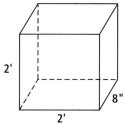

b. 8 in.: 4 edges; 24 in.: 8 edges **19.** 144 in^2

Lesson 9-9 (pp. 561–566)

Guided Example 2: 18; 4; 4; 3; 6; 4; 72

$12\frac{1}{2}$'
$6\frac{1}{2}$' back $6\frac{1}{2}$'
$9\frac{1}{2}$' left bottom right
$6\frac{1}{2}$' front $6\frac{1}{2}$'

Guided Example 3: $81\frac{1}{4}$ ft^2; $81\frac{1}{4}$ ft^2; $61\frac{3}{4}$ ft^2; $61\frac{3}{4}$ ft^2; $118\frac{3}{4}$ ft^2; $404\frac{3}{4}$ ft^2; 16; $404\frac{3}{4}$ ft^2; 16; 6,476
Guided Example 4: 6.5; 9.5; 12.5; 771.9 ft^3; 771.9 ft^3; 771.9 ft^3; 5,800 gal

Questions: **1. a.** 30 cubes **b.** 4 layers **c.** 120 in^3
3. Answers vary. Sample: Volume does not depend on the orientation of the box, so tipping it sideways still gives the same volume. **5.** 3,995.2 cm^2 **7.** 720 in^3
9. 106,280 mm^2 **11.** $lw + 2wh + 2lh$ **13.** 2,218.96 cm^2
15. a. 24 cm^3 **b.** 64 cm^2 (if we include the surface of the hole) **17.** Answers vary. Sample: $12 \times 4 \times 3$; $3 \times 3 \times 16$ **19.** 50,000 cm^2 **21.** 1,728 in^3 **23.** C
25. a. $\frac{1}{4}$ mi^2 **b.** 0.20 mi^2 **c.** 78.5%

Lesson 9-10 (pp. 567–572)

Guided Example 1: 3.25 cm; 3.25 cm; 33.2 cm^2; 33.2 cm^2; 12.5 cm; 415 **Guided Example 2:** 2 cm; 1.7 cm; 1.7; 1.7 cm^2; 8 cm
Questions: **1.** hexagonal prism **3.** cylinder **5.** $V = Bh$

	Solid from	Area of the Base	Height	Volume
7.	Question 2	21 in^2	8 in.	168 in^3
	Solid from	Area of Each Base	Area of Each Side	Surface Area
9.	Question 1	4 m^2	8.69 m^2	60.1 m^2
11.	Question 3	530.9 mm^2	4,002 mm^2	5,064 mm^2

13. Answers vary. Sample: Tiana is incorrect because she didn't include the area of one of the bases. The correct expression is $2\pi(4.25)^2 + 2\pi(4.25)(12.5)$.
15. 118,900 ft^2 **17. a.** The triangular bar is $0.33 per in^3 and the rectangular bar is $0.49 per in^3. **b.** the triangular bar **19. a.** 264 cm^2 **b.** 288 cm^3 **21.** 2 or 200%

Self-Test (pp. 576–577)

1. $\frac{1}{2}bh = \frac{1}{2}(25)(24) = 300\text{ in}^2$ 2. $bh = (3.5)(2) = 7\text{ ft}^2$ 3. a. $\pi r^2 = \pi(10)^2 \approx 314.16\text{ in}^2$ b. $2\pi r = 2\pi(10) \approx 62.83$ in. 4. $bh - \pi r^2 = (13.5)(10.5) - \pi(3)^2 = 141.75 - 28.27 = 113.5\text{ in}^2$ 5. $b_1h_1 + b_2h_2 = (0.5)(3) + (4)(7) = 1.5 + 28 = 29.5\text{ in}^2$ 6. a. $2\pi r_1 + 2\pi r_2 + 2\pi r_3 = 2\pi(3 + 4.5 + 5) \approx 78.5$ m b. $\pi r_1^2 + \pi r_2^2 + \pi r_3^2 = \pi(3^2 + 4.5^2 + 5^2) = \pi(54.25) \approx 170.4\text{ m}^2$ 7. $\frac{1}{2}b_1h_1 + b_1h_2 - b_2h_3 = \frac{1}{2}(18)(15 - 9) + (18)(9) - (10)(5) = 54 + 162 + 50 = 166\text{ ft}^2$

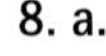

8. a.

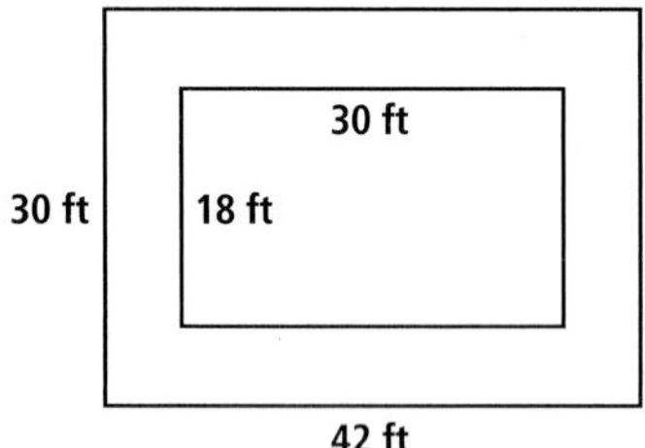

b. $A_{total} - A_{pool} = (30)(42) - (18)(30) = 1260 - 540 = 720\text{ ft}^2$

9. Answers vary. Sample: DC

10. Answers vary. Sample: H, D 11. Answers vary. Sample: $DCGH$ 12. Answers vary. Sample:

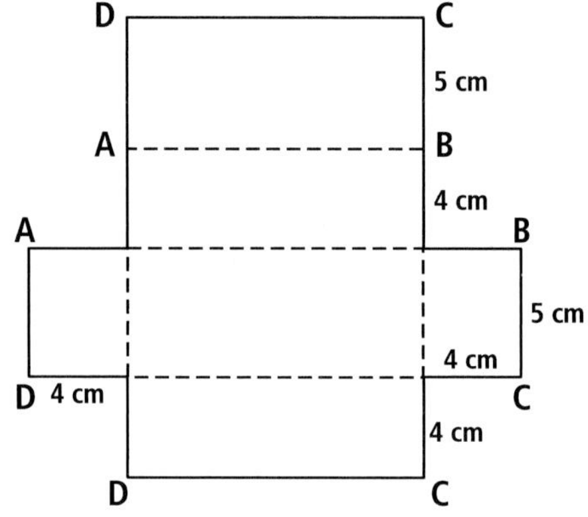

13. Answers vary. Sample:

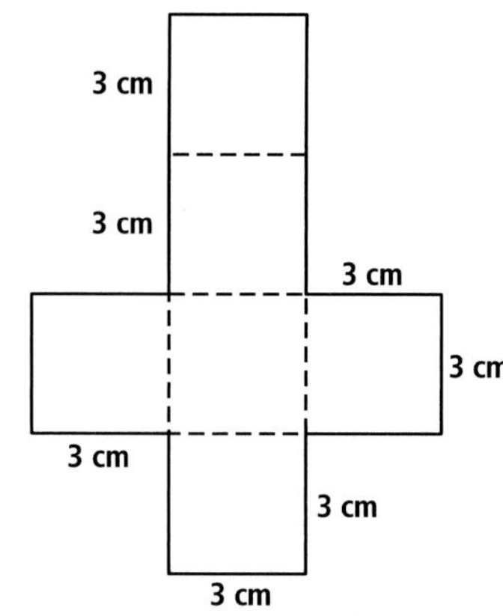

14. $6s^2 = 6(3)^2 = 54\text{ cm}^2$ 15. $s^3 = 3^3 = 27\text{ cm}^3$

16. Answers vary. Sample:

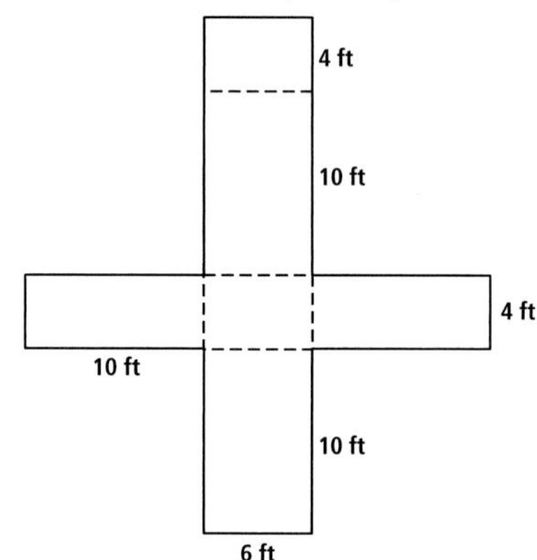

17. $2lw + 2wh + 2lh = 2(6 \cdot 4) + 2(10 \cdot 4) + 2(10 \cdot 6) = 48 + 80 + 120 = 248\text{ ft}^2$
18. $V = Bh = (4)(6)(10) = 240\text{ ft}^3$

19. $S.A. = 2(\frac{1}{2})(12)(6) + (12)(24) + 2(8.5)(24) = 72 + 288 + 408 = 768\text{ in}^2$; $V = \frac{1}{2}(12)(6) \cdot 24 = 864\text{ in}^3$
20. $2(4\pi) + 4\pi(1.5) = 25.13 + 18.85 \approx 43.98\text{ in}^2$
21. $\pi(2)^2\ (1.5) \approx 18.85\text{ in}^3$

Self-Test Correlation Chart

Question	1	2	3	4	5	6	7	8	9	10
Objective(s)	A	A	A, B	C	C	I, J	K	K	H	H
Lesson(s)	9-2, 9-3, 9-4	9-2, 9-3, 9-4	9-2, 9-3, 9-4	9-1, 9-4, 9-5	9-1, 9-4, 9-5	9-2, 9-3, 9-4	9-4, 9-5	9-4, 9-5	9-6	9-6
Question	**11**	**12**	**13**	**14**	**15**	**16**	**17**	**18**	**19**	**20**
Objective(s)	H	H	M	D	E	M	L	L	F	L
Lesson(s)	9-6	9-6	9-7	9-8, 9-9	9-8, 9-9	9-7	9-9, 9-10	9-9, 9-10	9-10	9-9, 9-10
Question	**21**	**22**								
Objective(s)	L	G								
Lesson(s)	9-9, 9-10	9-1, 9-3, 9-4								

22. Area($\triangle DEC$) $= \frac{1}{2}bh = \frac{1}{2}(DC)(AD)$; Area($\triangle ADE$) + Area($\triangle EBC$) $= \frac{1}{2}(AE)(AD) + \frac{1}{2}(EB)(BC)$; $BC = AD$, $\frac{1}{2}(AE)(AD) + \frac{1}{2}(EB)(AD) = \frac{1}{2}(AE + EB)(AD) = \frac{1}{2}(AB)(AD)$; $AB = DC$, $\frac{1}{2}(AB)(AD) = \frac{1}{2}(DC)(AD) =$ Area($\triangle DEC$) $= \frac{1}{2}$Area($ABCD$)

Chapter Review (pp. 578–583)

1. 44 ft^2 3. 48 cm 5. 12 in^2 7. 62.8 ft 9. 31.4 cm 11. $\approx$ 83.4 m^2 13. $\approx$ 53.4 yd^2 15. 156 m^2 17. 150 m^2 19. 172 cm^2 21. 312 in^3 23. 0.05 in^3 25. $S.A. =$ 108.8 m^2; $V = 52.5$ m^3 27. $S.A. \approx$ 35,186 m^2; $V \approx$ 502,655 cm^3 29. The area of $\triangle MNO$ is the difference of the areas of $\triangle MNP$ and $\triangle MOP$. 31. no 33. A 35. A, B, C, D, E, F, G, H 37. $ABCD$ and $EFHG$: 5×9; $ABFE$ and $DCHG$: 9×10; $AEGD$ and $BFHC$: 5×10 39. no 41. 56 cm 43. 1,963 ft^2 45. 45.5 in^2 47. 1,292 in^2 49. 10 cm^2 51. Karla is right. The sphere with a volume just under 400 in^3 has a radius of about 4.57 in. The box has an edge length of about 7.36 in., meaning that the largest sphere it could hold has a radius of 3.68 in. 53. $\approx$ 321.2 m^2 55. 45 m^2

57.

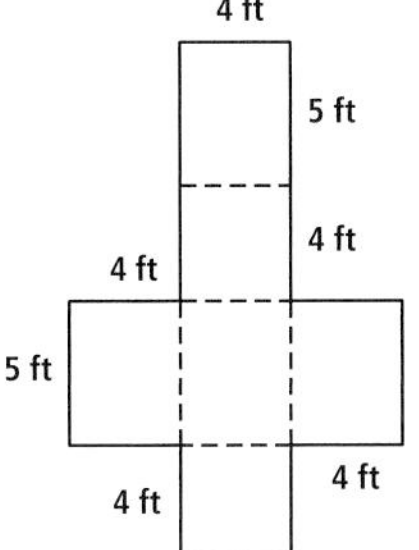

59.

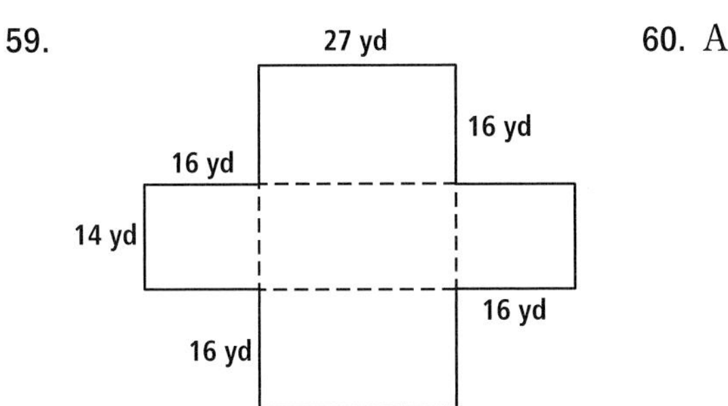

60. A

Chapter 10

Lesson 10-1 (pp. 586–590)

Guided Example 3: 26; 10; 26; 26; 26; 10; 10; 10; 17,576,000; 17,576,000

Questions:

1. a.

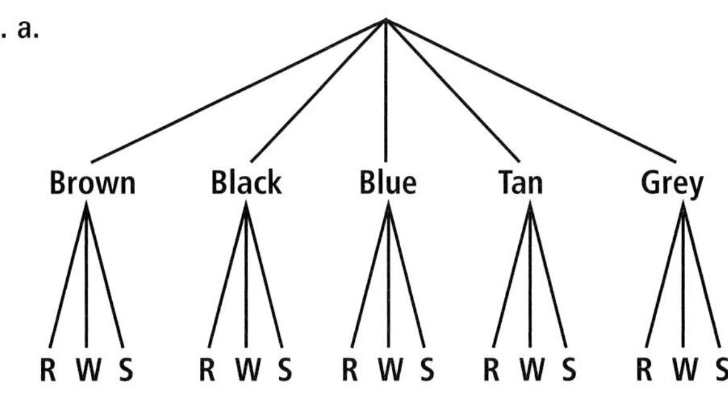

b. 15 3. No, it can only produce 72 possible pizzas. 5. 2,500 numbers 7. a. 360 days b. 90 meals c. 18 meals 9. 212, 213, 214, 221, 223, 224, 231, 232, 234 11.a.

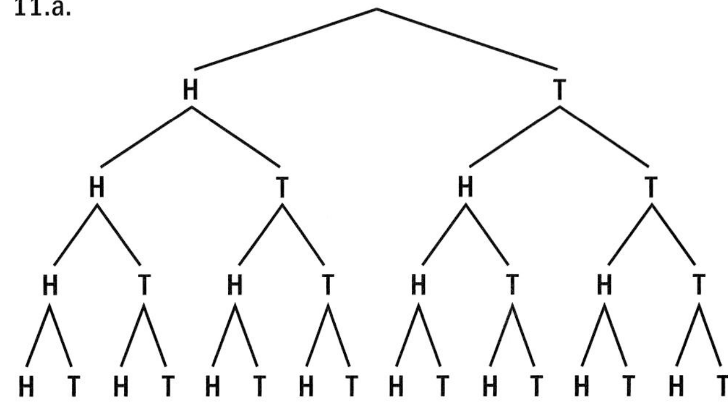

b. 16 outcomes c. $2 \cdot 2 \cdot 2 \cdot 2 = 16$ d. 5 e. 37.5% 13. a. 25 pairs b. (a, e), (a, i), (a, o), (a, u), (e, i), (e a), (e, o), (e, u), (i, a), (i, e), (i, o), (i, u), (o, a), (o, e), (o, i), (o, u), (u, a), (u, e), (u, i), (u, o) c. $5 \cdot 4 = 20$ 15. 9,261 in^3 17. $\frac{8}{15}$ 19. 30 sixth graders

Lesson 10-2 (pp. 591–596)

Guided Example 1: HTT; TTT; TTH; THT; THH; 8; 3; $\frac{3}{8}$

Guided Example 2: 10; 10; 10; 10; 10; 100,000; 1; 3; 5; 7; 9; 5; 5; 5; 5; 5; 3,125; $\frac{1}{32}$; 0.03125; 3.125%

Guided Example 3: 10; 24; 34; 34; 34; 34; 34; 34; 3,125; $\frac{3{,}125}{45{,}435{,}424}$

Questions: 1. the set of possible outcomes of a situation 3. a. HH, HT, TH, TT b. $\frac{1}{4}$ c. $\frac{1}{4}$ d. $\frac{1}{2}$ 5. a. 0.0625 b. $\frac{625}{1{,}336{,}336} \approx 0.00047$ c. sample space 7. a. 10 b. $\frac{1}{2}$ c. $\frac{3}{10}$ d. 0 9. a. $\frac{7}{365}$ b. yes 11. a. each letter of the alphabet b. $\frac{5}{26}$ c. $\frac{2}{13}$ d. $\frac{7}{26}$ 13. can 15. 38.48 in^2 17. $2^9 \cdot 5^9$

Lesson 10-3 (pp. 597–502)

Guided Example 3: $\frac{1}{4}, \frac{1}{8}, \frac{1}{8}, \frac{1}{8}$

Questions: **1. a.** $\frac{1}{6} \approx 0.167$ **b.** $\frac{2}{3} \approx 0.67$

3. a.

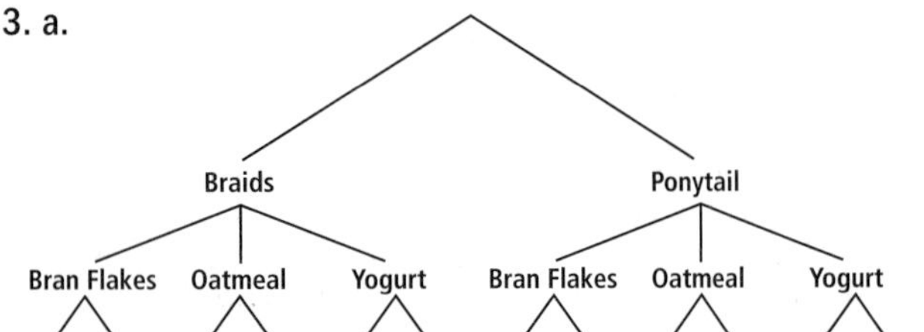

b. $\frac{1}{12} \approx 0.083$ **5.** $\frac{1}{16} \approx 0.063$

7. a.

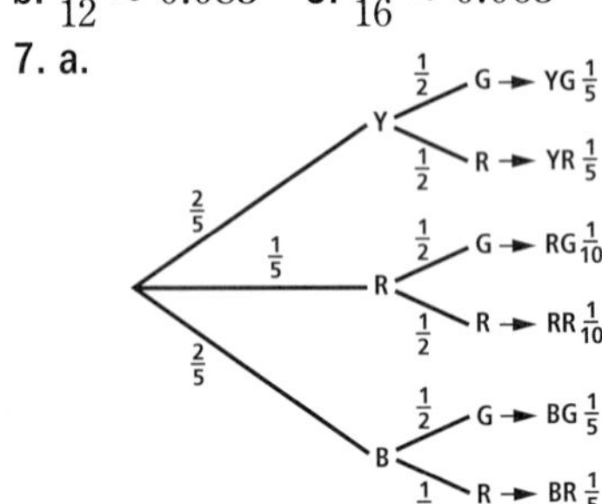

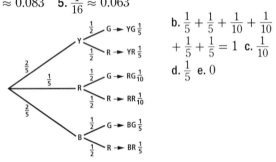

b. $\frac{1}{5} + \frac{1}{5} + \frac{1}{10} + \frac{1}{10} + \frac{1}{5} + \frac{1}{5} = 1$ **c.** $\frac{1}{10}$ **d.** $\frac{1}{5}$ **e.** 0

9. a.

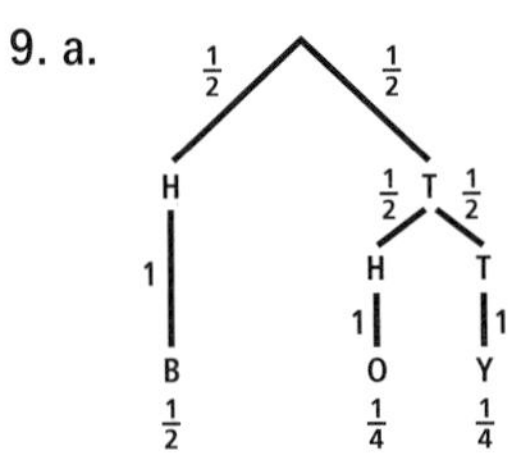

b. No. Since bran is chosen only after one coin toss instead of two, it would have a higher probability of being chosen.

11.

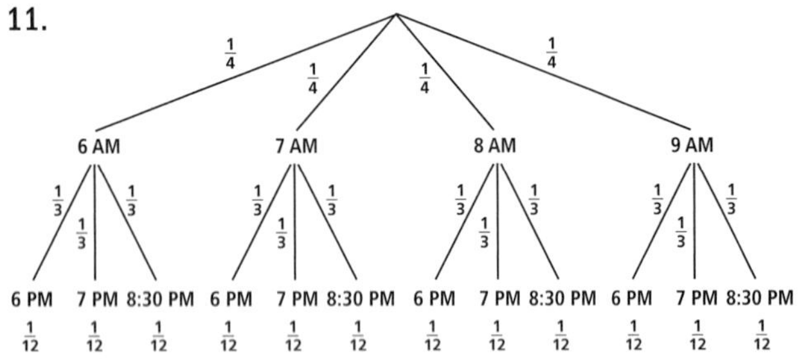

13. a. RRR, RRC, RCR, RCC, CCC, CCR, CRC, CRR
b. $\frac{1}{8} = 0.125$ **c.** $\frac{1}{8} = 0.125$ **d.** $\frac{1}{8} = 0.125$

15. 30 possible salads

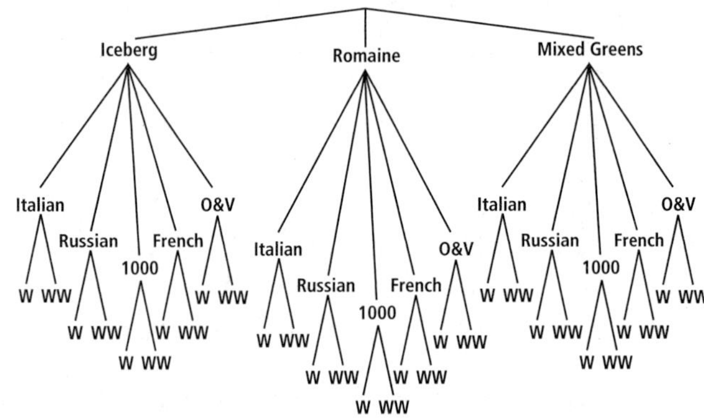

17. 37.5% **19.** false

Lesson 10-4 (pp. 603–609)

Guided Example 2:

Outcome	Who wins?	Outcome	Who wins?
RR	Tie	PS	Player 2
RP	Player 2	SR	Player 2
RS	Player 1	SP	Player 1
PR	Player 1	SS	Tie
PP	Tie		

$\frac{1}{3}; \frac{1}{3}$; 1; each player has an equal chance of winning

Guided Example 3:

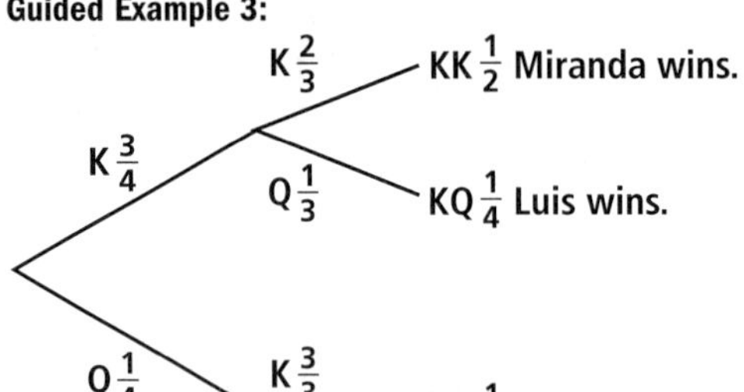

$\frac{1}{2}; \frac{1}{2}$; equal; is

Questions: **1.** A fair game is a game where each player has an equal chance of winning.

3.

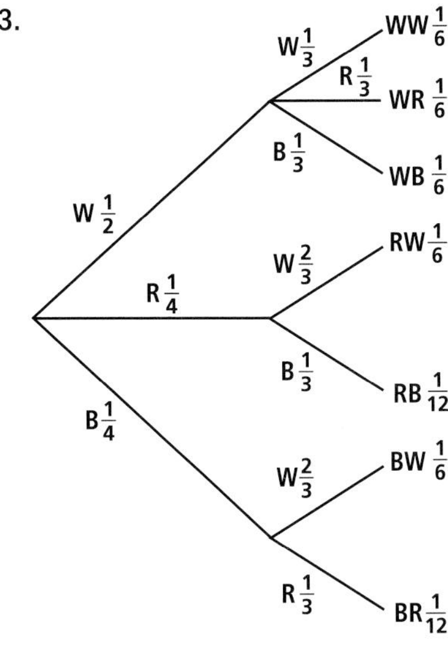

P(both are the same color) $= \frac{1}{6}$; P(one red and one blue) $= \frac{1}{6}$ **5.** i. = *count* **7. a.** $\frac{1}{3} \approx 0.33$ **b.** $\frac{1}{6} \approx 0.167$ **9. a.** $\frac{5}{22} \approx 0.23$ **b.** $\frac{5}{22} \approx 0.23$ **c.** $\frac{6}{11} \approx 0.55$ **d.** increase, because there is a bigger sample space **11.** Fedora Snowshoes, Fedora Sandals, Fedora Steel-toed Boots, Fedora Tennis Shoes, Bowler Snowshoes, Bowler Sandals, Bowler Steel-toed Boots, Bowler Tennis Shoes, Cowboy Snowshoes, Cowboy Sandals, Cowboy Steel-toed Boots, Cowboy Tennis Shoes, Porkpie Snowshoes, Porkpie Sandals, Porkpie Steel-toed Boots, Porkpie Tennis Shoes, Panama Snowshoes, Panama Sandals, Panama Steel-toed Boots, Panama Tennis Shoes, Boater Snowshoes, Boater Sandals, Boater Steel-toed Boots, Boater Tennis Shoes, Beret Snowshoes, Beret Sandals, Beret Steel-toed Boots, Beret Tennis Shoes **13. a.** 456,976 passwords **b.** 1,679,616 passwords

Lesson 10-5 (pp. 610–615)

Questions: **1. a.** 16 **b.** $\frac{16}{49} \approx 0.33$ **c.** $\frac{33}{49} \approx 0.67$ **3. a.** $\frac{1}{3} \approx 0.33$ **b.** $\frac{1}{3} \approx 0.33$ **c.** $\frac{1}{3} \approx 0.33$ **5.** Answers vary. Sample: The more trials of an experiment, the closer the relative frequency of an event will be to the event's probability. **7.** relative frequency; 0.5 **9.** probability; 0 **11.** Answers vary. Sample: Yes; Because Rick Barry shot thousands of free throws in his career, it is definitely possible that he may have missed four in a row. **13. a.** Answers vary. Sample: Relative frequency of winning = 0.36, Relative frequency of losing = 0.64. **b.** yes **c.** Answers vary. Sample: Find the probability of winning (0.5) and compare it to the probability of losing (0.5), and if they are equal, which they are, then it's a fair game. **15. a.** $\frac{1}{500{,}000} = 0.000002$ **b.** Answer vary. Sample: Yes, the probability of getting 10 heads in a row is extremely low.

17.

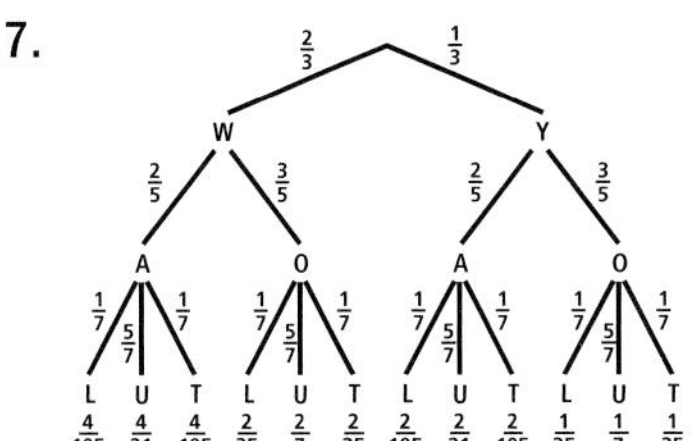

19. a. 14 **b.** 18 **c.** 4 **d.** 4

Lesson 10-6 (pp. 616–622)

Questions: **1.** $\frac{1}{3} = 0.\overline{3}$ **3.** Answers vary. Sample: It is possible, but not absolute. Probability only demonstrates the likelihood that something will occur, not that it will definitely occur a certain number of times. **5. a.** Answers vary. Sample: 4, 3, 1, 3, 3, 2, 5, 6, 3, 3, 2, 4, 4, 5, 5, 3, 6, 4, 3, 3, 5, 6, 2, 5, 3, 3, 2, 1, 3, 4
b.

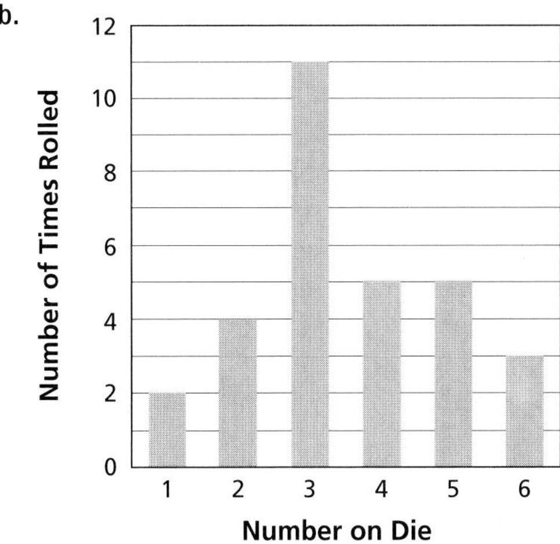

7. approximately 10 times **9.** Answers vary. Sample: Use a calculator and assign one of the random numbers to each of the salad choices. **11.** B **13.** 30% **15.** approximately 18 min

Self-Test (pp. 625–626)

1. Red: $7 \div 20 = \frac{7}{20} = 35\%$, Yellow: $3 \div 20 = \frac{3}{20} = 15\%$, Blue: $2 \div 20 = \frac{1}{10} = 10\%$, White: $2 \div 20 = \frac{1}{10} = 10\%$, Purple: $5 \div 20 = \frac{1}{4} = 25\%$, Orange: $1 \div 20 = \frac{1}{20} = 5\%$
2. Answers vary. Sample: I would guess that 7 or 8 purple marbles are in the bag. Assuming the relative frequency models the frequency of the purple marbles in the bag, then 25% of the 30 marbles in the bag is $0.25 \cdot 30 = 7.5$. **3.** Answers vary. Sample: I would guess the probability is 25% since that is the amount that was drawn in the experiment. **4.** Answers vary. Sample: I could increase the number of trials.
5. Answers vary. Sample: Carly's reasoning is not justified because she has only performed five trials.
6. Answers vary. Sample: Isabel's reasoning is not justified because she has only performed five trials.

7. a. i. **b.** iii. **c.** ii. **8. a.** RR, RG, RB, GG, GB, GR, BB, BR, BG **b.** $\frac{3}{9} = 0.\overline{3}$ **c.** $\frac{5}{9} = 0.\overline{5}$

9.

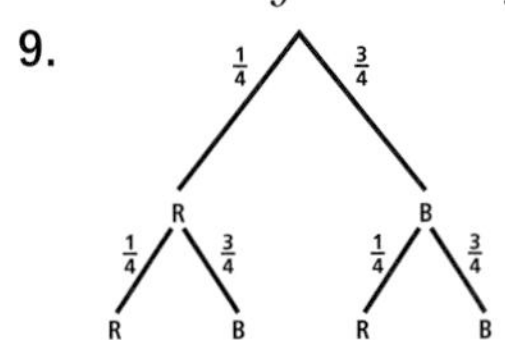

a. $\frac{1}{16} = 0.0625$ **b.** $\frac{9}{16} = 0.5625$ **c.** $\frac{3}{16} + \frac{3}{16} = \frac{3}{8} = 0.375$

10.

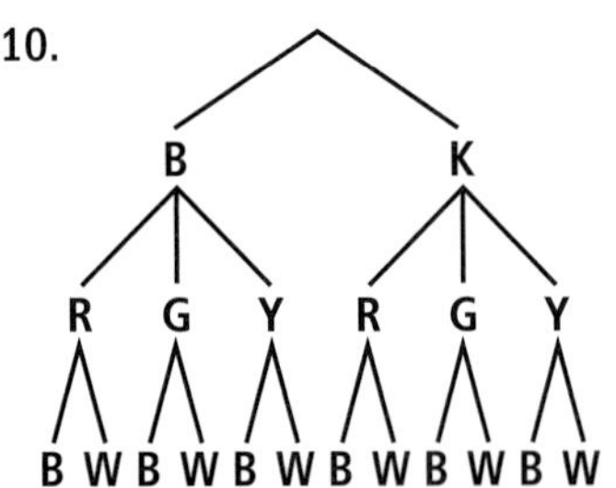

12 possible outfits

11. a.

×	1	2	3	4	5	6
1	1	2	3	4	5	6
2	2	4	6	8	10	12
3	3	6	9	12	15	18
4	4	8	12	16	20	24
5	5	10	15	20	25	30
6	6	12	18	24	30	36

b. $\frac{1}{18} = 0.0\overline{5}$ **c** 0 **d.** $\frac{1}{16} = 0.0625$ **12.** $30 \cdot 30 \cdot 30 = 27{,}000$

13.

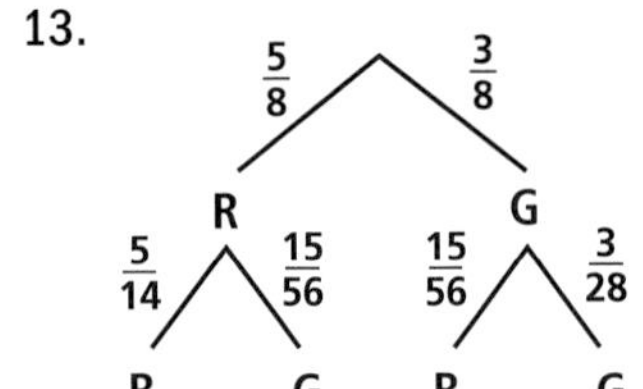

$\frac{15}{56} + \frac{15}{56} = \frac{30}{56} \approx 0.536$

14. a. $\frac{1}{2} \cdot \frac{1}{2} \cdot \frac{1}{2} \cdot \frac{1}{2} = \frac{1}{16} = 0.0625$ **b.** $4 \cdot \frac{1}{16} = \frac{1}{4} = 0.25$ **15.** Answers vary. Sample: Roll a fair die. **16.** Answers vary. Sample: No, Alfredo has the greatest chance of winning. The chance of winning any one game is $\frac{1}{2}$, so Alfredo has a $\frac{1}{2}$ chance of winning the championship, whereas the others have a $\frac{1}{4}$ chance of winning because they have to play two games and $2 \cdot \frac{1}{2} = \frac{1}{4}$.

Chapter Review (pp. 627–629)

1. $\frac{1}{2}$ **3.** $\frac{1}{3}$ **5.** Answers vary. Sample: 3, 1, 3, 3, 2, 5, 6, 3, 3, 2 **7.** Answers vary. Sample: 63, 57, 59, 66, 68, 55, 65, 59, 60, 54, 51, 57, 63, 52, 63, 50, 62, 55, 50, 69, 67, 55, 65, 55, 52, 65, 54, 62, 67, 69 **9.** 0 **11.** very unlikely **13.** Answers vary. Sample: I would expect the ratio to be closer to $\frac{1}{2}$ over the course of two weeks because there is a larger number of days. **15.** Answers vary. Sample: I would use Jane's results because her sample size was larger. **17.** 3,628,800 numbers **19.** 60 meals **21.** $\frac{1}{3}$ **23.** $\frac{1}{216}$ **25.** $\frac{5}{7}$ **27.** 48% **29.** The game is unfair because the number of odd and even choices is not equal. **31.** $\frac{3}{13}$ **33.** 1 **35.** MTW, TWR, WRF, RFSa, FSaSu, SaSuM, SuMT **37.**

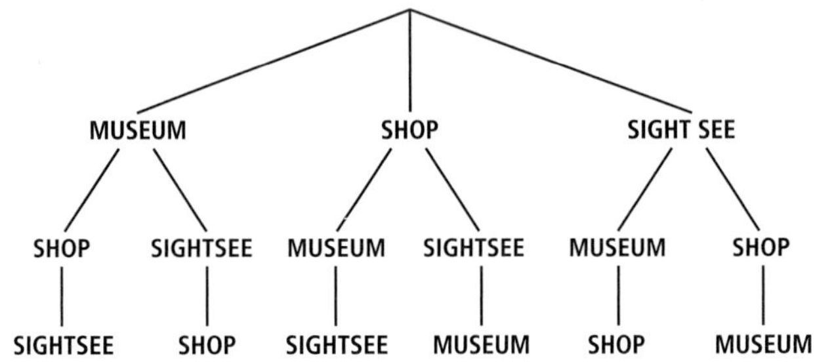

39. $\frac{1}{3}$

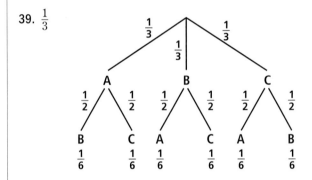

Self-Test Correlation Chart

Question	1	2	3	4	5	6	7	8	9	10
Objective(s)	I	D	G	D	D	D	C	A, F	K	J
Lesson(s)	10-5	10-5	10-4, 10-5	10-5	10-5	10-5	10-2	10-2	10-3, 10-4	10-1
Question	**11**	**12**	**13**	**14**	**15**	**16**				
Objective(s)	G	E	K	G	B	H				
Lesson(s)	10-4, 10-5	10-1	10-3, 10-4	10-4, 10-5	10-6	10-4				

41. $\frac{1}{9}$

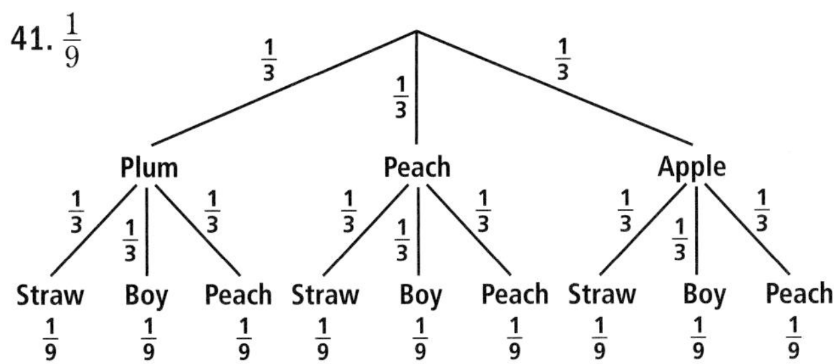

Chapter 11

Lesson 11-1 (pp. 632–637)

Questions: 1.

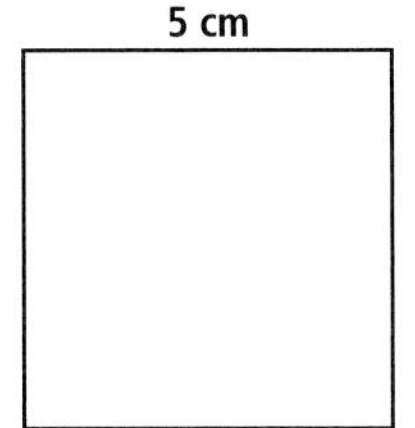

3. Step 1.

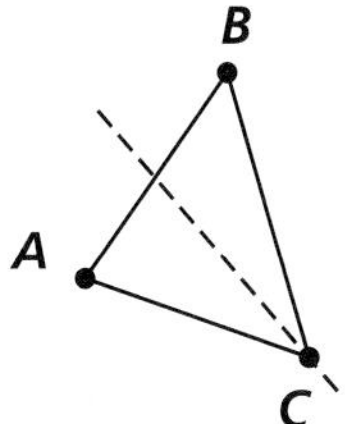

3. Step 2.

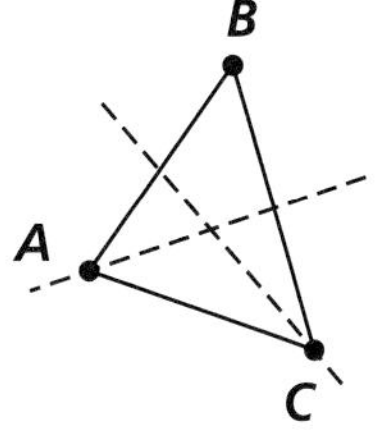

Step 3.

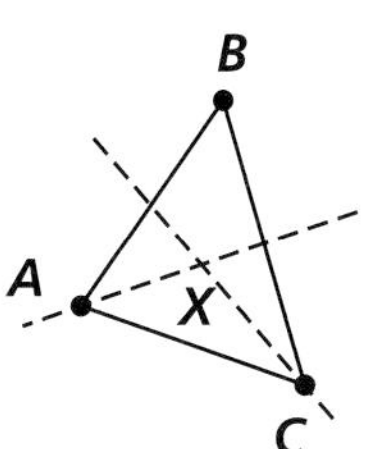

Step 4.

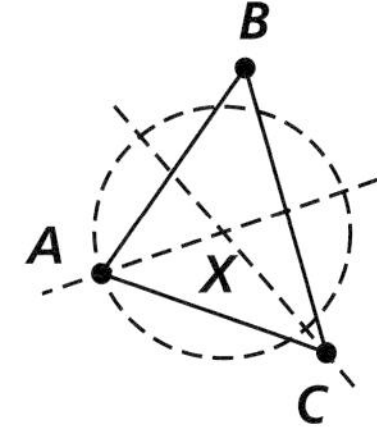

Both of the folds split the circle in half.

5.

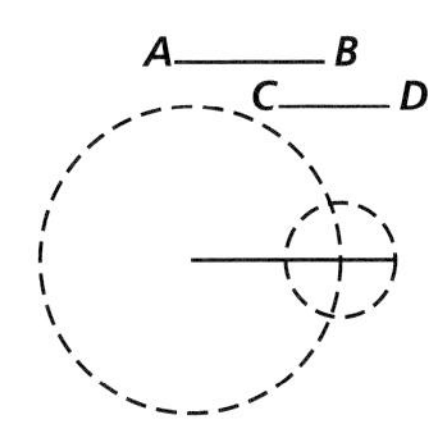

7.

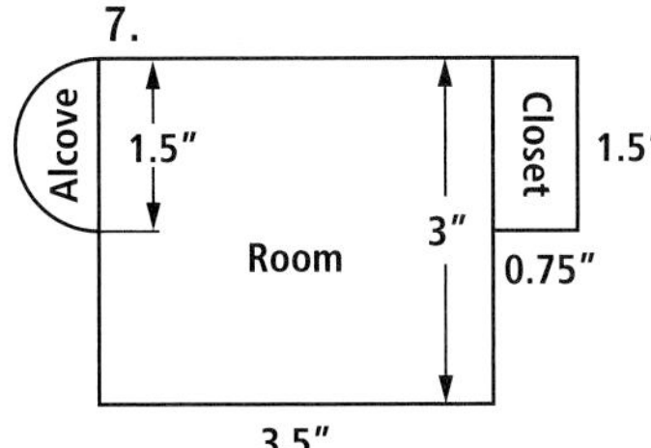

9.

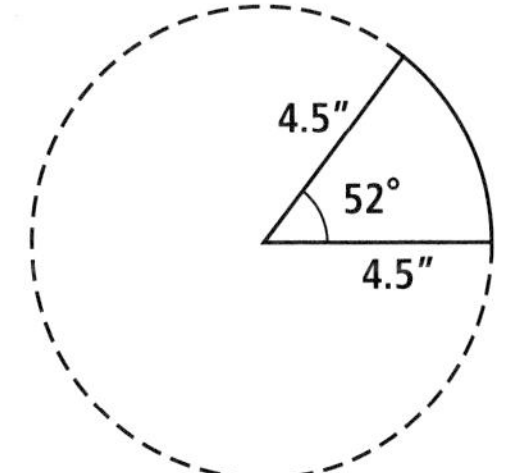

11.

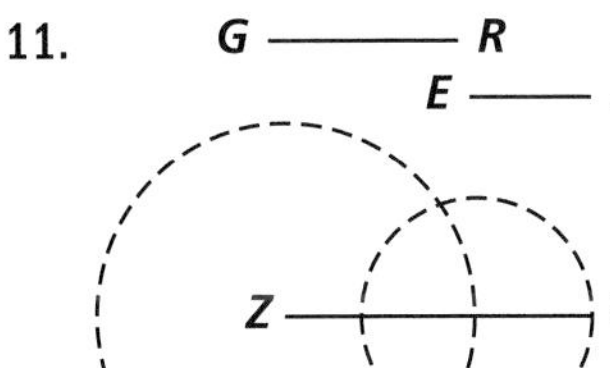

13.

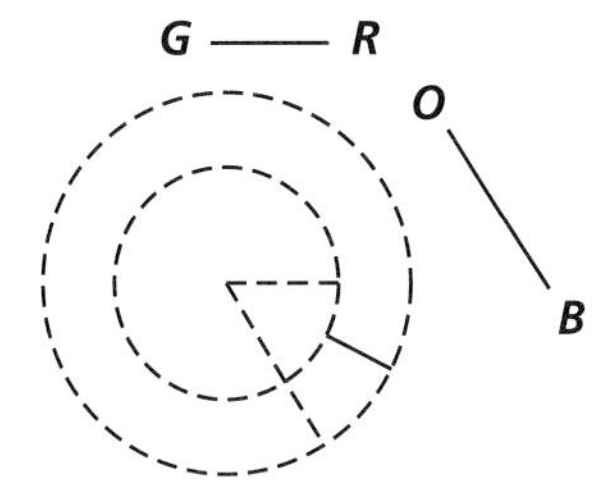

15. a. $\frac{25}{676}$ **b.** $\frac{441}{676}$ **c.** $\frac{105}{676}$ **17. a.** $\frac{9}{32}$ **b.** Answers vary. Sample: No. Although the relative frequency of his hitting a triple is zero, his probability of hitting a triple is probably more than zero, though it is still probably small. He was able to hit 1 double and 2 home runs, so he could likely hit a triple, if he had enough at-bats.

Lesson 11-2 (pp. 638–643)

Questions: 1. Answers vary. Sample: the edges of a book, most street intersections, posts of a soccer goal **3.** X

5.

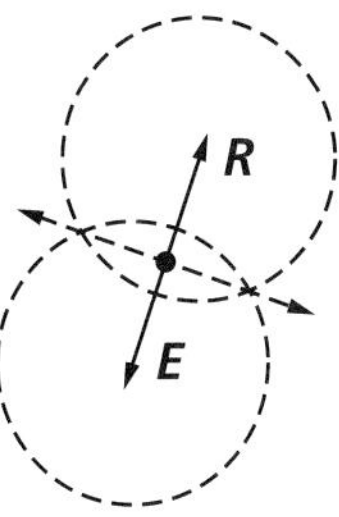

7a–b.

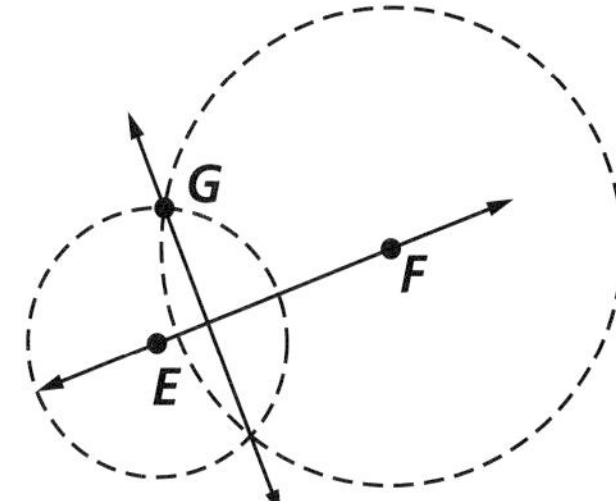

9. yes

11. a. Step 1.

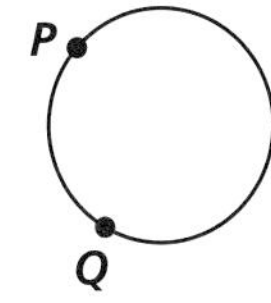

11. a. Step 2.

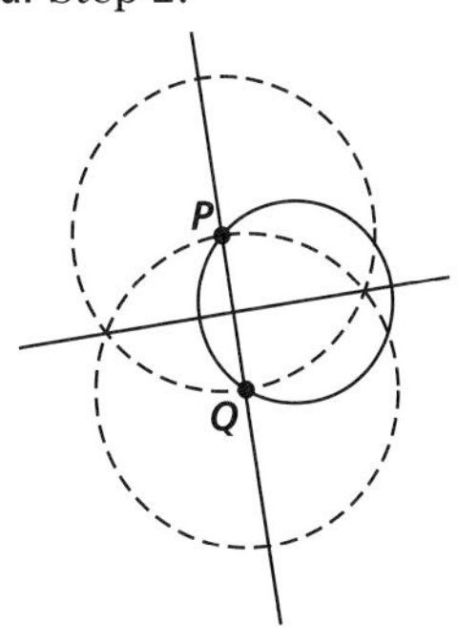

b. Answers vary. Sample: The perpendicular bisector passes through the center of the circle. If lines PC and PQ are drawn, then $\triangle PQC$ is isosceles.

13.

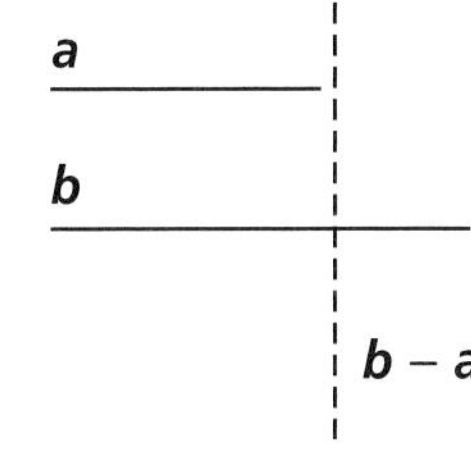

15. a. 0.9 **b.** 0.1

17.

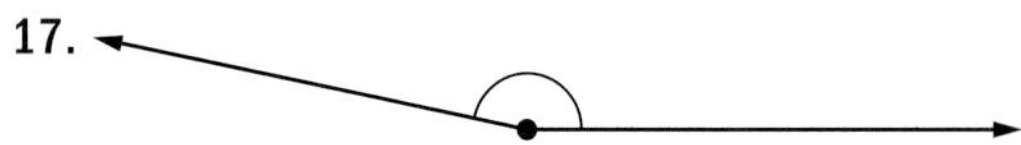

Lesson 11-3 (pp. 644–648)

Questions: 1. Answers vary. Sample: trees reflected in water, a face in the mirror

3.

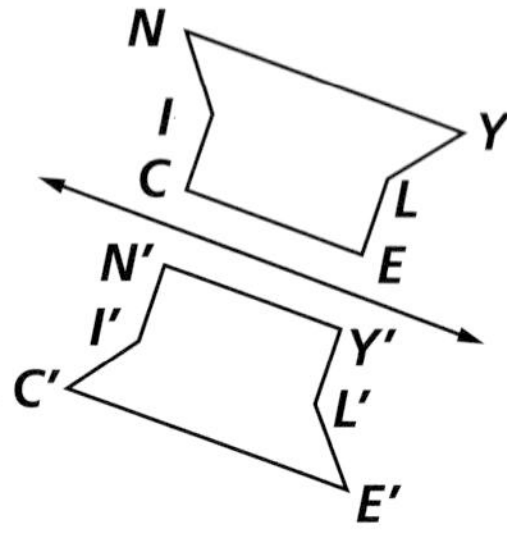

5.

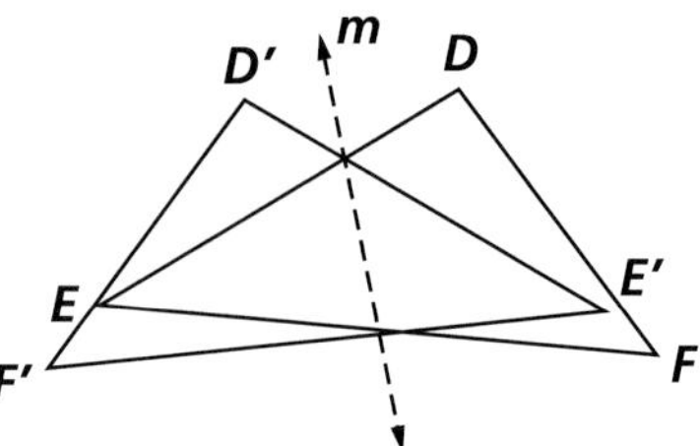

7. 9.

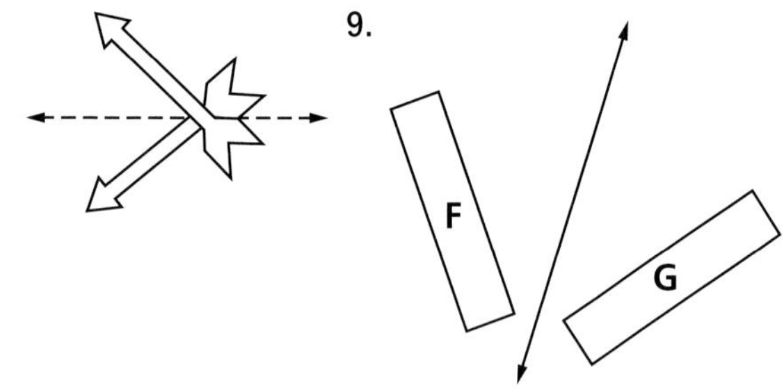

11. a. B'': (3, 2); R'': (-1, 3); A'': (-4, 0); V'': (-2, -2); E'': (0, -4) b. $(-x, y)$ 13. octagon

15.

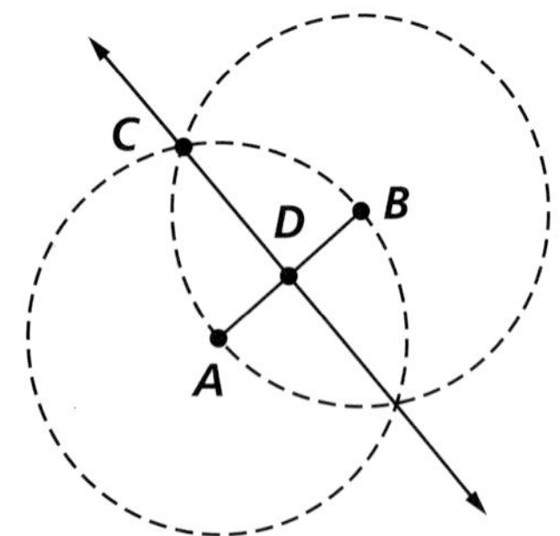

17. 2.25 km

Lesson 11-4 (pp. 649–654)

Questions:

1.

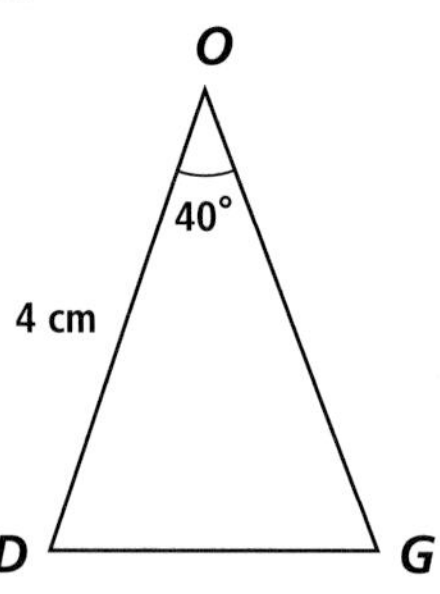

3.

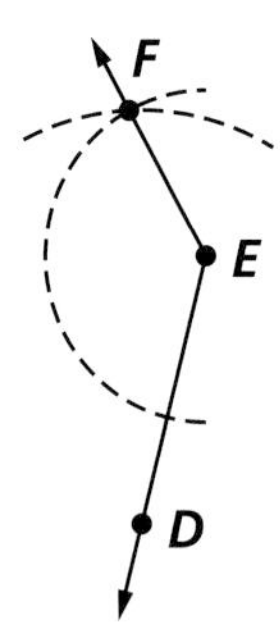

5. turn 7. the center 9. 7.5°

11.

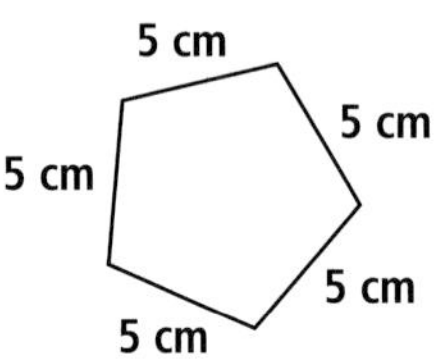

13.

R E A′ D A E′ R′

15.

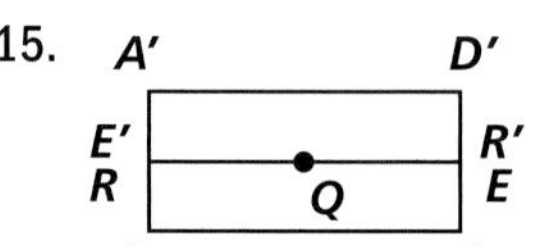

17. Step 2.

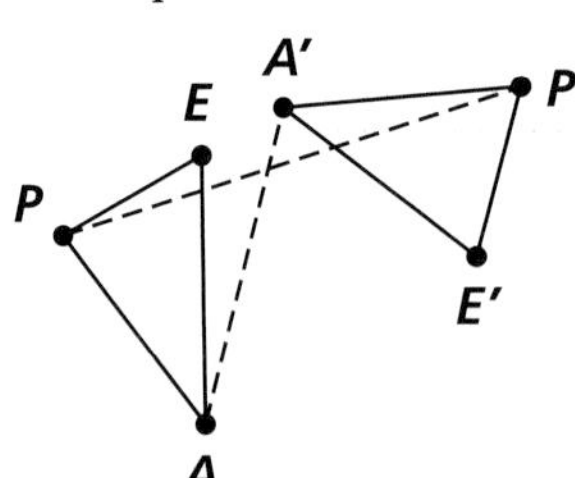

17. Step 3.

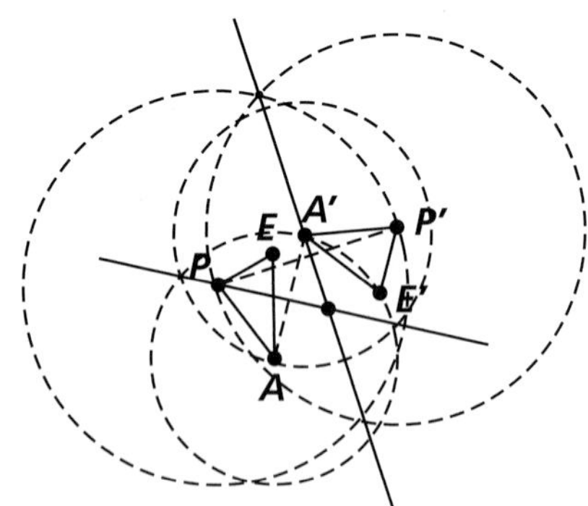

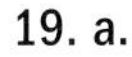

19. a.

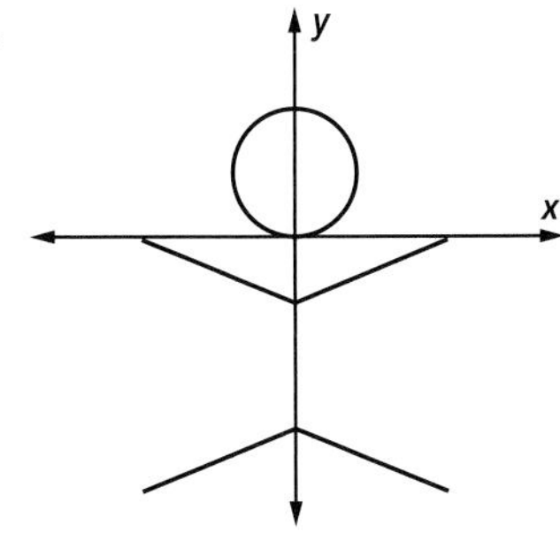

b.

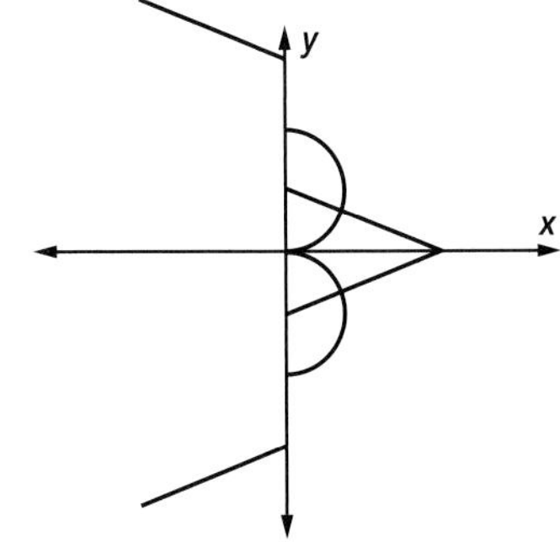

Lesson 11-5 (pp. 655–659)

Guided Example: 137°; 137°; 43°; ∠5; ∠5; 137°; linear pair; ∠3; ∠7; 43°; ∠4; 137°

Questions: 1. ∠1 and ∠6, ∠2 and ∠7, ∠3 and ∠5, ∠4 and ∠8 3. No; the measure of the corresponding angles of both of the labeled angles is 91°, so by the Corresponding Angles Property, they are not parallel.

5.

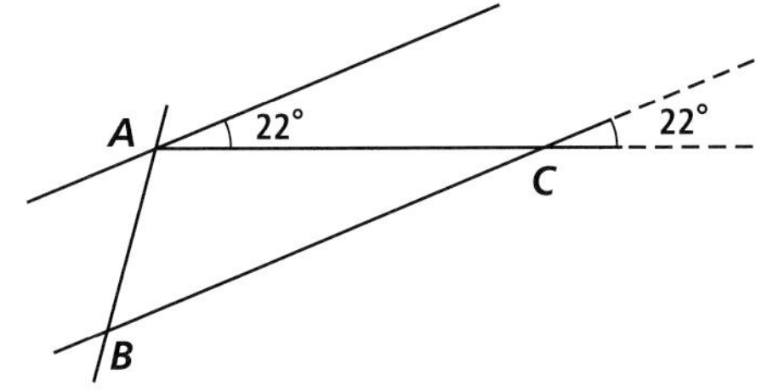

7. m∠*RSA*, m∠*TSB*, m∠*FWT*, and m∠*RWE* = 100°; m∠*RSB*, m∠*TSA*, m∠*TWE*, m∠*RWF* = 80°; m∠*JUT* = 30°; m∠*KUT* and m∠*JUR* = 150°; m∠*JGB*, m∠*KGA*, m∠*JIF*, and m∠*EIK* = 130°; m∠*JGA*, m∠*EIJ*, m∠*KIF* = 50° 9. m∠1, m∠2, m∠6, m∠8 = 46°; m∠3 = 44°; m∠4, m∠9 = 90°; m∠5, m∠7 = 134° 11. A 13. ∠3, ∠5, ∠7, ∠9, ∠12, ∠14, ∠16, ∠18, ∠20

15.

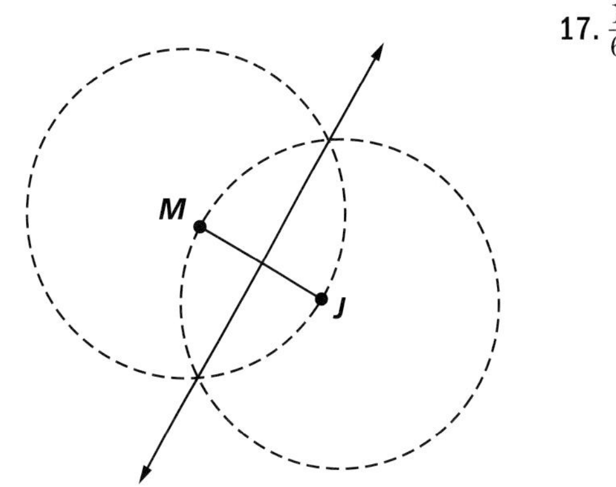

17. $\frac{1}{6}$

Lesson 11-6 (pp. 660–664)

Guided Example: 7; 5; 5; -15; 5; -5; 1; 10; 6; -5; 5; 5; 20; -15; 10; 5; 5; 15

Questions: 1. slide

3.

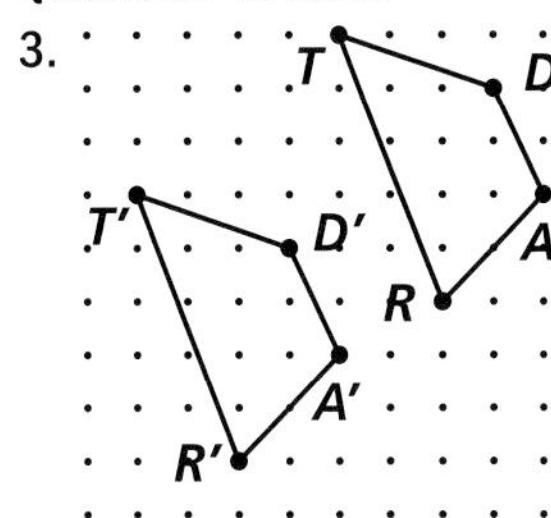

5.

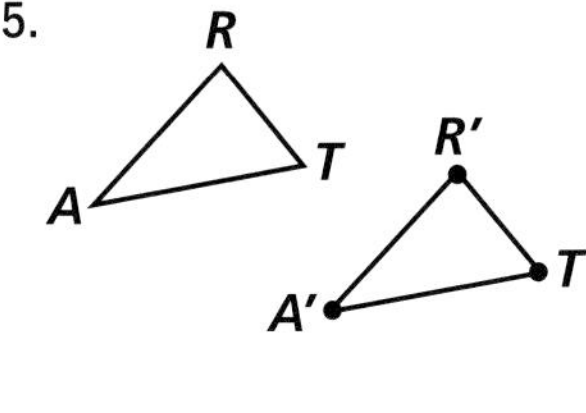

7. a.

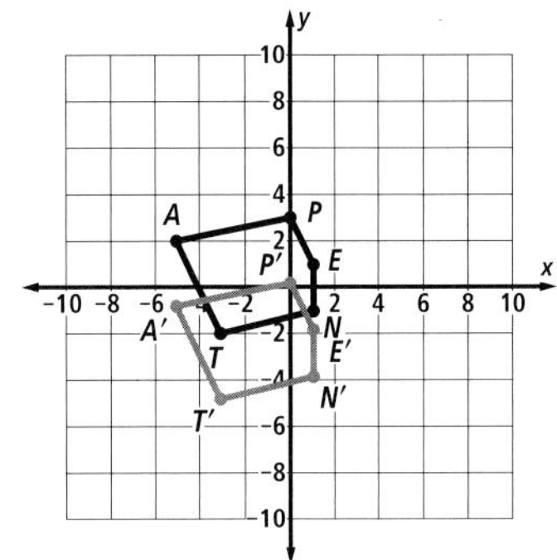

b. $P'' = (0, 0)$, $E'' = (1, -2)$, $N'' = (1, -4)$, $T'' = (-3, -5)$, $A'' = (-5, -1)$ c. $(x, y + b)$

9. a.

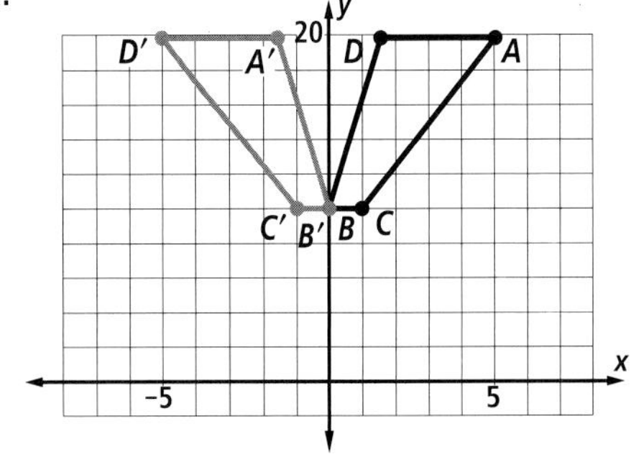

b. reflection over *y*-axis

11. 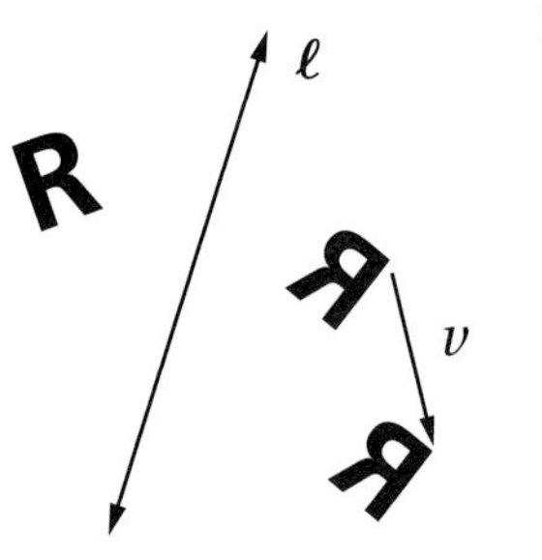

13. 

15. **a.** 63 tsp **b.** 21 tbs **c.** no

Self-Test (pp. 667–668)

1. **a., b.**

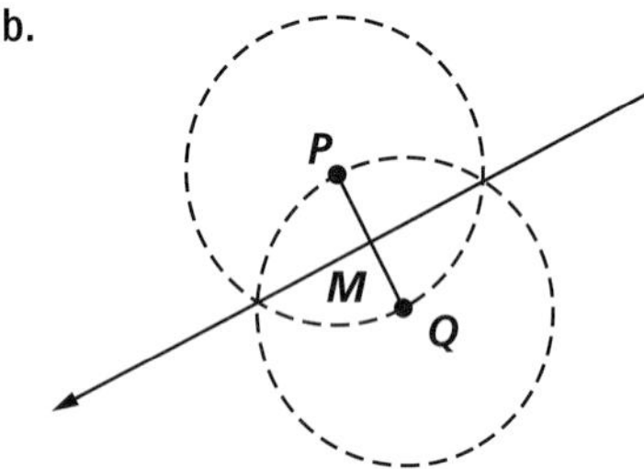

2. 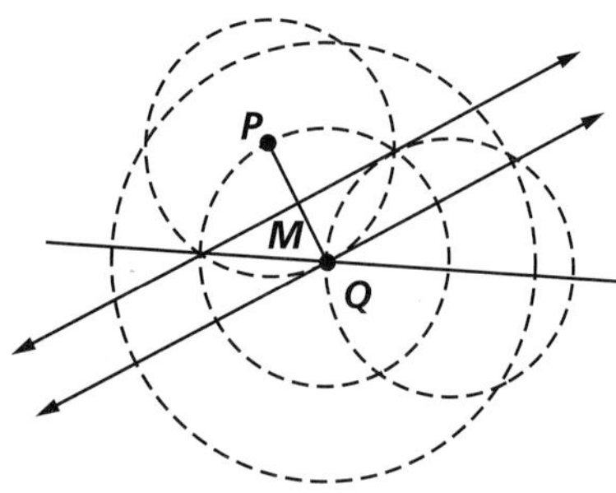

3. 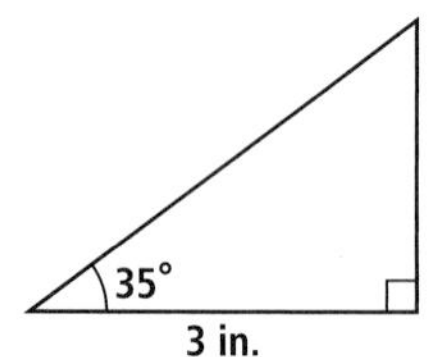

4. $m\angle 1 = 180° - 130° = 50°$, $m\angle 2 = 130°$, $m\angle 3 = 130°$, $m\angle 4 = m\angle 1 = 50°$, $m\angle 5 = m\angle 3 = 130°$

5. 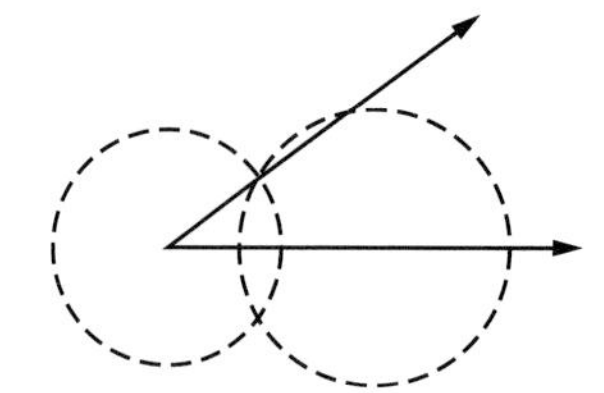

6. 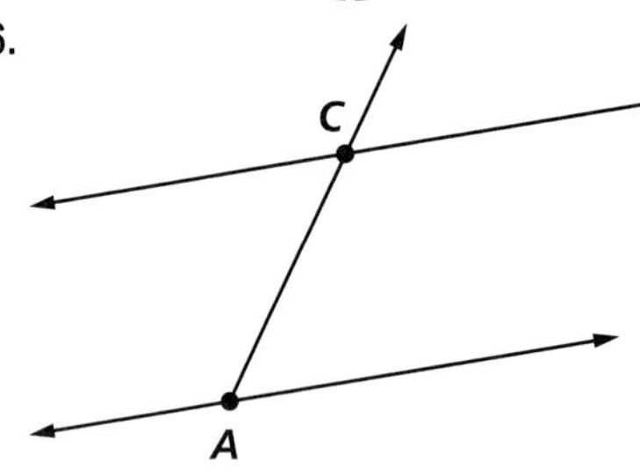

7. reflection **8.** rotation **9.** (-37, 5) **10.** rotation

11. $\angle 1$, $\angle 7$; $\angle 2$, $\angle 4$; $\angle 3$, $\angle 5$; $\angle 6$, $\angle 8$

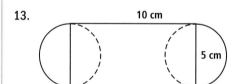

12. 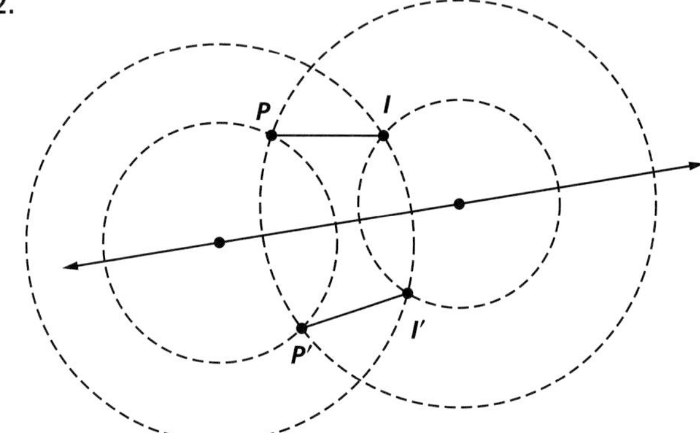

13. 

14. **a.** C or D **b.** C or D **c.** B

15.

Self-Test Correlation Chart

Question	1	2	3	4	5	6	7	8	9	10
Objective(s)	B	C	A	D	A	E	F	G	J	G
Lesson(s)	11-2	11-2	11-1, 11-4	11-5	11-1, 11-4	11-5	11-3	11-4	11-6	11-4
Question	**11**	**12**	**13**	**14**	**15**					
Objective(s)	H	F	A	I	F					
Lesson(s)	11-5	11-3	11-1, 11-4	11-3, 11-4, 11-6	11-3					

Chapter Review (pp. 669–673)

1.

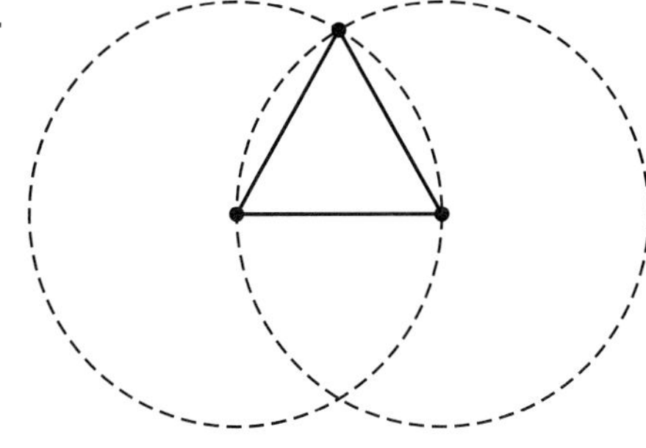

3.

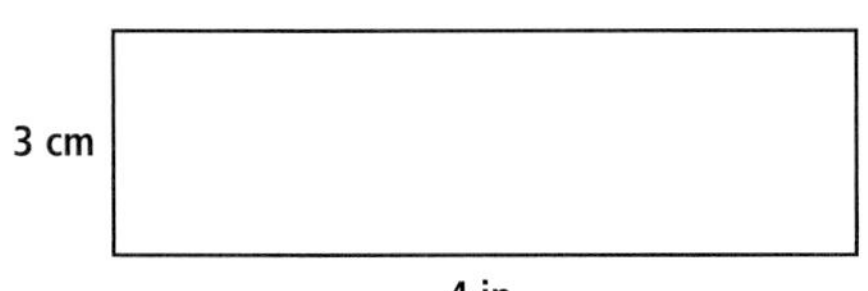

5.

7.

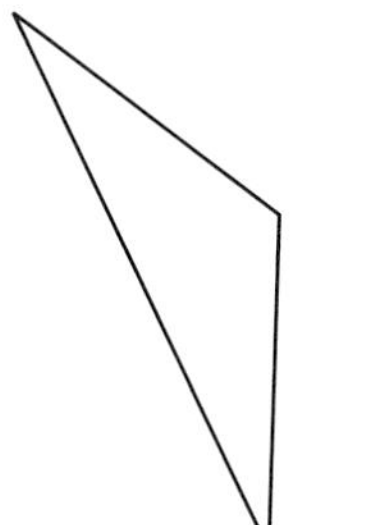

9.

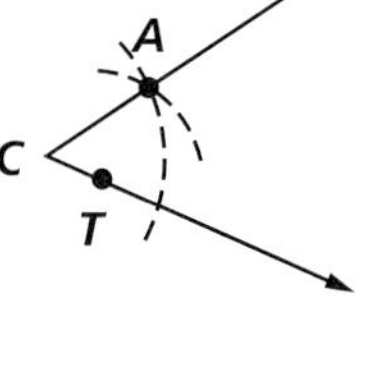

11. 13.

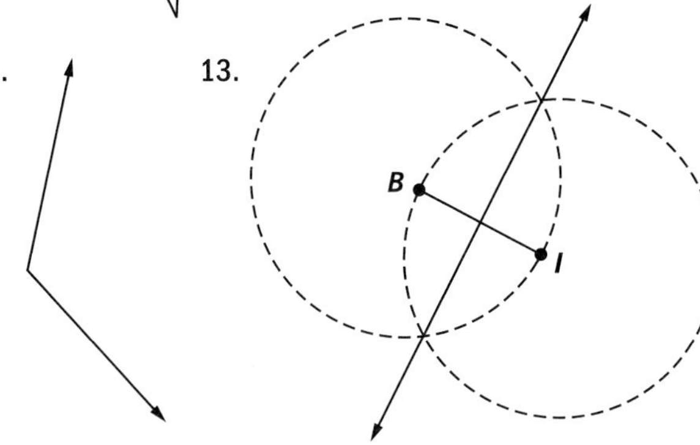

15.

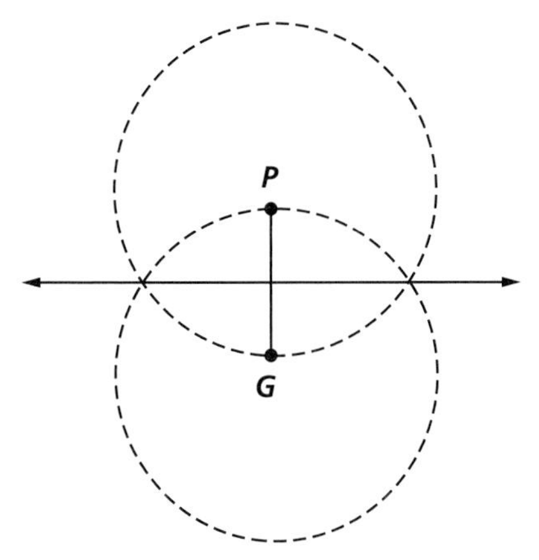

17.

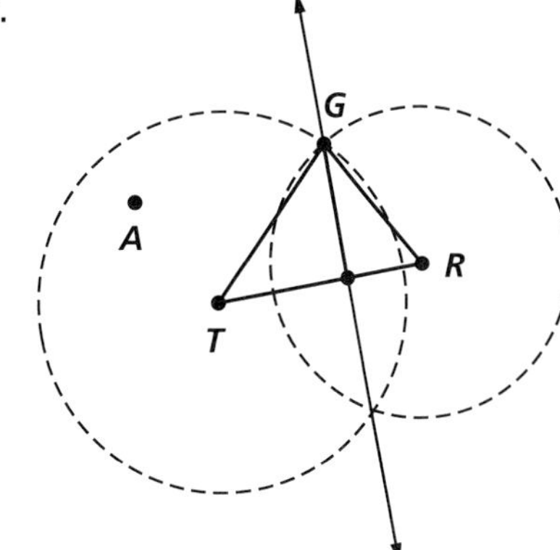

19.

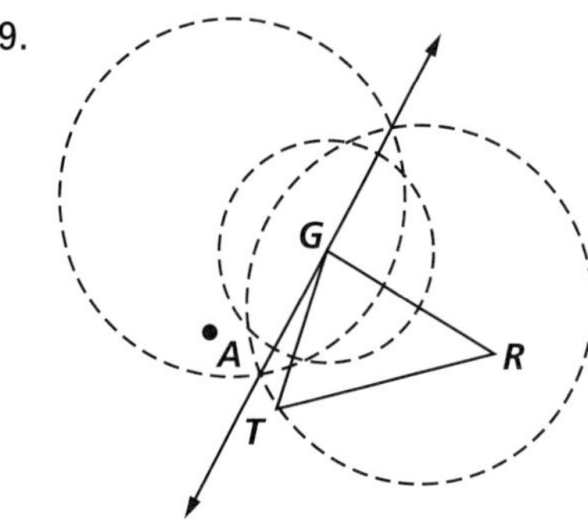

21. a. $125°$ b. $55°$ c. $125°$ d. $125°$

23. 25.

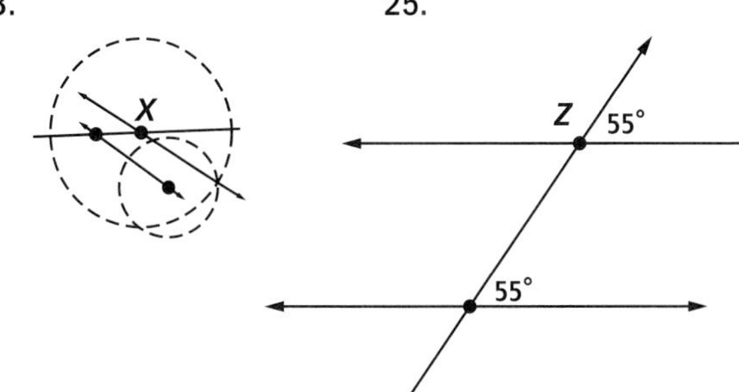

27. D

29.

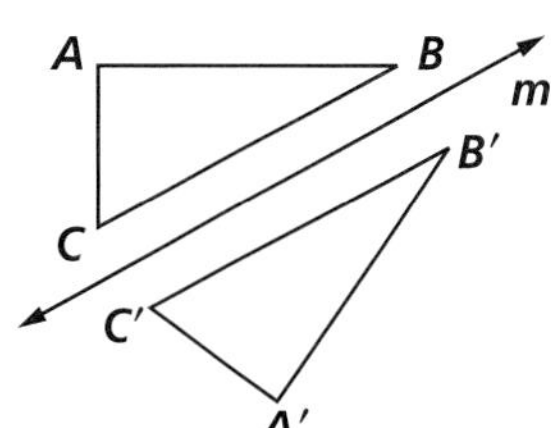

31.

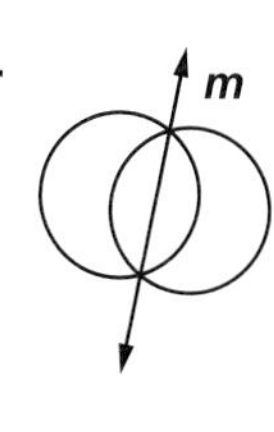

33.

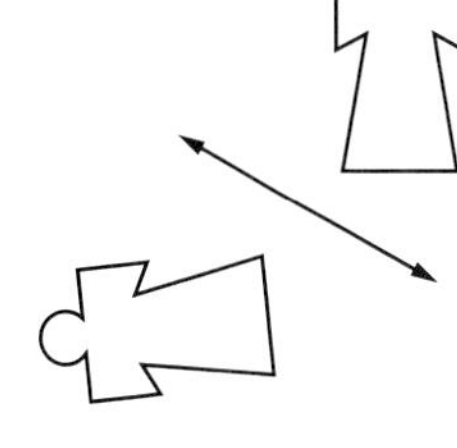

35.

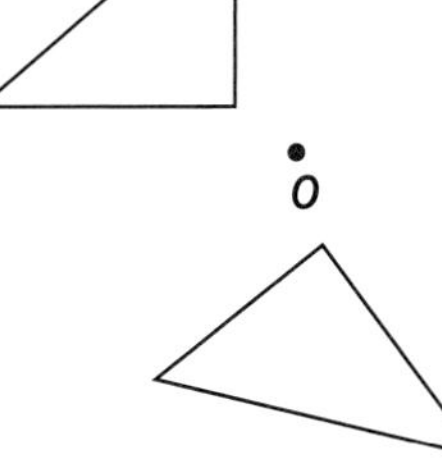

37. Answers vary. Sample: When rotated by a positive angle, the object moves counterclockwise, and when rotated by a negative angle, the object moves clockwise. Therefore, rotating an object 90° and –270° moves it to the same position.

39.

41. ∠7, ∠15; ∠5, ∠13; ∠6, ∠14; ∠8, ∠16; ∠1, ∠9; ∠ 3, ∠12; ∠2, ∠11; ∠4, ∠10
43. ∠6, ∠14, ∠15
45. 5, 7, 13, 14 **47.** 1, 9, 12

49.

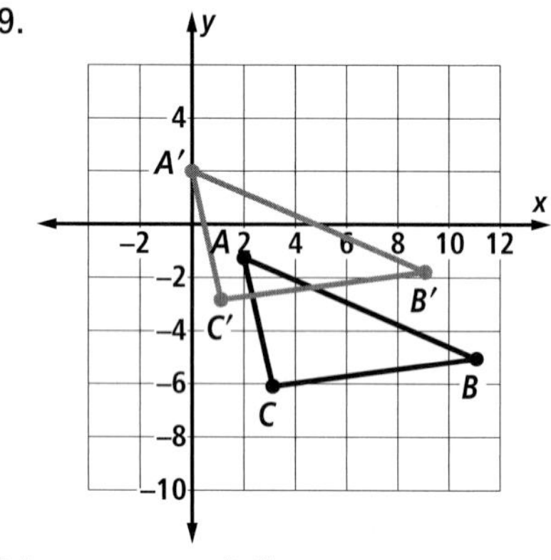

51. (1.5, 3)
52. $(2\frac{1}{2}, 3\frac{1}{4})$

Chapter 12

Lesson 12-1 (pp. 676–681)

Guided Example 2: 180°; 60°; 60°; 90°; 30°

Questions: **1.** reflection **3.** rotation

5.

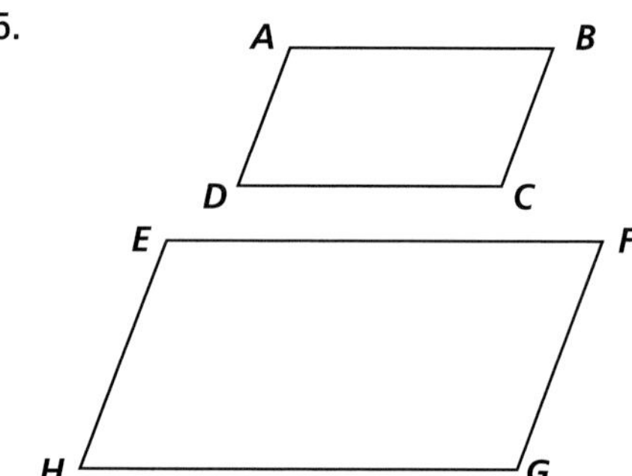

7. yes **9.** △*ABD* **11. a.** 4° **b.** 86° **c.** 176°
13. a. Answers vary. Sample: 5, 6, 9 and 5, 7, 8

13. b.

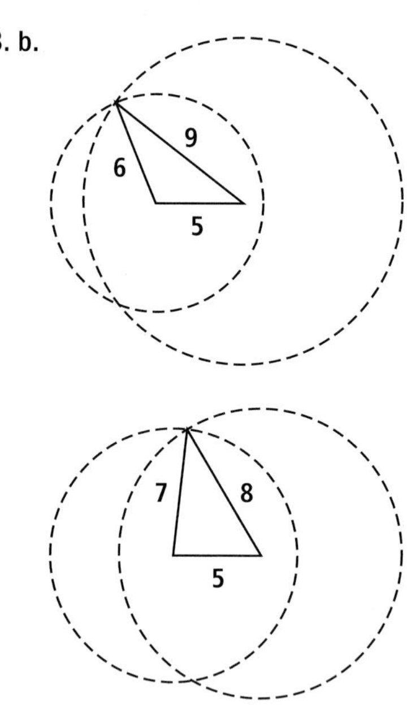

15. a. $\overline{A'N}$ **b.** $\overline{BC'}$ **c.** ∠*C'A'B'* **d.** △*CNB'* **17.** a line that intersects two or more lines **19.** Answers vary. Sample: The Law of Large Numbers states that the more trials, the more likely the probability of a coin landing on heads will equal 0.5. Six trials is not enough for the Law of Large Numbers to have an effect. **21.** $\frac{1}{5.2}$ **23. a.** Answers vary. Sample: A triangle has 180°. Obtuse angles are greater than 90°, so two obtuse angles would be greater than 180°.
b. yes; Answers vary. Sample:

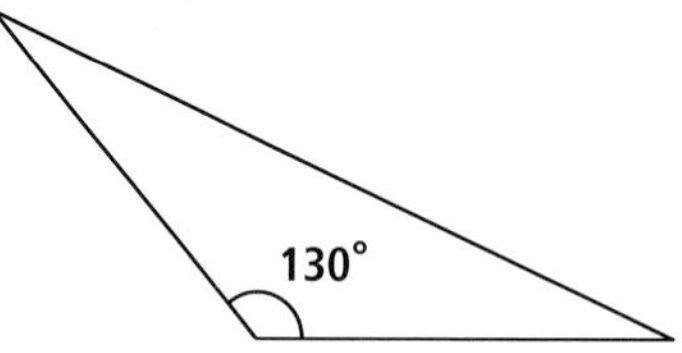

Lesson 12-2 (pp. 682–686)

Questions: **1.** isosceles **3.** D
5. Answers vary. Sample:

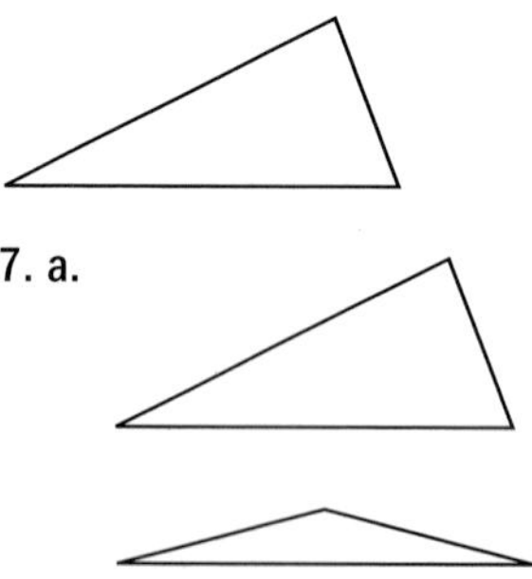

7. a.

b. Answers vary. Sample: They have the same shape.
9. no **11.** yes **13.** The right angle must equal 90° and the other angle must equal 19°.

15. yes

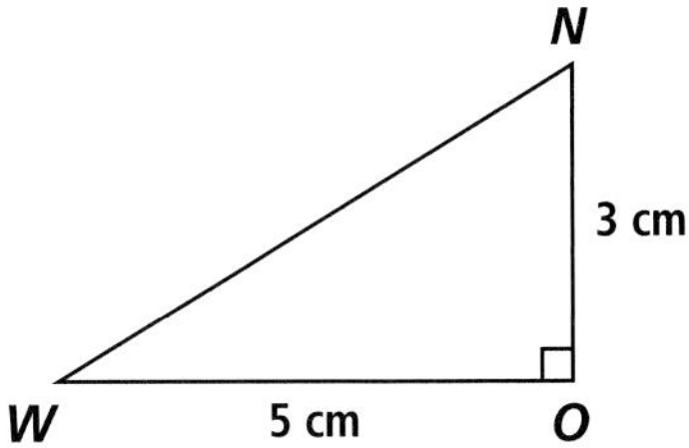

17. a. *IS* **b.** is **19.** ∠3, ∠6, ∠7

21. a. Step 1.

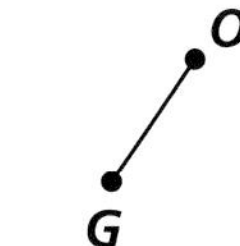

Step 2.

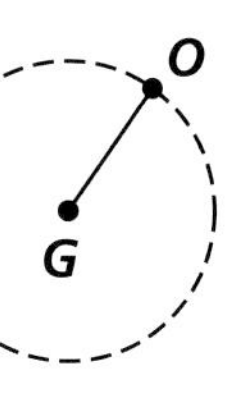

Steps 3–4.

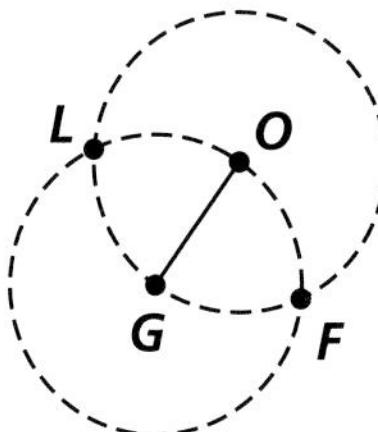

b. true **23.** 60°

Lesson 12-3 (pp. 687–691)

Guided Example: $\overleftrightarrow{QA}$; $\overrightarrow{QA}$;QU; $\overline{UA}$; UA

Questions:

1.

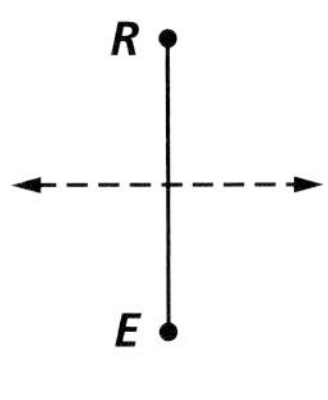

3.

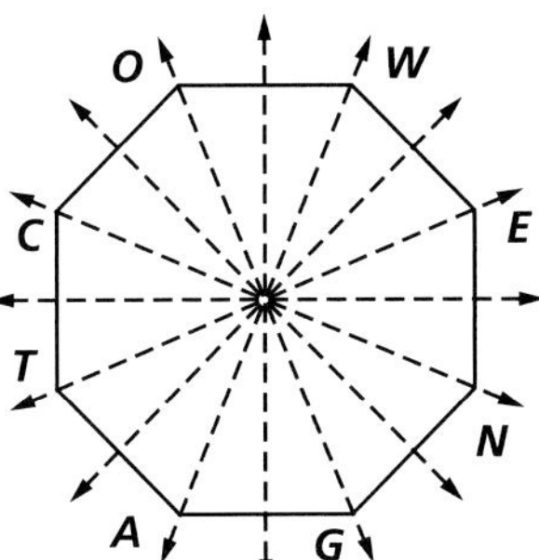

5.

A B C D
L M N E
K P O F
J I H G

7. 180°

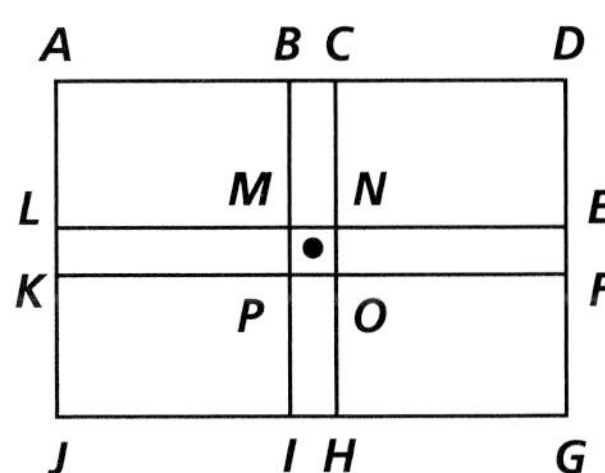

9. ∠*OFG*, ∠*MLA*, ∠*PKJ*

11. 30°

13. Answers vary. Sample:

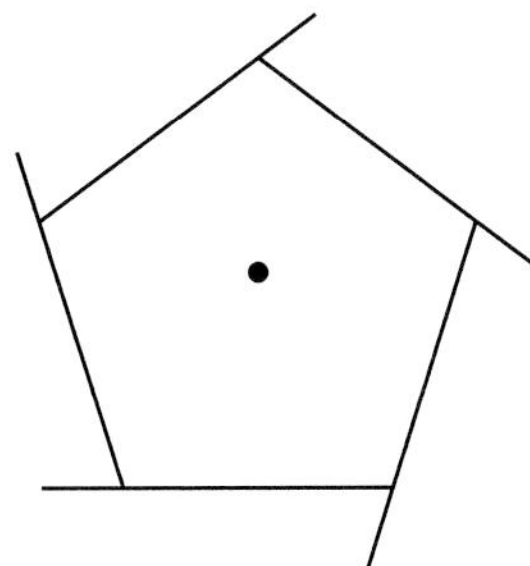

15. One angle must measure greater than 90°, while the other must measure less than 58°. **17.** 120 mm^2

19. $m = -173$

Lesson 12-4 (pp. 692–698)

Questions: **1.** yes

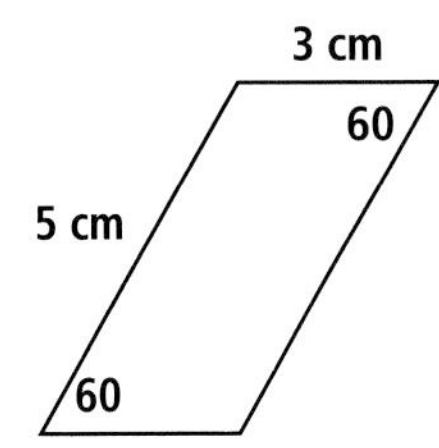

3. yes

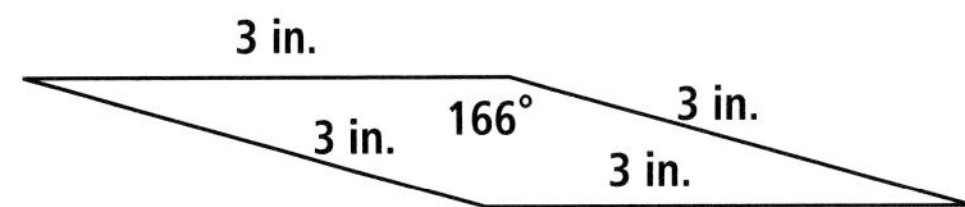

5. i. **7.** i.

9. a.

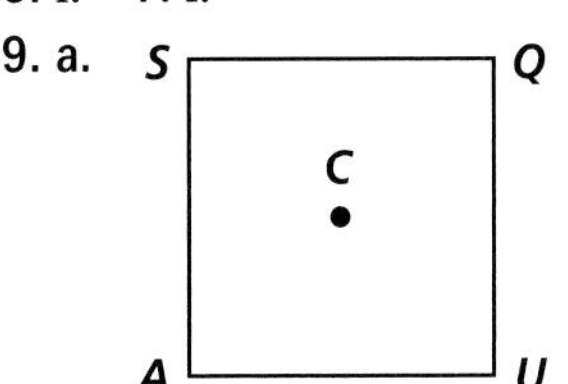

b. 90°

11. Answers vary. Sample:

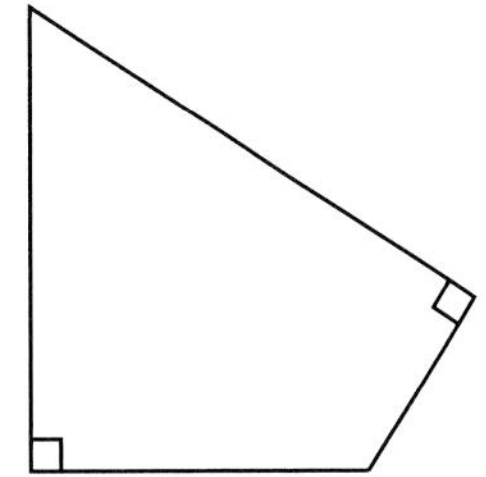

13. Answers vary. Sample:

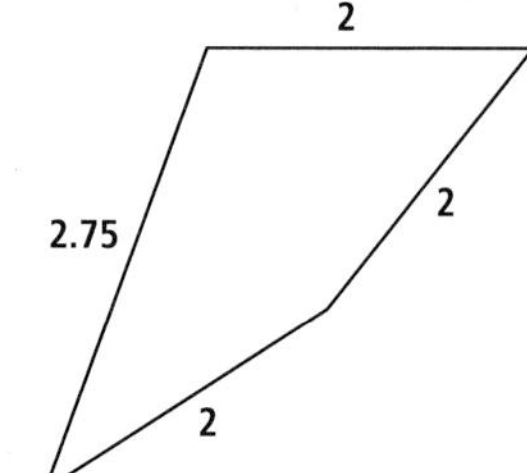

15.

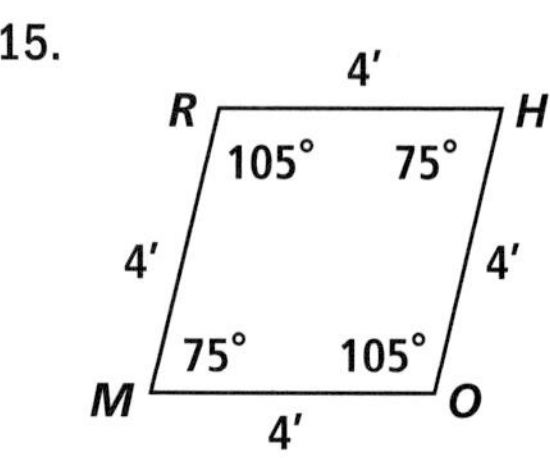

17. rectangle, square **19.** parallelogram, rhombus, rectangle, square **21.** always **23.** sometimes but not always **25.** Answers vary. Sample: Yes. All angles of a scalene triangle have a different measure. A right triangle can meet this definition. **27.** no

Lesson 12-5 (pp. 699–704)

Questions: 1. a. not a kite **b.** convex kite **c.** nonconvex kite

3.

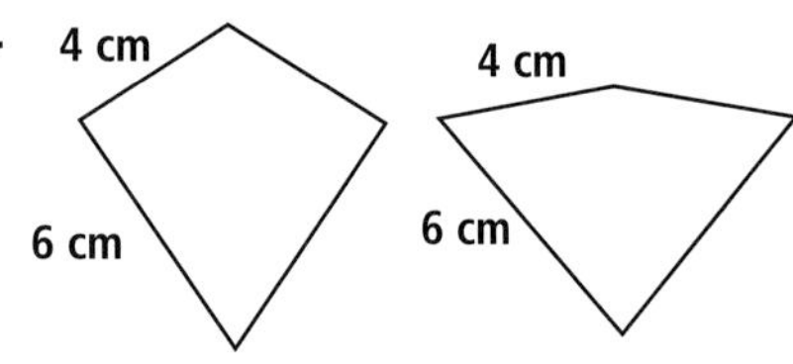

5. Answers vary. Sample: A rhombus is a quadrilateral with four sides of equal length, so every rhombus has two pairs of sides of equal length that are next to each other, therefore every rhombus is a kite.

7. a.

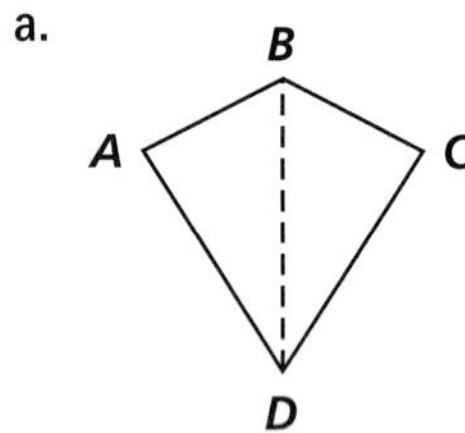

b. $AB = BC$, $AD = CD$, and BD bisects $\angle ABC$ and $\angle ADC$, so $m\angle ABD = m\angle CBD$ and $m\angle ADB = m\angle CDB$. Thus, $\triangle ABD$ and $\triangle CBD$ have sides of equal length and angles of equal measure, so they are congruent.

9. a.

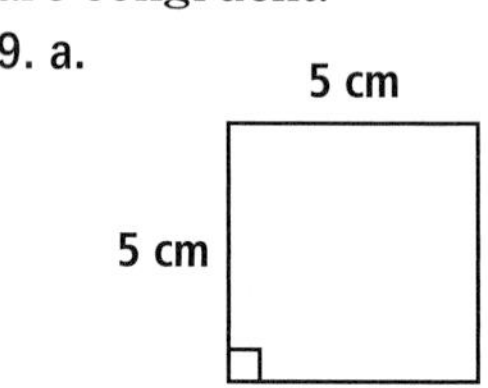

b. square **11.** kite **13.** rectangle **15.** parallelogram

17.

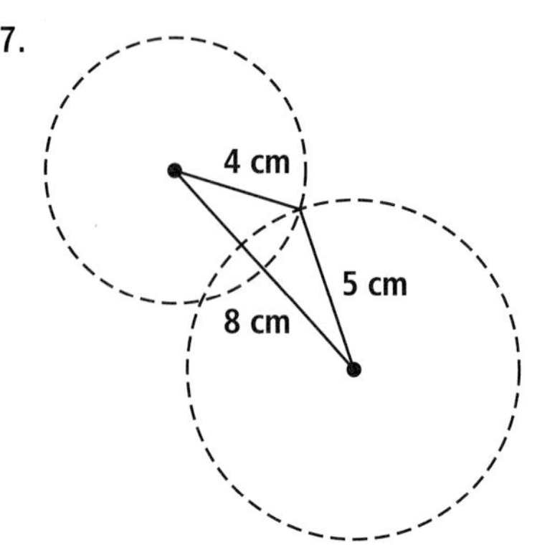

19. 1.77 in^2 **21.** $3^5 = 243$, $4^4 = 256$, $5^4 = 625$, $9^3 = 729$, $8^4 = 4{,}096$, $6^5 = 7{,}776$, $5^6 = 15{,}625$, $7^5 = 16{,}807$; geometry

Lesson 12-6 (pp. 705–709)

Guided Example: Answers vary.; 2; $\angle CED$; $m\angle CED$; $\angle C$; $m\angle C$

Questions: 1. Answers vary. Sample: A trapezoid is a quadrilateral with a pair of parallel sides. A parallelogram must have two pairs of parallel sides. Thus, it must also be a trapezoid.

3. **5.**

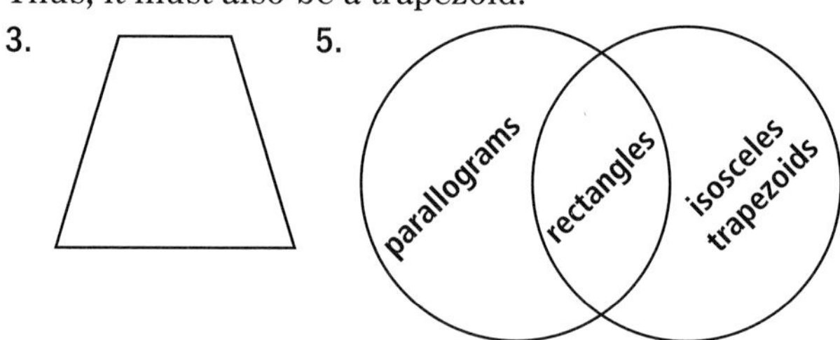

7. a.

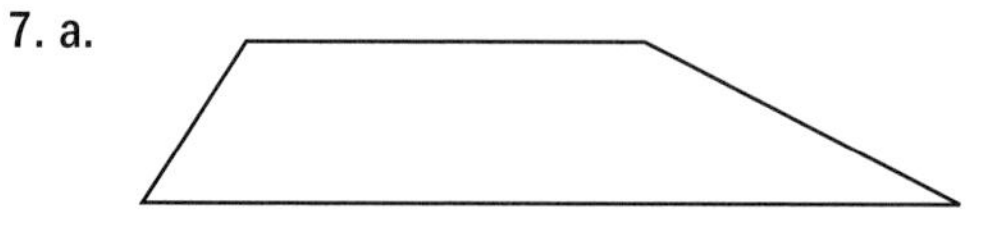

b.

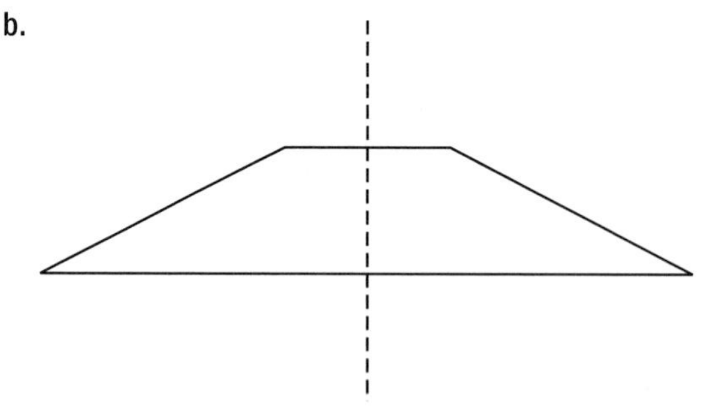

9. a.

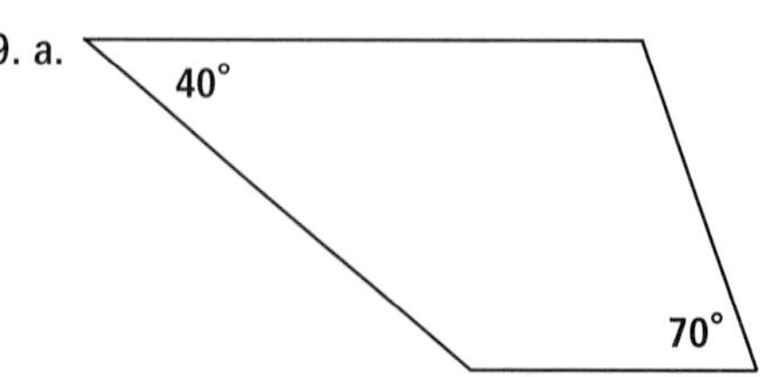

b. 110°, 140° **11.** R: 58°, O: 72°, A: 108°, D: 122°

13. a. yes **b.** no **c.** yes **d.** yes **e.** no
15. parallelograms, rectangles, rhombuses, squares
17. parallelograms, rectangles, rhombuses, squares
19. kites, rectangles, rhombuses

Self-Test (pp. 713–714)

1.

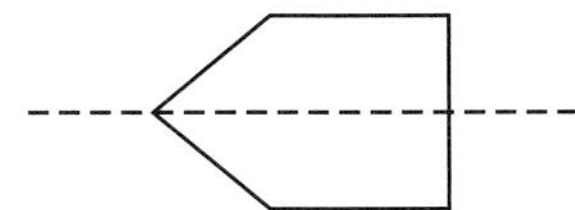

2. a. 60° **b.** 180° **c.** 60°

3. yes; exactly one triangle

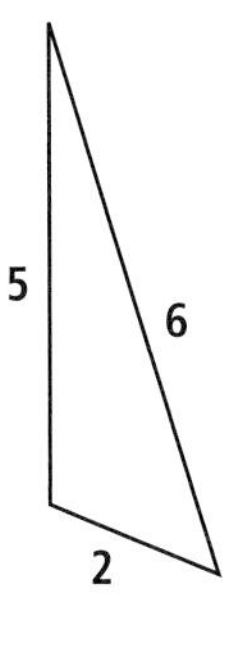

4. yes; more than one triangle

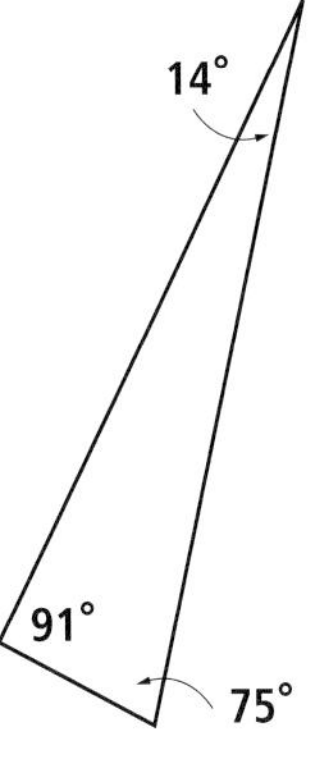

5. yes; exactly one triangle

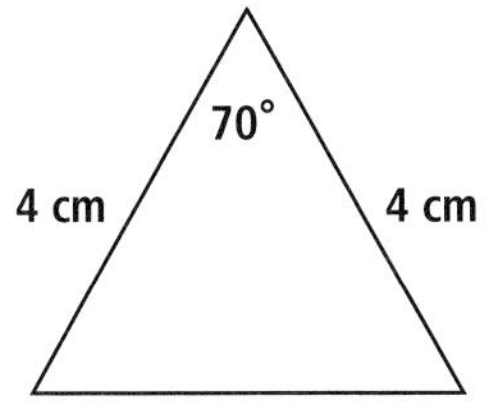

6. a. kite, rhombus, parallelogram, trapezoid **b.** trapezoid **c.** kite **7.** C **8.** square
9. a. $m\angle A = 50°$ **b.** $180° - 50° = 130°$ **c.** $AB = 3$ cm
10. $30° + 30° = 60°$; $360° - 60° = 300°$; $300° \div 2 = 150°$; 30°, 30°, 150°, 150°
11. parallelogram

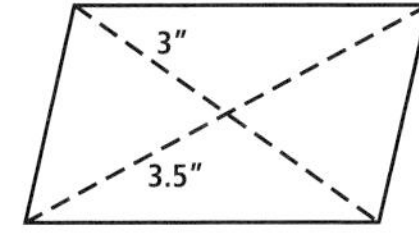

12. a.

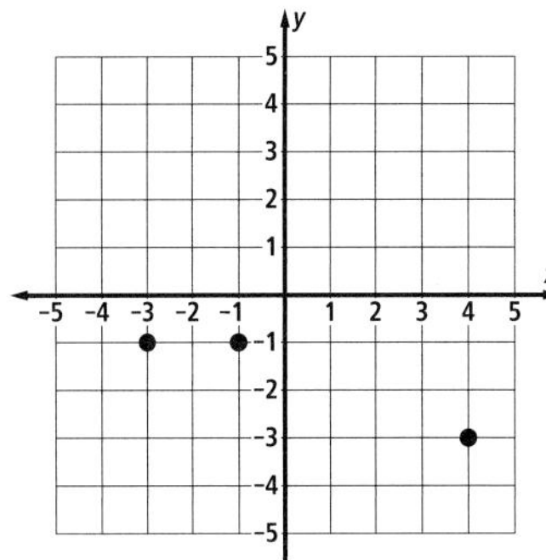

b. (2, -3)

13. a.

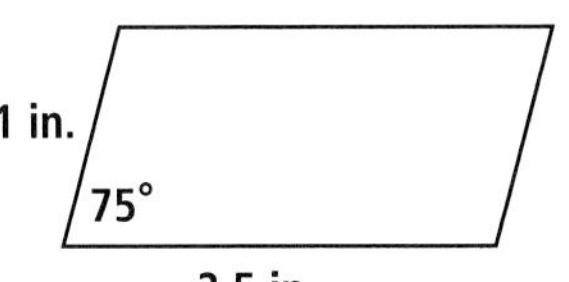

b. no **c.** yes

14. yes **15.** no **16.** false

Chapter Review (pp. 715–717)

1.

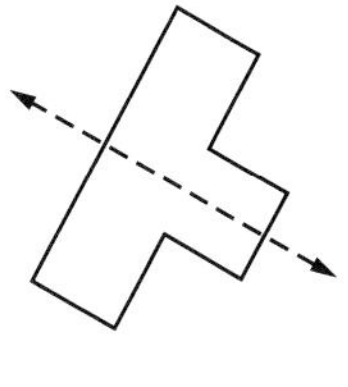

3. Answers vary. Sample:

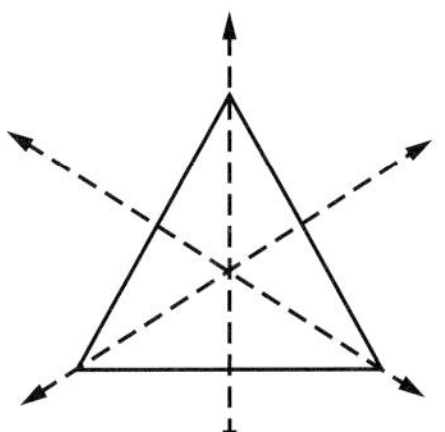

5. H, I **7.** 45°

9.

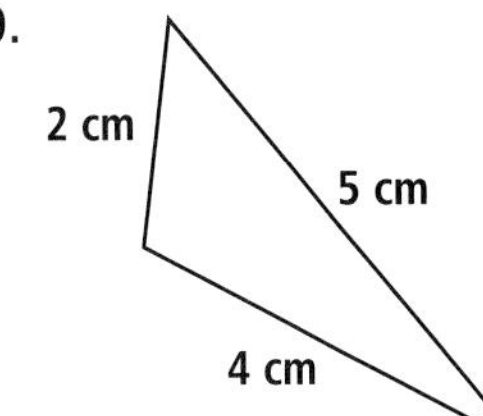

11.

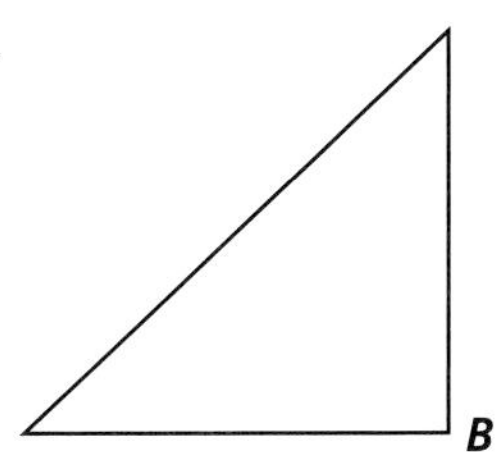

13. false

15.

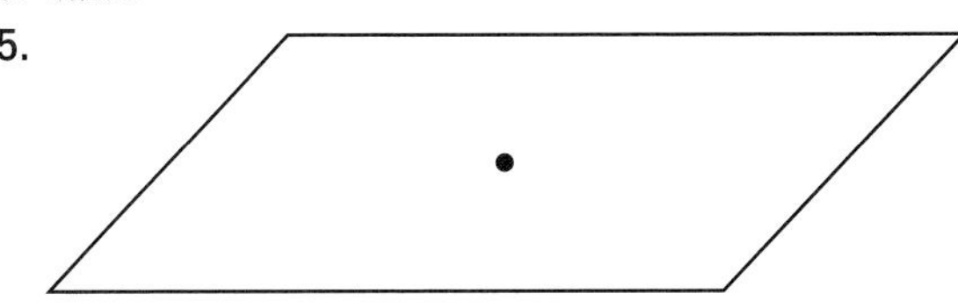

Self-Test Correlation Chart

Question	1	2	3	4	5	6	7	8	9	10
Objective(s)	A	B	C	C	C	G	G	G	E	G
Lesson(s)	12-3	12-3	12-1, 12-2	12-1, 12-2	12-1, 12-2	12-4, 12-5, 12-6	12-4, 12-5, 12-6	12-4, 12-5, 12-6	12-4	12-4, 12-5, 12-6

Question	11	12	13	14	15	16
Objective(s)	I	I	H	F	F	D
Lesson(s)	12-4, 12-5, 12-6	12-4, 12-5, 12-6	12-3	12-1, 12-2	12-1, 12-2	12-3

17. 35°, 145°, 145° **19.** $\overline{BC} = \overline{CD} = \overline{DA} = 7$; $m\angle C = 110°$, $m\angle B = m\angle D = 70°$ **21.** yes **23.** no **25.** yes **27.** no **29.** rectangles, squares **31.** squares, rectangles **33.** A parallelogram by definition has two pairs of parallel sides. A rectangle not only satisfies this requirement but also has four 90° angles.
35. a. no **b.** yes, 45° **37. a.** no **b.** yes, 120°

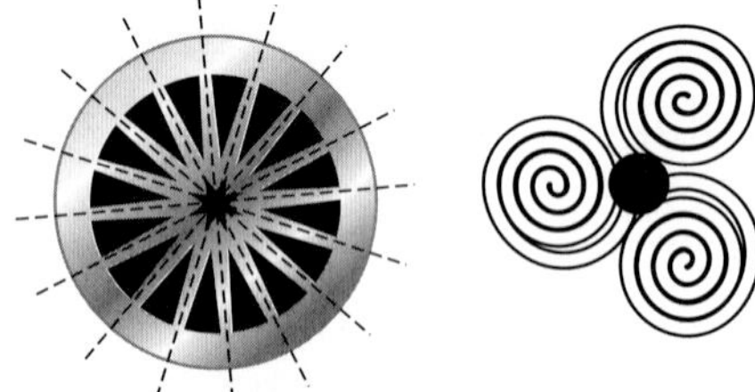

39. Answers may vary. Sample: right triangles: $\triangle ABC$, $\triangle BCD$, $\triangle CDA$, $\triangle DAB$; isosceles triangles: $\triangle AEB$, $\triangle DEC$, $\triangle AED$, $\triangle BEC$

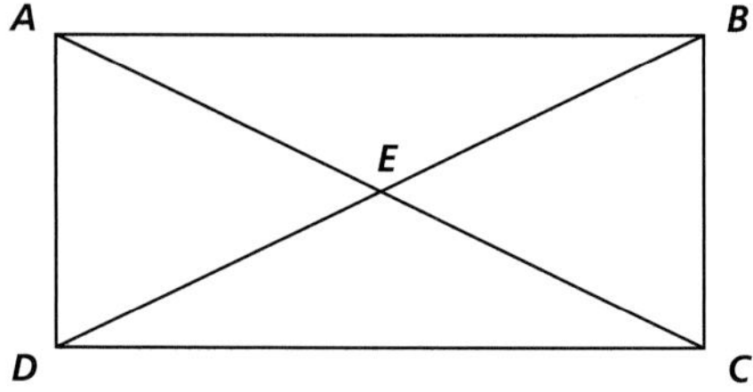

41. square, rectangle, rhombus
43. a.

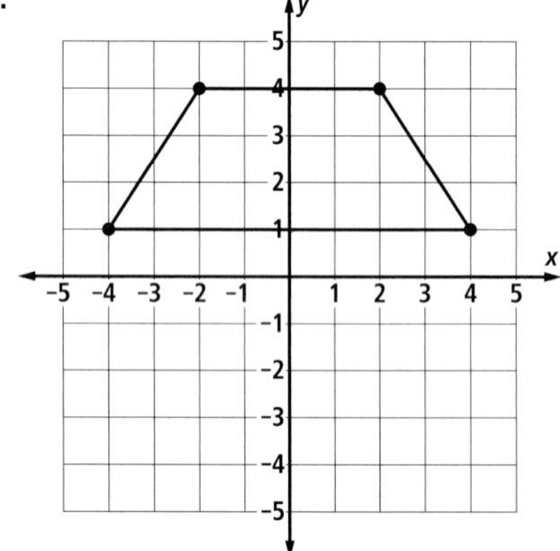

b. Isosceles trapezoid; there is one pair of parallel sides and the base angles are congruent.

Chapter 13

Lesson 13-1 (pp. 720–725)

Questions: 1. Japanese; paper folding
3. a.

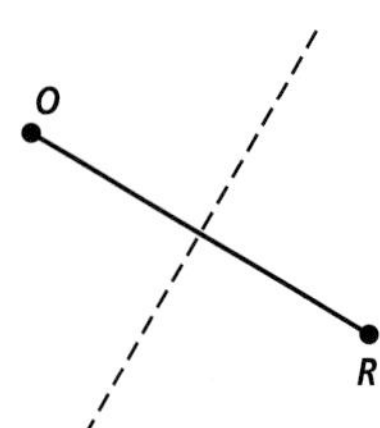

b. The fold is the perpendicular bisector of $\overline{OR}$.
5. a.

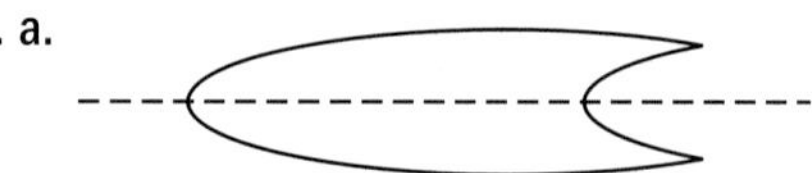

b. line of symmetry
7.

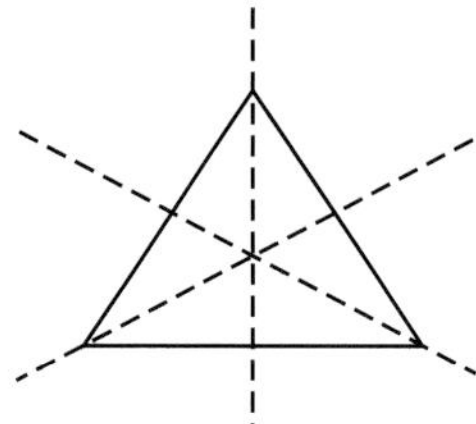

9 Check students' work.
11.

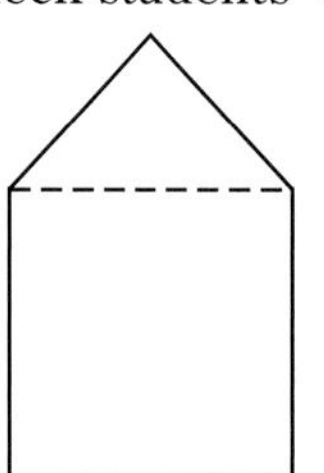

13. About 138.1 million

Lesson 13-2 (pp. 726–732)

Questions: 1. Answers vary. Sample: **a.** 16 cm **b.** 17 cm **c.** 10 cm **3.** Answers vary. Sample: **a.** 22.75 cm **b.** 23 cm **c.** 18 cm **5.** Answers vary. Sample: **a.** 11.3 cm **b.** 10 cm **c.** 17 cm **7.** Answers vary. Sample: In this case, the mean is the best way to compare a frog's jumping ability since the maximum jumping distance was used for each frog. **9.** Check students' work. **11.** about 9 times farther
13. $\frac{10}{21}$

Lesson 13-3 (pp. 733–741)

Questions: 1. about 10.5 million boys 3. 35–39 5. females 7. Answers vary. Sample: They might want to know if the children in their community are getting adequate nutrition (because malnutrition inhibits proper growth), or they may want to know what the average height is for someone in their community. 9. 135 cm 11. 163.5 cm 13. about 2.7 million males; about 3 million females 15. Answers vary. Sample: Canadian females are much more likely to survive to 80 years old or older than males. 17. Answers vary. Sample: Mexico, because a much greater proportion of the population is between the ages of 0 and 29 than 30 and 100+. 19. yes 15. 38 in., 96 cm 23. a. Jane b. Kate c. Kate d. Answers vary. Sample: Yes, the rules state the person with the longest jump wins. Jill was probably more aggressive with her jumps which is why she fouled 3 times, but her approach proved effective because she had the longest jump. 25. The distribution of heights for the class is a frequency distribution, and the distribution of heights by age for the US population is a relative frequency distribution.
27. a. Answers vary. Sample:

Boys:

4	8.5
5	1 6 7 8
6	0 0 1 3 4

Girls:

4	9
5	2 4 7 7.5
6	0 1 2 2.5 3

b. Answers vary. Sample: the double histogram because the intervals are 3 inches, instead of 10 inches 29. Answers vary. Sample: a. 140 cm, 152 cm, 151 cm, 149 cm b. 135 cm, 151 cm, 153 cm, 153 cm c. 134 cm, 150 cm, 154 cm, 154 cm d. 134 cm, 150 cm, 154 cm, 154 cm

Lesson 13-4 (pp. 742–747)

Questions: 1. Delaware, Rhode Island, and Kentucky 3. a. Georgia, North Carolina, and New York b. Maine, Rhode Island, and Vermont 5. There would be 16 more delegates; each state or territory would have one more delegate. 7. about 279,874 9. about 6,547,462 11. a. New York b. Georgia, about 99.06 13. a. about 5.1% b. about 75.2%

13. c.

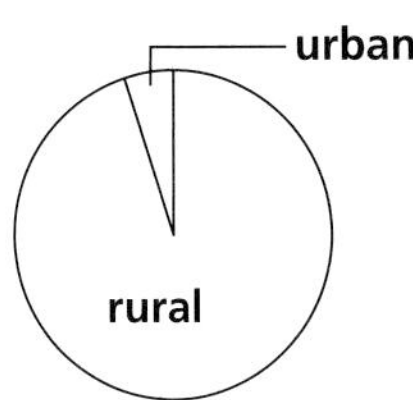

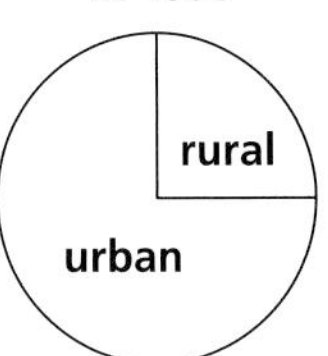

15. a. false

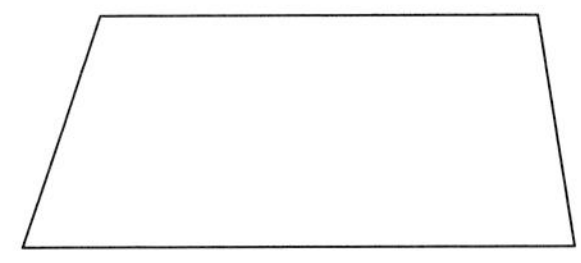

b. true; A parallelogram has 2 pairs of parallel sides. All rectangles have 2 pairs of parallel sides.
c. true

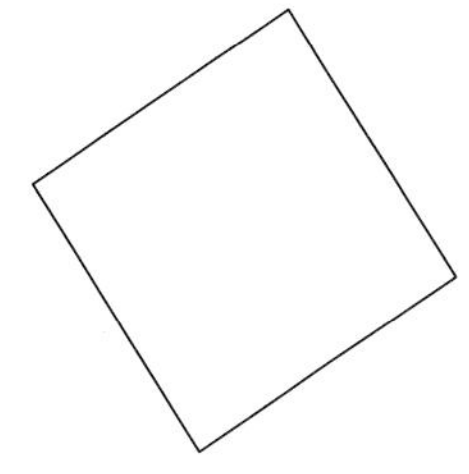

d. true; A trapezoid is a quadrilateral with at least one pair of parallel sides. All squares have 2 pairs of parallel sides. e. false; All rectangles are parallelograms.
17. about 78.5%

19.

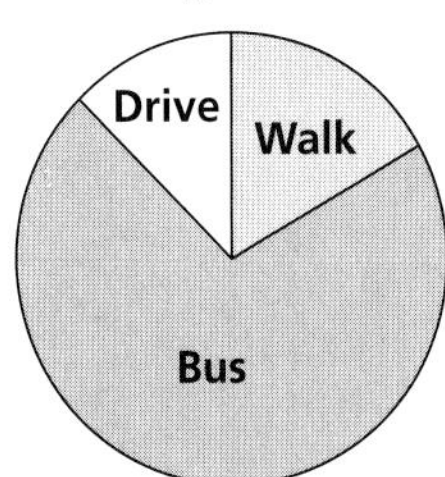

Lesson 13-5 (pp. 748–752)

Questions: 1. activity 3. good friends 5. Answers vary. Sample: cloudy 7. a. ii b. red, orange, yellow, green, blue, indigo, violet 9. Answers vary. Sample: Change choice D to "other." 11. Answers vary. Sample: not well written; Do you, on average, get 8 hours of sleep every night? 13. Answers vary. Sample: Where was the TV you own manufactured? 15. a. How old are you? b. How many people live in your house?

17. a.

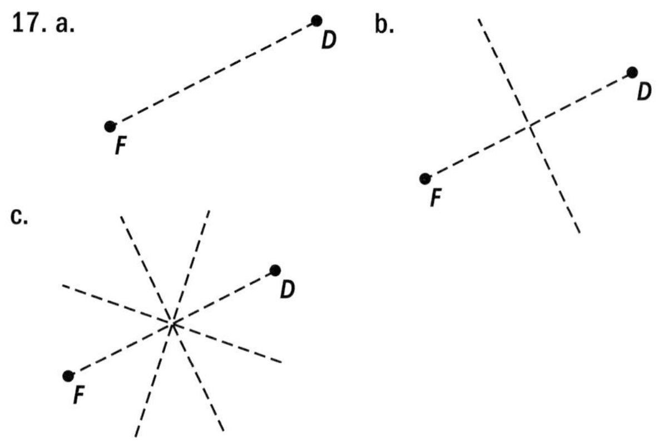

19. true **21.** Step 1: Commutative; Step 2: Associative

Lesson 13-6 (pp. 753–755)

Question: Check students' work.

Self-Test (pp. 759–761)

1. a. The filled bar indicates a change of party in the subsequent elections; an empty bar indicates no change in party. The shaded bar indicates an ambiguity—though the party did change, the popular vote was won by a member of the same party.

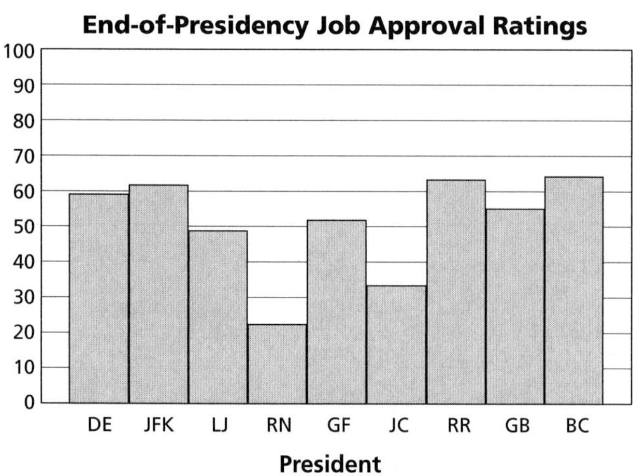

b. Answers vary. Sample: The data indicate that when a president's approval rate is above 60%, the subsequent election does not result in a change of party. This is because a popular president increases his party's popularity, making it likely that the next election will not result in a change of party. **2.** Check students' work. **3.** 2.36 **4.** $(3.35 + 2.18 + 2.36 + 1.56 + 1.63 + 2.72 + 2.20 + 2.22 + 3.57 + 3.00 + 3.05) \div 11 = 27.84 \div 11 \approx 2.53$

5. By folding the paper along a line including O such that $\overline{AO}$ and $\overline{BO}$ overlap, the angle formed by the fold and AO, as well the angle formed by the fold and BO, is $70°$.

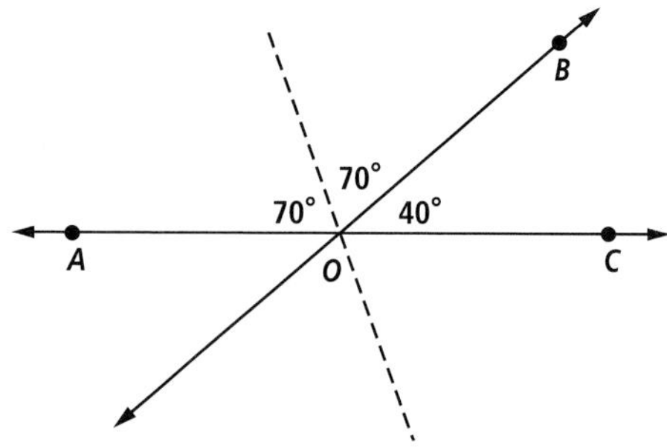

6. Answers vary. Sample: The question asks for one's favorite color, but only allows for one of two answers. A better question would be "What is your favorite color?" **7.** 1.3 million people are classified as "other" out of a total of 300 million people; thus, the percent of people classified as "other" is $100\,\frac{1.3}{300} \approx 0.43\%$.

8.

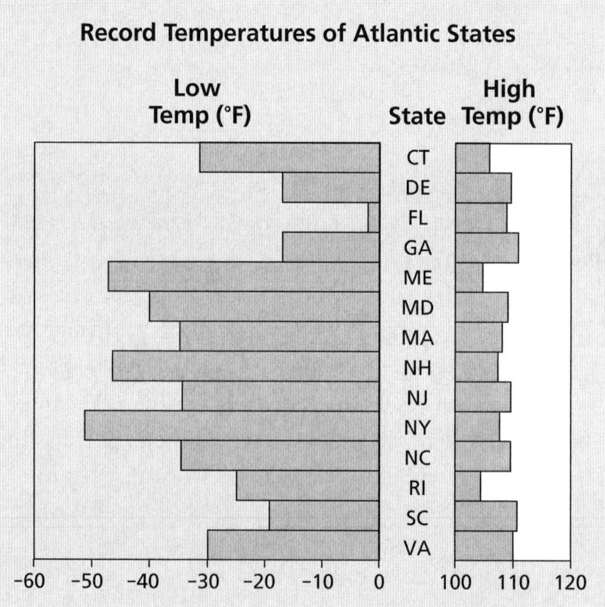

9. New York has the greatest range of temperatures with a range of $108 - (-52) = 160$.

10. a.

Money Earned by Leading
Money-Winner on PGA Tours

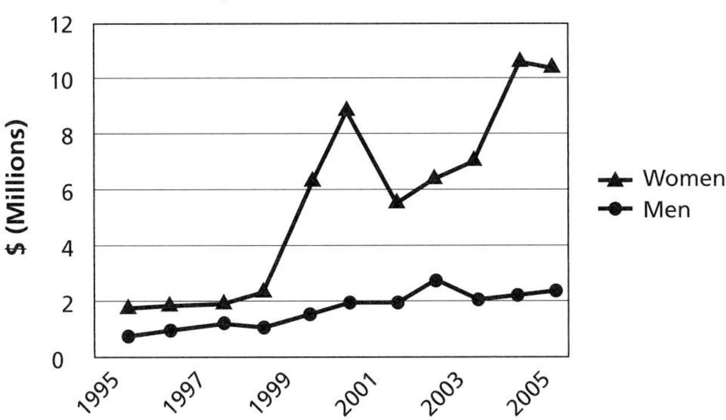

b. The amount of money earned by the women's leader has increased marginally; however, the men's leader has consistently made more money. **11.** Answers vary. Sample: Women: \$6 million, Men: \$18 million **12.** $100 \cdot \frac{986{,}002}{17{,}990{,}455} \approx 5.48\%$ **13.** Vermont had the least amount of population change from 1790 to 1990 with a change of 562,758 – 85,341 = 477,417.

27. a.

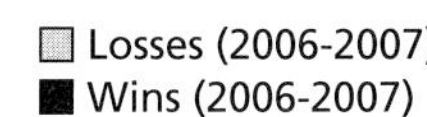

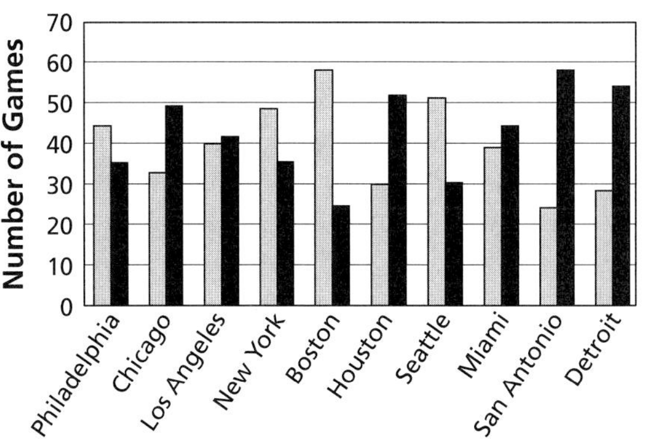

b. Answers vary. Sample: If you stack both bars, their height is the same for all of the teams, because all of the teams played the same number of games. **29.** Answers vary. Sample: LA won the most championships, but in the past season they only had the median record, so there is not necessarily any correlation. **31.** January **33.** January

Chapter Review (pp. 762–765)

1. wins: San Antonio; losses: Boston **3.** Answers vary. Sample: The distribution is uneven. **5.** somewhat true; The elephant is easily the heaviest at birth and as an adult. However, the other animals do not differ greatly in weight from each other as adults or as babies. The giant panda is the smallest at birth, but second heaviest as an adult. **7.** definitely true; Based on these data, the longer the animal, the heavier it is. **9.** Check students' work. **11.** B **13.** The fold is a parallel line halfway between the two lines **15.** Answers vary. Sample: There is no way to predict the possible responses to this survey. Rewrite as "Who do you think is greatest baseball team of all time?" **17.** Answers vary. Sample: Someone's favorite animal might not be represented by one of those four choices. Add choice "E" with "none of the above" as an option. **19.** 1790 **21.** by 11,847,443 people **23.** 25–44 **25.** 65 and older

35. a.

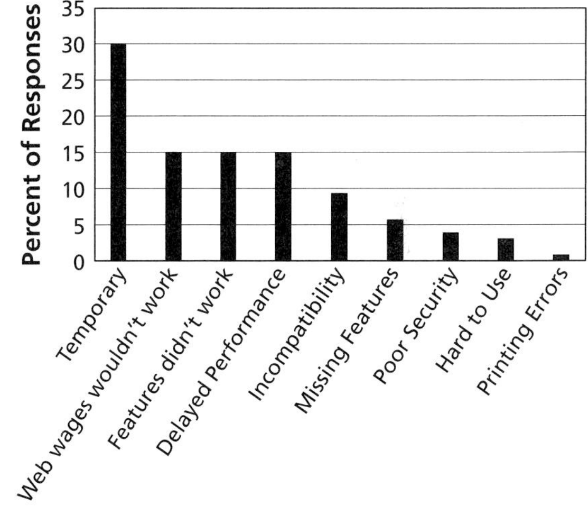

Self-Test Correlation Chart

Question	1	2	3	4	5	6	7	8	9	10
Objective(s)	H	B	A	A	C	D	E	F	A	G
Lesson(s)	13-2, 13-6	13-1, 13-2	13-2, 13-3	13-2, 13-3	13-1	13-5	13-4	13-2	13-2, 13-3	13-3

Question	11	12	13
Objective(s)	G	E	E
Lesson(s)	13-1	13-4	13-4

35. b. If the responses do not add up to 100%, some responses are unaccounted for.

37. **Reasons for Uninstalling**

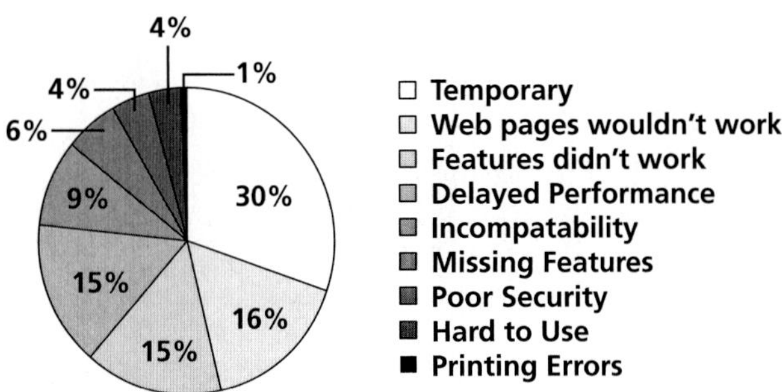

39. a.

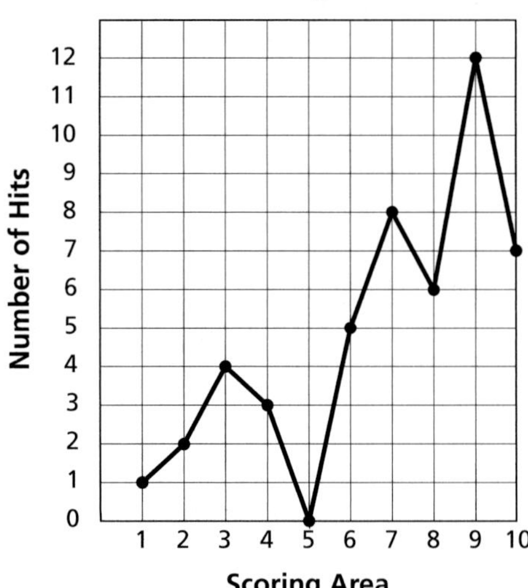

b. Answers vary. Sample: The archer hit the scoring areas farther away from the center more frequently. **41.** 187

Glossary

A

active cell The cell that is highlighted in a spreadsheet. (290)

acute angle An angle whose measure is between 0° and 90°. (239)

acute triangle A triangle in which the largest angle is acute. (682)

Adding Fractions Property For all numbers a, b, and c, with $c \neq 0$, $\frac{a}{c} + \frac{b}{c} = \frac{a+b}{c}$. (184)

Addition Property of Equality If $a = b$, then $a + c = b + c$. (256)

additive identity Zero, the number that can be added to a number without changing the value of the number. (159)

Additive Identity Property of Zero The sum of any number and zero is that number. For any number x, $x + 0 = x$. (159)

additive inverse The opposite of a number. The sum of a number and its additive inverse is zero. (160)

Additive Property of Opposites The sum of any number and its opposite is zero. For any number x, $x + {}^-x = 0$. (160)

Add-Opp Property See *Algebraic Definition of Subtraction.* (221)

adjacent angles Two angles that have a common side that is in the interior of the angle formed by the other two sides. (174)

Algebraic Definition of Division For any numbers a and b, $b \neq 0$, a divided by b equals a times the reciprocal of b: $\frac{a}{b} = a \cdot \frac{1}{b}$. Also called the *Mult-Rec Property.* (472)

Algebraic Definition of Subtraction For any numbers x and y, $x - y = x + {}^-y$. In words, subtracting y is the same as adding the opposite of y. Also called the *Add-Opp Property.* (221)

altitude of a parallelogram See *height of a parallelogram.* (527)

altitude of a triangle See *height of a triangle.* (521)

angle The union of two rays with the same endpoint. (165)

Angle Addition Property 1 The sum of the measures of all the non-overlapping angles about a point is 360°. (173)

Angle Addition Property 2 The sum of the measures of the two angles in a linear pair is 180°. (174)

Angle Addition Property 3 If a ray $\overrightarrow{CD}$ is between two rays $\overrightarrow{CA}$ and $\overrightarrow{CB}$, then $m\angle ACD + m\angle BCD = m\angle ACB$. (174)

angle bisector The line that divides an angle into two equal angles. (632)

arc A part of a circle that connects two points on the circle. (166)

Area Formula for a Circle The area A of a circle with radius r is given by the formula $A = \pi r^2$. (535)

Area Formula for Any Triangle The area A of any triangle is one half the product of the lengths of its base b and its height h: $A = \frac{1}{2}bh$. (522)

Area Formula for a Parallelogram The area A of a parallelogram is the product of the lengths of a base b and the height to that base h: $A = bh$. (528)

Area Formula for a Right Triangle The area A of a right triangle is one half the product of the lengths of its legs a and b: $A = \frac{1}{2}ab$. (520)

Area Model for Multiplication The area of a rectangle with length ℓ units and width w units is $\ell \cdot w$ (or ℓw) square units. (343)

Array Model for Multiplication The number of elements in a rectangular array with r rows and c columns is $r \cdot c$ or rc. (329)

Associative Property of Addition For any numbers a, b, and c, $(a + b) + c = a + (b + c)$. (145)

Associative Property of Multiplication For any numbers a, b, and c, $a(bc) = (ab)c$. (344)

average See *mean.* (273)

axis The horizontal or vertical number line containing the scale for a graph. Plural: *axes.* (290)

B

bar graph A data display in which the lengths of the bars correspond to the numbers in the data set. **(289)**

base In a power, the factor that is repeated. In x^n, x is the base. **(349)**

base line of a protractor The line containing the 0° mark on one side of a protractor and the 180° mark on the other side. **(167)**

base of a box The "bottom" of a box. Any face may be considered the base. **(562)**

base of a parallelogram Any side of a parallelogram to which an altitude, or height, is drawn. **(527)**

base of a triangle Any side of a triangle to which an altitude, or height, is drawn. **(521)**

bases of a trapezoid A pair of parallel sides of a trapezoid. **(705)**

base-10 system See *decimal system.* **(6)**

bisect Split into two parts of equal measure. **(234)**

bisector of a segment Any point, line, ray, or segment that intersects a segment at its midpoint. **(639)**

box A 3-dimensional surface with six faces that are all rectangles. **(545)**

C

capacity A measure of what a box, jar, or other container can hold. Also called *volume.* **(556)**

categorical data Data that can be sorted into non-numerical categories or groups. **(296)**

cell The intersection of a row and a column in a spreadsheet, identified by a column letter and a row number. **(290)**

census A sampling of an entire population. **(741)**

center of a protractor The midpoint of the segment from the 0° mark on one side of a protractor to the 180° mark on the other side. **(167)**

center of symmetry A point about which a rotation-symmetric figure can be turned to create an image that coincides with the original figure. **(689)**

centi- A prefix denoting $\frac{1}{100}$, or 0.01. **(83)**

circle graph A graph that uses sectors of a circle to show parts of a whole. **(115)**

circumference The perimeter of a circle. **(533)**

Commutative Property of Addition For any numbers a and b, $a + b = b + a$. **(140)**

Commutative Property of Multiplication For any numbers a and b, $ab = ba$. **(344)**

Comparison Model for Subtraction $x - y$ is how much more x is than y. **(214)**

compass A tool used for drawing circles and for copying and marking off lengths. **(633)**

complementary angles Two angles whose measures add to 90°. **(238)**

complex fraction A fraction with a fraction in the numerator or denominator or both. **(477)**

composite number A positive integer that has more than two factors. **(411)**

concentric circles Circles with the same center. **(540)**

Congruence Property 1 Two segments with the same length are congruent. **(677)**

Congruence Property 2 Two triangles with sides of the same three lengths are congruent. **(678)**

Congruence Property 3 If figures are congruent, then their perimeters, areas, and corresponding angles are equal in measure. **(678)**

Congruence Property 4 Two angles with the same measure are congruent. **(679)**

congruent figures Figures that are images of one another under a translation, rotation, reflection, or some combination of these transformations. **(676)**

construction See *Euclidean construction.* **(633)**

convex figure A figure in which the segment connecting any two points on the figure has all of its points on or inside the figure. **(699)**

coordinate axes A horizontal number line (x-axis) and a vertical number line (y-axis) that intersect at their zero points. Coordinate axes are used to locate points in the plane. **(307)**

coordinate Either of the two numbers in the ordered pair that locates a point on the plane. **(307)**

corresponding angles (1) Pairs of angles in similar locations in relation to a transversal. **(654) (2)** Angles in corresponding positions in congruent figures. **(676)**

Corresponding Angles Property When two lines are intersected by a transversal, corresponding angles have the same measure if and only if the lines are parallel. **(655)**

corresponding sides Sides in corresponding positions in congruent figures. **(676)**

counting unit In a count, the type of object that is counted. **(8)**

cube A box whose faces are all squares. **(547)**

cubed Raised to the third power. **(350)**

cylinder A 3-dimensional surface consisting of two circular bases lying in parallel planes and the points on the parallel segments connecting points on them. **(567)**

D

datum A piece of information. Plural: *data*. **(270)**

decimal system A number system in which any real number can be written as a sum of integer powers of 10. **(6)**

degree (°) A common unit for measuring angles; $\frac{1}{360}$ of a revolution. **(166)**

denominator The number b in the fraction $\frac{a}{b}$. **(13)**

depth of a box One dimension of a box. **(546)**

diameter A segment that connects two points on a circle and contains the center of the circle. **(173)**

difference The answer to a subtraction problem. **(209)**

dimensions of a box The lengths of the three mutually perpendicular edges of a box. **(546)**

dimensions of a rectangle The length and width of a rectangle. **(343)**

distribution The set of all possible outcomes of an experiment paired with their frequencies or relative frequencies. **(733)**

Distributive Property of Multiplication over Addition For any numbers a, b, and c, $a(b + c) = ab + ac$. **(377)**

dividend The number a in the division problem $a \div b$. **(400)**

divisor The number b in the division problem $a \div b$. **(400)**

double histogram Two histograms with the same scale but going in opposite directions from the scale line. **(734)**

double line graph Two line graphs on the same coordinate grid. **(301)**

duplicating an angle Creating a new angle with the same measure as a given angle. **(649)**

Dynamic Geometry System (DGS) Software used to draw, construct, transform, manipulate, and measure geometric figures. **(634)**

E

edge of a box Any of the sides of the faces of a box. **(545)**

endpoints The points at the ends of a line segment. **(12)**

Equal Fractions Property If the numerator and denominator of a fraction are both multiplied (or divided) by the same nonzero number, then the resulting fraction is equal to the original fraction. That is, if $k \neq 0$, then $\frac{ka}{kb} = \frac{a}{b}$. **(33)**

equation A mathematical sentence with an equals sign. Also called *equality*. **(249)**

equilateral triangle A triangle with all three sides the same length. **(682)**

equivalent fractions Fractions with the same value. Also called *equal fractions*. **(33)**

estimate A number that is close to another number. **(97)**

Euclidean construction A figure made using only a compass and straightedge. **(633)**

evaluating an expression Finding the value of an expression. **(373)**

event Any set of outcomes from a sample space. **(591)**

expanded notation A form of a number that shows all the place values of the number. **(64, 352)**

experiment A situation that is repeated again and again. **(610)**

exponent A raised number that indicates how many times a factor is repeated. In x^n, n is the exponent. **(349)**

exponential form A number written as a power. **(350)**

F

face of a box Any of the six rectangular regions that form the surface of a box. **(545)**

fact triangle A diagram that represents related addition and subtraction facts or related multiplication and division facts. The operation signs tell whether the triangle is an addition/subtraction triangle or a multiplication/division triangle. **(226)**

factor An integer that divides into another integer without a remainder. **(406)**

factor tree A method for identifying all the prime factors of a number by breaking it into pairs of factors, then breaking each of the non-prime factors into pairs of factors, and so on, until all factors are prime. **(412)**

fair Having outcomes that are equally likely. Also called *unbiased.* **(592)**

fair game A game in which each player has the same chance of winning. **(604)**

Formula for Circumference of a Circle In every circle with diameter d and circumference C, $C = \pi d$. **(534)**

frequency The number of times a data value or event occurs. **(290, 610)**

G

geometric mean The common value of the second and third terms of a true proportion when these terms are equal. **(493)**

gram (g) A unit of mass in the metric system. **(86)**

H

height of a box One dimension of a box. In the volume formula for a box, the length of an edge perpendicular to the base. **(546, 562)**

height of a parallelogram A segment from one side of a parallelogram perpendicular to a point on the opposite side, or the length of this segment. **(527)**

height of a triangle A segment from a vertex of a triangle, perpendicular to the opposite side (the *base*), or the length of this segment. **(521)**

histogram A bar graph in which each bar represents the frequency or relative frequency of data values within an interval. The intervals of a histogram do not overlap and, together, include all the values in the data set. **(290)**

hypotenuse The side of a right triangle opposite the right angle. **(519)**

I

improper fraction A simple fraction in which the numerator is greater than the denominator. **(40)**

included angle Given two adjacent sides of a triangle or other polygon, the angle they form. **(683)**

integer division A division in which the numbers in the problem and in the answer are integers, and the answer is given as a quotient and a remainder, rather than as a decimal or fraction. **(418)**

integer rectangle A rectangle with side lengths that are all whole numbers. **(147)**

integers The set of numbers that includes the whole numbers 0, 1, 2, 3, . . . and their opposites. **(46)**

interval On a ruler, the distance between two tick marks. **(20)**

is approximately equal to ($\approx$) Has nearly the same value as. **(98)**

is equal to ($=$) Has the same value as. **(121)**

is greater than ($>$) Has a greater value than. **(121)**

is less than ($<$) Has a lesser value than. **(121)**

isosceles trapezoid A trapezoid in which the two angles that contain a base are equal in measure. **(706)**

isosceles triangle A triangle with at least two sides of the same length. **(682)**

K

kilo- A prefix denoting 1,000. **(83)**

kilogram (kg) A unit of mass equal to 1,000 grams. **(86)**

kite A quadrilateral that has two distinct pairs of adjacent sides of equal length. **(700)**

L

Law of Large Numbers In general, the more trials of an experiment, the closer the relative frequency of an event will be to the event's probability. **(611)**

leaf The digits of a number to the right of the vertical segment in a stem-and-leaf plot. **(284)**

least common denominator The least common multiple of the denominators of two or more fractions. **(185)**

least common multiple The smallest positive integer multiple of two or more integers. **(185)**

leg Part of a trip. **(144)**

leg of a right triangle One of the two sides of a right triangle that form the 90° angle. **(519)**

length The distance along a line or a curve from one point to another. **(19)**

length of a box One dimension of a box. **(546)**

length of a rectangle One dimension of a rectangle. **(343)**

like denominators Denominators that are the same. **(184)**

line graph A graph of ordered pairs of numbers connected by segments in order from left to right. **(301)**

line segment Two points and all points on the line between them. **(12)**

line of reflection See *reflecting line.* **(645)**

linear pair Two angles that share a common side and whose other sides are rays on the same line in opposite directions. **(173)**

list A sequence of numbers. **(278)**

liter (L) A unit of capacity in the metric system. **(86)**

lowest terms A term used to describe a simple fraction for which no whole number greater than 1 is a factor of both the numerator and the denominator. **(34)**

M

maximum The greatest value in a set of data. **(273)**

mean The sum of the numbers in a set of data divided by the number of numbers. Also called *average.* **(273)**

median The middle number in a set of data when the numbers are ordered by size. If there is an even number of numbers, the median is the mean of the middle two numbers. **(273)**

meter (m) The basic unit of length in the metric system. **(83)**

metric system The international system of measurement in which like units are related by powers of 10. **(83)**

microgram The unit of mass equal to $\frac{1}{1{,}000{,}000}$ gram. **(88)**

midpoint The point that splits a segment into two segments of equal length. **(12)**

milli- A prefix denoting $\frac{1}{1000}$, or 0.001. **(83)**

milligram (mg) The unit of mass equal to $\frac{1}{1000}$ gram. **(86)**

milliliter (mL) The unit of capacity equal to $\frac{1}{1000}$ liter. **(86)**

minimum The least value in a set of data. **(273)**

minuend The number a in the subtraction problem $a - b$. **(209)**

mirror See *reflecting line.* **(645)**

mixed number A number that is written as the sum of a whole number and a fraction, with no addition symbol in between. **(20)**

mixed units A term used when two or more different units are used to write a single measure. **(27)**

mode The most common value in a set of data. **(273)**

multiple line graph A graph with two or more line graphs on the same coordinate grid. **(301)**

Multiplication Counting Principle If one choice can be made in m ways and a second choice can then always be made in n ways, then there are mn ways of making the first choice followed by the second choice. (587)

Multiplication of Fractions Property For all numbers a and c, and all nonzero numbers b and d, $\frac{a}{b} \cdot \frac{c}{d} = \frac{ac}{bd}$. (336)

Multiplication Property of Equality If $x = y$, then $ax = ay$. (484)

multiplicative inverses See *reciprocals.* (468)

Mult-Rec Property See *Algebraic Definition of Divison.* (472)

N

negative number A number less than zero. (45)

net A 2-dimensional pattern that, when folded, will create a 3-dimensional figure. (550)

nonbases of a trapezoid The sides of a trapezoid that are not bases. (706)

nonconvex figure A figure that is not convex. (699)

numerator The number a in the fraction $\frac{a}{b}$. (13)

numerical data Data that come from measurements. (296)

numerical expression An expression made up of numbers and operation symbols. (373)

O

obtuse angle An angle whose measure is between 90° and 180°. (239)

obtuse triangle A triangle in which the largest angle is obtuse. (682)

one-place decimal A number with one decimal place to the right of the decimal point. (64)

open-ended item On a survey, a question for which specific choices of responses are *not* given. (749)

open sentence An equation that has a variable. (249)

opposite See *additive inverse.* (46)

Opposite of a Difference Property For all numbers a and b, $a - b = -(b - a)$. (210)

Opposite of Opposites (Op-Op) Property The opposite of the opposite of a number is the number itself. For any number x, $-(-x) = x$. (160)

opposite angles of a quadrilateral A pair of angles of a quadrilateral that do not share a side. (692)

opposite sides of a quadrilateral A pair of sides of a quadrilateral that do not intersect. (692)

origami The art of folding a single sheet of paper following specific rules. (720)

origin The point $(0, 0)$ of intersection of the coordinate axes. (307)

P

parallel lines Lines in the same plane that have no points in common. (526)

parallelogram A quadrilateral in which both pairs of opposite sides are parallel. (526)

pentagon A five-sided polygon. (151)

percent circle A circle divided into 100 equal arcs, each representing 1%. (91)

percent sign (%) A symbol that means multiply by one hundredth, or 0.01. (114)

perimeter of a polygon The sum of the lengths of the sides of the polygon. (146)

perpendicular Lines, rays, or segments that intersect at right angles. (237)

perpendicular bisector of a segment The line that both bisects the segment and is perpendicular to it. (639)

pi (π) The ratio of the circumference of any circle to its diameter. Pi is an infinite, nonrepeating decimal that is approximately equal to 3.14159265. (533)

polygon A 2-dimensional figure formed when three or more points are connected in order so that the last point is connected to the first and no point is repeated, and so that (1) the segments intersect only at their endpoints and (2) no two segments with the same endpoint are on the same line. (145)

prime factorization The expression of a number as the product of its prime factors. (412)

prime number A positive integer that has exactly two integer factors—itself and 1. (411)

probability A number from 0 to 1 that describes the chance that something will happen. **(591)**

proper fraction A fraction in which the numerator is less than the denominator. **(40)**

Property of Reciprocals **(1)** For any nonzero number a, a and $\frac{1}{a}$ are reciprocals; **(2)** For any nonzero numbers a and b, $\frac{a}{b}$ and $\frac{b}{a}$ are reciprocals. **(468)**

proportion A statement that two fractions are equal. **(489)**

proportional terms The four terms in a true proportion. **(489)**

protractor A tool used to measure angles. **(167)**

Putting-Together Model for Addition Suppose something with measure x is put together with something that has measure y. If there is no overlap, then the result has measure $x + y$. **(138)**

Q

quadrant Each of the four regions into which the plane is split by the coordinate axes. **(307)**

quadrilateral A four-sided polygon. **(692)**

Quadrilateral-Sum Theorem In any quadrilateral with angles having degree measures a, b, c, and d, and both diagonals inside the quadrilateral, $a + b + c + d = 360°$. **(180)**

quotient The answer to a division problem. **(400)**

Quotient-Remainder Formula Suppose d and n are integers. Let d = divisor, n = dividend, q = integer quotient, and r = remainder. Then, when $n \div d = q$ Rr, it is also the case that $n = d \cdot q + r$. **(418)**

R

radius A segment from the center of a circle to any point on the circle, or the length of this segment. **(535)**

random outcomes A set of outcomes that have the same probability of occurring. **(616)**

random numbers Numbers selected using a random process, so that each possible number has the same chance of occurring at each selection. **(617)**

Randomness and Probability Property If an event has n outcomes that occur randomly, then the probability that any one of them will occur is $\frac{1}{n}$. The probability that one of m of the outcomes will occur is $\frac{m}{n}$. **(616)**

range The difference between the maximum and minimum values in a set of data. **(273)**

rate A division involving quantities with different units. **(401)**

rate unit The unit for a rate, which results from dividing quantities with different units. **(401)**

Rate Model for Division When two quantities with different kinds of units are divided, the quotient is a rate. **(401)**

ratio A comparison of two quantities with the same unit by division. A ratio has no unit. **(462)**

ratio comparison The use of division to compare two quantities with the same unit. **(462)**

Ratio Comparison Model for Division If a and b are quantities with the same unit, the $\frac{a}{b}$ compares a to b. **(462)**

rational number division Division in which the quotient is expressed as a fraction or a decimal. **(428)**

reciprocals Two numbers whose product is 1. Also called *multiplicative inverses*. **(468)**

rectangle A four-sided polygon (quadrilateral) with four right angles. **(146)**

rectangular array An arrangement of items with the same number of items per row and the same number of items per column. **(329)**

rectangular solid A box and all the points inside of it. **(545)**

reflecting line The line over which a point or figure is reflected. Also called the *line of reflection* or *mirror*. **(645)**

reflection image of *A* over the line *m* If A is not on m, the point A' such that m is the perpendicular bisector of $\overline{AA'}$. If A is on m, then A is its own reflection image. **(645)**

reflection-symmetric figure A figure that coincides with its reflection image. **(687)**

related facts Addition and subtraction equations or multiplication and division equations involving the same three numbers. If $a + b = c$, then $b + a = c$, $c - a = b$, and $c - b = a$. If $ab = c$, then $ba = c$, $c \div a = b$, and $c \div b = a$. **(226)**

Repeated Multiplication Model for Powers When n is a whole number greater than 1, then the nth power of x, $x^n = \underbrace{x \cdot x \cdot \ldots \cdot x}_{n \text{ factors}}$. (349)

remainder In an integer division $n \div d$, the whole number r such that $n = dq + r$. (405)

repeating decimal A decimal with an infinite, repeating pattern of digits. (105)

repetend In a repeating decimal, the digit or group of digits that repeat. (105)

rhombus A quadrilateral with all four sides of the same length. (694)

right angle An angle that measures 90°. (237)

right prism A 3-dimensional figure with two bases that are polygons of the same size and shape and other faces that are rectangles. (567)

right triangle A triangle in which the largest angle is a right angle. (682)

ring The region between two concentric circles, perhaps including one or both circles. (540)

rotation A turn around a fixed point. (650)

rotation-symmetric figure A figure that coincides with its image under a rotation with magnitude between 0° and 360°. (689)

round down Round to a lesser value. (90)

round to the nearest Round to the closer value. (97)

round up Round to a greater value. (90)

S

sample space The set of all possible outcomes of a situation. (591)

scale The ratio of the distance on a map or scale drawing to the true distance. (499)

scalene triangle A triangle with sides of three different lengths. (682)

sector A wedge-shaped piece of a circle, bounded by two radii and an arc, along with its interior. (92)

segment See *line segment*. (12)

semicircle An arc that has a measure of 180°. Half a circle. (173, 517)

sides of an angle The rays that form an angle. (165)

side of an equation The expression on either side of the equals sign in an equation. (249)

sides of a polygon The segments that make up a polygon. (145)

simple fraction A fraction with whole numbers in its numerator and denominator. (40)

simplifying a fraction Writing a fraction in lowest terms. (34)

simulation A process by which you examine a problem by using materials that are different from those in the actual problem. (619)

Slide Model for Addition If a slide x is followed by a slide y, the result is a slide $x + y$. (153)

Slide Model for Subtraction If a quantity x is decreased by y, the resulting quantity is $x - y$. (220)

solution A value of the variable that makes an open sentence true. (249)

solve a proportion Find the value of the variable that makes the proportion true. (490)

solve an equation Find all the values of the variable that make the equation true. (249)

spreadsheet A computer program used to organize information. (289)

squared Raised to the second power. (350)

stastistics **(1)** The science of the collection, organization, and interpretation of data. (270) **(2)** Numbers used to describe sets of numbers, including landmarks (minimum, maximum, and mode), measures of center (mean and median), and measures of spread (range). (272)

stem The digits of a number to the left of the vertical segment in a stem-and-leaf plot. (284)

stem-and-leaf plot A data display in which each number is split at a specific decimal place. The left digits of the numbers, called the *stems*, are listed vertically to the left of a vertical segment. The right digits of the numbers, called the *leaves*, are listed next to the corresponding stems to the right of the vertical segment. (284)

straight angle An angle whose sides are rays that form a line. A straight angle has a measure of 180°. (239)

straightedge An unmarked tool used to draw lines and segments. **(633)**

Substitution Principle If two numbers are equal, then one number can be substituted for the other in any computation without changing the results of the computation. **(73)**

Subtracting Fractions Property For all numbers a, b, and c, with $c \neq 0$, $\frac{a}{c} - \frac{b}{c} = \frac{a-b}{c}$. **(243)**

subtrahend The number being subtracted in a subtraction problem. **(209)**

supplementary angles Two angles whose measures add to 180°. **(231)**

surface area The sum of the areas of all the faces of a 3-dimensional figure. **(555)**

Surface Area for a Right Prism or a Cylinder The surface area of a right prism or cylinder is the sum of the areas of its two bases and the area of its sides. The area of its sides is the product of the perimeter of the base and the height. **(569)**

Surface Area Formula for a Cube The surface area $S.A.$ of a cube with edge length s units is $6s^2$ square units: $S.A. = 6s^2$. **(556)**

survey A question or set of questions used to collect data. **(741)**

symmetric figure A figure that coincides with its image under a transformation that does move some points. **(687)**

symmetry line A line over which the reflection image of a figure coincides with the figure. **(687)**

T

Take-Away Model for Subtraction If a quantity y is taken away from an original quantity x with the same units, the quantity remaining is $x - y$. **(208)**

terminating decimal A decimal that ends after a certain number of places. **(106)**

terms of a proportion In the proportion $\frac{a}{b} = \frac{c}{d}$, the numbers a, b, c, and d. **(489)**

translation A slide of a point or figure a certain distance in a certain direction. **(659)**

transversal A line that intersects two or more lines. **(654)**

trapezoid A quadrilateral with at least one pair of parallel sides. **(705)**

tree diagram A diagram used to represent outcomes in probability situations involving more than one stage. **(587)**

trial One repetition of an experiment. **(610)**

Triangle-Sum Theorem In any triangle with angles having measures a, b, and c, $a + b + c = 180°$. **(179)**

true proportion A proportion whose sides are equal. **(490)**

truncate A way of rounding decimals by cutting off the digits after a particular place. **(95)**

two-place decimal A number with two decimal places to the right of the decimal point. **(64)**

U

unbiased See *fair*. **(592)**

unit fraction A simple fraction with 1 in the numerator. **(433)**

unfair game A game in which players do not have the same chance of winning. **(604)**

unlike denominators Denominators that are not the same. **(185)**

V

value of a numerical expression The answer found by performing the arithmetic operations. **(373)**

variable A letter or other symbol that may stand for any one of a set of numbers or other objects. **(138, 249)**

vector An arrow that indicates the distance and direction of a translation. **(659)**

Venn diagram A diagram that uses circles or ovals to show relationships among sets of objects. **(694)**

vertex of a box A point common to two edges of a box. Plural: *vertices*. **(545)**

vertex of an angle The common endpoint of the rays that form the angle. **(165)**

vertical angles The two angles formed by intersecting lines and that do not share a common side. **(232)**

volume The amount of space inside a 3-dimensional figure. Also called *capacity.* (556)

Volume Formula for a Cube The volume V of a cube with edges of length s units is $s \cdot s \cdot s$ or s^3 cubic units: $V = s^3$. (557)

Volume Formula for a Prism or a Cylinder The volume V of a prism or cylinder equals the product of the area B of the base and the height h to that base: $V = Bh$. (568)

Volume of a Box Formulas (1) The volume V of a box is the area B of a base times the height h to that base: $V = Bh$. (2) The volume V of a box with dimensions ℓ, w, and h is the product of these dimensions: $V = \ell wh$. (563)

W

whole numbers The numbers 0, 1, 2, 3, 4, 5, ... (6)

width of a box One dimension of a box. (546)

width of a rectangle One dimension of a rectangle. (343)

X

***x*-axis** The horizontal number line in a coordinate grid. (307)

***x*-coordinate** The first number in an ordered pair, which tells how far the point is left or right from the y-axis. (307)

Y

***y*-axis** The vertical number line in a coordinate grid. (307)

***y*-coordinate** The second number in an ordered pair, which tells how far the point is up or down from the x-axis. (307)

Index

A

D

E

F

G

H

I

N

S

Photo Credits

Volume 1 Chapters 1–6

Cover: ©Peter Dazeley/Photographer's Choice/Getty Images, **front, back.**

vi (l) ©Baltimore Shakespeare Festival Archives, (r) Courtesy Monticello/Thomas Jefferson Foundation, Inc.; **vii** (l) ©VEER Jim Barber/Photonica/Getty Images, (r) ©Jeff Vanuga/Corbis; **viii** (l) ©Kevin Dodge/Corbis, (r) ©Karl Weatherly/Corbis; **ix** (l) ©Mario Lopes/Shutterstock, (r) ©Steve Allen/Brand X Pictures/Jupiterimages; **x** (l) ©William Manning/Corbis, (r) ©Chris George/Alamy; **xi** (l) ©Elisa Locci/Alamy, (r) ©Pixtal/SuperStock; **xii** ©Peter Menzel/drr.net; **1** ©Medioimages/Alamy; **3** ©Steve Allen/Brand X Pictures/Jupiterimages; **4** (b) David Coder/iStockphoto; **4-5** (t) ©Baltimore Shakespeare Festival Archives; **7** ©Yann Layma/The Image Bank/Getty Images; **9** ©Andreas Nilsson/Shutterstock; **10** "Wheel of Fortune" ©2008 Califon Productions, Inc., courtesy Sony Pictures Television. photo by Carol Kaelson; **14** ©Comstock/Punchstock; **16** ©John Warden/SuperStock; **17** ©Photolibrary; **18** ©Jim Whitmer; **19** (t) ©Ryan McVay/Photodisc/Getty Images, (b) ©Brand X Pictures/Punchstock; **22** ©David Young-Wolff/PhotoEdit; **23** ©Prisma/SuperStock; **25** ©Jeff Greenberg/eStockphoto; **28** ©Jeff Greenberg/PhotoEdit; **29** ©Associated Press; **30** ©Associated Press; **31** (t) ©cloki/Shutterstock, (b) Courtesy NASA; **37** ©Lynn Watson/Shutterstock; **39** ©The Granger Collection, New York; **41** Courtesy Furnitureland South, High Point, NC; **42** © Comstock Images/PictureQuest; **43** ©Rena Schild/Shutterstock; **44** ©Dave M. Benett/Getty Images Entertainment/Getty Images; **45** ©SuperStock, Inc./SuperStock; **47** ©Ross Kinnaird/Getty Images Sport/Getty Images; **48** ©Jennifer Lerman; **52** ©Wetgrass Images; **54** (t) ©Lisa F. Young/Shutterstock; (b) ©Mark Evans/iStockphoto; **55** (l) ©Blendimages/Tips Images, (r) ©David Lees/Corbis; 56 ©Floresco Productions/Corbis; **62-63** Courtesy Monticello/Thomas Jefferson Foundation, Inc.; **65** ©Ron Kuntz/AFP/Getty Images; **68** ©SuperStock, Inc./SuperStock; **69** ©Associated Press; **70** ©age fotostock/SuperStock; **73** ©Digital Vision/PunchStock; **74** ©Glowimages/Getty Images; **75** ©Christian Fischer/Bongarts/Getty Images; **79** ©Aman Ahmed Khan/Shutterstock; **80** ©Olav Wildermann/Shutterstock; **82** ©Nashville Zoo; **86** ©Anita Colic/Shutterstock; **87** ©Tony Freeman/PhotoEdit; **88** ©Nikola Bilic/Shutterstock; **91** ©Real Food by Warren Diggles/Alamy; **93** ©Dennis MacDonald/PhotoEdit; **94** ©Andrew Ward/Life File/Getty Images; **97** ©Digital Vision Ltd./SuperStock; **98** ©Stockbyte/Getty Images; **100** ©age fotostock/SuperStock; **101** ©Eleonora Kolomiyets/Shutterstock; **102** Michael-John Wolfe/Shutterstock; **103** © Ryan McVay/Photodisc/Getty Images; **105** ©BananaStock/Alamy; **107** ©Doug Menuez/Getty Images; **108** ©Designpics/Punchstock; **111** ©Comstock/Punchstock; **112** ©Michael Ledray/Shutterstock; **117** ©Jeff Greenberg/PhotoEdit; **118** ©image100/Corbis; **120** ©Associated Press; **123** ©Associated Press; **124** ©Magdalena Szachowska/Shutterstock; **125** ©Bettmann/Corbis; **127** ©Dennis MacDonald/Alamy; **128** Julian Rovagnati/iStockphoto; **136-137** ©VEER Jim Barber/Photonica/Getty Images; **140** ©Norbert Schaefer/Corbis; **141** ©Henry Course; **142** ©Sjwh Photography; **143** ©Steve Vidler/SuperStock; **149** ©Patti McConville/Photographer's Choice/Getty Images; **151** ©Hisham F. Ibrahim/Getty Images; **152** ©CMCD/Getty Images; **156** ©Brand X Pictures/Punchstock; **157** ©Associated Press; **159** ©Cleve Bryant/PhotoEdit; **161** ©J Silver/SuperStock; **162** ©Robert Holmes/Corbis; **163** ©David Young-Wolff/PhotoEdit; **165** ©Pixtal/age fotostock; **170** ©Joanne O'Brien/Photofusion Picture Library/Alamy; **171** (l) ©Nico Tondini/Corbis, (r) ©Michael Newman/PhotoEdit; **174** ©Brand X Pictures/Punchstock; **177** ©Tony Freeman/PhotoEdit; **183** ©M-A Studio; **185** ©Gustavo Andrade/Pixtal/Artlife Images; **187** ©Richard T. Nowitz/Corbis; **188** ©Karl R. Martin/Shutterstock; **195** ©Associated Press; **197** ©Brand X Pictures/Punchstock; **206-207** ©Jeff Vanuga/Corbis; **209** ©Robert W. Ginn/PhotoEdit; **211** ©James Baigrie/Jupiterimages; **212** ©age fotostock/SuperStock; **213** ©David Kelly Crow/PhotoEdit; **214** ©Associated Press; **215** ©Tony Duffy/Getty Images Sport/Getty Images; **217** ©Brand X Pictures/Punchstock; **218** ©PhotoLink/Getty Images; **220** ©Photodisc/Getty Images; **221** ©Bryan Busovicki/Shutterstock; **223** ©Michael Smith/Getty Images News/Getty Images; **224** ©Photodisc/Getty Images; **225** ©Shawn Thornsberry; **227** ©Andrew Ammendolia; **228** ©Touhig Sion/Corbis Sygma; **231** ©Marcos Carvalho/Shutterstock; **233** ©Ian McKinnell/Alamy; **236** ©BananaStock/Punchstock; **237** ©Photodisc/Getty Images; **238** ©Purestock/SuperStock; **242** ©Olga Vasilkova/Shutterstock; **243** ©Andersen Ross/Blend Images/Artlife Images; **246** ©James Steidl/Shutterstock; **247** ©Cathleen Clapper/Shutterstock; **252** ©Brand X Pictures/Punchstock; **258** ©Associated Press; **259** ©Marita Collins; **261** ©Associated Press; 262 (l) ©Hans Strand/Corbis, (r) ©Marc Golub; **270-271** ©Kevin Dodge/Corbis; **273** ©Tom & Dee Ann McCarthy/Corbis; **274** © Greg Fiume/NewSport/Corbis; **275** ©Lisette Le Bon/SuperStock; **276** ©Tony Mathews/Shutterstock; **278** ©The Granger Collection, New York; **281** ©Creatas/SuperStock; **282** ©Stocktrek Images/Alamy; **283** ©John Sevigny/epa/Corbis; **285** ©Sephen Waitkevich/Imagination Multimedia, Inc.; **288** ©Associated Press; **294** ©Robyn Mackenzie/Shutterstock; **297** ©Bob Daemmrich/PhotoEdit; **298** ©David Young-Wolff/PhotoEdit; **300** ©Franck Fife/AFP/Getty Images; **302** ©Jonathan Ferrey/Getty Images Sport/Getty Images; **306** ©Bob Rowan/Progressive Image/Corbis; **311** ©Claudio Lovo/Shutterstock; **312** ©Ezra Shaw/Getty Images Sport/Getty Images; **315** ©Brand X Pictures/Alamy; **317** ©Photo 24/Getty Images; **318** (l) ©Associated Press, (r) ©Leonard de Selva/Corbis; **326-327** ©Karl Weatherly/Corbis; **329** ©Michael Newman/PhotoEdit; **331** ©Marita Collins; **332** ©Corbis; **334** ©PhotoAlto/SuperStock; **337** ©Rick D'Elia/Corbis; **338** ©Telnova Olya/Shutterstock; **339** ©StockTrek/Getty Images; **340** ©Associated Press; **342** (tl) ©Tomasz Danul/Shutterstock, (tr) ©Marek Slusarczyk/Shutterstock, (br) ©StockTrek/Photodisc/Getty Images; **345** ©Corbis; **346** ©Tips Images; **347** ©Myrleen Ferguson Cate/PhotoEdit; **353** ©Associated Press; **354** ©Andresr/Shutterstock; **356** ©prism_68/Shutterstock; **358** ©Photodisc/Getty Images; **359** ©Tomasz Trojanowski/Shutterstock; **364** ©Creatas/SuperStock; **365** ©Royalty-Free/Corbis; **368** ©Marita Collins; **369** ©Rudy Sulgan/Corbis; **370** ©Richard Cummins/SuperStock; **378** ©fckncg/Shutterstock; **380** ©Matthew Jacques/Shutterstock; **381** ©Corbis/SuperStock; **382** ©Jupiterimages; **386** ©Brand X Picturess/Alamy; **388** ©Elena Elisseeva/Shutterstock; **389** ©The Granger Collection, New York; **390** ©StockTrek/Photodisc/Getty Images.

Volume 2 Chapters 7–13

398-399 ©Mario Lopes/Shutterstock; **402** ©Tony Freeman/PhotoEdit; **403** ©Associated Press; **409** ©Jeff Greenberg/Alamy; **410** ©Image Source/PunchStock; **415** ©Randy Faris/Corbis; **416** ©Danny Lehman/Corbis; **419** ©BananaStock/SuperStock; **420** ©Mark Aplet/iStockphoto; **421** ©Comstock Images/JupiterImages; **422** ©Terry W. Eggers/Corbis; **424** ©Gabe Palmer/Alamy; **426** ©Chris Clark/Alamy; **428** ©Enigma/Alamy; **429** ©Gualberto Becerra/Shutterstock; **430** ©Suzanne Tucker/Shutterstock; **435** ©Andrew Fox/Corbis; **437** ©Associated Press; **439** Courtesy Centers for Disease Control and Prevention; **440** ©Associated Press; **442** ©Natalie Fobes/Corbis; **444** ©Michael Newman/PhotoEdit; **446** ©Creatas/PunchStock; **450** ©Bob Krist/Corbis; **452** ©Brand X/SuperStock; **453** (l) ©Albert Lozano/Shutterstock, (r) ©Associated Press; **460-461** ©Steve Allen/Brand X Pictures/Jupiterimages; **464** ©Michael Newman/PhotoEdit; **466** ©Bonnie Kamin/PhotoEdit; **468** ©Bob Daemmrich/PhotoEdit; **470** ©BlendImages/TipsImages; **473** ©Judd Pilossof/FoodPix/Jupiterimages; **474** ©White Packert/Photonica/Getty Images; **475** ©Ron Brown/SuperStock; **476** ©Imagno/Contributor/Hulton Archive/Getty Images; **478** ©David Young-Wolff/PhotoEdit; **479** ©Envision/Corbis; **480** ©Blend Images/SuperStock; **481** ©Hein van den Heuvel/zefa/Corbis; **486** ©Carlos Santa Maria/iStockphoto; **487** ©Myrleen Ferguson Cate/PhotoEdit; **489** ©BananaStock/PictureQuest/Jupiterimages; **490** ©Corbis/Jupiterimages; **491** ©Associated Press; **492** ©Associated Press; **494** ©Comstock Images/Alamy; **495** ©David Young-Wolff/PhotoEdit; **496** ©Matt Trommer/Shutterstock; **498** ©Brand X Pictures/Punchstock; **499** ©maps.com; **501** ©Buccina Studios/Photodisc/Getty Images; **502** ©Pixtal/SuperStock; **504** ©Tan Kian Khoon/Shutterstock; **512-513** ©William Manning/Corbis; **519** ©Richard Cummins/SuperStock; **534** ©Jaimie Duplass/Shutterstock; **536** ©Eric Limon/Shutterstock; **537** ©Ernest D'Ambrosio/Painet Inc.; **543** ©Lisa Hubbard/Jupiterimages; **548** ©Maureen Collins; **553** ©patrik argast/Painet Inc.; **558** ©Joan Vicent/iStockphoto; **563** ©Hornbil Images Private Limited; **567** (tl) ©Sam Patrick/Shutterstock, (tc) ©Thinkstock/Index Stock, (tr) ©Steve Gorton/Dorling Kindersley/Getty Images, (br) ©Jerome Scholler/Shutterstock, (br) ©C Squared Studios/Getty Images; **571** ©Paul Toczynski/Emporis.com; **572** ©Tischenko Irina/Shutterstock; **573** (l) ©age fotostock/SuperStock, (r) ©Christie & Cole/Corbis; **574** ©Jamie Cross/Shutterstock; **584-585** ©Chris George/Alamy; **586** ©Creatas/PunchStock; **588** ©Michael Nelson/Taxi/Getty Images; **589** ©Michael Newman/PhotoEdit; **593** ©Larry Luxnor; **595** ©Joanna Zopoth-Lipiejko/Shutterstock; **596** ©Dariush M./Shutterstock; **602** ©Rachel Weill/FoodPix/Jupiterimages; **604** (l), (c), (r) ©Timothy R. Nichols; **607** ©Estelle Klawitter/zefa/Corbis; **608** ©Michael Newman/PhotoEdit; **609** ©Kruchankova Maya/Shutterstock; **612** ©Jack Hollingsworth/Corbis; **613** ©Focus On Sport/Contributor/Getty Images Sport/Getty Images; **619** ©Brand Z Food/Alamy; **620** ©C Squared Studios/Getty Images; **621** ©Valueline/Punchstock; **623** ©Robin Sachs/PhotoEdit; **630-631** ©Elisa Locci/Alamy; **637** ©Polka Dot Images/Punchstock; **638** (l) ©Diego Cervo/Shutterstock, (r) ©Byron W. Moore/Shutterstock; **644** ©Ronnie Howard/Shutterstock; **655** ©Corbis; **674** (b) ©Alan Schein Photography/Corbis; **674-675** (t) ©Pixtal/SuperStock; **675** (c) ©Mark Karrass/Corbis, (b) ©ARTEKI/Shutterstock; **676** ©Michael Brown/Getty Images News/Getty Images; **685** ©Digital Vision Ltd./SuperStock; **688** Wikimedia Commons; **690** (l) ©Petr Svarc/painet, (r) ©Brian Chase/Shutterstock; **705** (l) ©Virco, (r) ©Paul Hostetter/Shooting Star Agency; **711** ©Bob Mahoney/Time & Life Pictures/Getty Images; **718-719** ©Peter Menzel/drr.net; **720** (t), (b) ©Cadence Gamache/origami by Jerry Harris; **725** ©Ryan McVay/Getty Images; **732** ©0399778584/Shutterstock; **739** ©John Henley/Corbis; **743** Courtesy U.S. Census Bureau; **745** ©Paul Chesley/Stone/Getty Images; **746** Courtesy U.S. Census Bureau; **750** ©Brand X Photography/Veer; **751** BananaStock/PunchStock; **752** ©Tay Jnr/photolibrary; **756** (tl) Wikimedia Commons, (bl) ©Oleksiy Maksymenko/Alamy, (r) ©SuperStock, Inc./SuperStock; **757** ©age fotostock/SuperStock.

Illustrations: Garry Nichols

Symbols

Symbol	Meaning
$<$	is less than
$>$	is greater than
$\leq$	is less than or equal to
$\geq$	is greater than or equal to
$=$	is equal to
$\neq$	is not equal to
$\approx$	is approximately equal to
$\cong$	is congruent to
$+$	plus sign
$-$	minus sign
$\times, \bullet$	multiplication sign
$\div$	division sign
R	remainder
x	variable
$\frac{n}{d}$	n divided by d
$a:b$	ratio of a to b
%	percent
x^n	x to the nth power
$-p$	opposite of p
π	pi
$\sqrt{}$	radical sign
( )	parentheses
{ }	braces
$0.\overline{a}$	repetend bar
$\ldots$	continuing pattern
AB	length of segment from point A to point B
$\overleftrightarrow{AB}$	line through point A and B
$\overrightarrow{AB}$	ray with endpoint A containing B
$\overline{AB}$	segment with endpoints A and B
$\overset{\frown}{AB}$	arc AB
A'	image of point A
b°	b degrees
$\angle ABC$	angle ABC
$m\angle ABC$	measure of angle ABC
$\triangle ABC$	triangle ABC
$\perp$	is perpendicular to
$\parallel$	is parallel to
∟	right angle
(x, y)	ordered pair
$P(E)$	probability of event E